ROUTLEDGE COMPANION TO THE ISRAELI-PALESTINIAN CONFLICT

This companion explores the Israeli-Palestinian conflict from its inception to the present day, demonstrating the depth and breadth of the many facets of the conflict, from the historical, political, and diplomatic to the social, economic, and pedagogical aspects. The contributions also engage with notions of objectivity and bias and the difficulties this causes when studying the conflict, in order to reflect the diversity of views and often contentious discussion surrounding this conflict.

The volume is organized around six parts, reflecting the core aspects of the conflict:

- Historical and scholarly context of the competing narratives;
- Contemporary evolution of the conflict and its key diplomatic junctures;
- Key issues of the conflict;
- Its local dimensions;
- International environment of the conflict;
- The "other images" of the conflict, as reflected in public opinion, popular culture, the boycott, divestment and sanctions (BDS) movement, and academia and pedagogy.

Providing a comprehensive approach to the Israeli-Palestinian conflict, this companion is designed for academics, researchers, and students interested in the key issues and contemporary themes of the conflict.

Asaf Siniver is a reader in International Security at the University of Birmingham.

ROUTLEDGE COMPANION TO THE ISRAELI-PALESTINIAN CONFLICT

Edited by Asaf Siniver

Routledge
Taylor & Francis Group
LONDON AND NEW YORK

Cover image: © Getty Images

First published 2023
by Routledge
4 Park Square, Milton Park, Abingdon, Oxon OX14 4RN

and by Routledge
605 Third Avenue, New York, NY 10158

Routledge is an imprint of the Taylor & Francis Group, an informa business

British Library Cataloguing-in-Publication Data
A catalogue record for this book is available from the British Library

ISBN: 9780367135942 (hbk)
ISBN: 9781032249018 (pbk)
ISBN: 9780429027376 (ebk)

DOI: 10.4324/9780429027376

Typeset in Bembo
by Newgen Publishing UK

CONTENTS

ILLUSTRATIONS

Figures

Maps

Tables

NOTES ON CONTRIBUTORS

The Editor

Asaf Siniver is a reader in International Security at the University of Birmingham. His research focuses on the intersection of conflict resolution, diplomacy, international security, and the role of third parties in the settlement of territorial disputes. He has published extensively on the politics, history, and diplomacy of the Arab-Israeli conflict, the Israeli-Palestinian peace process, and the international relations of the Middle East. He is editor of the *Journal of Global Security Studies*, a Leverhulme Research Fellow, and a Fellow of the Royal Historical Society. His current research examines the role of international law in territorial disputes (*Oxford University* Press, forthcoming).

The Contributors

Uriel Abulof is an associate professor of politics at Tel Aviv University, teaching at Cornell University. Abulof studies the politics of fear, happiness and hope, legitimation, social movements, existentialism, nationalism, and ethnic conflicts. Abulof leads the PrincetonX award-wining online course, HOPE. In addition to over fifty academic journal articles, his recent books include *The Mortality and Morality of Nations* (Cambridge University Press) and *The Existential Uncertainty of Zionism* (Haifa University Press). Abulof is also the co-editor of *Communication, Legitimation and Morality in Modern Politics* (Routledge). He is currently working on his book *(a) Human Conflict: From Existential Clash to Coexistence in Israel/Palestine.*

Ayman K. Agbaria is a Palestinian researcher, poet, playwright, and social activist. He serves as senior lecturer and head of the MA program in Education, Society and Culture in the Department of Leadership and Policy in Education at the University of Haifa, and as senior honorary research associate at the Centre for Research and Evaluation in Muslim Education, University College London, UCL Institute of Education. He studies the policies and politics of citizenship education and Islamic political in minority contexts.

Susan M. Akram is a graduate of the University of Michigan, Georgetown University School of Law, Oxford University, and the Institut International des Droits del'Homme. She directs

Boston University Law's International Human Rights Clinic, supervising students engaged in international advocacy in domestic, international, and regional fora. She teaches courses in International Human Rights, Refugee and Migration law, United States Immigration law and Palestinian Refugees under International Law. Her research and publications include *Still Waiting for Tomorrow: The Law and Politics of Unresolved Refugee Crises*; *International Law and the Israeli-Palestinian Conflict: A Rights-Based Approach to Middle East Peace*; and "The Arab Israel Conflict," in the *Max Planck Encyclopedia of International Law*.

Marco Allegra is a principal investigator at the Institute of Social Sciences, University of Lisbon. His area of expertise includes Middle East politics, policy analysis, and political geography. His publications include articles in journals such as *Citizenship Studies, Mediterranean Politics, Urban Studies, Environment and Planning A, Dialogues in Human Geography, International Journal of Urban and Regional Research, Planning Theory and Practice, and European Planning Studies*. With Ariel Handel and Erez Maggor, he has edited a collection on Israel's settlement policy in the West Bank (Indiana University Press, 2017).

Seth Anziska is the Mohamed S. Farsi-Polonsky associate professor of Jewish-Muslim Relations at University College London. His research and teaching focuses on Israeli and Palestinian society and culture, modern Middle Eastern history, and contemporary Arab and Jewish politics. He is the author of *Preventing Palestine: A Political History from Camp David to Oslo* (Princeton University Press, 2018), which was awarded the British Association for Jewish Studies Book Prize in 2019. He is currently working on an international history of the 1982 Lebanon War, supported by the British Academy and Leverhulme Trust.

Derek Averre is a honorary reader in the Department of Political Science and International Studies, and former director of the Centre for Russian and East European Studies, at the University of Birmingham. His main research interests focus on Russian and Eurasian foreign and security policy. He has edited four books/special journal issues and written numerous journal articles and book chapters and has organized policy and academic conferences and presented at numerous events in the United Kingdom and overseas. From 1991 to 2018 he carried out research on a series of contracts funded by the United Kingdom and European Union. He is a member of the editorial board of the journal *European Security*.

Ahmad Barakat is a visiting lecturer in Middle East Politics at the University of Birmingham. His research examines the political economy in the Middle East, and his work has appeared in a number of leading journals. More broadly, he is interested in the politics and diplomacy of the Middle East. He completed his PhD in political science and international studies at the University of Birmingham. He is a former Syrian diplomat and human rights expert.

Shaiel Ben-Ephraim is Middle East correspondent for the *Asia Times*. He was a postdoctoral fellow at UCLA and received his PhD at the University of Calgary. He is the 2015 winner of the Baruch Kimmerling prize in Israel Studies.

Matthew Berkman is visiting assistant professor of Jewish Studies at Oberlin College. His research focuses on American Jewish political and philanthropic organizations, antisemitism, and US-Israel relations.

Ian J. Bickerton is honorary associate professor in the School of Humanities and Languages at the University of New South Wales. He has taught modern United States history and United States foreign relations with Israel and the Middle East at Pomona College (California) and UNSW. He was visiting scholar at the Johns Hopkins School of Advanced International Studies, in Washington, DC (twice), and the Oxford Centre of Hebrew and Jewish Studies, Oxford (twice). His most recent publications include *The Struggle for Peace in the Middle East* (Cengage, 2015); *A History of the Arab-Israeli Conflict,* 7th ed. (Pearson, 2015); *The Arab-Israeli Conflict: A Guide for the Perplexed* (Bloomsbury, 2012); and *The Arab-Israeli Conflict* (Reaktion, 2009).

Siobhan Byrne is associate professor and associate chair (Graduate Studies) in the Department of Political Science, and director of the Peace and Post Conflict Studies Certificate, at the University of Alberta. Her primary areas of research include feminist anti-war activism and peacebuilding in societies in transition from conflict. Her work has appeared in *International Feminist Journal of Politics*, *International Political Science Review*, *International Peacekeeping*, and elsewhere. She is also currently completing a book with Allison McCulloch on gender, peace, and power-sharing in deeply divided societies.

Neil Caplan received his PhD from the London School of Economics and Political Science. Since retiring from teaching he has held an affiliate position in the Department of History at Concordia University in Montreal. His publications include *Futile Diplomacy*, a documentary history of Zionist-Arab and Arab-Israeli negotiations, 1913–1956 (4 vols., reissued Routledge Library Edition, 2015), *The Israel-Palestine Conflict: Contested Histories* (2nd ed., John Wiley, 2019), *Negotiating Arab-Israeli Peace: Patterns, Problems, Possibilities,* co-authored with Laura Z. Eisenberg (3rd ed., Indiana University Press, forthcoming), and *My Struggle for Peace: The Diary of Moshe Sharett, 1953–1956,* co-edited with Yaakov Sharett (3 vols., Indiana University Press, 2019).

Alan Craig is visiting research fellow at the University of Leeds and at the University of Durham. He was the Pears Lecturer in Middle Eastern Politics at Leeds until 2018 and has recently served as the chair of the European Association of Israel Studies. He has advised various public bodies on policy issues connected with Israeli politics and security. His publications include *International Legitimacy and the Politics of Security* (Lexington Books, 2013). He is currently working on a book for Cambridge University Press on Israel as a securitized state.

Donna Robinson Divine is the Morningstar Family Professor of Jewish Studies and Professor of Government emerita at Smith College, where she taught a variety of courses on Middle East politics. Able to draw on material in Hebrew, Arabic, and Turkish, her books include *Women Living Change: Cross-Cultural Perspectives; Essays from the Smith College Research Project on Women and Social Change*; *Politics and Society in Ottoman Palestine: The Arab Struggle for Survival and Power*; *Postcolonial Theory and the Arab-Israeli Conflict*; *Exiled in the Homeland: Zionism and the Return to Mandate Palestine;* and *Word Crimes: Reclaiming the Language of the Israeli-Palestinian Conflict.*

Alan Dowty is professor emeritus of political science at the University of Notre Dame. In 1963–1975 he was on the faculty of the Hebrew University in Jerusalem, and since then he has been based at the University of Notre Dame, while also serving as the first Kahanoff Chair Professor of Israel Studies at the University of Calgary, Alberta, in 2003–2006. He was president of the Association for Israel Studies in 2005–2007. Among his books are *The Jewish*

State: A Century Later (1998) and *Israel/Palestine* (4th ed, 2017). In 2017 he received the annual Lifetime Achievement Award in Israel Studies from the Association for Israel Studies and the Israel Institute.

Jacob Eriksson is the Al Tajir Lecturer in Post-war Recovery Studies in the Department of Politics at the University of York. His research interests include conflict resolution, the Israeli-Palestinian conflict, Middle Eastern politics and security, and post-war recovery. His first book, *Small-state Mediation in International Conflicts: Diplomacy and Negotiation in Israel-Palestine* was published by IB Tauris in 2015, and he has published multiple journal articles and book chapters on various aspects of the Israeli-Palestinian conflict. He is the co-editor of *Iraq after ISIS: The Challenges of Post-war Recovery*, published by Palgrave in 2019.

Michael R. Fischbach is professor of history at Randolph-Macon College. His research interests include land and property issues related to the Arab-Israeli conflict. Among his publications are *Records of Dispossession: Palestinian Refugee Property and the Arab-Israeli Conflict* (Columbia University Press, 2003) and *Jewish Property Claims Against Arab Countries* (Columbia University Press, 2008).

Galia Golan is Darwin Professor emerita of the Hebrew University of Jerusalem, where she was chair of the Political Science Department. More recently, she was head of the Program in Diplomacy and Conflict Studies at the Interdisciplinary Center, Herzliya. She has authored 10 books, most recently *Israeli Peacemaking Since 1967: Factors for the Breakthroughs and Failures* (Routledge). She has co-edited with Gilead Sher *Spoilers and Coping with Spoilers in the Israeli-Arab Conflict*. Most of her academic work was on the foreign policy of the Soviet Union, for which she received the Israel Political Science Association 2007 Award for "Lifetime Contribution." She has also been the recipient of several other international academic prizes.

Oded Haklai is a professor in the Department of Political Studies at Queen's University in Kingston, Ontario. He is the author of *Palestinian Ethnonationalism in Israel* (University of Pennsylvania Press), recipient of the Shapiro Award for best book in Israel Studies, and co-editor of several books, including *Democracy and Conflict Resolution: The Dilemmas of Israel's Peacemaking* (2014), with M.F. Elman and H. Spruyt, and *Settlers in Contested Lands: Territorial Disputes and Ethnic Conflict* (2015), with N. Loizides. Haklai's research has been supported by several grants, including from Canada's Social Science and Humanities Research Council.

Maia Carter Hallward is a professor in the School of Conflict Management, Peacebuilding and Development at Kennesaw State University, Georgia, and editor of the *Journal of Peacebuilding and Development*. She is author or co-author of seven books, including *Understanding International Conflict Management* (Routledge, 2020), *Global Responses to Crisis and Conflict in Syria and Yemen* (Palgrave 2019), and *Understanding Nonviolence* (Polity, 2015), and over twenty peer-reviewed articles on topics including nonviolence, peacebuilding, human rights, the role of religion in politics, women's leadership, and civil resistance in Israel/Palestine. She is on the Fulbright Specialist Roster for Conflict Resolution and a Fulbright Scholar to Jordan.

Eran Halperin is a former dean of the School of Psychology at IDC–Herzliya and now professor in the Psychology Department at the Hebrew University in Jerusalem. His work develops new approaches for modifying the psychological roots of intolerance, exclusion, and intergroup violence. He has published more than 200 peer-reviewed papers in journals that include Science, PNAS, and Psychological Science and received competitive research awards totalling more than $6M in the last five years. He earned his PhD from Haifa University (summa cum laude) and was a postdoctoral researcher at Stanford University on a Fulbright scholarship.

Ariel Handel is director of the Lexicon for Political Theory project and academic co-director of the Minerva Humanities Center at Tel Aviv University. His research focuses on human mobilities in the West Bank and the Gaza Strip, the politics of housing and urban frontiers, gastropolitics, and the political philosophy of geography. Handel is the editor-in-chief of *The Political Lexicon of the Social Protest* (Hakibutz Hameuchad, 2012) and co-editor of *Normalizing Occupation: The Politics of Everyday Life in the West Bank Settlements* (Indiana University Press, 2017).

Menachem Klein is professor emeritus of political science at Bar Ilan University, Israel. Since 1996 he has been active in many unofficial negotiations with Palestinian counterparts, and in 2000 he was an adviser to Israel's Minister of Foreign Affairs for Jerusalem Affairs and Israel-PLO Final Status Talks, and a member of the advisory team in the office of Prime Minister Ehud Barak. His book *Lives in Common: Arabs and Jews in Jerusalem, Jaffa and Hebron* (Hurst and Oxford University Press, 2014), was recognized by the *New Republic* as one of the best non-fiction books in 2014. His latest book is *Arafat and Abbas: Portraits of Leadership in a State Postponed* (Hurst and Oxford University Press, 2019).

Ron Kronish is a Library Fellow at the Van Leer Jerusalem Institute. From 1991–2016 he served as the director of the Interreligious Coordinating Council in Israel (ICCI). He was educated at Brandeis University (BA), Hebrew Union College – Jewish Institute of Religion, and the Harvard Graduate School of Education. He is the editor of *Coexistence and Reconciliation in Israel: Voices for Interreligious Dialogue* (Paulist Press, 2015), and author of *The Other Peace Process: Interreligious Dialogue, A View from Jerusalem* (Hamilton Books, 2017). He has lived in Jerusalem for the past 41 years with his wife, Amy.

Oded Adomi Leshem is a fellow at the Truman Research Institute and the Psychology of Intergroup Conflict and Reconciliation Lab at the Hebrew University, Jerusalem. His research is located at the nexus of political psychology and conflict resolution with a specialization in protracted ethnonational conflicts. He has published numerous articles and book chapters on the political psychology of hope and despair and on how political power shapes people's interpretation of the concept of peace.

Erez Maggor is a postdoctoral fellow at the Edmond J. Safra Center for Ethics at Tel Aviv University. His broad interests include political economy, political sociology, and comparative-historical sociology. His research has appeared in *Socio-Economic Review*, *Politics & Society*, and *Israeli Sociology*. With Ariel Handel and Marco Allegra, he edited a collection on Israel's settlement policy in the West Bank (Indiana University Press, 2017).

Emily McKee is an associate professor at Northern Illinois University in the Department of Anthropology and the Institute for the Study of the Environment, Sustainability, and Energy. She specializes in environmental and Middle East anthropology, with a focus on political ecology. McKee is the author of *Dwelling in Conflict: Negev Landscapes and the Boundaries of Belonging* (Stanford University Press, 2016), which examines land conflicts in Israel, and she has also published articles on land and water relations and environmentalist campaigns in Palestine, Israel, and Jordan and on farming and food systems in the United States.

Aline Muff is a postdoctoral student in the Department of Leadership and Policy in Education at the University of Haifa. Her work focuses on citizenship education, education in conflict-affected societies, education of minorities, critical pedagogy, and the role of identity in education.

Costanza Musu is a associate professor at the Graduate School of Public and International Affairs at the University of Ottawa and Editor-in-Chief of the journal International Politics. She is the author of numerous publications on Western policies towards the Middle East, and of a book, *European Union Policy towards the Arab-Israeli Peace Process. The Quicksands of Politics*.

Maha Nassar is an associate professor in the School of Middle Eastern and North African Studies at the University of Arizona. She is the author of several academic articles and analysis pieces on Palestinian cultural history. Her first book, *Brothers Apart: Palestinian Citizens of Israel and the Arab World* (Stanford University Press, 2017), received a 2018 Palestine Book Award for academic titles. Her current book project explores the global history of the Palestinian people.

Wendy Pearlman is professor of political science at Northwestern University, where she also holds the Charles Deering McCormick Professorship of Teaching Excellence. A specialist in the comparative politics of the Middle East, she is the author of four books: *We Crossed A Bridge and It Trembled: Voices from Syria* (HarperCollins, 2017); *Violence, Nonviolence, and the Palestinian National Movement* (Cambridge University Press, 2011); *Occupied Voices: Stories of Everyday Life from the Second Intifada* (Nation Books, 2003); and *Triadic Coercion: Israel's Targeting of States that Host Nonstate Actors* (co-authored with Boaz Atzili, Columbia University Press, 2018). She has conducted research in Lebanon, Jordan, Turkey, Israel, and the West Bank and Gaza Strip.

Rob Geist Pinfold is a research fellow at the National Security Studies Centre, University of Haifa, the Department of War Studies, King's College London, and the Herzl Centre for Israel Studies at Charles University Prague. He holds a PhD in War Studies from King's College. His research intersects the study of strategy, security, and territorial conflict. His publications include articles in *Studies in Conflict and Terrorism*, *The Journal of Strategic Studies*, and *Mediterranean Politics*. He also jointly edited the book, *Understanding Israel: Political, Societal and Security Challenges*, published by Routledge in 2019.

Sahar Taghdisi Rad is a lecturer in Global Political Economy at the School of Politics and International Relations, University of Westminster. Her work focuses on the political economy of development, particularly in the fields of international development assistance, labour markets, conflict, and trade. She has previously taught political economy and development economics at the School of Oriental and African Studies and King's College London, and has worked as an economist at the United Nations Conference on Trade and Development, the African Development Bank, and the International Labour Organisation. She is author of *The Political Economy of Aid in Palestine: Relief from Conflict or Development Delayed?*

Oliver Ramsbotham is emeritus professor of Conflict Resolution at the University of Bradford and former head of the Department of Peace Studies. He is president of the Conflict Research Society, and former chair of the Oxford Research Group. He is series co-editor of the

Routledge Studies on Peace and Conflict Resolution. His main publications are, *Contemporary Conflict Resolution* (State University of New York Press, 2016), now in its fourth edition (co-author); *Transforming Violent Conflict: Radical Disagreement, Dialogue and Survival* (Routledge, 2010); and *When Conflict Resolution Fails: Engaging Radical Disagreement in Intractable Conflicts* (Polity 2017). In the field of practice with colleagues he has applied his "Collective Strategic Thinking" (CST) methodology for addressing radical disagreement in Israel/Palestine and in Yemen.

Jonathan Rynhold is a professor in the Political Studies Department at Bar-Ilan University. His research focuses on US-Israeli relations and Israeli foreign policy. His book, *The Arab-Israeli Conflict in American Political Culture* (Cambridge University Press, 2015) won the Israeli Association for Political Science book prize. In 2016, he co-edited a volume entitled, *US Foreign Policy and Global Standing in the 21st Century*.

Brent E. Sasley is associate professor of political science, the University of Texas at Arlington, where he teaches and writes on Israeli politics, foreign policy analysis, and international security. His disciplinary focus is on how language, emotions, and collective memories shape identity and foreign policymaking. He is the co-author with Harold M. Waller of *Politics in Israel: Governing a Complex Society* (Oxford, 2017).

Dahlia Scheindlin is a public opinion expert and strategic consultant who has advised eight national political campaigns in Israel and has worked in 15 other countries. She conducts research and policy analysis on the Israeli-Palestinian conflict, foreign policy, democracy, human rights, and civil rights, political analysis, and comparative conflict analysis. She has worked for civil society and political actors and has regional expertise in the Balkans and Eastern Europe as well. She holds a PhD in political science from Tel Aviv University and has been an adjunct lecturer at several universities. She is currently a non-resident fellow at The Century Foundation; and she co-hosts *The Tel Aviv Review* podcast.

Dag Henrik Tuastad is an internationally recognized anthropologist in Middle East Studies at the University of Oslo. He has extensive fieldwork experience in Arab and Palestinian society, including in Gaza, the West Bank, and Palestinian camps in Lebanon, Jordan, and Syria. He has published *Palestinske Utfordringer* (*Palestinian Challenges*, Cappelen Damm, 2014) and several journal articles on Palestinian politics, including on the relations between Hamas and the Palestine Liberation Organisation (PLO), the prospects for reforms in the PLO, and political representation of Palestinian refugees. He is currently the research leader of the Rebel Rule project of the University of Oslo.

Anastasia Valassopoulos is senior lecturer in World Literatures at the University of Manchester. Her research is on the postcolonial literature and culture of the Middle East. She is also very interested in the wider cultural production and reception of Arab film and music. Recent publications include work on the role of cinema in the Palestinian resistance movement, anti-colonial feminism in North Africa, as well as film, revolution and music in the Egyptian context (with Dalia Mostafa). She is currently working on a book-length project entitled *Palestine in the Popular Imagination*.

Imogen Watson is a political researcher with extensive experience working on matters of legislation and policy in the Westminster offices of Members of the United Kingdom Parliament. She completed her Bachelor's degree at the University of Exeter in politics and French and graduated from the University of Birmingham in 2019 with an MSc in Global Cooperation and Security. During her Master's degree, she focused her research on psychological barriers and rivalry termination theory in the Arab-Israeli conflict, alongside international cooperation, diplomatic history, and mediation.

Mohammed Saif-Alden Wattad is an associate professor and the Dean of Law at Zefat Academic College. Additionally, he serves as senior researcher at the Institute for National Security Studies at Tel-Aviv University; research fellow at the International Institute for Counter-Terrorism at Reichman University; and research fellow at the Minerva Center for the Rule of Law under Extreme Conditions at Haifa University. He is a legal scholar specializing in international and comparative criminal law, comparative constitutional law, international law, and legal issues surrounding war, torture and terrorism, Professional Ethics, and Medical Law. He is the 2020 winner of the prestigious Zeltner Young Scholar Award, and the 2015 winner of the Young Scholar Award on Israel Studies. Between 2003–2004, he served as a legal clerk at the Supreme Court of Israel under the supervision of Justice Dalia Dorner.

Taylor L. Williams is an MA candidate in the Department of Government at Georgetown University. Her research interests include state-sponsored ethnic cleansing in the twentieth-century Middle East.

INTRODUCTION

Asaf Siniver

One of the greatest conundrums of the Israeli-Palestinian conflict is the evident gap between the incomparable levels of diplomatic investment and assistance that the international community has directed at the parties since the historic launch of the Oslo peace process in 1993, and the pitiable results that have since followed. As one of the most protracted conflicts of our time, it has attracted dozens of mediation initiatives (the vast majority led by the United States) and received the backing of the international community, most notably following the formation of the Quartet on the Middle East in 2002 by the United Nations, the European Union, the United States, and Russia. Over the past three decades, the names, dates, and places of these initiatives seem to have all merged into a single inevitable pattern of high hopes and low returns. While the Declaration of Principles between Israel and the Palestine Liberation Organisation (PLO) in September 1993 was indeed historic for bringing an official end to the state of belligerency between the two parties, it was followed by a long succession of diplomatic efforts which, in the short term, may have contributed to an incremental progression in Israeli-Palestinian dialogue but, in the long term, failed to move the parties towards the ultimate goal of peaceful coexistence. These include, most significantly, Oslo II (1995), the Hebron Agreement (1997), the Wye River Memorandum (1998), the EU's 1999 Berlin Declaration, the Camp David Summit and the Clinton Parameters of 2000, the Taba Summit of 2001, the 2002 Arab Peace Initiative, the 2003 Geneva Initiative and the Quartet's "Road Map for Peace" of the same year, the 2007 Annapolis Conference, John Kerry's shuttle diplomacy of 2013–2014 and, most recently, the ill-conceived "deal of the century" (2020) of the Trump administration.

While these initiatives were led by different actors at different periods of time and were centred around different aspects of the conflict, they were all accompanied by an overpowering sense of ubiquitous, inevitable futility. This pessimistic outlook about the prospect of Israeli-Palestinian peace did not emerge in the aftermath of failure with the benefit of hindsight, but has been attached to every diplomatic effort before it had even started. This was perfectly demonstrated by one diplomat's assessment of the impressive credentials of US Secretary of State John Kerry's negotiation team and its likelihood of success before the launch of Kerry's Israeli-Palestinian shuttle diplomacy in 2013: At two-to-three times the size of previous State Department negotiation teams and including a mapping expert, "[t]his team has learned more, in greater depth, and with greater intellectual honesty what it will take to address the core

DOI: 10.4324/9780429027376-1

grievances than any effort previously in the American government. That's without any doubt. And they still only have maybe 10% chance of success" (Lewis and Sherwood 2014).

What explains this omnipresent pessimism? Is it just a case of an incremental realization that the conflict may be "beyond resolution" as one diplomatic failure follows another? How can we reconcile the fact that a majority of Israeli Jews (55%) and a large minority of Palestinians (44%) support the two-state solution, yet 71% of Israeli Jews indicate that Palestinians cannot be trusted, while 86% of Palestinians believe that Israeli Jews are untrustworthy? (PSR 2017). At a societal level, Israeli-Palestinian relations are no better today than they were three decades ago, while the political leadership on both sides are unable or unwilling (or both) to work constructively together to move from unilateralism to cooperation.

While such assessment may seem to lack the necessary spatial and temporal perspective to allow for some broader developments to have a pacifying effect on the conflict (e.g., the recent normalization agreements between Israel and the UAE, Bahrain, and Morocco, or the presidential election of Joe Biden in the United States), there is little reason to expect that these will fundamentally change the perceptions of Israelis and Palestinians of each other, or their motivations to forego their incompatible narratives about whose land it is, who is the victim and ultimately, who has history on their side.

The "war of narratives" presents the most indomitable challenge to Israeli-Palestinian reconciliation and has rightly attracted a large number of books, articles, and debates in academia and beyond. From Edward Said's "Permission to Narrate" (1984) and the historiographical debates between "Old" and "New" historians following the opening of Israeli state archives in the late 1980s (see ch. 1 by Neil Caplan), to more recent works which either present the narratives side-by-side or attempt to reconcile them (see, among others Scham, Salem, and Pogrund 2005; Tessler 2009; Adwan et al. 2012; Aly, Feldman, and Shikaki 2013; Caplan 2020), there is no doubting the importance of these narratives in building national identities, reaffirming legitimacy, informing policy, and ultimately, reinforcing communal images of "us vs. them" and the other as the enemy. Dismissing the conflict as "nothing more than a real-estate dispute between Israelis and Palestinians," in the words of Jared Kushner, former Middle East advisor to President Trump (Middle East Monitor 2021), is not only naïve and misinformed, but it also makes the prospect of a truly transformative change in Israeli-Palestinian relations an unlikely prospect. As the Israeli novelist Amos Oz noted, the conflict is not between a right narrative and a wrong narrative; both are equally valid, "and the definition of a tragedy is a clash between right and right. Or sometimes a clash between wrong and wrong" (Schmemann, Nusseibeh, and Oz 2010). Similarly, for Said,

> in a situation like that of the Palestinians and Israelis, hardly anyone can be expected to drop the quest for national identity and go straight to a history-transcending universal rationalism. Each of the two communities, misled though both may be, is interested in its origins, its history of suffering, its need to survive. To recognize these imperatives, as components of national identity, and to try to reconcile them, rather than dismiss them as so much non-factual ideology, strikes me as the task in hand.
> (Said 1984, 47)

This theme underpins the rationale of this edited volume. It does not intend to provide a "definitive" account of the evolution of Israeli-Palestinian relations from the inception of the conflict to the present, but rather to demonstrate the depth and breadth of the many facets of the conflict, from the historical, political and diplomatic to the social, economic and pedagogical – whilst recognising that each chapter (and the volume as a whole) reflects the personal choices and decisions of the author and thus cannot be considered truly "objective." To some degree, the format and content of the volume were also shaped by the choices of those who were invited to contribute but chose not to – some due to time constraints during a global pandemic, and others due to allegiance with the boycott, divestment, and sanctions (BDS) movement's aim of boycotting Israeli (or pro-Israel) academics. As such, this edited volume is very much an embodiment of the temporality of the conflict, especially as it concerns the steady demise in the appetite for scholarly collaboration between those who hold, or are seen as representative of, the opposing ends in the "war of narratives."

The volume is organised around six parts, reflecting the core aspects of the conflict: the historical and scholarly context of the competing narratives; the contemporary evolution of the conflict and its key diplomatic junctures; the key issues of the conflict; its local dimensions; the international environment of the conflict; and the "other images" of the conflict, as reflected in public opinion, popular culture, the BDS movement, and academia and pedagogy. The chapters in Part I place the origins of the conflict in the necessary historical, scholarly and psychological domains. As Neil Caplan points in his chapter on the historiography of the conflict (ch. 1):

> One basic lesson that all scholars learn is to appreciate the limits of objectivity; pure objectivity, they discover sooner or later, does not exist. Even the most neutral, unbiased scholars must necessarily employ some degree of selection (inclusion/exclusion) and emphasis in the course of constructing their chronological or analytical treatments of the past... Given that all historians consciously and unconsciously inject context and personal perspective into the bare bones of any story they are reconstructing from the past, the real questions are not about "bias" versus "no bias," but rather about which biases are in play and how readers ought to compensate for them in assessing authors and their works on this conflict.

Recognising that one's personal bias has some bearing on the writing of history or the analysis of current affairs is not a bad thing, but a necessary first step in acknowledging that the Israeli-Palestinian conflict is as much about narratives as it is about the prospects of power-sharing in Jerusalem or the dismantling of Israeli settlements. The modern roots of the conflict are commonly traced back to the late nineteenth century. In the face of increasing persecution and state-sponsored anti-Semitic attacks across Tsarist Russia and Eastern Europe in the 1880s, Zionism emerged as the ideological solution by calling for a homeland for the Jews in their ancestral home *Eretz Israel* or "Land of Israel." As Alan Dowty demonstrates in ch. 2, mirroring narratives of victimhood have not only accompanied the conflict since its inception but given the *civilizational divide* in Palestine between European-Jewish settlers on one side, and Turkish rulers and Arab residents on the other, "it is hard to see how the conflict could have evolved much differently. The die was cast." Between 1881 and 1948 the Jewish population in Palestine had risen from 5 per cent of the total (mostly Muslim) population to 33 per cent. A series of violent clashes between the Jewish and Arab communities in 1920, 1921, 1929 and 1936–1939 prompted Britain, which received a mandate over Palestine from the League of Nations at the end of the First World War, to find solutions to the incompatible demands of the Jewish and Arab communities; however its efforts did little more than exacerbate the nascent conflict and alienate the Arab and Jewish communities. Indeed, the British had played an important role in sowing the seeds of the conflict by promising the same land to the two peoples: first to Arab leader Hussein Bin Ali in 1916 in exchange for his help to defeat the Ottomans, while in 1917 the Balfour Declaration, issued by the foreign secretary, expressed the commitment of the

British Government to the establishment in Palestine of a national home for the Jewish people. By 1937 the British had concluded that the only solution was a surgical separation of the two communities when the Royal Peel Commission recommended the partition of Palestine into Jewish and Arab states.

While the "solution" of separating the communities along demographic lines had become the dominant paradigm in the minds of the international community, from Resolution 181 (29 November 1947) of the United Nations General Assembly to partition Mandatory Palestine between an Arab state and a Jewish state (with Jerusalem designated *corpus separatum*), to the Two-State Solution framework of the more recent peace process, the socio-psychological infrastructure of the conflict reinforces communal beliefs of injustice and victimhood, which make compromise impossible. As Oded Leshem and Eran Halperin show (ch. 3), "each group sees its goals as not only incompatible with those of the other group, but threatened by them and thus leading to a mutually-reinforcing negative image of each other." This innate belief in the group's unquestionable justness of its goals makes it very difficult to find a middle ground on which to agree. Ultimately, Leshem and Halperin conclude, "when groups are devoted exclusively to issues in the past (who was here first), they cannot focus on the future (how this conflict can be resolved)." This is perfectly illustrated in chs. 4 and 5 by Wendy Pearlman and Donna Robinson Divine on Palestinian Nationalism and Zionism, respectively. Both movements are motivated by historically shaped ideologies that in turn underpin two political legitimacies which are inherently opposed to each other. In ch. 6, Oliver Ramsbotham shows how radical asymmetry, made up of material, conceptual and strategic asymmetries, has repeatedly constrained conflict resolution efforts from the 1937 Peel Commission to the 2020 "deal of the century" of the Trump administration.

Part II of this volume builds on the foundations laid by earlier chapters to chart the contemporary evolution of the conflict from the first Arab-Israeli war of 1948 to the most recent diplomatic efforts and failures. In ch. 7, Michael Fischbach and Taylor Williams discuss the run-up to the 1948 war and the main consequences in its wake, including the permanent exile of approximately 750,000 Palestinian refugees and Israel's territorial expansion from 55 per cent of Mandatory Palestine as per the UN partition resolution to 78 per cent following the conclusion of four armistice agreements with Egypt, Syria, Lebanon, and Jordan (see map below). While the Palestinians were most directly affected by the war's end they remained very much on the sideline of Middle East diplomacy throughout the Cold War, as the conflict was viewed as an inter-state territorial struggle between Israel and her Arab neighbours, rather than one concerning Palestinian self-determination. For example, following the Six-Day War of June 1967, which saw Israel capturing additional territory from Egypt, Jordan and Syria, while a further 250,000 Palestinians were made refugees, UN Security Council Resolution 242 (22 November 1967) called for a "just and lasting peace" in the Middle East and a "just settlement" of the refugee problem; however, it contained no reference to the Palestinians. As Seth Azenska shows in ch. 8, the period from 1967–1991 was instrumental in shaping the Palestinian struggle for regional and international legitimacy and a seat at the negotiation table. The end of the Cold War and the triumph of the US-led coalition forces in the 1991 Gulf War had irreversibly changed the contours of Arab-Israeli diplomacy and for the first time in the history of the conflict, the Palestinians got their seat at the table (albeit as part of the Jordanian delegation) at the Madrid Peace Conference of October 1991 which was then followed by several rounds of talks in Washington. In September 1993, following months of secret talks facilitated by the Norwegian government, Israeli Prime Minister Yitzhak Rabin and Yasser Arafat, leader of the PLO (Palestine Liberation Organization) signed the historic Declaration of Principles, which officially ended the state of belligerency between the two peoples.

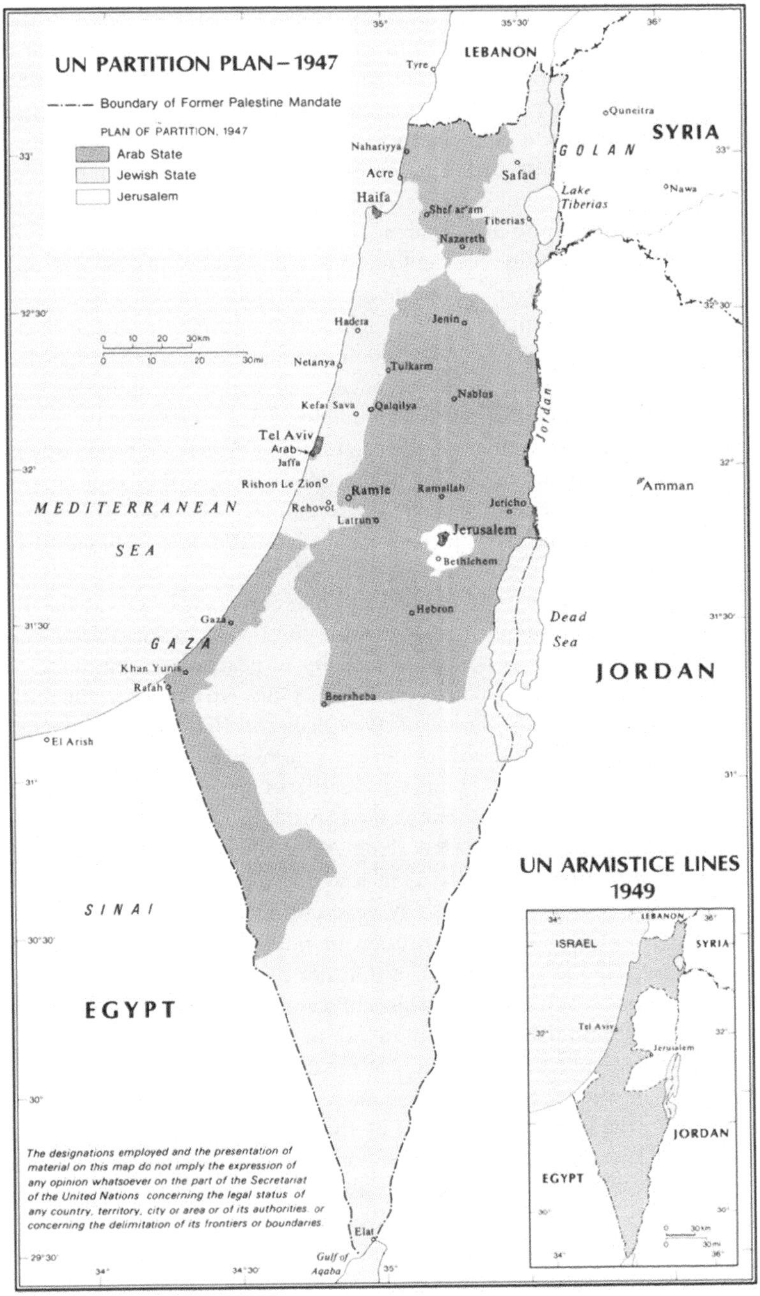

MAP NO. 3067 Rev. 1 UNITED NATIONS
APRIL 1983

Map 0.1 The 1947 United Nations Partition Plan and the 1949 Armistice Lines.

The remaining chapters in Part II discuss the many ebbs and rare flows in the peace process that followed this historic signing, from the intense diplomatic activity of the 1990s in the face of indefatigable domestic peace spoilers (ch. 9 by Ian Bickerton), through the disillusionment with the peace process and the turn to unprecedented levels of violence during the *Al-Aqsa Intifada* (2000–2005, ch. 10 by Brent Sasley), to what can only be described as the slow and somewhat inevitable demise of the peace process ever since (ch. 11 by Jacob Eriksson). Given the ubiquity of tragedy and despair in this period, any temptation (hope?) to cloak the occasional diplomatic breakthrough in a broader Fukuyama-esq "end of history" paradigm is inevitably short-lived. At the height of the Oslo peace process in the 1990s, in an article titled "The Arab-Israeli Conflict is Over," political analyst Barry Rubin celebrated the triumph of a two-state solution that would finally allow Israelis and Palestinians to live in peace. The diplomatic breakthrough of the Oslo Accords, Rubin maintained, was proof that the Palestinians had finally moved away from their futile insistence on liberating the entire land of Palestine to embrace compromise at the negotiation table, while Israel had abandoned its "more demanding policies of recent years." At the same time, the cementing of American hegemony following the end of the Cold War and the strengthening of the US–Israel special relationship helped ensure regional stability and strengthened moderate Arab regimes, who now had to come to terms with Israel's existence and legitimacy. In the final analysis, Rubin concluded, the Arab-Israeli conflict was now over (Rubin 1996).

Rubin's confident assessment was countered by the conservative David Bar-Ilan for being too "reasonable, sensible, and logical" in drawing a linear development from the early years of the Arab-Israeli conflict to a contemporary reality of peaceful co-existence. Such wishful thinking, Bar-Ilan cautioned, was akin to saying that the current peaceful relations among European nations began with the Peace of Westphalia of 1648, thus ignoring revolutions, civil wars and world wars that had cost the lives of more than 100 million people (Bar-Ilan 1996). History shows that violence, conflict and setbacks are more common than diplomatic breakthroughs (otherwise they would not be called "breakthroughs"), and this is nowhere truer than in the Israeli-Palestinian conflict. Recalling Abba Eban's over-worked adage that "men and nations behave wisely once they have exhausted all other alternatives," it is evident that Israelis and Palestinians have been remarkably persistent in demonstrating that they are better off with an ongoing hurting stalemate than they are with peace. Their various commitments to dialogue in the past (and in the future) can thus not be seen as the normal state of affairs in the conflict, but very much as momentary lapses of reason, which are the exception to the rule.

While Israelis and Palestinians have come close in the past to reaching a compromise on some parameters of the conflict (most notably at the 2000 Camp David Summit and following the 2007 Conference), they were never close enough to "end" the conflict. There are two reasons for this: First, the parties were bound by the Oslo formula of "nothing is agreed until everything is agreed," meaning that agreement on one of the permanent status issues (such as Jerusalem, settlements, refugees, and borders) was not considered binding and final until all other issues have been agreed upon. This "all or nothing" approach also meant that future negotiations would not start from where previous ones had ended. As Israeli Prime Minister Ehud Barak announced at the end of the Camp David Summit (which collapsed over disagreements over the status of Jerusalem), "Ideas, views and even positions which were raised in the course of the summit are invalid as opening positions in the resumption of negotiations, when they resume. They are null and void" (MFA 2000).

Second, and with the notable exceptions of the Camp David Summit and the post-Annapolis negotiations, much of the "peace process" has been just that – negotiations about the process rather than the endgame of peace. These "negotiations about negotiations" have often been used by both Israeli and Palestinian leaders as a delaying tactic to avoid making tough decisions whilst maintaining the appearance of a commitment to the peace process. In more recent years even this once-popular face-saving exercise is no longer employed, as the very idea of "peace" has become synonymous with "betrayal" and "weakness" after a decade of diplomatic stalemate compounded by the rise of ultranationalist right-wing politics in Israel and a crisis of leadership and a unilateral turn in Palestinian politics. Amidst these very inhospitable conditions for a revival of a "peace process," let alone a real diplomatic breakthrough, the tangible value and meaning of peace seem to have been lost. Could Israeli-Palestinian peace be tantamount to a "just" solution? Are peace and justice one and the same? Would an agreement between Israeli and Palestinian leaders over the core issues of the conflict mean that the conflict was "over" and, can the conflict be truly resolved, or can it at best be managed? Would Israeli-Palestinian peace mean the absence of direct violence (i.e., "negative peace"), or should it also aspire to incorporate social justice and quality, and the absence of structural and indirect violence as well? (Gatlung 1969). The Oslo Accords were quickly followed by an impressive programme of peacebuilding initiatives, funded by the international community and designed to complement the "resolution" of the conflict at the political level with the "transformation" of Israeli-Palestinian relations through inter-societal dialogue and cooperation. But three decades later, and notwithstanding some very impressive local initiatives, the conflict remains far from resolution, let alone transformation.

Amongst the plethora of reasons for this failure, three in particular are worth a mention here. First, while much attention has been devoted to resolving the conflict *between* the two communities, it is the impact of local cleavages and domestic peace spoilers *within* each community that has often played a significant role in the derailment and delegitimization of the peace process. These included, among others, the relentless terrorist attacks against Israeli civilians by Palestinian groups such as Hamas and Islamic Jihad, and the equally relentless incitement campaigns against Oslo and the Israeli government led by the right-wing Likud party and the powerful settler movement, which had directly led to the assassination of Israeli Prime Minister Yitzhak Rabin by a right-wing Jewish extremist in November 1995. Certainly for outside observers, amidst the general state of hyperbolic euphoria about historic breakthroughs and the conflict being "over," it was sometimes tempting to ignore the fragility of the Oslo paradigm – the most incongruous example being the ratification of the Oslo II agreement by the Knesset in October 1995, only weeks before Rabin's assassination, by a majority of 61:59 – and only after one right-wing parliamentarian agreed to support the government in return for the promise of a ministerial car and the promotion to the position of a deputy minister (Horovitz and Hirschberg 1997, 433–434; MFA 2012).

Alongside the considerable impact of domestic peace spoilers on the peace process, a different challenge to the Oslo framework had emerged from proponents of peace, who pointed that while diplomats and policymakers continued to negotiate over the "core issues" and exalted the goal of a "just and lasting peace," the realities on the ground and the asymmetry in relations between the parties had remained unchanged. Far from improving the lives of the Palestinians, critics argued, the Oslo peace process had in fact institutionalised the "normalisation" of the Israeli occupation; talking of "economic development" and "state-building" within a wider context of life under military occupation was thus seen as counter-intuitive and reinforcing the existing social, economic and political inequalities (Mi'Ari 1999; Roy 2012; Haddad 2018). Third, and related to the other points, this conflict is likely to remain resistant to resolution so long as leaders on both sides fail to develop and sustain a bilateral relationship that is built on trust and mutuality of interests. While interpersonal mistrust at the highest level cannot be separated from the wider inter-societal atmosphere of mistrust (as demonstrated in the survey cited above), the history of the conflict teaches us that convergence of national interests is sometimes sufficient to sustain political agreements despite the absence of a transformative "positive peace" between peoples. For example, Israel's peace treaties with Egypt (1979) and Jordan (1994) are commonly referred to as examples of "cold peace" (Elshinnawi 2011; Riedel 2019), while the more recent normalisation agreements between Israel and the UAE, Bahrain, and Morocco are the epitome of a *realpolitik* approach to peacemaking which not only has little to do with "peace," but it also shatters the decades-long mythology that Arab hostility toward Israel cannot be separated from the question of Palestine. The traditional wisdom that only the resolution of the Israeli-Palestinian conflict will lead to the wider normalisation of relations between Israel and the Arab world now seems less compelling. The agreements between Israel and the two Gulf monarchies were a public extension of a longer clandestine alignment against Iran's hegemonic ambitions in the region (and facilitated by the promise of sale of F-35 aircraft to the UAE by the Trump administration, the matchmaker of the agreements). Morocco, too, was quick to re-normalise its relations with Israel (after severing them during the 2000 Al-Aqsa Intifada) once the Trump administration agreed to recognise its claim to sovereignty over the disputed territory of Western Sahara.

That these agreements were facilitated by the United States is of course not surprising given Washington's hegemonic role in the Arab-Israeli conflict since the aftermath of the Yom Kippur War of October 1973. From the effective diplomacy of Henry Kissinger, through President Jimmy Carter's mediation of the Camp David Accords between Egypt and Israel in 1978, to the "New Middle East" vision of President George W. Bush following the 1991 Gulf War, and then as through the management of successive administrations of Israeli-Palestinian negotiations, it seems axiomatic that American leadership is indispensable for sustaining Arab-Israeli diplomacy. It follows, then, that while the disputants themselves should bear most responsibility for their failure to reach a peaceful compromise, some blame must nevertheless be apportioned to the United States as the principal third party in this relationship, most evidently for erecting and sustaining a diplomatic paradigm which is hinged on an almost visceral commitment to Israel's security. At the negotiation table, it meant that American officials have acted, in the words of former Middle East advisor Aaron Miller, as "Israel's attorney, catering and coordinating with the Israelis at the expense of successful peace negotiations" (Miller 2005).

As noted above, these negotiations have often revolved around what are commonly seen as the "core issues" of the conflict. These are covered in Part III of this volume, including the just resolution of the Palestinian refugees issue (ch. 12 by Susan Akram), the status of Jerusalem (ch. 13 by Menachem Klein), the future of Israeli settlements (ch. 14 by Ariel Handel, Marco Allegra, and Erez Maggor), and security (ch. 17 by Rob Pinfold). These issues are considered "core" because they represent the most protracted and contentious aspects of the conflict, underlined by competing historical, ideological, and religious narratives and, taken together, they create a seemingly impregnable barrier to a peaceful resolution, especially when reinforced and exacerbated by a rigid socio-psychological infrastructure of collective constructs of self-righteousness and victimhood. But other issues, too, are key to our understanding of the protracted nature of the conflict. For example, Sahar Taghdisi Rad (ch. 15) adopts a critical global political economy approach to demonstrate how neoliberal hegemony, practised through structures of international finance and development assistance, has reinforced the status quo of occupation as individual prosperity has been prioritised over collective development in the occupied territories. Similarly, Emily McKee (ch. 16) shows how access to water and its distribution is shaped by Israeli-Palestinian power relations. Finally, Ron Kronish (ch. 18) points to the dual role of religion in this conflict, first as a peace spoiler, hijacked by radical Judaism and extremist Islamism, and then as an important force for good in promoting interreligious dialogue and intercommunal peacebuilding.

Indeed, as the chapters in Part IV demonstrate, it is often the role of domestic actors – as well as socio-economic and political cleavages in Israeli and Palestinian societies – which has proven to be the most effective barrier to sustained cooperation. Dag Tuastad (ch. 19) shows how internal divisions between Palestinian factions over how best to end the Israeli occupation have for years prevented the creation of a unified political system that enjoys wider popular support, while Oded Haklai (ch. 20) points to how the increased fragmentation of the Israeli political system has effectively shattered the left-of-centre camp and provided opponents of territorial compromise with multiple opportunities to impede peacemaking efforts. Moreover, the rise of ultranationalist right-wing politics in Israel since the election of Benjamin Netanyahu in 2009 has directly contributed to the further marginalisation (and in some cases criminalisation) of Israel's Palestinian citizens, who are a fifth of the population. This has been most acutely manifested in the passing of the "Nakba Law" by the Knesset in 2011, which authorised the finance minister to revoke funding for institutions that reject the Jewish character of the state or mourn Israel's Independence Day as the *Nakba*, the catastrophe of the Palestinian exodus during the first Arab-Israeli war, and more recently the 2018 "Basic-Law: Israel – the Nation-State of the Jewish People," which removed Arabic as an official language, and established the development of Jewish settlement as a national value, among other clauses. As Maha Nasser notes in her chapter on the Palestinian citizens of Israel (ch. 21), such and similar policies have given rise to the framework of settler-colonialism to "make sense of the relationship between Palestinian citizens of Israel and the state, as well as to connect this group of Palestinians to the Palestinian people as a whole." For Israel, such policies raise fundamental challenges to the state's claim of being Jewish and democratic, as Mohammed Wattad discusses in ch. 22. Against this background of political fragmentation over the past two decades, Galia Golan (ch. 23) shows that while citizen-to-citizen diplomacy and civil society groups have grown in numbers, their "success" inasmuch as it concerns the revival of a peace discourse and intercommunal dialogue, has been limited to mostly single-issue and localised activities. An important aspect of such activities is the role of feminist peace and anti-occupation voices in Israel and Palestine. Unfortunately, as Siobhan Byrne demonstrates in ch. 24, although feminist cross-community coalitions have existed in the conflict for decades, women's peacebuilding initiatives have gradually dwindled following the demise of the peace process, in line with the general trend of declining peace activism across Israeli and Palestinian civil societies.

While primary blame for the continuation of the conflict should be firmly directed at the parties themselves and the socio-political domestic cleavages that encourage more unilateralism and less cooperation, it is nevertheless imperative to place Israeli-Palestinian relations in a broader context of their wider region and indeed the international system. Starting with the role of the Ottomans (see ch. 2 by Alan Dowty) and then the French and British colonial powers in carving up the region (the Sykes-Picot Agreement of 1916) and promising the same land to the two peoples (the 1915 McMahon-Hussein correspondence and the 1917 Balfour Declaration), the conflict had been shaped by outside intervention since its early days. The chapters in Part V of this volume review the role of external actors in shaping the conflict. Alan Craig (ch. 25) examines the changing function and approach of the UN to conflict through the prisms of Arab-Israeli wars and diplomacy, the Israeli-Palestinian peace process, and UN declaratory processes. In chapters 26 and 27, Ahmad Barakat and Costanza Musu (respectively) examine how the Arab world and the European Union (and its predecessors) have engaged with the Israeli-Palestinian conflict; while the means and methods of these actors' engagement with the conflict have varied considerably over time, it is noteworthy that both have struggled to truly assert their leverage and relevance beyond the rhetorical level, certainly compared to the ubiquity of the United States as the seemingly indispensable third party in the conflict (ch. 28 by Jonathan Rynhold), a position which has been sustained for decades with the help of the pro-Israel lobby in the United States and the "special relationship" between the two countries (ch. 29 by Shaiel Ben-Ephraim). Finally, Derek Averre (ch. 30) examines Russia's historic engagement with the conflict and especially its more recent attempts to position itself as a credible diplomatic alternative, certainly against the background of a gradual American withdrawal from its security commitments in the Middle East.

The final part of this volume is dedicated to several issues that shed a different light on the current state of affairs of Israeli-Palestinian relations. The chapters in Part VI address some of the "other images" of the conflict and show how they correspond to the "war of narratives" and the gradual demise of the peace process from the second decade of this century. Nowhere is this more acutely mirrored than in Palestinian and Israeli public-opinion polls. As Dahlia Scheindlin shows in ch. 31, both societies have exhibited similar patterns in their outlooks on the conflict and their support for the two-state solution, from hard-line/maximalist positions until the late 1980s, followed by increasing legitimacy for the two-state solution in the 1990s and 2000s, and then decline in support in the 2010s. Importantly, however, it remains the preferred solution in both societies compared to the alternatives of the one-state, binational solution, or the status quo. A more immediate picture of the daily realities of the conflict can be gained by examining the construction of Israeli and Palestinian identities in popular culture. As Anastasia Valassopoulos shows in ch. 32, television, music, documentaries, cinema, and short videos offer an unmitigated insight into pertinent themes in the contemporary political and cultural context, such as "the price of security; the relationship to the Diaspora; an intimate look at Palestinian-Israeli citizens; youth cultures and their interpolation of history; empowerment through alternative genres and ultimately, participation *in* and engagement *with* a *global* cultural economy."

One of the most contentious consequences of the demise of the peace process, coupled with the continuation of the occupation, was the launching of the Boycott, Divestment, and Sanctions (BDS) Movement in 2005, designed to appeal to international civil society to bring pressure on Israel to end its occupation of Palestinian territories, to achieve full equality for Israel's Palestinian citizens, and to ensure the right of Palestinian refugees to return to their homes. As Maia Hallward shows (ch. 33), the debates surrounding the motivations and aims of the BDS movement have become highly charged in recent years and reflect on, among others, "rival interpretations of international law, conceptions of justice, and varying understandings of root and contemporary causes of the conflict between Israelis and Palestinians." While BDS activities have so far failed to achieve any of the movement's stated aims, they have been more effective in challenging Israel's international image and delegitimizing its narrative as "the only democracy in the Middle East," doing so through more localised campaigns such as the calls to boycott the 2019 Eurovision song contest in Tel Aviv, or the targeted boycotting of Israeli artists, sportspeople, and academics abroad. The next three chapters touch more specifically on the role of academia and the education system as battlegrounds where the war of narratives often takes place in the most vociferous manner. As Matthew Berkman shows (ch. 34), campus contestation around the conflict (especially in the United States) and more specifically the policies and legitimacy of Israel dates back to the 1950s. However, the re-birth of Palestine solidarity activism following the demise of the peace process in the 2000s ushered in a new era in the antagonisation (some would say radicalization) of campus politics in relation to the conflict, supported on one side by the BDS movement and manifested through activities such as "Israeli Apartheid Week" and the boycotting of Israeli speakers on college campuses, and countered on the other side by individual donors and organisations committed to strengthening Jewish and pro-Israel groups on campus and delegitimizing anti-Israel campaigners as anti-Semitic and "dishonest purveyors of double standards."

The debates surrounding academic freedom and the delegitimization wars in the "conflict over the conflict" (Stern 2020) on university campuses cannot be separated from how the conflict is taught and studied, from primary to tertiary education (see ch. 35 by Ayman Agbaria and Aline Muff, and ch. 36 by Imogen Watson). As noted above, there are some notable attempts to teach the opposing narratives side by side, such as Neil Caplan's *Contested Histories*, Sami Adwan et al.'s *Side by Side* and Paul Scham et al.'s *Shared Narratives*, as well as the *Parallel Histories* project, which called on educators to not "shy away from competing narratives – seek them out, lay them side by side and challenge your students to immerse themselves in both" (Parallel Histories, n.d.). This "dual narrative" approach is, however, effectively absent in the civic and history curricula of both Israeli and Palestinian education systems. According to Adwan, Bar-Tal and Wexler (2016), books, maps, and illustrations on both sides present unilateral national narratives that show the other as an enemy (75% in the Israeli system and 81% in the Palestinian system), while information about the other's religions, culture, economic and daily activities is inadequate or absent. Moreover, only 4 per cent of maps in Palestinian textbooks label the territory beyond the West Bank as "Israel," while 76 per cent of maps in Israeli textbooks do not label the Palestinian territories. In both cases, the portrayed reality is that of a homeland where the "other" does not exist.

The concluding chapter, by Uriel Abulof (ch. 37), touches on many of the themes presented in this volume. Asking why Israelis and Palestinians have come to see peace as a "lost cause, an aspirational relic," he turns to the biblical stories about Judge Samson and King Solomon to reflect on four key emotions that underpin the Israeli-Palestinian conflict: the fantasy of power, the fault of trust, the fear of humiliation, and the faith-fuelled fury against enemies. He concludes that as long as both peoples are trapped in such a mindset, the prospects of an "emotional and moral awakening" seem rather distant.

This need for this self-realisation is evident in Sandy Tolan's *The Lemon Tree* (2006), a story of a thirty-year friendship between a Palestinian man (Bashir) and an Israeli woman (Dalia) amidst violence and political tensions. Reflecting on the fact that over the years their political differences had remained great while their personal relations were as warm as ever, Dalia reaches the inevitable conclusion about the tragedy of the conflict – and the hope for its resolution:

> "We couldn't find two people who could disagree more on how to visualize the viability of this land," Dalia said, standing and slipping on her sandals. "And yet we are so deeply connected. And what connects us? The same thing that separates us. This land."
>
> "Our enemy," she said softly, "is the only partner we have."

References

Adwan, S., D. Bar-On, E. Naveh, and Peace Research Institute in the Middle East. 2012. *Side by Side: Parallel Histories of Israel-Palestine*. New York: New Press.

Adwan, S., D. Bar-Tal, and B. E. Wexler. 2016. "Portrayal of the Other in Palestinian and Israeli Schoolbooks: A Comparative Study." *Political Psychology* 37:2, 201–217.

Aly, A. M. S, S. Feldman, and K. Shikaki. 2013. *Arabs and Israelis: Conflict and Peacemaking in the Middle East*. New York: Palgrave.

Bar-Ilan, D. 1996. "The Arab-Israeli Conflict Is Over: No, That's too Logical." *Middle East Quarterly* 3:3, 12–24.

Caplan, N. 2020. *The Israeli-Palestinian Conflict: Contested Histories*. Hoboken, NJ: John Wiley & Sons, 2nd ed.
Elshinnawi. M. 2011. "Egypt-Israel: A Cold Peace Could Get Colder." *Voice of America*. 19 September. Available at: www.voanews.com/middle-east/egypt-israel-cold-peace-could-get-colder.
Gatlung, J. 1969. "Violence, Peace, and Peace Research." *Journal of Conflict Resolution* 6:3, 167–191.
Haddad, T. 2018. *Palestine Ltd.: Neoliberalism and Nationalism in the Occupied Territory*. London: Bloomsbury.
Horovitz, D., and P. Hirschberg. 1997. [Israel]. *The American Jewish Year Book*, 97, 428–496.
Israel Ministry of Foreign Affairs (MFA). 2000. "Statement and Press Conference by Prime Minister Barak Regarding the Camp David Summit – 25 July 2000." 25 July. Available at: https://mfa.gov.il/MFA/ForeignPolicy/MFADocuments/Yearbook13/Pages/147%20%20Statement%20and%20press%20conference%20by%20Prime%20Minis.aspx.
Israel Ministry of Foreign Affairs (MFA). 2012. "Summary of Editorials from the Hebrew Press." 24 July. Available at: www.mfa.gov.il/mfa/pressroom/2012/pages/editorials-24-jul-2012.aspx.
Lewis, P., and H. Sherwood. 2014. "John Kerry in Final Push to Disprove Cynics on Middle East Peace Deal." *The Guardian*. 30 January. Available at: www.theguardian.com/world/2014/jan/30/john-kerry-israel-palestinian-ambitious-peace-deal-fade.
Middle East Monitor. 2021. "Kushner Describes Palestine-Israel Conflict as 'Real Estate Dispute'". 18 March. Available at: www.middleeastmonitor.com/20210318-kushner-describes-palestine-israel-conflict-as-real-estate-dispute/.
Miller, A. D. 2005. "Israel's Lawyer". Washington Post, 23 May. Available at: www.washingtonpost.com/wp-dyn/content/article/2005/05/22/AR2005052200883.html.
Mi'Ari M. 1999. "Attitudes of Palestinians toward Normalization with Israel." *Journal of Peace Research* 36:3, 339–348.
Palestinian Center for Policy and Survey Research (PSR). 2017. *Palestinian Israeli Pulse: A Joint Poll*. Available at: www.pcpsr.org/sites/default/files/Joint%20PAL-ISR%20Poll%202%20English%20Summary_9%20February%202017.pdf.
Parallel Histories. N.d. www.parallelhistories.org.uk/.
Riedel, B. 2019. "25 Years on, Remembering the Path to Peace for Jordan and Israel." *Brookings*. 23 October. Available at: www.brookings.edu/blog/order-from-chaos/2019/10/23/25-years-on-remembering-the-path-to-peace-for-jordan-and-israel/.
Roy, S. 2012. "Reconceptualizing the Israeli-Palestinian Conflict: Key Paradigm Shifts." *Journal of Palestine Studies* 41:3, 71–91.
Rubin, B. 1996. "The Arab-Israeli Conflict Is Over." *Middle East Quarterly* 3:3, 3–12.
Said, E. 1984. "Permission to Narrate." *Journal of Palestine Studies* 13:3, 27–48.
Scham, P., W. Salem, and B. Pogrund. 2005. *Shared Histories: A Palestinian-Israeli Dialogue*. Walnut Creek, CA: Left Coast Press.
Schmemann, S., S. Nusseibeh, and A. Oz. 2010. "Two States of Being." *New York Times*, 2 December. Available at: www.nytimes.com/2010/12/02/opinion/global/02iht-GA05nusseibeh.html
Stern, K. S. 2020. *The Conflict Over the Conflict: The Israel/Palestine Campus Debate*. Toronto: University of Toronto Press.
Tessler, M. 2009. *A History of the Israeli-Palestinian Conflict*. Bloomington and Indianapolis, IN: Indiana University Press, 2nd ed.
Tolan, S. 2006. *The Lemon Tree: An Arab, A Jew, and the Heart of the Middle East*. New York: Bloomsbury.
United Nations. *The 1947 UN Partition Plan and the 1949 Armistice Line*. Available at: www.un.org/unispal/document/auto-insert-208958/.

PART I

Setting the Context

1

THE HISTORIOGRAPHY OF THE ISRAEL-PALESTINE CONFLICT

Neil Caplan

While historians have many ways of portraying the clash between Zionism and the Arabs in Palestine and Israel, the two most frequently used are the colonial-settler-state paradigm and the clash-of-nationalisms model.[1]

According to the first, a conflict exists because the pre-1948 *yishuv* (Jewish settlement in Palestine) and later the state of Israel are an unwelcome modern-day, European "crusader" intrusion into a largely Arab homeland and Muslim Holy Land. Israel, created in 1948, is a colonial settler-state, and its motive force, Zionism, is a colonialist movement whose purpose is to populate this territory with foreign Jews, taking possession of the land by subjugating, dispossessing, or expelling the indigenous population. The conflict will persist until Palestinians achieve their national self-determination in a Palestinian state by defeating Israel, either by expelling Israelis and/or by de-Zionising the Jewish society living there (see, for example, Avnery 1971, ch.5; Ochsenwald 1976; Haddad 1992). This approach sometimes coincides with proposals for a "one-state solution" to the dispute.

The other approach posits a clash of nationalisms at the core of the conflict. It regards Zionism as a national liberation movement that sought to rally Jews from their increasingly vulnerable minority status in their dispersion (diaspora) and to facilitate their ingathering into their ancient, Biblical homeland. In the course of this quest, Zionist settlers encountered another people already inhabiting the land and seeking its own national liberation on the same territory. The clash is therefore between two valid national movements, each seeking fulfilment of its national aspirations over the same territory (see, for example, Talmon 1970; Tsur, 1977; O'Brien, 1986). Consistent with current advocacy of a "two-state solution," the conflict will persist until both parties are able to enjoy self-determination, each in a *part* of the disputed territory.

Many commentators gravitate towards one of these models to the exclusion of the other. Accepting exclusively the Zionist narrative of return contradicts the Palestinian narrative of being invaded and colonized, while subscribing exclusively to the colonialist interpretation undermines the legitimacy of Jewish nationalism and the Zionist case. Some analysts, however, view both as being simultaneously valid. Nascent Arab nationalism and emerging Zionism operated within the broader contexts of the rise of nation-states in Europe and a European thrust of economic, political, and cultural power over the declining 400-year-old Ottoman

DOI: 10.4324/9780429027376-3

Empire. Most Jews who moved to Palestine after 1882 saw themselves as fleeing persecution and returning to their ancient homeland; from the perspective of the mostly Muslim Arabic-speaking inhabitants of the land, however, these Zionist immigrants were foreign intruders.

Polemics and Academics

Discussion of these contrasting approaches often degenerates into partisan bickering. In recent decades the colonial-settler-state prism has enjoyed great and sometimes uncritical popularity among scholars around the world. In some circles, this portrayal is reinforced by an enumeration of the crimes and sins of Zionism and Israel, without nuance or weighing of evidence. To Ilan Troen (2007), a Brandeis-based expert on Israel, this way of presenting the conflict represented a "paradigm shift" from earlier scholarship, bypassing arguments that had at one time been convincing enough among Western governments and academia to produce a widespread consensus on Jewish-Zionist national rights. Others who reject the colonial-settler model have argued that Zionists and Israelis are not modern-day crusaders but rather an authentic indigenous people, restoring their deep roots in the area (see, for example, Shimoni 2007; Mansdorf 2010; Ohana 2012; Joffe 2017).

Some of these counterattacks also question the motives of those who promote the colonial-settler-state narrative. Noting the change in attitudes towards Israel in Western academe in the 1970s, Haifa University historian Yoav Gelber characterized the situation as follows:

> The same Palestinian slogans that had made little impression on European public opinion between the two world wars and in the aftermath of 1948 now found fertile ground in Europe's newfound postcolonial guilt. The process was encouraged by Arab petrodollars and other forms of funding and spread to American universities and later even to Israel. … Palestinians are portrayed as hapless objects of violence and Israeli oppression, Israeli–Transjordanian collusion, and treacherous British and Arab diplomacy. Some describe Israelis as intransigent, merciless, and needlessly callous usurpers who cynically exploited the Holocaust to gain world support for Jewish statehood at the expense of Palestinian rights to their country
>
> *(2007, 65; see also Gelber 2011)*

There are, no doubt, both noble and nefarious reasons why at any given time one paradigm becomes popular at the expense of another. But the colonial paradigm cannot simply be explained away as an artificial product of postcolonial guilt and shifts in academic and international politics. What gets lost in critiques like the one quoted above is the fact that the colonial-settler-state model of Zionism is not just a superimposed intellectual construct but also an integral part of actual Palestinian experience – just as the Jews' longing for a return to Zion is a genuine reflection of their diaspora experience and not merely a product of brainwashing. Unfortunately, too many scholars on both sides of this debate mimic the myopic belief held by the parties to the conflict that "*our* narrative tells the facts; *their* narrative is propaganda."

Contemporary treatments of Zionism as a colonial-settler movement are not new, but rather are the latest expression of claims and arguments that have been presented by Palestinian and Arab nationalists since the early 1920s, if not earlier. These arguments found their first powerful expression in George Antonius's influential book, *The Arab Awakening* (1938, esp. 386–412). Other major contributors to this approach in later decades have been French scholar Maxime Rodinson, in his seminal essay, "Israël: fait colonial?" (1967) and the dean of Palestinian historians, Walid Khalidi, whose publications include *From Haven to Conquest*

(1971) and *Before Their Diaspora* (1984). In 1979, Edward Said, the late Palestinian-American scholar and activist, published *The Question of Palestine* (1979) The chapter titles and subtitles used in this much-reprinted and oft-quoted book capture the essence of the anti-colonial critique. Part Two is entitled "Zionism from the standpoint of its victims," and is subdivided into two discussions: "Zionism and the attitudes of European colonialism" and "Zionist population, Palestinian depopulation." A more radical exponent of this approach is Columbia University's Joseph Massad, who has argued that the very phrase "Israeli–Palestinian conflict" is misleading because the word "conflict" implies a balance and symmetry between two equally legitimate contestants. For Massad, we should rather be talking about a colonial-settler invasion, an aggression perpetrated by one supremacist, racist party (Zionists) against another party (Palestinians) simply attempting to defend itself (2006, 143, 152–153, 161).

In a debate that patently fails to persuade those who subscribe to the view that Zionism is a form of colonialism, writers like Troen, Gelber, and others advance counterarguments that either reject the colonialist analogy outright or point to qualifications that would distinguish Zionism from "pure" forms of colonialism. Troen, for example, describes the Zionist attitude as one of building a new society that sought to reject, rather than reproduce, European realities in the Middle East:

> Adaptation, transformation and rejection of Europe reverberated throughout the intellectual and cultural reality of the Yishuv. It was patently clear that Zionism was not engaging in mere imitation or in direct transplantation. Zionists did not see themselves as foreigners or conquerors. For centuries in the Diaspora they had been strangers. In Eretz Israel they expended enormous creative energy to feel at home, as if they were natives. It was this rejuvenation that convinced a large portion of the world community that Jews were entitled to independence within that portion of the country they had so distinctively marked.
>
> *(2007, 875)*

Among the other arguments (Penslar 2007, 91, ch.5; Gelber 2007, 64–69. Cf. Shafir 2007; Pappé 2014, 102–104) advanced against the "Zionism = colonialism" model are that

- Zionist settlement and colonizing were nation-building activities of a people wishing to reintegrate themselves with the land, rather than create an outpost to exploit its resources for the benefit of a foreign metropolis.
- Zionists' use of force came about not as part of an original plan of aggressive conquest, but as a defensive response to Arab violence.
- Zionists purchased land, rather than conquered or stole it.
- Zionism contained a mixture of elements of "colonial, anti-colonial and post-colonial discourse and practice."

The debate over whether to view the conflict in accordance with the colonial-settler-state paradigm or the rival clash-of-nationalisms paradigm is one that probably can never be won. Well-intentioned dialogues among Palestinian and Israeli scholars, however open-minded to start with, tend to degenerate into inconclusive and at times heated tit-for-tat debates when the issue of Zionism-as-nationalism versus Zionism-as-colonialism is brought up (Scham, Salem, and Pogrund 2005, 75–91). Beyond the polemics, however, both these contested versions of the conflict deserve to be seen as authentic expressions of the protagonists' respective narratives. Some analysts have chosen to regard this not as an either/or choice, but rather as one of viewing

Zionism simultaneously as a movement of conquest (of Palestine) *and* of national liberation (of Jews). "There is no reason," concludes Columbia University's Rashid Khalidi, "why both positions cannot be true" (2006, xxxiii–xxxiv).

On the Shortcomings of "Myths versus Facts"

In both historical and contemporary arguments, Israelis and Palestinians and their respective supporters cling to their narratives and are quick to dismiss contesting versions as being based on myth, propaganda, or lies. Often this simplistic presentation of the history of the dispute – lining up and reinforcing one party's (true) "facts" against the other's (false) "myths" – provides vivid talking points used in debates and campus advocacy skirmishes.

The conflict's long history has been accompanied by the publication of many one-sided books, pamphlets, and articles, displaying varying levels of sophistication and often buttressed by legitimate scholarship. A sampling of titles through the decades is revealing: *Palestine: The Reality* (1939); *Palestine through the Fog of Propaganda* (1946); *Myths and Facts: A Guide to the Arab–Israeli Conflict* (2012 etc.);[2] *Battleground: Fact and Fantasy in Palestine* (1973, 1985); *Know the Facts* (1985). Critical readers soon discover that the real intention of these publications is less to enlighten than to score points in the ongoing debates between firm believers in either the Israeli-Zionist or the Palestinian-Arab point of view.

These publications are only one illustration of this battle which is as old as the conflict itself. Although communications technology and formats change, many of today's media and online debates replicate the old familiar pattern of our "facts" versus their "myths." On many college campuses, free and open discussion of controversial ideas is overtaken by heated, and sometimes toxic, clashes between passionate pro-Palestinian and pro-Israeli advocacy groups. The Internet abounds with similar binary ways of laying out the issues in dispute. Among the leading websites that foster this adversarial stance are the Jewish Virtual Library's "Myths & Facts" page (which comes up directly when clicking on a link called "Arab-Israeli Conflict"), "The Electronic Intifada" and "Palestine Remembered." Those seeking greater understanding of why the parties fight, and whether and under what conditions they may be able to reconcile their differences, would not be well served by excessive reliance on such one-sided resources. By its very essence, the myths-versus-facts approach marshals facts selectively and manipulates data using a wide gamut of rhetorical tools for the purpose of advancing one cause and discrediting its rival.

Objectivity and Bias in Academe

Professors and students of history and historical methodology are constantly faced with the challenges posed by bias, and more acutely so when the subject is the Israel-Palestine conflict. One basic lesson that all scholars learn is to appreciate the limits of objectivity; pure objectivity, they discover sooner or later, does not exist.[3] Even the most neutral, unbiased scholars must necessarily employ some degree of selection (inclusion/exclusion) and emphasis in the course of constructing their chronological or analytical treatments of the past. Writing of history is necessarily based on personal choices and decisions of the writer. Historians are not mere chroniclers; they not only report events, but often mirror and transmit the arguments and positions adopted by the conflicting parties they are studying. Given that all historians consciously and unconsciously inject context and personal perspective into the bare bones of any story they are reconstructing from the past, the real questions are not about "bias" versus "no bias," but rather about *which* biases are in play and how readers ought to compensate for them in assessing authors and their works on this conflict.

The halls of academe, where we would expect a strong measure of objectivity and accuracy, are often venues of partisanship, distortion, and advocacy when it comes to the Israel-Palestine conflict. A great responsibility falls to students and researchers to navigate through competing slanted versions of history. The quest for reliable, credible scholarship is hampered in this field of study by an overabundance of "nationalist historians," who were once defined by Sylvia Haim as those who devote their "abilities and scholarship to the greater glorification of [their] nation or community." Her main criticism was aimed at George Antonius, author of the classic *The Arab Awakening*. The author, she believed, needed

> to be assessed as a nationalist historian. Seeing that he deals with the actions of men in power, with right and wrong, and generally with what human beings do to each other, he is not permitted to set himself up as the defender of one imperfect cause against another – and all political causes are imperfect. Should he attempt to do so, this but shows a failure in his professional integrity.
>
> *(1953, 248–249)*

During the mid-1980s the editors of a compendium of articles on the conflict described the problems of academic bias in these terms:

> Even among scholars who are supposed to be objective observers, the conflict has engendered emotional intensity. … Scholars are not immune to the passions that animate the belligerents, who adhere to differing versions of history to support their respective claims. This tug-of-war between scholars … has manifested itself in contradictory arguments along the same lines which the belligerents themselves use.
>
> *(Lukacs and Battah 1988, 3)*

More recently, the editor of the *Encyclopedia of the Palestinians* has similarly lamented the "fusion of ideology and scholarship" in a field that "is dominated by partisans … who have used scholarship and journalism to galvanize their people, to gain world support, and as a weapon against one another in their struggle over Palestine" (Mattar 2005, xv).

In the last few years, academics dealing with the Israel-Palestine dispute have found themselves even more intensely embattled, as if to keep pace with the exacerbation of the unresolved conflict on the ground. The spillover from scholarship into advocacy in writing, lecturing, and on websites is more prevalent today than ever. It has become commonplace for bona fide scholars to willingly lend their academic credentials to the promotion of one version of the conflict while discrediting the other. Compare, for example, the pro-Palestinian "Faculty for Israeli–Palestinian Peace" with the pro-Israeli "Scholars for Peace in the Middle East." The first defines itself as an "Educational Network for Human Rights in Palestine/Israel," while the second calls itself "an international community of scholars dedicated to promoting academic integrity … with regard to the conflict between Israel and its Arab neighbours." Both promote what they call "educational" tours of the region and issue "research" publications, but their tours and publications are often sophisticated variants, in academic garb, of the problematic myths-versus-facts approach described above. Also, advocacy-inspired but more seriously oriented to research are two US-based organizations. The Palestinian American Research Center (PARC) is devoted to "improv[ing] scholarship about Palestinian affairs, expand[ing] the pool of experts knowledgeable about the Palestinians, and strengthen[ing] linkages among Palestinian, American, and foreign research institutions and scholars." The Israel Institute is mandated to "enhance knowledge about modern Israel through the expansion of accessible, innovative learning opportunities, on and beyond campus." Standing apart from the many partisan websites that advance the correctness of the Palestinian cause over the Israeli or vice versa, only a few online resources may be said to promote a genuinely even-handed approach to both the Palestinian and Israeli sides of the dispute.[4]

Israel's "New Historians"

With the opening of 1948 materials in many archives, a new generation of scholars eagerly probed the past through these primary sources, producing a wave of revisionist PhD theses and monographs on the Israel-Palestine conflict. Although not the first to challenge the sacred cows of official Zionist history, Benny Morris, Avi Shlaim, Ilan Pappé and others piloted a new wave of activist and committed archives-based scholarship in the late 1980s. Despite their differences in methodology and ideological leanings, they were lumped together by many critics as being on a "mission" or "crusade" under the banner of "new historians" (Morris 1988, 11–28; Penslar 2007, 23; M. Bar-On 1988, 23).

In *Collusion Across the Jordan* (1988) Oxford-based Avi Shlaim published ground-breaking research on Israel-Transjordan relations during the late 1940s, challenging the mainstream narrative of the Israeli War of Independence wherein little David (Israel) successfully fought off the giant Goliath (Arabs). Shlaim's account presented the emerging Jewish state as a tough negotiating partner, intoxicated by recent battlefield victories and seemingly uninterested in making sacrifices for peace.[5] Shlaim's iconoclastic conclusions flowed from his belief that the historian's "most fundamental task" is "to subject the claims of all the protagonists to rigorous scrutiny and to reject all those claims, however deeply cherished, that do not stand up to such scrutiny" (Shlaim 1999, 177).

Ilan Pappé, an admirer of American public intellectuals Edward Said and Noam Chomsky, went beyond merely debunking the Zionist narrative to openly embracing the rival narrative of the Palestinians as victims resisting Zionist colonial oppressors. Among his many publications is the provocatively titled *The Ethnic Cleansing of Palestine* (2006b). In an earlier work, *A History of Modern Palestine: One Land, Two Peoples,* Pappé defines his credo as follows:

> My bias is apparent despite the desire of my peers that I stick to facts and the "truth" when reconstructing past realities. I view any such construction as vain and presumptuous. This book is written by one who admits compassion for the colonized not the colonizer; who sympathizes with the occupied not the occupiers. … . He feels for women in distress, and has little admiration for men in command. … In short, mine is a subjective approach, often but not always standing for the defeated over the victorious.
>
> *(2006a, 11–12)*

Like Shlaim and Pappé, Benny Morris' career began with the publication of new findings that challenged many of the accepted Israeli and pro-Israeli views on 1948. His detailed research into the expulsion and flight of the Palestinian refugees undermined Israeli claims about the alleged voluntary, or Arab-inspired, exodus of Palestinians. From the files and from interviews, Morris (1987) reconstructed multiple episodes of crimes and misbehaviour by Zionist militias and Israeli soldiers, including intimidation, expulsions and looting, but fell short of concluding that there had been a Zionist master plan for ethnic cleansing.[6] Morris (2004) describes his own quest for objectivity as follows:

> [W]hile historians, as citizens, ha[ve] political views and aims, their scholarly task [is] to try to arrive at the truth about a historical event or process, to illuminate the past as objectively and accurately as possible. [Unlike Ilan Pappé,] I ... believe that there is such a thing as historical truth; that it exists independently of, and can be detached from, the subjectivities of scholars ... . When writing history, the historian should ignore contemporary politics and struggle against his political inclinations as he tries to penetrate the murk of the past.

While these intentions to keep personal views out of scholarship may be admirable as declared, Morris, Shlaim, Pappé and other new historians seem noticeably unable to insulate their historical research from their views on contemporary controversies.

Despite ideological and methodological divergences among themselves, this cohort of scholars shared a common mission to challenge a series of myths associated with the accepted narrative of the Israeli War of Independence. At the time, some inside Israel joined Palestinians and Israel's critics abroad in welcoming the findings of these new historians as vindicating their personal views. Some looked forward to the corrective effect this new scholarship could have in revising mainstream histories that had displayed an overdose of self-glorification or an unduly myopic perspective. In the view of many historians, the very launching of these debates could only be good for the professional study of the history of the conflict.

But many others in Israel and the Jewish world were taken aback to see their erstwhile heroes and heroines portrayed in such unflattering ways. Not many were happy to be told that the Zionist saga and the creation of Israel were tainted by "original sin" because of the way the first Israelis treated the Palestinians. Fresh research on 1948 seemed to show the state's very foundation as something less than the miraculous victory of beleaguered underdogs engaged in a life-or-death struggle against an implacable enemy dedicated to driving the Jews into the sea.

During the late 1980s and through the 1990s, Israeli public displeasure with the new historians (often mistakenly lumped together with "post-Zionist" and anti-Zionist scholars) provoked vigorous counterattacks. Some criticized the new historians for exploiting the imbalance in the availability of source materials, which disproportionately highlighted errors and omissions of Israeli-Zionist decision makers while having little or nothing to say about what their Arab and Palestinian counterparts were thinking and doing at the time. Others, less charitably, accused the new historians of engaging in an indiscriminate slaughter of sacred cows in a selfish pursuit of notoriety and career advancement. Still others challenged the accuracy of the newly revealed evidence.[7]

The "Missed-Opportunities" Approach

Beyond stirring up lively, sometimes nasty, public debates among Israelis and Jews, the phenomenon of the new historians had other repercussions for the historiography of the Israel-Palestine conflict. One of the immediate spin-offs of the appearance of the new historians was a surge in the use – and misuse – of the "missed-opportunities" approach to studying the elusiveness of Arab–Israeli peace. By this method, analysts and commentators review the history of the conflict with the aim of pointing out where protagonists have missed opportunities to resolve it. Many among Israel's new historians took to portraying the Israel-Palestine conflict as if it were primarily (or only) a series of opportunities for peace that Israel's leaders had unwisely missed.

The missed-opportunities approach relies heavily on counterfactual analysis, a complex field of inquiry pursued by philosophers and by international relations specialists.[8] But when research is driven by the goal of exposing and blaming those considered responsible for missing presumed opportunities, this approach risks losing its social-scientific integrity. This seems to be the case for many of the new historians, who have criticized Israeli leaders for not doing more to transform their limited armistice agreements, signed in 1949, into more stable peace treaties and for not responding more generously to overtures coming from the Arab side. This critique appeared first in Avi Shlaim's study of Syria's Husni Za'im (1986), and then in his later works, *Collusion Across the Jordan* and *The Iron Wall* (2014). Other researchers (Flapan 1987, 201–232; Segev 1986, 34–40; Pappé 1994, chs. 7–9; Shlaim 1999) buttressed Shlaim's critique, highlighting archival evidence that Israel's early leaders took conscious decisions demonstrating a preference for holding on to recently-acquired territory over a potential agreement with the defeated Arab states. These major historiographic debates over 1948 were followed by a similar flurry of academic controversy over whether Israeli leaders missed opportunities for peace with the Palestinians in 1967–1968, or with Egypt in the early 1970s (Gazit 1997; Finkelstein 2003; Shafir 2006; Raz 2012; Podeh 2015, ch. 10).

As with the second-guessing of Zionist and Israeli decision makers, there are also many writers who employ the missed-opportunities approach for the purpose of blaming the Arabs and Palestinians for the absence of peace. The late Israeli diplomat Abba Eban once quipped that the Arabs "never miss an opportunity to miss an opportunity," which became a stock phrase used by Israelis to condemn the other side whenever a window of opportunity was opened and slammed shut again. Most of those who quote this witty phrase do so in order to promote the view that, while Israel has always been ready to make sacrifices for peace, the Arabs and Palestinians were somehow unable to seize those opportunities – whether out of implacable enmity to Israel, inability to understand their own best interests, or incompetent leadership (for discussion, see Maoz 2006, ch. 10; Khalidi 2006, 291 fn.2; Podeh 2015, chs. 1–4). Some writers single out Palestinian rejection of the 1937 Peel and 1947 UNSCOP reports, both of which recommended a partition of the country, as evidence of a collective trait they call "extremism" and "rejectionism" (Schueftan 2008).

A number of scholars on both sides have sought to make more judicious use of newly opened archive material. One of the earliest examples of this effort at balance and nuance was Itamar Rabinovich's *The Road Not Taken: Early Arab–Israeli Negotiations* (1991), a work clearly intended as a corrective to the missed-opportunities approach as used by some new historians. In reviewing Israel's negotiations with Egypt, Syria, and Jordan in the wake of the 1948 fighting, Rabinovich spread the responsibility for the failure to achieve peace more evenly among the conflicting parties; his careful analysis can be tested, refined, or contradicted by further research and the integration of additional source materials as they become available.

Similarly, more nuanced and less accusatory critical scholarship asks whether Palestinians could realistically have been expected to endorse either of the partition proposals they rejected in 1937 and 1947. For example, would the boundaries proposed by Peel, restricting the proposed Jewish state to an enclave or mini-state in only 20 per cent of western Palestine, have remained on the table, given the Zionist leadership's energetic rejection of those boundary proposals? Would the Arab state proposed by Peel – areas of partitioned Palestine to be placed under the rule of Transjordan's Amir Abdullah – have been a viable one? And, perhaps most important, could the necessary population transfers have been successfully implemented? (see, for example, Wasserstein 2008, 109–114; Scham et al. 2005, 177–204).

Although unlikely to identify themselves as "new historians," Palestinian-Americans Philip Mattar and Rashid Khalidi are two scholars who have been developing their own critiques of the decisions taken by Palestinian leaders during the Mandate period and since. Mattar looks back to 1922–1923 to ask whether the Palestinian leaders' rejection of three successive British proposals for limited self-governing institutions deprived their people of a tool that might have slowed down the advance of Zionism and enhanced their own chances for statehood.[9] Khalidi's *The Iron Cage* (2006) is another example of an effective application of the missed-opportunities approach to Palestinian decision making. Khalidi raises a number of critical questions about what the Palestinians might have done differently:

- Could they have compromised before 1939 and agreed to some form of Jewish national home within the context of an Arab state in Palestine?
- Had they done so, would this have had any effect on the drive of the Zionist movement for an independent Jewish state in Palestine?
- Could they have benefited by reining in the violence of the revolt of 1936–1939 to win some political gains from it?

Reviewing the possible outcomes of these "what-if?" propositions in the circumstances of the 1930s and 1940s, Khalidi concludes that it would be "difficult or impossible" to imagine a successful trajectory either towards Palestinian statehood or reconciliation between Zionist and Palestinian national aspirations (2006, 33–34, 44–36, 64, 118–120). Similar careful counterfactual analysis could be used to examine whether the Palestinians should be blamed, or blame themselves, for missing another opportunity to contain or block the expansion of the Jewish national home when they decided after May 1939 to reject the MacDonald White Paper, rather than exploit its favourable clauses (Mattar and Caplan, forthcoming).

With notable exceptions like the work of Rabinovich, Khalidi, and Mattar, the missed-opportunities approach has not generally been conducive to producing solid scholarship about the nature of the conflict and the chances for its eventual resolution. Too many researchers have lapsed into simplistic certainties about what might have been, becoming part of a "blame game." A far better understanding of negotiation attempts can be had by examining a broader range of interwoven reasons why some fail and others succeed.[10]

Trends in Palestinian and Israeli Historiography

The early-1990s controversies sparked by Israel's new historians may have abated, but the historiography of the Israel-Palestine conflict continues to be plagued by highly polarizing intellectual disputes. Attacks on "new historians" and "post-Zionists" continue among right-wing and pro-Israel thinkers and writers, to the point where at least one post-Zionist historian has recently discerned a forceful "Neo-Zionist" reassertion of the classical Zionist narrative challenging the moral legitimacy of his own critical scholarship (Pappé 2014, esp. ch. 12).[11]

One remaining question deserves our attention: Why did critical, revisionist history of the conflict begin and flourish among Israelis while apparently bypassing Palestinian scholars? Why is there no Palestinian equivalent to the Israeli "new historians" phenomenon? Part of the explanation is structural. For a variety of reasons, primary sources in the form of diplomatic correspondence and memoranda are more plentiful and more easily accessible on the Israeli side. The Western institutionalization of open public archives is not generally replicated in the Arab world. The Palestinian community, stateless and dispersed, has lacked the structures and resources needed to facilitate and promote the accumulation of authoritative documentation on Palestinian history on the same scale as the rival Central Zionist Archives and Israel State Archives. For years, Palestinians relied on the PLO Research Center and the Institute for Palestine Studies, both based in Beirut, to collect and preserve these building blocks of their national heritage, but with much of the task of preservation of documents left to individuals and families. The relative scarcity of accessible written testimony is partially compensated for by a new generation of collectors of oral history.[12]

The asymmetrical power relationship between the two parties has also had implications for the writing of the history of the dispute. Ilan Pappé has claimed that Israel has not only colonized the Palestinians' land, but has also "colonized" the writing of their history. While Israel "had formed a state and employed the state's apparatus for successfully propagating its narrative in front of domestic as well as external publics," the weaker Palestinian party "was engaged in a national liberation struggle, unable to lend its historians a hand in opposing the propaganda of the other side" (2007, 2). Discounting such polemics, many Israelis involved in dialogue with Palestinians have nonetheless insisted that, now that they themselves have been subjected by their new historians to the painful process of myth-busting, it is time for the Palestinian side to do the same. Why, they ask, do we not see an equally energetic campaign to rewrite Palestinian history and subject its self-serving myths and narratives to rigorous scrutiny?

Palestinians offer several responses to this challenge by their Israeli counterparts. Within the context of the ongoing conflict, they point out, Israeli historians enjoy the luxury of criticizing their own side's "victor's history" with relative ease and impunity, risking only minor damage to the national self-image and (possibly, but not necessarily) personal career advancement. Palestinian academics cannot, they argue, be considered a parallel case. Being members of the weaker, defeated party and living largely under occupation or as guests in undemocratic host states, their historians cannot openly attack leaders or régimes, or engage in the slaughter of national sacred cows. They are loath, not unlike many Israelis, to engage in acts of self-criticism which may provide easy ammunition or comfort to the enemy.

There is another, perhaps more telling, reason why Palestinians do not find themselves replicating the crusading zeal of Israel's new historians. As Rashid Khalidi points out, the research findings of Israel's new historians have borne out the factual accuracy of "many elements of the standard Palestinian narrative" (2006, xxxiv; see also Kabha 2007, 301, 313–314) – thus leaving less to debunk on their own side. Some Palestinians take this point even further, viewing the emergence of Israel's new historians simply as a belated recognition of the non-tenability of the "old and distorted official history" of Zionism and Israel, and proof of the correctness and validity of their own Palestinian narrative. "The Palestinian historian," wrote poet Zakaria Mohammed (1999), cannot be "repentant," like Israel's new historians, "because he has nothing to confess to the 'priest of history'."[13]

Such sharply defined differences between the approaches of Israeli and Palestinian historians are a telling indication of how far apart scholars writing about the contested histories of Israel and Palestine remain. Similar dilemmas and disputes have occurred regarding the writing and revising of Israeli and Palestinian school textbooks.[14] Despite some interesting and original classroom experiments – notably the PRIME project's curriculum of parallel Israeli and Palestinian narratives aimed at children on both sides – the immediate results have been disappointing, largely owing to the effects of the conflict still being experienced on the street (see, for example, D. Bar-On and Adwan 2006; Jeffay 2010; Adwan et al. 2012; PRIME; Parallel Histories).

Several years before his death, Edward Said had welcomed the appearance of Israel's new historians, however imperfect their willingness to abandon parts of the Zionist narrative; he saw their work as an opportunity for both parties to engage in dialogue while scrutinizing their respective histories in a new critical spirit (Said 1998; Kabha 2007, 314–315; Pappé 2014, 131–132). But what is amply clear from many well-intentioned efforts during the last few decades to bring pro-Israeli and pro-Palestinian academics together is the extreme difficulty of arriving at a common project for revising their shared history, challenging myths, and criticizing both national narratives with even-handed rigour.

Notes

1 This chapter is adapted from the author's *The Israel-Palestine Conflict: Contested Histories*, 2nd ed., Wiley-Blackwell, 2020. The discussion limits itself to books and articles that have appeared in English.

2 A series begun by Wolf Blitzer under the title: *Myths and Facts: a concise record of the Arab-Israeli conflict* (Washington, DC.: Near East Report, 1964, 1976, 1982, 1985, 1992 etc.)

3 For discussions on the limits of objectivity, see, for example, Joyce Appleby, Lynn Hunt, and Margaret Jacob, *Telling the Truth about History* (New York: W. W. Norton, 1994), ch. 7; Richard J. Evans, *In Defense of History* (New York: W. W. Norton, 1999), ch. 8.

4 See, for example, "Parallel Histories: A New Way to Study Conflict," website accessed 19 May 2018 at www.parallelhistories.org.uk/; ProCon's page on this conflict at https://israelipalestinian.procon.org/; "Palestinian–Israeli Crossfire" at www.bitterlemons.net/; Peace Research Institute in the Middle East (PRIME) website at http://vispo.com/PRIME; Seeds of Peace website at www.seedsofpeace.org.

5 See also: Avi Shlaim, *The Iron Wall: Israel and the Arab World*, Updated and Expanded. (New York/ London: W. W. Norton, 2014), 51–55. For critiques see Neil Caplan, "From Powerlessness to Power: Zionism in Theory and Practice, 1882–1950," *The Historical Journal* 33:1 (March 1990), 177–188; N. Caplan, "Zionism and the Arabs: Another Look at the 'New' Historiography" (review essay), *Journal of Contemporary History* 36:2 (April 2001), 356–360.

6 See also Benny Morris, *The Birth of the Palestinian Refugee Problem Revisited*, Cambridge (UK / New York: Cambridge University Press), 2004. For the contrary view, see, for example, Walid Khalidi, "Plan Dalet Revisited: Master Plan for the Conquest of Palestine," *Journal of Palestine Studies* 18:1 (Autumn 1988), 3–37; Nur Masalha, *Expulsion of the Palestinians: The Concept of "Transfer" in Zionist Political Thought, 1882–1948* (Washington, DC: Institute for Palestine Studies, 1992); Pappé, *The Ethnic Cleansing of Palestine.*

7 On the new historians and the widespread controversies they initially aroused, see: Shabtai Teveth, "Charging Israel with Original Sin," *Commentary,* September 1989, available at: www.commentarymagazine.com/articles/charging-israel-with-original-sin/; *History & Memory* 7:1 (Spring/ Summer 1995), special issue: *Israeli Historiography Revisited*, ed. Gulie Ne'eman Arad; Penslar, *Israel in History*, chs. 1–2; M. Bar-On, "Historiography as an Educational Project," 21–38; Efraim Karsh, *Fabricating Israeli History: The 'New Historians'*, (London: Frank Cass, 2000, 2nd rev. ed.); Joseph Heller, *The Birth of Israel, 1945–1949: Ben-Gurion and His Critics* (Gainesville, FL: University Press of Florida, 2000), 295–307; *Israeli Historical Revisionism: From Left to Right*, eds. Anita Shapira and Derek J. Penslar, (London: Frank Cass, 2003).

8 For some of the challenges and limitations of counterfactual analysis, see: I. William Zartman, *Cowardly Lions: Missed Opportunities to Prevent Deadly Conflict and State Collapse* (Boulder, CO / London: Lynne Rienner, 2005), 3–5; Mordechai Bar-On, "Conflicting Narratives or Narratives of a Conflict: Can the Zionist and Palestinian Narrative of the 1948 War Be Bridged?" in *Israeli and Palestinian Narratives of Conflict: History's Double Helix*, ed. Robert I. Rotberg (Bloomington / Indianapolis: Indiana University Press, 2006), 157–158; Zeev Maoz, *Defending the Holy Land: A Critical Analysis of Israel's Security and Foreign Policy* (Ann Arbor: University of Michigan Press, 2006), 387–388.

9 Philip Mattar, unpublished manuscript. I am grateful to Dr. Mattar for sharing his draft with me.

10 For a study that explores historical patterns using seven interrelated factors affecting success and failure, see Laura Zittrain Eisenberg and Neil Caplan, *Negotiating Arab–Israeli Peace: Patterns, Problems, Possibilities* (2nd ed., Bloomington, IN: Indiana University Press, 2010). For political scientists' multifactor analyses of missed opportunities, see: Maoz, *Defending the Holy Land*, ch. 10; Podeh, *Chances for Peace*; Galia Golan, *Israeli Peacemaking Since 1967: Behind the Breakthroughs and Failures* (London: Routledge, 2015).

11 For recent critics of post-Zionism, see, for example, Avi Beker, "Exposing How Post-Zionists Manipulate History," *Post-Holocaust and Anti-Semitism* No. 100, 1 August 2010, available at: http://jcpa.org/article/exposing-how-post-zionists-manipulate-history/; Gelber, *Nation and History*. For a broad overview of recent currents of non-Zionist, post-Zionist and anti-Zionist thought, see Michael Brenner, *In Search of Israel: The History of an Idea* (Princeton University Press, 2018), ch. 6.

12 On the problems of Palestinian primary written and oral sources, see, for example, Saleh Abdel-Jawad, "The Arab and Palestinian Narratives of the 1948 War," in Robert I. Rotberg, ed., *Israeli and Palestinian Narratives of Conflict* (Bloomgton, IN: Indiana University Press, 2006), 72–114, esp. 95–103; Rashid Khalidi, *The Iron Cage*, xxxv–xxxviii; Scham et al., *Shared Histories*, 232–241, 265; Mattar, *Encyclopedia of the Palestinians*, xiv–xv; Nakba Archive, available at: http://nakba-archive.org/; Palestine Remembered website, available at: www.palestineremembered.com/.

13 See also the views of Wageh Kawthrani and Imad Abed al-Ghani, discussed in Kabha, "A Palestinian Look," 307, 313.

14 For some of the literature on the textbooks controversies, see Elie Podeh, "History and Memory in the Israeli Educational System: The Portrayal of the Arab–Israeli Conflict in History Textbooks (1948–2000)," *History & Memory* 12 (2000), 65–100, esp. 89–91; Nathan J. Brown, *Palestinian Politics after the Oslo Accords: Resuming Arab Palestine* (Berkeley, CA: University of California Press, 2003), ch. 6; Nathan J. Brown, "Contesting National Identity in Palestinian Education," in Robert I. Rotberg, ed., *Israeli and Palestinian Narratives of Conflict*, 225–243; Eyal Naveh, "The Dynamics of Identity Construction in Israel through Education in History," in Rotberg, ed., *Israeli and Palestinian Narratives of Conflict*, 244–270; Jennifer Miller, *Inheriting the Holy Land: An American's Search for Hope in the Middle East* (New York: Ballantine Books, 2005), 45–68.

Recommended Readings

Adwan, S., et al. 2012. *Side By Side: Parallel Histories of Israel-Palestine.* New York: The New Press.

Arad, G. N., guest ed. 1995. *Israeli Historiography Revisited.* Special Issue of *History & Memory: Studies in Representation of the Past*, 7:1.

Gelber, Y. 2011. *Nation and History: Israeli Historiography Between Zionism and Post-Zionism.* Portland, OR: Valentine Mitchell, 2011.

Karsh, E. 2000. *Fabricating Israeli History: The 'New Historians,'* 2nd rev. ed., London: Frank Cass.

Morris, B., ed. 2007. *Making Israel.* Ann Arbor, MI: University of Michigan Press.

Pappé, I., ed. 2007. *The Israel/Palestine Question: A Reader*, 2nd ed. London: Routledge.

Pappé, I. 2014. *The Idea of Israel: A History of Power and Knowledge.* London: Verso.

Rotberg, R. I., ed. 2006. *Israeli and Palestinian Narratives of Conflict: History's Double Helix.* Bloomington, IN: Indiana University Press, 2006.

Scham, P., W, Salem, and B. Pogrund, eds. 2005. *Shared Histories: A Palestinian–Israeli Dialogue.* Walnut Creek, CA: Left Coast Press.

Scham, P., B. Pogrund, and A. Ghanem, eds. 2013. *Shared Narratives – A Palestinian-Israeli Dialogue.* Special issue of *Israel Studies*, 18:2.

Shapira, A., and D. J. Penslar, eds. 2003. *Israeli Historical Revisionism: From Left to Right.* London: Frank Cass, 2003.

Questions for Discussion

(1) What are the main arguments that form part of the colonial-settler-state and clash-of-nationalisms paradigms? Which of the two paradigms do you find offers a more convincing understanding of the Israel-Palestine conflict?

(2) What are some of the factors affecting objectivity and bias in the writing and teaching of history, generally, and of this conflict in particular?

(3) What are some of the challenges facing academic scholarship dealing with the Israel-Palestine conflict?

(4) Why do you think writing and teaching about the Israel-Palestine conflict are so fraught with polemics and controversy over bias and objectivity?

(5) What are some of the advantages and drawbacks of focusing on "missed opportunities" of resolving the Israel-Palestine conflict?

(6) What are some of the positive contributions to the study of the Israel-Palestine conflict brought about by the emergence of the "new historians" in Israel? What are some of the main criticisms levelled against the "new historians"?

(7) Why has there been no "new historian" movement among Palestinian academics?

References

Abcarius, M. F. 1946. *Palestine through the Fog of Propaganda.* London: Hutchinson.

Adwan, S. et al. 2012. *Side By Side: Parallel Histories of Israel-Palestine.* New York: The New Press.

Antonius, G. 1938. *The Arab Awakening.* London: Hamish Hamilton.

Avnery, U. 1971. *Israel without Zionism: A Plan for Peace in the Middle East.* New York: Collier.

Bard, M. G., ed. 2012. *Myths and Facts: A Guide to the Arab–Israeli Conflict*. Chevy Chase, MD: American–Israeli Cooperative Enterprise. Available at: www.jewishvirtuallibrary.org/jsource/myths3/MythsEnglish2012.pdf.

Bar-On, D. and S. Adwan. 2006. "The Psychology of Better Dialogue between Two Separate but Interdependent Narratives," in *History's Double Helix*, ed. R. I. Rotberg. Bloomington, IN: Indiana University Press, 205–224.

Bar-On, M. 1988. "Historiography as an Educational Project: The Historians' Debate in Israel and the Middle East Peace Process," in *The Middle East Peace Process: Interdisciplinary Perspectives*, ed. I. Peleg. Albany: State University of New York Press, 21–40.

Electronic Intifada. https://electronicintifada.net/.

Evans, R. J. 1999. *In Defense of History*. New York: W. W. Norton.

Faculty for Israeli–Palestinian Peace. www.ffipp.org.

Finkelstein, N. G. 2003. *Image and Reality of the Israel–Palestine Conflict*. New York: W. W. Norton.

Flapan, S. 1987. *The Birth of Israel: Myths and Realities*. New York: Pantheon.

Gazit, M. 1997. "Egypt and Israel – Was There a Peace Opportunity Missed in 1971?" *Journal of Contemporary History* 32:1, 97–115.

Gelber, Y. 2007. "The History of Zionist Historiography: From Apologetics to Denial," in *Making Israel*, ed. B. Morris. Ann Arbor: University of Michigan Press, 47–80.

Gelber, Y. 2011. *Nation and History: Israeli Historiography Between Zionism and Post-Zionism*. Portland, OR: Valentine Mitchell.

Haddad, Y. 1992. "Islamists and the 'Problem of Israel': The 1967 Awakening." *Middle East Journal* 46:2, 266–285.

Haim, S. G. 1953. "'The Arab Awakening': A Source for the Historian?" *Die Welt des Islams*, n.s. vol. II.

Israel Institute. https://israelinstitute.org/.

Jeffay, N. 2010. "Banned Textbook Offers a Lesson in Mideast Politics," *Forward*, 3 December.

Jeffries, J. M. N. 1939. *Palestine: The Reality*. London: Longmans, Green and Company.

Jewish Virtual Library. Available at: www.jewishvirtuallibrary.org/jsource/myths/mftoc.html.

Joffe, A. 2017. "Palestinian Settler-Colonialism," *BESA Center Perspectives*, Paper No. 577 (3 September). Available at: https://besacenter.org/perspectives-papers/palestinians-settlers-colonialism/.

Kabha, M., 2007. "A Palestinian Look at the New Historians and Post-Zionism in Israel," in *Making Israel*, ed. B. Morris. Ann Arbor: University of Michigan Press, 299–318.

Karsh, E. 2000. *Fabricating Israeli History: The "New Historians,"* 2nd rev. ed., London: Frank Cass.

Katz, S. 1973. *Battleground: Fact and Fantasy in Palestine*, London/New York: W. H. Allen.

Katz, S. 1985. *Battleground: Fact and Fantasy in Palestine*, updated and expanded ed., New York/Jerusalem: Steimatsky.

Khalidi, R. 2006. *The Iron Cage: The Story of the Palestinian Struggle for Statehood*, Boston: Beacon, 2006.

Khalidi, W., ed. 1971. *From Haven to Conquest: Readings in Zionism and the Palestine Problem until 1948*. Beirut: Institute for Palestine Studies.

Khalidi, W. 1984. *Before Their Diaspora: A Photographic History of the Palestinians, 1876–1948*. Washington, DC: Institute for Palestine Studies.

Lukacs, Y., and A. M. Battah, eds. 1988. *The Arab–Israeli Conflict: Two Decades of Change*. Boulder, CO: Westview Press.

Mansdorf, I. J. 2010. "Is Israel a Colonial State? The Political Psychology of Palestinian Nomenclature," *Jerusalem Viewpoints* No. 576 (March-April). Available at: http://jcpa.org/article/is-israel-a-colonial-state-the-political-psychology-of-palestinian-nomenclature.

Maoz, Z. 2006. *Defending the Holy Land: A Critical Analysis of Israel's Security and Foreign Policy*. Ann Arbor: University of Michigan Press.

Massad, J. A. 2006. *The Persistence of the Palestinian Question: Essays on Zionism and the Palestinians*. London: Routledge.

Mattar, P., ed. 2005. *Encyclopedia of the Palestinians*, rev. ed. New York: Infobase Publishing.

Mattar, P., and N. Caplan. Forthcoming. *Missed Opportunities*.

Mohammed, Z. 1999. "New Palestinian Historians?" *al-Ayyam*, 4 November.

Morris, B. 1987. *The Birth of the Palestinian Refugee Problem, 1947–1949*. Cambridge: Cambridge University Press.

Morris, B. 1988. "The New Historiography: Israel Confronts its Past," in *Making Israel*, ed. B. Morris. Ann Arbor: The University of Michigan Press, 11–28.

Morris, B. 2004. "Politics by Other Means," *The New Republic*, 22 March. Available at: https://newrepublic.com/article/61715/politics-other-means-0.

Niv, D. 1985. *Know the Facts: A Historical Guide to the Arab-Israeli Conflict*. Department of Education and Culture, World Zionist Organization.
O'Brien, C. C. 1986. *The Siege: The Saga of Israel and Zionism*. New York: Simon and Schuster.
Ochsenwald, W. L. 1976. "The Crusader Kingdom of Jerusalem and Israel: An Historical Comparison." *Middle East Journal* 30:2, 221–226.
Ohana, D. 2012. *The Origins of Israeli Mythology: Neither Canaanites nor Crusaders*. Transl. David Maisel. New York: Cambridge University Press.
Palestinian American Research Center. http://parc-us-pal.org/.
Palestine Remembered. www.palestineremembered.com.
Pappé, I., ed. 2007. *The Israel/Palestine Question: A Reader*, 2nd ed. London: Routledge.
Pappé, I. 1994. *The Making of the Arab–Israeli Conflict, 1947–51*. London: I. B. Tauris.
Pappé, I. 2006a. *A History of Modern Palestine: One Land, Two Peoples*, 2nd ed., Cambridge: Cambridge University Press.
Pappé, I. 2006b. *The Ethnic Cleansing of Palestine*. Oxford: Oneworld Publications.
Pappé, I. 2014. *The Idea of Israel: A History of Power and Knowledge*. London: Verso.
Parallel Histories. www.parallelhistories.org.uk/
Peace Research Institute in the Middle East. http://vispo.com/PRIME
Penslar, D. J. 2007. *Israel in History: The Jewish State in Comparative Perspective*. London: Routledge.
Podeh, E. 2015. *Chances for Peace: Missed Opportunities in the Arab-Israeli Conflict*. Austin, TX: University of Texas Press.
Rabinovich, I. 1991. *The Road Not Taken: Early Arab–Israeli Negotiations*. New York: Oxford University Press.
Raz, A. 2012. *The Bride and the Dowry: Israel, Jordan, and the Palestinians in the Aftermath of the June 1967 War*. New Haven, CT: Yale University Press.
Rodinson, M. 1967. "Israël, fait colonial?" *Les Temps modernes* 22, 253bis, 17–88. [translated as *Israel: A Colonial Settler-State?*, by David Thorstad, introduced by Peter Buch, New York: Anchor Foundation, 1973].
Said, E. W. 1979. *The Question of Palestine*. New York: Times Books.
Said, E.W. 1998. "New History, Old Ideas," *al-Ahram Weekly*, no. 378, 21–27 May 1998, accessed online 4 July 2018 at http://weekly.ahram.org.eg/archive/1998/378/pal2.htm.
Scham, P., W. Salem, and B. Pogrund, eds. 2005. *Shared Histories: A Palestinian–Israeli Dialogue*. Walnut Creek, CA: Left Coast Press.
Scholars for Peace in the Middle East. www.spme.net.
Schueftan, D. 2008. "Historic Compromise and Historic Justice," in "The 1937 Peel Report Revisited," 14 January, edition 2, Palestinian–Israeli Crossfire. Available at: www.bitterlemons.org/previous/bl140108ed02.html#isr2.
Segev, T. 1986. *1949: The First Israelis*. New York: Free Press.
Shafir, G. 2006. "The Miscarriage of Peace: Israel, Egypt, the United States, and the 'Jarring Plan' in the Early 1970s." *Israel Studies Forum* 21:1, 3–26.
Shafir, G. 2007. "Zionism and Colonialism: A Comparative Approach," in *The Israel/Palestine Question: A Reader*, 2nd edition., ed. Ilan Pappé. London: Routledge, 78–93.
Shimoni, G. 2007. "Postcolonial Theory and the History of Zionism." *Israel Affairs* 13:4, 863–871.
Shlaim, A. 1986. "Husni Za'im and the Plan to Resettle Palestinian Refugees." *Journal of Palestine Studies* 15:4, 68–80.
Shlaim, A. 1988. *Collusion Across the Jordan: King Abdullah, the Zionist Movement, and the Partition of Palestine*. Oxford: Clarendon Press.
Shlaim, A. 1999. "The Debate about 1948," in *The Israel/Palestine Question*, ed. I. Pappé. London: Routledge, 171–192.
Shlaim, A. 2014. *The Iron Wall: Israel and the Arab World*, Updated and Expanded. New York: W. W. Norton.
Talmon, J. 1970. *Israel among the Nations*. London: Weidenfeld and Nicolson.
Troen, I. S. 2007. "De-Judaizing the Homeland: Academic Politics in Rewriting the History of Palestine." *Israel Affairs* 13:4, 872–884.
Tsur, J. 1977. *Zionism: The Saga of a National Liberation Movement*. New Brunswick, NJ: Transaction.
Wasserstein, B. 2008. *Israelis and Palestinians: Why Do They Fight? Can They Stop?* 3rd ed., New Haven, CT: Yale University Press.

2

HOW IT BEGAN

Origins of the Israeli-Palestinian Conflict

Alan Dowty

When did the Israeli-Palestinian (or Arab-Israeli) conflict begin? One might think that there would be a consensus on such a question, but answers differ as definitions of the conflict differ. On a state-to-state level, it began in 1948, but clearly there was a serious conflict between the Arab and Jewish communities in Palestine during the British Mandate period (1922–1948). One recent study, by Hillel Cohen, has defined 1929 as "year zero" in the conflict, since it marks the beginning of the first sustained organized clashes between the two sides (Cohen 2015). This makes sense given the definition used, but one could also make a case for the beginning of the Mandate with the first clear delineation of opposed parties and opposed aspirations.

But clearly these opposed forces also have earlier roots. To the extent that there is consensus on the conflict's onset, it has tended to focus on the decade before World War I (1905–1914). During this period, and especially after the Young Turk Revolution of 1908, Arab nationalism emerged as a visible force in the Palestinian arena, hostile to growing Jewish (Zionist) settlement there. At the same time, from 1905 the second wave of Jewish immigrants to Ottoman Palestine – labelled as the second *aliya* (ascent) – brought with them a more assertive attitude, deep-set opposition to the employment of Arabs in Jewish settlements, and thus direct competition with Arabs in their "conquest of labor" (Shafir 1989).

But what about the quarter century before this? The first wave of Jewish settlers, mostly from Eastern Europe – the first aliya – began in 1882 and established 28 new Jewish settlements in the Palestinian areas of the Ottoman Empire, doubling the Jewish population there. These achievements were, however, belittled by those who followed them, in the second aliya and later. The settlers of the first aliya, it was claimed, lacked a coherent program and a true sense of community. Worst of all, in this view, they lacked commitment to a return to the soil based on Hebrew labour, instead employing Arab workers in their fields and plantations. In the words of a later historian, "Settlers of the First Aliya did not bond with the land by working it with their own hands." (Neumann 2011, 18).

The denigration of the first aliya extends even to denying them "credit" for initiating the national conflict between Jews and Arabs. By inference, the first aliya did not constitute enough of a threat to the existing Arab population that it aroused organized Arab opposition. Whatever conflicts took place were not conflicts between two peoples: first aliya clashes with Arabs "did not have any bearing on political relations between the Arabs, as a national body, and the veteran Israeli settlers and residents, as part of another national body" (Asaf 1970, 37). In the years before a strong sense of Arab identity and an Arab national movement emerged, the clashes that

DOI: 10.4324/9780429027376-4

took place were, in this account, the usual quarrels among neighbours, similar to the clashes among the Arabs themselves. Of course, a serious test of this proposition would require close comparative analysis of the two sets of clashes, which no one has yet carried out. In the meantime, however, it is possible to take a closer look at Jewish-Arab relations during this period, based on the testimonies of those involved.

Palestine before Zionism

The area that later became the British Mandate of Palestine was, under Ottoman rule, divided into three districts. The southern district around Jerusalem, because of its religious importance, functioned from 1873 as an independent district reporting directly to the Sultan in Constantinople. The two northern districts were part of a province ruled either from Damascus or, after 1888, from Beirut.

Western travellers in Ottoman Palestine during the late nineteenth century described what they saw as bleak desolation, rampant lawlessness, and breath-taking misery. Typical was the 31-year-old Mark Twain, then known mainly for his short stories and travelogues, and whose 1867 visit was immortalized in *The Innocents Abroad*. Like other visitors from verdant lands of Europe and America, he was struck by the rocky aridity of the region: "Palestine sits in sackcloth and ashes. Over it broods the spell of a curse that has withered its fields" (Twain 2002, 462).

Such judgments lacked historical perspective. The Ottoman government had, beginning in 1839, enacted a series of far-reaching reforms (the *Tanzimat*) that had in many ways transformed areas it governed. In Palestine, by the time the early Jewish settlers arrived the population had actually doubled since 1800. New industries, such as citrus fruit, had appeared, foreign trade had greatly increased, and contemporary testimony points to broad improvements in basic law and order (Schölch 1993; Divine 1994). Among the improvements was a sweeping land reform, in 1858, that turned much of what had been state land into, essentially, private holdings. Much of this land was farmed by tenants under traditional rights of usage, but now this land could be sold, creating greater opportunities for foreign nationals – such as most Zionists – to acquire land.

The Tanzimat reforms did not, however, reverse the overall decline of an Ottoman Empire, facing serious challenges from without and within. Over the previous two centuries, the Ottomans had lost half of their territory to a combination of European imperialism and nationalist revolts. France and Great Britain now controlled former Ottoman North African provinces, while Christian minorities in the Balkans were in the last stage of achieving independence from their Turkish rulers. This hardly disposed the government in Constantinople to view the Zionist movement sympathetically since Zionism seemed to embody both threats. It was a European movement tied (in Turkish eyes) to the European powers, and it sought to insert yet another Western-oriented non-Muslim minority in the heart of what remained of the Ottoman Empire.

Furthermore, the Ottoman regime was already resisting European penetration of this Palestinian heartland. Driven by religious impulses, the Christian nations of Europe were competing among themselves to expand their sectarian, cultural, and economic presence there. The Ottomans depended on some European states to defend them from others: for example, in the Crimean War (1853–1856) Britain and France blocked Russian pressures. For this reason, the Ottoman government was often forced to concede to the demands of its protectors; for example, in allowing the first European diplomatic presence in Jerusalem since the Crusades. European states also had a powerful tool for intervening within the Ottoman Empire in the form of the "Capitulations," treaties that gave them jurisdiction over their own citizens within the Empire. European states often extended this protection to include co-religionists as well, France claiming the right to protect all Catholics, and Russia claiming all Orthodox Christians as protégés. Great Britain, having few Anglicans to protect, at one point took upon itself the protection of Jews in Palestine (Friedman 1986; Dowty 2019, 32–33).

European and American visitors to Palestine also noted a deep hostility to Westerners among both Arabs and Turks. When European states were allowed to open consulates in Jerusalem, for example, the consuls initially had to move around with armed escorts (Finn 1878, v. 2, 31, 362–363). On the other hand, the Ottoman Empire had traditionally been a haven for Jewish refugees, dating back to the expulsion of Jews from Spain in 1492. This tradition was sorely tested when Russian Jews fleeing persecution began arriving in 1881–1882. The official response, initially, was to continue the tradition, but in anti-Zionist mode. Jews were to be allowed anywhere in the Ottoman Empire *except* Palestine, they could come only as individuals and not as a group, and they would have to become Ottoman citizens, giving up their foreign passports and protection under the Capitulations (Mandel 1976, 2).

Russian Jews before Zionism

In some ways it seems odd that the movement to establish a Jewish state should come at the end of the nineteenth century, a period regarded as the era of Jewish emancipation. Beginning in France in 1791, Jewish populations in Europe and the Americas had made huge strides toward full civic equality and freedom from persecution. The road forward would seem to lead to assimilation *as Jews* in modern liberal democratic societies.

Of course, half the world's Jews lived in Tsarist Russia, which was hardly a beacon for democracy and human rights. But even in Russia, Enlightenment ideals had an impact. Under the "Liberator Tsar," Alexander II (1856–1881), broad reforms were carried out: the end of serfdom and the broadening of rights for minorities in this "Prison House of Nations." Jews were allowed to live outside the "Pale of Settlement" to which they had been restricted, gained more access to universities and closed occupations, and were encouraged to participate in the new order. In Western Europe, the general "Enlightenment" had sparked a Jewish Enlightenment, or *Haskala*, which sought to bring progressive liberal thinking into the Jewish world. By mid-century the Haskala had reached Russian Jews; over time it produced a significant corps of *maskilim* (followers of Haskala) devoted to integration as Jews into an enlightened Russian state and society. The ideal was expressed by the poet Yehuda Leib Gordon, a leading *maskil*:

> This Land of Eden [Russia!] now opens its gates to you …
> Become an enlightened people, speak their language …
> Be a man abroad and a Jew in your tent,
> A brother to your countrymen and a servant to your king.

It was, therefore, a cruel turn of fate when this emerging new order, on which so many pinned their hopes, came crashing down. The triggering event was the assassination of Tsar Alexander II on 1 March 1881, and the accession of his son Alexander III, who was dominated by reactionary advisors. Then, within weeks, came a wave of attacks on Jewish communities throughout southern Russia, the worst attacks in two centuries. It was these attacks that gave currency to the Russian word *pogrom*, meaning devastation. The role of the Russian government in instigating these attacks is debated among historians, but it did little to stop them, and it blamed the Jews themselves for having created the resentment of the mobs (Frankel 1981, 64). It also rescinded many of the reforms from which Jews had benefited.

Those who had the most invested in a liberalized Russia – the maskilim – not surprisingly became the most disillusioned. There is no surer recipe for revolution than to inspire hope and then snatch it away. Of course, the disillusionment was broad and deep among Russian Jews, and over the next forty years some four million of them, fitting the modern accepted definition of refugees, left Russia. But in the choice between Palestine or America (or elsewhere in the West) as a destination, the maskilim, in particular, chose Palestine. As they saw it, antisemitism would be prevalent everywhere except in the one place that Jews could call their own. Those who made this choice were thus self-selected for determination to secure their future in this one place where, as they saw it, they would not have to adjust to a host society.

First Encounters

The refugees who chose Palestine as a destination faced daunting obstacles from the first. As noted, the Ottoman government formally closed Palestine to Jewish immigration even before the first would-be settlers arrived. Any managing to enter despite this would probably not be allowed to purchase land, despite official Ottoman policy allowing land sales to foreign citizens. And if they did manage to acquire land, Ottoman authorities could and did refuse to grant them building permits and would demolish any structure built without a permit.

There were various ways of surmounting these obstacles. Some came as religious pilgrims – a traffic that the Ottoman Empire was forced to allow – and simply overstayed their visas. Others entered the Ottoman Empire at ports other than Jaffa, where the enforcement was most stringent, and then travelled overland to Palestinian areas (the two northern districts of "Palestine" being easier to enter than Jaffa and the Jerusalem district). Land was often bought in the name of Ottoman Jewish citizens. Building permits might be obtained through the widespread Ottoman practice of *baksheesh* (bribery), which might also be employed in border entry and land sales, at least on the lower levels of officialdom.

Often the last resort, however, was to evoke the intervention of European consuls acting under the Capitulations as protectors. The settlements supported by the French philanthropist Baron Edmund de Rothschild, for example, could usually count on French diplomatic intervention. The founders of Petah Tikva included one German citizen, and at one point the German Consul threatened to mobilize the Templers (German Protestant settlers) from nearby Sarona to prevent the demolition of "illegal" structures (Eliav 1981, v.2, 80; Ya'ari-Poleskin and Harizman 1929, 227–243).

The settlers in Gedera resorted to a different tactic when they could not get a building permit. Ottoman law provided that a structure with a roof could not be demolished; the problem was that Arabs living nearby would report any construction before it had a roof. The Gederans therefore dug a large pit, supposedly as a stable for their animals, and quickly roofed it over as a shelter for man and beast before the authorities could intervene (Laskov 1979, 241–242). As one settler recorded, when a Turkish officer appeared to demand the destruction of the stable, the settlers' response was: "You have undoubtedly forgotten, effendi, that you have no right to do that. We have a consul, and no one has the right to touch us without his permission" (Hisin 1976, 176).

There were, of course, other kinds of obstacles that the early settlers faced as well. They had to overcome an unfamiliar climate, rampant disease (especially malaria), and a severe scarcity of water. Above all, few of them had experience or any basic knowledge of agriculture, let alone agriculture in this new part of the world. Given these preoccupations, it is no surprise that they regarded the hostility of neighbouring Arabs as one of the least of their problems, and even as essentially not relevant to what they were doing. This was the one place in the world where they were not required to adjust to others, where they would determine their own course of action and let others adjust to them. When they became the majority, all would be well.

To the extent that the first settlers thought about the Arabs, they fell back on the belief that the settlers' presence would bring great benefits to the existing population. This can be seen vividly in the diary entries of young Eliezer Ben-Yehuda, known primarily for his role in the revival of Hebrew as a spoken language. Upon arriving in 1881, Ben Yehuda was initially dismayed by the reality he saw:

> My first meeting with our cousins Ishmael, was not a joyous meeting for me… I felt that they see themselves as citizens of the land that was the land of my fathers, and I, the son of these fathers, I come to this land as a stranger, as a foreigner.
>
> *(Ben-Yehuda 1993, 50)*

A few days later, however, Ben-Yehuda was able to cast the situation in an entirely different light:

> However, I also found a little comfort regarding the general position of the Arabs in Eretz Yisrael, which I have already managed to observe: that in general it is very lowly, that they are impoverished paupers and total illiterates. This fact … was for me the first ray of light since the moment that my foot trod on the land of our fathers.
>
> *(Ben-Yehuda 1993, 65)*

What Ben-Yehuda saw as the backwardness of Palestine was thus not an obstacle, but rather a reality that gave purpose to the Jewish return to Zion. This would become the central theme regarding relations with Arabs in Palestine: that Jews were bringing modernity to an unenlightened population. Ben-Yehuda's observations simply encapsulated within a few days an evolution of thinking that usually took longer.

The Civilizational Divide

Jews in Russia – or elsewhere in nineteenth-century Europe or the Americas – would not have thought to claim the label of "European" as their primary identity. But when they reached Palestine they magically became Europeans. They were seen as such by the existing residents of Palestine, and they saw themselves as such. The word "European" occurs frequently in their writings, whether in regard to culture, farming, education, law and order, technology – or to their relations with peoples of the Middle East.

By the late nineteenth century, European influence and control had penetrated most corners of the globe. The idea that this was a civilizing mission, bringing progress and modernity to other regions of the world, was widely accepted – at least in the West. It is hardly surprising that Jewish settlers in Palestine should consider themselves to be a part of this larger picture, and to believe that their presence would be a blessing to those among whom they were settling. A small expression of this was the practice, in settlements supported by Baron Rothschild, of providing free medical care to Arabs living nearby. In addition, the early settlements hired many Arab workers, basically out of a need for their labour but also explicitly as a way to build mutually beneficial ties.

Despite obvious hostility toward Europeans, some of the early settlers professed to believe that the benefits being bestowed on Arabs would earn their gratitude. Zalman David Levontin, the key figure in the founding of Rishon LeTsion, wrote:

> If the colonies are established in bonds of love and peace, then the holy land will be a land of freedom and liberty for them … and the Arabs who people the land will submit to them with the attitude of love and respect they show to all Europeans who work the soil and engage in commerce here.
>
> *(Laskov 1982, 190–191)*

Violent Clashes

The reality was that the Jewish settlements all had serious conflicts with their Arab neighbours at one time or another. Often this began at the very outset in disputes over property lines, given the deficiencies in Ottoman records and the clash between legal ownership and customary rights of usage.

All of the first few settlements had serious conflicts over delineation of their property lines; consequently, when Rehovot was founded a few years later, the Jewish settlers tried to pre-empt such conflict by carrying out a thorough survey and getting the signatures of local Arab leaders on the resulting maps. In the end, it was of little use; Arab villagers covered trenches and uprooted trees intended to mark the property lines. Beduin tenants on one parcel of land simply refused to leave, petitioning the Sultan "not to let the Jews chase us away" (Ben-Bassat 2013, 165). Despite serious efforts to avert conflict, Rehovot passed through the same history of violent encounters as the other settlements (Smilansky 1928–1929, 23–32; Dinur 1954, 98–99).

Another source of frequently violent clashes was the practice of Arab shepherds bringing their sheep, goats, cattle, or oxen to graze in newly planted Jewish fields. According to Arab custom, it was permissible to graze flocks and herds in any uncultivated field – but these fields were cultivated, testifying to an underlying hostility behind the act. Jewish settlers countered by seizing animals and holding them until restitution had been paid for the damage; needless to say, this often led to violent fights. Interestingly, even here European identity played a role. According to the young diarist Haim Hisin, it was difficult to round up animals being held for ransom because "the wild beast of the Arab stands in great awe of a European" (Hisin 1976, 116).

Over time the Jewish settlements developed strikingly similar narratives about the evolution of their relations with their Arab neighbours. This "standard narrative" was basically: they harassed us, we fought back and earned their respect, and eventually we developed a stable *modus vivendi* with our neighbours. Again, it was important to the entire settlement enterprise to minimize these clashes and to deny that there was a fundamental conflict of interest between the two sides. And there was some truth to the standard narrative on a strictly local level as Jewish settlements expanded and were able to defend themselves more effectively.

But in truth, the conflict was moving from localized incidents to broader confrontation. In 1886 came the first organized attack on a settlement, as an estimated 200 Arab villagers from al-Yehudia fell upon Petah Tikva on a day when most of the men had gone to Jaffa. To many observers this looked all too familiar; the word "pogrom" was invoked in the debate that followed. But to the settlers themselves, it was important to deny the comparison. They had not come to recreate the Diaspora model of a Jewish minority at the mercy of a hostile host population; this had to be different (Be'eri 1985, 60–62; Dinur 1954, 94; Laskov 1987, 157, 168).

But the attack on Petah Tikva was not an isolated event. It was followed by similar attacks on Gedera (1888), Yesud Hama'ala (1890), Rehovot (1892, 1893, 1899), Kastina (1896), Metula (1896–1904), and Hadera (1901). And in nearly all the new settlements, there were ongoing incidents of brawls, vandalism, thefts, and other clashes. It was becoming harder as time passed to deny the existence of a fundamental conflict.

Fighting Back

One of the mechanisms for denying a basic conflict between the two sides was to focus on the specific issues in each clash, that is, to see the trees but not the forest. In each clash there were immediate issues – land, grazing, cultural insensitivities – that were in theory soluble, and the fact that these clashes were part of an emerging pattern could be brushed aside. Even those who recognised a generalized Arab hostility toward Jewish newcomers could seek to explain this in terms of specific causes. Eliyahu Sapir, a teacher in Petah Tikva who knew Arabic language and culture, blamed the Catholic Church and, in particular, the Jesuit order, for instilling Western anti-Semitism among the Arabs (Sapir 1899). Sapir's choice of a culprit to be blamed reflected the prominence of Christian Arabs in the emergence of Arab nationalism, but as an explanation for Arab opposition to Zionism it gave the Jesuits far too much credit as an influence on their Muslim fellow countrymen.

But whatever the source of the hostility, for the Jewish settlers a huge part of the difference in this new situation was their readiness to fight back. Jews would no longer be constrained by Diaspora patterns of coexistence with a non-Jewish majority. They would no longer be weak and defenceless but would take pride in defending themselves.

In the earlier days when the main threats came from thefts and vandalism, the Jewish settlers employed Arabs as guards, particularly for night-time duty since the settlers found it difficult to take this on in addition to full-time farming – and in any event, Jews had little relevant experience in this sort of thing. Over the course of time, however, as the threats grew in scale, the settlers gradually took over the guard duties and established defence forces. In 1907 a small secret guard society, *Bar-Giora*, was organized in Sejera. Two years later, following a series of attacks in which two Jews had been killed, this group was rolled up in the first community-wide defence force, *HaShomer.* The slogan of the day was "By blood and fire Judea fell; by blood and fire Judea shall rise again." In their dress and comportment, HaShomer fighters copied the most martial image at hand, that of armed Beduin horsemen.

One index of the new assertiveness was the emergence of "muscle men," settlers known for their prowess and strength in physical confrontations. The standard history of Jewish fighting forces notes that "men like this were found in every settlement at its beginning, and they taught the Arabs to behave with respect to their new neighbours" (Dinur 1954, 69). In Rishon LeTsion, for example, there were three outstanding fighters who "taught the farmers ... how to deal with the Arabs who came to graze their herds in the fields of Rishon LeTsion" (Belkind 1983, 78). Indeed, the *Bilu* pioneer Haim Hisin wrote in his diary that "the youth of Rishon LeTsion earned the title of 'devils' among the neighbors, thanks to their ferocity in the frequent clashes with Arabs" (Hisin 1976, 114–115).

And when Ahad Ha'am criticized settler violence toward Arabs that he witnessed during his first visit in 1891, his fellow traveller (and future key figure) Menachem Ussishkin responded with a stinging defence of the new Jewish self-defence:

> And I rejoiced to see my brothers, who trembled from the sound of a falling leaf and kissed the whip with which their enemies lashed them, upon their return to the land of the Maccabees, taking a manly resolve to strike them, and no one will maliciously challenge their honor.
>
> *(Ussishkin 1891, 22)*

At this stage, however, assertive self-defence on the grassroots level did not yet translate into advocacy of organized military force (or for that matter, negotiation) in relations with Arabs on the national level. Arabs were not seen as a "nation" with whom either war or negotiation was relevant; to the extent that there was an interlocutor, it was the Ottoman Turks. Arabs would be treated fairly as individuals, and despite some rough passages sparked by their hostility, would, in the end, benefit from the building of the Jewish homeland as Jews became the majority. Once again, the eventual success of Zionism would in itself resolve the matter.

Recognizing a Problem

When was the first serious recognition of a fundamental conflict between Jews and Arabs as rival peoples with mutually exclusive claims to *Eretz Yisrael*/Palestine? On the Jewish side, the answer usually offered is Ahad Ha'am's 1891 article to which Menachem Ussishkin (above) was responding. Ahad Ha'am had emerged among early Zionists as a leading ideologue and as something of a gadfly, strongly critical of the movement's methods and direction. Summarizing his visit, he strongly attacked nearly every aspect of the early settlement, including their non-chalant optimism regarding Arabs: "If the time comes when the life of our people in *Eretz Yisrael* develops to the point of encroaching on the native population, they will not easily yield their place" (Ahad Ha'am 1891, 162).

As noted, the article also criticized the settlers harshly for "shamefully beating [the Arabs] for no good reason, and even bragging about what they do" (Ahad Ha'am 1891, 175). But the truth is that, apart from some incidental mentions, there are only two paragraphs in the entire article that deal with "the Arab question." In his discussion of the problems facing the Jewish settlements, the Arab issue was merely one in a long list of obstacles, and by no means the most difficult. In fact, Ahad Ha'am in the end subscribed to the same sanguine view held by others: by the time Arabs do rise against the Zionist project, "our brothers would be able to secure their position in Eretz Yisrael by the large number, their extensive and rich holdings, their unity and their exemplary way of life" (Ahad Ha'am 1891, 178). In essence, once again, the success of Zionism would itself solve the problem. Arabs would benefit as individuals, and there would be no need to deal with them on a collective level, either by force or negotiation. Ahad Ha'am clearly saw beyond what others saw at the time, but he did not challenge the prevailing optimism; his essay was the exception that proves the rule.

Yet there were already signs that the conflict was moving from local confrontations to the national level. Almost simultaneously with the publication of Ahad Ha'am's article, some five hundred prominent Arabs in Jerusalem sent a telegram to the Ottoman government in Constantinople demanding a complete ban on entry of, and land sales to, Russian Jews. The Sultan's response was unusually quick and categorical, announcing the closure of the entire Ottoman Empire (not just Palestine) to Russian Jews. And two months later the ban was extended to all foreign Jews. This directly contradicted commitments to non-discrimination that the Ottoman Empire had made following the Crimean War, giving leverage to the foreign consuls acting on behalf of their protégés, in addition to the usual problems the Ottoman government faced in trying to enforce such far-reaching decrees (Dowty 2019, 168–169).

In the following years, Arab opposition to Zionism testified to the fact that immigration and land sales were not totally cut off. The Mufti of Jerusalem, Muhammad Tahir al-Husayni, was head of a commission on land sales and did succeed in blocking land sales to Jews in the Jerusalem district for several years. In 1899 al-Husayni proposed to the Administration Council of the district that all foreign Jews who had entered since 1891 be expelled, if necessary by terror (Mandel 1976, 41).

The settler Yitzhak Epstein, who arrived in Palestine in 1886, formulated the first notable Jewish recognition of the emerging conflict, first as a lecture at the 1905 Zionist Congress and two years later as an article. Labelling the issue as "A Hidden Question," Epstein declared that "there is in our beloved land an entire people that has been attached to it for hundreds of years and has never considered leaving it" (Epstein 1907, 40). Moving beyond Ahad Ha'am, Epstein stressed the need to recognize Arabs as a nation and to negotiate with them on that basis:

> It must be admitted that up to now we had the "wrong address": in order to acquire our land we turned to all the powers that had some link to it, we negotiated with all the in-laws but forgot about the groom himself; we ignored the true masters of the land.
>
> *(Epstein 1907, 51)*

Epstein called for nothing less than a covenant (*brit*) – a sacred undertaking in Judaism – with the Arabs. He shared the still-prevailing view that Jewish development of Palestine could bring benefits to, and eventual partnership with, the Arabs. But he argued forcefully that this would not happen automatically with the success of Zionism; it would have to be based on far-reaching concessions in Zionist practices, including an end to land purchases that involved the eviction of tenant farmers. This would have forced the movement to make drastic changes in its program, and at the time there were few who were willing to go so far. In opposition to Epstein's integrative vision, most Zionists preferred to continue a separate path of development, without a partnership. This has, in essence, been the basis for conflicting approaches ever since.

Battle Lines: The Second Aliya and Arab Nationalism

The year 1905 also marks the onset of the second major wave of Jewish immigration to Palestine, the second aliya. This was to be the founding generation of the state of Israel, personified by its first prime minister, David Ben-Gurion. Second aliya immigrants had the same basic background: fleeing persecution in Eastern Europe and particularly in Russia. But by this time revolutionary ideologies and assertive self-defence were more influential forces in the Jewish world. The *kibbutz* – the commune – was the emblematic institution of the second aliya.

Settlers of the first aliya did, contrary to some claims, debate the wisdom of hiring Arab workers in their settlements. The goals of self-reliance and a return to the soil were important then as they were later. But the agricultural model they chose, focused on single-crop plantations, required intensive labour, especially seasonal labour, and due to Ottoman restrictions Jewish labourers were not available in requisite numbers. In addition, the theory of benefits to the Arab population helped to justify their employment and the development of mutual dependence.

Many of the refugees arriving in the second aliya were, however, workers with limited means and thus in competition with Arab workers. They were also more deeply imbued with the themes of socialism, self-reliance, manual labour, and a return to the soil. Their goal was defined as "conquest of labour," meaning they would replace Arab workers in Jewish enterprises. This of course sharpened the conflict between the two communities.

At almost the same time, Arab nationalism was emerging as an important force. Those whose first language was Arabic were usually referred to as Arabs, though the term was sometimes reserved for Beduin (the "true" Arabs) or inhabitants of the Arabian Peninsula. But Arabs in Palestine had in fact multiple other identities: as Muslims or Christians, as Ottoman citizens, as members of various tribes or clans, and (by the end of this period) as Palestinians. They were also beginning to be influenced by the *Western* idea of a nation-state that had framed much of nineteenth-century European history. As defined by language, on the model of German or Italian unification, Arabs might form a nation-state stretching from Morocco to Iraq. Christian

Arabs were prominent in this movement, since it made them members of an extensive majority rather than a small minority in an Islamic ocean.

As it happened, 1905 was also when the first "text" of Arab nationalism appeared. Najib Azouri was a Christian Arab, from what is now Lebanon, who served the Ottoman government in Jerusalem. Breaking with the governor, he fled to Egypt and then to Paris where he published *Le Reveil de la Nation Arabe* (The Awakening of the Arab Nation) in French. It is remarkable that this first manifesto of Arab nationalism begins with a broadside attack on Jews and Zionism:

> Two important phenomena ... are evident at this moment in Asian Turkey: these are the awakening of the Arab nation and the veiled effort of Jews to reconstitute on a very large scale the ancient monarchy of Israel. These two movements are destined to fight continually until one vanquishes the other. The fate of the entire world will depend on the final outcome of this battle between these two peoples representing two contrary principles.
>
> *(Azouri 1905, v)*

At the time Azouri wrote these words, neither Zionism nor Arab nationalism was all that visible. His book also included some classic antisemitic tropes – learned in France. In any event, it was clear that Arab nationalism, in whatever form it took, would inevitably clash with Jewish nationalism (Zionism) when it came to the future of the Ottoman Empire's Palestinian districts. This would become even clearer when Arab nationalism emerged, strongly following the Young Turk revolution of 1908. By 1914, there were voices on both sides speaking of the inevitability of armed conflict.

Conclusion

At its core, the clash between Arabs and Jews in Ottoman Palestine reflected the civilizational divide between West (Europe) and East (the Muslim world). While the Ottoman government did sometimes take measures that targeted all Jews, including Eastern (Sephardi) Jews, who were Ottoman citizens, the extent of the government's antipathy to Zionism (and that of their Arab citizens) can only be explained by reference to that movement's European character and centuries of deeply embedded enmity to the West.

This can best be seen, perhaps, by looking at test cases that isolate the various identities:

- *Sephardi (non-European) Jews.* Ottoman Jews in the Sephardi community were part of the dominant culture, spoke the language, and generally enjoyed a secure if unequal status politically and socially. While often helpful to their fellow Jews from Europe, they were also often extremely critical of them for refusing to assimilate to Arab culture and Turkish rule. In fact, (non-Palestinian) Ottoman Jews elected to parliament following the Young Turk Revolution were outspoken anti-Zionists. The two Jewish settlements in the new *yishuv* that were founded predominantly by Sephardi Jews, Mishmar HaYarden and Hartuv, suffered little of the hostility faced by the other new settlements (Dowty 2019, 185).
- *Non-Jewish Europeans.* On the other hand, the major group that shared a European origin with Zionists, despite serious differences, also had the same kind of conflicts with Arab neighbours and Turkish rulers. This was the German Protestant sect known as the Templers, who established seven settlements in Palestine beginning in 1868 with the aim of reclaiming the land for "God's people." Though their vision did not include a Jewish Restoration – in fact they were basically anti-Jewish – their role and aspirations were similar enough to the

Jewish movement that they have been labelled as "proto-Zionists." Their relations with the local authorities and with the Arab population were in any event as troubled as were those of the early Zionists (Yazbak 1999; Dowty 2019, 23–26).

- *Ashkenazi (European) Jews before Zionism.* Ashkenazi Jews had returned to Palestine in small numbers over the centuries; there was an organized community from 1687. But in line with their general attitude toward Europeans, Ottoman authorities regarded European Jews as an alien element. For over a century (1723–1836) they had barred European Jews from entering Jerusalem, and from the 1850s – well before the Zionist movement – they had tried to limit the influx of Jews from Europe. Their hostility was not directed toward Jews as such, but to those who chose to remain European in culture, refusing to assimilate or take Ottoman citizenship (Marmorstein 1982, 3–7; Ya'ari 1958, 29–35; Dowty 2019, 30–31).

All of this is confirmed in the numerous condemnations by Arabs and Turks – and *Sephardi* Jews – of the stubborn refusal of European Jewish newcomers to adjust to their new environment, or even to learn the language. At the first conference of Hebrew teachers, it was pointed out that "the natives of the land respect no one who does not speak Arabic" (Saposnik 2008, 70). On the other hand, a typical "European" rejoinder was that "there is nothing better for our brothers than to live far from the people of the land, and their children will not learn from the bad practices of this wild and destructive people" (Gur 1897, 350).

This civilizational divide thus runs through the entire history of Jewish Zionist activity in Ottoman Palestine. Given this divide, a clash was unavoidable. Several elements in the structure of the situation made any other outcome highly unlikely:

- *Changes in nineteenth-century Palestine made foreign access easier, but also strengthened the existing antipathy to European penetration among both Arabs and Turks.* Hostility to the West was deeply rooted in the Muslim world, and "opening up" Palestine only made European intrusions more visible and more deeply resented.
- *Most of the Jews who entered Palestine after 1882 were refugees by today's commonly accepted definition.* Like refugees generally, they came in an embittered state of mind and with a determination that the experience would never be repeated.
- *Despite having been persecuted in their native lands, Eastern European Jews who fled these lands still strongly identified with European civilization as an ideal.* If Russia had failed them, it was because Russia was not sufficiently European.
- *The early Jewish settlers set out to construct their own society, with little or no reference to the society among whom they settled.* The appeal of Palestine was that this was the one spot in the world where Jews would not have to adjust to others.
- *To the extent that they thought about relations with the Arab population of Palestine, Jewish settlers fell back on the "benefit theory."* Thinking in terms of benefits also focused attention on individuals rather than on Arabs as a national counterpart.

Given these points of departure, it is hard to see how the conflict could have evolved much differently. The die was cast.

Recommended Readings

Dowty, A. 2019. *Arabs and Jews in Ottoman Palestine: Two Worlds Collide.* Bloomington, IN: Indiana University Press.

Gorny, Y. 1987. *Zionism and the Arabs, 1882–1948.* Oxford: Clarendon Press.

Khalidi, R. 1997. *Palestinian Identity: The Construction of Modern National Consciousness*. New York: Columbia University Press.
Mandel, N. 1976. *The Arabs and Zionism before World War I*. Berkeley, CA: University of California Press.
Shapira, A. 1992. *Land and Power: The Zionist Resort to Force, 1881–1948*. Oxford: Oxford University Press.

Questions for Discussion:

(1) Does it matter when the Arab-Israeli conflict began? Why or why not?
(2) What part did official policies of the Ottoman Empire play in the development of the new Jewish community in Ottoman Palestine? Were these policies consistent? Were they effective in any respect, and if so, in what way?
(3) Was Arab opposition to Jewish immigration into Palestine based on opposition to Jews as such, or to Jews as representatives of European penetration? What is the evidence for or against either interpretation?
(4) If Yitzhak Epstein's proposals for changes in Zionist relations with the Arab population had been adopted, would it have made any difference? Why or why not?

References

Ahad Ha'am (Asher Ginzberg). 1891. "Emet Me'Eretz Yisrael" [Truth from the Land of Israel]. *HaMelitz*, June 19–30, trans. A. Dowty, "Much Ado about Little: Ahad Ha'am's 'Truth from the Land of Israel,' Zionism, and the Arabs." *Israel Studies* 5:2 (2000), 154–181.
Asaf, M. 1970. *HaYahasim ben Yehudim Ve'Aravim Be'Erets Yisrael* [Relations between Jews and Arab in the Land of Israel]. Tel Aviv: Mifalei Tarbut VeHinukh.
Azoury, N. (N. Azouri). 1905. *Le Reveil de la Nation Arabe* dans L'Asie Turque [The Awakening of the Arab Nation in Asian Turkey]. Paris: Librairie Plon.
Be'eri, E. 1985. *Reshit HaSikhsukh Yisrael-Arav, 1882–1911* [The Beginning of the Israel-Arab Conflict, 1882–1911]. Tel Aviv: Sifriat Po'alim and University of Haifa.
Belkind, Y. 1983. *BeNativ HaBiluiim: Zickhronot Yisrael Belkind* [On the Path of the Biluim: Memoirs of Yisrael Belkind]. Tel Aviv: Ministry of Defense Publications.
Ben-Bassat, Y. 2013. *Petitioning the Sultan: Protests and Justice in Late Ottoman Palestine, 1865–1908*. London: I. B. Tauris.
Ben-Yehuda, E. 1993. *A Dream Come True*, tr. T. Muraoka, ed. G. Mandel. Boulder, CO: Westview Press.
Cohen, H. 2015. *Year Zero of the Arab-Israeli Conflict: 1929*. Waltham, MA: Brandeis University Press.
Dinur, B., ed. 1954. *Sefer Toldot HaHagana* [History of the Hagana], vol 1, *MeHitgonenut LeHagana* [From Self-Defense to Defense]. Tel Aviv: Ma'arakhot.
Divine, D. R. 1994. *Politics and Society in Ottoman Palestine: The Arab Struggle for Survival and Power*. Boulder, CO: Lynne Rienner.
Dowty, A. 2019. *Arabs and Jews in Ottoman Palestine: Two Worlds Collide*. Bloomington, IN: Indiana University Press, 2019.
Eliav, M., ed. 1981. *Sefer Ha'Aliya HaRishona* [Book of the First Aliya]. 2 vols. Jerusalem: Yad Yitzhak Ben-Zvi and Ministry of Defense Publications.
Epstein, Y. 1907. "She'ela Ne'elama [A Hidden Question]. *HaShiloah* 17 (July–December): 193–206, tr. A. Dowty, "'A Question That Outweighs All Others,' Yitzhak Epstein and Zionist Recognition of the Arab Issue." *Israel Studies* 6:1, (2001): 34–54.
Finn, J. 1878. *Stirring Times: Or, Records from Jerusalem Consular Chronicles of 1853 to 1856*. London: C. Kegan Paul.
Frankel, J. 1981. *Prophecy and Politics: Socialism, Nationalism, and the Russian Jews, 1862–1917*. Cambridge: Cambridge University Press.
Friedman, I. 1986. "The System of Capitulations and Its Effects on Turco-Jewish Relations in Palestine, 1856–1897." In *Palestine in the Late Ottoman Period: Political, Social, and Economic Transformation*, ed. D. Kushner. Jerusalem: Yad Yitzhak Ben-Zvi and Leiden: E. J. Brill, 280–293.
Gur, Y. 1987. "From the Land of Israel." *HaShiloah*, 1 (January), 349–356.
Hisin, H. (C. Chissin). 1976. *A Palestine Diary: Memoirs of a Bilu Pioneer 1882–1887*, tr. F. Miller. New York: Herzl Press.
Laskov, S. 1979. *HaBiluiim* [The Bilu Movement]. Jerusalem: HaSifriya HaTsionit.

Laskov, S., ed. 1982 and 1987 *Ktavim LeToldot Hibat Tsion VeYishuv Erets Yisrael* [Documents on the History of Hibat Tsion and the Settlement of the Land of Israel]. Tel Aviv: HaKibuts HaMe'uhad. Vols. 1 & 4.

Mandel, N. J. 1976. *The Arabs and Zionism before World War I*. Berkeley, CA: University of California Press.

Marmorstein, E. 1982. "European Jews in Muslim Palestine." In *Palestine and Israel in the 19th and 20th Centuries*, ed. Eli Kedourie and Sylvia G. Haim. London: Frank Cass, 1–14.

Neumann, B. 2011. *Land and Desire in Early Zionism*. Waltham, MA: Brandeis University Press.

Sapir, E. 1899. "HaSina LeYisrael BeSiporet Ha'Aravit [Hatred of Israel in Arab Literature]." *HaShiloah* 6 (July-December), 222–232. Date of specific issue not available.

Saposnik, A. B. 2008. *Becoming Hebrew: The Creation of a Jewish National Culture in Ottoman Palestine*. New York: Oxford University Press.

Scholch, A. 1993. *Palestine in Transformation 1856–1882: Studies in Social, Economic, and Political Development*. Washington, DC: Institute for Palestine Studies.

Shafir, G. 1989. *Land, Labor and the Origins of the Israeli-Palestinian Conflict 1882–1914*. Cambridge: Cambridge University Press.

Smilansky, M. 1928–1929. *Rehovot*. Tel Aviv: Omanut.

Twain, M. 2002. *The Innocents Abroad*. New York: Penguin Books.

Ussishkin, M. 1891. "Bli Mara Sh'hora Yetera [Without Excessive Gloom]." *HaMelits*, July 17, 1.

Ya'ari, A. 1958. *The Goodly Heritage: Memoirs Describing the Life of the Jewish Community of Eretz Yisrael from the Seventeenth to the Twentieth Centuries*. Jerusalem: World Zionist Organization.

Ya'ari-Polskin, Y., and M. Harizman, eds. 1929. *Sefer HaYovel LeM'le'at Hamishim Shana LeYisud shel Petah Tikva* [Jubilee Book for Fiftieth Anniversary of the Founding of Petah Tikva]. Tel Aviv, Dfus A. Eitan and S. Shoshani.

Yazbak, M. 1999. "Templers as Proto-Zionists? The 'German Colony' in Late Ottoman Palestine." *Journal of Palestine Studies* 28:4, 40–54.

3

SOCIETAL BELIEFS, COLLECTIVE EMOTIONS, AND THE PALESTINIAN-ISRAELI CONFLICT

Oded Adomi Leshem and Eran Halperin

Will right-wing religious Jews living in ideological settlements in the West Bank agree to forsake the settlement project and evacuate their homes in return for a comprehensive peace agreement with the Palestinians? Will Islamist Palestinians from the West Bank be willing to abandon the idea of the Right of Return in exchange for an agreement with the Israelis? Most of the readers of this book, and possibly many more who have some basic knowledge of the conflict, will rightly guess that the answer is no. All-out opposition among ideologically committed Israelis and Palestinians to forgo their principled beliefs was also what Jeremy Ginges and his colleagues predicted when they designed their study, conducted among political hawks from both sides (Ginges et al. 2007). But what will happen if the same deals are proposed to the same people together with a lucrative offer: substantial monetary compensation granted by the international community? Will their opposition to peace remain the same once reparations are on the table? Will they acquiesce?

Ginges, a social psychologist from the New School, and his co-authors did not predict that their hawkish participants would take the offer, nor that their opposition would remain the same. In fact, the researchers hypothesized a third scenario. They predicted that participants' rejection of the proposals would *increase* once material compensation was offered and, as the results from the study revealed, the researchers were right (Ginges et al. 2007). When material reparations were on the table, participants' opposition to a comprehensive peace accord was higher than when compensations were not mentioned. The researchers explain that forsaking principled positions was not an option for the Israeli and Palestinian participants in the first place. When material compensation was offered, it violated sacrosanct values, insult was added to injury, and opposition to the peace agreements increased.

Traditional decision-making theories will not suffice to explain the seemingly irrational and impractical reactions of those who participated in the study. Indeed, the political behaviour of citizens (and elites) mired in decades of violent ethnonational conflict is hardly rational or pragmatic (Bar-Tal and Halperin 2013; Halperin and Bar-Tal 2011; Kelman 2018). Rather, conflict-related behaviour of those embroiled in intractable conflict can be better explained by what Daniel Bar-Tal and others call the socio-psychological infrastructure of intractable conflicts. During the formative stages of these prolonged disputes, a comprehensive set of

DOI: 10.4324/9780429027376-5

societal beliefs and collective emotions evolve regarding the adversary (i.e., the outgroup), one's own group (the ingroup), and the conflict itself (Bar-Tal 2013). In the course of the conflict, these beliefs and emotions solidify to form the rigid socio-psychological infrastructure through which citizens feel, think, and behave.

For example, to endure the material and psychological costs of the conflict and be willing to sacrifice their lives, group members must be convinced that their goals are just and rightful (Bar-Tal 2007; Klar and Baram 2014). Over time, self-justification becomes ingrained in society to the extent that society members become blind to their share of responsibility for the conflict's continuation. Another rigid belief held by those living in intractable conflict is that the outgroup is immoral and subhuman. Among other negative ramifications, denying the outgroup's humanity helps ingroup members justify past and contemporary atrocities committed against the outgroup (Bar-Tal et al. 2014; Oren 2019; Staub 1990). These and other beliefs and emotions that constitute the socio-psychological infrastructure of the conflict are shared by most group members and create one of the most challenging obstacles for public support for peace.

There is no doubt that the obstacles that stand in the way of resolution of the Israeli-Palestinian conflict are many. Some barriers are related to international and regional factors, others concern resources and security. There are also processes in the domestic politics of each society that hamper any movement towards conflict transformation in Israel-Palestine. However, intertwined in every macro-level cause is a powerful socio-psychological system of assumptions, beliefs, and emotions that influences leaders' and citizens' conflict-related decisions and behaviours. Israelis' and Palestinians' sense of vulnerability, support for armed action, and reluctance to compromise all stem, at least in part, from the socio-psychological infrastructure of the conflict. This socio-psychological infrastructure is highly functional when the conflict is at its peak. At times of relative calm, it inhibits group members' ability to identify opportunities for resolution. Distrust and resentment toward the outgroup coupled with a sense of self-righteousness and victimhood are powerful socio-psychological constructs that often override pragmatic decisions when it comes to resolution and reconciliation. Thus, even in the rare cases where international and regional factors align to enable conditions conducive to peace, the rigid socio-psychological infrastructure pulls the societies and their leadership back into antagonistic and hostile prepositions. For this reason, the socio-psychological infrastructure of the conflict serves as one of the biggest obstacles to conflict resolution.

Our aims in this chapter are twofold. We first wish to present the rationale behind the socio-psychological infrastructure of the Palestinian-Israeli conflict. In the last thirty years, significant advancements in the theoretical and empirical study of the socio-psychological infrastructure of the conflict boosted our knowledge on why it formed and how it contributes to the continuation of the dispute (for a comprehensive review, see Sharvit and Halperin 2016). Our second aim is to propose that resolving the Palestinians-Israeli conflict must entail a systematic challenge of the socio-psychological infrastructure of the conflict. In other words, we argue that the conflict is anchored in detrimental perceptions and emotions which, by nature, are subjective and that peace can only be attained by systematically challenging these subjective constructs.

The chapter continues as follows: We start by presenting how the social-psychological infrastructure is formed and becomes a major force propelling the dispute. We then discuss how the social-psychological infrastructure manifests itself in the context of the conflict in Israel-Palestine by focusing on four key societal beliefs; each group's unquestioned beliefs in the justness of their goals, their adversary's delegitimate existence, their own exclusive victimization, and the common belief that the conflict is innately irreconcilable.[1] We also describe the emotions associated with these beliefs. As will be presented, these beliefs and emotions are widespread and detrimental to the promotion of peace. We conclude by describing ways the socio-psychological infrastructure can be challenged and highlighting some implications of the socio-psychological approach to conflict resolution in Palestine-Israel.

As much as possible, we tried to include what is known on the socio-psychological infrastructure of both societies. However, research on the socio-psychological infrastructure of the conflict was conducted mainly among Jewish-Israelis while, regrettably, there are very few studies on the socio-psychological infrastructure of Palestinian society (for exceptions see: Canetti-Nisim et al. 2008; Halperin, Russell, Trzesniewski et al. 2011; Hasan-Aslih et al. 2019; Leshem and Halperin 2020a; Nasie and Bar-Tal 2012; Shaked 2016). Logistical, ethical, and political challenges make it difficult to obtain data from Palestinians living in the Occupied Palestinian Territories (OPT) (Leshem et al. 2020) and even from Palestinian citizens of Israel. This chapter is unique because it presents, side by side, what we know so far about the socio-psychological infrastructure of both societies.

The Socio-psychological Infrastructure of the Israeli-Palestinian Conflict

Intractable ethnonational conflicts, such as the one between Jews and the Palestinians, begin when groups' goals are understood as mutually incompatible (Bar-Tal, Kruglanski, and Klar 1989; Mitchell 1981). During the British Mandate, the perception of incompatible goals was quickly manifested through violence (Arieli 2013; Cohen 2015). Violence escalated, the number of casualties increased, and the costs of the conflict rose. In order to cope with the continuing state of hostility and loss while maintaining group members' commitment to their respective national struggles, Jews and Palestinians developed sets of positive beliefs (e.g., we are rightful) and emotions (e.g., pride) about their own group, and negative beliefs (the adversary is immoral) and emotions (e.g., hate) towards the outgroup. Together with a biased collective memory about the historical origins of the conflict, these emotions and beliefs evolved into the socio-psychological infrastructure of the conflict (Bar-Tal 2007; 2013).

The socio-psychological infrastructure provides Jews and Palestinians with a one-sided prism through which the conflict is experienced and interpreted (Bar-Tal and Halperin 2013; Magal et al. 2018). It offers simple answers to complex questions. Who is the victim? – We. Who is the perpetrator? – They. Why do we fight? – Because they want to eradicate us. The socio-psychological infrastructure also defines the emotional repertoire group members are expected to express towards the outgroup (e.g., fear, anger, and hate) and the ingroup (e.g., pride, empathy). The infrastructure is highly functional. It helps Palestinians and Jews justify the enormous costs its members are expected to endure and creates the psychological platform for mobilizing group members to engage in violent actions. Notably, the socio-psychological infrastructure creates *meaning* within the chaotic, unpredictable reality of the conflict (Sharvit 2016).

The widespread presence of the socio-psychological infrastructure in the media and public discourse results in its quick acquisition. Israeli Jews and Palestinians absorb the socio-psychological infrastructure as children and adolescents (Nasie 2016; Shalhoub-Kevorkian 2006; Teichman 2016; Teichman and Zafrir 2003). Its themes are disseminated through school textbooks (Bar-Tal 1998), films (Shohat 1989), mass communication outlets (Oren 2019), and leaders' speeches (Oren 2016; Shaked 2016). Both societies devote attention and resources to maintain the socio-psychological infrastructure and protect it from criticism (Bar-Tal 2013; Hameiri, Sharvit et al. 2016; Klar and Baram 2014; Shaked 2016). As the Palestinian-Israeli conflict progressed, the socio-psychological infrastructure ossified and became inseparable from how Jews and Palestinians feel, think, and behave (Kelman 2018).

The power of the socio-psychological infrastructure is vividly apparent in the numerous failed attempts to reach an agreement between Israel and the Palestinians. Detailed solutions that address most of the interests of both peoples have been suggested by the international community, with the needed guarantees to implement the agreements. Lines have been drawn, arrangements drafted, and assurances granted, yet the parties revert to their destructive positions prescribed by the socio-psychological infrastructure: Distrust, suspicion, and animosity.

To exemplify the formation and consequences of the socio-psychological infrastructure among Israelis and Palestinians, we will focus on societal beliefs and collective emotions. *Societal beliefs* are one of the three pillars of the socio-psychological infrastructure of intractable conflicts, alongside collective emotions and collective memory, and pertain to the set of truisms vehemently held by group members from rival parties (Bar-Tal 1998). *Collective emotions* such as hate, fear, and anger are conflict-related emotions that societies mired in conflict sanction as legitimate and appropriate. These widely shared emotions have a tremendous impact on group members' behaviours during conflict and, as such, pose a substantial barrier to conflict resolution (for a detailed review, see Halperin 2016).

Societal Beliefs and Collective Emotions among Jewish-Israelis and Palestinians

Societal beliefs constitute the perceived shared reality and the common point of reference shaping group members' interpretation of past, present, and anticipated future of conflict-related events (Bar-Tal, Sharvit et al. 2012). Palestinians' and Jewish Israelis' belief in the absolute justness of their goals, their profound sense of victimhood, and their perceptions of the "enemy" as inhuman are some of the societal beliefs common among citizens and elites alike. Apart from beliefs about the outgroup and the ingroup, citizens locked in an intractable conflict also hold rigid beliefs about the nature of the conflict itself. One of these beliefs is that the conflict is innately irresolvable.

As a whole, societal beliefs form a rigid and dogmatic ideology, which simplifies the complexities of the conflict and serves as a lens by which group members understand it (Bar-Tal, Sharvit et al. 2012). In times of escalation, societal beliefs intensify and become more salient in the public discourse (Hameiri, Sharvit et al. 2016; Klar and Schori-Eyal 2015). In turn, the intensification of these detrimental beliefs feeds the conflict's continuation. In this chapter, we focus on four core beliefs found in both societies. We describe each belief in detail, the way it is experienced in each society, and its negative ramifications for conflict resolution. We also highlight the collective emotions that complement and reinforce these core beliefs.

Justness of Goals

Possibly the most central societal belief held by Israelis and Palestinians is the belief in their exclusive right over the land between the Jordan River and the Mediterranean Sea (Sharvit 2016). This belief, adamantly held by both sides, is apparent in the maps hung on the halls of public schools in Israel and the OPT. Walk into any elementary school in Israel and look at the map. The internationally recognized Green Line will be absent, and "Israel" will be written over all the area between the "River and the Sea." Walk into any school in the West Bank; a similar map will be hung on the wall with "Palestine" written over the same area. Jewish-Israelis' and Palestinians' beliefs about their entitlement to the entire land are rooted in historical and religious arguments and modern political claims concerning the right to self-determination of ethnic collectives (Arieli 2013; Litvak 1994). As such, they are part of legitimate political beliefs and ideologies collectives might have. What makes this belief a socio-psychological barrier is its exclusiveness, namely, that it entails the complete negation of the outgroup's claims. Why do Israelis and Palestinians stress that their right to the Holy Land is exclusive? Is it only a matter of scant resources? Scarcity of land? Security?

The socio-psychological approach asserts that the problem is not about resources but rather concerns group members' innermost belief that acknowledging the outgroups' claims of indigenousness is a declaration that their own claims are not (Arieli 2013). In the formative years of the conflict, societal beliefs evolved such that they tied each group's claim for indigenousness to the negation of the other's indigenousness. Thus, to strengthen their own beliefs in "nativeness," both Israelis and Palestinians expend tremendous resources to refute their adversary's connection to the land (Kelman 2018).

Looking at the Jewish-Israeli society, 68 per cent agree or strongly agree with the proposition that "The Jews have an exclusive claim to the land as it has been their homeland for generations" (Leshem and Halperin 2020a). According to the hegemonic Zionist narrative, the historical and spiritual connections of Jews to the land coupled with the continuous persecution of Jews in the diaspora provide more than ample reasons why establishing a national home for the Jews in the Holy Land is a just and worthy endeavor (Oren et al. 2015). One of the ways the early Zionists justified the exclusiveness of their claims was by dismissing the fact that the land was already inhabited (Arieli 2013). The premise, "A land with no people for a people without a land," was conveniently accepted as a truism by supporters of Zionism. Furthermore, the conquest of the West Bank and the Gaza Strip in 1967 was, and still is, regarded by many as a direct continuation of the Zionist idea. As such, Israel's control over the Palestinian Territories is mainly seen as legitimate and just (Arian 1995; Halperin et al. 2010). By extrapolation, almost all violent actions carried out in the name of defending the idea of a Jewish State are justified. For instance, the three deadliest military operations in the Gaza Strip, "Cast Lead" (2008), "Pillar of Defense" (2012), and "Protective Edge" (2014), which amounted to 3,804 dead Palestinians (926 of them children), were seen by almost 90 per cent of Jewish-Israelis as fully justified (Magal et al. 2018).[2]

Palestinians also justify their exclusive rights over the land between the River and the Sea by referencing their indigenousness and dismissing Jewish connection to the land. Ninety-four per cent of Palestinians agree or strongly agree with the statement that "The Palestinians have an exclusive claim to the land as it has been their homeland for generations" (Leshem and Halperin 2020a). According to the Palestinian narrative, Palestinians have been dwelling on the land for centuries and constituted most of the population of Mandatory Palestine until they were forcefully expelled in 1948. The only reason their proportion in the population dropped from 95 per cent in 1920 to 70 per cent in 1946 is Britain's unjust policy to let the Jews immigrate to a land not theirs. Palestinians dismiss the historical connection of Jews to the land and stress that the Palestinian self-determination movement began before the Zionists started their settlement project (Shaked 2018). The arrival of the Jews to Palestine in the early twentieth century is thus seen as mere colonialism, an opportunistic attempt by the West to rob Palestinian land and resources. Therefore, all the historical efforts to grant land and resources to the Jews, from the Peel Commission plan proposed in 1937 to the "Two-State Solution," are unjust and wrongful (Arieli 2013).

One of the most profound expressions of Palestinians' belief in the justness of their goals is the idea of "Sumud," or steadfastness (Nassar and Heackok 1990). Sumud represents Palestinian perseverance, stubbornness, and commitment to the goal of self-determination in the land of Palestine, a commitment that did not wane throughout the decades of hardship (Shaked 2018).

No matter the cost or pain, Palestinians will always hold on to their claim to the land between the River and the Sea.

Anger is the collective emotion associated with justness of the goals, or more accurately, with its perceived violation. Anger towards the outgroup will be elicited when the group's goals are perceived as under threat, but more importantly, when this threat is perceived as unfair or unjust (Halperin 2011). In many cases, anger will be manifested in aggressive behaviours aimed at correcting the perceived injustice or eliminating the perceived threats to the goals of the ingroup. Anger is thus associated with group members' support for aggressive actions and military interventions against the "enemy" (Halperin 2011; Huddy et al. 2007; Skitka et al. 2006).[3]

Two related consequences stem from group members' belief in the unquestionable justness of their goals and the anger they feel when these goals are contested. The first is that any action against the outgroup, no matter how aggressive, is justified as an act of self-defence. After all, when the land is considered exclusively "ours," others' claims to the land are regarded as an outright assault requiring a severe response. The second has to do with the attention to the past rather than the future. When groups are devoted exclusively to issues in the past (like arguing about indigenousness), they cannot focus on the future (how this conflict can be resolved). Conflict resolution, by definition, requires a transition from dwelling in the past to planning for the future (Deutsch et al. 2006). This transition is almost impossible when each side is dedicated to proving its indigenousness and disproving the Other's.

Delegitimizing the Other

Like other groups involved in prolonged intergroup conflict, Israelis and Palestinians develop a stable set of negative perceptions about each other (Kelman 2018; Magal et al. 2018; Shaked 2018). These perceptions may include the belief that the other side is aggressive by nature, lacks morals and values, or that the outgroup members are inferior, backward, and primitive (Kteily et al. 2016). Negative stereotypes about the outgroup are common among Jewish-Israeli and Palestinian youths (Maoz 2000) and are openly expressed in the media and the public sphere (Kelman 1999; 2018). When aggregated, these negative perceptions may lead to the moral exclusion of the outgroup (Staub 1990). Moral exclusion is the omission of people, or groups of people, from the moral universe assumed to be shared by all human beings, and by extrapolation, from the rules and constraints these morals imply (Opotow 1990; Staub 2005). Excluding outgroup members from the moral universe makes fighting them more manageable and, through comparison, boosts ingroup members' convictions about their own worth and morality.

Many Israeli Jews view Arabs and Palestinians as aggressive, devious, and untrustworthy by nature (Oren 2019; Teichman and Zafrir 2003). In recent years, Israeli leaders have promoted the idea that Palestinians are morally inferior to Jews and depict them as primitive and having no respect for the value of life. These accusations are often presented in comparison to the high moral values that are a part of the Jewish tradition (Magal et al. 2018). In 2013, Minister of Defence Bogie Yaalon said, "We in the West, sanctify life, while many in the Arab societies sanctify death." Other Israeli Parliament members ridiculed Palestinians and mocked their existence as a social group. For example, speaking at the Knesset assembly, MK Oren Hazan (Likud Party) claimed in his infamous speech in 2017 that Palestinians are less worthy than cheap dish-washing detergent. Speaking from the same podium, MK Anat Barko (Likud Party) said there is no such thing as Palestinians because Arabs cannot pronounce the syllable "P." That same year, Benjamin Netanyahu referred to the Arabs surrounding Israel as animal predators. It is no wonder that 60 per cent of the Israeli public thinks that the moral standards of the Palestinians are lower than other societies (Pliskin et al. 2014).

Palestinian claims against the Zionist movement also use demeaning rhetoric, often building on anti-Semitic themes. Palestinian newspapers from the first half of the twentieth century depicted Jews as worthless lowlifes who control the world's money (Khalidi 1997). Some newspapers reported that Jews kidnapped Arab boys and used their blood to prepare for Passover (Shaked 2018). Since the First Intifada, degrading descriptions of Jews became widespread, with Jews depicted as liars, cowards, and mentally ill. Jews were accused of deliberately spreading diseases like AIDS and distributing drugs to Palestinians (Shaked 2018). Anti-Semitic themes are also found in formal documents. For example, article 22 of the 1988 Hamas Covenant reads,

> Their wealth permitted them to take control of the world media ... They also used this wealth to stir revolutions in various parts of the globe ... it has come to pass, and no one objects, that they stood behind WWI to wipe out the Islamic Caliphate ... They also stood behind WWII, where they collected immense benefits from trading with war materials and prepared for the establishment of their state. ... There was no war that broke out anywhere without their fingerprints on it.
>
> *(The Covenant of the Islamic Resistance Movement 1998)*

Finally, Israel and the Zionist movement are delegitimized by directly comparing them to Nazis (Shaked 2018). The use of Nazism and the swastika symbol to portray Israel and Zionism heightened during the Intifadas. The Israeli prisons were called the "Nazi camps," and the treatment of Palestinians by Israel was described as more brutal than the behaviours of Nazis during World War II (Shaked 2018).

The collective emotion tied to delegitimization is outgroup hate (Staub 2005). Hate is an enduring negative affective response directed at a particular individual or group (Halperin et al. 2012; Halperin, Russell, Dweck et al. 2011). In intergroup conflict, hate includes the fundamental denunciation of the outgroup accompanied by resentment and contempt towards the outgroup's cultural symbols. The behavioural reaction associated with outgroup hate is outgroup harm (Halperin, Russell, Dweck et al. 2011); that is, the willingness and desire to inflict pain on the outgroup. Outgroup hate is also the most dominant emotional antecedence of political intolerance (Halperin et al. 2009).

Hating members of the other party and delegitimizing them have grave consequences. First, delegitimizing the outgroup makes it much easier to aggress against its members because the moral boundaries that limit the use of force against others are impaired when the opponent is considered subhuman (Opotow 1990; Sharvit 2016; Staub 2005). In these cases, outgroup members are excluded from moral considerations, which, in turn, makes it permissible to harm them "on the premise that they are expendable, undeserving, exploitable, and irrelevant" (Maoz and McCauley 2008: 95). Second, hate and delegitimization create enormous barriers to conflict resolution. Negotiation and compromise would not be considered when the adversary is regarded as innately malign and morally deficient. Why should people reconcile with a group they abhor?

Victimhood

One of the most pervasive societal beliefs among Palestinians and Jews is that the ingroup is the only victim of the conflict (Bar-Tal, Sharvit et al. 2012). This notion is grounded in historical events where the ingroup was subject to excessive harm, persecution, or injustice (Schori-Eyal, Klar, Roccas et al. 2017; Shaked 2018; Volkan 1998). Another layer, comprised of exaggeration and myths surrounding the painful history, adds to the sense of group victimhood (Arieli 2013). Past, present, and imagined future events are then understood in light of the assumption that the ingroup is the weaker and more vulnerable side in the conflict (Noor et al. 2017; Schori-Eyal et al. 2014; Vollhardt 2009; Vollhardt and Staub 2011). For example, in one of our surveys conducted among a representative sample of Jewish-Israelis and Palestinians from the West Bank and Gaza Strip, we found that Palestinians and Jewish Israelis equally believe that they were "always subject to disproportional aggression from the other side," with only 7 per cent of Israelis and 12 per cent of Palestinians questioning this claim.

Palestinians' sense of victimization is grounded in what they believe to be a systemic attempt to expel them from their land (Rouhana and Bar-Tal 1998; Vollhardt 2009). From the Palestinian perspective, Zionism is a colonialist movement backed by the West (Arieli 2013), and, as in all colonialist endeavours, the true natives are those paying the price for the colonizer's greed. The Zionists are willing to use all means necessary to end Palestinians' presence in Palestine, as attested by their aggressive actions dating back to the beginning of the twentieth century. The Balfour Declaration of 1917 is one of the earliest expressions of international involvement in the attempt to grab the land from the Palestinians (Muslih 1988). Palestinians also see themselves as victims of the separation plan announced by the United Nations in 1947, which disproportionally divided the land in favour of the Jewish minority (Khalidi 1985). Victimhood is thus an inherent part of Palestinian history. The notion that Palestinians are the sole victims of the conflict is promoted by leaders, the media, and the educational system (Shaked 2018).

The most notable example of victimhood in the Palestinian collective memory is the 1948 *Nakba*, where hundreds of thousands of Palestinians were displaced (Said 1992; Shaked 2016). The second wave of Zionist expansions came in 1967 and involved another round of displacement. It marked the beginning of the military control of the Palestinians in the West Bank, the Gaza Strip, and East Jerusalem. Since then, Palestinians have been the victims of the Jewish settlement enterprise, where land and resources are being confiscated and given to the settlers (Shaked 2018). Violent acts against Palestinian civilians feed Palestinians' sense of victimhood and vulnerability. The Massacres of Dir Yasin (1948), Kayba (1953), Kafr Kassem (1956), Sabra and Shatila (1982), and The Cave of the Patriarchs (1994) strengthen the collective sense of victimhood (Morris 1999; Shaked 2018).

Though Israel has clear superiority in political, economic, and military capabilities, Jewish-Israelis' sense of victimhood is one of their most central and prevalent societal beliefs (Bar-Tal et al. 2009). In its core lies the idea that Jews have been the subject of persecution since biblical times (Klar et al. 2013). As the belief dictates, gentile nations and their leaders, from the Pharos to Hitler, tried to eliminate the Jews as a collective (Vollhardt 2009). The harm was and still is, intentional, and its roots lie in the deep hatred towards the Jewish people. On Passover night, Jewish households within and outside Israel recite the famous verse, "In every generation they rise against us to destroy us. And the Holy One, blessed be He, rescues us from their hands". Moreover, in the 1,877 years from the destruction of the Second Temple to the establishment of the State of Israel, the Jewish diaspora was not only severely persecuted but also completely defenceless. With no sovereignty or military force, Jews were subject to discrimination, harassment, and violence, culminating in the attempt to eradicate their entire race.

The Holocaust and other anti-Semitic events are omnipresent in the political discourse in Israel and have a powerful impact on politics and foreign affairs (Elon 2010). In speeches and ceremonies, Jewish-Israelis are reminded of their past as weak, defenceless people and the external threats of the present and the future. It is no wonder that almost two-thirds of

Jewish-Israelis believe that the "whole world is against us" and that this attitude will "never change regardless of Israel's policies" (Magal et al. 2018). With this prism, Jewish-Israelis interpret the conflict with the Palestinians. For example, even though the death ratio in the last twelve years is 1:23 (one Israeli fatality to twenty-three Palestinian fatalities), 80 per cent of Jewish-Israelis believe that they "have always been subjected to disproportionate aggression from the side of the Palestinians."

In the Israeli-Palestinian context, victimhood is a card that is often played to extort gains in the international arena. Palestinians claim that Israel uses the Holocaust and anti-Semitism to attain immunity for their crimes against the Palestinians. The rationale is that the West's guilt for its role in the Holocaust impedes its ability to condemn Israel's policies in the OPT (Shaked 2018). On the other hand, Jewish-Israelis blame the Palestinians for deliberately perpetuating the "Palestinian refugee problem" to exert the pity of the international community. The competition over who has suffered more is one of the defining features of the conflict, with each group confident in its entitlement to be labelled as the ultimate victim (Noor et al. 2012)

Victimhood is associated with the collective emotional response of fear. Collective fear arises when group members feel threatened by a real or perceived danger to the group and are unsure of their abilities to thwart the threat (Halperin et al. 2008). Fear is vital for the survival of humans, but in intractable conflicts, citizens become oversensitive to fear as they see threats even when threats do not exist. The excessive levels of fear "freezes" citizens' ideologies and reduces their motivation to take risks in the pursuit of a resolution (Bar-Tal 2001; Jarymowicz and Bar-Tal 2006). In the context of the conflict in Palestine-Israel, fear and threat are associated with support for military actions against the adversary and greater opposition to compromise (Arian 1989; Canetti et al. 2017; Canetti-Nisim et al. 2008, Leshem and Halperin 2021) as well as with a negative bias towards information favouring a peace proposal (Cohen-Chen et al. 2014a, 2014b).

Victimhood, in itself, is also a hurdle for conflict resolution (Vollhardt 2009). For instance, recent studies have demonstrated that those who see their group as victim are more likely to judge other groups as hateful towards one's own group (Schori-Eyal, Klar and Ben-Ami 2017). Moreover, an enduring sense of group victimhood is associated with aggressive attitudes and emotions toward the outgroup and less willingness to forgive and reconcile (Maoz and Eidelson 2007; Schori-Eyal, Klar, Roccas et al. 2017). In addition, when group members are convinced they are the sole victims of the conflict, they cannot see their own wrongdoings and take responsibility for past and present transgressions.

Belief in the Conflict's Innate Irreconcilability

Most Israelis and Palestinians believe that the conflict will never be resolved (Telhami and Kull 2013). This bleak conclusion derives from citizens' accumulated experiences of hostility and violence and the projection of these experiences onto the future. The low levels of expectation for peace are also based on the observation that the conflict has been, so far, resilient to negotiation attempts. Indeed, since the 1950s, international leaders of high calibre have visited the region in an effort to establish common ground for peace talks, but ultimately, to no avail.

Yet, the belief in the conflict's irreconcilability is so widespread because pessimism comes with psychological benefits. First, pessimism serves as a convenient excuse for passiveness. When people adopt a pessimistic stance, they find it easier to exonerate themselves from the taxing commitment to actively strive for peace. Another advantage of pessimism is that it protects against potential disappointments (Breznitz 1986). Simply put, believing that the conflict is irresolvable minimizes the chances that hopes will be dashed. Last, and quite ironically, perceiving the conflict as irreconcilable provides a sense of predictability and certainty for those enmeshed in decades of conflict because the reality of the dispute, however dire, is known and familiar (Fiske 2010; Thórisdóttir and Jost 2011). Peace, on the other hand, is unknown and entails significant uncertainty. Because people tend to avoid uncertainty, they might prefer, at least to some extent, the harsh but familiar reality of the conflict to the uncertain and unpredictable reality of peace (Leshem and Halperin 2020b).

Public polls and empirical studies show that Jewish-Israelis' expectations that peace will someday materialize are meager (Cohen-Chen et al. 2015; Maoz and Shikaki 2014; Rosler et al. 2017; Stone 1982; Telhami and Kull 2013). The percentage of Jewish-Israelis who believe that peace is probable is only 4.2 per cent (Leshem 2017). Looking at the difference between Jewish-Israelis' desires for the Two-state Solution and their expectations that it will materialize provides a valuable insight. Less than half of the Jewish-Israelis who do support the Two-State Solution think it will actually be realized (Leshem and Halperin 2020b). Recent studies revealed some of the socio-psychological factors that drive Jewish-Israelis' disbelief in the likelihood of peace. First, it seems that their pessimism is influenced by their extreme underestimation of Palestinians' actual desires for peace (Leshem and Halperin 2020a). In other words, Israelis do not believe that Palestinians want peace and therefore conclude that peace is impossible.

Threat perceptions also have an impact on Jewish-Israelis' low expectations for peace. The more Jewish-Israelis feel threatened by the likelihood of conflict-related harm (like suicide bombings and rockets), the less they think peace is possible (Leshem and Halperin 2021). Last, sceptical outlooks voiced by Israel's hard-line leaders promote pessimism among their constituents. Netanyahu's declaration from 2015 that Israelis will have to learn to "live on their swords" forever exemplifies the sceptical outlook Israelis are expected to endorse. Leaders' pessimistic predictions are attractive because they supposedly offer "realistic" interpretations of political reality rather than "naïve delusions" (Navot et al., 2017; Oakeshott, 1996). During conflicts, hawkish leaders can use pessimistic predictions about the possibility of resolution to secure citizens' support for hard-line policies and derail public pressure to strive for peace.

Palestinians' scepticism is also affected by their high levels of threat from the likelihood of violence (Leshem and Halperin 2021) and their underestimation of Israelis' actual desires for peace (Leshem and Halperin 2020a). In this regard, the two societies are similar. However, comparing the means, it seems that Palestinians' expectations for peace are higher than Jewish-Israelis'. For instance, Palestinians' estimation of the chances to "end the conflict" is significantly higher than Jewish-Israelis'. In addition, Palestinians' assessment of the likelihood of "achieving a peace agreement that assures independence for Palestinians and security for Jews" is also significantly higher than the assessments of Jewish-Israelis (Leshem and Halperin 2020a). This finding may seem counterintuitive because, compared to Israelis, Palestinians live under harsher conflict conditions. If anything, the dire situation in the West Bank and Gaza Strip is likely to cause deep scepticism among Palestinians. The relatively high optimism among Palestinians can be explained by the different strategies adopted by the two societies and their leadership (Navot et al. 2017; Oakeshott 1996). One of the ideas advocated by contemporary Israeli leaders is that the conflict can be managed but not resolved (Zanany 2018). Jewish-Israelis can readily endorse this approach because they live under relatively benign conditions of the conflict. In other words, as the high-power group, Jewish-Israelis can afford to be sceptical. Palestinians, however, cannot afford to be pessimistic. As a group struggling for self-determination, Palestinians are compelled to believe in the feasibility of peace and its assumed fruits: statehood and independence.

The collective emotional response related to the belief that the conflict is irreconcilable is despair. The emotion of despair is provoked when a sought-for goal, in our case, peace, seems unachievable. Despair is associated with passiveness and resignation (Breznitz 1986).

Despair may lead to withdrawal from any activity that can potentially promote peace among the high-power group. Among low-power group members, despair can lead citizens to partake in extreme violence. Butler (2002) cites despair as one of the chief sources driving young Palestinians to become suicide bombers. Eyad El Sarraj, the director of the Gaza Community Mental Health Program, argues that despair was a key factor propelling the escalation during the Second Intifada "Desperation is a very powerful force[;] … it propels people to actions or solutions that previously would have been unthinkable" (Butler 2002, 72).

Arguably, there may be many good reasons to be sceptical about the feasibility of peace in Palestine-Israel. The immense animosity and distrust between the groups, the toxic rhetoric of leaders, the new challenges in regional and international politics, and the rising death toll; are all good reasons to believe that peace in the Holy Land is improbable. In this chapter, we are not interested in providing evidence supporting or refuting this claim. What we are interested in, however, is examining scepticism as a psychological inhibitor of peace.

Empirical findings reveal the detrimental effect of political pessimism on social and political progress. For example, recent studies have shown that pessimism is one of the strongest predictors of reluctance to compromise for peace (Cohen-Chen et al. 2015). In other studies, Israelis' and Palestinians' pessimism predicted their opposition to peacebuilding initiatives, even after accounting for hawkish ideology (Leshem and Halperin 2020a). Stated differently, scepticism is not only an obvious conclusion stemming from the many obstacles for resolution but an obstacle in and of itself (Kelman 2018). Hopelessness leads parties to divest efforts and resources from the pursuit of resolution. There is simply no incentive to support negotiations, compromise, or peacebuilding if peace is assumed to be unachievable (Coleman 2003). When no attempt is being made in the direction of resolution, the conflict exacerbates and in turn, feeds back into the sense of pessimism (Kelman 2010; Pruitt 1997). Hopelessness is thus a self-fulfilling prophecy (Kelman 2018).

The four societal beliefs mentioned above and the collective emotional responses accompanying them are some of the most widely held beliefs and emotions pervading the "hearts and minds" of Palestinians and Jewish-Israelis. The fact that they are based on biased information, partial interpretations, and cognitive fallacies does not mean they are inconsequential (Porat et al. 2015). Research has revealed that the stronger Israelis and Palestinian adhere to these beliefs, the more they reject compromise (e.g., Bar-Tal, Halperin, et al. 2012; Cohen-Chen et al. 2014a; Porat et al. 2015), oppose peacebuilding (Leshem 2019; Leshem and Halperin 2020a), and support aggressive acts against each other (e.g., Schori-Eyal et al. 2019). If societal beliefs are so detrimental to conflict resolution, the question becomes: what can be done about them? Are there ways these beliefs can be challenged or even overturned? Can we mitigate their harmful ramifications?

Challenging Societal Beliefs Using Psychological Interventions

In the last decades, political psychologists studying intergroup conflicts pioneered a novel research agenda on using psychological interventions to mitigate intergroup conflicts. This line of research involves designing interventions and empirically testing their effectiveness in challenging the socio-psychological infrastructure of the conflict. Psychological interventions are stimuli that can come in many forms. They could be slogans, messages, activities, educational materials, or workshops designed to directly or indirectly challenge beliefs and emotions that serve as barriers to conflict resolution. The effectiveness of an intervention is assessed not only on whether the belief or emotion was altered but also on whether the change elicited attitudes and behaviours that are more conducive to conflict resolution.

The scope of this chapter only allows for a brief description of some of the psychological interventions found to facilitate conflict transformation in Palestine-Israel. Here, too, most of the studies were conducted among Jewish-Israelis (but see: Halperin et al. 2011). Further research using Palestinian samples is critical to understand how to best utilize psychological interventions among lower-power groups. However, studies on Jewish-Israelis are pivotal because, as members of the high-power group, Jewish-Israelis have more capacity and leeway to initiate conflict transformation.

In one study, Jewish-Israelis' belief in the absolute justness of their goals was challenged by exposing them to extreme versions of these goals, an intervention called "paradoxical thinking" (Hameiri, Porat, et al. 2016). In the study, Jewish-Israeli hawks who were exposed to a media campaign containing extreme versions of their own attitudes decreased their support for aggressive policies and increased their support for conciliatory policies, even one year after the participants were exposed to the intervention (Hameiri, Porat, Bar-Tal, et al. 2014). In another study, outgroup dehumanization was challenged by offering participants to take the perspective of their adversary using virtual reality technology (Hasson et al. 2019). The rationale is that once people experience the conflict from the perspective of their rivals, their ability to humanize the outgroup increases. In the study, Jewish-Israelis took the perspective of a Palestinian couple stopped at gunpoint by Israeli soldiers. This immersive experience significantly reduced participants' dehumanization of Palestinians and, in turn, increased their cautiousness to judge Palestinians as a threat. The positive effects of the virtual reality experience were observed even five months after the study ended.

Perceptions of victimhood were challenged by exposing participants to information that showed that both groups are victims of the conflict, thus reducing the exclusiveness of victimhood each group claims to have (Shnabel et al. 2013; Vollhardt 2009). In these studies, Jewish-Israelis' and Palestinians' willingness to forgive the other side was higher among those who learned that both groups are victims of the conflict than those who were not exposed to the psychological intervention (Shnabel et al. 2013). Last, the deeply held perception that the conflict is irresolvable was challenged in several studies that used hope-inducing interventions (Cohen-Chen et al. 2015; Cohen-Chen et al. 2014a, 2014b; Leshem 2019; Leshem et al. 2016). In these studies, Jewish-Israeli participants exposed to hope-inducing tasks (Cohen-Chen et al. 2015) or hope-inducing messages conveyed in a short video (Leshem 2019) increased their support for compromise and peacebuilding initiatives as a result of increased hope for peace.

These and other conflict interventions proved to effectively promote conflict resolution amidst high levels of tension and hostility. Respondents exposed to the interventions increased their support for forgiveness, compromise, and peacebuilding. Many of these interventions can serve as blueprints for media campaigns or policies aimed at changing the hearts and minds of Palestinians and Israelis locked in the deadly dispute in the Holy Land.

Conclusion

Given the high price they pay, it stands to reason that Palestinians and Israelis would have the greatest interest in opting for resolution. After all, even a partial solution to the conflict should be preferred over the continuation of anguish, violence, and death. A mutually agreed-upon solution should be the preferable choice for both parties, also because the extreme continuation of the conflict implies that absolute victory is improbable.

However, the Palestinian-Israeli conflict persists despite the enormous costs both parties endure and aggregated pain they are required to suffer. We have demonstrated that the Israeli-Palestinian conflict's widespread and rigid socio-psychological infrastructure enables this tragic situation. In this chapter, we have sketched only a brief and partial account of the socio-psychological infrastructure of the Israeli-Palestinian conflict and the way it influences the behaviours of those involved in the dispute. Researchers, practitioners, grassroots leaders, and policymakers will benefit from adopting a socio-psychological approach to not only enhance their ability to understand the conflict but also to create the conditions for transforming it.

Recommended Readings

Bar-Tal, D. 2013. *Intractable Conflicts*. Cambridge: Cambridge University Press.

Halperin, E. 2016. *Emotions in Conflict: Inhibitors and Facilitators of Peace-Making*. Routledge Studies in Political Psychology 2. New York: Routledge.

Kelman, H. C. 2018. *Transforming the Israeli-Palestinian Conflict: From Mutual Negation to Reconciliation*. Edited by P. Mattar and N. Caplan. Oxon: Routledge.

Sharvit, K., and E. Halperin, eds. 2016. *A Social Psychology Perspective on the Israeli-Palestinian Conflict: Celebrating the Legacy of Daniel Bar-Tal*. Vols. 1 and 2. New York: Springer International Publishing.

Notes

1 There are other core beliefs that have been identified as part of the socio-psychological infrastructure, but they are not the focus of this chapter.

2 Of course, there were Israeli fatalities as well in these operations (a total of 87, luckily none of them children) www.ochaopt.org/data/casualties.

3 It is important to note that under certain conditions, anger can result in constructive behaviors that facilitate conflict resolution (Halperin 2011).

Questions for the Discussion

(1) Are some socio-psychological components more detrimental to peace in Israel-Palestine?

(2) What can we learn from research on the political psychology of other conflicts that will help improve our understanding of the conflict in Israel-Palestine?

(3) Under what conditions can the rigid socio-psychological infrastructure of the Palestinian-Israeli conflict be overcome?

(4) What other interventions can we design to tackle the socio-psychological infrastructure of the Palestinian-Israeli conflict? How can we implement these interventions to create conditions more conducive to conflict resolution?

(5) Is the conflict beyond resolution as long as the socio-psychological barriers are not addressed?

References

Arian, A. 1989. "A People Apart Coping with National Security Problems in Israel." *Journal of Conflict Resolution* 33:4, 605–631.

Arian, A. 1995. *Security Threatened*. Cambridge: Cambridge University Press.

Arieli, S. 2013. *A Border Between Us*. Aliat Hagag (Hebrew).

Bar-Tal, D. 1998. "Societal Beliefs in Times of Intractable Conflict: The Israeli Case." *International Journal of Conflict Management* 9:1, 22–50.

Bar-Tal, D. 2001. "Why Does Fear Override Hope in Societies Engulfed by Intractable Conflict, as It Does in the Israeli Society?" *Political Psychology* 22:3, 601–627.

Bar-Tal, D. 2007. "Sociopsychological Foundations of Intractable Conflicts." *American Behavioral Scientist* 50:111, 1430–1453.

Bar-Tal, D. 2013. *Intractable Conflicts*. Cambridge: Cambridge University Press.

Bar-Tal, D., A. W. Kruglanski, and Y. Klar. 1989. "Conflict Termination: An Epistemological Analysis of International Cases." *Political Psychology* 10:2, 233–255.

Bar-Tal, D. and D. Antebi. 1992. "Siege Mentality in Israel." *International Journal of Intercultural Relations* 16:3, 251–275.

Bar-Tal, D. and E. Halperin. 2013. "The Nature of Socio-psychological Barriers to Peaceful Conflict Resolution and Ways to Overcome Them." *Conflict & Communication Online* 12:2, 1–16.

Bar-Tal, D., et al. 2009. "A Sense of Self-perceived Collective Victimhood in Intractable Conflicts." *International Review of the Red Cross* 91:874, 229–258.

Bar-Tal, D., K. Sharvit, et. al. 2012. "Ethos of Conflict: The Concept and its Measurement." *Peace and Conflict: Journal of Peace Psychology* 18:1, 40–61.

Bar-Tal, D., E. Halperin, et al. 2012. "Intractable Conflicts: Why Society Members Tend to Support their Continuation and Resist their Peaceful Resolution?" In *Social Psychology of Social Problems: The Intergroup Context*, ed. A. Golec de Zavala and A. Cichocka, eds. Houndmills, England: Palgrave Macmillan.

Bar-Tal, D., et al. 2014. "Sociopsychological Analysis of Conflict-supporting Narratives: A General Framework." *Journal of Peace Research* 51:5, 662–675.

Breznitz, S. 1986. "The Effect of Hope on Coping with Stress." In *Dynamics of Stress*, ed. M. H. Appley. New York: Plenum Press, 295–306.

Butler, L. 2002. "Suicide Bombers: Dignity, Despair, and the Need for Hope. An Interview with Eyad El Sarraj." *Journal of Palestine Studies* 31:4, 71–76.

Canetti, D., et. al., 2017. "Exposure to Violence, Ethos of Conflict, and Support for Compromise Surveys in Israel, East Jerusalem, West Bank, and Gaza." *Journal of Conflict Resolution* 61:1, 84–113.

Canetti-Nisim D., et al. 2008. "Life, Pocketbook, or Culture: The Role of Perceived Security Threats in Promoting Exclusionist Political Attitudes toward Minorities in Israel." *Political Research Quarterly* 61:1, 90–103.

Cohen, H. 2015. *Year Zero of the Arab-Israeli Conflict 1929*. Boston: Brandeis University Press.

Cohen-Chen, S., et al. 2014a. "Hope in the Middle East: Malleability Beliefs, Hope, and the Willingness to Compromise for Peace." *Social Psychological and Personality Science* 5:1, 67–75.

Cohen-Chen, S., et al. 2014b." The Differential Effects of Hope and Fear on Information Processing in Intractable Conflict." *Journal of Social and Political Psychology* 2:1, 11–30.

Cohen-Chen, S. 2015. "Perceptions of a Changing World Induce Hope and Promote Peace in Intractable Conflicts." *Personality and Social Psychology Bulletin* 41:4, 498–512.

Coleman, P. T. 2003. "Characteristics of Protracted, Intractable Conflict: Toward the Development of a Meta framework-I." *Peace and Conflict: Journal of Peace Psychology* 9:1, 1–37.

Deutsch, M., P. Coleman, and E. Marcus, eds. 2006. *The Handbook of Conflict Analysis and Resolution*, 2nd ed. San Francisco, CA: Jossey-Bass.

Elon, A. 2010. *The Israelis: Founders and Sons*. London: Faber and Faber.

Fiske, S. 2010. *Social Beings*, 2nd ed. Hoboken, NJ: Wiley.

Ginges, J., et al. 2007. "Sacred Bounds on Rational Resolution of Violent Political Conflict." *Proceedings of the National Academy of Sciences* 104:18, 7357–7360.

Halperin, E. 2011. "Emotional Barriers to Peace: Emotions and Public Opinion of Jewish Israelis about the Peace Process in the Middle East." *Peace and Conflict: Journal of Peace Psychology* 17:1, 22–45.

Halperin, E. 2016. *Emotions in Conflict: Inhibitors and Facilitators of Peace-Making*. Routledge Studies in Political Psychology 2. New York: Routledge.

Halperin, E., and D. Bar-Tal. 2011. "Socio-psychological Barriers to Peace Making: An Empirical Examination within the Israeli Jewish Society." *Journal of Peace Research* 48:5, 637–651.

Halperin, E., et al. (2008) "Emotions in Conflict: Correlates of Fear and Hope in the Israeli-Jewish Society." *Peace and Conflict: Journal of Peace Psychology* 14:3, 233–258.

Halperin, E., et al. 2009. "The Central Role of Group-Based Hatred as an Emotional Antecedent of Political Intolerance: Evidence from Israel." *Political Psychology* 30:1, 93–123.

Halperin, E., et al. 2010. "Socio-psychological Implications for an Occupying Society: The Case of Israel." *Journal of Peace Research* 47:1, 59–70.

Halperin, E., A. G. Russell, C. S. Dweck, et al. 2011. "Anger, Hatred, and the Quest for Peace: Anger Can Be Constructive in the Absence of Hatred." *Journal of Conflict Resolution* 55:2, 274–291.

Halperin, E., A. G. Russell, K. H. Trzesniewski, et al. 2011. "Promoting the Middle East Peace Process by Changing Beliefs about Group Malleability." *Science* 333:6050, 1767–1769.

Halperin, E., et. al. 2012. "In Love with Hatred: Rethinking the Role Hatred Plays in Shaping Political Behavior." *Journal of Applied Social Psychology* 42:9, 2231–2256.

Hameiri, B., R. Porat, D. Bar-Tal, et al. 2014. "Paradoxical Thinking as a New Avenue of Intervention to Promote Peace." *Proceedings of the National Academy of Sciences* 111:30, 10996–11001.

Hameiri, B., R. Porat, D. Bar-Tal, et al. 2016. "Moderating Attitudes in Times of Violence through Paradoxical Thinking Intervention." *Proceedings of the National Academy of Sciences* 113:43, 12105–12110.

Hameiri, B., K. Sharvit, et al. 2016. "Support for Self-Censorship Among Israelis as a Barrier to Resolving the Israeli-Palestinian Conflict." *Political Psychology* 38:5, 795–813.

Hasan-Aslih, S., et al. 2019. "A Darker Side of Hope: Harmony-Focused Hope Decreases Collective Action Intentions Among the Disadvantaged." *Personality and Social Psychology Bulletin* 45:2, 209–223.

Hasson, Y. et al. 2019. "The Enemy's Gaze: Immersive Virtual Environments Enhance Peace Promoting Attitudes and Emotions in Violent Intergroup Conflicts." *PloS one* 14:9, e0222342.

Huddy, L., et al. 2007. "On the Distinct Political Effects of Anxiety and Anger." In *The Dynamics of Emotion in Political Thinking and Behavior*, eds. A. Crigler, et al. Chicago, IL: University of Chicago Press, 202–230.

Jarymowicz, M., and D. Bar-Tal. 2006. "The Dominance of Fear over Hope in the life of Individuals and Collectives." *European Journal of Social Psychology* 36:3, 367–392.

Kelman, H. C. 1999. "The Interdependence of Israeli and Palestinian National Identities: The Role of the Other in Existential Conflicts." *Journal of Social Issues* 55:3, 581–600.

Kelman, H. C. 2010. "Interactive Problem Solving: Changing Political Culture in the Pursuit of Conflict Resolution." *Peace and Conflict: Journal of Peace Psychology* 16:4, 389–413.

Kelman, H. C. 2018. *Transforming the Israeli-Palestinian Conflict: From Mutual Negation to Reconciliation*. Mattar, P. and Caplan, N. (eds). Oxon: Routledge.

Khalidi, R. 1997. *Palestinian Identity – The Construction of Modern National Consciousness*. New York: Columbia University Press.

Khalidi, W. 1985. "A Palestinian Perspective on the Arab-Israeli Conflict." *Journal of Palestine Studies* 14:4, 35–48.

Klar, Y., and H. Baram. 2014. "In De *FENCE* of the In-Group Historical Narrative in an Intractable Intergroup Conflict: An Individual-Difference Perspective." *Political Psychology* 37:1, 37–53.

Klar, Y. and Schori-Eyal, N. (2015) "Gazing at Suffering Gaza from Suffering Sderot: Seeds of Forgiveness and Reconciliation Amidst the Turmoil?" *Group Processes & Intergroup Relations*: 1368430215570502. DOI: 10.1177/1368430215570502.

Klar, Y., et al. 2013. "The 'Never Again' State of Israel: The Emergence of the Holocaust as a Core Feature of Israeli Identity and Its Four Incongruent Voices." *Journal of Social Issues* 69:1, 125–143.

Kteily, N., et al. 2016. "They See Us as Less than Human: Metadehumanization Predicts Intergroup Conflict via Reciprocal Dehumanization." *Journal of Personality and Social Psychology* 110:3, 343–370.

Leshem, O. A. 2017. "What You Wish for is Not What You Expect: Measuring Hope for Peace during Intractable Conflicts." *International Journal of Intercultural Relations* 60, 60–66.

Leshem, O. A. 2019. "The Pivotal Role of the Enemy in Inducing Hope for Peace." *Political Studies* 67:3, 693–711.

Leshem, O. A., and E. Halperin E .2020a. "Hoping for Peace during Protracted Conflict: Citizens' Hope Is Based on Inaccurate Appraisals of Their Adversary's Hope for Peace." *Journal of Conflict Resolution* 64:7–8, 1390–1417.

Leshem, O. A., and E. Halperin. 2020b. "Hope During Conflict." In *Historical and Multidisciplinary Perspectives on Hope*, ed. S. Van den Heuvel. New York: Springer, 179–196.

Leshem, O. A. and E. Halperin. 2021. "Threatened by the Worst but Hoping for the Best: Unraveling the Relationship Between Threat, Hope, and Public Opinion During Conflict." Political Behavior, 20.

Leshem, O. A., et al. 2016. "Instilling Hope for Peace During Intractable Conflicts." *Social Psychological and Personality Science* 7:4, 303–311.

Leshem, O. A., et al. 2020. "Surveying Societies Mired in Conflict: Evidence of Social Desirability Bias in Palestine." *International Journal of Public Opinion Research* 32:1, 132–142.

Litvak, M. 1994. "A Palestinian Past: National Construction and Reconstruction." *History and Memory* 6:2, 24–56.

Magal, T., et al. 2018. "Why It Is So Difficult to Resolve the Israeli-Palestinian Conflict by Israeli Jews? A Socio-psychological Approach." In *Handbook of Israel: Major Debates*, eds. E. Ben-Rafael, et al. Berlin and Boston: De Gruyter Oldenbourg, 1211–1239.

Maoz, I. 2000. "An Experiment in Peace: Reconciliation-Aimed Workshops of Jewish-Israeli and Palestinian Youth." *Journal of Peace Research* 37:6, 721–736.

Maoz, I., and R. J. Eidelson. 2007. "Psychological Bases of Extreme Policy Preferences: How the Personal Beliefs of Israeli-Jews Predict Their Support for Population Transfer in the Israeli-Palestinian Conflict." *American Behavioral Scientist* 50:11, 1476–1497.

Maoz, I., and C. McCauley. 2008. "Threat, Dehumanization, and Support for Retaliatory Aggressive Policies in Asymmetric Conflict." *Journal of Conflict Resolution* 52:1, 93–116.

Maoz, I., and K. Shikaki. 2014. *Joint Israeli Palestinian Poll, December 2014.* Jerusalem, Ramallah: The Harry S. Truman Research Institute for the Advancement of Peace, The Hebrew University of Jerusalem.
Mitchell, C. R. 1981. *The Structure of International Conflict.* London: Macmillan.
Morris, B, 1999. *Righteous Victims: A History of the Zionist-Arab Conflict, 1881–1999.* New York: Knopf.
Muslih, M. 1988. *The Origins of Palestinian Nationalism.* New York: Columbia University Press.
Nasie, M. 2016. "Young Children's Experiences and Learning in Intractable Conflicts." In *A Social Psychology Perspective on The Israeli-Palestinian Conflict*, eds. K. Sharvit and E. Halperin. Cham: Springer International Publishing, 31–48.
Nasie, M., and D. Bar-Tal. 2012. "Sociopsychological Infrastructure of an Intractable Conflict Through the Eyes of Palestinian Children and Adolescents." *Peace and Conflict: Journal of Peace Psychology* 18:1, 3–20.
Nassar, J., and R. Heackok. 1990. *Intifada: Palestine at the Crossroads.* New York: Praeger.
Navot, D., et al. 2017. "The 2015 Israeli General Election: The Triumph of Jewish Skepticism, the Emergence of Arab Faith." *The Middle East Journal* 71:2, 248–268.
Noor, M., et al. 2012. "When Suffering Begets Suffering: The Psychology of Competitive Victimhood between Adversarial Groups in Violent Conflicts." *Personality and Social Psychology Review* 16:4, 351–374.
Noor, M., et. al. 2017. "The Social Psychology of Collective Victimhood: Collective Victimhood." *European Journal of Social Psychology* 47:2, 121–134.
Oakeshott, M. 1996. *The Politics of Faith and the Politics of Scepticism.* New Haven, CT: Yale University Press.
Opotow, S. 1990. "Moral Exclusion and Injustice: An Introduction." *Journal of Social Issues* 46:1, 1–20.
Oren, N. 2016. "The Jewish-Israeli Ethos of Conflict." In *A Social Psychology Perspective on The Israeli-Palestinian Conflict*, eds. K. Sharvit and E. Halperin. Cham: Springer International Publishing, 115–132.
Oren, N. 2019. *Israel's National Identity: The Changing Ethos of Conflict.* Boulder, CO: Lynne Rienner.
Oren, N., et al. 2015. "Construction of the Israeli-Jewish Conflict-Supportive Narrative and the Struggle Over Its Dominance." *Political Psychology* 36:2, 215–230.
Pliskin, R., et al. 2014. "Are Leftists More Emotion-Driven than Rightists? The Interactive Influence of Ideology and Emotions on Support for Policies." *Personality and Social Psychology Bulletin* 40:12, 1681–1697.
Porat, R., et al. 2015. "The Effect of Sociopsychological Barriers on the Processing of New Information about Peace Opportunities." *Journal of Conflict Resolution* 59:1, 93–119.
Pruitt, D. G. 1997. "Ripeness Theory and the Oslo Talks." *International Negotiation* 2:2, 237–250.
Rosler, N., et al. 2017. "The Distinctive Effects of Empathy and Hope in Intractable Conflicts." *Journal of Conflict Resolution* 61:1, 114–139.
Rouhana, N. N., and D. Bar-Tal. 1998. "Psychological Dynamics of Intractable Ethnonational Conflicts: The Israeli–Palestinian Case." *American Psychologist* 53:7, 761–770.
Said, E. W. 1992. *The Question of Palestine.* New York: Vintage Books.
Schori-Eyal, N., et al. 2014. "Three Layers of Collective Victimhood: Effects of Multileveled Victimhood on Intergroup Conflicts in the Israeli–Arab Context." *Journal of Applied Social Psychology* 44:12, 778–794.
Schori-Eyal, N., Y., Klar, and Y. Ben-Ami. 2017. "Perpetual Ingroup Victimhood as a Distorted Lens: Effects on Attribution and Categorization." *European Journal of Social Psychology* 47:2, 180–194.
Schori-Eyal, N., Y. Klar, S. Roccas. 2017. "The Shadows of the Past: Effects of Historical Group Trauma on Current Intergroup Conflicts." *Personality and Social Psychology Bulletin* 43:4, 538–554.
Schori-Eyal, N., et al. 2019. "Intergroup Commonality, Political Ideology, and Tolerance of Enemy Collateral Casualties in Intergroup Conflicts." *Journal of Peace Research* 56:3, 425–439.
Shaked, R. 2016. "Ethos of Conflict of the Palestinian Society." In *A Social Psychology Perspective on the Israeli-Palestinian Conflict*, eds. K. Sharvit and E. Halperin. Cham: Springer International Publishing, 133–148.
Shaked, R. 2018. *Behind the Kaffiyeh: The Conflict from the Palestinian Perspective.* Rishon le-Tsiyon: Yediʻot aḥaronot: Sifre ḥemed.
Shalhoub-Kevorkian, N. 2006. "Negotiating the Present, Historicizing the Future: Palestinian Children Speak about the Israeli Separation Wall." *American Behavioral Scientist* 49:8, 1101–1124.
Sharvit, K. 2016. "Sociopsychological Foundations of the Israeli-Palestinian Conflict: Applying Daniel Bar-Tal's Theorizing." In *A Social Psychology Perspective on The Israeli-Palestinian Conflict*, eds. K. Sharvit and E. Halperin. Cham: Springer International Publishing, 1–11.
Sharvit, K., and E. Halperin, eds. 2016 *A Social Psychology Perspective on the Israeli-Palestinian Conflict: Celebrating the Legacy of Daniel Bar-Tal.* Cham: Springer International Publishing.

Shnabel, N., S. Halabi, and M. Noor. 2013. "Overcoming Competitive Victimhood and Facilitating Forgiveness through Re-categorization into a Common Victim or Perpetrator Identity." *Journal of Experimental Social Psychology* 49:5, 867–877.

Shohat, E. 1989. *Israeli Cinema: East/West and the Politics of Representation*. Austin, TX: University of Texas Press.

Skitka, L. J., et al. 2006. "Confrontational and Preventative Policy Responses to Terrorism: Anger Wants a Fight and Fear Wants 'Them' to Go Away." *Basic and Applied Social Psychology* 28:4, 375–384.

Staub, E. 1990. "Moral Exclusion, Personal Goal Theory, and Extreme Destructiveness." *Journal of Social Issues* 46:1, 47–64.

Staub, E. 2005. "The Origins and Evolution of Hate. In *The Psychology of Hate*, ed. R. J. Sternberg. Washington, DC: American Psychological Association, 51–66.

Stone, R. A. 1982. *Social Change in Israel, Attitudes and Events*. New York: Praeger.

Teichman, Y. 2016. "Stereotypes and Prejudice in Conflict: A Developmental Perspective." In *A Social Psychology Perspective on The Israeli-Palestinian Conflict*, eds. K. Sharvit and E. Halperin. Cham: Springer International Publishing, 17–30.

Teichman, Y., and H. Zafrir. 2003. "Images Held by Jewish and Arab Children in Israel of People Representing their Own and the Other Group." *Journal of Cross-Cultural Psychology* 34:6, 658–676.

Telhami, S., and S. Kull. 2013. *Israeli and Palestinian Public Opinion on Negotiating a Final Status Peace Agreement*. Washington, DC: Saban Center at the Brookings Institution.

The Covenant of the Islamic Resistance Movement. 1998. Available at: https://avalon.law.yale.edu/20th_century/hamas.asp.

Thórisdóttir, H., and J. T. Jost. 2011. "Motivated Closed-Mindedness Mediates the Effect of Threat on Political Conservatism." *Political Psychology* 32:5, 785–811.

Vallacher, P. R. et al. 2010. "Rethinking Intractable Conflict: The Perspective of Dynamical Systems." *American Psychologist* 65:4, 262–278.

Volkan, V. D. 1998. *Bloodlines: From Ethnic Pride to Ethnic Terrorism*. Boulder, CO: Westview Press.

Vollhardt, J. R. 2009. "The Role of Victim Beliefs in the Israeli-Palestinian Conflict: Risk or Potential for Peace?" *Peace and Conflict: Journal of Peace Psychology* 15:2, 135–159.

Vollhardt, J. R., and E. Staub. 2011. "Inclusive Altruism Born of Suffering: The Relationship between Adversity and Prosocial Attitudes and Behavior Toward Disadvantaged Outgroups." *American Journal of Orthopsychiatry* 81:3, 307–315.

Zanany, O. 2018. *From Conflict Managing to Political Settlement Managing: The Israeli Security Doctrine and the Prospective Palestinian State*. Tel Aviv: Tami Steinmetz Center for Peace Research.

4
PALESTINIAN NATIONALISM

Wendy Pearlman

Scholars use the term *nationalism* to refer to several different dimensions of experience. At the level of group consciousness, nationalism is a kind of social identity grounded in a people's sense of common history and of boundaries that distinguish them from other peoples. At the level of ideology, nationalism is a set of assertions or aims constituting a program or vision of how politics should be organized. Most basically, that ideology is encapsulated in Ernest Gellner (1983)'s definition of nationalism as a principle of political legitimacy that holds that the political and national units should be congruent. At the level of mobilization, nationalism is a form of collective action. It is a social movement by those who see themselves as constituting a nation and who come together to advance the will and interests of that nation.

While Palestinian nationalism can be documented and analysed at all of these levels, this chapter focuses on the third.[1] From calls for Arab independence in the wake of World War I through varied types of action against occupation today, Palestinians' movement for national self-determination has evolved throughout the twentieth century and continues to evolve. This chapter examines this historical trajectory with particular attention to the movement's strategies, goals, and organizational forms.

From Ottoman to British Rule

Under the Ottoman Empire, the land between the Mediterranean Sea and the Jordan River spanned a number of administrative districts. At the close of the nineteenth century, the people who called this area home manifested layered local, familial, regional, ethnic, religious, and legal identities. Commercial, social, and cultural relations linked them to the rest of Greater Syria, ethnic identity created bonds to other Arabic-speaking areas, and commitment to protecting Islam fortified the Muslim majority's political allegiance to the Ottoman state. Though there was no entity called "Palestine," newspapers and other writings from the area express the inhabitants' sense of belonging to a unique place in the Arab world (Khalidi 1997) as well as their incipient reference to themselves as "Palestinians" (Mandel 1976).

This era also saw a literary and cultural revival of Arabism, which then became a political movement asserting Arab independence from both Ottoman colonialism and Anglo-French imperialism – what George Antonius (1946) dubbed the great "Arab Awakening." The

DOI: 10.4324/9780429027376-6

Palestinian national movement was the local manifestation of this popular and anti-colonial upsurge. Its trajectory, however, was set apart due to its confrontation with another national movement's claim to the same land. Beginning in the 1880s, successive waves of immigration increased the size of the Jewish population of Palestine exponentially. Arabs in Palestine protested Zionism with written declarations, and even a few clashes, as early as the 1880s and 1890s (Mandel 1976). Their concerns intensified in 1917, when the Balfour Declaration announced that the British government would

> view with favour the establishment in Palestine of a national home for the Jewish people and will use their best endeavours to facilitate the achievement of this object, it being clearly understood that nothing shall be done which may prejudice the civil and religious rights of existing non-Jewish communities in Palestine.

For the approximately 90 per cent of the population that was Muslim or Christian Arab, this policy not only prejudiced their civil and religious rights, but also precluded their political rights to their own national home in the land that they viewed as their patrimony for a millennium.

The first leaders of this Palestinian nationalist trend were the urban and landowning aristocrats, those who had functioned as elites throughout the Levant for decades (Hourani 1968). Though these notables acted as the default representatives of the Arab population, they disagreed on whether Palestine should be independent or unified with other Arab lands under the independent Arab Kingdom of Syria announced in Damascus in 1918 (Muslih 1989). In 1919, delegates from branches of the Muslim-Christian Association (MCA), the most prominent of elite-led social and political clubs in Palestine, held an "All-Palestine Congress." It declared rejection of Zionism, called for self-determination, and urged that "Southern Syria" be joined with its Arab neighbours.

The following year, Great Britain received a League of Nations mandate over Palestine, and France toppled Faysal's Arab Kingdom, dashing hopes for a united Greater Syria. The MCA convened a second Congress and called for recognition of Palestine as a distinct political entity to be governed by a parliament elected by the Arabic-speaking peoples' resident before the war. It rejected the right of the Jewish people over Palestine and called for ends to both Jewish immigration and the transfer of land to Jewish control (Porath 1974). Delegates elected an "Executive Committee of the Palestinian Arab Congress," which became known as the Arab Executive (AE). When colonial authorities expressed doubt that the AE represented the will of the population, organizations such as chambers of commerce and municipalities issued announcements asserting that it did (Muslih 1989). The AE established a permanent secretariat in Jerusalem and links to local MCA branches, as well as links to the other clubs and societies (Lesch 1977). Three more Palestinian Arab Congresses from 1921–1923 brought together larger numbers of delegates representing the country's various regions, associations, and religions.

This elite-led movement pressed for the national cause through an array of constitutional and nonviolent measures (Porath 1975, Lesch 1977). Nationalist societies presented protest notes and memoranda, convened congresses, delivered speeches, and published articles. They coordinated testimony before the King-Crane commission, dispatched by the United States, and organized delegations to the World War I peace conferences of 1919 and 1920, though the British ultimately forbade them from leaving Palestine. Upon its formation, the AE continued to submit memos, draft statutes, and petitions. It met with Colonial Secretary Winston Churchill, held conversations with the High Commissioner for Palestine, and dispatched delegations to London to meet with members of Parliament and government officers. Seeking international support, the AE sent representatives to make the Palestinian case before the pope, the Turkish government, and the League of Nations in Geneva. It organized demonstrations, delivered speeches, distributed leaflets, publicized its positions in the press, and reached out to the public in mosques, churches, and cafes.

These political efforts failed to realize Palestinian Arabs' nationalist goals. In this context, grassroots frustration with the expansion of the Jewish national home project fuelled major violent incidents in 1920, 1921, and 1929. While each had a unique trigger, they followed a pattern in which Arab civilians attacked Jewish life and property, British security forces intervened and killed nearly as many Arabs, and subsequent British commissions of inquiry concluded that violence was propelled by Arabs' anger and fear about being made strangers in their own homeland (see Great Britain 1921; Great Britain 1930). This trepidation intensified as Jews fled rising anti-Semitism in Europe, and the Jewish community grew from 11 per cent of the population of Palestine in 1922 to 28 per cent in 1936. Jewish land purchases not only increased in stride, but also increasingly shifted from sparsely-populated territories to the fields on which poor Arab peasants depended for survival (Stein 1984).

The Palestinian national movement needed strong, unifying institutions in order to face these formidable challenges, yet these remained elusive. Reflective of strategies of divide and conquer, the British tended to deal with Arabs as either Christians or Muslims, not as a single nation (Khalidi 2006). Indeed, the text of Britain's mandate did not endorse an official Arab agency to represent Palestine's Arab community, akin to the Jewish Agency authorized to represent the Jewish community. Beyond government policies, Palestinian Arab elites struggled with their own in-fighting. Amin al-Husayni, appointed by the British as Mufti of Jerusalem in 1921, emerged as the most popular figure in Arab Palestine (Mattar 1988). As he extended his influence, the rivalry between the Husayni and Nashashibi families splintered the traditional leadership so sharply that they did not convene a single Arab Congress between 1923–1928. At the same time, the elite's class interests were typically at odds with those of the peasantry and urban poor (Kanafani 1972). Peasants themselves were divided, as patron-client ties connected the various notable and rural clans, and thereby reinforced vertical rifts down to the grassroots (Tamari 1982). In this context of fragmentation, the country-wide network of MCA branches deteriorated. The AE neared bankruptcy and its work came to a standstill.

Meanwhile, socio-economic developments increasingly shifted the national movement from what Anne Lesch (1977) dubbed elite-led "mobilization from above" toward a more grassroots "mobilization from below." Expansions in literacy, education, urbanization, trade, and public health, as well as economic alternatives to subsistence agriculture, empowered novel forms of political engagement. A new generation of activists founded civil society groups such as sports and literary clubs, family-based societies, charitable associations, women's groups, chambers of commerce, and labour unions (Matthews 2006). Boy Scouts troops organized popular demonstrations and patrolled the coast for illegal Jewish immigration. New political parties and middle-class groups criticized traditional elites' failures to stop the Zionist project and called for more radical opposition to British policy. A preacher named Shaykh Iz al-Din al-Qassam began mobilizing Haifa's poorer residents in an armed struggle against Zionism and imperialism. His death in a 1935 battle against British troops inspired a religious and nationalist outpouring (Kanafani 1972, 70). Meanwhile, Britain's Parliament rejected the proposal for a legislative council encompassing all of Palestine's inhabitants, which was the national elites' last hope for political resistance against a seemingly imminent Jewish state

Against this backdrop, an April 1936 roadside incident provided the spark of what became the three-year "Grand Arab Rebellion." Arab gunmen shot Jewish travellers, and a Jewish paramilitary responded by shooting two Arabs. As rumours spread, Arabs rioted and attacked

Jews. Palestinian Arab activist professionals and merchants in major towns used the tension as a springboard for the organization of a grassroots protest effort. They called public meetings, formed popular "National Committees," and announced the commencement of a general strike (Zu'aytir 1980). These nationalists sought to seize the momentum to mobilize more radical opposition to British policies, yet also to obtain a measure of discipline to prevent events from spinning out of control. Within days, committees had emerged throughout Palestine. A countrywide general strike took hold, and the press responded with praise and calls for national unity behind the protest (Darwazah 1993).

As the rebellion cascaded across the country, different sectors of society participated, using non-violent means at their disposal (see Lesch 1977; Porath 1977). The Arab Car Owners' and Drivers' Association halted transport facilities, merchants and city labourers stayed home, prisoners refused to perform penal labour, and schools and factories closed. People participated in demonstrations and boycotted Jewish firms and products. Boy Scouts and urban young men enforced compliance with the strike and boycott at the neighbourhood level. Although civil servants in the mandatory apparatus did not go on strike, they donated a percentage of their salaries and submitted a memorandum to the government explaining Arab grievances and claims. Intellectuals demanded "no taxation without representation." The strike inspired a new popular unity that pushed hesitant elite politicians to form a coalition leadership body, the Arab High Committee (AHC) with Amin al-Husayni as president. The AHC announced that the strike would continue until the government ended Jewish immigration, banned land transfers from Arabs to Jews, and established a representative national government in Palestine.

The 1936 strike was accompanied by dozens of attacks on Jewish people and property, which increased as Britain refused to accommodate the strike's demands. The government sought to quell the rebellion with countermeasures that included the deportation and arrest of Arab activists, search and arrest without warrant, imposition of collective fines and curfew, and demolition of entire Arab neighbourhoods (Hughes 2010). As authorities cracked down, popular participation in civic protest receded, and bands of armed rebels formed in the countryside to carry out sniping and sabotage (Arnon-Ohanna 1981). After six months the AHC called off the strike, and the rebellion entered a hiatus.

In July 1937, Britain's Peel Commission issued its recommendation to partition Palestine into a Jewish state and an Arab state unified with Transjordan. Arab leaders rejected the plan, which would force nearly one third of the Arab population to come under Jewish rule or be transferred from their homes. Rebellion resumed and the number of guerrilla fighters swelled dramatically (Kimmerling & Migdal 2003). The British government poured thousands of troops into Palestine, declared martial law, and carried out repression that was not only severe, but often also collective or indiscriminate (Hughes 2010). It declared the AHC illegal, banned the National Committees, and arrested or deported many nationalist leaders.

Without leadership institutions to guide and discipline the nationalist movement, Arabs' social divisions became apparent. Armed bands used the rebellion as a guise for settling old scores, committing crimes, or expressing the resentment of the rural poor for the urban well-to-do (Swedenburg 1995). While, in Jerusalem, the Mufti threw his support behind continued rebellion, some Nashashibi affiliates accepted partition and others fled the country. As the rebellion intensified, Husayni forces vilified the Nashashibi opposition; the Nashashibi opposition supplied intelligence to the government, rebel bands assassinated oppositionists, and oppositionists organized bands against the rebels. By the rebellion's end, an estimated five thousand Palestinian Arabs had been killed, with approximately one quarter of their casualties inflicted by other Palestinians (Kimmerling & Migdal 2003). The national movement that emerged from the rebellion fractured, economically devastated, and leaderless. "The crippling defeat they had suffered in 1936–39," Rashid Khalidi (1997, 190) concludes, "was among the main reasons they failed to overcome it."

Exhausted by the end of World War II, Britain relinquished its Palestinian mandate to the United Nations in 1947. That November the General Assembly approved Resolution 181 partitioning Palestine into Arab and Jewish states, with international control over the Jerusalem-Bethlehem area. The Yishuv accepted the plan. The AHC and Arab states rejected it, and violence between Arabs and Jews began almost immediately. Jewish forces were better armed and organized, and quickly dominated the battlespace (Van Creveld 1998). On 14 May 1948, the state of Israel was declared. Arab state armies mobilized, and conventional combat ensued. By the time Israel signed armistice agreements with neighbouring Arab governments in 1949, it held approximately 78 per cent of mandatory Palestine, or 50 per cent more territory than was allotted by the United Nations partition plan. An estimated 700,000–760,000 Palestinian Arabs, some 60 per cent of the total Arab population, had fled or been forced from their homes as refugees (Morris 2004).

Coping with Catastrophe

The dissolution of Arab Palestine in the 1948 War, what Palestinians would call *al-Nakba* or "the Catastrophe," destroyed Palestinians' national life in nearly every respect. Villages were erased, families dispossessed of everything they owned, and the national community scattered across multiple states. From this incalculable shattering, however, unifying feelings of loss, exile, and historic injustice helped give rise to a new national consciousness. Commitment to the right of return, affirmed in United Nations Resolution of December 1948, became a defining national demand. Beyond that sense of purpose, discrimination in exile added to Palestinians' identities as a nation apart. The experience of being legally differentiated, economically marginalized, and socially stigmatized by host countries continually reminded refugees that they were Palestinian (see Turki 1972).

While rhetorically upholding the banner of Palestinian liberation, Arab states tended to view Palestinian refugees themselves as destabilizing, and thus restricted independent Palestinian political mobilization. Nevertheless, from 1959 to 1963, Palestinians managed to circumvent intelligence agencies to form some forty clandestine groups (Kimmerling and Migdal 2003, 238). More commonly, Palestinians joined existing Arab political parties. Many embraced Egyptian President Gamal Abdel Nasser and Arab nationalism. In the early 1950s, at the American University of Beirut, George Habbash spearheaded the Arab Nationalist Movement and asserted that anti-imperialism was the key to the recovery of Palestine. In Gaza, many young refugees joined the Muslim Brotherhood, but eventually became frustrated with its political conservatism. At the University of Cairo, a young Palestinian nationalist named Yasser Arafat argued that, rather than wait for Arab states to unite and attack Israel, Palestinians should rely primarily on themselves to liberate Palestine. This call gained popularity after Israel's four-month occupation of Gaza in 1956, an outgrowth of Great Britain, France, and Israel's invasion of Egypt in the Suez Crisis. Arafat and other "Palestine firsters" subsequently moved to Kuwait, where they formalized the "Palestinian National Liberation Movement," or Fatah (Cobban 1984; Sayigh 1997).

Fatah's clandestine organization grew into a network and began issuing a magazine, *Filastinuna* (Our Palestine), which facilitated contacts with Palestinians in other countries. In this and other publications, Fatah articulated a vision that challenged the reigning Arab order. In opposition to most regimes' inclination to subordinate Palestinians' struggle to their own government or party, Fatah stressed its ideological and organizational autonomy as an authentically popular organization (Khalaf 1981). Fatah's national liberation strategy centred on armed struggle. Fatah argued that guerrilla activity would not only wear Israel down by attrition, but also entangle Arab states in the conventional war that they preferred to postpone. Beyond this, Fatah endorsed the Fanonian view that by taking up arms Palestinians would overcome despair, transcend ideological differences, and reclaim their national honour.

Meanwhile, Nasser likewise recognized that the status quo of Arab representation of Palestinians was insufficient. In 1964 he led the first Arab League summit in authorizing Ahmed Shuqayri, the League's Palestinian delegate, to explore "the setting up of sound foundations for organizing the Palestinian people and enabling them to play their role in the liberation of their country and their self-determination" (Shemesh 1988, 37). Exceeding that mandate, the outspoken Shuqayri laid the foundations of a proto-state institution. He assembled 422 Palestinian personalities and declared the first session of the Palestinian National Council (PNC), which approved a Palestinian National Charter and announced the establishment of an overarching structure called the "Palestine Liberation Organization" (PLO). The PNC, confirmed as the PLO's parliament and highest authority, elected Shuqayri as chairman of an executive committee. The second Arab summit recognized the PLO and its military branch, the Palestine Liberation Army.

The Palestinian national movement thus proceeded along two tracks: guerrilla groups propelled from the bottom-up, and PLO-sanctioned institution-building from the top-down. These streams were mutually antagonistic: Shuqayri insisted upon his exclusive leadership of the Palestinian people, while Fatah viewed the PLO as an "envelope" by which Arab states sought to contain Palestinian nationalism (Sayigh 1997). In this context, Fatah pushed forward with its call for armed struggle. It carried out its first sabotage attack against Israel on New Year's Day 1965, issuing a statement in the name of Al-Asifa, which became known as its military wing. Fatah *fedayeen*, or "freedom fighters," continued to carry out such operations as planting roadside landmines and bombing pipelines, water pumps, warehouses, and power plants.

Accompanied by exaggerated pronouncements, Fatah's military activity garnered popular support and spurred the formation of other Palestinian groups eager to prove their nationalist credentials. The "Palestine Liberation Front" (PLF) was formed by Syrian army officers of Palestinian origin. Lest he fall behind, Shuqayri cooperated with the Arab Nationalists Movement and the PLF in establishing the PLO's own fedayeen squads. Guerrilla strikes against Israel doubled between 1966 and 1967 (Segev 2007, 143–144). Israel often targeted its reprisals against Arab states in the demand that they "take responsibility" and prevent cross-border attacks; the effectiveness of that strategy varied in accord with the politics of targeted states' own relations to the fedayeen, as well as their institutional and political capacity to restrict them (Pearlman and Atzili 2018). Eager to avert Israeli retaliation, Jordan, Lebanon, and Egypt worked to curb Palestinian military activity. By contrast, the revolutionary Ba'ath Party that seized power in Syria in 1963 aided Fatah with training, weaponry, and publicity. Competition among Arab states, tensions between them and Palestinian nationalists, and escalatory spirals engulfing Israel, Arab states, and Palestinian groups were some of the many factors leading the region to the brink of war by June 1967.

Nationalist Revival

Israel's defeat of Arab armies in the 1967 War, along with its occupation of the remainder of Mandate Palestine, represented both calamity and opportunity for the Palestinian national movement (Sayigh 1992). For many Palestinians the shocking outcome confirmed Fatah's position that Palestinians could not depend upon Arab states and must instead lead their own national struggle. As Arab state armies retreated from the frontlines, Palestinian fedayeen appeared to be the only force still committed to fighting Israel. The commandos' stature redoubled in March 1968, when Israel responded to Fatah attacks by invading its base near Karameh, Jordan. Palestinian and Jordanian forces launched an ambush that inflicted heavy Israeli losses. Though Arab casualties were greater, and Israel achieved its operational objectives, the Arab world heralded the "Battle of Karameh" as a mythic victory.

Against this backdrop, the Palestinian resistance movement rose "like a phoenix out of ashes" to reap "a harvest of hero-worship" (Sayigh 1979, 144). The word "Palestinian," for two decades associated with the downtrodden and displaced, came to conjure images of youth, intelligence, courage, and sacrifice (Peretz 1970, 327). Young refugees testified that the Palestinian revolution "gave me the answer to who I am" and "was the most important event … in all our lives" (Sayigh 1977, 34). Riding the wave of enthusiasm, dozens of new guerrilla groups formed, merged, splintered, and multiplied (Amos 1980; O'Neill 1978; Sayigh 1997). Fatah remained the largest faction with a deliberately mainstream appeal focused on Palestinian nationalism. The second-largest groups, the left-leaning Popular Front for the Liberation of Palestine (PFLP) and Popular Democratic Front for the Liberation of Palestine (PDFLP; later changed to DFLP), called for social revolution, Arab unity, and opposition to Arab regimes that they accused of being reactionary. When Shuqayri resigned in 1967, these and other commando groups agreed to join the PLO, with representation commensurate to their size. When the PNC convened in February 1969, Fatah formed the largest bloc and elected its spokesman, Yasser Arafat, as PLO chairman.

The restructured PLO was a milestone for contemporary Palestinian nationalism. It created an institutional framework within which the movement could deliberate policy, empower a single leadership, generate a clear set of symbols and slogans, and connect Palestinians across borders and ideological divides. While this was a fundamental step toward unifying a diasporic struggle, fragmentation was also built into the PLO's very structure. The PLO was not only an institution representing Palestinian nationalism, but also a political system within which Palestinian nationalist organizations adjudicated their different ideological and strategic approaches (Pearlman 2011). It was the umbrella under which Palestinian groups, as well as the states that stood behind them, bargained to determine least-common-denominator goals.

For Fatah-PLO leaders, the most basic goal was preserving the PLO's existence as the organ of independent Palestinian national decision-making, often referred to as *al-qarrar al-filastini al-mustaqeel*. To claim the right to represent all Palestinians, the PLO had to be open enough to accommodate the full range of Palestinian opinion and grant factions' demands to keep their own structures, programs, and alliances. PLO leaders used consensus decision-making, producing an annual political program through laborious back-door talks involving all factions. In practice, Fatah-PLO made the most pressing decisions in consultation only with each other (Khalidi 1986).

The fedayeen movement established its main operational base in Jordan, where it emerged as a parallel political system with its own police, courts, militias, and media. The long-standing tension between Palestinian nationalism and the Hashemite monarchy (Bailey 1984; Shlaim 1988) worsened as leftist factions called for the overthrow of King Husayn, and guerrilla attacks into the Israeli-occupied West Bank provoked harsh Israeli reprisals on Jordanian soil. Then, in September 1970, the PFLP landed four hijacked jetliners in Jordan and ignited them. The Jordanian army responded with an onslaught that became known as "Black September." By mid-1971, it had liquidated the last of the fedayeen from Jordan.

The PLO set up a new headquarters in Lebanon, where the government had already authorized it to maintain weapons and act as the governing authority in refugee camps. From the early 1970s, the Palestinian national movement continued to develop into something of a state-within-a-state in Lebanon (Brynen 1990). The fedayeen found support among Lebanese Muslims and leftists who wanted to transform Lebanon's confessional political system in which Christians held disproportionate state power, and wealthy elites neglected the country's poor periphery. The Palestinian movement's major detractors in Lebanon were defenders of that status quo. When these multifaceted tensions triggered a civil war in 1975, the Fatah-PLO leadership sought to avoid entanglement. Leftist PLO factions, by contrast, partnered with Lebanese allies demanding change. The Palestinian national movement struggled with this balancing act for months until Maronite Phalange militias' attacks on refugee camps made it even more untenable, and the PLO announced its official alliance with the Lebanese left (Sayigh 1997).

As civil war engulfed Lebanon, Palestinian factions' attacks continued across the border into Israel, as did Israel's retaliations against Lebanon. In 1978, Israel invaded south Lebanon and pushed PLO forces north of the Litani River. In 1982, Israel launched a major offensive to drive the PLO from its border once and for all. Troops reached the edge of Beirut and, after a three-month stand-off, the PLO leadership agreed to leave Lebanon and relocate to Tunis. The Israeli army entered Beirut and, under the shadow of its control, Lebanese Phalangist forces attacked the Sabra and Shatila camps and massacred an estimated 2,750 refugees.

Meanwhile, Egypt and Syria's surprise attack on Israel in 1973 had reshaped the regional environment in which the Palestinian national movement operated. In the war's aftermath, the United Nations hosted a first-ever Arab-Israeli summit as a step toward the pursuit of a peace settlement. Fatah-PLO leaders believed that the PLO needed to make political concessions on its stated goal of eliminating Israel if it were to gain states' recognition of its right to represent Palestinians in world diplomacy. If not, Jordan might manoeuvre to play that role and thereby advance its own claims to the West Bank. In this context, the 1974 PNC adopted a "Ten Point Transitional Program" that called for the establishment of a national authority in any Palestinian area liberated from or evacuated by Israel, as a phase toward total liberation. It also endorsed "all means of struggle," sanctioning diplomatic methods in addition to armed ones. Though radical factions took action to oppose the transitional plan, it stood as a monument in the national movement's gradual embrace of the principle of land for peace. In response, the Arab League declared the PLO to be the sole legitimate representative of the Palestinian people, and the United Nations granted it observer status. By the early 1980s, the PLO had formal representation in some 130 countries (Kirsci 1986).

Under and Against Occupation

Though the Palestinian national movement's centre of gravity solidified in exile, nationalist activity was never dormant in the West Bank and Gaza Strip. Between 1949 and 1967, Jordanian and Egyptian rulers prohibited, obstructed, or sought to control expressions of Palestinian nationalism. In 1967, activists in the West Bank and Jerusalem protested Israel's occupation with strikes and manifestos, while fighters in Gaza initiated a rebellion that only halted when Ariel Sharon imposed a sweeping crackdown in 1971 (Tessler 1994; Dakkak 1983).

In the years that followed, Israel curtailed Palestinian nationalist activism through a combination of repression and co-optation, while Jordan continued to vie for West Bankers' loyalty (Sahliyeh 1988). The "outside" PLO regarded the main task of Palestinians "inside" the occupied territories to be *sumud*, or remaining steadfast until armed struggle won liberation. Yet Palestinians under Israeli military rule created successive organizational structures to mobilize activism beyond that. First, in the West Bank, a network of underground "national committees" formed to address issues of both resistance and local welfare (Ahmad 1976). Building on that foundation, the Palestinian National Front became a semi-clandestine body coordinating various acts of nonviolent protest and non-cooperation (Sahliyeh 1988). In 1976, Israel held municipal council elections in the West Bank on the belief that their favoured personalities would win posts. Instead, pro-PLO nationalist candidates swept nearly every municipality (Ma'oz 1984). Thereafter, mayors and civil society activists came together in the National Guidance Committee to lead nationalist mobilization.

Meanwhile, similar to the 1930s, socio-economic developments spread nationalist consciousness throughout society and created a foundation for grassroots nationalist organizing. Labour in Israel hastened the transformation of the peasantry into a working class ready for political recruitment (Robinson 1997). Newly established Palestinian universities brought young people together in an activist student movement, while political imprisonment served as another kind of "school" in which a generation of Palestinians formed relationships with comrades from across the country, studied politics and philosophy, and redoubled their commitment to national liberation (Zeira 2019). At the same time, the Communist Party, mass organizations affiliated with PLO political factions, and other civic projects mobilized an increasingly large swath of the population in grassroots initiatives (Hiltermann 1991) Meanwhile, in Gaza, Muslim Brotherhood affiliates extended Islamist initiatives in civil society. Some Brotherhood affiliates demanded more forceful forms of resistance, and established a new group, "Islamic Jihad," to carry out armed operations (Abu-Amr 1994).

These developments brought an overwhelming number of Palestinians in the West Bank and Gaza Strip to identify with the larger Palestinian nationalist movement in general, and with the call to end the Israeli occupation, in particular. As that occupation entered its twentieth year with no end in sight, however, observers deemed the occupied territories to be a "pressure cooker ready to explode" (Nakle 1988, 210). In December 1987 an Israeli military truck in Gaza crashed into a car carrying Palestinian labourers, leaving four dead and seven injured. Riots ensued, and the Israeli army's violent response incited protests across the Gaza Strip and West Bank. Palestinians dubbed the budding uprising an *Intifada*, literally a "shaking-off" of the occupation.

The Intifada evolved into a grassroots revolt in which people of all walks of life sought to legitimate and rally behind the PLO, propel peace talks toward the goal of establishing a Palestinian state, and sustain everyday acts of defiance to force an end to the Israeli occupation (see Al-Madhoun 1989; Lockman and Beinin 1989; Schiff and Ya'ari 1989; Peretz 1990; Nassar and Heacock 1990; Rigby 1991; Ashrawi 1995). While there is no doubt various forms of social tensions remained in and even helped animate the uprising (Robinson 1997; Bucaille 2004), it also manifested a sense of national unity that struck many Palestinians to be as unprecedented as it was inspiring (Khalidi 1989). Hundreds of neighbourhood committees emerged throughout the occupied territories not only to organize protests at the local level, but also to meet communities' long-term needs necessary to sustain it. Representatives of Fatah, the DFLP, the PFLP and the Communist Party formed the United National Leadership of the Uprising (UNLU) as an underground, anonymous, consensus-based body. The UNLU issued communiqués, secretly printed and distributed throughout the West Bank and Gaza Strip, that both inspired the public and outlined a calendar of protest actions (see Mishal and Aharoni 1994).

While stone-throwing was a regular facet of confrontations between civilians and soldiers, the hallmark of the uprising was mass participation in deliberately unarmed forms of protest (King 2007; Pearlman 2011). Palestinians took part in demonstrations, defied soldiers on the streets, plastered walls with political graffiti, and displayed banned nationalist symbols such as the Palestinian flag. Youth erected barricades and declared their communities to be liberated. Merchants carried out a commercial strike. When Israel closed schools, educational committees organized underground classes. To varying degrees, communities boycotted Israeli goods and services, withdrew deposits from Israeli banks, refused to pay taxes or carry Israeli-issued identity cards, expanded local manufacturing and food production in the quest for self-sufficiency, complied with periodic strikes on labour in Israel, and minimized dealings with the Israeli Army's Civil Administration that governed the occupied territories.

The Intifada resulted in important achievements. It convinced many Israelis, including in the political and military leadership, that the status quo was unsustainable, and withdrawal from the Palestinian territories was in Israel's interests. In 1988, it encouraged and empowered the PLO to declare the independent state of Palestine next to Israel, and was part of the process leading to Palestinian attendance at the 1991 Madrid international peace conference (as part of the Jordanian delegation). In the two years following Madrid, Palestinian representatives from the West Bank and Gaza negotiated with Israel in unprecedented bilateral meetings in Washington.

The Intifada weakened under the toll of state repression, including deaths, injuries, imprisonment, deportations, and curfews (Al-Haq 1990). The failure of peace talks to yield results compounded exhaustion and frustration. In this context, mass participation waned and the rate of armed attacks rose, many carried out by the Islamic Resistance Movement, or Hamas, which had announced its formation during the first days of the Intifada (see Abu-Amr 1994; Hroub 2000; Mishal and Sela 2000). Palestinian national unity and optimism increasingly gave way to factional rivalries, crime, killings of alleged collaborators, and despair. The 1993 disclosure of a secret PLO–Israeli agreement marked the end of an uprising that had already begun to unravel. It thereby opened an entirely new phase in the national movement.

During and Against Oslo

On 13 September 1993, the PLO and Israel signed the Declaration of Principles (Oslo I) and committed themselves to a phased framework for negotiations. Subsequent agreements set forth the parameters according to which Israel would withdraw from parts of the West Bank and Gaza and transfer control over these areas to a new Palestinian self-governing apparatus, the Palestinian Authority (PA). Israel and the PLO pledged to commence permanent status talks on the issues of Jerusalem, refugees, settlements, water, and borders no later than May 1996 and conclude a final peace settlement by May 1999.

Few Palestinians believed that what became known as the Oslo peace process gave them their due. Fervent critics accused the PLO of accepting a reconfiguration of the occupation to save itself from isolation and bankruptcy, particularly after Arafat voiced support for Iraq after its 1990 invasion of Kuwait. Nevertheless, opinion polls from fall 1993 through spring 2000 showed that the large majority of Palestinians in the West Bank and Gaza Strip supported Oslo as the strategic choice of the national movement (see JMCC, n.d.). The PA, its building of state-like institutions, and robust participation in legislative and presidential elections in 1996, all helped transform a diasporic struggle into a national entity grounded in Palestinian society on Palestinian soil.

While most Palestinians had welcomed the PA as a national achievement, it was not long before many decried its authoritarianism and human rights violations. Arafat used corruption, patronage, tribalism, and competing security forces to divide, conquer, and co-opt (Brynen 1995; Hilal 1998). As the Palestinian Left waned and Islamists boycotted the PA, the once-pluralist national movement came to approximate something of a one-party regime. Yet even as Fatah dominated politics, divisions grew between returnee Fatah elites who dominated high national decision-making and younger activists who were raised in the occupied territories and called for reform and accountability (Usher 1995; Bucaille 2004). Meanwhile, the PA, though created as a subsidiary to the PLO, came to supersede the PLO as the international community's recognized interlocutor. Concurrently, the PLO institutions that had represented Palestinian nationalism since 1969 atrophied.

The negotiations process also disappointed Palestinians' hopes for statehood. Opposing the peace process, Hamas and Islamic Jihad initiated suicide bombings inside Israel after a settler's 1994 massacre of Palestinians in Hebron. Israel denounced Palestinian terror. Palestinians condemned Israel's continued settlement-building and new restrictions on freedom of movement. Interim negotiations were to have ended in a final settlement by 1999. That year, only 60 per cent of the Gaza Strip and 17 per cent of the West Bank were under Palestinian self-rule. The July 2000 Camp David II Summit not only failed to reach a final settlement but precipitated a crisis for the Palestinian national effort insofar as it crystalized a narrative that praised Israel's generous concessions and accused Arafat of unwillingness to make peace (Swisher 2004).

Against this backdrop, Ariel Sharon's September 2000 visit to the al-Aqsa Mosque triggered protests. Demonstrations began in Jerusalem and areas where Palestinian territory bordered Israeli military deployments in the West Bank and Gaza. Palestinians threw rocks and Molotov cocktails at Israeli soldiers, who responded with tear gas, rubber bullets, and live ammunition (Enderlin 2003). Palestinian gunfire was confirmed during the first week, as PA policemen stationed at demonstrations turned their weapons against the Israeli army. As demonstrations spread throughout the West Bank and Gaza, they became known as the Second or "al-Aqsa" Intifada. In the weeks that followed, Palestinian activists shot at Israeli military installations, settlements, and roads in the West Bank and Gaza. Israel deployed snipers, shelled Palestinian neighbourhoods, bulldozed homes and fields, and blocked movement with hundreds of new checkpoints. Palestinian casualties during the first three months were nearly equal to those of the entire first year of the first Intifada.

The new uprising brought to light the strategic divisions and organizational weaknesses mounting in the national movement since the start of Oslo (Sayigh 2002). Unlike in the first Intifada, there emerged no authoritative mechanism to coordinate varied political forces. Arafat, caught between his obligation to uphold Oslo and popular pressure against it, opted to "ride the wave" and let fragmentation take its course (Sayigh 2001). In this context, Israeli military repression drove popular calls for revenge that incentivized factions to take up arms in order to assert their national leadership and compete for popular support. After remaining on the sidelines during the uprising's first three months, Hamas carried out a suicide bombing on New Year's Day 2001. By year's end, an array of Palestinian factions had carried out more such bombings than they had during the previous seven years combined.

The second Intifada continued as a semi-war until Arafat's death in 2004 invited a transition in the Palestinian national movement. Mahmoud Abbas was elected President of the PA and Chairman of the PLO. He reached out to Hamas, which agreed to a ceasefire and participation in new PA parliamentary elections in 2006. Benefiting from a more effective electoral strategy, as well as the popular rebuff of Fatah incumbents, Hamas and its affiliated independents won 78 of 132 seats. Hamas formed a new government, but Israel refused to speak with it, the United States and European Union–imposed sanctions on it, and some Fatah leaders were eager to make it fall. A power struggle bubbled until June 2007 when Hamas, charging that Fatah was planning a coup, seized control of the PA in the Gaza Strip.

The Palestinian political system thus split between the Fatah-dominated PA in the West Bank and the Hamas-led government in the Gaza Strip. Israel tightened a blockade that imposed draconian limits on the Gaza Strip. Hamas and other groups fired rockets at Israel, a tactic it had initiated during the second intifada. Cycles of conflict between Israel and Hamas erupted into full-fledged wars in 2008, 2012, and 2014. Their brutal toll, exacerbating a long history of "de-development" (Roy 2016), brought the United Nations (2017) to declare Gaza on track to being "unliveable."

Conclusion

Since the turn of the twentieth century, Palestinian nationalism has succeeded in nourishing and preserving a common identity across a dispossessed and dispersed population, fought for and won international recognition, built an array of organizations and institutions to advance national goals, and defied numerous adversaries that would have preferred to see no Palestinian movement with a will of its own. These are accomplishments of historic proportions, against enormous odds.

Moving into the second decade of the twenty-first century, however, the national movement appears in crisis. Since 2007, repeated Fatah-Hamas reconciliation attempts have proved ineffective. So did Abbas's bids for United Nations recognition of Palestine's statehood. The toll of deleterious international interventions, Israeli policies, and Palestinian elites' own authoritarian practices have left Palestinian society "polarized and demobilized" (El Kurd 2019). Since the late 1990s, opinion polls reveal that the plurality of Palestinians choose "no one" as the faction that they trust most (JMCC, n.d.). Observers note that the political institutions built over decades, including the PLO, PA, and major factions, have decayed; they only persist due to inertia and absence of alternatives rather than moral and popular legitimacy (Brown and Nerenberg 2016). The situation is arguably even bleaker for Palestinian refugees in Lebanon and elsewhere, many of whom see themselves as forgotten and forsaken by a national movement focused only on struggles for power in the West Bank and Gaza Strip (Allan 2013).

Palestinian nationalism as an identity, ideology, and popular commitment is immeasurably stronger than the political institutions that ostensibly speak in its name. In this context, grassroots nationalist activism has never ceased. Since 2002, Israel's building of a 700-kilometer security fence/wall has confiscated and divided Palestinian lands in the West Bank, spurring villages in its route to sustain protests against it (Norman 2010; Qumsiyeh 2011). Launched in 2005 by 170 Palestinian civil society groups, the campaign for "Boycott, Divestment, and Sanctions" against Israel garnered attention around the globe (Barghouti 2011). Since late 2009, Palestinians have demonstrated against Israel's demolition of Palestinian homes and expansion of settlements in East Jerusalem. In the context of the Arab Uprisings, thousands gathered in the streets of Ramallah and Gaza City in March 2011, addressing Fatah and Hamas with the chant, "The people want an end to the schism." On 15 May "Nakba Day" that year, thousands of Palestinian refugees in Lebanon, Syria, and Gaza marched to their borders with Israel in a call for the right of return. On 20 March 2018 – "Land Day," which commemorates the 1976 killing of six Palestinian citizens of Israel who were protesting the expropriation of Palestinian land – Palestinians in Gaza launched the "Great Return March." In the weeks that followed, tens of thousands participated in demonstrations at Israel's border fence, even as the Israeli army's response left 260 Palestinians dead and more than 20,000 wounded.

These and myriad other examples demonstrate how the Palestinians' nationalist resolve continues and will continue as long as their individual and collective rights remain denied. The engine of the Palestinian national movement is, as it always has been, the Palestinian people's demand to live with freedom and dignity. Its ultimate expression is the everyday ways in which Palestinians near and far preserve their collective memory, practice their peoplehood, and work for a just future, as Palestinians.

Recommended Readings

El Kurd, D. 2019. *Polarized and Demobilized: Legacies of Authoritarianism in Palestine*. London: Hurst & Co Publishers.

Khalidi, R. 1997. *Palestinian Identity: The Construction of Modern National Consciousness*. New York: Columbia University Press.

Pearlman, W. 2011. *Violence, Nonviolence, and the Palestinian National Movement*. New York: Cambridge University Press.

Robinson, G. E. 1997. *Building a Palestinian State: The Incomplete Revolution*. Bloomington, IN: Indiana University Press.

Sayigh, Y. 1997. *Armed Struggle and the Search for State*. Oxford: Oxford University Press.

Note

1 This chapter is based on, and draws from, Wendy Pearlman, *Violence, Nonviolence, and the Palestinian National Movement*. New York: Cambridge University Press, 2011.

Questions for Discussion

(1) What is the relationship between Palestinian nationalism and other identities and allegiances that are either sub-national (such as local, partisan) or supra-national (such as Islam or Arab nationalism)?
(2) For the Palestinian movement, what is the relationship between the "nation" and the quest for a "state"? What does their experience suggest about how nations are created and can persist in the absence of a state?
(3) What explains the varied development in the internal politics of the Palestinian national movement, including its unity or divisions? How has the movement's structure affected its historical trajectory, and vice versa?
(4) What explains variation in the tactics, strategies, and goals of the Palestinian national movement over time?
(5) How have external actors and international institutions affected Palestinian nationalism? How has the relationship between the Palestinian movement and external actors changed over time?
(6) Ultimately, why has the Palestinian national movement been unable to achieve its goal of self-determination?

References

Abu-Amr, Z. 1994. *Islamic Fundamentalism in the West Bank and Gaza: Muslim Brotherhood and Islamic Jihad*. Bloomington, IN: Indiana University Press.

Ahmad, A. A. H. 1976. "Interview with the Palestine National Front." *MERIP Reports*, no. 50 (August), 16–21.

Al-Haq (Law in the Service of Man). 1990. *Punishing a Nation: Human Rights Violations during the Palestinian Uprising, December 1987–December 1988*. Boston: South End Press.

Allan, D. 2013. *Refugees of the Revolution: Experiences of Palestinian Exile*. Stanford, CA: Stanford University Press.

Al-Madhoun, R. K. 1989. *Al-Intifada al-filastiniyah: al-haykal al-tanthimi wa-asalib al-amal* [The Palestinian Uprising: Organizational Structure and Activities]. Acre: Dar al-Aswar.

Amos, J. W. II. 1980. *Palestinian Resistance: Organization of a National Movement*. New York: Pergamon Press.

Antonius, G. 1946. *The Arab Awakening: The Story of the Arab National Movement*. New York: GP Putnam's Sons.

Arnon-Ohanna, Y. 1981. "The Bands in the Palestinian Arab Revolt, 1936–1939: Structure and Organization." *Asian and African Studies*, no. 15, 229–247.

Ashrawi, H. 1995. *This Side of Peace*. New York: Touchstone.

Bailey, C. 1984. *Jordan's Palestinian Challenge, 1948–1983: A Political History*. Boulder, CO: Westview Press.

Barghouti, O. 2011. *Boycott, Divestment, Sanctions–The Global Struggle for Palestinian Rights*. Chicago: Haymarket Books.

Brown, N. J., and D. Nerenberg. 2016. *Palestine in Flux: From Search for State to Search for Tactics*. Carnegie Endowment for International Peace.

Brynen, R. 1990. *Sanctuary and Survival: The PLO in Lebanon*. Boulder, CO: Westview Press.

Brynen, R. 1995. "The Neopatrimonial Dimension of Palestinian Politics." *Journal of Palestine Studies* 25:1, 23–36.

Bucaille, L. 2004. *Growing Up Palestinian: Israeli Occupation and the Intifada Generation*. Princeton, NJ: Princeton University Press.

Cobban, H. 1984. *The Palestine Liberation Organization: People, Power, and Politics*. Cambridge: Cambridge University Press.

Dakkak, I. 1983. "Back to Square One: A Study in the Re-emergence of the Palestinian Identity in the West Bank 1967–1980." In *Palestinians over the Green Line: Studies on the Relations between Palestinians on Both Sides of the 1949 Armistice Line since 1967*, ed. A. Scholch. London: Ithaca Press, 64–101.

Darwazah, M. 'I. 1993. *Mudhakkirat Muhammad 'Izzat Darwazah, 1305 H–1404/1887 M–1984: Sijill hafil bi-masirat al-harakah al-'Arabiyah wa al-qadiyah al-Filastiniyah khilala qarn min al-zaman* [Autobiography of Muhammad 'Izzat Darwazah: Registrations alongside Arab Movements and the Palestinian Cause over a Century of History]. Beirut: Dar al-Gharb al-Islami.

El Kurd, D. 2019. *Polarized and Demobilized: Legacies of Authoritarianism in Palestine*. London: Hurst & Co Publishers.

Enderlin, Cs. 2003. *Shattered Dreams: The Failure of the Peace Process in the Middle East, 1995–2002*. New York: Other Press.

Gellner, E. 1983. *Nations and Nationalism*. Ithaca, NY: Cornell University Press.

Great Britain, Cmd. 1921. *1540: Palestine Disturbances in May 1921: Reports of the Commission of Inquiry … Haycraft, Chairman*. London: His Majesty's Stationery Office.

Great Britain, Cmd. 1930. *3530: Report of the Commission on the Palestine Disturbances of August 1929*. London: His Majesty's Stationery Office.

Hilal, J. 1998. *Al-Nizam al-Siyasi al-Filastini ba'ad Oslo: Dirasah Tahliliyah Naqdiyah* [The Palestinian Political Order after Oslo: A Critical Analytical Study]. Ramallah, West Bank: MUWATIN.

Hiltermann, J. 1991. *Behind the Intifada: Labor and Women's Movements in the Occupied Territories*. Princeton, NJ: Princeton University Press.

Hourani, A. 1968. "Ottoman Reform and the Politics of the Notables," in *Beginnings of Modernization in the Middle East*, eds. W. Polk and R. Chambers. Chicago: University of Chicago Press, 41–68.

Hroub, K. 2000. *Hamas: Political Thought and Practice*. Washington, DC: Institute of Palestine Studies.

Hughes, M. 2010. "From Law and Order to Pacification: Britain's Suppression of the Arab Revolt in Palestine, 1936–39." *Journal of Palestine Studies* 39:2, 6–22.

Iyad, A. (Salah Khalaf). 1981. *My Home, My Land: A Narrative of the Palestinian Struggle*, with Eric Rouleau, trans. L. B. Koseoglu. New York: Times Books.

JMCC. n.d. *Jerusalem Media & Communication Centre: Polls*. Available at www.jmcc.org/polls.aspx.

Kanafani, G. 1972. *Thawrat 36–39 fi Filisteen [The 36–39 Revolt in Palestine]*. Jerusalem: Abu Arifa Press Agency.

Khalidi, R. 1986. *Under Siege: P.L.O. Decision-making during the 1982 War*. New York: Columbia University Press.

Khalidi, R. 1989. "The Palestinian People: Twenty-two Years after 1967." In *Intifada: The Palestinian Uprising against Israeli Occupation*, eds. Z. Lockman and J. Beinin. Washington, DC: Middle East Research and Information Project, 113–126.

Khalidi, R. 1997. *Palestinian Identity: The Construction of Modern National Consciousness*. New York: Columbia University Press.

Khalidi, R. 2006. *Iron Cage: The Story of the Palestinian Struggle for Statehood*. Boston: Beacon Press.

Kimmerling, B., and J. Migdal. 2003. *The Palestinian People: A History*. Cambridge, MA: Harvard University Press.

King, M. E. 2007. *A Quiet Revolution: The First Palestinian Intifada and Nonviolent Resistance*. New York: Nation Books.

Kirsci, K. 1986. *The PLO and World Politics: A Study of the Mobilization of Support for the Palestinian Cause*. London: Frances Pinter Publishers.

Lesch, A. M. 1977. *Arab Politics in Palestine, 1917–1939: The Frustration of a Nationalist Movement*. Ithaca, NY: Cornell University Press.

Lockman, Z., and J. Beinin, eds. 1989. *Intifada: The Palestinian Uprising Against Israeli Occupation*. Boston and Washington, DC: Middle East Research and Information Project and South End Press.

Mandel, N. J. 1976. *The Arabs and Zionism before World War I.* Berkeley, CA: University of California Press.
Ma'oz, M. 1984. *Palestinian Leadership on the West Bank: The Changing Role of the Arab Mayors under Jordan and Israel.* London: Frank Cass.
Mattar, P. 1988. *The Mufti of Jerusalem: Al-Hajj Amin al-Husayni and the Palestinian National Movement.* New York: Columbia University Press.
Matthews, W. C. 2006. *Confronting an Empire, Constructing a Nation: Arab Nationalists and Popular Politics in Mandate Palestine.* London and New York: I.B. Tauris.
Mishal, S., and A. Sela. 2000. *The Palestinian Hamas: Vision, Violence, and Coexistence.* New York: Columbia University Press.
Mishal, S., and R. Aharoni. 1994. *Speaking Stones: Communiqués from the Intifada Underground.* Syracuse, NY: Syracuse University Press.
Morris, B. 2004. *The Birth of the Palestinian Refugee Problem Revisited*, 2nd ed. Cambridge: Cambridge University Press.
Muslih, M. Y. 1989. *The Origins of Palestinian Nationalism.* New York: Columbia University Press.
Nakle, E. 1988. "The West Bank and Gaza: Twenty Years Later." *Middle East Journal* 42:2, 209–226.
Nassar, J. R., and R. Heacock, eds. 1990. *Intifada: Palestine at the Crossroads.* New York: Greenwood Press.
Norman, J. M. 2010. *The Second Palestinian Intifada: Civil Resistance.* New York: Routledge.
O'Neill, B. 1978. *Armed Struggle in Palestine: A Political-Military Analysis.* Boulder, CO: Westview Press.
Pearlman, W. 2011. *Violence, Nonviolence, and the Palestinian National Movement.* New York: Cambridge University Press.
Pearlman, W., and B. Atzili. 2018. *Triadic Coercion: Israel's Targeting of States that Host Nonstate Actors.* New York: Columbia University Press.
Peretz, D. 1970. "Arab Palestine: Phoenix or Phantom?" *Foreign Affairs* 68:2, 322–333.
Peretz, D. 1990. *Intifada: The Palestinian Uprising.* Boulder, CO: Westview Press.
Porath, Y. 1974. *The Emergence of the Palestinian-Arab National Movement, 1918–1929.* London: Frank Cass.
Porath, Y. 1975. "The Political Organization of the Palestinian Arabs under the British Mandate," in *Palestinian Arab Politics*, ed. Moshe Ma'oz. Jerusalem: Jerusalem Academic Press, 1–20.
Porath, Y. 1977. *The Palestinian-Arab National Movement, from Riots to Rebellion, 1929–1939.* London: Frank Cass.
Qumsiyeh, M. B. 2011. *Popular Resistance in Palestine: A History of Hope and Empowerment.* London: Pluto Press.
Rigby, A. 1991. *Living the Intifada.* London: Zed Books.
Robinson, G. E. 1997. *Building a Palestinian State: The Incomplete Revolution.* Bloomington and Indianapolis, IN: Indiana University Press.
Roy, S. 2016. *The Gaza Strip: The Political Economy of De-development*, 3rd ed. Washington, DC: Institute for Palestine Studies.
Sahliyeh, E. D. 1988. *In Search of Leadership: West Bank Politics Since 1967.* Washington, DC: Brookings Institute.
Sayigh, R. 1977. "Sources of Palestinian Nationalism: A Study of a Palestinian Camp in Lebanon." *Journal of Palestine Studies* 6:4, 17–40.
Sayigh, R. 1979. *Palestinians: From Peasants to Revolutionaries.* London: Zed Books.
Sayigh, Y. 1992. "Turning Defeat into Opportunity: The Guerillas after the June 1967 War." *Middle East Journal* 46:2, 244–265.
Sayigh, Y. 1997. *Armed Struggle and the Search for State.* Oxford: Oxford University Press.
Sayigh, Y. 2001. "Anatomy of a Revolt." *Survival* 43:1, 47–60.
Sayigh, Y. 2002. "Palestine – Where to?" *PASSIA Roundtable Meeting and Discussion, 9 July.* Available at: http://188.166.160.81/passia_old/passia.org/meetings/2002/round0907.htm.
Schiff, Z. and E. Ya'ari. 1989. *Intifada: The Palestinian Uprising – Israel's Third Front*, trans. I. Friedman. New York: Touchstone.
Segev, T. 2007. *1967: Israel, the War, and the Year that Transformed the Middle East*, trans. J. Cohen. New York: Metropolitan Books.
Shemesh, M. 1988. *The Palestinian Entity 1959–1974: Arab Politics and the PLO, Part. 1.* London: Frank Cass.
Shlaim, A. 1988. *Collusion Across the Jordan: King Abdullah, the Zionist Movement, and the Partition of Palestine.* New York: Columbia University Press.
Stein, K. 1984. *The Land Question in Palestine, 1917–1939.* Chapel Hill, NC: The University of North Carolina Press.
Swedenburg, T. 1995. *Memories of Revolt: The 1936–39 Rebellion and the Palestinian National Past.* Minneapolis, MN: University of Minnesota Press.

Swisher, C. E. 2004. *The Truth about Camp David: The Untold Story about the Collapse of the Middle East Peace Process*. New York: Nation Books.

Tamari, S. 1982. "Factionalism and Class Formation in Recent Palestinian History." In *Studies in the Economic and Social History of Palestine in the Nineteenth and Twentieth Centuries*, ed. R. Owen. Carbondale, IL: Southern Illinois University Press, 177–202.

Tessler, M. 1994. *A History of the Israeli–Palestinian Conflict*. Bloomington, IN: Indiana University Press.

Turki, F. 1972. *The Disinherited: Journal of a Palestinian Exile*. New York: The Monthly Review Press.

United Nations Country Team in the occupied Palestinian territory. 2017. *Gaza Ten Years Later*. (July). Available at: https://unsco.unmissions.org/sites/default/files/gaza_10_years_later_-_11_july_2017.pdf.

Usher, G. 1995. *Palestine in Crisis: The Struggle for Peace and Political Independence after Oslo*. London and East Haven, CT: Pluto Press.

Van Creveld, M. 1998. *The Sword and the Olive: A Critical History of the Israeli Defense Forces*. New York: Public Affairs.

Zeira, Y. 2019. *The Revolution Within: State Institutions and Unarmed Resistance in Palestine*. Cambridge: Cambridge University Press.

Zu'aytir, A. 1980. *Yawmiyat Akram Zu'aytir: Al-harakah al-wataniyah al-Filastiniyah, 1935–1939* [Diary of Akram Zu'aytir: The Palestinian National Struggle, 1935–1939]. Beirut: Institute of Palestine Studies.

5
ZIONISM

Donna Robinson Divine

Zionism serves as Israel's foundational ideology. As an ideology, it is forged around an exodus story where people escaped death and destruction to rebuild a promised land, resurrect a language, and transform a culture through the sweat of their brows and the toil of their hands. Presumably a story of success, Israel's establishment in 1948 as a Jewish state is widely regarded as an achievement, albeit not a fulfilment, of Zionism's project for national transformation.

Zionism was one of several responses to the massive changes engulfing nineteenth-century Europe that widened opportunities but also posed special risks for Jews. Struggling to make sense of developments that beckoned them to become full citizens but simultaneously raised fears about their potential for undermining civilization, Jews could not help but wonder whether their own traditions and organizations were still relevant. Religious reformers revised doctrines, rituals, and liturgy. The newly-labelled Orthodox opposed innovations while doubling down on religious beliefs as the only means of halting collective Jewish decline. Both groups contended with proponents of emancipation as a means of integrating fully into state and society, and of ending discrimination. As high hopes for full acceptance remained unfulfilled, many turned to socialism and anarchism.

For those who laid the groundwork for Zionism, this century of political upheaval heralded catastrophe precisely because these several responses to modernity did nothing to stop the feeling that the Jewish future was spinning out of control. Not only a project for national revival, then, Zionism is also a strategy for survival. And while the preoccupation with survival forged neither unity against threats from without nor consensus within, it did produce a soul-searching language of moral inquiry as well as an inventory – imagined and real – of Jewish strengths and weaknesses.

Zionism has always attempted to frame Israel's understanding of itself, but the first question to raise is which Zionism? Israel's founding as a Jewish state in 1948 was curated as the work of nationalists who deemed themselves "secular" and who had led the Zionist movement from its establishment in the last decades of the nineteenth century. Some number of these Zionists, driven by a necessity to seek a political solution to the problems encountered in an age of nationalism and dictatorship, generated ambitions not simply for a state and society like all other nations but also for redemption, the hope that a Jewish state and society would provide a new kind of social order without hierarchy, without exploitation, and with justice and equality for all (Halpern and Reinharz 1998).

DOI: 10.4324/9780429027376-7

By tying a humanistic mission to a struggle for sovereignty, Zionist politics were frequently pulled in different directions. The tensions between the movement's utopian idealism and its capacity to set priorities meant having to come to terms with the fact that the promises of founding a Jewish state on the purest of Zionist visions could not be kept. Nor were Zionists disposed to dreaming up the same utopias. Perhaps because Israel was imagined long before it was founded – visions conjured in the religious canon, in utopian fantasies, and in political treatises – the country could never be entirely liberated from the idea of Zion no matter how far it departed from reality. For the standards generated by the Zionist imperatives to build a nation and homeland intended to be both "normal" and "exceptional" encouraged expectations that could not ever be met but could never be totally dismissed. And while the differences could often be hidden in abstractions or ambiguous language, they could not be entirely avoided. Never reluctant to champion their visions, Zionists displayed remarkable linguistic flexibility, particularly about foundational terms like homeland and state (Shumsky 2018; Brenner 2018). Still, Jews in Palestine knew they were participants in a story attracting intense global attention as well as in a risky political experiment marked by significant conflict and hardship.

"Shlilat Ha-Galut" (Negating the Diaspora)

The very core idea of the in-gathering of the Jews in the land of Israel and the ending of their exile illustrates the strains, if not the ruptures Zionism generated. The Zionist movement created its project around the idea of "Negating the Diaspora," aiming to transform a people not simply because their dispersion endangered their lives and culture but also because it was said to distort their values. Returning to the ancient homeland was proclaimed as an absolute rejection of exile. Emigration from Palestine was denounced as betrayal and dereliction of a sacred duty (Divine 2008).

Zionists insisted that only by casting off the culture and society of the Diaspora could the alchemy to liberate Jews be generated, essentially asking immigrants to see in their roots a past best discarded, and, in their new abode, a future worthy of commitment even if accompanied by substantial suffering. That stripping Jews of all that was familiar to them from the lands of their birth could easily hurt the prospects for the economic and political development of the Jewish Homeland is obvious. Telling those who arrived on Palestine's shores to reject all that once gave shape and meaning to their lives had to intensify their unease and magnify their difficulties in trying to integrate into the Jewish national home.

Proclaiming homeland and exile as bipolar opposites was intended to encourage immigrants to accept the process of nation building as the central task of their lives, but it could not camouflage questions both about the degree to which immigrants actually divested themselves of the cultures and customs of the lands of their birth, and the consequences for the society formed in the shadow of a narrative that did not fully correspond with the way ordinary men and women actually lived.

The Jews drawn to the land in order to redeem it and transform its people may have become Zionism's iconic leaders, holding fast to specific ideologies and/or representing particular economic and social interests. But not all who came to live in the land of Israel fell under the spell of such a radical program of social change requiring individuals to shed the customs and traditions of their ancestors. Many came to Palestine for the same reasons Jews moved to America – to raise their standard of living – and they were thus naturally inclined to replant their familiar religious and communal organizations across their new homeland (Alroey 2004).

Zionist leaders may have agonized over the remnants of what they deemed atavistic beliefs and rituals, but many newly arrived men and women thought their religious commitments fit seamlessly with their nationalist activities. Caught up in the excitement of building a homeland, many showed continued reverence for religious traditions, even as they shouted out their newly formed nationalist goals. Waving the Zionist flag at the Western Wall in 1928 may have displayed a measure of disdain for secular nationalism, but it brought forth so much reverence for Zionism's historic narrative that it could not be dismissed (Cohen 2005). Similar regard had to be accorded to the so-called ultra-orthodox whose members considered the very idea of Jewish sovereignty profane but whose population size kept Zionist claims on a firm footing.

Notwithstanding the multiplicity of its goals and values, Zionism managed to establish the coordinates of a widely accepted and highly regarded relationship between land, people, and language. Reviving the Hebrew language became an instrument to transform a people, once defined by their religious traditions and law, into a nation bound together by a shared, albeit often newly invented, set of mores forcing a sacred tongue to accommodate the language of politics and the hidden intimacies never fully addressed in Judaism's religious canon. The creation of a culture whose literature and ideas were expressed in Hebrew and whose ancient laws and rituals could be translated into national traditions was the groundwork for both a liberation Zionists sought from religious authority and for a state offering Jews something they believed could be found nowhere else – full rights and the opportunity to adapt and take advantage of the modern world.

A newly invented lexicon taken from the classical religious texts would seemingly show Jews how to criticize their tradition, yet create both a culture expressive of its deepest values and the confidence necessary to withstand the hardships to come in the course of building a Jewish state. Because Zionists presumed the march to enlightenment and equality would not necessarily or inevitably reach Jews – and if it did, the costs would be high and paid in the coin of their distinctive traditions – they argued for Jews to establish their own national home as a shield against the dangers coming from an increasingly unstable world. Zionism emerged in a transitional period, a time between centuries and eras when nothing seemed absolutely fixed. Those Jews raised within the piety of religious law and Rabbinic authority found themselves disoriented by their exposure to European culture. While developing Zionism's understanding of the world at a time when European philosophy posited that humans, treated as commodities in the modern economy or as cogs in a powerful bureaucracy, possessed little freedom of action, Zionists simultaneously insisted that these same impersonal forces could be harnessed to give Jews the capacity for both personal freedom and, most importantly, for collective transformation (Stanislawski 2001).

The collapse of Eastern European Jewish society, when the norms generated by synagogue and study hall lost their force, should have imparted an aura of apocalypse. Emigration unsettled families while political and economic changes disrupted customs and relations once taken for granted as eternal, raising the possibility that a collective Jewish existence would disappear. A tradition engaged through textual mastery and interpretation that guided behaviour and shaped social and economic relations was on the verge of collapse.

Where many saw the crumbling of faith as a fall, Zionists saw it as the beginning of liberation. The Zionist narrative supplied Jews with an answer in a familiar idiom replete with metaphors of a shared fate. But unlike the classic texts from which these words and ideas were drawn and reworked, Zionism's calls for a return to the land of Israel were not issued as religious imperatives. The national ideal, always implicit in the Jewish story, was not so much invented as re-focused away from the demands of Heaven and on to the brokenness of the Jewish Earth.

In proposing the building of a national homeland, Zionism provided Jews with a redemptive enterprise that would be authorized by their own work and the civic framework they were called upon to create.

The Jew who once focused on dwelling in the land of Israel as a religious ideal was always striving on behalf of a deferred, distant, and immeasurable Messianic goal. Zionists gave Jews a challenge intended to be experienced with successes and failures that could be calculated. Zionism thus gave voice to the power of the imagination, not simply to reinterpret history but, more importantly, to change it for the sake of creating a radically different future for Jews. Substituting action for prayers gave Zionism its purpose. What had been depicted in religious texts as an almost erotic longing for the Holy Land, as a craving for the flesh of the soil, the singularity of the landscape and its distinct vegetation was presented suddenly as something that could give instant and palpable gratification. Work, rather than textual study, legitimized possession and would be the vehicle for creating community and for transforming sites holy in scripture into a homeland. The discursive language that once connected a people to its sacred canon and ancient stories would be transformed to reflect the utilitarian and commonplace activities of the people now committed to returning it to the presumed birthplace of its collective identity. Hebrew expanded in the direction of action, and collective responsibilities focused more on obligations than on political rights. Zionists were builders empowered less as individuals than as members of a kind of collective construction team (Chowers 2012; Ohana 2012).

What is perhaps not surprising but ironic about Zionism and its commitment to the radical reform of what it meant to be a Jew was not simply that its ordinary adherents decided to remake their ancient culture – that is, of course, what ordinary people always do. What is remarkable is that what brought together people always at each other's throats because the stakes were cast as a matter of cultural life and death, is that among the first institutions set up by the World Zionist Organization in Ottoman Palestine were the very institutions central to sustaining Diaspora Jewry – schools – the Herzliya Gymnasium and Bezalel School of Art.

In the most unlikely of circumstances – Ottoman corruption, wars, a revolution, disease and epidemics – Zionists invented many of the indelible traditions associated with Israeli culture – the *tiyul* or knowing the land by walking across it; Jewish athletic contests; and parades to honour nature. Many Zionists saw themselves not so much creating a new Jewish calendar as infusing it with new meaning. Zionists who came to live in Palestine even before the land was mapped, expended their best energy on re-examining and reinterpreting every aspect of Jewish history and ritual: should Hanukkah be ignored because it marked the victory of religious fanaticism over the so-called enlightened proponents of Hellenism or was it rather to be celebrated as a class struggle, in the words of Labour Zionists, as the triumph of a peasant underclass (Saposnik 2008)?

The images inscribed in the conventional histories of Israel's founding tend to confirm the notion that a Jewish nation was remade, and a new collective identity formed. A land with no natural resources, claimed by a movement possessing too little capital for the tasks it undertook, Israel seems to have been established through commitment to the cause of national transformation. Zionist leaders pushed this notion to its extreme by presenting the agricultural collectives (*kibbutzim*) – never encompassing more than a tiny percentage of Israel's population (under 1 per cent in some years) – emblematic of the Jewish State. These communities were presumably bound together by a shared commitment to the principles of freedom, love of the land, physical labour, and of revitalizing the Hebrew language – all seemingly accomplished by sheer will. Unlike settler-colonial societies, Zionism was not predisposed to eliminating the so-called indigenous population. Hebrew literature is saturated with romantic notions of the Arab as overflowing with life in contrast to the Diaspora Jew, who is typically represented as withered and dying. Determined to transform the Jewish people, Zionism was at least, initially, more than willing to make room for the "other" (Shafir 1989; Locker-Biletzki 2018; Golan 2001).

The discourse that extolled agriculture also imagined the land as the site for transforming the people and their culture. The city, by contrast, came into focus as a place of social and cultural extremes, partly a product of unfettered capitalism and partly a consequence of the presence of immigrants uprooted from the Diaspora but still clinging to its values. The praise heaped on those working the land essentially indicted those in the cities with failure to cross the divide Zionists posited between Diaspora and national home (Divine 2008, ch.6). Stressing the presumed disparities between exile and homeland, the Zionist narrative gave its adherents great expectations of what coming to live in Palestine could mean for the collective life of the Jews. But instead of feeling empowered, immigrants often felt weakened by their move and more aware of the ruptures with their past than of the liberation in their future.

Because the strains of immigration could not be captured by any of Zionism's categories of analysis, they were almost never acknowledged and always exempt from scrutiny. At the level of first principles, Zionism seemed only capable of pursuing the pathway set out by its visions all the way to their ends. But although the visions remained, the logic underlying their realization grew increasingly complicated after Great Britain drove Ottoman troops out of Palestine and authorized both a geography and a set of political demands that bedevilled Zionists with tensions between the imperatives of nation-building and state-making.

Nation-Building versus State-Making

Zionism's ambition to transform the nation may have created the need to proclaim homeland and exile as binary opposites, but the project of creating a state could not afford to posit so radical a polarization. Without a genuine exchange between Diaspora and National Home, there would be too few Jews choosing Palestine if other options were available, and far fewer of Palestine's Jewish immigrants embracing Zionism's principles. State-making required consensus and compromise and familiarity with Jewish institutions in Europe; nation-building demanded absolute adherence to a newly designed set of principles and insulation from contamination by Diaspora organizations and values.

The devaluation of the Diaspora experience and the unquestioned presumption of exile and home as antinomies conferred a metaphorical order on seemingly unrelated or random developments. By reducing the many motivations for immigration to one of dedication to national transformation, Zionist leaders imagined that independence would not only liberate Jews from their marginal and subordinate existence, but it would also bestow on their community a harmony and moral purpose denied them in the Diaspora.

But the opposition Zionism posed in theory between Diaspora and Palestinian Jewish society was countered in practice by a variety of sustained contacts (Divine 2008, Conclusion). Sensitive to the fact that Jewish political power was widely dispersed, Palestine's Zionist political leaders travelled to Europe several times a year to consult with heads of various organizations in major Jewish population centres. Policies were often hammered out during meetings in Europe, where priorities with regard to the distribution of immigration certificates were fixed. These activities had an enormous effect on the social structure and economic development of Palestine's Jewish community. European Zionists shaped the creation of the new Jewish society in other ways as well. The shift in financial aid from the small to the large commune, or *kibbutz*, was decided by the World Zionist Organization and not by local activists. The kibbutz, itself, stabilized as an institution because of its association with a network of Diaspora organizations. Movements such as *he-halutz* gave the kibbutz a renewed sense of mission as a core state-building institution, and by recruiting new members, Zionists living in the Diaspora imbued kibbutz leaders with immeasurably greater confidence in its future.

An associational politics was created with Palestine's Jewish representatives – the community's up-and-coming leaders – invited to spend a year or more preparing Diaspora Zionists for life and work in the homeland. The practice of sending such activists to the Diaspora created a realm of intense political interaction for European and Palestinian Zionists. Palestinian teachers often learned political strategies from their European students, many of whom later immigrated and continued to exert a direct impact on the distribution of political power in Palestine's Jewish community.

Consider Zionist backing in the 1930s for the progressive cause of removing the so-called ghetto benches in Polish universities (Shiff 2019). Such Zionist interference in Diaspora politics could easily have triggered multiple rejoinders opposing efforts to improve conditions for the very people expected to leave the lands of their birth and add to the sorely needed Jewish population of Palestine. Instead, the discourse of civic equality in Poland soon threaded its way into the speeches of Ben-Gurion in his response to Britain's 1939 White Paper, which limited Jewish immigration to, and land purchase in Palestine.

Leaders of many Zionist political parties understood that the well-being of their institutions and organizations depended on their success in generating and maintaining loyalty in the Diaspora as well as in the Jewish National Home. Their more powerful branches in various countries of Europe sometimes overshadowed even the strongest of Palestine's political parties. Torn between conflicting needs, these political parties frequently had to respond to demands issued simultaneously from two different continents or sometimes had to establish priorities between them, often beholden to continental trends.

Finally, with all of the hoopla about economic independence and a productive Jewish economy, the national home relied on external financial aid and channelled large amounts of money into subsidies to control inflation and raise the standard of living. Capital accumulated in the lands of the Diaspora poured into real estate outstripping investments directed to industrial developments. In 1927 Chaim Arlosoroff warned against "dependency on Zionist philanthropy," which created what he called, "an artificially high standard of living in Palestine." "The *Yishuv*," he wrote, "had to learn to live within its means" (Divine 2008, 203). During the 1920s, private investment in the Jewish National Home exceeded that of public Zionist funds flowing into the country. Even some of the refugees fleeing from Bolshevism had capital. For them, Palestine represented an opportunity for private investment and individual affluence. Public funds were poured into building workers' apartments and also used to dampen inflationary pressures.

It is important to remember that the move from old world to new homeland contained an irony no immigrant anticipated. Although Zionists in Europe could take the idea of Jewish nationhood as a given, they were forced to see it as a problem in the homeland. To believe they had come home, immigrants had to negate the evidence of their senses because of their demographic relationship to the local population of Arabs as well as to the significantly larger stream of Jews who continued to move West until blocked either by United States law or by Soviet edict. The shortages of capital and natural resources that constrained economic development and added to the burdens of meeting individual and household needs could not help but raise further questions about Zionism's long-term prospects. Rebellions and riots reminded Palestine's Jews that their claims were contested and that their political objectives would be vigorously opposed. The outbreak of world war in 1939 confirmed Zionist views of the insecurities of life in the Diaspora, but it also deepened the sense of weakness among Palestine's Jews as relatives and a reservoir of potential immigrants were transported to death camps and not to the land of Israel.

What may have been repeatedly proclaimed in words – Negate the Diaspora – could not be implemented in deeds. The Diaspora could be rejected, in theory, but it could not be hallowed out in fact from homeland or from individuals. Imagining their homeland in the future, Zionist leaders, themselves, acknowledged the need to sustain British backing even as they tried to prepare the ground for the time when the Jewish National Home could stand on its own or for circumstances when it might be forced to dwell alone. Conscious of their own vulnerability, particularly while witnessing the collapse of European Jewry, Zionist leaders could not easily pursue or sometimes even proclaim goals that absolutely clashed with the interests of their British overlords in Palestine (Imber, Forthcoming).

Jewish immigrants to Mandate Palestine also carried their customs to the new land, developing the same kinds of ethnic neighbourhoods in their homeland as in the Diaspora and for the same reasons, to ease the turmoil of assimilation (Etkin, Forthcoming). Even those who embraced Zionism's romantic ideals often found themselves heavily burdened by trying to put theories literally into practice.

Disappointments that backbreaking physical labour did not produce a sense of fulfilment or feelings of intimacy with the land triggered profound feelings of melancholy and a deep sense of personal self-doubt. Acknowledged individual failures – missing home, lapsing into Yiddish, longing for the music of Beethoven and Chopin rather than for the sound of jackals – were typically scaled up from the personal to the social as violations of Zionism's sacred norms (Divine 2008, 123–125).

The Jewish consciousness of national belonging was forged in a crucible of insecurities. Many Zionist immigrants were young, separated from their families and birthplaces for the first time (Boord 2017). They felt loneliness in Palestine they did not know how to confront. How could they explain feeling alienated in the very land supposed to fulfil the redemptive Zionist vision they held sacred? Loneliness and insecurity caused Zionists to suspect that they could not measure up to the demands their visions imposed on them. Some number of young idealists killed themselves rather than relinquish the grip of a Zionist dream that had once given them such hope and infused their lives with such meaning.

For those caught in this complicated and consequential moment in Jewish history – the founding of a Jewish state – there was no single story, nor was there only one road to social and political transformation. Change was contested in families when children fought against the burdens of religious strictures while parents lived comfortably with those strictures. Immigrants from Germany carried their bourgeois family values – including abortion as a method of birth control – to the new land while some brought their non-Jewish spouses, foreshadowing trends to appear after Israel's founding (Rosenberg-Friedman 2017).

Although personal lives were entwined with the larger Zionist drama, the lifestyle patterns they forged were often not dramatically different from those formed by Jews living outside of the homeland. The colonization of Palestine brought men and women of diverse backgrounds together in the most unfamiliar of circumstances forcing them to confront the dissonance between Zionist theory and practice while generating a series of unexpected ruptures. It was one thing to imagine physical labour as the only way to achieve spiritual fulfilment, quite another to experience it as such. It was one thing to believe in equality and a communal life with no separation between public and private – another thing to live that way. It was one thing to do away with religion – another to live without the warmth of family and synagogue, particularly on holidays. It was easy to criticize traditional worship but hard to replace it with something genuine and appealing. It was one thing to denounce rabbis, another to marry without one. It was one thing to denounce religious rituals, another to bury loved ones without them. It was one thing to insist on speaking Hebrew; it was quite another thing to comply with the demand.

For Hebrew not only mobilized the impulses for revolutionary change, it also disciplined them. The revival of Hebrew was intended as a way of ordering the experience of immigrants, shape their outlook, and rationalize their place and identity in the developing community. For those who loved the language and loved hearing the rhythm and rhyme of antiquity, bringing Hebrew into daily life created a deep sense of home. But for most immigrants, the pressure to adopt Hebrew alienated them from the words that could give full expression to their experiences. The limited vocabulary of most in a Hebrew reborn meant that the losses people felt could neither be fully explained nor properly mourned. Language was expected to form the new Jew. Using one's original mother tongue was considered not only a form of laziness, but also condemned – wherever it was manifest – as an act of betrayal.

If the experience of social change kept the vast majority of Palestine's Jews distant from Zionism's utopian projects, most never conceded losing faith in their restorative powers. A silence was draped over the difficulties of living with radical social change even as its vision was turned into public metaphors leaving distinctive footprints on Palestine's Jewish culture and on the conventional or official history of how the Jewish National Home was developed. Students and the young generation of poets and writers in Tel Aviv took to its themes of land, nature, and love with great avidity. Young teens made a point of affirming and identifying with these values, not by joining communes, but rather by becoming familiar with the land of Israel by hiking and by singing the songs and reciting the poetry stirred by the reveries of the Zionist narrative. Illuminating this point is "Lo Sharti Lach Artzi"[1] written by Rachel, a young poet who described her homeland as gloried not by heroic deeds on a battlefield but rather by a tree planted on the Jordan's calm shores and by walking through its fields (Ezrahi 1992). To believe that Palestine could be conquered with the plough and simultaneously raised to glory through poetry was to believe that souls could be remade.

Only in song and poem could an independent Jewish society in the land of Israel be imagined as a vision of pure transcendence. Art was strengthened as the momentum for a weakened social change. The aesthetic quality of this culture, it might be argued, would be history's compensation for the social changes that had been lost. Transforming the actual Jewish people was, you might say, "Mishnah Impossible." The more the preconditions for transformation seemed beyond Zionist control, the more activities in the Jewish community fixed on language as a substitute for political action. And for this, there was plenty of warrant in Jewish history.

1948: Zionism Dispelled

Zionism's redemptive message, however powerfully it inspired songs and stories about how Jews in the land of Israel should live, did not set the strategic course that led to establishing a Jewish state in 1948. If Zionism's humanistic mission emerged out of the failures of the God of Abraham, Isaac, and Jacob, it soon triggered its own apostasies as a newly formed Jewish sovereignty seemed to lose its spiritual charge in trying to deal with the problems carried to the country by the millions of Jews who willingly and unwillingly gathered within its borders after 1948. Ordinary people coming to the country when it was still threatened from without were thrown into a cauldron they helped brew from within by joining the waves of immigrants who arrived without the resources necessary to sustain themselves and their households, and who deepened the cleavages among class, religion, and ethnicity. State institutions lacked the capacity to meet the needs of the country's growing population: an economy broken by war and overwhelmed by the numbers arriving without even the language to explain their problems. Epidemics killed young and old, running through the tents or huts hastily constructed to provide some protection from the weather that could be as brutal in the summer as in the winter.

The year 1948 gave Israelis occasions to celebrate, but it also brought them many reasons to fear. Profound economic disruptions and mass immigration threatened social upheaval. The stirring tales of heroic war that were so important for the imagination could not hide from view the discontent that absorbed the daily tasks of dealing with shortages and restrictions. Israel brought a multitude of people together, many of whom viewed one another as foreign and alien, but who lived side by side and encountered one another in ways that changed everyone and reshaped the nation's society and culture. All this frightened politicians and officials haunted as much by the prospect of social dislocation as by the possibility that the newly arrived would not be drawn into a full and firm commitment to the national cause (Rozin 2016).

Zionism's social- engineering imperatives continued to call on Israelis to shed their traditions; yet, multitudes sustained the customs of their families and/or of their countries of origin. Because such practices were still labelled an impediment to the country's advancement, Israel's foundational creed increasingly lost its vigour. Its idioms seemed both unpopular and a non-response to the country's serious problems.

To take just one example: even before the 1967 War, the storied socialist enterprises were running out of financing and energy, causing a very hard landing for the economy. Zionism's celebrated achievements – *kibbutz* and *moshav* – that which presumably stood as testimonials to the capacity of the political system to translate egalitarian ideals into reality, could not operate without generous subsidies from the nation's treasury. At a time of angry protests coming out of clear ethnic and social divisions, Zionism's public discourse seemed trapped in narrative paradigms – about the lingering effects of the weak and compromised Jewish life in the Diaspora – looking increasingly out of touch with events.

Israel may have moved toward its pivotal moment in 1948 buoyed by a record of Zionism's achievements, but the country also faced perils that the movement's cherished vocabulary could neither describe nor explain how to destroy, disable, or check. Israel's Proclamation of Independence spoke with eloquence but also with ambiguity on the question of sovereignty. Zionism had left no clear conceptual legacy on the meaning of the ultimate power of the state. Most importantly, in the process of structuring a government, Israel's political leaders had to find ways to transfer power from an array of pre-state organizations that not only professed primacy because of their nation-building goals – redeeming the land, transforming the people, rescuing Jews in danger – but also because some, like the Jewish Agency and Histadrut, operated with quasi-sovereign authority.

No wonder the issues of concern at the time of Israel's founding were less the rights of its citizens than the decentralized configuration of Jewish authority that served the community reasonably well in its colonial past but created the potential for a legitimacy crisis once Great Britain's officials withdrew. Nor could government ministries instantly supplant long-established voluntary organizations that had their own constituent and mythic status. The diversity of views about the idea of Jewish sovereignty as well as the rich institutional legacy representing and empowering it, at the beginning of statehood, thus convinced Israeli political leaders to create an inclusive electoral system, forging powerful incentives for even the most marginal of groups to compete for parliamentary seats (Sager 1985; Sasley and Waller 2017). Incorporating so many disparate positions into the political process inevitably had profound cultural ripple effects on public discourse, which became marked by contention, argument, and a heavy reliance on language in the struggle for political power.

Although Israel's establishment was believed by its founders to be a central and decisive phenomenon in the national life of the Jewish people and touched with universal significance, this did not enable politicians to reach a consensus on writing a constitution to mark a total break with Palestine's colonial past. For that reason, what began as a response to various crises ended up as a contentious process about the meaning of citizenship and the relevance of Zionism. That the tensions erupting during this tumultuous period continue to echo should not be surprising.

Once the state's existence seemed fragile; ironically, today its national identity seems less clear and, potentially, at risk.

The most enduring issue still arises from the seeming conflict between a national identity reflecting the corporate interests of the Jewish people and a notion of equal rights for all citizens irrespective of religious or ethnic identity. While the proclaimed Jewish state could be seen as reflective of the national conflict that had divided Jews and Arabs in Palestine during the decades preceding Israel's founding, the embrace of democracy projected an image of an undifferentiated and sovereign people dedicated to principles of common right (Gavison 1999; Waxman and Peleg 2011). But by simultaneously asking for peace from the Arab countries waging war against the Jewish state and promising to extend rights to its Arab citizens, the Proclamation implied both a condition for citizenship and a standard for measuring deviance.

It is important to remember that when Israel won its independence and armistice agreements were eventually signed, there were still deep cleavages within its Jewish population over borders, security, and how the costs would be borne for creating a political framework making ordinary life possible in this newly established nation. An array of associations, movements, institutions, and political parties had functioned for many decades, proposing a variety of strategies to address these issues. And while the establishment of a Jewish state gave rise to a host of new problems, it did not dissolve many of the old ones, nor did it shed past ways of handling these kinds of challenges.

That the obligations of citizenship were not placed upon the entire population, nor were they expected to devolve upon residents equitably, only added to the complications. Acknowledging that the ultra-orthodox challenged the legitimacy of a Jewish state, and that the Arabs were assumed hostile to its existence, Israel's democracy exempted both groups from the most onerous nation-building burden – serving in the military. Instead, both populations were granted a great deal of cultural and religious autonomy and not subjected to enormous pressure to assimilate to the dominant culture nor to accept its warrant for public service. Obeying laws and paying taxes would suffice. That Israel's citizens were not all enmeshed in identical obligations could be read as a sign of respect for the country's diversity; that such differences imposed on these communities a certain dependence could be interpreted as a portent of problems later encountered and the reason the country's discourse on citizenship continues to provoke dissent.

Citizenship for Israel's Arabs has produced tensions and contradictions since the country's policies have been forged to heed of a number of imperatives that often come into conflict with one another. Policies must expand opportunities and help shore up the economic well-being of the Arab population, but they must also ensure security. Almost all policies have been unequal to the demands placed on them and have achieved far less for Israel's Arab citizens than expected or desired. Israeli citizenship has brought the benefits of freedom and expanded opportunity even while it has triggered feelings of unease in those who have thought most deeply about what it means for a Palestinian to live in a Jewish state.

Zionism Revised

With an independent Jewish state since 1948 and generations achieving fluency in a Hebrew restored as a national language, one might ask whether the country's dominant culture is still framed by the same coordinates once elevated by the original Zionist vernacular into a national creed? Or has Zionism simply been remade by the new global forces Israel has rushed to embrace, thus necessarily making room, not only for other languages – English, Arabic, Russian, and even Yiddish – but also for religious resources once thought an expression of subordination and a metaphor for the stagnation of Jewish culture? If globalization beckons Israel to enter the world economy and benefit from its market forces, does it simultaneously undermine the predisposition to dismiss the culture of Jews living in other lands? Has the concept of a Diaspora once described as the place where Jews are scattered and live as outsiders, a place that is now filled with so many Israelis who cross oceans and continents for business, education, and careers, changed the discourse on homeland as much as on exile?

Adding urgency to these questions is Israel's recovery of the sacred sites of Jerusalem and the West Bank in the aftermath of the June 1967 War, a geographic and political change resonating backward and forward in time and meaning. Israel's public discourse has become at once more religious by building new categories of holiness around the territories conquered in 1967, and by Zionists having injected momentum into the Jewish nationalist mission for land.

The 1967 War, with its conquest of the West Bank territories, resurrected the long-dormant dream of building homes on the historic land of Israel and stirred a new religious awakening in the country. For most Israelis, their military victory in 1967 rescued the country from an existential threat; for some, it fostered a determination to revive and revise a Zionist goal that promised personal and collective redemption on a land made sacred by ancestors and one that could now be remade holy through the establishment of Jewish settlements.

Like the dominant visions of the past, this one, too, possessed an imaginative and moral power for many who embraced it as a substitute for the decline in public acclaim for Zionism's original egalitarian transformative mission (Kaplan 2015). A narrative of spiritual rebirth was crafted based on building homes on sites woven into Judaism's sacred story. These communities were intended to symbolize a strengthened dedication to Zionism and Judaism and to give both a new scale of expression.

In the past, Zionism's ambition to redefine what it was to be a Jew, lodged itself in the imagination even for many of those who abided by the traditions and religious rulings they carried from past generations. After 1967, Judaism began to refashion what it meant to be a Zionist by conveying an absolute conviction in the holiness of the territories now called by their biblical names, Judea and Samaria, and by converting what was asserted as a historic right into a powerful religious imperative. Any political calculation that deemed a withdrawal from these areas as congruent with Israel's national interest would confront not only the charge of violating critical Zionist principles but also the accusation of transgressing sacred obligations. Judaism entered the niche in public discourse once totally occupied by Zionism.

The many Jewish settlements and religious institutions dotting the hills and towns of the West Bank that often radiated from a reborn religious Zionism also tapped into ideals of individualism and personal fulfilment, sentiments that had in the past been marginalized or even buried by Israel's dominant Labour Zionist culture. After the 1967 War, the country's economic expansion enabled many Israelis to build their dream house and recast Israeli culture from a celebration of a Spartan labour ideal into a nation that could offer more opportunities to its citizens in their quest for prosperity and lifestyle satisfaction. The word settlement – once conjuring up images of a return to the soil, collective responsibilities, and to a labour imbued with an egalitarian ethic – became incarnated as a new spirit celebrating personal choice, inspired as much as burdened by a Zionist resonance for the land that set off alarms about where such trends were taking the Jewish state.

For the war that administered such a blistering defeat to Egypt, Syria, and Jordan and tripled the size of Israel's landmass, also gave the Jewish state responsibility for more than a million Palestinians living in the West Bank and Gaza Strip. The joy of military victory soon turned into a chronic entanglement in the tensions and difficulties produced by a dispossessed Palestinian population who have been victims of abuse by almost every government in whose jurisdiction they lived. And as the Palestinian issue festered, it took its toll on the Israeli political system. Governing coalitions were often stitched together to avoid rather than address a problem that, given past efforts, had much more potential for failure than for success. Although many political leaders endorsed the principle of two states for two peoples, few saw how it could work given regional instability and the persistence of violence against Israel defined by almost all Palestinian leaders as a legitimate form of resistance. Notwithstanding an international consensus on how to bring an end to the conflict, "two states for two peoples" still seems unworkable to many of the people expected to live within its auspices.

Thus, the religious messianic commitment to redeem the land of Israel has not abated, but it, too, is embattled – initially in the 1993 Oslo Accord, and finally, in the 2005 withdrawal from Gaza. Many could not keep faith with a religious message to settle the land, given that it was the sovereign Jewish state issuing the chilling order to evacuate the Gaza Strip and the Israeli army dismantling Jewish communities (Goodman 2018; Jacobson 2011).

Israelis know that what they see as a matter of life and death is often viewed differently across the globe. But in a country, where parents still send their children off to war, citizens sense that utopian dreams, not tempered by a reckoning with their costs, may stir the imagination but never withstand the ordeals of implementation.

And because Israel has become as much a freighted and dissonant symbol as a topic of study, the argument over Zionism is as much a part of public discourse as the Zionist argument. When Israel is cast as the nexus of current postmodern flashpoints – imperialism, nationalism, and terror – Zionism is indicted as the source of this toxic mixture. Not surprisingly, accusations levelled against Israel through this lens prompt both renewed assertions of the right of the Jewish people to national self- determination and of Zionism's core assumption that sovereignty is a necessary predicate for survival. "'If you will it, it is no dream,'" served as a foundational principle of Zionism but not a constituent of Israeli policies. Still, it hovers over public life in the Jewish state as a reminder of what is yet to be achieved.

Recommended Readings

Avineri, S. 2008. *Herzl: Theodor Herzl and The Foundation of the Jewish State*. London: Orion.

Chowers, E. 2012. *The Political Philosophy of Zionism: Trading Jewish Words for a Hebraic Land*. Cambridge: Cambridge University Press.

Dowty, A. 2020. *Arabs and Jews in Ottoman Palestine: Two Worlds Collide*. Bloomington, IN: University of Indiana Press.

Herzberg, A. 1997. *The Zionist Idea: A Historical Analysis and Reader*. Philadelphia: The Jewish Publication Society.

Laqueur, W. 1972. *A History of Zionism: From the French Revolution to the Establishment of the State of Israel.* New York: Holt, Rinehart and Winston.
Troy, G. ed. 2018. *The Zionist Ideas: Visions for the Jewish Homeland – Then, Now, Tomorrow.* Philadelphia: The Jewish Publication Society.

Questions for discussion

(1) Draft two letters, the first from a young Jew living in Russia in 1900 to a Palestinian in Jerusalem, on why Jews have a right to develop a homeland in Palestine and, the second, the response from the Palestinian.
(2) Was the idea of 'negating the Diaspora' useful for Zionism's success?
(3) Are Zionist norms and values part of Israel's national identity?
(4) What role has the creation of a Jewish State played in shaping how Jews are perceived and how they perceive themselves in the twenty- first century?
(5) To what extent did Zionism unite the Jewish people?

Note

1 I do not sing to thee, my homeland, tales of heroic deeds that brought you glory and fame; I rather planted a tree where Jordan's shore rests peacefully; my feet only conquered a path winding through the fields. Lo sharti lach artzi, ve-lo fearti shmach; be-allilot gevura, bishlal kvarot; Rak etz yadei natoo chofi yarden shoktim; Rak shvil kvshoo raglei al pnay sadot.

References

Alroey, G. 2004. *The Immigrants: Jewish Immigration to Palestine in the Early Twentieth Century.* Jerusalem: Yad Izhak Ben-Zvi Press. [in Hebrew].
Boord, M. 2017. "Creating the Labor-Zionist Family: Masculinity, Sexuality, and Marriage in Mandate Palestine." *Jewish Social Studies* 22:3, 38–67.
Brenner, M. 2018. *In Search of Israel: The History of an Idea.* Princeton, NJ: Princeton University Press.
Chowers, E. 2012. *The Political Philosophy of Zionism.* Cambridge: Cambridge University Press.
Cohen, H. 2005. *Year Zero of the Arab-Israeli Conflict 1929.* Waltham, MA: Brandeis University Press.
Divine, D. R. 2008. *Exiled in the Homeland: Zionism and the Return to Mandate Palestine.* Austin, TX: University of Texas Press.
Etkin, E. Forthcoming. "Neighborhood, Neighbors, and Neighborliness: Urban Life in the Jewish Community of Mandate Palestine/Eretz Israel." [in Hebrew].
Ezrahi, S. D. 1992. "Our Homeland, the Text ... Our Text, the Homeland: Exile and Homecoming in the Jewish Imagination." *Michigan Quarterly Review* 31:4, 463–497.
Gavison, R. 1999. "Jewish and Democratic? A Rejoinder to the 'Ethnic Democracy' Debate." *Israel Studies* 4:1, 1–30.
Golan, A. 2001. "European Imperialism and the Development of Modern Palestine: Was Zionism a Form of Colonialism?" *Space & Polity* 5:2, 127–143.
Goodman, M. 2018. *Catch-67: The Left, The Right, and The Legacy of the Six-Day War,* New Haven, CT: Yale University Press.
Halpern, B., and J. Reinharz. 1998. *Zionism and the Creation of a New Society.* New York: Oxford University Press.
Imber, E. (Forthcoming). "Thinking through Empire: Interwar Zionism, British Imperialism, and the Future of the Jewish National Home" [in Hebrew].
Jacobson, D. 2011. *Beyond Messianism: The Poetry of Second-Generation Religious- Zionist Settlers.* Brookline, MA: Academic Studies Press.
Kaplan, E. 2015. *Beyond Post-Zionism.* Albany: State University of New York Press.
Locker-Biltzki, A. 2018. "Rethinking Settler Colonialism: A Marxist Critique of Gershon Shafir." *Rethinking Marxism* 30:3, 441–461.
Ohana, D. 2012. *The Origins of Israeli Mythology: Neither Canaanites nor Crusaders.* Cambridge: Cambridge University Press.

Rosenberg-Friedman, L. 2017. *Birthrate Politics in Zion Judaism, Nationalism, and Modernity Under the British Mandate*. Bloomington, IN: Indiana University Press.
Rozin, O. 2016. *A Home for All Jews: Citizenship, Rights and National Identity in the New Israeli State*. Waltham, MA: Brandeis University Press.
Sager, S. 1985. *The Parliamentary System of Israel*. Syracuse, NY: Syracuse University Press.
Saposnik, A. 2008. *Becoming Hebrew The Creation of Jewish National Culture in Ottoman Palestine*. New York: Oxford University Press.
Sasley, B. E., and H. M. Waller. 2017 *Politics in Israel: Governing A Complex Society*. New York: Oxford University Press.
Shafir, G. 1989. *Land, Labor, and the Origins of the Israeli-Palestinian Conflict, 1882–1914*. Cambridge: Cambridge University Press.
Shiff, Ofer. 2019. "Exiles in the New Homeland: Diasporic Struggles for Civil Equality as Part of the 1930s Yishuv Agenda." Association for Israel Studies Conference.
Shumsky, D. 2018. *Beyond the Nation-State: The Zionist Political Imagination from Pincus to Ben-Gurion*. New Haven, CT: Yale University Press.
Stanislawski, M. 2001. *Zionism and the Fin de Siecle Cosmopolitanism and Nationalism from Nordau to Jabotinsky*. Berkeley, CA: University of California Press.
Waxman, D., and I. Peleg. 2011. *Israel's Palestinians: The Conflict Within*. New York: Oxford University Press.

6

RADICAL ASYMMETRY, CONFLICT RESOLUTION, AND STRATEGIC ENGAGEMENT IN THE ISRAELI-PALESTINIAN CONFLICT

Oliver Ramsbotham

Radical Material Asymmetry and Conflict Resolution

International attempts to resolve the Jewish/Arab conflict in Palestine go back to the 1937 British Palestine Royal Commission (Peel Commission) Partition Plan in response to the great 1936 Arab revolt. It failed because of the military asymmetry at the time, in which "the Jewish community was militarily weak and would have been easily defeated had Britain not intervened to restore law and order" (Shlaim, 2000, 20). The Jewish Agency accepted the partition plan. But, given their previous military preponderance and outrage at the whole idea of the imposition of a Jewish state in an Arab land, Arab leaders, notably Haj Amin al-Hassani, Grand Mufti of Jerusalem, rejected it. In the fighting British major-general Bernard Montgomery "broke the back of the Arab national movement" for the next decade. Conversely, part of the irregular Jewish *Haganah* (defence) was professionally armed and trained by the British in 1941–1942 to help defend Palestine from advancing German forces under Rommel (for example, the Palmach regiment). As a result, by the time of the next attempt at conflict resolution – the 1947 United Nations partition plan – the military asymmetry had been reversed. At the end of the 1947–1949 'War of Independence' Israel controlled 78 per cent of the mandate territory.

This astonishing outcome set the pattern for the next seventy years for Israel. The conclusion was that Israelis should rely on Ze'ev Jabotinsky's Iron Wall, not the inglorious and discredited conflict-resolution path of "negotiation and diplomacy":

> The State of Israel! My eyes filled with tears, and my hands shook. We had done it. We had brought the Jewish state into existence. ... From this day on we would no longer live on sufferance in the land of our forefathers. Now we were a nation like other nations, master – for the first time in twenty centuries – of our own destiny. The

DOI: 10.4324/9780429027376-8

dream had come true – too late to save those who had perished in the Holocaust, but not too late for the generations to come.

(Golda Meir 1975, 226)

[The 1948 victory] seemed to show the advantages of direct action over negotiation and diplomacy. ... The victory offered such a glorious contrast to the centuries of persecution and humiliation, of adaptation and compromise, that it seemed to indicate the only direction that could possibly be taken from then on. To brook nothing, tolerate no attack, cut through the Gordian knots, and create history by creating facts seemed so simple, so compelling, so satisfying that it became Israel's policy in its conflict with the Arab world.

(Goldmann 1969, 289–290)

This was compounded twenty years later in the 1967 Six-Day War (when Nahum Goldmann was writing his book) – another miraculous victory after a period of great doubt and foreboding in which even David Ben Gurion had suffered from "deep, almost irrational, anxiety" after the April 1963 Arab Federation between Egypt, Syria and Iraq:

To Israelis it was a war for survival, fought against a steady drumbeat of threats to Israel's very existence. Israelis never forget the fear of annihilation that prevailed on the eve of the war, or the digging of mass graves in anticipation of vast civilian casualties.

(Dowty 2012, 117)

Material asymmetry had now reached its limit. From 1967 onwards Israel was the 'possessor' of all the land in question – and more besides. Palestinians were dispossessed 'challengers', either living as citizens of Israel, or as stateless people in Gaza, the West Bank, and Jerusalem under Israeli control, or in other countries as diaspora/refugees.

Where was there a basis for conflict resolution now between Israel and the Palestinians given this extreme material asymmetry of power? The material asymmetry was qualitative – a struggle between a state actor and a non-state actor – as well as quantitative. Israeli military strength was progressively extended and transmuted to include all the other elements of Gramscian hegemonic control – economic, educational, bureaucratic, security, legal, physical, geographical. To illustrate this let us compare the situation in the Israeli/Palestinian conflict with the scope for conflict resolution in the wider Israeli/Arab conflict at the time – in particular, relations between Israel and Egypt.

Egypt had been the mortal enemy of Israel on the eve of the 1967 War:

If we were to enter a battle with Israel, with God's help we could triumph. ... The battle will be a general one and our basic objective will be to destroy Israel.

(Abdul Nasser: 26 May 1967, quoted in Lacquer and Rubin 2008, 99)

Nevertheless, eleven years later, after the Camp David talks brokered by United States President Jimmy Carter, conflict resolution succeeded in the guise of the March 1979 peace treaty between Israel and Egypt that has survived to this day.[1] The treaty with Egypt was negotiated when hard-line Israeli prime minister Menachem Begin's right-wing Likud party had just displaced the Israeli Labor Party as the biggest political party in Israel in the watershed 1977 national election. Why did this happen?

One answer is because the three aspects of radical asymmetry did not apply in this case: Radical qualitative material asymmetry did not exist between the two states, and quantitative material asymmetry had been to a large extent alleviated by the surprise – and considerable initial Egyptian success – of the October 1973 Yom Kippur War. Radical conceptual asymmetry did not exist because *Eretz Israel* (the Land of Israel) had never included the Sinai Peninsula. And radical strategic asymmetry (incompatibility of goals) did not exist because the gains for Israel in splitting the Arab world and ending the greatest external threat to its survival came to be seen to be self-evident by a majority of Israelis, especially after the historic visit to Israel and the Knesset by Egyptian president Anwar Sadat on 20 November 1977. As a result, conflict resolution worked.

But nothing similar happened in the parallel Israeli/Palestinian conflict, even after the historic and astonishing 1988 Palestinian declaration of statehood by the PLO on only 22 per cent of mandate Palestine and de facto recognition of Israel on 78 per cent that followed the March 1988 Palestinian National Council (PNC) meeting in Algiers, together with Yasser Arafat's public renunciation of violence in Geneva in December 1988. From a conflict-resolution perspective, this should have ushered in the well-known pattern of accommodation in asymmetric conflicts whereby challengers give up violent resistance in exchange for power-sharing by possessors – in this case in the form of "land for peace".

Despite high initial hopes in the early 1990s when, for example, delegates from Northern Ireland came to Israel/Palestine to learn how peace is made, and Israelis and Palestinians toured Northern Ireland to give them an answer, this never materialized.

To understand why, we must interrupt the chronological narrative about material asymmetry and take into account the other two dimensions of radical asymmetry as well – conceptual asymmetry and strategic asymmetry.

Radical Conceptual Asymmetry and Conflict Resolution

At this point let us also look at the other levels of conflict-resolution efforts – civil society and grassroots – which continue to be pursued with great determination and inventiveness to this day by Israeli, Palestinian, and international actors. This is a large and extremely varied field so the present account can only be indicative.

There are a number of ways of analysing these conflict-resolution approaches. Perhaps the simplest way is to distinguish between various forms of interactive problem-solving, dialogue for mutual understanding, and negotiation for mutual accommodation at societal level. Ronald Fisher explains the difference between interactive conflict resolution and dialogue:

> Unlike the more focused forms of interactive conflict resolution, such as problem-solving workshops, dialogue interventions tend to involve not influential, informal representatives of the parties, but simply ordinary members of the antagonistic groups. Furthermore, dialogue is primarily directed toward increased understanding and trust among the participants with some eventual positive effects on public opinion, rather than the creation of alternative solutions to the conflict.
>
> *(Fisher 1997, 121)*

A good idea of interactive problem-solving approaches in Israel/Palestine since the 1970s to the present day is provided in recent summative books by its most famous living exponent, Herbert Kelman (2017 and 2018). Recent examples of the range of dialogic approaches include

Maya Kahanoff's book *Jews and Arabs in Israel Encountering Their Identities: Transformations in Dialogue* (2016), and Rosemary Hollis' account of the long-standing 2004–2016 *Olive Tree* cross-conflict dialogue programme (2019). The best-known exposition of "principled" negotiation/mediation approaches that have fed into various contrasting "citizens diplomacy", "people-to-people". and "multi-track" levels remains Roger Fisher and William Ury's *Getting To Yes: Negotiating Agreement Without Giving In* (1981).

There are many other ways of analysing this rich and varied field, such as Ifat Maoz's distinction between the "coexistence model" based on exploring shared similarities, the "joint projects model" based on a search for shared superordinate goals, the "group identity model" based on discussion of confrontational roles and power relations, and the "narrative-story-telling model" based on interchanging life-stories (Maoz, 2011). In Robert Rotberg's edited volume, *Israeli and Palestinian Narratives of Conflict,* Ilan Pappe advocates "bridging the narrative gap", Daniel Bar-Tal and Gavriel Salomon promote "building legitimacy through narrative", Mordechai Bar-On recommends critical reappraisal by each side of its own historical record, and Dan Bar-On and Sami Adwan suggest a parallel text approach for better mutual understanding between two interdependent narratives that are intertwined "like a double helix" (Rotberg 2006). In their 2018 assessment of "planned contact interventions" (e.g., "citizens' dialogue" and "arranged encounters") between Jewish Israelis and Palestinians, Chuck Thiessen and Marwan Darweish analyse the tensions between peace and resistance workers about whether contact-based encounters should be supported because they help to reconstruct identities, explore contentious issues, and impact the peace process, or whether they should be opposed because they ignore the needs of the oppressed, neglect the injustices that constitute the roots of conflict, and normalize subjection and occupation (Thiessen and Darweish 2018). Thiessen and Darweish propose the idea of constructing an "emergent theoretical framework" in an attempt to combine the two.

And there are also a host of other approaches (too many and varied to outline usefully here) that creatively address the challenge of overcoming the conflict – including ideas of "two states one homeland", "parallel sovereignty", a future "confederation" between the State of Israel and a future State of Palestine (perhaps also including the State of Jordan). An innovative recent example is *The Holocaust and the Nakba: A New Grammar of Trauma and History* by Bashir Bashir and Amos Goldberg with its concomitant commitment to the idea of some form of "bi-nationalism" (Bashir and Goldberg 2019).

At the risk of gross over-simplification of a complicated field, why, despite their many local successes, have these various approaches so far not transformed prospects for conflict resolution in the Israeli-Palestinian conflict as a whole?

Undoubted successes include not only the immediate outcomes of particular projects and workshops and the transformations experienced by the individuals participating in them, but also long-term enterprises in communal living, such as the *Israeli-Palestinian School of Peace* project going back to 1972, when Arab and Jewish Israelis created a joint village – Neve Shalom/Wahat El Salam (Oasis of Peace) – which still thrives. Here, at first the emphasis was on individual relationships, but this was then extended to collective identities with Arabs and Jews meeting uni-nationally as well as bi-nationally (Halabi 2004). So why have enterprises like this not had more influence in transforming the wider conflict?

Explanations for this broader failure are no doubt to be found in the material and strategic aspects of radical asymmetry looked at in the previous and succeeding sections. There are also the fundamental changes that have taken place, and are taking place, within Israeli and Palestinian societies as noted in the final section of this chapter. But, in addition to the well-known problem of re-entry when local transformations are subsequently dissipated or lost as participants 're-enter' their wider communities and encounter the unchanged radical asymmetry of divided daily lives, and the problem that participants in conflict-resolution initiatives are often likely to be the more amenable members of both societies who perhaps least need transformation in the first place, the rest of this section focuses on the major challenge of conceptual asymmetry and radical disagreement.

To put it succinctly, the conceptual assumptions on which many, if not most, communicative conflict-resolution approaches rest – assumptions about reflexivity (that these are merely subjective narratives), functionality (that what is said does not refer to truth but only to internal interests and needs) and equivalence (that both narratives are symmetric and equivalent as such) – do not yet apply in conditions of conceptual asymmetry, linguistic intractability, and radical disagreement.

Interactive conflict resolution, dialogue, and interest-based negotiation/mediation approaches dismiss radical disagreement as competitive debate, adversarial debate and positional debate respectively (see Ramsbotham 2017, 29–45). Radical disagreement is rejected as an all-too-familiar dead end and terminus to dialogue that should, from the outset, be set aside or overcome, not learnt from. The minimal conflict-resolution aim is for each side to acknowledge the underlying interests and needs of the other, and to recognize and accept the functionality (and thereby "validity") of both narratives for their respective societies:

> The Israeli-Palestinian conflict for primacy, power, and control encompasses two bitterly contested, competing narratives. Both need to be understood, reckoned with, and analysed side by side in order to help abate violence and possibly propel both protagonists toward peace. This is an immensely tall order. But the first step is to know the narratives, the second to reconcile them to the extent that they can be reconciled or bridged, and the third to help each side to accept, and conceivably to respect, the validity of the competing narrative.
>
> *(Rotberg 2006, 1)*

But this is not yet the situation in conditions of extreme conceptual asymmetry. In radical disagreements, the conflicting parties do not just refer to their own subjectivity or reflexivity. They do not say that this is merely functional for their ongoing survival. And they do not describe the resulting quarrel as a mere co-existence of equivalent narratives or stories. That they do not say this is what makes it a radical disagreement. It is this that so far blocks attempts at communicative conflict resolution (see Ramsbotham 2017, 77–141, for extensive illustrations of this).[2]

For example – fully mindful of the great and passionately held differences of viewpoint within Jewish Israeli society – any time spent listening to what Israelis say in the process of radical disagreement makes it evident that most Jewish Israelis are not merely referring to the subjectivity, functionality and equivalence of their own 'story' but to the reality of lived experience, deep history and the security imperative.[3] Palestinians refer to the fused reality of fact (the *nakba*), value (its injustice), emotion (indignation) and will (determination to win back equality and freedom for their children and grandchildren). This is not just a "Palestinian narrative". What Palestinians say points at a lived reality, or collective nightmare, which continues – and deepens – to this day.[4]

There is only room for one short example of the conceptual asymmetry and radical disagreement that results from this. It is taken from Maya Kahanoff's book *Jews and Arabs in Israel*

Encountering Their Identities (2016), in which a Jewish Israeli (A) and an Arab Israeli (B) are arguing.

(A) As I see the conflict … it is a conflict between stories. Every person has their story. There are certain historic facts, but every person gives them their own meaning. … You have a story and I have a story. Neither story has … a true ontological status of "that is the story", but let's learn each other's stories.
(B) Listen, I know one thing. You will not convince me of that. *You took my land.* [Original italics]
(A) But that's your story.
(B) OK.
(A) But my story is a different story. |

(Kahanoff 2016, 66)

In this fragment of radical disagreement (A)'s account of the situation as "a conflict between stories" is contradicted by (B)'s insistence that "you took my land". It is not clear what (B)'s "OK" signifies here, but from later interjections it is clear that (B) stands by what he has said.

(A) later goes on to elaborate:

> But it goes to the root of the matter. That is … as far as you are concerned there is one story, the story … put very roughly and simplistically is: throughout history … there were placid Arabs here and one day the evil Jews came and expelled them. That is the Palestinian story in its rawest and bluntest form. Right? I can also simplify the Jewish story in the same way. We Jews, the persecuted and dispossessed minority, who were persecuted and killed and destroyed, came here because this is our homeland from which we were expelled and to which we are returning. That is also in the rawest and bluntest form of the story. Neither is truer than the other. There is one story and there is another story and neither story has a superior status.

What (A) says coincides with conflict-resolution assumptions about narrative reflexivity and equivalence. So, in rejecting (A)'s account, (B) is at the same time rejecting assumptions that also underpin most classic conflict-resolution approaches. (B) refuses to accept that what he says is merely reflexive, functional, and equivalent to what (A) says. (B) points at the *fact* of what happened – and is still happening – in Palestine. It is this reality that refutes (A) – and thereby also repudiates those conflict-resolution approaches that do not at the same time seek to rectify the asymmetry, inequality, and injustice to which (B) refers. Normalization tries prematurely to pacify what needs to be challenged and, by drawing a false veil of equivalence over an unequal situation, perpetuates inequality:

> From the moment Zionism was conceived, force has been a central component of its relationship with Palestinians. The seeds of protracted conflict are based in the relationship between colonizer and colonized, and thus are inherent to the dynamics of the encounter between the Zionist movement and Palestinians. It has always been naïve or self-serving to think that a Jewish state could be established in a homeland inhabited by another people except through the use of force.
>
> *(Rouhana 2006, 118)*

In this way, the radical conceptual asymmetry between possessors and challengers clearly reflects and reinforces the imbalances of radical material asymmetry.

Far from being a "terminus to dialogue" radical disagreement is its most characteristic aspect in intense political conflicts – namely what I call "agonistic dialogue", the dialogue of struggle (*agon*) (Ramsbotham 2010 and 2017). Agonistic dialogue is that part of radical disagreement in which conflicting parties directly address each other's utterances. If, instead of ignoring agonistic dialogue, we explore it with the protagonists, then we find that they are, not closer, but much further apart than was realized. Far from being "all-too-familiar" radical disagreement is perhaps the least familiar aspect of intractable asymmetric conflict. It is the main linguistic blockage to communicative conflict resolution. The disagreement involves what it is about, it reaches to the distant horizon, and it involves the distinctions invoked in the process of disagreeing – fact/value, opinion/reality, form/content, subject/object (Ramsbotham 2010 and forthcoming).

To sum all this up, radical disagreement is not a mere juxtaposition or co-existence of equivalent narratives (or discourses or world views). It is a life-and-death struggle to occupy the whole of discursive space – and to act accordingly. Radical disagreement is the war of words, as integral to the conflict as the war of weapons. Radical disagreement challenges conflict-resolution assumptions about neutrality, impartiality, and disinterestedness. Those who want to resolve radically asymmetric conflicts need to acknowledge and engage the radical disagreements at the core of those conflicts before they can hope to transform those conflicts.

Radical Strategic Asymmetry and Conflict Resolution

Strategic asymmetry follows from, and links together, the other two dimensions of radical asymmetry – material and conceptual asymmetry.

We return to the chronology of events between the 2000 Camp David talks between Israeli prime minister Ehud Barak and Palestinian leader Yasser Arafat, and the end of the Obama presidency in 2016 at the point where we broke off at the end of the first section. We are asking why conflict-resolution efforts at government level failed during this period. In addition to the 2000/2001 Camp David/Taba talks, there were negotiations as part of the Quartet "road map" between Israeli prime minister Ehud Olmert and Palestinian president Mahmoud Abbas in 2007–2008, and of the 2013–2014 Kerry initiative.

In radical strategic asymmetry the possessor (Israel) and the challenger (Palestinians) have entirely different strategic priorities, and this constitutes the final and critical blockage to conflict resolution.

The main strategic question for Israel as possessor is why Israel should give up anything at all. From a strategic perspective the only reason for doing this would be if Israel calculated that it would be more, rather than less, secure as a result. But the outbreak of the second intifada in September 2000, and Hamas's violent seizure of power in Gaza in June 2007, followed by indiscriminate rocket attacks on Israeli civilians, transformed the debate inside Israel and convinced most Israelis that withdrawal from the West Bank (Judea and Samaria) would be strategically suicidal:

> The Palestinians may have been provoked beyond endurance by the brutality of Israeli power. Nevertheless, resorting to firearms was a mistake of historic proportions. The key to success of the first intifada lay in its non-violent nature. By resorting to violence in 2000, the Palestinian leadership reneged on its principal pledge under the Oslo accord. Palestinian violence destroyed the Israeli peace camp; it persuaded

> Israelis from all points along the political spectrum that there is no Palestinian partner for peace.
>
> *(Shlaim 2009, 35–36)*

This was also seen as a death-knell to any further influence from Israeli "post-Zionist" new history after its brief flourishing in the 1990s:

> [A]lmost immediately after the outbreak of the Second Intifada a reinvigorated Zionist consensus, which had somewhat eroded at the height of the Oslo days, reasserted itself with force. Public discourse in Israel was reshaped along strictly consensual lines.
>
> *(Pappe 2012, 276)*

Israelis are outnumbered 50–1 by Arabs and 250–1 globally by Muslims. There is only one Jewish state. There are 22 Arab states. Withdrawing from the West Bank and handing it over to a weak Palestinian government would risk a repeat of what happened in Gaza after Israel's withdrawal in 2005. And a reading of the rabidly anti-Semitic Articles 22 and 23 of the 1988 Hamas Charter is enough to silence most Israeli critics of current strategy.[5]

In contrast, as the challenger, the main strategic question for Palestinians is how to dismantle the existing deepening status quo of oppression, occupation, illegal colonial settlement and apartheid and achieve full national liberation:

> Israel will have to face at least part of the truth that the country that they settled belonged to another people, that their project was the direct cause of the displacement and dismantling of Palestinian society, and that it could not have been achieved without this displacement. Israel will also have to confront the realities of the occupation and the atrocities it is committing, and will have to accept that Palestinian citizens in Israel are indigenous to the land and entitled to seek the democratic transformation of the state so that they have equal access to power, resources and decision making, and are entitled to rectification of past and present injustices.
>
> *(Rouhana 2006, 133)*

Since the unprecedented decision by the PLO in 1988 to accept a Palestinian state on only 22 per cent of the territory in question, the fundamental demand has been for full implementation of Palestinian national rights on this basis. Further compromise is not possible. The appeal is not to further never-ending concessions, as inappropriately expected in grossly asymmetric 'bilateral' negotiations with the Israeli state backed by its great-power guarantor, the United States, but to international support in implementing existing United Nations General Assembly and Security Council Resolutions, International Court of Justice Rulings, and Geneva Conventions – as well as the 2002 Arab Peace Initiative, still officially endorsed by all the members of the Arab League as well as the 57 member states of the Organization of Islamic Cooperation.[6]

This strategic radical disagreement engulfs interpretations of conflict-resolution efforts between 2000 and 2016. For example, in the view of United States Middle East envoy Dennis Ross at the time of the 2000 Camp David talks,

> [h]ad Nelson Mandela been the Palestinian leader and not Yasser Arafat, I would be writing now how … Israelis and Palestinians had succeeded in reaching an 'end of conflict' agreement.
>
> *(Ross, 2004, 756–757)*

This assertion is diametrically contradicted by a number of other analysts and commentators.[7]

Did the 2007–2008 negotiations "come close to success", as Ehud Olmert claims?

> We were very close, more than ever in the past, to completing an agreement in principle that would have led to an end of the conflict between us and the Palestinians.
>
> *(Olmert, 28 January 2011; quoted in Dowty 2012, 220)*

Or were prospects of a Palestinian state in any case delusional from the outset given the determination of successive Israeli prime ministers to prevent it, and the refusal, not just of the United States, but also of other members of the Quartet, notably the European Union, to challenge this? Despite lip-service paid to the idea of a Palestinian state in his 2009 Bar-Ilan speech, Israeli prime minister Binyamin Netanyahu openly promised to prevent this happening in successive pre-election appeals to the Israeli people over his long (second) period in office between 2009 and 2021. And were earlier Israeli prime ministers – including Yitzhak Rabin himself – also not seriously prepared to contemplate a fully independent Palestinian state? This is a complex debate. Palestinians point to the similarity between the Allon Plan for partitioning the West Bank in 1967, the Oslo II Interim Agreement of 1995, the so-called Naftali Bennett Plan of April 2014, and what looks like the current Trump deal. In this view the only inhibition against wholesale Israeli annexation of the West Bank has been the determination not to include large centres of Palestinian population (hence revived mention of the "Jordan option" whereby Jordan would absorb residual West Bank Palestinians).

Although there is no space to elaborate further here, during the 2013–2014 Kerry talks, despite initially high hopes among some members of the United States mediation team, in my experience few Israelis or Palestinians shared these expectations (Ramsbotham and Schiff, 2019).

In the face of these repeated conflict-resolution failures, my own work with Israeli and Palestinian partners during this period was to move away from attempts at conflict resolution between the conflicting parties when these efforts were premature. It was to start where the protagonists themselves were rather than from where third parties wanted them to be. This means shifting from *conflict resolution* to *strategic engagement* and, in the first instance, from efforts to promote dialogue and mediation *between* the contesting identity groups to the promotion of "collective strategic thinking" (CST) *within* them: Where are they? Where do they want to be? How can they get there? This can then be fed into the respective national debates at all levels, can animate strategic exchange across and between constituencies on both sides, and can inform would-be third-party peacemakers accordingly. This is a powerful, if little-developed, methodology for opening up new strategic possibilities in otherwise intractable conditions.[8]

In 2015, for example, collective strategic thinking reports by the *Israeli Strategic Forum* (ISF) and the *Palestine Strategy Group* (PSG) showed how beneath the surface of political polarization were a range of diverse constituencies within the identity groups with cross-cutting agendas, and a resulting complex mix of strategic issues and priorities, many of which were otherwise not on the radar screen.[9] For instance the possibility of a future confederation between Israel, Palestine and perhaps Jordan, often seen as a "one-state" variant, can in fact only be achieved via a "two-state" route. In other words, there was a much wider range of short-term, medium-term and long-term strategic possibilities than was contained in the decreasingly relevant "two-state solution/one-state solution" mantra.

In the March 2015 Israeli election these nuanced differences in Israeli politics, reflecting cross-cutting progressive-conservative social/economic issues, orthodox–secular tensions, and Misrahi–Ashkenazi antagonisms, were eclipsed by the security dimension exploited by Prime Minister Netanyahu supported by the organized settler-right (Lintl, 2015). Although more than half of Israelis polled said that they still favoured a Palestinian state in principle, a considerably higher percentage said 'not yet'. Progressive Left parties failed to find an effective counter-platform on security (for example that a negotiated Palestinian state would be in the long-term interest of Israel), while centrist parties attempted to match rightists in security toughness.

2017–2019: The End of the 1988–2016 International Consensus?

The last part of the chapter I briefly assess the impact of the events of the last three years on possibilities for conflict resolution at the time of writing.

It seems that any prospect of exploring new strategic spaces of the kind mentioned at the end of the last section – at government level – was abruptly shut down by the unilateral statements and actions of the new Trump Administration in the United States, and by the reactions (albeit at times uneasy about such forthrightness) of the Netanyahu government in Israel. This appears to amount to nothing less than the tearing up of the previous (admittedly often precarious) 1988 to 2016 international consensus about how best to end the Israel/Palestine conflict. We can see this by a brief review of the way in which the key elements of the former international consensus – as set out for example in the 2002 Arab Peace Initiative (API) quoted below – have been affected.

Between 2017 and 2019, instead of a "sovereign independent Palestinian state in the West Bank and Gaza Strip" (quotation from the API), any reference to a Palestinian state had already been cut from the United States Republican Party platform (O'Toole, 2016), and the Palestinian representative's office in Washington was closed down. Instead of "withdrawal from territories occupied since 1967" (API) the Israeli prime minister declared his intention to annex, not only major West Bank settlement blocks (declared "not illegal" by the United States on 18 November 2019), but "the Jordan Valley and northern Dead Sea" (Pfeffer 2019). This astonishing statement profoundly shocked Jordan, whose formal peace treaty with Israel, together with the peace treaty with Egypt, has been a bedrock of Israeli regional security. Instead of the Palestinian state having "East Jerusalem as its capital" (API), on 17 December 2017 the United States administration unilaterally recognized Jerusalem as the capital of Israel and moved its embassy there. Instead of an agreed "just solution to the Palestinian refugee problem" (API) the United States government withdrew its funding from UNWRA and demanded a redefinition of international treaty language that effectively eliminates the refugee issue. This complemented the likely impact of the 19 July 2018 Israeli 'Nation State Law'.[10] Instead of an equitable sharing of resources between two sovereign states, proposals for 'economic peace', such as those made at the 25–26 June 2019 Bahrein workshop, are seen by Palestinians, in the absence of political clarification, to reinforce and deepen permanent Israeli control.[11]

To the extent that United States/Israel political strategy is now set in this direction, it seems that it will generate an equal and opposite Palestinian strategic shift because the entire Palestinian national project now faces an existential threat. The middle ground will be removed, and with it any further talk of "one-state solution/two-state solution" strategic alternatives, since both were cancelled by the Trump/Netanyahu agenda.

Under this possible future (A) the existing "one-state reality" is made explicit and is accelerated towards its logical conclusion. It takes the form of a Jewish State of Israel with effective permanent jurisdiction/control over the whole of historic (mandate) Palestine. It includes the declared possibility of annexation of Area C on the West Bank, with the exclusion of major centres of Palestinian population, and perpetual military command of borders and airspace. This seems the culmination of the original concept of the "Iron Wall" – we may recall Nahum Goldmann's words: "[T]he advantages of direct action over negotiation and diplomacy". Its advocates, including the electorally powerful settler-rights lobby, point to Palestinian weakness and internal division, to Israeli success in realigning the interests of Arab regional leaderships in the face of threats from Iran, and to the reluctance of other members of the Quartet to challenge the United States. As a result, the expectation is that any future international protests will be short-lived, and that the younger generation of Palestinians will prefer transformed economic prospects to persistence in unrealistic dreams.

At the risk of over-simplification, many, if not most, Palestinians – particularly among the younger generation – responding to the existing "one-state reality" and its steady approximation in recent years towards "greater Israel" – have already some time ago written off the ideas of a "one-state solution" or a "two-state solution" as if they are meaningful alternatives, and advocate various forms of re-assertion of equal rights for Palestinians across the board and "from the river to the sea" (ECFR, 28 May 2019). Despite internal divisions, and current despondency and despair among many Palestinians, the existential threat of future (A) is likely to galvanize an equal and opposite shift in Palestinian strategy at leadership level in the same direction, as anticipated in the Palestine Strategy Group 2015 report *A Post Oslo Strategy* and the PSG 2020 report *Palestine 2030*. This is future (B). It includes a comprehensive rejection of, and resistance to, future (A) in its entirety, in which "smart resistance" minimizes the effectiveness of Israeli military force and adapts particular initiatives in accordance with their perceived efficacy in attaining specific strategic goals. Future (B) is centred on a reaffirmation of the Palestinian claim to equal rights across the board and throughout the territories in question. This includes equal individual citizenship rights, not just for Palestinians in Israel but for all Palestinians who are currently stateless (an as-yet underplayed strategic dimension), equal collective majority and minority rights, equal self-determination rights, and equal indigenous rights. All of these are seen to be complementary. The Palestinian strategic prerequisite is to overcome internal divisions sufficiently to have a capacity for collective strategic thinking in the first place, and to revitalize the legitimacy of governance to enable effective collective strategic action. This includes the core task of reanimating and inspiring the younger generations of Palestinians and of incorporating the interests and needs of the diaspora. This may seem a distant prospect given failure to do this in recent years, but the possibility of doing so is seen to be entirely in Palestinian hands.

Daunting though the task may be – given a capacity among Palestinians to reanimate unity and legitimate democratic authority – advocates of future (B) envisage eventual success, however long it may take, as a result of demography (larger Palestinian numbers), internal transformation within the United States (erosion of the Christian Zionist grip on Congress), the role of Palestinians in Israel (20% of the population and with the third-largest party in the Knesset), mounting international condemnation of Israeli policy and actions (illegal occupation, settlement, forcible separation, apartheid), overwhelming support for the Palestinian cause in international law (including the fact that Palestine is already a non-member United Nations state with a capacity to join international agencies and enter international treaties), the manifest contrast in international ethics between the idea under future (A) that Jewish Israelis have all rights and Palestinians no rights, and the idea under future (B) that both peoples have equal rights and, finally, the indomitable solidarity and unquenchable desire of Palestinians for national liberation in their own land. Under future (B) history is seen to show that military force cannot indefinitely withstand the legitimate demands of a great people for self-determination and freedom.

Overlapping these two "ideal-type" scenario clusters is a third alternative future – never-ending conflict (C). Future C stretches out to unpredictable outcomes that cannot be anticipated here, outcomes in a highly volatile region and an increasingly complex multi-polar world. In the most frightening scenarios hugely destructive weapons and means of delivery may be acquired by extreme factions impervious to traditional forms of deterrence. With hindsight, will Israelis come to regret not having accepted the 2002 Arab Peace Initiative as a basis for a lasting peace while it was at the peak of its relative strength? Will Palestinians come to regret not having accepted the offer of a Palestinian state in 1937, 1947 – and perhaps 2000? Or may future leaderships, after the Abbas, Netanyahu, and Trump governments have passed away, find more benign and unsuspected new configurations for ending the conflict than can be guessed at here? Who can tell? Predictions of what may happen, even in ten years' time, are highly unreliable.

Whatever the outcome, the conclusion of this chapter is that conflict resolution can only succeed in the Israeli/Palestinian conflict when the significance of the radical symmetry at its core – material (imbalance of power), conceptual (radical disagreement) and strategic (incompatibility of goals) – is understood, acknowledged, and fully incorporated into the very fabric of the peacemaking process.

Recommended Readings

Caplan, N. 2010. *The Israel-Palestine Conflict: Contested Histories*. Hoboken, NJ: John Wiley and Sons.
Dowty, A. 2012. *Israel/Palestine*, 3rd ed. Cambridge: Polity.
Montefiore, S.S. 2011. *Jerusalem: The Biography*. New York: Hachette.
Ramsbotham, O. 2017. *When Conflict Resolution Fails*. Cambridge: Polity, In particular, Part II, Case Study: The Israel-Palestine Conflict, 69–164.
Shlaim, A. 2000. *The Iron Wall: Israel and the Arab World*. New York: W. W. Norton.
Shlaim, A. 2009. *Israel and Palestine: Reappraisals, Revisions, Refutations*. London: Verso.
Tessler, M. 2009. *A History of the Israeli-Palestinian Conflict*, 2nd ed. Bloomington, IN: Indiana University Press.

Notes

1 Israel went on to sign a peace agreement with Jordan in 1994 – but not yet with Syria or Lebanon.
2 Ramsbotham (2017) chapters 5 and 6 give examples from successive strategy reports by the Israeli Strategic Forum (ISF) and the Palestine Strategy Group (PSG) – see fn. 9 below.
3 For many Israelis the "West Bank" is Judea and Samaria, historically more integral to *Eretz Israel* (the land of Israel) than the coastal plain where Tel Aviv has been built. "In Hebrew, emigrating to Israel is still *aliyah*, a going up. Jerusalem was unimaginable on the low fluvial plain. Rivers were murky with temptation; the sea was even worse" (Schama 2013, 3–4).
4 See, for example, the Palestine Strategy Group report, *Regaining the Initiative* (2008) and subsequent PSG strategy reports.
5 The 1988 text of the Hamas Charter is readily accessible via the Internet under "The Covenant of the Islamic Resistance Movement." A re-issue on 1 May 2017 made some adjustments, but not to Articles 22 and 23, and the original version is still seen to retain validity.
6 Arab Peace Initiative (2002) www.al-bab.com/arab/docs/league/peace02.htm.
7 See, for example, from almost the same time as Dennis Ross's version of events, the very different analysis in Jeremy Pressman (2003).
8 For a brief outline of the collective strategic thinking (CST) methodology in general, see Ramsbotham (2017, 49–60). On the application of CST in Israel/Palestine see the Oxford Research Group (ORG) website: Ramsbotham and Morgan (2017).
9 See Israeli Strategic Forum (2015), Palestine Strategy Group (2015) and Palestinian Citizens of Israel Strategy Group (2018).
10 Seen by Palestinians to apply to Palestinians in general, not just to Palestinians in Israel. See Nabulsi (2018).
11 For example, in the form of likely permanent Israeli political control over the passage of people and goods through a possible suggested future land link between Gaza and the West Bank.

Questions for Discussion

(1) Could the Israeli-Palestinian conflict have been avoided if Arabs had accepted the 1947 United Nations partition plan? Was this possible?
(2) Can the Israeli-Palestinian conflict be ended on a basis of equal rights?
(3) How important are continuing conflict-resolution initiatives at community and grass-roots levels in Israel/Palestine as preparation for possible future peaceful transformation at national level?
(4) To what extent do internal divisions among Israelis and among Palestinians block the path to a peaceful settlement between them? Can these be overcome?
(5) Does the 2002 Arab Peace Initiative still offer a basis for an end to the Israeli-Palestinian conflict? Would an Israeli Peace Initiative and a Palestinian Peace Initiative be likely to be compatible with this and with each other?

References

Arab Peace Initiative. 2002. Available at: www.al-bab.com/arab/docs/league/peace02.htm

Bashir, B., and G, Goldberg. 2019. "Introduction: The Holocaust and the Nakba: A New Syntax of History, Memory and Political Thought." In *The Holocaust and the Nakba: A New Grammar of Trauma and History*, des. B. Bashir and G. Goldberg. New York: Columbia University Press, 1–42.

Dowty, A. 2012. *Israel/Palestine*, 3rd ed. Cambridge: Polity.

European Council on Foreign Relations (ECFR). 2019. *The Future of Palestine: Youth Views on the Two-State Paradigm*. 28 May. Available at: www.ecfr.eu/article/commentary_the_future_of_palestine_youth_views_on_the_two_state_paradigm.

Fisher, R., and W. Ury. 1981. *Getting to Yes: Negotiation Agreement without Giving In*. Boston: Houghton-Mifflin.

Fisher, R. 1997. *Interactive Conflict Resolution*. Syracuse, NY: Syracuse University Press.

Goldmann, N. 1969. *The Autobiography of Nahum Goldmann: Sixty Years of Jewish Life*. New York: Holt, Reinhard and Winston.

Halabi, R., ed. 2004. *Israeli and Palestinian Identities in Dialogue: The School of Peace Approach*. New Brunswick, NJ: Rutgers University Press.

Hollis, R. 2019. *Surviving the Story: The Narrative Trap in Israel and Palestine*. London: Red Hawk.

Israeli Strategy Group. 2015. *Is There a Path to a More Equal Israel?* Van Leer Institute/Oxford Research Group. Unpublished.

Kahanoff, M. 2016. *Jews and Arabs in Israel Encountering their Identities*. Lanham, MD: Lexington Books/Van Leer Institute Press.

Kelman, H., and R. Fisher, eds. 2017. *'Interactive Problem Solving' in Conflict Resolution*. Heidelberg and New York: Springer International.

Kelman, H. 2018. *Transforming The Israeli-Palestinian Conflict: From Mutual Negation to Reconciliation*. London: Routledge.

Klug, T., and S. Bahour. 2014. "If Kerry Fails, What Then?" *Le Monde Diplomatique*. 8 April. Available at: https://mondediplo.com/outdidein/if-kerry-fails-what-then.

Lacquer, W., and B. Rubin, eds. 2008. *The Israel-Arab Reader: A Documentary History of the Middle East Conflict*, 7th ed. London: Penguin.

Lintl, P. 2015 "Understanding Coalition Formation in Israel: Party Positions and Cleavages in Light of the 2015 Elections." *Orient: German Journal for Politics, Economics and Culture in the Middle East* 56:3, 27–35.

Meir, G. 1975. *My Life*. New York: Putnam.

Maoz, I. 2011. "Does Contact Work in Protracted Asymmetric Conflict? Appraising 20 Years of Reconciliation-aimed Encounters between Israeli Jews and Palestinians." *Journal of Peace Research* 48:1, 115–125.

Nabulsi, N. 2018. *The Nationality Law: Targeting All Palestinians*. Ramallah: The Masarat Center.

O'Toole, M. 2016. "How Donald Trump and the GOP Dropped the Two-state Solution for Mideast peace." *Foreign Policy*. 14 July. Available at: https://foreignpolicy.com/2016/07/14/how-donald-trump-and-the-gop-dropped-the-two-state-solution-for-mideast-peace/.

Oxford Research Group. 2015 *Collective Strategic Thinking in Israel*. Available at: www.oxfordresearchgroup.org.uk/orgs-collective-strategic-thinking-model

Palestinian Citizens of Israel Strategy Group. 2018. *The Second Strategic Report: The Challenges Facing Palestinian Society in Israel and Ways to Confront Them* (co-ordinator: A. Jamal). I'lam Centre/Oxford Research Group.

Palestine Strategy Group. 2008. *Regaining the Initiative: Palestinian Strategic Options to End Israeli Occupation.* Available at: http://transparency.aljazeera.net/files/2706.PDF.

Palestine Strategy Group. 2015. *A Post Oslo Strategy: Parameters, Policy Implications, Actions.* Available at: www.palestinestrtegygroup.ps/wp-content/uploads/2015/A-POST-OSLO-STRATEGY-REPORT-2014-15.pdf.

Palestine Strategy Group. 2018. *Relations Between Palestinians Across the Green Line.* Available at: www.oxfordresearchgroup.org.uk/psg-report-relations-between-palestinians-across-the-green-line.

Pappe, I. 2012. *The Idea of Israel: A History of Power and Knowledge.* London: Verso.

Pfeffer, A. 2019. "Binyamin Netanyahu Vows to Annex West Bank Land in Late Poll Gamble." *The Times.* 11 September. Available at: www.thetimes.co.uk/article/binyamin-netanyahu-israel-vows-to-annex-west-bank-land-in-late-poll-gamble-kx9f5gxhw.

Pressman, J. 2003. "Visions in Collision: What Happened at Camp David and Taba?" *International Security* 28:2, 5–43.

Ramsbotham, O. 2010. *Transforming Violent Conflict: Radical Disagreement, Dialogue and Survival.* London: Routledge.

Ramsbotham, O. 2017. *When Conflict Resolution Fails.* Cambridge: Polity.

Ramsbotham, O., and M. Morgan. 2017. *ORG's Collective Strategic Thinking Model.* London: Oxford Research Group. Available at: www.oxfordresearchgroup.org.uk/orgs-collective-strategic-thinking-model.

Ramsbotham, O. (forthcoming). Taking Radical Disagreement Seriously: Filling the Discourse Analytic Gap in the Study of Intractable Asymmetric Conflicts. Amsterdam: John Benjamins.

Ramsbotham, O., and A. Schiff. 2019. "When Formal Negotiations Fail: Strategic Negotiation, Ripeness, and the Kerry Initiative." *Negotiation and Conflict Management Research* 11:4, 321–340.

Ross, D. 2004. *The Missing Peace: The Inside Story of the Fight for Middle East Peace.* New York: Farrar, Strauss and Giroux.

Rotberg, R., ed. 2006. *Israeli and Palestinian Narratives of Conflict: History's Double Helix.* Bloomington, IN: Indiana University Press.

Rouhana, N. 2006. "Zionism's Encounter with the Palestinians: The Dynamics of Force, Fear and Extremism. In *Israeli and Palestinian Narratives of Conflict*, ed. R. Rotberg. Bloomington, IN: Indiana University Press, 115–141.

Schama, S. 2013. *The Story of the Jews: Finding the Words: 1000 BCE – 1492 CE.* London: Bodley Head.

Shlaim, A. 2000. *The Iron Wall: Israel and the Arab World.* New York: W. W. Norton.

Shlaim, A. 2009. *Israel and Palestine: Reappraisals, Revisions, Refutations.* London: Verso.

Thiessen, C., and M. Darweish. 2018. "Conflict Resolution and Asymmetric Conflict: Competing Perceptions of Planned Contact Interventions between Jewish Israelis and Palestinians." *International Journal of International Relations* 66, 1–17.

PART II

Historical Evolution of the Conflict

7

THE 1948 WAR AND ITS CONSEQUENCES

Michael R. Fischbach and Taylor L. Williams

The 1948 Arab-Israeli War was a signal event in the history of the modern Middle East. The competing national visions of Palestine's Arab majority and its largely immigrant Jewish minority, the latter committed to the Zionist goal of creating a state for the Jewish people, were the background of the war. The British had established the borders of Palestine after they wrested the area from the Ottoman Turks in 1917–1918 during World War I, and then governed the country for three decades under the terms of the Mandate for Palestine assigned to them by the League of Nations in 1922. They formally supported the Zionist movement in its efforts to build a Jewish state in the country and failed to balance this commitment with the countervailing demands for independence lodged by the country's Arab Palestinian population.

Having at various points been confronted with communal violence as well as violence directed by both sides against them, the British, on 18 February 1947, announced their intention to withdraw from Palestine and to turn the matter of how to resolve conflicting Arab and Jewish visions for the country over to the newly established United Nations (UN). On 29 November 1947, the United Nations General Assembly voted to partition Palestine into a Jewish state and an Arab state of roughly equal size – even though Arabs outnumbered Jews two-to-one – as well as an international zone around Jerusalem and its holy shrines. The result, however, was an all-out war that ended in a massive Arab defeat, the establishment of a Jewish state called Israel on three-quarters of the country, the large-scale removal of the Palestinian Arabs who had lived within the boundaries of the new state, and huge political ramifications within the Arab World.

This chapter first notes how the pre-war nature of the Jewish and Palestinian-Arab societies contributed to the ultimate victory of Jewish military forces during the war and the concomitant Palestinian defeat. After enumerating the various military forces available to each side, it then charts the course of the fighting and the UN-brokered armistices that ended the fighting. It concludes by noting the tremendous consequences of the war, not just for Jews and Arabs in Palestine/Israel, but also for the surrounding Arab world.

Beyond the historical record, the entire subject of the 1948 Arab-Israeli War has been the source of heated debate among academics in recent decades. A new generation of mostly Israeli scholars such as Benny Morris, Avi Shlaim, and Ilan Pappé, anchoring their work in the careful parsing of archives and recently declassified documents, provided alternative interpretations of what happened in the 1948 war that challenged the "old history" previously produced by

DOI: 10.4324/9780429027376-10

journalists, soldiers, and other (largely Israeli and foreign Jewish) writers. That history had portrayed the war as a valiant Jewish struggle against a much stronger Arab enemy that led to an almost miraculous victory. Another part of the old history that the "new historians" challenged was the notion that Israel was not responsible for the flight of 725–750,000 Palestinian refugees. Palestinian scholars like Walid Khalidi, Rashid Khalidi, and Nur Masalha also challenged the old narrative about why the refugees fled (for a discussion of the war's historiography, see Ch. 1 in this volume). These debates continue.

Jewish and Palestinian-Arab Preparedness before the War

The pre-war Jewish community in Palestine, called the *Yishuv*, consisted of 554,000 persons by 1944 (*Survey of Palestine* 1991, 143), and it was highly organized and generally entered the war well prepared. Under the terms of the British Mandate, the Jewish Agency for Palestine (JA) was the official body that represented the Yishuv in dealings with mandatory authorities. Furthermore, secular Jewish life was coordinated through the *Va`ad Le'umi* (National Council), an executive body chosen from a nation-wide *Asefat ha-Nivharim* (Assembly of Representatives), and its various departments that dealt with health, education, and other communal matters.

Between the JA, the Va`ad Le'umi, and other national organizations such as the *Histadrut* labour federation, which played a major role in the economy, and the *Keren Kayemet le-Yisra'el* (Jewish National Fund; JNF), which possessed slightly over half of all Jewish-owned land in Palestine (Fischbach 2005, 294), the Yishuv had built up a type of state within a state. An additional factor in nationwide Jewish cohesiveness was that despite their differences and the existence of different political parties and factions, most Jews in the Yishuv were united around the Zionist dream of a Jewish state built along modern, Western lines. Finally, the influx of Jewish capital and expertise into the country meant that the Jewish economy was a multifaceted one characterized by agriculture, light industry, finance, and commerce (Metzer 1998).

The Yishuv was also prepared militarily by late 1947. Jewish armed forces consisted of three organizations. By far the largest was the *Hagana* ("Defense") militia, which was under the control of the JA and maintained about 17,000 fighters in the field plus 37,000 reservists organized on a territorial basis throughout the Yishuv (Dupuy 1978, 8). Shortly before the United Nations Partition vote, the JA announced conscription of all young men and women; in March 1948 this was extended to include older individuals. Moreover, in November 1947 the Hagana leadership ordered that the force be reorganized as a more conventional army subject to a high command. Chief-of-Staff Yisra'el Galili already had the basis for such a professional army: the Hagana's full-time strike force known as the PALMAH (a Hebrew acronym derived from the term "Strike Forces"), which maintained about 4,500 full-time fighters under its commander, Yigal Allon (Dupuy 1978, 8). The Hagana possessed some vehicles, mortars, and a nascent air service. Among its most important technological breakthroughs were its secret arsenals that produced duplicates of British sub-machineguns as well as an underground (literally) ammunition factory to manufacture cartridges for them (Morris 2008, 86–87).

Two other and much smaller Jewish fighting forces were operating in the country. The first was the *Irgun Tzva'i Le'umi* (National Military Organization), usually referred to as Irgun or by the Hebrew-language acronym ETZEL. Commanded by Menachem Begin, the Irgun had broken away from the Hagana before the war and was ideologically loyal to the opposition Revisionist Zionist movement rather than to the JA and mainstream Zionism. It maintained a force of 2,000–3,000 fighters. The other small Jewish fighting force existing at the time was the *Lohemei Herut Yisra'el* (Fighters for the Freedom of Israel), usually known by the Hebrew acronym LEHI, or sometimes as the Stern Gang, after its founder, Avraham Stern, who had broken with the Irgun before the war. The 200–300 fighters of LEHI were led by a troika consisting of Natan Yellin-Mor, Yitzhak Shamir, and Yisra'el Eldad (Morris 2008, 86).

In stark contrast, Palestinian-Arab society was not at all organized, cohesive, or ready for war (Khalidi 2001, 2020). There were 1.1 million Arabs living in Palestine in 1944 (*Survey of Palestine* 1991, 143). They were badly divided along a number of axes. One of the most significant was the huge socio-economic and cultural divide between those living in urban and those in rural areas. While integrated into global capitalist markets, the vast majority of Palestine's Arabs were small-scale peasant farmers living in hundreds of villages in the countryside in which tribal and religious connections, not necessarily national ones, were paramount (Tamari 2005, 448–454). Life in the large towns and cities, by contrast, was different. Here, the urban poor shared space with an educated, sometimes wealthy, elite consisting of landowners, merchants, scholars, and bureaucrats. Manufacturing generally was small scale (Metzer 1998).

Adding to the Arab urban-rural gulf was regionalism. Palestinians in different parts of the country maintained distinct accents and clothing styles, and long prior to British rule had been oriented toward different parts of the surrounding Arab world. Although Jerusalem became the capital of British Palestine, the city and the urban notable families that dominated its life, therefore, were not always recognized as national leaders by Palestinians in other parts of the country. Moreover, Palestinians sometimes were divided by religious identities. By the 1940s, close to 90 per cent were Sunni Muslims, with members of various Christian sects making up most of the rest (*A Survey of Palestine* 1991, 141). There also were a small number of people who followed the Druze religion in the Galilee region.

Palestinian Arab social fragmentation was reflected in its weak pre-war political structures. While the British Mandate formally recognized the JA as the institutional representative of the Yishuv, it did not recognize a comparable Palestinian Arab body. What passed for a national executive body in the 1940s was the Arab Higher Committee (AHC), headed by al-Hajj Amin al-Husayni, who also held the Islamic religious positions of mufti of Jerusalem and president of the Supreme Muslim Council (Mattar 1992). The AHC was established in 1936 to coordinate a nationwide Palestinian strike and, subsequently, an armed revolt that lasted until 1939. Yet here, too, factionalism crippled the AHC, notably in terms of the bitter rivalry between al-Husayni and his partisans and the supporters of another Jerusalem family, the Nashashibis. British authorities banned the AHC in October 1937, and its members either were arrested and deported or, like al-Husayni himself, escaped the country. Two more iterations of the AHC emerged in the 1940s but functioned in exile and not on the ground in Palestine (Khalaf 1991).

Complicating matters even more was the fact that British security forces crushed the 1936–1939 Palestinian revolt and effectively disarmed much of the population, which hindered Palestinian military preparedness in the 1940s. By late 1947 Arab fighting forces in Palestine consisted of three main types. The first were Palestinian town and village militias. These consisted of local defence forces made up of men, armed with an assortment of light infantry weapons, and who defended individual Palestinian Arab localities. The *Jaysh al-Jihad al-Muqaddas* (Army of the Holy Struggle) was the second armed Arab force in Palestine. Organized by the AHC, the Jaysh al-Jihad al-Muqaddas consisted of between 600 and 1,500 regular fighters in three main groupings, all commanded by al-Husayni's nephew, Abd al-Qadir al-Husayni. The force was assisted by local village militias in the areas where it operated, largely in the Jerusalem area and, further west, near Lydda. It lacked any heavy weaponry (Morris 2008, 89).

The third Arab fighting force was the largest and best-equipped: the *Jaysh al-Inqadh al-Arabi* (Arab Salvation Army), usually called in English the Arab Liberation Army (ALA). The ALA was formed by the Arab League, according to a November 1947 decision by its military committee, which was headed by a former Iraqi general, Isma`il Safwat. The Arab League knew that the regular Arab armies could not intervene to prevent the partition of Palestine while the British remained there, so they elected to raise the ALA instead by relying on volunteers and troops seconded by Arab armies. Trained in Syria and staffed largely by Syrians, Iraqis, Jordanians, and some Palestinians, the ALA fielded around five thousand troops and was led by a Lebanese fighter with previous military experience in Palestine, Fawzi al-Qawuqji (Morris 2008, 90). The bulk of its forces operated in the area of central Palestine that is today's West Bank, as well as in the northern Galilee region. The first ALA units crossed the border from Syria, Lebanon, and Jordan in late December 1947 and early January 1948. The best-equipped Arab force at that time, the ALA possessed some artillery pieces and even some armoured cars.

United Nations Partition Vote and Initial Fighting

The 1948 War actually began in late 1947. Almost immediately after the United Nations General Assembly adopted Resolution 181, the United Nations Palestine Partition Plan, on 29 November 1947, fighting between Jewish and Arab combatants and civilians broke out as everyone had expected. The early months of fighting saw the Jaysh al-Jihad al-Muqaddas successfully block Jewish traffic on the roads leading from Tel Aviv to Jerusalem. Some Jewish settlements in northern Palestinian also were cut off by Arab forces. Lifting the blockades imposed on Jewish communities, notably so that supplies could reach the besieged Jewish community in West Jerusalem, was a major objective for the Hagana in the first several months of 1948.

In early April the Hagana accordingly decided to go on the offensive and implement an operation known as Plan Dalet. Overseen by Chief of Operations Yigael Yadin, it consisted of a series of offensive actions designed to secure Jewish communities within and outside of the proposed Jewish state, gain control over the vital Tel Aviv-Jerusalem road, and eradicate places from which Palestinians could threaten Jewish populations. Part of the plan involved conquering Palestinian villages that were near to the borders of the proposed Jewish state and, if they resisted, expelling their inhabitants. Plan Dalet also called for destroying some villages to render them militarily useless, and local commanders were given a great deal of discretion in deciding what to do with conquered villages and their residents. Most of the military operations conducted under the plan occurred along the coastal plain, within the Tel Aviv-Jerusalem corridor, and both the western and eastern parts of Galilee, including the Galilee Panhandle (Khalidi 1961, 1988; Morris 2008, 116–121; Morris 2004, ch. 4; Masalha 2012; Pappé ch. 5).

An important goal of Plan Dalet was to open the roads. The battle for the Palestinian village of al-Qastal west of Jerusalem with its strategic castle overlooking the Tel Aviv-Jerusalem highway saw control of the village change hands several times before Jewish forces succeeded in holding it in early April. Significantly, Abd al-Qadir al-Husayni, commander of the Jaysh al-Jihad al-Muqaddas, was killed in the battle on 7 April. Two days later, ETZEL and LEHI units attacked another village west of Jerusalem, Dayr Yasin, even though the villagers had signed a non-aggression pact with the Hagana. When the village militia resisted the intrusion, the fighters called upon PALMAH troops to assist them. Over a hundred villagers died, most when ETZEL and LEHI forces swept through houses with grenades and small arms fire, but others were deliberately murdered. Surviving villagers were expelled, and several truckloads of them were paraded through the streets of Jewish areas of West Jerusalem (Morris 2008; McDaniel and Ellis 1998). Jews suffered a tragedy several days later on 13 April, when 78 died, mostly civilians, when Arab forces ambushed a medical convey and its armed Hagana escort vehicles travelling through East Jerusalem on their way to the Hadassah Hospital on Mount Scopus.

News of the brutality at Dayr Yasin spread quickly throughout Arab Palestine, and the fear of future massacres combined with the ongoing Hagana offensives in April prompted a massive flight of tens of thousands of Palestinians refugees. Some ran from the fighting; some fled out of fear of massacre; others were deliberately expelled by Hagana forces (Morris 2004; Pappé; Masalha 1992). The Palestinian refugee exodus intensified when more Palestinians fled after the Hagana captured four major cities with large Arab populations: Tiberias (18 April), Haifa (23 April), West Jerusalem (30 April), and Jaffa (13 May). Another misfortune to befall the Arabs was the defeat of the ALA at the hands of Hagana, PALMAH, and Irgun fighters at the Battle of Mishmar Ha-Emek in northern Palestine. A number of Palestinian villages in the area were depopulated as well; in some locales there were further atrocities, including the shooting of prisoners in `Ayn al-Zaytun by PALMAH troops on 1 May (Morris 1987, 102). Hundreds of thousands of Arab refugees were on the move by mid-May.

The first half of 1948 was not entirely successful for the Hagana and other Jewish forces. Units of the Jordanian army, the Arab Legion, conquered the four Jewish settlements of the Etzion Bloc between Bethlehem and Hebron that had been under siege by local Arab forces. Even though Jordan was not yet officially involved in the war, the British had brought units of the Legion into Palestine to assist with security during the waning days of the Mandate. The Legion's attack on the bloc was supported by ALA fighters and local militiamen, and Kfar Etzion eventually surrendered on 13 May. Most of the Hagana forces and kibbutz residents who survived were shot or otherwise killed following surrender; only four survived. The other three settlements in the bloc surrendered shortly thereafter and the over 350 inhabitants taken to Jordan as prisoners; the settlements were destroyed (Morris 2008).

End of the British Mandate and Arab Intervention

As the British had previously announced, High Commissioner for Palestine Allen Cunningham departed Haifa on 14 May 1948, and the mandate formally ended. That same day, JA head David Ben-Gurion proclaimed the independence of a Jewish state called Israel. Until that point Jewish forces by and large had been successful in securing the areas allotted to the Jewish state and even expanding their military control over surrounding Arab areas through Plan Dalet. The fighting immediately intensified when units from the armies of several Arab countries entered Palestine beginning 15 May. The Arab League had appointed Iraqi major general Nur al-Din Mahmud as overall commander of Arab military efforts, although to placate Jordan's King Abdullah, the latter was given the honorific title of "Supreme Commander" of the Arab expeditionary force.

The initial strength of these forces numbered approximately 5,500 Egyptian troops; 2,750 Syrians; 2,700 Iraqis; somewhere between 4,500 and 6,500 Jordanians; and a few hundred Lebanese, who mostly stayed north of the Palestine-Lebanon border (Morris 2008, 205). Saudi Arabia, Sudan, Yemen, and Morocco eventually also sent contingents of fighters over the course of the war. These Arab troops had more sophisticated weaponry at their disposal than did the ALA or the Jaysh al-Jihad al-Muqaddas: armoured cars, light tanks, and artillery pieces. The Egyptian, Iraqi, and Syrian units also had small air forces at their disposal that they were able to deploy, especially in their early engagements with Jewish forces in mid-1948.

The British departure, declaration of Israeli independence, and the entrance of regular Arab army troops into the war also led to immediate changes for Jewish forces. On 26 May, the provisional Israeli government, headed by Ben-Gurion, ordered that the Hagana, Irgun, and LEHI be merged into the new Israel Defense Force (IDF), the official army of the new state, with Lieutenant General Ya`akov Dori as chief of staff. Irgun and LEHI fighters operating in

Jerusalem remained independent, however. Like their opponents, Jewish forces also benefited from foreign intervention during the war. Approximately 4,500 foreign volunteers from over fifty countries, Jews and non-Jews and both ideological volunteers and mercenaries, served in Jewish military units, particularly after mid-May 1948. This foreign force came to be known by the Hebrew acronym MAHAL (World Machal). They proved most influential in the new Israeli air force (IAF), in which the majority of its pilots were Americans, Canadians, Britons, and South Africans who had flown in the Allied air forces during the World War II. Additionally, a number of the IDF's medical corps were foreigners. Beyond that, some 27,000 Jews, including Holocaust survivors, were recruited during the war from displaced persons camps in Europe and elsewhere to fight in the IDF as a force known by the acronym GAHAL (Yablonka 1999, 82; World Machal).

The intervention of regular Arab troops from the region's standing armies changed the balance of the fighting after 15 May to the initial detriment of Jewish forces. Egyptian troops under Major General Ahmad Ali al-Muwawi pushed northward from the Sinai Peninsula through Gaza and reached about two-thirds of the way from the border to Tel Aviv, which was bombed by the Egyptian air force. The Egyptians also advanced into the Hebron and Bethlehem areas south of Jerusalem. Syrians advanced both north and south of the Sea of Galilee (Lake Tiberias), while Iraqi forces advanced from Jordan into north central Palestine. Lebanon's small army only fought one real engagement with the IDF and that was not until 5 June.

The most capable Arab force was Jordan's Arab Legion, established by the British as a police force during World War II. Jordan's King Abdullah ordered the Legion only to gain control over the areas allotted to the proposed Arab State. The Legion was commanded by a Briton, Lieutenant General John B. Glubb, The Legion's field commander, Brigadier General Norman O. Lash, accordingly ordered his troops to move into the hilly regions of central Palestine. Yet the exodus of so many Palestinian refugees plus the widespread publicity given to what happened at Dayr Yasin prompted a change of course. Abdullah ordered the Legion into Jerusalem's Old City to control its Islamic and Christian shrines. Under the United Nations Partition Plan, Jerusalem was to become an international *corpus separatum*, part of neither the Jewish nor Arab states, but nevertheless both sides sought to occupy the Old City (Jewish forces already controlled West Jerusalem). After heavy fighting involving the Legion, ALA, and militia forces, surviving Hagana fighters and civilian inhabitants of the Old City's Jewish Quarter surrendered on 28 May. About 340 men of military age were imprisoned in Jordan and most of the rest of the quarter's Jews were allowed to leave for West Jerusalem. Much of the quarter was destroyed during and after the battle.

Hindering Arab military capabilities in Palestine in mid-1948 was a decided lack of coordination among the various fighting forces. Even prior to 15 May there was little centralized coordination among Arab fighting forces operating throughout Palestine. Indeed, such cooperation was hampered by bad blood between the ALA and the Jaysh al-Jihad al-Muqaddas, stemming from the poor relationship between al-Qawuqji and al-Hajj Amin al-Husayni. Adding to the friction was the fact that Jordan's King Abdullah long had harboured expansive regional ambitions, something that caused other Arab actors – notably al-Husayni, Syrian president Shukri al-Quwwatli, and Egypt's King Faruq – to view him with considerable suspicion (Gerges 2001; Landis 2001). They feared that Abdullah would use the opportunity of Jordanian intervention as the pretext to annex the Arab portions of Palestinian into his kingdom. Strongly opposed to an independent Palestinian Arab state emerging, particularly if it were headed by al-Husayni and the AHC, Abdullah had been in secret negotiations with the JA in November 1947 about Jordan taking over areas accorded to the proposed Arab state. Talks again were held on the eve of intervention in May (Shlaim 1988 and 1999; Bar-Joseph 1987; Gelber 2004). The only country whose forces coordinated closely with the Jordanians was Iraq (Tripp 2001).

Truces and Renewed Fighting

On 14 May the United Nations General Assembly adopted Resolution 186 creating the Office of the United Nations Mediator on Palestine. The mediator's mandate was to effect a truce, safeguard the welfare of the population of Palestine, and work toward a peaceful settlement of the conflict. Swedish diplomat Folke Bernadotte agreed to serve in this position and began work on 21 June. He was assisted by American Ralph S. Bunche, who previously had worked with the short-lived United Nations Palestine Commission during the first half of 1948.

Bernadotte was able to secure a four-week truce, as called for the United Nations Security Council on 11 June. By that point, Arab troops had secured much of the Palestinian majority regions in central Palestine and the northern part of the vast, desert region of the Negev/ Naqab in the south, while the IDF controlled most areas of the UN-proposed Jewish state (except for the Negev/Naqab) as well as parts of the UN-proposed Arab state. Both sides used the truce to improve their fighting capabilities. The Arab armies, however, had British and French equipment and weaponry and were hindered in their efforts to resupply themselves by an Anglo-French arms embargo put in place in February. Beyond that, the United States had imposed its own arms embargo on the region back in December 1947 and the United Nations Security Council later issued Resolution 50 of 29 May 1948, calling on the world community not to send arms to the combatants.

By contrast, the IDF benefitted from sophisticated and large-scale pre-war arms procurement arrangements and networks that had been set up by the Hagana and proved effective despite international embargoes. Israeli forces received shipments of Czech light infantry weapons, ammunition, and aircraft as well as aircraft smuggled in from the United States. The IDF also acquired heavy weapons and some tanks. These acquisitions were made possible through vigorous Zionist fundraising in the United States. The JA's Golda Meyerson (later, Meir) made a fundraising tour from January to March 1948 that secured $50 million for the Hagana; she made a second such tour in May and June and raised another $50 million (Morris 2008, 84). In addition to improving its fighting capabilities through training and weapons procurement, the IDF also managed to double its size by the time the truce ended on 8 July.

Bernadotte, assisted by officers of the new United Nations Truce Supervision Organization (UNTSO), supervised the truce and also sought to build on it by finding a political solution to the fighting (United Nations 1990). Informally, on 28 June, he proposed new partition lines in light of the changes that had occurred in the military situation since the 1947 partition plan, but both sides refused (Ben-Dror 2016). Fighting resumed on 8 July, one day before the truce was set to expire. During the subsequent ten days, the IDF blunted Egyptian offensives in the south and scored major victories when it captured the central Palestinian cities of Lydda on 11 July and nearby al-Ramla a day after the Arab Legion had withdrawn from them. The IDF expelled the population of the two cities, and between 40–60,000 Palestinians were trucked or forced to march eastward toward Jordanian lines. In the north, the IDF engaged the ALA and moved into much of central Galilee, including Nazareth the largest Palestinian town in the region, which was captured on 16 July. On the other hand, the IDF failed in its attempts to retake the Jewish Quarter in East Jerusalem and the former British police station at Latrun from Jordanian forces (Morris 2008).

The United Nations managed to secure a second, much longer truce ten days later on 18 July (Ben-Dror 2016). Once again, the IDF used the truce to its advantage, enlarging its ranks and securing additional weaponry from abroad. The IDF also used the opportunity to prevent the hundreds of thousands of Palestinian refugees who had been displaced from returning to their homes behind Israeli lines. As the weeks went by, various diplomatic quarters worked on a resolution to the fighting. From the Greek island of Rhodes, Bernadotte wrote a report on the situation in Palestine to the United Nations General Assembly on 16 September. He made several proposals, including that Jordan absorb the Arab parts of Palestine not under Israeli control. Bernadotte also was the first high-ranking official to focus international attention on the massive displacement of refugees. His report called for the United Nations to affirm their right to return to their homes in Israeli-controlled territory, called on Israeli authorities to take measures to protect refugee property left behind within its jurisdiction, and called for the payment of compensation for the property of those refugees who chose not to return to their homes (United Nations Mediator on Palestine, Progress Report).

The day after he issued his report, Bernadotte was back in Jerusalem, where he and a French military officer from UNTSO accompanying him were assassinated when a LEHI unit halted their car at a roadblock and fired into their vehicle. Seeking to distance itself from the assassination that it had ordered, LEHI issued a statement in the name of the "Fatherland Front" on 24 September claiming responsibility and denouncing Bernadotte's proposals. Bunche replaced him as United Nations Mediator on Palestine (Ben-Dror 2016).

On 22 September, a Palestinian government was formed in Egyptian-controlled Gaza: the All-Palestine Government. The Arab League had taken a decision earlier on 8 July 1948 to allow the formation of a civil Palestinian government. One of the major reasons was to check the ambitions of Jordan's King Abdullah. Under the titular leadership of Ahmad Hilmi Abd al-Baqi, the real authority behind the All-Palestine Government was the AHC and al-Husayni, who secretly left Cairo and arrived in Gaza on 28 September. The government convened a Palestine National Council and on 1 October declared the independence of Palestine with Jerusalem as its capital despite functioning only in Gaza and, with no budget or army, doing little more than issuing passports. With wider regional and international considerations in mind, the Egyptians forced al-Husayni to return to Cairo after only eight days in Gaza. Although the governments of Egypt, Iraq, Syria, Lebanon, and Saudi Arabia formally recognized the government later that month, the All-Palestine Government was effectively defunct by the end of 1948 (Shlaim 1990).

The second truce ended on 15 October with an IDF offensive against the Egyptians. The IDF's PALMAH captured the town of Beersheba on 21 October and expelled most its population. The Israeli offensive also managed to encircle about four thousand Egyptian troops in what came to be called the "Faluja Pocket." Two weeks after launching its attacks against the Egyptians, the IDF attacked the ALA and drove it out of north-central Galilee. The IDF even entered southern Lebanon and occupied 13 villages (Hughes 2005). More Palestinians were uprooted as refugees, and in several localities, including al-Dawayima, Hula, `Aylabun, Saliha, and Safsaf, IDF soldiers carried out massacres of Palestinian civilians (Morris 2008, 333, 344–345; Shavit 2004). Another United Nations ceasefire went into effect on 31 October that lasted until the IDF resumed its attacks on Egyptian forces south and west of Gaza on 22 December. The Egyptians called for a ceasefire on 7 January 1949, and the fighting throughout Israel-Palestine came to an end.

United Nations Armistice Agreements and Conciliation Efforts

The formal end of the fighting came as the result of four general armistice agreements forged between the warring parties in 1949 through the offices of United Nations Mediator Bunche.

Over several weeks of talks conducted on Rhodes, Bunche secured an armistice between Israel and Egypt on 14 February. This was followed by similar agreements between Israel and Lebanon on 23 March and between Israel and Jordan on 3 April. Talks between Israel and Syria did not begin until April and took place at the Daughters of Jacob Bridge that connected Syria and Palestine. An armistice eventually was signed there on 20 July (Ben-Dror 2016).

After the armistice agreements, Bunche's work as mediator was done and the charge to turn those ceasefire agreements into a permanent peace was left to another United Nations agency: the United Nations Conciliation Commission for Palestine (UNCCP). Following up a suggestion Bernadotte had made in his September 1948 report, the United Nations created the UNCCP by virtue of General Assembly Resolution 194 of 11 December 1948. The UNCCP brought together Arab and Israeli diplomats in Lausanne, Switzerland, from late April until mid-September 1949 for what the commission called an "exchange of views." No progress toward a final arrangement was made. Nor was a second conference, convened in Paris from September to November 1951, any more successful. On 19 November, the UNCCP announced to the parties that the meeting had failed and that it was unable to carry out its mission (Fischbach 2003, 91, 130–134). Formal peacemaking efforts were over.

By that time Israeli territory consisted of 20,330 square kilometres of pre-Palestine, 77.2 per cent of the country. Jordan controlled and eventually annexed 5,672 square kilometres (21.5 per cent), which became known as the West Bank. Egypt controlled the remaining 370 square kilometres (1.4 per cent) through a military administration in the small area of southwestern Palestine that came to be called Gaza or the Gaza Strip (Fischbach 2005, 294–295). Jerusalem also had been divided: Israel controlled the New City in the west, which became Israel's capital, while Jordan retained control of the Old City and its suburbs.

Depopulation of Palestine's Arab Lands

One of the most significant aspects of the war was the spatial and demographic revolution in the country wrought by the conflict. In the first instance, this involved the shattering of Palestinian-Arab society and the flight or expulsion of some 725,000 Palestinians – 80 per cent of those who had lived in what became the State of Israel. Israeli leaders rejoiced at this massive exodus. JNF official Yosef Weitz referred to the de-Arabization of Israel as "a gift from heaven" (Weitz 1950, 87). Israel's first president, Chaim Weizmann, called it a "miraculous simplification of our tasks" (McDonald 1951, 176). The "tasks" he had in mind were clear to Zionist leaders before the war: How could they build a Jewish state in a country with a clear Arab Palestinian majority? Provisional Foreign Minister Moshe Shertok (later, Sharett) referred to this as a "vexing problem" when he noted, in June 1948, that "The opportunities which the present position [the refugee exodus] open up for a lasting and radical solution of the most vexing problem of the Jewish State are so far-reaching as to take one's breath away" (Freundlich 1981, 163).

Yet the refugee exodus was neither "miraculous" nor a "gift from heaven." In fact, the war created the opportunity for some Zionist political and military leaders to deliberately uproot as many Arabs as possible and prevent their return, something known in Zionist circles as "transfer." The concept of transferring Palestine's Arabs out of the country to build a Jewish-majority state predated the war, and in fact represented a long historical tradition in Zionist thought going back to the earliest Jewish colonies in Palestine and the rise of political Zionism (Simons 1988; Masalha 1992, 1). Initially, some Zionists had spread the idea in Europe that Palestine was an empty land – it was a "land without a people, for a people without a land" (Masalha 1992, 5). However, it became clear to those on the ground that the land was indeed inhabited, and Zionist leaders began referring to the demographic imbalance between Jews and

Palestinian Arabs as "the Arab Question." As early as 1911, leading Zionists like Arthur Ruppin issued formal proposals to transfer Palestinians to other countries, while others from Theodor Herzl to Ben-Gurion also discussed the need to transfer Arabs to neighbouring countries if the Zionist project were to succeed in creating a Jewish-majority state. In 1937 the British Peel Commission even proposed a plan to partition Palestine between Arabs and Jews that included an "exchange of populations"; the plan never came to fruition (Morris 1999, 138–139).

Although the extent to which Jewish forces deliberately tried to expel as many Palestinians as possible during the war according to a master plan for transfer later became hotly debated (see below), it is clear that individual Zionist political and military leaders were motivated by what some have called the "transfer idea," and saw this as their aim during the war. As one Israeli historian noted,

> From April 1948, [David] Ben-Gurion is projecting a message of transfer. There is no explicit order of his in writing, there is no orderly comprehensive policy, but there is an atmosphere of transfer. The transfer idea is in the air. The entire leadership understands that this is the idea. The officer corps understands what is required of them. Under Ben-Gurion, a consensus of transfer is created.
>
> *(Shavit 2004)*

Weitz, for example, operationalized this by establishing a "transfer committee" that produced a plan called "Retroactive Transfer: A Scheme for the Solution of the Arab Question in the State of Israel" as the war was underway (Morris 1986; Morris 1987, 135–137; Golan 1995, 410–411). Weitz and his committee opined that the refugees who had fled should not be allowed back ("retroactive transfer") and ordered that eight abandoned villages be destroyed in June and July 1948 to prevent this (Morris 1987, 137).

The Hagana's Plan Dalet also included operational military orders that specified which Palestinian population centres were to be targeted (Khalidi 1959). The Hagana's intelligence service, known by the Hebrew acronym SHAI, had patiently surveyed over 600 Palestinian villages in the 1940s and created files on each, describing everything from roads, water sources, estimated numbers of weapons, tribal rivalries, and so forth (Fischbach 2011, 305–306). These files simplified the task of Plan Dalet and subsequent operations, the main objective of which, according to an Israeli historian, were "clear from the beginning – the de-Arabization of Palestine," although "the means to achieve this most effectively evolved in tandem with the actual military occupation of the Palestinian territories that were to become the new Jewish state of Israel" (Pappé 2006, 49).

Israel never allowed the vast majority of the refugees to return. United Nations General Assembly Resolution 194 of 11 December 1948 included a call for "refugees wishing to return to their homes and live at peace with their neighbours should be permitted to do so at the earliest practicable date" (United Nations General Assembly Resolution 194). However, as a result of an earlier 16 June 1948 Israeli cabinet meeting, the provisional government made it clear that it was not going to allow Palestinian refugees to return. At that meeting Ben-Gurion stated clearly, "I believe we should prevent their return," Shertok agreed, stating "Can we imagine a return to the status quo ante? … [T]hey will not return. [That] is our policy. They are not returning" (Morris 1987, 141; Morris 2008, 300–301).

Aftermath: Israel

The result of the 1948 War was that the Zionist dream had been accomplished: a Jewish state existed in Palestine/Israel and had been defended by force of arms. This led to tremendous demographic and spatial changes in the area that had been called British Palestine. The exodus of 80 per cent of the Palestinians who had lived within the borders of what became Israel meant there now was a Jewish state with a decided Jewish majority.

Beyond the massive expulsion of Arabs, significant demographic, spatial, and socio-economic earthquakes hit the new Jewish state. Israeli independence meant that pre-war British limits on Jewish immigration were gone, precipitating a huge influx of Jews into the country starting in May 1948. In addition to providing at least 20,000 troops for the IDF, this wave of immigrants helped to offset the Jewish losses in the war: about 5,800 persons killed, one-quarter of them civilians (Morris 2008, 406). This represented one per cent of the total Jewish population. Two years after the fighting ended, the right of virtually any Jew to immigrate and receive Israeli citizenship was enshrined in law under the 5 July 1950 Law of Return.

As a result, Israel's pre-war Jewish population doubled as some 688,000 new Jewish arrivals swelled the population during the years 1948–1951. By 1953, a total of nearly 725,000 Jews had arrived in Israel from two main sources. The first was Jews in Europe who either survived the Holocaust or who left Eastern European countries like Bulgaria, Romania, and Yugoslavia. The second was Jews who left Arab and other Islamic countries in the Middle East and North Africa (Hacohen 2003, 267; Segev 1986). The war significantly impacted Jews in the Arab World and was one of many factors explaining why they immigrated to Israel in such large numbers during and, especially after, 1948. Arabs' passions about Zionism sometimes were directed at the Jews living in their midst. Starting with the United Nations Partition Plan in November 1947 violent anti-Semitic outbreaks and/or property sequestrations beset the Jewish communities in several Arab countries. Approximately 260,000 left during the war or immediately afterwards, including most of the Jews of Iraq, Yemen, and Libya; tens of thousands also left Syria and Egypt for Israel and other destinations at that time (Fischbach 2008, 27).

On the spatial level, authorities from the new Israeli state and the JA decided to destroy Palestinian villages that had been emptied during the fighting. This served two purposes. First, this would forestall the possibility of Palestinian refugees trying to cross the borders and ceasefire lines and reoccupy their homes (Morris 2008, 300–301). Second, it would clear the ground so that Western-style housing and communities could be built for new immigrants. Eventually, somewhere between 369 and 450 villages, depending largely on the definition of a "village," were demolished (Morris 1987, xiv-xviii; Falah 1996, 256–285; Khalidi 1992; Nijim and Muammar 1984). In their place, settlements for new immigrants were built. By the end of 1953, 350 new Jewish communities had been erected on refugee land (Peretz 1958, 143).

With the majority of Palestinian Arabs gone and relegated to refugee status, efforts on the ground continued to ensure that Israel become a Jewish nation in every sense of the word, not just demographically. This was accomplished by a variety of means, including through changing place names. Empty Palestinian villages that remained standing after 1948 were renamed by the Israel Place-Names Committee (Cohen and Kliot 1992, 662). Renaming villages that were previously inhabited by Palestinians but that were now occupied by new Jewish immigrants secured their position as Jewish villages. In some instances, the new Hebrew names were quite similar to the previous Arabic names. For example, `Ayn Hawd became En Hod; Sa`sa became Sasa; Bayt Dajan became Bet Dagan; and Yazur became Azor. In other cases, completely new Hebrew names were given to former Palestinian villages and their lands: al-Dawayima became Amatzia, and al-Khalisa became Kiryat Shmona. Even names of valleys and natural formations were changed to Hebrew names (Benvenisti 2000).

Ultimately, roughly two-thirds to three-quarters of Palestinian settlement place names disappeared from the official maps and, therefore, from the topography of Israel (Cohen and Kliot 1992, 659). The map of Palestine had changed. Because cartographic knowledge is an inherently political power cloaked in scientific objectivity, maps are almost always unchallenged and frequently utilized as a means of understanding (Benvenisti 2000, 13). Maps, therefore, solidified the renaming and rebuilding of Israel, and newly made maps reconfigured the new political reality and aided in removing Palestinian identity from the area. With the formal erasure of many of Palestine's Arabs from the historic landscape, both demographically and culturally/linguistically, Israel was effectively a Jewish state in all forms after 1948.

Added to these immense changes in the physical and cartographic landscape of the new state were serious economic challenges. The post–1948 economic situation in Israel was dire. Even though the JA and Zionist corporations like the JNF and the Keren ha-Yesod (Foundation Fund) paid the costs of purchasing land and both bringing immigrants to Israel and settling them in housing, the state itself also incurred many costs associated with the war and the swelling of the country's Jewish population during and after 1948. Hindering Israeli economic growth was the fact that the surrounding Arab world refused to recognize Israel, and the Arab League initiated a boycott of the Jewish state. Thus, the Israeli economy was cut off from its natural, regional markets.

On the other hand, Israel benefitted economically from a huge windfall in terms of the vast amount of land, urban real estate, and other property left behind by the Palestinian refugees, which it subsequently confiscated. As early as 15 July 1948 the provisional Israeli government established a Custodian of Abandoned Property to secure refugee property, and on 2 December enacted the Emergency Regulations (Absentees' Property) law authorizing the state to confiscate property abandoned by "absentees"; the Absentees' Property Law of 14 March 1950 later replaced it (Fischbach 2003, 18–27). Values for this confiscated land vary. After a lengthy study in the 1950s and early 1960s, the UNCCP determined that the refugees left behind $824,780,808 (value in 1947) worth of land. Israeli estimates were lower, ranging between $328,445,000 to over $564,200,000. Arab estimates were as high as $2,580,006,000 (Fischbach 2006, 44). Beyond land, Israel confiscated valuable moveable property such as farm animals and equipment; the contents of warehouses, shops and factories; automobiles; furniture and other personal property; and grain and other agricultural products that had been left in the fields and on the vines and trees. Estimates of the value of such property ranged widely, from $70,122,000 to $453,375,000 (Fischbach 2006, 45).

Aftermath: The Arab World

The inability of both the Palestinians and the broader Arab world to prevent the partition of Palestine and defeat the new state of Israel represented a massive setback on a variety of levels. The most immediate and drastic effects of the war befell the Palestinians, who refer to 1948 as the *Nakba* ("Catastrophe"). No one knows how many Palestinians died, but figures as high as 12,000 have been suggested, totalling one per cent of the population (Morris 2008, 406). Somewhere between 725,000 and 750,000 were exiled from their homes – more than 50 per cent of all Palestine's Arabs, and a full 80 per cent of those who had lived in what became Israel. The United Nations assumed the obligation to provide social and economic services to the refugees and created the United Nations Relief and Works Agency for Palestine Refugees in the Near East (UNRWA) on 8 December 1949 by virtue of General Assembly Resolution 302.

Beyond that, no independent Arab Palestinian state emerged from the war. The result was that wherever they found themselves after the war, Palestinians were either stateless or citizens of other countries. The 120,00–150,000 Palestinians who remained in Israel – largely in the northern Galilee region, the central "Little Triangle" area, and the northern part of the expansive Negev/Naqab desert – eventually became Israel citizens but were subjected to a martial law regime restricting their movements that lasted until 1966 (Jiryis 1976; Lustick 1980).

The situation in the Arab world varied (Brand 1988). Following Arab League instructions, most Arab countries hosting Palestinian refugees did not grant them citizenship, thereby to protect their Palestinian identity. In Lebanon, the Christian-dominated state was quite happy not to extend citizenship to the largely Muslim refugees lest that upset the delicate confessional balance undergirding both society and the state. Instead, refugees were issued Lebanese travel documents that did not convey citizenship. The government also restricted Palestinians' ability to purchase land and enter into a variety of professions (Sayigh 1994). Syria also issued travel documents for its refugees, but otherwise afforded them the same treatment as its citizens. Egyptian authorities who governed refugees crammed into the Gaza Strip subjected them to military rule and eventually issued them travel documents as well.

By contrast, Jordan made all Palestinians residing there and in the West Bank Jordanian citizens. As early as 1 October 1948, King Abdullah sought to block the ambitions of the All-Palestine Government when he convened a gathering in Amman attended by several Palestinian refugees. The attendees called for the convening of a second Palestinian congress for the purpose of requesting Jordan to annex the areas of Palestine it controlled. In Jordanian-occupied Jericho on 1 December. the Palestinian congress was convened, at which Palestinian notables denounced the All-Palestine Government and called for annexation by Jordan. Other similar conferences were staged in major West Bank cities, and Jordan's parliament formally approved the annexation on 24 April 1950 (Mishal 1978).

Beyond what happened to the Palestinians, the broader Arab world was rocked by the 1948 defeat. Government mismanagement of the war effort and scandals involving substandard supplies sold to the army by corrupt contractors led to immense political instability in Syria. On 30 March 1949 the Syrian army's chief of staff, Colonel Husni al-Za`im seized power in a military coup d'état. He declared himself president of the republic, only to be overthrown by a second coup on 14 August. This coup was engineered by, among other officers, Colonel Adib al-Shishakli (who had fought in the war as part of the ALA) and Brigadier General Sami al-Hinnawi. The latter became the titular head of the new junta. Instability continued, however, when al-Shishakli pushed aside al-Hinnawi in yet another coup on 19 December – the third to befall Syria during the eventful year of 1949. Jordan suffered instability shortly after the war ended as well (Seale 1987). Many Palestinian refugees blamed King Abdullah and the Arab Legion for their fate. On 20 July 1951, a Palestinian shot and killed Abdullah as he entered East Jerusalem's al-Aqsa Mosque for Friday prayers (Wilson 1987). Abdullah's son, Talal, emerged as Jordan's new king, but Palestinian resentments against Jordan and its royal family would fester for decades thereafter.

Political discontent over the war also would lead to dramatic political changes further afield in Egypt and Iraq, although not immediately. Egyptian army officers who served in the war were bitter over the government's poor military leadership as well as by accusations of corrupt contractors who supplied substandard equipment to troops during the war. The leading figure in a clique called the "Free Officers Movement" was Lieutenant Colonel Jamal Abd al-Nasir (Gamal Abdel Nasser), who had been wounded in the war and had been in the besieged Faluja Pocket. He and other Free Officers staged a military coup on 23 July 1952 and sent King Faruq into exile the following day. Major General Muhammad Najib (Naguib), a respected war veteran, emerged as the public face of the coup even though Abd al-Nasir was really in charge. The following year the officers abolished the monarchy and established a republic, with Najib as president (Gordon 1992). Iraqi army officers' grievances against their government for the country's poor performance during the 1948 war were some of the many factors that later drove them to emulate their Egyptian comrades by overthrowing the royal government in a bloody coup six years later, on 14 July 1958, and similarly establishing a republic under Brigadier General Abd al-Karim Qasim who, like Abd al-Nasir and Najib, had fought in the 1948 war (Batatu 1978).

Conclusion

The 1948 Arab-Israeli War marked the victory of Zionism: despite being a minority before the war, one that owned a small percentage of the land, Palestine's Jewish community emerged from the war having declared and defended a Jewish state that at war's end occupied 77 per cent of pre-1948 Palestine. Furthermore, the war led to a virtual revolution in terms of the demographic and spatial nature of the country: the first and foremost being the removal of 80 per cent of the Palestinians from the area, the destruction of the vast majority of the villages they left behind, and the immediate influx of hundreds of thousands of new Jewish immigrants. The landscape and even the placenames of the country seemingly have been forever changed. Moreover, the war led to permanent exile of the Palestinian refugees whose fates thereafter would be intimately tied up with the Arab host states where they found themselves, states that themselves underwent tremendous political turmoil as a result of the pan-Arab defeat in the war.

Recommended Readings

Khalidi, R. 2020. *The Hundred Years War on Palestine: A History of Settler Colonialism and Resistance, 1917–2017*. New York: Metropolitan Books.

Masalha, N. 2012. *The Palestine Nakba: Decolonising History, Narrating the Subaltern, Reclaiming Memory*. London and New York: Zed Books.

Morris, B. 2004. *The Birth of the Palestinian Refugee Revisited*. Cambridge: Cambridge University Press.

Morris, B. 2008. *1948: A History of the First Arab-Israeli War*. New Haven, CT: Yale University Press.

Rogan, E. L., and A. Shlaim, eds. 2001. *The War for Palestine: Rewriting the History of 1948*. Cambridge: Cambridge University Press.

Segev, T. 1986. *1949: The First Israelis*. Arlen Neal Weinstein, English language editor. New York: The Free Press.

Questions for Discussion

(1) What factors led to Israel's victory in the war?
(2) What factors led to the Arabs' defeat in the war?
(3) What factors led to the exodus of so many Palestinian refugees?
(4) How can one characterize the role of the United Nations in the 1948 war?
(5) What are some of the legacies of the 1948 war?

References

Bar-Joseph, U. 1987. *The Best of Enemies: Israel and Transjordan in the War of 1948*. London: Frank Cass.

Batatu, H. 1978. *The Old Social Classes and the Revolutionary Movements of Iraq: A Study of Iraq's Old Landed and Commercial Classes and of Its Communists, Ba`thists, and Free Officers*. Princeton, NJ: Princeton University Press.

Ben-Dror, E. 2016. *Ralph Bunche and the Arab-Israeli Conflict: Mediation and the UN, 1947–1949*, trans. D. File and L. Schramm. Abingdon and New York: Routledge.

Benvenisti, M. 2000. *Sacred Landscape: The Buried History of the Holy Land Since 1948*. Berkeley, CA: University of California Press.

Brand, L. A. 1988. *Palestinians in the Arab World: Institution Building and the Search for State.* New York: Columbia University Press.

Cohen, S. B., and N. Kliot. 1992. "Place-Names in Israel's Ideological Struggle over the Administered Territories." *Annals of the Association of American Geographers* 82:4, 653–680.

Dupuy, T. 1978. *Elusive Victory: The Arab-Israeli Wars: 1947–1974.* Garden City, NY: Military Book Club.

Falah, G. 1996. "The 1948 Israeli-Palestinian War and Its Aftermath: The Transformation and De-Signification of Palestine's Cultural Landscape." *Annals of the Association of American Geographers* 86:2, 256–285.

Fischbach, M. R. 2003. *Records of Dispossession: Palestinian Refugee Property and the Arab-Israeli Conflict.* New York: Columbia University Press.

Fischbach, M. R. 2005. "Land." Philip Mattar, ed. *Encyclopedia of the Palestinians*, revised edition. New York: *Facts On File*, 291–298.

Fischbach, M. R. 2006. *The Peace Process and Palestinian Refugee Claims: Addressing Claims for Property Compensation and Restitution.* Washington, DC: United States Institute of Peace Press.

Fischbach, M. R . 2008. *Jewish Property Claims against Arab Countries.* New York: Columbia University Press.

Fischbach, M. R. 2011. "British and Zionist Data Gathering on Palestinian Arab Landownership and Population during the Mandate." In *Surveillance and Control in Israel/Palestine: Population, Territory, and Power*, eds. E. Zureik, D. Lyon, and Y. Abu-Laban. London and New York: Routledge, 297–312.

Freundlich, Y., ed. 1981. *Documents on the Foreign Policy of Israel Vol. 1.* Jerusalem: Israel State Archives.

Gelber, Y. 2004. *Israeli-Jordanian Dialogue, 1948–1953.* East Sussex, UK: Sussex Academic Press.

Gerges, F. A. 2001. "Egypt and the 1948 War: Internal Conflict and Regional Ambitions." In *The War for Palestine: Rewriting the History of 1948*, eds. E. L. Rogan, and A. Shlaim. Cambridge: Cambridge University Press, 150–175.

Golan, A. 1995. "The Transfer to Jewish Control of Abandoned Arab Lands during the War of Independence." In *Israel: The First Decade of* Independence, eds. I. S. Troen, and N. Lucas. Albany: State University of New York Press, 403–440.

Gordon, J. 1992. *Nasser's Blessed Movement: Egypt's Free Officers and the July Revolution.* Oxford: Oxford University Press.

Hacohen, D. 2003. *Immigrants in Turmoil: Mass Immigration to Israel and its Repercussions in the 1950s and After*, trans. G. Brand. Syracuse, NY: Syracuse University Press.

Hughes, M. 2005. "Lebanon's Armed Forces and the Arab-Israeli War, 1948–49." *Journal of Palestine Studies* 34:2, 24–41.

Jiryis, S. 1976. *The Arabs in Israel*, trans. I. Bushnaq. New York: Monthly Review Press.

Khalaf, I. 1991. *Politics in Palestine: Arab Factionalism and Social Disintegration, 1938–1948.* Albany: State University of New York Press.

Khalidi, R. 2001. "The Palestinians and 1948: The Underlying Causes of Failure." In *The War for Palestine: Rewriting the History of 1948*, eds. E. L. Rogan, and A. Shlaim. Cambridge: Cambridge University Press, 12–36.

Khalidi, R. 2020. *The Hundred Years War on Palestine: A History of Settler Colonialism and Resistance, 1917–2017.* New York: Metropolitan Books.

Khalidi, W. 1959. "Why Did the Palestinians Leave?" *Middle East Forum* 24:6, 21–24.

Khalidi, W. 1961. "Plan Dalet: The Zionist Master Plan for the Conquest of Palestine." *Middle East Forum* 37:9, 22–28.

Khalidi, W. 1988. "Plan Dalet: Master Plan for the Conquest of Palestine." *Journal of Palestine Studies* 18:1, 4–33.

Khalidi, W. 1992. *All That Remains: The Palestinian Villages Occupied and Depopulated by Israel in 1948.* Washington, DC: Institute for Palestine Studies.

Landis, J. 2001. "Syria and the Palestine War: Fighting King `Abdullah's 'Greater Syrian Plan.'" In *The War for Palestine: Rewriting the History of 1948*, eds. E. L. Rogan, and A. Shlaim. Cambridge: Cambridge University Press, 176–203.

Lustick, I. 1980. *Arabs in the Jewish State: Israel's Control of a National Minority.* Austin, TX: University of Texas Press.

Masalha, N. 1992. *Expulsion of the Palestinians: The Concept of "Transfer" in Zionist Political Thought 1882–1948.* Washington, DC: Institute for Palestine Studies.

Masalha, N. 2012. *The Palestine Nakba: Decolonising History, Narrating the Subaltern, Reclaiming Memory*. London and New York: Zed Books.

Mattar, P. 1992. *The Mufti of Jerusalem: al-Hajj Amin Al-Husayni and the Palestinian National Movement*, rev. ed. New York: Columbia University Press.

McDaniel, D. A., and M. Ellis, eds. 1998. *Remembering Deir Yassin: The Future of Israel and Palestine*. New York: Olive Branch Press.

McDonald, J. G. 1951. *My Mission in Israel 1948–1951*. New York: Simon and Schuster.

Metzer, J. 1998. *The Divided Economy of Mandatory Palestine*. Cambridge: Cambridge University Press.

Mishal, S. 1978. *West Bank, East Bank: The Palestinians in Joran 1949–1967*. New Haven and London: Yale University Press.

Morris, B. 1986. "Yosef Weitz and the Transfer Committee, 1948–49." *Middle Eastern Studies* 22:4, 522–561.

Morris, B. 1987. *The Birth of the Palestinian Refugee Problem, 1947–1949*. Cambridge: Cambridge University Press.

Morris, B. 1999. *Righteous Victims: A History of the Zionist-Arab Conflict, 1881–1999*. New York: Alfred A. Knopf.

Morris, B. 2004. *The Birth of the Palestinian Refugee Problem Revisited*. Cambridge: Cambridge University Press.

Morris, B. 2008. *1948: A History of the First Arab-Israeli War*. New Haven: Yale University Press.

Nijim, B. K., with B. Muammar. 1984. *Toward the De-Arabization of Palestine/Israel 1945–1977*. Dubuque, IA: Kendall-Hunt Publishing Co.

Pappé, I. 2006. *The Ethnic Cleansing of Palestine*. Oxford: Oneworld Publications, Ltd.

Peretz, D. 1958. *Israel and the Palestine Arabs*. Washington, DC: Middle East Institute.

Rogan, E. L., and A. Shlaim. 2001. *The War for Palestine: Rewriting the History of 1948*. Cambridge: Cambridge University Press.

Sayigh, R. 1994. *Too Many Enemies: The Palestinian Experience in Lebanon*. London: Zed Books.

Seale, Patrick. 1987. *The Struggle for Syria: A Study of Post-War Arab Politics 1945–1958*. New Haven and London: Yale University Press.

Segev, T. 1986. *1949: The First Israelis*. Arlen Neal Weinstein, English language editor. New York: The Free Press.

Shavit, U. 2004. "Survival of the Fittest." *Haaretz* English internet edition, 8 January. Available at: www.haaretz.com/1.5262454.

Shlaim, A. 1988. *Collusion Across the Jordan: King Abdullah, the Zionist Movement, and the Partition of Palestine*. New York: Columbia University Press.

Shlaim, A. 1990. "The Rise and Fall of the All-Palestine Government in Gaza." *Journal of Palestine Studies* 20:1, 37–53.

Shlaim, A. 1999. *The Politics of Partition: King Abdullah, the Zionists, and Palestine 1921–1951*. Oxford: Clarendon Press.

Simons, C. 1988. *International Proposals to Transfer Arabs from Palestine 1895–1947: A Historical Survey*. Hoboken, NJ: Ktav Publishing House.

Survey of Palestine. 1991. *Prepared in December 1945 and January 1946 for the Information of the Anglo-American Committee of Inquiry, Vol. 1*. Jerusalem, 1946; rep. ed. Washington, DC: Institute for Palestine Studies.

Tamari, S. 2005. "Society." In *Encyclopedia of the Palestinians*, rev. ed., P. Mattar, ed. New York: Facts On File, 448–465.

Tripp, C. 2001. "Iraq and the 1948 War: Mirror of Iraq's Disorder." In *The War for Palestine: Rewriting the History of 1948*, eds. E. L. Rofan, and A. Shlaim. Cambridge: Cambridge University Press, 125–149.

United Nations. 1990. *The Blue Helmets: A Review of United Nations Peacekeeping*, 2nd ed. New York: United Nations.

United Nations General Assembly Resolution 194. 11 December 1948. Available at: https://unispal.un.org/DPA/DPR/unispal.nsf/0/C758572B78D1CD0085256BCF0077E51A.

United Nations Mediator on Palestine. "Progress Report," 16 September 1948. Available at: https://unispal.un.org/UNISPAL.NSF/0/AB14D4AAFC4E1BB985256204004F55FA.

Weitz, Y. 1950. *The Struggle for the Land*. Tel Aviv: Lion the Printer.

Wilson, M. C. 1987. *King Abdullah, Britain and the Making of Jordan*. Cambridge: Cambridge University Press.

World Machal. "About Machal." Available at: www.machal.org.il/index.php?option=com_content&view=article&id=302&Itemid=357&lang=en.

Yablonka, H. 1999. *Survivors of the Holocaust: Israel after the War*, trans. O. Cummings. Basingstoke and London: Macmillan.

8

THE PALESTINIANS AND ARAB-ISRAELI DIPLOMACY, 1967–1991

Seth Anziska

In examining the origins of the Palestinian national movement and its influence on the broader dynamics of Arab-Israeli diplomacy, a focus on the pursuit of political self-determination sits uneasily alongside a history of prolonged statelessness. One reason for this tension is that as Palestinians successfully organized around a unified political message of independent statehood, the possible space in which their national home could be built was fast disappearing under Israeli sovereignty. The history of the Palestinian demand for collective rights also extends well beyond the wave of mid-century decolonization, a temporal twist of fate that has posed innumerable challenges for the achievement of national aims. By considering the Palestinian role in Arab-Israeli diplomacy from 1967 until the formal onset of the "peace process" in the early 1990s, this chapter highlights the central paradox in a longstanding struggle for recognition. Just as Palestinians were gaining international attention as a political question requiring a diplomatic solution – marked by acceptance of the Palestine Liberation Organization (PLO) in Europe, the United States, and eventually Israel – on the ground, the possibility of a resolution in territorial terms was narrowing considerably. This left a political movement disconnected from the successful fulfilment of its statist project, a challenge that continues to shape the Palestinian struggle.

During the early years of the Arab-Israeli conflict, the Palestinian issue was often elided by interstate and regional rivalries. Israel's creation in 1948, and the simultaneous dispossession of over 700,000 Arab inhabitants of Palestine, known as the *Nakba*, initially cast the Palestinian question in humanitarian terms. Efforts to address the plight of the refugees included the creation of the United Nations Relief and Works Agency (UNRWA) and local struggles to contain border conflicts growing out of Palestinian efforts to return to their homes in the new state of Israel (Morris 1993). This humanitarian prism shifted considerably over subsequent decades, with the emergence of the PLO in 1964 and regional wars in 1967 and 1973 crystallizing the Palestinian dimension of the conflict.

Widespread Israeli and Western hostility to Palestinian self-determination reflected a deep-seated denial of their national political expression that extended back to the early twentieth century. This opposition intensified in response to the armed struggle that put Palestinian political claims on the international map, as well as Cold War considerations that cast the PLO as a Soviet proxy in the Middle East. For Israel, the opposition also emerged from a deeper fear about Palestinian claim-making over 1948, a reminder that the birth of the Israeli state was

DOI: 10.4324/9780429027376-11

predicated on the dispossession of the local Arab population. The demand for restitution or rights undermined the Zionist narrative of state creation and posed a demographic threat to the Jewish majority of the state. As the PLO shifted tactics towards diplomacy in the aftermath of the 1973 War, Palestinians gained greater recognition but also continued the opprobrium from their harshest critics, Israel and the United States. The deep cultural affinity for Zionism and a budding strategic alliance contributed to a policy of non-engagement, formalized by United States Secretary of State Henry Kissinger in 1975.

Shifting sympathies in Europe throughout the late 1970s, coupled with the rise of human-rights discourse in the United States, ultimately drew the Palestinians into the diplomatic arena. It was a fitful journey, however, with public calls by President Jimmy Carter for a Palestinian "homeland" coupled with secret talks to secure PLO acceptance of United Nations resolution 242, and the triumph of the Camp David Accords, which enabled a bilateral Egyptian-Israeli peace treaty in 1979 but ensured lasting Palestinian statelessness. The 1980 Venice Declaration by the European Economic Community (EEC) called for an acknowledgement of the right of Palestinian self-government, but the United States resisted formal engagement until President Ronald Reagan's recognition of the PLO in 1988. In the interim, the outbreak of the 1982 Lebanon War recast the Palestinian struggle and drove the PLO into wider exile, as the national movement was revived in the occupied territories themselves. The 1987 outbreak of the first *Intifada* underscored the staying power of the Palestinian cause on a global scale, leading to official recognition and diplomatic engagement. Not all segments of the Palestinian national movement were in agreement, however, as the birth of *Hamas* (the Islamic Resistance Movement) in this period ultimately challenged the diplomatic track of the PLO.

The end of the Cold War and resurgent United States intervention in the Middle East in the early 1990s coincided with this reorientation of the Palestinian struggle, underpinned by the emergence of a "peace process" with the 1991 Madrid Conference and subsequent diplomatic talks in Washington. But even as Palestinian, American, and Israeli diplomats in the United States were negotiating the extent of possible Palestinian self-determination, PLO leaders sought to leverage their return to the Palestinian territories via secret talks in Oslo. The 1993 Oslo Accords and the division of the territories that followed with the creation of a Palestinian Authority (PA) ultimately put an end to the meaningful pursuit of political sovereignty in part of historic Palestine. Protracted efforts that followed revealed the paradox of the Palestinian role in Arab-Israeli diplomacy: the demand for political rights, which had evolved from a maximalist position for reclaiming all of historic Palestine to the endorsement of territorial partition, would continually be called into question. The demand for a separate independent state in the West Bank and Gaza Strip with East Jerusalem as a Palestinian capital has increasingly been seen as a mirage since Oslo; rather, many Palestinians now advocate for equal rights and equal citizenship across all of Israeli-controlled territory, framing their struggle as a fight against structural discrimination and political exclusion by one sovereign power. This signals a return to some of the same impulses that first animated the Palestinian struggle in the aftermath of Israel's creation.

The Quest for Legitimacy

Just over a decade after 1948, a new vanguard of Palestinian activists created *Fatah* in 1959, an acronym for the Palestinian National Liberation Movement. The movement was conceived by diaspora Palestinian professionals in the Gulf States – many of whom had once been students in Cairo and Beirut and hailed from Gaza – formalizing a political party in 1965. Under the influence of leading figures that included Yasser Arafat, Salah Khalaf (Abu Iyyad) and Khalil al-Wazir (Abu Jihad), *Fatah* challenged Arab governments to put the question of Palestine back on the political map after the Nakba. In an effort to curb the impact of these brash nationalists, Egypt encouraged the formation of the Palestine Liberation Organization (PLO) as a vehicle to exercise control over Palestinian national expression. In June 1964, the Arab League Summit in Cairo announced the creation of the PLO with a national charter that declared the

> Palestinian Arab people has the legitimate right to its homeland and is an inseparable part of the Arab Nation. It shares the sufferings and aspirations of the Arab Nation and its struggle for freedom, sovereignty, progress and unity.
>
> *(1964 PLO National Charter)*[1]

This interplay between pan-Arab liberation politics and Palestinian demands would gradually shift towards a national framing. The Palestinian historian Rashid Khalidi argues that "the PLO under the leadership of Fateh was broadly seen in terms of a teleology of evolution from a liberation movement to a para-state that would eventually lead the Palestinians to full-fledged statehood and independence" (Khalidi 2006, 150). Initially, the PLO and its constituent factions advocated direct armed struggle against Israel and did not officially endorse the notion of an independent Palestinian state until the mid-1970s. In part, this was due to Jordanian and Egyptian territorial angling in the West Bank and Gaza Strip, a dynamic quickly transformed by the June 1967 Arab-Israeli War. Israel's conquest of the West Bank, Gaza Strip, East Jerusalem, Sinai Peninsula and Golan Heights was a startling development across the Arab world, reorienting regional politics on Palestine. A large wave of newly exiled Palestinian refugees and the onset of Israeli control over those who remained behind in the occupied territories served to strengthen the PLO's nationalist drive (Raz 2012; Khalidi 2017). The growth of illegal Israeli settlements in the wake of the 1967 War, as well as the ideological influence of the *Gush Emunim* movement, directly challenged these national aspirations.

Regionally, the destruction of Egyptian president Gamal Abdel Nasser's credibility as a guarantor of Palestinian rights buoyed the rise of the younger Fatah nationalists under Arafat's leadership. Uniting factional organizations under a fully independent PLO, Fatah gained control of the organization's executive bodies, and Arafat was appointed chairman, a role he maintained until his death in 2004. The PLO implemented intensive guerrilla warfare as part of its strategy, bringing Palestinian militants into armed confrontation with Israel during the War of Attrition (1969–1970), and organizing further strikes, hijackings, and armed attacks that garnered international attention and recast the Palestinian struggle in global terms (Sayigh 1997; Chamberlin 2012).

Disagreements soon erupted between Fatah and the Popular Front for the Liberation of Palestine (PFLP), founded by the physician George Habash, as well as the Democratic Front for the Liberation of Palestine (DFLP), led by Nayef Hawatmeh. The PFLP and DFLP supported armed confrontation to overthrow Arab regimes unsympathetic to the Palestinian cause, while Fatah remained less enthusiastic. These internal splits shaped the Palestinian national movement throughout its history, as did regional pressures (Sayigh 1997). The advent of "Black September" in Jordan in 1970 and the expulsion of the PLO from its base shifted the locus of power to Damascus and Beirut, where the PLO would remain until it was driven out during the 1982 Israeli invasion of Lebanon. While Arab League recognition of the PLO "as the sole legitimate representative of the Palestinian people" came in 1974, the Lebanese Civil War in 1975 further highlighted how regional tensions continually shaped their struggle.

By the mid-1970s, Palestinians had managed to gain regional and international prominence through a combination of diplomatic overtures and violent acts of militancy on the global stage, shifting from a strategy of armed struggle to political engagement.[2] Moderate voices within the national movement had also steadily grown more influential, generating measured support for a negotiated settlement with Israel (Baumgarten 2005; Sela 2014). As Mohammad Muslih argues, from 1969–1973 the PLO political platform moved from an exclusively ethnic state towards a secular democratic entity allowing for the presence of Jews and other minorities. This secular democratic platform of the early 1970s endured until the twelfth meeting of the Palestinian National Council (PNC) in June 1974, where the PLO made its first steps towards what would be known as a "two-state solution." The PNC approved the Ten Point Program, which included important steps formulated by Fatah leaders calling for the establishment of a national authority over "any piece" of liberated Palestinian land. It was a break with past rejections of the principle of partition, and set the stage for later negotiations with Israel (Muslih 1990).

The crucial development that drove this shift in the PLO's strategy was the October 1973 Arab-Israeli War. In a bid to force a settlement to the Arab-Israeli conflict, Egyptian president Anwar al-Sadat sought to create a "crisis of détente" (Daigle 2012) to break the status quo in the region. A massive American airlift of tanks and aeroplanes reversed Egyptian and Syrian advances and further solidified close US–Israeli relations. With United States president Richard Nixon distracted by the Watergate scandal, Secretary of State Henry Kissinger negotiated the terms of agreement to end the war. They were passed as United Nations Security Council Resolution 338, which called for a "just and durable peace in the Middle East" along the lines of United Nations Security Council Resolution 242 after the 1967 War. It remained unclear, however, to what extent territorial concessions might include the Palestinians.

Kissinger, as Nixon's envoy and later as Secretary of State to President Gerald Ford, pursued a step-by-step approach to achieve a diplomatic solution between Israel and its neighbours. But these attempts at negotiating a comprehensive solution favoured piecemeal stages that separated the Palestinian issue from broader regional concerns. Palestinian national aspirations, which were emerging as a central point of contention between Israel and the Arab states, were ignored by Kissinger's diplomatic initiatives (Yaqub 2008). In contrast, at the Arab League Summit in 1974, the PLO was officially recognized as the representative voice of Palestinian concerns in the Arab world. The organization's efforts at a dialogue with the United States was stymied by a 1975 ban on direct talks with the organization put in place by Kissinger (Khalil 2016).

United States officials began to revisit relations with the Palestinians after Jimmy Carter's victory in the 1976 presidential election. A small number of policymakers recognized the necessity of limited Palestinian rights, fuelled by the broader sweep of decolonization in the Global South (Nemchenok 2009; Pressman 2013; Jensehaugen 2014). The PLO's Information Bulletin, *Palestine*, noted the movement's growing international prominence during this period.[3] The organization was making quiet inroads with Western diplomats. British Embassy officials in Europe, the United States and the Middle East had regular "discreet and informal contact with the PLO," including monthly lunches between the Middle East desk officer in London and Said Hammami, the PLO representative in the city.[4] British officials were mindful of Israeli opposition to these contacts but stressed the importance of hearing their ideas. In France and Belgium, the PLO had attained some official recognition, and the organization was gaining ground with the German and Austrian governments as well.

Among European governments, there was a growing consensus to support the organization, increasingly seen as the legitimate vehicle for achieving Palestinian self-determination. This would be formalized with the Venice Declaration of 1980, which stated that

> [a] just solution must finally be found to the Palestinian problem, which is not simply one of refugees. The Palestinian people, which is conscious of existing as such, must

> be placed in a position, by an appropriate process defined within the framework of the comprehensive peace settlement, to exercise fully its right to self-determination. … These principles apply to all the parties concerned, and thus to the Palestinian people, and to the PLO, which will have to be associated with the negotiations.
>
> *(Venice Declaration, 1980, in Laqueur and Rubin, 2008, pp 232–233)*

While the process of diplomatic engagement with Palestinians was clear in Europe, the United States took a more uneven approach under Carter, compounded by pressures from domestic supporters of Israel and the new Likud government of Menachem Begin that came to power in 1977 (Anziska 2018).

Camp David and the Triumph of Autonomy

The rise of the right-wing Likud party in Israel followed soon after Jimmy Carter had taken office as the 39th United States president. A former Democratic governor of Georgia, Carter was eager to break with the dominant Cold War approach of his predecessors. In the Middle East, this yielded a regional strategy that was concerned with local dynamics and recognized the necessity of addressing the Palestinian issue in political terms. At a May 1977 town hall meeting in Clinton, Massachusetts, Carter remarked "there has to be a homeland provided for the Palestinian refugees who have suffered for many, many years."[5] The frank language and insistence on accommodating Palestinians fit with Carter's decisive rhetorical embrace of human rights. But it also elicited a great deal of public criticism from Cold War hawks as well as Israeli and American Jewish leaders, all of whom opposed the emergence of a Palestinian state.

As for the PLO leadership in Beirut, they had praise for Carter's new approach, but also scepticism. Palestinians had moved away from using the term "homeland" in favour of the phrase "independent national state," which reflected a grudging willingness to live side by side with Israel (Tanner 1977). The PLO's *Information Bulletin* recalled a history of declarations that had not brought substantive change on the ground, while seeing Carter's statement as a "step forward in U.S. Middle Eastern policy, and an encouragement for the Palestinian people in their resistance to Zionist expansion and settler colonialism."[6] PLO chairman Arafat relayed a message to President Carter "implying the PLO's willingness to live in peace with Israel." His condition was a "U.S. commitment to the establishment of an independent Palestinian "state unit entity."[7] Although the form of such an entity remained a matter of fierce disagreement, the principle of Palestinian diplomatic engagement was clear.

The new Israeli government, however, was firmly opposed to Carter's stance. Menachem Begin was a revisionist Zionist with deep-seated ideological opposition to Palestinian territorial rights. He was also a believer in settlement expansion in the occupied territories, which he pursued with the help of Ariel Sharon, his agriculture minister and later defence minister. Begin arrived in the United States for his first face-to-face meeting with President Carter on 19 July 1977. During their initial discussion in the White House cabinet room, Carter laid out the central principles of his approach to the Middle East conflict, which included a comprehensive peace based on United Nations resolutions 242 and 338, a resolution of territorial boundaries, and the question of the refugees.

The absence of official Palestinian participation in the efforts spearheaded by the Carter Administration was conspicuous. The PLO leadership was hamstrung by the official United States ban on political contact with the organization that Kissinger and the Israelis had agreed upon in 1975. To circumvent this ban, extensive secret United States backchannel conversations were held with leading Palestinians, intended to clarify the organization's possible acceptance of United Nations Security Council Resolution 242. Palestinian leaders were hesitant to recognize Israel along the lines of the resolution without some indication of substantive promises in return. There was external pressure on the organization as well, with Saudi Arabia, Egypt, and the Soviet Union pushing the leadership to sign, while the Syrians were strongly advising the PLO against such a move.

In his secret outreach to American diplomats, Yasser Arafat spoke of the PLO's legitimacy and willingness to accept 242 as long as it dealt with the Palestinians "as a people with national rights and aspirations and not as refugees." This insistence on the Palestinians as a nation was fuelled by the PLO's suspicion of American diplomacy and the Israeli position on the PLO. During an intensive effort over the summer of 1977, the PLO Executive Committee decided against acceptance of 242, even as some within the Fatah faction wanted to begin a dialogue with the United States.[8] It was not, however, the end of the matter. Attempts to meet the American requirements continued with further secret talks, and the disagreements reflected a wide range of internal voices within the PLO, who offered divergent strategies for advancing the political aims of the national movement (Anziska 2018, 66–68).

Against the backdrop of American efforts, the Egyptian president Anwar al-Sadat looked to solidify his country's alliance with the West. Egypt had been looking to the United States as a patron since the acceptance of the Rogers Plan for Arab-Israeli peace in 1970. But Sadat's growing frustration over the lack of movement towards a comprehensive regional peace precipitated an unprecedented visit to Jerusalem in November of 1977. In a remarkable speech in front of Israel's Knesset, Sadat declared "there can be no peace without the Palestinians" (Lukacs 1991, 143–144). The Egyptian president argued that the establishment of a Palestinian state and an Israeli withdrawal to the Green Line was essential for regional peace. Members of the Carter Administration, watching in utter amazement from the sidelines, largely supported Sadat's decisive move while finally acknowledging that their own comprehensive peace plans would never come to pass. Sadat's speech also increased the internal debate among PLO leaders about the possibility of statehood, with some figures ready to embrace a small Palestinian state on the West Bank and Gaza Strip, while others resisted this idea. There was concern that the bilateral focus between Egypt and Israel would not serve Palestinian political interests.

As subsequent negotiations between the United States, Israel, and Egypt faltered, Jimmy Carter invited Sadat and Begin to the presidential retreat in Camp David for 13 days of negotiations. The Camp David Accords were reached on 17 September 1978, and led to a formal Egyptian-Israeli peace treaty signed by Sadat and Begin on 26 March 1979. The Camp David agreement affirmed United Nations Security Council Resolution 242 as the basis for any negotiated settlement and stated that "Egypt, Israel, Jordan and the representatives of the Palestinian people should participate in negotiations on the resolution of the Palestinian problem in all its aspects" (Lukacs 1991, 157). It also outlined mechanisms to include the Palestinians in a political process, calling for some form of self-government and including specific language to "recognize the legitimate rights of the Palestinian people and their just requirements." But rather than inaugurate diplomacy that may have led to a possible Palestinian state, Menachem Begin unveiled a detailed autonomy plan for what he called the "Arab residents of Judea and Samaria," proffering limited self-rule rather than full political or territorial sovereignty (Anziska 2017).

For Carter, the Camp David summit was a great diplomatic victory, but also an incomplete one. His ambitious aim to tackle Palestinian aspirations and resolve the wider Arab-Israeli conflict had given way to a narrower bilateral agreement. The 1979 Egyptian-Israeli peace treaty secured the return of the Sinai Peninsula to Egypt in exchange for recognition, relieving military pressure on Israel's southwest border and bringing the major phase of interstate Arab-Israeli conflict to an end. Begin's price was the retention of the West Bank, Gaza Strip, and

East Jerusalem. Roughly five thousand Jewish settlers lived in the occupied territories when Begin entered office, and the number of settlers continued to rise steadily in the wake of the Accords, reaching over eighty thousand by the late 1980s. Additionally, the agreement included more United States military and economic aid to Israel than had been given under any previous administration: $10.2 billion over four years, a little less than half in grants. Egypt and Saudi Arabia also received military aid and security guarantees, highlighting the emerging spectrum of United States allies in the Middle East.

In the eyes of the PLO leadership, the implications of a separate peace between Egypt and Israel and an emerging autonomy plan in the West Bank and Gaza Strip were distressingly clear. Arafat conveyed his views to the United States government via a secret back channel. The PLO chairman described the Camp David Accords as nothing more than "meaningless negotiations about some permanent colonial status for the Palestinians under Israeli rule." Arafat warned of the "massive build-up of U.S. arms to both Israel and Egypt, and preparations of another Arab-Israeli war which Begin is doing everything to provoke through his attacks on South Lebanon. That is not a treaty for peace – it is a treaty for war."[9]

Arafat was equally dismissive of Begin's autonomy plans, which he called "a farce," suggesting instead an alternative path. "If there is a clear platform for serious, comprehensive peace negotiations," the PLO leader remarked to United States officials, "we will of course take part." In Arafat's view, that platform should include three major points:

(1) Human rights for the Palestinians;
(2) The principle of the right of return for the Palestinians;
(3) The right of the Palestinians to have our own state.[10]

In the wider context of an emerging discourse on human rights in the 1970s, the PLO demands echoed similar political struggles across the globe. The diplomatic context in which these demands arrived would change considerably with Carter's defeat and the election of Ronald Reagan to the United States presidency.

The Lessons of Lebanon

During the 1980 United States presidential campaign, former California governor Ronald Reagan was asked whether he thought the PLO was a terrorist organization. He answered affirmatively while also making an important distinction. "I separate the PLO from the Palestinian refugees. None ever elected the PLO."[11] Reagan's victory signalled a return to global Cold War geopolitics, reconstituting the Middle East as a site of contestation between the United States and the Soviet Union. Given this new reality, relations with Israel were granted strategic priority, while the Palestinians were deemed a Soviet proxy. At the same time, there was direct low-level contact between the American government and the PLO, especially in the context of the Lebanese civil war. By the end of Reagan's second term in office, the United States would officially open a dialogue with the organization. In the interim, the Israeli invasion of Lebanon would overturn regional politics and the fate of the Palestinian national movement, while drawing the United States further into the conflict (Anziska 2018).

Ever since their expulsion from Jordan in 1970, the PLO had regrouped in Lebanon, building para-state institutions and putting the Palestinian question back at the centre of regional politics. The Cairo Accords of 1969, brokered between the Lebanese Army and Yasser Arafat, authorized actions on behalf of the Palestinian Resistance Movement and guaranteed

Palestinian civic rights in Lebanon. Paramilitary training and mass mobilization by Palestinians was seen in some quarters as an encroachment upon Lebanese sovereignty. The PLO solidified its hold in the south of the country, venturing outside refugee camps and launching border skirmishes with Israel. Alongside internal rivalries that had contributed to the outbreak of the 1975 Lebanese civil war, Syria was also drawn into the fighting, while Maronite politicians promoted an alliance with Israel in their fight against the PLO and leftist allies.

New evidence suggests a United States green light for Israel's invasion of its northern neighbour, which was initially portrayed as an attempt by Israel to contain Palestinian attacks on its Galilee border towns. The June 1982 incursion quickly escalated into a full-scale effort to remake Lebanon as Israel's Christian ally. Unlike the wars in 1948, 1967, or 1973, Israel was unequivocally engaged in what Prime Minister Begin called a "war of choice." An unprecedented siege and saturation bombing of Beirut unfolded in the summer of 1982, and the war resulted in the deaths of at least 5,000 Lebanese and Palestinian civilians – over 19,000 by Lebanese estimates that counted combatants as well, in addition to over 600 Israeli soldiers (Anziska 2018). This included the notorious massacre of Palestinian civilians in the Sabra and Shatila refugee camp in south Beirut by Christian Phalange militiamen, supported by the Israeli army along with the unwitting complicity of the American government (Anziska 2012).

With the involvement of United States diplomats, American officials helped facilitate the departure of Yasser Arafat and thousands of PLO fighters from Lebanon to other Arab countries as a means of ending the conflict in August 1982. Reagan soon unveiled his administration's new peace plan in a primetime address on 1 September 1982. Building on Carter's Camp David framework, he acknowledged that implementation of the Camp David Accords had been slow. The central question, he said, was "how to reconcile Israel's legitimate security concerns with the legitimate rights of the Palestinians." The Reagan Plan reflected a return to the notion of comprehensive peace; however, it did not support outright the creation of a Palestinian state, opting instead for Palestinian self-government in association with Jordan. It was also a short-lived initiative, rejected swiftly by the Israeli cabinet and the last serious United States effort to broker a resolution to the conflict in the 1980s (Quandt 2005).

Throughout the 1982 War, Palestinian leaders asserted the PLO's willingness to accept binding United Nations resolutions and the possibility of a negotiated settlement. In the aftermath of the PLO's August evacuation from Beirut, ABC News hosted an episode of "This Week with David Brinkley" on the situation in the Middle East, inviting Bassam Abu Sharif of the Popular Front for the Liberation of Palestine (PFLP) to discuss the political repercussions of the departure. Brinkley asked the Palestinian spokesman whether he would be satisfied with a Palestinian state in the West Bank and Gaza, and Abu Sharif remarked that it was "satisfactory" to have a state on "any part of Palestine." In a follow up, he was asked "does that mean that the Palestinians, in your view, the PLO, in your view, can accept the simultaneous existence of Israel as a Jewish state?" Abu Sharif replied, "This is the PLO program. It was very clear … it is to establish a Palestine independent state on any part of Palestine." Brinkley asked if such an outcome were to materialize, "would that be the end of your hostility to Israel?" Abu Sharif replied that "this would be probably a start for simultaneous cooperation between Palestinians and Jews."[12]

Israel's invasion of Lebanon radically altered global perceptions of the Zionist movement and United States actions in the Middle East, as well as the broader context in which Palestinian nationalism was viewed. The Palestinian quest for self-determination was rendered visible once again on a global scale, despite Israeli hopes that it would disappear from view. One unintended consequence was the strengthening of calls for a national solution to the Palestinian question. A special National Intelligence Estimate prepared by the CIA in the aftermath of the war described this altered climate. "Israel has been surprised to discover that its military victory has not produced the expected political dividends and seems to have strengthened its antagonists' political hand."[13] This analysis cohered with the view of one Israeli Knesset member, who remarked, "In Beirut, we created a Palestinian state."[14] But the PLO itself was now in exile, with Arafat banished to the forlorn Hotel Salwa in Tunis, where he struggled to rebuild national unity. Far away in North Africa, the PLO was further cut off from the West Bank and Gaza, "working clandestinely to build institutional ties to the population" in the occupied territories (Khalidi 2006, 158). While Israel's short-term aim of defeating the PLO in Lebanon was successful, the long-term implications reignited the national movement and drove a shift in the locus of power to the occupied territories.

From *Intifada* to Recognition

Given the pivotal role of Jordan as a gateway back to the West Bank, Palestinians debated the value of reconciling with the Hashemite regime in order to further ties with Palestinians living under occupation. But relations between Jordan's King Hussein and Arafat deteriorated considerably in the mid-1980s, with factional violence within the PLO continuing and Hussein's political vulnerabilities taking an enormous toll on the alliance (Khalidi 2006, 148; 260–265). In a scathing address in February 1986, Hussein announced the end of any joint initiative with the PLO (Laqueur and Rubin 2008, 299–313). He blamed the Palestinian leadership for continued intransigence in not accepting United Nations resolution 242, and his remarks signalled "the end of an era in which Jordan was the leading actor in the search for a peaceful solution to the Middle East conflict" (Shlaim 2007, 433).

By December 1987, Israel's twenty-year control over the Palestinian territories was seen as intolerable, and protests erupted in the Gaza Strip after an incident in the Jabalia refugee camp, quickly spreading to the West Bank. Demonstrators unfurled Palestinian flags, burned tires, and threw stones and Molotov cocktails at Israeli cars, and the Israeli security forces responded with force. The first Intifada had erupted. This largely non-violent protest, which lasted through the early 1990s, fundamentally altered the landscape of Palestinian politics and the PLO's relations with Israel as well as the United States (Lockman and Beinin 1999). Supporters of Israel, already distressed by the events in Lebanon, were acutely aware of negative perceptions of the state, increasingly seen as a biblical Goliath fighting a lone David. The PLO was taken by surprise with the uprising, watching it unfold from a distance. The Intifada was entirely generated from within the territories, a spontaneous unplanned eruption. Seeing an opportunity to capitalize on popular discontent in order to secure political clout, the PLO began to assert a leadership role.

The detrimental impact of the occupation, which had largely failed to penetrate the consciousness of most Israelis or their supporters abroad, was now indisputably apparent. As the Israeli journalist Amos Elon wrote, "the occupation has held 1.5 million Palestinians as pawns, or bargaining chips, and as a source of cheap menial labor, while denying them the most basic human rights. The pawns have now risen to manifest their frustration, their bitterness and their political will" (Elon 1988).

Among the 14 demands outlined by West Bank and Gaza Palestinian leaders in January 1988 was a call to abide by the Fourth Geneva Convention, a demand for the cessation of settlement activity and land confiscation, and the removal of restrictions on political contacts between inhabitants of the territories and the PLO (Laqueur and Rubin 2008, 319).

Prominent figures within the PLO began to publicly embrace negotiations with Israel, and a decisive move towards a negotiated settlement came in Algeria that fall. At the November 1988 Palestine National Congress in Algiers, Yasser Arafat won a majority of votes for the historic decision to accept relevant United Nations resolutions 242 and 338 (Laqueur and Rubin 2008, 349–353). The leading national poet Mahmoud Darwish was asked to craft a Palestinian Declaration of Independence, and it proclaimed an independent Palestinian state alongside Israel on the basis of United Nations Resolution 181, which had enshrined the idea of partition in 1947. "This was the first official Palestinian recognition of the legitimacy of the existence of a Jewish state," explained a leading historian of Palestinian nationalism, "and the first unequivocal, explicit PLO endorsement of a two-state solution to the conflict" (Khalidi 2006, 194–195). The notion that a state of Palestine could exist side by side with a state of Israel, near heresy in the 1970s, had emerged as the preferred Palestinian position at the close of the 1980s.

In light of these developments, United States officials slowly entertained an official dialogue with the PLO. At a Geneva press conference in December 1988, Arafat read out a statement highlighting the PLO's approach to diplomacy. "Self-determination means survival for the Palestinians," Arafat explained, "and our survival does not destroy the survival of the Israelis, as their rulers claim." The PLO leader responded directly to critics who continued to marginalize or dismiss the national movement. "The intifada will come to an end only when practical and tangible steps have been taken towards the achievement of our national aims and establishment of our independent Palestinian state." Arafat's insistence on statehood, however, remained a one-sided pledge. Israeli and American officials were opposed to such an outcome, a reminder that the quest for self-determination did not inevitably lead to national sovereignty. In announcing the beginning of an official American dialogue with the PLO, statehood was explicitly not endorsed. "Nothing here may be taken to imply an acceptance or recognition by the United States of an independent Palestinian state," Secretary of State George Shultz declared. "The position of the United States is [that] the status of the West Bank and Gaza [strip] cannot be determined by unilateral acts of either side, but only through a process of negotiations. The United States does not recognize the declaration of an independent Palestinian state" (Rabie 1995, 180–182).

By the end of 1988, the Palestinians had finally begun to achieve the international diplomatic recognition that had eluded them for so long. The failed attempts to bypass Palestinian nationalists in the late 1970s and 1980s had actually served to legitimate the PLO and force Israel, the United States, and the wider Arab world to reckon with their quest for national self-determination. This recognition was the culmination of years of diplomatic efforts, armed struggle, and backchannel negotiations. That such a development took place in the last months of a Republican administration ideologically opposed to Palestinian nationalism, viewing the PLO as a Soviet proxy, was certainly a surprising turn of events. PLO recognition did not, however, denote the attainment of political sovereignty. The form and content of a possible Palestinian political future remained unclear in the closing months of the 1980s. The newly inaugurated US-PLO dialogue was fitful, and was suspended in June 1990 after an attack by the Palestine Liberation Front, a splinter group backed by Iraq. It was only with the end of the Cold War and the onset of the Madrid Talks in 1991 that a possible future based on political sovereignty for the Palestinians was more sharply delineated (Anziska 2018, 260–266).

The election of George H. W. Bush precipitated new opportunities and challenges for the Palestinians. During Bush's tenure, and with the help of Secretary of State James Baker, an Israeli-Palestinian "peace process" was situated as a key foreign policy goal for the United States. The context for this re-emergence was largely geopolitical: the end of the Cold War had removed the Soviet threat, and the outbreak of the first Gulf War in 1990 had reshaped United States interests in the Middle East. President Bush and Secretary Baker launched the Madrid Peace Conference in October 1991, the first official face-to-face gathering that included representatives from Israel, Lebanon, Syria, Jordan, and the Palestinian Territories. The Palestinians were part of a joint Jordanian delegation coordinating closely with the PLO leadership in Tunis, who were prevented from attending the conference by Israel. President Bush and Soviet President Mikhail Gorbachev co-chaired direct multilateral negotiations, while the bulk of negotiations happened in Washington between 1991 and 1993. This was the first time the Palestinians were directly negotiating their own political fate, and the discussions reveal the extent to which meaningful political sovereignty in the occupied territories was debated and considered a plausible outcome for the future (Anziska 2018, 267–282).

Unbeknownst to the delegates in Washington, however, the PLO leadership had begun secret talks with Israeli leaders in the Norwegian capitol of Oslo. The resulting Oslo Accords, which were signed on the south lawn of the White House on 13 September 1993, were considered a breakthrough in the Israeli-Palestinian conflict. Alongside Israeli recognition of the PLO and Palestinian recognition of Israel, the Accords marked the start of a multi-year peace process between the parties. But the peace process launched by the Oslo Accords was nowhere near as picture perfect as the famous handshake between Arafat and Israeli Prime Minister Yitzhak Rabin suggested. At the time, critics warned that the Accords set aside the most contentious issues left unresolved from earlier efforts while enshrining limited autonomy rather than statehood for Palestinians (Rabbani 2012; Said 1993).

In September 1995, Arafat and Rabin signed the Interim Agreement on the West Bank and Gaza Strip, or Oslo II, establishing the Palestinian Authority (PA) and dividing the West Bank into three separate zones of control. There was enormous scepticism of Arafat's move in the Arab world, where he was seen as selling out meaningful Palestinian sovereignty for the sake of his own return to the West Bank and subsequent appointment as president of the PA. Oslo II granted the PA limited self-government, for an interim period of time, providing the vestiges of statehood without actual content. The process around Oslo lulled its proponents into the false belief that real issues like Jerusalem, refugees' right of return, settlements, and security were being dealt with. In this regard, Oslo serves as a bookend to the Palestinian national struggle, inaugurating a period of stalemate and calling into question the concessions that led the PLO towards diplomacy without an outcome of sovereign statehood.

Conclusion: The Limits of Self-Determination

What then is the legacy of Palestinian engagement with Arab-Israeli diplomacy between the 1967 War and the peace process of the 1990s? Can real lasting political accomplishments be delineated? Scholars of the Palestinian national movement in the post-1948 era have long argued that the PLO's major political achievement was rooted in a restoration of Palestinian identity and the insistence on maintaining a focus on the struggle for self-determination. While a confluence of factors kept the Palestinian cause ingrained in global consciousness in the aftermath of the Nakba, the PLO was the driving force for advancing the Palestinian national struggle in military, and then diplomatic, terms. Having coordinated years of armed struggle, it worked to create a vehicle for the achievement of national recognition in political terms. By 1988, this took the form of the endorsement of a state in the West Bank and Gaza Strip with East Jerusalem as the capital, along the 1967 lines and in accordance with United Nations resolution 242.

While Israel opposed the statist claims of Palestinians, Europe and the United States gradually accepted these terms, and the PLO did manage to establish a legitimate address for diplomatic engagement by the end of the twentieth century. Moreover, the organization parlayed recognition of the Palestinian national movement to Arab states and the international community, through United Nations recognition and bilateral agreements. Mindful of the pitfalls of exile, it worked to return the political centre of the Palestinian struggle back to the Palestinian territories. Yet despite these important accomplishments, the PLO failed in one central political aim: it could never shift from para-statehood to national independence. This crucial failure of the PLO may say more about the limited horizon for a diplomatic resolution that affected the Palestinians more broadly, whether through the formal channels of the national movement or among informal activists and factions across the Palestinian diaspora.

In the struggle for moral recognition, the Palestinians have largely succeeded; but in the struggle for political rights and sovereignty, the outcome remains quite grim. Critics have pointed to the PLO's embrace of the Oslo Accords as a key moment in this diplomatic failure, but as the present chapter has suggested, the difficulties far predate the 1990s. As the Palestinian national movement gradually came to endorse the concept of statehood in part of Palestine, the physical territory had been transformed by Israeli settlements and the erasure of the 1967 boundaries. What remains to be seen is whether an alternative mode of politics, one that moves away from state building and towards the achievement of equal citizenship and belonging inside Israel and the occupied territories, can open a new space for a just resolution of the Palestinian question.

Recommended Readings

Al-Hout, Shafiq. 2011. *My Life in the PLO: The Inside Story of the Palestinian Struggle*. London: Pluto.

Cobban, H. 1984. *The Palestinian Liberation Organisation: People, Power, and Politics*. Cambridge Middle East Library. Cambridge: Cambridge University Press.

Khalidi, R. 2020. *The Hundred Years' War on Palestine: A History of Settler Colonial Conquest and Resistance*. London: Profile Books.

Pearlman, W. 2012. "The Palestinian National Movement," in *The 1967 Arab-Israeli War: Origins and Consequences*, eds. Wm. R. Louis and A. Shlaim. Cambridge: Cambridge University, 126–148.

Quandt, W. B. 2005. *Peace Process: American Diplomacy and the Arab-Israeli Conflict since 1967*. Washington, DC: Brookings Institution Press.

Smith, C. D. 2007. *Palestine and the Arab-Israeli Conflict: A History with Documents*, 6th ed. Boston: Bedford/St Martins, 2007.

Notes

1 Reproduced in the Primary Resources in International Affairs, ETH Zurich, www.files.ethz.ch/isn/125413/2123_Palestinian_National_Charter.pdf.

2 On the revolutionary movement itself, see the extensive resources compiled in *The Palestinian Revolution* website: http://learnpalestine.politics.ox.ac.uk/.

3 "Twelve Years … Palestine Lives," Editorial, *Palestine: PLO Information Bulletin*, 3.1 (January 1977): 4–5. All copies of *Palestine* were accessed in the library of the Institute for Palestine Studies, Beirut, Lebanon [hereafter IPS].

4 "Contacts with the PLO," Confidential Memo, Roger Tomkys, 14 January 1977, "Status of the PLO in the UK," FCO 93/1134, United Kingdom National Archives, Kew, London.

5 Carter made this comment at a press conference in Clinton, Massachusetts, on 12 May 1977. For the full text see www.presidency.ucsb.edu/ws/index.php?pid=7495.
6 "The Palestinian Homeland," *Palestine*, 3 (May 1977), IPS.
7 See Memorandum from Brzezinski to Carter, undated, *Foreign Relations of the United States, 1977–1980* [hereafter FRUS], Vol. 8, Arab-Israeli Dispute, January 1977–August 1978. Ed. Adam M. Howard. Washington, DC: US GPO, 2013, Doc 51.
8 "CIA Intelligence Information Cable," 20 August 1977, FRUS, Doc 97.
9 "Summary of two evenings of talk with Yasir Arafat – July 24, 25, 1979," undated report, NSA Brzezinski Material, Box 49, File 6, Palestine Liberation Organization 5/79-10/80, Jimmy Carter Library [hereafter JCL].
10 See "Summary of two evenings of talk," NSA Brzezinski Material, Box 49, File 6, JCL.
11 "*Msibat Itonaim-Reagan*" [Reagan's Press Conference], 6 November 1980, MFA-8652/3, Israel State Archives.
12 "Full Text: Middle East," This Week with David Brinkley, 29 August 1982, 11:30AM, CIA Records Search Tool [CREST], (CIA-RDP88-01070R000100330006-3), National Archives and Records Administration.
13 Special National Security Intelligence Estimate, "PLO: Impact of the Lebanese Incursion," 8 November 1982. CREST (CIA-RDP85T00176R001100290014-5).
14 This was Shevach Weiss; see transcript of Knesset meeting, 22 September 1982, Abraham D. Sofaer Collection, Box 8, Hoover Institution Archives.

Questions for Discussion

(1) When did the Palestinian demand for self-determination first get a global hearing in the post-1948 era?
(2) What role did the United States play in Arab-Israeli diplomacy during the Cold War?
(3) Examine the origins of the Palestine Liberation Organization (PLO). Why was it founded and how did it shape the Palestinian national struggle?
(4) Discuss the role of Arab states in addressing Palestinian political demands since 1967.
(5) To what extent did diplomatic initiatives between 1967–1991 limit Palestinian sovereignty?

References

Anziska, S. 2012. "A Preventable Massacre," *The New York Times*, 17 September.

Anziska, S. 2017. "Autonomy as State Prevention: The Palestinian Question after Camp David, 1979–1982." *Humanity: An International Journal of Human Rights, Humanitarianism, and Development*, 8:2, 287–310.

Anziska, S. 2018. *Preventing Palestine: A Political History from Camp David to Oslo*. Princeton, NJ: Princeton University Press.

Baumgarten, H. 2005. "The Three Faces/Phases of Palestinian Nationalism, 1948–2005." *Journal of Palestine Studies* 34:4, 25–48.

Chamberlin, P. 2012. *The Global Offensive: The United States, the Palestine Liberation Organization, and the Making of the Post Cold War Order*. New York: Oxford University Press.

Daigle, C. 2012. T*he Limits of Détente: the United States, the Soviet Union and the Arab-Israeli Conflict, 1969–73*. New Haven, CT: Yale University Press, 2012.

Elon, A. 1988. "From the Uprising," *The New York Review of Books*, 14 April.

Jensehaugen, J. 2014. "Blueprint for Arab-Israeli Peace? President Carter and the Brookings Report." *Diplomacy & Statecraft* 25:4, 492–508.

Khalidi, A. 2017. "Ripples of the 1967 War," *The Cairo Review*. Available at: www.thecairoreview.com/essays/ripples-of-the-1967-war/.

Khalidi, R. 2006. *The Iron Cage: The Story of the Palestinian Struggle for Statehood*. Boston: Beacon Press.

Khalidi, R. 2020. *The Hundred Years' War on Palestine: A History of Settler Colonial Conquest and Resistance*. London: Profile.

Khalil, O. 2016. "The Radical Crescent: The United States, the Palestine Liberation Organisation, and the Lebanese Civil War, 1973–1978." *Diplomacy and Statecraft* 27:3, 496–522.

Laqueur, W., and B. Rubin. 2008. *The Israel-Arab Reader: A Documentary History of the Middle East*. New York: Penguin.

Lockman, Z., and J. Beinin, eds. 1999. *Intifada: The Palestinian Uprising Against Israeli Occupation*. Cambridge, MA: South End Press.

Lukacs, Y. 1991. *The Israeli-Palestinian Conflict: A Documentary Record*, 2nd ed. Cambridge: Cambridge University Press.

Morris, B. 1993. *Israel's Border Wars: 1949–1956*. Oxford: Oxford University Press.

Muslih, M. 1990. *Towards Coexistence: An Analysis of the Resolutions of the Palestine National Council*. Washington, DC: Institute for Palestine Studies.

Nemchenok, V. V. 2009. "'These People Have an Irrevocable Right to Self-Government': United States Policy and the Palestinian Question, 1977–1979." *Diplomacy and Statecraft* 20:4, 595–618.

Pressman, J. 2013. "Explaining the Carter Administration's Israeli-Palestinian Solution." *Diplomatic History* 37:5, 1117–1147.

Quandt, W. B. 2005. *Peace Process: American Diplomacy and the Arab-Israeli Conflict since 1967*. Washington, DC: Brookings Institution Press.

Rabbani, M. 2012. "In Honor of Titans," *Jadaliyya*, 10 December. Available at: www.jadaliyya.com/Details/27588/In-Honor-of-Titans.

Rabie, M. 1995. *U.S.-PLO Dialogue: Secret Diplomacy and Conflict Resolution*. Gainesville, FL: University of Florida Press.

Raz, A. 2012. *The Bride and the Dowry: Israel, Jordan, and the Palestinians in the Aftermath of the June 1967 War*. New Haven, CT: Yale University Press.

Said, E. 1993. "The Morning After." *The London Review of Books*, 15.20–21. Available at: www.lrb.co.uk/the-paper/v15/n20/edward-said/the-morning-after.

Sayigh, Y. 1997. *Armed Struggle and the Search for State: The Palestinian National Movement 1949–1993*. Oxford: Clarendon Press.

Sela, A. 2014. "The PLO at Fifty: A Historical Perspective." *Contemporary Review of the Middle East* 1:3, 269–333.

Shlaim, A. 2007. *Lion of Jordan: The Life of King Hussein in War and Peace*. London: Allen Lane.

Tanner, H. 1977. "Why Not a Homeland or a State for the Palestinian Refugees?" *New York Times*, 10 April, E1.

Yaqub, S. 2008. "The Weight of Conquest: Henry Kissinger and the Arab–Israeli Conflict," in *Nixon in the World: American Foreign Relations, 1969–1977*, eds. F. Logevall and A. Preston. Oxford: Oxford University Press, 227–248.

9

THE OSLO PEACE PROCESS AND THE CAMP DAVID SUMMIT, 1993–2000

Ian J. Bickerton

The multiple agreements generally referred to as the Oslo Accords or the Oslo Peace Process began in September 1993 with the signing of the first Oslo Accord and ended in July 2000 with the failure of the Camp David II negotiations and the start of the Second *Intifada* in September 2000.[1] This chapter briefly outlines the course of events during these years and offers an explanation as to why the so-called "peace process" failed. From the outset, leaders of all the parties involved – Israelis, Palestinians, Syrians, Jordanians, Lebanese, regional Arab states, and the United States – were very familiar with the long-standing substantive issues at stake between Israel and its neighbours and the positions each of them held at this point in the conflict. There were essentially two separate, but related, "streams" of events: one involved Israel and the Palestine Liberation Organization (PLO); the other involved Israel and its neighbours, Syria, Jordan, and Lebanon. In addition, the United States and the Soviet Union were both, to differing degrees, observers to and participants in both these streams. The focus of this chapter is the relationship between Israel and the PLO.

The hotly contested, frequently violent, issues over which the participants fought included, for Palestinians, Israel's continued occupation of, and military presence in, the West Bank and Gaza Strip; the growth and disposition of Jewish settlements located therein; the future establishment of an independent Palestinian state; the status of Jerusalem, and the return of refugees. Israel's key concerns were ensuring secure and recognized boundaries, gaining recognition of its legitimacy by Palestinians and neighbouring Arab states – together with corresponding peace treaties – protecting its population from Palestinian attacks, validating the status of Jerusalem as its undivided capital, and preventing the return of Palestinian refugees.

Oslo I

On Monday, 13 September 1993, in a carefully staged event on the White House lawn in Washington, Israeli foreign minister Simon Peres and PLO representative Mahmoud Abbas signed the "Declaration of Principles on Interim Self-Government Arrangements" (DOP) for the Palestinians of the West Bank and Gaza Strip while United States president Bill Clinton, PLO chairman Yasser Arafat, and Israeli prime minister Yitzhak Rabin stood looking on. United States secretary of state Warren Christopher and Russian foreign minister Andrei Kozyrev added their signatures as witnesses. Arafat then extended his hand to Rabin, who

DOI: 10.4324/9780429027376-12

reluctantly shook hands with the man up until that time he had viewed as the leader of a terrorist organization. Clinton remarked: "A peace of the brave is within our reach."[2] This document was to become known as the Oslo Peace Accord, or Oslo I – the first of two such named accords.

Although tentative feelers had been initiated by Norwegian deputy foreign minister, Jan Egeland, in the summer of 1992, the first definite steps leading to this truly historic moment began in December 1992 in London, when PLO representatives Ahmed Qurie (Abu Ala) and Hassan Asfour met with Israeli academics Yair Hirschfeld and Ron Pundak to launch a diplomatic process they hoped would end the conflict between Israel and Palestinians. The first move in this direction had been taken in October 1991 following the end of the First Gulf War, when, pressed by the United States and the Soviet Union, leaders of Middle Eastern countries gathered in Madrid for a direct, face-to-face round of meetings in an ambitious attempt to explore options to end the regional conflict. The conference, co-chaired by President George H. W. Bush and Soviet President Mikhail Gorbachev, was attended by Israeli, Egyptian, Syrian, and Lebanese delegations, as well as a joint Jordanian-Palestinian delegation. For the first time, all the parties to the Arab-Israeli conflict had gathered to hold direct negotiations – a historically unprecedented event. Conversations were based on the "Framework for Peace in the Middle East" document signed at Camp David in 1978, using as starting points United Nations Resolutions 242 (essentially an exchange of land for peace formula) and 338 (calling for direct negotiations).

Two parallel tracks of negotiations followed. Bilateral talks were aimed at achieving peace treaties between Israel and its three neighbour states: Jordan, Lebanon and Syria, as well as with the Palestinians. A multilateral track addressed shared regional issues such as water, environment, arms control, refugees, and economic development. Although the conference was brief and little progress was made in bilateral and multilateral talks, the momentum created at Madrid was the catalyst that motivated a renewal of talks in December 1992.

December 1992 had been a particularly turbulent month in the region. On 1 December, Israeli troops in the Gaza Strip had shot at Palestinian demonstrators, killing a twelve-year-old boy and wounding forty demonstrators. In response, Hamas militants killed three Israeli reserve duty soldiers, and on 11 December they kidnapped a border policeman, Nissim Toledano, demanding that Israel release their jailed-for-life leader, Sheikh Ahmed Yassin. Two days later, after Hamas's deadline had expired, Toledano's body was found in the West Bank. In turn, Israel arrested and deported 415 Hamas and Islamic Jihad activists to Lebanon. As the month progressed, violence increased. It was in this context that diplomatic negotiations began, culminating in the signings in Washington nine months later.

On 9 September 1993, Arafat and Rabin exchanged letters. Arafat declared that the PLO "recognizes the right of the state of Israel to exist in peace and security[,]... renounces the use of terrorism and other acts of violence" and accepted United Nations Security Council Resolutions 242 and 338. In his letter of reply, Rabin stated that the government of Israel recognized "the PLO as the representative of the Palestinian people" and agreed to commence negotiations with the PLO "within the Middle East peace process." Four days later the Oslo I Accord was signed in Washington.[3] This was the first time in the conflict that an Israeli leader had negotiated directly with a Palestinian leader.

The primary aim of this accord was to establish a Palestinian Interim Self Government Authority (the Council) to be elected by Palestinians in the West Bank and Gaza Strip for a transitional period up to five years, which (in the third year) would enable negotiations to proceed between Israel and the PLO leading to a permanent status based upon the implementation of United Nations Security Council Resolutions 242 and 338. Faced with the increasing influence of Hamas among Palestinians, one of Rabin's objectives was to hand-over the responsibility for reducing anti-Israeli violence among the Palestinian population to the more moderate PLO, with the promise of handing over territory. Arafat saw an opportunity to increase his and the PLO's support among his frustrated people at the expense of Hamas by demonstrating that he could gain concessions from Israel. He also sought to gain legitimacy and much-needed financial support from the United States through his recognition of Israel and renunciation of violence.

Article V of the accord stipulated that the process would begin upon the withdrawal of Israeli military forces from Jericho and the Gaza Strip and the subsequent establishment of a Palestinian police force to maintain law and order. An annex to the DOP further stipulated that Israel would retain responsibility for external security and the internal security of Israeli settlements within the Gaza Strip and Jericho areas (including border crossings into the Gaza Strip and the Allenby/King Hussein Bridge crossing into Jordan). The status of Jerusalem and other outstanding issues would be left to the final status negotiations. It was anticipated that Israel would complete its troop redeployments and withdrawals by the middle of April 1994. Talks on the final status of the occupied territories were scheduled to begin by December 1995, with a permanent settlement to come into effect by December 1998. The principle of "early empowerment" would apply to the rest of the West Bank, where authority would be transferred from the Israeli military government and civil administration to "authorized Palestinians" who would take control of health, education and culture, welfare, tourism, and direct taxation. An interim agreement would specify the structure and powers of the Palestinian council that would replace the Israeli administration, and elections for the council were to be held no later than 13 July 1994. For the embattled Arafat, Gaza and Jericho provided some territory over which to preside right away. In accepting an immediate but partial solution, he gained recognition and resumed dialogue with the United States on 10 September 1993.

Israel made it clear that an undivided Jerusalem would continue to be its capital (the "eternal capital" of the Jewish people, as Rabin stated in his speech at the Washington signing), while the Palestinians made it equally clear that they would claim East Jerusalem as the capital of Palestine. It was not clear if Jewish settlers would cooperate with the Israeli government and what would happen to the settlements after the five-year period. It was also not clear whether Palestinian leaders would be able to deal with the many factions within their population. There were grave risks all around, for Israel, for Arafat, and for those supporting the accord, but the general consensus was that a continuation of the status quo was intolerable and that the risks for peace were worth taking.

Although both the Knesset and the newly established Palestine National Council ratified the September 1993 accord, and despite many months of almost non-stop negotiations to implement the DOP, violence did not decrease following the signing. Dissatisfied Israeli settlers were unwilling to countenance the surrender of any West Bank territory to the Palestinians. On 25 February 1994 an Israeli settler, Baruch Goldstein, a member of a small extremist group, the *Kach* party, entered the Ibrahimi Mosque within the Tomb of the Patriarchs in Hebron and shot and killed 29 Muslim worshippers. Several more died in the ensuing chaos. Arafat also seemed unable or unwilling to control Palestinian dissatisfied and extremist factions, In April, members of the Palestinian group Hamas, in revenge attacks, carried out suicide bombings on two buses within Israel, killing more than fifteen Israelis. Despite these setbacks, on 4 May 1994, Rabin and Arafat signed a 300-page agreement in Cairo, setting out the security, legal, civilian and economic details of terms agreed to relating to the Gaza Strip and Jericho. After considerable disputation – including a last-minute hastily-arrived-at solution over a map of the Jericho area – agreements were reached over the size of the Jericho area and the numbers of Israeli troops that would be redeployed and Palestinian police that would be permitted. Nine days later, on 13 May, the Israelis completed troop withdrawals from Jericho and from the Gaza Strip on 18 May. On 1 July, Arafat departed his headquarters in Tunis and entered the Gaza Strip to considerable fanfare, and on 5 July he entered Jericho and swore in members of the Palestine National Authority (PNA, later known as the Palestinian Authority or PA).

Lacking organization and underfunded, the PLO found creating an administrative structure difficult. They lacked the financial and personnel resources to take over the health welfare, judicial, and tax collection functions previously performed by the Israeli military government which, by December 1994, had been handed over to the PNA. Moreover, Israel refused to significantly reduce its military presence around border crossings and in East Jerusalem. The situation was further complicated by the fact that Israeli settlements and citizens in the Palestinian self-rule areas remained under Israeli legal jurisdiction. Furthermore, Arafat was reluctant to delegate power. It was also apparent that although some Hamas political leaders were willing to forgo violence, its military wing was not. Further suicide bus bombings took place in Ramat Gan in July and Jerusalem in August. Hamas militants claimed that the attacks were part of a new campaign intended to bring down the current Israeli government, and they vowed to continue their activities until the Israeli elections.

It was not only militant Islamists who wished to undermine efforts to keep the peace. Israeli settlers motivated by religious and nationalist ideologies became increasingly angry and disillusioned with Rabin's attitude toward them and toward their objective of retaining all of *Eretz Yisrael*. Rabin denounced the settlers as a "burden" on the army in its fight against radical Palestinians. "Settlements add nothing, absolutely nothing, to Israel's security," he said. "They are a liability rather than an asset." (Haberman, 1995.) Determined settlers had begun staking out claims to hilltops and lands they thought would be returned to the Palestinians, and they and their supporters blocked Israeli highways to protest the planned expansion of Palestinian self-rule. As the Israeli government continued to control demonstrators, sometimes harshly, the Likud and other right-wing opposition parties stepped up their rhetoric against Rabin and the peace process.

Some progress was made. Key differences were reached on security and division of control over land, and a compromise was reached on water allocation, with Israel officially recognizing Palestinian rights (in principle) to water sources in the West Bank. Israel agreed that Palestinians in East Jerusalem would be allowed to vote in Palestinian elections. The Palestinians accepted that an IDF presence would remain in the predominantly Arab city of Hebron near the five Jewish pockets of population separated by roads in the area, and that Israel would continue to be responsible for security at the Tomb of the Patriarchs and for the traffic route between the Jewish settlement of Kiryat Arba and Hebron. Palestinian police would cover the rest of the city. Rabin also made it clear that Israel had no intention of removing the Jewish settlers from around Hebron. In one of the many ironies of the conflict between Israel and Palestinians, even as violence escalated in late 1994 and early 1995 at the hands of those on both sides opposed to the so-called peace process, Arafat, Rabin, and Peres were awarded the Nobel Peace Prize in Oslo on 10 December 1994.

Oslo II or the Taba Accord

Talks continued through the first half of 1995 and, by September of that year, Israeli and PA negotiators had agreed on a number of civil and security issues. On 24 September – the eve of the Jewish new year – a second agreement between Israel and the PLO (almost 400 pages in length) was reached at Taba (an Egyptian resort on the Red Sea) and four days later, on

28 September, in a low-key ceremony in Washington, Arafat, Rabin, Peres, Egyptian president Hosni Mubarak, and Jordan's King Hussein signed a second Israeli-Palestinian Interim Agreement on the West Bank and Gaza Strip, quickly tagged Oslo II, or the Taba Accord, the aim of which was to set the stage for the final status talks to begin by May 1996.

This agreement broadened Palestinian self-government in the West Bank and paved the way for Palestinian elections. It established three areas in the West Bank (see Map 9.1): Area

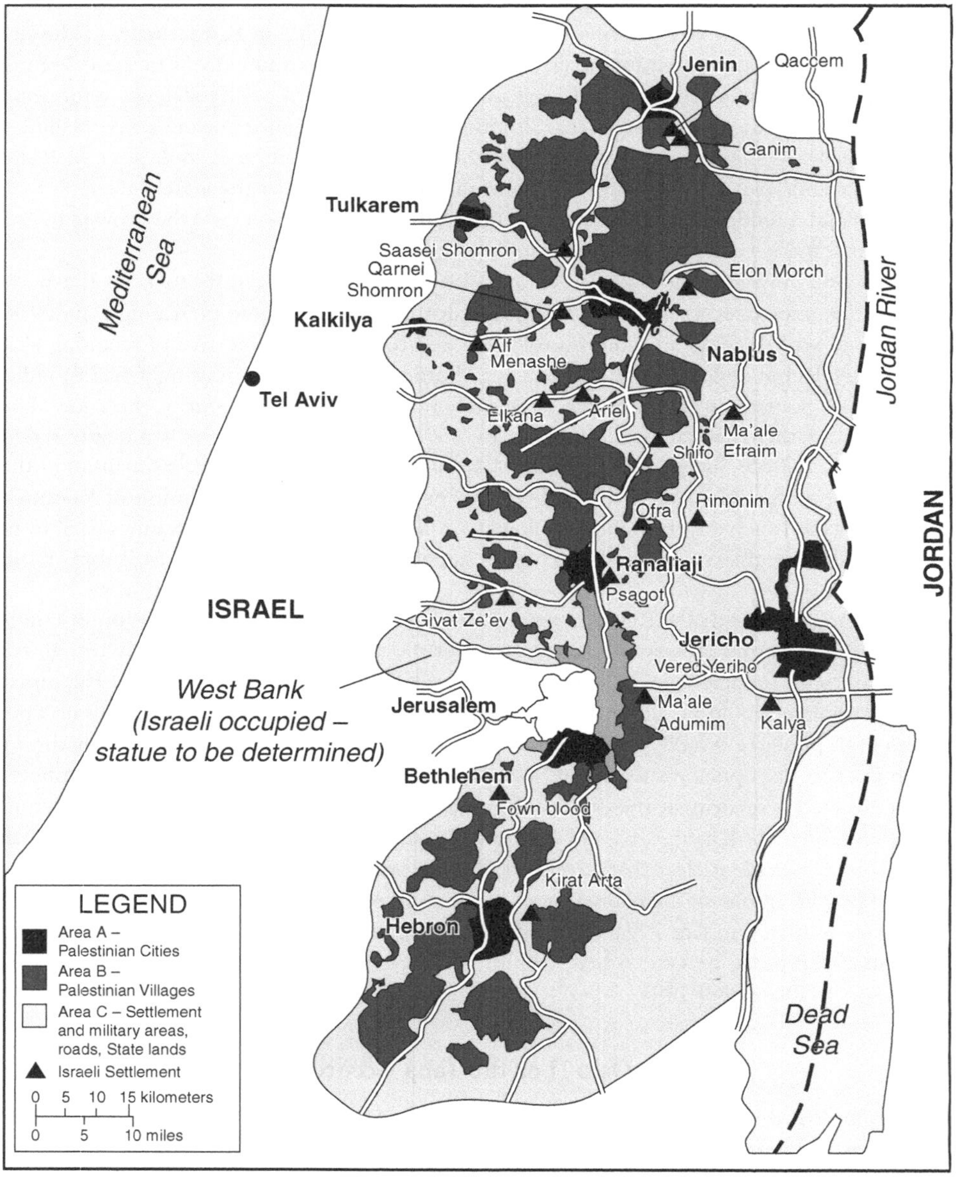

Map 9.1 Areas A, B, and C of the West Bank.

A, which would consist of territory to be placed under direct Palestinian control; Area B, jointly controlled territory, in which the Palestinians would exercise civil and police authority, but Israel would retain security responsibility; and Area C, territory in which Israel would have exclusive control. Accordingly, the agreement provided for the IDF to redeploy from the major cities of Jenin, Tulkarm, Qalqilya, Nablus, Bethlehem, and Ramallah (to be included in Area A), and from about 450 Palestinian villages and smaller communities (to be included in Area B). Areas A and B, consisting of approximately 3 per cent and 24 per cent respectively of the West Bank, contained the majority of the Palestinian population. Area C consisted of sparsely or unpopulated areas, Israeli military installations, and Jewish settlements. After the Israeli withdrawal from the populated areas, elections would be held for a Palestinian legislative council and the head of the council. In Hebron, the army would redeploy, but special security arrangements would apply. Further redeployments from parts of Area C would occur in three phases at six-month intervals and be completed within eighteen months from the inauguration of the council. Other provisions concerned prisoner releases, the allocation of water resources, and a commitment by the PLO to amend its Covenant within two months after the inauguration of the Palestine council. Israel began its pull-out from some smaller West Bank villages, and, on 25 October, the IDF began to withdraw from Jenin, the first large Arab population centre named in the agreement. On 24 April 1996, the PNC met in Gaza and voted 504 to 54 to cancel those parts of the Palestinian National Covenant that denied Israel's right to exist, and it set up a legal committee to redraft the Covenant.

Militants on both sides vowed to continue to use force to achieve their goals. On 4 November 1995, just a week after the signing of Oslo II, a Jewish zealot, Yigal Amir, assassinated Israeli prime minister Yitzhak Rabin, whom he viewed as a traitor. Amir, from the town of Herzliya and a law student at Bar-Ilan university, said that he was acting on God's orders to prevent the land of Israel from being turned over to the Palestinians. In yet another irony, Rabin's murder occurred just after he had addressed a huge peace rally in Kings of Israel Square in Tel Aviv, where over 100,000 Israelis had gathered to support the peace process and to sing a song of peace. The nation mourned his death and leaders from around the world, including a number from Arab states, attended his funeral on Mount Herzl (the burial place of Theodor Herzl, regarded as the founder of modern political Zionism) on 6 November. Yasser Arafat personally expressed his condolences to Rabin's widow, Leah Rabin.

Known as "Mr. Security," Rabin had been elected in June 1992 promising "peace with security." He had devoted his life to the defence of Israel. He had fought in the elite commando unit, Palmach, during Israel's war for independence; was army chief of staff in 1967; had authorized Israel's raid on Entebbe in 1976; and was defence minister during the Intifada. Jewish extremists, however, were infuriated by his "conversion," from a defence minister, who not so long ago had advocated breaking the bones of the young rock-throwers of the Intifada, to the prime minister who came to believe that Israel could not preserve its Jewish and democratic character while continuing to rule over almost two million Palestinians who detested Israeli occupation and sought to determine their own destiny.

Nevertheless, moderates on both sides saw no option but to continue with negotiations. Shimon Peres promised to continue the process, but the acting prime minister faced stiff opposition within the Knesset from Benjamin Netanyahu and the Likud party. Although polls suggested that around 70 per cent of Israelis were in support of the peace process, political divisions increased in the coming months. Following Israeli troop withdrawals from Tulkarm, Qalqilya, Nablus and Bethlehem in December 1995, elections were held on 20 January 1996, for the Palestinian Legislative Council. Arafat was overwhelmingly elected president with 88 per cent of the vote, in which between 70 and 80 per cent of Palestinians participated. The newly formed legislature convened for the first time on 7 March.

Sharm al-Sheikh

Efforts to maintain momentum in implementing the accords were hampered by deadly attacks and assassinations perpetrated by both sides. Seemingly intractable political rivalries within the ruling parties on both sides and highly emotional responses among the populations added to the complexity of maintaining a steady course. Militant members of Hamas and Islamic Jihad refused to accept the authority of the PLO and the premises of Oslo, while fundamentalist parties aligned to Likud rejected the approach of Rabin, Peres and the Labour Party. Israelis also soon realized that the military wing of Hamas was not ready to bend on their principles and even denied Jewish historical claims in Jerusalem. On 13 March 1996, in an attempt to break the cycle of terrorist violence, Egyptian president Hosni Mubarak convened at Sharm al-Sheikh a "summit of peacemakers" which, in addition to himself, Peres and Arafat, was attended by the presidents and prime ministers of the United States, Russia, France, and Turkey as well as leaders from over twenty nations. Although little concrete came out of the summit, it served as a reminder of the increasing economic and developmental cooperation between the nations of the Middle East, North Africa and Europe that had taken place since the first Oslo Accords of September 1993.

However, in March and April 1996, Israel's major security concern related to missile attacks on northern Israel by the Islamic militant group, *Hezbollah*, coming out of southern Lebanon. Israel's brief but bloody military incursion into southern Lebanon added to Arab and Palestinian distrust of Israel's long-term goals. It also provided the opportunity for Israeli opponents of the negotiations with the PLO to oust Peres and Labour. The victory of Likud party leader Benjamin Netanyahu in general elections called by Peres in May 1996, did not bode well for the peace process. On all the outstanding issues, Netanyahu was hard-line. In his campaign speeches he had stated he wanted peace, but it was not a peace that left the PLO with much, if any, room to move. Netanyahu formed a government with the support of the religious and ultra-nationalist parties. One of the first decisions of his government was to lift the freeze on additional West Bank settlements that had been in place since 1992. Netanyahu also offered financial incentives to settlers.

Wye River Plantation

Later, in mid-January 1997, at the insistence of newly elected United States president Bill Clinton, and the personal intervention of Jordan's King Hussein, Israel and the PLO signed an agreement that included the withdrawal/redeployment of Israeli troops from Hebron (scheduled for September 1997) by May 1998. Although it indicated that Netanyahu was prepared to accept the Oslo formula and Arafat's acceptance of a continuation of Jewish settlers in Hebron, in many ways it was a problematic agreement, in that 1,000 Israeli troops would remain to protect the 100 Israeli settlers who lived in the city of 160,000 Palestinians, and it did not address other ongoing issues.

Faced with increasing dissent within his coalition, Netanyahu resisted pressure from Washington to set a deadline for the withdrawal of Israel from the West Bank. Arafat entered Hebron on 19 January 1998 and soon after began talking about a unilateral declaration of a Palestinian state by May 1999. Under considerable pressure from Clinton and Secretary of State Madeleine Albright, Netanyahu and Arafat reluctantly agreed to meet at the Wye River plantation, Maryland, in mid-October 1998 in an effort to reach an acceptable land for peace agreement. Despite a last-minute intervention by King Hussein, the distrust and dislike of the two men for each other prevented any significant outcome from a week of negotiations.

The resulting Wye River (interim) memorandum signed in Washington on 23 October 1998 detailed minor adjustments agreed to on areas and times for Israeli withdrawals and contained a commitment by Israel to release a limited number of non-Hamas Palestinian prisoners. Israel insisted upon proof that the Palestine National Covenant had been amended to nullify articles in the calling for the destruction of Israel. In clauses dealing with security, limitations were placed on the size and activities of Palestinian forces. As had been the case with previous agreements, the most critical issues were deferred. And, as had also been the case previously, radicals and rejectionist groups on both sides regarded the memorandum as a betrayal of their side. The Knesset approved the Wye agreement on 17 November and shortly thereafter Israel handed over pockets of the West Bank to Palestinian control. On 14 December the PNC, meeting in Gaza with Clinton in attendance, revoked the clauses of the Covenant offensive to Israel.

The victory of a Labour party coalition led by highly decorated former general Ehud Barak in Israeli general elections in June seemed to promise new momentum in the peace process. At first, there was little change in the positions of Israelis and Palestinians toward each other. Even as some Israeli West Bank outposts were dismantled, more settlements were expanded, and militant Palestinian groups threatened violence to sabotage existing agreements. Nevertheless, Arafat and Barak established a more cooperative and functional relationship than had existed during the Netanyahu regime.

For the first five months of 2000, Israel was preoccupied with the process of withdrawing its 1,200 troops from Southern Lebanon, where they had been in occupation since 1982, and it was not until the end of May that serious negotiations began again between Israel and the Palestinians. Israeli and Palestinian negotiators met in Jericho to discuss the release of 1,650 Palestinian prisoners held in Israeli jails, and Israel agreed to some concessions although there was no immediate resolution of this issue. On 5 June United States Secretary of State Madelaine Albright travelled to the Middle East and met with Barak and Arafat and Syrian and Egyptian officials in Cairo. Barak intimated that he could consider relinquishing over 90 per cent of the West Bank, including at least part of the Jordan River Valley, to the Palestinians, and also would consider granting them municipal authority over part of Jerusalem. Contrary to the views espoused by his predecessors, Barak did not believe that territorial concessions were a major threat to Israel's future. He regarded the Jewish state as the strongest country in the region militarily, strategically. and economically and, because it enjoyed the support of the United States, also diplomatically. News of Barak's thinking prompted a majority of the Knesset to support a move to dissolve the government.

Events continued with a logic of their own. A frustrated Arafat renewed his earlier threats of a unilateral declaration of statehood and warned that violence could erupt if the 13 September 2000 deadline for a final peace agreement was not met. Such a unilateral declaration of statehood would have almost certainly led to Israeli annexations of large areas of the West Bank followed by an inevitable violent reaction.

Camp David II, 2000

Confronted by these developments, on 5 July 2000, President Clinton announced that he would invite Barak and Arafat to Camp David for a summit to negotiate a framework agreement for a final peace settlement. In Israel, Barak's religious and nationalist coalition parties immediately defected, leaving him with a minority government of 42 of 120 members. He narrowly escaped a no-confidence vote in the Knesset. Arafat faced similar pressures not to accept significant concessions from Israel that fell short of declared Palestinian positions on Jerusalem and the return of refugees.

On 11 July, Clinton, Arafat and Barak gathered at Camp David to begin talks. The negotiations lasted 15 days. Barak made what most Israelis considered a generous offer for a final agreement on three contentious issues: the return of Palestinian refugees, the borders of a future Palestinian state, and the disposition of the Israeli settlements. Israel agreed to accept a limited number of refugees, but would not agree to the principle of any unlimited Palestinian "right of return." Palestinian negotiators reluctantly accepted this formula. There was more or less agreement on Israeli annexations in the West Bank, which would incorporate 80 per cent of all Israeli settlers in return for the return of a roughly equivalent amount of land inside pre-1967 Israel.

However, the issue of Jerusalem – especially the status of Temple Mount/Haram al-Sharif – remained intractable. The United States put forward the notion of a form of shared sovereignty. Israel interpreted this as a proposal for Palestinian sovereignty over most outlying Arab neighbourhoods in East Jerusalem in return for Israeli annexation of the Jewish communities surrounding the city. Palestinians would have limited authority over Arab neighbourhoods in the Old City under Israeli military control, and continued control over the Al Aqsa Mosque, and guaranteed free access to all Muslim and Christian holy places. The PLO countered with a demand for Palestinian sovereignty over all of East Jerusalem, with Israeli control of the Jewish quarter and safe passage to the holy site of the Western Wall. This was totally unacceptable to Israel. There was nowhere to go. On 25 July, with no solution in sight, the conference ended, and both men returned home.

The talks collapsed because neither Barak nor Arafat would, or indeed could, compromise over the issue of Jerusalem. Barak's endangered minority government would have fallen had he agreed to a Jerusalem partitioned or divided in any way, and had Arafat approved anything less than Palestinian sovereignty over all of East Jerusalem his leadership and authority would have been challenged by Hamas.

Given the stalemate and collapse of the Camp David talks and the fractured politics of both sides, the extremists took control and resorted once again to violence. In late September 2000 the Second Intifada erupted. In December 2000 Clinton in a desperate last-minute effort to salvage something from the debris left by the failed talks of the past year, put forward more proposals to Barak and Arafat (termed the Clinton parameters) who met at Bolling Air Force Base in Washington DC. The two agreed to meet again in the new year. However, at their meeting at the Egyptian resort town of Taba in late January 2001, the two men and their teams failed to find sufficient common ground on the main issues that had divided them from the beginning; the return of Palestinian refugees, Israeli security, the division of territory, and Jerusalem.

Conclusion: The War of Narratives

The Oslo-Camp David process produced neither a peace agreement nor a Palestinian state. Despite what seemed to be a promising step toward the implementation of peace between Israel and the Palestinians, from the outset there was little likelihood that the Oslo Accords would bring about a peaceful resolution of the conflict. There can be little doubt that Israel was the major beneficiary of the Oslo Accords, both in terms of the actual principles and provisions set out, and as decisions on vital matters were postponed. In addition, the government of Israel remained the major arbiter as to whether or not the circumstances were such that the steps agreed to could or should be implemented. Israeli leaders and Arafat had very different agendas. Although both sides recognized that the notion of partition was implicit in the negotiations, they interpreted the two interim agreements quite differently. Palestinians believed the DOP promised them a state in all but name, while the-Israelis regarded Palestinian self-rule in much narrower terms, as indicating merely "autonomy" rather than self-government. Rabin made it clear that he did not envisage a future independent Palestinian state. On 5 October 1995, he told the Knesset that the Palestinian political entity he envisaged alongside Israel, west of the Jordan River, would be "less than a state and will independently manage the lives of the Palestinians under its rule."[4] It was equally clear that, as leader of the PLO, Arafat could not accept anything less than full sovereignty. Nor did Rabin have any intention of relinquishing or sharing control of Jerusalem with the Palestinians. And Israeli settlers had no intention of giving up what they regarded as ancestral Israeli territory to Palestinian control. Foreign Minister Peres noted that under the accord, Israel would maintain control of 73 per cent of the land, 80 per cent of the water, and 97 per cent of the security arrangements – a statement that only intensified Palestinian anxiety. These were irreconcilable differences.

At the time Oslo I was signed there were over two hundred Israeli settlements situated throughout the West Bank and Gaza Strip, many of them located on hills, promontories and other strategic points. The largest were designed for permanence. They were connected to Israel by an independent system of roads, creating disabling discontinuities between population centres of Palestinians. The total area of the occupied territories in the West Bank controlled by Israel was in the vicinity of 55 per cent. Greater Jerusalem alone, annexed by Israel, comprised at least 25 per cent of the total amount. Encouraged by successive Israeli administrations, by 1993 the number of Israeli settlers in the West Bank had risen from around 12,500 in 1980 to over 116,000. In the Gaza Strip, where around 4,800 settlers lived among the one million Palestinian inhabitants, there were three settlements in the north, two in the middle and thirteen in the region along the coast south of Khan Yunis toward the Egyptian border. These settlements constituted at least 30 per cent of the Strip. In addition, Israel had tapped into all the aquifers on the West Bank and used about 80 per cent of the water there for the settlements and for Israel proper.

In terms of internal security, during a period of increasingly harsh Israeli military occupation, the PLO agreed to collaborate with Israeli security forces. The Oslo process made the Palestinians responsible for policing themselves in the West Bank, which led to vast improvements in Israeli security from terrorism at little cost to Israel. The PLO thus became Israel's enforcer, an unsatisfactory situation for most Palestinians. The idea was that this arrangement would deter Palestinians from demonstrating against the presence of the Israelis, whose troops, numbering around 15,000, were not withdrawing, simply redeploying. In any event, Israeli settlers remained under Israel's jurisdiction. Economically, the Oslo arrangement served Israel's interests: the Palestinian Authority's foreign donors subsidized government services on the West Bank, relieving Israel of the obligation to provide these services. However, Palestinians remained dependent upon Israeli goods, food, fuel, and electricity. The accords gave the Palestinian Authority responsibility for providing services like sanitation and hospitals that would otherwise cost Israel, as the occupying power, hundreds of millions of dollars. The situation was not helped by Arafat's refusal to share or delegate power, to say nothing of the financial assets he alone controlled and siphoned off to buy loyalty and build militias. However, the accords did lead to the lasting substantive achievement of the establishment of the Palestinian Authority as an interim self-government. Although widely accused of corruption and increasingly autocratic, the PA provided basic services and created jobs for roughly a quarter of the work force.

The Oslo-Camp David II peace process, like most aspects of the conflict has, not surprisingly, become a rhetorical battleground between the two protagonists. There have been countless books and articles on the events of this period by scholarly analysts, ex-negotiators, lobbyists, and partisans of both sides. Most, of course, are self-serving and blame the other side for failure to reach the goals set out in the Oslo Accords. The differing accounts developed into a full-scale historiographical "war." The absence of archival material presents a further difficulty in evaluating the accuracy of the various versions. Truth is elusive – some might say even imaginary – and given the differences of opinion expressed about the events under consideration, separating reality from fantasy is a near impossible task.

Initially, both sides celebrated the September 1993 DOP – at least publicly. Yitzhak Rabin and Shimon Peres applauded Oslo. Peres believed that in signing the Oslo Accords, Arafat and the PLO had become partners with Israel in a journey toward peace. The process, he stated, had transformed Arafat from the most hated person in Israel into a partner that Israeli leaders could sit with, and made him acceptable to the people (Eisenberg and Caplan 2010, 168, see also 357). Israeli negotiator Yossi Beilin was also confident it was possible to negotiate with Arafat. Oxford historian Avi Shlaim optimistically described the DOP as a triumph of pragmatism over ideology. In his view, both sides had addressed practical issues relating to the division of the land. And Israeli academic Ron Pundak, who had played an important role in initiating the negotiations, wrote that the Oslo process created an Israeli-Palestinian consensus on a two-state solution that would lay the foundation for a comprehensive and lasting peace (Eisenberg and Caplan 2010, 180, 183). Not all Israelis agreed, of course. There were many who believed Arafat and the PLO harboured the desire to destroy Israel and would continue to use violence and terrorism to achieve their goals. They cited the creation and arming of a Palestinian police force permitted by the accords as an example of a dangerous betrayal (Karsh 2004).

Palestinians also celebrated the DOP. Ahmed Qurie (Abu Ala) wrote that the Oslo agreement "added a new dimension to the geographic, demographic, and political scene in the region. It was, in fact, nothing less than the cornerstone of a new regional political climate" (Qurie 2006, 1). Mahmoud Abbas also believed that the accords had "set out people on the road to independence and glory" (Qurie 2006, 4). But the narratives soon moved beyond optimism and, as the reality of the facts on the ground unfolded, it soon became obvious that the two sides were not singing from the same songbook. On the very month the accords were signed, noted Jerusalem-born Palestinian-American scholar Edward Said, a prominent independent member of the Palestine National Council from 1977 until his resignation in 1991. Said wrote the first of a series of articles published throughout the Arab world and (in 1996) in the United States. In these articles, he launched a scathing attack on the recently signed accords and the actions of Yasser Arafat.

In Said's view (1996, 74–84), Arafat had capitulated to all Israel's demands. Israel had gained recognition, legitimacy and acceptance from the PLO without conceding any sovereignty over Arab land, including annexed East Jerusalem. Said was furious that the right of Palestinians to self-determination, future sovereignty, the return of refugees, and control of Jerusalem had been negotiated away in return merely for limited autonomy, early empowerment of the Palestinian people, and recognition of the PLO and Arafat as its chairman. In the meantime, Said argued, Israel would remain in control of the land, water, overall security and foreign affairs in the "autonomous" areas. In another essay (1996, 7–20) he described the agreement as essentially a Palestinian surrender, a Palestinian Versailles. He contended that in return for Israel's recognition of the PLO, by accepting that questions of land and sovereignty be postponed till "final Status negotiations," Arafat, in effect, had discounted the unilateral and internationally acknowledged Palestinian claim to the West Bank and Gaza Strip. Those areas had subsequently become "disputed territories.' Said quoted the remarks of the Israeli "dove" Amos Oz, who reportedly told the BBC, that the agreement was "the second biggest victory in the history of Zionism (1996, 8)."

Following the failure of the Camp David II negotiations (and the January 2001 Taba talks), the opposing narratives focused on two questions: What did Israel offer the Palestinians? And what was the PLO response? On 8 July 2001, the *New York Times* published an article by Robert Malley, titled "Fictions About the Failure at Camp David." Malley had been special assistant to the president for Arab-Israeli Affairs and director for Near East and South Asian Affairs on the National Security Council staff from September 1998 to January 2001, and had participated as an American delegate in the July 2000 Camp David talks. His purpose was to expose what he called "dangerous myths" about the Camp David summit. The first myth, Malley stated, was that Camp David was "a test that Mr. Barak passed and Mr. Arafat failed." Malley noted that the prevailing narrative in the United States asserted that the Palestinians were offered close to 99 per cent of their dreams, but rejected the offer and chose to hold out for more. The second myth Malley identified was that the Palestinians did not present any concession of their own. Instead, they adopted "a no-compromise attitude that unmasked their unwillingness to live peacefully with a Jewish state by their side." Malley argued that both these claims were simply not true (Malley 2001).

Three weeks later, on 24 July 2001, Lee Hockstader, in an opinion piece in the *Washington Post*, "A Different take on Camp David Collapse," supported Malley's position, reporting that Ahmed Qurie, the Palestinians' top negotiator at Camp David had recently told a group of journalists that "The biggest lie of the last three decades is … that [then-Israeli prime minister Ehud] Barak offered everything [and] the Palestinians refused everything." Qurie further insisted that the Palestinians, who regarded their demands for refugee rights and the return of the Israeli-occupied West Bank and Gaza Strip as firmly rooted in United Nations resolutions, were under no obligation to respond to Israel's ideas with counter offers. He added that Israel's insistence on retaining control of Palestinian border crossings to Egypt and Jordan made a mockery of Palestinian sovereignty. Finally, Qurie stated, Israel never clarified any plan to share Jerusalem with the Palestinians, displaying neither documents nor maps but instead floating vague proposals through the American mediators (Hockstader 2001).

Two days later, on 26 July 2001, Deborah Sontag responded with an article "Quest for Mideast Peace: How and Why it Failed," also published by the *New York Times* (Sontag 2001). Sontag restated the claim that Barak generously offered Arafat everything he wished for, but the Palestinian leader refused the offer, resorting instead to the path of violence. Sontag concluded that Arafat's actions revealed that the Israeli-Palestinian conflict was insoluble. Malley, together with Palestinian advisor Hussein Agha, then wrote an extended reply, "Camp David: The Tragedy of Errors," in the *New York Review of Books,* on 9 August 2001. They argued that the Palestinians did not regard Israel's offer as generous, or, indeed, as an offer at all, and believed both Israel and the United States were seeking to blame Arafat for their own unwillingness to make realistic concessions to the PLO (Malley and Agha 2001a).

Dennis Ross, who headed the United States negotiating team at Camp David, joined the debate on 20 October 2001 with a letter to the editors of the *New York Review of Books* (NYRB). To Ross, the issue was, "[D]id Yasser Arafat respond at any point – not only at Camp David – to possibilities to end this conflict when they presented themselves? Any objective appraisal would have to conclude he did not." Ross acknowledged, "History may not have been kind or fair to the Palestinians. They have suffered and been betrayed by others. They are, surely, the weakest player with the fewest cards to play." But, he argued, the major problem they faced was their inability to recognize their own failures and to always blame others for their misfortunes. This, Ross asserted, was why there was no permanent status deal concluded at Camp David. Ross was joined in these views in an accompanying letter by Gidi Grinstein of the John F. Kennedy School at Harvard University. Grinstein added the idea that although Arafat was the greater offender, both leaders were frustrated by their respective domestic political restraints. The same issue of the NYRB contained a somewhat conciliatory reply from Malley and Agha, suggesting that it was somewhat unrealistic to expect all the problems surrounding a final settlement deal could be reached in a couple of weeks of negotiating at Camp David (Malley and Agha 2001b).

The battle for public opinion continued. Eight months later, on 15 March 2002, Saul Singer, editorial editor and columnist at the *Jerusalem Post,* published a long piece for the Jerusalem Center for Public Affairs, "Whose Fault Was the Failure of Camp David" analysing these two narratives. Singer acknowledged that the principals involved – Ehud Barak, Bill Clinton, and Yasser Arafat – had not given comprehensive, blow-by-blow accounts of what happened at Camp David, but three of the top-tier negotiators – Israeli foreign minister Shlomo Ben Ami, United States mediator Dennis Ross, and Palestinian negotiator Mahmoud Abbas (Abu Mazen) – had all given somewhat detailed accounts. Not surprisingly, Singer concluded that Barak was flexible in his negotiating stance, and Arafat was the intransigent one, refusing to negotiate. To support this view, Singer quoted Clinton's reported statement to Arafat: "If the Israelis can make compromises and you can't, I should go home. You have been here fourteen days and said no to everything" (Singer 2002).

The debate surrounding responsibility for the failure at Camp David reached new levels in late June 2002 when it was joined by Ehud Barak himself who, supported by noted Israeli historian Benny Morris, collaborated with a vitriolic rebuttal to Malley and Agha published in the 27 June 2002 issue of the *NYRB* attacking Arafat and the Palestinian "terroristic onslaught" (Barak and Morris 2002). This was a joint article in response to Malley and Agha following an interview of Barak by Morris in the 13 June 2002 issue of the NYRB. Morris and Barak describe the arguments of Malley and Agha as fantasy and propaganda. They describe Arafat as a serial liar and urge Western leaders "to treat Arafat and his ilk in the Palestinian camp as the vicious, untrustworthy, unacceptable reprobates and recidivists that they are." Malley and Agha replied in equally hostile terms describing Morris and Barak as engaging in "hollow demagoguery" and accused Barak through his words and actions of setting in motion "the process of delegitimizing the Palestinians and the peace process" (Malley and Agha 2002).

The rhetorical battle between pro-Israeli and Pro-Palestinians commentators over the failure of the Oslo Peace Process and Camp David has continued into the present. Among the recent analyses that discuss the implications of the Oslo process for both sides is that of Efraim Karsh, director of the conservative think tank, the Begin-Sadat Centre of Strategic Studies at Bar Ilan University. In a lengthy critique of the Oslo Accords titled "The Oslo Disaster," he asserted that the Oslo diplomatic process was "the starkest strategic blunder in Israel's history" and was "one of the worst calamities ever to have afflicted Israelis and Palestinians." The Oslo "peace process," he claimed, substantially worsened the position of both parties and made the prospects for peace and reconciliation ever more remote (Karsh 2016). Karsh had been a longtime critic of Yasser Arafat (Karsh 2004).

As far as Israel is concerned, Karsh argued that the Oslo Accords "led to establishment of an ineradicable terror entity on Israel's doorstep, deepened Israel's internal cleavages, destabilized its political system, and weakened its international standing." In strategic and military terms, he maintained that the Oslo Accords allowed the PLO to achieve its strategic vision of transforming the West Bank and the Gaza Strip into terror hotbeds that would disrupt Israel's way of life, and that politically and diplomatically they transformed the PLO (and, to a lesser extent, Hamas) into an internationally accepted political actor that remained committed to Israel's destruction. Even worse in Karsh's view was that the Jewish state was still subject to international opprobrium for what he called Israel's "non-existent occupation." In addition, Oslo radicalized Israel's Arab minority, nipping in the bud its decades-long "Israelization" process and, no less importantly, making Israeli politics captive to the vicissitudes of Palestinian-Israeli relations, with the PLO and the militant groups becoming the effective arbiters of Israel's political discourse and electoral process (Karsh 2016).

Karsh maintained that Oslo was also a disaster for West Bank and Gaza Palestinians. It brought about subjugation to a corrupt and repressive PLO and eventually a Hamas regime in the Gaza: "These regimes reversed the hesitant advent of civil society in these territories, shattered their socioeconomic well-being, and made the prospects for peace and reconciliation with Israel ever more remote." Palestinian leadership saw the accords not as a pathway to a two-state solution but to the subversion of the State of Israel. He blamed the decades of "dispersal and statelessness" experienced by the Palestinian population on the PLO/PA leadership's zero-sum approach to Israel, and the predication of Palestinian national identity on hatred of the "other," rather than on a distinct shared legacy (Karsh 2016).

Many contemporary Palestinian commentators also believe that the Oslo agreements were a catastrophe for the Palestinian people. Arafat dominated Palestinian politics for more than a quarter of a century and was responsible for the revitalization of the Palestinian cause, but by the end of his life in 2004 many Palestinians held him responsible for the failures of the Oslo Accords. Rashid Khalidi, for example, argued that Arafat made a mistake when he agreed to defer talks on core issues of the conflict – permanent borders, the fate of the Palestinian refugees and the Palestinian demand for a capital in Jerusalem – until final-status negotiations (Khalidi 2006, 141–145). This echoes the views expressed at the time by PLO legal advisor Raja Shehadeh (1997), leading Palestinian activist and politician Hanan Ashrawi (1995) and other participants in the process. Arafat should have insisted, they argue, upon an explicit clause in the interim agreements freezing further Israeli settlement expansion where the Palestinians envisaged their state. The accords allowed Israel to postpone, seemingly indefinitely, a broader withdrawal from the West Bank. And, they conclude, the PLO chairman miscalculated when he bargained away recognition of the state of Israel's right to exist and a renunciation of violence for little more than Israeli recognition of the Palestine Liberation Organization as the legitimate representative of the Palestinian people.

Palestinian Authority officials contend that Israel achieved virtually total control over the lives of Palestinians, and that Israeli occupation obstructed Palestinian economic growth and steps toward democracy (Khalidi 2006, 164–172). But the Authority's supporters argue that for all its faults, the Authority improved life for most Palestinians. Despite the failure of PA leadership, and despite its nepotism and corruption, many Palestinians accepted the Authority as the least-bad option open to them. Propped up with around $500 million a year in foreign aid, about 12 per cent of its budget, the Authority was the biggest Palestinian employer, providing livelihoods for around 150,000 workers and their dependents, roughly a quarter of the population. After the chaos of two uprisings, many credited it with restoring law and order.

The reality is that both sides failed to pursue or engage meaningfully in peace talks, thereby undermining the fragile agreements. Both sides deeply distrusted the other and neither was prepared to move on their "red line" issues – and they regarded most of the issues as red lines. Furthermore, both were restricted and restrained by divisive internal political divisions. Pressed by right-wing extremists and settlers, successive Israeli governments halted agreed-upon withdrawals from occupied territory, leaving itself in full control of more than 60 per cent of the West Bank. Settlements were expanded, more land was seized, further demoralizing its Palestinian neighbours. The PA was unable to effectively rule the Gaza Strip, or to contain challenges from militant factions after Israel redeployed its troops from the area in 1996 as part of the Gaza-Jericho Accord.

Both sides resorted to violence. The Second Intifada, which began in September 2000 and did not subside until September 2005, caused immense havoc to both sides and destroyed any hope for a peaceful resolution anytime soon. Israel and the United States had vainly hoped that Arafat would prove at least a capable strongman, only to watch as he failed to suppress violence by Hamas and other militant factions. As far as Israelis were concerned, Arafat did not do enough to stop terror, either because he could not, or because he did not see it as important enough at the time. Israel's decision in June 2001 to begin construction of what it called a security barrier/wall entrenched some land grabs. The wall bred resentment, and – in achieving the desired goal of reducing terrorist attacks – allowed Israelis to largely ignore the desperate situation of the Palestinians caused by Israel's occupation. In 2002, Israel reinvaded the West Bank cities, destroying much the Palestinian Authority had built. In addition, when Israel withdrew the last Jewish settlers from Gaza in 2005, a showdown between the Fatah and Hamas factions resulted in a Hamas takeover in 2007. Whatever the justification, Palestinian terrorism substantially contributed to crippling the peace process. In Israel, the peace camp that backed Oslo withered from waves of Palestinian violence.

The on-again, off-again approach of the United States had little real influence over the outcome. Despite claiming to be an "honest broker," the United States sought to provide support for Israel's policies without alienating neighbouring moderate Arab states in the region. Accordingly, between 1973 and 1993, following Israel's lead, the United States had refused to acknowledge, or to negotiate with, the Palestine Liberation Organization until it recognized Israel, thereby depriving Palestinians of any effective negotiating voice. That policy, together with United States unwillingness throughout the negotiations to sympathetically consider the Arab position on the Israeli occupation of the territories captured in 1967, contributed significantly to the failure of the peace talks.

Finally, the accords did not succeed in countering Islamic extremism. The rise of Islamic militancy throughout the Middle East has become a major threat not only to Israel but also to secular and moderate Arab governments, including the Palestinian Authority. The Palestinian people remain stateless, their prospects as remote as ever. In 2019, most Israelis believe that a Palestinian state would be a threat to Israel's security and/or identity. Israel's dominant right-wing coalition parties debate whether merely to manage the occupation in perpetuity or to declare victory and annex much of the West Bank. The number of Israeli settlers there, in what much of the world considers a violation of international law, has tripled, to about 400,000. Another 200,000 live in Israeli-annexed East Jerusalem, which the Palestinians claim as their future capital. The Palestinian body politic is divided, perhaps irrevocably, between the Palestinian Authority, led by President Mahmoud Abbas and his Fatah faction, on the West Bank, and the Islamic militant group Hamas in the Gaza Strip. Efforts to unify the two bodies keep failing. In office since 2005, Abbas is increasingly repressive of dissent, ruling his dwindling domain by decree.

The accords did not fail solely because the negotiators could not reach agreement. Admittedly, the disparity in the balance of power between the two parties presented an almost insurmountable obstacle for the diplomats to overcome – assuming they genuinely wished to do so. The accords failed because "facts on the ground" derailed the arrangements reached around the conference tables. These "facts" were created by those on both sides who were committed to the use of armed force rather than relying on the success of their quietly spoken diplomats. The extremist settlers and religious nationalists on the Israeli side, and Islamic religious extremists on the Palestinian side cared little for peace. Ultimately, the central question is whether or not Israeli and/or PLO leaders were complicit in creating, or allowing, the circumstances to develop they knew would sabotage the diplomatic agreements reached. In other words, to what extent were they engaged in an elaborate game of smoke and mirrors? In the words of Zhou Enlai: "It is too soon to say."

Notes

1 The chronological narrative of this chapter draws from chapters 10–12 of I. Bickerton and C. Klausner, 2018, *A History of the Arab-Israeli Conflict*, 8th ed. London: Routledge, 2018. I am greatly indebted to Carla.

2 For the full text of President Clinton's speech, see: www.jewishvirtuallibrary.org/president-clinton-speech-at-the-signing-ceremony-for-the-israeli-palestinian-declaration-of-principles-september-1993.

3 For the texts of these documents and other documents cited in this chapter see the relevant chapters in Bickerton and Klausner, *A History of the Arab-Israeli Conflict*.

4 For the full text of Rabin's speech, see: https://mfa.gov.il/mfa/mfa-archive/1995/pages/pm%20rabin%20in%20knesset-%20ratification%20of%20interim%20agree.aspx.

Recommended Readings

In addition to the works cited in this chapter, for a comprehensive and detailed study on this topic, consult L. Z. Eisenberg and N. Caplan, 2010, *Negotiating Arab-Israeli Peace: Patterns, Problems, Possibilities*, 2nd ed. Bloomington, IN: Indiana University Press, 2010. The bibliographic endnotes in this volume contain not only most published sources but also extensive comments on them. Another very useful and thorough exploration of the peace process is D. C. Kurtzer, et al., 2017, eds., *The Peace Puzzle: America's Quest for Arab-Israeli Peace, 1989–2011*, Ithaca: Cornell University Press.

Questions for Discussion

(1) To what extent is Article 1 of the Israel-PLO Declaration of Principles: " to establish a Palestinian Interim Self Government Authority," a significant change from previous Israeli policy?

(2) Discuss the reason why such issues as Jerusalem, refugees, settlements, security arrangements, and borders were not discussed in the Declaration of Principles or the Oslo Accords and held over for five years.

(3) Evaluate the impacts of Israeli and Palestinian domestic politics on the outcome of the peace process.

(4) In your considered judgement, did the parties engaged in what we call the Oslo Peace Process really give peace a chance? Explain in detail, giving specific examples, how and why you reached your conclusion.

(5) "The historian is, we are told, not a judge but a detective; he/she provides the evidence, and the reader ... can form what moral conclusions he/she likes" (Isaiah Berlin). What do you think of this proposition? Discuss the interpretation of historian of the Oslo Peace Process you have read in relation to this statement, and indicate the conclusions you have reached, and explain why others might disagree with you.

References

Ashrawi, H. 1995. *This Side of Peace: A Personal Account*. New York: Simon and Schuster.

Barak, E., and B. Morris. 2002. "Camp David and After – Continued." *The New York Review of Books*, 27 June, 46–49.

Eisenberg, L. Z., and N. Caplan. 2010. *Negotiating Arab-Israeli Peace, Patterns, Problems, Possibilities*, 2nd ed. Bloomington, IN: Indiana University Press.
Haberman, C. 1995. "Rabin Renews Denunciation of Settlers as 'Burden.'" *New York Times*, 28 January, 3.
Hockstader, L. 2001. "A Different Take on Camp David Collapse." *Washington Post*, 24 July, 24.
Karsh, E. 2004. *Arafat's War: The Man and His Battle for Israeli Conquest*. New York: Grove Press.
Karsh, E. 2016. "The Oslo Disaster." *Mideast Security and Policy Studies No. 123*, Begin-Sadat Centre of Strategic Studies, Tel Aviv, 4 September, 1–21.
Khalidi, R. 2006. *The Iron Cage: The Story of the Palestinian Struggle for Statehood*. Boston: Beacon Press.
Kurtzer, D. C., et al., eds. 2013. *The Peace Puzzle: America's Quest for Arab-Israeli Peace, 1989–2011*. Ithaca, NY: Cornell University Press.
Malley, R. 2001. "Fictions about the Failures at Camp David." *New York Times*, 8 July, 11.
Malley, R., and H. Agha. 2001a. "Camp David: The Tragedy of Errors." *The New York Review of Books*, 9 August, 59–65.
Malley, R., and H. Agha. 2001b. "A Reply." *The New York Review of Books*, 20 October. Available at: www.nybooks.com/articles/2002/06/13/camp-david-and-after-an-exchange-2-a-reply-to-ehud/.
Malley, R., and H. Agha. 2002. "Camp David and After: An Exchange (2. A Reply to Ehud Barak)." *The New York Review of Books*, 27 June. Available at: www.nybooks.com/articles/2001/09/20/camp-david-an-exchange/.
Qurie, A. 2006. *From Oslo to Jerusalem; The Palestinian Story of the Secret Negotiations*. London: I. B. Tauris.
Ross, D. 2001. "Camp David: An Exchange [with Malley and Agha]." *The New York Review of Books*, 20 October.
Said, E. 1996. *Peace and its Discontents: Essays on Palestine in the Middle East Process*. New York: Vintage.
Shehadeh, R. 1997. *From Occupation to Interim Accords: Israel and the Palestinian Territories*. Leiden: Brill Publishing.
Singer, S. 2002. "Whose Fault was the Failure of Camp David." *Jerusalem Letter*, Center for Jerusalem Public Affairs, 15 March. Available at: www.jcpa.org/jl/vp474.htm.
Sontag, D. 2001. "Quest for Mid-East Peace: How and Why it Failed." *New York Times*, 26 July, A1.

10

THE END OF OSLO AND THE SECOND *INTIFADA*, 2000–2005

Brent E. Sasley

The 2000–2005 period is epitomized by two iconic images. The first one is a video, though frames of it are also often presented as a series of photographs, of 12-year-old Muhammad al-Durrah, cowering behind his father, Jamal al-Durrah, as they were trapped in the crossfire between Israeli soldiers and Palestinians in the Gaza Strip, on 30 September 2000. Muhammad was killed, with most observers blaming Israel for his death. The second image is of a Palestinian displaying his blood-stained hands after a mob murdered and then celebrated over the corpses of two Israeli reserve soldiers, Vadim Nurzhitz and Yosef Avrahami, in el-Birah, in the West Bank on 12 October 2000.

Though other events took place in this period – the Camp David (2000) and Taba (2001) summits, the Arab Peace Initiative (2002), the construction of Israel's security barrier (2002), and the presentation of the internationally sanctioned Roadmap for Peace (2003) – the photos and videos of these two moments represent the primary development that dominated these years, the Second *Intifada*, or what Palestinians call the *al-Aqsa Intifada*. These images not only captured for many the violence, rage, and despair of the era, but also continue to represent competing interpretations of the origins, motivations, and responsibility for the violence and subsequent breakdown in peace talks. Even more, they have been used by Israelis and Palestinians to promote their own interpretations of the conflict and to present the case for their different goals and objectives. In his study of the role of the media in the Second Intifada, Gadi Wolfsfeld found an "increasingly powerful belief on both sides of this conflict that the struggle over the [international] news media can be just as important as the battle on the ground" (2001, 113). The two images have served as pithy statements toward this end.

For most Israeli Jews and Palestinians, these icons were and remain clear proof that the other side cannot be reasoned with and, therefore, cannot be trusted in negotiations. The Second Intifada has haunted all efforts at peacemaking, by creating an entire generation of Israeli Jews and Palestinians who have lived under a shadow of hatred and violence, and who have often demanded a harder line in negotiations. This, in turn, has convinced Israeli leaders and *Fatah* to avoid hard compromises out of fear of their publics and of trapping their people in a condition of weakness.

DOI: 10.4324/9780429027376-13

Breakdown of the Oslo Peace Process

The Second Intifada emerged out of the failures of the peace process of the 1990s. Though some specific successes did come from the agreement – such as the redeployment of the Israel Defense Forces (IDF) from areas in the West Bank, the creation of the Palestinian National Authority (PA), and limited Palestinian self-government – the Oslo process soon broke down under the weight of a series of counter-efforts by opponents of the process and the difficulties both sides had in overcoming decades of hostility and suspicion, which slowed down the implementation of the various agreements signed under its auspices. Not surprisingly, Israelis and Palestinians blamed each other for the breakdown, absolving themselves of their own responsibility and thus laying the groundwork for the anger and animosity that characterized the Second Intifada period.

The Declaration of Principles, often referred to as the Oslo Accords, signed on 13 September 1993 by Israel and the Palestine Liberation Organization (PLO), ushered in a period of optimism and hope for many in the region. The Declaration was negotiated in secret, on the Israeli side by Yair Hirschfeld, Yossi Beilin, and Ron Pundak, and overseen by Foreign Minister Shimon Peres. But it required Prime Minister Yitzhak Rabin's stamp of approval, both because of his position as prime minister and his security credentials as a former IDF Chief of Staff. If he thought an Israeli withdrawal from parts of the territories and the implementation of limited Palestinian autonomy was not a threat to Israel, then many were prepared to believe him.

The beginning of the end of the Oslo process occurred on 4 November 1995, when Yigal Amir, a religious Zionist who believed no Israeli government had the right to give away Jewish land, assassinated Rabin. Opponents of Oslo had insisted that Rabin was violating Jewish tradition and law by signing away sovereignty over ancient Jewish land, "going soft" on Palestinian terrorism, and embracing the worst Palestinian terrorist of all, Yasser Arafat. During protests against the Accords, Rabin had been presented on posters in a Nazi *SS* uniform, and sometimes with his head in an image of crosshairs. The leader of the right-wing Likud party, Benjamin Netanyahu, spoke at several rallies where these images and rhetoric were present, without condemning them, which in turn seemed to give them at best a wink of encouragement, at worst a stamp of approval. There were reports that some rabbis from the national-religious community proclaimed that *din rodef* could be applied to Rabin. This concept refers to an individual chasing after a person in order to kill them. If the pursuer has been warned to stop and does not, then anyone is permitted to kill them to save the life of the pursued. At his confession, Amir referenced the concept as a motivation for his murder of Rabin.

Peres took over as prime minister. Though adherents of Oslo actively supported Peres's efforts to continue the process, the political atmosphere in Israel was already poisoned by the political right, the far-right, and the settler movement that had demonized Rabin (and Peres) during their protests. Buoyed by sympathy for Rabin that translated into widespread, but not total, support for the Oslo process, in February 1996 Peres called an election for 29 May. Within a week of calling the election, the Palestinian Islamist group *Hamas* initiated an aggressive campaign of terrorism, carried out by suicide bombers. Major attacks took place on 25 February 1996, when 26 Israelis were killed when their bus was blown up; on 3 March, when 19 were killed the same way; and on 4 March, when 13 people were killed near Tel Aviv's popular Dizengoff Center. In April, Peres oversaw a mismanaged attack on *Hizbullah* in Lebanon, which led to the shelling of a United Nations compound where Lebanese civilians were sheltering. Over one hundred non-combatants were killed.

As a result of these events, Jewish-Israelis worried Peres was weak on security. His association with the Oslo process, which was seen as undermining Israel's security control in the West

Bank, further tainted him for many Israelis. The 1996 election was also the first time Israel's new split-ticket voting system was used: voters now cast one ballot for prime minister, and one ballot for their preferred party or list for the Knesset. This reform was meant to strengthen the prime minister at the expense of the parties. But it had the opposite effect. Smaller parties were strengthened at the expense of the big parties, such as Labour and Likud. Voters felt they could select their preferred candidate for prime minister according to their place on the political spectrum – left or right – and then also vote for the party they felt best represented their narrower ideological or sectarian interests. This led to a drop in seats for Labour and Likud – from a combined 76 in 1992 to 66 in 1996 – and an increase for smaller parties, which in turn were now better able to challenge and constrain the prime minister during the policymaking process. In the end, Benjamin Netanyahu, leader of Likud, was elected prime minister, beating Peres by just under 30,000 votes. Though his Likud party, in an electoral alliance with two other parties, received only 32 seats to Labour's 34, Netanyahu had the support of more Jewish parties than Labour did, and was thus able to form the government.

Netanyahu's government lasted until June 1999, when he was replaced as prime minister by Ehud Barak of the Labour party and the new government was led by Labour. Although he had railed against the Oslo Accords, Netanyahu continued to negotiate with Arafat in order to implement its requirements, including redeploying Israeli soldiers in the West Bank city of Hebron (in January 1997) and signing the Wye River Memorandum for further redeployments (in October 1998). Though the memorandum was widely supported in Israel, Netanyahu immediately slowed down its implementation. In September 1996, he authorized the opening of a tunnel alongside the base of the Western Wall, which many Palestinians viewed as damaging the ancient site and undermining their claim to the Noble Sanctuary/Temple Mount. This led to three days of riots by Palestinian civilians and security forces that resulted in many dead and injured on both sides, but especially among Palestinians. And in September 1997 Netanyahu authorized the assassination of Hamas leader Khaled Mashal in Jordan. The strike team used Canadian passports to enter the country, but the attack was botched, and two of the five team members were captured by Jordanian police while three sheltered in the Israeli embassy. This led to diplomatic crises with both Canada and Jordan. Jordan's King Hussein demanded Israel supply the antidote, which United States President Bill Clinton supported. Israel then had to release over 60 prisoners, including Sheik Ahmad Yassin, a founder and prominent spiritual leader of Hamas. During this entire period, Israel was subjected to continued suicide bombings, from which Netanyahu had promised to secure Israelis again.

Finally, he and his wife Sara were accused of venality and hit by several scandals, culminating in a police recommendation that he be charged with corruption. Forced to call new elections for 17 May 1999, Netanyahu was trounced by Ehud Barak of the Labour Party, losing the race for prime minister by almost 400,000 votes, while Labour, at the centre of a new electoral alliance, won 26 seats to Likud's 19 and formed the new government. After his defeat, Netanyahu resigned as head of the Likud and retired for a short period from politics. In the subsequent leadership race, Ariel Sharon defeated two other candidates and became chairman of the party in September 1999.

Barak's time in office was marked by mismanagement, too. Focused on his goals of ending the Israeli-Palestinian conflict, Barak hastily withdrew the IDF from its security zone in southern Lebanon in May 2000, leading to Hizbullah's takeover of the area and putting all of northern Israel under its military shadow. Barak also aggressively pursued negotiations with Arafat at Camp David in July 2000 and at Taba, Egypt, in January 2001. The concessions he offered at both summits made many Israeli Jews nervous and uncertain. In fact, one right-wing party (*Yisrael B'Aliyah*) and two religious parties (*Shas* and the National Religious Party) withdrew

Table 10.1 New Construction Starts in Settlements, 1991–2005

1991	*1992*	*1993*	*1994*	*1995*	*1996*	*1997*	*1998*	*1999*
7,750	6,180	2,240	1,320	2,854	1,982	2,564	4,337	3,491
2000	*2001*	*2002*	*2003*	*2004*	*2005*			
4,958	1,701	1,567	2,069	1,944	2,028			

(Source: Peace Now Settlement Watch, Construction Starts in Settlements by Year. https://peacenow.org.il/en/settlements-watch/settlements-data/construction)

from the coalition just before Barak left for Camp David, leaving him with a minority government dependent on support from parties outside the coalition. Barak also alienated many of his supporters by his autocratic decision-making style, and his neglect of key constituencies, particularly the Palestinian-Israeli community.

On the Palestinian side, Fatah was dominant throughout this period in the two main Palestinian decision-making bodies, the PLO and the PA. It did face challenges from other factions, particularly Hamas and from a number of groups associated with Fatah and the PLO that were led by a younger generation of Palestinians, such as the *Tanzim*. Arafat, though nominally the final authority, often allowed different factions and groups to conduct their own affairs, including attacks against Israelis, without trying to stop them.

A bigger problem for the Palestinian leadership was the constrained nature of its autonomy. During the Oslo period, the PA's ability to rule over the territory granted to it by the Oslo agreements was hindered by unrestricted access that the IDF had to the territory, and the mesh of roads, military checkpoints, and settlements throughout the West Bank and Gaza, all of which were under full Israeli security and administrative control. The PA regularly accused Israel of violating the Oslo Accords in both principle and in letter, including not ending the occupation, expanding settlements, not releasing political prisoners or opening up a route between Gaza and the West Bank, restricting Palestinian movement, and not prosecuting Jewish settlers who committed violence against Palestinians.

Most galling for the Palestinians, and the most egregious from their perspective regarding advancement of the peace process, was the growth of settlements. From 1992, the year that Rabin and Labour came to power, to 2000 the population of Israeli settlers grew steadily from 105,400 to 198,300 (Peace Now n.d.b). According to Peace Now's Settlement Watch program,[1] the number of construction starts dropped from 7,750 in 1991 to 1,324 in 1994, but then maintained a steady if uneven rate of building, with considerable increases by the end of the decade (Peace Now n.d.a). Table 10.1 shows the number of new construction starts from 1991 to 2005. The number of outposts – small settlements not authorized by the government – also increased. In 1996, four new outposts were established; in 1998 it was 14, while in 1999 it was 19. In 2001 the number rose to 20, and in 2002 it was 23 (Peace Now n.d.b). Each outpost was later supported with infrastructure and supplies, and then incorporated into the IDF's defence plans. Thus, though each outpost is small, they incorporate more territory than their buildings account for and require more land for the Israeli military to access in order to protect them.

The Second Intifada

The Second Intifada and the intense violence that characterized it was the result of a convergence of several factors and conditions. First, building off the lack of progress in the Oslo process, the failure of the Camp David and Taba summits created a sense of frustration, anger, and despair among both Israelis and Palestinians – despair that facilitated a willingness to lash out violently. A fact-finding mission sponsored by the United Nations, the Sharm el-Sheikh Fact-Finding Committee (commonly known as the Mitchell report, after the Committee's chair, American politician and diplomat George Mitchell) stated that the cause of the violence of the Second Intifada was rooted in

> a profound disillusionment with the behaviour of the other in failing to meet the expectations arising from the peace process launched in Madrid in 1991 and then in Oslo in 1993. Each side has accused the other of violating specific undertakings and undermining the spirit of their commitment to resolving their political differences peacefully.

These positions, it continued,

> have hardened into divergent realities. Each side views the other as having acted in bad faith; as having turned the optimism of Oslo into the suffering and grief of victims and their loved ones. In their statements and actions, each side demonstrates a perspective that fails to recognize any truth in the perspective of the other.
>
> *(Sharm El-Sheikh Fact-Finding Committee 2001)*

Second, the ongoing Israeli occupation and continued expansion of settlements convinced many Palestinian leaders, especially among the "young guard," that negotiations were not going to lead to Palestinian independence, and that armed struggle was needed again. Third, Arafat's unwillingness to stop militants within Fatah or Hamas from attacking Israeli civilians. Fourth, Israel's commitment to a harsh coercive response to Palestinian protests at the start of the clashes.

Barak's concessions and Arafat's reactions at Camp David and Taba are the subject of intense scholarly and popular disagreement.[2] From the dominant Israeli and American perspective, Israel offered unprecedented and very generous concessions to the Palestinians, but they – especially Arafat – chose to walk away without even presenting a counter-proposal. In a subsequent interview, Barak proclaimed that Arafat believed Israel "has no right to exist, and he seeks its demise" (Morris 2002). Dennis Ross also laid most of the blame for lack of progress on Arafat, contending that Arafat was "not capable of negotiating an end to the conflict because what is required of him is something he is not able to do. It's simply not in him to go the extra yard" (Haberman 2001). Instead, according to this narrative, the Palestinians started the Second Intifada and hoped the violence would push Israel out of the West Bank and Gaza, if not out of the region entirely.

For Palestinians, Arafat was subject to bullying by Barak and Clinton, there was no advance preparation necessary for a successful leadership summit, and the so-called "generous" Israeli concessions were not miserly in the details and, anyway, were a cover for continued Israeli occupation since what was left for a Palestinian state would be broken in small pieces, bifurcated by Israeli territory, Israeli roads, and Israeli security installations and bases. Similar to the blame that many Israelis placed squarely on Arafat, some Palestinian leaders have contended the opposite for Barak. Ghassan Khatib, a former minister in the Palestinian Authority, argued that Barak had only two goals at Camp David: "[E]ither to reach a final settlement ending the Palestinian-Israeli conflict and achieving Israel's objectives … without compromising on Jerusalem, the refugees or many of the settlements, or to end the entire peace process and place the blame squarely on the other side" (Khatib 2002). What is clear is that the mutual recriminations and blame intensified the hostility that helped lead to the outbreak of the violence.

At the popular level, there was widespread discontent, frustration, and anger among Palestinians in the West Bank and Gaza (WBG), and among Israelis, both Jewish and Arab citizens. For WBG Palestinians, the failure of the Oslo process to lead to a substantial increase in Palestinian independence after the formation of the PA was a major issue. The Israeli military continued to control the two territories, frequent incursions into Palestinians towns and homes alongside continued expansion of settlements and incorporation of more land into settlement infrastructure and road systems for Israeli civilians and security forces, and the extensive system of checkpoints throughout the West Bank was were humiliating and signalled that Israel had no intention of giving up control. Under conditions that were viewed as unbearable, negotiations were increasingly seen as a waste of time. A public opinion poll taken at the end of December 2001 found that while 71 per cent of respondents supported an immediate return to negotiations, 61 per cent believed that "armed confrontation" would help improve the Palestinian position (Palestinian Center for Policy and Survey Research 2001). Though these represent an increase and a decrease, respectively, they still reflect majority opinions that the Palestinian leadership could not ignore, and indeed dovetailed with the views of the "young guard" in Fatah. About a year later, in November 2002, 66 per cent of Palestinians said they believed that armed confrontations had, in fact, helped the Palestinian cause (Palestinian Center for Policy and Survey Research 2002).

For Israeli Jews, the perceived failure of Arafat to engage seriously with Barak at Camp David was proof of Palestinian perfidy and commitment to the destruction of Israel. The ongoing attacks by Hamas and other Palestinian groups against Israeli civilians and soldiers throughout the 1990s and the fact that Arafat rarely tried to constrain Hamas underlined a presumed commitment to violence. In 1999, survey research found that 63 per cent of Israeli Jews believed that "most Palestinians want peace." That number fell to 37 per cent in 2002, though it went up to 46 per cent in 2003 (Ben Meir and Bagno-Moldavsky 2010, 78). To questions about Arab (though not specifically Palestinian) goals, Israeli Jews increasingly believed that the objective was to "conquer Israel and destroy a large part of the Jewish population" – 19 per cent in 1999, 28 per cent in 2000, 31 per cent in 2001, 42 per cent in 2002, and 37 per cent for the next two years (Ibid., 79).

Palestinian domestic politics also contributed to the outbreak. One of the main disputes in Fatah and the PLO was between a younger generation of Palestinians who had grown up during and participated in the First Intifada, and spent many years in Israeli prisons, and an older faction comprised of Arafat and others who had led Fatah and the PLO for decades and had lived outside the WBG until they returned under the Oslo Accords in the mid-1990s. The young guard challenged Arafat and the old leaders over their corruption and lack of institution-building, but by 2000, they also came to disagree with the emphasis on negotiations. One of the main leaders of the Second Intifada was Marwan Barghouti, a popular organizer of the young guard and the head of the Tanzim. Barghouti was convinced that the previous years of talks had deepened Israeli occupation and nearly foreclosed the possibility of Palestinian statehood. For him, the Intifada was, as he told a reporter at the end of October 2000, "for peace and will create better conditions for the talks and for the peace" (NPR 2000). In November he stated that "We are not against negotiations, but we want the Intifada to continue simultaneously," and called for the continuation of the Intifada "till we achieve independence" (Lahoud 2000).

Despite Israeli accusations, the evidence does not indicate that the PA or its supporters planned the violence in advance (see Pressman 2006, 117), but it does show that the PA did not try to stop attacks against Israelis. The protests and violence in reaction to Ariel Sharon's visit to the Temple Mount/Noble Sanctuary, as Likud's candidate for prime minister (see below), was immediate, but that may be because the PA had advance warning of the tour and word of it very likely spread, prompting outrage against the assertion of Israeli authority and against Sharon himself, due to his role in the 1982 Sabra and Shatila massacres. However, the visit took place on a Thursday; on Friday large numbers of Palestinian Muslims gathered, as they always did, on the platform on which the Dome of the Rock and the al-Aqsa Mosques are located. Protests after Friday prayers in Jerusalem were common in that period, and rock-throwing had, since the First Intifada, become a symbol of Palestinian defiance and action. Arafat did not restrain the protests once they began or try to stop Palestinian groups from attacking Israelis. In part this is because Arafat himself believed that some force was needed to prod the Israelis into better concessions; this had been his modus operandi for decades. The demands for military action were widespread, too, so that Arafat did not want to appear to be at odds with popular opinion at the beginning. In Yezid Sayigh's words, Arafat's actions reflected an "*absence of any strategy*. His political management has been marked by a high degree of improvisation and short-termism, confirming the absence of an original strategy and of a clear purpose" (2001, 47; emphasis in original).

The key factor was that Arafat's authority among Palestinians was not total. Though he was head of the PLO and the PA, a handful of factions within these entities ignored him when he disagreed with their approach, such as the Tanzim. Hamas, which was not a member of either organization, had no loyalty to Arafat and did not recognize his authority. Both of these groups had demanded institutional and policy changes and were willing to challenge Arafat in order to see them through. As the Tanzim, the al-Aqsa Brigades,[3] and Hamas continued to launch attacks against Israeli military and civilian targets, Fatah was unwilling to be seen as a stooge of the Israeli occupation by rejecting the violence. As Helga Baumgarten notes, "At Oslo, [Fatah] agreed to renounce violence in its conflict with Israel, but with the second Intifada that restraint no longer held" (2005, 43). Instead, Fatah and the PA were found to have actively contributed financial and military support to groups associated with them.

If some Palestinian leaders believed the use of force was a tool for prompting negotiations, Israel's security officials were similarly committed. The redeployment in the West Bank and Gaza as a result of the various agreements in the Oslo process had deprived Israeli intelligence of some of its networks, which in turn undermined Israel's ability to stop militant and terrorist groups from carrying out some of their attacks. The Western Wall tunnels riots in 1996 also caught the security forces unprepared. Both of these, it was felt, had undermined Israel's deterrent capability. The simmering discontent at the lack of progress in the peace process had convinced Israeli military and intelligence leaders that an outbreak of violence was coming, and they were confident that an immediate and aggressive response would keep the violence from spreading. Like Barghouti, some Israeli officers believed that the Palestinians had to be brought back to the negotiating table by being forced into submission; Israeli might would be "burned into [their] consciousness" (Pedatzur 2004). This helps explain why 1.3 million bullets were fired by Israeli forces in the first few days of the uprising.

Under these conditions, many Israeli troops and Palestinian fighters eagerly embraced violence. Based on a large-N study of Israeli soldiers who served in the IDF between 1999 and 2006, Devorah Manekin (2013) found that the longer soldiers were deployed among Palestinian civilians during the Second Intifada, as a method of crowd control and to stop terrorist activities, the more likely they were to engage in "opportunistic violence" against Palestinians – unplanned violence against civilians without any benefit to overall military goals. Bader Araj (2012) conducted in-depth interviews with close friends and family of 42 Palestinian suicide bombers who carried out their attacks during the Second Intifada. He found that the two most prominent motivations for carrying out suicide bombings were revenge against Israel, particularly because of its harsh response to Palestinian protests, and religious inspiration.[4]

The specific trigger of the Second Intifada was Ariel Sharon's visit to the Temple Mount/Noble Sanctuary. On 28 September 2000, Sharon, escorted by over a thousand police, toured the platform for about 45 minutes. Palestinian protestors followed the entourage, throwing stones and other items, and police responded with tear gas and rubber bullets. Whether or not Sharon's visit was approved by the Palestinian Authority is disputed. Shlomo Ben-Ami, the Israeli minister of Internal Security, said that Jibril Rajoub, head of the Palestinian Preventative Security Force, told him Sharon could visit the platform provided he did not enter any of the mosques there. Rajoub has denied the claim. The Mitchell report found that "The Sharon visit did not cause the 'Al-Aqsa Intifada.' But it was poorly timed and the provocative effect should have been foreseen; indeed it was foreseen by those who urged that the visit be prohibited" (Sharm El-Sheikh Fact-Finding Committee 2001).

Sharon's visit to the compound had two aims: First, to enhance his position in Israel's domestic political struggles. Sharon wanted to assert Israel's claim to the holy sites in the face of Barak's concessions at Camp David and to undermine Barak's bargaining position. He also wanted to enhance his hard-line credentials against Netanyahu, whom he was contesting for leadership of the political right. Second, the visit was meant to challenge Palestinian expectations about what they could achieve through the peace talks. The message was clearly received. As Faisal Husseini, the former top PA official in Jerusalem, said at the time, the visit was "a direct attempt to derail the peace process and an attempt to inflame the whole region" (Greenberg 2000).

The next day the violence intensified. Israeli police replaced rubber bullets with live ammunition, and in the clashes that followed Friday prayers four Palestinians were killed and over two hundred injured. From there Palestinian protests and attacks and an Israeli military response spread across the West Bank, and even into Israel. By the end of the Intifada, over four thousand people had been killed, including murders committed by non-combatants (BBC 2005b). About 3,200 were WBG Palestinians. The majority of the dead on both sides were civilians.

In thinking about the Second Intifada, several key moments stand out. As the protests and riots spread from Jerusalem, Israeli police and security forces moved to contain them. On 30 September at the Netzarim junction in Gaza, Jamal al-Durrah and his 12-year-old son Muhammad arrived at the site just as shooting began between Palestinians and Israelis. Caught in the crossfire, the two took cover behind a concrete drum for about 45 minutes. A cameraman for France 2, Talal Abu Rahme, filmed about half of this time. At some point Muhammad was shot; film footage shows him lying in his father's lap, and raising his hand. He later died of his wounds. The image of a sobbing boy, cowering behind his father, represented for Palestinians (and their international supporters) the cruel nature of the Israeli occupation, and the efforts Israel will go to in order to prevent Palestinian independence. It became an iconic image around which Palestinians rallied.[5]

Protests spread into Arab-Israeli communities. In the first week and a half of October, demonstrations against the government's violent approach, combined with frustration at government neglect, took place across northern Israel. Some turned into riots, while mobs of Jewish citizens attacked Arab citizens. Israeli police responded harshly to the Arab crowds, but not the Jewish ones. 13 Palestinian citizens of Israel were killed in the clashes. The killings had a profound effect on Arab-Jewish relations within Israel and led to a reassessment among Arab community leaders about their place in Israel.

If the death of Muhammad al-Durrah provided Palestinians with an image to represent their cause, then the lynching of two Israeli reservists on 12 October in el-Bireh in the West Bank did the same for Israeli Jews. Vadim Nurzhitz and Yosef Avrahami were called up for duty, and drove toward the West Bank settlement of Beit El. They were stopped at a Palestinian roadblock and taken to the el-Bireh police station. As word spread, hundreds of Palestinians gathered around the station, eventually breaking in and mutilating and killing the two Israelis. One of the murderers, Aziz Salha, held up his blood-stained hands at a station window, and the crowd cheered. One of the bodies was then thrown out the window, and mutilated again. Both bodies were then dragged to a city square and celebrated over. The images convinced many Israelis that the Palestinians were out for blood, not independence, and could not be trusted. In response, the IDF destroyed a number of Palestinian government buildings.

Talks between Israel and the PA continued throughout this period, leading to the Taba summit between Barak and Arafat from 21–27 January 2001. By then, Barak's government was a minority one. With the Second Intifada already raging, the political right in Israel argued that diplomacy and concessions to the Palestinians were foolish and only brought more violence. This undermined Barak's signature foreign policy goal, a final peace agreement with the Palestinians. Forced to call a special election for prime minister on 6 February, Barak was defeated by an even greater margin than his victory over Netanyahu three years earlier; he lost to Ariel Sharon by over 670,000 votes. This poll also had the lowest voter turnout rate in Israeli history, in part because many Arab citizens refused to vote in the aftermath of the October events and to protest Barak's abandonment of their community.

Sharon had a reputation for toughness, a willingness to buck authority, and a relentless focus on Jewish security. He was also known as a strong supporter of the settlement enterprise. His previous nickname was "the Bulldozer," in reference to his determination to achieve a policy goal, however controversial or brutal in its implementation. His reputation was equally one of violence. During the 1956 and 1967 Arab-Israeli wars he commanded military units in bold but controversial (and sometimes unauthorized) missions. He had also commanded Unit 101, a military group tasked with retribution against Palestinian and Arab forces that attacked Israelis. His forced evacuation of Israeli settlers from the Sinai Peninsula showed that he could apply his determination against Israeli Jews, too. For Palestinians, most demeaning was his role as defence minister and one of the planners on the 1982 invasion of Lebanon, which led to the massacres by Christian forces in the Sabra and Shatila refugee camps, but for which an Israeli government inquiry found Sharon to bear "personal responsibility" for ignoring the likelihood of such an attack.

The joint statement issued by Israel and the PA at the end of the summit noted that the talks "were unprecedented in their positive atmosphere and expression of mutual willingness to meet the national, security and existential needs of each side," and that "The sides declare that they have never been closer to reaching an agreement and it is thus our shared belief that the remaining gaps could be bridged with the resumption of negotiations following the Israeli elections" (Israeli-Palestinian Joint Statement, 2001). After his electoral victory, however, Sharon rejected continuation of the talks and focused instead of the use of force to defeat the Second Intifada.

The clashes and killings continued. On 3 January 2002, the IDF intercepted the *Karine A*, a ship sailing in international waters in the Red Sea. The vessel was carrying 50 tons of weapons, including short-range rockets and anti-tank missiles. Israel produced evidence that showed the weapons were provided by Iran and were meant for the PA, and that Arafat himself had provided some funds for the purchases. Others have disputed a direct Palestinian link and contended that the weapons were meant for longtime Iranian client Hizbullah, in Lebanon. The incident convinced United States President George W. Bush that Arafat could not be trusted, which in turn helped persuade Bush to support Sharon's later invasion of the West Bank.

Israeli forces killed hundreds of Palestinian civilians during protests and riots. For their part, Palestinian terrorists attacked Israeli civilians throughout the period. Two particularly terrible assaults stand out. On 21 June 2001, an Islamic Jihad suicide bomber struck the Dolphinarium nightclub, killing 21, most of whom were teenagers. On 27 March 2002, at the Park Hotel in the seaside city of Netanya, a suicide bomber from Hamas blew himself up at a *seder*, the traditional meal eaten at the beginning of the holiday of Passover. 30 people were killed, most of them senior citizens. The attack was the proximate motivation for Operation Defensive Shield, in which the IDF launched a number of strikes against targets in the West Bank, eventually leading to the isolation of Arafat and his loss of power.

As part of the military effort to contain the violence, Israel began targeting leaders of the Palestinian militant groups, particularly of Hamas. On 22 March 2004, Israeli helicopters fired Hellfire missiles at Sheikh Ahmed Yassin, a quadriplegic leader of Hamas who rejected Israel's existence and supported armed force against it, including terrorism.[6] His successor, Abdel Aziz al-Rantisi, was assassinated in the same way on 17 April.

Operation Defensive Shield

While the violence raged, negotiations with the Palestinians continued, conducted through American special envoy General Anthony Zinni. Sharon, however, was increasingly worried about attacks against Israeli civilians and about his own slipping popularity. He was already inclined to use even more force to end the uprising, but the 27 March Park Hotel bombing was the final motivation. On 29 March Israel launched Operation Defensive Shield, the biggest mobilization of the IDF since 2006. The purpose of the assault was, according to the Cabinet communique on the invasion,

> a wide-ranging operational action plan against Palestinian terror [to] defeat the infrastructure of Palestinian terror in all its parts and components; to this end, broad action will be undertaken until this goal is secured. Arafat – who set up a coalition of terror against Israel – is an enemy; at this stage, he will be isolated.
>
> *(Cabinet Communique 2002)*

In his own statement on the operation, Sharon singled out Arafat as solely responsible for Palestinian terror: "This [Palestinian] terror is operated, directed and initiated by one man – Palestinian Authority Chairman Yasser Arafat ... The PA Chairman is an enemy of Israel in particular and the entire free world in general" (Sharon 2002).[7]

Israeli forces invaded six major Palestinian cities: Ramallah, Tulkarm, Qalqilya, Bethlehem, Jenin, and Nablus. Checkpoints and military cordons were set up around these and other towns and villages, curfews were imposed, and military raids were regularly conducted to search for and arrest militants and terrorists. Arafat's headquarters in Ramallah, called the *Muqata*, was placed under a near-constant siege, which ended only when Arafat, extremely ill, was allowed to leave at the end of October 2004 for a hospital in Paris, where he later died.

From 1 to 11 April, fierce fighting took place in Jenin, identified as a major source of terrorism. The urban warfare led to the destruction of significant sections of the city and the fleeing of thousands from Jenin. Having walked into ambushes and booby-traps, the IDF turned to the use of helicopter missiles and bulldozers to flatten buildings in the path of ground troops. The intense fighting in the middle of an urban area meant little information was available to outside analysts, but Palestinians accused Israel of a committing a "massacre."

Five hundred was mentioned as the number of Palestinian fatalities, and international media soon picked it up, while human-rights organizations accused Israel of atrocities, including torture and summary executions. The struggle over how many were killed in Jenin fit with the use of images from Netzarim and el-Bireh, and with Wolfsfeld's finding that the global media was a major battleground between the two sides. A United Nations fact-finding mission later put the number of Palestinians killed at 52, about half of whom were civilians. 23 Israeli soldiers were killed.

Another battle took place around the same time in Bethlehem. From 2 April to 10 May, Israeli forces surrounded the Church of the Nativity, where several militants wanted by Israel had hidden. Israel claimed the monks who had been in the building were held hostage by the Palestinian fighters, though the clerics said they had stayed voluntarily, and the militants denied the claim outright. Regular exchanges of fire broke out, with Israeli snipers shooting directly into the church. The Vatican expressed concern over the place of a church at the centre of a war. Negotiations continued until 13 wanted men walked out and, under an agreement, were exiled to Europe and to Gaza.

Constructing Israel's Security Barrier

In 1992 Prime Minister Rabin had proposed building a barrier to separate Israel from West Bank Palestinians as a way to cut down on terrorists slipping from the territory into Jerusalem and Israel proper. Some concrete slabs were put in place in 1994, but little else was done. When he became prime minister, Barak publicly committed to building a barrier. But it was Sharon's government that embraced the idea and began large-scale construction of it. The Israeli government refers to it as a separation fence or a security barrier, while Palestinians call it the apartheid wall or simply "the wall."

Public support for the barrier increased during the Second Intifada. It was widely viewed as both a physical impediment, and a symbol of separation from the Palestinians. Sharon himself was reluctant, fearing that it might become a political border; in the event, when the route of the barrier was published, some in the settler movement came out against it since it did not incorporate all settlements in the West Bank and might be used by Palestinians as proof of an international border with Israel.

The cabinet approved the construction of the barrier on 23 June 2002, and construction began immediately. The route itself has changed several times; though some of it follows the Green Line, as of this writing about 85 per cent of the barrier runs into the West Bank. Challenges to the legality of the route began almost immediately, as Palestinians and others brought suits against it both in Israeli courts and in the International Court of Justice. In the context of Israeli-Palestinian relations, the barrier constitutes another component of the turn toward unilateralism in Israeli policy. The idea that Arafat and his successor Mahmoud Abbas, and the Palestinians as a people, have no interest in peace or willingness to make hard compromises is reflected in other policy decisions, such as the Gaza disengagement plan.

Diplomatic Efforts During the Second Intifada

There were two major diplomatic pushes to contain the violence of the Second Intifada and lay the groundwork for a comprehensive agreement: the Arab Peace Initiative, adopted on 27 March 2002, and the Roadmap for Peace, released on 30 April 2003. The two plans shared a number of similarities but were promoted by different international actors. Though both were part of the continuation of the diplomatic process that began with Oslo, and in that sense were useful for maintaining diplomatic channels, neither achieved their goals.

The Arab Peace Initiative (API) was the result of a proposal put forward by Saudi Arabia. Riyadh was concerned about instability emanating from the Second Intifada and from the threat of an Iranian challenge to the Sunni Arab states. On 27 March 2002, the Arab League, meeting in Beirut, adopted the API. A short document, it called for a final end to the Israeli-Palestinian conflict by Israel's withdrawal to the 4 June 1967, lines; a "just solution" to the Palestinian refugee problem; and a sovereign Palestinian state with its capital in East Jerusalem. In return, the API promised that League members would establish "normal relations" with Israel. The Sharon government rejected the effort, while the PA under Abbas expressed careful acceptance.

The Roadmap for Peace, officially titled *A Performance-Based Roadmap to a Permanent Two-State Solution to the Israeli-Palestinian Conflict*, was released on 30 April 2003. It was created by the Quartet, comprised of the United States, the European Union, Russia, and the United Nations, formed to bring an end to the Israeli-Palestinian conflict. It emerged out of a speech by President Bush on 24 June 2002, in which he called for the establishment of a Palestinian state alongside Israel. The key to this, he argued, was the creation of better Palestinian institutions of governance, which in turn required new Palestinian leadership; in effect, the end of Arafat's authority. At the time, conditions in Israel/Palestine seemed amenable to it: Sharon won the January 2003 election and became prime minister again, Operation Defensive Shield appeared to have been largely successful, and Arafat was weakened to the point that in March he had appointed Mahmoud Abbas as prime minister under him. Abbas was more popular in the international community and seen as less of a liability than Arafat.

The Roadmap laid out a three-stage process based on the "performance" of the two sides. It was to culminate, in 2005, in an end to the conflict, a two-state solution, and the normalization of Israel in the Middle East. Sharon expressed several major reservations and instead announced his Gaza disengagement plan on 18 December 2003. The plan called for a unilateral Israeli effort, in coordination with the United States, to withdraw all soldiers and civilians from Gaza and from part of the northern West Bank. Internecine fighting in the PA and between Fatah and Hamas also intensified. Under these pressures, the Roadmap was ignored.

The End of the Second Intifada

The attacks and killings continued throughout 2004 and 2005, but by the end of 2004 a series of developments occurred that laid the groundwork for the end of the Second Intifada. On 11 November 2004, Yasser Arafat died. Mahmoud Abbas was elected chairman of the PLO that same day, and president of the Palestinian Authority and the State of Palestine on 15 January 2005. Where Arafat had either actively encouraged or winked at the use of force, Abbas explicitly tried to contain it and to focus on the diplomatic process.

Under pressure from the disengagement plan and the Roadmap, and worn out from the bloodshed and fighting, Sharon, Abbas, Egyptian president Hosni Mubarak, and Jordan's King Abdullah II met at Sharm el-Sheikh on 8 February 2005. They agreed to end the violence and work again toward a diplomatic solution to the conflict. Given the hostility that remained in place, both Sharon and Abbas in their final statements reiterated their viewpoints, but also made references to ending the fighting and moving on, and their hopes for a peaceful future. Sharon repeated his focus on terror as the cause of the violence and on the need to "dismantle the terrorist infrastructure," but proclaimed,

> we must all announce here today that violence will not win, that violence will not be allowed to murder hope. We must all make a commitment not to agree for a temporary solution, not to allow violence to raise its head.
>
> *(Sharon 2005)*

Abbas was more conciliatory, focusing on Palestinian aspirations and the diplomatic process, and declaring, "We have agreed with Prime Minister Ariel Sharon to stop all acts of violence against Israelis and Palestinians, wherever they are" (BBC 2005a).

Consequences of the Second Intifada

The Second Intifada had ground normal life to a halt for both Israelis and Palestinians. Israelis were fearful of going out of their homes even to a restaurant, while Palestinians were subject to curfews and checkpoints that made it difficult if not impossible to leave the immediate vicinity of their homes. The security barrier divided some Palestinian villages and cut others off from their agricultural fields. Individuals and families suffered not just by loss of life but due to tens of thousands injured and, for Palestinians, destruction of homes, neighbourhoods, and urban infrastructure. The Intifada devastated the Palestinian economy, as Israel placed severe restrictions on trade and movement within the West Bank and between Israel and the WBG. Palestinians who had previously worked regularly in Israel were prevented from doing so, leading to a loss in remittances that made up a substantial portion of Palestinian gross national income. Poverty rates increased significantly. The PA faced a series of budgetary crises.

The Israeli economy also suffered, though not as much as the Palestinian economy. Loss of Palestinian labour, loss of tourism revenue, and an increase in defence expenditures (including for the security barrier) led to a recession. Israel did recover quickly once the Intifada ended, but the Palestinian economy did not.

The conflict had a deleterious effect on the peace process. Hostility, mistrust, and anger lingered. In Israel, particularly, a younger generation of Jews who had experienced the Intifada came to hold deeply rooted negative feelings about the Palestinians. This has been reflected in voting patterns throughout the 2010s, as the political left – those parties more likely to negotiate an end to the conflict and the establishment of a Palestinian state – was weakened in part because the right was now seen as better on security (Sasley 2015). Unlike the First Intifada, which convinced Rabin that direct talks between Israel and the PLO were necessary and could produce an agreement, the Second Intifada convinced many people on both sides of the opposite: that neither could be trusted.

Recommended Readings

Dowty, A. 2017. *Israel/Palestine*, 4th ed. Cambridge: Polity Press.

Pearlman, W. 2003. *Occupied Voices: Stories of Everyday Life from the Second Intifada*. New York: Nation Books.

Pressman, J. 2003. "Visions in Collision: What Happened at Camp David and Taba?" *International Security* 28:2, 5–43.

Schulze, K. E. 2001. "Camp David and the Al-Aqsa Intifada: An Assessment of the State of the Israeli-Palestinian Peace Process, July-December 2000." *Studies in Conflict and Terrorism* 24:3, 215–233.

Shamir, J., and K. Shikaki. 2010. *Palestinian and Israeli Public Opinion: The Public Imperative in the Second Intifada*. Bloomington, IN: Indiana University Press.

Notes

1 All figures exclude population and building in eastern Jerusalem neighborhoods.
2 For a good comparison of the different versions of events, see Pressman (2003).
3 A newly formed militia within Fatah, classified by the United States, European Union, and others as a terrorist organization. In April 2002, Barghouti was arrested by Israel for being its leader. He was convicted of five counts of murder and been imprisoned since then.
4 The latter is underlined by the name Palestinians give the uprisings: the al-Aqsa *Intifada*, referring to the mosque on the Haram al-Sharif.
5 The film footage and the event are controversial. Palestinians and many other accuse Israeli soldiers of having killed Muhammad. Israel argues that, given the angle of the shooting, it is not possible and that Palestinian snipers had done the killing, and the video was doctored. Others contend there is no way to know for sure who killed Muhammad.
6 Yassin had been imprisoned in Israel in 1989, but was released in 1997 as part of the penance Netanyahu had to pay for the Israeli attack on Khaled Mashal.
7 In cabinet discussions about the invasion, Sharon had initially also called for the permanent expulsion of Arafat from the area.

Questions for discussion:

(1) How important is history in shaping contemporary peace negotiations between Israelis and Palestinians?
(2) Explain how Israeli and Palestinian political institutions have shaped the goals, strategies, and behaviours of the two sides during this period.
(3) Given the emotional attachments to both the land itself and to their own narratives of victimhood, what would it take to move Israelis and Palestinians toward compromise?
(4) What is the relative weight of emotional/psychological factors versus material factors in leading to the outbreak of the Second Intifada, and more broadly in maintaining the conflict?
(5) Do individual leaders have a great effect on the contours of the conflict? Or do history, institutions, and social forces push the two sides toward specific activity regardless of who is in power?

References

Araj, B. 2012. "The Motivations of Palestinian Suicide Bombers in the Second Intifada (2000 to 2005)." *Canadian Review of Sociology* 49:3, 211–232.

Available at: www.nytimes.com/2001/03/25/magazine/dennis-ross-s-exit-interview.html.

Baumgarten, H. 2005. "The Three Faces/Phases of Palestinian Nationalism, 1948–2005." *Journal of Palestine Studies* 34:3, 25–48.

BBC. 2005a. "Full Text of Abbas Declaration." 8 February. Available at: http://news.bbc.co.uk/2/hi/middle_east/4247327.stm.

BBC. 2005b. "Intifada Toll 2000–2005." 8 February. Available at: http://news.bbc.co.uk/2/hi/middle_east/3694350.stm.

Ben Meir, Y. and O. Bagno-Moldavsky. 2010. "The Second Intifada and Israeli Public Opinion." *Strategic Assessment* 13:3, 71–83.

Cabinet Communique, Israel. 2002. 29 March. Available at: https://mfa.gov.il/MFA/PressRoom/2002/Pages/Cabinet%20Communique%20-%2029-Mar-2002.aspx.

Greenberg, J. 2000. "Sharon Touches a Nerve, and Jerusalem Explodes." *New York Times*, 29 September.

Haberman, Clyde. 2001. "Dennis Ross's Exit Interview." *New York Times Magazine*. 25 March.

Israeli-Palestinian Joint Statement. 2001. 27 January. Available at: https://mfa.gov.il/MFA/MFA-Archive/2001/Pages/Israeli-Palestinian%20Joint%20Statement%20-%2027-Jan-2001.aspx.

Khatib, G. 2002. "A Palestinian View: Camp David: An Exit Strategy for Barak." www.bitterlemons.org Edition 26. 15 July. Available at: www.bitterlemons.org/previous/bl150702ed26.html.

Lahoud, L. 2000. "Barghouti Calls to Continue Intifada." *The Jerusalem Post*. 8 November.

Manekin, D. 2013. "Violence Against Civilians in the Second Intifada: The Moderating Effect of Armed Group Structure on Opportunistic Violence." *Comparative Political Studies* 46:10, 1273–1300.

Morris, B. 2002. "Camp David and After: An Exchange." *New York Review of Books*. 13 June. Available at: www.nybooks.com/articles/2002/06/13/camp-david-and-after-an-exchange-1-an-interview-wi/.

NPR. 2000. "Fatah Party Leader Marwan Barghouti." *All Things Considered*. 30 October.
Palestinian Center for Policy and Survey Research. 2001. "Palestinian Public Opinion Poll No.3." 19–24 December. Available at: www.pcpsr.org/sites/default/files/Palestinian%20Public%20Opinion%20Poll%20No%20%283%29%20with%20Table.pdf.
Palestinian Center for Policy and Survey Research. 2002. "Palestinian Public Opinion Poll No.6." 13–24 November. Available at: www.pcpsr.org/sites/default/files/Palestinian%20Public%20Opinion%20Poll%20No%20%286%29%20with%20table.docx.pdf.
Peace Now. N.d.a. "Construction." Settlement Watch Data. Available at: https://peacenow.org.il/en/settlements-watch/settlements-data/construction.
Peace Now. N.d.b. "Population." Settlement Watch Data. Available at: https://peacenow.org.il/en/settlements-watch/settlements-data/population.
Pedatzur, R. 2004. "More Than a Million Bullets." *Haaretz*. 29 June. Available at: www.haaretz.com/1.4744778.
Pressman, J. 2003. "Visions in Collision: What Happened at Camp David and Taba?" *International Security* 28:2, 5–43.
Pressman, J. 2006. "The Second Intifada: Background and Causes of the Israeli-Palestinian Conflict." *Journal of Conflict Studies* 23:2, 114–141.
Sasley, B. E. 2015. "Israel's Right Turn." *Foreign Affairs*. 24 March. Available at: www.foreignaffairs.com/articles/israel/2015-03-24/israels-right-turn.
Sayigh, Y. 2001. "Arafat and the Anatomy of a Revolt." *Survival* 43:3, 47–60.
Sharm El-Sheikh Fact-Finding Committee. 2001. 30 April. Available at: https://avalon.law.yale.edu/21st_century/mitchell_plan.asp.
Sharon, A. 2002. "PM Sharon's Address to the Nation." 31 March. Available at: https://mfa.gov.il/MFA/PressRoom/2002/Pages/PM%20Sharon-s%20Address%20to%20the%20Nation%20-%2031-Mar-2002.aspx.
Sharon, A. 2005. "Statement by PM Ariel Sharon at the Sharm el-Sheikh Summit." 8 February. Available at: https://mfa.gov.il/mfa/foreignpolicy/peace/guide/pages/statement%20by%20pm%20sharon%20at%20sharm%20el-sheikh%20summit%208-feb-2005.aspx.
Wolfsfeld, G. 2001. "The New Media and the Second Intifada: Some Initial Lessons." *Harvard International Journal of Press/Politics* 6:4, 113–118.

11
THE DEMISE OF THE PEACE PROCESS

Jacob Eriksson

While the 1993 Oslo Agreement marked a breakthrough in the Israeli-Palestinian conflict, continuing to progress towards a final peace agreement between Israelis and Palestinians has proved significantly more difficult. Reaching a compromise on the core final-status issues – borders, Israeli settlements, Jerusalem, the Palestinian refugee problem, security – would require sustained and intensive negotiations, made all the more difficult by the sensitivity of the issues and the ongoing violent conflict. The mere prospect of a peace agreement galvanized spoilers on both sides who were insufficiently addressed, and interim agreements failed to be implemented (Pundak 2001). In the summer of 2000, United States president Bill Clinton and his peace team undertook the first official effort at final-status negotiations at Camp David. It was to become the first of many such unsuccessful attempts, with recriminations for the failure coming from all sides (Malley and Agha 2001 and 2002; Morris 2002; Morris, Malley, and Agha 2002).

This chapter chronicles the story of the subsequent mediation attempts by the administrations of Presidents George W. Bush, Barack Obama, and Donald Trump. It presents each administration's policies towards peace and how they sought to approach the issue, and seeks to explain why each effort to date has failed. Although the role of the mediator is central, this chapter also reflects on the parties, their positions on substantive and procedural issues, their relationship with the mediator, and their relationship with each other. This chapter focuses exclusively on United States efforts as the pre-eminent mediator of the conflict. This is not to suggest that other actors have not played a role, but they have at most played a secondary part. One such case in point is the European Union, an actor that has been a primary funder of the Palestinian Authority and the peace process, but which Israel has a contentious political relationship with and does not accept as a mediator (Del Sarto 2019; Persson 2015).

For Israel, the prospect of peace with the Palestinians is viewed through the lens of security. Surrendering control of the occupied Palestinian territories as part of the "land for peace" formula presents risks, both in terms of Palestinian actions and deep domestic divisions, as the assassination of Prime Minister Yitzhak Rabin by a religious extremist in 1995 illustrated. Palestinians believe they have already made the most significant concession by acknowledging Israeli sovereignty over roughly 78 per cent of Mandatory Palestine when Yasser Arafat and the Palestine Liberation Organisation (PLO) recognized the state of Israel as part of the unequal mutual recognition element of the Oslo Agreement. This chapter argues that while this is a

DOI: 10.4324/9780429027376-14

story of the failure of the mediators, it is also a story of the failure of the parties to find common ground and to internalize the need for a compromise to coexist as equals. Much like the conflict itself, a zero-sum war of narratives continues over the failure of the peace process, with each side blaming the other.

The Bush Administration

At the beginning of his first presidential term, it quickly became clear that George W. Bush had no desire to get embroiled in the Israeli-Palestinian conflict in the same way his predecessor had. As he remarked to Martin Indyk, the former United States ambassador to Israel and member of Clinton's peace team, "There's no Nobel Peace Prize to be had here" (Indyk 2009: 379). Clinton had warned Bush not to trust Palestinian President Yasser Arafat, whom he deemed culpable for the failure of the Camp David summit in 2000 and for the subsequent start of the second *Intifada*, and Bush heeded the advice. Contrary to the wishes of Secretary of State Colin Powell, the administration explicitly vetoed any diplomatic initiative and avoided using the term "peace process" (Indyk 2009, 379–380; Kurzter et al. 2013, 164, 169). Dominant neo-conservatives like Vice President Dick Cheney, Secretary of Defence Donald Rumsfeld, and national security advisor Elliott Abrams opposed negotiations, viewing Arabs generally and Palestinians specifically as unwilling to ever make peace with Israel on terms the Israelis could accept (Ross and Makovsky 2009, 91–113; Thrall 2014).

In the wake of 9/11, however, the Middle East and the Israeli-Palestinian conflict acquired a greater significance amid the reframing of United States foreign policy towards the "war on terror". Bush identified with Israeli prime minister Ariel Sharon's uncompromising stance against Palestinian terrorism, but also made it clear that progress on the conflict was important to ensure Arab support for his new agenda. Mindful of the need to maintain strong relations with President Bush, which was an "obsession" for Sharon, he unexpectedly endorsed the concept of a Palestinian state in a speech on 23 September 2001 (Ross and Makovsky 2019, 259). In his address to the United Nations General Assembly on 10 November 2001, Bush followed suit, becoming the first United States president to officially refer to a Palestinian state as a desired outcome.[1] He then reiterated the message in his "Rose Garden" speech on 24 June 2002, where he laid out his vision of two democratic states living side by side. However, he stipulated that this required institutional reform "to build a practising democracy based on tolerance and liberty", and the election of new leadership untainted by terror on the Palestinian side to show that they were ready to assume the responsibility of statehood (Bush 2002). As Abrams has explained,

> There would be an independent state of Palestine, but only if and when terrorism was abandoned, and Arafat was gone. The key, then, was not diplomacy, not international conferences, nor was it Israeli concessions – it was Palestinian action.
>
> *(Abrams 2013, 37)*

In response to the ongoing violence of the Intifada, Powell and other envoys were sent to the region to try to negotiate a cease-fire at different stages, but these efforts were hampered by limited political support from the White House and a lack of coherent policy, as evidenced by mixed messages emanating from the executive branch and the State Department (Abrams 2013, 33). This duality was exemplified by the United States approach to the international Quartet's *Road Map for Peace*, launched in April 2003. A "performance-based and goal-driven" peace plan, the Road Map envisaged three phases: Phase I focused on an end to terrorism and violence, Israeli redeployment from positions in the West Bank, Palestinian institution-building, political and security reform, and a full Israeli freeze in settlement construction; Phase II focused on the creation of a provisional Palestinian state; and Phase III envisaged permanent status negotiations to end the conflict (United Nations 2003). The plan was based on three key principles – parallel rather than sequential or conditional implementation, monitoring, and accountability, and a defined end game – but it failed to abide by the first two and only partially fulfilled the third (Elgindy 2012, 9). Parallel implementation ran contrary to the White House view and the Israeli position – expressed in one of their 14 reservations to the plan which, in practice, conditioned their acceptance (Zoughbie 2014, 63) – that any Israeli obligations were conditional on Palestinian security improvement and reform (ECF 2003). A United States implementation monitoring position was created but accomplished little, as it never received political support, and no effective Quartet monitoring mechanism existed (Elgindy 2012, 11–14; Feldman and Shikaki 2007, 4). In terms of a defined end game, the plan stipulated the creation of a Palestinian state but left the key final-status issues, such as borders, settlements, Jerusalem, and refugees to negotiations envisioned for 2005, though subject to performance (Elgindy 2012, 10).

This plan was upended on 18 December 2003, when Sharon announced his intention to unilaterally withdraw both the Israeli military and settlers from the Gaza Strip. Having been staunchly opposed to the idea in the past, Ross and Makovsky (2019, 258–259, 265) argue that this was guided by Sharon's military conviction that it is better to take the initiative than to react. In a domestic debate on the Road Map, Sharon publicly acknowledged that there was an "occupation" (a term anathema to his fellow Likud party members) which was bad for Israel, and argued that separation from the Palestinians was necessary to preserve Israel as a Jewish state (Ross and Makovsky 2019, 261–262). The "disengagement", as it became known, allowed him to pursue separation on Israel's terms, effectively sidelining the Road Map and other international peace initiatives such as the Arab Peace Initiative of 2002 and the Geneva Initiative of 2003. As Sharon's lawyer and advisor Dov Weisglass explained, disengagement was "actually formaldehyde" to ensure "the freezing of the peace process":

> when you freeze that process, you prevent the establishment of a Palestinian state, and you prevent a discussion on the refugees, the borders and Jerusalem. Effectively, this whole package called the Palestinian state, with all that it entails, has been removed indefinitely from our agenda. And all this with authority and permission. All with a presidential blessing and the ratification of both houses of Congress.
>
> *(Shavit 2004)*

This logic, however, did not resonate with Sharon's traditional right-wing constituency, particularly the settlement movement that he had long supported. Opposition within Likud was so strong that Sharon was forced to break away and create a new centrist party, *Kadima* (meaning "forward"), to implement the policy. To the right wing, the withdrawal of 21 settlements in the Gaza Strip and four outposts in the northern West Bank, completed in September 2005, was a betrayal. To support Sharon domestically, President Bush wrote him a letter of assurance, stating that Israel could not be expected to return to the precise 4 June 1967 lines, that larger settlement blocs would be incorporated into Israel, and that Palestinian refugees would be resettled in a new Palestinian state, effectively pre-empting negotiations on these final-status issues (Bush 2004). Sharon reportedly considered this strengthening of the Israeli negotiating position one of his greatest diplomatic achievements (Ross and Makovsky 2019, 269).

Continuing Palestinian terrorist attacks as part of the Intifada had cemented Sharon's belief that there was no partner for peace, which became a prominent part of the Israeli narrative (Del Sarto 2017, 46–49). Although Arafat had appointed as prime minister Mahmoud Abbas (Abu Mazen), a senior PLO member who had been integral to the earlier peace process and rejected violence, Arafat disempowered him and refused to cede control, to the point where in September 2003 Abu Mazen resigned in frustration (Rumley and Tibon 2017, 93–99). Upon Arafat's death in November 2004, Abu Mazen inherited the leadership of the PLO and was elected president in January 2005. Despite their professed desire for new Palestinian leadership, the Bush administration failed to effectively support it when the opportunity arose (Kurtzer et al. 2013, 195–196). The disengagement was not coordinated with Abu Mazen, and the unilateral nature of the withdrawal let Palestinians draw their own conclusions as to what prompted this dramatic development. Many considered it the product of armed resistance, which boosted Abu Mazen's Islamist rivals, Hamas. This, together with their campaign against the rampant corruption in Fatah, paved the way for Hamas to win the January 2006 elections for the Palestinian Legislative Council (PLC). With "Fatah's inability to come to terms with the loss of hegemony over the political system coupled with Hamas' inability to come to terms with the limitations of its own power" (ICG 2007, i), political contestation turned to violent competition and, following a brief period of civil war, Hamas took control of the Gaza Strip in June 2007.

This political and geographical split within the Palestinian community was and remains a prominent obstacle to any negotiated resolution to the conflict. Multiple Egyptian, Qatari, and Saudi attempts at reconciliation and forming a national unity government between the two groups have failed (ICG 2011). The absence of a coherent position towards Israel reduces confidence that any agreement reached would represent all Palestinian parties and be able to be implemented, worsening the existing lack of trust between the two sides. Simultaneously, however, Israel has refused to negotiate with a Palestinian unity government that includes Hamas, creating a dynamic which is not conducive to effective negotiation.

Ironically, American insistence on democracy had legitimized and strengthened the very forces who rejected a negotiated two-state solution with Israel. To respond to Hamas' election victory, new United States secretary of state, Condoleezza Rice, decided that Abu Mazen and moderate Palestinian forces needed to be strengthened, and lobbied President Bush to endorse a diplomatic initiative in a stark departure from his first-term policy. In March 2006, new Kadima leader Ehud Olmert was elected in Israel, following Sharon's incapacitation due to multiple strokes. Olmert had campaigned on a peace platform, pledging to negotiate with the Palestinians and, if these failed, to apply Sharon's strategy of unilateral withdrawal to the West Bank by evacuating settlements outside the main blocs that Israel sought to retain (Kurtzer et al. 2013, 203).

In her early conversations with Olmert, Rice expressed a preference for a negotiated solution over his unilateral *hitkansut* ("convergence") policy: "I didn't like the sound of that term but thought it could be shaped to mean a negotiated solution – not a unilateral one – to the Palestinian question" (Rice 2011, 414). Rice argued that the Palestinians needed a "political horizon" in order to encourage them and generate hope. Bush later reflected, "At first I was skeptical. … But I came to like the idea. If wavering Palestinians could see that a state was a realistic possibility, they would have an incentive to reject violence and support reform" (Bush 2011, 408). Although Abrams argued that this "horizon" already existed through American and Israeli endorsement of a Palestinian state, this remained vague and gave no indication of what that state would look like and whether or not it would have full sovereignty (Abrams 2013,

203–204). With Rice's encouragement, Abu Mazen and Olmert began meeting directly in December 2006 and would continue to meet, both with and without Rice present.

On 16 July 2007, Bush announced that he would convene an international meeting of Israelis, Palestinians, and Arab states in Annapolis, Maryland, to support a return to negotiations. While Rice had worked hard to ensure Israeli and Palestinian commitment, but also that of key regional states such as Egypt, Jordan, and Saudi Arabia, there remained confusion as to exactly what Annapolis would be and what it would generate. Was it to be a crowning event to present a negotiated document, or a launching pad for future negotiations? (Feldman and Shikaki 2007). The Palestinians wanted the former to present a framework agreement on the final-status issues, while the Israelis wanted the latter (Rice 2011, 612). Abrams, who opposed Annapolis and preferred to focus on supporting new Palestinian prime minister Salam Fayyad's state-building reforms, describes this period as one of Rice "substituting motion for progress", creating "the appearance that something positive was happening" with meeting after meeting: "One can caricature this activity as reminiscent of Peter Pan: The peace process was like Tinkerbelle, in that if we all just believed in it firmly enough it really would survive" (Abrams 2013, 226). Ross and Makovsky (2009, 110–111, 141) and Schiff (2013) are similarly critical of Annapolis, arguing that the event was poorly prepared, while a number of former United States diplomats urged Bush and Rice to be more assertive and take the opportunity to present the principles of a final-status agreement to be endorsed (Brzezinski et al. 2008).

The Annapolis Conference took place on 27 November 2007, and although there was little of substance in the joint declaration, the parties did agree to a timetable for final-status negotiations across multiple tracks. These included direct talks between Abu Mazen and Olmert, in addition to those between negotiating teams led by Israeli Foreign Minister Tzipi Livni and long-time Palestinian negotiator and former prime minister Ahmed Qurie (Abu Ala). Negotiations on both tracks proceeded throughout 2008 and reached a pinnacle on 16 September, when Olmert verbally outlined a proposal to Abu Mazen and presented an accompanying map. Abu Mazen asked to take the map with him in order to study it further, but Olmert refused, insisting that he sign it then and there (Avishai 2011). President Bush has explained that the idea was then for Olmert to deposit his proposal with him on a November trip to Washington, DC, Abu Mazen would follow in December to agree the deal, and it would be finalized in January 2009 before Bush left office (Golan 2015, 184, 194; Abrams 2013, 292–293; Avishai 2011). However, this chain of events did not materialize.

The United States team elected not to present a bridging proposal based on Olmert's verbal offer. Their mediation strategy of allowing the parties to largely negotiate bilaterally throughout 2008 was logical, as the leaders were engaging constructively, and both sides preferred dealing with the other directly, but at the crucial point when more assertive and coercive United States mediation would have been necessary to finalize an agreement, Bush and Rice failed to adapt (Eriksson 2019, 404–405). Although United States commitment to this process was significantly greater than the Road Map earlier in the Bush administration, once again the divisions between those in the State Department who believed in diplomacy and the neo-conservatives who did not were stark, and the president's reluctance to get involved reflected his predilection toward the latter.

This episode has come to form a part of the Israeli narrative that the Palestinians "never miss an opportunity to miss an opportunity" and that there is no partner for peace, but Abu Mazen did not actually reject Olmert's offer (Del Sarto 2017, 50–51). As Abrams (2013, 291), Kurtzer and colleagues (2013, 231–232), and Thrall (2017, 181–183) have argued, the Palestinians had a number of questions about the offer that were never answered, and there were multiple details that remained to be clarified. A number of contextual factors also contributed to the failure of the Annapolis process. Throughout 2008, Olmert was dogged by allegations of corruption, leading to his effective resignation in July and official resignation in September, not long after his verbal proposal to Abu Mazen. His mandate to negotiate as caretaker prime minister and, above all, his ability to deliver on any deal were thus questionable. Abu Mazen, too, was a weak and domestically unpopular leader struggling to cope with the challenge from Hamas. He was reluctant to make an agreement with a counterpart on his way out of office, and the politics of succession affected negotiating dynamics – with Livni and others suggesting to Abu Mazen that they wait until she was elected to finalize a better deal (Golan 2015, 184, 188; Rice 2011, 724). Moreover, Livni avoided discussing sensitive issues like Jerusalem lest any leaks should damage her election prospects (Kurtzer et al. 2013, 230; Abrams 2013, 279).

Although ultimately unsuccessful, the Annapolis process was a serious attempt by committed yet weak leaders to resolve the conflict. With the benefit of hindsight, it certainly constitutes, to use Podeh's framework, a "missed opportunity" (Podeh 2016), but it was a failure shared by all sides. Without any type of proposed framework agreement deposited with President Bush, the progress that had been made was lost, and relations between the parties once again deteriorated as a result of the 2008–2009 Gaza war between Hamas and Israel.

The Obama Administration

Like Bush before him, President Barack Obama came to office in January 2009 keen to distinguish himself clearly from his predecessor. In a speech at Cairo University on 4 June, he declared that he sought "a new beginning between the United States and Muslims around the world" to repair relations damaged due to the war on terror. Addressing the Israeli-Palestinian conflict, Obama acknowledged the history of suffering on both sides, underscored the need to reject terrorism and violence with a pointed message to Hamas, and endorsed the two-state solution as a necessity, describing the Palestinian situation as "intolerable". On one issue, Obama was very clear: "The United States does not accept the legitimacy of continued Israeli settlements. This construction violates previous agreements and undermines efforts to achieve peace. It is time for these settlements to stop" (Obama 2009). The primary difference, however, was one of tone rather than substance. On key issues such as the need for a negotiated two-state solution, the need for Palestinian institution-building, and the cessation of Israeli settlement construction (which was part of the Road Map), there was greater continuity than difference (Siniver 2011; Gerges 2013).

Nonetheless, one prominent procedural difference rapidly became apparent: unlike Bush, Obama demonstrated a willingness to exert pressure on Israel over settlements, pushing for a complete freeze in settlement activity. This had been a central recommendation of George Mitchell, Obama's new special envoy to the peace process, in the 2001 fact-finding report he led to address the violence of the Second Intifada (EEAS 2001). Like Sharon at the time, the new Israeli government of Prime Minister Benjamin Netanyahu rejected this approach, and it became the primary issue that initially defined a combative relationship between Obama and Netanyahu. In response to United States pressure, Netanyahu agreed to a ten-month moratorium on new settlement construction and the expropriation of additional land, but insisted that this did not include natural growth within existing settlements or apply to East Jerusalem or the large settlement blocs (Kurtzer et al. 2013, 252–253).

Perceived as a significant concession by Israel and insufficient by the Palestinians, the partial moratorium satisfied no one and failed to build momentum towards renewed negotiations (Ruebner 2013, 99). A generous United States offer of additional military assistance and political guarantees of protection at the United Nations Security Council to Netanyahu in exchange for a three-month extension of the moratorium was made and then withdrawn, as the Israelis had serious reservations and the offer itself became the subject of negotiation (Rogin 2010). As Siniver (2011, 681) argues, Mitchell's efforts to secure a settlement freeze in effect focused on the preconditions to negotiation rather than the substance of final status. In other words, the administration was more committed to managing the conflict than resolving it. United States State Department spokesman P. J. Crowley seemed to acknowledge this at the time:

> We thought that this [the settlement moratorium] had, in a sense, become an end in itself rather than a means to an end. … We're going to focus on the substance and to try to begin to make progress on the core issues themselves. And we think that will create the kind of momentum that we need to see – to get to sustained and meaningful negotiations.
>
> *(Rogin 2010)*

However, the two parties remained far apart, both on substance and on process. Whereas the Palestinians wanted to resume the negotiations from where they had left off with Olmert, Netanyahu declared that Israel would not be bound by the terms of Olmert's offer, which was not to serve as a basis for further negotiations (Kurtzer et al. 2013, 247, 249, 252). Shortly after Obama's Cairo speech, Netanyahu endorsed the concept of a Palestinian state in a speech at Bar-Ilan University, but with multiple preconditions: that Palestinians recognize Israel as the nation state of the Jewish people, that the Palestinian refugee problem be solved outside Israel's borders, that a Palestinian state would have circumscribed sovereignty by being demilitarized with "ironclad" security provisions for Israel, and that Jerusalem remain the undivided capital of Israel (Netanyahu 2009; Lochery 2016, 278–281).

For Palestinians, Obama's push for a complete settlement freeze was then adopted as a precondition for the resumption of negotiations (Rumley and Tibon 2017, 182). Although direct negotiations were launched in Washington, DC on 1–2 September 2010, with Egyptian president Hosni Mubarak, Jordan's King Abdullah II, and Quartet envoy Tony Blair in attendance, these did not extend beyond a second meeting in Sharm el-Sheikh in mid-September. A lack of detailed terms of reference for the negotiations, the impending end of the partial settlement freeze and sensitivities associated with it, and an increase in Palestinian terrorist attacks combined to derail these talks before they had even really started (Ruebner 2013, 104–108; Kurtzer et al. 2013, 259–260).

Dan Kurtzer, a former United States ambassador to Israel and Egypt and member of President Clinton's peace team, argues that the United States approach was driven by tactics rather than strategy. Mitchell and his team engaged in "a kind of billiard-ball diplomacy", trying confidence-building measures, then indirect negotiations, and then direct negotiations, without an underpinning strategy:

> The question is, why did we not start with a strategy and then decide how these various tactics might fit in? … The issue is not to seek the confidence-building measure, but rather to embed it in a strategy so that you can market it in a sustainable process in which there are going to be gains and challenges for both sides, but the gains hopefully will outweigh the risks that the two sides have to take.
>
> *(Kurtzer et al. 2014, 3)*

After years of stalemate amidst the Arab Spring, the newly re-elected President Obama travelled to Israel in March 2013 in a bid to reset the bilateral relationship. John Kerry, the new secretary of state, accompanied him to resurrect the moribund peace process as a key foreign policy issue. Convinced that the window for the two-state solution was closing – "in one to one-and-a-half to two years – or it's over" (Gerstein 2013) – Kerry was determined to re-engage the parties in direct bilateral negotiations. Mistrust between the parties, however, remained high, with multiple waves of attacks in 2012 between Israel and Hamas in Gaza. Since the collapse of the last United States-sponsored talks, rather than merely wait for external actors to pick up the peace portfolio again, the Palestinian Authority had embarked upon a strategy of internationalization, seeking international recognition of their unilaterally declared statehood and commensurate membership of international organizations. Without support of the majority in the United Nations Security Council, the Palestinians had to settle for the status of "non-member observer state" bestowed by the General Assembly in 2012, but continued to use the prospect of membership in international organs such as the International Criminal Court to pressure Israel.

After months of talks with each side, Kerry announced the resumption of final-status negotiations on 30 July, 2013, aimed at achieving a full final-status agreement on all the core issues in nine months (Kerry, Livni and Erekat, 2013). To get the parties back to the table, Kerry had agreed a package of confidence-building measures. In exchange for the release of 104 Palestinians imprisoned by Israel for murder prior to the 1993 Oslo Agreement, a "major slowdown" in Israeli settlement construction, and United States commitment that any future borders be based on the 4 June 1967 lines, the Palestinians agreed to cease their internationalization campaign for the duration of the talks. Although a majority of the Palestinian leadership was against returning to the table on these terms due to deep scepticism about the prospect of any deal with Netanyahu and concern about the political cost of returning to negotiations without a full settlement freeze, Abu Mazen overrode them and decided to return to the table. On the Israeli side, Netanyahu was concerned about being held responsible by the United States for the continued impasse, and mounting European Union threats not to do business with entities that operated in the occupied territories (Birnbaum and Tibon 2014).

The difficulty Netanyahu faced in getting these highly sensitive confidence-building measures approved by his right-wing cabinet created problems that would ultimately precipitate the collapse of the talks. The Palestinian prisoners were to be released in four tranches over the course of the talks rather than all at once, and Netanyahu told Kerry he would need to approve more than two thousand new settlement units in order to appease his coalition partners. As Birnbaum and Tibon (2014) argue, these elements generated misunderstandings and conflicts between the sides that Kerry could not solve. Kerry thought Netanyahu had agreed to release all 104 prisoners, whereas he had agreed to only approximately 80, and did not clarify where the new settlement units would be, with East Jerusalem being particularly sensitive to both sides.

Once again, there were significant differences on both substance and process. According to Schiff (2018), the Israelis sought to discuss all issues in parallel, while the Palestinians wanted to start discussing borders and security. Of these issues, Israel insisted on first agreeing on security arrangements and guarantees, such as a continued Israeli military presence in the West Bank for decades, which Palestinians opposed. On the most sensitive issues of Jerusalem and the Palestinian "right of return", the same traditional differences existed. Israel rejected the idea of a Palestinian capital in East Jerusalem and any responsibility for the refugee issue, insisting that refugees could only return to a Palestinian state. A combination of violence and Israeli announcements of new settlement plans created a difficult negotiating environment, worsened further due to Palestinian anger at Netanyahu's erroneous suggestion that Abu Mazen had accepted new construction in return for the prisoner release (Indyk 2014). The dynamics between the negotiators was also reportedly complicated by the presence on the Israeli side of Netanyahu's attorney, Yitzhak Molho, who seemed intent on avoiding details and insisted that no maps be discussed until security arrangements had been agreed (Birnbaum and Tibon 2014). As it became clear towards the end of 2013 that a full agreement was impossible in the proposed timeframe, Kerry and his envoy, veteran diplomat Martin Indyk, focused instead on a framework agreement on the core issues.

Of the two leaders, Kerry focused his attention on Netanyahu, who had historically fought against the Oslo Agreement and sought to limit its implementation while he was prime minister (1996–1999) (Eriksson 2015, 147–163). Security had always been Netanyahu's foremost concern, so the United States team decided this was a logical place to start, and it put together a security package that they presented to the Israelis in early December. While Netanyahu saw it as a basis for discussion, Minister of Defence Moshe Ya'alon did not and rejected the package, with his private criticism of the American team, and Kerry personally, as "obsessive" and "messianic" generating headlines (Birnbaum and Tibon, 2014). Despite this setback, Kerry continued to work with Netanyahu on a framework agreement and generated some movement. On the right of return, Israel would, at its own discretion, admit some refugees on a humanitarian basis, and on borders, Netanyahu accepted that these would be negotiated based on the 4 June 1967 lines with mutually agreed swaps, language which he had previously decried Obama for using (Kurtzer et al. 2013, 263–265). Jerusalem, however, remained a key sticking point, together with Palestinian recognition of Israel as a Jewish state. When Kerry took elements of this framework to Abu Mazen in February 2014, the Palestinian leader was disappointed with the lack of clarity on Jerusalem. Although certain elements were improved in a later draft discussed in a March meeting between Obama and Abu Mazen at the White House, the Palestinian leader did not respond definitively to it, either positively or negatively (Tibon 2017).

With Israel unwilling to release the final tranche of Palestinian prisoners on 29 March, Kerry appealed unsuccessfully to Abu Mazen for a delay. If Israel could not be compelled to release the final 26 prisoners, then there was no way they could be compelled to agree to a Palestinian capital in East Jerusalem, he reasoned (Birnbaum and Tibon 2014; Rumley and Tibon 2017, 189). Kerry tried to devise a grand bargain for an extension of the talks involving the United States release of convicted spy Jonathan Pollard to Israel, but the Palestinians wanted the prisoner release they had been promised and which Kerry was under the impression Netanyahu had agreed to. On 1 April, instead of a prisoner release, Israel announced the approval of over 700 new homes in the East Jerusalem settlement of Gilo, which prompted Abu Mazen to sign 15 United Nations conventions. American attempts to salvage the talks throughout April were definitively ended when news emerged of a unity government between Hamas, Fatah, and Islamic Jihad, prompting the Israelis to officially suspend the talks (Schiff 2018, 17; Birnbaum and Tibon 2014).

In subsequent testimony to the Senate Foreign Relations Committee, Kerry explained that both sides bore responsibility for the failure of the talks, but seemed to emphasize the Gilo settlement announcement as the key turning point, much to the annoyance of the Israelis (Landler 2014; Kershner 2014). As Ramsbotham has reflected, each party had their disagreements with the United States effort: for Palestinians, it was an issue of process and prioritizing Israeli demands, while for the Israelis, it was an issue of substance, as the unofficial United States position on a number of final-status issues was deemed to be more aligned with the Palestinians (Ramsbotham 2016, 156). Although Kerry considered releasing proposed United States parameters for a framework agreement, much like President Clinton had done in 2000, he opted against such an approach and instead publicly outlined six principles of final status that echoed the 1995 Beilin-Abu Mazen Understandings (Eriksson 2015, 136–137), the

Clinton parameters, and the 2003 Geneva Initiative (Kerry 2016). Once again, this meant that what had been discussed did not create an official baseline for future peace talks or United States policy (Kurtzer et al. 2014, 6).

The Trump Administration

Even if a framework or set of principles had been passed from the Obama Administration to the Trump Administration, it is not clear that Trump would have felt bound by them. During his campaign, Trump was forthright about his desire to do things differently. Already during the transitional period, Trump's team was actively lobbying against United Nations Security Council Resolution 2334, which condemned illegal Israeli settlement construction in the West Bank, on behalf of Netanyahu, in an effort to undermine the Obama Administration, which later abstained on the resolution and allowed it to pass (Lynch 2017; Beaumont 2017a). The Trump Administration subsequently broke a number of longstanding precedents in United States policy towards the conflict and adopted a one-sided approach that prioritised Israeli needs over Palestinian ones. While this is not necessarily novel – former United States mediator Aaron Miller (2005) famously described the Clinton peace team as having acted as "Israel's lawyer" – the scale of Trump's shift was unlike anything seen previously.

Trump appointed Jason Greenblatt, a lawyer for the Trump Organisation, as his special envoy for Middle East peace, who together with the president's son-in-law and advisor, Jared Kushner, was tasked with putting together "the ultimate deal". Whereas Kerry's final address on the conflict as secretary of state emphasized the shared Israeli, Palestinian, and United States interest in a two-state solution (Kerry 2016), the Trump Administration did not clearly commit to this goal. Rather, Trump vacillated between a one-state and two-state solution, saying in February 2017, "I could live with either one" (Trump 2017a). On 6 December 2017, Trump announced the United States recognition of Jerusalem as the capital of Israel, altering their traditional position that the city's status should be subject to negotiation between the two parties (Trump 2017b). Although the announcement lacked specifics, Trump failed to mention Palestinian claims to East Jerusalem, noting only that specific borders were to be the subject of negotiations between the parties. In response, Abu Mazen announced that the Palestinians would no longer accept any United States-sponsored peace initiative and called for more systemic change in the mediation of the conflict to include other mediators (Beaumont 2017b; Melhem 2017).

Whatever constructive ambiguity the Trump Administration preserved by omitting specifics in their announcement was not used to effectively mediate and engage with the Palestinians (Eriksson 2018, 54–56). Rather than address Palestinian needs, the Trump Administration's strategy focused on rewarding Israel and taking further punitive actions against the Palestinians, including halting funding for the United Nations Relief and Works Agency (UNRWA) responsible for the provision of services to Palestinian refugees, trying to redefine which Palestinians can be classified as refugees, closing the PLO representative office in Washington, DC, and reducing funding to the Palestinian Authority (Hirsh and Lynch 2019; Calamur 2018). Zartman and Rubin (2000, 288) argue that biased mediators are only useful if they deliver the party toward whom they are biased, but the Trump Administration refused to exert any leverage to do so.

Kushner unveiled the first component of the administration's plan at the Peace to Prosperity workshop in Bahrain, 25–26 June 2019. Billed as a presentation of the economic opportunities that the administration sought to offer the Palestinians, the event was widely criticized for failing to move beyond broad economic aid aspirations, for including projects that already exist or projects that have been proposed in the past, and for ignoring Israel's occupation which remains the major obstacle to Palestinian economic growth (Makovsky 2019; Morris

2019; Lee 2019). Trump presented the full Peace to Prosperity plan at the White House on 28 January 2020, accompanied by Netanyahu but no Palestinian representative. These were fitting optics, as the plan was heavily tilted towards the Israeli perspective on all final status issues. Under the plan (The White House, 2020), Israel would not evacuate any illegal settlements but rather annex substantial portions of the West Bank, in return for land swaps surrounding Gaza and in the Negev desert along the Israeli border with Egypt. A Palestinian capital would be created in areas east of the current security barrier around Jerusalem, such as Kafr Aqab, Abu Dis, and parts of Shuafat, rather than all Arab areas of East Jerusalem. Israel would accept no responsibility for the Palestinian refugee problem, and no refugees would be re-settled in Israel.

Although the Trump plan called for the establishment of a Palestinian state after negotiations based on their vision, the plan was a non-starter for the Palestinians, with the conditionalities included effectively emptying any proposed sovereignty of meaning. By effectively seeking to normalize the one-state status quo rather than mediate, the most consequential impact of the Trump Administration's plan may well be the final death of the two-state solution (Eriksson 2018, 58–59). The prospect of Israeli unilateral annexation of parts of the West Bank has been widely criticized, with EU foreign policy chief Josep Borrell stating that such a move "could not pass unchallenged" (Emmott et al. 2020). While multiple individual EU member states have announced that they will not recognize any unilateral Israeli annexation, a lack of consensus among all members has made it difficult for the EU to effectively act on Borrell's words (Eriksson 2020; Lovatt 2020; Del Sarto 2019).

As countless international and Israeli officials have repeatedly warned, the abandonment of the two-state solution will have detrimental effects on Israel, and imperil the notion of a Jewish and democratic state (Kerry 2016; Ross and Makovsky 2019, 268–269, 273–290; Guardian 2020). In an interview with German broadcaster Deutsche Welle (Schmitt 2017), former Israeli prime minister Ehud Barak warned that continued Israeli occupation of the Palestinian territories meant that Israel would "inevitably" become "either non-Jewish or non-democratic", putting Israel on "a slippery slope toward apartheid".

Conclusion

Although the basic guiding principles of a two-state solution have been clear for over two decades, an agreement to end the conflict has not been achieved despite multiple attempts. This chapter has critically evaluated these mediation efforts in terms of strategy, engagement, and execution. Former officials like Martin Indyk and Dennis Ross have argued that the United States needs to reassure Israel in order to generate progress in negotiations (Thrall 2014), but it must also take into account the needs of both sides. However, as Thrall and others have argued, the United States must also pressure the parties to compromise and be willing to use the substantial leverage it holds (Thrall 2014; Thrall 2017, 39–40; Eriksson 2019). A key lesson Kurtzer and Lasensky (2008, 43–47) identified during the Oslo process was the need for accountability and ensuring the implementation of agreements reached. The same was true of the efforts detailed here (Kurtzer et al. 2014, 5–6), but the United States has always been reluctant to fulfil this role, despite its unique position to do so.

To use a well-worn expression often heard during the case studies examined in this chapter, a mediator cannot want peace more than the parties themselves. They are the ones who will have to implement peace, and they have to own it. Both parties bear responsibility for this catalogue of failure. Neither side has adequately prepared its people for the nature and scale of the sacrifices an equitable two-state solution would require. Both sides are riven with division between pragmatists and extremists, those who are willing to compromise and those who are not, and facing up to these differences runs the risk of generating internal conflict. On the Palestinian side, this is already evident in the continuing rift between Hamas and Fatah, while on the Israeli side, the vast political polarization evident in the murder of Prime Minister Yitzhak Rabin in 1995 continues through competing visions of the nature of the state of Israel and its future.

An alternative argument, however, would be that the failure of previous efforts suggests a deficiency in the concept of a two-state solution, and that other solutions such as the one-state solution are preferable. Indeed, this is the position of the Israeli right wing, and Palestinians have also increasingly adopted this view, seeking to reframe the struggle as one for equal rights within one state. However, just as with the two-state solution, there are wildly different visions of what a one-state solution would look like in practice. Would it be a Jewish state, or would it be a bi-national state with equal rights for all citizens, regardless of identity? Neither solution would fully satisfy the twin nationalisms that have developed and consolidated over time. Consequently, a one-state solution is no guarantee of a peaceful future, merely a different form of conflict.

Recommended Readings

Abrams, E. 2013. *Tested by Zion: The Bush Administration and the Israeli-Palestinian Conflict*. New York: Cambridge University Press.

Eriksson, J. 2019. "Coercion and Third-party Mediation of Identity-based Conflict." *Review of International Studies* 45:3, 387–406.

Golan, G. 2015. *Israeli Peacemaking since 1967: Factors Behind the Breakthroughs and Failures*. London: Routledge.

Kurtzer, D., et al. 2013. *The Peace Puzzle: America's Quest for Arab-Israeli Peace, 1989–2011*. New York: Cornell University Press.

Thrall, N. 2017. *The Only Language They Understand*. New York: Metropolitan Books.

Note

1 The Clinton parameters of December 2000 referred to a Palestinian state, but these were proposals rather than official government positions, and they expired when he left office.

Questions for Discussion

(1) What were the strengths and weaknesses of the Annapolis process?
(2) Was the Obama Administration correct to focus on Israeli settlements as the main obstacle to peace?
(3) How has the Trump Administration's peace plan differed from previous plans? How has it impacted the prospects for peace?
(4) Why has United States mediation failed to produce a peace agreement?

References

Abrams, E. 2013. *Tested by Zion: The Bush Administration and the Israeli-Palestinian Conflict*. New York: Cambridge University Press.

Avishai, B. 2011. "A Plan for Peace that Still Could Be." *The New York Times Magazine*, 7 February, 36.

Beaumont, P. 2017a. "Were Other Trump Aides Lobbying for Israel Illicitly Alongside Michael Flynn?" *The Guardian*, 1 December. Available at: www.theguardian.com/us-news/2017/dec/01/michael-flynn-israel-lobbying-russia-united-nations

Beaumont, P. 2017b. "Palestinians No Longer Accept US as Mediator, Abbas Tells Summit" *The Guardian*, 13 December. Available at: www.theguardian.com/world/2017/dec/13/recep-tayyip-erdogan-unite-muslim-world-trump-east-jerusalem

Birnbaum, B., and A. Tibon. 2014. "The Explosive, Inside Story of How John Kerry Built an Israel-Palestine Peace Plan – and Watched It Crumble." *The New Republic*, 20 July. Available at: https://newrepublic.com/article/118751/how-israel-palestine-peace-deal-died.

Bush, G. W. 2002. "President Bush calls for new Palestinian leadership", Speech on 24 June. Available at: https://georgewbush-whitehouse.archives.gov/news/releases/2002/06/20020624-3.html.

Bush, G. W. 2004. "Letter from President Bush to Prime Minister Sharon", Speech on 14 April. Available at: https://georgewbush-whitehouse.archives.gov/news/releases/2004/04/20040414-3.html.

Bush, G. W. 2011. *Decision Points*. New York: Broadway Books.

Brzezinski, Z. et al. 2008 "Letter on Middle East Peace Conference to President George W. Bush and Secretary of State Condoleeza Rice, 10 October 2007." *Journal of Palestine Studies* 37:2, 198–200.

Calamur, K. 2018. "The US Is Sidelining Itself in the Middle East." *The Atlantic*, 31 August. Available at: www.theatlantic.com/international/archive/2018/08/trump-palestinians-unrwa-funding/569167/.

Del Sarto, R. 2017. *Israel Under Siege: The Politics of Insecurity and the Rise of the Israeli Neo-Revisionist Right*. Washington, DC: Georgetown University Press.

Del Sarto, R. 2019. "Stuck in the Logic of Oslo: Europe and the Israeli-Palestinian Conflict." *Middle East Journal*, 73:3, 376–396.

Economic Cooperation Foundation (ECF) .2003. "Government of Israel's Reservations to the Road Map (2003)." Available at: https://ecf.org.il/issues/issue/96.

Elgindy, K. 2012. "The Middle East Quartet: A Post-mortem." Analysis paper, *The Saban Centre for Middle East Policy at Brookings*, no. 25, February.

Emmott, R., et al. 2020. "Vexed by Annexation: The Battle Inside the EU over Israel." *Reuters*, 23 June. Available at: https://reut.rs/37W8osM.

Eriksson, J. 2015. *Small-state Mediation in International Conflicts: Diplomacy and Negotiation in Israel-Palestine*. London: IB Tauris.

Eriksson, J. 2018. "Master of None: Trump, Jerusalem, and the Prospects of Israeli-Palestinian Peace." *Middle East Policy* 25:2, 51–63.

Eriksson, J. 2019. "Coercion and Third-party Mediation of Identity-based Conflict." *Review of International Studies*, 45:3, 387–406.

Eriksson, J. 2020. "The European (Dis)Union on Jerusalem and the Israeli-Palestinian Conflict." In *Trump's Jerusalem Move: Making Sense of US Policy on the Israeli-Palestinian Conflict*, eds. K. Üstün and K. Kanat. Washington, DC.: SETA, 145–168.

European External Action Service (EEAS) .2001. "Sharm el-Sheikh Fact-Finding Committee Report: 'Mitchell Report.'" 30 April. Available at: http://eeas.europa.eu/archives/docs/mepp/docs/mitchell_report_2001_en.pdf.

Feldman, S. and K. Shikaki. 2007. "Is It Still Fall in Annapolis? Thinking About a Scheduled Meeting." *Crown Center for Middle East Studies Middle East Brief*, no. 21, November, 1–8.

Gerges, F. 2013. "The Obama Approach to the Middle East: The End of America's Moment?" *International Affairs*, 89:2, 299–323.

Gerstein, J. 2013. "Kerry: 1–2 years for Mideast peace 'or it's over.'" *Politico*, 17 April. Available at: www.politico.com/blogs/politico44/2013/04/kerry-1-2-years-for-mideast-peace-or-its-over-161945.

Golan, G. 2015. *Israeli Peacemaking since 1967: Factors Behind the Breakthroughs and Failures*. London: Routledge.

The Guardian. 2020. "Grave concern about US plan to resolve Israel-Palestine conflict." 27 February. Available at: www.theguardian.com/world/2020/feb/27/grave-concern-about-us-plan-to-resolve-israel-palestine-conflict

Hirsh, M., and C. Lynch. 2019 "Jared Kushner and the Art of Humiliation." *Foreign Policy*, 12 February. Available at: https://foreignpolicy.com/2019/02/12/jared-kushner-and-the-art-of-humiliation/.

Indyk, M. 2009. *Innocent Abroad: An Intimate Account of American Peace Diplomacy in the Middle East*. New York: Simon & Schuster.

Indyk, M. 2014. "The Pursuit of Middle East Peace: A Status Report." Keynote address to the Washington Institute for Near East Policy's 2014 Weinberg Founders Conference, 8 May. Available at: www.washingtoninstitute.org/uploads/Documents/other/IndykKeynote20140508.pdf

International Crisis Group (ICG). 2007."After Gaza." *Middle East Report*, no. 68, 2 August. Available at: www.crisisgroup.org/middle-east-north-africa/eastern-mediterranean/israelpalestine/after-gaza.

International Crisis Group (ICG). 2011. "Palestinian Reconciliation: Plus Ça Change," *Middle East Report*, no. 110, 20 July. Available at: www.crisisgroup.org/middle-east-north-africa/eastern-mediterranean/israelpalestine/palestinian-reconciliation-plus-ca-change.

Kerry, J. 2016. "Remarks on Middle East Peace." US Department of State, 28 December. Available at: https://2009-2017.state.gov/secretary/remarks/2016/12/266119.htm.

Kerry, J., T. Livni, and S. Erekat. 2013. "Remarks on the Middle East peace process talks." US Department of State, 30 July. Available at: https://2009-2017.state.gov/secretary/remarks/2013/07/212553.htm.

Kershner, I. 2014. "Israel Says It Is 'Deeply Disappointed' by Kerry's Remarks on Peace Talks." *New York Times*, 9 April. Available at: www.nytimes.com/2014/04/10/world/middleeast/middle-east-peace-effort.html.

Kurtzer, D., and S. and Lasensky. 2008. *Negotiating Arab-Israeli Peace: American Leadership in the Middle East.* Washington, DC: United States Institute of Peace.

Kurtzer, D., et al. 2013. *The Peace Puzzle: America's Quest for Arab-Israeli Peace, 1989-2011.* New York: Cornell University Press.

Kurtzer, D., et al. 2014. "The Israeli-Palestinian Conflict: Has the US Failed?" *Middle East Policy*, 21:4, 1–31.

Landler, M. 2014. "Mideast Frustration, the Sequel." *New York Times*, 8 April. Available at: www.nytimes.com/2014/04/09/world/middleeast/israeli-settlement-plan-derailed-peace-talks-kerry-says.html.

Lee, M. 2019. "Investors at Bahrain workshop say peace is the missing piece in US Mideast plan." *The Times of Israel*, 26 June. Available at: www.timesofisrael.com/investors-at-bahrain-workshop-say-peace-is-the-missing-piece-in-us-mideast-plan/.

Lochery, N. 2016. *The Resistible Rise of Benjamin Netanyahu.* London: Bloomsbury.

Lovatt, H. 2020. "Israel's West Bank annexation: Preparing EU policy for the day after." European Council on Foreign Relations, 14 May. Available at: www.ecfr.eu/article/commentary_israels_west_bank_annexation_preparing_eu_policy_for_the_day_aft.

Lynch, C. 2017. "Flynn pressured UN on Israel vote before taking office." *Foreign Policy*, 17 February. Available at: http://foreignpolicy.com/2017/02/17/logan-trump-israel-flynn-pressured-u-n-on-israel-vote-before-taking-office/.

Makovsky, D. 2019. "Jared Kushner's All-or-Nothing Mistake in the Middle East." *The Washington Post*, 1 July. Available at: www.washingtonpost.com/opinions/global-opinions/jared-ku...27f-ed2942f73d70_story.html?noredirect=on&utm_term=.c1c9ce7701a7.

Malley, R. and H. Agha. 2001. "Camp David: Tragedy of Errors", *New York Review of Books*, 9 August (13).

Malley, R. and H. Agha. 2002. "Camp David and After: An Exchange (2. A Reply to Ehud Barak)." *New York Review of Books*, 49(10), 46–49.

Melhem, A. 2017. "PA Rejects US, Seeks New Sponsors for Talks." *Al Monitor*, 27 December. Available at: www.al-monitor.com/pulse/originals/2017/12/palestine-new-peace-process-sponsor-us-jerusalem-move.html.

Miller, A. 2005. "Israel's Lawyer." *The Washington Post*, 23 May. Available at: www.washingtonpost.com/wp-dyn/content/article/2005/05/22/AR2005052200883.html.

Morris, B. 2002. "Camp David and After: An Exchange (1. An Interview with Ehud Barak)." *New York Review of Books*, 49(10), 42–45.

Morris, B., Malley, R. and Agha, H. 2002. "Camp David and After – Continued," *New York Review of Books*, 27 June, 49(11).

Morris, L. 2019. "Kushner Presents Vision of a Middle East at Peace but No Details How to Get There." *The Washington Post*, 25 June. Available at: www.washingtonpost.com/world/middle_east/trump-administ...-9692-11e9-9a16-dc551ea5a43b_story.html?utm_term=.604a82f59f2d.

Netanyahu, B. 2009. "Full Text of Netanyahu's Foreign Policy Speech at Bar Ilan." *Ha'aretz*, 14 June. Available at: www.haaretz.com/news/full-text-of-netanyahu-s-foreign-policy-speech-at-bar-ilan-1.277922.

Obama, B. 2009, "Remarks by the President at Cairo University." The White House, 4 June. Available at: https://obamawhitehouse.archives.gov/the-press-office/remarks-president-cairo-university-6-04-09.

Persson, A. 2015. *The EU and the Israeli-Palestinian Conflict, 1971–2013.* Lanham, MD: Lexington Books.

Podeh, E. 2016. *Chances for Peace: Missed Opportunities in the Arab-Israeli Conflict.* Austin, TX: University of Texas Press.

Pundak, R. 2001. "From Oslo to Taba: What Went Wrong?", *Survival*, 43:3, 31–45.

Ramsbotham, O. 2016. *When Conflict Resolution Fails: An Alternative to Negotiation and Dialogue.* Cambridge: Polity.

Rice, C. 2011. *No Higher Honour: A Memoir of My Years in Washington.* New York: Random House.

Rogin, J. 2010. "Why the U.S.-Israel Settlement Deal Fell Apart." *Foreign Policy*, 9 December. Available at: https://foreignpolicy.com/2010/12/09/why-the-u-s-israel-settlement-deal-fell-apart/.

Ross, D., and D. Makovsky. 2009. *Myths, Illusions, and Peace: Finding a New Direction for America in the Middle East.* London: Viking.

Ross, D., and D. Makovsky. 2019. *Be Strong and of Good Courage: How Israel's Most Important Leaders Shaped Its Destiny.* New York: Public Affairs.

Ruebner, J. 2013. *Shattered Hopes: Obama's Failure to Broker Israeli-Palestinian Peace.* London: Verso.

Rumley, G., and A. Tibon. 2017. *The Last Palestinian: The Rise and Reign of Mahmoud Abbas.* Buffalo, NY: Prometheus Books.

Schiff, A. 2013. "The 'Annapolis Process': A Chronology of Failure." *Israel Affairs*, 19:4, 660–678.

Schiff, A. 2018. "The Kerry Peace Initiative in the Israeli-Palestinian Conflict: When Hope and Good Intentions Are Not Enough." *International Negotiation*, 23:1, 8–41.

Schmitt, C. 2017. "Former PM Barak: Israel on 'Slippery Slope' towards Apartheid." *Deutsche Welle*, 21 June. Available at: www.dw.com/en/former-pm-barak-israel-on-slippery-slope-towards-apartheid/a-39356087.

Shavit, A. 2004. "The Big Freeze." *Ha'aretz*, 7 October. Available at: www.haaretz.com/1.4710587.

Siniver, A. 2011. "Change Nobody Believes In: Obama and the Israeli-Palestinian Conflict." *Diplomacy and Statecraft*, 22:4, 678–695.

Thrall, N. 2014. "Israel and the US: The Delusions of Our Diplomacy." *New York Review of Books*, 9 November. Available at: www.nybooks.com/articles/2014/10/09/israel-us-delusions-our-diplomacy/.

Thrall, N. 2017. *The Only Language They Understand.* New York: Metropolitan Books.

Tibon, A. 2017. "Exclusive: Obama's Detailed Plans for Mideast Peace Revealed – and How Everything Fell Apart." *Ha'aretz*, 8 June. Available at: www.haaretz.com/israel-news/.premium-1.794292?=&ts=_1496932209512.

Trump, D. 2017a. "Remarks by President Trump and Prime Minister Netanyahu of Israel in Joint Press Conference." The White House, 15 February. Available at: www.whitehouse.gov/briefings-statements/remarks-president-trump-prime-minister-netanyahu-israel-joint-press-conference/.

Trump, D. 2017b. "Statement by President Trump on Jerusalem." The White House, 6 December. Available at: www.whitehouse.gov/briefings-statements/statement-president-trump-jerusalem/.

United Nations (UN). 2003. "A Performance-based Road Map to a Permanent Two-state Solution to the Israeli-Palestinian Conflict." 30 April. Available at: https://peacemaker.un.org/israel-palestine-roadmap2003.

The White House. 2020. "Peace to Prosperity: A Vision to Improve the Lives of the Palestinian and Israeli People." January 2020. Available at: https://trumpwhitehouse.archives.gov/wp-content/uploads/2020/01/Peace-to-Prosperity-0120.pdf.

Zartman, I. W., and J. Z. Rubin. 2000. "Symmetry and Asymmetry in Negotiation." In *Power and Negotiation*, eds. I. W. Zartman and J. Z. Rubin. Ann Arbor, MI: University of Michigan Press, 271–293.

Zoughbie, D. 2014. *Indecision Points: George W. Bush and the Israeli-Palestinian Conflict.* Cambridge, MA: MIT Press.

PART III

The Key Issues of the Conflict

12
PALESTINIAN REFUGEES

*Susan M. Akram**

Introduction

The Palestinian refugee issue is the fault line of the Palestinian-Israeli conflict, and resolving it is key to finding solutions for the outstanding issues between the parties. Globally, Palestinians number approximately 13 million persons, of which about 9 million have been forcibly displaced, including refugees. It is more accurate to refer to most Palestinians as 'forcibly displaced persons,' as the international treaty-based definitions of refugees or stateless persons to Palestinians do not readily apply to them, and there is more than one definition that applies to Palestinians in these categories. Nevertheless, available data includes the 5.55 million Palestinians registered as 'Palestine refugees' from the 1948 conflict with the United Nations Relief and Works Agency for Palestine Refugees (UNRWA), as well as another unregistered over a million Palestine refugees in UNRWA areas; 1.24 million 'displaced Palestinians' from the 1967 conflict also registered with UNRWA; and another million internally displaced Palestinians within the Occupied Palestinian Territories (OPT) and within Israel itself (American Friends Service Committee, n.d.). However, UNRWA-registered 'Palestine refugees' comprise only about 64 per cent of the population of Palestinians who have been displaced from the start of the conflict, and continue to be displaced today (BADIL 2016–2018, ix). Identifying and defining who is a Palestinian refugee or a stateless person, and who among them is entitled to the benefits of the durable solutions required under international law, are critical to determining the beneficiaries of a negotiated settlement in any forthcoming peace process. This chapter summarizes the historical–legal background to the Palestinian refugee problem, how the United Nations has responded to it over time, the establishment of relevant United Nations agencies, and the complex definitional issues. It reviews the situation for Palestinians in the main host states today, the trajectory of peace negotiations, and the main issues to be resolved for a just and comprehensive solution.

Historical and Legal Background to the Palestinian Refugee Problem

Forced displacement of Palestinians began well before the establishment of the State of Israel on 15 May 1948. Following the passage of United Nations Resolution 181 on 29 November 1947 that recommended partitioning Palestine into two states, conflict broke out between the Jewish

DOI: 10.4324/9780429027376-16

and Palestinian communities (United Nations General Assembly 1947). The organized Zionist militias forced out, terrorized or massacred large numbers of Palestinians, and about 350,000 of the approximately 1.2 million pre-war Palestinian population were forcibly displaced from their homes by May 1948. Upon the declaration of the Israeli state, another 380,000 Palestinians were expelled or fled the fighting, and the 700–800,000 Palestinian refugees sheltered in encampments in the West Bank, Gaza Strip, Lebanon, Jordan, and Syria (Akram and Lynk 2011, 27–28). In the aftermath of the 1967 Arab-Israeli conflict, Israel occupied East Jerusalem, the West Bank, Gaza, the Syrian Golan and the Egyptian Sinai Peninsula, forcing another 350–400,000 Palestinians to flee their homes. In addition to those who were displaced, approximately 60,000 Palestinians who were outside the area during the conflict were prevented from returning home (BADIL 2015).

Responsibility for the forced displacement of Palestinians is heavily contested. The official Israeli view is that the refugees fled on their own, while a number of Israeli historians claim that Palestinians were encouraged to leave by the Arab leadership, or that there was an 'exchange of populations' between Arabs from Palestine and Jews from Arab states (Artz 1997). In his report to the General Assembly (GA) in September 1948, the United Nations Mediator for Palestine stated that 'the exodus of Palestinian Arabs resulted from panic created by fighting in their communities, by rumours concerning real or alleged acts of terrorism, or expulsion' (United Nations Mediator for Palestine 1948). Historical evidence based on Israeli and Jewish archives reveals that 'transfer committees' were established by Zionist leadership in May 1948, to carry out Plan Dalet, which was a set of policies to expel Palestinians from their homes, destroy their houses, expropriate their property, settle Jews in their places, and pass regulations and laws to prevent their return (Pappé 2006; Morris 1989). Plan Dalet was approved at the highest level, by the heads of the Zionist militias (Morris 1989).

Closely related to the question of the right of Palestinians to return is the issue of restitution of the massive property losses Palestinians suffered as a consequence of their displacement and of Israeli law that confiscated their properties. By the end of 1947, there were 1.2 million Palestinians residing in all of Palestine, comprising two-thirds of the population, while the other one-third were Jews, about 610,000. The Jewish population at the time owned no more than 7 per cent of the land in Palestine, while Palestinians owned the rest under individual or communal title or usufruct: homes, villages, holy places, cultivated and uncultivated lands, citrus and olive groves, cemeteries, and national, municipal and local official and other buildings throughout Palestine. As early as June 1948, the provisional Israeli government put a series of policies in place to prevent the refugees from returning and to confiscate their properties, expanding confiscations Jewish militias had already been carrying out when they took over Palestinian villages in the fighting. In July 1948, the Ministerial Committee for Abandoned Property and Custodian of Abandoned Property centralized the taking of Palestinian homes and lands and leased them to Jews to live in and to use for agricultural purposes. In a series of successive regulations and laws, Israel confiscated refugee properties, froze refugee bank accounts in Israel, and put in place the mechanisms for permanent expropriation.[1]

Building on prior legislation, the most extensive law affecting Palestinian property was the 1950 Absentees' Property Law (Laws of the State of Israel 1950). The law defined an 'absentee' as anyone who, as of 29 November 1947 (the date of the Partition Resolution), was a citizen of an Arab state, was in an Arab country, was in any part of Palestine that was not under Jewish control, or had left his habitual residence, even briefly.[2] The law authorized Israel to confiscate the property of any person defined as an 'absentee' and transfer it to the State Custodian of Absentee Property who controlled all use of Palestinian land, including the right to lease or sell. At the same time, Israel created the Development Authority, a public body authorized to acquire land for the Israeli state, and regulate public land use (Laws of the State of Israel 1950). The Custodian of Absentee Property was given almost unfettered discretion to confiscate, lease, or sell Palestinian land to the Development Authority, and the Israeli Supreme Court has affirmed this broad discretion in the face of decades of challenge by Palestinian landholders.[3] The Development Authority also purchased large amounts of Palestinian refugee property from the Jewish National Fund (JNF) – land which is restricted by JNF charter for exclusive use and benefit of Jews. In 1960, Israel passed the Basic Law that defined the lands of the state, the Development Authority and the Jewish National Funds as 'Israel Lands', for the exclusive use of the Jewish people in perpetuity. Through these and other mechanisms, including more recent laws confiscating Palestinian properties in the West Bank, Jewish pre-1948 ownership of 7 per cent of Palestine has been transformed to ownership of 92 per cent of the lands and properties of historic Palestine. The vast majority of these lands can never be leased or otherwise alienated to or for the use of non-Jews.

In addition to the land laws designed to prevent Palestinians from reclaiming their properties, Israel passed laws to prevent Palestinians from returning and stripped them of citizenship in the new state. The 1950 Law of Return provided automatic citizenship to Jews from anywhere in the world who exercise their 'right of return' (performing *aliyah*), granting them the status of 'Jewish nationals.'[4] Two years later, Israel passed the Nationality Law, which created two separate citizenship statuses: one for 'Jewish nationals' (as defined under the 1950 Law of Return) and one for 'Israel nationals.' Under Israeli law, only Jewish nationals can lease, own or benefit from all the lands claimed as 'Israel lands' (Lehn 1974; Bisharat 1993; Kedar 2001). To acquire the status of 'Israel national,' an individual had to fulfill very stringent requirements, including unbroken residence and registration with Israeli authorities between 14 May 1948 and the date of the Law's passage on 14 July 1952 (Laws of the State of Israel 1952). None of the Palestinians forced out during the conflict could satisfy the requirements, and many of the internally displaced Palestinians in Israel could not meet them either. Finally, the Nationality Law retroactively repealed Palestinian citizenship to the date Israel was declared a state. Thus, the vast majority of Palestinians were rendered stateless under the provisions of Israeli law.

From a legal perspective, the reasons for flight are not relevant to the rights of refugees to return to their homes, obtain restitution of their properties and compensation for losses, as these rights are grounded in international law that makes no distinction between forcible and voluntary displacement. As for the claim of population exchanges, there is no historical evidence of any agreement between Arab states and Israel that Arab Jews would be 'exchanged' for Palestinians. Moreover, forcible population exchanges were prohibited as a matter of customary international law well before 1948. The political debates over these issues, however, mostly fail to take international law into account, and the negotiations between the parties thus far have focused almost exclusively on contesting moral and political responsibility for the refugee problem.

United Nations Response, the Problem of Definitions and United Nations Agency Mandates

In the aftermath of the passage of Resolution 181 and the violence that ensued, the United Nations was intensely engaged with the Arab-Israeli conflict in general and with the refugee issue in particular. As the refugees were fleeing by the thousands from Palestine, the General Assembly passed Resolution 194 on 11 December 1948, the most important resolution on the rights of the refugees and international legal consensus for implementing them (United Nations General Assembly 1948). In Resolution 194 the General Assembly established the first of several agencies with varying mandates towards the Palestinian refugees, the United Nations Conciliation Commission on Palestine (UNCCP). The UNCCP was authorized to mediate and resolve the outstanding issues between the warring parties, and to provide international protection to, and implement durable solutions for, the refugees. In its key paragraph, 11, Resolution 194 required that the refugees were to be permitted to return to their homes 'at the earliest practicable date,' and obtain compensation for loss or damage to their properties (United Nations General Assembly 1948, 11). The UNCCP was required to implement the durable solutions embodied in paragraph 11 for the refugees within its mandate.

Resolution 194 did not include a definition of the 'refugees' whose 'rights properties and interests' the UNCCP was entrusted to protect. However, in a series of notes and authoritative interpretations, the United Nations Secretariat and Legal Advisor to the UNCCP clarified the categories of persons to be considered 'refugees' for purposes of the resolution and the scope of UNCCP's mandate. Although the categories were very specifically laid out, the refugees were generally defined as all habitual residents and citizens of Palestine – recognized as such by Palestinian Nationality law under the terms of the Lausanne Treaty – who left, or were forced to leave, that territory between 6 August 1924 and up through the 1947–1949 conflict.[5]

Under the terms of the Lausanne Treaty at the end of World War I, Turkish subjects residing in Palestine became Palestine nationals when the treaty was ratified on 6 August 1924 (Treaty of Lausanne 1923). Subsequently, Britain codified the Lausanne Treaty's nationality provisions through the Palestine Citizenship Order of 1925, which conferred citizenship on approximately one million Palestinians by birth or parentage, the overwhelming majority of whom were Arab. As a matter of international law, Palestinian nationality was recognized by ratification of the treaty, and Resolution 194's definition of 'refugee' encompassed all these Palestine nationals.[6] The obligations that the UNCCP was entrusted to implement were not solely for 'refugees' as generally understood, but for the entire national population of Palestinians who had been forcibly displaced from Palestine.

With the UNCCP established as the agency to provide international protection for the Palestinian refugees, the General Assembly realized that until the UNCCP could fulfil its mission, the urgent humanitarian needs of thousands of refugees would have to be addressed and, one year later, the General Assembly passed Resolution 302 (IV) establishing UNRWA for that task (United Nations General Assembly 1949). UNRWA was set up as a short-term agency with an initial three-year term to provide food, clothing and shelter to the refugees in the five major areas of their displacement – the West Bank, Gaza, Syria, Jordan, and Lebanon. UNRWA's initial task was to define the 'refugees' for whom it was to provide its services, as it had inherited various lists from several humanitarian agencies that had been responding to the crisis. UNRWA's 'Palestine refugee' definition was based on the UNCCP definition (Palestine nationals) but included only those who were 'in need', who had fled the 1948 conflict and had found themselves within UNRWA areas. In addition to the category of 'Palestine refugees,' UNRWA extended coverage to individuals who had been registered with predecessor aid agencies and were grandfathered onto the UNRWA rolls. However, registration with UNRWA was, and remains, voluntary.

The General Assembly acknowledged that the refugee problem was not going to be resolved through international efforts, and continued UNRWA's mandate, usually for five-year periods. When Israel invaded and occupied the West Bank and Gaza in June of 1967, it forced another 350–400,000 Palestinians to flee to neighbouring countries. The General Assembly responded by passing Resolution 2252 to include Palestinian 'displaced persons' from the 1967 conflict as eligible for UNRWA's services – a category that has been renewed by the GA since then, along with others from 'subsequent hostilities.'[7]

Today, UNRWA defines 'Palestine refugees' as

> Persons whose normal place of residence was Palestine during the period 1 June 1946 to 15 May 1948, and who lost both home and means of livelihood as a result of the 1948 conflict. Palestine Refugees, and descendants of Palestine refugee males, including legally adopted children, are eligible to register for UNRWA services.
>
> *(UNRWA 2009)*

In addition to the 1967 'Palestinian displaced' category, UNRWA includes other beneficiaries in its Consolidated Eligibility and Registration Instructions (CERI's) based on emergency situations or extreme hardship. These include 'Jerusalem poor', 'Gaza poor,' orphans and non-refugee wives. Descendants of Palestine refugees and 1967 displaced Palestinians continue to be registered, but services to other categories do not extend to subsequent generations (UNRWA 2009; Bartholomeusz 2009, 457–460).

Just one week before establishing UNRWA, the General Assembly passed Resolution 319 (IV) creating the United Nations High Commissioner for Refugees (UNHCR)(United Nations General Assembly 1949). UNHCR was established to provide international protection and assistance to all groups and individuals defined as refugees in its Statute, and to search for and implement durable solutions for them.[8] However, the Statute was passed on 14 December 1950, after the creation of UNRWA, and included a provision stating that 'the competence of the High Commissioner ... shall not extend to a person ... (who) continues to receive from other organs or agencies of the United Nations protection or assistance.'[9] Although not explicitly mentioned in the Statute, Palestinians were the only 'persons' who were excluded from UNHCR's mandate under the terms of this provision.

Between January 1950 and September 1954, the General Assembly debated and drafted two treaties: one that became the Convention on the Status of Refugees (Refugee Convention), and one that became the Convention on the Status of Stateless Persons (Stateless Persons Convention). In both these treaties, similar though not identical language appears as in the UNHCR Statute, excluding Palestinians from the benefits of the Refugee Convention under its Article 1D,[10] and from the benefits of the Stateless Persons Convention under its Article 1 (Convention Relating to the Status of Stateless Persons. 1954). The reasons for excluding Palestinians from the benefits of the Refugee Convention and the Stateless Persons Convention, as well as from the mandate of UNHCR, are explained in the drafting history of these instruments (Takkenberg 1998, 68–83). In essence, the United Nations delegates agreed that since Palestinians had become refugees as a result of the United Nations's own action in partitioning their homeland (by passing Resolution 181), the United Nations had a special responsibility towards their care and protection. In addition, the United Nations had already established a 'special regime' for them by the creation of two agencies, the UNCCP to provide them international protection, and UNRWA to provide for their humanitarian assistance. As such, there was no need for a third agency (UNHCR) to have overlapping competence with UNCCP and UNRWA. Finally, the delegates proposing these provisions were concerned that the focus of the new treaties was on placing greater responsibility on host states to absorb or resettle refugees and stateless persons, while the United Nations had already formulated a specific durable solution for Palestinians focused on return to their homes. The delegates wanted to ensure the ongoing commitment of the United Nations as a whole on implementing Palestinians' right to return, to restitution of their properties and compensation for their losses, as formulated in paragraph 11 of Resolution 194.

However, it soon became clear that the UNCCP would be unable to fulfil either aspect of its mandate: to resolve the conflict between the parties, or to implement the required durable solutions for Palestinian refugees. By the early 1960s, the General Assembly had reduced the UNCCP's funding so that it was unable to carry out most of its responsibilities, and reduced its work to recording Palestinian property losses.[11] With the UNCCP no longer providing the full scope of protection to Palestinian refugees or displaced persons, and with UNRWA mandated to provide assistance but not international protection – including access to durable solutions – many experts consider Palestinian refugees to have fallen into a 'protection gap.'[12]

Although the existence and consequences of the protection gap are hotly debated along with a range of interpretations of the relevant 'exclusion clauses,' some important conclusions can be drawn.[13] The Arab host countries where UNRWA operates have refused to accede to the refugee or stateless treaties, and confine UNHCR's activities to non-Palestinian refugees in their territories. Thus, in the areas where the majority of forcibly displaced Palestinians reside, they are neither legally defined as 'refugees' or 'stateless persons' for purposes of United Nations Agency protection, do not have access to durable solutions, and have limited forms of protection from UNRWA due to host state and other constraints. Moreover, outside the Arab host states, there is a wide range of interpretations of the 'exclusion clauses,' with the majority of states failing to provide the benefits of the Refugee Convention to Palestinian refugees as the drafters intended.[14] Additional serious consequences of the lack of agreement on what definition applies to Palestinians as refugees and stateless persons are discussed below with regard to how the refugee issue has been framed in the peace negotiations to date. Nevertheless, the General Assembly has reaffirmed Resolution 194 every year since its passage, confirming the rights of Palestinians to return, property restitution and compensation, but leaving them with no United Nations mechanism for implementation.[15]

Status and Conditions of Palestinians in Host States

The status and conditions of Palestinians in the host territories vary significantly and have also fluctuated over time depending on politically driven decisions. Jordan has been the most generous of the host countries, as it granted full citizenship to the majority of the 1948 refugees, who have been fairly well-integrated into the community. However, in Jordan as in the rest of the Arab states, refugee-related definitions do not necessarily designate a legal status, as there is little conformity in definitions and terms used for Palestinians. In Jordan, over 2 million Palestinians are registered 'Palestine refugees' with UNRWA, even though the majority are also Jordanian citizens with national ID numbers. However, most Palestinians displaced from the West Bank and Gaza during and after the 1967 conflict have only temporary Jordanian passports, without national ID numbers, that are essentially travel documents but not confirmation of citizenship (Tiltnes and Zhang 2013).[16] In 1988, during the First *Intifada*, when Jordan relinquished all claims to the West Bank, it denationalized thousands of Palestinians and began issuing temporary passports to West Bankers.

About 300–360,000 Palestinian refugees live in the ten official UNRWA camps and the informal camps in Jordan. While Palestinians who are citizens of Jordan enjoy full rights and privileges, the socio-economic conditions of those living outside from those inside refugee camps differ markedly, and high levels of poverty and insecurity prevail in the camps (Tiltnes and Zhang 2013). The situation for Palestinians in Jordan became far more precarious after the 1970–1971 civil war of 'Black September' between the Palestine Liberation Organization (PLO) and the Hashemite kingdom, when the PLO was expelled from the country, along with thousands of fighters and their families. The Jordanian government has retained files on all the

Black September fighters, their families and affiliates, bars them from entering the country, and arrests those it finds on its territory. Since the Syrian conflict began in 2011, the Jordanian government has placed new restrictions on entry of Palestinians, despite its initial generosity to Syrians (including Palestinian refugees from Syria) fleeing the war. Over ten thousand Palestine refugees from Syria have entered Jordan and are receiving assistance from UNRWA (BADIL 2016–2018).

Palestinians in Syria, including the pre-2011 populations of 552,000 refugees, enjoyed the most extensive civil and economic rights without distinctions between the types of status they held until the start of the uprising and civil conflict in 2011. They had full employment, education, medical and other benefits on par with Syrian citizens with the exception of the ability to vote or to own more than one piece of real property. Palestinians in Syria could obtain travel documents on the basis of their UNRWA refugee registration. However, as with Syrian citizens, Palestinians faced extreme political censorship and repression under the Assad regime, and have suffered thousands of casualties from the violence of the civil conflict. Several of the Palestinian refugee camps have been completely destroyed, and UNRWA has struggled to provide basic services to the 430,000 Palestinian refugees remaining in the country (UNRWA 2021).

Lebanon has been the least hospitable host country for Palestinians, and most of the over 470,000 Palestine refugees registered with UNRWA live in poverty-stricken camps. Lebanon has instituted a series of laws and regulations that severely restrict the rights of Palestinians to work in a host of professions, to have access to higher education, and obtain other government benefits For a short time, Lebanon allowed some Palestinians to obtain citizenship, but few succeeded in becoming citizens. UNRWA has recorded 29,000 Palestinian refugees from Syria for assistance, but due to Lebanon's 'no-camps' policy, Palestinians from Syria have been forced to live in the already-overcrowded Palestinian refugee camps, or struggle to find scarce living accommodations in urban areas or informal encampments. (UNRWA 2009).

Palestinians in Lebanon have also suffered extreme forms of discrimination and targeted violence due to the history of the PLO's involvement in the Lebanese civil war and its operations as a 'state within a state' until the PLO was forced out of Lebanon in 1982. Palestinians and Lebanese have bitter memories of the brutal war: Lebanese partially blame the Palestinians for the Israeli invasion and occupation of Lebanon from 1982–2000, while Palestinians blame the Lebanese for destruction of their camps and for colluding with Israel in the Sabra-Shatila camp massacre of thousands of unarmed refugees in 1982 (Suleiman 2006).

In the West Bank, UNRWA has registered about 775,000 Palestine refugees, about a quarter of whom live in 19 camps, and the rest in towns and villages. All Palestinians in the West Bank came under Israeli occupation in 1967 and have been subject to Israeli military law since then, while 500,000 Jewish settlers receive all the benefits of full Israeli citizenship in the same area. Palestinians in the West Bank and in East Jerusalem lack Israeli citizenship and have various forms of residency status regulated by Israel through an arbitrary and discriminatory permit system. After the Oslo Accord and establishment of the Palestinian Authority (PA) based in Ramallah in 1994, Palestinians in part of the West Bank have enjoyed some limited autonomy. Under Oslo, the West Bank was divided into three administrative areas, of which only one (Area A), covering 18 per cent of the West Bank, is under full PA control. Despite the Oslo arrangements, all of the West Bank remains under de facto Israeli occupation, as Israel has divided it into over a hundred fragments through the concrete wall that cuts off Palestinian towns and villages and through a system of checkpoints, permits and segregated roads that allow unrestricted travel for Jewish settlers but are prohibited for Palestinian use. At the same time, Israel has continued policies of mass administrative detention of thousands of Palestinians – including children – property seizures and house demolitions, seizure of resources and discriminatory allocation of water favouring Jewish settlers but depriving Palestinians of sufficient water for basic needs, and separation of Palestinian families through the discriminatory residency permit system (United Nations Office for the Coordination of Humanitarian Affairs).

Conditions for Palestinians in Gaza are the most dire of the areas where Palestinians reside. Almost 1.4 million Gazans are registered refugees with UNRWA out of the approximately 2 million Palestinians living in the Gaza Strip – that is, over half of the Gazan population are refugees. Gaza has been under almost total blockade by Israel since 2007, ostensibly in response to Hamas' overwhelming electoral win there in the Palestinian national elections. Israel enforces the blockade by preventing any entry or egress to or from Gaza by air, sea or land, restricting internal movement through barred areas within Gaza and snipers targeting Palestinians coming close to those areas or for other reasons. According to United Nations data, 80 per cent of the population of Gaza now depends on international assistance, with 50 per cent of Gazans unemployed, 95 per cent of the population without access to potable water, electricity available only 4–5 hours per day on average while sometimes unavailable for up to 12 hours per day – all of which are regulated by Israel. All of these shortages have severe effects on Gazans' health, education, access to medical care, and essential services (UNCTAD 2018).

Conditions for Gazans have also deteriorated as a result of Israel's full-scale attacks on Gaza in 2006, 2007, 2008–2009, 2012 and 2014. In July 2014, as a result of Israel's 50-day bombardment of Gaza, UNRWA declared a humanitarian emergency to address the massive loss of life, destruction of houses, schools and other property, and widespread displacement across the Gaza Strip. On 30 March 2018, Gazans launched the 'Great March of Return,' a weekly peaceful protest near the border between Israel and Gaza, demanding an end to the blockade and implementation of their right to return. Israel has responded by killing almost 200 Palestinians, injuring approximately 25,000, including 3,000 children with live ammunition and other means. In 2018, the United Nations issued a report on conditions in Gaza, concluding that it would be 'unlivable by 2020' (UNCTAD 2018).

Efforts at Negotiations and Key Issues to be Resolved

Just as the Palestinian refugee issue is the core of outstanding issues to be resolved in any negotiated settlement between Israel, the Palestinians and the Arab states, the Palestinian demand for implementation of their right to return is the core to resolving the refugee issue. However, the right of return is itself complex, involving competing claims of nationality between Palestinians and Jews; competing claims of property and restitution rights; and competing claims for compensation for losses and wider reparations. The legal claims are also bound up with contested narratives of historic and moral responsibility for the population displacement, of a link between the Holocaust and the need for a 'Jewish homeland' in Palestine, and of religious entitlement. This brief overview unpacks the legal rights from non-legal claims, and reviews how these have been addressed in negotiations thus far.

Right of Return: For Whom and to Where?

Palestinians, the PLO and the host Arab states have consistently maintained that Palestinians have a right to return to their homes, that successive generations of Palestinian refugees continue to have that right, and that this right must be implemented according to international law as embodied in Resolution 194. Israel, on the other hand, has steadfastly refuted a Palestinian right of return, particularly if implementing such a right would in any way undermine the claim to a Jewish state.

The Palestinian position focuses on the language of paragraph 11 of Resolution 194, stating that

> [t]he refugees wishing to return to their homes and live at peace with their neighbours should be permitted to do so at the earliest practicable date, and that compensation should be paid for the property of those choosing not to return and for loss or damage to property which, under principles of international law or in equity, should be made good by the Governments or authorities responsible.

Their position is that Resolution 194 guarantees all Palestinians displaced from their homes the right to return to them, to obtain restitution of the properties they held, and to obtain compensation for those homes or properties lost or destroyed. Israel has claimed that Resolution 194 is non-binding, since it is a General Assembly and not a Security Council resolution. As for its language, Israel has contested the provisions of 194: that Palestinians are not willing to 'live at peace with their neighbours;' that 'the earliest practicable date' refers to a comprehensive solution to the conflict (which has not been reached); and that, in any case, Israel is not 'responsible' for Palestinian losses. In addition, Israel claims that the internationally recognized right of return applies only to nationals of a territory, and since Palestinians are not Israeli nationals, they have no right to return there. Finally, Israel claims that the right of return applies only to individuals and does not require the return of masses of refugees.

Examining these competing arguments requires a short excursus into the legal sources of the right of return. The internationally recognized 'right of return' rests on four distinct bodies of law and is not limited to the right of refugees to return home. The first and earliest law guaranteeing return to one's home is found in humanitarian law, codified in 1907 in the Hague Regulations, and recognized by the Permanent Court of International Justice (PCIJ) as customary international law in 1939.[17] Today, the humanitarian law principle of the right of every person displaced by conflict to return to his/her own home appears in one of the most widely ratified international law instruments, the Fourth Geneva Convention of 1949 (Geneva Convention (IV) 1949). Israel has reaffirmed the binding nature of the Hague Regulations, and that it applies the Fourth Geneva Convention.[18] The second body of law that guarantees the right to return is the law of nationality and state succession. The two core principles of nationality and state succession law are that persons who are nationals of a territory have an absolute right to return there, and habitual residents of a territory that undergoes a change of sovereignty must be granted citizenship in the new state, to which they have an absolute right to return. These principles were considered customary international law – and codified – as early as 1923.[19] The General Assembly has adopted the principles in its Article on Nationality of Natural Persons in Relation to the Succession of States, affirming their status as customary international law (United Nations General Assembly 2000).

Related to the law of state succession and nationality is human rights law, which has incorporated the above principles in two of the core human rights treaties. Israel is a party to both of the main treaties that codify the principles on right of return of nationals and habitual residents in the context of state succession, the Civil and Political Rights Convention (ICCPR) and the Racial Discrimination Convention (CERD).[20] Finally, the law on refugees, forced displacement, and stateless persons incorporate parallel principles prohibiting mass expulsion, arbitrary deprivation of nationality, and deprivation of citizenship that causes individuals of the territory to become stateless. Mass forcible expulsion is absolutely prohibited, and under humanitarian law constitutes a war crime.[21] Since mass forcible expulsion is prohibited, mass return is an absolute obligation on a state from which mass expulsion has occurred – in other words, the right of return is guaranteed, whether for an individual or for masses of displaced persons.

This reading of the right of return was reinforced in one of several authoritative working papers issued by the United Nations Secretariat interpreting the provisions and legal bases of each of the key provisions in Resolution 194. In its Analysis of Paragraph 11, the Secretariat clarified the intentions of the drafters on key points on the right of return: (1) that the language 'return to their homes' meant to the exact places from which they had been displaced, and that several amendments were rejected that did not make that clear; (2) that 'the earliest practicable date' meant the date of cessation of conflict (i.e., the Armistice Agreements), consistent with the requirements of humanitarian law; (3) and that the decision whether to return, whether to obtain restitution of his/her property, or obtain compensation must be the voluntary choice of each individual refugee.[22]

Restitution of Property and Compensation for Losses

Palestinians claim that in addition to their right to return to their homes, they have a right to restitution of all their lost or abandoned properties in Israel, and to compensation for the losses they have suffered. They also ground these claims on Resolution 194 and on international law more generally. Israel claims that Palestinians abandoned their properties voluntarily, or that these properties have been 'exchanged' for properties Jews left behind in Arab countries. Israel also claims that it has complete discretion to legislate the use and takings of properties in its territory, and that it has been willing to compensate Palestinians for such takings. However, both parties have hotly contested the scope and value of Palestinian refugee properties, the legal rights underlying claims to restitution and/or compensation, and, of course, who owns legitimate title to the properties left behind.

Palestinians maintain that Israel's expropriation of their properties, the land and nationality/citizenship laws that denationalized them and deprived them of citizenship in their homeland, were all illegal acts. They claim that they remain the holders of title to all the private and communal property in historic Palestine, and that their properties must be restored to them. Israel's position on Palestinian properties paralleled the position on Palestinians' demands to return: that Palestinians had abandoned their properties, which Israel had legally expropriated and were now inhabited by Jews. Israel claimed from the outset that it was prepared to pay compensation for the property Palestinians had left behind, but that such compensation would be offset by the value of properties Jews had left behind in Arab countries.

Palestinians rest their position primarily on Resolution 194 and the law underlying rights to restitution and compensation. Resolution 194's language 'refugees ... wishing to return to their homes ... should be permitted to do so[,] ... and compensation should be paid for the property of those choosing not to return,' implies that both return to homes and restitution of their homes are to be implemented *as well as* compensation for properties lost or damaged. The United Nations Secretariat's working papers explaining the language chosen and the legal basis, support such a reading.[23] In addition, they claim that all benefits from Palestinian land, from the time the lands were taken until the present, must be paid in the form of compensation. The United Nations shares the Palestinian position on land restitution and compensation, and the General Assembly has repeatedly passed resolutions consistent with this view.[24] In a detailed working paper, the United Nations Secretariat gave an exhaustive review of the law supporting the claim that 'return' also meant 'property restitution.'(United Nations Secretariat 1950)

The law underlying the right to restitution of property for persons whose property was confiscated has been firmly established since at least 1928, when the Permanent Court of

International Justice (PCIJ) found that to be a binding principle of customary international law. In the *Chorzow Factory (Indemnity) Case*, the PCIJ stated that to remedy wrongful property takings, the state responsible must restore the exact property to the victim – and compensation for the full value of the property can only be paid if it is 'impossible' to restore the property itself to the owner (PCIJ 1928).[25] The successor to the PCIJ, the International Court of Justice (ICJ), has reiterated this principle in Palestinian property takings by Israel in its 2004 Advisory Opinion on the Wall (ICJ 2004). This principle as customary international law is incorporated in humanitarian and human rights law, as well as widespread state practice and, increasingly, in peace agreements involving return of refugees in many parts of the world.[26]

Summary of Negotiations over the Key Issues

As early as 1948, an Israeli government committee to assess possibilities for Palestinians to permanently resettle in Arab countries, appointed by Prime Minister Ben Gurion, produced a report estimating the scope and value of 'Abandoned Land' in Israel. In line with Israel's perspective on who owned the land, this report only included their estimates of privately owned refugee property, and excluded the vast amounts of village, communal, uncultivated and municipal properties Palestinians owned and used throughout Palestine.[27] For its part, the UNCCP pursued its mandate to protect the rights, properties, and interests of the refugees by also studying the scope and value of Palestinian refugee property. It produced a 'Global Estimate' in 1951, concluding that Palestinian abandoned land amounted to 16.3 million dunums valued at 100.4 million British pounds. The 'Global Estimate', however, also included movable property, valued at 20 million British pounds.[28]

In 1952, the UNCCP undertook a Technical Program to document Palestinian property based on land records, title and other property documents (where available). It aimed at a complete record of Palestinian landholdings in Israel up until 14 May 1948, to assess both individual and collective holdings. The Technical Program was completed in 1964, but only the global data was released; individual property data has remained in the UNCCP offices, unavailable to the public. The release of the UNCCP estimates was met with immediate criticism by Palestinians and Arab states as being inaccurate on various grounds and far too low. Palestinian and Arab experts had begun working on their own estimates as early as 1948.[29] The two most widely cited studies for the Palestinians are those by economist Yusuf Sayigh, published in 1966, and by Sami Hadawi and Atif Kubursi, in 1988. Sayigh's study covered overall losses for Palestinians, estimating them at a value of 752.7 million British pounds, while Hadawi and Kubursi's focused on land losses, calculating their value at 528.9 million British pounds (Fishbach 2006).[30] The gap between the various estimates and valuations produced in the early years while the United Nations was still actively engaged in seeking resolution to the conflict over the refugees, has only grown wider. Since then, there have been more recent efforts at mapping refugee properties and losses produced by the United Nations, the PLO, governments, and independent experts, particularly for purposes of the various rounds of negotiations.[31]

On the key issues of concern for the refugees – return, restitution, and compensation – little progress had been made in all the peace negotiations to date. Negotiations for settlement of the conflict began with the Camp David Accords and the Egyptian-Israeli peace treaty of March 1979. Jordan and Israel participated in the Madrid Conference in October 1991, which led to the Israel-Jordan peace treaty in October 1994. The Madrid Process set up five multilateral working groups, including a Refugee Working Group that met between 1992–1995. Although Palestinian participants maintained their demands of return and property restitution, these issues were not discussed in detail, and efforts were focused on the conditions for refugees in host communities. No real progress was made by the Working Groups when the multilateral process ended with the 2000 Intifada (Brynen 2013).

For the first time, Palestinians and Israelis negotiated face-to-face during the Oslo process that began in September 1993 and concluded with the failed Camp David II meetings in September 2000. The Oslo process postponed the refugees to 'final status' issues, and the refugee issue was not included in the agreements that emerged from the process, the Declaration of Principles (DOP), the Gaza-Jericho Agreement, and the Interim Agreement between Israel and the PLO.[32] Notably, the only references to legal frameworks in these documents are to Security Council Resolutions 242 and 338;[33] there is no reference to Resolution 194. The Oslo agreements also established what was to be the foundations of a Palestinian state, with the Palestine Authority in full control of Area A, Israeli-Palestinian joint administration of Area B, and full Israeli control continuing over Area C.[34]

The Camp David Summit of July 2000 was intended to address the issues postponed from the Oslo process. At the talks, the focus was on territory, settlements, Jerusalem, and security, and the refugee issues were given short shrift, with each side reiterating their positions. The Palestinians demanded Israel acknowledge the right of refugee return, restitution, and compensation before any modalities of implementation could be discussed. They also insisted that Israel must bear primary responsibility for reparations for Palestinian losses. Israel responded that it bore no responsibility for the refugee problem, and that Israel would recognize a right for Palestinians to 'return' only to a Palestinian state in the West Bank and Gaza. It did not agree that Resolution 194 created any obligation to accept Palestinian return or any related rights. However, it would agree to a limited number of Palestinians into Israel as part of a phased 'family unification' program over several years, but only for a few thousand individuals. Israel also claimed that any compensation would be through a compensation fund to be established and paid for by the international community. In return for a final agreement, Israel would require an 'end of claims' clause to all issues relating to the refugees. Israel also sought to link the claims of Jewish refugees' property in Arab states to resolution of Palestinian claims (Brynen and El-Rifai 2007).

In December 2000, President Clinton proposed a compromise on refugee return within the context of a two-state solution. His proposal was, in essence, that the 'right of return' be accepted in principle, but that it would encompass 'return' primarily within the West Bank and Gaza, resettlement in host and third countries, and acceptance by Israel of a limited number of Palestinian refugees as family unification. According to Clinton, these arrangements would fulfil Resolution 194. The only outcome of the negotiations was a trilateral statement that the parties aimed to achieve a 'just and lasting peace' based on UNSC Resolutions 242 and 338 (Clinton Parameters cited in Brynen and El-Rifai 2007). Although the Clinton Parameters did not end in agreement, they were the basis of the subsequent Taba negotiations.

In January 2001, Israeli and Palestinian negotiators met again at Taba, produced two separate papers, but did not reach an agreement. The Taba talks were the first time Palestinian refugee rights were discussed in significant detail, and clear reference was made to the principles underlying Resolution 194. The Palestinian proposal set out categories of claimants and their entitlements: returning refugees would obtain restitution of their properties and compensation for losses for movable property; refugees who did not return would be compensated for both land and movable properties; and refugees for whom it would be 'impossible' to provide restitution would receive substitute property in Israel. The proposal included establishing a compensation commission with an international fund towards which Israel would contribute, and that would calculate losses and distribute compensation to all Palestinian refugees for all their losses over the decades. In contrast, the Israeli proposal set out five 'options' to resolve the refugee issue: a limited number of refugees 'returning' to Israel; resettlement primarily in the Palestinian 'state'; absorption and rehabilitation for the majority of the refugees in the Arab states; a land swap between the Palestinian and Israeli territories; and some resettlement in third states. The Israeli proposal did not accept responsibility for the refugee problem, claiming 'indirect responsibility ... with all those parties directly or indirectly responsible' (cited in Brynen and El-Rifai 2007).

After the Taba talks, several other 'Track II' or unofficial negotiations took place, notably the July 2002 People's Voice Initiative and the October 2003 Geneva Accord. Subsequent official proposals such as the 'Road Map,' the 'Arab Peace Initiative,' and the 'Kushner plan,' have not produced much detail or been taken up by the parties to the conflict (United States Department of State 2003; European Parliament 2002; Trump 2020).

Conclusion

To date, Israel has not exhibited a willingness to recognize a right of Palestinian refugees to voluntarily return to their homes, to offer restitution of Palestinian properties, or to bear more than token responsibility for paying compensation for their losses. On the other hand, Palestinians have retreated significantly from their initial position demanding the right of all Palestinian refugees to return to their homes and lands from where they were forcibly displaced, whether in present-day Israel or in the West Bank and Gaza, as their proposals during the Oslo and Taba processes indicated.

From a legal point of view, the unresolved political issues relate directly to dramatically opposing perspectives on what the parties are entitled to and what obligations they bear. On the right to return, Israel claims that its Nationality Law and Law of Return were valid exercises of the new state's sovereignty, and Palestinians who could not meet the criteria of those laws never became nationals of the new state. Hence, they have no right to return to Israel. Israel also claims no responsibility for the displacement, that Palestinians voluntarily abandoned their homes, which Israel legally expropriated, so title to Palestinian property has lawfully transferred to Israel and the current inhabitants.

Palestinians maintain that these Israeli laws violate Israel's international legal obligations, that Palestinians remain 'nationals' of the territory and the rightful holders of the homes and lands that were dispossessed. The claim to nationality is based on Palestinians' international legal status from the Lausanne Treaty onwards as nationals of Palestine. The ramifications of this are not trivial. If the Palestinian position is correct, then all Palestinians tracing their ancestry to the Lausanne Treaty provisions are the 'persons' towards whom the UNCCP (and the international community) are responsible for implementing the solutions of return, restitution, and compensation under Resolution 194. This interpretation would cover between 10–13 million Palestinians worldwide. In contrast, all the negotiations so far have contemplated that only those Palestinians falling under UNRWA categories would be eligible for the agreed resolution to the refugee problem – that is, 5.5 million persons today.

Both sides dispute which United Nations Resolutions establish the legal framework for resolution of the refugee question. Israel has thus far successfully excluded reference to UNGA Resolution 194, the key resolution on individual refugee rights from negotiations (other than at Taba), while insisting that only Security Council resolutions are binding, and that the guiding resolutions are UNSC Resolutions 242 and 338. The latter resolutions have no reference to individual refugee rights and establish the 'land for peace' formula – that is, in exchange for establishing a Palestinian state alongside an Israeli one, that Palestinians agree that refugee (and all other outstanding) rights are satisfied. This is the exchange intended to be binding in an 'end of claims' clause. The UNSC framework substitutes a collective agreement for the individual rights of the refugees, while the General Assembly framework puts individual refugee rights at the core of the required solution.

The lack of consensus on definitions extends to Palestinians in Arab host states as well as to Palestinians outside the Arab world. Whether they are refugees or stateless persons, foreigners or displaced persons affects their ability to access fundamental rights and, in particular, their access to temporary or permanent protection from third states. The factors underlying the protection gap affecting Palestinian refugees relate, as well, to whether Palestinians as refugees or stateless persons have access to an international agency that can ensure and promote their legal rights. UNRWA acknowledges it does not have a mandate to seek and implement durable solutions for Palestinian refugees, nor does it have a mandate towards Palestinians as stateless persons. UNHCR has no mandate towards Palestinians as either refugees or stateless persons within the UNRWA areas and has not exercised its protection authority towards Palestinians as stateless persons outside UNRWA areas, other than in exceptionally urgent situations.

Finally, the future of UNRWA as the main agency representing the will and obligations of the international community to the ongoing welfare of Palestinian refugees has never been more precarious. In August 2018, the Trump Administration terminated all United States contributions to UNRWA, which had been the largest single source of UNRWA funding. The United States Administration's actions were consistent with its position that UNRWA was prolonging the Palestinian refugee problem and should be eliminated. The United Nations and majority of the world's governments have not agreed, and they have renewed UNRWA's mandate as well as stepped-up contributions to make up for the United States shortfall.[35]

Legal rights and political positions are inextricably intertwined, and a durable solution to the Palestinian refugee problem requires agreement on both. The 2020 Trump-Kushner 'Deal of the Century' announced on 28 January 2020, was remarkable in the total absence of Palestinian participation. The 'Deal' would legitimize Israeli annexation of one-third of the West Bank including all of the Jordan Valley, Israeli claims to all of Jerusalem as its capital, and the creation of a Palestinian 'state' in non-contiguous, separated areas in pockets of the West Bank and Gaza. There is no provision for return of Palestinian refugees or compensation for their properties by Israel (Trump 2020). Not surprisingly, the 'Deal' has been rejected by the Palestinians and has precipitated widespread protests across the Middle East and beyond. Meanwhile, Palestinians continue to suffer ongoing forced displacement, not only from within the Occupied Territories due to Israeli settlement expansion, land expropriation, and the siege of Gaza, but from renewed conflict in Syria, Iraq, Libya, and elsewhere in the Arab world. As the largest and longest displaced population in the world, resolution to the Palestinian refugee problem is more urgent than ever, but appears no closer today than when it began over seven decades ago.

Recommended Readings

Akram, S., and M. S. Lynk. 2011. "Arab-Israeli Conflict." *Max Planck Encyclopedia of Public International Law.*

Fishbach, M. R. 2003. *Records of Dispossession: Palestinian Refugee Property and the Arab-Israeli Conflict.* New York: Columbia University Press.

Brynen, R., and R. El-Rifai. 2007. *Palestinian Refugees: Challenges of Repatriation and Development.* London: IB Tauris.

Pappé, I. 2006. *The Ethnic Cleansing of Palestine.* Oxford: One World Publishing.

Morris, B. 1989. *The Birth of the Palestinian Refugee Problem.* Cambridge: Cambridge University Press.

Notes

* The author thanks Boston University law student Kristina Fried for her excellent research assistance on this chapter.

1 Among these laws and regulations were the Emergency Regulations for the Cultivation of Fallow Land and the Use of Unexploited Water Sources, 5709-1948, 2 Laws of the State of Israel (henceforth LSI) 71 (1948); Emergency Regulations (Cultivation of Waste Lands) (Extension of Validity) Ordinance, 5709-1949, 2 LSI 70 (1949).

2 Emergency Regulations Concerning Absentee Property, 5708-1948, 1 LSI 8 (1948); Absentee's Property Law, 5710-1950, 4 LSI 68 (1950).

3 For a thorough review of cases affirming the Custodian of Absentee Property decision on Palestinian property confiscations, see A. H. Hussein and F. McKay, *Access Denied: Palestinian Land Rights in Israel* (London: Zed Books, 2003).

4 Law of Return, 5710-1950, 4 LSI 114 (1950). For explanation of the ramifications of this law, see Nancy C. Richmond, "Israel's Law of Return: Analysis of Its Evolution and Present Application," *Dickinson Journal of International Law* 12:99 (1993), 109.

5 See United Nations Conciliation Commission for Palestine (UNCCP), Analysis of paragraph 11 of the General Assembly's Resolution of 11 December 1948, A/AC.25/W/45 (15 May 1950); United Nations Conciliation Commission for Palestine (UNCCP), Definition of a "Refugee" under paragraph 11 of the General Assembly Resolution of 11 December 1948, A/AC.25/W/61 (9 April 1951); United Nations Conciliation Commission for Palestine (UNCCP), Addendum to Definition of a "Refugee" under paragraph 11 of the General Assembly Resolution of 11 December 1948, A/AC.25/W/61/Add.1 (29 May 1951).

6 Order defining Boundaries of Territory to which the Palestine Order-in-Council does not apply, 1 Sept. 1922 (Legislation of Palestine, Vol. II, p. 405). The population of 847,000 persons who met the Citizenship Order criteria included foreign residents entering Palestine between 1920–1922 who did not meet the Lausanne Treaty requirements, while excluding thousands of Palestinians who did meet the Treaty criteria.

7 United Nations General Assembly, Resolution 2252 (ES-V), A/RES/2252 (4 July 1967). See also United Nations General Assembly, Resolution 63/92, A/RES/63/92 (18 Dec. 2008) (referring to persons displaced as a result of the June 1967 conflict and subsequent hostilities); United Nations General Assembly, Resolution 63/93, A/RES/63/93 (5 Dec. 2008), ¶ 7 (referring to persons displaced in the OPT and Lebanon).

8 The durable solutions of voluntary return, host country integration and third country resettlement are set out in the Statute. United Nations General Assembly, Resolution 428(V), Statute of the Office of the United Nations High Commissioner for Refugees, A/RES/428 (14 Dec. 1950), Annex.

9 The General Assembly passed UNHCR's Statute as an Annex to Resolution 428(V) on 14 December 1950.

10 Convention Relating to the Status of Refugees, 28 July 1951, 189 U.N.T.S. 137. Art 1D states in full: "This Convention shall not apply to persons who are at present receiving from organs or agencies of the United Nations other than the United Nations High Commissioner for Refugees protection or assistance. When such protection or assistance has ceased for any reason, without the position of such persons being definitively settled in accordance with the relevant resolutions adopted by the General Assembly of the United Nations, these persons shall *ipso facto* be entitled to the benefits of this Convention."

11 See United Nations Conciliation Commission for Palestine (UNCCP), Progress Report of the United Nations Conciliation Commission for Palestine for the Period 23 January to 19 November 1951, A/1985 (20 Nov. 1951).

12 For the range of conflicting views on the interpretation of Article 1D and related provisions, see, e.g., Bartholomeusz, "The Mandate of UNRWA at Sixty"; N. Morris, "Towards a Protection Strategy for UNRWA," *Refugee Survey Quarterly* 28:550 (2009); B. Goddard, "UNHCR and the International Protection of Palestinian Refugees," *Refugee Survey Quarterly* 28:2–3 (2009), 475–510; M. Kagan, "Is There Really a Protection Gap? UNRWA's Role vis-à-vis Palestinian Refugees," *Refugee Survey Quarterly* 28: 2–3 (2009), 511–530; S. M. Akram, "Palestinian Refugees and Their Legal Status: Rights, Politics, and Implications for a Just Solution," *Journal of Palestinian Studies* 31:3 (2002), 36–51.

13 For UNHCR's interpretations of the 'exclusion clauses' of art. 1D of the Refugee Convention, art. 1(2) and UNHCR Statute ¶ 7(c), see UNHCR 2009. "Revised Note on the Applicability of

Article 1D of the 1951 Convention relating to the Status of Refugees to Palestinian Refugees." www.un.org/unispal/document/auto-insert-205174/; UNHCR, Guidelines on International Protection No. 13: Applicability of Article 1D of the 1951 Convention Relating to the Status of Refugees to Palestinian Refugees, HCR/GIP/16/12 (Dec. 2017).

14 For European Court of Justice (CJEU) jurisprudence on these provisions, Case C-31/09, Nawras Bolbol v. Bevándorlási éáársági Hivatal, 2010 E.C.R. I-05539, ¶ 53. Mrs. Bolbol, a Palestinian from Gaza, was not registered with UNRWA, and thus had not "availed herself of [UNRWA's] protection or assistance." Ibid. ¶¶ 27, 41, 55. See also Case C-364/11, Mostafa Abed El Karem El Kott and Others v. Bevándorlási és Állampolgársági Hivatal, 2012 ECLI:EU:C:2012:826, ¶ 82. This was a case involving stateless Palestinian refugees who fled Lebanon for Hungary due to threats and arson. The CJEU found that the reasons a Palestinian could be considered to have lost protection or assistance against his/her volition include when his/her personal safety is at serious risk, and it was impossible for the organ or agency to guarantee his living conditions commensurate with its mission. Ibid ¶¶ 63, 65. For a thorough review of the jurisprudence over thirty countries on the interpretation of art 1D and related provisions and an analysis of compatibility with the drafting history of the instruments (see Akram and Al-Azza 2015).

15 See, e.g., General Assembly, Resolution 64/87, A/Res/64/87 (10 Dec. 2009).

16 Most Palestinians displaced from Gaza in 1967 have two-year temporary passports, while most Palestinians from the West Bank who have not obtained Jordanian citizenship hold five-year temporary passports. About 80,000 Gazans ('ex- Gazans') have Egyptian travel documents but no status or Jordanian ID's and are considered 'foreigners' by the Jordanian government. See A. A. Tiltnes and H. Zhang, "Progress, Challenges, Diversity: Insight into the Socio-economic conditions of Palestinian Refugees in Jordan," *Fafo Report* 42 (2013).

17 Hague Convention (IV) Respecting the Laws and Customs of War on Land, and Annex: Regulations Respecting the Laws and Customs of War on Land, 18 Oct. 1907, T.S. 539.

18 Israel has consistently maintained that it is bound to the Hague Regulations. See, e.g., CrimA 336/61Attorney-General of the Government of Israel v. Adolf Eichmann 16 PD 2033; HCJ 606/78 Ayyoub v. Minister of Defence 33(2) PD 113 (The 'Beit El' case). While Israel has claims that it is not bound by Geneva Convention IV in the occupied territories, the International Court of Justice declared in its advisory opinion, Legal Consequences of the Construction of a Wall in the Occupied Palestinian Territory, that Geneva Convention IV applies in the Occupied Palestinian Territories. Legal Consequences of the Construction of a Wall in the Occupied Palestinian Territory, Advisory Opinion, 2004 I.C.J. Rep. 136 (9 July), ¶ 101. For a detailed discussion on Israel's position with regard to the Hague Regulations and Geneva Convention IV, see Akram and Lynk 2011, ¶¶ 85–95.

19 For jurisprudence affirming these principles, see Tunis and Morocco Nationality Decrees, Advisory Opinion, 1923 P.C.I.J. (ser. B) No. 4 (7 Feb.); Panevezys-Saldutiskis Railway (Est. v. Lith.), Judgment, 1939 P.C.I.J. (ser. A/B) No. 76 (28 Feb.); Nottebohm (Liech. v. Guat.), Second Phase, 1955 I.C.J. Rep. 4 (6 April). The Convention on Certain Questions Relating to the Conflict of Nationality Laws incorporated the principles in 1930, and the widely ratified International Convention on Civil and Political Rights and the Convention on the Elimination of Racial Discrimination have codified the principles in contemporary form. See Convention on Certain Questions Relating to the Conflict of Nationality Laws, 13 April 1930, 179 L.N.T.S. 89; International Covenant on Civil and Political Rights, 16 Dec. 1966, 999 U.N.T.S 171; International Convention on the Elimination of all Forms of Racial Discrimination, 7 March 1966, 660 U.N.T.S. 195.

20 ICCPR, art. 12(4); CERD art. 5(d)(ii).

21 See Geneva Convention (IV), arts. 49, 147; see also Additional Protocol I, 7 Dec. 1978, 1125 U.N.T.S. 3, art. 85(4)(a) and Additional Protocol II, 7 Dec. 1978, 1125 U.N.T.S. 609, art. 17. Under the Rome Statute, the unlawful deportation or forcible transfer of a population can be either a war crime or a crime against humanity. Rome Statute of the International Criminal Court, 17 July 1998, 2187 U.N.T.S. 3, arts. 7(1)(d), 8(2)(a)(vii), 8(2)(b). The prohibition against mass expulsions of nationals, habitual residents, aliens or refugees on a territory appears in the 1951 Refugee Convention (art. 33), the European Convention on Human Rights (art. 3; art. 4 of Protocol 4), the African Convention on Human Rights (art. 22) and the American Convention on Human Rights (art. 22). Jurisprudence in the regional human rights courts have consistently confirmed the prohibition.

22 See United Nations Conciliation Commission for Palestine (UNCCP), Analysis of Paragraph 11 of the General Assembly Resolution of 11 December 1948, Working Paper Prepared by the United Nations Secretariat, A/AC.25/W.45 (15 May 1950).

23 See, in particular United Nations Secretariat, Working Paper, Compensation to Refugees for Loss of or Damage to Property to be Made Good under Principles of International Law or in Equity, A/AC.25/W/30 (31 Oct. 1949), ¶¶1–2. See also, United Nations Secretariat, Working Paper, Returning Refugees and the Question of Compensation, A/AC.25/W/36 (7 Feb. 1950).

24 See United Nations General Assembly, Resolution 36/146 (C), A/RES/36/146 (C) (16 Dec. 1981). The General Assembly has passed similar resolutions affirming the demand to return the refugees' properties each year. See, e.g., United Nations General Assembly, Resolution 62/105, Palestine refugees' properties and their revenues, A/RES/62/105 (10 Jan. 2008) (reaffirming that Palestine refugees are entitled to their property and to the income derived therefrom … and requests the Secretary-General to take all appropriate steps, in consultation with the UNCCP, for the protection of Arab property, assets and property rights in Israel).

25 Factory at Chorzów (F.R.G. v. Pol.), Judgment, 1928 P.C.I.J. (ser. A) No. 17 (13 Sept.). The Court construed 'impossible' strictly in order not to benefit the state responsible for unlawful takings.

26 Hague Convention (IV), Annex, arts. 28, 46, 47, 56; Geneva Convention (IV); ICCPR; CERD; International Covenant on Economic, Social, and Cultural Rights, 16 Dec. 1966, 993 U.N.T.S. 3; United Nations General Assembly, Resolution 217 (A) (III), Universal Declaration of Human Rights, A/RES/217 (10 Dec. 1948). Peace agreements around the world include the right of property restitution as part of durable solutions post-conflict, along with return of refugees. For a thorough review of these agreements, see Scott Leckie, *Housing, Land, and Property Restitution Rights of Refugees and Displaced Persons* (Cambridge University Press, 2007).

27 The Committee's Report estimated 2 million dunums of land were abandoned by Palestinians, with a net value of 81.5 million Israeli pounds. See M. R. Fishbach, *The Peace Process and Palestinian Refugee Claims* (United States Institute of Peace, 2006), 22–23 (citing Israel State Archives (ISA) (138) 2445/3 "Report on a Settlement of the Arab Refugee [Issue] (25 November 1948, and Central Zionist Archives (CZA) A246/57, "Comments on Value Assessments of Absentee Landed Property (12 November 1962)).

28 Fishbach *The Peace Process and Palestinian Refugee Claims, 36–39* (citing UNSA DAG 13-3, UNCCP; Subgroup: Office of the Principal Secretary. Series: Records Relating to Compensation/Box 18/1949051/Working Papers; document: W/60, "Sampling Study of Abandoned Property Claimed by Arab Refugees" (12 April 1951)).

29 See M. R. Fishbach, *Records of Dispossession: Palestinian Refugee Property and the Arab-Israeli Conflict*, (Institute for Palestine Studies Series, 2003), 28–30 (citing Tannous, Izzat. 1951. *Value of Refugee Property According to Izzat Tannous and the Arab Refugee Property Owners in Palestine*, 216; Baydas, Sa'id. 1951. *Scope and Value of Refugee Land According to Sa'id Baydas*, 217; Arab Higher Committee. 1955. *Value of Refugee Property According to the Arab Higher Committee*, 225; Arab League. 1956. *Value of Refugee Property According to the Arab League*, 225).

30 See Fishbach, *The Peace Process and Palestinian Refugee Claims*, 31–35 (citing Sayigh, Yusuf. 1966. *Al-Iqtisad al-Isra'ili (The Israeli Economy)*. Cairo: League of Arab States, Institute for Higher Arab Studies; S. Hadawi, *Palestinian Rights and Losses in 1948: A Comprehensive Study* (London: Saqi Books, 1988).

31 Estimates range from just under $3 billion to approximately $327 billion, depending on the losses considered, how they are valued, and how 1948 losses are converted to current values. See, e.g., R. Brynen, "Palestinian Refugees," in *Routledge Handbook on the Israeli-Palestinian Conflict*, eds. J. Peters and D. Newman (Routledge, 2013), 115; A. A. Kubursi, "Palestinian Losses in 1948: Calculating Refugee Compensation," *Palestinian Refugee ResearchNet*, 3 Aug. 2001, https://prrn.mcgill.ca/research/papers/kubursi.htm.

32 Declaration of Principles on Interim Self-Government Arrangements (Oslo I), O.P.T.-Isr., 13 Sept. 1993; Agreement on the Gaza Strip and the Jericho Area, O.P.T-Isr., May 4, 1994; Israeli-Palestinian Interim Agreement on the West Bank and the Gaza Strip (Oslo II), O.P.T.-Isr., 28 Sept. 1995.

33 United Nations Security Council, Resolution 242, S/RES/242 (22 Nov. 1967) (requiring the withdrawal of Israeli armed forces from the OPT and the "[t]ermination of all claims or states of belligerency and respect for and acknowledgment of the sovereignty, territorial integrity and political independence of every State in the area and their right to live in peace within secure and recognized boundaries free from threats or acts of force"); United Nations Security Council, Resolution 338, S/RES/338 (22 Oct. 1973) (calling upon all parties to cease firing and terminate all military activity, and to immediately apply the terms of United Nations Security Council Resolution 242).

34 Area A is under full civil and security control of the Palestine Authority. Although Israeli citizens are formally prohibited from entering Area A, the Israeli armed forces retain the right to enter and

conduct regular raids in the area. Area B is under Palestinian civil control and join-Israeli-Palestinian security control. As in Area A, Israeli armed forces retain the right to enter at all times. Israeli and partial Palestine Authority control. Area C is under full Israeli civil and security control. Palestinians are restricted from building on or accessing much of the land and resources (including water) in Area C. United Nations Office for the Coordination of Humanitarian Affairs, Occupied Palestinian Territory. n.d. "Area C." www.ochaopt.org/location/area-c; Economic Cooperation Foundation. n.d. "Israeli-Palestinian Interim Agreement (Oslo II, 1995)." http://ecf.org.il/issues/issue/818.

35 United Nations General Assembly, Resolution 74/83, A/RES/74/83 (26 Dec. 2019); Fourth Committee, Press Release, UNRWA Faces Greatest Financial Crisis in Its History Following 2018 Funding Cuts, Commissioner-General Tells Fourth Committee, GA/SPD/684 (9 Nov. 2018).

Questions for Discussion

(1) How is the situation of Palestinian refugees different from or similar to that of other protracted refugee groups, such as the Kurds or Bedouin? Why do Palestinians fall under 'special' protection and why are they excluded from UNHCR protection, when these other groups are not?

(2) What is the difference between the claims to Palestine nationality and Jewish nationality? How does international law address these competing claims to national rights?

(3) To what extent are host states (e.g., Lebanon, Jordan, Syria) responsible for helping to fill in the gaps in international protection for Palestinian refugees? Do the obligations of these states to provide Palestinian refugees greater protection, or even citizenship, supersede the obligations of Israel to accept Palestinians returning to their homes?

(4) How does the legal perspective presented in this chapter affect your view of how the Palestinian refugee problem should be resolved? If the 'right of return' is grounded in international legal obligations, what is the difference between Palestinian refugees' right of return and Arab Jewish refugees' right of return to their countries of origin? Are they linked? Should they be linked in an ultimate resolution?

(5) There are a number of different perspectives regarding how to calculate losses for which Palestinians are entitled to restitution. Discuss the possible legal and political reasons for the different means of calculating losses and restitution, and who should be responsible for paying compensation.

(6) What are the implications of the various claims that have been put forward in the negotiations for the possibility of a durable solution for the refugee problem?

References

Akram, S. M. 2002. "Palestinian Refugees and Their Legal Status: Rights, Politics, and Implications for a Just Solution." *Journal of Palestinian Studies* 31:3, 36–51.

Akram, S. M., and N. Al-Azza. 2015. *Closing Protection Gaps: Handbook on Protection of Palestinian Refugees in States Signatories to the 1951 Refugee Convention.* Bethlehem: BADIL Resource Center for Palestinian Residency and Refugee Rights.

Akram, S., and M. Lynk. 2011. "Arab-Israeli Conflict." *Max Planck Encyclopedia of Public International Law*, paragraphs 1–110.

American Friends Service Committee. n.d. "Palestinian Refugees and the Right of Return." Available at: www.afsc.org/resource/palestinian-refugees-and-right-return.

Artz, D. 1997. *Refugees into Citizens: Palestinians and the End of the Arab-Israeli Conflict.* New York: Council on Foreign Relations Press.

BADIL Resource Center for Palestinian Residency and Refugee Rights. 2015. *Closing Protection Gaps: Handbook on Protection of Palestinian Refugees.* Al-Ayyam Printing, Press, Publishing and Distribution Company.

BADIL Resource Center for Palestinian Residency and Refugee Rights. 2016–2018. *Survey of Palestinian Refugees and Internally Displaced Persons.* Vol. IX. Al-Ayyam Printing, Press, Publishing and Distribution Company.

Bartholomeusz, L. 2009. "The Mandate of UNRWA at Sixty." *Refugee Survey Quarterly* 28: 2–3, 452–474.

Bisharat, G. 1993-94. "Land, Law, and Legitimacy in Israel and the Occupied Territories," American University Law Review 43: 467.

Brynen, R. 2013. "Palestinian Refugees." in *Routledge Handbook on the Israeli-Palestinian Conflict*, eds J. Peters and D. Newman. London: Routledge.

Brynen, R., and R. El-Rifai. 2007. *Palestinian Refugees: Challenges of Repatriation and Development*. London: IB Tauris.

Convention Relating to the Status of Stateless Persons. 1954. 360 U.N.T.S. 117, art. 1(2)(i), 28 Sept.

Economic Cooperation Foundation. n.d. "Israeli-Palestinian Interim Agreement (Oslo II, 1995)." Available at: http://ecf.org.il/issues/issue/818.

European Parliament. 2002. "Arab Peace Initiative." 28 March. Available at: www.europarl.europa.eu/meetdocs/2009_2014/documents/empa/dv/1_arab-initiative-beirut_/1_arab-initiative-beirut_en.pdf.

Fishbach, M. R. 2003. *Records of Dispossession: Palestinian Refugee Property and the Arab-Israeli Conflict*. New York: Columbia University Press.

Fishbach, M. R. 2006. *The Peace Process and Palestinian Refugee Claims*. Washington, DC: United States Institute of Peace.

Geneva Convention (IV) Relative to the Protection of Civilian Persons in Time of War. 1949. 75 U.N.T.S. 287, 12 Aug.

Goddard, B. 2009. "UNHCR and the International Protection of Palestinian Refugees." *Refugee Survey Quarterly* 28: 2–3, 475–510.

Hadawi, S. 1988. *Palestinian Rights and Losses in 1948: A Comprehensive Study*. London: Saqi Books.

Hussein, A. H., and F. McKay. 2003. *Access Denied: Palestinian Land Rights in Israel*. London: Zed Books.

ICJ. 2004. "The Legal Consequences of the Construction of the Wall in the Occupied Palestinian Territory, Advisory Opinion," 9 July, I.C.J. Rep. 136.

Kagan, M. 2009. "Is there Really a Protection Gap? UNRWA's Role vis-à-vis Palestinian Refugees." *Refugee Survey Quarterly* 28: 2–3, 511–530.

Kedar, S. 2001. "The Legal Transformation of Ethnic Geography," New York University Journal of International Law and Politics 33: 923.

Kubursi, A. A. 2001. "Palestinian Losses in 1948: Calculating Refugee Compensation." *Palestinian Refugee ResearchNet*, 3 August. Available at: https://prrn.mcgill.ca/research/papers/kubursi.htm.

Laws of the State of Israel 1950. "The Absentee Property Law 5710-1950." 20 March.

Laws of the State of Israel 1950. "Development Authority (Transfer of Property) Law 5710-1950." 31 July.

Laws of the State of Israel. 1952. "Nationality Law 5712-1952."

Lehn, W. 1974. "The Jewish National Fund," Journal of Palestine Studies 3:87-88.

Leckie, S. 2007. *Housing, Land, and Property Restitution Rights of Refugees and Displaced Persons*. Cambridge: Cambridge University Press.

Morris, B. 1989. *The Birth of the Palestinian Refugee Problem*. Cambridge: Cambridge University Press.

Morris, N. 2009. "Towards a Protection Strategy for UNRWA." *Refugee Survey Quarterly* 28: 2–3, 550–560.

Pappé, I. 2006. *The Ethnic Cleansing of Palestine*. Oxford: One World Publishing.

PCIJ. 1928. "Factory at Chorzów" (F.R.G. v. Pol.), *Judgment*, (ser. A) No. 17, 13 Sept.

Richmond, N. C. 1993. "Israel's Law of Return: Analysis of Its Evolution and Present Application." *Dickinson Journal of International Law* 12, 95.

Suleiman, Jaber. 2006. "Marginalised Community: The Case of Palestinian Refugees in Lebanon." Development Research Center on Migration, Globalisation and Poverty, University of Sussex, 20–21. Available at: https://assets.publishing.service.gov.uk/media/57a08c4be5274a31e0001112/JaberEdited.pdf.

Takkenberg, L. 1998. *The Status of Palestinian Refugees in International Law*. Oxford: Clarendon Press.

Tiltnes, Å. A. and H. Zhang. 2013. "Progress, Challenges, Diversity: Insight into the Socio-economic conditions of Palestinian Refugees in Jordan." *Fafo Report* 42.

Treaty of Lausanne. 1923. 28 L.N.T.S. 11, 24 July.

Trump, D. 2020. "Peace to Prosperity." *Washington, DC: White House*. 28 January. Available at: www.whitehouse.gov/wp-content/uploads/2020/01/Peace-to-Prosperity-0120.pdf.

United Nations Conciliation Commission for Palestine (UNCCP). 1950. "Analysis of paragraph 11 of the General Assembly's Resolution of 11 December 1948. 15 May, A/AC.25/W/45.

United Nations Conciliation Commission for Palestine (UNCCP). 1951. "Definition of a 'Refugee' under paragraph 11 of the General Assembly Resolution of 11 December 1948." 9 April, A/AC.25/W/61.

United Nations Conciliation Commission for Palestine (UNCCP). 1951. "Addendum to Definition of a 'Refugee' under paragraph 11 of the General Assembly Resolution of 11 December 1948." 29 May, A/AC.25/W/61/Add.1.
United Nations Conference on Trade and Development (UNCTAD). 2018. "Annual Report 2018." Available at: https://unctad.org/annualreport/2018/Pages/index.html.
United Nations General Assembly. 1947. Resolution 181(II), Concerning the Future Government of Palestine, A/RES/181, 29 November.
United Nations General Assembly. 1948. Resolution 194(III), A/RES/194, 11 December.
United Nations General Assembly. 1949. Resolution 31(V), A/RES/319, 3 December.
United Nations General Assembly. 1949. Resolution 302(IV), A/RES/302, 8 December.
United Nations General Assembly. 2000. Resolution 55/153, 1/RES/55/153, 12 December, arts. 5, 6, 14.
United Nations Mediator for Palestine. 1948. "Progress Report of the United Nations Mediator on Palestine delivered to the General Assembly." 16 September, A/648.
United Nations Office for the Coordination of Humanitarian Affairs. n.d. "Area C." Available at: www.ochaopt.org/location/area-c.
United Nations Secretariat. 1949. "Working Paper, Compensation to Refugees for Loss of or Damage to Property to be Made Good under Principles of International Law or in Equity." 31 October, A/AC.25/W/30.
United Nations Secretariat. 1950. "Working Paper, Returning Refugees and the Question of Compensation." 7 February, A/AC.25/W/36.
United Nations Secretariat. 1950. "Working Paper, Historical Precedents for Restitution of Property or Payment of Compensation to Refugees." 18 March, A/AC.25/W/41.
United Nations Security Council. 1967. Resolution 242, S/RES/242, 22 November.
United Nations Security Council. 1973. Resolution 338, S/RES/338, 22 October.
UNHCR. 2017. "Guidelines on International Protection No. 13: Applicability of Article 1D of the 1951 Convention Relating to the Status of Refugees to Palestinian Refugees." December, HCR/GIP/16/12.
UNHCR. 2002. "Note on the Applicability of Article 1D of the 1951 Convention relating to the Status of Refugees to Palestinian Refugees." *International Journal of Refugee Law* 14.
UNHCR. 2009. "Revised Note on the Applicability of Article 1D of the 1951 Convention relating to the Status of Refugees to Palestinian Refugees." Available at: www.un.org/unispal/document/auto-insert-205174/.
UNRWA. 2009. "Consolidated Eligibility and Registration Instructions (CERI)." Available at: www.unrwa.org/sites/default/files/2010011995652.pdf.
UNRWA. 2021. *Syria: 10 Years of Multiple Hardships for Palestine Refugees*. Available at: www.unrwa.org/newsroom/press-releases/syria-10-years-multiple-hardships-palestine-refugees
United States Department of State. 2003. "A Performance-Based Roadmap to a Permanent Two-State Solution to the Israeli-Palestinian Conflict," 30 April. Available at: https://2001-2009.state.gov/r/pa/prs/ps/2003/20062.htm.

13
JERUSALEM

Menachem Klein

Introduction

Jerusalem is known for its holy sites and rich history, as well as for being a platform for many wars and occupations (Sebag-Montefiore 2012). This chapter does not deal with wars but with attempts to settle the conflict over the city since the second half of the 20th century. During this period the Jewish/Israeli side struggled with the Palestinians over ruling Jerusalem. Consequently, many settlement proposals were raised, not a few with the help of international actors. Hereafter, the most known ones are presented, both by the two struggling peoples and worldwide. The chapter starts with the 1947 Partition Plan and continues with the division of the city between Israel and Jordan. The main part of the chapter deals with post-1967 War Jerusalem.

The chapter does not deal with urban life, municipal boundaries, and city development, unless they relate to the struggle. It shows how these issues are related to the conflict and to its solution; in other words, the conflict is not limited to violence and bloodshed but how it influences the city's development. In charting the most well-known negotiations and proposals over Jerusalem, it becomes clear that no proposed solution can ignore the reality on the ground.

From the 1947 United Nations Partition Plan to the 1948 War and the Partition of Jerusalem

Jerusalem's high historical and religious status in the three monotheistic religions brought the United Nations General Assembly, on 29 November 1947, to create a special international regime in the city (*Corpus Separatum*) that would take effect when the British Mandate ended. Outside the city, Palestine would be divided into two states, one Jewish and the other Arab. The Zionists accepted the resolution, but not the Arabs, which led to the outbreak of the first Arab-Israeli war.

The issue of Jerusalem was raised during the years 1947–1948 in contacts between King Abdullah of Jordan and the head of the Political Department of the Jewish Agency, Golda Meyerson (Meir). Although the Jewish Agency and the Jordanian emir arrived at some sort of understanding about non-belligerency and a quiet partition of Palestine between them, they did not come to an agreement regarding Jerusalem. When the fighting began, the Jordanian

DOI: 10.4324/9780429027376-17

Legion sought – for political reasons – to refrain from military involvement in the city itself (in contrast to its northern and eastern approaches and the Arab quarters surrounding it), assuming that the Israeli army would also abstain from occupying the city. This assumption was realistic as far as the Old City of Jerusalem was concerned, but not with regards to West Jerusalem (Klein 2002).

The leadership of the Jewish Agency, and later the Israeli government, decided to mould the future of West Jerusalem as the capital of Israel by force of arms. However, Israel did not invest the same effort toward the conquest of the Old City as it directed toward West Jerusalem. It assumed that a conquest of the eastern part of Jerusalem, with its Christian and Islamic holy sites, would eventually lead to the ousting of Israel from the western city as well. The Jordanian Legion entered the Old City on 19 May 1948 and conquered the Jewish Quarter ten days later. Following the conquest of the Old City, King Abdullah turned Jerusalem into the religious-spiritual capital of his kingdom. Israel's foremost aim directly after the fighting ceased was to be accepted as a member of the United Nations, thereby bolstering the political status of the newborn state. Israel's leaders faced a dilemma: its acceptance to the United Nations required that it agree to some form of internationalization of the whole of Jerusalem, in keeping with the decision of the 1947 Partition Resolution of the United Nations General Assembly. However, the Israeli leaders wished to preserve the achievements of the war: to establish the partition of the city between Israel and Jordan and to declare West Jerusalem the capital of Israel. Blocking the internationalization of Jerusalem suited the intentions of King Abdullah, whose primary aim was to maintain his sovereignty over the areas he had occupied during the war: the West Bank of the Jordan River and Eastern Jerusalem (Klein 2002).

Thus, between 1948–1967, Jerusalem was divided between Israel and Jordan, both of which grew to accept this partition. The annexation of Eastern Jerusalem to the Kingdom of Jordan occurred on 13 December 1948, along with Jordan's annexation of the whole of the West Bank. It was a *de jure* annexation, which became de facto in May 1950. Only Pakistan and Great Britain recognized the annexation, the latter declaring that it did not recognize Jordan's sovereignty over Jerusalem, only its practical governing of it. Israel worked the other way around. First, on 2 August 1948 it annexed de facto the areas it controlled under its military rule. Later, on 4 February 1949, with the official annexation, civil administration replaced the military rule. According to the Israeli–Jordanian Armistice Agreement of April 1949, Israel kept a small enclave on Mount Scopus (Klein 2002).

International recognition of the reality of a divided Jerusalem was granted in 1952, when the United Nations General Assembly decided that Israel and Jordan would be responsible for an arrangement on Jerusalem in accordance with previous United Nations resolutions on the internationalization of the city, without stating how the two would implement a decision which both opposed. In other words, the United Nations recognized Israel and Jordan as the governing authorities in Jerusalem, and tacitly accepted the demise of the idea of internationalization.

On 13 July 1951, elections were held in the municipality of Jordanian Jerusalem, and on 1 April 1952 the borders of the Jordanian city were extended to include adjacent areas (e.g., Silwan and Ras-al-Amud). The area of the Jordanian city was thus 6.5 sq. km., while the built-up area was only half of that – 3 sq. km. In February 1958, the Jordanian municipality of Jerusalem initiated an extension of the city's area northward towards the airport of Qalandia. This plan was not implemented, nor was the 1963 plan to extend the city's area to 75 sq. km. Discussions concerning these plans ceased in 1967, with the outbreak of the war. On the other side, West Jerusalem occupied at that time an area of 38 sq. km., after an Israeli extension of its area westwards – reflecting the difference in status between the capital of Israel and Jordanian Jerusalem, which remained an outlying town with symbolic-religious importance only. West

Jerusalem's status in Israel was higher than East Jerusalem's status in Jordan, although the centre of Israeli economic, cultural, and social life, as well as the political parties, trade unions and main newspapers, were all in Tel-Aviv. Judaism's holiest sites – the Western Wall and Temple Mount, both remnants of the Second Temple, which was destroyed in 70 AD – had been inaccessible to Israelis during the 19 years of Jordanian rule (Klein 2002).

The 1967 War and the Israeli Annexation

Israel ruled Jerusalem longer than the British Mandate or the Jordanian kingdom, or both combined. During this period, Israel dramatically changed Jerusalem's physical and demographic environments. In no other place in the occupied territories did Israel invest so many legal, material, and symbolic resources. The decisive demographic balance between Jewish settlers and Palestinian natives that Israel achieved in East Jerusalem does not exist anywhere in the West Bank. 38 per cent of the overall populations in East Jerusalem are Israeli settlers, compared to 62 per cent Palestinian Arabs. However, Jews compose 61 per cent of Jerusalem's total population. East Jerusalem was the jewel of the territories that Israel captured in less than a week of war in June 1967. It was followed by legal annexation, in the form of imposition of Israeli law and administration on a territory twice as large as the western city. 6.5 sq. km. of Jordanian Jerusalem, as well as an additional 64.4 sq. km. of adjacent West Bank territory were added to the 38.1 sq. km. of the Israeli city. Israel unilaterally declared this new entity to be "United Jerusalem, the Eternal Capital of Israel," making Jerusalem the largest city in Israel and the urban centre of West Bank Palestinians. Jerusalem has the largest Jewish population in Israel, 559,800 according to 2019 data, as well as the largest Arab population, 341,500, forming about 10 per cent of Palestinian population in the West Bank and Gaza Strip. Never in history did the city have so many residents (Klein 2001:18–84, Klein 2008; JIFR 2019).

Unsurprisingly, maintaining Israeli sovereignty over all of East Jerusalem, or at least its historical core and the settlements surrounding it, is a vital Israeli–Jewish interest. Moreover, for most Israeli Jews, ruling East Jerusalem is a self-identity definer, connecting them to their biblical origins in the Holy Land of their ancestors, to the Western Wall and Temple Mount. The Palestinians, of course, hold an opposite identity and national liberation aspirations. They are attached to the city that their ancestors ruled almost uninterruptedly from 632 to 1918 with its Muslim and Christian holy sites, first and foremost al-Haram al-Sharif/Temple Mount. Hence, the contest between Israel and the Palestinians over the future of the Israeli annexation moved along two tracks: facts on the ground and negotiations. Israel, the powerful side, thought that by imposing facts on the ground she would determine Jerusalem's future. But, after 20 years, when the First *Intifada* broke out in 1987, Israel acknowledged the limits of her power and turned to negotiations at Oslo. Below, these two interrelated tracks are examined.

The Israeli annexation opened the door to waves of construction that changed the Jordanian-Palestinian city's physical and demographic landscape. Israel did this in three stages. First, it expunged the painful memory of its loss of the Jewish Quarter to the Jordanian army in the war of 1948. In the 1970s, Israel rebuilt and enlarged the Jewish Quarter and constructed a chain of neighbourhoods that connected West Jerusalem with Mount Scopus: Ma'alot Dafna, Sanhedria Murhevet, Ramot Eshkol, Giv'at HaMivtar, and HaGiv'a HaTzarfatit. This dissipated the fears that had caused the country's military planners sleepless nights in the two decades following 1949 – the loss of Israel's sovereign enclave on Mount Scopus. Furthermore, in the 1970s Israel began to build settlements in the area of the West Bank close to Jerusalem. These settlements became part of the Jerusalem metropolitan area, physically connected by new roads to the city.

The 1980s saw construction projects on the hilltops around the Old City basin – Gilo, East Talpiot, Ramot, and Neve Ya'akov. These new neighbourhoods surrounded East Jerusalem and were built to render impossible the return of the city to Arab control. Upon completing this stage, Israel believed that it had ensured its control of the basin. It then turned its attention farther eastward, in part because Arab East Jerusalem had, under Israeli rule, begun to expand. This led, in the 1990s, to the construction of new Israeli settlements: Pisgat Ze'ev, Ramot Shlomo, and Har Homa (Klein 2008).

In no other populated Palestinian territory has Israel reached the same level of achievement – annexation and the creation of near demographic parity with the original population. But this is a mixed blessing. The sheer amount of Jewish construction in former Jordanian territory, and the waves of tourists who have visited Jerusalem since 1967, turned the city into a metropolitan area that provides income and work to hundreds of thousands of Palestinians, and to a centre of services for the inhabitants of the central West Bank.

Mayor Teddy Kollek was the author of the view that everyday life could win the battle for a united Jerusalem, even though the Arabs and the rest of the world opposed the annexation. Kollek sought to put this view into effect in two complementary ways. He promoted the vision of Jerusalem as a multi-ethnic and multi-confessional mosaic in a single urban fabric under Israeli rule, and he sought to create a fabric of urban life that crossed Jewish-Arab boundaries. Kollek believed that only a democratic and enlightened Israeli rule could ensure coexistence, freedom of worship, and the city's rich cultural and historical heritage. Over time, he maintained, the Arabs would acquiesce and adjust to life under Israeli rule. He stressed that, to achieve this, Israel had to find the right balance between conquest and enlightenment, between oppression and tolerance, between restrictions and freedom, human rights, and provision of services. Jerusalem's Arabs, Kollek maintained, needed to realize that they had something to lose if they were to rise up against Israeli rule, and something to gain if they accepted it de facto. Kollek hoped to mitigate the contradiction by indulging the conflict into latency. He therefore promoted an ambitious plan to bring East Jerusalem municipal services – schools, social welfare, roads, sewage, and other essential infrastructure – close to the levels enjoyed in West Jerusalem. However, Israel's national government consistently refused to provide the necessary funds and institutional support for this plant. Most of what improvements the East Jerusalem Palestinians enjoyed were the side effects of the development of infrastructure for the new Jewish neighbourhoods in their midst. The national government's first priority was to control Jerusalem's Arab residents and counter the "demographic threat" it believed they presented to the city's Jewish majority. This took precedence over improving day-to-day life. As a result, Jerusalem remained a frontier city and never became the multicultural city of many faiths that Kollek envisioned. Israeli rule imposed containment on Jerusalem's Palestinians and restricted development and construction in their part of the city. Some 35 per cent of the territory of East Jerusalem was appropriated by Israel. Palestinians have faced great obstacles when requesting permits to build on the remaining land. The housing shortage impelled many Palestinians to build illegally or to move to villages outside the official boundaries of the eastern city as annexed by Israel. The Palestinian villages grew and became suburbs. This, along with the development of central East Jerusalem, rendered the annexation boundary functionally meaningless. When the First Intifada (1987–1993) reached Jerusalem, Israelis discovered that the city's public spaces were not empty but were in fact full of Palestinians whom they had not noticed before. Israel, it turned out, had swallowed East Jerusalem but failed to digest it. The First Intifada put the Palestinian population in the occupied territories on the road that led from passivity to activism. The conflict changed their self-perception and the perception of the international community (Klein 2008; Cheshin et al. 1999).

Essentially, a separate Palestinian metropolitan centre came into being alongside the Israeli metropolitan city – two cities back-to-back. Israeli-Jewish Jerusalem faces west, towards its natural hinterland in Israel. Palestinian Jerusalem faces east, towards the West Bank. Interaction takes place, for the most part, in defined geographical areas, or in certain functional areas that can be described as areas of encounter.

Multi-border City

Since 1967, Jewish West Jerusalem has been the dominant city. It is there that political and municipal decisions are taken, and there that resources are distributed, and it dominates the eastern city economically and socially. Advanced industry is located in the western and not the eastern city, as are the city's first-rate research institutes and universities. Arab East Jerusalem is a source of blue-collar workers and service providers – mechanics, construction workers, taxi drivers, waiters, cooks, and cleaning and sanitation workers for the dominant city. These workers do not live in the dominant city but rather in separate neighbourhoods in the dominated city or its periphery. Some of these suburbs and neighbourhoods may be defined as the city's neglected slums with no law and order (Dumper 2014).

Deep ethnic-national, political, community, religious, historical, and cultural differences separate the Jewish side of the city from the Arab side. One may also add the element of language, in particular the Arabic spoken in the East. These are primordial barriers. Except for the instrumental use of Hebrew in the labour market or in daily life when coming into contact with a Jewish Westerner, the Easterner speaks Arabic and consumes Arab culture and media. With regard to education, there is an arrangement whereby on the symbolic level and on the organizational level the public schools in East Jerusalem are tied to Israel, while Jordan (until 1994) or the Palestinian Authority (since then) determines most of the curriculum, chooses textbooks, and supervises diploma examinations. The religious Islamic (*Sharia'*) courts of East Jerusalem are not under the jurisdiction of Israel's Ministry of Religious Affairs under which the *Sharia'* courts in Israel operate. The state of Israel does not recognize the rulings of the East Jerusalem *Sharia'* courts for the purpose of registration of personal status unless they have been ratified by the *Sharia'* court in West Jerusalem or Jaffa. The latter automatically issue the required document without considering itself a superior bench to the East Jerusalem court.

Israeli state apparatus controlls only to a small degree what is done in these areas in East Jerusalem. Israeli law sets the standards and licensing procedure for vehicles and traffic but its enforcement in East Jerusalem is very limited. Israel is not interested in maintaining law and order in East Jerusalem, with the exception of anti-Israeli nationalist demonstrations. There is no real war on crime by the Israeli Police in East Jerusalem. With this regard, its concern is to contain the crime inside Palestinian neighbourhoods (Klen 2008; Shlomo 2017).

As permanent residents of Israel, Palestinians are allowed to participate in Jerusalem's municipal elections both as voters and as candidates, but since 1967 only ever-shrinking minorities go to the voting stations. In the 1995 Oslo agreement (Oslo II), Israel agreed with the Palestinian Authority that East Jerusalem's Palestinians would take part in the elections of 1996 and 2006 for the Palestinian national governing institutions but in a different form than in the rest of the Palestinian territories (Klein 2001, 214–246).

The Oslo Agreements

Following the Oslo Accord of 1993, and as the deadline of five years to reach a comprehensive permanent status agreement including Jerusalem approached, in the years 1999–2000 each side sought to establish as many facts on the ground and to obtain as many bargaining chips as it could. In the city hall, Ehud Olmert, of the hawkish Likud party, who replaced Teddy Kollek as mayor in 1993, sought to subjugate the Palestinians once and for all, and to scuttle the 1993 and 1995 Oslo Accords. The Palestinians tried to erode Israel's hold on Arab Jerusalem. Israeli-Palestinian competition for open spaces also had political motives.

First, Israel tried to address the demographic and political problems with brutal bureaucratic measures. In the mid-1990s, Israel began a campaign of demolishing buildings constructed without permits. It also began confiscating the identity cards that testified to Palestinians' status as residents of Jerusalem from those who, according to the annexation law, had lost their right to live in the city. The Israeli government hoped to impel a large number of Palestinians to leave the territory it had annexed. These initiatives were, however, largely unsuccessful.

Second, in the 1990s Israel commenced a campaign to take possession of land and build settlements in a belt encircling the Palestinian neighbourhoods and the Palestinian suburbs outside the city limits. Israel sought to link Jerusalem with the settlements on its periphery – Ma'aleh Adumim in the east, Pesagot in the north, Giv'at Ze'ev in the northwest, and Beitar Ilit and Gush Etzion in the south. It also sought to sever East Jerusalem from its social, political, and economic hinterland in the West Bank.

Third, in the 1990s Israeli governmental institutions began supporting settler non-profit organizations that bought up homes in Palestinian neighbourhoods with the intention of shattering Palestinian ethnic homogeneity. Settlers built isolated compounds of their own in the Old City's Muslim, Christian, and Armenian quarters and in the neighbourhoods of Ras al-Amud, Silwan, al-Tur, and Sheikh Jarah. Jewish settler penetration into Palestinian neighbourhoods is not aimed at changing the demographic balance between settlers and Palestinians: settlers constitute only about 1 per cent of the Arab population in the eastern city (about 2,000 settlers among about 200,000 Palestinians). Rather, they insert a wedge that will prevent a political solution based on the division of the city along territorial lines, a concept envisioned in President Clinton's parameters (2000) and the Geneva initiative (2003). An Israeli-Jewish compound in the heart of a hostile Palestinian neighbourhood, with the armed protection it requires, is a sharp reminder of who are the conqueror and who are the conquered. By raising the Israeli flag and giving a Hebrew name to the entire neighbourhood, they express aggression and domination of the others' territory with the aim of changing its identity.

Fourth, Israel shut down Palestinian governing institutions in East Jerusalem. As long as it was talking to the Palestinian Authority and the PLO, Israel could act against only a few of these Palestinian institutions. Israel was forbidden by the Oslo Accord of 1993 to interfere with the activities of the PLO's headquarters in the eastern city. The *Al-Aqsa Intifada* of 2000 removed these constraints and, in the summer of 2001, the Israeli government closed Orient House, headquarters of the PLO in the 1980s and 1990s. Fifth, Israel erected permanent roadblocks at the boundary between the West Bank and East Jerusalem. The roadblocks first appeared in the context of the first Gulf War of 1991 and became more numerous and institutionalized when Palestinian terror increased in the mid-1990s. They escalated the competition over permanent settlement. Ten years after it was first set up in the early 1990s, the provisional roadblock became a wall and a chain of physical barriers – the "separation fence" that divides the Palestinians of East Jerusalem from the Palestinians in the country's interior (see below) (Klein 2001: 247–293; Klein 2008).

Terror attacks during the Second Intifada (2000–2005) and the subsequent militarization of daily life in the city created mutual mistrust, and each community's self-isolation within its own boundaries. The disappearance of tourists from Jerusalem during the two intifadas caused economic recession and unemployment in both economies and advanced the segregation of the two ethno-national communities. The First Netanyahu government (1996–1999), which opposed the Oslo Accords, battled the Palestinians in East Jerusalem principally along the above methods. In contrast, the Barak government (1999–2001), which prepared to negotiate a permanent status agreement to improve the demographic balance between Jews and Arabs in Jerusalem, moved this competition to the metropolitan area and built settlements there at an increased pace. Within the city, the Barak government arrived at a quiet understanding with the Palestinian representatives on a form of activity engaged in by Palestinian institutions and individuals in the area annexed by Israel. However, under the governments of Ariel Sharon (2001–2006), which have opposed the Oslo Accords and a permanent status agreement, there were renewed attempts to subjugate the Palestinians, both within the city and in the metropolitan area. Like predecessor administrations, the Sharon governments have acted in the areas of building, residence, and land ownership, concentrating on closing Palestinian political and cultural institutions that operated in East Jerusalem and on encouraging Jewish settlement in the heart of Palestinian neighbourhoods (Klein 2008).

On top of that, the Sharon governments approved in August 2003 and February 2005 the construction of the separation wall. The principal purpose of the separation wall in Jerusalem is not only defence nor the factor used to determine its course. The wall's path aims to break the East Jerusalem metropolitan city from its natural hinterland, to police its population, and to take over East Jerusalem by dividing it into smaller sections. Moreover, the wall further establishes the Jerusalem metropolitan area by including several settlements on the Israeli side of the fence, principally Ma'aleh Adumim and Giv'at Ze'ev, respectively east and north of Jerusalem, and Har Giloh, Beitar Ilit and Etzion Block south of the city. In the Palestinian metropolis, the wall envelops suburbs such as 'Anata, Hizma, Al Za'im, Al Ram, and Dahiat Al Barid, leaving them only a narrow link with the West Bank hinterland in the form of a cramped road or tunnel under Israeli control. Moreover, the fences exclude about 70,000 original East Jerusalem residents living in Kafr 'Aqab in the north, Arab al-Sawahara and Sheikh Sa'ad in the East. These residents have to cross at very busy and humiliating checkpoints in order to continue enjoying their rights for national health and social insurance, free public education, access to the job market in West Jerusalem, to visit family members or patronize downtown services. To avoid these checkpoints, many of them choose to return to the city and live in densely populated neighbourhoods. In sum, Israel tries to contain both the Palestinian territory and the population without equaling the Palestinians to the Jews, instead of sharing rule with the Palestinians, as the Barak government proposed (Shtern 2018).

First, such right-wing policies lead to further deterioration in East Jerusalem. According to 2019 data, 72 per cent of all Palestinian families live below the poverty line, compared to 26 per cent of Jewish families; 81 per cent of Palestinian children live below the poverty line, compared to 36 per cent in the Jewish community. An average of six Arab persons dwell in a home compared to 3.2 among the Jews. Such a gap in an urban fabric is a recipe for social conflicts and rising criminality (ACRI 2019; JIFR 2019). Second, with growing challenges to maintaining contacts with the West Bank, more Palestinian Jerusalemites turn toward the west for employment. Since 2010, about 47 per cent of the Palestinian labour force in East Jerusalem, more than 35,000 young men, work in West Jerusalem, mostly in construction, cleaning, low-tech industries, transportation, hotels, and services. 71 per cent of construction workers in West Jerusalem, 57 per cent in transportation, and 40 per cent in the food industry and hotel employees are from East Jerusalem. More than ever, Jerusalem's Palestinians visit West Jerusalem's shopping centres, enjoy West Jerusalem parks, work in Jewish pharmacies, or study in Israeli universities and colleges. More East Jerusalemites are employed in or benefit from Israeli health services, both in East Jerusalem clinics and West Jerusalem hospitals or surgeries.

Several hundreds of them even rent apartments in East Jerusalem Jewish neighbourhoods/settlements (Shtern 2018).

Permanent Status Negotiations

In their peace talks, the parties have gradually shifted the discourse from slogans and myths to a practical and detailed discussion. They brought up a range of topics that comprise the issue: demography and the urban composition of the city, holy places, symbolic and national status, and social and geographical integration of its neighbourhoods, security, borderlines and border regimes, planning and zoning, employment and economic interests. Based on unofficial and unauthorized discussions made on Track Two negotiations since 1994, mainly on Jerusalem, where these subjects were discussed at length, the official negotiators made an effort to outline points of understanding. Track Two negotiators used, first and foremost, a method of differentiating among the various geographical areas in the city. They drafted different solutions to different areas, acknowledging the situation on the ground and leaving the sovereignty question to decision makers. Thanks to open communication channels between Track Two negotiators and the official delegates, Track Two has had a meaningful impact on the formal talks (Lehris 2013, Klein 2019b).

During the talks, only East Jerusalem – occupied by Israel since 1967 – had been on the negotiation table. It was officially introduced into the negotiations for the first time during the Camp David Summit in July 2000. The Israelis set the agenda, defined the city borders, had more room for manoeuvre, were more sophisticated in presenting their arguments, and could display more flexibility. Their positions were modular, as opposed to the one-dimensional and firm Palestinian position. Israeli delegation members enjoyed superior professional teams and better working methods, whereas the Palestinians were dysfunctional, did not prepare well, and their delegation was more divided in opinion than the Israelis were. Israel considered East Jerusalem areas inhabited by Jews as part of her sovereign city. The Palestinians did not reject that, provided they would get equal territorial compensation from Israel within the pre-1967 war borders. Israel was prepared to come to terms with Palestinian sovereignty in outer East Jerusalem neighbourhoods like Sho'afat, Beit Hanina, Azariya, Abu-Dis, and Sur Baher. For the inner neighbourhoods, Israel proposed municipal autonomy, limited to the neighbourhood level. Overarching responsibility for the security of the inner arc of neighbourhoods, including the Old City, would remain in Israeli hands. The Palestinians, for their part, demanded that all the Arab neighbourhoods come under their sovereignty. The two sides were also divided over the Old City. Israel wanted the entire area within the city walls to remain under its sovereignty, with the Christian, Muslim, and Armenian quarters receiving municipal autonomy. Alternatively, it proposed that the decision on sovereignty be deferred, or that the two sides agree that both claim sovereignty and that in the meantime the Old City would be under an autonomous administration. The American compromise offered at the end of the Camp David summit was that the Old City be divided between Israeli and Palestinian sovereignty. The Muslim and Christian quarters would be Palestinian, while the Jewish and Armenian quarters would be Israeli. Israel was prepared to accept this as part of a package deal in which the Palestinians accept Israel positions on the Old City and Temple Mount. The Palestinians firmly rejected the compromise (Lehris 2013, Klein 2019b).

Israel's proposals on the Old City were part of a concept of the Holy Basin that includes the Old City and its adjacent historical and religious sites such as Silwan and Mount of Olives. As a first possibility, Israel proposed that the Holy Basin be under Israeli supreme sovereignty, with the Palestinians living there enjoying municipal autonomy. Their religious bodies would administer the Christian and Muslim holy sites, and the Palestinians would receive full sovereignty over several compounds of homes in the Muslim Quarter, through which would run a road linking al-Haram al-Sharif to Palestinian sovereign territory. The Palestinian state could locate its president's office in these homes. A second possibility Israel suggested was that both sides declare that the issue of sovereignty over Temple Mount was unresolved, and that resolution of the issue would be deferred to an unknown date. A third Israeli alternative was that Israel retain supreme sovereignty over Temple Mount, but that Palestine would have religious custodianship of the site under the aegis of an international body to be established by the Muslim states and the United Nations. This arrangement would permit the use of national flags and symbols on Temple Mount. To balance the picture, Israel insisted at Camp David that a Jewish prayer compound be set aside on the site, thus changing the status quo by establishing an official division of sovereignty, so that Israel would have sovereignty-expressing powers. It should be noted that Israel did not treat Temple Mount as a single unit that included the Western Wall, as was accepted practice in Judaism and Islam. It claimed the Western Wall entirely for itself, and a part of Temple Mount. In addition, Israel was not prepared to give full recognition to sole Palestinian sovereignty over the site (Lehris 2013, Klein 2019b).

The Palestinians rejected all the Israeli proposals. They demanded full and exclusive sovereignty over Temple Mount, while agreeing to Israeli sovereignty over the Western Wall and the Jewish Quarter. The American compromise proposed towards the end of the summit was that Palestine would have sovereignty over the Temple Mount plaza, while Israel would enjoy sovereignty under the surface, where Israel claimed the ruins of the Temple lay. Israel accepted this proposal, but the Palestinians rejected it. In the negotiations conducted at the end of the summit, Israel withdrew its demand for a Jewish prayer compound on Temple Mount. On the other issues, its position remained the same. It proposed a special regime for the Old City and Holy Basin, in which administrative powers would be divided between the two sides, with the question of sovereignty to be deferred. Alternatively, an agreement could state that both sides maintained mutually exclusive claims to sovereignty. According to the Israeli proposal, these incompatible claims would not prevent the two sides from agreeing to an end to their mutual claims. The Palestinians rejected this idea because an end to claims would prevent them seeking to change a fundamental state of affairs that they opposed – the lack of Palestinian sovereignty over al-Haram al-Sharif and the Old City's Arab quarters (Lehris 2013, Klein 2019b).

Israel suggested another possibility – agreeing that God would have sovereignty over the area. However, from an administrative point of view, Israel proposed institutionalizing the status quo, which granted the Palestinians limited powers while Israel retained supreme authority. The Palestinians perceived this as a trick that sought to enlist God to justify their limited authority on Temple Mount and to give Israel preferred status. It seemed to them unfair and inequitable. Israel also reiterated its proposal from Camp David that Temple Mount be placed under the sovereignty of an international body that would in turn grant the Palestinians custodianship of the site. But under this proposal Palestinian authority would also be limited (Lehris 2013, Klein 2019b).

The two sides made progress during the 2001 Taba talks, and the areas of agreement expanded. As in the Camp David talks, Israel proposed viewing Jerusalem as a metropolitan area only to justify the annexation of settlements in East Jerusalem periphery such as Ma'ale Adumim and Giv'at Zeev that Israel calls 'Greater Jerusalem'. There was no discussion of the possibility that both municipalities, Israeli and Palestinian, upgrade the status of their respective parts of Jerusalem. Both sides agreed on the establishment of a committee that would coordinate between the two municipalities, rather than an umbrella municipality for 'Greater Jerusalem'. For the first time, Israel raised the idea of creating a permeable partition between the two cities – a barrier containing several crossing points. Authorized inhabitants of Jerusalem and of al-Quds (the future Palestinian capital in East Jerusalem) would be allowed free passage between the two cities. Everyone else would require visas. The Old City would be open, and people could enter it freely. Control would take place at the exits. The Palestinians did not accept the Israeli proposal – they wanted to maintain a completely open city. In keeping with this, the Palestinian delegation proposed to place the checkpoints outside both municipalities. Alternatively, they demanded a "hard" border that would completely separate the Palestinian and Israeli municipal areas, with no free passage for the residents of al-Quds and Jerusalem between the two sides. Disagreements on other Jerusalem issues prevented developing these initial ideas.

The discussion of the sovereignty issue at the Taba talks was based on President Clinton's parameters – all Jewish neighbourhoods would be Israeli, and all Arab neighbourhoods Palestinian. Israel accepted this idea with reservations. Its argument with the Palestinians focused, first, on the Har Homa neighbourhood. Israel considered this neighbourhood an established fact and claimed that, according to the Clinton parameters, the neighbourhood should fall under Israeli sovereignty. The Palestinians refused to apply the Clinton parameters to the then-small existing part of the neighbourhood because it had been built after and in violation of the Oslo Accords. For its part, Israel was unenthusiastic, to put it mildly, about applying the Clinton parameters to the Holy Basin and the Old City. President Clinton's proposal about Temple Mount recognized that each side felt a connection to the site, which was central to their religion. Hence, he proposed to grant Palestine sovereignty over the compound and Israel sovereignty underneath. Alternatively, Clinton proposed that Israel receive functional sovereignty in the issue of excavations under Temple Mount compound (on the Clinton parameters and Taba talks, see Klein 2003, 199–214).

The Palestinians were extremely indisposed to these proposals and demanded full sovereignty over the site – which Israel was utterly unwilling to accept. Because of these diametrically opposed positions, the issue of Temple Mount was not discussed in length at Taba. As an alternative, Israel proposed the establishment of a special regime, or division of sovereignty, in the Old City in accordance with its proposal at Camp David. Palestine would be sovereign in the Muslim and Christian quarters, whereas Israel would be sovereign in the Armenian and Jewish quarters, the archaeological parks in the City of David neighbourhood and along the Temple Mount wall, as well as the Mount of Olives and its access road. Israel also offered options familiar from the previous stage of negotiations – suspension of the sovereignty issue and joint administration of the Old City, in accordance with the parameters Israel presented at Camp David; or giving sovereignty to an international body that would grant the Palestinians co-administrative powers, so that the source of authority would not be Israeli. The Palestinians, however, stuck tenaciously to the Clinton parameters according to their understandings them (Klein 2003, 199–214).

Several years later, at the Annapolis talks (2007–2008, see ch. 10 in this volume), the sides agreed that East Jerusalem areas outside the Old City inhabited by Jews will be under Israeli sovereignty and their size included in the territorial land swap. The rest (areas populated by Palestinians and empty areas) will be part of the state of Palestine. However, they continued to debate over the Har Homa settlement. To bridge the disagreement on the Old City and the Holy Basin, Israeli Prime Minister Ehud Olmert proposed an administration of the Holy Basin by an international trusteeship composed of Israel, the Palestinian state, the United States, Jordan, and Saudi Arabia. In other words, the Holy Basin (Temple Mount included), will be neither under Israeli nor under Palestinian sovereignty, but managed by a special international custodianship.

The Palestinian president neither accepted nor rejected Olmert's proposal. He asked for further clarifications to meet his concerns on the impact of including tens of thousands of Palestinian citizens within the international regime. In addition, Olmert did not elaborate on the international custodianship management principles: Which areas will be under exclusive Palestinian or Israeli management, if at all, and which under a joint one? These questions, Abbas thought, needed clear answers given their national and religious symbolic importance. Olmert did not provide Abbas any further clarification; it was a take-it-or-leave-it proposal. Beyond the Holy Basin, the sides disagreed over the question of the open or physically divided cities. The Palestinians wanted to maintain the two capitals open, whereas Israel preferred to divide them and establish controlled crossing points (Zanany 2015).

Although the two sides did not produce an agreement in Camp David, Taba, or Annapolis, and were guided by the Oslo understanding that "nothing is agreed until everything is agreed," meaning that all the core issues, including Jerusalem, were interrelated and could not be settled independently, the understandings reached during these negotiations over Jerusalem could have constituted terms of reference in future negotiations. However, they were subsequently rejected by the United States, first mildly during the Obama administration by Secretary of State John Kerry, and then more forcefully by President Trump.

From Secretary Kerry's Failure to Trump's Breaking of United States Commitments

Between 2012 and 2014, Secretary of State John Kerry tried to resume the peace process. In order not to bring Netanyahu to reject his proposal, the document Kerry presented to Abbas in 2014 did not include the principle that Jerusalem would be the Palestinian capital. Instead, it stated that each of the two sides wished to achieve international recognition of Jerusalem as their capital. Abbas reacted angrily. Consequently, the American team presented him with a new paper. Accordingly, East Jerusalem would be the capital of Palestine but that the status of the Old City, the Holy Sites and the Israeli settlements in Jerusalem would remain open for future negotiations. In other words, Kerry's document did not include the guiding principle which featured in President Clinton's parameters, that Jewish areas would be under Israeli control, and Arab areas, including in the Old City, under Palestinian control. In his meeting with Obama in March 2014, Abbas rejected the American document (Klein 2019a, 62–71). In his farewell speech, in December 2016, Secretary Kerry presented the principles that guided his mission: "Provide an agreed resolution for Jerusalem as the internationally recognized capital of the two states, and protect and assure freedom of access to the holy sites consistent with the established status quo." In so doing, Kerry also publicly withdrew from President Clinton's parameters providing for the division of sovereignty in Jerusalem, including in the Old City and Temple Mount (Times of Israel 2016).

President Trump went much beyond any of his predecessors' policies. He recognized Jerusalem as the capital of Israel; decided to move the American embassy from Tel Aviv to Jerusalem; and declared that Jerusalem had therefore been taken off the Israeli–Palestinian negotiation table. For Palestinians, as well as Arabs and Muslims worldwide, this signified that the United States had sided unequivocally with Israel, not only on the issue of Jerusalem, but also on maintaining the occupation of the 1967 territories. Trump emphasized that the United States would support two states "if agreed to by both sides," thus giving Israel the right to veto any solution it deems unsuitable. In other words, Trump was aligned with Netanyahu's intention to grant the Palestinians a "State minus," meaning autonomy, and only in part of the West Bank (Klein 2019a: 71–76; see also ch. 10 in this volume).

While previously the United States had always been closer to Israel than to the Palestinians, it had always been openly committed to the principles of a peace process based on international law and previous United Nations resolutions. This allowed the Palestinians to accept the United States as a broker, despite its clear support for Israel, since it accepted a legal and international framework that also provided support for the Palestinian position. Trump, however, exempted the United States and Israel from all commitments to international law and United Nations Security Council resolutions, which had established that annexing Jerusalem and the continued construction of settlements were both illegitimate and unlawful.

Recommended Readings

Benvenisti, M. 1998. *City of Stone: The Hidden History of Jerusalem*. Berkeley, CA: University of California Press.

Cohen H. 2013. *The Rise and Fall of Arab Jerusalem – Palestinian Politics and the City since 1967*. London: Routledge.

Lemire V. 2017. *Jerusalem 1900: The Holy City in the Age of Possibilities*. Chicago: University of Chicago Press.

Oren, Y., and H. Yacobi. 2004. "Urban Ethnocracy Ethnicization and the Production of Space in an Israeli Mixed City." *Environment and Planning D: Society and Space* 21:6, 673–693

Sebag-Montefiore, S. 2012. *Jerusalem: The Biography*. London: Vintage.

Questions for Discussion

(1) What have been the main diplomatic achievements and failures over the years regarding the status of Jerusalem?
(2) In what ways do negotiations on Jerusalem reflect the asymmetric power balance between the sides? What would you suggest to overcome this problem?
(3) Is Jerusalem a political or a religious core issue in the conflict?
(4) What makes Jerusalem an intractable issue?

References

Cheshin, A., B. Hutman, and A. Melamed. 1999. *Separate and Unequal: The Inside Story of Israeli Rule in East Jerusalem*. Cambridge, MA: Harvard University Press.

Dumper, M. 2014. *Jerusalem Unbound: Geography, History and the Future of the Holy City*. New York: Columbia University Press.

Jerusalem Institute for Policy Research (JIFR). 2019. "Jerusalem Fact and Trends 2019." Available at: https://jerusaleminstitute.org.il/en/publications/facts-and-trends-2019/.

Klein, M. 2001. *Jerusalem: The Contested City*. New York: New York University Press.

Klein, M. 2002. "Rule and Role in Jerusalem: Israel, Jordan and the PLO in a Peace Building Process." In *Jerusalem: Essays Towards Peacemaking*, eds. M. J. Breger and O. Ahimeir. Syracuse, NY: Syracuse University Press, 137–174.

Klein, M. 2003. *The Jerusalem Problem: The Struggle for Permanent Status*. Gainesville, FL: University of Florida Press.

Klein, M. 2008. "Jerusalem as an Israeli Problem – A Review of Forty Years of Israeli Rule Over Arab Jerusalem." *Israel Studies* 13:2, 54–72.

Klein, M. 2019a. *Arafat and Abbas, Portraits of Leadership in a State Postponed*. London: Hurst, and New York: Oxford University Press.

Klein, M. 2019b. "Jerusalem in the Peace Process." In *Routledge Handbook on Jerusalem*, eds. S. A. Murad, N. Koltun-Fromm, and B. Der Matossian. London and New York: Routledge, 408–414.

Lehris, L. 2013. *Peace Talks on Jerusalem: A Review of the Israeli–Palestinian Negotiations Concerning Jerusalem 1993–2013*. Jerusalem; The Jerusalem Institute for Israel Studies.

Sebag-Montefiore, S. 2012. *Jerusalem: The Biography*, London: Vintage.

Shlomo, O. 2017. "The Governmentalities of Infrastructure and Services Amid Urban Conflict: East Jerusalem in the Post–Oslo Era." *Political Geography* 61 (November), 224–236.

Shtern, M. 2018. "Towards 'Ethno-National Peripheralisation'? Economic Dependency Amidst Political Resistance in Palestinian East Jerusalem." *Urban Studies* 56:6, 1129–1147.

The Association for Civil Rights in Israel (ACRI). 2019. "East Jerusalem Facts and Figures, May 2019." Available at: www.english.acri.org.il/east-jerusalem-2019.

Times of Israel. 2016. "Full text of John Kerry's speech on Middle East peace, December 28, 2016." 28 December. Available at: www.timesofisrael.com/full-text-of-john-kerrys-speech-on-middle-east-peace-december-28-2016/.

Zanany, O. 2015. *The Annapolis Process (2007–2008): Negotiation and Its Discontents*. Tel Aviv: Tami Steinmetz Center for Peace Research, Tel Aviv University.

14
THE ISRAELI SETTLEMENTS
Past, Present, and Future

Ariel Handel, Marco Allegra, and Erez Maggor

Introduction

Among all the various manifestations of Israel's occupation of the West Bank, none has had a more profound impact on the region and its inhabitants than Israel's settlement project. The steady growth of the settlements in the last five decades transformed them into what is widely considered as the most significant "fact on the ground" established by Israel in the territories it conquered in 1967. It is therefore fitting that for decades the political, territorial, and demographic consequences of the settlements have been subject to intense debate in the international media.

Despite the importance of the issue for the past, the present, and the future of Israel/Palestine, it is rather surprising that the conventional wisdom on the settlements is often misleading rather than illuminating. In the international media, Jewish settlers are often uniformly portrayed as religious nationalists imbued with radical ideology, while the settlements themselves are depicted as small hilltop communities located in the heart of the West Bank and near Palestinian cities or villages. But, in fact, the majority of development efforts in the West Bank have remained concentrated near or around the Green Line (the 1949 armistice line, separating the state of Israel from the territories it occupied in 1967).

In contrast to the common emphasis on ideology and messianic faith, this chapter argues that the best way to understand the persistent growth and robustness of Israel's settlement project is to consider its development in light of a broader range of factors, and as an ongoing process of *banalization* of Jewish presence in the West Bank – which we have defined elsewhere as "normalization" (Allegra et al. 2017). Thus, factors such as urban and regional planning, rising inequality, and the retreat of the welfare state within Israel proper, as well as the changing political economy of industry and employment in the region, have all played a crucial, yet conventionally underappreciated role in determining the on-going expansion and resilience of Israel's settlement project. Illuminating these processes does not aim to ignore the ideological and strategic drivers behind Israel's colonization of the West Bank, but rather places them in a wider perspective.

The Settlements – Historical Background and Terminology

Before proceeding further, however, some historical background and terminological clarifications are needed. In the 1967 War, Israel occupied several territories at the expense of

DOI: 10.4324/9780429027376-18

its Arab neighbours: the Sinai Peninsula and the Gaza Strip (previously controlled by Egypt); the West Bank, including the eastern part of the city of Jerusalem (Jordan); and the Golan Heights (Syria). Following the Camp David Accords and the subsequent peace treaty between Egypt and Israel, the Sinai was returned to Egypt in 1982; all the other territories remain under different scales of Israeli control to this day.

Immediately after the 1967 War, Israel began establishing in the conquered territories communities commonly known as "Jewish settlements." These communities, some of which are now more than fifty years old, vary considerably in nature (from agricultural villages and small exurban communities, to full-fledged towns and urban neighbourhoods, to "single-building" settlements established in densely inhabited Palestinian urban areas); in size (from a few dozens of residents to the more than 60,000 of the ultra-orthodox settlement of Modi'in Illit); in genesis (from state-sponsored planned towns to the "unauthorized outposts" established by activist groups formally functioning outside the boundaries of Israeli law); and in administrative status within the Israeli system of local authorities. Throughout the years, a limited number of these communities have been evacuated by Israel. This is the case of the settlements in the Sinai (and notably of the town of Yamit in the northern part of the peninsula) in 1982, following the Israeli-Egyptian agreement; and of the communities of the Gaza Strip and three smaller settlements in the northern West Bank evacuated in 2005 as part of the "Disengagement Plan" implemented by the then Israeli Prime Minister Ariel Sharon. Overall, however, the settler population has experienced steady and significant growth in the past five decades. Counting settlers is difficult (Hirsch-Hoefler and Shitrit 2020), but a rough estimate would put the current number of Israeli settlers in the West Bank at 650,000 (out of a total population of some nine million), of which more than 200,000 are in East Jerusalem (CBS 2019; B'Tselem 2020; PeaceNow 2020).

Throughout this chapter, the term "settlements" identifies all the Jewish communities (towns, villages, neighbourhoods) established in the areas conquered by Israel during the 1967 War, irrespective of their status in international and Israeli law and their geographical location – although the chapter exclusively focuses on those in the West Bank and Gaza. It is specifically worth stressing this point in regard to East Jerusalem. In the aftermath of the 1967 War, the Israeli government created in the West Bank the territorial entity that is now commonly known as "East Jerusalem," an area of some seventy square kilometres that includes the Old City of Jerusalem and tens of square kilometres of its surroundings. With the Golan Heights, East Jerusalem is the only area that Israel has formally annexed and constitutes today an integral part of the Israeli municipality of Jerusalem. In Israeli official and daily discourse, the settlements in East Jerusalem are thus referred to as "neighbourhoods" (rather than "settlements") and their inhabitants are considered "residents" (rather than "settlers").

As of today, we can count 270–280 settlements, including some 30 communities located in Golan Heights and between 240 and 250 settlements in the West Bank, of which about 100 are "unauthorized outposts." Various estimates have shown that the vast majority of settlers, between two-thirds and four-fifths, depending on the definitions adopted, live in large suburban communities around Jerusalem (Allegra 2013). A large part of this population is constituted by the residents of East Jerusalem and, of the five main "settlement blocs," – as they are usually referred to – namely the clusters around the communities of Ma'ale Adumim, Modi'in Illit, Giv'at Ze'ev, and the Gush Etzion in the area of Jerusalem, and the cluster around the city of Ariel in the northern West Bank.

Although the definition of these "blocs" has no administrative or legal standing, it loosely alludes, on the one hand, to the sociopolitical fabric of the resident population, which is by and large constituted by the "quality of life settlers" and "out of necessity settlers" – that is, by Israelis who moved beyond the Green Line for material rather than ideological concerns. On the other hand, the notion of "settlement bloc" largely coincides with the idea of "consensus settlements" – the settlements whose status is regarded as relatively non-controversial by the vast majority of Israeli public opinion. Since the inception of Israeli-Palestinian diplomatic talks in the early 1990s, the maintenance of control over these settlement blocs, as well as over East Jerusalem, has constituted Israel's non-negotiable condition for the definition of a border with a future Palestinian entity – although it should be noted that the vague definition of "bloc" does leave considerable scope for ambiguity in this respect.

While our definition of settlements refers, strictly speaking, to human habitation, it should be noted that over time Israeli governments established an extended network of infrastructure of varying nature, destined to service the Jewish communities in the Occupied Territories and the population of Israel proper. Major examples in this respect are the system of military bases and surveillance artefacts (walls, checkpoints, etc.) and the network of dedicated roads connecting them to one another and to the Israeli road system. Furthermore, in the West Bank we also find several infrastructure developments catering to the interests of a wider audience: this is the case, for example, of the several industrial areas, and of the touristic infrastructures established within and around the Old City of Jerusalem (such as the tourist park of the City of David). Parallel with material infrastructure, and especially since the second half of the 1970s, Israel has gradually extended its legal and administrative system onto the Jewish West Bank. Today, the structure of the local government of the settlements is virtually indistinguishable from the one established in Israel proper – although local authorities in the settlements tend to receive a larger proportion of public funds compared to their equivalent in Israel. It is worth noting that even the "unauthorized outposts" are in fact heavily funded by the Israeli authorities, from connection to infrastructures and massive military protection, to direct subsidies to agriculture, small industry and tourist initiatives.

Our last point refers to the status of the settlements in relation to international law. Most of the international community, including the United States and the European Union, considers the areas conquered by Israel in 1967 as "occupied territories," and therefore sees Israel as bounded by the provisions of international law governing the conduct of states during and after an armed conflict. Under international law (e.g., the Hague and Geneva conventions of 1907 and 1949, respectively, and United Nations Resolution 242 of November 1967) all areas conquered in 1967 remain under a regime of military occupation, and the Geneva Convention (of which Israel was a signatory) would oblige Israel to maintain the status quo in the occupied areas and therefore refrain from establishing civilian settlements there. Israel, as a signatory of the Geneva Convention, has consistently rejected the applicability of these norms to the West Bank and Gaza, arguing that these areas constitute "contested" rather than "occupied" territories – an argument that has never been accepted by the international community or most legal experts (Kretzmer 2002; Galchinsky 2005).

The First Steps

The conquest of the West Bank and Gaza in 1967 constituted a significant quagmire for the Israeli leadership of the time. On one hand, the war brought under control areas of utmost strategic and symbolic importance (e.g., East Jerusalem and the main sites of the biblical landscape); on the other, the incorporation of these territories into Israel's posed significant logistic, political, and diplomatic challenges. Central to these challenges was the trade-off between territorial gains and demographic balances; as Levi Eshkol (then Israeli prime minister) succinctly put it at the time, Israel did "covet the dowry [the conquered land], but not the bride [the Palestinians]" (Gordon 2008, 29).

In order to bridge the inherent contradictions between territorial and demographic goals, Israel adopted a set of policies that have been defined as "non-decision" (Ranta 2015). Israel formally annexed the area of East Jerusalem and established a system of military administration in the rest of the territory. At the same time, arrangements with Jordan and local Palestinian communities were put in place to grant some form of municipal and religious autonomy to the population of the occupied territories.

The same ambiguity surrounded Israel's settlement policy. Israel did define an explicit settlement policy for East Jerusalem, where large-scale, state-funded development projects were started in the years immediately following the war in the so-called new neighbourhoods of Jerusalem: Ramat Eshkol, Ma'alot Dafna and French Hill, Atarot, Gilo, Neve Ya'akov, East Talpiyyot and Ramot. The land reservoir of these large residential and infrastructural schemes was constituted through the establishment of the new municipal borders of Jerusalem, which were expanded to include 72 km^2 of West Bank territory – a much larger area than the 6.5 km^2 of the previous Jordanian municipality. It is worth underlining the importance of this administrative act as a key statement about Israel's territorial policies, which expressed the will to fully incorporate a large area of the West Bank as part of the capital of the state.

The new boundaries were designed to include large areas that would permit the development of a Jewish hinterland for Jerusalem, while at the same time leaving densely inhabited Palestinian suburbs such as Abu Dis and el-Eizariya outside the city limits (Benvenisti 1995, 53; Gazit 2003, 246; Allegra 2013). Once again, while no formal planning doctrine was spelled out as far as Jerusalem's development was concerned, these territorial and demographic considerations were reflected in the adoption of a "dispersed" (versus "compact") model of urban development. This allowed for the rapid mobilization of resources to build large-scale residential projects on greenfield sites (Schweid 1986; Faludi 1997; Rokem and Allegra 2016). A decade after 1967, the Jewish population in East Jerusalem already counted 40–50,000 residents.

Labour governments did not establish an official set of rules and guidelines for the rest of the areas under their control, and to what extent settlement activities there can be considered as "policy" is disputed by scholars (Harris 1980; Demant 1988; Eldar and Zertal 2004; Gorenberg 2006; Ranta 2015). In general terms, we can say that Israeli settlement activities outside East Jerusalem were debated mainly by committees rather than by government meetings, and on an ad hoc basis rather than as general policy. The success of each settlement project depended on the support of political factions and influent individuals (most prominently, at the time, influential Labour figures such as Yigal Allon, Shimon Peres, Moshe Dayan, and Yisrael Galili), and on the participation of various agencies and groups (ministries and government agencies, Zionist institutions, parties, non-affiliated groups) providing resources, manpower and logistic capabilities.

It is in this light that we should look at territorial blueprints such as the so-called Allon Plan. The plan, presented for the first time in July 1967 by Yigal Allon, then minister of labour, called for the annexation of wide areas of the West Bank (along the Jordanian border, around Jerusalem, and between the city and the Dead Sea; the Gaza Strip was also to be annexed, but only after resettling the Palestinian population). In the annexed territory Israel would establish settlements and military bases, while in the other areas the Palestinians would enjoy municipal autonomy. The plan was never formally approved by the government, but it is traditionally understood as representing a sort of "unofficial government policy" – in part because its emphasis on maintaining Israel's control over the Jordanian border and the area of Jerusalem reflected a consensus across parties and factions; and in part because Yigal Allon and Yisrael

Galili, among the key sponsors of early settlement activity, controlled the inter-ministerial Settlement Committee.

Indeed, most of the settlements built outside Jerusalem between 1967 and the mid-1970s fell approximately within the territorial scope of the Allon Plan. This was the case of the settlements that would eventually constitute the Gush Etzion bloc, southwest of Jerusalem (Kfar Etzion; Rosh Tzurim; Alon Shvut; Har Gilo; Elazar); of the first nucleus of the settlement of Ma'ale Adumim in the eastern periphery of the city; and of a dozen military-agricultural settlements established in the Jordan Valley. Other settlements, however, were established during the same time span outside Allon's boundaries. This is the case of the first settlements established by the national-religious group Gush Emunim (Ofra and Kedumim) (Newman 1984 and 1985); and of the settlements of Kiryat Arba near Hebron, which remained for a long time the largest settlement outside East Jerusalem. A decade after 1967, these settlements hosted some five thousand residents (CBS 2019).

The examination of these cases gives us a glimpse of the dynamics of settlement activities outside East Jerusalem. Different rationales and contextual dynamics were reflected in each settlement: quasi-official government policy informed by strategic and security consideration; activist mobilization that openly advocated a more maximalist territorial policy than did the Allon Plan; less politically charged initiatives conducted in the area of Jerusalem by non-affiliated groups of settlers (e.g., Kfar Etzion and Ma'ale Adumim). At the same time, all these initiatives invariably could only succeed thanks to the support of the key figures in the Labour Party – indeed, Allon himself was instrumental in the establishment of settlements outside the scope of the Allon Plan.

The Suburbanization of Settlement Policy

By the mid-1970s, Israel's settlement policy proceeded in a landscape quite different from that in the years immediately following the war. First, by the mid-1970s, settlement operations had already grown to a significant scale, especially in East Jerusalem, and Labour governments had officially approved the establishment of several settlements outside the scope of the Allon Plan. As time passed, consensus grew around the idea that Israel would keep control over at least part of the West Bank and Gaza for the foreseeable future, alongside some limited form of Palestinian autonomy. Opinions in the political elite differed as to the temporal nature of these arrangements (with the exception of the annexation of East Jerusalem, which was considered permanent), and on the role that Jordan or Egypt might have in this respect; however, while negotiation with Egypt brought about Israel's withdrawal from the Sinai in 1982, no real discussion was ever held on the status of the West Bank and Gaza until after the First Intifada, which began in 1987. Between the late 1970s and the early 1980s, Israel further consolidated the legal framework of settlement policy (Shehadeh 1993) by, for example, introducing the Israeli legislation to local authorities in the occupied territories through a number of military orders; by mid-1980, "the pre-June 1967 borders [had] faded for almost all legal purposes that reflect[ed] Israeli interest" (Benvenisti 1989, preface), de facto obliterating any meaningful administrative difference between the settlements established in areas annexed by Israel (such as East Jerusalem and the Golan) and those outside them.

Second, the general tone of the settlement policy reflected the political dynamics at play. The Labour Party was undergoing a serious internal crisis due to factional rivalries and high-profile scandals such as the "Lavon Affair" as well as social unrest led by second-generation Jewish immigrants from North Africa and Middle Eastern countries (*Mizrachim*), which led traditional Labour Party voters to shift their allegiance to the right-wing Likud Party. Labour's reputation had been tarnished by the Yom Kippur War (1973), which had caused the resignation of Golda Meir and brought forth a government led by Yitzhak Rabin. The Likud Party would turn out to be the main beneficiary of Labour's crisis: in 1973, at the general elections held immediately after the war, Likud obtained a third of the vote, and then proceeded to win the next election in 1977, when Menachem Begin became the first Israeli prime minister to break the three decades of Labour's hegemony over Israeli politics. Likud would stay in power practically uninterrupted until 1992. While the Labour Party has had a strong tradition of its own in this respect (represented by figures such as Allon and Galili), the Likud and the national-religious Gush Emunim were more straightforwardly defiant against any restriction to colonization. This is reflected in the semi-official territorial blueprints from this period, such as the ones produced by the World Zionist Organization's Settlement Department (Drobles 1978), and by Likud founder and agriculture minister, Ariel Sharon (Weizman 2007), as well as in the settlements campaigns conducted by the Gush Emunim. All in all, between 1977 and 1989, some one hundred new settlements were established outside East Jerusalem (compared to a couple of dozen in the period 1967–1977) – most of them relatively small communities built outside the areas earmarked by the Allon Plan.

Despite the reluctance of the maximalist right to accept limits to colonization, continuity prevailed in that the area of Jerusalem remained at the centre of the settlement policy of the Likud. Indeed, it could be argued that the key traits of the settlements operations in East Jerusalem in the early 1970s constituted the main axis of Israel's settlement policy until the late 1980s. First, the development of an initial belt of satellite towns in East Jerusalem (the "new neighbourhoods") constituted the basis for the subsequent establishment of a large Jewish hinterland outside the municipal boundaries. By the mid-1970s, planning for the first metropolitan belt of the city was well underway (Rokem and Allegra 2016). In 1974 the Labour government had approved the establishment of Jerusalem's new industrial area of Mishor Adumim, on the Jerusalem-Jericho road, and of the attached "workers camp"; in 1977 it approved the establishment of the 5,000 residential units in the new town of Ma'ale Adumim (Allegra 2013; Allegra and Handel 2017). In the following decade, the Likud continued to build relatively large settlements there, such as Efrat, Givaat Ze'ev, Geva Binyamin, Beitar Illit, Hashmonaim, Kochav Ya'akov, Har Adar, and Talmon. By the late 1980s, East Jerusalem's new neighbourhoods and the network of satellite towns around the city constituted the overwhelming majority of settler population.

Second, some key features of the settlements of East Jerusalem were replicated on a larger scale, and in other territorial areas. Jerusalem's "new neighbourhoods" were relatively large, state-sponsored residential projects, usually detached from the inner urban core of the city. They catered to a mixed audience of prospective residents, who expected to rely on the inner city as far as work services and leisure were concerned. Finally, despite the contested nature of Israel's control on the land, these settlements were fully integrated into Israel administrative, economic, and infrastructural fabric. The same key traits marked several settlements established by the Likud in the hinterland of Tel Aviv between the late 1970s and the late 1980s, which constitute today the second largest territorial concentration of settler population (Elkana, Ariel and Karnei Shomron, Beit Arye, Alfei Menashe, Sha'arei Tikva, and Oranit). Suburban settlements proved to be attractive housing opportunities for a much larger audience that did not necessarily connect with the ideological side of settlement policy – such as the ultra-orthodox community, which today provides the population of the two largest settlements in the West Bank: Beitar Illit in the Gush Etzion area, and (later on) Modi'in Illit, sitting between Jerusalem and Tel Aviv (Cahaner 2017).

This "suburban turn" in settlement policy reflected social and economic trends operating in contemporary Israel, and a broader shift in policy paradigms towards a neoliberal model of economic development. In the mid-1970s Israeli policies started to abandon the principles of balanced regional growth and population dispersal and embraced instead an approach based on the consolidation of metropolitan regions, the concentration of modern industry in a limited number of core areas, the provision of infrastructures – with the overall goal of laying the ground for market-oriented economic development (Allegra et al. 2017; Schwake 2020a and 2020b).

To Israel's planners and policymakers, the West Bank offered significant potential resources in this respect. Suburban settlements did offer a solution to overcrowding in Jerusalem and Tel Aviv. Their "double centrality" (Newman 1996), that is, the combination of decisive locational advantages with the financial and fiscal benefits awarded by the government to settlements, exerted a considerable power of attraction over prospective residents and the business community, and their size allowed for an efficient provision of services on the part of the Israeli administrative system (Maggor 2015). Indeed, even the Likud and the leaders of the settlers' movements were quick to grasp their importance as territorial and demographic facts on the ground (Benvenisti 1984; Newman 2017), while some have argued that the whole system of financial benefits underlying the settlement policy worked as a "compensatory mechanism" for the retrenchment of the welfare state (Gutwein 2017).

The Settlements between the Two Intifadas

Between the mid-1970s and the mid-1980s, Israel's settlement policy underwent a process of administrative, territorial, and demographic consolidation. Retrospectively, we can look at the years between the first and the second Intifada (1987–2000) as a continuation and consolidation of earlier trends, which is reflected in record rates of demographic growth of the settler population. However, this smooth expansion took place in a rapidly changing landscape marked by three key elements: the explosion in 1987 of the first Intifada, a large Palestinian uprising in the West Bank and Gaza, which continued to rage for several years; the start of diplomatic talks between Israel and the PLO in 1993; and the large inflow of Jewish immigrants from the former Soviet Union.

The Intifada re-opened the debate on the future of the West Bank and Gaza, which was discussed for the first time by Israeli and Palestinian representatives at the Madrid Conference of 1991, and then during the negotiations that preceded the signing of the Oslo Accord in 1993 by PLO president Yasser Arafat and Israeli prime minister Yitzhak Rabin. Various rounds of negotiation and several agreements followed as Labour and Likud alternated in power. The development of a US-sponsored Israeli-Palestinian peace process implicitly called into question Israel's settlement policy. Israel's control over the West Bank and Gaza and the annexation of East Jerusalem had never been officially sanctioned by the international community, not even by the United States. However, the influence of the Oslo process over Israel's settlement policy was limited and mostly indirect.

None of the agreements signed during the 1990s directly addressed the issue of settlements, a "final status issue" reserved for the conclusive peace agreement to be reached by 1999. In 1994, the Palestinian National Authority (PNA) was established as a provisional Palestinian autonomous government, but its limited power and jurisdiction could not challenge settlement expansion. Negotiations on final-status issues only started a few months before the Camp David summit (2000), convened by the United States in a desperate attempt to solve the impasse that had stalled the peace process since 1995, and to broker an agreement. The summit eventually failed, and no official record exists of the proposals presented, but there is consensus that Israel's final proposal would imply the annexation of some 10–15 per cent of the West Bank (i.e., the main settlement blocs around Jerusalem and Tel Aviv, representing an estimated total of some 80–90 per cent of the settler population) in the context of a land swap; Israel's control over a narrow strip of land alongside the Jordanian border; and partial Palestinian sovereignty over some of the Arab neighbourhoods of East Jerusalem (Enderlin 2003; Swisher 2004; Ross 2005).

The combined impact of the first Intifada and the Oslo agreements was instead more effective in bringing about the end the relative freedom of movement that had previously characterized the relations between Israel, the West Bank, and Gaza – and therefore between the settlements and the surrounding Palestinian communities. After the outbreak of the Intifada, Palestinian areas became, for the first time, off limits for Jewish Israelis and, in 1991, the Israeli government forbade the Palestinians from the territories to enter Israel without an official permit. This system was further institutionalized by the Oslo agreements, which introduced a "zone system" of separate jurisdictions over the West Bank. Throughout the 1990s a system of permanent checkpoints and bypass roads started to be established to filter access to specific areas and to separate Palestinian and Israeli traffic (Berda 2017). In a context of growing inter-communal violence (from the Intifada to the waves of terrorist attacks of the 1990s), a large part of these measures were implemented to protect the settlements and guarantee smooth circulation between Jewish communities on both sides of the Green Line, resulting in disastrous effect on the mobility of the Palestinian population (Handel 2014).

In terms of the territorial and demographic expansion of Israel's settlement policy, however, other factors had a more direct impact. The first, exogenous factor was the sudden influx of Jewish immigration from the Soviet Union – 330,000 arrivals between 1990 and 1991, with a total of 870,000 between 1990 and 2000. The scale of immigration flows remained a key factor in Israel's settlement policy for more than a decade because of the exceptional pressure it exerted on the housing market. The housing crisis further increased the appeal on both old and new Israelis of the large suburban settlements established a few years earlier in the metropolitan areas of Jerusalem and Tel Aviv (Weiss 2017). At the end of the Oslo process some 350,000 settlers lived in the West Bank (including some 150,000 in East Jerusalem); in the key years of Russian immigration (1990–2000) annual population increase outside East Jerusalem more than doubled compared to the previous decade (CBS 2019).

The second factor was internal to the political and administrative dynamics of settlements policy and rested on the inability (or the unwillingness) by successive Israeli governments to restrain colonization activities. After construction starts in the settlements had skyrocketed during the last years of Shamir's tenure as prime minister (1986–1992), the government of Yitzhak Rabin committed to a freeze in the establishment of new settlements and, at least theoretically, to allow just the "natural growth" of existing ones. This commitment, however, did not include pre-approved projects or construction in East Jerusalem, and settler population continued to grow much more rapidly than Israel's population. Rabin's tenure was tragically brought to an end by his assassination in November 1995, and his successor, Shimon Peres, would lose the election to Binyamin Netanyahu's Likud in June the following year. Under Netanyahu, settlement activities regained momentum, with new tenders approved for the expansion of existing settlements and the implementation of old plans for the last of Jerusalem's "new neighbourhoods," Har Homa. Likud lost the general elections in 1999 to Ehud Barak's Labour, which stayed in power for less than two years (July 1999 to March 2001), during which the pace of settlement expansion remained by and large unchanged.

After the Intifadas

The failure of the Camp David Summit in 2000 marked the end of a decade of Israeli-Palestinian negotiations: a few months after the summit the second Intifada started in East Jerusalem and rapidly propagated to the rest of the West Bank and Gaza. In a few weeks demonstrations and clashes in the street rapidly escalated into a full-blown confrontation between armed Palestinian militias and Israeli security forces, with repeated Israeli incursions into Palestinian cities that also resulted in a long siege of Yasser Arafat's presidential compound in Ramallah.

Such catastrophic failure of the peace process had long-term consequences. First, it spelled the political eclipse of the Labour Party and inaugurated the long reign of the right, with the tenures of Ariel Sharon (2001–2006), Ehud Olmert (2006–2009), and the return to power by Netanyahu (2009–2021). Second, Israeli-Palestinian relations sank to a historical low. By the start of the second Intifada, the region had lived through 15 years of economic crisis, increasing cantonization, and inter-communal violence – which included repeated terrorist campaigns by the Palestinian Hamas but also instances of right-wing Jewish terrorism, such as the Hebron massacre by settler Baruch Goldstein (who killed 29 Palestinian worshippers in the Cave of Patriarchs in 1994) and the assassination of prime minister Rabin by Yigal Amir (November 1995). The second Intifada, however, brought inter-communal violence to yet unseen levels. Third, the situation on the ground brought about a readjustment of Israel's territorial policies, which resulted in its withdrawal from Gaza (2005) and the construction of the so-called "wall of separation."

The dynamics of Israel's settlement policy reflected in part this reality. The more immediate consequences stemmed from the flare-up of inter-communal violence, peaking between 2000 and 2003. The settlements were mostly barricaded behind fences, security was tightened, and the system of bypass roads and checkpoints was expanded. Violence brought about a temporary halt in construction activities and slowed down immigration to settlements due to the perceived danger in the area. In the long run, however, established trends continued. The settler population continued to experience the steady growth inaugurated at the end of the 1980s, from approximately 350,000 (2000) to 500,000 (2010), to 650,000 today (East Jerusalem included, B'Tselem 2020).

Most of this demographic growth took place in existing communities. Since Rabin's "settlement freeze" almost no new officially sanctioned settlement had been established in the West Bank and Gaza – with the notable exceptions of Modin Illit (1996) and Har Homa (1997). Entirely new settlements started to be established in the form of "outposts," small communities that received no official approval from the government (Sasson 2005) – some 40–50 outposts were built between 1997 and 2000, and 70–80 more in the following years (B'Tselem 2020; PeaceNow 2020). Although the outposts are not authorized under Israeli law, in practice these communities receive full support from various government agencies.

The outposts are extremely diverse: some offer modernity, quality of life and bourgeois education; some emphasize freedom, organic farming, wine and artisanal production; others are the ideological communities of right-wing activists, the so-called "hilltop people" (Handel et al. 2015; Tzfadia 2017). Most of the outposts are tiny, and their combined population does not exceed a few thousand people, but their influence on the territory has been great (Handel 2009 and 2014). The impact of outposts (and settlements in general) on Palestinian mobility and access to land came to be especially significant after the second Intifada, with the tightening of security and with movement restrictions imposed on the Palestinian population. The restrictions imposed on the Palestinians were fully in line with the settlement map: the physical fortification of the settlements and the road system were first and foremost intended to enable the settlers' freedom of movement; at the same time, the hundreds of checkpoints, ditches, earth mounds, and concrete blocks that dotted the occupied territories increased the separation between the two populations, as economic relations waned and Palestinians' work in settlements was largely stopped or confined to industrial areas cut off from the inhabited parts of the settlements. Despite their lack of demographic weight, the outposts' spread over large areas considerably affected Palestinian movement. Furthermore, ideological outposts in the areas of Mount Hebron, Nablus, and the northern Jordan Valley became flashpoints of inter-communal tension, as settler violence against Palestinians increased in the form of the so-called "price tag" attacks, ranging from racial graffiti and tire punctures to physical violence, assault, and murder.

Apart from a generalized tightening of security, the years after the second Intifada brought about two main turns in Israel's territorial strategy for the West Bank and Gaza. The first was Israel's decision, in 2002, to build a separation barrier in the West Bank. The barrier – partly a system of fences and partly a concrete wall eight meters high – was presented as a "security fence" that would prevent Palestinian infiltrations into the Jewish areas. Its route departs in many places from the Green Line, in order to include on the "Israeli side" the main settlement bloc (Ma'ale Adumim, Modi'in Illit, Giv'at Ze'ev, Gush Etzion in the area of Jerusalem, and the cluster around the city of Ariel in the northern West Bank); as of today, however, only about two-thirds of the planned 700-kilometre route has been built, with large gaps remaining open – for example, around Ma'ale Adumim and Gush Etzion in the area of Jerusalem, and around Ariel in the northern West Bank.

The second main turn directly related to Israel's settlement policy: in 2003 Prime Minister Sharon announced a plan for an Israeli withdrawal from Gaza. The plan was implemented in the summer of 2005, when some eight thousand settlers were evacuated from the 21 settlements existing in the Gaza Strip (and three small settlements in the West Bank). Despite the minor demographic and territorial significance of the settlements that were abandoned – as well as reiterated signals from the government that the disengagement was part of a plan for consolidating Israel's hold on the territories – the disengagement has left significant marks in Israeli society. For the settler community, in particular, this turn of events was seen as proof that even after almost forty years (some of the communities in Gaza had been founded in the early 1970s) their status was not at all certain (Dalsheim 2011).

Retrospectively, we can look at the construction of the wall and to the disengagement from Gaza in terms of a process of entrenchment of the status quo post-Oslo. Indeed, the last few years have seen the first open calls since the Allon Plan for Israel's unilateral annexation of areas of the West Bank, also thanks to favourable international conditions. In recent years United States president Donald Trump broke longstanding taboos in American foreign policy by moving the United States embassy in Israel to Jerusalem, recognizing the city as the united capital of Israel; by recognizing Israel's sovereignty over the Golan Heights; and by publishing the outline for an Israeli-Palestinian peace plan that foresaw Israel's annexation of some 30 per cent of the West Bank, including most of the settlements in the area (Newman 2020).

Conclusion: Settlements as the Production of Territory

The previous sections have reconstructed the history of Israel's settlement policy. In this final section, we present some concluding remarks regarding key questions that implicitly arise from this reconstruction: Who are the settlers? How did the settlements come into being and proliferate across five decades? And, what is the relationship between the settlements, Israel, and the Palestinian territories?

We argue in this respect that much of the conventional wisdom on the settlements – as expressed by international media and, to a certain extent, by the scholarly contributions on the subject – is often misleading rather than illuminating. The common view of the Jewish settlements in the Occupied Territories is clearly presented by Adam LeBor's (2007) depiction of an alleged "two Israels":

> There are two Israels: one inside the Green Line, the 1967 border, the other an occupying power extending beyond it. The first is a vibrant democracy, with Arab members of Parliament, university professors and lawyers, beauty queens and soldiers, and even a Muslim cabinet minister ... Across the Green Line, the West Bank, captured in 1967, is another country, neither Israel nor Palestine, but a lawless place, where the Jewish settler, rifle in one hand and prayer book in the other, is undisputed king.
>
> *(LeBor 2007)*

Indeed, as Erez Tzfadia (2017) has noted, entering "Jewish settlers" or "Israeli settlers" into web search engines typically returns images of armed bearded men (or armed women), usually depicted during demonstrations or tense confrontations with Palestinians or the Israeli military. Often, as David Newman (2017) notes, settlements are depicted as "small hilltop communities, populated only by groups of settlers imbued with a radical ideology." This stereotypical image of the settlers is reinforced by the overemphasis expressed in the scholarly literature, which has by and large looked to the expansion of settlements as driven exclusively by religious ideology and strategic considerations – or, less often, restrained by diplomatic concerns. Thus, in an influential contribution on the subject, Israeli anthropologist Michael Feige went so far as to argue that "it would be hardly an exaggeration to claim that [Gush Emunim] has changed the history of the Middle East" (Feige 2009, 35).

Within this perspective, settlers (or at least, the settlers who have spearheaded the colonization of the West Bank) are the national-religious activists; Israel's settlement policy is nothing but a national-religious ideological product; and the settlements are "exceptional" with respect to key features and trends of Israeli society – that is, they remain outside Israel's political, social, and territorial fabric.

We argue that the history of Israel's settlement policy suggests otherwise. Indeed, as anthropologist Hadas Weiss points out in her review of Feige's book, the emphasis on Gush Emunim and the small ideological-religious settlements attributes a "disproportionate agency to a nationalist theology" (Weiss 2009, 757), and has therefore prevented gaining a thorough understanding of Israel's settlement policy. Our argument is that the best way to understand Israel's settlement project is to consider its development in relation to broader trends and changes that originated from within Israeli society – a process that we have referred to elsewhere (Allegra et al. 2017) in terms of "normalization," that is, of progressive banalization of a Jewish presence in the West Bank.

This approach, in the first place, places a great emphasis on the more "banal" motivations that drew the settlers to take part in the settlement project. Generations of activists and politicians committed to Zionist ideology and the idea of "Greater Israel" have significantly contributed to the proliferation of settlement. Yet, equally, if not more important, has been the largely overlooked contribution of state planners and bureaucrats, employers, and real estate developers, and of course, the tens of thousands of Israelis who did not necessarily care about the "redemption of the land," but choose to migrate to Jewish communities beyond the Green Line for much more banal reasons. To understand Israel's settlement policy means therefore investigating the interplay between the different factors, discourses, strategies, and rationalities underlying the colonization policy, and the formation of different, often paradoxical coalitions of actors advocating for it.

In the second place, we argue that the settlements' enterprise has not been an exceptional phenomenon contradictory to other trends in Israeli society – something happening, politically and geographically, "outside" Israel, in a distant frontier territory. From the very start, the banalization of Jewish life in the West Bank has been a crucial feature of colonization, a historical pattern that was shaped by long-term structural transformations such as marketization of the economy, retrenchment of the welfare state, and suburbanization that were occurring at both the national and global scale. Illuminating these processes does not aim to ignore the ideological and strategic drivers behind Israel's colonization of the West Bank, but rather to place them in a wider perspective, rejecting one-dimensional explanations of the proliferation of settlements. The history of the colonization of the West Bank cannot be reduced to the mechanical implementation of a century-old Zionist agenda, nor can it be understood as a coup, single-handedly conducted by a fundamentalist faction mobilizing in opposition and against the wishes of the otherwise sane body of the Israeli nation.

In other words, the establishment of the West Bank settlements and their consolidation over time is not due to ideological factors alone (e.g., the political persuasion of the various governments ruling from 1967 onwards, or the action of national-religious activists), but rather to the convergence of the various interests and preferences of many different actors (politicians, activists, bureaucrats, planners, private developers and "ordinary settlers").

Settlement strategies, as well as single communities, have been therefore successful only to the extent that they were able to relate to a wide Israeli audience, and to shepherd broad coalitions of actors in their support. Suburban settlements such as Ma'ale Adumim, Ariel, Karnei Shomron, Alfei Menashe, and Givat Ze'ev (and, more recently, Beitar-Illit and Modi'in Illit) have been especially successful because, by and large, they served the interests and rationales of Israelis of (almost) every political persuasions and backgrounds. Planners saw them as the appropriate answer to the challenges of planning the development of urban regions; bureaucrats considered them as an efficient way to allocate resources and services to the local communities; developers, contractors, and real estate agents recognized them as a new opportunity for profit; certain politicians viewed them as a mechanism through which they can compensate their constituencies; and maybe most important for tens, and later hundreds of thousands, of "ordinary" Israelis crossing the Green Line, these new, state-subsidized localities in the West Bank serve as an opportunity to build their houses and lives, as well as a springboard to upward mobility. In the context of extreme retrenchment of public spending anywhere else within the Green line, this choice could be seen as a rational decision that did not require being driven by religious or fundamentalist ideology (Gutwein 2017).

At the same time, even the more ideologically minded activists saw several advantages in establishing suburban communities in the West Bank. Such a choice was in part directly instrumental to their political goals, as suburban settlements could cater to a wide Israeli audience, resulting in fast-growing communities that represented solid facts on the ground. The existence of mundane pull factors for colonization has in fact greatly expanded the audience of potential settlers beyond the boundaries of the national-religious camp – itself a diverse community (Harel 2017). The settler population includes today both a large (and growing) component of non-Zionist *haredim* (Cahaner 2017) and of largely secularized immigrants from the former Soviet Union (Weiss 2017) – two communities that can hardly be assimilated to the standard characterization of the national-religious camp. More recent scholarship has also criticized the traditional literature on the settlements for ignoring the large presence – at least since the 1980s – of a diverse Mizrachi population beyond the Green Line (Dalsheim 2004; Gillis 2016), as well as Jewish immigrants from the United States (Hirschhorn 2017). Finally, the heterogeneity of the settler population was not lost even on Palestinians, who – as is captured by Honaida Ghanim (2017) – differentiate between groups of settlers based on their history of relations with the local population.

In LeBor's quote on the "two Israels," the Green Line is presented as the boundary dividing the sane, democratic Israeli polity from the settlements' exotic, lawless and dangerous country. It sees Israel/Palestine as composed of distinct, separate (or at least, separable with some future efforts) territorial entities. According to this argument, Israel's settlement policy created in the West Bank a distant, alien "Settlersland" which is completely removed from the reality of Israel and contradicts its fundamental values. Settlements are, however, in no way an enclosed society existing outside the "rational" or "sane" body of the Israeli nation.

To be sure, negating the existence of a clear-cut division between the two sides of the Green Line, and describing the banal and mundane drivers of Israel's settlement policy, does not legitimize colonization, but rather exposes its underlying mechanisms and dynamics. Doing so, we believe, means to shed light on the everyday or banal violence that exists in the "normal" settlements. Challenging the idea that settlements could be conceptually separated from Israel allows us to see their continuous interactions with the other territorial and demographic components of Israel/Palestine, and the complex political, social, and territorial landscapes that those interactions create.

The establishment of Jewish communities in the West Bank, we believe, should be analyzed as a multi-faceted process of "production of territory" (Brenner and Elden 2009; Allegra 2013 and 2017). In this respect, the mundane and banal routines and artifacts that make up the daily life of the residents of Israel/Palestine – building yourself a career, commuting to work, shopping at the mall, sending the kids to school, visiting friends and families, driving on the highway, obtaining a mortgage – are of no less importance than activists' campaigns or generals' strategies. The territory is made and re-made by the interplay of laws and regulations, planning and economic policies, political campaigns, symbols and discourses, against the background of broader social, political and economic trends. Acknowledging this multifaceted and ever-changing pattern, and the variety of agents and instruments involved in it, is crucial for a deep understanding the region's past, present, and future.

Recommended Readings

Allegra, M., A. Handel, and E. Maggor, eds. 2017. *Normalizing Occupation: The Politics of Everyday Life in the West Bank Settlements*. Bloomington: Indiana University Press.

Dalsheim, J. 2011. *Unsettling Gaza: Secular Liberalism, Radical Religion, and the Israeli Settlement Project.* Oxford: Oxford University Press.

Eldar, A., and I. Zertal 2007. *Lords of the Land: The War over Israel's Settlements in the Occupied Territories, 1967–2007*. New York: Nation Books.

Gorenberg, G. 2006. *The Accidental Empire: Israel and the Birth of Settlements, 1967–1977.* New York: Times Books.

Hirschhorn, S. Y. 2017. *City on a Hilltop: American Jews and the Israeli Settler Movement.* Cambridge, MA: Harvard University Press.

Lustick, I. 1988. *For the Land and the Lord: Jewish Fundamentalism in Israel.* New York: Council on Foreign Relations.

Weizman, E. 2007. *Hollow Land: Israel's Architecture of Occupation.* London and New York: Verso.

Questions for Discussion

(1) What explains the bipartisan commitment of successive Israeli governments to the settlements project?
(2) What is the status and significance of East Jerusalem in Israel's settlement policy?

(3) The "Green Line" separates Israelis who live in "Israel proper" from Jewish settlers who live in the West Bank. Some argue these two groups are uniquely different, while others have highlighted their shared commonalities. Which view would you support and why?
(4) Do you agree that the settlements are the most fundamental obstacle to peace? Or are they only the most visible?
(5) Is the settlement process irreversible? In case of a peace agreement between Israel and Palestine, what would be the most significant barriers to separation and which policies can be implemented to overcome them?

References

Allegra, M. 2013. "The Politics of Suburbia: Israel's Settlement Policy and the Production of Space in the Metropolitan Area of Jerusalem." *Environment and Planning A*, 45, 497–516.

Allegra, M. 2017. "Outside Jerusalem – Yet So Near": Ma'ale Adumim, Jerusalem, and the Suburbanization of Israel's Settlement Policy. In *Normalizing Occupation: The Politics of Everyday Life in the West Bank Settlements*, eds. M. Allegra, A. Handel, and E. Maggor. Bloomington, IN: Indiana University Press, 48–63.

Allegra, M., and A. Handel. 2017. "Colonizzazione per consenso: la nascita di Ma'ale Adumim (1967–1975) e la politica degli insediamenti israeliana in Cisgiordania." *Passato e Presente*, 102, 47–67.

Allegra, M., A. Handel, and E. Maggor. 2017. "Introduction." In *Normalizing Occupation: The Politics of Everyday Life in the West Bank Settlements*, eds. M. Allegra, A. Handel, and E. Maggor. Bloomington, IN: Indiana University Press, 1–17.

B'Tselem. 2020. "Statistics on Settlements and Settler Population." Available at: www.btselem.org/settlements/statistics.

Benvenisti, M. 1984. *The West Bank Data Project: A Survey of Israel's Policies*. Washington, DC: American Enterprise Institute for Public Policy Research.

Benvenisti, E. 1989. *Legal Dualism: The Absorption of the Occupied Territories into Israel*. Boulder, CO: Westview Press.

Benvenisti, M. 1995. *Intimate Enemies: Jews and Arabs in a Shared Land*. Berkeley, CA: University of California Press.

Berda, Y. 2017. *Living Emergency: Israel's Permit Regime in the Occupied West Bank*: Stanford University Press.

Brenner, N., and Elden, S. 2009. "Henri Lefebvre on State, Space, Territory." *International Political Sociology*, 3(4), 353–377.

Cahaner, L. 2017. "Between Ghetto-politics and Geo-politics: Ultra-orthodox Settlements in the West Bank." In *Normalizing Occupation: The Politics of Everyday Life in the West Bank Settlements*, eds. M. Allegra, A. Handel, and E. Maggor. Bloomington, IN: Indiana University Press, 112–128.

CBS. 2019. "Statistical Abstract of Israel 2019 - No. 70." In *Statistical Abstract of Israel* (Vol. 70). Tel Aviv: Central Bureau of Statistics.

Dalsheim, J. 2004. "Settler Nationalism, Collective Memories of Violence and the 'Uncanny Other.'" *Social Identities* 10:2, 151–170.

Dalsheim, J. 2011. *Unsettling Gaza: Secular Liberalism, Radical Religion, and the Israeli Settlement Project*. Oxford: Oxford University Press.

Demant, P. R. 1988. *Ploughshares Into Swords: Israeli Settlement Policy in the Occupied Territories, 1967–1977*. Amsterdam: Amsterdam University Press.

Drobles, M. 1978. "Masterplan for Developing Settlement in Judea and Samaria for the Years 1979–1983." *Jerusalem: World Zionist Organization, Rural Settlement Division, 12*.

Eldar, A., and I. Zertal. 2004. *Lords of the Land: The Settlers and the State of Israel 1967–2004*. Or-Yehuda: Kinneret.

Enderlin, C. 2003. *Shattered Dreams: The Failure of the Peace Process in the Middle East, 1995–2002*. New York: Other Press.

Faludi, A. 1997. "A Planning Doctrine for Jerusalem?" *International Planning Studies* 2:1, 83–102.

Feige, M. 2009. *Settling in the Hearts: Jewish Fundamentalism in the Occupied Territories*. Detroit: Wayne State University Press.

Galchinsky, M. 2005. "The Jewish Settlements in the West Bank: International Law and Israeli Jurisprudence." *Israel Studies* 9:1, 115–136.

Gazit, S. 2003. *Trapped Fools: Thirty Years of Israeli Policy in the Territories*. Portland, OR: Frank Cass.

Ghanim, H. 2017. "From Kubaniya to Outpost." In *Normalizing Occupation: The Politics of Everyday Life in the West Bank Settlements*, eds. M. Allegra, A. Handel, and E. Maggor. Bloomington, IN: Indiana University Press, 151–171.

Gillis, R. 2016. "The Question of Ethnic Identity in the Israeli Settlements." *Theory and Criticism* 47:1, 41–63.

Gordon, N. 2008. *Israel's Occupation*. Berkeley, CA: University of California Press.

Gorenberg, G. 2006. *The Accidental Empire: Israel and the Birth of Settlements, 1967–1977*. New York: Times Books.

Gutwein, D. 2017. "The Settlements and the Relationship between Privatization and the Occupation." In *Normalizing Occupation. The Politics of Everyday Life in the West Bank Settlements*, eds. M. Allegra, A. Handel, and E. Maggor. Bloomington, IN: Indiana University Press, 21–33.

Handel, A. (2009). "Where, Where to, and When in the Occupied Territories: An Introduction to Geography of Disaster." In Ophir, A., Hanafi, S. and Givoni, M. eds. *The Power of Inclusive Exclusion: Anatomy of Israeli Rule in the Occupied Palestinian Territories*, 179–222.

Handel, A. 2014. "Gated/gating Community: The Settlement Complex in the West Bank." *Transactions of the Institute of British Geographers* 39:4, 504–517.

Handel, A., G. Rand, and M. Allegra. 2015. "Wine-washing: Colonization, Normalization and the Geopolitics of *Terroir* in the West Bank's Settlements." *Environment and Planning A*, 47, 1351–1367.

Harel, A. 2017. "Beyond Gush Emunim: On Contemporary Forms of Messianism among Religiously Motivated Settlers in the West Bank." In *Normalizing Occupation: The Politics of Everyday Life in the West Bank Settlements*, eds. M. Allegra, A. Handel, and E. Maggor. Bloomington, IN: Indiana University Press, 128–150.

Harris, W. W. 1980. *Taking Root: Israeli Settlement in the West Bank, the Golan, and Gaza-Sinai, 1967–1980*. Chichester, UK, and New York: Research Studies Press.

Hirsch-Hoefler, S., and L. B. Shitrit. 2020. "So, How Many Settlements Are There?" In *POMPES Studies 41 - Israel/Palestine: Exploring A One State Reality*, eds. M. Lynch, M. B. Barnett, and J. Nathan. Washington, DC: POMEPS Publications, 43–49.

Hirschhorn, S. Y. 2017. *City on a Hilltop: American Jews and the Israeli Settler Movement*. Cambridge, MA: Harvard University Press.

Kretzmer, D. 2002. *The Occupation of Justice: The Supreme Court of Israel and the Occupied Territories*. Albany: State University of New York Press.

LeBor, A. 2007. '"Over the Line." *New York Times*, 14 October. Available at: www.nytimes.com/2007/10/14/books/review/LeBor-t.html.

Maggor, E. 2015. "State, Market and the Israeli Settlements: The Ministry of Housing and the Shift from Messianic Outposts to Urban Settlements in the early 1980s." *Israeli Sociology* 16:2, 140–167.

Newman, D. 1984. "The Development of the Yishuv Kheillati in Judea and Samaria: Political Process and Settlment Form." *Tijdschrift Voor Economische En Sociale Geografie*, *75*, 140–150.

Newman, D. 1985. *The Impact of Gush Emunim: Politics and Settlement in the West Bank*. London: Croom Helm.

Newman, D. 1996. "The Territorial Politics of Exurbanization: Reflections on 25 Years of Jewish Settlement in the West Bank." *Israel Affairs* 3:1, 61–85.

Newman, D. 2017. Settlement as Suburbanization: The Banality of Colonization. In *Normalizing Occupation. The Politics of Everyday Life in the West Bank Settlements*, eds. M. Allegra, A. Handel, and E. Maggor. Bloomington, IN: Indiana University Press, 34–47.

Newman, D. 2020. "The Changing Geopolitics of Settlements and Borders in Trump Deal of the Century – It is Time to Think Beyond the Territorial Box." *The Arab World Geographer* 23:1, 29–38.

PeaceNow. 2020. Settlement Watch – Data. Available at: https://peacenow.org.il/en/settlements-watch/settlements-data.

Ranta, R. 2015. *Political Decision Making and Non-Decisions: The Case of Israel and the Occupied Territories*. London: Palgrave Macmillan.

Rokem, J., and M. Allegra. 2016. "Planning in Turbulent Times: Exploring Planners' Agency in Jerusalem." *International Journal of Urban and Regional Research* 40:3, 640–657.

Ross, D. 2005. *The Missing Peace: The Inside Story of the Fight for Middle East Peace*. New York: Farrar, Straus and Giroux.

Sasson, T. 2005. "Unauthorized Outposts. Report for the Prime Minister." In *Behind the Settlements*, by D. Kurtzer, Spring 2010. Available at: www.jmcc.org/documents/Behind_the_Settlements.pdf.

Schwake, G. 2020a. "Settle and Rule: The Evolution of the Israeli National Project." *Architecture and Culture*. DOI: 10.1080/20507828.2020.1730624.

Schwake, G. 2020b. "Supply-side Territoriality: Reshaping a Geopolitical Project According to Economic Means." *Space and Polity*. DOI: 10.1080/13562576.2020.1788930.
Schweid, J. 1986. "The Planning of Jerusalem before and after 1967: Attitudes toward Uncertainty." In *Planning in Turbulence*, eds. D. Morley, and A. Shachar. Jerusalem: Magnes Press, 107–113.
Shehadeh, R. 1993. *The Law of the Land: Settlements and Land Issues under Israeli Military Occupation*. Jerusalem: PASSIA.
Swisher, C. E. 2004. *The Truth about Camp David: The Untold Story about the Collapse of the Middle East Peace Process*. New York: Nation Books.
Tzfadia, E. 2017. "Informal Outposts in the West Bank." *In Normalizing Occupation: The Politics of Everyday Life in the West Bank Settlements*, eds. M. Allegra, A. Handel, and E. Maggor. Bloomington, IN: Indiana University Press, 92–111.
Weiss, H. 2009. "Settling in the Hearts: Jewish Fundamentalism in the Occupied Territories by Michael Feige. "*Cultural Anthropology* 24:4, 755–757.
Weiss, H. 2017. "Embedded Politics in a West Bank Settlement." In *Normalizing Occupation: The Politics of Everyday Life in the West Bank Settlements*, eds. M. Allegra, A. Handel, and E. Maggor. Bloomington, IN: Indiana University Press, 75–91.
Weizman, E. 2007. *Hollow Land: Israel's Architecture of Occupation*. London and New York: Verso.

15
ECONOMIC LIBERALISATION VERSUS NATIONAL LIBERATION

Sahar Taghdisi Rad

The Israeli occupational strategies, combined with the policies of international organisations, have together restricted the development of the Palestinian economies of the West Bank and Gaza Strip and inside Israel through the dispossession of key economic resources and rights, the forced integration of Palestinian land and economic resources to Israel, sharing and outsourcing the costs of the occupation to local Palestinian and international institutions and actors, and through co-option of segments of the Palestinian political elite through offers of personal prosperity at the expense of collective development and statehood. As a result, decades after the signing of the Oslo Accords, the Palestinian economy suffers from a weak and diminishing productive capacity.

The importance of the question of Palestine in global politics and international relations – its endurance under a prolonged occupation, and its subjugation to neoliberal economic policy experimentation – all highlight the need for a global political economy approach to analyse the complex trajectory of Palestinian economic development. Such an approach accounts for the historical, political and economic determinants as well as the multiplicity of actors, interests, and instruments at national, regional, and international levels that have shaped Palestinian lives and livelihoods. A growing number of studies over the last decade have pushed for a critical political economy approach to the study of Palestinian economic development, focusing on various topics from state formation to the Israeli occupation, the role of international organisations and civil society (see, e.g., Da'na 2014; Haddad 2018; Hanieh 2016; Khalidi and Samour 2011; Khalidi and Taghdisi-Rad 2009; Khan 2014; Turner and Shweiki 2014; Taghdisi-Rad 2011).

This chapter aims to build on this body of work by bringing together these interconnected aspects of the Palestinian development experience. By adopting a neo-Gramscian framework, the chapter demonstrates how the global economic and ideological hegemony, compounded by the prolonged Israeli occupation, have resulted in the subjugation of independent and endogenous development, whereby individual prosperity has been prioritised over collective development, and economic liberalisation has taken precedent over national liberation. Following a brief overview of the neo-Gramscian approach to political economy, the chapter demonstrates how neoliberal hegemony, practised through structures of international finance, has shaped key actors and processes, perpetuating the status quo of the occupation and a gradual yet consistent distancing from the materialisation of Palestinian self-determination.

DOI: 10.4324/9780429027376-19

A Neo-Gramscian Political Economy Approach

A neo-Gramscian approach investigates the link between political and economic evolutions at the national level and the structures of power and production at the international level. Central to this approach is the concept of hegemony developed by the Italian revolutionary Antonio Gramsci, whose work was primarily concerned with class and national political processes, where hegemony of dominant forces is maintained by the state and civil society through the use of strategies of consent and coercion. The Gramscian "state" is "the entire complex of practical and theoretical activities with which the ruling class not only justifies and maintains its dominance, but manages to win the active consent of those over whom it rules" – the latter referring to the "civil society" (Morton 2003, 158). Hegemony is established when "a consensus, or form of consent between the ruling class and the subordinate 'class' is in place, resulting in creation of a 'historic bloc,'" a "solid structure that is produced by an existing hegemonic order" (Bieler and Morton 2003, 2). Therefore, hegemony is viewed as a negotiated process since the "dominant groups must secure the consent of the subordinate social forces in order to guarantee the legitimate rule of the former" (Conteh-Morgan 2002, 59).

Neo-Gramscian approaches, based chiefly on the pioneering work of Robert Cox in the 1980s, offer an application of this framework to the international level, beyond the dominating role of the state (Cox 1981). The latter focuses on the global hegemony of ideas and the dominant global mode of production that creates an international social, economic, and political structure that penetrates all countries.

> Therefore, the conception of hegemony is extended to the international level based on a coherent conjunction or fit between a configuration of material power, the prevalent collective image of world order (including certain norms) and a set of institutions which administer the order with a certain semblance of universality.
>
> *(Cox 1981, 139)*

Therefore, a neo-Gramscian hegemony extends beyond the dominance of a state to the dominance of a consensual global order, in which the state is only "a semi-autonomous intermediary in social relations between global and local social forces" (Morrison 2010, 8). Based on this dynamic conception of hegemony, Cox defines three definitive historical stages in which "the hegemonic relationship between ideas, institutions, and material capabilities varied, and during which different forms of state and patterns of production relations prevailed": the liberal international economy (1789–1873); the era of rival imperialisms (1873–1945); and the neo-liberal world order (post-World War II) (Cox 1987, 109).

As Morrison (2010, 8) argues, the "neo-Gramscian hegemony is a matrix of power, ideas, and institutions." For hegemony to form, Cox argues, it requires a combination of

> *ideas*, understood as intersubjective meanings as well as collective images of world order; *material capabilities*, referring to accumulated resources; and *institutions*, which are amalgams of the previous two elements and are means of stabilising a particular order.
>
> *(Bieler and Morton 2003, 2)*

Here, the international institutions play a "very important role in representing and expanding hegemony ideologically and tangibly" as they offer mechanisms and produce consensuses through which universal values, norms, and consent are manufactured and reproduced, consolidating the hegemony of neoliberalism's particular mode of social relations of production (Morrison 2010, 12).

In this context, the role of the state does not disappear, but it is instead transformed in line with international norms – referred to by some as the "internationalisation of the state," making it a "transmission belt from the national to global economy" (Morrison 2010, 13). The role of the Bretton Woods Institutions, such as the International Monetary Fund (IMF) and World Bank, are critical instruments through which structures of international finance ensure conformity of behaviour and suppression of anti-hegemonic tendencies across the world. The restructuring of the developing country policies in line with the macroeconomic stabilisation and Structural Adjustment Programmes of the International Financial Institutions (IFI), something that Gill calls "disciplinary neo-liberalism," has resulted in transnationalisation of these countries' production structures and a restructuring of their states' priorities away from meeting the needs of their citizens to meeting the conditions of "market civilisation" (Gill 1995, 399).

The above processes are facilitated by the formation of a 'historical bloc' through which leading social forces within a specific national context establish a relationship over contending social forces. The historical bloc is composed of a variety of actors with a "unison of economic and political aims, but also intellectual and moral unity … on a 'universal' plane" (Gramsci 1971, 181–182). This is an important concept for understanding how global social relations of production are internalised in the national context, shaping state-society relations, resulting in new structures of exploitation, prompting class-consciousness and various modes of resistance (Morton 2003; Bieler and Morton 2003). The interplay of the internal and the international is essential to the contemporary explanations of development, democratisation, and decolonisation. As Khalidi and Samour point out, "the African National Congress's embrace of neoliberalism and neoliberal "shock therapy" and the rise of an 'oligarchy' in countries of the former Soviet Union," as well as the experience of Palestinian state-building, all point to the process of neoliberalisation that followed formal independence (Khalidi and Samour 2011, 7).

The neo-Gramscian notion of passive revolution is of relevance in understanding the above examples. Defined as a process of change presided over by established elites whose use of "revolutionary" change helps to consolidate their power and maintain the existing social order, passive revolution is the means through which international institutions "transmit their ideological currents to the periphery," for example during the post-independence state-building processes. During this process, potential leaders of hostile groups or subordinate classes are incorporated into elite networks to prevent the formation of possible counter-hegemony. This concept can be used to understand the nature of the Palestinian state, civil society, and elite formation after Oslo, and their contribution to replacing a discourse of colonisation and liberation with that of accommodation and cooperation. What determines the "passiveness" of this revolution is the "organizational competence and political will of subordinates" and the extent to which they are vulnerable to concessions and co-optation (Conteh-Morgan 2002, 2). Fragmentation is an important ingredient of passive revolution. As will be seen further below, by fracturing the Palestinian society – its aims, desires, and priorities – along class, regional, and identity lines, the neoliberal hegemony has paved the way for easier acceptance and implementation of its universal norms and values.

Neoliberal Hegemony in post-Oslo Palestine

In recent decades, neoliberal hegemony, beyond the Israeli occupation, has been the most important reality shaping the trajectory of Palestinian economic development and state-building experience. Through promotion of the dominant neoliberal discourse, international institutions and their policies have penetrated all facets of Palestinian life and economy. This process, as has been documented widely, has not only resulted in the de-development of the Palestinian economy, but has also contributed to disguising and reinforcing the reality of settler–colonial relations that exist there. The neoliberal agenda has played a critical role, particularly since the signing of the Oslo Accord in Palestine in 1993, with an unprecedented number of international organisations involved in the peace negotiations. The World Bank's six-volume publication of *Developing the Occupied Territories: An Investment in Peace*, published only weeks after the signing of the Oslo Accords, set in motion the shape and parameters of a future Palestinian economy and policymaking framework (World Bank 1993).

Ever since, the World Bank has played its usual role of harmonising Palestinian economic policies with the "established" neoliberal values through support of sympathetic domestic social forces (World Bank 2011). Since the early 1990s, the IMF has also worked closely with the Palestinian Authority (PA), the Palestinian Central Bureau of Statistics (PCBS) and the Palestine Monetary Authority (PMA), on public-sector institutional development, management, and reform. While the World Bank has been more focused on the promotion of private sector development and growth in the Palestinian economy, the IMF has focused more on formulating the fiscal, monetary, and trade policies of the PA. The deep involvement of such IFIs is closely intertwined with their key patrons' geopolitical interests in the region, characterised by Lagerquist (2003, 17) as "colonial prerogatives in the … context of globalization." Of particular significance in this context is the United States desire to reinforce its hegemony in the Middle East through neoliberal peace dividends – something that Beinin (1998) refers to as 'Pax Americana' – an alliance between the United States and strategic and militarily strong partners such as Israel.

With two-thirds of the budget of the new post-Oslo Palestinian government, the Palestinian Authority, dependent on donor financing and transfer of VAT remittances and customs duties from Israel,[1] the Palestinian government and its policies have, since their inception, been subject to the conditions set out by donors and the Israeli authorities – who, by default, also have extensive leverage over Palestinian livelihoods. The aid industry that has emerged at the juncture of donors and transnational capital has created a very powerful mechanism of consent in favour of hegemony of advanced capitalist economies. The aid conditionalities, in the form of a standardised "laundry list" of neoliberal policy recommendations, are premised on greater market centrality and the rolling back of the state, privatisation, trade and financial liberalisation, and promoting foreign direct investment. State sovereignty is redefined to facilitate the free flow of capital and commodities across the world and enable private capital accumulation. This 'rationality' of the neoliberal economic framework is premised on the separation of economics from politics, whereby a political settlement or an end to the Israeli occupation is not deemed essential for economic development and emergence of market-driven private-sector-led economic prosperity. By disregarding the political realities and occupational legacies, such development frameworks end up reinforcing and strengthening them.

The neoliberal depoliticisation of development, and its overwhelming emphasis on the individual as an economic agent, have had broad implications for Palestinian economic development. With politics being treated as "policies rather than structural inequalities," the Israeli occupation is viewed by donors, for example, in terms of measurable "closures" and "restrictions" that can be managed and worked with, through a series of "occupation-proof" policies and without the need to challenge Israel's right to movement control. The donor-financed "closure-proof trade routes" around industrial estates and free zones are one of many examples of this (Morrison 2010). Therefore, the neoliberal economic approach hides the reality of Israeli settler colonialism while "incorporating the structures of Israeli occupation into official Palestinian development strategy … promoting an economic perspective that views development as an objective and disinterested process operating above (and outside) power relations" (Hanieh 2016, 33). Development is, instead, defined by (and valued as) a politically neutral technical and technocratic process that can happen in the context of resource (aid) availability and the right institutional and governance (not political) environment. Encompassing the security, the rule of law, accountable institutions, efficient service delivery, and fiscal discipline, the good governance agenda has been "elevated to the status of a national goal in and of itself" and as a proof that development can take place under or despite the occupation (Khalidi and Samour 2011, 10).

Moreover, this depoliticisation of development goes hand in hand with its support of the individual entrepreneur as the 'rational' actor in the economy. Through promotion of privatisation of commonly held assets, donors have contributed to a loss of collective capacity to resist. Individuals become "free agents" acting individually in various markets, rather than as members of communities knit together through social networks. As such, they will be more easily persuaded and coerced. As Hanieh puts it,

> development has become a problem internal to the individual (or the community), which can best be solved through the mysterious mantra of empowerment. Underdevelopment thus becomes the fault of the oppressed themselves, not a situation primarily conditioned by the prevailing structures of power.
>
> *(Hanieh 2016, 35)*

Neoliberal emphasis on the individual also makes it easier to manage any challenge to the hegemonic order through offers of personal gains, material concessions, and co-opting of moderate groups into the "coalition of the hegemonic bloc while marginalizing more radical elements" to ensure no fundamental change in social relations of power (Conteh-Morgan 2002, 59).

Palestinian State Formation under Neoliberalism

An important actor whose consent and co-option are critical for maintaining the neoliberal hegemony of transnational capital is the state. The state is seen as an important "intermediary" in charge of implementing the neoliberal policy prescriptions aimed at maintaining "stability" and the status quo. However, by virtue of its dependence on supranational institutions and capital, the state (particularly in developing countries) is often in the subordinate position. As several works have shown (Haddad 2018; Hanieh 2016; Khan 2004; Khalidi and Samour 2011), the evolution of the Palestinian Authority since Oslo highlights how, through 'coerced consent' the state has acted increasingly on behalf of the IFIs, which have, in return, ensured the PA's legitimacy on the international stage (Conteh-Morgan 2002, 61). The PA has, as expected, also displayed the same donor desire to adopt a technical approach to development by avoiding politics and the key political factors behind the question of Palestine (Khalidi and Samour 2011).

This takes place in the context of many decades of containment and forced integration into the Israeli economy that have deprived the PA of any real power to challenge the external obstacles to Palestinian economic development.[2] In return, the state focuses on "internal" obstacles to statehood, as demonstrated by the large and growing PA focus and expenditure on policies of "good governance, accountability, rule of law, fiscal consolidation and a non-ending programme of reforms. This reinforces the notion that the 'right' sort of state and free-market economy can be built while the occupation continues and the Palestinian polity remains divided politically and geographically" (Khalidi and Samour 2011, 17). The fast-rising PA (and effectively donor) allocation of expenditure to policing and security activities, particularly since the 2006 parliamentary election that resulted in the victory of Hamas,[3] is a further indication of the PA's desire of rooting out anti-hegemonic and noncompliant actors in the society through coercive means disguised within the notion of "good governance."

The PA's own non-compliance with the donor agenda is punishable and reversible through the instrument of aid conditionality. An example of this is the PA's bid for Palestine's non-member status at the United Nations, which in retaliation resulted in reductions in IFI funding and a halt in the transfer of tax revenues from Israel. In another instance, in 2009 then United Nations Secretary General Ban Ki-moon called PA president Mahmoud Abbas a "credible partner for peace" after the latter, under pressure from the "international community"[4] dropped the campaign for the United Nations General Assembly to adopt the Goldstone Report that accused Israel of war crimes during the 2008–2009 war in Gaza (Turner 2014). Both occasions resulted in a public outcry to which the PA responded through the familiar patrimonial functions of service delivery, employment generation, and new financial facilities for investors. It seems then that the PA's economic crisis is often tolerated (if not, from time to time, instigated) by donors as it ensures greater PA dependence on and vulnerability to donor finance, and a bigger scope for secondary rents being used by the PA vis-à-vis the Palestinian public.

Caught in the above "process of political rent extraction," the PA has used the rent proceeds as a powerful instrument of manufacturing consent around the political status quo and a "business as usual" environment. These rents were used to pacify the growing resentments against the preferential economic licences and import monopolies granted to the capitalist elites, and the pressure that increased imports, a consequence of trade liberalisation, exerted on domestic Palestinian producers. Therefore, "symbolic and material" rewards have been offered to appease potential resentment; these include public employment, "higher wages attainable in growth sectors and steady government salaries and also … the promise of social mobility for university graduates or those who hope eventually to benefit from economic growth" (Khalidi and Samour 2011, 20). As such, over time, political liberation has been presented as material contentment of individuals, a social contract provided by donors and the PA. This is evident in the proliferation of banking facilities, mortgage underwriting and micro-finance schemes, facilitated and financed by donors. According to the Palestinian Monetary Authority, loans to individuals in the West Bank and Gaza Strip more than doubled from $1 billion in 2010 to $2.2 billion by the of 2015, spent mostly on residential real estate, automobile purchases, and consumer loans (Hanieh 2016, 41). This debt-based financial deepening, often disguised under donors' "inclusive finance" strategy, is a powerful means of manufacturing consent as it turns citizens into consumers concerned with their individual financial stability and debt repayment. As Nir and Wainwright (2018, 351) put it, this process "has empowered the formation of distinct social forces whose material interests, with every new paycheck, housing loan, and consumer fad, appear less and less dependent on and concerned with a successful national liberation."

Formation of a "Historical Bloc"

The PA rents to those that matter to and benefit from the state-building agenda, namely "the upper echelon of the PA hierarchy, the NGO-sector, and the portion of the capitalist class that benefits from the security reform-enabled, Israeli-sanctioned economic revival in the West Bank are of great strategic importance to the PA's survival" (Khalidi and Samour 2011, 19). These groups form the "historic bloc" that is required for sustenance of the PA hegemony and the continuation of the status quo. This is in line with David Harvey's conceptualisation of neoliberalism as "a type of governance that selects spaces to be privileged and excludes others from state's protection" (Barata 2017, 3).

The political aftermath of the 2006 parliamentary elections was a major reaffirmation of the role of the "historical bloc" in shaping the trajectory of the Palestinian political economy. In the context of the PA's increasing realisation of dissenting forces after the second *Intifada* and then again after 2006, the PA further intensified its security apparatus and operations in response to various forms of domestic protests, entering "a more directly coercive phase" that designated Hamas as a "radical threat incompatible with development and democracy" (Leech 2015, 1017).[5] With the aim of marginalising Hamas in the Gaza Strip, Salaam Fayyad, a US-trained economist that previously worked at the World Bank and IMF was appointed as the Prime Minister in the West Bank, ordering some 70,000 PA public servants in the Gaza Strip to refrain from reporting to duty under the new Hamas leadership, or else risk losing their salaries (Qarmout and Béland 2012, 39). Simultaneously, Israel released 256 mostly-Fatah prisoners from Israeli jails, increased entry permits for senior PLO officials, and started to remit some of the clearance revenue back to the PA that it had been withholding as part of the Hamas boycott. Donors, in return, supported the Palestinian Reform and Development Plan 2008–2010 which proposed a comprehensive plan of neoliberal reform and development in the Palestinian territories, while Jordanian capital[6] investors geared up for increasing FDI in the West Bank. This configuration of domestic and international social forces further reaffirmed the "role of international elite social forces in conceptualizing Palestine" (Morrison 2010, 55).

Fragmentation is an important instrument of reinforcing consent and coercion – something that has been done in a variety of ways, at multiple levels, and for so long in Palestine. Firstly, by failing to challenge the territorial fragmentation of the Palestinian territories, donors have contributed to Israel's objective of normalisation of the occupation. Secondly, this fragmentation is sustained by an uncritical and de-historicised developmental strategy that gives materiality to Israeli power. The nurturing of two different economic realities financed by donors, one of institution-building and business development in the West Bank (consent creation) and isolation, punishment and limited humanitarianism in the Gaza Strip (coercion), has reinforced this fragmentation while serving the Israeli occupational objectives. Together with a disregard for the Palestinian Citizens of Israel and refugees, this contributes to a loss of collective identity among Palestinians. This happens alongside the growing endorsement of a discourse of "cooperation" with Israel, increasingly incorporated into the activities of international organisations and NGOs, disregarding the "structural relations of exploitation and domination between Israel and the Palestinian population … mean[ing] that Israeli colonialism becomes part of the process of Palestinian development itself" (Hanieh 2016, 39).

Furthermore, the gradual geographical disintegration of the Palestinian territories, caused by the occupation and the artificial separation of the West Bank and Gaza Strip, first in 1948, have become legitimate and standard categorisations in the development discourse and policy formulation, further lending materiality to Israeli power and sustaining fragmentation (Hanieh 22016). Referred to as "statistical nomenclature" by Haddad, this categorisation has provided "hard data" for donors to use as "tools of analysis and policy formulation that would enable their political and economic interventions" (Haddad 2018, 271). This divide-and-rule strategy, implemented through the support of the PA's apparatus of a donor-funded product and suppression of any signs of a delimited national agenda or even democratic elections, has deepened intra-Palestinian class and political conflict (ibid).

Palestinian Globalised Elites

Of significant role in the neo-Gramscian political economy given their importance in institutionalising neoliberalism and serving the global hegemony, and as an important component of the "historical bloc," are the globalised elites. This transnational network of capitalists gains even more importance as the role of the state is diminished and redefined under neoliberalism as the guardian of equal rules of the game in particular geographical locations for the purposes of a growing influence of capital accumulation and continuation of the status quo. These elites, as Haddad argues, are connected via "vertical linkages" with Israel and the international donors, which "tie these actors to a specific political economic arrangement erected by Oslo that is fundamentally dependent on political transfer rent that could stop if the arrangement were politically or militarily challenged" (Haddad 2018, 273). In this process, various classes of Palestinian capitalist elites have emerged from among the PA as well as civil society, including high-ranking PA officials, the NGO-sector, and the portion of the capitalist class (located domestically or regionally) that benefits from the security reform-enabled, Israeli-sanctioned economic revival in the West Bank.

The "system of patrimonial capitalism" led by the PA, brought together an array of business elites from inside the Palestinian territories, Israel, and the diaspora during the 1990s, all with the intention of investing in an international vision of Palestine as the "Singapore of the Middle East" (Bouillon 2004). These business elites have been critical in implementing a debt-based neoliberal economic model that prioritises private sector development through financialisation and regulatory reforms – although much of their activities was either disconnected from the realities of the disenfranchised Palestinians or worked to the detriment of the national liberation struggle. An example of this is that the mortgage market founded in 1996 worsened the housing crisis in the Palestinian territories, already under severe strain from the spread of settlements, with investors instead opting for the construction of luxury apartments in Ramallah, accessible only to the leaders of the PA and their associates, along with Palestinian capitalists who spend most of their time in Jordan or the Gulf (Haddad 2018).

The PA has also created its own monopolies, which by virtue of being neither public rather than private, are subject neither to public scrutiny nor to regulatory laws (Samara 2020). This is facilitated by the donor-funded initiatives – such as the establishment of industrial zones, designated customs, and duty-free, export-processing zones, with access to cheap Palestinian labour – that aim to attract foreign direct investment and facilitate joint ventures. Highly popular with investors, they are an embodiment of the neoliberal jobless growth strategy. Their enclaved "zones" make them a perfect development project choice for donors who opt for shutting out political realities, while promoting cooperation of Palestinian and Israeli investors in these zones. That they were given the special status of being "closure-free zones" demonstrates their significance even to the Israeli investors. The dynamics of these zones, such as the Jenin Industrial Estate (JIE) "normalise and legitimise the existing structures of occupation" as, for example, the land for JIE was confiscated twice from Palestinian farmers (Hanieh 2008). The donor-financed investment conferences that have been a regular fixture of PA policy, particularly since 2007 and conducted on the basis of close security cooperation with Israel, have over the years brought together domestic, regional and international capitalists to engage in economic activities that often have very few linkages with, or spill-over effects to, the Palestinian economy.

Closely tied into the political economy of neoliberal state-building in Palestine, the strata of Palestinian economic and political elite are central components of a historical bloc that flourishes despite growing dependency on the Israeli economy and at the expense of an oppressed people's dreams and aspirations for justice and liberation. Together they have constructed what Haddad (2018, 280) refers to as

> Palestine Ltd. … A dystopian product of an elaborate arrangement of political and economic actors operating within discordant visions and interests … in their currency of preference: power, money, security and logistical support, conducive to their interests and reproduction.

The Professionalisation of Palestinian Civil Society

As discussed in the first part of this chapter, the neo-Gramscian approach to political economy offers a new conception of the state – one which reflects the "underlying configuration of social forces" (Bieler and Morton 2003). Therefore, according to Gramsci, the state should be understood "not just as the apparatus of government operating within the 'public' sphere (government, political parties, military) but also as part of the 'private' sphere of civil society (church, media, education) through which hegemony functions" (Bieler and Morton 2003). As such, the neo-Gramscian conception of the state is closely connected to that of civil society. This is distinct from the liberal understanding of civil society, based on the works of Alexis de Tocqueville, "as the sphere of pluralism and associational life where common interests can be pursued, and citizens can protect themselves from both the despotic state and the 'tyranny of the majority'" (Da'na 2014, 119). As such, civil society is seen as a "transmission belt" between the individual and the state, tasked with protecting the citizens, and a critical component of a democratic society. By contrast, the Gramscian civil society is "an arena of struggle and contestation, segmented along lines of class and other forms of social identity, where hegemony and power relations are legitimated and reproduced, but which can also offer the possibility for counterhegemonic formations" (ibid). Given the *counter*-hegemonic potential of Gramscian civil society, the neoliberal discourse has adopted instead the liberal definition of civil society.

The nature of civil society in Palestine underwent substantial changes at key historical junctures; whereas for much of the pre-Oslo period, civil society was deeply intertwined with the national liberation movement, the 1990s began to see a professionalisation and "NGOisation" of civil society facilitated by the donors and the PA. While earlier civil society took the shape of traditional charitable societies, the 1967 occupation marked a move towards grassroots organisations that provided support to those whose lives and livelihoods were damaged by the occupation. The central mission of these organisations – which took many institutional forms, from trade unions to voluntary committees and cultural centres – was political self-determination through the creation of an independent and self-sufficient state, "free from occupation[, and] coupled with the right of return for refugees" (Arda and Banerjee 2019, 6). Although in the late stages of the Intifada a number of factors weakened these organisations, their activities always had an innate political mission and a local educational element: for example, agricultural services were linked to mobilisation against land confiscations, while poverty was seen as a direct outcome of occupation.

Since the 1990s, civil society has become an important component of development policy discourse. Support of the civil society is in line with the good governance mantra that promotes institutional and regulatory reforms to enhance service delivery and democratic participation. The status of the civil society is further elevated as a channel for maintaining checks and balances on the state, contributing to service delivery where the state fails, and containing any destabilising and anti-hegemonic forces. The neoliberal civil society offers a set of standardised tools through which citizens are supposed to represent themselves and their demands. However, as Da'na argues these "invited spaces" of representation are different from the "created spaces" for the exercise of citizenship. Where the latter is often the result of grassroots political and social struggle, the former are formal channels, often offered by donor-financed NGOs, often used as means of control, social fragmentation and deepening of inequalities between those who fall inside or outside their networks. Therefore, under neoliberalism NGOs as physical institutions are being equated with civil society, with their strength judged by their numbers and by their connections to the globalised elites – a definition that leaves out other forms of civil society such as trade unions, social movements, grassroots organisations, and cooperatives.

Since the 1990s, the mushrooming of NGOs around the world, particularly in developing countries, has been financed mainly through international organisations, further removing them from the grassroots nature of civil society and closer to the powerful networks of capital. This has limited the NGOs' ability to induce a bottom-up process of social change as they prioritise meeting donor requirements and demands over the needs of their disenfranchised constituents. Although non-elected bodies themselves, NGOs have in recent decades entered all facets of political life, from democracy-promotion to peacebuilding and human rights, providing them an insight into the host country's popular mobilisation and mass movements (Da'na 2014). As Harvey points out, the "nonelected (and in many instances elite-led)" nature of these NGOs and advocacy groups fulfils the "markets plus elections" neoliberal agenda (in Da'na 2014, 123–124). The growing professionalisation of NGOs has resulted in the creation of "local elites of professionals and technocrats who are close to the global actors," widening the gap with the marginalised sections of society that have fallen outside of the NGOs' "invited spaces" (ibid). As actors within the globalised Palestinian elites, this category of (often young and well-paid) professional local elites are similarly preoccupied with ensuring maintenance of their salaries, renewal of funding contracts, identifying new projects in line with donor guidelines, and targeting communities prioritised by donors (Arda and Banerjee 2019).

The civil society scene that emerged after Oslo had little in common with that of pre-Oslo. The flourishing of the aid industry in the Palestinian territories intensified the NGOisation process, combined with growing donor conditionalities imposed on their activities. After Oslo, therefore, NGOs became more embedded in the web of competitive donor financing, fulfilling donor conditionality, which often emphasised 'civic' modes of activity and service delivery and adherence to reporting practices based on pre-defined matrices and quantitative criteria. This was also reflected in major structural changes in NGOs, shifting from governance through popular committees to more hierarchical forms. Evaluation of NGOs' performance also changed from a focus on deep-rooted bottom-up social change to quantitative indicators, such as the number of workshops or training programs carried out regardless of what they have actually achieved (Arda and Banerjee 2019).

The role of donor conditionalities has been fundamental to the systematic depoliticisation of NGOs. For example, USAID's requirement for all organisations receiving its funding to furnish an Anti-Terrorism Certificate (ATC), is so restrictive that any resistance or engagement with nationalist politics could be construed as terrorism, effectively criminalising any form of resistance (Arda and Banerjee 2019, 9). To maximise the chances of receiving funding, NGO proposals need to demonstrate apolitical attitudes and behaviours and avoid reference to the vocabulary of resistance such as "military occupation," "apartheid," and "colonialism" (Arda and Banerjee 2019, 27). In doing so, NGOs after Oslo have lent themselves as important manufacturers of consent with the status quo of occupation. In the field of human rights, NGOs have gradually shifted from reporting Israeli violations to focusing on the violations by, and corruption of the PA, or shifted their focus from traditional but politically significant issues, such as agricultural development, to the "flavour of the month" themes such as democracy promotion and gender (Da'na 2014). This has resulted in a disconnect from both local constituencies as well as the older generation of activists leading the pre-Oslo grassroots organisations (Arda and Banerjee 2019). This disconnect from the frustrations and aspirations of ordinary Palestinian was demonstrated clearly through the conscious lack of NGOs' involvement in the second Intifada.

As Da'na (2014, 134) argues, NGOs' "depoliticization does not mean an absence of politics but … a shift in relations of power where collective interests can only be voiced through private individualistic and market-driven mechanisms." This approach, in line with neoliberal parameters, instead offers "efficient market-based solutions to poverty and social welfare suppressing alternate political ideologies that could be seen as a threat to neoliberal development policies" (Arda and Banerjee 2019, 27). This, according to Arda and Banerjee (2019, 3) has entailed "a shift from provision of social welfare to promotion of social entrepreneurship … [indicating] a new technology of power that creates private authority regimes of governance." The PA has been complicit in this shift and in the ideological containment of NGOs. Given the potential role that civil society could have in mobilising and politicising local communities, the PA has displayed a suspicious and coercive attitude towards civil society, including close monitoring and strict regulation of their activities. This is a departure from the pre-Oslo alliance between political and social forces – something that, as Alashqar argues, sustained the Palestinian national struggle during that phase (Alashqar 2018).

Conclusion

The above analysis has brought together a number of key determinants of the Palestinian economic development trajectory over the last few decades. In doing so, it has used a neo-Gramscian perspective to help make sense of the interlinkages between the local and the global, the economic and the political, the liberalisation and liberation. The analysis has demonstrated how the neoliberal hegemony that represents the interests of big capital and the political machinations of Western economies has penetrated all facets of Palestinian development and state-building experience, ultimately exerting firm limits on the struggle for national liberation. International financial institutions, through their conditional aid contributions and packages of policy reforms, have played an important role in creating a coercive consent around the neoliberal parameters of development and governance in the Palestinian territories. Reiterating the economic "rationality" of neoliberal thinking, they have institutionalised the practice of separating development from politics, and in doing so, have contributed to maintaining the status quo of the Israeli occupation.

Through employing various instruments to manufacture consent, the neoliberal hegemony has shaped the objectives, structures, and policies of important realms in the Palestinian society, most importantly the state and civil society. By nurturing a Palestinian state highly dependent on various forms of rent from the international donors and the Israeli authorities, the IFIs have reconfigured the state in such a way that, on the one hand, strives to provide the right regulatory and institutional environment for private sector development and, on the other, controls any potential anti-hegemonic challenges that may arise. To maintain its own legitimacy and hegemony, the Palestinian government itself has used the distribution of rents, in the form of employment, consumer loans and credit, to buy the consent of otherwise disenfranchised Palestinians. Alongside this, civil society has also been restructured into a plethora of professionalised NGOs, operating within the globalised discourse on civil society and focused on responding to the requirements and conditions of their increasingly international sources of funding. While caught up in the web of fulfilling donor requirements and reporting standards, NGOs are expected to pursue an apolitical line of work, resulting in their growing separation from the needs and grievances of the local constituencies they are supposed to represent. The depoliticisation enforced by the state and civil society, under international pressure, has enforced a sense of passive revolution through patronage and coercive consent, so distinct from the pre-Oslo nature of the Palestinian struggle for self-determination, where the civil society was not the "sphere through which hegemony is diffused, but ... the terrain upon which resistance to hegemony, or counter-hegemonic projects" was formulated (Pratt 2004, 318).

Key players within these transformed structures of state and civil society, together with the growing influence of a Palestinian globalised elite, have formed the type of Gramscian "historical bloc" that is instrumental in maintaining and exerting global hegemony in the Palestinian territories. The Palestinian business elites, with their close connections to both the PA, Arab, Israeli, and global capital, are the embodiment of the very private sector that the neoliberal paradigm aims to nurture and celebrate. Through establishing transnational networks of capital, this globalised elite prioritises investment returns and capital accumulation over national liberation, contributing to the conceptualisation of development and growth as the new peacebuilding mantra, rather than resistance against the Israeli occupation.

As stated earlier, hegemony is understood as a contested and negotiated terrain. Prior to Oslo, the Israeli occupation and associated international hegemony were directly contested through an alliance of grassroots organisations and movements. In the lead up to, and after, Oslo, this changed into a situation whereby hegemony negotiated its way through facets of Palestinian state and society, through offers of international legitimacy, material rewards, and personal prosperity. This has firmly positioned the Palestinian state-building experience within the transnational hegemonic structures and international Palestinian development discourse. Therefore, the "regimes of international aid" have transformed the economic and social realities and power relations in the Palestinian territories, where politics is professionalised into preferably quantitative development indictors and projects that can be implemented regardless of the ongoing occupation. This discourse ignores the root causes of Palestinian de-development and dispossessions – allowing unchallenged continuation of the Israeli occupation.

Recommended Readings

Cox, R. W. 1987. *Production, Power and World Order: Social Forces in the Making of History*. New York: Columbia University Press.

Hanieh, A. 2016. "Development as Struggle: Confronting the Reality of Power in Palestine." *Journal of Palestine Studies* 45:4, 32–47.

Khalidi, R., and S. Samour. 2011. "Neoliberalism as Liberation: The Statehood Program and the Remaking of Palestinian National Movement." *Journal of Palestine Studies* 40:2, 6–25.

Taghdisi-Rad, S. 2011. *The Political Economy of Aid in Palestine: Relief from Conflict or Development Delayed?* New York and London: Routledge.

Notes

1 According to the Paris Economic Protocol, the economic annex to the Oslo Accords, the Israeli authorities continued to be in charge of collecting customs duties and import taxes, which were transferred to the PA only in the case of direct Palestinian imports. However, given that most imports into the areas under PA control were re-exported from Israel, the bulk of the collected customs duties would remain in the Israeli treasury (Bouillon 2004).

2 After all, under the terms of the Oslo Accords, the PA was intended to be a transitional institution with restricted power, with no control over its borders or natural resources.

3 Notably, after the 2006 elections, the United States security assistance was channelled through the Office of the President and Fatah to bypass Hamas administration. In 2011, 25 per cent of the PA's budget was spent on "public order and safety," more than double that spent on "social protection" and more than 11 times that spent on "economic affairs" (Turner 2014, 42).

4 The unchallenged conceptualisation of the term "international community" has been challenged by many, including Hanieh (2016, 39), who argues that the term "empties the global economy of its sharply hierarchical power relations, presenting it as a neutral, homogenous, and disinterested body concerned simply with the welfare of the Palestinian people."

5 This was also in line with the PA's integration as an agent on the United States side of the so-called "War on Terror" that had begun in 2001.

6 This Jordanian capital, derived from Palestinian origin with its main "seat of operations, regulation and accommodation [being] Amman and indirectly the Gulf, not Ramallah," played the role of the "Arab partner" benefiting from lucrative economic opportunities presented by the occupation-induced Palestinian economic structure (Haddad 2018).

Questions for Discussion

(1) How do neo-Gramscian concepts of consent and coercion help the analysis of the Palestinian development trajectory in the context of global neoliberal hegemony?
(2) What role have donors played in shaping the Palestinian political economy since 1993?
(3) How has Palestinian civil society evolved over time? And how can it play a more constructive role in the economic, social and political life of Palestinians?
(4) Is it possible to envision an alternative economic development model for Palestine – one that is more in line with goals of justice and national liberation?

References

Alashqar, Y. 2018. "The Politics of Social Structures in the Palestinian Case: From National Resistance to Depoliticization and Liberalization." *Social Sciences* 7:4, 69.

Arda, L., and S. Banerjee. 2019. "Governance in Areas of Limited Statehood: The NGOization of Palestine." *Business & Society*. DOI:10.1177/0007650319870825.

Barata, P. 2017. "Colonialism, Neoliberalism and the Political Economy of Exception in the Occupied Palestinian Territories." Available at: https://cabodostrabalhos.ces.uc.pt/n14/documentos/08_PauloBarata.pdf.

Beinin, J. 1998. "Palestine and Israel: Perils of a Neoliberal, Repressive, Pax Americana." *Social Justice* 25:4, 20–39.

Bieler, A. and A. Morton. 2003. "Theoretical and Methodological Challenges of Neo-Gramscian Perspectives in International Political Economy." *International Gramsci Society*. Available at: www.internationalgramscisociety.org/resources/online_articles/articles/bieler_morton.shtml.

Bouillon, M. E. 2004. "Gramsci, Political Economy, and the Decline of the Peace Process." *Critique: Critical Middle Eastern Studies* 13:3, 239–264.

Conteh-Morgan, E. 2002. "Globalization and Human Security: A Neo-Gramscian Perspective." *International Journal of Peace Studies* 7:2, 57–73.

Cox, R. W. 1981. "Social Forces, States and World Orders: Beyond International Relations Theory." *Millennium: Journal of International Studies* 10:2, 126–155.

Cox, R. W. 1987. *Production, Power and World Order: Social Forces in the Making of History*. New York: Columbia University Press.

Da'na, T. 2014. "Disconnecting Civil Society from its Historical Extension: NGOs and Neoliberalism in Palestine." In *Human Rights, Human Security, National Security: The Intersection*, ed. S. Takahashi. Westport, CT: Praeger Security International, 117–138.

Gill, S. 1995. "Globalisation, Market Civilisation and Disciplinary Neoliberalism." *Millennium: Journal of International Studies* 24:3, 399–423.

Gramsci, A. 1971. *Selections from the Prison Notebooks of Antonio Gramsci*. New York: International Publishers.

Haddad, T. 2018. *Palestine Ltd: Neoliberalism and Nationalism in the Occupied Territory*. London: I.B. Tauris.

Hanieh, A. 2008. "Palestine in the Middle East: Opposing Neoliberalism and US Power." *LINKS: International Journal of Socialist Renewal.* Available at: http://links.org.au/node/524.

Hanieh, A. 2016. "Development as Struggle: Confronting the Reality of Power in Palestine." *Journal of Palestine Studies* 45:4, 32–47.

Khalidi, R. and S. Samour. 2011. "Neoliberalism as Liberation: The Statehood Program and the Remaking of Palestinian National Movement." *Journal of Palestine* Studies 40:2, 6–25.

Khalidi, R., and S. Taghdisi-Rad. 2009. T*he Economic Dimensions of Prolonged Occupation: Continuity and Change in Israeli Policy towards the Palestinian Economy. UNCTAD.* Available at: https://mpra.ub.uni-muenchen.de/21808/1/MPRA_paper_21808.pdf.

Khan, M. 2004. *State Formation in Palestine: Viability and Governance during a Social Transformation.* Abingdon: Routledge.

Khan, M. 2014. "Learning the Lessons of Oslo: State-building and Freedoms in Palestine." In *Decolonizing Palestinian Political Economy: De-Development and Beyond*, eds. M. Turner and O. Shweiki. Basingstoke: Palgrave Macmillan, 238–256.

Lagerquist, P. 2003. "Privatizing the Occupation: The Political Economy of an Oslo Development." *Journal of Palestine Studies* 32:2, 5–20.

Leech, P. 2015. "Who Owns 'the Spring' in Palestine? Rethinking Popular Consent and Resistance in the Context of the 'Palestinian State' and the 'Arab Spring.'" *Democratization* 22:6, 1011–1029.

Morrison, S. 2010. *Configuring Palestine: A Neo-Gramscian Perspective of International Institutions in Palestinian.* American University in Cairo.

Morton, A. D. 2003. "Social Forces in the Struggle over Hegemony: Neo-Gramscian Perspectives in International Political Economy." *Rethinking Marxism* 15:2, 153–179.

Nir, O., and J. Wainwright. 2018. "Where Is the Marxist Critique of Israel/Palestine?" *Rethinking Marxism* 30:3, 336–355.

Pratt, N. 2004. "Bringing Politics Back In: Examining the Link between Globalization and Democratization." *Review of International Political Economy* 11:2, 311–336.

Qarmout, T., and D. Béland. 2012. "The Politics of International Aid to the Gaza Strip." *Journal of Palestine Studies* 41:4, 32–47.

Samara, A. 2000. "Globalization, the Palestinian Economy, and the 'Peace Process.'" *Journal of Palestine Studies* 29:2, 20–34.

Taghdisi-Rad, S. 2011. *The Political Economy of Aid in Palestine: Relief from Conflict or Development Delayed?* New York and London: Routledge.

Turner, M. 2014. "The Political Economy of Western Aid in the Occupied Palestinian Territory Since 1993." In *Decolonizing Palestinian Political Economy: De-development and Beyond.* Basingstoke: Palgrave Macmillan, 32–52.

Turner, M., and O. Shweiki. 2014. *Decolonizing Palestinian Political Economy: De-development and Beyond.* Basingstoke: Palgrave Macmillan.

World Bank. 1993. *Developing the Occupied Territories: An Investment in Peace.* Washington, DC: The World Bank.

World Bank. 2011. *Building the Palestinian State: Sustaining Growth, Institutions, and Service Delivery: Economic Monitoring Report to the Ad Hoc Liaison Committee.* Working Paper No. 76019. Available at: https://openknowledge.worldbank.org/handle/10986/27796?show=full.

16
THE POWER OF WATER IN PALESTINIAN-ISRAELI RELATIONS

Emily McKee

Israel, Jordan and Palestine are scarce in natural water resources by world standards.
(EcoPeace, "A Water and Energy Nexus as a Catalyst for Middle East Peace")

Palestine is a geographic area that is rich with water. It's not a dry area.
(Palestinian schoolteacher)

To many readers, the assertion in the first epigraph may seem to be indisputably factual, while the second may seem false. This region's scarcity of fresh water is often raised as a key factor in Israeli-Palestinian conflict and, indeed, Israel and Palestine are typically referred to as arid and semi-arid drylands (Tal 2013). However, a closer look at water and its role in Palestinian-Israeli relations shows us that neither the designation of scarcity nor the grouping of Israel, Jordan, and Palestine into the same condition of scarcity can be so easily taken for granted (Alatout 2008; Trottier 2008). There is great variation in the average rainfall of areas across the region. Israel's far south may average only 20 mm of rainfall annually, but parts of the West Bank mountains and the Galilee receive close to 800 mm (Fanack Water 2016). Compared to London – a city that conjures images of fog and rain – Ramallah, Palestine, has a higher average annual rainfall (Met Office 2016). Furthermore, "scarcity" is neither fixed nor objective. This region is more arid than many places on the planet, but water scarcity is shaped by inequitable distribution, the domination of water by some at the expense of others. And what counts as scarcity is a socially and politically malleable concept, the declaration of which can be used to political advantage (Trottier 2008; Barnes 2014; Alatout 2008).

To understand the role of water in people's lives, we must focus not only on the presence or absence of water but also on water *access*. Though there is disagreement about the precise amounts, it is generally agreed that Israelis enjoy higher per capita access to water than Palestinians. But what explains this disparity? "The problem is that people are not allowed to reach the water," I was told by Hamza, a Palestinian date farm manager and holder of a PhD in political economics. "Our homeland is rich in water. … Because of the Israeli occupation and their policies, we are not allowed to reach the water." However, just a few months earlier, I sat across the desk from an Israeli Water Authority official as he insisted, "The infrastructure in … the areas of the Palestinian Authority, are very old, and the leakages there and the thefts there

DOI: 10.4324/9780429027376-20

are very high. They lose between forty and sixty per cent of the water. If they fix that, they have more water per capita than Israel has. And it's only in their hands!"

How do differently situated people across Israel and Palestine view the same, seemingly natural phenomena and arrive at such different conclusions? How have these disparate conclusions mattered for Israeli-Palestinian relations of conflict, cooperation, and disengagement over the years, and for life within these territories? Control over water access can be used to influence a wide variety of key flashpoints in Palestinian-Israeli relations, including but not limited to territorial expansion efforts, the economic viability of villages and cities, public opinion of local and national governments' efficacy, the symbolic and material centrality of agriculture, diplomatic relations, and international recognition (or denial) of sovereignty. This makes water a key lever of power.

Furthermore, water can be most forcefully applied to these flashpoints when people understand it as a scarce resource. Water is a material necessity, and Israel dominates water access in the region, while many Palestinians are left in dire need of more and cleaner water. However, while pronouncements of scarcity-driven water wars – past and impending – are frequent among the region's residents and scholarly analysts alike (e.g., Amery 2002; Ward 2003), speaking of "water wars" can be misleading. It is most accurate to focus not on overall water availability, but on how water access is shaped and manipulated. This includes examining both control over water sources and the ways that the concepts of scarcity and stewardship are mobilized.

This chapter outlines the current situation of water access across the region and addresses key geographical, political, and technological developments that have raised the stakes of water within Israeli-Palestinian relations. Because water relations and politics in the region are dynamic, the chapter gives readers the tools to understand the interconnectedness of water use with political flashpoints and to identify the importance of water-related developments as they continue to unfold. This analysis is based on a survey of scholarly literature and original ethnographic field research on land conflict in southern Israel from 2007–2010 and on cross-border water use, conservation, and desalination in Palestine, Israel (and to a lesser extent, Jordan) from 2012–2020.

A Contemporary Snapshot

Water Sources and Access Control

Palestinians and Israelis pull fresh water from several sources (see Map 16.1). The Coastal Aquifer lies under 18,370 sq. km of the densely populated region of the Gaza Strip and greater Tel Aviv, Israel, as well as eastern Egypt (UN-ESCWA and BGR 2013). The aquifer is rain recharged, but extensive withdrawals have led to an annual net deficit ranging from 150–200 MCM (million cubic meters) (UN-ESCWA and BGR 2013, 486, 494–495), while seawater intrusion and contaminated recharge water have made 96 per cent of water extracted from the aquifer unfit for human consumption by World Health Organization standards (UNEP 2020). The Mountain Aquifer system consists of Eastern, Western, and Northern portions that are recharged by rainfall. These are primarily in the mountainous areas of the West Bank, but also small parts of Israel, and flow to lower-altitude areas that feed springs and wells in the West Bank and Israel. Lesser amounts are pulled from the other small basins. The salinity levels of these aquifers vary, and overdrawing is raising the salinity of many. The Jordan River system includes tributaries from Syria, Lebanon, Jordan, Israel, and Palestine, which flow into the Jordan River and the Sea of Galilee. Withdrawals from this system are also high, such that of the 1.3 billion cubic meters that

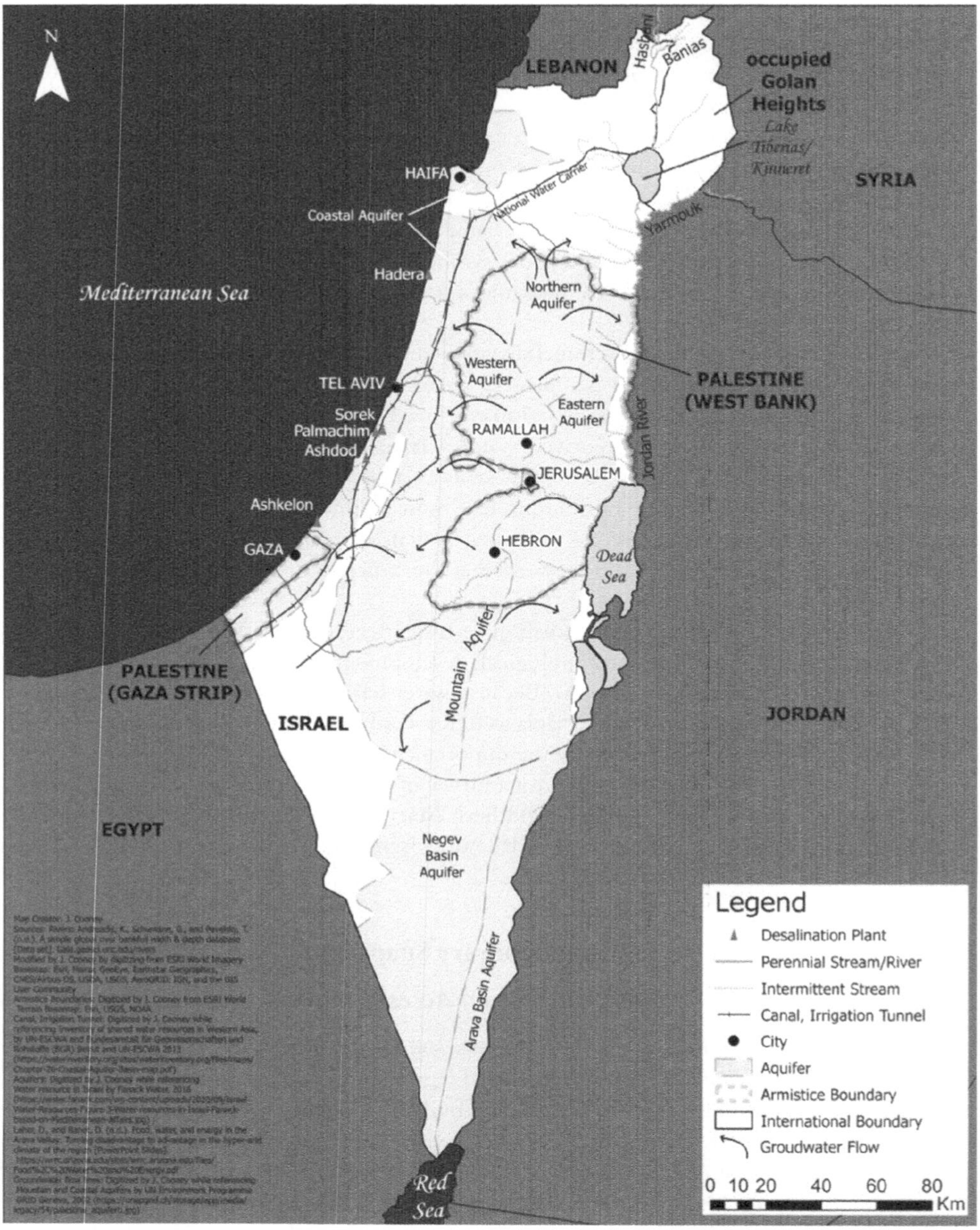

Map 16.1 Map of Water Sources and Major Water Infrastructure in Israel-Palestine.

historically flowed through the lower Jordan River annually, between 3 and 15 per cent now flows (see Fig 16.1). (UN-ESCWA and BGR 2013; Becker, Helgeson, and Katz 2014).

Often, an upstream political entity can use its position along a shared water source to exert control over that water and, as a result, over downstream political entities, as well. However, water access is determined by much more than geographic position. While Israel is upstream of the Palestinian Territories along the Jordan River, the Palestinian Territories cover the "upstream," or recharge, areas of the Mountain Aquifer. Yet, Israel dominates the entire Palestinian-Israeli water system through a combination of military, judicial, economic, and technological measures (Zeitoun et al. 2013; Selby 2013; McKee 2019). Contested sovereignty shapes the governance of water.

Within the State of Israel, all water, whether falling from the sky, flowing in streams or lakes, or existing in aquifers, is legally public property, to be managed by the state for "the needs of its residents and the development of the country" (State of Israel 1959). Since the inception of the State of Israel, the national government has set water regulations, and water has been managed by Mekorot, Israel's national water company. Water within the occupied Palestinian Territories is likewise legally defined as public property, to be managed by the Palestinian Water Authority (PWA) (Palestinian National Authority 2002). In practice, however, water in these territories is controlled by a complicated array of overlapping powers (McKee 2019).

Since 1967, Israel has occupied the West Bank and controlled water access there. Though the Jordan River flows along its eastern border, Palestinians have no direct access to this, the largest surface water source in their territory, because Israel has designated its banks a closed military zone. To apportion Mountain Aquifer water, the Oslo II Accord, signed in 1995 and intended to be a five-year interim agreement, set water withdrawal allocations and established a Joint Water Committee (JWC) consisting of Palestinian and Israeli representatives. The JWC holds authority over well permitting and other water development projects in the West Bank, but it has been functional only intermittently, and its balance of power has been decidedly weighted toward Israel (Selby 2013; World Bank 2009). As a result, water access has been skewed. For example, from 1995 to 2009 only 19 per cent of Palestinian-proposed well-drilling projects gained approval while, from 2005 to 2008 all Israeli projects submitted to the JWC gained approval. Overall, only 29 per cent of Palestinian water projects were approved (World Bank 2009, 49). This means that even in areas where the Palestinian Authority ostensibly holds jurisdiction over civil affairs and infrastructure, its efforts to manage piped water networks and institute pricing reforms depend on Israeli governmental and military decisions. In addition, any water project involving Oslo-established Area C, which constitutes the vast majority of non-urban land in the West Bank, is in practice dominated by the Israeli military body that controls bureaucratic affairs across the occupied West Bank. Faced by these layers of obstructions, some Palestinian residents drill unlicensed wells, but these are all at risk of demolition.

In the Gaza Strip, Israeli forces and settlements withdrew unilaterally in 2005, and Palestinian authorities have managed groundwater use since 2007. However, because Israel continues to control Gaza's borders, it also controls the flow of supplies necessary for well rehabilitation, the laying of pipes, and filtration and reuse facilities. Gaza residents draw the vast majority of the water they use from the Coastal Aquifer, despite its high degree of contamination, and the PWA purchases about 7 per cent of consumed water from Mekorot (PWA 2018).

Facing high demand on these water sources, both Palestinians and Israelis also look to "unconventional" sources, namely from seawater desalination and wastewater recycling. Israeli government bodies and private companies have been working since the 1950s to develop these technologies. As of 2019, Israel was recycling 86 per cent of its wastewater, much of which is reused in farming, and about 80 per cent of its drinking water came from seawater desalination.[1] Palestinian private and governmental initiatives have also been expanding in recent decades, with small desalination plants on the Gaza coast and plans for a new large plant. The PWA also oversees facilities treating wastewater in Gaza, which recharges the

Coastal Aquifer, and in the West Bank, which flows to streams. Its goals for more widespread connection of residents to sewage networks and more treatment facilities have faced many obstacles from Israeli occupation and from insufficient funds (Stamatopoulou-Robbins 2020). Israeli settlements in the West Bank have also built treatment plants, despite Palestinian objections over land seizures, which supply date plantations and other agricultural projects (Trottier, Leblond, and Garb 2020).

Water as a Lever of Power

Thus, Israel dominates the physical water system. And while water is a valuable material, it is also more than simply an object to be monopolized. To understand water's complexity, it is helpful to think of it as a "total social fact" (Orlove and Caton 2010), that is, to attend to the ways that water connects diverse domains of life. Anthropologists understand total social facts to involve "a very large number of institutions," if not "the totality of society and its institutions" (Mauss 2002, 100). People shape economic practices, laws, family relations, ethical norms, and other social institutions in response to variations in water's material qualities and its relative accessibility for human and nonhuman inhabitants. The arrangements made in these domains are also interwoven such that if a change is made – for example, in the economic treatment of water – this change reverberates through legal, familial, ethical, and other realms of life. Because of this integration, understanding the role(s) of water in Israeli-Palestinian relations requires a systemic approach. Manipulating water access can contribute to profound experiences of success (or hardship) and privilege (or discrimination) that ripple across many domains of life and across scales from the individual to the state.

One measure of differential access is in the gross volumes of water used by Palestinians and Israelis. According to the Oslo II Accord, Israel may extract four times more water from the Mountain Aquifer than the Palestinian Authority (*Annex III* 1995). On average, Palestinians in Gaza and the West Bank consume well below the WHO recommended minimum of 100 litres per capita per day, while Israelis' per capita consumption is three to four times that of Palestinians (B'Tselem 2018; PCBS, PWA, and PMD 2020; Avgar 2018). Hidden within these average figures are greater disparities, whereby Israeli settlers in the West Bank consume more than the average Israeli, while Palestinian households not connected to the water grid consume as little as 20 litres per day, and Gazans obtain only 22 litres per day of water that meets WHO criteria for human consumption (B'Tselem 2018; ARIJ 2012). Furthermore, whereas government-recognized towns in Israel enjoy regular, reliable water access, Palestinian citizens of Israel living in villages not recognized by the state often have no running water (Adalah 2006).

While water is a necessity in and of itself, it is also a tool for directing wealth and political influence. Water is most clearly necessary for farmers to grow their crops and earn a living. Other industries also rely heavily on water, including tourism, which depends on a reliable supply of safe drinking water to attract visitors and has become an increasingly significant economic sector in both Israel and Palestine. While agriculture's economic centrality is declining, the farmer is still a potent national symbol of strength, independence, and connection to the land for both Palestinians and Israelis, and agriculture's role in food security remains a significant concern, particularly in Palestine.[2]

While water access provides opportunities, the withholding of water can also have significant economic and political impacts: for example, by pushing those lacking water into subservient positions. Aversion to such dependence on a national scale has driven a great deal of political decision-making, including Palestinian objections to relying on Mekorot for water provisioning (Zeitoun 2008). The power of withholding is also exercised against marginalized populations within a state. One case in point is in the Naqab region of southern Israel. There, state agencies use control over water access as one of several levers of power, including the outlawing of Bedouin shepherding practices and restrictive definitions of legal land ownership, to move Bedouin citizens of Israel off lands they claim and into government-planned townships (Abu-Saad and Creamer 2013; McKee 2016).

The power that water holds, both as a presence and an absence, draws from water's integration across realms of life. Residents of the region often expressed this integration with phrases like "water is life" or "as long as there is fresh water, we will be here and can keep going in life." Integration is also evident in the land–water–food nexus by which Israeli occupation shapes lives and livelihoods in the West Bank (McKee 2021). While the Israeli military has seized or cordoned off more than two million dunams of land (approximately half a million acres) from Palestinians to transfer it to Israeli settlements and create military zones and nature reserves (OCHA 2012), Palestinians' lack of water access has led to the removal of even more land from agricultural production.

The following example from ethnographic field research in the Jordan Valley village of al-Auja demonstrates how shifts in water access can push far-reaching changes across people's lives. Throughout the West Bank, and particularly in the arid Jordan Valley that used to be "sallat falastin," the bread basket of Palestine, farmers are heavily reliant on irrigation water, but they face restrictions on well-drilling and the increasing salinity of shallow groundwater.[3] When canals and wells go dry, farmers cannot raise crops, yet if they stop working their land, it is more vulnerable to seizure as abandoned land. Some feel compelled to sell off their land to finance new careers, and much of this land has been converted to housing. Meanwhile, seized lands surrounding al-Auja have been transferred to Jewish settlers, who receive abundant irrigation water.

For communities like al-Auja, the demise of farming ripples into all aspects of life. Formerly green landscapes have gone brown. Many rue the precarity and dependence of the wage-labour jobs, often in settlements, that they turn to when independent farming is no longer possible (McKee 2021). As a former local council member from the village told me, "Al-Auja used to export bananas and vegetables to all the areas, to Jordan and here and there." But their access to water has declined precipitously in recent years. "So now we import," he continued.

> We now buy vegetables and fruits from the Israelis, and we became workers for the Israelis, and this is what the Israelis want. They pumped out our water and stole it; they took everything. We – our workers, our youth – all became workers for the settlements.

While some farmers cope with the decreasing water access by investing in drip irrigation and greenhouses, this capital-intensive approach is out of reach for those most in need of the income. Reliance on salt-tolerant date palms, another capital-intensive endeavour, is also growing across the Jordan Valley, which is further concentrating wealth and raising concerns about the precarity of monocrops (Trottier, Leblond, and Garb 2020).

How Did This Situation Arise?

Whole tomes have been written on the development of water conflict in the Middle East. To understand how Israelis and Palestinians have arrived at these circumstances requires at the very least attention to geography, political history, and technological change. Climate or geography are not truly deciding factors, but rather variables that can be mobilized by those with power. Likewise, technology alone decides little. These categories are useful thinking tools that, in reality, meld together in numerous ways. Power hierarchies crosscut these categories, allowing some individuals and groups to mobilize resources more readily than others and, sometimes, accumulate greater power during times of crisis.

Colonialism

> *The Negev is a great Zionist asset. … [It] is a desolate area which is currently empty of people, and therein lies its importance. What it lacks is water and Jews. It has the potential to be densely populated, even amounting to millions.*
>
> *(David Ben Gurion, "The Renewed State of Israel.")*

Colonialism has been a fixture on this landscape for centuries, though its players and its socio-political dynamics have changed. Over a period of four hundred years, Palestinians' status as subjects of the Ottoman Empire shaped their farming practices and other livelihoods to an increasing degree. Most notably, land ownership reforms of the late 1800s, known as *tanzimat*, encouraged the concentration of ownership and enhanced the strategic importance of agricultural settlements (Abu Hussein and McKay 2003; Reilly 1981). British and French colonial ambitions left their mark through their boundary-carving practices across the Levant (Segev 2000). Their interventions laid the groundwork for Palestinian-Israeli conflict more broadly, and they directly affected water disputes by splitting the Jordan River watershed across four countries and the Palestinian Territories.

More recently still, and following a pattern familiar to colonial projects around the world, Zionism reimagined the purpose, and value, of land toward more intensive productivity (Davis and Burke 2011). In the name of creating a Jewish homeland, Zionism called for modernization in the form of accelerated capitalist extraction, which prompted profound interventions in the region's hydrology (Gasteyer et al. 2012). Over the years, this has meant redirecting lakes and rivers, draining swamps, and pumping aquifers. The Zionist project has also made its mark on water systems by moving more than three million Jews from around the world to the region (both before and after Israeli statehood). Ongoing militarily backed occupation of the West Bank supports settlement towns and cities housing approximately 450,000 settlers, as well as the domination of Gaza (Federman 2019).

All the people who now call this region home need water for their households and businesses. Most well-known is the centrality of agriculture to both Palestinian and Israeli nationalisms. The pre-state Zionist settlement project relied on Jewish farming communities to claim and hold territory, and farmers continued to sway water planning and policy for decades following statehood (Shuval 2013). In Palestine, too, farming has long been an economic mainstay and a large consumer of water. Water consumption also has been significant and increasing in other industries and in homes.

This rising demand raises the stakes of scarcity-backed bids for managerial control over water. Furthermore, control over water sources is one key means through which sovereigns exercise power. Because all main water sources for the lands claimed by Israelis and Palestinians are shared, all projects and policies involving water extraction are also necessarily territorial moves and signals of sovereignty. As a result, water has been one of the thorniest issues for peace agreements. Negotiators managed to arrive at a five-year interim agreement in 1995 … but there has been no replacement for 25 years.

Geography and Environmental Imaginaries

> *The truth is, there is water scarcity in Israel. We do not have [a] water scarcity issue in the West Bank, in Palestine. We have groundwater. Enough for Palestine for today and for tomorrow. But it's being taken by Israel.*
>
> *(Palestinian water regulator)*

It is not the geography or climate per se that make water available for human use. Rather, water flows in a hydrosocial cycle, a cycle governed by physical, biological, and social power (Linton and Budds 2014). Political arrangements, technological interventions, and even the environmental imaginaries through which people interpret particular landscapes and plan environmental projects are all part of this hydrosocial cycle.[4]

As part of this hydrosocial cycle, colonialism has deeply imprinted not only relationships among people, but the very landscapes of this region. For example, while the West Bank (itself an area defined by the political boundaries of the 1967 ceasefire) may have an advantageous hydrological cycle, boasting abundant aquifer water and rainfall compared to many parts of Israel, Palestinian residents have access to significantly less water. All of the following determine where water actually flows and ebbs: Israel's military occupation since 1967, Palestinian negotiators' weak position when bargaining over allocations under the Oslo Accords (Selby 2013), the Israeli-built separation barrier that winds inside the Green Line and ensnares many Palestinian wells, Palestinians drilling and pumping from non-permitted wells, and the greater ability of an established state (Israel) than an aspiring state (the PA) to build and maintain water infrastructure.

Likewise, water becomes a powerful lever within Palestinian-Israeli relations, not because of the arid climate per se, but rather through the mobilization of the two interlocked concepts: scarcity and stewardship. Disagreements about the scarcity or abundance of this region's natural water resources have had dramatic diplomatic, economic, and social consequences over the past century. In the 1920s, when the British Mandate authorities adopted the concept of "carrying capacity" to guide debates about Jewish immigration to Palestine, much of the disagreement centred around water availability. Zionists denied pronouncements of water scarcity by proffering hydrological studies they had conducted suggesting high groundwater capacity, and they touted the ability of technological developments to advance water efficiency (Alatout 2009). However, during Israel's early statehood, Zionist leaders' claims of abundance turned to warnings of scarcity. During this period, water experts and policymakers of the new state divided into scarcity advocates versus abundance advocates, and the scarcity camp, with its strongly statist approach to water management, eventually won influence (Alatout 2008). Water management debates envelop politically important issues, including individual versus collective rights, competing nation-building projects, and group identity. During both pre-state and statehood eras, directing these debates to the seemingly depoliticized, measurement-focused notions of scarcity and capacity gave an advantage to those with greater control over scientific research and technical expertise.

Climate patterns and hydrology have never been static, but global climate change raises new challenges for the Middle East. Rainfall and temperatures in this region are growing increasingly unreliable. While degrees and rates of change are under debate, some researchers are already finding evidence of rising temperatures, harsher droughts, and less predictable rainfall. Multiple models forecast that this region will suffer both rising temperatures and declining precipitation at rates faster than global averages (Mason, Zeitoun, and Mimi 2012).

Technology

The quickness with which this country just adapts and believes in technology is quite remarkable, and can be somewhat dangerous.

(Israeli environmentalist)

Technological change is the third major factor that has led to the currently fractious role of water in Israeli-Palestinian relations. For as long as people have been vying over these shared water sources, amongst co-nationals as well as between Palestinians and Israelis, they have used technologies to redirect water flows and change the material qualities of water.

During Ottoman rule and much of the British Mandate, water management across Palestine was decentralized. Councils of water users constructed and maintained irrigation networks. Palestinian farmers working on steep mountain slopes developed terracing strategies that direct water at the right pitch to soak into gardens of grapes, olives, and other hillside crops (Tesdell, Othman, and Alkhoury 2018). Early Zionist settlers likewise managed water at a relatively local scale (Shuval 2013).

However, in the 1900s Zionist settlers and donors, and later the Israeli state, mustered the technologies necessary to realize their vision of productive, "modern" landscapes. They invested in larger-scale agriculture, often bringing intensive farming methods to previously unirrigated lands (Tal 2002). This was most starkly the case in the Naqab/Negev desert, where David Ben Gurion and other Zionist leaders saw great potential to settle Jews in this purportedly empty area by "making the desert bloom." As in many parts of the world, the expansion of export agriculture and state-building brought a trend of high modernist water management that sought to reshape landscapes to fit national (political and economic) goals. Indeed, the lack of intensive agriculture and extensive irrigation systems to support it were frequently cited justifications for the claim that the Naqab was uninhabited, despite the large population of Palestinian Bedouins calling it home (McKee 2016). And Israeli leaders dedicated a huge proportion of the nascent state's meagre resources to irrigation infrastructure as state-building.

Beginning with the Yarkon-Negev pipeline in 1955 and culminating with the completion of the National Water Carrier (NWC) in 1964, Israel built a massive network of canals and pipes that then redirected nearly half a billion cubic meters of water annually from northern Israel to the south (Tal 2002). The NWC reshaped water management models in the region, sidelining watershed-based arguments for water management and instead channelling water according to profitable use and national interests (Alatout 2011). The project spread agriculture and population growth to all of Israel, shifting water demand for generations to come. And as it accorded with high modernist ideas of water management favoured in international circles at the time, the NWC also boosted Israel's international image as a leader in water management.

While Palestinian approaches to water management prior to the rise of Zionist settlement had been more localized and less intensively interventionist, the PA and Israeli government now share ideologies regarding water. Both favour the centralization of management and the implementation of full cost recovery, with the aim of supporting capitalist expansion.[5] Since 2001, Israeli law has legally required municipalities and other local water managers to transfer their services to regional water authorities, and consumer prices have been set to recover the full cost of water provisioning. Water industry leaders and government officials in Israel regularly tout these management approaches as the key to good water stewardship. Cost recovery in infrastructure projects and other tenets of neoliberalism also have grown increasingly central to PA nation-building efforts (Khalidi and Samour 2011; Trottier 2007). During interviews, Palestinian water industry and government officials repeatedly stressed the need to build a single water distribution grid and manage it through a unified national water company.

Desalinated seawater and recycled wastewater have been the stars of the latest chapter in the development of water technology, not least for their ability to make water no longer a zero-sum issue. The quantity available is not simply set by rainfall and aquifer capacity, which may ease the discussion of water allocations in Palestinian-Israeli negotiations. Israel now procures 600 MCM of drinking water annually from five large desalination plants, which are privately owned, but supervised by the Water Authority. Two more plants, now in planning stages, would boost the annual total to more than 1,000 MCM. Wastewater treatment plants recycle 700 MCM annually, which provides much of Israel's agricultural water. In the Gaza Strip, small desalination plants provide a trickle of water, and a proposed 110 MCM-capacity plant is being planned with international donors.[6]

However, because desalination and wastewater treatment expertise and capacity are unevenly distributed, with Israel dominating both, these technologies can become a new mechanism for domination. Indeed, many Palestinians worry about becoming overly dependent on Israel for this vital resource and are also concerned that desalination, in particular, may change the terms of debate over water rights. They worry that concentrating on "producing new" water for purchase shifts the focus away from national rights to environmental resources, including aquifer water and the Jordan River, which would constitute a threat to Palestinian sovereignty (see also Stamatopoulou-Robbins 2018).

Furthermore, while many industry and government officials, as well as the foreign press, describe Israel as being "years ahead" and "a role model" in its technological sophistication, these technological developments have also brought negative environmental consequences. For example, the draining of the Huleh Valley, justified by its proponents in the 1950s as the transformation of dangerous swamp into productive farmland, later sparked an environmental movement to restore this valuable wetland (Anton 2008). The NWC has altered the nutrient content of the Sea of Galilee (Tal 2002, 215), reduced the lower Jordan River to a trickle of agricultural runoff, and contributes to the recession of the Dead Sea (Becker, Helgeson, and Katz 2014). Likewise, despite claims of an "unlimited" supply of water from the sea, the costs of desalination include not only the price tag of plant construction, but also the greenhouse gas emissions and uncertain ecological impacts of their operation.

Scarcity, Stewardship, and Power

Today, scarcity is a key watchword of government and water industry leaders. During interviews with me, Israeli government officials often argued that because water in the region is so scarce, centralized management and price mechanisms must be used to encourage efficient use. Likewise, the centralization and commodification of water are also key tenets of the PA's nation-building efforts (Trottier 2007), but the same obstacles preventing the establishment and operation of a functioning Palestinian state have also prevented the PA from exercising robust power over the water system (Stamatopoulou-Robbins 2019). Israel has a many-decades head start in implementing these strategies, and this head start is powerful in commanding international respect and in using water as a lever of power and state-building. In addition, every Palestinian government official and hydrologist I spoke with attempted to walk a fine line between, on one hand, asserting the scarcity of water and the need for conservative use and, on the other, maintaining focus on Israeli domination of existing water supplies as the cause of Palestinians' water deprivation (Stamatopoulou-Robbins 2018).

This balancing act is so difficult because claims of scarcity, stewardship, and wise management are often used as justifications for Israel maintaining control over the entire Palestinian-Israeli water system. Israeli government and industry representatives regularly highlight Israel's track record in recycling water and minimizing leakages in water networks, projecting an image of Israelis as leading water experts, not only in the region, but around the world. The Watec international water conference hosted by Israel in 2019, for example, featured declarations of Israel as "a water empire" and a "world leader." One government minister asserted "the global reputation that Israel has acquired as a leader in the heart of innovation in the water sector," then continued,

> There is a phrase in the Jewish heritage, ... *tikkun olam*, which [means], to make the world a better place. We see the role of the state of Israel is to improve the life of humanity, and to make the world a better place.

Given the mixed environmental implications of water management in Israel, and the gaping disparities in Palestinian and Israeli water access, Israel's claims of expertise and water authority in the region strike many as paternalistic. As one Palestinian hydrologist stated, "they have built a technology, which I believe they are proud of, and they are selling that technology all over the world, especially in Africa. So this is not peace!" While Israeli representatives cited rising rates of household water connections for Palestinians under its jurisdiction and high rates of water recycling as examples of its goodwill, Palestinian experts and laypeople alike pointed to Israel's refusal of well-drilling permits, their bulldozing of rainwater cisterns, and the financial advantage gained by selling desalinated water as evidence that Israel used its water expertise as a tool of power.

Climate change concerns are likely to further entrench existing power dynamics. The climate crisis has already magnified scarcity concerns and intensified the focus on water stewardship (Stamatopoulou-Robbins 2018; Lautze and Kirshen 2009). While there are some calls for localization and the wider distribution of management authority to cope with this crisis, the proponents of centralization and of efficiency through monetization, who are already in seats of power, call more loudly for a deepening of their approaches. Even Palestinian climate planners who want to prioritize Israeli acknowledgment of Palestinian water rights feel compelled to focus on technical interventions to achieve efficient use in order to garner support from the United Nations Framework Convention on Climate Change (UNFCC) and potential donors (Stamatopoulou-Robbins 2018).

Conclusion

It is not surprising, given the interconnectedness of water with so many Palestinian-Israeli flashpoints, that there has been much discussion about "water wars" ravaging this region. However, while it is true that struggles over physical and symbolic control of water have been key to Israeli-Palestinian battles, boiling this complex conflict down to the simple moniker "water war" ignores too many other critical factors. Palestine-Israel is both a parched and water-needy place *and* a place of abundance and fertility. Furthermore, there is no straight line between water scarcity and conflict. Rather, power mediates water access through forms of governance, such as colonialism; through technology, such as diversion canals and desalination plants; and through ideologies, such as arguments for cost recovery and centralized control in the face of scarcity.

Water is shaped by power, as existing power struggles guide the flows of water. And water is also a tool of power; those controlling access can use water's interconnectedness to shape lives and political outcomes. Understanding these relationships of water to power is necessary for just negotiations of water rights. Outdated interim agreements are insufficient to meet current water needs. Meanwhile, water's interconnectedness in society makes it a challenging – and constantly changing – final-status issue for peace brokering between Palestinians and Israelis. However, like all the final-status issues, water disputes are not waiting for final negotiations to impact people's lives in the region in profound ways. Water equity is both urgent and elusive.

Recommended Readings

Alatout, S. 2008. "'States' of Scarcity: Water, Space, and Identity Politics in Israel, 1948–59." *Environment and Planning D: Society and Space* 26:6, 959–982.

Orlove, B., and S. C. Caton. 2010. "Water Sustainability: Anthropological Approaches and Prospects." *Annual Review of Anthropology* 39, 401–415.

Trottier, J. 2007. "A Wall, Water and Power: The Israeli 'Separation Fence.'" *Review of International Studies* 33:1, 105–127.

Zeitoun, M., et al. 2013. "Hydro-Hegemony in the Upper Jordan Waterscape: Control and Use of the Flows." *Water Alternatives* 6:1, 86–106.

Notes

1 Interviews with Uri Shor, Rashut HaMayim spokesperson (23 July 2019) and David Muhlgay, Director of Hadera Desalination Plant (28 July 2019).

2 The value and importance of agriculture across the region is hotly contested, and both Palestinian and Israeli farming advocates decry agriculture's neglect for the sake of urban water supply. Meanwhile, reform advocates prioritize water efficiency and contend that farmers need to adapt or cease irrigating.

3 The Jordan Valley contains more than 40 per cent of the total Palestinian-held irrigated land in the West Bank (PCBS 2011).

4 Environmental imaginaries are the ideas that groups of people have about particular landscapes, including how those landscapes came to be and how they should be adapted or changed (Davis and Burke 2011).

5 This has been driven in large part by the favoured approaches to water management and economic development among the international aid and loan organizations upon which the PA relies for funding.

6 Planned capacity figures in Israel and Palestine are drawn from interviews with water regulators.

Questions for Discussion

(1) Why is water access a contentious issue for Palestinians and Israelis?

(2) What does it mean to say, as McKee does, that "what counts as scarcity is a socially and politically malleable concept"?

(3) The relationships of water to power are complex. On the one hand, how is the flow of water shaped by existing Palestinian-Israeli power relations, and on the other hand, in what ways does water serve as a tool of power?

(4) Given your readings about water and Israeli-Palestinian conflict, what currently unfolding political flashpoints are likely to affect water access in the region in the near future?

(5) If you were a facilitator sitting down with Israeli and Palestinian negotiators trying to settle disputes over water, how would you frame the conversation? Where would you start?

References

Abu Hussein, H., and F. McKay. 2003. *Access Denied: Palestinian Land Rights in Israel.* London: Zed Books.

Abu-Saad, I., and C. Creamer. 2013. "Socio-Political Upheaval and Current Conditions of the Naqab Bedouin Arabs." In *Indigenous (In)Justice: Human Rights Law and Bedouin Arabs in the Naqab/Negev*, eds. A. Amara, I. Abu-Saad, and O. Yiftachel. Cambridge: Harvard University Press, 19–66.

Adalah. 2006. "'Unrecognized Villages' in Israel – CHR – NGO Statement." United Nations Commission on Human Rights. Question of Palestine. 13 February. Available at: www.un.org/unispal/document/auto-insert-186018/.

Alatout, S. 2008. "'States' of Scarcity: Water, Space, and Identity Politics in Israel, 1948–59." *Environment and Planning D: Society and Space* 26:6, 959–982.

Alatout, S. 2009. "Bringing Abundance into Environmental Politics: Constructing a Zionist Network of Water Abundance, Immigration, and Colonization." *Social Studies of Science* 39:3, 363–394.

Alatout, S. 2011. "Hydro-Imaginaries and the Construction of the Political Geography of the Jordan River: The Johnston Mission, 1953–56." In *Environmental Imaginaries of the Middle East and North Africa*, eds. D. K. Davis and E. Burke. Athens, OH: Ohio University Press, 218–245.

Amery, H. A. 2002. "Water Wars in the Middle East: A Looming Threat." *The Geographical Journal* 168:4, 313–323.

Annex III: Protocol Concerning Civil Affairs. 1995. *The Israeli-Palestinian Interim Agreement on the West Bank and the Gaza Strip*. Available at: https://unispal.un.org/DPA/DPR/unispal.nsf/1ce874ab1832a53e852570bb006dfaf6/4607cabebc559b7085256f18006c8447?OpenDocument.

Anton, G. 2008. "Blind Modernism and Zionist Waterscape: The Huleh Drainage Project." *Jerusalem Quarterly*, no. 35, 76–92.

ARIJ. 2012. "Water Resource Allocations in the Occupied Palestinian Territory: Responding to Israeli Claims." Bethlehem: Applied Research Institute - Jerusalem. Available at: www.arij.org/files/admin/latestnews/water.pdf.

Avgar, I. 2018. "Israeli Water Sector: Key Issues." The Knesset Research and Information Center. Available at: www.knesset.gov.il/mmm/data/pdf/mmmeng250218.pdf.

Barnes, J. 2014. *Cultivating the Nile: The Everyday Politics of Water in Egypt*. Durham, NC: Duke University Press.

Becker, N., J. Helgeson, and D. Katz. 2014. "Once There Was a River: A Benefit–Cost Analysis of Rehabilitation of the Jordan River." *Regional Environmental Change* 14:4, 1303–1314.

B'Tselem. 2018. "Statistics: Water Crisis." 4 July. Available at: www.btselem.org/water/statistics.

Davis, D. K., and E. Burke, eds. 2011. *Environmental Imaginaries of the Middle East and North Africa*. Athens, OH: Ohio University Press.

Fanack Water. 2016. "Water in the Middle East and North Africa." 21 November. Available at: https://water.fanack.com/

Federman, J. 2019. "West Bank Settlers Report Surge in Population Growth." Associated Press, 5 February. Available at: https://apnews.com/article/305751a5ca13491a8f6e2f8cf1b74615.

Gasteyer, S., et al. 2012. "Water Grabbing in Colonial Perspective: Land and Water in Israel/Palestine." *Water Alternatives* 5:2, 450–468.

Khalidi, R., and S. Samour. 2011. "Neoliberalism as Liberation: The Statehood Program and the Remaking of the Palestinian National Movement." *Journal of Palestine Studies* 40:2, 6–25.

Lautze, J., and P. Kirshen. 2009. "Water Allocation, Climate Change, and Sustainable Water Use in Israel/Palestine: The Palestinian Position." *Water International* 34:2, 189–203.

Linton, J., and J. Budds. 2014. "The Hydrosocial Cycle: Defining and Mobilizing a Relational-Dialectical Approach to Water." *Geoforum* 57 (November), 170–180.

Mason, M., M. Zeitoun, and Z. Mimi. 2012. "Compounding Vulnerability: Impacts of Climate Change on Palestinians in Gaza and the West Bank." *Journal of Palestine Studies* 41:3, 38–53.

Mauss, M. 2002. *The Gift: The Form and Reason for Exchange in Archaic Societies*. Trans. W. D. Halls. New York: Routledge.

McKee, E. 2016. *Dwelling in Conflict: Negev Landscapes and the Boundaries of Belonging*. Stanford, CA: Stanford University Press.

McKee, E. 2019. "Water, Power, and Refusal: Confronting Evasive Accountability in a Palestinian Village." *Journal of the Royal Anthropological Institute* 25:3, 546–565.

McKee, E. 2021. "Divergent Visions: Intersectional Water Advocacy in Palestine." *Environment and Planning E: Nature and Space*. 4:1, 43–64.

Met Office. 2016. "Southern England: Climate." Available at: www.metoffice.gov.uk/binaries/content/assets/metofficegovuk/pdf/weather/learn-about/uk-past-events/regional-climates/southern-england_-climate---met-office.pdf.

OCHA. 2012. "How Dispossession Happens: The Humanitarian Impact of the Takeover of Palestinian Water Springs by Israeli Settlers." *East Jerusalem: United Nations Office for the Coordination of Humanitarian Affairs Occupied Palestinian Territory*. Available at: www.ochaopt.org/content/how-dispossession-happens-takeover-palestinian-water-springs-israeli-settlers-march-2012.

Orlove, B., and S. C. Caton. 2010. "Water Sustainability: Anthropological Approaches and Prospects." *Annual Review of Anthropology* 39, 401–415.

Palestinian National Authority. 2002. *Water Law*. Available at: www.pwa.ps/userfiles/file/water-law-App_-E1.pdf.

PCBS. 2011. "Land Use 2010/2011." *Palestinian Central Bureau of Statistics*. Available at: www.pcbs.gov.ps/Portals/_Rainbow/Documents/LandUse-2011-05e.htm.

PCBS, PWA, and PMD. 2020. "Press Release on the Occasion of World Water Day and World Meteorological Day." *Palestinian Central Bureau of Statistics*. Available at: www.pcbs.gov.ps/site/512/default.aspx?lang=en&ItemID=3690.

PWA. 2018. "Environmental and Social Assessment (ESIA) for Associated Works of the Gaza Sustainable Water Supply Program." *Palestinian Water Authority*. Available at: www.pwa.ps/userfiles/server/reports/Final_Draft_ESIA_Report_revised_10_5_2018_and_Annexes.pdf.

Reilly, J. 1981. "The Peasantry of Late Ottoman Palestine." *Journal of Palestine Studies* 10:4, 82–97.

Segev, T. 2000. *One Palestine, Complete: Jews and Arabs under the British Mandate*. London: Little Brown.

Selby, J. 2013. "Cooperation, Domination and Colonisation: The Israeli-Palestinian Joint Water Committee." *Water Alternatives* 6:1, 1–24.

Shuval, H. 2013. "The Agricultural Roots of Israel's Water Crisis." In *Between Ruin and Restoration: An Environmental History of Israel*, eds. D. E. Orenstein, A. Tal, and C. Miller. Pittsburgh: University of Pittsburgh, 129–145.

Stamatopoulou-Robbins, S. 2018. "An Uncertain Climate in Risky Times: How Occupation Became like the Rain in Post-Oslo Palestine." *International Journal of Middle East Studies* 50:3, 383–404.

Stamatopoulou-Robbin, S. 2019. *Waste Siege: The Life of Infrastructure in Palestine*. Stanford, CA: Stanford University Press.

Stamatopoulou-Robbin, S. 2020. "Failure to Build: Sewage and the Choppy Temporality of Infrastructure in Palestine." *Environment and Planning E: Nature and Space*.

State of Israel. 1959. *The Water Law (1959)*. Available at: www.knesset.gov.il/review/data/heb/law/kns3_water.pdf.

Tal, A. 2002. *Pollution in a Promised Land: An Environmental History of Israel*. Berkeley, CA: University of California Press.

Tal, A. 2013. "Combating Desertification: Evolving Perceptions and Strategies." In *Between Ruin and Restoration: An Environmental History of Israel*, eds. D. E. Orenstein, A. Tal, and C. Miller. Pittsburgh: University of Pittsburgh Press, 106–128.

Tesdell, O., Y. Othman, and S. Alkhoury. 2018. "Rainfed Agroecosystem Resilience in the Palestinian West Bank, 1918–2017." *Agroecology and Sustainable Food Systems* 43:1, 21–39.

Trottier, J. 2007. "A Wall, Water and Power: The Israeli 'Separation Fence.'" *Review of International Studies* 33:1, 105–127.

Trottier, J. 2008. "Water Crises: Political Construction or Physical Reality?" *Contemporary Politics* 14:2, 197–214.

Trottier, J., N. Leblond, and Y. Garb. 2020. "The Political Role of Date Palm Trees in the Jordan Valley: The Transformation of Palestinian Land and Water Tenure in Agriculture Made Invisible by Epistemic Violence." *Environment and Planning E: Nature and Space* 3:1, 114–140.

UNEP. 2020. "State of Environment and Outlook Report for the OPt 2020." *UN Environmental Program Report*. Nairobi: United Nations Environmental Programme. Available at: www.un.org/unispal/document/state-of-environment-and-outlook-report-for-the-opt-2020-un-environmental-program-report/.

UN-ESCWA and BGR. 2013. "Inventory of Shared Water Resources in Western Asia." Beirut: Institute for Geosciences and Natural Resources.

Ward, D. R. 2003. *Water Wars: Drought, Flood, Folly, and the Politics of Thirst*. New York: Riverhead Books.

World Bank. 2009. "Assessment of Restrictions on Palestinian Water Sector Development." 47657-GZ. Washington, DC. Available at: http://siteresources.worldbank.org/INTWESTBANKGAZA/Resources/WaterRestrictionsReportJuly2009.pdf.

Zeitoun, Mark. 2008. *Power and Water in the Middle East: The Hidden Politics of the Palestinian-Israeli Water Conflict*. London: I.B.Tauris.

Zeitoun, M., et al. 2013. "Hydro-Hegemony in the Upper Jordan Waterscape: Control and Use of the Flows." *Water Alternatives* 6:1, 86–106.

17

SECURITY IN THE ISRAEL-PALESTINE CONFLICT

Applying a Territorial Prism

Rob Geist Pinfold

Introduction

The pursuit of security has long shaped the Israeli-Palestinian conflict. The multitude of proposed solutions to this stubbornly persistent territorial and ethno-religious struggle have varied significantly. What has not changed, however, is the omnipresence of security in any and all negotiations that have sought to resolve the conflict. Traditionally, the international community's well-worn peace-making formula has sought to create 'security for Israel and a state for the Palestinians' (Nusseibeh 2020). Nevertheless, both parties have security concerns. On a state level, insecurity has exacerbated the many outbreaks of organised violence that has characterised the Israeli-Palestinian conflict from its beginnings. Similarly, human security, or the ability to live one's life free of existential fears, has frequently proved elusive for both Israelis and Palestinians. As a result, their publics distrust each other's intentions whilst their leaders often use force to mitigate threats, which in turn only perpetuates the violence and insecurity.

Throughout Israel and the Palestinian territories, the prevalence of security concerns is immediately obvious. Within the West Bank, checkpoints cause regular friction between Israeli security forces and local Palestinians. Within Israel, foreign visitors are often shocked at the extensive security checks that pervade regular civilian life. Many Palestinians feel directly threatened by Israel's military operations and see sovereignty as an antidote to their insecurity. Politicians on both sides persistently fixate on security and militarised discourse. It is no coincidence that Benjamin Netanyahu, who has cultivated an image of himself as 'Mr Security', is Israel's longest-serving prime minister, whereas the iconic Palestinian leader, Yasser Arafat, never appeared in public without his trademark military uniform. During their active service, Israel's security personnel exhibit significant influence over policy-making. Many enter politics after their military service concludes (Peri 2006). Thus, within Israeli and Palestinian polities, the distinction between military and civilian spheres is often blurred.

Yet, how to pursue the elusive concept of 'security' has long divided Israelis and Palestinians alike. Within the Palestinian territories, supporters of groups such as Hamas and Islamic Jihad emphasise a maximalist territorial strategy of violence. Backers of Fatah and the Palestinian Authority, on the other hand, largely favour a moderate approach that emphasises diplomacy

DOI: 10.4324/9780429027376-21

as a tool to achieve statehood. Similarly, Israel's victory in the Six-Day War of June 1967 exacerbated a dissensus between 'doves' and 'hawks': whether security is best pursued by trading 'land for peace' with Arab rivals, or perpetuating occupation over the territory Israel captured in the conflict. When debating security with 'hawkish' settlers, the 'dovish' Israeli author Amos Oz captured this dichotomy by stating, 'You think that letting go of the West Bank will pose an existential danger to the state of Israel. I think that annexing these lands will pose an existential danger to the state of Israel' (Gavron 2019). Security is both a national priority and a deeply contested concept, with competing visions tied to territory in a debate that has long constituted the most salient divide in Israeli and Palestinian politics.

Scholars have argued that 'tangible' and 'intangible' factors affect conceptions of what constitutes security-generating territorial policy (Geist Pinfold 2019). Tangible factors span a territory's geography and topography. Intangible factors are more subjective and include ideational attachment to a territory. Illustrating the high stakes involved, disputed territory in the Israeli-Palestinian conflict includes both these factors. For instance, a West Bank mountain range overlooks the greater Tel Aviv area, whilst hundreds of missiles fired from the Gaza Strip are a persistent security threat. The scarceness of territory further exacerbates the conflict's security problems: Israel, the West Bank, and Gaza Strip constitute less than 27,000 square kilometres – by comparison, the United Kingdom is over 240,000 square kilometres in size. Israelis also have a deep ideological connection to the West Bank. Referencing two ancient Jewish kingdoms, Israelis refer to the territory as 'Judea and Samaria', ensuring that history and values affect divergent conceptions of the security–territory relationship. Many Palestinians, conversely, believe that they have a sovereign right over all of modern-day Israel.

Employing the prism of territory, this chapter scrutinises how contested conceptions of security affected the Israel-Palestinian conflict. Specifically, it focuses on Israel, for two key reasons. Firstly, it is Israel's security concerns that have largely shaped bilateral conflict dynamics. Secondly, Israel has long justified its occupation of the West Bank and Gaza Strip in *securitized* (in Hebrew, *Bithonist*) language and logic. Israeli grand strategy has consistently pursued three goals: security, territory, and peace. This chapter examines how the relationships within this triumvirate has changed over time. First, it clarifies how competing Israeli and Palestinian conceptions of security have prolonged the conflict. Second, this chapter narrows its focus and illustrates why security is a core Israeli concern. Third, the security-territory-peace triad is unpacked entirely. Israeli policies in two radically divergent case studies – the West Bank and the Gaza Strip – are then compared. The chapter ends by delineating why Israel felt secure enough to leave the Gaza Strip but not the West Bank, where its continuing occupation represents a significant impasse to conflict resolution.

Israel and Palestine: Two Conflicting Conceptions of Security

For a prospective Palestinian state, the end of Israel's occupation of the West Bank and Gaza Strip is an inherent *sine qua non*. Statehood requires that an administration monopolise its power within the territory it claims sovereignty over. Additionally, states project power in the international system by defending and advancing their national interests. But Israel's occupation has blocked these external and internal criteria for Palestinian statehood. The Israel Defence Forces (IDF) continue to control the borders and airspace of the West Bank and Gaza Strip alike. Israel's 'facts on the ground', notably the West Bank barrier and its settlements, deprive a Palestinian state of territory over which it might exercise authority. Within supra-national organisations such as the United Nations, Israel has strenuously lobbied to prevent recognition of a Palestinian state. Israel argues that its settlements, military bases, and walls are essential for its own protection, whilst a declaration of Palestinian statehood would deny the IDF operational freedom within the West Bank and Gaza Strip. Thus, Israel's perceived security needs prolong its occupation, which itself constitutes an ongoing, real, and existential security challenge to Palestinian statehood.

Many Palestinians also perceive that the end of Israel's occupation is essential for their human security. Throughout the West Bank, checkpoints, ever-expanding settlements and Israel's labyrinthine bureaucracy and security network choke and constrain individual, economic, cultural, and social Palestinian daily life. Palestinians see Israeli soldiers and settlers as tangible threats to their own security. Despite the Israeli troop presence, the lack of a strong local authority often means that unaccountable criminal gangs and militias exercise de facto power. Palestinian individuals, businesses, and organisations rarely receive building permits from the Israeli authorities; their access to resources is curtailed, and the Palestinian economy is heavily constrained. When Palestinians challenge these decisions, the military authorities deny them the due process that Israel affords to its own citizens. Israeli authorities have castigated the Palestinians for employing violence, yet have suppressed non-violent indigenous movements. Israel argues that these controls are essential to safeguard its own human and state-level security. It is little surprise, though, that the Palestinians seek statehood for not only ideological and normative reasons, but also because of pragmatic security considerations.

In sum, both Israelis and Palestinians see the ongoing bilateral conflict and each of their collective conceptions of security-generating policy through a zero-sum lens. Israel has long prioritised its security needs in every round of talks and in its strategic planning. As a result, Israel has sought to either prevent, or reduce the scope of, a Palestinian state. The Palestinians, in turn, have sought sovereignty as a route to achieve human and state-level security. Whereas Israel perceives that its control over the West Bank and Gaza Strip makes it safer, the Palestinians feel the very same policies deprive them of sovereignty and therefore security. These established perceptions encapsulate the tragic nature of the Israeli-Palestinian conflict and its prolonged impasse. In practice, the perpetuation of this paradigm has ensured that Israel has failed to mitigate its security concerns, whilst the Palestinians remain a people without a state.

Security as a Core Israeli Concern

If the Palestinians seek statehood and sovereignty to promote national and human security, why does Israel maintain its control over them? Though the reasons for the occupation's extraordinary endurance are complex, one core concern has persistently characterised Israeli policy: security. Scholars have claimed that Israel's pursuit of security and its 'concern with insecurity at times verges on a national obsession' (Klieman and Cohen 2019, 2). Israeli domestic actors have securitised a range of seemingly unconnected and relatively benign topics, such as the economy, the environment, and healthcare. At the same time, Israel has been in a state of emergency since 1948, with the Knesset approving its extension every year with virtually no debate. Thus, critics have argued that securitisation stifles the rule of law and degrades Israel's liberal and democratic status. What factors, then, precipitates the unusual predominance of security in Israel's praxis, public perceptions, and discourse?

One factor driving Israel's contemporary quest for security is a collective national recollection of a traumatic past. The pre-state Zionist movement gathered strength as a direct result of insecurity in the diaspora, where Jews were frequently scapegoated and persecuted. The Israeli saying, 'I fight the Nazis at night and lose; I fight the Arabs during the day and win', illustrates how history affects perceptions and policy today (Miller 2008). Several Israeli prime ministers, including Menachem Begin and Golda Meir, referred to the Palestinians as 'Nazis', whilst every year the IDF's newest batch of conscripts are taken to Jerusalem's Yad Vashem Holocaust memorial for a blunt reminder of insecurity's dire costs. Security and statehood are inherently linked in Zionism and seared into the national consciousness as an antidote to the insecure, non-sovereign, and unrooted 'wandering Jew' of the diaspora.

But the 'return to Zion' failed to mitigate existential insecurity. As soon as mass Jewish emigration to historic Palestine began, Arab hostility met the Zionist pioneers and inculcated a need for collective self-reliance to promote security. Connecting historical experience to the struggle for statehood, hard-line Zionists adopted the slogan, 'In blood and fire, Judea fell, in blood and fire, Judea will rise'. Indubitably, the transition to statehood in 1948 was accompanied by internecine violence between Jews and Palestinians and a full-scale regional war between Israel and neighbouring Arab states. This First Arab-Israeli War determined Israel's borders, with the nascent state annexing the territory it captured in the fighting.

That 1948 was only the start of a series of near-incessant and currently largely unresolved conflicts between Israel and its Arab neighbours exemplifies another key factor that makes Israeli security a core concern: regional realities. Israel has gone to war with every single one of its neighbours and remains in a state of war with a number of other regional actors. As such, Israel is a small state, dwarfed numerically and geographically by surrounding hostile entities. Though the IDF defeated armies from Jordan, Egypt, Syria, and Iraq in June 1967, Israel could not convert its tactical success into a political victory, as the Arab powers afterwards declared a joint policy of 'no peace, no negotiations and no recognition' of Israel. Resultantly, Israel has often limited its goal to pursuing 'quiet'. Even this modest objective has proved elusive, since relative stability has always been temporal and followed by further violence.

Israel's security threats have changed over the years, yet insecurity, instability, and a lack of a long-term solution remain the norm, particularly vis-à-vis the Palestinians. Whilst Iran is a powerful regional foe, Israel's main adversaries have shifted from Arab states to non-state actors on its borders. This change did not reduce violence, however: despite their limited capacities, non-state actors have often inflicted more Israeli casualties than in major state-level wars. Hamas and Hezbollah continue to reject not only negotiations with Israel, but they deny Israel's very existence. Israelis have also been traumatised by the upsurge in violence and civilian casualties during the 1990s and the Second Palestinian *Intifada*. More recently, low-intensity terrorism emanating from the West Bank remains a threat, whilst outbreaks of fighting between the IDF and Hamas in and around the Gaza Strip regularly confines the civilians of Israel's south to bomb shelters for days. Security in contemporary Israel remains a salient topic for politicians and the public alike, precisely because it remains so elusive.

Security, Territory, and Peace: Israel's Awkward Triumvirate

Alongside security, territory is another scarce, though valuable, resource for Israel. The State of Israel is 20,000 square kilometres in size and 15 kilometres wide at its narrowest point, with half its population concentrated within a coastal strip bordering the Mediterranean Sea and the West Bank. These 'tangible' realities have led Israel to seek 'strategic depth': additional territory to push fighting away from its urban heartlands, mitigating its small size. Concurrently, Israel has treated withdrawal with suspicion. When Israel left the Sinai Peninsula between 1978 and 1982 in exchange for peace with Egypt, Defence Minister Ezer Weizman refused to use the term 'withdrawal' because he claimed the term 'burns my ear' (IMFA 19 September 1978). This reluctance to actually say 'withdrawal' is unsurprising because for much of Israel's history territory and security were a dyad: more of the former facilitated the latter, by proving a physical base for strategic depth and national sovereignty.

Whilst changing Israel's security situation and its territorial holdings, the Six-Day War of June 1967 precipitated the pursuit of peace. In capturing the West Bank, Gaza Strip, Golan Heights, and the Sinai Peninsula, Israel possessed a surfeit of territory for the first time in its history. Domestically, the conflict provoked a bitter divide over whether Israel should keep the territory and pursue conflict management or withdraw in a conflict-resolution framework that leads to peace with its Arab neighbours. Each side argues that their own approach would enhance Israel's security, but that the other's approach represents a dire or even existential threat. This divide is not absolute, since 'hawkish' and 'dovish' Israeli governments alike have given up some land in return for peace, whilst maintaining control over other territories deemed particularly valuable for security and ideational reasons. In its simplest terms, though, this debate can be reduced to a binary question: Is withdrawal or occupation the best long-term guarantor of Israel's security?

The international community has expressed a preference for withdrawal, as illustrated by United Nations Security Council Resolution 242. Passed in November 1967, Resolution 242 acknowledges Israel's security needs by stressing 'the territorial inviolability … of every state in the area' and the Arab and Palestinian demand for security through sovereignty, by calling for the 'withdrawal of Israeli armed forces from territories occupied in the recent conflict'. Resolution 242 advocates peace as the best strategy to pursue these goals, thereby establishing the 'land for peace' bargaining equation and calling for

> [t]ermination of all claims or states of belligerence and respect for and acknowledgement of the sovereignty, territorial integrity and political independence of every state in the area and their right to live in peace within secure and recognised boundaries free from threats.

Nevertheless, Resolution 242's deliberately vague wording has ensured that Israel and the Arab world have interpreted it differently. Because the resolution calls for withdrawal from 'territories', Israel claims it is only required to withdraw from some of the land occupied in 1967, in exchange for full peace. Many Arab states have argued the resolution requires 'termination of belligerence' rather than peace and recognition, in exchange for a full Israeli withdrawal. Correspondingly, recognising the security risks inherent in withdrawal from particularly valuable or sensitive territories, Israel seeks to replace its pre-war boundaries with 'defensible borders', whilst the Arab states demand withdrawal to 'recognised borders'. Accordingly, Israel's assertion that more territory increases its security has scuppered bilateral and multilateral attempts to arrive at a long-term, negotiated peace deal.

Synchronously, other factors affected the perceived territory–security relationship after 1967. For instance, Israel rapidly built settlements along the Gaza Strip and West Bank's borders to entrench its presence in certain territories deemed to possess extraordinary security value. Right-wing governments then built settlements throughout the West Bank and Gaza Strip, creating 'facts on the ground' that deliberately seek to hinder withdrawal and deny Palestinian statehood. The issue of where to build settlements and whether they provide security has divided Israel's domestic political arena. Though 'hawkish' Israelis often emphasize withdrawal's security risks, many reject territorial compromise within any of the 'Land of Israel' for ideological reasons. In practice, this combination of 'tangible' and 'intangible' factors affecting Israeli policy works to deny Palestinians their own sovereignty and security.

Accompanying these domestic divides, Israel's interactions with hostile and friendly actors alike in the international system transformed its perceptions of security-enhancing policy. Frequently, Israel has prioritised strategic depth to constrain rivals. On other occasions, enemy violence caused many Israelis to perceive that control over foreign territories and peoples actually precipitated insecurity. Interactions with third-parties, particularly the United States, has sometimes presented Israel with a dilemma: whether to prioritise territorial control, or relations with a superpower as the best guarantor of security. When Israel refused to leave parts of the Sinai Peninsula in 1975 in exchange for Egyptian non-belligerency guarantees, the United States – then serving as a mediator – threatened a 'reassessment' of relations with Israel if the latter did not moderate its positions. Israel then agreed to withdraw, in exchange for increased security and political cooperation with the United States (Geist Pinfold 2015).

Overall, Israel has pursued three sometimes-contradictory objectives: territory, security, and peace. Israel has sometimes perceived territory as a panacea, whilst at other times it has pursued 'land for peace', based on changing domestic, international, and local distributions of power and perceptions. In public opinion surveys taken in late 1967, 82 per cent of Israelis sought to annex the Sinai Peninsula (Israel Democracy Institute, 2017). Israel then built settlements in parts of the peninsula and entrenched itself locally. Yet, in late 1978, Israel's right-wing prime minister, Menachem Begin, agreed to leave the entire Sinai, in an ideological about-turn that led to a peace treaty with Egypt. If Israel successfully operationalised 'land for peace' with a long-term adversary, with no security loss, why has it failed to do with the Palestinians? In addressing this question, it is necessary to analyze Israel's policies and the security-territory-peace triad in two different case studies: the Gaza Strip and the West Bank.

Two Occupations, Two Outcomes: The West Bank and Gaza Strip

Israel's policies towards both the West Bank and Gaza Strip have been affected by 'intangible' factors that suggest withdrawal and annexation alike could constitute security threats. First, both territories formed part of the 'Land of Israel' and are connected to Jewish identity and history. Many Israelis see each territory not as foreign, occupied territory, but as an integral part of the state itself. Withdrawal would therefore imperil Israel's existence (Lustick 1995). Conversely, annexation would precipitate an unparalleled 'demographic threat' to Israel's national identity as a Jewish and democratic state, because the West Bank and Gaza Strip together are populated by up to five million Palestinian Arabs. Israel would either have to grant the territory's residents citizenship or deny it on an ethno-religious basis. Because of these contradictory, twin 'intangible' factors, Israel has sought long-term control over much of the West Bank and Gaza Strip, whilst proposing 'autonomy' for their residents.

Additionally, both territories possess 'tangible' security challenges that disincentivise withdrawal. Palestinians have crossed the Gaza Strip's northern and eastern borders into Israel and smuggled in arms and equipment from Egypt. Likewise, non-state actors have infiltrated Israel from the West Bank's western, northern, and southern borders, since before 1967 until the present. The West Bank's eastern border – the Jordan Valley – is equally salient, because policy-makers fear that Arab hostiles could enter the territory via Jordan and threaten Israel's urban heartlands. The Gaza Strip's and West Bank's proximity to major Israeli urban centres, spanning Sderot, Ashkelon, and Ashdod to Tel Aviv and Jerusalem, ensure any security threats from either territory are elevated. Thus, from cross-border raids by Palestinian *fedayeen* in the 1950s to Hamas' recent rocket attacks, the West Bank and Gaza Strip have long been a security headache for Israel.

Since 1967, Israel has entrenched itself in the West Bank and Gaza Strip to mollify these security threats. Though seeking to operationalise 'land for peace' with Jordan soon after the war ended, Israel sought full peace for limited withdrawal, scuppering a deal by refusing to cede control over the West Bank's western and eastern borders. In the Gaza Strip, Israel launched a counter-insurgency campaign to pacify its residents and rejected returning the territory to Egyptian control. Israel's 'hawks' and 'doves' alike always saw sustained occupation and control over the West Bank and Gaza Strip's Palestinian residents to constitute a security problem, but less of a threat than withdrawal would bring. Indeed, Moshe Dayan termed the Gaza Strip a 'hornet's nest' and then paradoxically ordered its occupation in 1967 (Catignani 2008, 170).

The First Palestinian Intifada's eruption in December 1987 smashed the Israeli consensus that occupation best advanced national security. Civil disorder in the West Bank and Gaza Strip descended into a full-blown uprising and caused the status quo's costs to skyrocket. Between 1968 and 1975 there were, on average, 350 violent incidents each year between Israelis and Palestinians. During the Intifada's first six months alone, the IDF recorded 42,355 Palestinian attacks (Harms and Ferry 2012, 142). The Intifada legitimised 'dovish' Israeli calls for 'separation' from the Palestinians, whilst the IDF advised decision-makers that no military solution existed (Peri 2006). When faced with popular discontent rather than a conventional army, Israel's well-trained and equipped IDF failed to restore security. The occupation appeared to provoke violence, with Israeli settlers and soldiers caught in a quagmire. Therefore, the Israeli desire for security and the Palestinian quest for statehood and sovereignty dovetailed for the first time and appeared complementary, rather than mutually exclusive.

After sustained violence and an internal Israeli dissensus about how to mitigate this security threat, the Intifada ended when both sides signed the Oslo Accords in September 1993. Though the Palestine Liberation Organisation (PLO) had attacked Israel from the West Bank and the Gaza Strip, both sides now agreed to implement 'land for peace', with the PLO freezing its armed struggle and Israel committing to withdrawal. Reversing decades of policy, Israel now sought to promote its security by cooperating with the Palestinians and providing them with increased autonomy, albeit short of the full sovereignty and statehood they desired (Ross 2005). The Oslo Accords began the Oslo Process, a series of multiple limited agreements that sought to mitigate Israel's security concerns as it slowly withdrew from the West Bank and Gaza Strip, by establishing a state-like Palestinian Authority (PA) to fill the power vacuum. As part of this process, Israel left 80 per cent of the Gaza Strip; by mid-2000, only 40,00 of the West Bank's two million Palestinians lived under full Israeli occupation (Tessler 2009).

Yet the Oslo Process failed to secure either a full Israeli withdrawal from the West Bank and Gaza Strip or Palestinian statehood and security for either side. Though the PLO cooperated with Israel, 'spoiler' groups opposed to the peace process, such as Hamas and Islamic Jihad, upped their attacks. Israel, in turn, created insecurity for Palestinians by retaliating harshly and expanding its settlements. After a US-mediated summit at Camp David in July 2000 that was supposed to engender a final-status deal ended without an agreement, the Second Intifada superseded negotiations. Bilateral violence spread throughout the West Bank and Gaza Strip and killed over a thousand Israelis and three thousand Palestinians, more than during the Oslo Process and the First Intifada combined (Mnookin, Eiran and Gilad 2014). Palestinian groups – spanning both spoilers and PLO-affiliated groups – employed terrorist tactics, particularly suicide bombings, to exact a hitherto unforeseen toll on Israel's civilian home front.

In response, Israel eschewed cooperation with the Palestinians and acted increasingly unilaterally to restore security. The violence's dire impact on society, politics, and the economy convinced most Israelis the Palestinians were not a sincere partner. Israel cut off negotiations, built a 700-kilometre 'separation barrier' to wall off the West Bank and sent the IDF to re-occupy territory it had withdrawn from during the Oslo Process. Though 'Operation Defensive Shield' blunted the worst excesses of the violence by degrading the Palestinian militant groups' infrastructure and capabilities, Israel still sought to withdraw from both the West Bank and the Gaza Strip, albeit 'unilaterally'. The perception that occupation no longer provided security drove this new consensus policy of 'unilateral withdrawal', because: 'security came first, and if 'Greater Israel' threatened this, as Israelis increasingly believed, then it must be abandoned' (Waxman 2008, 85). Israel was apparently abandoning its pursuit of peace and territory alike, breaking up the long-established triumvirate to achieve security.

Though leaving the entire Gaza Strip 'unilaterally' in September 2005 and announcing a pending exit from 90 per cent of the West Bank in 2006, Israel never withdrew from the latter. Whilst the Intifada subsided in 2005, the West Bank remains frozen in the 'interim' stages of the Oslo Process: limited Palestinian self-government, with Israel retaining overall control. Despite the 'tangible' and 'intangible' commonalities between the West Bank and the Gaza Strip delineated above, Israel operationalised a radically divergent territorial policy in each. To explain this incongruency requires exploring how different Israeli perceptions of security and territory vis-à-vis the Gaza Strip and West Bank created contrasting policies.

Questioning the Security-Territory Dyad: Israel Leaves Gaza

Though the Second Intifada made the West Bank and Gaza Strip less secure for Israelis and Palestinians alike, both territories differed in their geographies of violence. Most West Bank Palestinian militants infiltrated into Israel to carry out their attacks, whereas Gazan militants mainly attacked Israeli targets within the Gaza Strip, itself, rather than within Israel (Ben-Sasson Gordis 2016). Concurrently, Israel had already left 80 per cent of the Gaza Strip during the Oslo Accords. Violence was therefore concentrated in the 20 per cent of the territory that Israel still controlled, where the IDF were defending small settlements and access roads surrounded by dense urban topography. Between September 2000 and September 2005, Palestinians killed 54 Israelis on roads or crossings into Gaza alone, whilst an entire infantry company and armoured platoon defended an isolated settlement of 26 settler families (Byman 2011; Ben-Sasson Gordis 2016). Resultantly, Israel's truncated Gaza Strip occupation caused substantial tactical difficulties and apparently harmed security by providing the enemy opportunities to inflict casualties on soldiers and settlers.

Israel's tactics also changed in response to the Second Intifada and because of technological advances, which together suggested territory was less essential for security. Gaza's militant groups did not limit their attacks to this territory out of choice. The IDF deterred and denied hostiles through a system of high-tech physical boundaries monitored by drones and cameras that prevented infiltration. Hence, Israel's decision-makers believed that leaving the Gaza Strip entirely could further reduce friction and stop hostiles from imposing costs. Innovations in targeting and ordnance ensured the IDF shifted to employing airpower. Ground forces, by contrast, were relatively easy targets for Palestinian militants. Israel's air force had proven effective in carrying out 'targeted killings' of militant leaders during the Intifada, which successfully pressured hostile groups to reign in their activities (Bregman 2015).

The above trends escalated demands from within the IDF to change the status quo. With the Intifada at its height, 600 IDF personnel refused to serve in the occupied territories (Byman 2011). In May 2004, paratroopers guarding the Gaza Strip's civilian settlement of Netzarim publicly declared the settlement's existence damaged national security (Agence France Presse, 30 May 2004). Criticism extended to the heart of the security establishment, when four former heads of the Mossad and Shin Bet warned that the Intifada and the accompanying occupation existentially threatened Israel's security (Geist Pinfold 2019).

Conversely, Israel's decision-makers saw the proposed plans to end the Intifada as more dangerous for national security than the violence itself. Domestic and foreign actors were urging Israel's government to adopt either the Geneva Initiative or the Arab Peace Initiative. Both these plans promised to end the violence and improve Israel's relations with the Arab World. These benefits notwithstanding, Israel rejected them, since they mandated withdrawal from all or most of the West Bank and Gaza Strip. Increasing the tangible pressure, the United States secretly warned Israel in 2003 that it must change the status quo. Israeli officials were concerned that the United States, a superpower and staunch ally, could endorse the Geneva or Arab Peace Initiatives (Geist Pinfold 2019). The combination of violence and political pressure on multiple fronts concerned Prime Minister Ariel Sharon, who argued that 'only an Israeli plan will keep us from being dragged into [the] dangerous … Geneva and Saudi initiatives' (Peters 2010, 36).

Sharon then shocked observers in early 2004 by announcing that Israel would withdraw from the Gaza Strip. The 'unilateral disengagement plan' was propelled by macro-level pressure to change the status quo and an increasingly dominant perception that occupying the Gaza Strip now harmed national security. Realising he would be compelled to withdraw from somewhere, Sharon left Gaza to mitigate pressure to change the status quo, whilst perpetuating Israel's control over 'strategic' parts of the West Bank with significant perceived security value. Sharon's chief-of-staff, Dov Weisglass, argued that the 'unilateral disengagement … supplies the amount of formaldehyde necessary so there will not be a political process with the Palestinians' (Shavit 2004). The plan created a new domestic Israeli consensus that spanned 'doves' and 'hawks' by merging suspicion of the Palestinians, the search for security, territorial withdrawal, and fears of a 'demographic threat'.

Yet, the 'unilateral disengagement' was not strictly unilateral, with the United States determining the withdrawal's contours and providing Israel with concessions. The Israelis at first sought to only leave Gaza, but the United States demanded that the plan include parts of the West Bank.[1] Furthermore, in April 2004, the United States publicly praised the plan and declared that as a reward for the 'bold' move, it would 'prevent any attempt by anyone to impose any other plan' on Israel. The United States further decreed it was 'unrealistic' to expect a return to the pre-Six Day War borders, whilst Palestinian refugees should not be re-settled in Israel. Altering its policy of ambiguity on these issues, the United States mollified Israel's fears of the Geneva and Arab Peace initiatives, the 'demographic threat' and withdrawal to the '1967 borders'. Indubitably, Israel's Gaza withdrawal did not constitute 'land for peace'. It was instead a non-unilateral 'land for security' exchange (Geist Pinfold 2019). By offering superpower guarantees against perceived existential threats, the United States compensated Israel with greater security benefits than territory could.

Nevertheless, Israel's withdrawal from the Gaza Strip in August 2005 generated significant domestic criticism. Settlers vigorously protested their uprooting and the government's disavowal of the 'Land of Israel'. Right-wing 'hawks' charged that Israel's withdrawal was an irrational act undertaken 'under fire' because societal resilience was in freefall, which in itself constituted a security threat in a dangerous and violent Middle East. Sharon's finance minister, Benjamin Netanyahu, resigned over the withdrawal and called for Israel to stop 'rewarding terror' and to 'get back to the policy we abandoned, the policy of asking for something in exchange' (Susser 2005).

However, Israel's withdrawal was not unilateral, irrational, or non-compensatory. Enemy action ensured the occupation of Gaza required rising costs, whilst technological and tactical changes made it appear superannuated. Interactions with third parties also affected Israeli perceptions; international pressure made policymakers realise the status quo was unsustainable, whilst the United States then offered substantial incentives that advanced Israel's national interests, in exchange for withdrawal from a territory with little perceived security value. Whereas, previously Israel prioritised peace *or* territory to advance security, the 'unilateral disengagement' represented an unprecedented break from either of these two options. Israel withdrew to promote security through 'separation'. Many Israelis were shocked that the right-wing Ariel Sharon implemented withdrawal from Gaza. Israeli president Reuven Rivlin, however, argued that '[A]ll Sharon cares about is whether settlements serve Israeli security' (Aronoff 2010, 154). That the pursuit of security overcame strategic depth, prestigious peace plans and the 'Land of Israel' illustrates the potency of national security in shaping Israeli policy.

On the other hand, Israel's reassessment of the security-territory relationship was not holistic and was apparently limited to the Gaza Strip. Sharon left Gaza to retain parts of the West Bank with heightened security value, particularly the Jordan Valley and the territory's western borderlands. As such, tactical and technological changes, international pressure, and enemy action did not cause Israel to re-assess its perceived security need to control parts of the West Bank. Why, then, did these factors cause Israel to re-assess the status quo's effectiveness at advancing security in the Gaza Strip, but not, ostensibly, in the West Bank?

Security and Territory Reunited: Why Israel Retains the West Bank

One factor explaining Israel's non-withdrawal is that the West Bank possesses significantly more 'tangible' value than the Gaza Strip, ensuring that the perceived security risks of changing the status quo in the West Bank have always been higher. The Israel-West Bank border is 307 kilometres long and snakes around central, southern, and northern Israel, whereas the 51-kilometre-long Gaza border only intersects southern Israel. Moreover, Israel's borders with Gaza are located on its relatively sparsely populated periphery, whereas the West Bank border – the so-called 'Green Line' – surrounds and divides Jerusalem and runs parallel to Israel's central urban heartland, where its main airport and industries are concentrated. Central Israel is the country's narrowest point, whilst a mountain range is located just within the West Bank's western border. Thus, any hostile army operating within the West Bank could easily cut Israel in two and would possess significant tactical and topographical advantages.

Israel's West Bank security concerns are not hypothetical. Before the Six-Day War, Palestinian attacks from the Jordanian-controlled West Bank were frequent and led to multiple deaths in Israel's urban centres, disrupting civilian life. Israel launched raids into the West Bank in retaliation, which led to confrontations with the Jordanian army and international condemnation. Palestinian groups continued to use the territory as a safe haven, beyond the IDF's reach. The division of Jerusalem, with Israel controlling the city's western neighbourhoods and the Jordanians in the east, caused a plethora of security and economic problems. In the territory's east, Arab armies from countries such as Iraq crossed into the West Bank with Jordan's consent in June 1967, threatening Israel's heartlands.

Consequently, after capturing the territory, 'doves' and 'hawks' alike feared a full West Bank withdrawal would imperil Israel's security. Israeli statesman Abba Eban – though a 'dove' – referred to the Green Line as 'Auschwitz borders'. In the first ten years after the Six-Day War, Israel's Labour-led governments offered to leave around 60 per cent of the territory (Raz 2012). Subsequently, more 'hawkish' Likud-led governments rejected any withdrawal whatsoever. Whilst Israel softened its position at the Camp David summit and afterward, no government has ever been willing to leave more than 94 per cent of the West Bank.[2] The Arab Peace Initiative proves that the entire Arab world has provided a tangible offer of peaceful, full diplomatic relations in exchange for a withdrawal to the Green Line. Israel's rejection of the offer suggests it perceives certain 'strategic' parts of the West Bank as more valuable for national security than ending its conflict with the Arab world.

This perception that a full withdrawal would imperil Israeli national and human security has actually been reinforced by previous attempts to operationalise 'land for peace' in the West

Bank. Though the peace process was supposed to reduce violence, Palestinian groups killed more Israelis during the Oslo Process than in the First Intifada. Whereas the First Intifada largely involved mass civil disobedience and isolated violent acts in the West Bank, the 1990s saw organised, hard-line Palestinian rejectionist groups conduct mass-casualty suicide bombings within Israeli cities. After talks between Israel and the PLO collapsed at Camp David in 2000, leading to the Second Intifada, more moderate Palestinian groups and PA police officers became involved in the violence. In a single month, 'Black March' 2002, 135 Israelis were killed. Palestinian leadership turned to violence as a result of a strategic calculation, attempting to use force where dialogue had failed to engender an Israeli withdrawal from the entire West Bank up to the Green Line (Catignani 2008).

This Palestinian shift away from negotiations and towards violence was a strategic mistake. Previously, Israelis were divided as to whether peace or territory would best advance security. But the Second Intifada's shocking violence made normal civilian life impossible, with Israel public demanding the immediate restoration of security by any means necessary. In response, the IDF launched 'Operation Defensive Shield' and aggressively pursued Palestinian militant groups by re-taking the West Bank territory it left during the Oslo Process. In the First Intifada, the IDF could provide no military solution when faced with riotous crowds, whereas during the Second Intifada, the IDF faced organised cells of non-state actors. As a result, the IDF successfully employed its overwhelming military advantage: in 2002, Israel suffered 53 suicide attacks, whilst in 2006 there were only six (Byman 2011, 153). The Palestinian escalation, therefore, had the opposite effect than they had intended, causing many Israelis to assert that territory brings security, whereas withdrawal from the West Bank is dangerous.

Concurrently, Israel still sought to retrench its presence in the West Bank by applying the same methodologies that had quelled and geographically limited the violence in the Gaza Strip. In 2006, after Israel constructed a system of walls and fences on its border, Prime Minister Ehud Olmert outlined his 'convergence plan' to unilaterally withdraw from most West Bank territory east of the new 'separation barrier'. Ostensibly, the Palestinians had successfully employed violence to compel Israel to re-frame the territory-security relationship. In fact, the Palestinians did not receive a better offer than they had already rejected in negotiations and failed to force Israel to abandon the West Bank territory to which it associated extraordinary security value. The convergence plan called for Israel to leave 93 per cent of the West Bank but keep control over the Jordan Valley and the territory's western borders. Modelled on the 'unilateral disengagement' from Gaza, the plan would have seen Israel leave the West Bank's Palestinian-populated areas in order to mitigate the 'demographic threat' and Palestinian violence.

The 'convergence plan', however, was never implemented. In 2000, the IDF ended its 15-year occupation of southern Lebanon. Initially, Israel's local rival – the non-state Islamist Hezbollah – reduced its violent activities, signifying that withdrawal provided more security than did the costly and ineffective occupation. In summer 2006, though, conflict erupted and up to 1,500 people were killed on both sides in 34 days of fighting. Before the Lebanese escalation, Israel was contending with increased instability within and rocket attacks from the Gaza Strip, following the 'unilateral disengagement'. In June 2006, Palestinian groups kidnapped an IDF soldier, Gilad Shalit; one year later, Hamas violently ousted the Palestinian Authority from the entire Gaza Strip. Increased conflict on Israel's northern and southern borders engendered a growing sense of communal insecurity. Faced with the fallout of these salient security threats, Olmert indefinitely postponed his planned West Bank withdrawal.

Unlike Gaza and Lebanon, the West Bank remains relatively calm. Despite the IDF's technological and air superiority, Israel has been unable to prevent hostiles from using territory in Gaza and Lebanon to employ long-range ordnance to paralyse Israeli civilian life. On the other hand, Hezbollah and Hamas increased the quality and quantity of their weaponry and inflicted heavy casualties whenever the IDF raided territory under their control. In the West Bank, by contrast, the IDF has prevented rocket launches, helped secure the PA's stability, and maintained an intricate web of human intelligence and technological surveillance, and a physical presence. Simultaneously, by contracting civil governance and policing responsibilities to the PA, Israel has masked its presence and reduced friction between occupier and occupied. These comparative realities brought a strategic re-assessment. Whereas planners previously believed technology and airpower could deter and deny hostiles from afar, senior figures within Israel's military and political elites have resuscitated the belief that control of territory is essential to mitigate threats and to promote national security.

In sum, Israel's conflicts in Gaza and Lebanon, and the West Bank's relative stability, prompted another collective re-calculation of the perceived territory-security dyad. Opponents of withdrawal regularly contrast Israel's relatively favourable perceived security situation in the West Bank to other territories. For instance, in 2014, Defence Minister Moshe Ya'alon argued withdrawal would create a Hamas-led quasi-state in the territory, a *Hamastan* (Ginsburg 2014). Previously, Israeli public and elite opinion supported the Oslo Process, the 'unilateral disengagement' and the 'convergence plan'. Today, however, a growing majority of Israelis back maintaining the West Bank's status quo or even annexing particularly 'strategic' parts of the territory. Hence, Israel retains its West Bank occupation because of a hegemonic internal perception that withdrawal is a greater security risk than perpetuating the status quo. At the time of writing, a question mark remains as to how proposed plans to break the impasse, such as President Donald Trump's 'deal of the century', could make Israel give up some territory, without losing any perceived security.

Conclusion

The pursuit of security has been a persistent staple of Israeli and Palestinian policy-making. Just as early Zionist pioneers saw sovereignty as an antidote to the instability of Diaspora Jewish life, the Palestinians seek security via statehood, thereby removing the violence and controls that characterise Israel's occupation. Conversely, both Israel's 'doves' and 'hawks' have formulated policy under the influence of a perceived territory-security dyad, where more of the former inherently best guarantees and enhances the latter. Territory is therefore integral to both Israeli and Palestinian visions of security. Nonetheless, differing perceptions of how to achieve security and its relationship with territory have prolonged the conflict. Israel has entrenched its occupation in order to achieve its own security, thereby denying the Palestinians theirs. Palestinian violence, in turn, has deprived Israel of security and often made it less willing to consider territorial concessions, trapping both sides in a vicious cycle.

This chapter demonstrated that security is an incredibly powerful determinant of Israeli policy, with divergent conceptions of how to promote it re-shaping the conflict. Security is an all-encompassing, but contested, concept in Israel, feeding into broader debates about settlements, negotiations, strategic depth, ideology, and 'tangible' and 'intangible' policy determinants, amongst others. Consequently, one Israeli administration can perceive a potential policy as an existential threat, whereas another may frame it as an unparalleled opportunity. From Israel's founding in 1948, an awkward triumvirate has shaped its grand strategy: security, peace, and territory. Israel has been divided over whether to best pursue security through peace, or via territory and perpetuating its occupation, particularly since its 1967 victory.

The salience of each of these contrasting approaches is non-static and has responded to shifts in perception and in the local and international distribution of power. The First Intifada's instability encouraged Israel to leave territory, whereas the Second Intifada's shocking violence precipitated the opposite. Influences as far apart as international pressure and relations, to technological and tactical changes have all shaped Israel's perceived territory-security dyad. As well as seeing the same territory differently in divergent time periods, Israel has attributed dissimilar security values to diverse territories, as illustrated by the withdrawal from the Gaza Strip but the persistent refusal to leave all of the West Bank. In short, Israel was more willing to leave territory when it perceived the status quo damaged security. When withdrawal was perceived to harm security, Israel perpetuated the status quo, as remains the case at the time of writing.

Equally, this chapter illustrated that Israel's current position of ruling out any West Bank withdrawal is unlikely to be permanent. Although the perceived negative consequences of previous withdrawals and the failure of the Oslo Process have prolonged the occupation, Israel has historically been willing to leave most of the West Bank. If faced again with international and hostile pressure, the status quo will not remain permanent. The one territory that Israel has refused to part with, no matter how extensive the pressure, is between six and ten per cent of the West Bank with extraordinary perceived security value. Given that neither the Second Intifada's violence nor the Arab Peace Initiative's game-changing offer could cause a policy reassessment, it is unlikely that Israel will ever willingly withdraw to the Green Line. When asked to choose between peace or security, Israelis have often chosen the latter. Thus, any final-status peace plan must mitigate Israel's security needs and fears, whilst providing the Palestinians with sufficient sovereignty and autonomy to meet their own aspirations.

Recommended Readings

Bregman, A. 2015. *Cursed Victory: A History of Israel and the Occupied Territories*. London: Penguin.

Byman, D. 2011. *A High Price: The Triumphs and Failures of Israeli Counter Terrorism*. New York: Oxford University Press.

Catignani, S. 2008. *Israeli Counter-insurgency and the Intifada: Dilemmas of a Conventional Army*. London: Routledge.

Freilich, C. D. 2012. *Zion's Dilemmas: How Israel Makes National Security Policy*. New York: Cornell University Press.

Klieman, A., and S. A. Cohen, eds. 2019. *The Routledge Handbook of Israeli Security*. Oxon: Routledge.

Notes

1 Israel's West Bank withdrawal was comparatively small. However, it involved the removal of four settlements: Homesh, Ganim, Kadim, and Sa-Nur, each of which was located in the northern West Bank, between the Palestinian cities of Nablus and Jenin.

2 Exactly how much of the West Bank Israel is truly willing to leave is disputed. At Camp David in 2000, Israel proposed withdrawing from 92 per cent of the West Bank. Critical observers, however, noted that Israel would still have de facto security control over much more of the territory. For instance, Israel would surrender the Jordan Valley to Palestinian sovereignty, but would 'lease' the territory and keep it under its indefinite control, whilst controlling all of the West Bank and Gaza Strip's airspace and sea access.

Questions for Discussion

(1) What security issues stopped Israel withdrawing from further territory, since 2005?

(2) From an Israeli perspective, how has the relationship between security and territory changed over time, and what factors have affected it?

(3) Is Israel's territorial policy guided by security, or ideology, or both?

(4) Does withdrawal or occupation best enhance Israel's security?

References

Agence France Presse. 2004. "Israeli Soldiers Urge Immediate Withdrawal from Flashpoint Gaza Settlement." 30 May.

Aronoff, Y. S. 2010. "From Warfare to Withdrawal: The Legacy of Ariel Sharon." *Israel Studies* 15:2, 149–172.

Ben-Sasson Gordis, A. 2016. *The Strategic Balance of Israel's Withdrawal from Gaza*. Tel Aviv, Molad: The Center for Renewal of Israeli Democracy. Available at: www.molad.org/images/upload/files/Disengagement-Eng-report-full_final-for-website.pdf.

Bregman, A. 2015. *Cursed Victory: A History of Israel and the Occupied Territories*. London: Penguin.

Byman, D. 2011. *A High Price: The Triumphs and Failures of Israeli Counter Terrorism*. New York: Oxford University Press.

Catignani, S. 2008. *Israeli Counter-insurgency and the Intifada: Dilemmas of a Conventional Army*. London: Routledge.

Gavron, A. 2019. "Ofra, The Mayflower of the Settlements." *Tablet Magazine*. 4 December. Available at: www.tabletmag.com/jewish-arts-and-culture/295015/ofra-israeli-settlements-amos-oz.

Geist, P. R. 2019. "Territorial Withdrawal as Multilateral Bargaining: Revisiting Israel's 'Unilateral' Withdrawals from Gaza and Southern Lebanon." *The Journal of Strategic Studies*. DOI: 10.1080/01402390.2019.1570146.

Ginsburg, M. 2014. "Ya'alon Rules Out Notion of West Bank Withdrawal." *The Times of Israel*. 30 September. Available at: www.timesofisrael.com/yaalon-rules-out-notion-of-west-bank-withdrawal/.

Harms, G., and T. M. Ferry. 2012. *The Palestine-Israel Conflict: A Basic Introduction*. London: Pluto Press.

Israel Democracy Institute. 2017. "Surveys: 50 Years Since the Six Day War." 23 May. Available at: https://en.idi.org.il/press-releases/14606.

Israel Ministry of Foreign Affairs (IMFA). 1978. "Press Conference with Foreign and Defence Ministers Dayan and Weizman upon their return from Camp David." 19 September. Available at: http://mfa.gov.il/MFA/ForeignPolicy/MFADocuments/Yearbook3/Pages/196%20Press%20Conference%20with%20Foreign%20and%20Defence%20Mini.aspx.

Klieman, A., and S. A. Cohen, eds. 2019. *The Routledge Handbook of Israeli Security*. Oxon: Routledge.

Lustick, I. 1995. *Unsettled States, Disputed Lands: Britain and Ireland, France and Algeria, Israel and the West Bank-Gaza*. New York: Cornell University Press.

Miller, A. D. 2008. *The Much too Promised Land: America's Elusive Search for Arab-Israeli Peace*. New York: Bantam Dell.

Mnookin, R. H., E. Eiran, and S. Gilad. 2014. "Is Unilateralism Always Bad? Negotiation Lessons from Israel's 'Unilateral' Gaza Withdrawal." *Negotiation Journal* 30:2, 131–156.

Nusseibeh, L. 2020. "Why Human Security is Relevant to the Israeli-Palestinian Conflict." *The Palestine-Israel Journal*. Available at: www.pij.org/articles/1194.

Peri, Y. 2006. *Generals in the Cabinet Room: How the Military Shapes Israeli Policy*. Washington, DC: United States Institute of Peace.

Peters, J. 2010. "The Gaza Disengagement: Five Years Later." *The Israel Journal of Foreign Affairs* 4:3, 33–44.

Pinfold, R. G. 2015. "It's the 'Special Relationship', Stupid: Examining Israel-US Relations Through the Prism of Israeli Territorial Withdrawals." *Strife Journal*, Special Issue I, 48–57.

Raz, A. 2012. "The Generous Peace Offer that was Never Offered: The Israeli Cabinet Resolution of June 19, 1967." *Diplomatic History* 37:1, 85–108.

Ross, D. 2005. *The Missing Peace: The Inside Story of the Fight for Middle East Peace*. New York: Farrar, Straus and Giroux.

Shavit, A. 2004. "The Complete Interview with Dov Weisglass." *Haaretz* [Hebrew]. 7 October. Available at: www.haaretz.co.il/misc/1.1004558.

Susser, L. 2005. "Netanyahu Plots a Challenge to Sharon." *Jewish Telegraphic Agency*, 11 April. Available at: www.jta.org/2005/04/11/lifestyle/netanyahu-plots-a-challenge-to-sharon.

Tessler, M. 2009. *A History of the Israeli-Palestinian Conflict*. Bloomington, IN: Indiana University Press.

United Nations Security Council. 1967. "Resolution 242." 22 November. Available at: https://unispal.un.org/DPA/DPR/unispal.nsf/0/7D35E1F729DF491C85256EE700686136.

Waxman, D. 2008. "From Controversy to Consensus: Cultural Conflict and the Israeli Debate over Territorial Withdrawal." *Israel Studies* 13:2, 73–96.

18

THE ROLE OF RELIGION AND INTERRELIGIOUS DIALOGUE IN THE ISRAELI-PALESTINIAN CONFLICT

Ron Kronish

This chapter provides an overview of the role of religion and interreligious dialogue in the Israeli-Palestinian conflict. The negative role played by Radical Judaism and by Extremist Islam is examined. Certain fundamentalist versions of Judaism and Islam, which have dominated the headlines in recent decades, have turned the conflict – once essentially a nationalist conflict – into a religious as well as a nationalist conflict. These distortions of authentic Judaism and Islam have not only misled the world to think that they are the normative outlooks of these religions, but they have also greatly exacerbated the ongoing conflict between Israelis and Palestinians. In contrast, there is some hope on the horizon via some positive developments in interreligious dialogue in Israel and Palestine. Some courageous individuals and movements have used dialogue as a method of peacebuilding between the two main religious communities in conflict – Jews and Muslims. The pioneering and groundbreaking ideas and actions of Rabbi Michael Melchior and the Religious Peace Initiative and the work of Professor Mohammed Dajani via the Wassatia movement are portrayed, with an eye to how these initiatives point the way towards a better future for Israeli Jews and Palestinian Arabs alike.

This chapter provides an overview of the role of religion and interreligious dialogue in the Israeli-Palestinian conflict. The first part reviews the role of Jewish-Muslim relations in exacerbating the conflict, while the second part sheds light on positive developments in the field of interreligious dialogue as a form of peace-building. The third part reflects on the possible role that religion (and interreligious dialogue) can play in mitigating the conflict in the future.[1]

The Negative Role Played by Radical Judaism and Extremist Islam in the Conflict

There is no doubt that the struggle between Judaism and Islam is often portrayed as playing an important part in the Israeli-Palestinian conflict. However, in reality, there are certain fundamentalist and ultra-nationalist versions of these religions that dominate the headlines in the media and create the mistaken perception of true representations of what the two religions preach and teach. This conflict, which was initially a conflict between two nationalisms – Zionism, as the national liberation movement of the Jewish People, and Palestinian Nationalism,

DOI: 10.4324/9780429027376-22

largely as a reaction to Zionist settlement in the land of Israel – has always contained religious undertones. While it is still essentially a conflict about how two collectivities who both see themselves as "peoples" – the Jewish People and the Palestinian People – are trying (or not) to share the land of Israel/Palestine, in recent decades the religious undertones have turned to overtones. With the rise of the messianic nationalist Jewish settler movement known as *Gush Emunim* ("The Bloc of the Faithful") and the growth of religious right-wing political parties in Israel, and with the rise of extremist Muslim groups in Palestine and in the region, such as Hamas, Islamic Jihad, Hezbollah, Iran, ISIS, Al Qaeda and the like, the conflict has become a religious conflict as much as a national one. In fact, two extremist religious nationalisms, both of which ideologically believe that the Land (of Israel or Palestine) belongs only to them, have become increasingly uncompromising and rejectionist of any peace plans, leading to ongoing violence, wars, terror, counter-terror and all-or-nothing ideologies or theologies, which sustain and even exacerbate the conflict.

Religious Nationalist and Ultra-orthodox Judaism

There are two main forms of religious Judaism that are dominant in Israeli society. One is known as "Religious Nationalism" (in Hebrew, *Dati Leumi*) and the other is known as "Ultra-Orthodoxy" (in Hebrew, *Yahadut Haredit).* The Religious Nationalist camp – which has its origins in religious (orthodox) Zionism via the *Mizrachi* faction of the Zionist movement in Europe and in pre-state Israel – has changed and developed from a once-moderate, tolerant, compromising group to a collection of extremist, uncompromising, zealous and intolerant expressions of Judaism in the State of Israel, especially in "the Territories", that is, the West Bank, which they refer to by its biblical names of "Judea and Samaria". Over time, the Religious Nationalist camp has gained more and more political power. They have four political parties, three[2] of which joined together in one slate to run together in the Israeli elections of March 2020, and an extreme one, known as "Jewish Power" (in Hebrew, *Otzmah Yehudit*), which consists of the most extreme fringe of these groups, and whose followers support the outright racist ideas of a deceased rabbi named Meir Kahane, whose party *Kach* was banned from the Knesset (Israel's Parliament) in 1988 due to its incitement and its racist platform (Burack 2019).

All four political parties have an ultra-nationalist agenda, highly influenced by Jewish theological radicalism, which sees the land of Israel as belonging only to the Jewish People by divine right, an ideology which is represented by many rabbis in this sector of Israeli "religious" society. For "religious" and "nationalist" reasons, they all reject any compromise on "the territories", and they seek to annex all or most of them, with no regard for what the Palestinians who live on these lands or the international community think about this, and with no concern for international law. They are led by rabbis and nationalist leaders who cater to the growing number of religiously right-wing voters in Jewish society, including and especially settler Jews, who live in the West Bank and who number approximately 463, 000, as of 1 January 2020, not including about 200,000 Israeli Jews who live in Jewish communities in East Jerusalem, which was annexed to Jerusalem following the June 1967 war (Jewish Virtual Library, n.d.).

The second major camp in Religious (i.e., Orthodox) Judaism in Israeli society is known as the *Haredi* ("God-fearing" camp), sometimes referred to in the media as "Ultra-orthodox Judaism". This camp contains many subgroups. The most extreme ones are anti-Zionist factions such as the *Neturei Karta* and the Satmar Hasidic communities, who reject Zionism since they believe that God will bring the Messiah in His time, and that Jews should not "push the end" by advancing the Messianic era on their own, which is one of the main tenets of the Zionist movement, including both religious and secular Zionists. In their minds, these Jews live in the "land of Israel" and not "the State of Israel", and they do not support many of the institutions of the state, such as the armed forces, the tax authorities, and the police (against whom they often violently demonstrate). The majority of the ultra-orthodox Jews could be classified as "non-Zionist", that is, they do not support the idea of a Jewish state theologically, but since they live in the land of Israel, which for them is holy, they are willing to compromise and cooperate with the institutions of the state, but with limitations. For example, they do not agree to be ministers in Zionist governments, but only deputy ministers. However, they will agree to have one of their politicians become chairman of the Finance Committee of the Knesset, which helps them ensure that state funds will flow to their institutions, particularly schools and *yeshivas* (adult learning centers), where young ultra-orthodox Jewish men can study for many years, thus avoiding service in the Israeli army.

In recent years, these non-Zionist parties have been represented in the Knesset via two major parties – *Agudat Yisrael*, which is mostly Ashkenazi, that is, of Western European descent, and *Shas* – Sephardic Torah Guardians, which is mostly comprised of Jews who are originally from Middle Eastern countries and have remained religiously observant. In recent years, such as in the Knesset after the September 2019 elections, they have significant political power, with *Agudat Israel – United Torah Judaism* holding seven seats (6.06%) and *Shas* holding nine seats (7.44%), with a combined 16 seats out of 120 in the Parliament, representing 13.5 per cent of the total vote in Israel (Jerusalem Post 2019). And, in recent elections they have joined the "religious-nationalist bloc" of parties, along with the Likud, at the insistence of Prime Minister Netanyahu, the leader of the Likud Party.

For the most part, these non-Zionist ultra-orthodox parties have little concern for foreign policy, issues of war or peace, or justice for the Palestinians. Their main concerns are the welfare of their constituents and maintaining their mostly separatist way of life in Israel. (They tend to live in self-imposed "ghettoes" or neighbourhoods, where they control who can or cannot enter on Shabbat and other religious Jewish holidays.). Yet, since they believe in the divine right of the Jewish People to possess all of the Land of Israel, they go along with the nationalist religious parties in opposing any compromise with the Palestinians that would lead to yielding any parts of the land to anyone other than Jews, which puts them in the ultra-nationalist camp.

Another large group of ultra-orthodox Jews is *Habad*, or the *Lubavitch* Hasidic group. They, like most of the other ultra-orthodox groups in Israel, originated in Europe, in this case in Eastern Europe. They are a growing force in the ultra-Orthodox community in Israel (and the world) because of their policy of outreach, by which they reach out to other Jews to influence them to become more observant of Jewish rituals. They do not have a political party and they used to vote mainly for the Agudat Yisrael Party. Many of the members of this group believe that their deceased leader, Rabbi Schneerson (often known as "the Rebbie"), who died in 1994, is the messiah and will one day return to Israel and lead Israel in an old-new form (their version) of religious Judaism. In the elections of September 2019, large numbers of their followers voted for the most extreme right-wing "religious" political party known as Otzmah Yehudit, Jewish Power (see above). This demonstrated that this popular ultra-Orthodox Jewish group in Israel is just as anti-peace and anti-justice, as other ultra-Orthodox groups (Maltz 2019).

In sum, the main forms of religious Judaism in Israel are anti-peace, anti-Arab, and anti-Palestinian. They are therefore mostly an obstacle to peace, and they do not engage very much in peace-building activities. (There are some rare exceptions, such as the work of Rabbi Michael Melchior and Rabbi Daniel Roth, discussed below). They generally join with the ultra-nationalist religious and secular Jewish groups who oppose peace and favour annexation of "the territories", that is the biblical lands of Judea and Samaria, which they regard as holy and totally belonging to the State of Israel.

Extremist Islam in Palestine and the Region

The main Palestinian Muslim group that mixes religion and nationalism into a dangerous anti-peace cocktail is Hamas, which is an acronym for *Harakat al-Muqqawamah al-Islamiyyah* – the Islamic Resistance Movement. A militant Islamic Palestinian nationalist movement in the West Bank and Gaza Strip, it was founded in 1987 in opposition to the secular approach of the Palestine Liberation Organization (PLO) to the Israeli-Palestinian conflict. It rejected, and continues to reject, any attempts by Palestinian leadership to compromise on any parts of the Land of Palestine for peace. In December 1987, at the beginning of the uprising known as the First Palestinian *Intifada* (Arabic for "shaking off the Israeli occupation"), Hamas (which is also an Arabic word for "zeal") was established by members of the Muslim Brotherhood and by some members of religious factions of the PLO. With the outbreak of the uprising, this new movement became popular in parts of Palestine, especially in the Gaza Strip. As a religious movement, Hamas's leaders claimed that it is a religious obligation for Muslims to regain control of all of the Land of Palestine.

Since 1987, Hamas has grown and developed with the help of many outside sources of funding, including and especially from Iran and Qatar. In 1996, it established a military wing known as the *Izz al-Din al Qassam* Forces, which became a mini-army in the Gaza Strip. In addition, Hamas rejects any direct peace process with Israel, since it does not formally recognize the existence of the State of Israel and says that it will never do so and opposes any compromises by the PLO or Palestinian leadership with the State of Israel (Scham and Abu-Irshaid, 2009).

It is important to emphasize that Hamas is not just a Palestinian nationalist movement but also a fundamentalist Muslim movement, similar to Muslim extremist religious groups in the region, such as the Ayatollahs in Iran and Hezbollah in Lebanon. In the charter of the Hamas movement from August 1988, it is made abundantly clear that it is a religious Islamic movement: "The Islamic Resistance Movement draws its guidelines from Islam; derives from it its thinking, interpretations and views about existence, life and humanity; refers back to it for its conduct; and is inspired by it in whatever step it takes" (Horowitz and Khalel 2017).

In September 2000, the Hamas movement led the Second Intifada, which became known as the *Al Aksa Intifada*, named after one of the two main mosques on Harem El Sharif, Temple Mount, which according to Hamas activists, was in danger of destruction by the State of Israel. This uprising was characterized by hundreds of suicide bombings against Israeli civilians in the name of Allah (the Muslim name for God), attacks that killed hundreds of Israelis and wounded thousands. In August 2005, Israel unilaterally disengaged from the Gaza Strip, withdrawing all its settlers, demolishing all the settler communities and removing their army from the Strip. This disengagement was seen as a direct result of the Hamas terror campaign. Following this, Hamas won a surprise victory in the elections for the Palestinian Legislative Council. This was a great shock to Fatah, which had been the dominant force within the PLO for a long time.[3] This led to clashes between Fatah and Hamas in 2006 and 2007, and in June 2007 the PLO's president, Mahmoud Abbas, dissolved the Hamas-led government and declared a state of emergency. As a result, Hamas assumed control of Gaza while the PLO remained in control of the West Bank. This has been the case since then, even though there have been many attempts at reconciliation between these two major parts of the Palestinian people, all of which have failed so far. Since this time, Hamas and the State of Israel have engaged in three mini-wars: Operation "Cast Lead" (December 2008–January 2009), Operation "Pillar of Defense" (November 2012), Operation "Protective Edge" (July–August 2014) and many actions of terror and counter-terror in an ongoing unresolved hot conflict, with no resolution in sight.

For Israeli Jews, Hamas's version of Islam dominated their life and the media, and for most of them, it was the only form of Islam that they had come to know. Accordingly, for the majority of Israeli Jews and Jews worldwide, Islam became the religion of suicide bombers, martyrs, jihadists, terrorists, fanatics, and rejectionists. It must be noted, however, that it was not, and is not, the Islam that is practised by the majority of Muslims who are citizens of the State of Israel, whose version of their religion is quite moderate. Therefore, for many Israeli Jews, Hamas is seen as a religious enemy who could only be defeated, not comprised with, since their hatred of Israel and Jews is uncompromising and theologically based. As a result, Israel never negotiated directly with Hamas, since it did not recognize the State of Israel, although there have often been indirect negotiations, through third parties, such as Egypt, to end hostilities after mini-wars or other violent confrontations.

While Hamas rules in Gaza, the PLO continues to rule in the West Bank, with security cooperation with the State of Israel. Indeed, the PLO often arrests Hamas operatives in the West Bank and puts them in Palestinian jails, as a way of preventing terror and counter-terror. Moreover, one of the reasons that the PLO leadership has not held elections in many years is that it is worried Hamas might win in the West Bank and thereby try to turn the West Bank into a fundamentalist religious reactionary society, which is opposed to the Fatah vision of Palestine as a secular democratic state.

It is important to point out that while there is an Islamic Movement within Israel – with a northern branch that is more extreme in its rhetoric and a southern branch that is more moderate – neither wing of the movement accepts the Hamas charter. Both branches of the Movement in Israel are non-violent, although one could say that the northern branch is often verbally violent. On the other hand, the southern branch of the Islamic Movement in Israel participates in local and national elections and is part of the fabric of Israeli democracy. Furthermore, most Muslims in Israel (who represent about 20% of the citizens of Israel) are non-violent Sunni Muslims, law-abiding citizens who seek to practice their religion in reasonable ways in mosques all over Israel, most of which are funded by the State of Israel, and through their Shari'a courts, which handle matters of personal status via modern Islamic jurisprudence, and under the auspices of Israel's Ministry of Justice (Zahalka 2015).

Nevertheless, the perception that has been created by Hamas, especially in Gaza but also in the West Bank, is that Islam is a violent, anti-democratic, anti-peace religion, which when fused with extreme nationalism, does not leave much room for peacebuilding and coexistence ideologies. Thus, this form of radical Islam, which has unfortunately dominated the consciousness of most Israeli Jews in recent decades through ongoing violence and even some wars, has been a severely negative and rejectionist factor that has inhibited the peace process between Israelis and Palestinians from moving forward.

Some Positive Developments in Interreligious Dialogue as a Form of Peacebuilding[4]

Interreligious dialogue has been a force for good in conflicts around the world. It has led to much mutual understanding and cooperation between parties in conflict, and in many places has become an important part of peacebuilding efforts among key actors in civil society. Indeed, interreligious dialogue, cooperation and action as a form of peacebuilding has been supplementing the work of the political peacemakers for a long time and has become increasingly important, especially in places where religion has been playing a major role in the conflict (Lederach 1997; Smock 2002; Gopin 2002).

It is important to make the distinction between peacemaking and peacebuilding. Peacemaking is the work of the lawyers, politicians and diplomats. The goal of those who engage in such work is to create peace treaties between governments, what one could call *pieces of paper*. Professionals who do this work are usually trained in legal studies and international relations. While acknowledging the importance of these political and diplomatic processes, we need to be mindful of their limitations. They do not solve all the problems of a conflict. Rather, they prepare a legal framework for agreement on principles and practices to resolve the conflict (Kronish 2017). On the other hand, peacebuilding is not the work of the diplomats or politicians. Rather, it is the work of rabbis, imams, priests, educators, social workers, psychologists, architects, urban planners, youth workers, women, and other actors in civil society, especially in countries and regions of conflict. It is these people – not the lawyers and politicians – who bring people together to enter into dialogue and engage in educational programs aimed at helping people in these societies to learn to live in peace with each other now, and for the future. These processes – which are sometimes called *track-two diplomacy* (*track one* being the political-diplomatic track) or simply *people-to-people programs* – involve long-term psychological, educational, and spiritual transformation (Kronish 2017, 45).

Most of the work for peace via interreligious dialogue in Israel and Palestine in recent years has been part of *peacebuilding*, rather than *peacemaking*. Rather than surveying all the efforts in this area, this section will focus on some of the most impactful initiatives in interreligious dialogue.

The Religious Peace Initiative

There is one major interreligious initiative that has courageously and systematically tried to achieve both peacemaking and peacebuilding at the same time. It is known as the Religious Peace Initiative, and has been going on for several years, mostly under the radar, but sometimes with some public international gatherings and recognition. It was the brainchild of Rabbi Michael Melchior and his colleagues in an organization known as Mosaica, which operates in Israel, Palestine, and the wider region (The Religious Peace Initiative, n.d.).

Rabbi Michael Melchior is without doubt the leading Jewish interreligious peacebuilder in Israel. For many years now, he has been bringing religious leaders together from within Israel and the region, as well as internationally, and more recently he has been witness to significant results and much positive progress. A descendant of seven generations of rabbis in Denmark, Rabbi Melchior was born in Copenhagen in 1954. He studied at *Yeshivat Hakotel* in Jerusalem and received rabbinic ordination from the Chief Rabbinate of Israel. Soon afterwards, he returned to Scandinavia to serve as Rabbi of Oslo and later as the Chief Rabbi of Norway. In 1986 he immigrated to Israel and settled down with his family in Jerusalem, where he serves until the present day as the rabbi of an Orthodox synagogue, while still holding the title of Chief Rabbi of Norway. He was a supporter of the Israeli-Palestinian peace process from the beginning of the Oslo meetings in 1993, during which time he was involved with and close to Norwegian policymakers. He did this even though he had reservations about the secular nature of the process, which left religious leaders out of it:

> Without religious authorities involved talking openly about their respective narratives and without religious teachings which compel us to make compromises for the sake of peace, there will be no way that society as a whole, on either side of the conflict, will see the peace process as credible or acceptable.
>
> *(Melchior 2015, 117–118)*

Rabbi Melchior was one of the founders of the moderate religious Zionist political party known as *Meimad* (which no longer exists as a party, only a movement). Melchior entered politics with this party in 1995. When Rabbi Yehuda Amital was appointed minister without portfolio after the assassination of Prime Minister Yitzhak Rabin in November 1995, Melchior served as Rabbi Amital's aide. Following that, he was selected chairman of the managing committee of the Meimad Party in early 1996. In the 1999 elections in Israel, Meimad ran as part of the *One Israel* alliance, along with the Labour Party and the *Gesher* Party. He won a seat in the Knesset and was appointed Minister of Social and Diaspora Affairs in August 1999, under Prime Minister Ehud Barak, a post he held until Ariel Sharon was elected prime minister in February 2001. Melchior was re-elected to the Knesset as a member of the joint list in 2003 and 2006, as Meimad continued its alliance with the Labour Party. In 2008, Meimad broke away from the alliance and ran in partnership with the Green Movement in the 2009 elections, but failed to win a seat. Rabbi Melchior also served in several important ministerial positions in Israeli governments: as Deputy Minister of Foreign Affairs from August 1999 until November 2002, Deputy Minister of Education, Culture, and Sport from January to June 2005, and Deputy Minister for Social and Diaspora Affairs from June 2005 until November of that year.

Rabbi Melchior became famous in the world of interreligious peacebuilding after he catalyzed the publication of the famous Alexandria Declaration in January 2002, at the height of the First Intifada (Palestinian uprising). In more recent years, he and colleagues have issued new proclamations that his group of distinguished religious leaders have issued, especially their Madrid Declaration, was published in Spain at the end of 2016, and which was brought to the United Nations Alliance of Civilizations for international approval in July 2017. Through this unique coalition, Rabbi Melchior has brought together an influential group of Jewish, Muslim, and Christian religious leaders not only to *dialogue* for peace but to *act* for peace.[5]

In addition to the various interreligious peace summits Rabbi Melchior has planned and implemented successfully with vision and vitality, he and his colleagues have also been asked to help resolve hot issues, especially concerning tensions on Temple Mount/Haram El Sharif. In recent years, they have been successful in preventing crises from developing into violent confrontation (Kronish 2018a). They are able to be effective, in his opinion, because they have developed a high level of trust among important religious leaders.

What does Rabbi Melchior mean by a *religious peace*?

> A religious peace is a peace of values, where the values of the belief systems -- such as that we are all created by and in the image of the same God, that crushing the other is crushing the Divine in the other --are part of the fabric of peace. I believe that if we believe that it was God's plan for us to come back to the Holy Land and establish a Jewish state again as part of the fulfillment of our prophecies, then it was also part of God's plan that there is another people living here. It is very important to make this theological statement.
>
> *(Melchior 2015, 122)*

Through his many years of dialogue and cooperation with Muslim religious leaders, Rabbi Melchior has insisted that there has been an immense change taking place in the Muslim world towards peace with Israel. In his view, a paradigm shift has been taking place among many religious Jews and religious Muslims toward peace: "This is the test of our religions, that is, the ability to transform the world from war to peace" (Melchior 2015, 126). In the early months of 2020, under the new leadership of Rabbi Daniel Roth, the *Religious Peace Initiative* has developed a new strategic plan for the years ahead, based on more outreach activities in religious communities (Religious Peace Initiative, n.d.).

A Muslim Palestinian Approach to Peacebuilding

On the Palestinian side, the most persistent interreligious peacebuilder over many years has been, and still is, Professor Mohammed Dajani Daoudi. A prolific author, sought-after lecturer and a relentless activist, he has been vocal in his call for peace and reconciliation for the past few decades. He is the author of many articles and monographs, including one that he wrote with me and others for the Frankfurt Peace Research Center in Germany (Baumbart-Ochse, et al, 2014).

Dajani was not always an interreligious peacebuilder. In his youth, he was active in the Fatah movement in the West Bank and then in Lebanon. In 1993, after several years in the United States, (where he earned two doctorates at two different universities) and Jordan, he returned to Jerusalem to reunite with his family (Barakat 2017). In the late 1990s Dajani trained Palestinian civil servants for the United Nations Development Program and for different Palestinian organizations. In 2001, he was asked to teach at Al Quds University in East Jerusalem and in the following year he founded and directed the American Studies program at Al Quds. While at the university, Dajani and his brother Munther Dajani became the founders of the moderate Muslim Palestinian organization called *Wasatia*, Arabic for "the middle way", which has been promoting interreligious dialogue, peace and reconciliation in Palestinian and Israeli societies, as well as internationally (Barakat 2017).

In 2014, following a trip with his students to the concentration camp of Auschwitz in Poland, Dajani was forced to resign from Al Quds University. This was due to protests by Palestinian students and professors and anti-normalization activists in Palestinian society who did not appreciate his controversial decision to teach Palestinian students about Jewish suffering and Jewish Israeli students about Palestinian suffering. Even though there are divergent accounts of why he was forced to resign, Dajani insists that the administration of the university did not support his academic freedom at that time, and therefore he decided to discontinue his relationship with the university.[6]

Over the years, Dajani's organization, *Wasatia*, has educated hundreds, perhaps thousands, of Palestinian religious leaders, adults, and youth in the classic texts of Islam that clearly speak in favour of moderation, reconciliation, and peace. He has conducted many workshops for these target audiences in East Jerusalem and in the West Bank. Dajani does not believe in giving in to despair, which is all too prevalent in Palestinian (and Israeli) society, or drifting with the crowd. He has brought his message to regional and international conferences, and his organization has published more than thirty publications in a variety of languages, which are distributed freely to readers (Kronish 2018b).

What is his message?

> Moderation in times of extremism is a revolutionary idea. It is a positive, courageous value, as opposed to a defeatist attitude. It is swimming against the tide, rather than following the crowd on a path obviously leading to the abyss. We need to create our own vision rather than just copy the vision of others. ... We are standing with a voice of reason, so that people don't only hear the voice of extremism. ... We want to reverse this trend by arguing against the dominant paradigm that Islam comes to replace other religions that preceded it such as Judaism and Christianity by explaining

> and showing that Islam, according to its foundational Quranic texts, was sent to complement other faiths and calls for cooperation and coexistence with other religions.
> *(Kronish 2018b)*

In recent years, Dajani has devoted much of his efforts to setting up a new graduate program in Peace and Reconciliation Studies, in cooperation with universities abroad. This new program offers doctoral studies in Palestine and Israel, and then abroad, for Israeli and Palestinian students who would want to specialize in this field. Graduates would return to their homelands to teach in universities and schools, and promote dialogue and peace education in many settings, to help both peoples, Israelis and Palestinians, build bridges between them. In February 2020 Professor Dajani announced that the European Inter-disciplinary College at the European University in Flensburg has established the Wasatia Graduate School for Tolerance and Reconciliation (WGS) to grant a doctorate in tolerance, peace, and conflict-resolution studies. The program is designed to respond to a growing demand for academic skills and knowledge and professional training that addresses the complex issues of tolerance, reconciliation, peace, and conflict resolution.[7]

In his lectures and writings on this theme, Dajani often likes to end with a story that he learned from a Jewish friend and colleague, whose theme comes from the Talmud:

> A king walking in the fields came across an old man planting a tree. He asked him: *Old man, why are you planting a tree when you are too old to eat its fruit?* The old man responded, *Oh my king, our grandparents planted trees and we ate their fruit and we plant so that our grandchildren would eat its fruit.*

Dajani adds his own reflection to this story:

> *Sadly, we have inherited this conflict from our grandparents and we owe it to our grandchildren to leave them a heritage of peace so they may live in security and prosperity.*
> *(Kronish 2018b)*

An Interfaith Youth Movement of Palestinian Arabs and Israeli Jews

Many of the organizations that used to bring Palestinian Arab and Israeli Jewish Youth together in East Jerusalem and the West Bank have given up. This is a sad reflection of the despair that has set in over the decades as the Palestinian-Israeli Conflict remains intractable, with no solution in sight. Both security concerns and anti-normalization sentiments have become serious obstacles in attempting to bring Palestinian and Israeli youth together. One organization that has bucked this trend for many years and remains active in Jerusalem to this day is "Kids4Peace", which in 2020 became part of the larger and well-established organization known as "Seeds for Peace".

Founded in 2002, originally as part of the peacebuilding activities of St. George's Cathedral (Anglican) in Jerusalem, Kids4Peace is a movement of youth and families, dedicated to ending conflict and inspiring hope in divided societies in Israel/Palestine and other parts of the world, such as France, Spain, and the United States. This is a grassroots community-based organization, bringing together people from a wide variety of cultures, religions, national identities, economic status, and political points of view. Through dialogue, action programs, and other activities, Palestinian Arab and Jewish Israeli youth from Jerusalem gain skills that help them bridge the gaps between their communities, promote mutual understanding among the disparate populations, and seek social justice in their schools and communities. The mission of

Kids4Peace is to educate future influencers and activists for social justice and peacebuilding in Israel and Palestine. As an interfaith movement, it aims to bring to bear the best values of Judaism, Christianity ,and Islam to inspire peaceful coexistence in the long term.[8]

Some Thoughts for the Future

There is no doubt that religions, especially Judaism and Islam, will continue to play a major role in the Israeli-Palestinian conflict. Unfortunately, religions' role is likely to be mostly negative, as it has been in recent decades, since the extremist Islam propagated by Hamas, Islamic Jihad, and other groups will continue to dominate in Gaza and in parts of the West Bank, and certainly in the media. And radical Judaism, which already dominates most of the West Bank settlements and much of right-wing ultra-nationalist and ultra-orthodox Jewish society, appears only to be growing and getting more and more support from successive Israeli governments. This is not a good omen for the possibility of a renewed peace process, since these groups represent narrow tribal ideologies that fundamentally reject the existence of the other and oppose not only political peace processes but peaceful coexistence on almost every level. It would be helpful if more moderate religious movements within Islam and Judaism could gain more currency, but this is unlikely to happen in the foreseeable future.

There is a great need for interreligious dialogue, especially Jewish-Muslim Dialogue. Movements like Rabbi Melchior's Religious Peace Initiative and Professor Dajani's Wasatia organization, and the interfaith youth movement of Kids4Peace point the way for a better future. However, they will take time to grow and develop and attract more adherents. They are, nevertheless, a beacon of hope in an otherwise rather dark situation, and they should be given support and encouragement (and funding!) to grow and develop. In any event, interreligious dialogue will be needed for a long time, creating relationships and goodwill in both Palestinian and Israeli societies. However, it alone will not resolve the conflict. Without fundamental political change, it can only mitigate and moderate the conflict in the short run by creating less hatred, leading to less violence and more possibilities of peaceful coexistence. In the long run, interreligious dialogue and joint action will be a necessary component of what I have often called "the other peace process" (Kronish 2017).

Third, there is still a need for a political peace process that will attempt to resolve the conflict, not just to manage it. Without a real "peace process", all the attempts at religious, cultural, and social peacebuilding will be insufficient, and inter-communal trust is unlikely to develop. Unfortunately, for this to happen a new generation of leaders on both sides will need to emerge. If intractable conflicts were resolved in Northern Ireland, South Africa, and Yugoslavia, then the Israeli-Palestinian conflict can be resolved as well. And then the peacebuilders – including the interreligious peacebuilders and many other actors in civil society – will need to work together across the divide to realize the possibilities and benefits of peaceful coexistence. It will not be easy, nor will it be quick. But as one of the great rabbinic sages of the Jewish Tradition said a long time ago, "Rabbi Tarfon taught: 'It is not your responsibility to finish the work [of perfecting the world], but you are not free to desist from it either'" (Ethics of the Fathers, n.d.).

Recommended Readings

Dajani, M. D., ed. 2009. *Wasatia: The Spirit of Islam.* Jerusalem: Wasatia Publications.

Kronish, R., ed. 2015 *Coexistence and Reconciliation in Israel. Voices for Interreligious Dialogue.* Mahwah, NJ: Paulist Press.

Kronish, R. 2017. *The Other Peace Process: Interreligious Dialogue, a View from Jerusalem*. Lanham, MD: Hamilton Books.
Melchior, M. 2015. "Establishing a Religious Peace." In *Coexistence and Reconciliation in Israel*, ed. R. Kronish. Mahwah, NJ: Paulist Press, 117–129.
Smock, D. 2002. *Interfaith Dialogue and Peacebuilding*. Washington, DC: United States Institute of Peace Press.

Notes

1 The American government created a program called CMM--Conflict Mitigation and Management to fund cooperative programs between Israelis and Palestinians in 2004. Note that they did not use the term "resolution" in their title for this program. USAID West Bank/Gaza and the United States Embassy in Israel jointly invest in Conflict Management and Mitigation (CMM) grants, which support Israelis and Palestinians, as well as Jewish and Arab citizens of Israel, working on issues of common concern. The CMM program is part of a worldwide effort to bring together individuals of different backgrounds from areas of conflict in people-to-people reconciliation activities. These activities provide opportunities to address issues, reconcile differences, and promote greater understanding and mutual trust by working on common goals such as economic development, environment, health, education, sports, music, and information technology. Since the program's start in 2004, USAID and the U.S. Embassy have invested in 136 CMM grants. https://il.usembassy.gov/education-culture/conflict-management-and-mitigation-program-fact-sheet/.
2 The three political parties are The New Right, *Bayit Yehudi* (Jewish Home) and National Union.
3 The Fatah movement (*Harakat al-Tahrir al-Watani al-Filastini,* Palestinian National Liberation Organization) is a Palestinian national movement that since the 1970s has been the dominant faction in the PLO, the sole legitimate representative of the Palestinian people. From the establishment of the Palestinian Authority (PA) in 1995 and until the recent elections to the Palestinian Legislative Council (PLC) (1/06), in which it lost its majority and the right to form the government, the Fatah movement was the most dominant political party in the PA (Reut Institute 2006).
4 I have written about this topic extensively in *The Other Peace Process, Interreligious Dialogue, A View from Jerusalem* (Hamilton Books, 2017), and on my blog for *The Times of Israel*. https://blogs.timesofisrael.com/author/ron-kronish/, especially in my series on "peacebuilders" in recent years.
5 For Rabbi Melchior's biography, see www.rabbimichaelmelchior.org/biography.
6 Author's conversations with Dajani.
7 Author's interview with Dajani, 26 February 2020.
8 Interview with Udi Cohen, Director General, Kids4Peace in Jerusalem, 5 March 2020.

Questions for Discussion

(1) What is the difference between peacemaking and peacebuilding? How do they influence each other?
(2) Why are religious fundamentalism and extremist nationalism obstacles to moving forward with the peace process between Israelis and Palestinians?
(3) Are you inspired by the examples of Rabbi Michael Melchior and his "Religious Peace Initiative" and Professor Mohammed Dajani and his Wasatia program? Do they give you hope for the future?
(4) How can religions – and interreligious dialogue – be a force for good in the Israeli-Palestinian conflict, now and in the future?

References

Barakat, Z. M. 2017. *From Heart of Stone to Heart of Flesh: Evolutionary Journey from Extremism to Moderation*. Munich: Herbert Utz Verlag GmbH.
Baumgart-Ochse, C., et al. 2014. "The Practice and Promise of Inter-faith Dialogue and Peacebuilding in the Israeli-Palestinian Conflict." Policy Brief No. 35, *Peace Research Institute Frankfurt (PRIF)*. Available at: http://academicpeaceorchestra.com/?p=policybriefs.
Burack, E. 2019. "Rabbi Meir Kahane and Israel's Far Right, Explained." *The Times of Israel*. 1 March. Available at: www.timesofisrael.com/rabbi-meir-kahane-and-israels-far-right-explained/.

Ethics of the Fathers. N.d. Chapter 2, Verse 16. Available at: www.chabad.org/library/article_cdo/aid/2011/jewish/Chapter-Two.htm.

Gopin. M. 2002. *Holy War, Holy Peace: How Religions Can Bring Peace to the Middle East*. New York: Oxford University Press.

Horowitz, A., and S. Khalel. 2017. "Read the full translated text of the leaked Hamas charter." *Mondoweiss*, 5 April. Available at: https://mondoweiss.net/2017/04/translated-leaked-charter/.

Jerusalem Post. 2019. "CEC announces 'almost final' results, Gantz leads by two seats." 20 September. Available at: www.jpost.com/Israel-Elections/Israel-elections-results-based-on-counted-ballots-12-am-602045.

Jewish Virtual Library. N. d. *Total Population of Jewish Settlements (1970–Present)*. Available at: www.jewishvirtuallibrary.org/jewish-settlements-population-1970-present.

Kronish, R. 2017. *The Other Peace Process: Interreligious Dialogue, a View from Jerusalem*. Lanham, MD: Hamilton Books.

Kronish, R. 2018a. "Rabbi Michael Melchior and his Religious Peace Initiative." *The Times of Israel*, 24 April. Available at: https://blogs.timesofisrael.com/rabbi-michael-melchior-and-his-religious-peace-iniative/.

Kronish, R. 2018b. "Moderation in times of extremism: Mohammed Dajani Daoudi." *The Times of Israel*, 22 February. Available at: https://blogs.timesofisrael.com/moderation-in-times-of-extremism-mohammed-dajani-daoudi/.

Lederach, J. P. 1997. *Building Peace: Sustainable Reconciliation in Divided Societies*. Washington, DC: United States Institute of Peace.

Maltz, J. 2019. "Election Results: Israel's Most Far-right Community Is Only a 10-minute Drive From Tel Aviv." *Haaretz*, 25 September. Available at: www.haaretz.com/israel-news/elections/.premium-israel-election-results-israel-s-most-far-right-community-is-a-10-minute-drive-from-tel-aviv-1.7898099.

Melchior, M. 2015. "Establishing a Religious Peace", in *Coexistence and Reconciliation in Israel. Voices for Interreligious Dialogue*, ed. R. Kronish. Mahwah, NJ: Paulist Press, 117–129.

Religious Peace Initiative. N. d. http://religiouspeaceinitiative.org/en/about/

Reut Institute. 2006. "Sole Legitimate Representative of the Palestinian People." 20 March. Available at: http://reut-institute.org/en/Publication.aspx?PublicationId=1169.

Scham, P. P., and O. Abu-Irshaid. 2009. "Hamas: Ideological Rigidity and Political Flexibility." *United States Institute for Peace*, Special Report 224. Available at: www.usip.org/publications/2009/06/hamas-ideological-rigidity-and-political-flexibility.

Smock, D. 2002. *Interfaith Dialogue and Peacebuilding*. Washington, DC: United States Institute of Peace Press.

Zahalka, I. 2015. "Development of Islamic Jurisprudence in Israel." In *Coexistence and Reconciliation in Israel. Voices for Interreligious Dialogue*, ed. R. Kronish. Mahwah, NJ: Paulist Press, 168–183.

PART IV

The Local Dimensions of the Conflict

19

THE PALESTINIAN NATIONAL MOVEMENT AND THE STRUGGLE WITHIN

Dag Henrik Tuastad

Introduction

Two unsolved political problems continue to paralyse Palestinian politics. The first is the role of violence as a means in the struggle against the Israeli occupation. Article 9 of the National Covenant of the Palestine Liberation Organization (PLO) states that: "Armed struggle is the only way to liberate Palestine. This is the overall strategy, not merely a tactical phase" (YLS 2008). Through the 1993 Oslo Accords, the PLO annulled this clause: "The PLO renounces the use of terrorism and other acts of violence and will assume responsibility over all PLO elements and PLO personnel in order to assure their compliance, prevent violations and discipline violators" (Dajani 1994, 7; Ferziger 1993). The problem is that when the decision to renounce violence was taken, not everyone was on board. This, not everyone being on board, constitutes the second unresolved problem: No national institution exists that include all the main Palestinian national groups. The armed Islamist groups Palestinian Islamic Jihad (PIJ) and Hamas, both with the military capacity to spoil PLO decisions while also having considerable support in the Palestinian street, are not part of the PLO, the organization internationally recognized as the "sole legitimate representative of the Palestinian people" (Dajani 1994, 19).

The internal Palestinian division, with Hamas ruling Gaza and Fatah and the PLO the West Bank, is a consequence of the problems of violence and representation remaining unresolved. The division is unprecedented in the history of the Palestinian national movement. As will be elaborated upon below, the PLO's system of representation had in fact been designed to prevent any of its militant member-groups from breaking away.

The National Institutions

The Palestine Liberation Organization

When the Arab League established the PLO in 1964, a motive was to contain the activities of Palestinian guerrilla groups popping up inside Palestine and the Palestinian refugee communities in diaspora (Baconi 2018, 14). The Arab states needed to control the Palestinians before the weapons of the militants were used against their own authoritarian regimes. One consequence

DOI: 10.4324/9780429027376-24

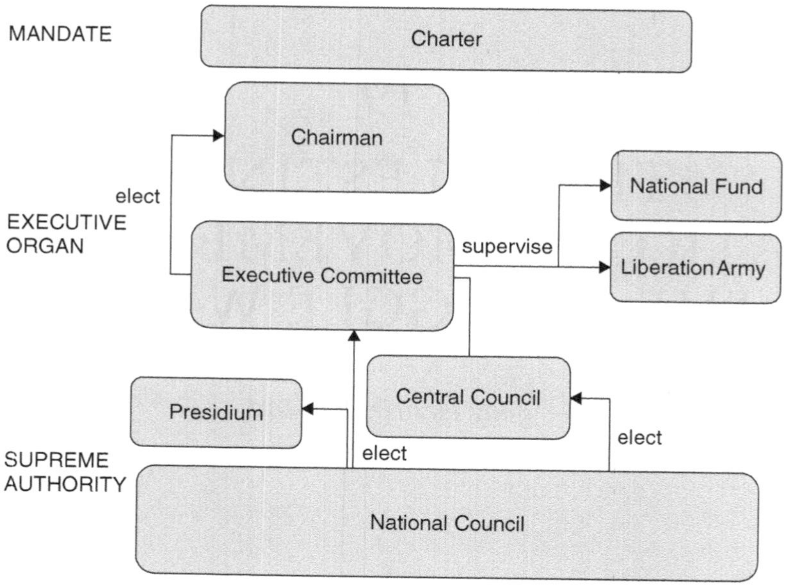

Figure 19.1 PLO's political structure.

of being founded by the Arab League was that the PLO's organizational structure became modelled after a full-grown state rather than a liberation organization. The PLO had a constitution, an army (the Arab Liberation Army), a treasury (the National Fund), a government (the Executive Committee, EC) and a parliament (the Palestinian National Council, PNC) (see Figure 19.1). The PNC was the PLO's principle institution. According to the PLO constitution it should be democratically elected, should elect the chairman of the PLO, and confirm the members of the EC (Tuastad 2012, 10).

The Palestinian guerrilla groups did not want to be part of the PLO initially, knowing it had been established to contain their militancy. But as the Israeli occupation of the West Bank and Gaza in 1967 shattered the belief in a pan-Arab front against Israel, it became of paramount interest for Fatah and the guerrillas to unite their efforts and have a common political and military organizational framework. Fatah and the armed Palestinian groups consequently took control over the PLO in 1968–1969. While elections for the PNC never took place, the organizational structure of the original PLO remained intact. For Yasser Arafat, the Fatah leader and PLO leader from 1969 until his death in 2004, it was crucial to avoid internal splits (Sayigh 1997, 236). The PNC was thus needed to hammer out strategies and unite the Palestinian groups behind a joint, national program. Moreover, to avoid splits, Arafat was conscious of his own group, Fatah, not overtly dominating the PLO. This paved the way for the quota system as the principle for representation within the PLO, where the constituent PLO groups were represented irrespective of their size or popularity among the Palestinian people at large. The quota system meant that the question of political representation – in the PNC, the Executive Committee, and down to the refugee camp committees controlled by the PLO – became an issue of negotiation between the various guerrilla groups, each having the right to their quota.

From all angles, save the one that really mattered for them, the military one, PLO was a success story. The PLO was well funded, mainly through an agreement with Arab states in the Gulf of taxing Palestinians working there (Rubenberg 1983, 60). And in its heyday, the

PLO was so strong that it threatened the power of Arab regimes hosting them. This eventually led Jordan to crack down upon and expel the PLO in 1970. The PLO then established its base in Lebanon where their military strength was by far stronger than that of the state, until 1982 when it was once again driven out following an Israeli invasion aimed at destroying the organization. The PLO then evacuated to Tunisia, being forced to rethink its strategy of armed resistance that, no matter how hard it was to admit, had not brought the PLO closer to liberating the homeland.

Despite their military defeats, the PLO enjoyed wide support among the Palestinians. The organization had the civil and military apparatus of a mini-state in exile but, more important, it had created a cultural revolution, especially in the Palestinian refugee camps (Parsons 2013, 214). The PLO changed the self-perception among the Palestinians from one of humiliation to one of pride, from helpless refugees to feared guerrilla fighters. Moreover, although not elected, its "parliament", the PNC, would be more active and transparent than most Arab ruling bodies, engaging publicly in regular and substantial discussions on political issues and strategies. But with the Oslo Accord in 1993 and the establishment of the Palestinian Authority in 1994, this came to an end.

The Palestinian Authority and the 2006 Election Bombshell

The Palestinian Authority (PA) was tasked to govern autonomous areas in the West Bank and Gaza, established as part of the Oslo Accords between Israel and the PLO. The focus on PA governance meant a marginalization of the PLO, which formally was the supreme authority. Most strikingly, as the Palestinian Authority established itself, the PNC was not convened to ratify the Israel–PLO agreements through which the Palestinian Authority was founded (Parsons 2005, 129; Dajani 1994, 8).[1]

The 1996 elections were held for president of the Palestinian Authority and the members of the Palestinian Legislative Council (PLC). This was the first time the Palestinians elected a national leadership. Although the Islamist factions boycotted, seeing the elections as part of the Oslo Accords that they were bitterly against, the voter turnout was as high as 72 per cent. Yasser Arafat, already chairman of the PLO and leader of Fatah, was elected President of the Palestinian Authority. In 2004 Arafat died and was replaced by Mahmoud Abbas as leader of Fatah, the PLO, and as President of the Palestinian Authority through elections in 2005. Abbas had been an early member of Fatah and, as head of the PLO's international department since the 1970s, he had been instrumental in forging relationships with peace-oriented Israelis.

In 2006 the second elections for the PLC were held. These elections were special because the Islamic resistance movement, Hamas, chose to participate and, in one of the largest political bombshells in Palestinian history, crushed Fatah and the PLO parties, winning 74 of 132 seats. With the Hamas victory, a crisis of legitimacy was born in Palestinian politics. In the most representative election ever held among the Palestinians, the people had chosen a party not part of the PLO, while six PLO groups, members of the Executive Committee, had won only two out of 132 seats. These small parties – Arab Liberation Front (ALF), Democratic Front for the Liberation of Palestine (DFLP), Palestine Liberation Front (PLF), Palestine Popular Struggle Front (PPSF), Palestine Peoples Party (PPP), and the Palestinian Democratic Union (FIDA) – had a plurality of the party seats in the EC but had together won only 1 per cent of the seats in the PLC (see Table 19.1). At the same time, Hamas, not a member of the PLO, had won a plurality of seats for the PLC, 57 per cent (see Figure 19.2). If the people voted for Hamas in the elections, and Hamas was not part of the PLO, while the PLO had never held any election, how could the PLO legitimately claim to represent the Palestinian people?

Table 19.1 Number of Seats in the Executive Committee of the PLO and the PLC

Party	*Seats in EC*	*Seats PLC*
Fatah	5 (28 %)	45 (41%)
Popular Front for the Liberation of Palestine (PFLP)	1 (5.5 %)	3 (4 %)
Arab Liberation Front (ALF)	1 (5.5 %)	0[1]
Democratic Front for the Liberation of Palestine (DFLP)	1 (5.5 %)	1 (1 %[2])
Palestine Liberation Front (PLF)	1 (5.5 %)	0
Palestine Popular Struggle Front (PPSF)	1 (5.5 %)	0
Palestine Peoples Party	1 (5.5 %)	1 (1 %[3])
FIDA	2 (5.5 %	0[4]
Independents	5 (28 %)	4 (--)
Hamas	0	74 (44 %)
Third Way/PNI	0	4 (5 %)

1 ALF did not run; result is for the Palestinian Arab Front which has roots in ALF.
2 Result for the Badeel coalition divided by three, from PLC elections, 2006.
3 Result for the Badeel coalition divided by three, from PLC elections, 2006.
4 Result for the Badeel coalition divided by three, from PLC elections, 2006. FIDA gained 0.2 % in the PLC elections in 1996, when the party ran on a separate list.

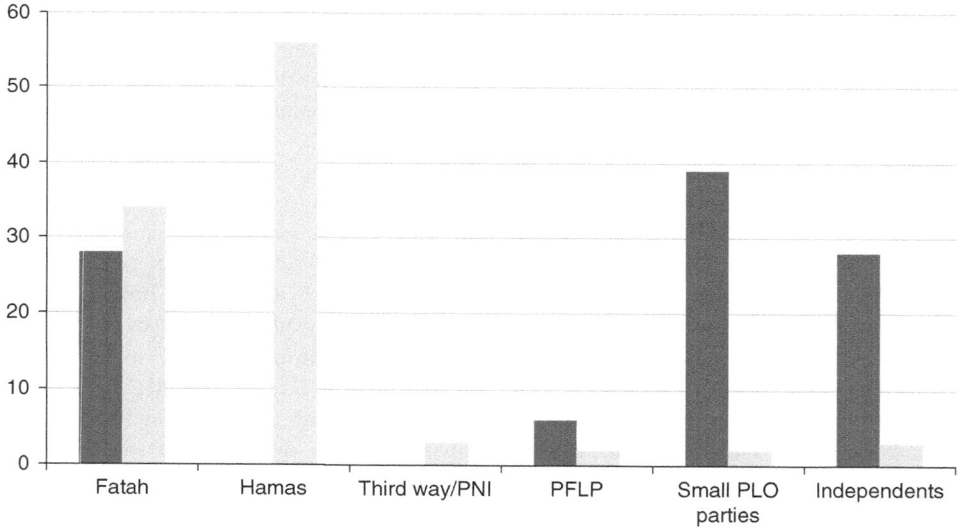

Figure 19.2 Percentage of PLO representation (black) versus elected representation for the PLC (grey).

The Road to Division

If possible, the consequences of the Hamas victory were even worse for the Palestinian Authority than for the PLO. The main donors of the Palestinian Authority – the United States and the European Union – refused to recognize – or fund – any authority Hamas was part of, including a unity government with Fatah, as long as Hamas did not recognize Israel and renounce the armed struggle. Hamas refused to relent. For Fatah and the PLO the situation was catastrophic (Macintyre 2017). The whole political project after the Oslo Accords – state-building in Gaza and the West Bank – was threatened. The Palestinian Authority institutions employed 140,000 people, one out of every four Palestinian employees, funded by international donors. Without this funding, the Palestinian Authority would collapse (Le More 2008, 179).

The semi-presidential system of the Palestinian Authority, with a prime minister responsible to the legislature, while the president retained the power to dismiss him/her, was designed for anything but a situation with one party controlling the parliament (Hamas), and another the presidency (Fatah) (Cavatorta and Elgie 2009, 22). After repeated armed skirmishes, the situation ended with Hamas ousting Fatah from Gaza in a violent, efficient military operation on 14 June 2007.

The same day as the internal fighting in Gaza ended, the President of the Palestinian Authority declared a state of emergency in the West Bank town of Ramallah. Abbas declared the formation of a new emergency government and that the Gaza government had been dissolved. In Gaza, Hamas refused to back down. The Hamas prime minister, Ismail Haniyeh, replaced the six ministers of Hamas who were from the West Bank and were unable to travel to Gaza, while the portfolios of Fatah ministers (a unity government had been in place since March 2007) were distributed among 11 Hamas ministers. From a legal point of view, Abbas could dismiss the prime minister according to the Palestinian Basic Law. However, the same law said that a sacked prime minister and his cabinet should remain in place until a new government received the confidence of an absolute majority of the legislative council. This was impossible for the Ramallah government, having lost the PLC elections. The dismissal of the Gaza government and establishment of a new government in the West Bank was thus unconstitutional (Brenner 2017, 42).

The Quartet (United Nations, Russia, European Union, and the United States) recognized the Fatah government and boycotted Hamas in Gaza. Additionally, Israel established a blockade against Gaza, letting in only the minimum needed to avoid starvation. One consequence of the boycott was that the 77,000 Palestinian Authority employees in Gaza – teachers, health workers, policemen, judges and others – were ordered to leave work if they were to receive salaries from the Palestinian Authority in Ramallah, not being permitted to work for the Hamas government (Hovdenak 2010, 23). While Hamas gradually replaced these workers with their own staff, Hamas struggled to pay their salaries. The issue of how to unite two parallel employed governmental administrative staff later became one of the obstacles in unsuccessful reconciliation talks between Fatah and Hamas.

Thus, since 14 June 2007 the Palestinians have had two governments, a Hamas-controlled government in Gaza, with a mandate from the 2006 PLC elections, and a Fatah-controlled government in the West Bank, with a mandate from the 2005 presidential elections. The 2007 confrontation created wounds in the Palestinian political community, still not healed. In fact, 2007 was the first time in 40 years, since the Israeli occupation, that more Palestinians were killed in the occupied territories as the result of Palestinian internal fighting (490), than from Israeli attacks (396) (HRW 2008, 18).

Palestinian Rule of Gaza and the West Bank after the Division

Hamas's first priority after "14/6", the date that became the reference to Hamas seizing control in Gaza, was to establish order. The armed wing of Hamas, the Izz al-din al-Qassam brigades and "the Executive Force", the police unit Hamas had established, became active in disarming the forest of armed groups and clans in Gaza. Hamas's new security forces were rendered unconstitutional by the Palestinian president in Ramallah, but for Gazans they achieved wonders; finally, peace and order came to the streets of Gaza as Hamas brought a brutal but welcome end to the "chaos of the weapons" that had plagued Gaza since the second *Intifada* (2000–2004). "The performance of the police was very bad with regard to respect for the legal procedures", said a human rights lawyer from the International Committee of Human Rights, "but citizens were glad when a thief was arrested" (HRW 2008, 61).

Once order was established, Hamas started focusing on developing its own form of rule. In September 2007 the Hamas government asked the new Palestinian legislative council to start preparing for holding its first session in Gaza. The council faced a number of challenges following Fatah boycotting it and the fact that 43 of the 74 elected Hamas members of the council had been arrested by Israel. However diminished, Hamas considered the council the legitimate and supreme authority in Palestine. To cope with the challenges of the Fatah boycott and Israeli arrests a system was organized where the names and photos of the arrested councillors were placed on their chairs during sessions. Those jailed were to be represented in one of two ways, by proxy or by present PLC members being giving the right to vote on their behalf.

On 7 November 2007, the PLC held its first session since the Hamas takeover. Although Fatah was boycotting, the Hamas-dominated PLC started working regularly, holding sessions every two weeks, subcommittee meetings every week. The government proposed bills to be discussed by the legislators, who then referred them to committees and subcommittees, where they were debated, returned to chamber, and voted on (Brenner 2017, 43). From 2007 until 2019, 50 laws were issued, most dealing with efficient governance rather than on Islamizing society.

While Hamas leaders in Gaza increasingly used legal discourse and the language of democracy to defend their right to rule, they lambasted Abbas as an authoritarian dictator out of touch with reality by not conceding that Hamas had won the 2006 election. Even harsher was the criticism of the PLO. "The Arab Liberation Front, established by Saddam Hussein, how many members do they have?" asked the Hamas veteran, Mahmod Zahar, "five or six? And then, these small groups, they have one seat each on the PLO's Executive Committee" (Tuastad 2017, 163).

But the Hamas rule, too, was criticized by opponents. In turn, Hamas crushed any opposition, especially from Fatah. According to Fatah leaders remaining in Gaza, Fatah members were, after 2007, treated as if they were members of a prohibited organization, activists being arrested, abused, and humiliated. While the situation improved slightly over the years, Fatah would not be permitted to arrange seminars, conferences, or celebrations, but it still happened that Fatah activists could be summoned by the authorities for writings on Facebook.[2]

In the West Bank, as Palestinian president Abbas lacked support in the PLC, the rule became marked by the issuing of presidential decrees. From 2007 until 2018 the president issued 230 decrees. This is more than double the number of laws issued by the first Palestinian legislative council, from 1994 until 2006 (110 laws). In December 2018 the president even ordered the dismantling of the PLC (Kuttab 2018). A week later the amputated PLC convened in Gaza and declared that the Palestinian president had lost his "legal, constitutional, moral and humanitarian capacity to continue in his post" (Asad 2019).

The Abbas regime's rule by decree pacified the West Bank political system, as no institutions, parliamentary committees and the like were convened to prepare, debate, and control laws created by decrees. The Abbas regime thus became increasingly authoritarian. But the regime was also stable and relatively peaceful, with the Palestinian security apparatus largely managing to stop efforts from the West Bank to attack Israeli targets. The challenge for Abbas, however, was not only from Hamas. It also came from within Abbas's own party, the first and historically largest Palestinian guerrilla group, Fatah.

The Main Palestinian Groups

Fatah

Fatah, a reversed acronym for *harakat al-tahrir al-watani al-filastini* (the Palestinian National Liberation Movement) was established in 1957. Since its founding and until today it has been the largest and leading guerrilla organization of the PLO and the dominant party of the Palestinian Authority. Fatah was founded with one goal: to take the lead in the armed struggle to liberate Palestine. Mobilization, not ideology, was thus what distinguished Fatah. It was a movement (*haraka*), rather than a party (*hizb*), where both communists and Muslim Brothers should feel at home (Sayigh 1997, 84). Over the years the lack of a clear ideological belonging became Fatah's strength. It meant that its leaders could make radical decisions without being bound by religious or ideological dogmas. Thus, it was Fatah who first opined for a two-state solution among the Palestinian groups, and also Fatah who became the protagonist on the Palestinian side of the Oslo process.

But Fatah also epitomizes the crisis of the PLO and the secular Palestinian national movement. When it recognized Israel and abandoned the armed struggle in 1993 it did not reform itself accordingly, still being organized as a guerrilla organization rather than a party running a mini-state. Its original internal organization combined a highly centralized hierarchal model, influenced by Leninist principles of democratic centralism with a small-scale, cell-based local structure, all combined with seniority as the principle to climb in the internal power structure. The more years in Fatah, the more "points" a person would get, with higher positions in the internal power hierarchy requiring progressively more points. The principle of seniority to climb up the power hierarchy worked when the need for secrecy was crucial, but after the return of Fatah and the PLO to Palestine it was anachronistic, with Fatah's leadership now older and increasingly out of touch. By 2020 Fatah and PLO leader Mahmoud Abbas was 85 years old; Fatah's general secretary, Farouk Kaddoumi, was 89 years old; and Fatah's speaker of the PNC, Salim Zanoun, was 86 years old.

These features created rifts inside Fatah, not only between Fatah's old guard and its crown princes, but also among the old guard themselves. Thus Farouk Kaddoumi, the general secretary, claimed in a press conference in Jordan in 2009 that he could prove that Mahmoud Abbas had poisoned Yasser Arafat to death in 2004 (Lynch 2009). Abbas, for his sake, later claimed that his rival for the leadership in Fatah and frontrunner in the 2006 elections, the former intelligence chief in Gaza Mahmoud Dahlan, had been behind the alleged killing (Hass 2014). The accusations against Dahlan, who found it safest to leave Palestine for the United Arab Emirates in 2009, appeared to be related to Dahlan's role in leading the internal opposition in Fatah against Abbas. Dahlan, together with Salam Fayad, the prime minister of the Palestinian Authority between 2007 and 2013, the most popular Palestinian politician among Western diplomats, and Yasser Abed Rabbo, the general secretary of the PLO, were accused by Abbas of preparing a coup against him. Fayad and Abed Rabbo were consequently fired by Abbas. Abed Rabbo responded by saying that Abbas suffered from "hallucinations" and wanted to establish a one-man-rule in the West Bank (Magid 2015).

Even more challenging for Abbas was the situation inside Fatah in Gaza. With most of the Fatah elite evacuating Gaza during the Hamas takeover in 2007, Fatah members in Gaza, especially in the refugee camps where Fatah members had always been radical and hard to control, found themselves equally alienated by Hamas and the Abbas regime in Ramallah. Many would follow Dahlan's initiative, the Democratic Reform Current (DRC). The DRC was meant to work within Fatah, for democratic reforms and to end the division, said Ibrahim al-Musadar from DRC in Gaza.[3] But without such reforms, Fatah could be split, al-Musadar warned: "Our principles and culture are Fatah, and we want one unified list representing Fatah in the next Palestinian elections. But if this is not done we will be forced to run a separate list".

If anything, the experienced Abbas knew how to handle internal challenges. As internal discontent and complaints gained momentum, he finally called for the convening of Fatah's sixth national congress. According to the statutes of Fatah the congress was supposed to take place every fifth year. However, 20 years had gone by since the last Fatah congress when it convened in Bethlehem in 2009 with 1,400 delegates. Seven years later, in 2016, the seventh Fatah congress was held in Ramallah with 2,000 delegates. The congresses revitalized Fatah's wide apparatus through a comprehensive internal elections process to choose delegates in constituencies inside and outside Palestine. The process largely renewed the legitimacy of the Fatah leadership in Ramallah, despite Fatah's problems in Gaza (Melhem 2016). In the West Bank, after the 2016 congress, the support for Dahlan and the DRC dwindled.

The congresses also gave Abbas the mandate to continue Fatah's diplomatic strategy on the international stage that had replaced the armed struggle. The strategy produced some results, as Palestine in 2011 became a full member of UNESCO (the United Nations Educational, Scientific and Cultural Organization) and a non-member observer state of the United Nations in 2012. This enabled Palestine to engage with the International Criminal Court and to seek accountability for Israeli actions in the Occupied Territories. These achievements came at the expense of the relationship with the United States, which strongly disliked Palestinian unilateralism. The relationship further deteriorated under the Trump Administration. In 2017 Abbas decided to severe all contacts with United States diplomats, calling Trump a "lost cause" (*Times of Israel* 2017). The Trump Administration had cut aid to Palestinian refugees, recognized Jerusalem (including the occupied east part) as Israel's capital, and closed the PLO's Washington offices, while the United States ambassador to Israel had publicly supported the settlement movement. In 2019 Abbas announced that the Palestinian boycott of the United States administration would continue.

Abbas remained popular in Europe. His autocratic tendencies were largely forgiven as he remained consistent in renouncing the armed struggle. But with Abbas in power, prospects for Fatah reconciling with its Islamist nemesis, Hamas, remained meagre.

Hamas

When the Islamic resistance movement, Hamas, was formally founded in January 1988 (Baconi 2018, 20), it was as an armed Islamist movement with roots in the Muslim Brotherhood (MB). Sheikh Ahmed Yassin, co-founder and first leader of Hamas, was the preeminent figure of the Muslim Brotherhood in Gaza after 1967. Yassin had learnt from the experiences of the Egyptian Muslim Brotherhood that as long as focus was on preaching and education, authorities would leave the Islamists alone. As Yassin saw it, the liberation of Palestine could only result from a phased struggle. A period of *dawa*, of Muslim preaching and education, and a subsequent period of Islamic institution building, had to predate the launching of armed jihad (Mishal and Sela 2000, 18–19).

Dawa implied social work, establishing the Islamic Center in Gaza, (*al-mujamma' al-Islami*), to help the poor and the ones in need. This made Islamists popular at the grassroots level. But dawa also meant fighting secularism in all its shapes. Not only could females be attacked over lack of modesty, or shops in Gaza attacked for selling alcohol, but also communists, PFLP and other PLO members would be confronted by affiliates of the Islamic Center (Filiu 2012, 64). Some of the enduring scepticism within Fatah and the PLO towards Hamas has its roots in these experiences.

With the outburst of the Intifada in December 1987 the Islamists could no longer be bystanders, jihad eventually replacing the period of dawa. Hamas largely followed their own, more violent track, during the Intifada, without coordinating with the PLO-affiliated Unified National Leadership. The lack of coordination exploded after the 1993 Oslo Accords, widely regarded an act of treason within Hamas. Hamas would use all means to destroy the Oslo process, most infamously by launching suicide bombings inside Israel. The violence made Hamas targeted by security forces from the Palestinian Authority and Israel alike. In March 2004 Israel assassinated Ahmed Yassin, the leader of Hamas, and a month later his successor, Abdel Aziz al-Rantisi, both in Gaza. The leader of Hamas's politburo, based in Damascus to reduce the risk of all the leadership being wiped out, Khaled Mishal, then became the new Hamas leader.

After 2005 a more pragmatic Hamas emerged, pursuing internal Palestinian politics and not only armed struggle against Israel (Hroub 2006). Thus, Hamas decided to participate in the 2006 PLC elections, which it had boycotted in 1996. After their election victory and subsequent ousting of Fatah from Gaza in 2007, Hamas found itself in a position that looked embarrassingly similar to the one they had criticized Fatah for: having to balance governing and resistance, and having to control the violence and armed resistance of others.

When Hamas changed positions, like participating in elections, the decisions seemed to be well-anchored within the movement. Every four years, Hamas regularly elected its higher council (*shura*), politburo, and leader through secret elections in Gaza, the West Bank, and in the prisons inside and outside Palestine (Gunning 2007, 102).

This did not, however, spare Hamas of internal tensions. With its leader and politburo based in Damascus after the assassinations of Yassin and al-Rantisi, the distance and different priorities between local operatives and commanders in exile started to wear on their relationship. The rift was further deepened with the Hamas takeover of Gaza in 2007 and the 2011 "Arab Spring", where Hamas aligned with the losing sides in Egypt and Syria, the Muslim Brotherhood and the democratic opposition in Syria, respectively. This alienated Iran, the main sponsor of Hamas's armed branch, the Izz ad-Din al-Qassam Brigades. Inevitably, the power centre inside Hamas was pulled back to Gaza.

In the 2017 internal elections the prime minister of the Hamas government in Gaza, Ismail Haniyeh, was elected the new Hamas leader, replacing Mishal. In addition, Yahia Sinwar, a leader of the al-Qassam brigades, who had served 22 years in Israeli prison until released in the 2011 prison swap for the captive Israeli soldier Gilad Shalit, was elected the new Hamas leader of Gaza (Saleh 2018, 59). Khaled Mishal, head of Hamas from 2004 to 2017, had been a respected leader in Hamas, with analytical, diplomatic and political skills largely unrivalled inside the movement. But he lacked the street credentials of Sinwar and Haniyeh, both sons of Gazan refugee camps (Khan Younis and Beach camp) where they still lived. It also meant that the Gaza-based leadership of Sinwar and Haniyeh would have stronger authority over Hamas's armed forces of which Sinwar was the commander.

The year 2017 saw another significant development inside Hamas. For the first time since its infamous 1988 charter, notorious for its many anti-Semitic references, a new political program was launched (Hroub 2017). Two of the most striking points in the program were, first, the acceptance of a Palestinian state within the 1967 borders, which Hamas hoped would improve its relations with the West. Second, Hamas rebranded itself as an Islamist national movement rather than a branch of the Muslim Brotherhood. The MB was considered a terrorist organization by the new Egyptian regime, and Hamas hoped to remove this main hurdle in their relationship with Egypt.

With the change of the Hamas leadership, the issue of reforming the PLO, a high priority of the former leader Khaled Mishal since the beginning of the 2010s, appeared a secondary priority. The priority was rather to end the division between the West Bank and Gaza and reconcile with Fatah. Yahia Sinwar, the new Gaza leader, said he would "break the neck of all those who do not want reconciliation, from Hamas or others" (Saleh 2018, 53). One asset in reconciliation efforts was that Sinwar was an old acquaintance of Muhammad Dahlan, the leader of the Fatah reformist movement, both born and raised in the Khan Younis camp in Gaza. With money from the United Arab Emirates, Dahlan agreed with Sinwar on an initiative to heal some of the wounds of the 2007 Fatah-Hamas violence. Through the reconciliation project families of victims would receive $50,000 in compensation money, in public reconciliation ceremonies (*sulha*) between Hamas and the families in Gaza.

For Hamas the red line of reconciling with Fatah was "protection of the resistance". Hamas was reportedly willing to follow the approach of Hezbollah in Lebanon, being out of government but without giving up its weapons. Since its takeover of Gaza, Hamas's armed forces had been considerably strengthened and transformed. The armed forces were divided into the artillery forces (offensive) of mortars and rockets, and the ground forces. The ground forces numbered 15,000 to 20,000 men, divided into three geographic brigades in the north, centre and south of the Gaza Strip (Cohen and White 2009). Three wars with Israel, in 2008, 2012, and 2014, where three to four thousand Gazans were killed, had further developed Hamas's military experience and capabilities (Eldar 2014). Military strength was also an implicit part of the Hezbollah-model. In Lebanon, the state was simply not strong enough to challenge Hezbollah. Equally, however, as much as Fatah and Abbas were against applying the Hezbollah-model in Palestine, they would hardly have any choice but to accept it. Ironically, the Hamas regime has in recent years come to face its own version of the Hezbollah challenge in Gaza, with the increasingly strong Palestinian Islamic Jihad.

Palestinian Islamic Jihad

When Hamas seized power in Gaza and confiscated the weapons of all groups to end the chaos on the streets, it made an exception for the Palestinian Islamic Jihad (PIJ). The consequence was a tremendous growth in PIJs strength in Gaza. PIJ had capitalized from Iran's ceasing to support Hamas after their break with the Syrian regime. The PIJ did not break with Syria and thereby experienced a massive increase in support. From Iran.

The PIJ was founded in Egypt by Palestinian students in late 1979. Fathi Shaqaqi, founder and its first leader, inspired by the Iranian revolution and Egyptian Islamist radicalism, left the Muslim Brotherhood to form an Islamist, jihadist, and at the same time nationalist armed resistance group (Skare 2019). In 1981, after the murder by the Egyptian Islamic Jihad of the Egyptian president, Anwar Sadat, Shaqaqi and the PIJ left for Gaza. After the first PIJ operation in 1984, it later engaged in attacks inside Israel. The PIJ was responsible for what is regarded as the first Palestinian suicide attack in Israel, a bus attack in 1989 killing 16 civilians.

In spite of its recent growth, the PIJ distinguished itself from Hamas and Fatah by not intending to be a mass movement. Its ideology was inspired by the idea of the Islamist ideologist Sayyid Qutb on the Islamic vanguard, that is, of an elite front group that paved the way for the masses to join. The PIJ called for immediate jihad against Israel, parting with the MB thinking of a phased struggle. Where Hamas saw Islamization as necessary to have liberation, the PIJ saw liberation as necessary to have Islamization (Skare 2019).

As a vanguard organization, the PIJ was vulnerable to setbacks. Thus, when the PIJ leader Shaqaqi was assassinated by Israel in Malta in 1995, the PIJ struggled to survive, especially in the West Bank, where its cells were disclosed and its members arrested. Ramadan Shallah, a professor of economics at the University of South Florida, replaced Shaqaqi. Shallah established himself and the PIJ headquarters in Beirut and Damascus. In Gaza, with Fatah's weakened position, the PIJ became the second-largest Palestinian group. At its peak, a month after the 2014 Gaza-Israel war, 31 per cent of Gazans said they supported the PIJ (al-Ghoul 2014).[4] As the PIJ grew larger, growth pains inevitably followed. Reports started surfacing of internal discontent with non-transparent internal procedures for appointments to positions, hierarchical decision-making mechanisms, and mismanagement of funds. The PIJ consequently changed its organizational structure by establishing a politburo and in 2014 started preparations for a general conference (Balousha 2014). The conference was called off as the PIJ entered a crisis following a request from Iran for the PIJ to express their support for the Houthis and denounce the Saudis in Yemen, which the PIJ declined to do. Iran then cut its aid to the PIJ. While the PIJ had never had so many fighters on its payroll, all of a sudden it was unable to pay them (Balousha 2015). The coffers were later gradually opened following efforts of the exile leadership, including PIJ's new leader, Ziad Nakhalah, who replaced Shallah, who had suffered a stroke in 2018.

In October 2019 the PIJ angered Israel and Hamas alike, when they fired rockets at Israel while Hamas were in Cairo negotiating a long-term ceasefire with Israel, and after Egypt had just released a number of imprisoned PIJ members. Israel subsequently assassinated the PIJ military commander, Abu Ata, responsible for the rocket attack. In response, the PIJ fired 500 mostly makeshift rockets against Israel. It was the first time Israel responded to a massive rocket attack by not bombing Hamas targets.

The PIJ has accumulated an enormous amount of rockets in Gaza, reportedly having a larger arsenal than Hamas. Hamas, however, has more than five times as many armed men as the PIJ in Gaza. The PIJ thus needed to balance its relations with the Islamist rulers in Gaza and its wish of pursuing the armed struggle against Israel. Part of PIJ's success formula had been the image of an organization that was above the internal Palestinian skirmishes, one that publicly insisted on mending the divided Palestinian house. The PIJ leadership liked to call it principled pragmatism, but opponents criticized the group for having so-called "yes, but" positions (Al-Ghoul 2015). The PIJ would pay lip service to what otherwise was agreed with Hamas and other Palestinian factions but would nevertheless act unilaterally.

Challenges with balancing opposite demands were also something the second-largest PLO group, the Popular Front for the Liberation of Palestine (PFLP), experienced from time to time.

The Popular Front for the Liberation of Palestine

The Palestinian political scene has had a number of new parties established in the West Bank, but these have mostly been connected to personalities – like the Palestinian National Initiative of Mustapha Barghuti – and have failed to become larger political movements. Moreover, old member groups, like the Iraqi-founded Arab Liberation Front, has remained PLO members and also members of the Abbas government in the West Bank, while lacking popular support and being completely dependent on PLO funds for their political survival. An exception to this picture is the PFLP, which has maintained its initial political program of support for armed struggle while also being part of the Palestinian political order, being active in both the PLC and the PNC.

The Marxist-Leninist PFLP was founded in 1967 by George Habash, its leader until 2000. Habash, a Christian working as a doctor in Palestinian camps in Jordan, had been a founder of the Arab National Movement (ANM) in 1951 (Strindberg 2000). The ANM strongly supported Egyptian president Gamal Abdel Nasser and regarded radical Pan-Arabism as the way to liberate Palestine. After the Israeli occupation of the West Bank and Gaza in 1967, Palestinians lost their belief in pan-Arabism and that the ANM would liberate Palestine. The founders and members of the PFLP, however, were distinguished by still believing in wakening the Arab masses to topple reactionary Arab regimes and unite the Arabs against Israel. The PFLP saw it as their mission to lead this struggle, and their recipe for popular mobilization was violence. The PFLP became the group closest associated with violent Palestinian operations: radical, left-wing terrorism, including assassinations, also of civilians and prisoners, and spectacular aeroplane hijackings. While becoming a pariah on the international stage, the PFLP, rivalled only by Fatah, made the Palestinian *fedayee* (guerrilla soldier) the hero of the impoverished Palestinian underclass found in the Palestinian refugee camps throughout the Middle East, while at the same time appealing to radical youth and students. Their offices in the various Middle East Palestinian refugee camps could hardly absorb all those who came to join the struggle. When the PFLP survived the dissolution of the Soviet Union and the fading attraction of Marxist ideology in the 1990s, it was not because they reformed but rather because they stayed true to their ideals. This included calling for democratization of the PLO, but also for continuing the armed struggle against Israel, as formulated by the PFLP.

In August 2001 Israel assassinated Abu Ali Mustafa, the leader of PFLP who had replaced Habash, who had retired due to ill health in 2000. Three months after the killing of Ali Mustafa a PFLP cell assassinated the right-wing Israeli minister, Rehavam Ze'evi in a Jerusalem hotel. This internationally condemned killing led to considerable admiration in the Palestinian street and from Palestinian armed factions. It was the first time a Palestinian faction had killed a serving Israeli minister. As a result of the assassination PFLP leader Ahmad Sadat was arrested by Palestinian Authority forces and transferred to their prison in Jericho. In 2006 the prison came under attack from Israel, shelling the compound and eventually capturing Sadat. The surrender of the Palestinian Authority's security forces during the capture inflicted a deep wound in the PFLP's relationship with Fatah and the Palestinian Authority, regarding the lack of resistance as an act of betrayal (JPS 2014, 49). Sadat was sentenced by an Israeli military court to 30 years in prison, and is today one of the most vocal leaders of the Palestinian prisoners' movement.

In 2006 Sadat was one of three PFLP candidates elected to the PLC. The PFLP won 4.5 per cent, being much stronger in urban than rural areas, winning 10 per cent in Bethlehem. The PFLP's elected representatives were, in addition to the imprisoned Sadat, Jamil Majdalawi in Gaza and Khalida Jarrar from Ramallah. Jarrar gained wide media attention and sympathy among Palestinians after being arrested by Israel and imprisoned for 15 months in 2014 over PFLP membership and alleged "incitement". In 2019 she was imprisoned yet again, then released in 2021 following 20 months in administrative detention without trial.

According to Jarrar, the main political issues for PFLP was the renewal of the PLO, including elections for the PNC, the president, and the PNC to elect a new executive committee. A reformed PNC should not shy away from radical decisions, said Jarrar, such as abandoning the Oslo Accords and even dissolving the Palestinian Authority if it failed to serve national Palestinian interests (JPS 2017, 43).

Although the PLO needed the PFLP for its legitimacy, the PFLP's criticism of the PLO leader and Palestinian Authority president Mahmoud Abbas was occasionally met with repercussions. When the PFLP urged Abbas to resign in 2016, he blocked disbursements to the PFLP from the PLO's National Fund, a main income source of the PFLP. When the PFLP renewed criticism in 2017, Abbas again suspended disbursements (Saleh 2018, 62). The cutting of funds was indicative of a form of rule that also distinguished the relationship between the PLO leader in Ramallah and Fatah and PLO groups in exile. If criticism of the leadership became too harsh, the funds paying the salaries of PLO exiles would be cut. This had a strong impact especially on the loyalty of the smallest PLO parties that had kept their quotas in the refugee camp committees, despite diminishing support within the refugee communities where they operated.

Refugee Representation

The Palestinian refugees have, since the Oslo Accords, largely been lacking specific representation to fight for their interests, with the PNC dormant and the PLO in the shadow of the Palestinian Authority. Within the camps outside Palestine, the refugees are only allowed to organize freely in Lebanon, although their civil and legal rights are far more restricted outside the camps than in Syria and Jordan.

The camp leadership, the so-called popular committees, were originally established in 1969 following an agreement with the Lebanese government granting the PLO autonomy over the camps. These committees are today either the old PLO groups or of the so-called Alliance of Palestinian Forces, composed of Hamas, PIJ and pro-Syrian groups not being members of the PLO (Strindberg 2000). The resistance-rhetoric of both forms of committees have increasingly alienated camp residents, sensing that the committees do not care about their daily lives and struggles. This has led to demonstrations inside camps, calling for elected camp leaderships. There have also been regular outbursts of violence, especially in Ain al-Hilwe, the largest and most unruly camp in Lebanon. Attempts at establishing a joint security apparatus of all armed groups in the camp, including al-Qaida-supporting jihadist groups, have been only partially successful (Sogge 2017).

Conclusion

The importance of having all main political actors integrated into the same political system to avoid internal violent conflict can hardly be overestimated. A political elite is a group or formation with the power to influence political outcomes (Higley and Burton 2006). When a political elite is excluded from participating in the political process, this almost always leads to violent political conflict, as in Iraq when the Ba'ath party was excluded by the Americans after the invasion in 2003. If violent internal conflicts are to be avoided there must be agreement on the decision-making process, elections, procedures for change of power, and the like. Most important is to agree that on some issues one simply cannot agree. One nevertheless has to find a solution.

With Hamas and the PIJ out of the PLO, Fatah fearing to lose control if the Islamists are admitted – and with the national Palestinian Authority being divided with one government in Gaza and one in the West Bank – Palestinian politics is deeply fragmented. The Palestinians have clearly not found a way to agree on how to not agree. The most obvious way out of the current stalemate is to have the PLO reformed, have the Islamic groups included through elections for the Palestinian National Council or another formula like the quota system. This is easier said than done. For Fatah, no new group can enter the PLO without accepting its program and its agreements, including recognizing Israel and abandoning the armed struggle.

One alternative to immediate PLO membership is an alternative framework where all the main Palestinian political groups are members. In fact, such a framework already exists. In 2005 the so-called Activation and Development Committee (ADC) was established, composed of the Executive Committee of the PLO and the Islamist factions, PIJ and Hamas, with all their general secretaries participating in regular meetings. These meetings led to the breakthrough Cairo agreement in 2005, opening for elections for the PLO and PA, with Hamas participation, although the PNC elections were suspended. With the Arab Spring in 2011, after being suspended due to the 2007 division, the ADC reactivated its work. Again, a substantial agreement on political inclusion and democratization of the Palestinian Authority and PLO was produced. This agreement, too, was not implemented, but the fact remained that inclusion and participation could increase unity and lead to political settlements. The former Palestinian Authority prime minister, Salam Fayad, as well as Hamas and PIJ, later advocated related ideas of a permanent transitory committee of the main Palestinian groups until the PLO has been reformed. But for this to happen, Hamas waits for the replacement of the 85-year old Fatah, Palestinian Authority and PLO leader Mahmoud Abbas, whom they regard as the main obstacle to the transitory committee starting to work. Until then the "managing of failure", with both sides blaming each other, is likely to continue (Saleh 2018, 49).

Recommended Readings

Kimmerling, B., and J. S. Migdal. 2003. *The Palestinian People: A History*. Cambridge, MA: Harvard University Press.

Macintyre, D. 2017. *Gaza: Preparing for Dawn*. New York: Simon and Schuster.

Sayigh, Y. 1997. *Armed Struggle and the Search for State: The Palestinian National Movement, 1949–1993*. Oxford: Oxford University Press.

Tamimi, A. 2011. *Hamas: A History from Within*. Northampton, MA: Olive Branch Press.

Notes

1 PNC did not convene until spring 1996, but then it was to change the charter of the PLO. Insufficient adherence to procedure has contributed to doubts about the legality of the Gaza PNC session in 1996.

2 Elected PLC member and Fatah revolutionary council member Faisal Abu Shahla, interview with Hani al-Dada, Gaza, December 2019.

3 Interview with Hani al-Dada, Gaza, November 2019.

4 In Gaza 31% supported the PIJ, 44% supported Hamas and 19% supported Fatah according to the poll carried out by the Watan Center for Studies and Research in the Gaza Strip: https://paltoday.ps/ar/post/215762/ارتفاع-نسبة-المؤيدين-لأداء-حركة-الجهاد-الاسلامي-خلال-العدوان-على-غزة

Questions for Discussion

(1) What are the main barriers against achieving Palestinian reconciliation?

(2) Fatah and Hamas have both gone through some important changes throughout their history. What are the main changes? Discuss similarities and differences between the changes within the two groups.

(3) What is the problem of violence in Palestinian politics, and why is the question of violence so divisive?

(4) What have been the PLO's greatest successes and failures?

(5) What is "the Hezbollah-model" and how is it relevant in the Palestinian context?

References

Al-Ghoul, A. 2014. "Islamic Jihad's popularity grows after Gaza war." *Al-Monitor*, 25 September. Available at: www.al-monitor.com/pulse/originals/2014/09/islamic-jihad-movement-gaza-palestine.html.

Al-Ghoul, A. 2015. "Islamic Jihad takes mediator role between Hamas, Fatah." *Al-Monitor*, 26 January. Available at: www.al-monitor.com/pulse/originals/2015/01/palestinian-gaza-islamic-jihad-mediation-hamas-fatah.html.

Asad, M. 2019. "Palestinian Legislative Council votes to end Abbas' mandate." *Memo, Middle East Monitor*, 9 January Available at: www.middleeastmonitor.com/20190109-palestinian-legislative-council-votes-to-end-abbas-mandate/.

Baconi, T. 2018. *Hamas Contained: The Rise and Pacification of Palestinian Resistance* Stanford, CA: Stanford University Press.

Balousha, H. 2014. "Islamic Jihad members push for internal reform." *Al-Monitor*, 15 April. Available at: www.almonitor.com/pulse/originals/2014/04/islamic-jihad-internal-reform-elections-palestine.html.

Balousha, H. 2015. "Islamic Jihad's coffers run dry." *Al-Monitor*, 2 June. Available at: www.al-monitor.com/pulse/originals/2015/06/palestine-islamic-jihad-financial-crisis-money-iran-hezbolla.html.

Brenner, B. 2017. *Gaza under Hamas*. London: I.B. Tauris.
Cavatorta, F., and R. Elgie. 2009. "The Impact of Semi-presidentialism on Governance in the Palestinian Authority." *Parliamentary Affairs* 63:1, 22–40.
Cohen, Y., and J. White. 2009. *Hamas in Combat*. Policy Focus #97, October. Washington, DC: The Washington Institute for Near East Policy. Available at: www.washingtoninstitute.org/media/3416.
Dajani, B. 1994. "The September 1993 Israeli-PLO Documents: A Textual Analysis." *Journal of Palestine Studies* 23:3, 5–23.
Eldar, S. 2014. "Hamas, the first Palestinian army." *Al-Monitor*, 23 July. Available at: www.al-monitor.com/pulse/originals/2014/07/hamas-terror-organization-recruit-army-gaza-is-idf-tunnels.html.
Ferziger, J. 1993. "Israel recognizes PLO, which renounces violence." *UPI archives*, 9 September. Available at: www.upi.com/Archives/1993/09/09/Israel-recognizes-PLO-which-renounces-violence/4937747547200/.
Filiu, J. P. 2012. "The Origins of Hamas: Militant Legacy or Israeli Tool?" *Journal of Palestine Studies* 41:3, 54–70.
Gunning, J. 2007. *Hamas in Politics: Democracy, Religion, Violence*. New York: Columbia University Press.
Hass, A. 2014. "Internal Rift Rattles Abbas' Fatah (Yet Again)." *Haaretz*, 17 March. Available at: www.haaretz.com/.premium-internal-rift-rattles-fatah-again-1.5334615.
Higley, J., and M. Burton. 2006. *Elite Foundations of Liberal Democracy*. Oxford: Rowman & Littlefield Publishers.
Hovdenak, A. 2010. *The Public Services under Hamas in Gaza: Islamic Revolution or Crisis Management?* Oslo: PRIO.
Hroub, K. 2006. "A 'New Hamas' through Its New Documents." *Journal of Palestine Studies* 35:4, 6–27.
Hroub, K. 2017. "A Newer Hamas? The Revised Charter." *Journal of Palestine Studies* 46:4, 100–111.
HRW. 2008. *Internal Fight: Palestinian Abuses in Gaza and the West Bank*. New York: Human Rights Watch.
JPS. 2014. "Interview with Ahmad Sadat: Leading from Prison, Ending Negotiations, and Rebuilding the Resistance." *Journal of Palestine Studies* 43:4, 40–56.
JPS. 2017. "Interview with Khalida Jarrar: The Israeli Occupation Must End." *Journal of Palestine Studies* 43:4, 40–56.
Kuttab, D. 2018. "Why Was the Palestinian Legislative Council Dismantled?" *Al-Monitor*, 30 December. Available at: www.almonitor.com/pulse/originals/2018/12/palestinian-legislative-council-abbas-dismantle-hamas.html.
Le More, A. 2008. *International Assistance to the Palestinians after Oslo*. Oxon: Routledge.
Lynch, M. 2009. "PLO Official: Did Abu Mazen Conspire to Kill Yasir Arafat?" *Foreign Policy*, 14 July. Available at: https://foreignpolicy.com/2009/07/14/plo-official-did-abu-mazen-conspire-to-kill-yasir-arafat/.
Macintyre, D. 2017. *Gaza. Preparing for Dawn*. New York: Simon and Schuster.
Magid, A. 2015. "Dismissed PLO leader denies Dahlan coup plot." *Al-Monitor*, 24 July. Available at: www.al-monitor.com/pulse/originals/2015/07/palestine-plo-yasser-abed-rabbo-mahmoud-abbas.html.
Melhem, A. 2016. "Abbas Comes Out of Fatah Congress Stronger than Ever." *Al-Monitor*, 14 December. Available at: http://December 14 2016. www.al-monitor.com/pulse/originals/2016/12/fatah-congress-abbas-senior-leaders-no-change.html.
Mishal, S., and A. Sela. 2000. *The Palestinian Hamas*. New York: Columbia University Press.
Parsons, N. 2005. *The Politics of the Palestinian Authority*. New York: Routledge.
Parsons, N. 2013. "The Palestine Liberation Organization." In: *The Routledge Handbook on the Israeli-Palestinian Conflict*, eds. J. Peters and D. Newman. New York: Routledge, 209–222.
Rubenberg, C. 1983. "The Civilian Infrastructure of the Palestine Liberation Organization." *Journal of Palestine Studies* 12:3, 54–78.
Sayigh, Y. 1997. *Armed Struggle and the Search for State: The Palestinian National Movement, 1949–1993*. Oxford: Oxford University Press.
Saleh, M. M. 2018. *The Palestine Strategic Report 2016–2017*. Beirut: Al-Zaytouna Centre for Studies and Consultations.
Skare, E. 2019. *Faith, Awareness, and Revolution: A History of Palestinian Islamic Jihad*. PhD dissertation. Oslo: Department of Culture Studies and Oriental Languages, Faculty of Humanities, University of Oslo.
Sogge, E. L. 2017. *No One Can Rule Us. Politics of Exile in Refugee Camp 'Ayn al-Hilwe, Capital of Palestinian Diaspora (1993–2017)*. PhD dissertation. Oslo: Department of Culture Studies and Oriental Languages, Faculty of Humanities, University of Oslo.

Strindberg, A. 2000. "The Damascus-Based Alliance of Palestinian Forces: A Primer." *Journal of Palestine Studies* 29:3, 60–76.

Times of Israel. 2017. "Seeing Trump as 'Lost Cause,' Abbas Said to Widen Boycott to US Consular Staff." 24 December. Available at: www.timesofisrael.com/seeing-us-as-lost-cause-abbas-said-to-extend-boycott-to-low-level-officials/.

Tuastad, D. 2012. *Democratizing the PLO: Prospects and Obstacles*. Oslo: Peace Research Institute Oslo (PRIO).

Tuastad, D. 2017. "The Violent Rise of Palestine's Lost Generation." *Middle East Critique* 26:2, 159–169.

YLS. 2008. "The Palestinian National Charter: Resolutions of the Palestine National Council July 1–17, 1968." *The Avalon Project, Documents in Law, History and Diplomacy*. Yale Law School. Available at: https://avalon.law.yale.edu/20th_century/plocov.asp.

20

ISRAELI DOMESTIC POLITICS AND THE CHALLENGES OF PEACEMAKING

Oded Haklai

> Israel has no foreign policy, only domestic politics.
>
> *Henry Kissinger, 1975 (Sheehan 1976, 53)*

Although overstating the absence of a formulated approach towards foreign relations, Henry Kissinger's often-cited observation serves to highlight the profound constraints that domestic politics impose on Israel's conduct in international affairs in general, and in the Palestinian-Israeli conflict in particular. Although influential in many other countries, Kissinger found the dynamics of domestic Israeli politics to present a particularly exigent hindrance for conflict resolution. There are several reasons why Israeli domestic politics have been consequential for peacemaking. First, there are divergent worldviews within Israeli society about its appropriate borders. Furthermore, the threshold for translating these worldviews into political power is relatively low due to Israel's electoral rules and multi-party political system. Finally, the fragmented political system has provided hardliners and opponents of compromise with a veto power throughout most of the time that has passed since the 1967 War.

This chapter is organized as follows. First, the main worldviews of the relevant political actors are described. The chapter then proceeds to describe the domestic political institutions in Israel. On this basis, the subsequent section discusses how the action taken by relevant political actors is explored, paying particular attention to the period since the Declaration of Principles on Palestinian Self-Rule, commonly known as the "Oslo Accord", signed between Israel and the Palestine Liberation Organization (PLO) in September 1993.

Domestic Actors and Their Worldviews

No society is monolithic, and Israeli society is no different. When it comes to worldviews on the Israeli-Palestinian conflict, it is possible to distinguish between two broad political camps: those who support compromise over the territories Israel conquered from Jordan in the 1967 War (the West Bank/Judea and Samaria) and those who support holding on to the entire territory.

To a large extent, these diverging worldviews are premised on different ways of approaching competing values and ideological commitments. In a nutshell, Jewish nationalism, or Zionism, has always faced a challenge trying to reconcile (1) the objective of redeeming the

DOI: 10.4324/9780429027376-25

putative ancient homeland with (2) the desire to express Jewish national self-determination in a state that has a Jewish majority and a democratic regime. The tension between the two arose because of the large Palestinian Arab population inhabiting territory presumed to be the homeland. The need to consider trade-offs between redeeming the "Whole Land of Israel" and a Jewish democracy pre-dates the establishment of the state. Zionist leaders in the 1930s and 1940s had to make decisions about partition plans proposed by members of the international community, such as the Peel Plan of 1937 (Biger 2008; Galnoor 2009). When the United Nations General Assembly passed Resolution 181 in November 1947, calling for the partition of Palestine into a Jewish state and an Arab state, the decision of the leadership of the Zionist movement to embrace the resolution did not receive unanimous support, as many, including the Revisionist Zionists (progenitor of the Likud political party), objected to territorial partition, prioritizing territorial wholeness over other values. Nevertheless, in the period between Israel's Declaration of Independence in 1948 and the 1967 War, this issue was not salient because Jordan conquered much of the land designated by the United Nations partition plan for the Arab state, annexed it, and labelled it the West Bank (of the Jordan River).

The outcome of the 1967 War – which saw Israel capture the West Bank from Jordan, the Gaza Strip and the Sinai Peninsula from Egypt, and the Golan Heights from Syria – awakened the dormant discussion in Israeli society about the appropriate location of Israel's borders. These debates have been particularly pertinent for the West Bank because historically all Zionist streams recognized this territory as part of the putative homeland (Shelef 2010). Now that Israel exercised territorial control over this disputed land, however, the question of what to do with the territories gained concreteness.

Speaking in broad strokes, three main blocks of opinion can be identified. The first is the Israeli centre-left, led for many decades by the Labor Party, which typically viewed the acquired territories as a bargaining chip that could be traded away in a peace agreement. The party's approach followed the "land-for-peace" formula that premised United Nations Security Council Resolution 242 for the resolution of the Arab-Israeli conflict, adopted in November 1967. Indeed, according to Alan Dowty, this resolution "has been the point of departure for all subsequent Arab-Israeli diplomacy" (Dowty 2017, 117).

Although historically not willing to concede the entire conquered territories, Laborites have traditionally viewed at least those parts populated by the local Palestinians as dispensable, indeed undesirable. Levi Eshkol, prime minister at the time of the 1967 War, expressed this sentiment in a famous quote to his colleagues: "I get it. You want the dowry, but you don't like the bride" (Gordon 2007, 453), relaying that the Palestinian "bride" would significantly change the demographic character of the state and potentially lead to tension between the Jewishness and the democratic character of the state. That reflected how the Labor Party, governing until 1977, calculated the challenge of reconciling (1) the demographic Jewishness of the state, (2) democracy, and (3) control over the entire territory perceived as the homeland. If Israel was to retain control over the entire territory, it would need to compromise on one of the other two values. Labor and the political parties to its left prioritized a Jewish democracy over territorial aggrandization.

On the political right-of-centre, on the other hand, the worldview has been different. Led by the Herut Party, precursor of the Likud, the prioritized objective of this political camp has been territorial maximalization, or the Whole Land of Israel ideology, even at the cost of ruling over a Palestinian population without citizenship rights in Israel. Indeed, from the perspective of the Likud Party, a painful concession had already been made by accepting the severing of Transjordan from the Land of Israel by the British mandate in 1921. Ultimately, this camp came to accept the borders of the British mandate of Palestine west of the River Jordan as the appropriate borders of Israel (Shelef 2010, 89–96). When Israel captured the West Bank, Herut leader Menachem Begin viewed it "as a correction of a major historical error" (Steinberg and Rabinovitz 2019, 3).

Alongside the Likud, the religious Zionists also embrace the vision of the Whole Land of Israel. This stream makes a religious claim to the disputed territories and views them as part of the biblical promised land. According to this religious view, the conquest of the West Bank, or what the claimants term Judea and Samaria, is a part of a messianic redemptive process. The very fact that Israel managed to redeem the land with such an emphatic triumph on the battlefield is seen as a sign of their righteousness, signalling that God wanted the Jewish people reunited with their promised land (Newman 2005; Inbari 2012). For many decades, the party claiming to represent the religious Zionists was the National Religious Party (NRP). In the late 1990s, a competing party, *Haichud Haleumi* (the National Union), was established, claiming the NRP was not sufficiently stringent in adhering to the religious-Zionist worldview. The NRP was reincarnated in the 2010s in the *Bayit Yehudi* (Jewish Home). More often than not, the NRP/Jewish Home and the National Union run together on a joint list in Knesset elections despite technically being distinct political parties.

Importantly, alongside the established political parties, the religious-Zionist stream has produced a powerful extra-parliamentary movement that has been responsible for establishing many of the Jewish settlements in the disputed territories. This movement, *Gush Emunim* ("Bloc of the Faithful"), was established in 1974 after concluding that the Labor government at the time was not resolute in holding on to the territories, indeed even mulling whether to trade them in return for peace. As a result, it set out to establish Jewish settlements at the heart of the Palestinian populated territories, against the policy of the Labor-led government (Shafir and Peled 2002, 165–172). Although the movement was formally abolished in the 1980s, after the Likud came into office, it managed to lay the foundations for a very powerful settlers' movement that operated along multiple tracks, including penetrating political parties and government and advancing their objectives from "within" the state apparatus (Haklai 2007); lobbying and organizing rallies and protests (Haklai 2003); settling the territory, often against official government policies; and public advocacy, aiming to change the "minds and hearts" of Israelis at large (Feige 2009).

Although the numbers of the religious Zionists have been relatively small, their impact has been large (Haklai 2015). One of the reasons, as the subsequent section will demonstrate, has been the fragmented structure of the Israeli political system and state institutions.

Israel's Political Institutions

Israel has a multi-party parliamentary democracy. The Israeli legislature, the Knesset, contains 120 members (MKs). Elections to the Knesset are conducted using a proportional representation system whereby the country as a whole constitutes a single electoral district. Because the barriers for representation in the Knesset have historically been very low under this system, numerous political parties representing the interests of narrowly defined constituencies as well as single issues have been formed, including religious Zionists, *Haredi* (ultra-orthodox) Jews of *Ashkenazi* and *Sephardi* descents, Arabs, new immigrants from the former Soviet Union, and more. As a by-product, the so-called "catch-all" parties – parties that appeal to multiple constituencies over multiple issues – have typically been weak in Israel. No catch-all party has ever mastered a parliamentary majority in Israel on its own, therefore, requiring coalition partners to reach a Knesset majority and retain the confidence of the legislative body. The dependence on coalition partners has made main governing parties susceptible to pressure from junior coalition partners.

Since 1967, the electoral system has been tinkered with several times in an attempt to strengthen the executive and weaken the niche parties. First, a direct election of prime minister by popular vote was introduced for the 1996 elections, although this experiment was abandoned by 2003. Second, the electoral threshold has been raised several times, from 1 per cent in 1967 to 1.5 per cent prior to the 1992 elections, 2 per cent in 2003, and eventually 3.25 per cent in the lead-up to the 2015 elections. A higher threshold incentivizes pre-election coalitions of disparate parties running on joint electoral lists, thereby reducing the number of electoral lists represented in the Knesset. However, as Table 20.1 shows, these changes have not had a profound impact on the fundamental structure of multi-party coalitions whereby almost any party leaving the coalition could bring down the government, thus empowering the smaller parties.

As Hendrik Spruyt has noted, the structure of the system does not provide niche parties with incentives to appeal to voters outside their identified voter constituencies. Therefore, they have no incentives to compromise on or moderate issues central to their voting base (Spruyt 2005, 245). Likewise, voters have no reason to steer away from parties that cater to their particularistic interests considering that such parties are not only likely to pass the threshold but also yield disproportionate political power if they join the coalition.

This fragmented institutional configuration has made it very difficult to pursue Israeli-Palestinian conflict resolution based on the land-for-peace formula. To put it succinctly, an Israeli government pursuing a two-state solution with borders roughly along the pre-1967 War frontiers needs an absolute majority supportive of this solution in the 120-member Knesset and relative convergence of worldviews on other issues. By contrast, a government supportive of territorial maximalization does not need an absolute majority in support of annexation to prevent territorial withdrawal. Rather, as shall be explained later on, by holding onto the territory while leaving its status formally unresolved, the fragmented domestic institutional configuration has provided opponents of territorial compromise with opportunities to advance entrenching Israel's hold on the disputed territory and stall peacemaking efforts.

Indeed, fragmentation is a critical point in this analysis. As Spruyt has observed, a fragmented system provides veto points for opponents to inflict a heavy cost on the government (Spruyt 2014). When preferences within the government converge, it is easier for the government to pursue a territorial compromise. However, when they diverge, even with a single party, that party has a veto power that could allow it to spoil peace-making efforts. This is the main reason why the Oslo Accords could only have been pursued when they did (as will be discussed in the next section), whereas at other times, peacemaking on the basis of land-for-peace was not pursued.

Domestic Politics and Peacemaking at the End of the Twentieth Century

During most of the 1980s, Israeli politics was characterized by a stalemate between the Israeli Right, led by the Likud Party, and the Israeli Left, led by Labor, with an occasional advantage to the Right. Thus, the period of 1984–1990 saw so-called National Unity governments in which Likud and Labor shared power.

In 1987, Shimon Peres, Israel's minister of foreign affairs and leader of the Labor Party, met with King Hussein of Jordan in London to negotiate an agreement about finding a path toward resolving the Arab-Israeli conflict. The London Agreement envisioned an international conference, sponsored by the United Nations Security Council, in which a regional peace agreement

Table 20.1 Number of Electoral Lists Represented in the Knesset and Governing Coalitions after the 1967 War

Year of election	*Threshold in percentage*	*Number of electoral lists in Knesset*	*Number of lists in coalition government**
1969	1	13	3–4
1974	1	10	3–4
1977	1	13	5
1981	1	10	6
1984	1	15	6–9
1988	1	15	6–9
1992	1.5	10	2–3
1996	1.5	11	6
1999	1.5	15	6–7**
2003	2	13	Varied**
2006	2	12	4–5
2009	2	12	6
2013	2	12	4
2015	2	10	5–6
2019a	3.25	11	no government-elect
2019b	3.25	9	no government-elect
2020	3.25	8	5–7**

* In the majority of cases, the number of coalition parties varied as political parties left and joined the coalition in the middle of the term.

** These Knessets saw changing governments, the Likud Party split, and several instances of parties leaving and joining the coalition.

would be negotiated on the premises of the land-for-peace formula stipulated in Security Council Resolution 242. Of particular significance was section C of the agreement, which stipulated that the Jordanians would effectively represent the Palestinians in a joint Jordanian-Palestinian delegation (Peres-Hussein London Agreement 1987). The agreement was seen as particularly favourable by the Labor leadership because (1) it entailed negotiating with Jordan over the future of the territories rather than with the Palestinians, and (2) it allowed for a bilateral agreement that did not necessitate consent from others in the Arab world. The first point was viewed as especially significant because, given the significant geographical size of Jordan, Israeli political elites could envision the Jordanians compromising on some of the territories in the West Bank.

The agreement, however, required the approval of the Israeli government. Prime Minister Yitzhak Shamir of the Likud vetoed it, ultimately preventing its materialization. In December 1987, a Palestinian uprising, the *Intifada*, erupted and shortly thereafter, the Jordanian king retracted Jordan's claims to the West Bank, leaving Israel to deal with the Palestinians directly (Kifner 1988). Thus, it was the fragmented governmental structure that hindered this peacemaking effort while leading to a profound recalibration of the conflict, refocusing it on the Israeli and Palestinian parties.

In 1992, the Labor Party, led by retired General Yitzhak Rabin, and the Israeli left, recorded a scarce electoral victory. Winning 46 Knesset seats, Labor formed a coalition government with the left-wing Meretz Party, which won 12 seats, and the Orthodox *Shas* Party, which gained 6 seats. Although Shas itself was not ideologically committed to pursuing a land-for-peace deal with the Palestinians, it was not strongly antagonistic to it either. Significantly, the coalition was backed from the outside by the five members of the Arab bloc of parties, who were enthusiastic supporters of territorial partition. It was this unique configuration that enabled Rabin's government to pursue the Oslo Accord with the Palestine Liberation Organization (PLO) in September 1993.

However, after Shas withdrew from the coalition in 1993, the government effectively relied on the support of the thinnest of margins, supported by 61 MKs. This majority included the five MKs from the Arab bloc, who were not formal participants in the government. When two Labor MKs broke ranks over peace negotiations with Syria, the government lost its majority support. As a result, Labor persuaded two members of the right-wing Tzomet Party to defect to its camp, thus regaining its parliamentary majority. In-and-of themselves, these parliamentary manoeuvres were highly revealing of the fragility of the central government and the challenges this presented to the pursuit of the peace process.

Furthermore, opponents began questioning the government's legitimacy to pursue a land-for-peace deal without having a clear Jewish majority. Beginning in 1993, thousands of protesters sympathetic to the Whole Land of Israel ideology mobilized in turbulent protests, rallies, and a civil-disobedience campaign (Haklai 2003). They not only objected to the idea of territorial compromise but questioned the very legitimacy of the government to withdraw from territory given to the Jewish people by religious ordain without having a clear Jewish majority. Dov Waxman has argued that territory was such an important component of this constituency's national identity that their opposition to territorial concessions was spurred by underlying identity anxiety (Waxman 2014). Opponents of the Oslo process felt that the very core of their national identity was being challenged by a government that did not enjoy the support of the Jewish majority in the Knesset (Haklai 2003, 797–798). Tensions intensified and, on 4 November 1995, at the end of a mass pro-peace rally in Tel Aviv, Prime Minister Yitzhak Rabin was assassinated by a 25-year-old Jewish law student, Yigal Amir. Subscribing to the view that the government was illegitimate, Amir sought to bring an end to the peace process through this act.

The 1996 elections saw Benjamin Netanyahu of the Likud Party become prime minister. Netanyahu's coalition included six parties commanding a total of 66 MKs. Three of Netanyahu's coalition partners held more than six seats, thus essentially giving them veto power over the peace process. Among these three was the National Religious Party (NRP), whose niche constituency included the ideological religious settlers and their supporters. Other powerful allies included the hawkish *Yisrael Be'aliya*, which claimed to represent the interests of recent immigrants from the former Soviet Union, and the Orthodox Shas, claiming to represent the impoverished classes of Middle Eastern and North African origins.

After stalling for over two years and facing sustained international pressure, particularly from President Bill Clinton, Netanyahu signed the Wye River Memorandum in October 1998. The agreement, which faced intense opposition from within his party and coalition partners, promised to uphold Israeli commitments made in previous agreements ("Oslo II" in 1995 and the "Hebron agreement" in 1997) as well as to transfer additional West Bank territory to Palestinian control. Himself skeptical about the Oslo peace process, Netanyahu found himself lacking support in the Knesset when only 29 members of the parties in his coalition, including the Likud, voted in favour of the Wye agreement. Ultimately, the agreement was approved with the support of the left-of-centre opposition. However, the coalition collapsed shortly thereafter, and early elections were called for May 1999.

The elections of May 1999 brought a new government led by Ehud Barak of the Labor Party. Barak faced an even more fragmented Knesset and an unstable coalition. Barak's coalition initially consisted of seven electoral lists, commanding 75 Knesset seats. Barak's own Labor Party ran on a joint list named *Yisrael Ahat* ("One Israel") with the right-of-centre *Gesher*,

Table 20.2 Prime Minister Barak's 1999 Coalition According to Position on the Peace Process

Dovish positions	*Centrist positions*	*Hawkish positions*
Labor + Meimad (One Yisrael) (24) Meretz (10)	Shas (17) Centre Party (6) United Torah Judaism (5) Gesher (One Yisrael) (2)	NRP (5) Yisrael Be'aliyah (6)

which had defected from the Likud in 1998, and *Meimad*, a dovish religious party. The coalition further included the leftist *Meretz*, a party enthusiastically supportive of the peace process, with 10 seats, the newly formed Centre Party (6 seats), Shas (17 seats), Yisrael Be'aliya (6 seats), the orthodox United Torah Judaism (5 seats), and the NRP (5 seats). The latter 4 were all partners in Netanyahu's earlier coalition. With 75 MKs, the coalition seemed stable, essentially preventing any single party aside from Shas from having veto power. In practice, however, the coalition was highly divided between supporters and opponents of the territorial partition premised process.

Barak declared finalizing peace agreements with the Palestinians as well as Syria to be the centrepiece of his tenure. Yet, as Table 20.2 reveals, he could only count on the support of three parties in his coalition, amounting to less than one-third support in the Knesset. Even Gesher, which had coalesced with Labor in a joint electoral list, had reservations about the extent of compromise with the Palestinians.

Indeed, Barak's coalition did not last much longer than a year. The need to reconcile between Barak's secular, liberal, and dovish voter base and the religious coalition partners led to the departure of the United Torah Judaism Party barely four months into the government's tenure following a conflict over the transfer of a large oil container on the Sabbath. In the summer of 2000, Barak went to Camp David for a summit with Palestinian Authority Chairman Yasser Arafat, to reach an agreement on the final status of the West Bank and Gaza. As a result, he lost the support of Gesher, Yisrael Be'aliya, and the NRP. Shas also formally left the coalition although, thanks to a side deal, it provided the government with external support until December 2000. Ultimately, Barak's government collapsed, and early elections were called for 2001.

Yet, the story of the impact of political fragmentation during Barak's government does not conclude here. In the first place, in order to join the coalition, the settlement-friendly NRP demanded control over the Ministry of Housing and Construction. This ministry is particularly important for the Jewish settlers in the West Bank because it has the capability of providing resources for the construction of settlements there, even without the formal approval of government (Haklai 2007). Thus, even though neither the Barak government nor its predecessor approved the construction (as required by Israeli law) of new settlements in the disputed territories, the ministry, controlled by settler sympathizers had enabled the construction of dozens of unauthorized settlement outposts in the late 1990s and early 2000s. Furthermore, under pressure from his coalition partners, Barak then negotiated with the settler movement leadership the retroactive legalization of some unauthorized settlements. The story of the unauthorized outposts shall be returned to later in this chapter.

Domestic Politics and Peacemaking in the Twenty-First Century

The elections of 2003 were won by the Likud, headed by Ariel Sharon. Sharon's approach to the conflict had traditionally been hardline. He was highly suspicious of the Palestinian leadership and regarded PA Chairman Yasser Arafat as an arch-terrorist. Moreover, Sharon was a long-time ally of the settlers and "more than any other Israeli politician, helped create much of the settlement network and infrastructure" (Newman 2005, 192–193).

In the first stage, Sharon's coalition included the Likud (38 seats), the centrist-secularist *Shinui* Party (15 seats), the National Union (seven seats, and the most hardline party in the Knesset), and the NRP (six seats). In total, this right-of-centre coalition enjoyed the support of 66 MKs. As with Barak's government, the important Ministry of Housing and Construction was handed over to the settler-friendly NRP.

Shortly after coming to power, however, Sharon's approach changed. He started to refer to Israel's control over the Palestinian population as "occupation", a term particularly abhorred by proponents of the Whole Land of Israel ideology, who regard the territories as liberated. Furthermore, to the disgruntlement of his settler allies, Sharon's government did not approve the construction of new settlements. At the same time, Sharon retained his traditional animosity toward the Palestinian leadership in general and Arafat in particular. He was skeptical about the utility of bilateral negotiations.

The tension between, on the one hand, distrust of the Palestinian leadership and, on the other, the challenges involved with the existing situation – including the second Palestinian uprising that had erupted earlier in the decade – led Sharon to adopt a new approach, namely *unilateralism*. A plan was adopted for unilateral disengagement from the Gaza Strip, including the withdrawal of all Israeli troops and civilian settlers and the forfeit of any claims Israel had to the territory. The disengagement further included removal of four settlements in the northern West Bank. The Gaza Strip was inhabited by approximately 1.5 million Palestinians at the time. The plan specifically identified improving the demographic situation as a primary purpose, demonstrating how the demographic consideration continued to retain its relevance in the calculus of state leaders.

The disengagement was approved by the Israeli government in June 2004. However, the composition of Sharon's coalition did not provide support from the majority of the ministers. To reshape the balance in his government, Sharon dismissed the ministers of the most hawkish party in his government, the National Union. The NRP also departed the coalition, leaving the government with the backing of only 53 MKs. The plan was ultimately approved by the Knesset with the support of the left-of-centre opposition parties, Labor and Meretz. Disengagement from the Gaza Strip was implemented in the summer of 2005.

At the beginning of 2005, Labor joined Sharon's coalition, increasing its tally to 72. However, this did not bring about stability. In the aftermath of the disengagement, and with no further diplomatic moves on the horizon, the newly elected leader of the Labor Party, Amir Peretz, led his party out of the coalition in November, less than a year after Labor had joined the government. Furthermore, facing a rebellion from within his own Likud Party and a possible unseating as a result of the disengagement, Sharon chose to secede with one-third of the Likud parliamentary faction. His newly created political party, called *Kadima* ("Forward"), incorporated a handful of defectors from the Labor Party. Ultimately, however, the coalition was unsustainable and, yet again, early elections were called for March 2006.

In January 2006, Sharon became incapacitated after suffering a stroke. His successor, Ehud Olmert, led the Kadima Party to victory, winning 29 seats to Labor's 19 and Likud's 12. Kadima's main platform promise was an additional unilateral withdrawal from the bulk of the West Bank, leaving the settlements concentrated in approximately three settlement blocks on 7 per cent of the West Bank territory. Given the magnitude of the withdrawal, it was estimated that the planning phase alone would only be complete in 2008.

Olmert's plan was labelled *hitkansut*, formally translated as "convergence", but literally meaning "gathering together", thereby insinuating yet again the significance of consolidating territorial borders that would ensure a solid Jewish majority. As Alan Dowty rightly observes, "Olmert's position, based primarily on demographic considerations, was almost indistinguishable from arguments long made by dovish advocates of Israeli withdrawal" (Dowty 2017, 171–172). Olmert's coalition included Labor (19 seats) as well as the Orthodox Shas (12), which had traditionally been willing to support territorial concessions if its demands serving its niche constituency were met, the hawkish Yisrael Beitenu (11 seats), and the surprise of the elections, the Pensioner's Party (seven seats). The oversizing of the coalition at 78 MKs was not incidental. It was meant to ensure that no single coalition partner aside from Labor could veto the government's policies. Olmert would have likely hoped that, by addressing the particularistic demands of his coalition partners on behalf of their constituencies, he could appease them and gain their support on the diplomatic front.

The problem Olmert faced, however, was that by the end of 2006, the regional dynamics had transformed. The so-called Second Lebanon War against *Hezbollah* in the summer of 2006 was widely seen as unsuccessful after the Shiite militia was able to continuously launch rockets into civilian centres in Israel despite the Israeli military incursion into Lebanon (Dowty 2017, 189). Furthermore, the Gaza Strip was taken over by Hamas, following violent turmoil between supporters of the Palestinian Authority and Hamas. Finally, on 25 June 2006, Hamas militants penetrated into Israel from Gaza, captured an Israeli soldier, and dragged him to the Gaza Strip. In light of these turns of events, an additional withdrawal from the West Bank lost some of its support amongst Israelis (Dowty 2017, 189).

Still, with a 78-member coalition, Olmert's government enjoyed relative stability as no party had an incentive to bolt the coalition. In January 2007, however, the police opened a criminal investigation against Olmert and, in September 2008, recommended Olmert be charged with corruption (Weiss 2008). By this time, Olmert was already making offers to Palestinian Authority Chairman, Mahmud Abbas, that exceeded those of any previous Israeli governments (Avishai 2011). And yet, at this point, he was already a lame-duck prime minister, under pressure from Labor to resign due to the criminal investigations against him. Indeed, with its 19 seats, the Labor Party was the only coalition partner with sufficient clout to bring down the government. Labor did issue an ultimatum, and Olmert was forced to resign (Bronner 2008). Thus, yet another government was unable to complete a full term as a result of pressure from coalition partners.

In 2009, Benjamin Netanyahu was re-elected as Israel's prime minister, serving continuously throughout the subsequent decade. Netanyahu has taken a harder line than any of his three predecessors. Although he was always more skeptical of territorial partition, his approach in the twenty-first century has been even more uncompromising than the one he took in his first term in office. Some pundits have speculated that Netanyahu had reached the conclusion that his political survival hinges on appeasing his support base rather than appealing to the median voter. For example, in an expansive documentary, Amit Segal, senior correspondent of Channel 12 news, Israel's most widely watched TV station, claimed that following decades of experience, Netanyahu had realized he had "natural partners" in the Orthodox parties, the national religious community, and the generally hawkish community of Russian speakers (Segal 2019). These constituencies are seen as inherently more inclined to support him even if they vote for a party other than his Likud. By ensuring their inclusion in his coalition, Netanyahu could essentially create a solid block of support that would remain stable as long as he attended to their particularistic interests. It is this tactic, according to Segal, that has enabled him to complete full terms in office, something that none of his predecessors in the twenty-first century managed to do, and indeed retain power for over a decade. And when he did not manage to win parliamentary elections, as in 2019 and 2020, he still got his "right-wing bloc" to commit to eschewing any other coalition. Retaining a consolidated base in this way has entailed appeasing the Israeli Right. Thus, under Netanyahu's rule, the Palestinian-Israeli peace process practically came to a halt.

Settlements and the Consolidation of Territorial Control

Whereas political fragmentation has hindered the capacity of interested Israeli governments to pursue peacemaking on the basis of the land-for-peace formula, it did not have the same impact on those wishing to preserve Israeli control over the territories. This is because such control has not required a formal government proclamation of annexation, something that could have been vetoed by dovish coalition partners. Rather, fragmentation has provided opportunities to entrench Israeli control, primarily through the expansion of Israeli settler presence in the West Bank.

To be clear, since the signing of the Oslo II protocols on 28 September 1995, this expansion has been done mostly informally, meaning without official government authorization or with retroactive government approval. According to Israeli law, the construction of a new Israeli settlement in the West Bank requires a formal government decision, followed by an approved urban (or rural) master plan with zoning and approved municipal boundaries, and also a land title (Sasson 2015, 43). Even though this process has not been followed since the mid-1990s, the number of Israeli settlements has grown as over a hundred unauthorized settlement outposts emerged from 1995 to 2005. After a lull of several years, about forty more unauthorized settlement outposts were erected in the second decade of the twenty-first century, according to the Peace Now settlement-watch team (Peace Now 2020). In total, the number of settlers in the West Bank (excluding East Jerusalem) has increased from about 134,000 in 1995 to over 425,000 by the end of the second decade of the twenty-first century (although the majority have been overwhelmingly in already existing settlements).

The story of the unauthorized settlement outposts is particularly revealing of the impact of domestic politics on territorial control. In a nutshell, it is a story of the political mobilization of settlers and their penetration into political parties either by having themselves elected or by electing allies. The emerging political power, in turn, has translated into political appointments favourable to the expansion of the settlement enterprise and access to the broader corridors of power unparalleled by any other social movement in Israel's history (Newman 2013, 261). Settlers have become active in political parties on the right, such as the NRP/Jewish Home, the Likud, and the National Union. While the number of parliamentarians living in settlements has varied over the years, since the early 1990s it has always been larger than their relative size in the population.

One of the key demands that settler sympathizers have made during coalition negotiations has been control over ministries that have a direct influence over settlement construction, with one of the most conspicuous examples being the Ministry of Housing and Construction. The NRP, for example, demanded from Labor prime minister Ehud Barak this particular portfolio in return for joining his otherwise left-of-centre government. The NRP held onto the ministry until withdrawing from the government altogether in 2000 due to the Camp David summit. Likewise, the NRP received control over the Ministry of Housing and Construction under Sharon's government in 2003 until leaving the government in objection to the Disengagement Plan. Under Netanyahu's 2013 government, Uri Ariel (Jewish Home-National Union faction), previously a leading activist in the settlement movement and Secretary-General of the Judea and Samaria Settlement Council, served as Minister of Housing.

The issue of government ministries facilitating unauthorized settlement construction became a thorn in the government's side in the early 2000s. As a consequence, in July 2004, Prime Minister Sharon tasked Talia Sasson, a former senior attorney from the State Attorney's Office, with compiling an investigative report on the phenomenon. Sasson identified that between 1996 to 2005, 105 new outposts – which she identified as foundations for new settlements – were established (Sasson 2015, 41). Sasson found that during that period, the Ministry of Housing and Construction spent over 72 million shekels (approximately $18 US million) on providing construction infrastructure, paving roads, connecting to hydro, electricity, and sewage systems, and so forth (Haklai 2007, 730). To be sure, Sasson's report found complicity in other branches of the bureaucracy, including the military and pre-existing Israeli local councils in the West Bank/Judea and Samaria. Following the report, the Israeli government committed to the administration of George W. Bush that it would take steps to dismantle the unauthorized settlements. And between 2006 and 2011, no new unauthorized settlements were established, although only two were ever removed, Migron and Amona.

However, after coming to power, Benjamin Netanyahu relented to pressure from his coalition partners and commissioned a counter-report, authored by former supreme court judge, Justice Edmund Levi, known for his sympathy to Israel's claims to the territory. The Levi report posited that Israel is not an occupier in the West Bank because there was never an undisputed sovereign with a legal claim over the disputed territories (Levi et al. 2012, 6). As a result, the report concluded that, in contrast to Sasson's assertion, the process of new settlement construction does not require a formal government decision or any process that is different from construction within the pre-1967 borders of Israel. Consequentially, the report concluded that because of the complicity of government ministries, the unauthorized settlements should not be seen as illegal and, instead, the government needs to take steps to standardize them (Levi et al. 2012, 84–88). In February 2017, Benjamin Netanyahu's fourth government passed the Law for Regulating the Settlements in Judea and Samaria, which standardized a process for retroactive approval of the unauthorized settlements. Possessing a solid right-wing majority in the coalition and Knesset, opponents of territorial expansion had no veto capacity.

Conclusion

There is little doubt that international factors are influential in the Israeli-Palestinian conflict. There is also no question that actions by the Palestinians and Palestinian domestic politics have aroused skepticism amongst Israelis regarding the sincerity of Palestinian intentions. At the same time, domestic politics in Israel have played a decisive role in shaping the contours of the conflict. When preferences of the majority of parliamentarians converge on the centre-left, pursuing a land-for-peace approach has been feasible. More often than not, however, the fragmented Israeli political system has provided opponents of territorial compromise with multiple opportunities to impede peacemaking efforts premised on the land-for-peace principles. Without a cohesive left-of-centre majority in the Knesset and the coalition, prime ministers supportive of territorial withdrawals have found it challenging to pursue territorial compromise. At the same time, actions toward consolidation of Israeli control over the territories short of formal annexation, primarily the expansion of settlements in the West Bank/Judea and Samaria, have not required the same type of consensus. Strategic action by settler activists and sympathizers, and control over relevant government ministries, has proven sufficient for advancing their ends.

Recommended Readings

Eiran, E. 2019. *Post-Colonial Settlement Strategy*. Edinburgh: Edinburgh University Press.
Pedahzur, A. 2012. *The Triumph of Israel's Radical Right*. Oxford: Oxford University Press.
Sasley, B. E., and H. M. Waller. 2017. *Politics in Israel: Governing a Complex Society*. Oxford: Oxford University Press.
Del Sarto, R. A. 2017. *Israel Under Siege: The Politics of Insecurity and the Rise of the Israeli Neo-Revisionist*. Washington, DC: Georgetown University Press.

Questions for Discussion

(1) Which attributes of the Israeli political system facilitate the pursuit of peacemaking, and which make it more difficult?
(2) How does the Israeli electoral system influence the propensity to advance a two-state solution to the Israeli-Palestinian Conflict? What kind of an electoral system would better help advance peacemaking?
(3) Who are the main opponents to the land-for-peace formula in Israel, and how might they be persuaded to abandon their opposition?
(4) What factors beyond the domestic politics of Israel influence the prospects of Israeli-Palestinian peacemaking?

References

Avishai, B. 2011. "A Plan for Peace That Still Could Be." *The New York Times Magazine*. & February. Available at: Retrieved: www.nytimes.com/2011/02/13/magazine/13Israel-t.html.
Biger, G. 2008. "The Boundaries of Israel-Palestine Past, Present, and Future: A Critical Geographical View." *Israel Studies*, 13:1, 68–93.
Bronner, E. 2008. "Olmert Quits Post, and Political Maneuvering Begins." *The New York Times*. 21 September. Available at: www.nytimes.com/2008/09/22/world/middleeast/22olmert.html.
Dowty, A. 2017. *Israel/Palestine*, 4th ed. Cambridge: Polity Press.
Feige, M. 2009. *Settling in the Hearts: Jewish Fundamentalism in the Occupied Territories*. Detroit: Wayne State University Press.
Galnoor, I. 2009. "The Zionist Debates on Partition (1919–1947)." *Israel Studies* 14:2, 74–87.
Gordon, N. 2007. "Of Dowries and Brides: A Structural Analysis of Israel's Occupation." *New Political Science*, 29:4, 453–478.
Haklai, O. 2003. "Linking Ideas and Opportunities in Contentious Politics: The Israeli Nonparliamentary Opposition to the Peace Process." *Canadian Journal of Political Science*, 36:4, 791–812.
Haklai, O. 2007. "Religious-Nationalist Mobilization and State Penetration: Lessons from the Jewish Settlers' Activism in Israel and the West Bank." *Comparative Political Studies* 40:6, 713–739.
Haklai, O. 2015. "The Decisive Path of State Indecisiveness: Israeli Settlers in the West Bank in Comparative Perspective." In *Settlers in Contested Lands: Territorial Disputes and Ethnic Conflicts*, eds. O. Haklai and N. Loizides. Stanford: Stanford University Press, 17–39.
Inbari, M. 2012. *Messianic Religious Zionism Confronts Israeli Territorial Compromises*. Cambridge: Cambridge University Press.
Kifner, J. 1988. "Hussein Surrenders Claims on West Bank to the P.L.O.; U.S. Peace Plan in Jeopardy." *New York Times*, Section A, 1 August, p. 1. Available at: www.nytimes.com/1988/08/01/world/hussein-surrenders-claims-west-bank-plo-us-peace-plan-jeopardy-internal-tensions.html.
Levi, E. et. al. 2012. *Report on the Status of Construction in Judea and Samaria*. Jerusalem.
Newman, D. 2005. "From Hitnachlut to Hitnatkut: The Impact of Gush Emunim and the Settlement Movement on Israeli Politics and Society." *Israel Studies* 10:3, 192–224.
Newman, D. 2013. "Gush Emunim and the Settler Movement." In *Routledge Handbook on the Israeli-Palestinian Conflict*, eds. J. Peters and D. Newman. London: Routledge.
Peace Now. 2020. Peace Now Settlement List. Available at: https://peacenow.org.il/en/settlements-watch/settlements-data/population.
Peres-Hussein London Agreement. 1987. "A Three-Part Understanding Between Jordan and Israel." Retrieved from the Economic Cooperation Foundation (ECF), The Israeli-Palestinian Conflict: An Interactive Database. Available at: https://ecf.org.il/media_items/556, Retrieved 12/12/2019.

Sasson, T. 2015. *On the Brink of the Abyss: Is the Triumph of the Settlements the End of Israeli Democracy?* Jerusalem: Keter [in Hebrew].

Segal, A. 2019. "Yemei Binyamin" (Benjamin's Days). *Mako*, 15 December Available at: www.mako.co.il/news-politics/benjamin_days/Article-f20f893981a0f61027.htm?Partner=searchResults.

Shafir, G., and Y. Peled. 2002. *Being Israeli: The Dynamics of Multiple Citizenship*. Cambridge: Cambridge University Press.

Sheehan, E. R. F. 1976. "How Kissinger Did It: Step by Step in the Middle East," *Foreign Policy*, no. 22, 3–70.

Shelef, N. G. 2010. *Evolving Nationalism: Homeland, Identity, and Religion in Israel, 1925–2005*. Ithaca, NY: Cornell University Press.

Spruyt, H. 2005. *Ending Empire: Contested Territory and Territorial Sovereignty*. Ithaca, NY: Cornell University Press.

Spruyt, H. 2014. "Territorial Concessions, Domestic Politics and the Israeli-Palestinian Conflict." In *Democracy and Conflict Resolution: The Dilemmas of Israel's Peacemaking*, eds. M. Elman, O. Haklai, and H. Spruyt. Syracuse, NY: Syracuse University Press, 29–66.

Steinberg, G. M., Z. Rabinovitz. 2019. *Menachem Begin and the Israel-Egypt Peace Process: Between Ideology and Political Realism*. Bloomington, IN: Indiana University Press.

Waxman, D. 2014. "Identity Matters: The Oslo Peace Process and Israeli National Identity." In *Democracy and Conflict Resolution: The Dilemmas of Israel's Peacemaking*, eds. M. Elman, O. Haklai, and H. Spruyt. Syracuse, NY: Syracuse University Press, 133–156.

Weiss, E. 2008. "The Police Recommends Indicting Olmert for Accepting a Bribe and Fraud." *Ynet, Calcalist*. 7 September. Available at: www.calcalist.co.il/local/articles/0,7340,L-3114627,00.html.

21
PALESTINIAN CITIZENS OF ISRAEL

Maha Nassar

During the 1948 *Nakba*, not all Palestinians fled or were expelled from their homes in areas that became the state of Israel. A small minority of roughly 156,000 Palestinians remained, and most were eventually granted Israeli citizenship. These Palestinian citizens of Israel have constantly fought for access to land, economic development, educational investment, and political freedom. Scholars have used various conceptual frameworks to understand these dynamics between a non-Jewish minority and a self-declared Jewish state, including modernization, fragmentation, and exclusion (Sa`di 1997; Lustick 1980). More recently, scholars have turned to the framework of settler-colonialism to make sense of the relationship between Palestinian citizens of Israel and the state, as well as to connect this group of Palestinians to the Palestinian people as a whole. Understanding Palestinian citizens of Israel within a settler-colonial framework allows us to more fully see how their conditions and struggles fit in with those of other Palestinians. This chapter begins with an overview of the current conditions of Palestinian citizens of Israel in socio-economic and political terms. It then shows how the framework of settler-colonialism helps explain the Israeli state's policies to try to gain exclusive control over the land and eliminate the indigenous Palestinian population (Wolfe 2006). The chapter also shows how Palestinians have historically resisted these policies and how they continue to do so, despite the daunting obstacles they face.

Palestinian citizens of Israel number approximately 1.6 million, making up about 18 per cent of all Israeli citizens (Israeli Central Bureau of Statistics 2019a). Roughly two-thirds live in the north of the country: 49 per cent live in the Northern District, including the Galilee region and the city of Nazareth, and 17 per cent live in the Haifa District, which includes the city itself, surrounding towns and villages, and large towns further inland such as Um al-Fahm and Baqa` al-Gharbiyya (Israeli Central Bureau of Statistics 2019a). An additional 17 per cent live in the Southern District, including in numerous Bedouin communities in the Naqab (Negev) Desert, while smaller percentages live in the Central (11 per cent) and Jerusalem Districts (5 per cent) (Israeli Central Bureau of Statistics 2019a). About 83 per cent of the population are from Muslim backgrounds, while 10 per cent are from Christian backgrounds, and 7 per cent are from Druze backgrounds (Israeli Central Bureau of Statistics 2019b).

Israel's claim to be a "Jewish and democratic state," has led to a duality in terms of how the state treats its Palestinian citizens. On the one hand, Israel's Declaration of Independence calls for the state to "ensure complete equality of social and political rights to all its inhabitants

DOI: 10.4324/9780429027376-26

irrespective of religion, race or sex" ("Declaration" 1948), and the Israeli High Court has generally recognized the principle of equality under the law (Kretzmer 2019). Palestinian citizens of Israel can form political parties, serve as parliamentarians and judges, and advance in professional fields, leading some observers to see this as evidence of Israel's vibrant democracy. On the other hand, in order to maintain the state's Jewish character, government officials have developed a complex legal and political system of segregation and unequal treatment of Palestinian citizens, especially when it comes to accessing land and housing, obtaining employment opportunities, receiving social services, and being able to express their identity as Palestinians. These discriminatory policies have led other observers, and especially Palestinian citizens themselves, to question the sincerity of Israel's self-professed democratic ideals.

Despite comprising nearly one-fifth of the population, Palestinian citizens of Israel have very limited access to land. During the early years of the state, Israel confiscated approximately 70 per cent of the land owned by Palestinians who remained in Israel (Abu Hussein and McKay 2003, 136–137), in addition to confiscating land that was privately owned or communally shared by Palestinians who became refugees. As a result, today roughly 93 per cent of the land in Israel (4,820,500 acres/7,532 sq. miles/19,508 sq. km) is owned by either the state, the Jewish National Fund (JNF), or the Development Agency. This land is managed by the Israel Land Authority (ILA), which grants "leasing rights" to citizens for a period of 49 or 98 years. Since the land cannot be sold or transferred except between the three entities, and because the JNF officially prohibits the land it owns from being leased to non-Jews, Palestinian citizens of Israel are effectively barred from leasing land and properties in large swaths of the country (Forman and Kedar 2004).

In addition, Palestinian towns and villages in Israel are hemmed in by state planning commissions that narrowly define their municipal boundaries, which leads to overcrowding and housing shortages in those areas. Similarly, Bedouin Palestinians in the South have been forced into overcrowded townships, while their ancestral lands have been confiscated by the state (Nasasra 2017; Kedar et al. 2018). Upwardly mobile Palestinian citizens who wish (and can afford) to move into more spacious Jewish townships often find themselves excluded through admissions councils and other forms of covert discrimination aimed at keeping them out (Shafir 2018).

These policies of segregation have hindered Palestinian economic development in Israel. The restrictive municipal boundary allocations severely limit access, not only to agricultural land that is available to Palestinian municipalities, but also to land that could be used for commercial or industrial development. Palestinian localities are often excluded from consideration as "development zones" and therefore deprived of the government subsidies, tax breaks and favourable grants and loans that have helped Jewish municipalities develop commercially (Khamaisi 2013). In addition, industrial facilities are often sited near Palestinian towns and cities, yet zoned outside their jurisdiction, leading those communities "to share in pollution hazards, but not the revenues which industry generates" (Shmueli 2008, 2389).

Labour practices further impede both the development of an independent Palestinian economic sector and its integration into the Israeli economy. Since its inception, the Israeli state has played a dominant role in managing the economy, which includes regulating the labour market. Israel's self-definition as a Jewish state has led to the "subjugation of the economy to what is ideologically conceived as representing the 'common good' of the Jewish majority," rather than the common good of all citizens. Discriminatory hiring practices are usually cloaked in other terms, such as requiring that job candidates for skilled labour positions have had military service (most Jewish Israelis serve in the military while most Palestinian citizens do not), or that they reside in Jewish towns (Sa`di 1995, 429). As a result, Palestinian citizens as a whole have been pushed into more precarious, lower-wage unskilled and semi-skilled jobs, and are more likely to lose their jobs in an economic downturn (Sa`di 1995). They also are more likely to have to commute long distances to their jobs in predominantly Jewish municipalities, further impeding their economic prospects (Schnell and Shdema 2016). This is particularly true for Palestinian women, who have a difficult time entering the labour market (Yonay and Kraus 2013). As a result, the poverty rate among Palestinian citizens is more than double that of the poverty rate in Israel as a whole. In 2016, for example, poverty among families in Israel stood at 18.5 per cent overall, but was 49.2 per cent for Arab families (National Insurance Institute of Israel 2016).

This economic marginalization is further exacerbated by a fragmented and unequal educational system. There are four school subsystems in Israel: government schools for the Jewish secular population; government schools for the Jewish religious population; government schools for the Palestinian Arab population, and an independent school system for ultra-religious Jews. Most Palestinian students attend government-funded "Arab schools." On average, per student expenditure in Arab schools is 78 per cent of the per capita allocation to Jewish students in secular schools and only 68 per cent of the per capita allocation to Jewish students in religious schools (Taub Center 2019, 18). As a result of this underfunding, many schools in the Arab sector struggle with large class sizes, dilapidated infrastructure, a shortage of teachers and classrooms, a scarcity of educational counsellors and special education resources, as well as a lack of vocational and technical training opportunities (Abu-Saad 2004). Inadequate schooling also results in greater high-school dropout rates and lower university admission test scores (Israeli Central Bureau of Statistics 2019c). While in recent years these achievement gaps have narrowed significantly between middle-class Palestinian citizens and their Jewish counterparts, in part due to the rise of private education, Palestinians in lower socio-economic groups continue to fall behind (Taub Center 2020, 40).

Regardless of their socio-economic status, Palestinian citizens routinely face racist treatment by both the state and Jewish Israelis (Lentin 2018). Considered a "suspect minority" that could, at any moment, turn against the Israeli state and its Jewish citizens, Palestinian citizens are subjected to bureaucratic and technological surveillance methods that limit their political and social activities (Halabi 2011; Zureik 2015). At the cultural level, the government-mandated school curriculum perpetuates stereotypes about Palestinians, Arabs, and Muslims, thereby "endorsing strong ethno-religious ethos and narratives that widen the chasm between the Jewish 'us' and the Palestinian 'them' thereby contributing to the rise of right-wing politics in Israel" (Agbaria 2018, 18). In addition, Palestinians who have entered skilled and technical professions often face prejudicial treatment from their Jewish co-workers and supervisors (Mjdoob and Shoshana 2017).

Much of this discrimination has been enshrined in the Israeli legal system, despite official proclamations that all citizens are equal. In the absence of a ratified constitution, the Knesset has passed a series of Basic Laws that together serve as the foundational legal infrastructure. While the Basic Law on Human Dignity and Liberty, enacted in 1992, was interpreted by the Israeli Supreme Court as prohibiting discrimination, the Israeli legislature (Knesset) has chipped away at this principle through laws aimed at undermining the rights of Palestinian citizens. According to Adalah – The Legal Center for Arab Minority Rights in Israel, there are already 65 active laws that discriminate against Palestinian citizens of Israel (Adalah 2017). This legal discrimination was given additional legal weight with the 2018 passage of "Basic Law: Israel as a Nation-State of the Jewish People" (Benvenisti and Lustig 2018). By asserting Israel's special connection to the Jewish people and omitting any mention of equality between citizens, rights groups are concerned that Israeli lawmakers will pass additional laws that violate even more explicitly the principle of equality among citizens (ACRI 2018).

In sum, despite making up nearly 20 per cent of the population, Palestinian citizens of Israel continue to face multiple forms of official and unofficial discrimination. To understand how these conditions came to be – and to see how Palestinian citizens have resisted their ongoing marginalization within Israeli society – we turn to the frameworks of settler-colonialism and indigenous resistance.

Settler-colonialism, Indigenous Resistance, and the Palestinian Citizens of Israel

Settler-colonialism differs from other forms of colonialism in that the primary purpose of settler-colonialism is not to exploit land using indigenous labour, but rather to conquer the land and replace the natives with the settlers altogether. This conquest of land is therefore accompanied by what Patrick Wolfe calls a "logic of elimination of the native" (2006, 387). While this logic of elimination is commonly associated with campaigns of mass murder, it can also include other forms, such as the attempted physical transfer of indigenous people from their lands to other locations, and the attempted erasure of their distinct and collective political identity by folding them into the settler-colonial state as depoliticized and minoritized communities.

Since its inception in the nineteenth century, the dominant strains of the Zionism movement adopted this logic of elimination by constructing the indigenous Palestinian population as foreign interlopers who needed to be removed for Jews to redeem *Eretz Israel* (Pappé 2012). This logic of an essential Jewish "us" against a Palestinian "them" served as the basis for what historian Fayez Sayegh laid out as three dimensions of Zionist colonial ideology: "racial self-segregation, racial exclusiveness and racial supremacy" (Sayegh 2012). As a result, Palestinians were construed in the Zionist imaginary as backwards, racially inferior, and lacking both a modern political identity and an attachment to the land.

These racialized stereotypes of Palestinians continued after the establishment of the state of Israel in 1948 and shaped the early scholarship on those Palestinians who eventually became citizens (Sa`di 1997; Rabinowitz 2002). Meanwhile, critical scholars showed how Israel discriminated against the Palestinian minority by imposing a military government, confiscating their land, and passing discriminatory laws (Jiryis 1968). Sociologist Elia Zuriek argued that these discriminatory structures, coupled with the use of rhetoric that dehumanizes Palestinians in order to justify the Zionist project, amounted to a form of "internal colonialism" (Zureik 1979). Subsequent studies set out to determine the methods by which Israeli policies effectively controlled, marginalized, and excluded the Palestinian minority from meaningful participation in the Jewish state (Lustick 1980; Rabinowitz 1997; Yiftachel 2006), while other studies were primarily concerned with the extent to which their identification with the Palestinian people more broadly might undermine Israel's Zionist underpinnings (Bligh 2003; Reiter 2009; Peleg and Waxman 2011; Haklai 2011).

In recent years, scholars have increasingly turned their attention to the ways in which the framework of settler-colonialism helps elucidate the various dynamics between Zionists/Israelis and Palestinians (Salamanca et.al 2012; Zureik 2015). Palestinian citizens of Israel – and the scholars who study them – are increasingly turning to settler-colonialism as a conceptual tool for making sense of their conditions and treatment within the Jewish state (Nasasra 2017; Zureik 2015). Nadim Rouhana and Areej Sabbagh-Khoury (2015, 219) argue that although Palestinian citizens have routinely called upon Israel to live up to its self-proclaimed democratic values by treating them as equal citizens, "in critical moments, [Israel] treated them openly as subjects of a settler-colonial project." As a result, they have increasingly come to see themselves as having "settler-colonial citizenship." In response, many of them are framing their efforts to decolonize their lands and to live *as Palestinians* in their land in terms of indigenous resistance against the settler-colonial rule (Jamal 2011; Pappé 2018).

While scholars and activists may be using the terminology of settler-colonialism and indigenous resistance more frequently today, the relationship between the Israeli state and its Palestinian citizens has long fit into this paradigm. In the sections below, we see how Palestinians' twin struggles to resist displacement by remaining on their land and to resist erasure by identifying themselves as part of the Palestinian people continue to shape their existence today.

The Struggle to Remain

"The struggle to remain" on their lands and in their homes is a phrase coined by historian Adel Manna to challenge the notion that the Palestinians who stayed in Israel were simply "allowed" to do so (Manna 2019). During the 1948 war, many Palestinians who fled or were expelled from their homes in the coastal and central areas of Palestine took refuge in Nazareth and the Galilee, believing they were safe from expulsion since those areas were part of the "Arab state" proposed in the 1947 United Nations Partition Plan. As Israeli forces conquered Nazareth and the Galilee that summer and fall, they continued to expel many Palestinian residents, sometimes even after surrender agreements were signed with villages, and the fighting had stopped. But the uncertain status of those areas meant that the expulsions were not as systematic as they were in other parts of the country. As it became clear that Israel did not have the international sanction to continue conducting widescale expulsions, as it had done earlier, Israeli officials looked for other ways to gain control of the land while inducing the remaining Palestinians to leave and/or preventing their return (Manna 2019; Robinson 2013).

To do so, the Israeli government issued a series of emergency regulations that were based on British Mandate emergency regulations. One of the most significant, Regulation 125, imposed military rule on any area, allowing military commanders to prevent Palestinians from entering the designated area. While outwardly declaring that these policies were necessary security measures, internally Israeli leaders concluded that

> military rule was the best mechanism at the state's disposal to block the return of Palestinian refugees (from both inside and outside the country) to their lands; to depopulate other Arab villages whose land they sought to expropriate immediately; and to bring in Jewish immigrants to replace the original residents.
>
> *(Robinson 2013, 41)*

Initially, the legal status of the Palestinians who remained within the Green Line was unclear. A census was hastily conducted on 11 November 1948 to determine which Palestinians were present within the Armistice Lines and therefore could be eligible for legal recognition by the Israeli state. But the upheavals of the war meant that hundreds of Palestinians were not counted in the census, even though they were often just a few miles from their villages. Palestinians uncounted in the census were deemed to be "infiltrators" and therefore ineligible to receive permanent legal status. These bureaucratic obstacles prompted Palestinians in Israel to launch a series of legal and popular challenges demanding that they receive a permanent ID, which would (in theory, at least) protect them from expulsion. Israel was reluctant to do so, seeking to minimize the number of Palestinians in the country (Robinson 2013; Manna 2019).

Over the next few years, Israel faced mounting pressure to provide permanent legal status to the roughly 156,000 Palestinians who had managed to stay in – or return to – the areas under Israeli control. Drawing on the discriminatory citizenship laws of the United States, Australia, and South Africa, in April 1952 the Israeli Knesset passed the Citizenship Law, which granted formal citizenship to most of the Palestinians within the Green Line (Tatour 2019). But unlike Jewish immigrants who were automatically deemed citizens upon their arrival, Palestinians needed to produce several documents establishing residency (many of which were lost during the war) in order to receive citizenship. As a result, approximately 15,000 internal refugees were denied the legal security that citizenship offered. While most of the internal refugees (referred to euphemistically by the Israeli authorities as "present absentees") were eventually granted Israeli citizenship, during the early years they were subjected to ongoing expulsions and were systematically denied access to their land, which was subsequently confiscated by the state (Masalha 2003, 142–158).

Yet even those Palestinians who were counted in the census often found it impossible to reclaim their lands. The emergency regulations passed in 1948–1949 allowed the government to seize millions of dunams of Palestinian land, often by declaring them to be "abandoned" or "absentee" properties after having banned Palestinians from returning to them. In March 1950 the Israeli Knesset passed the Absentee Property Law, followed in July by passage of the Development Authority (Transfer of Property) Law. These two laws made permanent the state expropriations of Palestinian-owned land that had been carried out over the previous two years. While, in theory, Palestinian citizens whose land was confiscated by the state could appeal to the Custodian of Absentee Property for restoration of their ownership rights, in reality, Palestinian petitions were repeatedly denied (Abu Hussein and McKay 2003, 71). As a result, by 1950 the Israeli state had permanently acquired "more than 10,000 shops, 25,000 buildings (housing 57,000 family dwellings), and nearly 60 per cent of all fertile land in the country. These holdings, which included 95 per cent of existing olive groves and nearly one half of all citrus groves, increased the land available for Jewish settlement by 250%" (Robinson 2013, 47).

Despite the state's acquisition of land, the population of the Galilee and northern regions remained overwhelmingly Palestinian. For the Israeli state to further solidify its conquests and prevent the return of confiscated land, it introduced plans to "Judaize the Galilee." During the 1950s and 1960s over a hundred new Jewish settlements were established in the Galilee, many of them built on expropriated Palestinian land (Falah 1991, 72). Beginning the 1970s, Israel established an additional 40 Jewish "lookout settlements" scattered on hilltops throughout the Galilee, leading to the seizure of additional Palestinian-owned land (Shafir 2018).

Palestinian citizens of Israel have undertaken numerous methods to resist these policies of expulsion and land expropriation. Indeed, reclaiming their land has been a central political cause for Palestinian citizens of Israel since the establishment of the state. As early as 1951, the former inhabitants of northern border villages Kafr Bir`im and Iqrit filed petitions with the Israeli High Court arguing that they had been unjustly prevented from returning to their villages, despite being assured that their evacuation in 1948 was temporary and that they would be allowed to return (Masalha 2003, 158–63). Their efforts were supported by the Israeli Communist Party, which organized public protests and other mobilizing campaigns against the state's seizure of land. In 1959 a group of nationalist-minded Palestinians established the *Ard* (Land) group that called for, among other things, a halt to land seizures and the return of Palestinian refugees who had been expelled in 1948 (Dallasheh 2010). And on March 30, 1976, thousands of Palestinians in the Galilee organized a general strike and demonstrations, called Land Day, to protest the government's announcement that it would be seizing over 20,000 dunums of Palestinian-owned land to establish Jewish-only lookout settlements. Violent police crackdowns on the protesters led to six Palestinians being killed, 50 injured, and about 300 arrested (Nakhleh 2011). Since then, Palestinians in Israel and around the world have commemorated Land Day as a sign of their ongoing struggle to remain on their land in the face of repeated Israeli attempts to remove them.

Meanwhile, in the South, Palestinian Bedouin communities have also struggled against expulsions, land seizures, and forced relocation. Over the course of the 1948 war, the majority of this semi-nomadic community of approximately 90,000 was expelled from the Naqab (Negev) Desert, mainly into neighbouring Jordan and Egypt. In the early 1950s, most of the remaining 13,000 Palestinian Bedouins were placed under Israeli military rule and forced into a restricted zone (Arabic *siyaj*/Hebrew *sayeg*) that was roughly one-tenth the size of their traditional lands (Abu-Saad 2011). By the end of the decade, Bedouins had launched numerous political campaigns and petitioned the state to be allowed to return the lands they needed for grazing and herding, yet their petitions were repeatedly denied (Nasasra 2017). Instead, a 1962 Israeli Supreme Court decision gave the government wide latitude to consider Bedouin grazing and farming land to be "dead land," and thereby available for confiscation (Kedar et al. 2018). The government also introduced urbanization schemes aimed at forcing the Bedouin to abandon their traditional lands. About half of the Bedouin population was eventually settled into seven planned townships within the *siyaj*; the other half continue to live in 35 "unrecognized villages" as well as in 11 newly "recognized villages," none of which receive municipal services from the state (Nasasra 2017, 227–229).

In sum, since 1948 Palestinian citizens of Israel have struggled to remain on their lands in the face of expulsions, land confiscations, and planning schemes. At the same time, they have also been waging a more existential struggle: to maintain and pass on their identity as Palestinian Arabs who are proud of their heritage and are connected to the rest of the Arab world. We turn to that struggle next.

The Struggle Against Elimination

The Palestinian struggle to remain on their land has been deeply intertwined with their struggle to develop, maintain, and disseminate self-narratives of their identity as Palestinian Arabs who have deep historical roots in their land and strong political ties to the Arab world and beyond. In doing so, they have faced a formidable Israeli state apparatus that has sought to eliminate their identity as Palestinians and cast them instead as a transient, depoliticized amalgamation of ethnic and religious groups that could be folded into the state. Those who resisted this casting – and asserted their identity as Palestinians who have a right to an equal presence on their homeland – have been treated as a fifth column that needs to be surveilled and controlled.

This casting has drawn on a history of orientalist portrayals of Palestinians that permeated early Zionist thought and carried over into the post-1948 period (Eyal 2006). In 1952, the newly established Central Council for Arab Affairs held that the country's non-Jewish population consisted of several disjointed minority communities, including: "Arab Christians (further divided into different sects); non-Arab Christians (Armenians and Greeks); Arab Muslims (the majority among the minorities); non-Arab Muslims (Circassians); and non-Muslim Arabs (Druze)" (Cohen 2010, 174). Similar to the divide-and-conquer approach found in other colonial contexts, Israeli authorities hoped to present themselves as a protector of the smaller, "non-Arab" and "non-Muslim" populations while at the same time mitigating against the possibility that the Palestinian communities would work together to fight against Israeli discriminatory practices, particularly the loathsome military government and the ongoing confiscation of land (Sa`di 2014, 69–92).

Palestinian citizens of Israel responded to these policies in different ways, ranging from more accommodationist positions to more confrontational ones (Dallasheh, 2015). Those who adopted more confrontational stances challenged, through various means, Israel's claim that it was a Jewish democracy with a content Arab minority. They included Arab nationalists (most of whom were forced underground during the early years of the state), as well as members of the Israeli Communist Party (ICP). As the only legally recognized non-Zionist political party that accepted Arabs as equal members, the ICP became the political home for many Palestinian intellectuals who wanted to push for greater social, political, and economic rights within the state. To be clear, the ICP was not anti-Zionist: in keeping with Soviet formulations of the time, the party officially recognized the Israeli state and the Jewish people's right to self-determination. Those stances, coupled with Israel's ties to the Soviet Union, gave the ICP a measure of legitimacy that Arab nationalists did not enjoy. Yet the ICP nonetheless faced crackdowns from the state, including restrictions on the distribution of its Arabic newspapers and the revocation of work permits for Palestinians who were members of the party (Robinson 2013; Nassar 2017).

Arab nationalists faced even harsher repression. In 1959, the al-Ard group, which espoused a pan-Arab nationalist outlook and called for Palestinian self-determination, was denied a permit to print its newspaper, and several leaders were arrested and accused of incitement. Their numerous court appeals seeking formal recognition were ultimately denied by the High Court in 1964 on grounds that their advocacy for Palestinian rights threatened the legitimacy of the Jewish state. (Dallasheh 2010; Nassar 2017).

In order to counteract the influence of communist and Arab nationalist groups, Israeli state authorities went to great lengths to show – to themselves and others – that the "Arab Israelis" were a content minority in the Jewish state. One tactic they used throughout the 1950s and 1960s was to induce Palestinian citizens to perform acts of allegiance, especially during the annual Israeli Independence Day celebrations – which coincided with the anniversary of the Palestinian *Nakba*. School teachers, whose jobs depended on being in the good graces of the state, rehearsed patriotic songs and poems with their students, which they then performed during the public festivities. Amid heavy police presence, those who refused to participate – or who displayed insufficient enthusiasm in doing so – faced economic and political repercussions (Robinson 2013; Cohen 2010). Still, Palestinians quietly took advantage of the lifted travel restrictions to visit loved ones and return to their destroyed homes and villages.

The police presence on display at the annual Independence Day celebrations also reflected the deep levels of state surveillance that permeated the lives of Palestinians in Israel. By 1949, fears that the multiple "minority communities" would consolidate into a single national minority led the government to place most aspects of Palestinian life under the control of the military, which constructed the Palestinians as a security threat that needed to be surveilled and controlled (Korn 2018). This surveillance was facilitated in part by Palestinians who felt they had no other choice but to become informants. As Nadera Shalhoub-Kevorkian (2017, 346) explains,

> Many Palestinians who had managed to survive and remain on their land sought minor benefits from the state such as telephone lines, travel permits, licenses to open their businesses and so on. Israel deliberately exploited these needs to extract concessions such as various forms of information and requests to spy on families and neighbors in order to attain the most basic services.

These dynamics of surveillance and control also extended into the realm of education. Ismael Abu-Saad (2004, 116) explains that "the hiring of teachers, principals and supervisory staff ultimately lies in the hands of the Ministry of Education Deputy Director for Arab Education, who is actually an official of the General Security Services." Even after they are hired, teachers face constant surveillance and can be terminated if the Minister of Education determines that "the teacher inculcated a provocative, unloyal and immoral education or oriented to harm in another manner." As a result, numerous teachers have been fired from their positions for criticizing Israeli policies or showing insufficient obeisance to the state (Al-Haj 1995, 163–168). With no appeal mechanism for those who are denied positions or fired, the result is a school system that alienates teachers and students.

Another alienating dimension has been a state-imposed curriculum that celebrates Jewish cultural identity while downplaying Palestinian identity. The 1953 Law of State Education called for state-sponsored education in Israel

> to base education on the values of Jewish culture and the achievements of science, on love of the homeland and loyalty to the state and the Jewish people, on practice in agricultural work and handicraft, on pioneer training and on striving for a society built on freedom, equality, tolerance, mutual assistance, and love of mankind.
>
> *(Cited in Abu-Saad 2006, 1088)*

No parallel learning outcomes have been laid out for Palestinian students to appreciate or celebrate their own culture. Instead, Palestinian students are required to study Jewish culture and history even more so than Palestinian history and culture. As a result, Palestinian students "are required to develop identification with Jewish values and further Zionist aspirations at the expense of the development of their own national awareness and sense of belonging to their own people." (Abu-Saad 2006, 1091).

With an educational system that downplays Arab civilization and erases Palestinian identity from the consciousnesses of students, many young Palestinians in Israel have turned to other forms of cultural production in order to push back against these attempted erasures. During the early years of the State of Israel, with travel to neighbouring states forbidden and regional publications very difficult to bring in, broadcasts from the Arab world, such as the popular *Sawt al-`Arab* Egyptian radio program, helped them feel connected to the region. In addition, the local Arabic publications of the ICP – particularly its semi-weekly newspaper *al-Ittihad* and its monthly literary journal *al-Jadid* – played a key role in exposing Palestinian intellectuals and activists to anticolonial concepts (Nassar 2017). Initially, the reach of these publications remained limited: the government sponsored rival Arabic publications (which state employees were pressured to read) that sought to convince readers that the Israeli state was a force for good in the lives of its Arab minority citizens. These publications further argued that Arab citizens should be grateful for the benevolence of the state, even if there were occasional shortcomings in its treatment of the Arabs. This framing was accompanied by surveillance and coercion mechanisms that rewarded Palestinian citizens who were deemed loyal to the state and punished those (including communists and Arab nationalists) who were deemed disloyal. As a result, throughout the early decades of the state, "most members of Arab society did not dare to openly show that they listened to radio programs from Arab countries or that they read *al-Ittihad*" (Jamal 2009, 41).

But some did. Beginning in the late-1950s, a small, dedicated group of Palestinian activists, intellectuals, and writers increasingly challenged Israeli attempts to isolate them from the political and cultural trends of the Arab and decolonializing worlds. Comprised of high-school and college students, teachers, poets, journalists, and party activists, they called upon Palestinians to celebrate the anti-colonial and independence movements taking place in Algeria, Iraq, the Congo, and elsewhere, even as the Israeli authorities took a dim view of those movements. In the mid-1960s, this group increasingly identified with the growing Palestinian national movement as well. Some of the most famous figures associated with these intellectual circles, including Tawfiq Zayyad, Rashid Husayn, Samih al-Qasim, and Mahmoud Darwish, faced persecution for their activities from the Israeli authorities, in the form of imprisonment, torture, and house arrest, adding to their reputations as "resistance poets." While their reputation inside Israel grew steadily over the course of the 1960s, they were largely unknown outside the Green Line until after the June 1967 War (Nassar 2014, 2017).

Following the formal removal of the military government in December 1966 and the shockwaves that accompanied the June 1967 War, a younger, even more assertive generation of Palestinian activists in Israel came onto the scene. Raised under the coercive forces of the military government and inspired by the Palestinian resistance fighters, by the early 1970s many of them began to shed the fear that had gripped their parents' generation. In this climate of growing political activism, the communists continued to be prominent among the ranks of oppositional political action; they condemned Israel's ongoing occupation of Arab territories and were early champions of the establishment of a Palestinian state in the West Bank, East Jerusalem, and Gaza Strip under the slogan of "two states for two nations." But they were increasingly challenged by a younger cohort of Arab nationalists who formed the Abna' al-Balad (Sons of the Village) group, which was more directly influenced by the Palestinian nationalist movement (Moustafa 2018a).

Overall, the communists and nationalists agreed on many issues, especially the need for greater Palestinian rights in Israel. As a result, they worked together on campaigns that had an immediate impact, such as the 1976 Land Day strike and protests. And since Abna' al-Balad refused to participate in Knesset elections, these campaigns did not threaten the communist party electorally. But the two camps had fundamentally different ideas about how they should understand and confront Israel's settler-colonial project. The communists, despite their language of decolonization, publicly accepted Israel as a Jewish state and framed their campaigns in terms of holding Israel up to its self-professed democratic ideals. In contrast, the nationalists insisted that Israel was fundamentally a colonial state whose colonial structures needed to be dismantled in order for true equality to take hold.

These political developments were accompanied by important social changes that were taking place in Palestinian communities during the 1970s and 1980s. With the ongoing loss of agricultural land, the social pressures exerted by extended families (*hamulas*) loosened, allowing younger Palestinians to leave their villages to pursue higher education and employment opportunities elsewhere in the country and abroad. The younger generation of intellectuals established various civil-society associations and groups, such as the National Union of Arab University Students, the National Union of Arab Secondary School Students, and the Regional Committee for the Defense of Arab Lands (Moustafa 2018b). In addition, women's organizations, most notably the Democratic Women's Movement, grew considerably during this period as they sought to raise awareness about various challenges that Palestinian women faced, both within patriarchal societies and from the Israeli state itself (Abu-Baker 2018). These developments were accompanied by a significant rise in women's education, especially higher education, and their partial integration into the Israeli workforce (Daoud 2009). However, even with these social changes, Palestinian women have continued to face added marginalization within Israeli society as compared to Palestinian men (Abdo 2011).

This period also saw growing social and political connections between Palestinians in Israel and those in occupied East Jerusalem, the West Bank, and the Gaza Strip. Coming into more regular contact with one another meant that new ways of thinking about the struggle against elimination could travel across the Green Line. Palestinians under occupation were inspired by the resistance poets in Israel, such as Mahmoud Darwish and Samih al-Qasim, who spoke up defiantly against the political structures that ruled over their lives (Nassar 2017). Meanwhile, Palestinians in Israel increasingly met with supporters of the Muslim Brotherhood in the West Bank and beyond, leading to the establishment of the Islamic Movement in Israel in 1971. The Islamic Movement's activities focused on social programs, such as the establishment of highly regarded schools, welfare initiatives for the poor, and infrastructure improvements in areas where they have municipal authority (Ali 2018). While their activities were locally based, their overall message – that Palestine would be liberated when more Palestinians adopted visible aspects of Islamic practice – echoed the message of other Palestinian Islamist groups. In doing so, these Palestinians resisted Israeli efforts to isolate them from the rest of the Palestinian people.

Despite these growing connections, the First *Intifada* (1987–1993) and the Palestinian Declaration of Independence (1988) marked a rift between Palestinians in Israel and those in the occupied territories. Palestinians in Israel generally supported the uprising, but they saw the struggle to end the occupation as distinct from their own struggle to remain on their land and be recognized as equal citizens. In addition, the PLO's formal adoption of the two-state solution effectively excluded Palestinian citizens of Israel from its national project and "brought into sharp focus the difference between the two [Palestinian] communities in terms of status, collective goals and collective future" (Rouhana 1990, 72). Meanwhile, Israeli officials were worried that the unrest of the Intifada could spill over into Israel, so they increased budget allocations for the Arab sector and initiated new economic projects to try to narrow the socio-economic gaps between Jewish and Palestinian citizens (Hitman 2019).

The 1993 signing of the Oslo Accords marked the arrival of a two-state consensus. Coupled with several Israeli initiatives, this consensus aimed at narrowing the socio-economic gap between Arab and Jewish sectors. As a result, some Palestinian citizens joined Zionist parties to seek greater integration within the state, believing that their future lay in trying to integrate more fully into Israeli society (Hitman 2019). At the same time, a growing number of Jewish Israelis, including many on the Zionist left, began demanding that Palestinians recognize Israel more explicitly as a "Jewish state" (Jabareen 2013). In response, a number of Palestinians formed the National Democratic Assembly (NDA) party (also known by its Arabic name, *Hizb al-Tajammu` al-Watani*, and its Hebrew acronym, *Balad*) in 1995. The NDA demanded equal rights for Palestinians within Israel at the civic and national levels, thereby challenging the trend toward greater Palestinian integration into an Israel that was increasingly defining itself as a Jewish state. Instead, the party called for Israel to become "a state of all its citizens" (Sultany 2018, 218), a sign of greater Palestinian political assertiveness.

In sum, Palestinian citizens of Israel have not only struggled to remain on their land, but they have also fought against a web of Israeli state mechanisms aimed at denying their political identity as Palestinians while keeping them subordinated within the state and isolated from the Palestinian people as a whole. In response, Palestinian citizens have utilized various political, social, and cultural strategies of resistance to maintain their Palestinian identity while advocating for greater political, social and economic equality in the state. These struggles have intensified in recent years.

Dual Struggles Since 2000

Since 2000, Palestinian citizens of Israel have continued to fight to remain on their lands and assert their identity as Palestinians amid growing pressures from the state and an increasingly right-wing Jewish Israeli body politic. A key turning point in this struggle occurred on 28 September 2000, when Likud leader Ariel Sharon walked onto al-Haram al-Sharif (the

Temple Mount), triggering Palestinian protests in the Occupied Territories that erupted into the Second (al-Aqsa) *Intifada*. To signal support for their people on the other side of the Green Line, Palestinian citizens of Israel declared a general strike on 1 October and launched a wave of protests. Over the following week, Israeli security forces killed 13 unarmed Palestinians (12 citizens of Israel and one from the West Bank). The killings were a major blow to the idea that equality could be achieved by integrating into Israeli society, and they were followed by an increase in Jewish Israeli expressions of racism toward Palestinians and the introduction of several discriminatory laws (Waxman 2012). In response, a growing number of Palestinian citizens began positioning themselves more explicitly as an indigenous people resisting Israeli settler-colonial rule.

This shift can be clearly seen in a set of statements issued by civil society organizations in 2006–2007. Collectively dubbed the "Future Vision Documents," they sought to "redefine the relationship of Arab society with the Israeli state, demanding the transformation of Israel from an ethnic to a democratic state" (Jabareen 2008). Significantly, the documents asserted Palestinians citizens' long-standing connection to their homeland and to the Palestinian people much more directly than did past statements. The "Haifa Declaration," for example, asserts

> [o]ur national identity is grounded in human values and civilization, in the Arabic language and culture, and in a collective memory derived from our Palestinian and Arab history and Arab and Islamic civilization. … It is continuously nourished by our uninterrupted relationship to our land and homeland, by the experience of our constant and mounting struggle to affirm our right to remain in our land and homeland and to safeguard them, and by our continued connection to the other sons and daughters of the Palestinian people and the Arab nation.
>
> *("Haifa Declaration" 2007, 7–8)*

The Haifa Declaration's framing is part of a broader set of developments in which Palestinian citizens of Israel have more assertively positioned themselves as an integral part of the native Palestinian people. This included initiating more wide-scale and organized commemorations of the Nakba, in which participants affirm that they are part of the Palestinian people who were forcibly removed from their lands (Rouhana and Sabbagh-Khoury 2015; Sorek 2015). This development coincided with a Jewish-Israeli shift to the right, signalled by the repeated re-election of Benjamin Netanyahu as prime minister, beginning in 2009. In 2011 a coalition of right-wing parties in the Knesset passed a "Nakba Law," aimed at deterring Palestinians' commemoration of their displacement in 1948 (Adalah 2011). Yet Palestinians have nonetheless continued commemorating this day, indicating their growing confidence and a refusal to have their memories erased (Sorek 2015).

Meanwhile, the Palestinian struggle to remain on their lands endures as well. Palestinians in Arab municipalities and in mixed cities have undertaken public protests and legal appeals to resist ongoing Israeli bureaucratic manoeuvres aimed at segregating and limiting where they can live (Plonski 2017; Shafir 2018; Shdema et al. 2018). These dynamics are especially noticeable in the South as Bedouin have continued to defy Israeli attempts to further enclose them and confiscate their land. For example, in June 2013 the Knesset approved a bill that, if enacted, would lead to the destruction of up to 35 unrecognized Bedouin villages in the Naqab and the forced displacement of up to 70,000 Palestinians. Dubbed the Prawer Plan, it drew widespread condemnation from the Bedouin Palestinians, who spearheaded a series of campaigns against it. The campaigns drew international attention and support, leading the government to shelve the plan (Nasasra 2017; Plonski 2017).

Conclusion

Since 1948, Palestinian citizens of Israel have confronted an Israeli settler-colonial project that has sought to displace them from their land and erase their identity as part of the native Palestinian people. Palestinian citizens' ongoing confrontation with the state has centred on the twin struggles of remaining on their land and asserting their identity as Palestinians who are entitled to equal rights in their homeland. During the early decades of the state, these struggles were often framed in terms of calling upon Israel to live up to its self-professed democratic ideals – a framing that became even more prominent during the Oslo years (1993–2000). However, the killing of unarmed Palestinian protesters in October 2000 – coupled with the increase in anti-Palestinian rhetoric, the passage of more blatantly discriminatory laws, and the continued restrictions on accessing land and resources – have led Palestinian activists in Israel to frame their struggle more explicitly in terms of indigenous resistance against the settler-colonial rule. Meanwhile, over the last two decades, the conceptual framework of settler-colonialism has become increasingly theorized in the academic literature, leading to comparative studies of settler-colonialism that de-exceptionalize the Israeli-Palestinian case. As Palestinian citizens of Israel increasingly understand their current conditions in terms of settler-colonialism, any future solution must take into account both their historical grievances as well as the current unequal conditions under which they live and find ways to redress them.

Recommended Readings

Nasasra, M. 2017. *The Naqab Bedouins*. New York: Columbia University Press.

Nassar, M. 2017. *Brothers Apart: Palestinian Citizens of Israel and the Arab World*. Stanford, CA: Stanford University Press.

Robinson, S. 2013. *Citizen Strangers: Palestinians and the Making of Israel's Liberal Settler State*. Stanford, CA: Stanford University Press.

Rouhana, N., and A. Sabbagh-Khoury, eds. 2011. *Palestinian Citizens of Israel: Readings in History, Politics and Society*, vol. 1. Haifa: Mada al-Carmel.

Rouhana, N. N. and Areej Sabbagh-Khoury, eds. 2018. *Palestinian Citizens of Israel: Readings in History, Politics and Society*, vol. 2. Haifa: Mada al-Carmel.

Questions for Discussion

(1) What are some similarities and differences between the conditions of Palestinian citizens of Israel and the conditions of other Palestinians?

(2) Which example of settler-colonialism and/or indigenous resistance was most surprising to you? Why?

(3) Compare and contrast the conditions of Palestinian citizens of Israel before and after 2000. Do you think things have gotten better or worse? Why?

(4) Palestinian citizens of Israel are not a monolith. What are some differences (social, political, economic) among the different subgroups of Palestinian citizens of Israel?

References

Abdo, N. 2011. *Women in Israel: Race, Gender and Citizenship*. London: NBN International.

Abu-Baker, K. 2018. "The Palestinian Women's Movement: Palestinian Feminism in Israel." In *The Palestinians in Israel: Readings in History, Politics and Society*, vol. 2, eds. N. Rouhana and A. Sabbagh-Khoury. Haifa: Mada al-Carmel, 230–248.

Abu Hussein, H., and F. McKay. 2003. *Access Denied: Palestinian Land Rights in Israel*. London: Zed Books.

Abu-Saad, I. 2004. "Separate and Unequal: The Role of the State Educational System in Maintaining the Subordination of Israel's Palestinian Arab citizens." *Social Identities* 10:1, 101–127.

Abu-Saad, I. 2006. "State-Controlled Education and Identity Formation Among the Palestinian Arab Minority in Israel." *American Behavioral Scientist* 49:8, 1085–1100.

Abu-Saad, I. 2011. "The Indigenous Palestinian Bedouin of the Naqab: Forced Urbanization and Denied Recognition." In *The Palestinians in Israel: Readings in History, Politics and Society*, vol. 1, eds. N. Rouhana and A. Sabbagh-Khoury. Haifa: Mada al-Carmel, 120–127.

ACRI – The Association for Civil Rights Groups in Israel. 2018. "Nation-State Law." Available at: https://law.acri.org.il/en/2018/07/20/nation-state-law/.

Adalah – The Legal Center for Arab Rights in Israel. 2011. "The *Nakba* Law: Amendment No. 40 to the Budgets Foundations Law." Available at: www.adalah.org/en/law/view/496.

Adalah - The Legal Center for Arab Rights in Israel. 2017. The Discriminatory Laws Database. Available at: www.adalah.org/en/content/view/7771.

Agbaria, A. 2018. "The 'Right' Education in Israel: Segregation, Religious Ethnonationalism, and Depoliticized Professionalism." *Critical Studies in Education* 58:1, 18–34.

Al-Haj, M. 1995. *Education, Empowerment and Control: The Case of the Arabs in Israel*. Albany: SUNY Press.

Ali, N. 2018. "The Islamic Movement in Israel: Historical and Ideological Development." In *The Palestinians in Israel: Readings in History, Politics and Society*, vol. 2, eds, N. Rouhana and A. Sabbagh-Khoury. Haifa: Mada al-Carmel, 199–214.

Benvenisti, E., and D. Lang. 2018. "We the Jewish People: A Deep Look into Israel's New Law." *Just Security*. 24 July. Available at: www.justsecurity.org/59632/israel-nationality-jewish-state-law/.

Bligh, A. 2003. *The Israeli Palestinians: An Arab Minority in the Jewish State*. Abingdon, UK: Routledge.

Cohen, H. 2010. *Good Arabs: The Israeli Security Agencies and the Israeli Arabs, 1948-1967*. Trans. Haim Watzman. Berkeley, CA: University of California Press.

Dallasheh, L 2010. "Political Mobilization of Palestinians in Israel: The al-'Ard Movement." In *Exiled at Home: Ethnicity and Gender among Palestinians in Israel*, eds. R. A. Kanaaneh and I. Nusair. Albany: SUNY Press, 21–38.

Dallasheh, L. 2015. "Troubled Waters: Citizenship and Colonial Zionism in Nazareth." *International Journal of Middle East Studies* 47:3, 467–487.

Daoud, S. A. 2009. *Palestinian Women and Politics in Israel*. Gainesville, FL: University Press of Florida.

"Declaration of the Establishment of the State of Israel." 1948. Available at: https://mfa.gov.il/mfa/foreignpolicy/peace/guide/pages/declaration%20of%20establishment%20of%20state%20of%20israel.aspx.

Eyal, G. 2006. *The Disenchantment of the Orient: Expertise in Arab Affairs and the Israeli State*. Stanford, CA: Stanford University Press.

Falah, G. 1991. "Israeli 'Judaization' Policy in the Galilee." *Journal of Palestine Studies* 20:4, 69–85.

Forman, G., and A. Kedar. 2004. "From Arab Land to 'Israel Lands': The Legal Dispossession of the Palestinians Displaced by Israel in the Wake of 1948." *Environment and Planning D: Society and Space* 22:6, 809–830.

"Haifa Declaration." 2007. Haifa: Mada al-Carmel. Available at: www.adalah.org/uploads/oldfiles/newsletter/eng/may07/haifa.pdf.

Halabi, U. 2011. "Legal Analysis and Critique of Some Surveillance Methods Used by Israel." In *Surveillance and Control in Israel/Palestine: Population, Territory and Power*, eds. E. Zuriek, D. Lyon and Y. Abu-Laban. Abingdon, UK: Routledge, 199–218.

Haklai, O. 2011. *Palestinian Ethnonationalism in Israel*. Philadelphia: University of Pennsylvania Press.

Hitman, G. 2019. "Israel's Policy towards Its Arab Minority, 1990–2010." *Israel Affairs* 25:1, 149–164.

Israeli Central Bureau of Statistics. 2019a. "Locations and Population, by Population Group, District, Sub-District and National Region." In *Statistical Abstract of Israel 2019, No. 70*. Available at: www.cbs.gov.il/he/publications/doclib/2019/2.shnatonpopulation/st02_17.pdf.

Israeli Central Bureau of Statistics. 2019b. "Population, by Religion." In *Statistical Abstract of Israel 2019, No. 70*. Available at: www.cbs.gov.il/he/publications/doclib/2019/2.shnatonpopulation/st02_02.pdf

Israeli Central Bureau of Statistics. 2019c. "Students in Grades 1–12 by Age, Sex and Population Group." In *Statistical Abstract of Israel 2019, No. 70*. Available at: www.cbs.gov.il/he/publications/doclib/2019/4.shnatoneducation/st04_15.pdf.

Jabareen, H. 2008. "The Political Ethos of Palestinian Citizens of Israel: Critical Reading in the Future Vision Documents." *Israel Studies Forum* 23:2, 3–28.

Jabareen, H. 2013. "20 Years of Oslo: The Green Line's Challenge to the Statehood Project." *Journal of Palestine Studies* 43:1, 41–50.

Jamal, A. 2011. *Arab Minority Nationalism in Israel: The Politics of Indigeneity*. Abingdon, UK: Routledge.

Jamal, A. 2009. *The Arab Public Sphere in Israel: Media Space and Cultural Resistance*. Indianapolis, IN: Indiana University Press.

Jiryis, S. 1968. *The Arabs in Israel, 1948–1966*. Beirut: The Institute of Palestine Studies.

Kedar, A., et al. 2018. *Emptied Lands: A Legal Geography of Bedouin Rights in the Negev*. Stanford, CA: Stanford University Press.

Khamaisi, R. 2013. "Barriers to Developing Employment Zones in the Arab Palestinian Localities in Israel and Their Implications." In *Palestinians in the Israeli Labour Market: A Multi-Disciplinary Approach*, eds, N. Khattab and S. Miaari. New York: Palgrave Macmillan.

Korn, A. 2018. "Between the Military Government and the Minority Affairs Ministry: The Construction of the Palestinian Minority as a Security Threat during the First Years of the Existence of Israel." *Journal of Historical Sociology*, 31:1, e1–e15.

Kretzmer, D. 2019[1990]. *The Legal Status of the Arabs in Israel*. New York: Routledge.

Lentin, R. 2018. *Traces of Racial Exception: Racializing Israeli Settler-colonialism*. London: Bloomsbury Academic.

Lustick, I. 1980. *Arabs in a Jewish State: Israel's Control of a National Minority*. Austin, TX: University of Texas Press.

Manna, A. 2019. "Resistance and Survival in Central Galilee, July 1948–July 1951." *Jerusalem Quarterly* 79 (Summer), 28–38.

Masalha, N. 2003. *The Politics of Denial: Israel and the Palestinian Refugee Problem* London: Pluto Press.

Mjdoob, T., and A. Shoshana. 2017. "Palatable Arabs: Palestinian Professionals in Work Organizations in Israel." *The Sociological Quarterly* 58:2, 163–181.

Moustafa, M. 2018a. "Sons of the Village Movement." In *Palestinian Citizens of Israel: Readings in History, Politics and Society* vol. 2, eds. N. Rouhana and A. Sabbagh-Khoury. Haifa: Mada al-Carmel, 149–159.

Moustafa, M. 2018b. "The Student Movement and Palestinian Activism in Israel." In *Palestinian Citizens of Israel: Readings in History, Politics and Society* vol. 2, eds. N. Rouhana and A. Sabbagh-Khoury. Haifa: Mada al-Carmel, 249–262.

Nakhleh, K. 2011. "*Yawm al-Ard* (Land Day)." In *The Palestinians in Israel: Readings in History, Politics and Society*, eds. N. Rouhana and A. Sabbagh-Khoury. Haifa: Mada al-Carmel, 83–89.

Nasasra, M. 2017. *The Naqab Bedouins*. New York: Columbia University Press.

Nassar, M. 2014. " 'My Struggle Embraces Every Struggle': Palestinians in Israel and Solidarity with Afro-Asian Liberation Movements." *Arab Studies Journal* 22:1, 74–101.

Nassar, M. 2017. *Brothers Apart: Palestinian Citizens of Israel and the Arab World*. Stanford, CA: Stanford University Press.

National Insurance Institute of Israel. 2016. "Poverty and Social Gaps Report of the National Insurance Institute of Israel." Available at: www.btl.gov.il/English%20Homepage/Publications/Poverty_Report/Documents/oni2016-e.pdf.

"Palestinian Declaration of Independence." 1988. Available at: www.paljourneys.org/en/timeline/historictext/9673/palestinian-declaration-independence.

Pappé, I. 2012. "Shtetl Colonialism: First and Last Impressions of Indigeneity by Colonised Colonisers." *Settler Colonial Studies* 2:1, 39–58.

Pappé, I. 2018. "Indigeneity as Cultural Resistance: Notes on the Palestinian Struggle within Twenty-First-Century Israel." *South Atlantic Quarterly* 117:1, 157–178.

Peleg, I., and D. Waxman. 2011. *Israel's Palestinians: The Conflict Within*. Cambridge: Cambridge University Press.

Plonski, S. 2017. *Palestinian Citizens of Israel: Power, Resistance and the Struggle for Space*. London: I.B. Tauris.

Rabinowitz, D. 1997. *Overlooking Nazareth: The Ethnography of Exclusion in the Galilee*. Cambridge: Cambridge University Press.

Rabinowitz, D. 2002. "Oriental Othering and National Identity: A Review of Early Israeli Anthropological Studies of Palestinians." *Identities: Global Studies in Culture and Power* 9: 305–324.

Reiter, Y. 2009. *National Minority, Regional Majority: Palestinian Arabs versus Jews in Israel*. Syracuse, NY: Syracuse University Press.

Robinson, S. 2013. *Citizen Strangers: Palestinians and the Making of Israel's Liberal Settler State*. Stanford, CA: Stanford University Press.

Rouhana, N. 1990. "The Intifada and the Palestinians of Israel" Resurrecting the Green Line." *Journal of Palestine Studies* 19:3, 58–75.

Rouhana, N., and A. Sabbagh-Khoury. 2015. "Settler-Colonial Citizenship: Conceptualizing the Relationship between Israel and Its Palestinian Citizens." *Settler Colonial Studies* 5:3, 205–225.

Sa`di, A. 1995. "Incorporation without Integration: Palestinian Citizens in Israel's Labour Market." *Sociology* 29:3, 429–451.

Sa`di, A. 1997. "Modernization as an Explanatory Discourse." *British Journal of Middle Eastern Studies* 24:1, 25–48.

Sa`di, A. 2014. *Thorough Surveillance: The Genesis of Israeli Policies of Population Management, Surveillance and Political Control towards the Palestinian Minority*. Manchester: Manchester University Press.

Salamanca, O. J., et al. 2012. "Past is Present: Settler-colonialism in Palestine." *Settler Colonial Studies* 2:1, 1–8.

Sayegh, F. 2012. "Zionist Colonialism in Palestine (1965)." *Settler Colonial Studies* 2:1, 206–225.

Schnell, I., and I. Shdema. 2016. "The Role of Peripherality and Ethnic Segregation in Arabs' Integration into the Israeli Labour Market." In *Socioeconomic Inequality in Israel: A Theoretical and Empirical Analysis*, eds. N. Khattab, S. Miaari, and H. Stier. New York: Springer, 207–224.

Shafir, Gershon. 2018. "From Overt to Veiled Segregation: Israel's Palestinian Arab Citizens in the Galilee." *International Journal of Middle East Studies* 50:1, 1–22.

Shalhoub-Kevorkian. 2017. "Settler-colonialism, Surveillance, and Fear." In *Israel and Its Palestinian Citizens: Ethnic Privileges in the Jewish State*, eds. N. Rouhana and A. Sabbagh-Khoury. Cambridge: Cambridge University Press, 336–366.

Shdema, I., et al. 2018. "The Social Space of Arab Residents of Mixed Israeli Cities. *Geografiska Annaler. Series B, Human Geography*, 100:4, 359–376.

Shmueli, D. F. 2008. "Environmental Justice in the Israeli Context." *Environment and Planning A* 40, no. 10, 2384–2401,

Sorek, T. 2015. *Palestinian Commemoration in Israel: Calendars, Monuments, and Martyrs*. Stanford, CA: Stanford University Press.

Sultany, N. 2018. "The National Democratic Assembly." In *Palestinian Citizens of Israel: Readings in History, Politics and Society* vol. 2, eds. N. Rouhana and A. Sabbagh-Khoury. Haifa: Mada al-Carmel, 215–229.

Tatour, L. 2019. "Citizenship as Domination: Settler-colonialism and the Making of Palestinian Citizenship in Israel." *Arab Studies Journal* 27:2, 8–39.

Taub Center. 2019. "The Education System: An Overview." Available at: http://taubcenter.org.il/wp-content/files_mf/theeducationsystemanoverview2019eng.pdf.

Taub Center. 2020. "Achievements and Gaps: The Status of the Israeli Education System." Available at: http://taubcenter.org.il/wp-content/files_mf/achievementsangapseng.pdf.

Waxman, D. 2012. "A Dangerous Divide: The Deterioration of Jewish-Palestinian Relations in Israel." *The Middle East Journal* 66:1, 11–29.

Wolfe, P. 2006. "Settler-colonialism and the Elimination of the Native." *Journal of Genocide Research* 8:4, 387–409.

Yiftachel, O. 2006. *Ethnocracy: Land and Identity Politics in Israel/Palestine*. Philadelphia: University of Pennsylvania Press.

Yonay, Y., and V. Kraus. 2013. "Ethnicity, Gender, and Exclusion: Which Occupations Are Open to Israeli Palestinian Women?" In *Palestinians in the Israeli Labour Market: A Multi-Disciplinary Approach*, eds. N. Khattab and S. Miaari. New York: Palgrave Macmillan, 87–110.

Zuriek, E. 1979. *Palestinians in Israel: A Study in Internal Colonialism*. London: Routledge and Kegan Paul.

Zureik, E. 2015. *Israel's Colonial Project in Palestine: Brutal Pursuit*. Abingdon, UK: Routledge.

22

ISRAEL AS A JEWISH AND DEMOCRATIC STATE

Mohammed Saif-Alden Wattad[*]

Introduction

What is the meaning of a "Jewish and Democratic State"? This term of dual and ambiguous values is of utmost significance, particularly following the recent enactment of the controversial Basic Law: Israel – the Nation-State of the Jewish People (hereafter, the Nation-State Law). This law is arguably perceived as an attempt by the right-wing nationalists and religious parties to erode Israel's pledge to establish a "Jewish and democratic state," as embodied and most precisely defined in Israel's Declaration of Independence (The Knesset 1948) and in the later Basic Law: Human Dignity and Liberty (The Knesset 1992) and the Basic Law: Freedom of Occupation (The Knesset 1994), and as an attempt to shake the fragile balance between both values by giving Israel's Jewish values supremacy over Israel's democratic commitments (Wootliff 2018).

Prima facie, Israel's conceptual, political, and legal features as a modern democratic nation-based state were already and clearly set forth[1] in Resolution 181(II) of the United Nations General Assembly (UNGA), which explicitly elaborated its resolution and vision to establish two independent democratic nation-based states in Mandatory Palestine (Al-Kayyali 1985, 37),[2] that is, Arab and Jewish states (hereafter, the Partition Plan) (Resolution 181, 1947).

However, while exclusively emphasizing Israel's religious and national values and rights, the recently enacted version of the Nation-State Law has failed to mention, let alone protect, the non-Jewish minorities' democratic values and rights (Wootliff 2018).

This chapter does not aim to challenge the legitimacy of the Israeli parliament's lawful decision to define itself as a "Jewish and democratic state,"[3] but rather seeks to comprehend what exactly are the meaning and the implications of the enacted version on the significant part of Israel's non-Jewish population. In other words, what is the legal, political, reasonable, proportionate, and just balance that must be struck between Israel's national identity, as a Jewish state, and its civil identity as a democracy?

The major insight one can deduct from this chapter is that in order to project a vision for the future of Israel, it is vital for Israel to move, without further delay, towards what the Partition Plan explicitly defined and anticipated to happen. The Partition Plan perceived both the Arab and the Jewish inhabitants of Mandatory Palestine as Palestinian citizens who should be recognized by the international community as two entities with venerable national and

DOI: 10.4324/9780429027376-27

cultural identities, whereby the obvious comprehension of the need to establish two separate nation-based independent states: one, a Jewish state, and the other, an Arab state (Resolution 181, 1947, Sec. B, Part 1, ch. A, art. 3). Moreover, each state was expected to establish a constitutional democratic regime (Resolution 181, 1947, Sec. B, Part 1, ch. B, art. 10, para. (1), which provides protection of civil and political rights to all citizens alike (Resolution 181, 1947, Sec. B, Part 1, ch. B, art. 10, sub-paras. (a), (d), and (e), Sec. C, ch. 2, arts. 1–8), as well as a special set of mutual collective rights for national minorities, the Arab national minority of the Jewish state and the Jewish national minority of the Arab state (Resolution 181, 1947, C, ch. 2, art. 6).

However, an objective and independent examination of Israel's current political and legal structure demonstrates that Israel has so far not adhered to the Partition Plan's initial aspirations.[4] The mere historical fact that the Partition Plan was ultimately accepted solely by the Jewish Agency for Palestine but rejected by all the Arab leaders and their governments (Al-Kayyali 1985, 284; Morris 2008, 66–67, 72–73, 75; Hadawi 1989, 76; Resolution 181, 1947, ch. 2) cannot, for two reasons, afford Israel to maintain such a position; first, the plan provides the fundamental international legal justification for the establishment of Israel (Janis 2003, 208–209);[5] and second, it is in force and effect even today because Israel officially adopted the legal and political structure of governance expressed in the Partition Plan in its 1948 Declaration of Independence (Declaration of Independence, 1948).

The core question then becomes that of examining the nature and the characteristics of Israel's democracy in light of the existing theories on liberal democracy and liberal-substantive democracy. In furtherance to the enactment of the Nation-State Law's endorsed version, Israel cannot be described as the liberal democracy one would expect it to be – particularly as this governing structure was officially secured in the Partition Plan and the Declaration of Independence.

The Partition Plan

Insofar as international law is concerned, the Partition Plan was the first official international document to adopt the 1917 Balfour Declaration's interpretation as "the establishment of a national home for the Jewish people" (The Balfour Declaration, 1917),[6] thus distinguishing between Jewishness as a national identity (Ram 1995, 91; Anidjar 2003),[7] and Judaism as a religious identity,[8] a prerequisite to recognize and justify granting self-determination rights to any nation (Montevideo Convention, 1933, art. 1; United Nations Charter, 1945; ch. 1, art. 1, para. 2; Dunoff et al. 2002, 109–111).

Consequently, the idea of establishing a nation-based state is already anchored in the constitutive document that legally justifies the establishment of Israel as a Jewish state. Therefore, the question then is not, and cannot be, whether Israel may define itself as a "Jewish state," but rather what is the meaning of "Jewish state." This is not an easy question, as Israel's Jewish national and civil identity might be confused with the concept of Judaism as a strictly observed religious identity.

This chapter cannot, and has no such aspiration to, provide an ultimate and satisfactory solution to the question of "who is a Jew," neither from a national nor a religious perspective. Rather, this chapter seeks to understand – from the firmly depicted collective and national perspective provisions of the Partition Plan, which stipulate the establishment of a Jewish "and democratic" state, and not solely "a Jewish state," – what being a "Jewish state" means.

As anticipated from a truly democratic regime, the Partition Plan rightfully expected the new nation-based state to apply a constitutional democratic regime that provides legal protection for a very wide range of individual, civil, political, social and economic rights, as well as collective rights. The Partition Plan's provisions, under which Israel was accepted by the international community, were based on three elements; first, it must be a nation-based state, namely, a Jewish state; second, it has to be a constitutional democratic state; and third, a mutually respectful and proper balance between Israel's renown and historical Jewish identity and democracy, and the expectations that its national indigenous minorities would become full legal citizens of the new Jewish state.

Israel's Declaration of Independence

When then will Israel, if at all, adopt the conceptual grounds of the Partition Plan as a model for good governance? As a matter of fact, the merits and terminology anticipated by the Partition Plan, regarding the nature of Israel, have already been adopted in its Declaration of Independence. Therefore, the question here is not of their adoption, but of their prompt, faithful, and impartial fulfilment.

In view of Israel's historical desire to be admitted to the United Nations and recognized by the international community, it did not have much choice but to compromise and accept the Partition Plan's firm demands. First, the Partition Plan itself had set forth the supreme values that should be included in the Declaration of Independence (Resolution 181, 1947, Sec. C) and second, for Israel's Founding Fathers, who considered this historical document as the realization of a two-thousand-years' dream, it was crucial to venerate that document, being the first international and official recognition ever, of the Jewish nation's right for self-determination, and more specifically the Jewish people's right to establish a state of their own as an "irrevocable" right (The Declaration of the Establishment of the State of Israel, para. 9).[9] Accordingly, one would rightfully expect the Declaration to be in full harmony with the Partition Plan on the nature of Israel, not only as a Jewish and democratic state, but a Jewish and constitutional democratic state (The Declaration of the Establishment of the State of Israel, paras. 12–13).

While its well-selected and weighed wording clearly indicates that Israel would be a true democracy, it must be noted that the Declaration of Independence failed to include the terms "Jewish and democratic state" and refrained altogether from including the term "democracy." However, as correctly held by the Supreme Court of Israel (hereafter, the Court), a plausible interpretation of the Declaration's reading leaves no doubt as to the democratic nature of Israel (Kol Ha'am 1953, 876–878). It took 44 years for the joint terms "Jewish and Democratic" to appear in Israel's laws. First in article 1A of the 1992 Basic Law: Human Dignity and Liberty, as amended in 1994, and then again in article 2 of the 1994 Basic Law: Freedom of Occupation, both of which provide that "[T]he purpose of this Basic Law is to protect [,] ... in order to establish in a Basic Law the values of the State of Israel as a "Jewish and democratic state." Additionally, article 1 of both Basic Laws states that the "[F]undamental human rights in Israel ... shall be upheld in the spirit of the principles set forth in the Declaration of Establishment of the State of Israel." This dramatic change in the wording of Israel's Basic Laws leads us to the sole decisive conclusion that, according to the values set forth in the Declaration, Israel is a Jewish and democratic state. This has been aptly thought of as

> a dramatic change in the status of the Declaration of Independence: It is no longer a mere source of interpretation but has become an independent source of human rights.
> *(Clal 1994, 465)*[10]

The Nature of Israel's Democracy

On the Concept of Liberal Democracy

Based on the detailed description of the Partition Plan's vision, it is asserted that the plan acknowledges the conceptual distinction between formal and liberal-substantive democracy and eventually emphasizes its adoption of the latter one. Liberal democracy is commonly defined as a form of government in which the political power belongs to the public as a whole and not merely to a single person or a particular group of people. A state is democratic, not "if," but "when" the majority of the population can exercise an effective influence on the decision-making process. Whereas democracy is a matter of degree and not a fixed concept, it would be more practical to think in terms of a scale rather than laying down the preconditions to be defined as a democracy.

The earlier liberalism had to vindicate the elements of personal, civil and economic freedom, and in doing so it took a stand on the rights of the individual and the desirable harmony of the natural order (Hobhouse 1945, 54). The preservation of individual rights and the emancipation of the individual from public control mean that all, without exception, enjoy the same equal rights. No group is favoured over another. The majority may decide the identity of government, but should, under no pretext undermine the basic democratic value of equal rights for all. Liberalism, in opposition to feudalism, placed the individual on a legal equality status and challenged the right of the monarchy to govern while ignoring the interests of its citizens (Macpherson 1977, 12; Hayek 1955, 36–43).

The philosophy of a free society is grounded on the concept that every human being is an autonomous individual, whose actions are the product of his/her own (and free) will, choice, and purpose. The liberal society aims to equally provide the common good not to only a privileged class but to all, insofar as the capacity of each permits the individual to share it. The object of such a society, according to this view, is to increase the capacities by which the individual can contribute to the common good.

In a democracy, irreconcilable and incommensurable conceptions of the good often occur. Given that people lead different ways of life, having diverse ideals is the normal condition. Furthermore, this variety is conceived to be a good thing. Liberal states afford their citizens the freedom to develop their own subjective conceptions of the good. In order to ensure that every person is able to pursue his/her conception, neutrality refrains from identifying essential interests with a particular conception of the good and decreases the possibility that the government, being inevitably associated with one or more segments of society, might impose its prioritized values and ideals on others, either by propagation or by force. Methodologically, the idea of neutrality is placed within the broader concept of anti-perfectionism. The implementation and promotion of the conceptions of the good, though worthy in themselves, are not considered as a legitimate matter for governmental action (Raz 1986, 110; Cohen-Almagor 1994b, 217–236). Governments ought to publicly acknowledge each person's unconditional liberty to act according to his/her own convictions, enjoy autonomy, and be free to materialize his/her ideals.

Whereas in every democracy the range of norms that society can respect has limitations, certain norms and moral codes must be shared by all people despite their cultural differences; the most basic norms a democracy has to secure are respecting others as human beings (under the Kantian Respect for Others Argument), and not inflicting harm upon others (under the Millian Harm Principle) (Cohen-Almagor 1993; 1994a, chs. 3,7,8; 2017).

Within the concept of liberal democracy, it is possible to distinguish between formal and substantive democracies. Formal democracy is only interested in the opinion of the majority and seeks to enforce the majority's decisions, whether they are good or bad, whereas substantive democracy respects the opinion of the majority, yet, it simultaneously guarantees that minorities (weakened groups) are protected, particularly in circumstances where the majority misuses its power to abuse these minorities. Formal democracy acts in accordance with the rule of the legislature, no matter how right, decent, just, and fair the legislature might be; whenever the legislature says "the law is" it becomes binding law. Any abuse of power inherently contradicts the basic ideal of Democracy. However, in substantive democracy, the legislature's actions are scrutinized for their compatibility with the fundamental principles of fairness, reason, justice, and good. This is a healthy and desirable democracy, where political power is always limited, supervised, and scrutinized.

The distinction between formal and substantive democracy is represented by the meaning attributed to the Rule of Law, as being binding, not because it has been enacted in a proper formal procedure by a duly elected legislature, but because it is just and proper (*Recht* in German, *droit* in French, and *derecho* in Spanish) (Henkin 1990).[11] In this context, the rule of law deals with the aspiration for governmental actions to comply with certain fundamental requirements, which are intended to guarantee the internal morality of the law. This was exactly what might have inspired Plato's mind in offering *The Republic* (Plato 2003), that is, the challenge of providing a true definition of justice; for him, democracy is the rule of Law, namely, the rule of good and justice.

In *The Law of Peoples,* John Rawls draws a distinction between liberal and non-liberal societies. Liberal societies are pluralistic and peaceful; they are governed by reasonable people who protect basic human rights. These rights include providing a certain minimum to means of subsistence, security, liberty, personal property as well as to formal equality and self-respect as expressed by the rules of natural justice (Rawls 2002, ch. 2; Rorty 2005). Liberal people are reasonable and rational. Their conduct, laws, and policies are guided by a sense of political justice (Rawls 2002, 25). In contrast, non-liberal societies fail to treat their people as truly free and equal. They adopt norms based on compulsion and coercion. Authoritarian societies aggressively fight to undermine political opponents while liberal societies encourage pluralism and provide avenues to empower opposition. Theocracy attempts to provide strict answers to all questions and concerns whereas liberal societies have no qualms about presenting questions with no definite answers, to challenge common truisms, to present competing ideas, to admit human infallibility, and celebrate heresy.

Featuring Israel's Democracy

Israel is a Jewish-ethnic democracy (Smooha 2002a, 2002b and 2018). The framework of governance is democratic, but its underpinning concepts give precedence to Judaism over the Respect for Others principle and the Harm Principle. Consequently, by preferring Jews over others, Israel is bound to adopt non-liberal policies and practices that are discriminatory in nature and critically weaken the democratic values it has vowed to respect.

By defining itself as a "Jewish and Democratic State," Israel should remain as was originally anticipated by the international community and reflected in the Declaration of Independence and Israel's ensuing Basic Laws. As mentioned above, the Declaration did not include the terms "Jewish and democratic state" and also omitted the binding term "democracy." However, as correctly held by the Supreme Court of Israel, a plausible interpretation of the Declaration leaves no doubt as to the democratic nature of Israel (Kol Ha'am 1953, 876–878). Yet, in order to materialize this policy, a proper balance must be struck between Israel's Jewish identity and its democratic nature. This will be possible only when Israel acknowledges that democracy and Jewishness (and/or Judaism) are not contradictory values in themselves but, rather, equal means to achieve both of them. Each of them can bring about destructive consequences if abused by governmental power, but each can also establish constructive hopes if substantively adhered to.

Considering the tense and fragile balance between the two supposedly equivalent – Jewish and/or democratic – values, Israel could have chosen to satisfy its Jewish identity through the right of return (The Law of Return, 1950) the observance of official Jewish holidays and sanctioning Hebrew as the official state language (The Palestine Order in Council, 1922, art. 82; Pinto 2007). From a historic point of view, Israel is the sole homeland of the Jewish nation, thus entitling all its members a special key to come back "home." Being an integral part of the Jewish nation, the right of return for Jews, as such, is this golden key that grants them, after two millennia in harsh exile, the indisputable right to return to their holy homeland. Notwithstanding, every legal citizen who lived in that homeland, whether a Jew or not, must be treated fairly and equitably (*Qa'adan* 2000, para. 31).

As for its democracy, one would expect Israel to promote principles of substantive democracy by lending itself to liberal values. Recalling the distinction between formal and substantive democracies, it is notable that especially during recent years there have been several official governmental voices that perceive democracy as nothing but a means to fulfil the needs and the wishes of the electoral majority, notwithstanding how immoral they might be. To many Israeli politicians' dismay, the Israeli judiciary, represented by the Supreme Court, has played an important role in advancing and protecting the values of substantive democracy and in protecting the rights and liberties of minorities against any possible abuse of power by the democratically elected majority (Ely, 1980).

The international community originally anticipated Israel to become a Jewish and democratic state, as promised in the Declaration of Independence as well as in subsequent human rights Basic Laws. Yet Israel has a long way to go before it achieves a proper balance between its Jewish identity and its democratic nature. Presently, it is in Israel's discretion to decide, as a matter of principle, to adopt the positive universal peculiar pillars of each of these identities – hence, actively acknowledge that democracy and Jewishness (and/or Judaism) are not values in themselves but rather means to achieve other idealistic values.

Epilogue: Israel's Democracy and the Arab Minority Citizens

Like Israeli citizens on the one hand, and Arab nationals on the other,[12] the Arab minority, as full and legal citizens of Israel (Peleg and Waxman 2011, 19–26; Kimmerling and Migdal 2003, 240–273; Sachar 2002, 615–739),[13] should have a better and clearer understanding of their multiple identities. The geographic, historic, and cultural nexus between Israeli Arabs and the Arab Palestinian citizens of Mandatory Palestine does not make them Palestinians; otherwise, one would deem the indigenous Jewish citizens of Mandatory Palestine, some of whom nowadays have become Israeli citizens, Palestinians as well.

In order to be considered as loyal to the Israeli state, Arab minority citizens of Israel are not necessarily expected to be Zionists, nor do they have to be patriotic to Israel. Patriotism expresses solidarity, which crosses all political, national, and international boundaries, whereas loyalty embodies a contractual relationship between the state and its citizens. Israeli Arabs' nationality as Arabs does not (and must not) undermine their citizenship as Israelis, nor does their citizenship vis-à-vis their nationality. Israel, in turn, must be loyal to its Arab citizens and refrain from treating them as a "fifth column" whenever, even in times of war, they oppose any governmental policy.

Being loyal to Israel does not negate or lessen Israeli Arabs' absolute and inherent right to feel solidarity toward their Arab brothers and sisters from other Arab countries and. in particular, the Palestinian Arabs. In the course of expressing their solidarity, Israeli Arabs may (and should be allowed to) invoke all legitimate legal, social and political means. But still, they may not raise an arm against Israel, exactly as Israel should not have raised an arm against them in October 2000 (see Ch. 20 in this volume).

Israel's democratic citizens agree that the Jewish state's flag and national anthem do not represent all Israelis. Were Israel's flag and anthem symbols of the state, they should have reflected the statehood identity of Israel, namely, its Israel-ness, not its national and/or religious identity as a Jewish state. Since Israel is defined as a Jewish and democratic state, there is a responsibility to embrace all Israeli citizens alike, and in doing so, Israel does not negate the essence of its being Jewish. To this extent, for example, the anthem must speak of the "Israeli spirit [not the Jewish spirit]" as "yearning deep in the heart" (Flag, Emblem, and National Anthem Law, 1949).[14]

The recent enactment of the Nation-State Law – which seems to give Israel's Jewish values supremacy over Israel's democratic commitments – raises fundamental questions regarding the future of Israel as originally defined as a "Jewish and Democratic" state. Without a prompt and effective change in its application of the Nation-State Law, Israel's future might be either close to "Utopia" (More 1984)[15] or to "Dystopia" (Mill, 1988).[16] Patching up the gaps between the majority and other minorities is not solely the concern of minorities who, day and night, must give up their rights, suffocate their freedoms, and limit their liberties. This must primarily be of the utmost concern to the majority, who must strike a balance between its own interests and the rights of minorities; thus, expressing tolerance and compassion toward the latter. Moreover, in diverse states, such as Israel, the urgent involvement of governmental power is required for all means of reconciliation to be achieved.

Recommended Readings

Kimmerling, B., and J. S. Migdal. 2003. *The Palestinian People: A History*. Cambridge, MA: Harvard University Press.

Morris, B. 2008. *1948: A History of the First Arab-Israeli War*. New Haven, CT: Yale University Press.

Navot, S. 2014. *The Constitution of Israel: A Contextual Analysis*. Oxford: Hart Publishing.

Peleg, I., and D. Waxman. 2011. *Israel's Palestinians: The Conflict Within*. New York: Cambridge University Press.

Sachar, H. S. 2002. *A History of Israel: From the Rise of Zionism to Our Time*, 2nd rev. ed. New York: A. A. Knopf.

Questions for Discussion

(1) Can Israel be a Jewish and democratic state?
(2) What is the legal status of Israel's Declaration of Independence?
(3) What are the characteristics of Israel's democracy?
(4) What is the legal status of the Arab citizens of Israel?
(5) Is the Nation-State Law a racist statute?

Notes

* I would like to thank Mr. Yehuda Levy for reading an early version of this chapter, as well as for providing his very helpful comments, suggestions, reservations and edits. Many thanks as well to my research assistant Dana Salameh for her assistance. I owe special thanks to my father, Saif-Alden Wattad, a lawyer, who has educated me on principles of proportionality and reasonableness; I owe him a lot.

All opinions and errors (and, if applicable, errors of opinion) are my own. I would like to dedicate this chapter to my wife Lana and to my daughters Lady Lorraine and Emily; I wish us a good future together. Note: Several arguments of this chapter are borrowed from an earlier contribution of mine (Cohen-Almagor and Wattad 2019).

1 The chapter concerns the conceptual grounds of governance as stipulated in the Partition Plan. Nothing in the chapter suggests routing Israel's geographic borders as set forth in the Partition Plan. The latter issue falls outside the scope of the subject matter of this chapter.

2 The term "Mandatory Palestine" refers to the geographical area that was administered by the Mandate of the United Kingdom (hereafter, the British Mandate), and was the area carved out of the Southern area of Great Syria under the Ottoman Empire, e.g. the territory of nowadays Jordan and Israel, as well as the West Bank and the Gaza Strip of the Palestinian Authority (Mandate for Palestine, 1922).

3 Human Dignity and Liberty, 1992, art. 1A; Freedom of Occupation, 1994, article 2; the Knesset, 1958, article 7. Additionally, on arguments against Israel's definition as a "Jewish and democratic state," consider Adalah 2006; Bishara, 1993, 7; Tibi, 2005. Compare: I contend that the day Israel will cease being both a "Jewish" and "democratic" state; it will lose the fundamental legal and political justification for its existence, and so there will be no legal and political justification for the establishment of the Palestinian state as an "Arab and democratic" state. The inception for the official recognition of the national aspirations of the Arab citizens of Mandatory Palestine was set forth at first in the Partition Plan (UNESCO 1989, 3). Note: In the Partition Plan the word "Palestinian" is used to describe the citizenship identity of both the Arab and the Jewish citizens of Mandatory Palestine. See United Nations General Assembly, "The Future Government of Palestine," at Sec. B, Part 1, ch. B, art. 9, para. 2, which states: "Qualified voters for each State for this election shall be persons ... who are: (a) Palestinian citizens ...]." To elaborate, Al-Kayyali, in his article, uses the term "the Arab Palestinians" while referring to the Arab citizens of Mandatory Palestine, which reflects, in my opinion, the distinction between the Arab nationality and the Palestinian citizenship (Al-Kayyali, 1985, 38; Kimmerling and Migdal, 2003, 135). Accordingly, I do not agree with the position that provides that the Partition Plan recognizes Palestinian nationalism. This cannot be true, as the Partition Plan speaks of the establishment of an independent Arab, not a Palestinian, state. Furthermore, the political activity of the Arab citizens of Mandatory Palestine against the Ottoman Empire in particular, but also against the British Mandate, was perceived as a desire to receive recognition for their Arab national identity (Al-Kayyali, 1985, 39–41, 46–47, and 234–238). However, to make this clear: I am not asserting that, since 1947, Palestinian nationalism has not evolved. However, I do not purport to discuss the issue of Palestinian nationalism as distinguished from Arab nationalism. This topic is too complicated, thus deserves to be discussed in a separate chapter. For general reading, see Ayyad, 1999; Khalidi, et al., 1991.

4 For example, Israel has not succeded to adopt a full written constitution as mandated by the Partition Plan (Resolution 181, 1947, B, Part 1, ch. B, art. 9, para. 1). Eventually, by means of a political compromise, Israel has adopted a series of incomplete Basic Laws intended, once enacted, to compose the constitution for Israel. Whereas the Knesset has never decided when such a project will be completed, thus establishing the full and final constitution, the contemporary Basic Laws that deal with human rights, severely fail to include a straightforward constitutional protection for very basic human rights, otherwise included in the Partition Plan, e.g. freedom of expression and the right to equality. On the normative constitutional status of the basic laws, see Navot 2014, 4–12; Wattad 2015, 213, 221–226.

5 As such, resolutions of the United Nations General Assembly are not binding. Its power is restrained to discussing matters within the scope of the United Nations Charter (hereafter, the United Nations Charter). In addition, its power to make recommendations is limited "with matters about which the Security Council "is exercising' its 'functions'" (United Nations Charter, 1945, arts. 10–17). The Partition Plan was never adopted by the United Nations Security Council, hence, its present status as an unbinding resolution of the UNGA that was accepted by the Jewish Agency for Palestine but rejected by the Arab states' leaders and governments.

6 What constitutes "people" for the purposes of international law is a very complicated question, especially nowadays, where societies are composed of a very complicated texture of multiple identities. Vita Gudeleviciute argues that in cases of non-self-governing peoples, e.g. colonized, "a people" is deemed the entire population of the occupied territorial unit, no matter their other differences (Gudeleviciute, 2005, 48).

7 The accurate title should be "the Hebrew nation," thus distinguishing it from the Jewish religion.

8 Had it been otherwise, it is only plausible then that the Partition Plan would have proposed the establishment of a Muslim state beside the Jewish state, yet not necessarily an Arab state.

9 Further historical, national, and religious justifications for the establishment of Israel are also included in the Declaration.

10 However, note that the legal status of the Declaration of Independence, has remained, by majority voices of the Court's justices solely as expressing the credo of Israel as a Jewish and democratic state, thus in the absence of a complete constitution, the Declaration has remained relevant, yet only "as a document that can bridge the divides in Israeli society" (Navot 2014, 13; Clal 1994; Ziv 1948, 89; Rogozinsky 1971).

11 I do not refer to the concept of law in its narrow sense, i.e., *Gesetz* in German, *loi* in French, and *ley* in Spanish.

12 Nation is not a synonym for state; there must be a clear distinction between nationhood and statehood. Nationhood refers to ordinary people who may or may not share the same state; in nationhood, something stronger than a state binds the people together. A nation encompasses the factors that constitute each individual – the language, the history, the culture, and the bond between geography and self – and it is what people feel part of, rather than what they belong to. The nation acts in history, achieving greatness and committing crimes, for its glory as well as its shame. This is the Shakespearian notion of brotherhood. Unlike the nation, the state is what people belong to, but not necessarily what they feel part of. If the people are part of the nation, it follows that the nation comes first, and thus legitimizes the establishment of the state. The state is not about death and birth, but about organization of power; it is a political entity.

13 The Arab minority citizens of Israel constitute around 20 per cent of Israel's entire population.

14 Israel's anthem contains the phrase, "[A]s long as in the heart within, the Jewish soul yearns."

15 Utopia means "*NOPLACIA*," namely, "no place."

16 The term represents the concept of "Not a Good Place," or a society that is undesirable or frightening. It is believed that one of the early uses of this word was made by John Stuart Mill in one of his parliamentary speeches.

References

Adalah. 2006. "The Future Vision of the Palestinian Arabs in Israel." Available at: www.adalah.org/uploads/oldfiles/newsletter/eng/dec06/tasawor-mostaqbali.pdf.

Al-Kayyali, A. 1985. *Tareekh Falastin al-Hadeeth* (Beirut: al-Mu'assasat al-Arabiyya.

Anidjar, G. 2003. *The Jew, The Arab: A History of the Enemy*. Stanford, CA: Stanford University Press.

Ayyad, A. 1999. *Arab Nationalism and the Palestinians, 1850–1939*. Jerusalem: The Palestinian Academic Society for the Study of International Affairs.

Bishara, A. 1993. "On the Question of the Palestinian Minority in Israel." *Theory and Criticism* 3:1, 7–20.

Cohen-Almagor, R. 1993. "Harm Principle, Offence Principle, and the Skokie Affair." *Political Studies* 41:3, 453–470.

Cohen-Almagor, R. 1994a. *The Boundaries of Liberty and Tolerance*. Gainesville, FL: University Press of Florida.

Cohen-Almagor, R. 1994b. "Between Neutrality and Perfectionism." *Canadian Journal of Law and Jurisprudence* 7:2, 217–236.

Cohen-Almagor, R. 2017. "JS Mill's Boundaries of Freedom of Expression: A Critique." *Philosophy* 92:4, 565–596.

Cohen-Almagor, R. and M. S. Wattad. 2019. "The Legal Status of Israeli-Arabs/Palestinians in Israel." *GNLU Law & Society Review* 13:1.

Dunoff, J. L., et al. 2002. *International Law: Norms, Actors, Process: A Policy-Oriented Approach*. New York: Aspen Law and Business.

Ely, J. H. 1980. *Democracy and Distrust*. Cambridge, MA: Harvard University Press.

Gudeleviciute, V. 2005. "Does the Principle of Self-determination Prevail over the Principle of Territorial Integrity?" *International Journal of Baltic Law* 2:2, 48–74.

Hadawi, S. 1989. *Bitter Harvest: A Modern History of Palestine*. New York: Olive Branch Press.

Hayek, F. A. 1955. *The Counter-Revolution of Science*. Glencoe, IL: Free Press.

Henkin, L. 1990. *The Age of Rights*. New York: Columbia University Press.

Hobhouse, L. T. 1945. *Liberalism*. Oxford: Oxford University Press.

Janis, M. W. 2003. *An Introduction to International Law*, 4th ed. New York: Aspen Publishers.

Khalidi, R., et al., eds. 1991. *The Origins of Arab Nationalism*. New York: Columbia University Press.

Kimmerling, B., and J. S. Migdal. 2003. *The Palestinian People: A History*. Cambridge, MA: Harvard University Press.

League of Nations. 1922. "Mandate for Palestine." United Nations Information System on the Question of Palestine Documents Collections, 24 July. Available at: https://lb.archive.org/lb/20131125014738/http://unispal.un.org/UNISPAL.NSF/0/2FCA2C68106F11AB05256BCF007BF3CB.

Macpherson, C. B. 1977. *The Life and Times of Liberal Democracy*. Oxford: Oxford University.

Mill, J. S. 1988. *Public and Parliamentary Speeches*, vol. 1, eds. J. M. Robson and B. L. Kinzer. Toronto: University of Toronto Press.

More, T. 1984. *Utopia*, trans. P. Turner. London: Penguin Books.

Morris, B. 2008. *1948: A History of the First Arab-Israeli War*. New Haven, CT: Yale University Press.

Navot, S. 2014. *The Constitution of Israel: A Contextual Analysis*. Oxford: Hart Publishing.

Peleg, I., and D. Waxman. 2011. *Israel's Palestinians: The Conflict Within*. New York: Cambridge University Press.

Pinto, M. 2007. "On the Intrinsic Value of Arabic in Israel – Challenging Kymlicka on Language Rights." *Canadian Journal of Law & Jurisprudence* 20:1, 143–172.

Plato. 2003. *The Republic*, trans. H. D. Lee. London: Penguin Classics.

Ram, U. 1995. "Zionist Historiography and the Invention of Modern Jewish National Identity: The Case of Ben Zion Dinur." *History and Memory* 7:1, 91–124.

Rawls, J. 2002. *The Law of Peoples*. Cambridge, MA: Harvard University Press.

Raz, J. 1986. *The Morality of Freedom*. London: Clarendon Press.

Rorty, R. 2005. "Justice as a Larger Loyalty." *Ethical Perspectives* 4:3, 139–151.

Sachar, H. S. 2002. *A History of Israel: From the Rise of Zionism to Our Time*, 2nd ed., rev. New York: A. A. Knopf.

Smooha, S. 2002a. "The Model of Ethnic Democracy: Israel as a Jewish and Democratic State." *Nations and Nationalism* 8:4, 475–503.

Smooha, S. 2002b. "Types of Democracy and Modes of Conflict-management in Ethnically Divided Societies." Nations and Nationalism 8:4, 423–431.

Smooha, S. 2018. "Israel 70: The Global Enigma." *Fathom*, July. Available at: http://fathomjournal.org/israel70-the-global-enigma/.

"The Balfour Declaration." 1917. *Israel Ministry of Foreign Affairs*. Available at: www.mfa.gov.il/mfa/foreignpolicy/peace/guide/pages/the%20balfour%20declaration.aspx.

"The Declaration of the Establishment of the State of Israel" 1948. 14 May, available at: www.mfa.gov.il/mfa/foreignpolicy/peace/guide/pages/declaration%20of%20establishment%20of%20state%20of%20israel.aspx#:~:text=14%20May%201948&text=On%20May%2014%2C%201948%2C%20on,of%20the%20State%20of%20Israel.

The Knesset. 1949. "Flag, Emblem, and National Anthem Law." Available at: https://knesset.gov.il/holidays/eng/hatikva_eng.htm.

The Knesset. 1950. "The Law of Return." Available at: www.knesset.gov.il/laws/special/eng/return.htm.

The Knesset. 1958. "Basic Law: the Knesset." Available at: https://knesset.gov.il/laws/special/eng/BasicLawTheKnesset.pdf.

The Knesset. 1992. "Basic Law: Human Dignity and Liberty." Available at: http://knesset.gov.il/laws/special/eng/BasicLawLiberty.pdf.

The Knesset. 1994. "Basic Law: Freedom of Occupation." Available at: http://knesset.gov.il/laws/special/eng/BasicLawOccupation.pdf.

"The Palestine Order in Council – 1922." 1922. *United Nations Information System on the Question of Palestine Documents Collections*. Available at: https://unispal.un.org/DPA/DPR/unispal.nsf/0/C7AAE196F41AA055052565F50054E656.

Montevideo Convention on the Rights and Duties of States (1933).

Tibi, A. 2005. "Medinat Kol Leumeha." *NRG*. 10 May. Available at: www.nrg.co.il/online/1/ART/932/352.html.

United Nations Charter. 1945. Available at: www.un.org/en/sections/un-charter/un-charter-full-text/.

United Nations General Assembly. 1947. "Resolution 181." United Nations Information System on the Question of Palestine Documents Collections, 29 November. Available at: https://unispal.un.org/DPA/DPR/unispal.nsf/0/7F0AF2BD897689B785256C330061D253.

UNESCO. 1989. "Request for the Admission of the State of Palestine to UNESCO as a Member State." Available at: http://unesdoc.unesco.org/images/0008/000827/082711eo.pdf

Wattad, M. S. 2015. "Israel's Laws on Referendum – A Tale of Unconstitutional Legal Structure." *Florida Journal of International Law* 27:2, 213–260.

Wootliff, R. 2018. "Final text of Jewish nation-state law, approved by the Knesset early on July 19." *The Times of Israel*. 19 August. Available at: www.timesofisrael.com/final-text-of-jewish-nation-state-bill-set-to-become-law/.

Legal Cases

Clal Insurance Co. Ltd. v. Minister of Finance, HCJ 726/94, 48(5) PD 441 (1994), Nevo. Available at: https://portal.zefat.ac.il/f5-w-68747470733a2f2f7777772e6e65766f2e636f2e696c$$/psika_word/elyon/padi-ng-5-441-l.pdf#xml=http://www.nevo.co.il/Handlers/Highlighter/PdfHighlighter.ashx?index=0&type=Main.

Kol Ha'am Co., Ltd. v. Minister of the Interior, HCJ 73/53 and HCJ 87/53; 7(2) PD 871 (1953), Nevo. Available at: www.nevo.co.il/Psika_word/elyon/5300073.pdf.

Qa'adan et al. v. Israel Lands Administration et al., HCJ 6698/05, 54(1) PD 258 (2000).

Rogozinsky v. State of Israel, CA 450/70, 26(1) PD 129 (1971), Nevo. Available at: https://portal.zefat.ac.il/f5-w-68747470733a2f2f7777772e6e65766f2e636f2e696c$$/psika_word/elyon/KE-1-129-L.pdf#xml=http://www.nevo.co.il/Handlers/Highlighter/PdfHighlighter.ashx?index=0&type=Main.

Ziv v. Gubernick, HCJ 10/48, 1 PD 85 (1948), 89, Nevo. Available at: https://portal.zefat.ac.il/f5-w-68747470733a2f2f7777772e6e65766f2e636f2e696c$$/psika_html/elyon/4800010.pdf#xml=http://www.nevo.co.il/Handlers/Highlighter/PdfHighlighter.ashx?index=0&type=Main.

23

CIVIL SOCIETY AND CITIZEN-TO-CITIZEN DIPLOMACY

Galia Golan

Introduction

This chapter examines the history and emergence of today's large and active civil society in Israel. Reference is made to the tradition of politically related organizations and the general absence of a multifaceted civil society until relatively late in the history of Israel. The primary focus is on Jewish and joint Jewish and Arab organizations in civil society, with a particular look at organizations engaged in peace or coexistence activities. These became increasingly active in the period of the Oslo Accords. Yet, it will be noted, the plethora of Jewish and even joint Jewish and Arab organizations and activities did not result in significant changes in Israeli governmental policies regarding coexistence or peace. Arab civil society also experienced steady growth, which will be referred to in connection with changes that occurred in the communities of Palestinian citizens of Israel.

Israeli and Palestinian Civil Society: A Brief Overview

Civil society and civil society activism are relatively new concepts in Israel, despite the many religious, ethnic, social, and economic rifts in the country. President Reuven Rivlin referred to these schisms as tribes, referring to four major groups (Lewis 2015). He addressed the socio-demographic transformation that is remaking Israel's society, arguing that Israel is now composed of four increasingly equal-sized "tribes" – secular, national religious, ultra-orthodox (*Haredi*), and Arab. Historically this was not always the case, given the different sizes of the groups. Still, in the early years of the country, and since the 1950s, there were conflicts, occasional confrontations, and protest demonstrations. Nonetheless, a social justice demonstration by underprivileged citizens in Jerusalem in the late 1960s was still an anomaly barely understood by the Israeli public. Indeed, the prime minister at the time, Golda Meir, said the demonstrators were "not nice people" (CIE, n.d.).

Israeli society and politics, for decades centred on political parties. Labour organizing was commonplace both before and subsequent to the creation of Israel, which was established as a welfare state. However, the founding generation hailed from Eastern Europe and Russia, for the most part, and its leaders had little acquaintance with liberal (or social) democracy or political pluralism, nor with organized public activity beyond political parties. Neither the European

DOI: 10.4324/9780429027376-28

nor the slightly later immigrant populations from the Middle Eastern countries brought with them a tradition or political culture born of Western liberalism. To their credit, the early leaders installed a system more or less modelled on democratic institutions, but the absence of a political culture suited to such a system can be felt to this day. Civil society units existed – such as labour unions, sports teams, women's groups, youth movements, and so forth – but they, including even schools, were linked to political parties. In time, service groups multiplied, forming the largest segment of civil society. Still, for the most part, if not exclusively, public activity, pressure groups, and public demands tended to focus on the parties. This was within Jewish Israeli society, while Arab society in Israel was even less organized, revolving more around family clans and focusing on services.

That said, over the years a large, and very active, civil society has gradually emerged in Israel (Gidron, Bar, and Katz 2004). As the country shifted from a welfare state to a liberal economy including extensive privatization, the non-profit – third – sector grew significantly. In many instances, organizations have partnered with the government or fully replaced the government. Some 80 per cent of the not-for-profit Israeli organizations are engaged in activities related to religion, education, social services, cultural and leisure activities, and philanthropy (Reut Institute 2008). As in earlier years, these are concentrated mainly among the Jewish sector of Israelis. Today there are 39,819 "Jewish organizations" – Jewish-led and working within Jewish society; 3,895 "Arab organizations" – Arab-led and working in Arab or mixed communities to benefit Arab society. Of these, 10 are defined as "mixed organizations" – having Jewish management but working within Arab society via chapters managed by local residents but defined as minority; 29 are "Joint Jewish-Arab organizations" (IATS 2019).

Within the Jewish sector, the organizations generally do fall into the three of the tribal categories suggested by President Rivlin, namely, religious, ultra-orthodox, and secular, with the religious sector accounting for the largest number of organizations. The smaller number of organizations in the Arab sector of society (in relation to the proportion of the whole populations) are also divided among the more traditional, often religious, and secular, but the increase may not be so clearly defined in these terms. Until 1993 an average of forty new Arab organizations registered per year, later rising to over fifty per year. After the year 2000, over a hundred registered per year and, in recent years, this number has grown to two hundred new organizations registering annually. The periods of greatest increase coincided with the Oslo period and the Second *Intifada* (IATS 2019).

According to a recent study, there are a number of factors behind the growth of civil society among the Arab population. Internal factors, such as the weakening of traditional structures and also of the role of Arab political parties in community life, along with the rise in educational levels and human rights discourse of the younger generation of Arabs, are all important contributing factors (IATS 2019). Greater political awareness and independence of the younger generation has inspired involvement to deal with the socio-economic areas habitually neglected by the Israeli government, or those areas in which there has not been significant government investment, and even lacking attention by the Arab political parties (Jabareen 2007).

An important Arab civil society group, perhaps the most important, is the Higher Monitoring Committee of Arab Citizens of Israel (founded in 1982). It includes all the community and political organizations of Israeli Arab society and deals with all areas, from education to sport and health matters. The Islamic Movement also exists, alongside the Monitoring Committee, and deals with welfare and education, but also matters of health, culture, and sport, as well as religious matters. Several organizations have also been founded to protect the human and civil rights of the Palestinian minority in Israel. One of these, primarily a legal organization, the Mosaswa ("equality") Advocacy Center for Arab Citizens of Israel, engages in litigation and occasional political protest as well as advocacy on behalf of Palestinian citizens of Israel. A second Arab organization concentrating on legal rights is Adalah ("justice"); it often handles land issues, as well as human rights issues, representing Palestinians in the occupied territories as well. Alongside these fully Arab groups, there are a number of joint non-governmental organizations (NGOs) that focus on serving the Arab community in Israel. Sikkuy, the Association for the Advancement of Civic Equality, was created as a joint organization in 1991 and devotes much attention to economic equality in addition to matters of equality in the areas of health, education, and social welfare. It is run by two directors, an Arab and a Jew, and seeks to remove barriers in all walks of Israeli society, including the public sector. The Abraham Fund Initiatives deals with coexistence, coordinating a large network of coexistence groups and projects, but it also pursues equality in the fields of the economy, planning and culture. A major funder for the Arab and joint Arab/Jewish groups in Israel is the New Israel Fund (NIF). An international group created by Jewish American philanthropists in 1982, the NIF provides funds for many Israeli groups engaged in social change, and its section, Shatil, provides organizational and other training for the groups that the NIF assists financially.

Citizen-to-citizen Diplomacy and the Israeli-Palestinian Conflict

While service and self-help groups have continued generally to dominate in Israeli society, over the years protest groups, not limited to economic or social grievances, have emerged and expanded. This has occurred among both the Jewish and Arab publics, but primarily amongst the Jewish population. Alongside these, political protest groups have multiplied, constituting an ever-growing peace and human rights sector. Over the years, the Israeli-Arab conflict and more specifically the Israeli-Palestinian conflict, often alternated between hot and cold, violent and quiescent, and expressed greater or lesser animosity between Jews and Arabs within the new state. Yet, throughout all this, and for many years, contacts between citizens, civil society organizations, and even former officials did take place behind the scenes, in "Track Two" meetings. Not only do they seek communication, but often they seek to change the realities on the ground, maybe even to promote resolution. The advantage of such contacts is that they do not commit their respective official leaders regarding the ideas, initiatives, or actions adopted or proposed by the participants. But, in addition to keeping channels of communication open, often during violent times, they also inform the other side of red lines, what is possible and what is not possible, what might work and what definitely will not work. And those who engage in more than talking, that is, those who engage in actually working together, have the hope, perhaps even the goal, of changing minds and hearts between and within adversaries. Thus, they may even hope to make peace possible between the two peoples.

Track Two meetings, namely the many meetings between former officials, decision makers, and opinion makers, have been going on for many years. However, in order to maintain the freedom to discuss, and also to avoid committing their leaderships to positions or to public pressure, such meetings are generally secret. Thus, few of these encounters are open to research or public scrutiny. The few that are known are some of those that were in fact semi-official (sometimes even called "Track One and a Half," rather than Track Two). The governments behind those involved tended to know what was going on, and even to use the encounters for their own ends. One of the earliest, and most important, Track Two frameworks were the Pugwash meetings, which became the venue for discussions between the Soviet Union and the United States in search of an ending to the Vietnam War. In fact, Pugwash was awarded the Nobel Peace Prize for this accomplishment, without having to reveal officially that governments, especially the Soviet government, were behind the people who participated.

In later years, Pugwash as an international organization, brought in personalities from many conflicts, from Afghanistan and Iran, and local protagonists, including Israelis and Palestinians.[1] Often created as fronts, either by the Soviet Union or the United States (or other countries), these organizations nonetheless played a role in bringing adversaries together across the lines of the Cold War, and served as something of a model for Israelis and Palestinians, among others.

A less famous, but quite effective, Track Two framework that went on for years was the Aix Group, consisting mainly of Israeli and Palestinian economists, who met for years in France and eventually published its joint analyses and proposals for economic cooperation. Beyond these known frameworks, there were many, many others, meeting regularly or just once or twice, but nonetheless fulfilling the task of maintaining channels of communication and bringing together adversaries and their allies in a common search for understanding and possibly peace.

In Israel, Track Two, and citizen-to-citizen diplomacy, namely Jewish–Arab meetings and dialogues, blossomed in the period following the signing of the Oslo Accords in 1993. Both Arabs and Jews sought communication, dialogue, and joint ventures. As a result, numerous new NGOs were formed, including many that were mixed, Arab and Jew, or sought joint endeavours. Part of this could be linked to clauses in the Oslo Accords that encouraged people-to-people activities, but the phenomenon most likely reflected the enthusiasm of both publics for the era of peace and cooperation promised by Oslo.

In addition to dialogue and joint activities, there have also been a number of more direct avenues of cooperation between civil-society groups, including NGOs, between adversaries in the Israeli-Arab, Israeli-Palestinian, conflict over the past few decades. Some of this has simply been cooperation on the edges – for example, cooperative ventures on scientific matters, the environment, or health issues – that bring people together professionally without directly seeking resolution of the conflict. The idea has often been that, by working together, the participants may create empathy or understanding that generally eludes politicians and officials. During the 1990s, in the period of the Oslo Accords, joint work and even joint NGOs were almost the norm. Innumerable new groups were organized; existing Israeli and Palestinian NGOs (and institutions and businesses) made contact and began working together. Women's groups, such as the Jerusalem Link (later the International Commission for a Just Peace in the Middle East, sponsored by UNIFEM, the United Nations Development Fund for Women), and professional groups such as social workers, town planners, and others took advantage of the new atmosphere and began working together. In some ways, this was the untold story of Oslo.

However, most of these joint ventures disappeared or fell apart as Oslo itself disintegrated and violence returned in the Second *Intifada*. Not only did it become virtually impossible to meet, but one side, the Palestinian side, disdained cooperation, and the Palestinian Association of NGOs condemned cooperation with Israelis as "normalization." The explanation was that one could not work with the enemy as if everything were normal. In fact, the anti-normalization position became quite strong and has continued until this day. Thus, the few groups that continue or seek to work across conflict lines have also declined in number. They have to combat opposition to such work even from within their own communities. Despite this public response, the Palestinian leadership, namely the PLO, has continued to appreciate the need to reach and influence the Israeli public. Therefore, in 2012 the PLO created the Committee for Interaction with Israeli Society, which not only condones, but even occasionally assists, NGO cooperation between Israelis and Palestinians from the occupied territories.

For example, Women Waging Peace, an Israeli group of women (including Arab women citizens of Israel) received assistance from the PLO for its massive women's march in the West Bank in 2017. There are still a few, although not many, examples of dialogue groups or at least encounters, organized by peace NGOs and others. However, today there are only two joint peace NGOs, the Family Forum-Parents Circle, and Combatants for Peace. Both groups were created – and remain – as totally joint organizations, with both Palestinian and Israeli individuals in all the staff and leadership positions and events. Both are unique. The Family Forum, created in 1995, brings together family members of persons lost in the conflict, conducting dialogue and public joint mourning. Combatants for Peace brings together former fighters from both sides to work together, repairing damage caused by the Israeli army or settlers, protecting local Palestinian shepherds and the like. It was nominated for the Nobel Peace Prize in 2019 as the only organization of fighters from both sides to work together while their conflict is still ongoing.

Upon occasion, the two NGOs work together, most notably in their annual joint Memorial Ceremony at the time of Israel's official Remembrance Day. A joint Israeli and Palestinian memorial is, of course, a controversial event in the eyes of many Israelis and Palestinians, since it is viewed as implying equality of suffering or equality of victimhood and absence of guilt on one side or the other as perpetrators. Nonetheless, Israelis in these groups are often former combat officers, and the Palestinians former resistance fighters. Combatants for Peace was founded in 2006 by former Israeli combat officers and Palestinians who had spent years in Israeli prisons for violent actions.

While these are the only fully joint peace movements, there are other NGOs in which there are ad hoc joint activities or significant cooperation. *Ta'yush*, for example, is an Israeli NGO that brings both Israelis and Palestinians to protests or service in the occupied territories. *B'teslem*, which records and protests human rights abuses perpetrated by Israel in the occupied territories, employs Palestinian field workers as well as Israeli Jews in their research and activities. Of course, virtually any NGO active in the occupied territories, such as Rabbis for Human Rights, or Physicians for Human Rights, will receive assistance from local Palestinians, sometimes on more than an ad hoc basis, but these are not joint movements as such.

Other organisations work on specific issues of the conflict. For example, *B'Tseelem* is dedicated to documenting human rights violations in the occupied territories, *Bimkom* deals with construction plans, *HaMoked* deals with rights of Palestinian workers in Israel, *Yesh Din* deals with legal issues, particularly related to land expropriation and settlements. These tend to be Israeli groups, composed of Israeli Jews and Arabs, but often aided by Palestinians in the occupied territories or solicited to help Palestinians in the occupied territories. *Gisha* is similar; it deals with Gaza, concentrating on restrictions on freedom of movement. Another group that deals with Gaza, A Different Voice, is composed of Palestinians living in Gaza and Israeli Jews living on the Israeli borders of the Gaza Strip (what is known as the Gaza envelope). They initiate dialogues and play an important role in promoting peace and understanding in an area often subject to Israeli military attack (on Gaza) and to Palestinian rockets on Israel.

Most of these organizations also seek not only to prevent or protest actions related to the occupation, but also to try to protect local Palestinians from such actions. At the same time, these and others also promote peace and seek to influence public opinion within Israel. They do this by publicizing information related to land confiscation, house demolition, and so forth. One relatively newer organization is Breaking the Silence, devoted explicitly to changing Israeli public opinion. They publicize testimonies of Israeli male and female soldiers, following their required military service or reserve duty, in connection with violent or illegal actions by the IDF that they have personally witnessed or in which they even participated. This group has attracted the ire of the right wing in Israel, perhaps even more than any other peace group, and the government has banned appearances by them in the Israeli school system.

What Combatants for Peace, Breaking the Silence, and the older, once mass-movement Peace Now have in common is their relationship to former Israeli soldiers and officers.

Peace Now was founded in 1978 by reserve soldiers and officers as, later, were the other two movements, Combatants for Peace and Breaking the Silence. The use of the military motif was deliberate, invoking the legitimacy (in Israel) and veracity of their peace advocacy. While the centrality of the Israeli Defense Forces (IDF) in Israel (natural in a country engaged in an ongoing violent conflict), and the enormous respect for the army, have eroded somewhat since the 1982 Lebanon War (which was opposed by many Israelis at the time), the fact of having served still connotes legitimacy. The mother motif has also been used by women's peace groups, such as Women Waging Peace and the much earlier Four Mothers group, but demonstrating mothers of soldiers have not had the same appeal as that of soldiers themselves among the Israeli public.

A group that does not employ the mother motif directly, but is nonetheless composed of women, is Machsom Watch. Created during the Second Intifada, when violence and killings of Palestinians at checkpoints were at a high, women undertook the task of observing first- hand the activities at checkpoints. Implied in this was the idea that, perhaps, the presence of women would have a moderating effect on the soldiers serving there – perhaps even suggesting a role as surrogate mothers. The group, nonetheless, stages protests and conducts activities clearly advocating peace, as distinct from limiting their work to calming checkpoints.

Many other peace groups have come and gone, and at various times (Hermann 2009). The First Intifada, which was generally non-violent, saw the rise of tens of peace NGOs in Israel. Many of these, and some that came earlier, during the 1982 Lebanon War, or later, were created to address a specific public or to deal with specific topics. Thus, as noted above, groups like B'Tselem and Yesh Din each sought to deal with a specific issue, while religious peace groups like *Oz v'shalom* addressed the religious public, and the earlier, short-lived *Mizrach l'Shalom* believed it could address the *Mizrahi* public in Israel more effectively than the largely *Ashkenazi* movements like Peace Now. Peace Now itself created a group to work specifically on the issues related to East Jerusalem; this group, *Ir Amim*, later became independent and continues to work on issues of land expropriation and settlement construction in East Jerusalem and surrounding areas of the West Bank. A Russian-speaking group was created in the 1990s to work, not only with human-rights–minded new immigrants from the former Soviet Union, but also with Russian-speaking Arabs in Israel (who had once studied in the Soviet Union).

Assessing the Impact of Civil Society

This is by no means a complete list of the many peace NGOs in Israel or the civil society groups engaged in dialogue or coexistence or education for peace.[2] Yet, despite the large number of such groups, they encompass only a very small proportion of Israeli society. In fact, while most movements can boast a regular influx of new, young adherents, polls have indicated that the vast majority of Israeli young people are not of the peace persuasion (Hexel, Nathanson, and Tzameret-Kertcher 2010). Given the obligatory military service at the age of 18 for all Jewish citizens (with the exception of the ultra-orthodox), Jewish Israeli youth have undergone not only a nationalist education but also a militaristic experience (army service) as they enter adulthood. Moreover, young people today did not have the experience or memory of the Oslo period. The very possibility of peace is rarely mentioned, and opinion polls among both younger and older Israelis reflect decided scepticism about the possibility for peace in the near future. Opinion polls also indicate greater "dovishness," for example, willingness to compromise for peace, or left-wing opinions regarding the conflict, as much higher among the over-sixties than the younger cohorts (IDI, 2019.).[3] The rule of right-wing governments for nearly twenty years, and the impact of the religious and right-wing parties over the education system in Israel, have also had an effect. To this one might add: manipulation of fears, linked to Jewish history and present-day anti-Semitism abroad, the growing power of Iran, and the BDS campaign, as contributing factors to the stable, even growing numbers of right-wing voters among Jewish Israelis.

Moreover, despite the many peace NGOs, dialogue groups, and the like, the Israeli public tends to vote in far greater numbers for right-wing or centre-right parties than the left. Even the Arab public appears to prefer conservative parties when faced with a choice among Arab parties (Sharir 2021). Thus, the elections of 2021 saw an increase in support for the conservative Islamist party among Palestinian citizens of Israel, as well as support among Jewish voters for the extremist, openly racist parties on the right. These may be trends reflecting the fact that little to no progress toward peace has occurred in the last twenty years. Nationalist sentiment has risen within both publics. Moreover, neither peace, nor the occupation, is an issue in Israeli elections; nor has either of the two been a central topic even in social conversation for many years. This would seem to attest to the ineffectiveness of Israeli civil society regarding the conflict; this segment of civil society can no longer even claim, modestly, to have impacted public discourse, if nothing else.[4]

It is, of course, difficult to gauge the success of peace NGOs. Government leaders are not prone to acknowledge the contribution of civil society to moves towards peace, more often preferring to claim full credit for themselves. Or, in some cases, given the unpopularity of peace groups, some leaders – for example, Yitzhak Rabin – strove to prevent any mention of the role of peace groups in the Oslo process; he would not permit a Peace Now speaker, for example, at the 1995 rally despite the fact that Peace Now was one of the organizers, and the rally was clearly intended to demonstrate support for the peace process. Similarly, Ariel Sharon, as prime minister, also ignored the peace camp despite its support for his 2005 disengagement from Gaza. Menachem Begin was an exception to this when he acknowledged the role played by the large rally staged by Peace Now prior to the 1978 Camp David Israel-Egypt peace conference. He said that, in light of the rally, he could not return empty-handed. Yet, Ezer Weizman, also a participant in the 1978 conference, later said quite explicitly, that Peace Now and the rally had no effect whatsoever on their positions at Camp David (Golan 2014, 40). Nor do opinion polls indicate a direct relationship between peace rallies and peace activism, on the one hand, and public opinion regarding the conflict, on the other.

At most, it may be said that civil society activities, especially the large demonstrations, and perhaps some of the publicity, changed the public discourse to some degree. Government action, ironically, also occasionally helped, as was the case of governmental condemnation of activities conducted by B'Tselem (especially abroad) and Breaking the Silence. Similarly, government condemnation and actions to prevent Palestinians from attending the joint memorial held by Combatants for Peace and the Family Forum, in 2019 brought unexpected free publicity for the event.

Service NGOs, as expected, have a better record; they often receive government funding or other help as they replace some of the activities formerly conducted as part of the welfare state, prior to privatization. Human rights groups tend to fall more often into the category of peace groups, suffering criticism from the government and right-wing parties or organizations. In addition, there are some co-existence groups, often ad hoc. The largest and oldest coexistence group is Sikkuy, which generally deals with grievances from Arab citizens of Israel, alongside *Givat Haviva* (belonging to the left-wing kibbutz movement, *HaShomer ha-Zair*) that organizes meetings, dialogues, languages classes, and the like. There is also a joint cooperative Arab–Jewish village, *Neve shalom/Wahat as-Salam* that runs its own elementary and high schools, alongside workshops and dialogues for its residents and also for the broader public.

Since these human rights organizations and some co-existence groups receive financial support from the New Israel Fund, created and funded by progressive Jews mainly from abroad, the NIF is a favourite target for right-wing NGOs. The right-wing NGOs that have been particularly harsh and outspoken are *Im Tirtzu* and *NGO Monitor*. The latter runs a public campaign against peace, but especially against the human rights groups, both within Israel and abroad. Im Tirtzu had been relatively successful, not only in its public campaigns but also in the Israeli Knesset, criticizing other NGOs, especially the peace and human rights organizations, but also the political science departments of most Israeli universities. Both organizations have sought to ways to limit or disparage their funding sources, even succeeding in obtaining legislative action to limit funding from abroad.

Inasmuch as peace has not been achieved, one might easily conclude that the peace NGOs have failed. Circumstances and events such as the lethal Second Intifada (2000–2004) greatly reduced the so-called peace camp and the numbers of left-wing voters in the country. Nonetheless, these groups can point to a few successes. More common than not, peace actions against settlement and outpost building have secured postponements if not actual prevention. Combatants for Peace and the Rabbis for Human Rights, often joined by other groups, staged a long vigil at Chan al Achmar in 2018 in protest to government plans to evacuate the small, makeshift Bedouin village in the desert east of Jerusalem. The sit-in attracted international attention, and the orders to evacuate (and destroy) the village were suspended; the village remains in place to this day despite Netanyahu's promises to resume the previous plans. Earlier there were similar suspensions, although temporary, when Peace Now protested settlement plans for Ras al Amud in East Jerusalem or Efrat to the south. The peace NGO, Ir Amim, originally an offshoot of Peace Now, continues to campaign against government plans for settlements in the East Jerusalem neighbourhood of Silwan, sometimes attracting enough attention to delay such plans. The right-wing NGO, *Amana*, however, has been quite successful in aiding Israeli settler encroachment in Silwan and other parts of East Jerusalem. Perhaps the most notable success of the peace NGOs was the massive protest organized by Peace Now against the 1982 killings in the Lebanese refugee camps Sabra and Chatilla. Peace Now organized a number of protests once news of the Lebanese Christian actions in the camps became known, with the reports of assistance rendered by the Israeli army (indirect, not direct, involvement in the massacre). The protests built up to a massive rally in Tel Aviv, estimated by the police at 400,000 protestors (out of an Israeli population at the time of just 4 million). The demand was for an official commission of inquiry into Israel's role in the massacre. And in response, a commission was indeed created by the government, the Kahan Commission. When, some months later, Peace Now rallied in Jerusalem to demand that the commission's findings (resignation of Defense Minister Ariel Sharon and more), a hand grenade was thrown on the demonstrators, killing one, Emile Greensweig, and injuring seven others. The killing shocked the country; even the Prime Minister Menachem Begin condemned the action and acknowledged that Peace Now was not a fifth column as claimed by some right-wing politicians and groups (Sher, Sternberg, and Ben-Kalifa 2019; also Golan 2014).

Far more successes can be chalked up by the Association for Civil Rights in Israel (ACRI). A primarily Israeli organization, but not exclusively, of lawyers and legal specialists, both Jewish and Arab, ACRI has been occasionally successful in cases it has taken to the Israel Supreme Court. It often joins with other NGOs, for example the Israel Women's Network or Israeli Arab Human Rights NGO such as Adalah (Justice), both for public as well as legal campaigns. One of the most notable examples of NGO cooperation was the 1995 Alice Miller case, petitioned by ACRI and the Israel Women's Network, together. The petition resulted in a ruling allowing women to volunteer for the IDF air force. This groundbreaking decision in turn led to the opening of combat roles for women in the Israeli army. ACRI remains one of the few, relatively successful, bulwarks of Israeli democracy, although it has been generally less successful in cases it has brought against settlement construction, and has had very few successes defending or obtaining rights for persons seeking asylum (Sfard 2018; Kretzmer 2002, 31–46).

Conclusion

Human rights groups, such as ACRI, have the advantage of promoting specific cases of wrong-doing. And rectification can be obtained, often, in the courts. Demands or protests by other types of civil society groups are often more amorphous, eluding purely judicial resolution. Aside from delays, even prevention of certain actions such as evacuations, land expropriations or settlement construction can be approached via the courts, but peace itself must rely on political action of the government, encouraged perhaps by public opinion. Thus, one may turn to public opinion polls to demonstrate positive changes over the years that may, at least in part, be attributed to the efforts of peace NGOs. No direct relationship can be drawn, and, in fact, other factors, domestic, regional and international have played major roles even as Israeli public opinion moved toward support for the two-state solution. Indeed, it may even be argued that globalization, with the domestic shift to a liberal economy and privatization, played as great a role as ideology or peace activism. As neo-capitalism replaced the welfare state, Israeli citizens shifted to values such as individualism, related to competition rather than ideology (Ben Porat 2006). Ideology did not disappear, but the former ethos of social solidarity gave way to individualism and, possibly, to less interest in the general good. as distinct from a desire to get on with one's own life. Such a shift could, it has been argued, lead to greater willingness to compromise in the context of the Israeli-Arab conflict in the interests of simply getting on with one's life. Yet, the vacuum left by the former social democratic values appears to have been filled by more exclusive values related to nationalism and expressed by populist rhetoric. Thus, civil society did not contract, but the phenomenon of right-wing, conservative NGOs emerged. Im Tirtzu and NGO Monitor were prime examples of this, along with settler groups like the Women in Green and other organizations that replaced the former Gush Emunim in promoting and protecting settler interests. They were eventually accompanied by new, right-wing political parties, but the right-wing NGOs mobilized many Jewish – especially religious Jewish Israelis – not interested in direct involvement in party politics. Their impact on public opinion could be felt in the Knesset elections, especially in 2021, but the activities of right-wing groups extended far beyond the political parties. Religious institutions, the *yeshivas*, often formed the backbone of such groups, mobilizing and organizing their activities, thereby contributing to civil society. In fact, the contribution of religious institutions and organizations may warrant further research as one of the newer, more important phenomena in Israeli society.

In conclusion, Israeli democracy may have become more robust with the expansion of civil society. There are more NGOs today and far more citizen activity than in the earlier years of the country. But activity, and numbers, are not necessarily indicators of greater democracy. The nature of the groups, and the nature of their activities, their demands, as born of their ideologies, would provide a more accurate characterization. The election or elevation of greater numbers of women, or Arabs, to political office would tell us something about a society, and perhaps the evolution of equality. Yet, the election or elevation of such groups would not necessarily mean increased response to the interests or the needs of these groups, if the individuals involved did not see themselves as representing the interests of these parts of society.[5] In political studies this is called the difference between descriptive and substantive representation. The key may well be ideology. Numbers may be important; one may consider the more groups participating and active, the better. But one must also look at what the groups are advocating, and how, in order to reach any conclusion about the role of civil society and its contribution to democracy.

Recommended Readings

Galnoor, I. and D. Blander. 2018. *The Handbook of Israel's Political System*. Cambridge: Cambridge University Press, 659–663.

Gidron, B., M. Bar, and H. Katz. 2004. *The Israeli Third Sector: Between Welfare State and Civil Society*. New York: Kluwer Academic/Plenum.

Golan, G. 2004. "The Impact of Peace and Human Rights NGOs on Israeli Policy." In *Non-state Actors in the Middle East: Factors for Peace and Democracy*, eds. G. Golan and W. Salem. London: Routledge, 28–41.

Golan, G. Z. Kamal. 1999. "Bridging the Abyss: Palestinian-Israeli Dialogue." In *Public Peace Process: Sustained Dialogue to Transform Racial and Ethnic Conflicts*, ed. H. Saunders. New York: St. Martin's Press, 197–220.

Hermann, T. 2009.*The Israeli Peace Movement*. Cambridge: Cambridge University Press.

Notes

1 The Dartmouth Group was similar to Pugwash in that it provided a venue for disarmament talks, and PEN international brought together writers.

2 See Hermann (2009) for a fairly exhaustive list and treatment of the peace groups.

3 And unpublished data provide by Dahlia Scheindlin.

4 This was at least an accomplishment I noted in my "The Impact of Peace and Human Rights NGOs on Israeli Policy," in Golan and Salem, eds., *Non-State Actors in the Middle East: Factors for Peace and Democracy*, Routledge, 2014, 28–41.

5 Unpublished research by Galia Golan and Lavi Melman demonstrated the greater relevance of ideology (feminisms) than numbers in their study of legislative activity of both men and women in the 18th Knesset with regard to issues of particular interest to women and issues of women's rights. Feminist men were often more active than non-feminist women on such matters so that numbers were not necessarily a good indication of the nature of legislative initiatives.

Questions for Discussion

(1) What is the relationship between government and civil society?
(2) What factors have contributed to the growth of civil society in Israel?
(3) What factors have contributed to the growth of civil society in the Arab sector in Israel?
(4) What factors account for the relative success or failure of civil society?

References

Ben Porat, G. 2006. *Global Liberalism, Local Populism: Peace and Conflict in Israel/Palestine and Northern Ireland*. Syracuse, NY: Syracuse University Press.

Center for Israeli Education (CIE). N.d. "Israeli 'Black Panthers' Meet with Prime Minister Meir to Discuss Mizrahi Jews, April 13, 1971." Available at: https://israeled.org/israeli-black-panthers/.

Gidron, B., M. Bar, and H. Katz. 2004. *The Israeli Third Sector: Between Welfare State and Civil Society*. New York: Kluwer Academic/Plenum.

Golan, G. 2014). "The Impact of Peace and Human Rights NGOs on Israeli Policy." In *Non-State Actors in the Middle East: Factors for Peace and Democracy*, eds. G. Golan and W. Salem. London: Routledge, 28–41.

Hermann, T. 2009. *The Israeli Peace Movement*. Cambridge: Cambridge University Press.

Hexler, R., R. Nathanson, and H. Tzameret-Kertcher. 2010. *All of the Above: Identity Paradoxes of Young People in Israel*. The 3rd Youth Study of the Friedrich-Ebert-Stiftung Changes in National, Societal, and Personal Attitudes. Tel Aviv: MACRO: The Center for Political Economics.

IATS (Interagency Task Force on Israeli Arab Issues). 2019. "Arab Civil Society Organizations in Israel: A Review of Trends, Growth, and Activities." 1 October. Available at: www.iataskforce.org/activities/view/965.

IDI (Israel Democracy Institute). 2019. *Surveys and Polls*. Available at: https://en.idi.org.il/tags-en/1465.

Jabareen, Y. T. 2007. "NGOs as a Political Alternative: A Critical Perspective." In *The Arab Minority in Israel and Election of the 17th Knesset: Start of a New Era?*, ed. E. Rekhess. Tel Aviv: University of Tel Aviv, 93–99 [in Hebrew].

Kretzmer, K. 2002. *The Occupation of Justice*. New York: SUNY Press.

Lewis, A. 2015. "Tribal Schisms Tearing Israel Apart, Rivlin Cautions." *The Times of Israel*, 7 June. Available at: www.timesofisrael.com/israel-divided-along-tribal-lines-rivlin-warns/.

Reut Institute. 2008. *Non-Profit Sector in Israel*. 18 May. Available at: http://reut-institute.org/en/Publication.aspx?PublicationId=3240.

Sfard, M. 2018. *The Wall and the Gate*. New York: Henry Holt Metropolitan Books.

Sharir, I. 2021. "'There's an Attempt to Change the Jewish Monopoly on Power.'" *Haaretz*, 19 April. Available at: www.haaretz.com/israel-news/.premium-there-s-an-attempt-to-change-the-jewish-monopoly-on-power-1.9722326.

Sher, G., N. Sternberg, and M. Ben-Kalifa. 2019. "The Delegitimization of Peace Activists in Israeli Society." INSS, *Strategic Assessment*, Vol. 22, Issue 2, July 2019. Available at: www.inss.org.il/publication/the-delegitimization-of-peace-advocates-in-israeli-society/.

24

FEMINIST ACTIVISM AND THE ISRAELI-PALESTINIAN CONFLICT

Siobhan Byrne

This chapter charts the evolution of feminist peace and anti-occupation activism in Israel and the occupied West Bank, East Jerusalem, and Gaza Strip, focusing on current conditions of conflict and the deepening occupation. The Palestine/Israel case has served as an exemplar of radical women-led peace and anti-occupation activism and coalitions in the gender and peace literature. Along with a few other select cases, including Bosnia-Herzegovina (BiH), Cyprus, and Northern Ireland (for example, see: Deiana 2016; Murtagh 2008; Cockburn 2007; Hadjipavlou 2006; Yuval-Davis 1997), scholars typically understand this case as a model of how women can forge cross-community peace coalitions that defy deep ethnonational division. Whereas the feminist peace literature of the 1980s and 1990s tends to exalt such cross-community peace coalitions, called 'transversal' peace groups, the field of activism has always been more varied than indicated in this literature. Given that Palestine/Israel has reached the end of the Oslo-era peace process, this has perhaps never been truer than today.

Moreover, insights from the growing body of feminist intersectional scholarship and new thinking around identity politics in feminist political movements can better capture the diversity of emergent forms of feminist peace activism in the Middle East. In this chapter, I argue that feminist intersectional approaches that engage theories of identity and identity politics can bring into view changes in feminist peace politics. This is important for writing feminist voices into the politics of the Israeli-Palestinian conflict. Further, it is critical to inform effective transnational solidarity practices and realize the goals of international instruments such as the United Nations-led Women, Peace and Security (WPS) agenda.

The first section of the chapter maps the impact of the current post-peace-process context on feminist peace and anti-occupation movements. Nearly three decades since the signing of the Oslo Accords, there is now a permanent occupation of Palestinian territories, tight control of Gaza's borders, rightist political leadership in Israel, and deep political division and discord amongst Palestinian leaders. While the end of the peace process has limited some forms of feminist peace activism, this period is also characterized by a rise in new political movements and commitments. Examples include the Palestinian-led Boycott, Divestment, and Sanction (BDS) movement gaining international traction, and new groups coalescing around the UN-led Women, Peace and Security agenda.

The second section focuses on a more extended history of feminist peace and anti-occupation activism in the Israeli-Palestinian conflict. Palestinian and Israeli activists and academics

DOI: 10.4324/9780429027376-29

have written and recorded excellent feminist histories of women's peace and anti-war occupation movements (for example, see: Kuttab 2008; Taraki 2006; Hermann 2002; Jad 1999; Abdulhadi 1998; Sharoni 1995; Mayer 1994; Freedman 1990; Svirsky 1996).[1] This section chronicles some of this history to show changes in feminist activism over time while also signalling the centrality of this history of Middle East politics. As this history shows, there is continuity between current formations of feminist peace and anti-war movements and early women's movements. For example, feminist peace groups continue to organize around themes such as maternal politics and people-to-people dialogue. However, there are also important ruptures with the past, indicating renewed and reimagined modes of activism.

Section three examines the implications of changes in women's peace and anti-occupation activism in the post-peace-process era. Modes of feminist peace and anti-occupation activism have changed. In particular, the peace process's failure undermines the rationale for mass mobilization organized around demands for women's inclusion in the peace process. However, Palestinian feminists and Israeli feminists are forging intersectional coalitions within their national communities and building transnational solidarity outside of strict people-to-people modes of activism.

The final section reviews the implications of the analysis beyond the Palestine/Israel case. In the feminist peace literature, intersectional analysis is closely tethered to consciously cross-community peace coalitions. Likewise, the WPS agenda reproduces an idea of women peacebuilding coalitions that are imagined to stand outside of national identitarian conflicts. However, shifts in activism in this case demonstrate the diversity of ways that feminists understand and realize intersectional activism and build solidarity that is sometimes deeply rooted in national identity politics. Further, it reveals how international instruments such as United Nations-led WPS resolutions, which privilege a particular vision of women's peace coalitions, may both help and hinder feminist activism. If we think more expansively about intersectional coalitions and understand that nationalism and national liberation can be a source of radical feminist peace and anti-occupation activism, then we are better positioned to view the ways women build coalitions and articulate peace and social justice politics. Understanding coalitions as cross-community only may miss important ways that feminists negotiate differences to build solidarity movements.

Assessing the Current Context

Through the 1990s and early 2000s, peace movements were operating in a peace-process context, marked by regular high-level political talks, tentative agreements, and occasional public engagement. Such movements worked within and across ethnonational communities to persuade political leaders to sit at the negotiating table; to demand gender representation and public transparency of peace talks; to call-out Israeli policies that deepened the occupation, such as the expansion of settlements or arbitrary arrest and detention of Palestinians living under occupation; and to protest state and paramilitary violence. However, nearly thirty years since the signing of the Oslo Accords, the Israeli-Palestinian conflict is no closer to resolution; the Oslo-track peace process is dead.

Within Israel, new harsh restrictions and laws target particular forms of activism, such as support for the Boycott, Divestment and Sanction (BDS) movement. The status of Palestinian citizens of Israel has shifted, too; the 2018 Basic Law, Israel as the Nation-State of the Jewish People, limits Palestinians' national standing within Israel. Further, Palestinians living in the occupied West Bank are subject to arbitrary arrest, pre-dawn raids on their homes, and – in the case of prominent feminist Palestinian activists like Khalida Jarrar, and Khitam Saffin, head of the Union of Palestinian Women's Committees – interminable and repeated episodes of administrative detention (Associated Press 2021; *WAFA* 2020). These local conditions provoke peace and anti-occupation activists to consider how impactful their decades of activism have been in moving political leaders to a peace agreement.

At the international level, improved support and partnerships for peace are unlikely to materialize anytime soon. For example, the United States, which has engaged in shuttle diplomacy and peace brokerage for decades, radically shifted its Middle East policy under the Trump Administration. Defunding the United Nations Relief and Works Agency for Palestinian Refugees (UNRWA), moving the United States embassy from Tel Aviv to Jerusalem, and closing the de facto Palestinian embassy in Washington, DC, were all provocative moves that undermined the US's role as a Middle East peace broker. Trump's peace plan, titled "Peace to Prosperity: A Vision to Improve the Lives of the Palestinian and Israeli People" (2020), which proposed expanding Israeli sovereignty over sections of the West Bank and Jerusalem, was roundly rejected by Palestinians. Despite the changeover in the United States administration, there is no good reason to believe that President Joe Biden will prioritize the Middle East peace process. As such, activists continue to struggle to find an international audience to help resurrect the peace process.

Given the new local and international context in the post-peace process, the locus of peace and anti-occupation activism have shifted. Organizations tend to be smaller, multiple, and sometimes transitory as activists target the day-to-day conditions of violence that come with living in an active conflict zone that has no peace agreement on the horizon. Transnational groups are targeting their governments' policies that support the occupation. National groups are organizing on either side of the occupation to inform and influence their respective political leadership. For women in Israel – including Jewish and Palestinian women – this means targeting state and party policies that maintain and deepen the occupation. This means organizing separately for women in occupied Palestine to target their political leadership and building solidarity with regional and transnational organizations. While this marks a change in feminist peace and anti-occupation activism from the joint Palestinian-Israeli cross-community encounters of the 1990s and early 2000s, it is emblematic of a long history of evolution and change in the Palestinian and Israeli women's movements.

A History of Feminist Peace and Anti-occupation Activism

The Palestinian women's movement is rooted in Palestinian nationalism and national liberation politics. After World War I and the imposition of the British mandate, women became politicized in early women's conferences and demonstrations as part of the development of a strong Palestinian national consciousness (see Jad 1999). Palestinian women continued national liberation activism through the establishment of Israel, the Jordanian annexation of the West Bank, and Egyptian rule of Gaza – providing services and delivering education in refugee camps. In 1964, the Palestinian Liberation Organization (PLO) formed, followed by the General Union of Palestinian Women (Jad 1999, 219–220). After the 1967 War and subsequent occupation, women continued to organize as part of women-led charities and as part of the General Union of Palestinian Women. Women participated in armed revolutionary action through the 1970s as part of Palestinian national committees, unions, and student groups, and they were imprisoned for their resistance. In the late 1970s and early 1980s, women formed PLO party-affiliated committees, including the Union of Palestinian Working Women's Committees, the Palestinian Women's Committee, and the Women's Committee for Social Work. These women saw that "emancipating Palestinian women" was central to the national liberation movement (Jad 1999, 223). Palestinian women's groups were forming what we now call intersectional coalitions that included urban and rural women representing different political perspectives, organizing en masse to empower Palestinian women in the national struggle (see Jamal 2015, 238). For Palestinian feminist scholars, it was the experience of grassroots organizing from the 1970s, focused on taking care of the community and national politics, that made the First *Intifada* possible (see Hammami 2000, 16; Jamal 2015, 239).

Early National and Women's Liberation Politics, 1970s and 1980s

The First Palestinian Intifada, in 1987, was a critical period of activism for Palestinian women (Jad 1999, 224–225). Women's mass participation in street protests and public demonstrations were opportunities to challenge the occupation, counter patriarchal society, and define their place in the Palestinian national movement (see Hiltermann 1990, 34–35). Some women's mobilizations continued through Palestinian party-affiliated women's unions (Hiltermann 1991, 50). Throughout this period, Palestinian women's activism took many forms, from militancy to petition writing. As Rabab Abdulhadi (2012, 20) remarks, "as there are many sources of oppression, there are many paths to consciousness and liberation." Women's mass participation in the First Intifada – where women's liberation and national liberation came together in an active struggle against the occupation – stands as a critical historical movement in Palestinian feminist activism.

Like the Palestinian women's movement, the Israeli women's movement follows a similar historical trajectory: predating Israel's establishment and developing in the 1970s mass women's movement and through various feminist movements in the 1980s and 1990s (Herzog 2008). Tamar Hermann (2002, 94, 101) dates the origins of a distinct peace movement in Israel to the late 1960s. These groups grew in the wake of the 1973 Arab-Israeli War, receiving wider recognition with the creation of *Shalom Achsav*, or Peace Now, in 1978. Hermann describes the "particularistic style" of peace group that developed in the 1980s, including movements like Parents Against Silence, which wanted a withdrawal from Lebanon; *Mizrachi* peace groups, like East for Peace (Ha'mizrach Le'shalom); and women's peace groups, like the Four Mothers Movement (Hermann 2002, 102). Like Palestinian women's movements, these groups were intersectional coalitions of women negotiating ethnic, linguistic, and other differences.

Women in Black (WiB) is among the most recognizable of the early Israeli women's anti-occupation peace groups. It started as a women's vigil in West Jerusalem in January 1988. Participants met weekly for one hour, dressed in black and holding signs that read "end the occupation." Twice nominated for a Nobel Peace Prize, the movement went on through the 1990s to inspire peace vigils in other Israeli cities and around the world, including Belgrade, Brussels, Edmonton, London, and Toronto. In Israel, WiB was largely an Israeli-Jewish movement, according to Gila Svirsky (2005), a long-time participant (Interview with author 2005). Hannah Safran (2005) locates the origins of the movement in feminist meetings in the 1980s at the *Kol-Ha-Isha* women's centre in Jerusalem. As Safran remembers, participants represented diverse political and identity constituencies, including Zionist and anti-Zionist women, working-class and middle-class women, lesbian and straight-identifying women, and to a much smaller extent, Palestinian women.

Herzog notes that securing diversity and sustaining dialogue across differences was not always easy. Some participants perceived the women's movement in Israel as "elitist," dominated by a "secular *Ashkenazic* bourgeoise" and "middle-class, heterosexual feminism." Lesbian, *Mizrahi*, and working-class women were not always represented in women's movements. While these divisions were always there, according to Herzog, they grew in the late 1980s and 1990s. During this period, feminists began to form, for example, separate Mizrahi groups and Palestinian women's associations. Herzog writes, "The feminist peace movement, despite being split into many voices, has some common ground; it draws a connection between protracted occupation and oppression in its various aspects: national, gender, class, ethnic, and religious" (Herzog 2008, 272).

The Oslo Peace Process and Feminist Transversal Coalitions, 1990s

The signing of the 1993 Oslo Accord, Declaration of Principles (DOP), ushered in a new phase of institutionalized 'people-to-people' (P2P) initiatives supported by sponsoring partners such as Norway and the European Union. Donors supported such endeavours across diverse sectors in Israel and occupied Palestine, including health, education, the arts, and women's peace movements. As Julie M. Norman notes, the DOP specifically and directly called for P2P strategies to encourage dialogue and build relations to support future peace negotiations around final status issues like the status of Jerusalem, the Palestinian right of return, and the status of settlements (Norman 2010, 104).

Such peacebuilding initiatives were intended to hold the Oslo Accords' nascent peace and build the foundation for a final settlement. These were well-funded programs, receiving as much as $35 million in the post-Oslo period (see Herzog and Hai 2005, 31; Jamal 2015, 246; Richter-Devroe 2018, 35–36). The underlying ethos of these programs was that dialogue could produce the conditions of reconciliation.

According to Hermann (2002, 103–104), hundreds of grassroots cross-community dialogue groups began to seed in this period. For example, Palestinian and Israeli women formed the Jerusalem Link in 1994 as a cross-community partnership that included the prominent Israeli women's peace group *Bat Shalom* and the Palestinian Jerusalem Center for Women. While the Jerusalem Link was founded after the Oslo Accords, it represented inter-community dialogue amongst members of the respective peace movement that began at international conferences through the mid-1980s to early 1990s.

The Jerusalem Link describes itself as a

> cooperative model of coexistence between our respective peoples. Each organization is autonomous and takes its own national constituency as its primary responsibility – but together we promote a joint vision of a just peace, democracy, human rights, and women's leadership.
>
> *(n.d.)*

Israeli feminist peace activist Galia Golan describes the dialogue between women in women-led peace groups as different from groups that included men and women. Golan recalls that,

> [t]he women in the women's groups (on the Israeli side) are much more radical, in my opinion, than the men or the mainstream in the peace movement. And I think frankly the women, if I look at our various groups, we are very much on the fringes of society and maybe we can permit ourselves to be radical because no one is going to pay too much attention to us anyway.
>
> *(Golan, author interview, 2005)*

Like Norwegian partners and the European Union, the United Nations was keen to support women's cross-community peace efforts. The International Women's Coalition (IWC), which included elite women from Palestine, Israel, and the international community, was the most high-profile example of a cross-community group that lobbied the United Nations (Richter-Devroe 2018, 39). The Charter of Principles (International Women's Commission 2005) defines its mission as one that: "brings together Palestinian, Israeli and international women dedicated to an end of the Israeli occupation and a just peace based on international law [including relevant United Nations resolutions], human rights and equality."

Women-led, dialogue-based cross-community groups became an object of study and garnered broad international attention among those keen to support people-to-people dialogue. Nira Yuval-Davis (1997, 125) first introduced a theory of transversal politics to capture these kinds of dialogic engagements. Transversal politics was the term Yuval-Davis adopted to describe a dialogue encounter between Palestinian and Israeli women in Bologna, Italy, in 1993. Transversal politics is "a counter to identity politics." As Yuval-Davis explains, "What unites us is not the 'identity' of the oppressed, as in 'rainbow politics', but a shared normative value system" (Merck et al. 2016, 107). In transversal dialogue, women recognize each other's distinct ethnic and national "rootedness," but "shift" or transcend their differences through dialogue. Yuval-Davis understands transversalism as guided by an intersectional mode of analysis:

> Transversal dialogical political solidarity does not fall into the trap of 'oppression olympics' (Hancock 2011), in which contested unidimensional constructions of oppression compete with each other, but rather uses dialogical collective knowledge, imagination and judgment, aided by intersectional analysis, in its ongoing political struggles.
>
> *(Yuval-Davis 2012)*

In this rendering, identity politics can lead to an oppression olympics, divisive and antithetical to building feminist solidarity.

The term *intersectionality* was coined by critical legal scholar Kimberle Crenshaw (1989, 149; 1991) to capture, by way of analogy, how Black women are harmed by multiple and intersecting forms of discrimination, such as those based on race, sexual orientation, gender, disability, and class. As an analytic concept, intersectionality considers the impossibility of distinguishing forms of discrimination based on singular axes of identity. In this sense, intersectionality is, according to Crenshaw (2015), "a way of thinking about identity and its relationship to power."

Following Yuval-Davis's gender and transversal scholarship (1994, 1997, 1999, 2006, 2009, 2010, 2011, 2012, 2016; also Einhorn 2006: 208; Grünell and Saharso 1999: 211) and the empirical work of scholar-activists like Cynthia Cockburn (1998, 1999, 2000, 2004, 2007; Cockburn and Hunter 1999; Cockburn and Mulholland 2000), feminist peace scholars argue that women in cross-community peace coalitions are uniquely able to talk with each other across contested ethnicized boundaries and develop a shared politics of peace (see Golan 1997: 585; Hadjipavlou 2006; Kilmurray and McWilliams 2011; Korac 2006: 515; Murtagh 2008; Porter 2000; Roulston 1999, 2000). While transversal theory helped capture the special place of intersectional feminist cross-community dialogue in the 1990s and early 2000s, it is less able to capture new forms of intersectional coalitions, organized around identity and identity politics, that re-emerged in the wake of the Oslo Accords.

Feminist Activism in the Post-peace Process Period

As the Oslo-track peace process moved into its second decade, optimism for a final settlement waned. The physical infrastructure of the occupation made it impossible for Israeli and

Palestinian women to meet face-to-face. With Israeli's construction of a new wall encircling the West Bank in 2004, the eruption of the Second Palestinian Intifada in 2000, and the rapid expansion of settlements through the West Bank – peace remained elusive. Groups like the Jerusalem Link were already beginning to fall apart by the Second Intifada's start in 2000, but especially following the 2008–2009 Gaza War. There was a perception amongst Palestinian women that their Israeli counterparts in Bat Shalom were not appropriately rebuking Israel for the war (see Aggestam and Strömbom 2013, 118). The IWC, which was formed in 2005, officially disbanded in 2011 due to divisions between Palestinian and Israeli women (see Richter-Devroe 2018; Farr 2011). Palestinians living in the occupied West Bank and Gaza, too, were embroiled in the internal political division between Hamas leadership in Gaza and Fatah leadership in the West Bank, which meant that reconciliation efforts were needed amongst Palestinians, and not just between Palestinian leaders and Israel.

In this context, it was a burden on all sectors to bundle services and products in a cross-community package (see Aggestam and Strömbom 2013). For example, an open letter signed by 20 Palestinian organizations, including women's committees, unions, health providers, and educational institutions, objected to what the letter termed "Palestinian-Israeli cooperation schemes" that promote the view that "cooperation can achieve much in ongoing conflict, especially when justice for Palestinians has not been achieved" (Open Letter 2005). Some Palestinian women worried that collective action had moved from the realm of grassroots national liberation to internationally funded and less politically oriented non-governmental organization (NGO) style movements (Kayali 2020, 2). Hammami writes critically of this shift from grassroots movements to salaried positions in the NGO sector where, "Speaking English, dressing well and maintaining a nice office are all part of this new culture. The entrance of waves of young professionals into the NGO sector has further de-politicized it." (2000, 27). For Norman, Palestinians were challenging "peacebuilding," defined as dialogue during this period (Norman 2010, 113). Running through assessments by Hammami, Norman, Kayali, and others is a desire to return to a period before NGOs' institutionalization.

Some Israeli scholars and feminist coalition participants offer a different take on the "NGOisation" of women's peace activism. For example, Herzog (2008, 276) acknowledges that while "NGOization has the potential to depoliticize the women's movement and co-opt women to serve the needs of the state and/or funding agencies," the formal organization of women can also "empower women and lead to new opportunities," including skill-development around mentorship and negotiation. Chazen (2018, 146) finds that while the new millennium marked a shift to the professionalization in some segments of the women's movement in Israel, it also emphasized identity politics and intersectional organizing in others. Chazen (2018, 147) notes that the Coalition of Women for Peace, the IWC, and Women Wage Peace were all "Concerned with developing their unique identity and with empowering women in their particular groups." She writes, "these initiatives looked inwards in order to achieve greater societal inclusion on their own terms."

For a subset of both Israeli and Palestinian feminist activists, the Women, Peace and Security (WPS) agenda also formed the foundations of new activism to ensure women were included in peace negotiations and security matters. In brief, WPS refers to a range of local, national, and international policies and social movement affirmations designed to improve women's representation in peace processes. The agenda is repeated in a basket of ten United Nations Security Council resolutions, dozens of state-level national action plans, and reflected in the organizational ethos of women's peace movements worldwide. Across these policies and statements, the category "woman" features not just as an analytic category to assess, for example, equality measures in peace processes or the gender impacts of war. Rather, the category "woman" also features as an agential category whereby women attain "empowerment in peacebuilding" (UNSCR 1889 2009), or otherwise hold a unique role as peacebuilders "in the prevention and resolution of conflicts" (UNSCR 1325 2000) and at the helm of "women-led peacebuilding organizations" (UNSCR 2493 2019). Indeed, "women's organizations" are a constituency with which "national and international decision makers" in conflict can be in "consultation and dialogue" (UNSCR 2122).

Women's organizations in Israel formed a coalition in 2012 to demand a national action plan (NAP) on UNSCR 1325. Members included prominent activists like Anat Saragusti, executive director of Agenda; Naomi Chazan, Center for the Advancement of Women in the Public Sphere, and former member of the Knesset; and Eti Livni, former member of the Knesset and 1325 activist. Coming together at bi-monthly meetings, participant Maki Haham Neeman says, "The process allowed a very diverse group of women to take part in drafting this important document." In December 2014, Israel passed a resolution to create a NAP on UNSCR 1325. Noor Falah captures the ambition and enthusiasm for the NAP: "My greatest fantasy is that this process will eventually bring about peace agreements" (Itach Maaki 2015).

Palestinian feminist activists were successful in pushing the Palestinian leadership to adopt a NAP, too. In October 2020, the PA implemented a second NAP on 1325 (2020–2023), which falls under Palestine's Ministry of Women's Affairs. The first NAP was adopted in 2016. UNSCR 1325 has been championed in Palestine by the Higher National Committee on UNSCR 1325 and the General Union of Palestinian Women-led National Civil Society Coalition on UNSCR 1325 (see United Nations Women 2020).

The Women, Peace and Security (WPS) agenda also provided the context for new forms of cross-community coalition-building projects. For example, the Israeli-based Women Wage Peace (WWP) group emerged in 2004 at the time the Jerusalem Link was folding. Today, it describes itself as "the largest grassroots movement in Israel." It is committed to a political settlement to the conflict and to supporting the aspirations of 1325 (Women Wage Peace n.d., About). Some of its notable actions include a 30,000-gathering of people in the March of Hope 2016, and a staged camp outside the Knesset and prime minister's residence (Women Wage Peace n.d., About).

Like previous cross-community schemes, WWP is led by Israeli and Palestinian women. The mission statement describes WWP as a broad-based, non-partisan and diverse movement (Women Wage Peace n.d., Mission Statement). As with some of the early women's peace movements in the 1980s and 1990s, the group appeals to women's shared experiences as mothers. For example, Israeli Jewish musician Yael Deckelbaum wrote a song that became the anthem of the 2016 march, titled, "Prayer of the Mothers" (Deckelbaum and Eilabouni 2018). While WWP is intended to be cross-community, representatives admit that the regular membership of 26,000 comprises mostly urban, middle age, Ashkenazi-Jewish women (Maltz 2017). WWP focuses on issues that women agree on and not the challenging discussions that can divide communities. For example, Yahaloma Zakut, a member of the steering committee, writes that the group purposely does not use terms like "occupation." She explains, "Our movement is all about using language that unifies people – not language that divides them" (Maltz 2017). As such, Palestinian women who define their struggle as anti-occupation are not represented in this movement.

While women-led and consciously cross-community, WWP is less relevant for Palestinian women living under occupation. Palestinian feminists are also committed to pushing for change at the level of the Palestinian leadership, improving the representation of women in politics, and ending the occupation. One such group that illustrates these concerns is *Tal'at* – which means "stepping out" or "rising up" – a Palestinian feminist movement that started in September

2019. According to Tal'at activists Hala Marshood and Riya Al-sanah (2020), the group started as a thousands-strong march of Palestinian women in response to the murder of Israa Ghrayeb, a 21-year-old woman from Bethlehem who was killed by family members in August 2019 (see Marshood and Alsanah 2020; Bakria and Khoury 2019). Tal'at is a diverse and intersectional movement that targets a "matrix of oppression," including colonialism, occupation, and patriarchy.

For these activists, national liberation must include women's liberation. Riya Al-sanah explains: "We're told [it is] national liberation first and [only then is it time for] women's emancipation. We do not accept this separation anymore. What kind of liberation are we talking about if it doesn't include women?" (Deprez 2019). Al-sanah describes Ta'alt this way: "Currently, Tal'at is the only Palestinian feminist movement that seeks to unite Palestinian women – despite their fragmented geographies and varied lived experiences – under a single, explicitly political feminist umbrella" (Al-Sanah and Harb 2020). For Marshood (2019), women of Tal'at build feminist solidarity amongst Palestinian women who have been displaced through the conflict "so that they can fight together to build a just, safe Palestinian struggle."

This linking of women's liberation and national liberation is evident through the long history of Palestinian women's activism. The gender and peace literature, as international donors and sponsors, tend to look at nationalism as an impediment to peace. As Sharoni and Abdulhadi observe:

> For years, feminists in the Global North have failed to understand why Palestinian women insist on linking their struggles for gender equality to national liberation. As a result, Palestinian women have been at the receiving end of well-intentioned but misguided initiatives, which have disregarded their agency, needs and resilience.
>
> *(Sharoni et al. 2015, 654)*

While intersectional, the feminist coalition does not follow the cross-community model of peace activism of the 1990s and early 2000s. Marhsood (2019) explains: "As we prepared for the demonstrations, we again ran up against the arrogance of Israeli feminists who cannot tolerate a Palestinian voice that does not seek their approval or participation."

Feminists are also finding transnational and regional coalition-building valuable modes of activism. For example, the Palestinian-led Boycott, Sanctions and Divestment (BDS) movement, which took off in 2005, reflects a growing sense among Palestinians that working in coalition with Israelis – even in peace groups – may normalize rather than challenge the occupation (see Palestinian Civil Society 2005). Modelled on the South African apartheid-era boycott movement, BDS calls on the international community to put political and economic pressure on Israel to end the occupation. For some feminist scholars, BDS is part of a broader and intersectional "transnational feminist solidarity" response to the occupation (Sharoni et al. 2015). Sharoni and Abdulhadi explain:

> Supporting BDS is an opportunity to address the root causes of Palestinians' oppression as we center our intersectional analysis on the links between interlocking systems of domination, and foreground the transnational movements that are determined to dismantle them.
>
> *(Sharoni et al. 2015, 666)*

The BDS movement also includes diasporic Jewish participants. For example, reflecting on her contribution to BDS, feminist academic-scholar Ronit Lentin explains: "Although I have lived and worked in Ireland since 1969, I feel an added duty to support Palestinian feminists as an Israeli citizen – but, importantly, not through speaking *for* them" (Sharoni et al. 2015, 663). These emergent forms of transnational feminist solidarity, which are inclusive of differently situated participants, are an important part of the story of feminist peace and solidarity politics.

The urgency of the 2020–2021 COVID-19 pandemic has provoked other forms of regional and transnational feminist peace coalitions, too. According to the World Health Organization (WHO, 2021), the Palestinian Ministry of Health began vaccinating Palestinians in the West Bank in early February 2021, a month and a half after Israel began an intensive vaccination campaign throughout Israel and Israeli West Bank settlements. With limited financial resources and weak public health infrastructure, Palestinians do not enjoy the same access to the vaccine as Israelis; instead, they depend on the international emergency COVAX Facility for vaccine doses (see Krauss 2020).

For Israeli feminist scholar-peace activists Sarai Aharoni and Amalia Sa'ar (2020), the public-health emergency makes plain that Israeli and Palestinian feminists must find opportunities to forge "cross-border feminist peace activism"; they worry that growing support for BDS runs counter to this imperative. In the context of the pandemic, however, Palestinian women seek out other forms of cross-border coalitions, albeit regional ones. For example, a group of Palestinian civil society organizations in Arab states issued a call for unity and a ceasefire to address COVID-19. The joint statement reads:

> If we allow this virus to spread further in our war-torn countries, it would ravage us with no regard to our national, ethnic, religious, or political differences ... So, we need to put our differences aside and fight this common enemy before it is too late.
>
> *(Women's Civil Society 2020)*

The appeal calls for solidarity and coalition with women from Palestine, Syria, Yemen, Libya and Iraq.

Israeli-Jewish women are also forging transnational and intersectional alliances with Jewish women outside of Israel. For example, the Jewish-American group IFNOTNOW describes its platform as "a call for every American public official to join the next generation of Jews in fighting for a better future." (IfNotNow 2020). The organization aims to defund the occupation and fight both anti-Semitism and white nationalism. IFNOTNOW is cofounded by American Simone Zimmerman, current director of B'Tselem USA. One of this group's actions was to share letters of solidarity from Jewish Americans with the family of Palestinian teen Ahed Tamimi (Plachta 2018). When Tamimi was 17 years old, the Israeli military removed her from the West Bank, and she was put on trial for slapping and kicking a soldier after her younger cousin was shot in the face.

Beyond the value of regional and transnational organizing, the political conditions in Israel, the West Bank, and Gaza are such that participating in traditional cross-community groups or any other form of cross-community solidarity can be dangerous. Today, it is illegal for Israelis to travel into Palestinian-controlled areas of the West Bank and to Gaza; most Palestinians are restricted from travelling to Israel. Even within each political jurisdiction, cross-community dialogue is fraught. For example, Hamas detains Palestinian activists for speaking with Israelis, even via Zoom (for example, see *Algemeiner* 2020; Abu Toameh 2020). In Israel, all forms of resistance are met with extreme censure by the state. For example, Dareen Tatour, a Palestinian poet with Israeli citizenship, was arrested and imprisoned after writing a poem titled, "Resist, my people resist them" (see Pen America n.d.; Ahituv 2018; Shpigel 2018). The Ministry of Strategic Affairs is also fighting a propaganda war and legal battle to delegitimize BDS and BDS activists (Jaffe-Hoffman 2018; Patir 2019). Israel published a "blacklist" in 2018 of groups banned from Israel due to BDS support, which follows an earlier March 2017 travel ban targeting anyone who supports BDS (Landau 2018; Lis 2017).

In many of these examples, from BDS to the Arab women's civil society coalition, to Tal'at, to IfNotNow, feminists participate in intersectional coalitions that extend beyond the logic of earlier Israeli-Palestinian women's people-to-people campaigns. However, these are rich sites of intersectional solidarity that include Palestinians, Jews, diasporic communities, and other allies. Each venture's aims are a little different – sometimes sharing regional experiences of war and deprivation, sometimes pressuring foreign governments to oppose the occupation, and sometimes working to enlighten and persuade diasporic communities of the urgency to act.

Identity, Intersectionality, and Feminist Coalitions

From early development within Israeli and Palestinian national movements, through women's rights, peace, and anti-occupation activism, the history of Israeli and Palestinian feminist activism is one of large-scale shifts in organizational formation and strategy. Israel's occupation of the West Bank and Gaza Strip and annexation of East Jerusalem in 1967, emergent wars in the region, and Palestinian resistance stirred popular women-led peace and anti-occupation activism through the 1970s to today. The 1973 Arab-Israeli War, Israel's 1982 invasion of Lebanon, and the 1987 Palestinian Intifada compelled feminist activists to forge new peace coalitions. The 1993 Oslo peace process provided the context for cross-community women's peace coalitions, and the international community enthusiastically promoted these types of initiatives through new funding and support. The passage of UNSCR 1325 in 2000 marked the beginning of the UN-led WPS agenda, which further entrenched an international normative commitment to the kinds of women's peace initiatives that took off in Israel/Palestine in the post-Oslo period. The Oslo peace process's failure, the eruption of the Second Palestinian Intifada, a marked shift to rightist political leadership in Israel, and new wars in Gaza strained peace movements. Cross-community groups, in particular, were unable to traverse the hardening borders of an ever-deepening occupation. For Palestinians, an anti-normalization ethos and new attention to transnational solidarity-building eroded the rationale for people-to-people engagement.

In the literature on peace groups, intersectionality is sometimes conflated with cross-community forms of activism whereby feminist transversal engagements are viewed as intersectionality par excellence. Sometimes intersectional coalitions in Israel/Palestine have been consciously cross-community. However, this is not the only form of intersectional coalition-building, and it is not the dominant form amongst feminist activists today. As critical feminist observers, if we focus on or otherwise exalt only one model of intersectional coalition-building, we risk missing all of the critical ways in which feminists in the occupied West Bank, Gaza, and Israel are forging solidarity, challenging the occupation, and developing new ideas about peace.

For some intersectionality scholars, identity politics can be a source of "empowerment," and collective identity can be a source of solidarity, dialogue, and mobilization (Collins and Bilge 2016, 173–174). For example, Patricia Hill Collins and Sirma Bilge write that while identity politics can get a bad rap, "a more productive approach lies in examining how understandings of the politics of identity can constitute a *starting point for intersectional inquiry and praxis and not an end in itself*" (Collins and Bilge 2016, 177). Collins and Bilge emphasize that identities are already intersectional, such as men and women organizing together within communities of colour (Collins and Bilge 2016, 177–179). Carastathis (2013, 941), following Crenshaw, writes that when we view identities as a form of coalition, we escape the charges that identity politics are at odds with coalitional politics. Understanding identities as coalitions means recognizing that identities are "internally heterogeneous, complex unities constituted by their internal differences and dissonances and by internal as well as external relations of power" and that this "enables us to form effective political alliances that cross existing identity categories and to pursue a liberatory politics of interconnection" (2013, 942).

In the history of Palestinian and Israeli activism above, we can see how coalitions of predominantly Israeli women, such as WWP, or coalitions of Palestinian women, such as Tal'at, are also intersectional – bringing together diverse Israeli and Palestinian women around a common politics of peace and/or anti-occupation. This opens up the possibilities for understanding diverse forms of feminist activism in Israel/Palestine and beyond – sometimes organized as more explicitly identity-coalitions, and other times as cross-community or transversal-style coalitions. In both forms, identities and differences are still negotiated through dialogue to build feminist solidarity.

Conclusion

A long history of Palestinian and Israeli feminist activism has influenced the development, demise, and restructuring of peace and anti-occupation coalitions over the last five decades. The occasion of internal and regional wars and violence, shifts in Israeli and Palestinian political leadership, the capricious interest and influence of external political actors, on and off again peace talks, and the deepening occupation have all provoked new and innovative forms of feminist peace and anti-occupation activism.

In this chapter, I reviewed early Israeli and Palestinian women's liberation movements in the 1960s and 1970s that were closely tethered to their respective nation-building projects. The 1982 Israeli invasion of Lebanon inspired Israeli women to forge autonomous peace coalitions rooted in their identities as Israelis and, in some instances, as mothers. Palestinian women were active in national party-affiliated women's unions and their communities through the 1970s and 1980s. Later, the 1987 Palestinian Intifada provided the context for new women's peace and anti-occupation activism throughout Israel, East Jerusalem, the West Bank, and Gaza Strip. Once again, the Oslo Peace Accords in 1993 marked another shift in feminist peace and anti-occupation activism. This time women were not only forming separate coalitions of Israeli and Palestinian women but inter-community feminist projects. International enthusiasm and sponsorship of cross-community ventures, along with new scholarly attention to these unique feminist coalitions, elevated their visibility and stature as a key mode of feminist peace politics. Such international attention was reflected in international instruments like the UN-led WPS agenda.

Despite enthusiasm for women's peacebuilding initiatives, the peace process's failure strained cross-community coalitions through the 2000s. While people-to-people schemes were no longer in the ascendant, women continued to build new strategic coalitions. For example, Israeli women formed peace coalitions within Israel and transnationally to challenge Israeli occupation policies and build solidarity with diaspora communities. Likewise, Palestinian women built feminist coalitions within the occupied West Bank and Gaza, with regional women sharing everyday experiences of war and deprivation and new transnational activist communities.

This historical review of changing modes of peace and anti-occupation movements reveal the multiple ways feminist activists have been reimagining and rebuilding intersectional feminist coalitions. These shifts are not always captured in the feminist peace literature or reflected in UN engagements with WPS in the last 20 years. Cross-community partnerships tend to be the primary way the feminist peace literature and the WPS agenda imagine women's activism in Israel/Palestine. Further, intersectionality is typically deployed in a quite restrictive way: to uncover and promote the kinds of cross-community solidarity coalitions popularized in the

1990s and early 2000s. While these were important political engagements, they do not represent the many ways feminists build intersectional coalitions of women and allies within and beyond Israel's borders and occupied Palestine.

This has important implications for considering what role – if any – UNSCR 1325 and the WPS agenda has for the Israeli-Palestinian conflict. In the post-peace process context, the WPS agenda may be less relevant and potentially less effective in the short to medium term if its primary goal is to increase women's participation in a peace process. Further, while in the 2000s WPS helped feminist peace groups promote cross-community organizing and the internationalization of women's peace politics, this mode of organizing has been less enduring as the occupation deepened. If we look at the landscape in Israel/Palestine through the women-as-peacebuilder lens only, it might lead us to conclude that there is little in the way of feminist peace politics happening today. More problematically, it might suggest that the international community and transnational feminist solidarity movements must offer more funding and support for those limited cross-community ventures that continue to exist today. While people-to-people exchanges are not the mainstay of feminist peace and anti-occupation politics in Israel/Palestine today, international enthusiasm for such projects persists. For example, the United States Congress recently approved $250 million for USAID-administered funding to support "coexistence initiatives" and "dialogue programs" for Israeli-Palestinians groups (United States Congress 2020). The United Kingdom is also actively considering enacting a similar fund (United Kingdom 2020).

This means we may miss seeing and elevating the many other ways feminists are organizing to end conflict on the ground and imagine new political futures. A more expansive conception of intersectional coalition politics – one that does not eschew identity politics or focus on cross-community forms of engagement only – better captures the changing modes of feminist peace and anti-occupation activism in Israel/Palestine today. This will mean moving beyond a figuration of the woman-as-peacebuilder model in the literature and the international imaginary to a new valuation of the different forms of political contestation that characterize feminist politics in war.

Recommended Readings

Carastathis, A. 2013. "Identity Categories as Potential Coalitions." *Signs* 38:3, 941–965.

Cockburn, C. 2007. *From Where We Stand: War, Women's Activism and Feminist Analysis*. London: Zed Books.

Hammami, R. 2000. "Palestinian NGOs since Oslo: From NGO Politics to Social Movements?" *Middle East Report* 214, 16–48.

Kayali, L. 2020. *Palestinian Women and Popular Resistance: Perceptions, Attitudes and Strategies*. Abingdon, Oxon: Routledge.

Richter-Devroe, S. 2018. *Women's Political Activism in Palestine: Peacebuilding, Resistance, and Survival*. Urbana: University of Illinois Press.

Yuval-Davis, Nira. 1997. *Gender and Nation*. London: Sage Publications.

Note

1 For example, feminist archives of selected feminist movement pamphlets, books, articles and other documents are maintained by the Institute of Women's Studies, Birzeit University, West Bank, Palestine and Isha L'Isha – Haifa Feminist Center, Haifa, Israel.

Questions for Discussion

(1) What is the role of nationalism and national identity in Palestinian and Israeli feminist peace and anti-occupation activism today? Are nationalism and national liberation impediments to building feminist coalitions, or resources for robust feminist solidarity movements?

(2) What is the UN-led Women, Peace and Security (WPS) agenda? To what extent does WPS risk essentializing women as peace-builders? As critical feminist scholars, how can we understand political activism such as women-led peace movements in ways that recognize women's agency without essentializing the category women?
(3) Yuval-Davis advocates "transversal politics," or a coalitional mode of activism that includes Israeli and Palestinian women. What is transversalism or transversal politics? In your view, to what extent can careful transversal practices transcend deep ethnonational divisions?
(4) Identify an example of a feminist intersectional coalition in the context of the Israeli-Palestinian conflict. What makes the coalition "intersectional"?
(5) Are identities and identity politics necessarily at odds with feminist peace and anti-occupation politics?
(6) How do external political factors and internal political conditions impact feminist peace and anti-occupation movements over time in the Israeli-Palestinian conflict?

References

Abdulhadi, R. 1998. "The Palestinian Women's Autonomous Movement: Emergence, Dynamics, and Challenges." *Gender and Society* 12:6, 649–673.

Abdulhadi, R. 2012. "Gender, Resistance and Liberation in 1960s Palestine: Living Under Occupation." *Against the Current* July/August, 15–20.

Abu Toameh, K. 2020. "Coronavirus: Hamas Arrests Palestinians for Video Chats with Israelis." *The Jerusalem Post*, 9 April.

Aggestam, K. and Strömbom, L. 2013. Disempowerment and Marginalisation of Peace NGOs: Exposing Peace Gaps in Israel and Palestine. *Peacebuilding* 1:1, 109–124.

Aharoni, S. and Sa'ar, A. 2020. "A View from Within the Fortress," Blog Entry. *International Feminist Journal of Politics*. Available at: www.ifjpglobal.org/blog/2020/10/28/a-view-from-within-the-fortress.

Ahituv, N. 2018. "I Didn't Report my Rape Because I was 7. I Could be Murdered for This, but I Can't Stay Silent." *Haaretz*, 4 November. Available at: www.haaretz.com/israel-news/.premium.MAGAZINE-i-didn-t-report-my-rape-because-i-was-7-i-can-no-longer-stay-silent-1.6615112.

Al-Sanah, R. and Harb, S. 2020. "Part of the Revolutionary Feminist Tradition: A Discussion about the New Palestinian Feminist Initiative, Tal'at." *Rosa Luxemburg Stiftung*, 23 March. Available at: www.rosalux.de/en/news/id/41813/part-of-the-revolutionary-feminist-tradition?cHash=52de355b26af99a6b0555c3f84d08d14.

Algemeiner. 2020. "Hamas Arrests Palestinians in Gaza for Zoom Video Chat with Israelis." 10 April. Available at: www.algemeiner.com/2020/04/10/hamas-arrests-palestinians-in-gaza-for-zoom-video-chat-with-israelis/.

Associated Press. 2021. "Israel Sentences Palestinian Lawmaker to Two Years in Prison." 2 March. Available at: https://apnews.com/article/israel-3a1e20a42d5fc434ac487ae08422ed6e.

Bakria, Y. and Khoury, J. 2019. "'Free Homeland, Free Women': Palestinians Take to the Streets to Protest Femicide." *Haaretz*, 27 September. Available at: www.haaretz.com/israel-news/.premium-free-homeland-free-women-palestinians-take-to-the-streets-to-protest-femicide-1.7914855.

Carastathis, A. 2013. "Identity Categories as Potential Coalitions." *Signs* 38:4, 941–965.

Chazen, N. 2018. "Israel at 70: A Gender Perspective." *Israel Studies* 23:3, 141–151.

Cockburn, C. 1998. T*he Space between Us: Negotiating Gender and National Identities in Conflict*. London: Zed Books.

Cockburn, C. 1999. "Crossing Borders: Comparing Ways of Handling Conflictual Differences." *Soundings* 12, 99–114.

Cockburn, C. 2000. "The Anti-Essentialist Choice: Nationalism and Feminism in the Interaction between Two Women's Projects." *Nations and Nationalism* 6:4, 611–629.

Cockburn, C. 2004. The Line: Women, Partition and the Gender Order in Cyprus. London and New York: Zed Books.

Cockburn, C. 2007. *From Where We Stand: War, Women's Activism and Feminist Analysis*. London: Zed Books.

Cockburn, C. and Hunter, L. 1999. "Transversal Politics and Translating Practices." *Soundings* 12, 88–93.

Cockburn, C. and Mulholland, M. 2000. "What Does a Feminist Action Research Partnership Mean in Practice?" In *(Re)searching Women: Feminist Research Methodologies in the Social Sciences in Ireland*, eds. A. Byrne, R. Lentin, Dublin: Institute of Public Administration, 119–139.

Crenshaw, K. 1989. "Demarginalizing the Intersection of Race and Sex: A Black Feminist Critique of Antidiscrimination Doctrine, Feminist Theory and Antiracist Politics." *University of Chicago Legal Forum*, 1989 (1), Article 8.

Crenshaw, K. 2015. "Opinion: Why Intersectionality Can't Wait." *The Washington Post*, 24 September. Available at: www.washingtonpost.com/news/in-theory/wp/2015/09/24/why-intersectionality-cant-wait/.

Deckelbaum, Y. and Eilabouni, M. 2018. "The Israeli-Palestinian Conflict: Women on the March for Peace." Interview by B. Serra. International Journalism Festival, 14 April 2018. Video, 57:34. Available at: https://youtu.be/0GlpvTpebXM.

Deiana, M. 2016. "To Settle for a Gendered Peace? Spaces for Feminist Grassroots Mobilization in Northern Ireland and Bosnia-Herzegovina." *Citizenship Studies* 20:1, 99–114.

Deprez, M. 2019. "Rights Now: Why Palestinian Women do not Want to Wait for Liberation." *Al-Monitor*, 7 October. Available at: www.al-monitor.com/pulse/originals/2019/10/palestinian-women-fight-for-their-rights.html.

Einhorn, B. 2006. "Insiders and Outsiders: Within and Beyond the Gendered Nation." In in *Handbook of Gender and Women's Studies*, eds. K. Davis, M. Evans, and J. Lorber. London: Sage, 196–213.

Farr, V. 2011. "UNSCR 1325 and Women's Peace Activism in the Occupied Palestinian Territory." *International Feminist Journal of Politics*. 13:4, 539-556.

Freedman, M. 1990. *Exile in the Promised Land*. Ithaca, NY: Firebrand.

Golan, G. 1997. "Militarization and Gender: The Israeli Experience." *Women's Studies International Forum* 20:5/6, 581–586.

Golan, G. 2005. Interview by the author. Herzliya, Israel. 5 June 2005.

Grünell, M. and Saharso, S. 1999. "State of the Art: bell hooks and Nira Yuval-Davis on Race, Ethnicity, Class and Gender." *European Journal of Women's Studies* 6:2, 203–218.

Hadjipavlou, M. 2006. "No Permission to Cross: Cypriot Women's Dialogue across the Divide." *Gender, Place and Culture* 13:4, 329–351.

Hammami, R. 2000. "Palestinian NGOs since Oslo: From NGO Politics to Social Movements?" *Middle East Report* 214, 16–48.

Hancock, A-M. 2011. *Solidarity Politics for Millennials: A Guide to Ending the Oppression Olympics*. New York: Palgrave Macmillan.

Hermann, T. 2002. "The Sour Taste of Success: The Israeli Peace Movement, 1967–1998." In *Mobilizing for Peace: Conflict Resolution in Northern Ireland, South Africa, and Israel/ Palestine*, eds. B. Gidron, S. N. Katz, and Y. Hasenfeld. Oxford: Oxford University Press, 94–129.

Herzog, H. 2008. "Re/Visioning the Women's Movement in Israel." *Citizenship Studies* 12:3, 265–282.

Herzog, S. and Hai. A. 2005. "The Role of People-to-People Programs in the Current Israeli-Palestinian Reality." Friedrich-Ebert-Stiftung, Israel Office. Available at: https://library.fes.de/pdf-files/bueros/israel/04093.pdf.

Hill Collins, P. and Bilge, S. 2016. *Intersectionality*. Cambridge: Polity Press.

Hiltermann, J. R. 1991. "The Women's Movement During the Uprising." *Journal of Palestine Studies* 20:3, 48–57.

Hiltermann, J. R. 1990. Trade Unions and Women's Committees: Sustaining Movement, Creating Space. *Middle East Report* 164/165, 32–36+53.

IfNotNow Education Fund. 2020. The IfNotNow 2020 Platform. Available at: www.ifnotnowmovement.org/2020-platform.

International Women's Commission for a Just and Sustainable Palestinian-Israeli Peace. 2005. Charter of Principles. 27 July. Available at: www.un.org/unispal/document/auto-insert-200863/

ItachMaaki. 2015. "Our Journey to Implement UNSCR Resolution 1325 in Israel." YouTube Video, 13 July. Available at: www.youtube.com/watch?v=3yxvaEUog_s&feature=youtu.be.

Jad, I. 1999. "From Salons to the Popular Committees: Palestinian Women 1919–89." In *The Israel/ Palestine Question*, ed. I. Pappé. London and New York: Routledge, 217–233.

Jaffe-Hoffman, M. 2018. "Strategic Affairs Ministry to Form Anti-BDS Legal Network." *The Jerusalem Post*, 20 December.

Jamal, M. A. 2015. "Western Donor Assistance and Gender Empowerment in the Palestinian Territories and Beyond." *International Feminist Journal of Politics* 17:2, 232–252.

Jerusalem Link, The. (n.d.). "Who We Are" Available at: www.batshalom.org/files/about_us.html.

Kayali, L. 2020. *Palestinian Women and Popular Resistance: Perceptions, Attitudes and Strategies*. Abingdon, Oxon: Routledge.

Kilmurray, A. and McWilliams, M. 2011. "Struggling for Peace: How Women in Northern Ireland Challenged the Status Quo." *Solutions Journal* 2:2, 32-41.

Korac, M. 2006. "Gender, Conflict and Peace-Building: Lessons from the Conflict in the Former Yugoslavia." *WSIF* 29:5, 510–520.

Krauss, J. 2020. "Palestinians Left Waiting as Israel is Set to Deploy COVID-19 Vaccine." *PBS News Hour*, 17 December. Available at: www.pbs.org/newshour/health/palestinians-left-waiting-as-israel-is-set-to-deploy-covid-19-vaccine.

Kuttab E. 2008. "Palestinian Women's Organizations: Global Cooption and Local Contradiction." *Cultural Dynamics* 20:2, 99–117.

Landau, N. 2018. "Israel Published BDS Blacklist: These Are the 20 Groups Whose Members Will Be Denied Entry." *Haaretz*, 7 January. Available at: www.haaretz.com/israel-news/israel-publishes-bds-blacklist-these-20-groups-will-be-denied-entry-1.5729880.

Lis, J. 2017. "Israel's Travel Ban: Knesset Bars Entry to Foreigners Who Call for Boycott of Israel or Settlements." *Haaretz*, 7 March. Available at: www.haaretz.com/israel-news/.premium-israel-bars-entry-to-foreigners-who-call-for-boycott-of-settlements-1.5445566.

Maltz, J. 2017. "'We're Part of This Society Too': In Israel, Arab Women are Joining Jewish Activists in Fight for Peace." *Haaretz*, 28 September. Available at: www.haaretz.com/israel-news/.premium-in-israel-arab-women-are-joining-jewish-activists-in-fight-for-peace-1.5453620.

Marshood, H. 2019. "Tali'at: Putting Feminist at the Centre of Palestinian Liberation." *Mada Masr*, 26 October. Available at: https://madamasr.com/en/2019/10/26/opinion/u/taliat-putting-feminism-at-the-center-of-palestinian-liberation/.

Marshood, H. and Alsanah, R. 2020. "Tal'at: A Feminist Movement that is Redefining Liberation and Reimaginging Palestine." *Mondoweiss*, 25 February. Available at: https://mondoweiss.net/2020/02/talat-a-feminist-movement-that-is-redefining-liberation-and-reimagining-palestine/.

Mayer, T. (ed). 1994. *Women and the Israeli Occupation: The Politics of Change*. London: Routledge.

Merck, M., et al. 2016. "Feminism and 'the S-word.'" *Soundings: A Journal of Politics and Culture* 61, 95–112.

Murtagh, C. 2008. "Transient Transition: The Cultural and Institutional Obstacles Impeding the Northern Ireland Women's Coalition (NIWC) in Its Progression from Informal to Formal Politics." *Journal of International Women's Studies* 9:2, 41–58.

Norman, J. M. 2010. *The Second Palestinian Intifada: Civil Resistance*. London: Routledge.

Open Letter to the Palestinian and International Community. 2005. "Palestinian Campaign for the Academic and Cultural Boycott of Israel, 6 May 2005." Available at: www.pacbi.org/etemplate.php?id=45.

Palestinian Civil Society. 2005. "Palestinian Civil Society Calls for BDS, Open Letter." The Palestinian BDS National Committee, 9 July. Available at: www.bdsmovement.net/call.

Patir, Y. 2019. "Opinion: Who Needs the Strategic Affairs Ministry?" *Haaretz*, 20 October. Available at: www.haaretz.com/opinion/.premium-who-needs-the-strategic-affairs-ministry-1.8009618.

Pen America. (n.d.). "Writers at Risk: Dareen Tatour, Israel." Available at: www.pen.org/advocacy-case/dareen-tatour/.

"Peace to Prosperity: A Vision to Improve the Lives of the Palestinian and Israeli People." 2020. January. Available at: https://trumpwhitehouse.archives.gov/wp-content/uploads/2020/01/Peace-to-Prosperity-0120.pdf.

Plachta, A. 2018. "Hundreds of Young U.S. Jews Send Birthday Wishes to Jailed Palestinian Teen Ahed Tamimi Ahead of Trial." *Haaretz*, 5 February. Available at: www.haaretz.com/israel-news/.premium-700-young-u-s-jews-send-birthday-wishes-to-jailed-palestinian-teen-1.5786303.

Porter, E. 2000. "The Challenge of Dialogue across Difference." In *Gender, Democracy and Inclusion in Northern Ireland*, eds. C. Roulston and C. Davies. New York: Palgrave, 141–163.

Richter-Devroe, S. 2018. *Women's Political Activism in Palestine: Peacebuilding, Resistance, and Survival*. Urbana: University of Illinois Press.

Roulston, C. 1999. "Feminism, Politics, and Postmodernism." In *Contesting Politics: Women in Ireland, North and South*, eds. Y. Galligan, E. Ward, and R. Wilford, Boulder, CO: Westview Press, 1–17.

Roulston, C. 2000. "Democracy and the Challenge of Gender." In *Gender, Democracy and Inclusion in Northern Ireland*, eds. C. Roulston and C. Davies. New York: Palgrave, 24–46.

Safran, H. 2005. "Alliance and Denial: Lesbian Protest in Women in Black." In *Sappho in the Holy Land: Lesbian Existence and Dilemmas in Contemporary Israel*, eds. C. Frankfort-Nachmias and E. Shadmi. Albany: SUNY Press, 191–209.

Sharoni, S. 1995. *Gender and the Israeli-Palestinian Conflict: The Politics of Women's Resistance*. Syracuse, NY: Syracuse University Press.

Sharoni, S., et al. 2015. Transnational Feminist Solidarity in Times of Crisis. *International Feminist Journal of Politics* 17:4, 654–670.

Shpigel, N. 2018. "Israel Convicts Palestinian Poet Dareen Tatour of Incitement to Violence, Supporting Terror." *Haaretz*, 3 May. Available at: www.haaretz.com/israel-news/.premium-israel-convicts-palestinian-poet-dareen-tatour-of-incitement-1.6052973.

Svirsky, G. 1996. "*Standing for Peace: A History of Women in Black in Israel*." Unpublished. Available at: www.gilasvirsky.com/wib_book.html.

Svirsky, G. 2005. Interview by the author. Jerusalem, Israel. 21 January 2005.

Taraki, L., ed. 2006. *Living Palestine: Family Survival, Resistance, and Mobility under Occupation*. Syracuse, NY: Syracuse University Press.

United Nations Security Council (UNSC) Res 1889 (5 October 2009) UN Doc S/RES/1889(2009).

United Nations Security Council (UNSC) Res 1325 (31 October 2000) UN Doc S/RES/1325(2000).

United Nations Security Council (UNSC) Res 2493 (29 October 2019) UN Doc S/RES/2493(2019).

United Nations Security Council (UNSC) Res 2122 (18 October 2013) UN Doc S/RES/2122(2013).

United Nations Women. 2020. "Palestine Moves Forward in Promoting Women's Participation in Peace and Security – UN Women Press Release." 28 October. Available at: www.un.org/unispal/document/palestine-moves-forward-in-promoting-womens-participation-in-peace-and-security-un-women-press-release/.

United States Congress .2020. H.R.3104 – Partnership Fund for Peace Act of 2019. Available at: www.congress.gov/bill/116th-congress/house-bill/3104/text.

United Kingdom Parliament House of Commons. 2020. 17 November Debate (vol. 684, col. 82WH) Available at: hansard.parliament.uk/Commons/2020-11-17/debates/1E3EC84E-81DC-4068-A1E6-1143FAF36B2D/InternationalFundForIsraeli-PalestinianPeace.

WAFA News Agency. 2020. "Prominent Woman Activist among Eight Palestinians Detained by Israel in the West Bank." 2 November. Available at https://english.wafa.ps/Pages/Details/120802.

WHO. 2021. "Coronavirus disease (COVID-19) Situation Report 63 (11 February)." Available at: https://who18.createsend.com/campaigns/reports/viewCampaign.aspx?d=j&c=99FA4938D049E3A8&ID=2FD5411B238B33562540EF23F30FEDED&temp=False&tx=0&source=Report.

Women's Civil Society. 2020. "On the Occasion of Eid al-Fitr, Women Civil Society Organizations in the Arab States Region join UN Secretary-General António Guterre's Call for Ceasefire and Unity in the Face of COVID-19." Available at: www2.unwomen.org/-/media/field%20office%20arab%20states/attachments/2020/05/ceasefire%20declaration/update%204%20june/2020-06-03_declaration-csos-en.pdf?la=en&vs=4825.

Women Wage Peace. n.d. About Us, Webpage. Available at: https://womenwagepeace.org.il/en/about-eng/

Women Wage Peace. n.d. Mission Statement, Webpage. Available at: https://womenwagepeace.org.il/en/mission-statement/.

Yuval-Davis, N. 1994. "Women, Ethnicity and Empowerment," *Shifting Identities, Shifting Racisms, Special Issue of Feminism and Psychology* 4:1, 179–197.

Yuval-Davis, N. 1997. *Gender and Nation*. London: Sage Publications.

Yuval-Davis, N. 1999. "What Is 'Transversal Politics?'" *Soundings* (12), 1294–1298.

Yuval-Davis, N. 2006. "Human/Women's Rights and Feminist Transversal Politics." In Ferree, M. M. and Tripp, A. M. (eds) *Global Feminism: Transnational Women's Activism, Organizing and Human Rights*. New York: New York University Press, 275–295.

Yuval-Davis, N. 2009. "Women, Globalization and Contemporary Politics of Belonging," *Gender Technology and Development* 13:1, 1–19.

Yuval-Davis, N. 2010. "Theorizing Identity: Beyond the 'Us' and 'Them' Dichotomy." *Patterns of Prejudice* 44:3, 261–280.

Yuval-Davis, N. 2011. *The Politics of Belonging: Intersectional Contestations*. London: Sage.

Yuval-Davis, N. 2012. "Dialogical Epistemology – An Intersectional Resistance to the 'Oppression Olympics.'" *Gender and Society* 26:1, 46–54.

Yuval-Davis, N. 2016. "Power, Intersectionality and the Politics of Belonging." In *The Palgrave Handbook of Gender and Development: Critical Engagements in Feminist Theory and Practice*, ed. W. Harcourt. New York: Palgrave Macmillan, 367–381

PART V

The International Dimensions of the Conflict

25
THE UNITED NATIONS AND INTERNATIONAL LAW

Alan Craig

Without the United States, Israel would be chopped liver at the United Nations.

Ron Prosser, Israel's Permanent Representative to the UN[1]

Introduction

In 2019 the Pew Research Centre Global Attitudes Survey found that 65 per cent of Israelis surveyed held negative views of the United Nations (Pew 2020). With a median of 32 per cent adverse responses across 32 countries, the Israeli polling was by far the most negative. This finding is in line with every Pew polling of Israeli attitudes since 2007, which have consistently recorded a high proportion of negative responses (2007 58%, 2009 65%, 2011 69%, 2013 70%, 2019 65%). This was not, however, always the case, particularly in the early years, when the United Nations (UN) played a central role in the creation and recognition of the state in 1947. After all, admission to the UN and the processes that preceded it laid the foundation for Israel's international legitimacy as a sovereign state among the other states that make up international society.

The UN had been established in 1945 to prevent recurrence of wars between states. In accordance with established International Law, the UN Charter mandated that inter-state military action was restricted to self-defence, and that states under threat of attack could expect the help of the UN. Chapter VII gave the organisation an enforcement role with Article 39 empowering the Security Council to "determine the existence of any threat to peace, breach of the peace or act of aggression," and Article 42 empowering the UN to

> take such action by air, sea, or land forces as may be necessary to maintain or restore international peace and security. Such action may include demonstrations, blockade, and other operations by air, sea, or land forces of Members of the United Nations.
>
> *(UN 1945)*

These were high expectations of the new international institution, which itself had only been in existence for three years when Israel declared independence. On the face of it, as a sovereign Israeli state with membership of the UN, Israel was expressly entitled to defend itself and to expect UN help should the need arise. In fact, Israel came to rely on the right of self-defence

DOI: 10.4324/9780429027376-31

rather than the right to UN help. This was partly from choice, with Prime Minister David Ben-Gurion preferring Israeli unilateral action to international diplomacy, and partly out of necessity as the UN showed itself to be an unreliable security guarantor. The pattern of Israel's arm's-length relationship developed over time as Israel established its military superiority through the Arab-Israel wars and committed to United States sponsorship of the peace process that left little room for UN involvement. Behind the scenes at Geneva and New York, the UN served an important role in enabling Israeli diplomats to communicate "under the radar" with states that did not recognise Israel and who could not be seen to be talking in public (Washington Institute 2017). But these valuable benefits were private and seemed insubstantial compared to the very public anti-Israel rhetoric that emerged as the UN grew from a select group of 51 states to its current membership of 193 and steadily including within its ranks more states that were committed to anti-Israel positions. Of course, steadfast support from the United States, especially since the 1970s, with its permanent seat on the Security Council and its willingness to veto anti-Israel Resolutions, has for the most part limited UN anti-Israel initiatives to declarations of the General Assembly and its various subsidiary organs. The frequency and severity of UN condemnations of Israel reinforced the Israeli view of the organisation as biased and impervious to Israeli argument (Navoth 2006, 2014; Neuer 2012; Resnik 2018; UN Watch 2006, 2019; Steinberg 2012). In these circumstances Israel adopted a policy of downplaying the importance of the UN, distancing itself from its deliberations and working to exclude the UN from the peace process. This included a policy of non-cooperation with UN investigations into Israeli military operations – a policy that came under increasing internal Israeli challenge in the aftermath of the 2008 War in Gaza (Operation Cast Lead) when the UN was seen to be at the epicentre of international condemnation.

Stung by the potency of these allegations of war crimes, Israel began to take the threat to its legitimacy very seriously, reasoning that unrelenting UN criticism could reach a level where Israel would be increasingly isolated and constrained from making the best use of its military superiority (Cohen and Freilich 2015, 2018; Craig 2013; Ravid 2010; Wajner 2019). UN bias was raised to an existential threat and incorporated into its National Security Strategy (Craig 2013; Eisenkot and Siboni 2019). This process of securitisation (Olesker 2019) of the UN has framed the UN both as acting to delegitimise the Israeli state and, as a forum for the promulgation of delegitimating discourses promoted by hostile states and international NGOs, underpins the consistently negative Pew survey results. Yet, despite this and, indeed, as will be argued in this chapter, *because* of this centrality of the UN to Israel's legitimacy battles, Israel has seen the danger of ignoring the organisation and is taking an increasingly active role at the UN.

This chapter examines the evolving relationship between the UN and the Israeli-Palestinian conflict in three parts: (1) the Arab-Israeli wars of 1948, 1956, 1967, and 1973; (2) the UN role in the Israel-Palestine Peace process; and (3) UN declaratory processes from the perspective of their impact on Israel's international legitimacy. Given the enormous scope and complexity of these issues, this cannot be a complete account of the relationship between Israel and the UN. Rather, an examination of several key moments grounds an analysis that charts the development of the role of the UN and explains why, despite the decline in Israel-Arab state conflict and apparent absence of the UN from the peace process, Israel has for the last decade been developing a closer relationship with the UN than ever before.

The Arab-Israeli Wars

The struggle for a Jewish state in Palestine is a long and complex story and, of course, predates the UN but, ultimately, it was the UN that was instrumental in the creation of the state.

Britain as the former mandatory power had relinquished the Palestine mandate and handed the UN the problem. The UN response was to establish the United Nations Special Committee on Palestine (UNSCOP) in May 1947. In September 1947 UNSCOP published its report, recommending the partition of the remainder of Mandate Palestine (much having already been hived off to create modern-day Jordan) between a Jewish state, an Arab state and an independent Jerusalem (UNSCOP 1947). This early iteration of a "two-state solution" was adopted on 29 November 1947 by General Assembly Resolution 181 calling for the establishment of two states in Palestine, thereby conferring international legitimacy on the Zionist project of a Jewish state in Palestine. On 14 May 1948, the final day of the British Mandate, Israel declared the establishment of the state on the territory allocated to it under the Resolution 181. This in itself did not create the state, which was borne in bloodshed following the rejection of the Partition Plan by the Arab League. The 1948 Arab-Israel War began immediately after Israel's Declaration of Independence, when a coalition of Egypt, Syria, Jordan, Lebanon, Iraq and Saudi Arabia declared war on Israel, leading to ten months of conflict. It was not until 15 July 1948, when the tide had turned in favour of Israel, that the Security Council finally invoked Chapter VII with UNSC Resolution 54 declaring the situation to be a threat to international peace and security. Under threat of enforcement action, the parties agreed to a ceasefire to be supervised by the UN. The final armistice left Israel with substantial territorial gains and borders that were to remain largely unaltered until 1967. The UN had been unable to prevent the conflict but, with the assistance of UN Mediator Ralph Bunche, did orchestrate the 1949 Armistice Agreements.[2] This facilitation of the Armistice Agreements was an important contribution to preventing further bloodshed but, in truth, UN intervention had been largely ignored until it suited the parties to take notice.

Israel's first application to the UN for membership was rejected by the Security Council on 17 December 1948. The subsequent application succeeded on 4 March 1949 but, as a harbinger of what was to come, was conditional on Israel allowing the return of the refugees. The confirmatory vote of the General Assembly through Resolution 273 was greeted by dancing in the streets in Israel. This undoubtedly represents the high point of Israeli popular support for the UN. Events had shown the enormous legitimating power of the UN in the state-creation process, but at the same time had exposed its weakness as a security guarantor. It had been powerless to prevent war, with its role being limited to assisting armistice negotiations. The UN had legitimated Zionism in accepting both the concept and the reality of the Jewish state but, in Israeli eyes, the institution had not acted to protect it. The very early lessons for Israel reinforced the push for both self-reliance through military strength and Great Power patronage.

These themes converged during the 1956 Suez Crisis. In July 1956 Egyptian President Gamal Abdel Nasser had nationalised the Anglo/French–owned Suez Canal, and his aggressive promotion of Arab Nationalism threatened British and French interests in the region. Israel acted covertly with Britain and France to support their seizure of the Suez Canal and in the process attempt to unseat the Egyptian president. These outcomes were in Israel's interest but, more pressingly, would also bring Israeli territorial expansion into the Sinai and secure maritime access to Israel's Red Sea port of Eilat. Israeli forces captured large swathes of the Sinai, with British and French forces occupying the canal zone, but United States opposition, with potentially devastating economic consequences to war-weakened Britain and France, was fatal to the plan. The UN was the instrument for the mobilisation of international condemnation: On 2 November 1956 the UN General Assembly passed Resolution 997 demanding a withdrawal of forces, requiring Israel to relinquish the captured territory.[3] Israeli Prime Minister Ben Gurion angrily rejected the resolution, delaying withdrawal until March of the following year. Within the Israeli political echelons there was a strengthening of the activist position that Israel should act unilaterally to harden the borders and to respond harshly to Arab *Fedayeen* incursions, and a weakening of the moderate or diplomatic school that placed reliance on international support. Ben Gurion's successful rejection of Foreign Minister Moshe Sharett's calls for constructive diplomacy during the 1950s and 1960s established an Israeli conventional wisdom that the UN was irrelevant (*oom shmoom*) if not malignant (Caplan 2020).[4] Ben Gurion's much-quoted aphorism demanded Israeli independence of action: "[I]t is not important what the Goyim [i.e., Gentiles] think, rather, what the Jews do."

Prior to the 1967 War, the UN had not spent disproportionate time on the Arab-Israeli Conflict. There had been resolutions over the provision of aid for the refugees and, after the 1956 War, the establishment of the United Nations Emergency Force (UNEF) to help 'maintain quiet' along the armistice lines between Israel and Egypt (General Assembly Resolution 1001). Within the institution itself, 1961 had seen the establishment of five regional groups at the UN: the Asia Group, African Group, Eastern European Group, Latin America and Caribbean Group, and the Western European and Others Group. With Israel excluded by Arab and Muslim states from the Asia group, Israel could not sit on any UN body where membership in a regional group was required. Equally, Israel could not count on group support for any UN initiatives. As the 1960s progressed with Egyptian President Nasser building an apparently formidable coalition of forces against Israel, the Jewish state was very much the outsider, both in the region and at the UN.

There was steadily mounting tension in the months prior to the June 1967 war with the closure of the Straits of Tiran to Israeli shipping and the mobilisation of Egyptian forces along the border with Israel. This had been achieved by the simple expedient of requesting the withdrawal of the United Nations Emergency Force. In Israel, where municipal parks were hurriedly being consecrated as cemeteries, popular fear of being overrun had reached hysterical proportions. The tame withdrawal of UN forces from the border was seen as a betrayal that was to colour Israeli perceptions of the UN for generations to come. This was the height of the Cold War and, with the Soviet Union now supporting Egypt, the Security Council was paralysed. Israel took successful pre-emptive action, ultimately capturing substantial territory, which it proceeded to occupy, marking the beginning of the Occupation that has continued to this day. After the war, five months of intensive diplomacy and numerous draft resolutions produced the November 1967 Security Council Resolution 242, which established the "Land for Peace" paradigm of peace with Israel's Arab neighbours in return for an Israeli withdrawal, generally understood as a return to the 1949 Armistice Green Line (UNSC 1967). Although the welfare of Palestinian refugees was a concern, the debates centred on the rights of Israel and the Arab states rather than those of the Palestinian population. The land-for-peace formulation assumed that the Palestinians would benefit in the process rather than be the priority.

The UN Resolution called for withdrawal of Israeli armed forces from territories occupied in the recent conflict:

ii. Termination of all claims or states of belligerency and respect for and acknowledgement of the sovereignty, territorial integrity and political independence of every State in the area and their right to live in peace within secure and recognised boundaries free from threats or acts of force.

And it also affirms the following necessities:

a. For guaranteeing freedom of navigation through international waterways in the area;
b. For achieving a just settlement of the refugee problem;

c. For guaranteeing the territorial inviolability and political independence of every state in the area; through measures including the establishment of demilitarised zones.

The deliberate creative ambiguity over whether withdrawal from *the* territories occupied meant *all* territories occupied has enabled the Resolution to stand as the basis of all serious efforts to resolve the conflict.

Meanwhile, Israel remained in Sinai, with its forces encamped on the Suez Canal. This amounted to a dangerous fault line between Soviet and United States influence in the region. The Cold War paralysis of the UN, the failure of several US-sponsored peace initiatives and the Soviet arming of Egypt in the aftermath of the 1967 War kept low-level warfare rumbling. This War of Attrition[5] culminated in the 1973 Arab-Israeli War (Siniver 2013). Israel had clear warnings of the impending attack by Egypt and Syria but failed to act. Israeli refusal to negotiate a return of Egyptian territory while failing to strengthen its defences led to the country paying a high price in casualties. On Yom Kippur, Israel's principal Holy Day, Egypt launched an attack across the Canal, quickly overrunning Israel's poorly defended positions, while the new Soviet ground-to-air missile systems deprived the Israel Air Force of its accustomed command of the skies. These were costly losses that have lived long in the memory of the Israeli public, as has the criticism of Prime Minister Golda Meir's apparent capitulation to international pressure not to take pre-emptive military action. Ultimately, Israel regained the military initiative and was within striking distance of Cairo before a ceasefire halted hostilities. The collapse of the Egyptian army led to a congruence of American and Soviet interest in ending the conflict and ended the UN paralysis, allowing the Security Council to pass a succession of ceasefire resolutions and despatch an observer mission. Security Council Resolution 338 was jointly proposed by the United States and the USSR, and demanded that, "immediately and concurrently with the ceasefire, negotiations start between the parties concerned under appropriate auspices aimed at establishing a just and durable peace in the Middle East" (UNSCR 1973). In short, the ceasefire was more the result of American and Soviet de-escalation to avoid direct confrontation than UN intervention, but the UN provided the vital institutional role of managing the de-escalation.

The December 1973 Geneva Peace Conference was convened following the war under the auspices of the UN Secretary General but was chaired by the United States and the USSR. Little was achieved at the conference with Israel and the United States opposing direct Palestinian participation and a Syrian boycott, but its importance lay in kickstarting negotiations between Egypt and Israel. This was facilitated by Egypt distancing itself from the USSR and moving into the United States orbit, allowing the United States to take sole leadership of a process that ultimately led to an Israeli withdrawal and a peace treaty between the two countries. The 1979 Egypt-Israel Peace Treaty came about as a result of United States mediation at Camp David in 1978. The UN response was General Assembly Resolution 34/70 condemning the treaty – an expression of the wider Arab condemnation of Egypt for negotiating a separate peace that ignored the interests of other Arab states and the Palestinians (UNGA 1979).

The 1973 War is seen as the closure of an era of Arab-Israeli state conflict. Subsequent wars in Lebanon and Gaza are better understood as asymmetric warfare against non-state actors and the product of a failure to resolve the conflict with the Palestinians, although the distinction is less clear where the non-state actor is located in another state. Israel's 1978 invasion of Lebanon was designed to expel the PLO from the country but with long term ambitions of installing Israel's Maronite Christian allies as a new government. The invasion was condemned at the UN with the Security Council Resolution 425 calling for immediate withdrawal. Unabashed, Israel remained in Lebanon, increasingly in conflict with an emerging *Hezbollah*, until its unilateral withdrawal in 2000. This developed into a pattern that repeated itself with the 2006 Lebanon War, with UN Security Council Resolution 1701 (UNSC 2006), whereby Israel relied on its military superiority to mount operations against its perceived state and terrorist opponents, and the UN passed condemnatory resolutions. UN action became structured around ceasefires, armistices, and supervision of compliance – but only when it suited the parties to disengage.

It would be misleading to suggest that the failure of the UN to prevent or curtail the Arab-Israeli wars left the UN without a significant role. When the parties to the conflict and their Great Power patrons were ready to de-escalate, the UN provided the mechanisms for agreement and implementation, particularly when it came to supervising the separation of forces. The 1948 United Nations Truce Supervision Organisation supervised the armistice. The United Nations Emergency Force was deployed in 1956 and remained on the Egyptian border before exiting the field in the run-up to the 1967 War. The United Nations Interim Force in Lebanon was deployed in 1978 to monitor Israel's phased withdrawal from Lebanon and expanded in the aftermath of the 2006 Second Lebanon War in an effort to prevent border violations (Feltman 2020). Additionally, since 1948 the UN has actively supported the Palestinian refugees, principally through the United Nations Relief and Works Agency for Palestine Refugees in the Near East (UNRWA), which was established in 1949 as a subsidiary body reporting directly to the General Assembly.

The Israel-Palestine Peace Process

The Palestinian voice was largely excluded from the wars between Israel and her Arab neighbours, and from their resolution. The issues were territorial; justice for the Palestinians was the language of Arab conflict rather than its driving force. True, the peace with Egypt was expressly linked to resolving Palestinian claims, but both the war and the peace were about Egyptian recovery of the Sinai. Pledges to address Palestinian claims amounted to loose linkage designed to bolster the prestige of the agreement and of Egyptian president Sadat. Similarly, intensive negotiations between Israel and Syria in the 1990s concerned Syrian efforts to recover territory lost in 1967, and the negotiations ultimately collapsed over Syrian access to Lake Kinneret rather than the rights of Palestinian refugees. On the other hand, Israel's 1994 peace treaty with Jordan, with its large Palestinian population, only became possible after tangible progress in the Oslo Israel-Palestinian negotiations. That said, separating the Arab-Israeli wars from the Israel-Palestine Conflict allows examination of the role of the UN in the Israel-Palestinian peace process, separately from a consideration of its role in the inter-state conflict.

A distinction can be made between, on the one hand, the occasions when the UN has played an active role in facilitating the peace process and, on the other, its declaratory role. This latter function has been through resolutions and statements of its officers and organs conferring and denying legitimacy to the parties and their policies. The high point of UN involvement has been declaratory, to legitimate the "Two-state Solution" as the structure of a comprehensive resolution of the conflict. This was actively promoted by the UN through the adoption of Resolution 181 approving the Partition Plan and has since been constructed through the interconnection between three Security Council resolutions:

UNSCR 242 (1967), Israeli withdrawal from territory occupied in 1967;
UNSCR 338 (1973), a just and durable peace; and
UNSCR 1397 (2002), affirming a vision of a region where two states, Israel and Palestine, live side by side within secure and recognised borders.

The importance of resolution 1397 lies in its framing of a Security Council call for a Palestinian state. That said, beyond passing resolutions, there has been a marked absence of the UN from the negotiations between Israel and the Palestinians. In the two decades following the 1967 War, this can be explained to a large part by a general paralysis of the organisation caused by the Cold War. After 1967 and until the 1990s, the Cold War dividing lines across the Middle East saw the Soviet Union and its allies supporting the Palestinian cause and disrupting United States pro-Israel initiatives. Equally, the United States blocked Soviet efforts to give the PLO a voice in UN deliberations. This institutional weakness played into the Israeli policy of holding onto its 1967 gains, denying Palestinian national rights, and favouring exclusively United States sponsorship of the process. As Israel's relationship with the United States strengthened from the 1970s, so the United States grip on the process tightened. While the United States made no serious denial of its partiality towards Israel, it had emerged as the dominant power in the region and was seen by many Palestinians as the only authority capable of providing the security guarantees essential to reaching an enduring resolution. Equally, it was generally supposed that the United States was best placed to extract Israeli concessions. To be sure, there were other actors involved in the process, including from time to time, the European Union, the Arab League, Russia, individual European states, regional neighbours, and informal negotiators – most notably during the Oslo years. This was accompanied by a growing belief that direct negotiations, often held in secret, were more likely to succeed than grand UN interventions. Added to this, the constant outpourings of UN condemnations of Israel reinforced an Israeli determination to exclude the organisation from the process.

The collapse of the 1990s Oslo process and the outbreak of the Second *Intifada*, characterised by a spiral of terrorism and Israeli incursions into the Occupied Territories, led to the formalisation of a rare active role for the UN. With the Bush Administration concentrating its energies on the "War on Terror," the absence of direct US-sponsored bilateral negotiations created space for multilateral engagement. At the same time, the European Union was looking for its own active role beyond bankrolling the Palestinian Authority, while a post-Soviet Russia was seeking a role in the region. The idea of the "Quartet" emerged from the joint United States and Russian 1991 Madrid Peace Conference, with the European Union, the United States, and Russia turning to the UN to give institutional structure to their combined intervention in the peace process. The Middle East Quartet was formally constituted in 2002, consisting of the UN, the European Union, the United States and Russia. UN involvement was not through agreement of the Security Council. Rather, the parties invited the Secretary General to be a member of the group.[6] Its official mandate was to help mediate Middle East peace negotiations and to support Palestinian economic development and institution-building in preparation for eventual statehood. This was entirely consistent with UN resolutions promoting a Two-State Solution and facilitated rather than replaced the United States role in mediating a settlement. This seemed to be a necessary function and a welcome departure from failed strategies. The Quartet has taken the lead from the United States in policy formation, with much of the implementation being driven by the European Union. The production of the "Roadmap," which was endorsed by Security Council Resolution 1397 (UNSC 2002), set out a process leading to a Two-State Solution, beginning with a focus on reform of Palestinian institutions (Quartet 2003). The European Union took a lead role in placing conditions on the Palestinian Authority and on Hamas in Gaza. Ultimately, the Roadmap stalled on the failure to meet the preliminary requirements of Palestinian reform, Hamas's recognition of Israel and transparency, with the Quartet increasingly concentrating instead on providing on-going support for Palestinian development and institution building. The deep divisions between Palestinian political factions, the Hamas takeover in Gaza in 2007 (having won the 2006 parliamentary elections; see Ch.

18 in this volume), Israel's repeated incursions into Gaza and the realities of an economy under occupation have combined to limit the impact of the Quartet's development strategies. Former British prime minister, Tony Blair, was active as Special Envoy of the Quartet between 2007 and 2015, promoting reconciliation and developmental initiatives but, in reality, the resumption of negotiations in their various forms since 2006 have been US-led, albeit with diplomatic use of the Quartet to add multilateral legitimacy to resumed United States mediation. In this way, the Quartet has used the UN to structure and give authority to its deliberations while at the same time distancing itself from the organisation. Equally, the United States has gained the benefit of multilateral credentials while remaining in the driving seat (Tocci 2013). All in all, in terms of actions rather than declarations, the UN role in the peace process has remained a facilitator rather than an instigator.

UN Declarations and Investigations: From Legitimation to Delegitimation

Beyond taking an active role in the Arab-Israeli wars and the Israel-Palestine peace process, the UN and its subsidiary bodies generate a constant stream of resolutions, statements, reports, and investigations concerning Israel and Palestine. The prestige of the UN gives force to these statements, which operate to enhance or undermine the status of the parties under scrutiny. Rather than seeing UN support for the Palestinian cause as an appropriate response to the Occupation and abuse of Palestinian rights, Israel views that support as biased and unjustified. Since 2008 Israel has increasingly understood UN criticism as impacting Israel's right to equal treatment as a sovereign state alongside others in the international state system – its international legitimacy (Reut Institute 2010). This process of delegitimation carries with it the risk of increased international isolation and an undermining of the ability to use military force to defend itself. But it is not just the status of the parties to the peace process that is enhanced or undermined, it is also the practices and policies that make up the peace process itself. Viewed from this perspective, the UN statements matter – whether emanating from the Security Council, the General Assembly or across the UN system of subsidiary institutions and spokespersons.

Security Council

It cannot be denied that the UN gives greater attention to Palestine than to any other issue, both in the Security Council, where Israel has the protection of the United States veto, and elsewhere across the UN system. On 18 December 2017, the United States vetoed a draft Security Council resolution sponsored by Egypt that sought to reverse Israel's claim to Jerusalem as its capital and the Trump Administration's relocation of the United States embassy.[7] The vote in the Security Council was 14 in favour with only the United States veto counting against. The resolution had not been expected to pass, given the strength of the United States bi-partisan commitment to Israel. Rather, the vote was designed to expose the United States and Israeli isolation at the Security Council. The issue was then moved to the floor of the General Assembly, where similarly worded Resolution GA/1195 was carried by an overwhelming 128 votes to 9 with 35 abstentions (UN Meetings 2017). Israeli and United States diplomacy had garnered support only from Guatemala, Honduras, Marshall Islands, Micronesia, Nauru, Palau, and Togo. These very different outcomes in the Security Council and the General Assembly demonstrate the extent to which Israel is sheltered in the Security Council and exposed in the General Assembly.

An examination of the Security Council voting record shows the United States vetoed 44 anti-Israel resolutions between 1972 and 2020 (Dag Hammarskjold Library). But there are limits to United States protection, as was seen in 2016 with the adoption of Security Council Resolution 2334, which condemned Israeli settlements as a "flagrant violation of International Law" (UNSC 2016). Reflecting the strains of Israel's relationship with the departing Obama administration in the aftermath of the failed 2014 Kerry peace initiative, and United States frustration with Israel's acceleration of settlement construction, the United States abstention allowed the resolution to pass unopposed, thereby charting a low point in the relationship between the two countries. True, United States diplomacy had succeeded in removing the blunter language of illegality, but the passing of the resolution unopposed by the United States allowed a rare Security Council condemnation of Israeli policy and serves as a reminder that the United States can choose when Israel is beyond the reach of the Security Council and when it is not.

General Assembly

As has been seen, the United States veto can shield Israel from hostile Security Council Resolutions but not from General Assembly Resolutions. Israel's relationship with the UN, which had been steadily deteriorating since 1967, reached a historic low with the adoption of General Assembly Resolution 3379 on 10 September 1975 (UNGA 1975). The resolution, which had been promoted by the Soviet bloc, "Determines that Zionism is a form of racism and racial discrimination." This went beyond condemnation of Israel's wars and its occupation of Arab lands. Popularised as "Zionism = Racism" and effectively equating Israel with Apartheid South Africa, this was an attack on the concept of a Jewish state and as such its right to exist in its current constitutional form. The resolution stood until its revocation in 1991, which came about at the height of United States power in the aftermath of the collapse of the Soviet Union. However, it is the original 1975 resolution rather than its revocation that lives long in the Israeli memory. In fact, despite the overturning of the resolution, the UN has continued to condemn Israel and Zionism, demonstrating a concern with Israel that can best be understood as an acceleration of the switch from its early legitimation of the state to contemporary delegitimation.

While Israel's advocates are quick to demonise the UN, it cannot be denied that the sheer volume of General Assembly Resolutions criticising Israel far exceeds those directed towards all other states or international issues. Between January to November 2020, the General Assembly has passed 18 resolutions critical of Israel, compared to seven concerning the whole of the rest of the world (UN Watch 2019). The expansion of the UN to include many more Arab, Muslim, and African states together with the anti-Israel policies of the Soviet Union gave impetus to the growth of anti-Israel sentiment in the General Assembly. The cooperation between the Arab group and the Eastern Bloc ensured a continuing focus on Israeli policies and a guaranteed majority in the General Assembly. Equally, since 1967 the enduring Occupation and its humanitarian consequences have encouraged an acceptance of the Palestinian narrative. This has advanced with the policy of the PLO and the Palestinian Authority of renouncing violence, pursuing state recognition and an ever-closer diplomatic engagement with international institutions, particularly the UN.

In 1974 Yasser Arafat was invited to address the General Assembly in the debates leading to the adoption of General Assembly Resolutions 3236 and 3237. Adopted in November 1974, these two resolutions formalised UN support for the Palestinian cause and brought the PLO into the UN system. Resolution 3236 recognised the right of the Palestinian people to self-determination, national independence and sovereignty in Palestine. It also recognised the PLO as the sole legitimate representative of the Palestinian people. The Secretary-General was requested to "establish contacts with the Palestine Liberation Organization on all matters concerning the question of Palestine." Resolution 3237 accorded the PLO observer status in the UN (UNGA 1974). This was a momentous step-change in Palestinian access to the UN at a time when Israel was denouncing the PLO and Arafat as terrorists and refusing direct contact. In 1977 the General Assembly proclaimed 29 November the International Day of Solidarity with the Palestinian People with annual events in New York and Geneva. These were big advances that guaranteed the PLO a voice at the UN, but an observer role is necessarily a long way from full membership, which is only open to states.

The PLO first declared a Palestinian state in 1988. This was triggered by Jordan's ceding its claim to the West Bank, but the day-to-day reality of the Occupation made the declaration illusory. It was only after 1994, when the Oslo Accords formalised a limited governmental role for the Palestinian National Council within clear territorial limits, that there could be a meaningful declaration. Even then, there was no rush to a further declaration. Any unilateral declaration of a state would be a radical departure from the long-standing framework for a negotiated settlement and was steadfastly opposed by both the United States and Israel. The process was further disrupted by the 2007 Hamas takeover of Gaza. It was only in 2011, after another collapse in the peace process and some semblance of Fatah-Hamas reconciliation that the Palestinian campaign for state recognition, with full membership of the UN, gathered momentum, leading to President Mahmoud Abbas formally applying in November 2011 for the state of Palestine to be admitted as a member of the UN. Under its Charter, UN membership needs a vote of two-thirds of the General Assembly and then only on the prior recommendation of the Security Council. In the face of United States opposition and a clear willingness to deploy their veto, the Palestinians explored but did not proceed with a Security Council vote.[8] Instead, the strategy was to enhance their Observer *Entity* status to that of Non-member Observer *State* status, which did not need Security Council approval and could be achieved through a resolution of the General Assembly.

On 29 November 2012 the General Assembly adopted Resolution 67/91 by 138 votes to 9, upgrading the status of Palestine to Non-member Observer State – a position shared only with the Vatican. This mechanism has been used by the UN to allow Palestine a voice across the UN without actual membership. Although falling short of state recognition, the resolution has led to the admission of Palestine to several international institutions, including the jurisdiction of the International Criminal Court. In this way, the UN has intervened in the peace process to enhance a Palestinian unilateral declaration of statehood that had not been agreed by negotiation between the parties. The fact that in the absence of UN membership the outcome is incomplete should not detract from the huge significance of the contribution. This process of legitimation of Palestine and the Palestinian narrative, despite Israeli and United States opposition, is in sharp contrast with Israel's experience of diminishing legitimacy in both in the General Assembly and the UN subsidiary organs that report to the General assembly.

Subsidiary Organs and the International Criminal Court

The bodies that make up the UN system beyond the General Assembly and Security Council (UNGA 2020) share what can be seen as an anti-Israel culture across the UN. This is not the place for a comprehensive analysis of all organs of the UN, but two examples illustrate the point. First, the UN Educational, Scientific, and Cultural Organisation (UNESCO) admitted Palestine as a state member as early as 2011 and has since produced a number of reports and recommendations supporting Palestinian cultural rights to sites in Jerusalem and Hebron while denying Israeli cultural claims, leading to the United States and Israel resigning from the organisation in 2019 (Ahren 2019). Second, in March 2017 the UN acceptance of the South African apartheid analogy took a significant step forward when the UN Economic and Social Commission for Western Asia released a report on "Israeli Practices Towards the Palestinian People and the Question of Apartheid," effectively branding Israel an "apartheid state" (UNESCWA 2017). But the discussion cannot be concluded without considering the United Nations Human Rights Council (UNHRC), which has long been the engine of UN criticism of Israel and plays a central role in the Israeli narrative of UN bias and delegitimation.

In 2006 the UNHRC replaced the United Nations Commission on Human Rights, which had been widely discredited through allegations of bias in its selection of human rights abuses, particularly regarding its unrelenting criticism of Israel (UN Watch 2006). A key objection was a predominance of serial human rights abusers among the Commission membership, which came to a head in 2004 when Sudan was elected to the Commission despite the ongoing war crimes investigation of the Sudanese president. The new UNHRC was designed to avoid bias through the introduction of a Universal Periodic Review whereby the human rights record of each member of the UN is examined in turn. This hope was dashed when as one of its first acts, the Council voted to make the investigation of Israeli breaches of human rights a permanent agenda item for every council session. At each session, "agenda item 7" requires consideration of "human rights violations and implications of the Israeli occupation of Palestine and other occupied Arab territories" and consideration of the right to self-determination of the Palestinian people. No other state has its own permanent agenda item. The Council is empowered to mandate reports on major situations from experts and from its special rapporteurs, including a special rapporteur on the Israel-Palestine Conflict.[9] Unsurprisingly, the Council has not departed from its predecessor's intense focus on allegations of Israeli human rights abuses (Navoth 2006, 2014; Resnik 2018). The NGO UN Watch recorded 61 UNHCR condemnations of Israel between 2006 and 2015 (UN Watch 2019). This was six more than the rest of the world combined. The Israeli response has been to angrily distance itself as much as possible from the Council proceedings while reluctantly participating in the periodic reviews. While the regular UNHRC condemnations of Israel's human rights record act to reinforce negative perceptions of Israel, since 2006 the Council's most impactful criticism of Israel has been in the form of high-level commissions of enquiry. These enquiries have produced a succession of highly critical reports, particularly in relation to Israeli military operations in Gaza. Two reports illustrate important aspects of the impact of the UN through the production of these UNHRC reports. First, the 2009 Goldstone Report into the 2008–2009 war in Gaza propelled international criticism of Israel to new heights and acted as a tipping point forcing a change in Israeli understanding of the power of the UN and a recognition of the need to act to counter the impact of UN delegitimation of the state (UNHRC 2019). Second, the 2019 report into Israel's response to the 2018 Gaza border protests revealed a new dynamic between the UNHRC and the International Criminal Court (UNHRC 2019).

The 2008–2009 War in Gaza (Operation Cast Lead), saw Israel deploy devastating airpower over a three-week period from 27 December 2008 until 18 January 2009. Israeli aerial attacks were broadcast to an international audience through rolling 24hr TV news reporting, prompting mounting international consternation. The UNHRC quickly became involved, adopting Resolution S-9/1 to send a fact-finding mission

> to investigate all violations of international human rights law and international humanitarian law by the occupying Power, Israel, against the Palestinian people throughout

> the Occupied Palestinian Territory, particularly in the occupied Gaza Strip, due to the current aggression, and calls upon Israel not to obstruct the process of investigation and to fully cooperate with the mission.
>
> *(UN Resolution S-9/1)*

The resulting Goldstone Report was a damning indictment of Israeli wrongdoing, amounting to a catalogue of deliberate and/or disproportionate attacks on civilians and civilian institutions. The authors listed war crimes and urged international prosecution of the Israelis involved. The report was taken up by state and civil society groups intensifying the mounting international criticism that demanded justice for Gaza. Israel hurried to reveal its decision-making processes and targeting identification and to issue its own report (IMFA 2019) asserting the legality of its operations. At the same time, it mounted an international publicity campaign to counter the multiple NGO reports into the conduct of the war. Ultimately, Goldstone reviewed the new evidence (Goldstone 2011) and rolled back from the main findings of illegality. But the process had been very damaging to Israel's international standing. The Goldstone Affair marks the point where the utility of the policy of non-cooperation with UN investigations started to be seriously eroded. (Cohen and Freilich 2015,2018; Craig 2013 189–205; Steinberg 2012).

Goldstone had called for states to prosecute Israelis involved in the planning and execution of the alleged war crimes under the Universal Jurisdiction, which allows states to prosecute war crimes committed beyond their shores. While these proceedings were an irritation for Israeli elites travelling in Europe, where there had been some high-profile attempted arrests, Israelis accused of war crimes had remained beyond the reach of the courts. In short, the UN had investigated Israeli actions, given its authority to calls for prosecution for war crimes, but without tangible results other than the further degradation of Israel's international legitimacy. This was because Israel was beyond the reach of the International Criminal Court (ICC), which had been set up to investigate and prosecute war crimes. The Court has jurisdiction on the territory of state signatories of the Rome Statute, where states have voluntarily given the court jurisdiction or where the Security Council allows the court jurisdiction. In 2008 Israel had not acceded to the Rome statute or voluntarily submitted to its jurisdiction, and since the United States veto guarded against any Security Council authorisation, Israel was operating beyond the reach of the Court.[10] The UN could urge prosecutions, but the ICC was not in a position to deliver, at least while Palestine was unable to ratify.

Palestine applied to join the Court in 2009, but was rejected as not being a state. A second application in 2015 was successful with the Court giving weight to Palestine's enhanced UN status. On 16 January 2015, the Prosecutor announced the opening of a preliminary examination into the situation in Palestine while at the same time accepting that, "since Palestine was granted observer State status in the UN by the UNGA, it must be considered a 'State' for the purposes of accession to the Rome Statute" (ICC 2016). Palestine, aware of its own vulnerability to war crimes allegations, chose only to agree to the Court's jurisdiction from 2014 onwards, leaving "Cast Lead" still off the table.

With the ICC jurisdiction now extending to Palestine, the UNHRC reports take on added importance as an authoritative call for ICC involvement. The 2018 Gaza border protests showed the relationship at work. In May 2018 Palestine submitted a referral pursuant to Article 14 of the Rome Statute cataloguing the events on the Gaza border, requesting the ICC Prosecutor to investigate "crimes involving murders and unlawful attacks on civilians, including through excessive use of force and unlawful killings of Palestinians, including demonstrators exercising their right to protest" (State of Palestine 2018). At the same time the UNHRC adopted Resolution S-28/1 mandating an inquiry to investigate Israeli "military assaults on the large-scale civilian protests." In March 2019 the Commission reported that there was evidence of Israeli war crimes and crimes against humanity by lethal targeting of demonstrators (UNHRC 2019). As with previous investigations, the report called for the arrest of perpetrators under the Universal Jurisdiction, but with the additional call for the UN High Commissioner for Human Rights to pass dossiers on alleged perpetrators to the ICC. Put simply, the presence of Israel in Gaza, the West Bank, and East Jerusalem gives the UNHRC an effective enforcement mechanism and forces Israel to engage with its investigations. On 22 January 2020, the ICC Prosecutor concluded her investigation, reporting that there is a reasonable basis to believe that the IDF had committed war crimes when firing on the demonstrators (ICC 2020). This very low burden of proof is sufficient to open an investigation, which at the time of writing has yet to be concluded. Three points can be made: first, the UN action to enhance the status of Palestine has led directly to an ICC investigation of alleged Israeli war crimes, which had previously been unthinkable; second, the interaction between the UNHRC and the ICC enhances the status of the UN as a meaningful actor in the peace process; and, third, these processes – whether or not they lead to criminal convictions – impact on the legitimacy of the Israeli state and its policies demanding Israeli responses in defence of its legitimacy (Wajner 2019).

In fact, Israel has gone further than responding to UNHRC investigations. Israel no longer derides the UN as being irrelevant. As Yaron Salman observes, this has been evident in Israel's promotion of its technological advances in furthering the UN Millennium Development Goals, its humanitarian contributions, its courting of African, Asian, and South American states in order to influence their voting patterns (frequently measured in absences and abstentions rather than pro-Israel votes), and its efforts to take positions in UN bodies (Salman 2020). Of course, it has not all been plain sailing with Israel exiting UNESCO in 2019, but even this was after a long process of negotiation with the organisation. But the trend has been for closer engagement that has built on Israel's admission to the Western European and Others Group (WEOG) in 2000 and progressed in 2017 with the election of Israeli representative Danny Danon as a vice president of the UN General Assembly.

Conclusion

The analysis in this chapter reveals a complex UN role that has changed significantly over time. Several themes assist our understanding. From the perspective of Israel's international legitimacy, we can chart a downwards trajectory from a high of UN admission and recognition of the Zionist state, to a steady decline following the start of the Occupation in 1967 and rapidly progressing with the adoption of the Palestinian narrative and the quasi-recognition of Palestine through the upgrade to state observer status. This trajectory from legitimation to delegitimation accounts for changes in Israeli policy towards the UN. Initially, the UN was essential to Israel as the route to statehood. Then as UN criticism of Israel's policies towards its neighbours and the Palestinians intensified, Israel rejected UN initiatives as biased and not worthy of close engagement. This policy changed, particularly after the Goldstone Affair, when Israel recognised the power of UN criticism to impact on the security of the state – all the more so with Palestine joining the ICC. However, although examining the Israel-UN relationship from the perspective of international legitimacy is helpful, it only reveals a small part of this complex picture. Widening the focus to include the Arab-Israel wars and the Israel-Palestine peace process reveals other important aspects of the relationship.

The Arab-Israeli wars reveal an early Israeli understanding that the UN could not guarantee Israeli security. UN diplomacy soon took a back seat to security through Israeli military strength, Great Power patronage and Israeli unilateral action. As the state established its military superiority over its neighbours it sought to maximise its freedom of action by distancing itself from the UN. To be sure, the UN served useful purposes when it came to a ceasefire, an armistice agreement, or a neutral disengagement force, but only when Israel was ready for it. In any event, from the perspective of the UN, the Cold War paralysis allowed little opportunity for a more active role.

The accepted view is that the UN has played an even lesser role in the Israel-Palestine peace process. From 1948, when Israel resisted UN facilitation of a return of the refugees, through to contemporary times, Israel has worked to block UN initiatives. Indeed, as pressure mounted from the 1970s for Israel to end its occupation, Israel and the United States worked to maintain semi-exclusive control of the negotiations. Even when the UN joined the Quartet, its role was to structure and institutionalise the process rather than to actively seek change. But the argument here is that the absence has been overstated; UN declarations, whether critical of the parties or otherwise, are themselves a part of the peace process. The adoption of the Palestinian narrative informing a constant outpouring of support for the Palestinian cause – expressed as a demand for an end to the occupation, illegal settlements, Israeli human rights abuses, war crimes and for a return of the refugees – alters the power dynamics between the parties. This operates, however imperfectly, to exert pressure on Israel to accept a Palestinian state or at least preserve the viability of the Two-State Solution. Equally, the promotion of Palestinian rights acts to empower the Palestinians and strengthen the Palestinian factions that advocate resistance through international diplomacy. The status of non-member observer state is misleading. Palestine does not observe; where it matters, Palestine participates albeit by invitation and has done so very effectively. From this perspective, the UN has played an active role in the peace process by enhancing the status of Palestine and by giving vocal support to Palestinian claims. This *legitimation* of Palestine and the Palestinian narrative is lost when UN declarations are viewed only from a perspective of UN delegitimation of Israel.

To be sure, Israel continues to seek security through military strength and unilateral action rather than rely on the UN, continues to see the organisation as institutionally biased, and continues to work to deny the UN a role in the peace process. But despite these efforts, a thematic analysis of the Arab-Israel wars, the Israel-Palestine peace process, and legitimacy, reveal a greater UN role than is generally recognised. This goes a long way towards explaining why, despite an overwhelming popular Israeli dislike of the UN, Israel has begun to take the UN very seriously and to play a much greater role in New York and Geneva.

Recommended Readings

Cohen, M. S., and C. D. Freilich. 2015. "The Delegitimization of Israel: Diplomatic Warfare, Sanctions, and Lawfare." *Israel Journal of Foreign Affairs* 9:1, 29–48.

Navoth, M. 2006. "From a UN Commission on Human Rights to a Human Rights Council: A Structural Change or Human Rights Reform?" *Israel Journal of Foreign Affairs* 1:1, 112–118.

Salman, Y. 2020. "The UN and Israel: From Confrontation to Participation." *Strategic Assessment*, July, 23:3. Available at: https://strategicassessment.inss.org.il/wp-content/uploads/2020/07/Adkan23.3Eng_5.pdf#page=39.

UN Charter. 1945. Available at: https://legal.un.org/repertory/art1.shtml.

Notes

1 Washington Institute, Policy Analysis, 8 December 2017, "For Israel at the UN, Quiet Respect and Continued Public Hostility." Available at: www.washingtoninstitute.org/policy-analysis/view/2017-scholar-statesman-conversation.

2 The first UN mediator, Count Bernadotte of Sweden, was assassinated by Jewish terrorists in September 1948.
3 The resolution was tabled in the General Assembly because the United Kingdom and France vetoed Security Council Resolutions.
4 Israel's first foreign minister and architect of Israel's admission to the UN. He had served briefly as prime minister (26 January 1954–3 November 1955). He was sacked by Ben-Gurion from his post as foreign minister in June 1956 in the run-up to the war, ending his political career. *oom shmoom* was Ben-Gurion's dismissive trivialisation of the UN.
5 The period between the 1967 and 1973 wars involved repeated low-intensity conflict particularly on the border between Israel and Egypt, with the War of Attrition technically proclaimed by Nasser in 1969.
6 In practice this role is undertaken by the UN Special Co-ordinator for the Peace Process.
7 Draft resolution S/2017/1060, asserted that, "any decisions and actions which purport to have altered the character, status or demographic composition of the Holy City of Jerusalem have no legal effect, are null and void and must be rescinded in compliance with relevant resolutions of the Security Council."
8 A two-thirds majority in the Security Council is required for membership, which seemed unlikely at the time, which would have obviated the need for a United States veto.
9 Richard Falk attracted intense Israeli criticism for his anti-Zionist views and allegations of Israeli war crimes while UN Special Rapporteur on the "situation of human rights in the Palestinian Territories since 1967" from 2008 till 2014. In 2012 he was expelled from Human Rights Watch's advisory committee after comparing Israelis to Nazis (UN Watch 2012).
10 The exception was in relation to the 2010 Gaza Flotilla, since the Mavi Marmara was registered to Comros, which joined the ICC leading to several years of ICC examination but ultimately a finding that the alleged crimes were not sufficiently serious to merit prosecution.

Questions for Discussion

(1) How effective has the UN been in resolving the Arab-Israeli conflict and the Israel-Palestine conflict?
(2) What have been the major challenges to effective UN interventions?
(3) Is there any substance to the Israeli charges of UN bias?
(4) What does the concept of delegitimisation add to an understanding of UN power?

References

Ahren, R. 2019. "69 years after Joining, Israel Formally Leaves UNESCO; So, too, Does the US." *Times of Israel*, 1 January. Available at: www.timesofisrael.com/69-years-after-joining-israel-formally-leaves-un-cultural-body/.

Cohen, M. S., and C. D. Freilich. 2015. "The Delegitimization of Israel: Diplomatic Warfare, Sanctions, and Lawfare." *Israel Journal of Foreign Affairs* 9:1, 29–48.

Cohen, M. S., and C. D. 2018. "War by Other Means: The Delegitimisation Campaign against Israel." *Israel Affairs* 24:1, 1–25.

Craig, A. 2013. *International Legitimacy and the Politics of Security*. Lanham, MD: Lexington Books.

Eisenkot, G., and G. Siboni. 2019. "Guidelines for Israel's National Security Strategy." *Washington Institute*, Policy Focus 160, 2 October. Available at: www.washingtoninstitute.org/policy-analysis/guidelines-israels-national-security-strategy.

Feltman, J. 2020. "Debating UN Peacekeeping in Lebanon." *Brookings Institute*, 15 June. Available at: www.brookings.edu/blog/order-from-chaos/2020/06/15/debating-un-peacekeeping-in-lebanon/.

Goldstone, R. 2011. "Reconsidering the Goldstone Report on Israel and War Crimes." *Washington Post*, 1 April.

ICC. 2016. "The Prosecutor of the International Criminal Court, Fatou Bensouda, Opens a Preliminary Examination of the Situation in Palestine." *ICC Press Release*, 16 January. Available at: www.icc-cpi.int/Pages/item.aspx?name=pr1083.

ICC. 2020. "Prosecution Request Pursuant to Article 19(3) for a Ruling on the Court's Territorial Jurisdiction in Palestine." ICC-01/18, 22 January. Available at: www.icc-cpi.int/Pages/record.aspx?docNo=ICC-01/18-12.

Israel Ministry of Foreign Affairs (IMFA). 2019. "Israel's response to UNHRC Commission of Inquiry Report, 21 March 2019." Available at: https://mfa.gov.il/MFA/InternatlOrgs/Issues/Pages/Israel-s-response-to-UNHRC-Commission-of-Inquiry-report-21-March-2019.aspx.

Israel vs. Oom-shmoom: Ben-Gurion vs. Sharett," *Israel Studies* 25:1 (Spring 2020), 26–46.

Navoth, M. 2006. "From a UN Commission on Human Rights to a Human Rights Council: A Structural Change or Human Rights Reform?" *Israel Journal of Foreign Affairs* 1:1, 112–118.

Navoth, M. 2014. "Israel's Relationship with the UN Human Rights Council: Is There Hope for Change?" *Jerusalem Center for Public Affairs*, May–June, No. 601. Available at: https://jcpa.org/article/israels-relationship-un-human-rights-council/.

Neuer, H. 2012. "The Demonization of Israel at the United Nations in Europe Focus on the Human Rights Council and Specialized Agencies." *Jerusalem Centre for Public Affairs*, June, No. 27. Available at: http://jcpa.org/overview_palestinian_manipulation/ demonization_of_israel_at_the_united_nations/.

Olesker, R. 2019. "Delegitimization as a National Security Threat." *Israel Studies Review* 34:2, 33–54.

Pew Research Centre. 2020. "Global Indicators Data Base." *Global Attitudes and Trends*, March. Available at: www.pewresearch.org/global/database/indicator/26/.

Quartet. 2003. "A Performance-based Roadmap to a Permanent Two-state Solution to the Israeli-Palestinian Conflict." 30 April. Available at: www.un.org/unispal/document/auto-insert-186742/.

Ravid, B. 2010. 'Delegitimization of Israel Must be Delegitimized." *Haaretz*, 23 October. Available at: www.haaretz.com/1.5250761.

Resnik, U. 2018. "Bias at the Human Rights Council: A Quantitative Approach." *The Arena*, 28 September. Available at: www.eng.arenajournal.org.il/single-post/2018/09/28/Resnick-UNHRC-ENG.

Reut Institute. 2010. "Building a Political Firewall against Israel's Delegitimization: Conceptual Framework." 10 March. Available at: https://20a1ea9b-cbf6-4da3-88fd-ab21d8ba06cc.filesusr.com/ugd/1bfcb5_d59cc682a61444439b12462b75e1fbb5.pdf.

State of Palestine. 2018. "Referral by the State of Palestine Pursuant to Articles 13(a) and 14 of the Rome Statute." 15 May. Available at: www.icc-cpi.int/itemsDocuments/2018-05-22_ref-palestine.pdf.

Salman, Y. 2020. "The UN and Israel: From Confrontation to Participation," *Strategic Assessment*. July, 23:3. Available at: www.inss.org.il/publication/the-un-and-israel-from-confrontation-to-participation/.

Siniver, A. ed. 2013. *The Yom Kippur War: Politics, Diplomacy, Legacy*. New York: Oxford University Press.

Steinberg, G. M. 2012. "From Durban to the Goldstone Report." *Israel Affairs* 18:3, 372–388.

Tocci, N. 2013. "The Middle East Quartet and (In)effective Multilateralism." *The Middle East Journal* 67:1, 29–44.

UN Charter. 1945. Available at: https://legal.un.org/repertory/art1.shtml

UNESCWA. 2017. "Israeli Practices towards the Palestinian People and the Question of Apartheid." *Palestine and the Israeli Occupation*, No. 1. Available at: www.middleeastmonitor.com/wp-content/uploads/downloads/201703_UN_ESCWA-israeli-practices-palestinian-people-apartheid-occupation-english.pdf.

UNGA Resolution 3379. 1975. "Elimination of All Forms of Racial Discrimination." 10 November. Available at: https://unispal.un.org/UNISPAL.NSF/0/761C1063530766A7052566A2005B74D1.

UNGA Resolutions 3236. 1974. "Question of Palestine." 22 November. Available at: www.securitycouncilreport.org/atf/cf/%7B65BFCF9B-6D27-4E9C-8CD3-CF6E4FF96FF9%7D/IP%20A%20RES%203236.pdf.

UNGA Resolution 34/70. 1979. Available at: https://web.archive.org/web/20140111145137/http://unispal.un.org/UNISPAL.NSF/0/6118CF31EC9EB7FB852560DA006E47F3

UNHRC. 2019. "Report of the United Nations Fact Finding Mission on the Gaza Conflict." 25 September. Available at: www.ohchr.org/EN/HRBodies/HRC/SpecialSessions/Session9/Pages/FactFindingMission.aspx.

UN Meetings. 2017. "General Assembly Overwhelmingly Adopts Resolution Asking Nations Not to Locate Diplomatic Missions in Jerusalem." 21 December. Available at: www.un.org/press/en/2017/ga11995.doc.htm.

UN Resolution S-9/1. Available at: https://web.archive.org/web/20180617093013/https://unispal.un.org/DPA/DPR/unispal.nsf/0/404E93E166533F828525754E00559E30.

UNSC Resolution 242. 1967. "Resolution 242 (1967) of 22 November 1967." Available at: https://unispal.un.org/unispal.nsf/0/7D35E1F729DF491C85256EE700686136.

UNSC Resolution 338. 1973. "Resolution 338 (1973) of 22 October 1973." Available at: http://unscr.com/en/resolutions/338.
UNSC Resolution 1397. 2002. "The Situation in the Middle East, Including the Palestinian Question." 12 March. Available at: http://unscr.com/en/resolutions/1397.
UNSC Resolution 1701. 2006. Available at: https://peacemaker.un.org/israellebanon-resolution1701
UNSC Resolution 2334. 2016. "Resolution 2334 (2016)." 23 December. Available at: www.un.org/webcast/pdfs/SRES2334-2016.pdf.
UNSCOP.1947. "Report A/364 to the UN General Assembly." 3 September. Available at: www.jewishvirtuallibrary.org/united-nations-special-committee-on-palestine-unscop.
UNGA. 2020. "Subsidiary Organs of the General Assembly." General Assembly of the United Nations. Available at: www.un.org/en/ga/about/subsidiary/councils.shtml.
UN Watch. 2006. "The Struggle against Anti-Israel Bias at the UN Commission on Human Rights." Issue 138, 4 January. Available at: https://unwatch.org/9009-2/
UN Watch. 2012. "Human Rights Watch Expels Top U.N. Official Richard Falk," 18 December. Available at: https://unwatch.org/human-rights-watch-expels-top-u-n-official-richard-falk/#more-3023.
UN Watch. 2019. "2019-2020 UN General Assembly Resolutions Singling Out Israel–Texts, Votes, Analysis." 19 November. https://unwatch.org/2019-un-general-assembly-resolutions-singling-out-israel-texts-votes-analysis/.
Wajner, D. 2019. "Battling for Legitimacy: Analysing Performative Contests in the Gaza Flotilla Paradigmatic Case." *International Studies Quarterly* 63:4, 1035–1050.
Washington Institute. 2017. "For Israel at the UN, Quiet Respect and Continued Public Hostility." *Policy Analysis*, 8 December. Available at: www.washingtoninstitute.org/policy-analysis/view/2017-scholar-statesman-conversation.

26

THE ARAB WORLD AND THE PALESTINIAN-ISRAELI CONFLICT

Ahmad Barakat

Introduction

The Palestinian-Israeli conflict has long been a central issue to the Arab world, with attitudes to the conflict underpinned by intra-Arab cleavages and interests. While the 'Arab world' is not a monolithic actor, it is possible to speak of broad views on the conflict, views that are shared by the majority of Arab states, if not all, most pertinently in relation to the right of the Palestinians to statehood – although the means of achieving this goal, as well as the level of normalisation of relations with Israel, have been the subject of much disagreement on the Arab street and between Arab capitals.

This chapter begins by dividing the Arab world's attitudes towards the Palestinian-Israeli conflict into five broad phases: Pan-Arabism, Palestinian particularism, the 1967 War and its aftermath, the Oslo peace process, and post-Oslo period. This followed by an analysis of the three levels of engagement with the conflict's different phases, namely the national, regional, and international. The chapter then examines the role of the Arab League and its key resolutions in relation to the conflict, and concludes with general observations on the future direction of the Arab world's engagement with the conflict.

The Arab World and the Conflict: Five Phases

The Palestinian-Israeli conflict has been at the forefront of the wider Arab-Israeli conflict since the first Arab-Israeli war of 1948. Over the years, Arab attitudes toward the conflict have evolved through five broad phases: Pan-Arabism during most of the 1950s and early 1960s; Palestinian particularism in the mid-1960s; Palestinian nationalism, which followed the 1967 war; the Oslo peace process; and the post-Oslo period. Each phase had its unique characteristics and marked a significant transformation in the nature of the conflict from the Arab world's standpoint.

Pan-Arabism prevailed during most of the 1950s and early 1960s, under the leadership of Egypt's Gamal Abdel Nasser (1918–1970). Nasser believed that the Arabs constitute a single nation, and that the Arab world should be unified because they shared a common culture, religion, and language. Nasserism (Hamid 2017) was able to attract support in the Arab world because it shared Arab sympathy for the exiled Palestinian Arabs and hostility towards Zionism

DOI: 10.4324/9780429027376-32

(Mansfield 1973). It transferred, if only partially, to the Arab world itself, the centre of decisions concerning the future of that world. This change inspired self-confidence in the Arab community, which was particularly welcome after the recent shock over the loss of Palestine (Laqueur 1958, 125).

The creation of the Palestine Liberation Organisation (PLO) by the Arab League in 1964 saw a shift in how the Arab world viewed the Palestinian-Israeli conflict, from pan-Arabism to a notion of Palestinian particularism, which recognised that Palestinian self-organisation, rather than under the umbrella of pan-Arabism, was essential in the struggle for self-determination (Khalidi 1985). Years of experience in wars and diplomacy have taught the Palestinian people a lot, and systematically produced two parallel processes: self-reliance and self-organisation through numerous political and popular initiatives and organisational structures (Barghouti 2018). The organisation of the refugee camps by various resistance movements in the mid-1960s such as Fatah, the Popular Front for the Liberation of Palestine (PFLP), the Democratic Front for the Liberation of Palestine (DFLP), and others, emerged because of the despair engendered by the failure of the international community and Arab states, in particular, to support the Palestinian claims for repatriation and self-determination (Nabulsi 2014).

The June 1967 war altered geographic borders and political fortunes in the Middle East, and with it the Arab world's support for Palestinian nationalism. While Israel quadrupled its territory to include East Jerusalem, the West Bank, the Gaza Strip, the Golan Heights, and the Sinai Peninsula, for the Arab states it meant crushing military and reputational defeat, leading to a unified refusal to negotiate, recognise or make peace with Israel. For the Palestinians, the war's outcome meant the occupation of more than one million inhabitants in the West Bank and the Gaza Strip, and another quarter of a million refugees, but it also gave rise to more organised and popular calls in the Arab world in support of Palestinian nationalism. This phase marked the first time in the conflict that the Palestinians broke away from the guardianship of the Arab states and made their national claims as a people (Abu Sharif 2005, 25). This became more pronounced, particularly following the sudden death of Nasser in 1970, which left Pan-Arabism, and the Arab world more broadly, without a clear leader (Ajami 1978).

The growing support of the international community for the Palestinian cause in the subsequent two decades, together with the dramatic events of the end of the Cold War and the first Gulf War, eventually led to the Oslo peace process, which began in 1993. The process brought the Israeli and Palestinian leaders together for the first time. It included the first formal mutual recognition between Israel and the PLO and specified that bilateral negotiations were the only viable path to Palestinian statehood, but it ended in a spectacular failure at the 2000 Camp David summit. The Arab states did not have a unified stance towards the peace process. Some, like Jordan and Egypt, supported the Oslo Accords and saw them as an opportunity to settle the conflict, while others, like Syria, criticised the accords for not going far enough in terms of securing the rights of the Palestinians, and called for a total Israeli withdrawal from the Arab lands occupied in the June 1967 war. Syria (aided by Iran) rejected the agreement and worked to undermine it by supporting the Palestinian factions opposed to the agreement, especially Hamas and Islamic Jihad and some of the PLO factions (Bouez 1994, 263–270).

The failure of the 2000 Camp David summit was characterised by a return to violence, unilateralism, and securitisation of the Palestinian-Israeli discourse (Ross 2018; Shah 2003). It was a recognition that the peace process had reached a deadlock (Shlaim 2005). Following years of diplomatic deadlock, briefly interspersed by diplomatic failures such as the Annapolis Conference (2007) and the mediation efforts of United States Secretary of State John Kerry (2013–2014), Palestinian president Mahmoud Abbas announced in 2015 that the Palestinians were no longer bound by the Oslo Accords (Global Conflict Tracker, 2020). By then, and against the background of the Arab Spring and the Syrian civil war, the role of the Arab League as a collective decision-making body had diminished significantly, and the Palestinian cause had received considerably less attention in the Arab world, while Israeli clandestine relations with many Arab states, especially the Gulf monarchies, had become common knowledge (Hatuqa 2019).

The Arab World and the Conflict: Levels of Analysis

The five broad phases of the Arab world's engagement with the conflict can be analysed through national, regional, and international levels of analysis. The context has evolved considerably since the first Arab-Israeli war and resulted in significant changes in the position of the Arab world from non-recognition to normalisation by some Arab states (Alhelou 2020). To some extent, the cosying up of the Gulf monarchies with Israel has led to a measured decline in rhetorical and diplomatic support to the Palestinian cause, compared to the first decade of the millennium.

On the national level, disunity between Palestinian factions led to a lack of a unified voice representative of a consensual Palestinian position in peace talks. Feuding between the Palestinians' two main rival political factions, Fatah and Hamas, and their inability or unwillingness to bridge their internal divisions are widely seen as primary obstacles to Palestinian unity (Alhelou 2020; Dalloul 2019). Divisions and political disengagement between Palestinians hindered efforts for a settlement to the conflict and sometimes alienated traditional allies, leading to a decline in support for the Palestinian cause. The political alignments of the Palestinians have complicated the scene. Some Palestinian political factions' decisions to strengthen relations with Iran, for example, or oppose peace talks with Israel, put them in conflict with other Arab states.

Arab policies towards the conflict have also been affected by domestic politics in individual states, and the centrality of the Palestinian cause as an Arab national responsibility has been contested. It has been overwhelmed, especially in recent years, by other issues that have been prioritised by the Arab states, and the Zionist threat was no longer perceived as a major threat to Arab national security. As explained by the secretary-general of the Arab League, Ahmed Abu al-Gheith, the priority of the Palestinian cause – resisting Israel and pushing for a Palestinian state – has been somewhat reduced, which he attributed to the drastic changes in the internal, regional, and international context. Abu al-Gheith added that the Arab world now faces other pressing concerns, such as political instability and failed states, resulting from mistakes made by Arab rulers, inflicting tragedies upon the region (Abumaria 2019).

On the regional level, events such as the Arab Spring and the civil war in Syria shifted attention in the Arab street towards internal reflection and analysis, as well as towards regional rivalries between pro-Assad and anti-Assad regimes, at the expense of demonstrations of Arab unity in support of the Palestinian cause (Asseburg 2012; Katz 2013). Similarly, the diplomatic crisis between the Gulf monarchies, which led to the isolation of Qatar, weakened its support for Hamas and contributed to further discord between Arab capitals over the Palestinian cause (Wang 2017).

On the international level, too, progress on the Palestinian-Israeli conflict has often been conditioned on the trajectory of global events and the policies of external parties. For example, the American-led discourse of the war on terror following the 9/11 attacks immediately placed Israelis and Palestinians in opposing camps and further compounded the mothballing of the peace process against the background of the Second *Intifada* (2000–2005). Similarly, Palestinian efforts to internationalise the conflict by appealing to bodies such as the United Nations and the International Criminal Court only led to unilateral Israeli moves in the West

Bank, such as the build-up of new settlements, leading to widening the gap between the parties' positions and further removing them from the negotiation table (Vick 2014). The policies of the United States under Donald Trump towards the conflict, such as the cutting of aid to the Palestinian Authority and the United Nations Relief and Works Agency for Palestinian Refugees (UNRWA), moving the United States embassy from Tel-Aviv to Jerusalem and recognising Jerusalem as Israel's capital, brought the American role as the indispensable mediator in the conflict to an historic nadir, leading the Palestinians to refuse to negotiate via the United States, while driving Israel further towards intransigence and religious-national zeal (Kirshner 2019).

The Arab League and the Conflict

More often than not, the position of the Arab League on the conflict lacked consistency and unity, which affected its ability to influence in the long term. Differences between the oil-rich states and less affluent states – between monarchies and republics, between proponents and detractors of Arab nationalism, and between 'moderate' and 'radical' regimes –invariably hindered the League's capacity to speak with one voice and to lend its considerable leverage in aid of the Palestinian cause. Nevertheless, the Palestinian cause had been permanently fixed to every League summit since the first in 1946, which affirmed the Arabism of Palestine as the heart of the Arab people, and that its fate is linked to the fate of all Arab states. From its outset, the Arab League considered confronting the danger of Zionism as a duty of all Arab and Islamic states. It continued to affirm the centrality of the Palestinian cause as the cause of all Arabs and considered that the struggle for the restoration of Palestine to the Palestinians was a general national responsibility, which all Arabs must adhere to.

Formed in Cairo on 22 March 1945, the League's main goal was to coordinate the policies of the Arab states, to deliberate on matters of common concern, to settle intra-Arab disputes, and to promote Arab unity internationally. The League's original pact noted that the recognition of Palestine, and its independence among the nations, be no more questioned *de jure* than the independence of any of the other Arab states (Avalon, 1945). As soon as the League was established, it called for an organised boycott of the *Yishuv* (the pre-state Jewish community in Palestine), which had remained in place for decades after the establishment of the state of Israel. The boycott was designed to weaken Jewish industry in Palestine and deter Jewish immigration to the region. A secondary boycott was later imposed to boycott non-Israeli companies that did business with Israel, and a later tertiary boycott involved the blacklisting of firms that did business with other companies that did business with Israel (Turck 1977; Miller 2016; Weiss 2017).

The feasibility of the boycott remained disputed. While it undoubtedly hurt Israel to some extent, it failed to cripple its economy. On the contrary, it forced Israeli industry to become more innovative and develop new technologies, as well as to seek new markets in Asia, sub Saharan Africa, and Latin America. Moreover, Israel's signing of peace treaties with Egypt (1979) and Jordan (1994), and the peace process with the Palestinians in the 1990s, significantly eroded the effects of any boycott (Weiss, 2017). With the notable exceptions of Syria and Lebanon, the Arab states no longer enforce the secondary and tertiary dimensions of the boycott. Despite the Arab moral justification behind the boycott, it affected at least some Arab states more adversely than it did Israel. According to the Arab Council for Regional Integration, the primary victims of the Arab boycott of Israel are the Palestinians and Arab states that could not trade with Israel and benefit from its advanced industries and technological innovations (El-Dessouki and Gheita 2019).

The League held 42 Arab summits on the Palestinian cause between 1946 and 2019. Its resolutions persisted on principal issues and were escalating in response to the development of the conflict, beginning with the publication in Lausanne of the Anglo-American Committee of Inquiry's report on Palestine on 20 April 1946, which recommended that the British Mandate authorities allow the entry of 100,000 European Jews into Palestine, and abolish the 1939 White Paper's restrictions on the purchase of lands by Jews. It also recommended that Palestine shall be neither a Jewish nor an Arab state. Over its 75-year history, the League issued a series of resolutions to support the Arabs of Palestine by all means: It considered Israel a primary danger that the entire Arab nation must resist, and called for the creation of a unified Arab leadership for the armies of Arab states (League of Arab States, Cairo Summit 1964); approved an Arab Collective Action Plan for the liberation of Palestine, adopted the PLO as a representative of the Palestinian people, and decided to raise, fund, and equip what became known as the Palestinian Liberation Army (League of Arab States, Alexandria Summit 1964). And the League agreed on an Arab Solidarity Pact and a unified Arab Plan to defend the Palestinian cause at the United Nations and international forums (League of Arab States, Casablanca Summit 1965). The League's resolutions were accompanied by a series of steps taken by the Arab states, such as, in the run-up to the 1967 war, the concluding of a Syrian-Egyptian military pact that Jordan and Iraq later joined, the expulsion of the United Nations Emergency Force (UNEF) from the Sinai Peninsula, the concentration of Egyptian forces there, and mobilising Arab forces towards the Israeli borders. Israel viewed the Arab response as provocative and a casus belli (IMOFA 2013).

The Arab states found themselves in a precarious position, politically and militarily, in the aftermath of defeat in the June 1967 war. On 1 September the League convened a summit in Khartoum – what became known as the 'Summit of the Three No's'. The summit resolved that could be no peace with Israel, no recognition of Israel, and no negotiations with Israel (League of Arab States, Khartoum Summit 1967). In addition, an oil embargo targeted nations perceived as supporting Israel during the 1967 war and. while it was ineffective and too costly (Stocking 1970), it laid the ground for the much more effective Arab oil embargo, which followed the October 1973 war where, for the first time the Arab states decided to use oil strategically as an economic weapon in line with League resolutions of Arab solidarity and a unified Arab plan (Daoudi and Dajani 1984, 65–90).

The October war of 1973 was an attempt by the Arab states to restore the territories they lost in the 1967 war. Egyptian and Syrian forces launched a coordinated attack against Israel on Yom Kippur, the holiest day in the Jewish calendar. The Arab oil embargo was targeted at nations perceived as supporting Israel during the war and, by March 1974 the price of oil had risen nearly 400 per cent, leading to the worst global economic crisis since 1929 (Daoudi and Dajani 1984; Department of State 2017). The embargo contributed to a global recession and increased tension between the United States and its European allies, who criticised the United States for provoking an embargo by supplying arms to Israel during the war (Hughes 2008). However, the effectiveness of the Arab oil embargo remained contested. It did not force an Israeli withdrawal to the 1949 Armistice borders, and the states targeted by the embargo did not change their policies on the conflict (Licklider 1988). From a different perspective, the oil embargo remade the international economy (MERIP 1974). Over the long term, the oil embargo changed the nature of policy in the West towards increased exploration, alternative energy searches, energy conservation, and more restrictive monetary policies to better fight inflation. In America, various legislative acts during the 1970s sought to redefine its relationship to fossil fuels and other sources of energy. As part of the movement towards energy reform, efforts were made to stimulate domestic oil production as well as to reduce American dependence on fossil fuels and find alternative sources of power (Lifset 2014).

The oil embargo of 1973 reflected Arab coordination and solidarity, but also aspects of differences in theory and practice, which reflected on its applicability and durability. Some members of the Organisation of Arab Petroleum Exporting Countries (OAPEC), such as Algeria, Iraq, and Libya, were supportive of the use of oil as a weapon to influence the political outcome of the conflict. However, the embargo lasted only a few months because other OAPEC members (such as Saudi Arabia) were strong proponents of separating oil from politics and were wary of the availability of oil from non-Arab oil-producing countries (Ahrari 2015). Moreover, in the decades leading up to the crisis, the region's monarchies had grown dependent on Western support to ensure their continued survival as Nasserism gained traction.

The 1978 Camp David Accords between Egypt and Israel were a turning point in the conflict. As Henry Kissinger put it, you cannot make war in the Middle East without Egypt, and you cannot make peace without Syria (Fischer 2014). The Egypt-Israel peace treaty that followed in 1979 was not only a sign of disintegration in the Arab regional system, but also a sign of a regional imbalance of power. Egypt acted outside the Arab Solidarity Pact and the unified Arab Plan. As a key figure in the Middle East, President al-Sadat's decision to distance Egypt from the conflict contributed to the erosion of the Palestinian cause. The Arab states looked at the agreement as a betrayal that ignored the Arab states and the PLO. The oil-producing Arab states pledged to provide annual assistance for ten years to support the PLO and the struggle of the Palestinian people in the occupied lands (League of Arab States, Baghdad Summit 1978). Multiple attempts at negotiations stalled over the question of Jerusalem after the Israeli government passed its Basic Law, declaring Jerusalem, complete and undivided, as the capital of Israel (Knesset 1980). The Arab League blamed the Israeli Basic Law on the Camp David Accords, which divided the Arab front, weakened the Arab stance, and enabled Israel to avoid negotiating with the Arabs as one bloc. The League adopted the Arab Joint Program of Action, National Economic Action Charter, and vowed to cut all relations with any state that recognised Jerusalem as the capital of Israel or moved its embassy there (League of Arab States, Amman Summit 1980).

The outbreak of the Intifada in Gaza and the West Bank provided another opportunity for the Arab League to demonstrate its solidarity with the Palestinian cause. The League called on the United Nations Security Council to work on an immediate end to the Israeli occupation and to provide protection for the Palestinians (League of Arab States, Extraordinary Algiers Summit 1988). The Intifada marked a significant transition in the conflict from Arabic to the Palestinian-led, and from leaders to people. It was an expression of popular dissatisfaction with the Arab engagement in the conflict and with Palestinian leadership. The Arab summits were disappointing and did not offer any solutions. Unlike the Arab intellectuals and peoples, the Arab and Palestinian leaders in exile did not feel the pain of the Palestinians and their deteriorating conditions. In addition to heightening international recognition of the centrality of the Palestinian cause to a Middle East peace settlement, the Intifada also contributed to a shift in the political gravity of the national movement from the exile community to West Bank Palestinians and an official moderation of the movement's political position from military struggle and liberation of the whole of historic Palestine to a negotiated two-state solution (Alin 1994).

The League supported the PLO's agreement in Israel in September 1993 and, when Jordan signed its peace treaty with Israel in October 1994 it was not ostracised by the League as Egypt had been following its peace treaty with Israel in 1979 (The Arab League, Extraordinary Cairo Summit 1996). By the end of the decade, however, with the collapse of the peace process and the outbreak of the *Al-Aqsa Intifada*, the Arab street across the Middle East demonstrated in support of the Palestinians, showing levels of political activism never seen in many Arab states, especially the Gulf monarchies, which reflected the gap between ordinary Arabs and their leaders.

In its Beirut summit of 2002, under the initiative of Saudi Crown Prince Abdullah, the Arab League adopted what became known as the Arab peace initiative, which, for the first time in the history of the conflict, laid out its outlook for the normalisation of relations with Israel. It called for a complete Israeli withdrawal from all Arab territories occupied in 1967 (including East Jerusalem), a just solution to the Palestinian refugee problem based on United Nations General Assembly Resolution 194, and the establishment of an independent Palestinian state in Gaza and the West Bank and with East Jerusalem as its capital. In return, the Arab states would consider the conflict with Israel over, sign peace treaties with Israel and establish normal relations (The Arab League, Beirut Summit 2002). However, as Israel viewed the initiative as a non-starter given the maximalist demand for withdrawal, as well as its refusal to negotiate while Palestinian attacks continued during the Intifada, the Arab League's initiative failed to gain momentum, despite being re-adopted at the 2007 summit.

As the conflict continued to escalate, the League issued a number of resolutions: It condemned the Israeli aggression in Gaza Strip in the summer of 2014 (League of Arab States, Sharm el-Sheikh Summit 2015; Reuters 2014); confirmed the invalidity and illegitimacy of the Trump administration's decision to recognise Jerusalem as the capital of Israel (League of Arab State, Dhahran Summit 2018); and denounced the United States Department of State's suspension of funding for UNRWA (League of Arab States, Tunis 2019). However, the attitude of the Arab states towards Trump's 'deal of the century' marked a significant change. Rather than convening a summit, officials from the 22 member states issued a joint communique saying that the deal would not lead to a just peace between the Palestinians and the Israelis, and that the League would not cooperate with the United States to implement it (Al Jazeera 2020a).

Throughout the history of the Arab League, some Arab states did not adhere to the spirit of the League's resolutions on the Arab-Israel conflict, but instead pursued policies that were incompatible with several resolutions. Some Arab states acted outside the League's framework of collective Arab responsibility and contradicted the decisions of several Arab summits. Most notable were Egypt's signing of a peace treaty with Israel in 1979, the PLO's agreement with Israel in 1993, and Jordan's peace treaty with Israel in 1994. In addition, Syria negotiated bilaterally with Israel throughout the 1990s, while several Arab states began to normalise their relations with Israel, at least clandestinely, despite the 2002 Arab Peace Initiative, which explicitly conditioned normalisation with Israel on the resolution of the Palestinian issue.

The Arab states did not adhere to the resolutions of the 1980 Arab summit and did not cut all relations with any state that recognised Jerusalem as the capital of Israel or transferred its embassy to Jerusalem. For example, none of them severed relations with the United States following the Trump Administration's moves over Jerusalem, while the United Arab Emirates (UAH), Bahrain, Sudan, and Morocco readily accepted United States mediation to normalise relations with Israel, despite none of these agreements being explicitly tied to progress on the Palestinian issue (Ephron, 2020). In response, Palestine rejected its scheduled six-month chairmanship of Arab League meetings, with Foreign Minister Riyad al-Maliki claiming that "There is no honour in seeing Arabs rush towards normalisation during [Palestine's] presidency' of the Arab League's council of foreign ministers (Al Jazeera 2020b).

Alongside the League's failure to act upon its own resolutions, it has also repeatedly failed to respond effectively to looming intra-Arab crises. These include, among others, the Egypt-Yemen conflict in the 1960s, the 1970 confrontation between Jordan and the PLO, the territorial dispute between Morocco, Algeria, and Mauritanian over Western Sahara in 1975, the 1990 Iraq–Kuwait dispute, which led to the first Gulf War and, more recently, the civil wars in

Libya, Syria, and Yemen, and the diplomatic crisis between Qatar and Saudi Arabia, the UAE, Bahrain, and Egypt (Arab Center Washington DC 2020).

Conclusion

The failure of the Arab states to develop concerted action against Israel partly reflected intra-Arab disarray, but also a sense of growing pragmatism in more than one Arab capital (Khalidi 1985). The decision by four Arab states to forge ties with Israel in 2020 was never about peace, but it reaffirmed that many Arab states were always guided by *realpolitik*. The Arab world seems more divided than ever, with each state motivated by narrow national interests that are not always subservient to the historic loyalty to the Palestinians cause, and at times may even dictate a more pragmatic approach toward Israel (Alhelou, 2020). Some Arab leaders changed course to improve their relations with the United States to obtain international support for their regimes, while others did so to alleviate their political and economic troubles. As a result, many Arab governments have been pursuing a dual policy of rhetorically denouncing the Israeli occupation and American support for Israel while continuing to cooperate with the United States (and sometimes Israel), with little or no tangible support to the Palestinians. For these Arab governments, keeping their publics focused on the conflict still plays a useful role in distracting domestic attention from internal problems (Katz 2013).

The current landscape in the Middle East is bringing new policy priorities to the fore. The Arab world has not decided to withdraw support for the Palestinian cause, but the nature of that support has become fragmented. With some states still reeling from the aftershocks of the Arab Spring, a resultant prioritisation of domestic security and economic concerns on the part of key states such as Syria and Egypt – as well as intra-Arab disputes that continue to simmer or intensify the geopolitical bandwidth of many Arab states – downgraded political attention to, and diplomatic investment in, the Palestinian cause (Feuer and Zilber 2018).

In recent years, with the growing regional challenge posed by Iran, and with other opportunities for security, economic, and technological cooperation, Israel and 'moderate' Arab states have been gradually normalising their relations irrespective of the Palestinian-Israeli conflict. Nevertheless, while not as central as it once was in the Arab world, and despite the chequered history of Arab-Palestinian relations, the Palestinian cause still resonates widely. Arab leaders, from Syria's al-Assad, to Egypt's Sisi, to Jordan's Abdullah, to Saudi's Salman, consistently emphasise the need for a two-state solution based on the 2002 Arab Peace Initiative, with East Jerusalem as the Palestinian capital. Arab leaders are still heavily engaged with the Palestinian cause, precisely because they view it as important for their domestic politics and societies (Feuer and Zilber 2018).

On the popular level, the conflict remains of great importance to the vast majority of the 'Arab street'. In contrast with the perception that younger generations in the Arab world are more concerned with issues pertaining to their daily lives, such as unemployment and poverty, a recent survey showed that 80 per cent of Arab youth care about the Palestine-Israel conflict. According to ASDA'A 2019 Arab Youth Survey of 3,300 15–24-year-olds in 15 Arab states in the Gulf region, 79 per cent of Arab youth said they were concerned about the conflict, with the younger generation showing a greater commitment to the right of return of Palestinian refugees than older generations. The Palestinian cause was also ranked among the top five biggest obstacles facing the Middle East, together with the rising cost of living, unemployment, lack of Arab unity, and slow economic growth (Al-Tamimi, 2019).

In the final analysis, the Arab world has failed to force Israel to withdraw to the pre-1967 lines or to halt the construction of new settlements, or bring pressure on Israel's allies to change their policies. This is partly because of the national, regional, and international context and challenges that did not favour the Palestinians and the Arab states, but also because of a persistent lack of Arab unity and lack of will to act upon the anti-Israel, pro-Palestine rhetoric. Instead, Arab leaders have demonstrated pragmatism in their approach to the Palestinian-Israeli conflict, which at times elevated bilateral opportunities to cooperate with Israel over the declaratory support for Palestinian statehood. Given such recent trends, and while many Arab governments still do not recognise Israel officially, and popular support for Palestine remains high, the 'Arab-Israeli conflict' seems to have lost much of its essence as the Palestinian-Israeli conflict is seen more as a 'localised' conflict rather than a proxy of a wider conflict between Israel and the Arab world.

Recommended Readings

Daoudi, M., and S. Dajani. 2009. "The Arab Peace Initiative: Lost in the Translation." *CrossCurrents* 59:4, 532–539.

Dawisha, A. 2016. *Arab Nationalism in the Twentieth Century: From Triumph to Despair.* Princeton, NJ: Princeton University Press.

Erakat, N. 2020. *Justice for Some: Law and the Question of Palestine.* Redwood City, CA: Stanford University Press.

Khalidi, R. 2007. *The Iron Cage: The Story of the Palestinian Struggle for Statehood.* Boston: Beacon Press.

Said, E. 1992. *The Question of Palestine.* New York: Vintage.

Questions for Discussion

(1) What effect did the Arab League have on the Palestine-Israel conflict and Arab-Israeli diplomacy?

(2) To what extent has the position of the Arab states on the conflict been affected by the position of the United States?

(3) How effective has the Arab League's support for the Palestinian cause been?

(4) Do you agree that Arab governments often have emphasised the Palestine-Israel conflict to distract attention from their own domestic and foreign policy failures? If yes, to what extent?

(5) To what extent has the effectiveness of the Arab states' position been hindered by the national, regional, or international contexts?

References

Abu Sharif, B. 2005. *Yasser Arafat.* Beirut: Dar Aladdin.

Abumaria, D. 2019. "Arab League says importance of Palestinian cause has been 'reduced.'" *The Medialine.* 20 January. Available at: https://themedialine.org/news/arab-league-says-importance-of-palestinian-cause-has-been-reduced/.

Ahrari, M. E. 2015. *The Oil Embargo.* Lexington, KY: University Press of Kentucky.

Ajami, F. 1978. "The End of Pan-Arabism." *Foreign Affairs* 57:2, 355–373.

Alhelou, Y. 2020. "Does the Palestinian cause still matter to Arabs and Muslims?" *The Arab Weekly.* 19 January Available at: https://thearabweekly.com/does-palestinian-cause-still-matter-arabs-and-muslims.

Alin, E. 1994. "Dynamics of the Palestinian Uprising: An Assessment of Causes, Character, and Consequences." *Comparative Politics* 26:4, 479–498.

Al Jazeera. 2020a. "Arab League Rejects Trump's Middle East plan." 1 February. Available at: www.aljazeera.com/news/2020/2/1/arab-league-rejects-trumps-middle-east-plan.

Al Jazeera. 2020b. "Palestine Quits Arab League Role in Protest over Israel Deals." 22 September. Available at: www.aljazeera.com/news/2020/9/22/palestine-quits-arab-league-role-in-protest-over-israel-deals.

Al-Tamimi, J. 2019. "Why Palestine Still Matters to Arab Youth." *Gulf News.* 2 May. Available at: https://gulfnews.com/world/mena/why-palestine-still-matters-to-arab-youth-1.63694282.

Arab Center Washington DC. 2020. "The Arab League's Many Failures." 8 October. Available at: http://arabcenterdc.org/policy_analyses/the-arab-leagues-many-failures/.

Asseburg M. 2012. "The Arab Spring and the Arab-Israeli Conflict: A Vicious Circle of Mutually Reinforcing Negative Repercussions." In *An Arab Springboard for EU Foreign Policy*, eds. S. Biscop, R. Balfbour, and M. Emerson. Brussels: Egmont, 83–90.

Avalon. 1945. "Pact of the League of Arab States." Available at: https://avalon.law.yale.edu/20th_century/arableag.asp.

Barghouti, M. 2018. "Post-Oslo: What Was Written 20 years ago?" *Middle East Monitor*. 12 September. Available at: www.middleeastmonitor.com/20180912-post-oslo-what-was-written-20-years-ago/.

Bouez, F. 1994. "The Peace Process in the Middle East: The View from Lebanon." *The Brown Journal of World Affairs* 2:1, 263–270.

Chatham House. 2019. "A Call for Freedom." 27 January 2022. Available at: www.chathamhouse.org/sites/default/files/2019%20Arab%20Youth%20Survey.pdf.

Dalloul, M. A. 2019. "After Three Decades, Hamas Remains a Popular Democratic Movement." 27 January 2022. Available at: www.middleeastmonitor.com/20210224-after-three-decades-hamas-remains-a-popular-democratic-movement/.

Daoudi, M. S., and M. S. Dajani. 1984. "The 1967 Oil Embargo Revisited." *Journal of Palestinian Studies* 13:2, 65–90.

Department of State. 2017. "Oil Embargo, 1973–1974." *Office of the Historian*. Available at: https://history.state.gov/milestones/1969-1976/oil-embargo.

El-Dessouki, M., and E. Gheita. 2019. "Arabs against Boycotting Israel." *Wall Street Journal*. 20 November. Available at: www.wsj.com/articles/arabs-against-boycotting-israel-11574293923.

Ephron, D. 2020. "How Arab Ties with Israel Became the Middle East's New Normal." *Foreign Policy* 21. Available at: https://foreignpolicy.com/2020/12/21/arab-ties-israel-diplomacy-normalization-middle-east/.

Feuer, S., and N. Zilber. 2018. "What Happened to the Arab Support for the Palestinians?" *The Washington Institute*. 16 November. Available at: www.washingtoninstitute.org/policy-analysis/view/what-happened-to-arab-support-for-the-palestinians.

Fischer, L. 2014. "Turning Point on the Road to Peace: The Government of Yitzhak Rabin and the Interim Agreement with Egypt (Sinai II)." *Israel Studies* 19:3, 55–80.

Global Conflict Tracker. 2020. "Israeli-Palestinian conflict." Available at: www.cfr.org/interactive/global-conflict-tracker/conflict/israeli-palestinian-conflict.

Hamid, S. 2017. "50 Years: Legacies of the 1967 War." *Brookings*. 5 June. Available at: www.brookings.edu/blog/markaz/2017/06/05/the-end-of-nasserism-how-the-1967-war-opened-new-space-for-islamism-in-the-arab-world/

Hatuqa, D. 2019. "How the Gulf States Got in Bed with Israel and Forgot about the Palestinian Cause." *Foreign Policy*. 28 March. Available at: https://foreignpolicy.com/2019/03/28/how-the-gulf-states-got-in-bed-with-israel-and-forgot-about-the-palestinian-cause-netanyahu-oman-chad-uae-saudi-arabia-mohammed-bin-salman-qatar-bahrain/.

Hughes, G. 2008. "Britain, the Transatlantic Alliance, and the Arab-Israeli War of 1973." *Journal of Cold War Studies* 10:2, 3–40. www.muse.jhu.edu/article/237150.

IMOFA. 2013. "Events Leading to the Six-Day War (1967)." Available at: https://mfa.gov.il/mfa/aboutisrael/maps/pages/events%20leading%20to%20the%20six%20day%20war-%201967.aspx#:~:text=The%20immediate%20causes%20for%20the,forces%20there%2C%20and%20finally%20the.

Katz, M. 2013. "The Arab Spring and the Israeli/Palestinian Conflict: International Implications." *Global Affairs*, January/March. Available at: https://eng.globalaffairs.ru/articles/the-arab-spring-and-the-israeli-palestinian-conflict-international-implications/.

Khalidi, W. 1985. "A Palestinian Perspective on the Arab-Israeli Conflict." *Journal of Palestine Studies* 14:4, 35–48.

Kirshner, I. 2019. "Palestinian Leader Abbas Brushes off Trump Plan for Investment." *New York Times*. 23 June. Available at: www.nytimes.com/2019/06/23/world/middleeast/palestinians-trump-mahmoud-abbas.html.

Knesset. 1980. "Basic Law: Jerusalem, Capital of Israel." Available at: www.knesset.gov.il/laws/special/eng/basic10_eng.htm.

Laqueur, W. 1958. *Political Trends in the Fertile Crescent by Walid Khalidi*. New York: Praeger.

League of Arab States. 1946–2019. "Arab Summits Courses." Available at: www.lasportal.org/ar/summits/Pages/ArabicSummits.aspx?Stype=1&imgLib=ArabicSummit&RID=41.

Licklider, R. 1988. *Political Power and the Arab Oil Weapon*. Berkeley, CA: University of California Press.
Lifset, R. D. 2014. "A New Understanding of the American Energy Crisis of the 1970s." *Historical Social Research* 39:4, 22–42.
Mansfield, P. 1973. "Nasser and Nasserism." *International Journal* 28:4, 670–688.
MERIP. 1974. "A Political Evaluation of the Arabic Oil Embargo." *MERIP Report* 28, 23–25.
Miller, W. J. 2016. "Arab Boycott." *Lawin*. Available at: https://lawin.org/arab-boycott/.
Nabulsi, K. 2014. "Being Palestinian." *Government and Opposition* 38:4, 479–496.
Reuters. 2014. "Arab League Calls Israeli Attack in Gaza 'War Crime.'" *Reuters*. 20 July. Available at: www.reuters.com/article/us-palestinians-israel-arableague/arab-league-calls-israeli-attack-in-gaza-war-crime-idUSKBN0FP0GY20140720.
Ross, D. 2018. "Did Camp David Doom the Palestinians", *Foreign Policy*. 19 October. Available at: https://foreignpolicy.com/2018/10/19/did-camp-david-doom-the-palestinians-israel-palestine-yasser-arafat-menachem-begin-jimmy-carter-reagan-bush-clinton-middle-east-peace/.
Shah, A. 2003. "Oslo Dead? Violence and Palestinian Uprising in 2000." *Global Issues*. 16 January. Available at: www.globalissues.org/article/113/palestinian-uprising-in-2000.
Shlaim, A. 2005. "The Rise and Fall of the Oslo Peace Process." In *International Relations of the Middle East*, ed. L. Fawcett. Oxford: Oxford University Press, 245–261.
Stocking, G. W. 1970. *Middle East Oil: A Study in Political and Economic Controversy*. Nashville, TN: Vanderbilt University Press.
Turck, N. 1977. "The Arab Boycott of Israel." *Foreign Affairs* 55:3, 472–493.
United Nations. 2007. "Annapolis Conference." 27 January 2022. Available at www.un.org/unispal/document/auto-insert-205805/.
Vick, K. 2014. "Middle East Peace Talks Hang by a Thread." *Time*. 2 April. Available at: https://time.com/46729/israel-palestine-peace-talks-abbas/.
Wang, C. 2017. "Gaza a Victim of Gulf Rift." *Strait Times*. 19 June. Available at: www.nst.com.my/opinion/columnists/2017/06/250274/gaza-victim-gulf-rift.
Weiss, M. A. 2017. "Arab League Boycott of Israel." *Congressional Research Service*. 25 August. Available at: https://fas.org/sgp/crs/mideast/RL33961.pdf.

27
THE EUROPEAN UNION AND THE CONFLICT

Costanza Musu

This chapter analyses and evaluates the long history of Europe's involvement with the Arab-Israeli conflict and the subsequent Israeli-Palestinian peace process. These have been among the most strongly debated issues by member states, not only since the creation of the Common Foreign and Security Policy (CFSP) in 1991, but since the establishment of the European Political Co-operation (EPC) in 1970. The peace process has been the subject of innumerable joint declarations and joint actions on the part of the EC/EU and has always remained a high priority issue in the European foreign-policy agenda. The Middle East has also often represented a problematic issue in EU-US relations, given on the one hand Europe's double dependence on the United States as a security guarantor and on Middle East oil and, on the other hand the strategic American interests in the region and the United States' desire to maintain control over the development of the peace process, which has frequently clashed with Europe's attempts to shape a role for itself in the negotiations.

Background

In the first years of its life, the then European Economic Community (EEC) made small progress in the field of political integration. By 1967 economic integration was proceeding steadily, while a European common foreign policy remained little more than a project.

In late May 1967, amid an international crisis on the eve of the Six-Day War, an EEC Summit of the Six Heads of State or Government took place in Rome, primarily to discuss the prospect of the UK's accession to the Community. The international situation called for a common Community declaration on the Middle East crisis, but positions were so irreconcilable that the Six went nowhere near such an achievement: "I felt ashamed at the Rome summit. Just as the war was on the point of breaking out, we could not even agree to talk about it", were German Chancellor Kiesinger's words following the summit.[1]

But this failure to reach a common position was only a prelude to what would happen a few days later, when the June 1967 war broke out. Indeed, the Six achieved the remarkable result of expressing each a different position, following their traditional national policy and privileging what was perceived to be the national interest: attitudes ranged from France's strong condemnation of Israel and support for the Arabs, to Germany's support of Israel, disguised behind a formal neutrality. The member states' different traditions and interests in the Middle East, the

DOI: 10.4324/9780429027376-33

differing intensity of their ties with Israel and with the Arab world, and the inability to agree on a political role for Western Europe alongside the United States, all contributed to the failure to reach an agreement on that occasion.

The following two years saw hardly any attempt to harmonise the member states' policies towards the Middle East conflict; however, the inability of the EC to respond adequately and, if not unanimously, at least in harmonious coordination to major world crises, was becoming increasingly evident and was a striking contrast to the increasing economic weight of the Community – especially in view of the likely imminent enlargement of the Community to include the United Kingdom, Denmark and Ireland.

The Six increasingly felt the urgency to promote an enhanced political role for Europe in the world. Arguably their failure to adequately face the Middle East crisis in 1967 was one of the main triggers of the new developments that were to take place shortly thereafter in the process of European integration. In December 1969, with a few lines unobtrusively located at the end of the official communiqué of the Conference of the Heads of Government held at The Hague – known as The Hague Summit Declaration – the Ministers of Foreign Affairs of the European Community member states were instructed to "study the best way of achieving progress in the matter of political unification, within the context of enlargement".[2] In turn, the six Foreign Ministers instructed the Belgian Political Director, Vicomte Davignon, to prepare a report which would serve as the basis for the future European Foreign Policy. The report, known as the Davignon or Luxembourg Report, was finally presented and approved at the Luxembourg Conference of Foreign Ministers on 27 October 1970.

The Hague Summit Declaration and the Davignon Report sanctioned the official birth of European Political Co-operation – the nucleus of what more than twenty years later would become the Common Foreign and Security Policy – and defined its initial structure. The rationale behind the creation of the EPC was, to use the Luxembourg Report's words, "to pave the way for a united Europe capable of assuming its responsibilities in the world of tomorrow and of making a contribution commensurate with its traditions and its mission".[3] The activities of EPC were kept as separate as possible from those of the Commission and of the Parliament. This model of political co-operation basically "relied on the principle of official collegiality to build up the consensus in preparation for foreign ministers' intergovernmental decisions".[4]

The member states, in other words, were torn between two different aspirations: on the one hand, that of responding to international crisis more adequately, trying to project in the international arena the combined political weight of all the Community members through foreign policy coordination; and on the other hand, that of retaining national control over crucial foreign policy decisions that were perceived to be of a State's exclusive competence. After The Hague Summit Communiqué, EPC progressively developed, and new instruments of political co-operation were slowly added, mainly in an informal and incremental fashion. In this framework the Middle East was very often used by the member states as a testing ground for these instruments.

The first EPC ministerial meeting took place in Munich in November 1970, and the Arab-Israeli conflict and the necessity to harmonise the Six's policy towards it was one of the topics chosen to be discussed. At the time of the meeting, though, the member states' positions were still too divergent and distant from each other for an agreement to be reached over a common public document. What is of interest here, however, is the fact that since that first meeting in Munich, the Arab-Israeli conflict has been an almost permanent feature of EPC discussions, regardless of the very limited success obtained by the EC in dealing with the matter. It can be said that certain principles of today's European Union Middle East policy took shape as far back as in the years of EPC, and particularly between 1970 and 1980.[5]

In the years leading up to the signing of the peace treaty between Israel and Egypt in 1979, the EC supported the United States' mediating efforts, underlining however that it did so "as a first step in the direction of a comprehensive settlement".[6] After the treaty was signed the EC became more critical of the Camp David agreements, as it became convinced that this process would not solve the Palestinian problem, which the EC members viewed as the core of the Middle East problem.

France and Britain in particular put pressure on the other member states to launch an autonomous European peace initiative for the Middle East that would clearly distinguish itself from the American-led Camp David process. But the project met with the strong opposition of both Israel and the United States: Israel launched a vigorous diplomatic campaign to block the European initiative, and the United States exerted its influence to make sure that the content of any EC declaration would not harm the Camp David process, and to play down European aspirations of acting independently in the Middle East.

On 13 June 1980, the Heads of State and Government of the Nine met at the European Council in Venice and finally issued a joint resolution, known today as the Venice Declaration. As a result of American pressures, the text of the declaration was significantly watered down, even if it did contain some very relevant points. Paragraph 6 of the Declaration states: "The Palestinian people, which is conscious of existing as such, must be placed in a position, by an appropriate process defined within the framework of the comprehensive peace settlement, to exercise fully its right to self-determination"; and in paragraph 7 it declares that "the PLO will have to be associated with the negotiations".[7]

The Venice Declaration is considered a landmark in Europe's Middle East policy, as it contained some crucial principles that still constitute the basis of the EU's policy towards the Arab Israeli peace process more than forty years later. These principles include the centrality of the Palestinian question, the need to achieve a two-state solution, the importance attached to United Nations resolutions and to the principles of international law and the insistence on the need for all the relevant issues to be taken on simultaneously through the convening of an international peace conferences where regional actors could meet in a multilateral framework.

These principles (particularly the centrality of the Palestinian question and the goal of achieving a two-state solution of the Israeli-Palestinian dispute) were embraced only years later by Israel and the United States, and it was only in 1991 that the first international conference on the Middle East peace process was convened in Madrid. What became clear early on, however, were also the limits of European policy coherence, the contradictions of different member states' positions and the serious tensions that the development of a European autonomous stance in the Middle East created between Europe and the United States.

The Limits to Coherence

European countries are directly implicated in the Arab-Israeli conflict because of their geographic proximity, their dependence on oil and their security needs, as well as the historical role played by several of them in the region. Harmonising the EU's member states' viewpoints on the Arab-Israeli conflict, however, is a task which has always proved difficult.

As a brief overview of some member states' approach to the Middle East peace process demonstrates, the specific individual interests of the member states are some considerable way apart, despite the common interest and common efforts in finding a just and lasting solution to the conflict. It can be argued that very often policy coordination has been obtained, not on the basis of policy convergence, but rather on the basis of congruence, that is, of a sufficient compatibility of member states' preferences allowing the elaboration of a common policy.

French policy in the Middle East has privileged France's relations with the Arab world, even if it has tried at the same time to maintain good relations with Israel. Paris has often promoted an independent French policy in the area, and this independence has mainly implied that it is conducting a policy that is independent from that of the United States. At times, such a policy has gone so far as to cause tensions with other EU member states, with autonomous French initiatives in the Middle East seemingly taken without any prior consultations with its European allies.[8]

For some European countries, such as Germany and the Netherlands, the sensitivities of relations with Israel are such that their governments have hesitated to criticise Israeli policy. For these countries the possibility of shifting national positions under the guise of a search for a common European position has proven attractive: it has allowed them to initiate a rapprochement to the Arab world while claiming this to be an "unavoidable price" in striving for the superior objective of reaching a unified European position and at the same time avoiding upsetting their own internal public opinions. Great Britain has tended to go along the lines of American Middle East policy: on the British foreign policy agenda, transatlantic relations are a much higher priority than Middle East policy, despite the long historical involvement of the United Kingdom in the area. London has been inclined to favour a policy that secures American approval and avoids direct confrontation with US policy in the name of Europe taking on an independent role in the peace process. Italy's policy, on the one hand, has supported a European involvement in the peace process in the framework of a broader "Mediterranean policy" which has to be, from the Italian point of view, one of the top European priorities and must not be neglected in favour of a policy more concentrated on enlargement problems and on the "northern dimension"; on the other hand, Italy's internal political divisions tended to make its Middle East policy unsteady and unclear.

To summarize, it is fair to say that all EU member states continue to have their own foreign policy agendas and to set their own priorities within these agendas with regard to their Middle East policies.

Transatlantic Relations

In analysing EU policy towards the Israeli-Palestinian peace process, one cannot avoid the crucial problem: is EU Middle East policy at all *separable* from transatlantic relations?

The Middle East has indeed always been a highly controversial issue in transatlantic relations, sparking off some of the harshest instances of confrontation between the United States and Europe: this was the case in 1973 during the oil crisis, when Europe's Arab policy in response to the oil boycott outraged an American administration that considered it an interference in both its step-by-step strategy towards the Arab-Israeli conflict and in its construction of an "oil consumers front" by means of a new International Energy Agency; and contrasts arose again less than ten years later, in 1980, when the EC's Venice Declaration on the Arab-Israeli conflict caused discontent – to say the least – in Washington, where Europe's emphasis on the centrality of the Palestinian question and on the legitimacy of the PLO were seen as extremely untimely and potentially damaging to the peace process that had started at Camp David.

It may be argued that some of the patterns of US-European interaction in the Middle East already began taking shape at the time of the events mentioned above, with the United States progressively deepening its engagement in the region and becoming the main mediator in the Arab-Israeli conflict, and the EC confined to a subordinated role, constrained and conditioned in its action by internal divisions, institutional inadequacies and a heavy dependence on Middle Eastern oil, but also by American reluctance to share the driving seat in the peace process and by the rigid dynamics of the Cold War – of which the Middle East was hostage – which allowed Europe very little leeway, caught as it was in the middle of a confrontation between superpowers.

The end of the Cold War changed the world's balance of power and security order: the United States emerged as the only surviving superpower, and the new Russia failed to fill the gap left by the Soviet Union. The Middle East was no longer viewed in a Cold War perspective. Global intervention in the Middle East no longer projected bipolar superpower rivalry in the region, and the Gulf War transformed the dynamics of inter-regional relations, creating a window of opportunity for a resolution of the Arab-Israeli dispute and strengthening the role of the United States as the only accepted mediator. Post–Cold War global intervention took on a unipolar form, with a dominant United States using its influence in the region to protect its interests, which include ensuring the free flow of oil at reasonable prices; regional stability and prosperity, which would help protect oil supplies, create a market for American products, and reduce the demand for US military involvement in the area; the security of the State of Israel; and the consolidation of the Arab-Israeli peace process that could guarantee Israel's security and at the same time contribute to the stability of the entire region.

The end of the Cold War also led to a redefinition of EU interests and foreign policy priorities: the fall of the Berlin Wall marked the dissolution of the political cement of the communist threat and, following the reunification of Germany, integration became an even more important issue for European stability. With the Maastricht Treaty and the formal creation of the Common Foreign and Security policy of the EU (CFSP), the European Union aimed to achieve a common foreign policy able to project onto the international arena the combined power of its member states, whose weight and influence in international affairs was hoped to be stronger than that exercised by each state individually. The creation of the CFSP marked an acceleration in the process of European political integration and in the transformation of the EU into a global actor, increasing its aspirations – and its chances – of playing a more relevant role in the Middle East.

In the Middle East, the EU shares many interests with the United States: the promotion of the region's stability and prosperity, as well as the protection of the flow of oil supplies on which it depends heavily. Due to its geographical proximity and strong economic ties with the region, the EU risks being seriously affected by problems arising in the Middle East, such as an instability spill-over, uncontrolled migration flows, proliferation of weapons of mass destruction, and the spread of terrorism.

The consolidation of the Middle East peace process is a crucial EU interest, as it aids stability and enhances the chances of resources and efforts being directed to the economic and political development of the region. On the other hand, Europe must balance its support for the search of a just and lasting solution to the conflict between the Palestinians and Israel with its interests in the Arab world. The end of the Cold War and the subsequent collapse of the Soviet Union created a political vacuum in the Middle East that could have represented a political opening for the EU. Theoretically, there was the opportunity to redefine EU-US interaction and the dynamics of burden-sharing in the region, and Europe could potentially increase its role and influence in the Middle East peace process. This opportunity came about over the 1991–1993 period, following the end of the Cold War and the redefinition of the balance of power in the Middle East, the start of the peace process with the Madrid Peace Conference and the redefinition of Europe itself and of its role in the international arena at the Maastricht conference, with the call for a Common Foreign and Security Policy.

The start of the peace process, however, saw the United States as the only mediator (considering the inexorable decline of the Soviet Union) accepted by both the Arabs and the

Israelis and able to exert a definite political influence, and Europe as a guest, invited as a normal participant to the Peace Conference and whose potential role as additional mediator was refused by the main actors involved in the process.

Although initially cut out from the core negotiations and diplomatic efforts of the peace process initiated at Madrid,[9] the European Union nevertheless gradually expanded its role, at least in its area of comparative advantage, that is, the economic area. The EU's economic role in the peace process increased progressively, to the point that the EU became the major single aid donor to the Palestinians. In the year 2000 the EU donated 225 million euro to the Palestinians, a figure that had increased to 486 million euro in 2008.[10] The logic of the peace process – in the EU's view – was that trade and co-operation were to underpin peace, Palestinian economic development being Israel's best long-term guarantee of security. This assumption was the justification behind the European Union's massive financial assistance to the consolidation of the peace process, the underlying logic being that this was a necessary precondition for keeping the peace process on track.[11]

Together with direct aid to the Palestinians, the EU also promoted regional dialogue and co-operation through the so-called Barcelona Process – from which the United States was excluded – which saw the EU engaged in a political and economic relationship with 12 Mediterranean states (including Israel) in a context that, at least in the European intentions, was parallel and separate from the peace process itself.

On the other hand, Europe's enhanced economic role in the peace process has not for many years been matched by a similar increase of its political influence: the United States remained the only mediator between the parts and the EU played a diplomatically and politically complementary role to that of the United States. In a way, the EU provided the basic economic foundation of the peace process, but for most of the 1990s it lacked the military instruments and security institutions to make a contribution on the front of security – which remained the domain of the United States – and also lacked that unitary dimension of action that in such negotiations necessarily qualifies an effective mediator.

The American position was ambivalent: on the one hand the United States wanted to keep its primary role in the peace process so as to protect its interests however it saw fit; on the other hand it was happy to delegate a relevant part of the financial assistance to the Palestinians to the EU, as it was not willing to accept a free-riding European Union that exploits the security coverage offered by the United States without offering at least the limited assistance it is able to provide (limited, diplomatically speaking, but substantial in economic terms). The United States was as well aware of the fact that economic growth of the Palestinian Authority (PA) was a necessary precondition for the consolidation of the peace process, and was willing to recognise a prominent role by the EU in this field, as long as it remained politically in line with United States plans.

At a collective level, all EU member states benefited from US presence in the region and from the security guarantees that stemmed from that presence. The United States keeps the Sixth Fleet stationed in the Mediterranean, has substantial military assets in the region and provides enormous military assistance to friendly countries there (like Egypt and Israel); all this, while protecting US security interests guaranteed a security coverage to Europe as well, and at the same time contributed to deferring the problem of a European defence capacity. Member states had come to realise, especially following the experience of the Gulf War, that the EU was not yet able to guarantee security, either in the region, or of its own territory from the dangers deriving from instability. Under the US security umbrella, the EU was able to postpone tackling the potentially highly divisive issue of how Europe should protect itself from dangers deriving from an insecurity spill-over from the Middle East.

Some member states, like Britain, Germany, the Netherlands and Italy, remained highly aware of the risk that an EU move from a declaratory policy towards active diplomacy would risk a crisis in transatlantic relations: these countries were inclined to favour a low-profile EU policy, complementary to that of the United States and limited mainly to providing economic aid to the region, and particularly to the Palestinian Authority; a contribution that the United States itself welcomes for its stabilising effects. Some countries however, in particular France, were not satisfied with a US-dominated peace process and continued to push for a more active EU policy.[12]

From Camp David to the Creation of the Quartet: the Middle East in Flux

In July 2000 a summit took place in Camp David, involving Palestinian leader Yasser Arafat, Israeli Prime Minister Ehud Barak, and US President Bill Clinton. During the talks all the core issues were discussed, including the protracted questions on the status of Jerusalem and the right of return of Palestinian refugees, but none of them were resolved. The breaking down of the peace process also influenced the Barcelona Process negatively: Lebanon and Syria refused to attend the fourth Euro-Mediterranean conference of foreign ministers in Marseilles in September 2000, and the EU had to drop any attempt to sign a Charter of Peace and Stability for the Mediterranean, as the Arab participants were not prepared to discuss the issue and no agreement was possible. Ultimately, economic co-operation could not prove conducive to a political settlement.

After the failure of the Camp David Summit the situation between Israel and the Palestinians deteriorated rapidly. At the end of September the Second Intifada – also called Al-Aqsa Intifada – started, and a vicious cycle of Palestinian violence and Israeli retaliation began. In October 2000 – in a last attempt to bring peace to the region before the end of his mandate – President Clinton convened a peace summit in Sharm-el-Sheikh, where he met with representatives of Israel, the Palestinian National Authority, Egypt, Jordan, the UN, and the EU. At the summit the decision was taken to appoint a fact-finding commission with the task of proposing recommendations to end the violence, rebuild confidence and resume the negotiations. The commission was to be chaired by former US Senator George Mitchell and included EU CFSP High Representative Javier Solana.

The Sharm-el-Sheikh (or Mitchell) Committee presented its report in April 2001 to the new president of the United States, George W. Bush, but the new administration (at least until September 11) was showing relatively little interest in the Middle East and was deliberately disengaging from the previous administration's detailed involvement as main mediator between Arab states and Israel. The Bush Administration felt particularly strongly about differentiation on the Middle East, where – from their perspective – Clinton's overactive diplomacy had demeaned the presidency without achieving a settlement. They were committed to a much more "selective engagement" in global diplomacy, to what Richard Haass, the new head of policy planning in the State Department, called in July 2001 "à la carte multilateralism".[13]

In June 2001, after having vetoed a UN Security Council resolution to establish a UN observer mission, Bush dispatched CIA Director George Tenet to the Occupied Territories to negotiate a ceasefire plan. Hamas and the Islamic Jihad, however, rejected the plan, arguing that it failed to address the root of violence. The terrorist attacks of 11 September 2001 forced a change in American policy. In order to secure the "coalition against terrorism" the United States had once again to concentrate on the Israeli-Palestinian peace process: Bush declared his support for a Palestinian state, and in November 2001 retired Marine Corps general Anthony Zinni was appointed as senior adviser to work towards a cease-fire and to implement the Tenet plan and the Mitchell Committee Report. His mission, however, failed like the previous ones, as violence continued to escalate.

The State Department decided to pursue a multilateral approach to the peace process, with co-operation with European governments as a key factor. On April 10th 2002, Colin Powell announced the formation of a Madrid "Quartet", reviving the agenda of the 1991 Madrid conference with the UN Secretary-General, the EU High Representative for Common Foreign and Security Policy, Javier Solana, and the Russian foreign minister. The cumbersome structures of EU diplomacy, however, also squeezed the Commissioner for External Relations and the foreign minister of the member state holding the Council presidency into the "single" EU seat. The focus of this approach was on pursuing a two-state solution to the Israeli-Palestinian conflict, with the active engagement of outside actors.[14]

In a communiqué issued in New York in September 2002, the Quartet announced that it was working with the parties and consulting key regional actors on a three-phase implementation "roadmap" that could achieve a final settlement within three years.[15]

In 2002 tensions had arisen between the EU and Israel as the Israeli army, in retaliation for Palestinian terrorist attacks, proceeded to systematically destroy Palestinian infrastructure, most of which had been paid for by the EU, and because Israel continued to export to the EU goods manufactured in the Palestinian Territories (the so-called problem of the "rules of origin"). When Israel halted the payments of tax revenues to the Palestinian Authority, the EU approved a series of replacement loans and, in response to the "rules of origin" problem, it threatened to withdraw the preferential tariffs that Israel enjoys. The threat, however, remained such, and in general the EU's action did not show great incisiveness.

Arguably, the collapse of the peace process left the EU unable to react in a co-ordinated and effective fashion: notwithstanding High Representative Solana's participation in the October 2000 Sharm-el-Sheikh Peace Summit and in the Mitchell Committee, and the uninterrupted behind-the-scenes diplomatic activity of both the High Representative and the Special Envoy Moratinos, the EU's contribution to ending the violence in the area was not particularly effective. In 2002, after a number of clashes among member states, who were unable to agree on a common strategy for the peace process, and after a failed diplomatic mission during which the CFSP High Representative and the Spanish presidency were prevented by Israel to meet Arafat in Ramallah, the EU finally decided to renounce launching an independent peace plan and to back the US peace initiative that led to the creation of the Madrid Quartet. The EU hoped that participation in the Madrid Quartet would gain the EU more visibility and influence in the peace process and would provide Europe with a tool for influencing American policies as they were formulated.

The Quartet has been praised for its "multilateral" nature, which officially brought other actors – particularly the European Union – into the peace process in addition to the traditional actors, such as the United States and the UN, but the Quartet was also criticised for its inability to bring about a breakthrough in the negotiations. The EU had played an increasingly important role in the peace process since the Madrid Conference, but participation in the Quartet arguably gave the European role a higher political relevance and resonance. The EU's presence was particularly welcomed by the Palestinians, who saw it as a potential counterbalance to an American position they perceive as permanently biased in favour of Israel. Conversely, the creation of the Quartet met with less enthusiasm in Israel, where multilateralism is seen as a means to impose unwelcome decisions, and the EU is perceived as a less than friendly actor.

In parallel with this multilateral approach, however, the US administration elaborated new policy guidelines that, in light of the 2001 9/11 attacks, favoured unilateralism in dealing with perceived threats from the region and from rogue states.

The American approach to the region was set out by President Bush in his "Axis of Evil" speech in January 2002, which linked the efforts of Iraq and Iran (and North Korea) to acquire weapons of mass destruction to their sponsorship of terrorism. Though there was no evidence linking any of these states directly to al-Qaeda, this conceptual framework transmuted the war on terrorism into the pre-existing framework of rogue states and WMD, and thus into a potential war on Iraq. Iranian and Iraqi support for terrorist groups attacking Israel was an important part of their inclusion in this category, indicating how closely the Arab-Israeli conflict and the war on terrorism were linked in American minds. The priority for Western Middle East policy, in this formulation, was regime change in Iraq, combined with continued containment of Iran. The removal of a regime that encouraged Palestinian intransigence would in itself ease the Israeli-Palestinian conflict. The European allies would be invited to play supporting roles in the "coalition of the willing" assembled to enforce disarmament – and/or regime change – on Iraq, and to pay for subsequent social and economic reconstruction.

European governments, on their part, sympathised with the suffering and felt the outrage that the 9/11 attacks had generated in America. But they placed this new scale of trans-national terrorism within the context of the lower level of trans-national terrorism their countries had suffered in the past. As observers, too, of American strategy towards the region over previous years, largely without influence over that strategy and often critical of its sweep, there was an unavoidable undercurrent of differentiation: a feeling that the United States and the Muslim world were locked into a confrontation that both jeopardised European security and ignored European views.

In Europe's eyes, what was needed after 9/11 was a broad diplomatic approach to the region, including an active and concerted attempt to bring the Israel-Palestine conflict back to the negotiating table and a dialogue with "friendly" Arab authoritarian regimes. In terms of power projection and political influence, however, European governments were acutely conscious of their limited capabilities in the face of American regional hegemony.

2002–2007: Crises and Opportunities

In 2002 the clash between the European approach to the Middle East, which traditionally favours multilateralism and negotiation, and the increasingly unilateral American approach, became more and more evident, bringing about a deterioration of transatlantic relations and generating mutual distrust.

The United States' decision to launch an attack against Iraq in 2003 (and the preceding diplomatic struggles at the UN) highlighted the rift between the transatlantic allies, while at the same time making painfully obvious Europe's own internal division and the persistence of national agendas that make the elaboration of a common foreign policy strenuous and at times impossible.

With the creation of the Quartet, however, the EU and US approaches had formally converged, at least on the aspect of Middle East policy related to the peace process. It remained, however, unclear whether the US administration beyond the State Department was seriously committed to this exercise, or whether national governments within the EU were fully behind their collective representatives.

Since its creation, the Quartet has been intermittently protagonist toward the peace process, mainly with the elaboration of the "Roadmap to a Permanent Two-State Solution to the Israeli-Palestinian Conflict", and given up for dead, especially when the bilateral track of negotiations between Israel and the Palestinians – with the United States as sole mediator, or at least facilitator – seemed to be the only active track, or even more so in the numerous occasions in which violence escalated and the international community seemed unable, or unwilling, to play a constructive role in helping the parties to reach a settlement.[16]

The Quartet was instrumental in the conclusion of the "Agreement on Movement and Access" between Israel and the Palestinian Authority, which included agreed principles for the Rafah crossing between Gaza and Egypt. On 21 November 2005, the Council of the EU welcomed the Agreement and concurred that the EU should undertake the Third Party role proposed in the Agreement. It therefore decided to launch the EU Border Assistance Mission at Rafah, named EU BAM Rafah, to monitor the operations of this border-crossing point. The operational phase of the Mission began on 30 November 2005 and was meant to have a duration of 12 months. On 13 November 2006, the mission's mandate was extended for 6 months, and it still remains in existence (albeit with limited capabilities) as of 2022.[17]

This limited initiative was unprecedented in nature at the time of its inauguration: for the first time, EU military personnel under the command of an Italian general, supervised an area of security concern for Israel. Only a few months before, such a proposal would have been unthinkable: the EU had long voiced its wish to be involved more directly in the security dimension of the peace process but, as already underlined, both Israeli and American opposition had rendered this by and large unfeasible. In the particular circumstances created by Israel's withdrawal from Gaza however, the EU was better suited to carry out the task of supervising the Rafah crossing, and American assurances contributed to convincing Israel to accept the EU's offer. Arguably, such a development was partly made possible by the EU's membership of the Quartet, which creates a formal framework for the EU's role, tying it to the US one, thus easing Israel's deep-seated reservations with regard to the EU's involvement. It was also rendered possible by the significant changes that had taken place within the EU itself, with the creation of security and military institutions that contribute to reinforce Europe's credibility as a global actor.

If the creation of EUBAM can be seen as a success – albeit limited – in promoting the EU's role in the security dimension of the peace process, the difficulties that the EU faces remain enormous. The peace process and the Middle East as a whole pose challenges that the cumbersome structure of the EU27 foreign policy making has great difficulties in facing. Proof of this, arguably, is the tendency developed in the last few years by member states of attempting to use a variable geometry of "directoires" to address the problems arising from the region. The EU3 for example, composed of the UK, France, and Germany, has been at the forefront of the diplomatic negotiations with Iran over its nuclear programme (a window of opportunity opened partly by the absence of US-Iran diplomatic relations).

In the summer of 2006, on the other hand, while the war between Israel and Hezbollah was raging in Lebanon, France and Italy took a leading role in attempting to resolve the crisis. In August, Israel accepted (and encouraged) the deployment of a large interposition force to reinforce the existing UN mission to Lebanon (UNIFIL) as a condition for a ceasefire. On 25 August 2006, EU foreign ministers met for a so-called troop-generating conference and agreed to deploy a total of almost seven thousand troops to Lebanon as a peace-keeping force. The mission was to continue to be run under the aegis of the UN, but the most significant military presence was going to be European.

France had a central role in helping to negotiate the text of the UN Security Council resolution aimed at ending the conflict. Having initially committed to send up to five thousand troops to Lebanon as a contribution to UNIFIL, France became very hesitant, however, when the moment came to put "boots on the ground". Wariness of the unclear rules of engagement resulted in France changing its offer to only two hundred troops. Only after several days, and lengthy diplomatic discussions with Italy, did France announce that it would send up to three thousand troops.[18]

Italy also committed a large number of troops – between two thousand and three thousand – and offered to take over from France the command of the operation in early 2007. This initiative was clearly in line with Italy's ambition to play an important role in the region, and efforts to ensure that the Mediterranean remain a high priority on the agenda of the EU's policy-making.[19]

Yet another example of the attempted use of structures alternative to the formal EU foreign policy mechanisms was the announcement by France, Italy, and Spain, in November 2006 of a new Middle East peace plan. The proposal came after a major Israeli ground offensive in the Gaza Strip, which was aimed at ending militant rocket fire into Israel. In the words of Italy's President Prodi "Italy, France, and Spain – taking their presence in Lebanon as a starting point – intend to develop the operational and concrete aspects of a wider initiative in the Middle East in order to give a real contribute to the pacification of the whole area".[20] The initiative – which did not have the formal support of the Council – was short-lived and underlined once again the limits of EU's coordination.

The Collapse of the Peace Process and the Challenges Ahead

The victory of Hamas (which is included in the list of terrorist organisations of both the EU and the United States) in the Palestinian elections of January 2006 heightened Israel's feeling of insecurity and its need to receive reassurances that the international community will not support the Palestinian Authority financially if this means supporting a government that organises terrorist attacks on Israel's soil.

The Palestinian elections' results also highlighted divergences within the Quartet itself: if the EU and the United States froze – albeit temporarily – economic support to the PA and refused to deal directly with Hamas until it recognises Israel's right to exist, and Russia (also a member of the Quartet) invited members of the Hamas leadership to Moscow for talks, such developments could undermine the credibility of the Quartet as a coherent actor.

The victory of Hamas exposed the EU to a double set of pressures: on the one hand the EU's policy had long been characterised by its preference for engagement rather than isolation of difficult interlocutors (as proved by EU's policy towards Iran), and on the other both the United States and Israel insisted on the necessity to sabotage the government of an organisation that had neither recognised Israel's right to exist nor renounced violence.

Despite its decision to boycott the Hamas government, the EU maintained – and even increased – its high level of economic support to the Palestinian Authority. What changed was that the funds began to be given directly to the intended recipients through a "Temporary International Mechanism" created ad hoc, instead of being channelled through the PA.

The situation worsened rapidly, however: Palestinian institutional reforms stalled, EUBAM was rendered largely inoperable, and the EU's other Civilian Crisis Management Mission, COPPS (Coordination Office for Palestinian Police Support) met the same destiny.[21]

With the beginning of the Obama presidency there was a shift in the American discourse about the Middle East. During a 2009 speech in Cairo, entitled "A New Beginning", President Obama emphasized the need for a relationship between the United States and Muslims around the world based "upon mutual interests and mutual respect." In reference to the peace process, he underlined that

> Israelis must acknowledge that just as Israel's right to exist cannot be denied, neither can Palestine's. The United States does not accept the legitimacy of continued Israeli settlements. This construction violates previous agreements and undermines efforts to achieve peace. It is time for these settlements to stop.[22]

The Cairo speech raised hopes in Europe that Washington would start putting more pressure on Israel to stop the construction of new settlements, which many European leaders view as an insurmountable obstacle on the path to peace. After the Cairo speech the Obama Administration attempted to reopen the peace negotiation, asking Israel to stop settlement construction and demanding Hamas renounce violence and embrace previous agreements. However, a new peace plan presented by the Quartet, as well as various American peace initiatives, failed, as violence continued to flare up between Israel and Hamas, with major confrontations taking place in 2008–2009, in 2012, and in 2014, and violent clashes flaring up regularly at the Israel-Gaza border thereafter.

The EU continued to provide vast economic support for the Palestinian Authority (between 2017 and 2020, for example, the EU donated 1.3 billion euros directly to the Palestinian Authority under the banner of the Joint Strategy[23]), but its role remained rather limited, and new initiatives were taken mostly through the Quartet. Divisions among member states' positions also remained evident, as highlighted, for example, by the reaction to the Palestinian Authority's 2011 bid for an upgrade of their status at the UN to 'non-member state', a bid for which most states voted in favour, but others (Germany, the United Kingdom, and the Netherlands) abstained.

During the Trump presidency years, the peace process between Israel and the Palestinians remained stalled, even as the Abraham Accords normalized relations between the United Arab Emirates and Bahrain and Israel. President Trump's unabashed support of Israel to the detriment of Palestinian aspirations, and his decision to move the American Embassy from Tel Aviv to Jerusalem were met with intense criticism in Europe.[24] However, besides generic declarations asking for violence to cease on the ground and for parties to return to the negotiating table, the EU has been unable to contribute anything substantial to a peace process that seems hopelessly hostage to, and overshadowed by, complex dynamics, including the growth of the terrorist threat, the continuation of the occupation and growth of the settlements, the rise of Iran's aspirations, and the evolving interests of powerful players in the region, such as Russia and China. In this context it is likely that the EU will continue to play a secondary role in the peace process, given also the limits to its foreign policy initiatives imposed by the intergovernmental framework and by the need to constantly harmonize the policy preference of twenty-seven members.

Notes

1 Quoted in Greilsammer, I., *Israël et l'Europe*, Fondation Jean Monnet pour l'Europe, Centre des Recherches Européennes, Lausanne, 1981. Pg. 64.

2 Communiqué of the Conference of the Heads of State and Government of the Member States of the European Community (The Hague Summit Declaration), The Hague, 2 December 1969. Paragraph 15.

3 Communiqué of the Conference of the Heads of State and Government of the Member States of the European Community (The Hague Summit Declaration), The Hague, 2 December 1969. Paragraph 3.

4 Hill, C. and Smith, K. E., *European Foreign Policy: Key Documents*, Routledge, 2000. Pg 75.

5 Musu, C. '*European Union Policy towards the Arab-Israeli Peace Process. The Quicksands of Politics.*' Palgrave Studies in European Union Politics, Palgrave Macmillan, paperback ed. 2015.

6 Statement of the Nine Foreign Ministers on the Egyptian-Israeli Peace Treaty, Paris, 26 March 1979.

7 Declaration by the European Council on the Situation in the Middle East (Venice Declaration), Venice, 12–13 June 1980.

8 See for example Chirac's 1996 trip to the Occupied Territories: www.washingtonpost.com/archive/politics/1996/10/23/chirac-angered-by-tight-israeli-security/38bfe48f-0ed2-4568-afa8-abd4ce022df3/

9 While excluded from the bilateral negotiations, which were based on direct talks between the parties, the EU played a more relevant role in the multilateral negotiations, as gavel holder of the Regional Economic Development Working Group (REDWG).

10 www.europarl.europa.eu/meetdocs/2009_2014/documents/budg/dv/2010_fayyad_eu_financial_assistance_/2010_fayyad_eu_financial_assistance_en.pdf

11 See Select Committee on European Union (Sub-Committee C), Ninth Report: *The Common Strategy of the European Union in the Mediterranean Region*, House of Lords Reports, London, 2001.

12 Author's interview with Sir Brian Crowe, Former Director-General for External and Politico-Military Affairs, General Secretariat of the Council of the European Union, and with Sir Malcolm Rifkind, former British Minister of Defence and Secretary of State for Foreign and Commonwealth Affairs.

13 www.cfr.org/blog/multilateralism-la-carte-new-world-global-governance

14 See Musu, C. and Wallace W., 'The Focus of Discord? The Middle East in US Strategy and European Aspirations' in Peterson J. and Pollack M.A. (eds.): *Europe, America, Bush: Transatlantic Relations After 2000*, Routledge, 2003

15 Communiqué issued by the Quartet, New York, 17 September 2002 available at www.un.org/press/en/2002/Quartetpc.doc.htm

16 See Musu, C., 'The Madrid Quartet. An Effective Instrument of Multilateralism?', in Nathanson R. and Stetter S. (eds.) '*The Monitor of the EU-Israel Action Plan*', IEPN – Israeli European Policy Network, Friedrich-Ebert-Stiftung, Berlin/Tel Aviv, 2006

17 www.eubam-rafah.eu/en/node/5048

18 www.theguardian.com/world/2006/aug/18/syria.israelandthepalestinians

19 www.repubblica.it/2006/11/sezioni/esteri/medio-oriente-25/iniziativa-italia/iniziativa-italia.html

20 www.repubblica.it/2006/11/sezioni/esteri/medio-oriente-25/iniziativa-italia/iniziativa-italia.html

21 See Richard Youngs, *'The EU and the Middle East Peace process: Re-engagement?'*, FRIDE Comment, March 2007.

22 https://obamawhitehouse.archives.gov/issues/foreign-policy/presidents-speech-cairo-a-new-beginning

23 https://ec.europa.eu/neighbourhood-enlargement/european-neighbourhood-policy/countries-region/palestine_en

24 See www.timesofisrael.com/european-countries-blast-us-embassy-move-to-jerusalem/

Recommended reading

Del Sarto, Raffaella A., ed. (2015). *Fragmented Borders, Interdependence, and External Relations: The Israel-Palestine-European Union Triangle*. Houndsmill: Palgrave.

Musu, Costanza (2015). *European Union Policy towards the Arab–Israeli Peace Process. The Quicksands of Politics*. 2nd edition; Basingstoke: Palgrave Macmillan.

Pardo, Sharon, and Peters, Joel (2010). *Uneasy Neighbors: Israel and the European Union*. Lanham, MD: Lexington.

Persson, Anders (2015). *The EU and the Israeli–Palestinian Conflict 1971–2013: In Pursuit of a Just Peace*. Lanham: Lexington Books.

Questions for discussion

1. Why has the conflict been an important issue for the European Union?
2. What have been the main obstacles for the EU in formulating a coherent policy towards the Arab-Israeli dispute?
3. How has the enlargement of the EU to new members changed the way the EU formulates its policy toward the conflict over the years?
4. What role has the United States played in influencing the development of an EU policy towards the conflict?
5. Does the EU have anything unique to offer to the peace process, or is it destined to remain just a payer, never a player?

28

AMERICAN APPROACHES TO THE ISRAELI-PALESTINIAN CONFLICT

Jonathan Rynhold

Introduction

President Sadat of Egypt had a well-known saying that the United States holds 99 per cent of the cards in the Middle East. Israeli Prime Minister Menachem Begin was less certain. In response to an offer of an American security guarantee in exchange for an Israeli withdrawal, he opined, 'There is no guarantee that can guarantee a guarantee!' (Quandt 1986, 50, 80). In reality, the United States has held considerably less than 99 per cent of the cards, nonetheless it has been the most important international actor involved in the Israeli-Palestinian conflict. Clearly, American policy matters. Consequently, it is important to understand how America has approached the Israeli-Palestinian conflict. Below, the parameters of United States policy to the Israeli-Palestinian conflict are outlined. Then four approaches to the conflict are presented and delineated according to their characteristics and their underpinnings. Finally, the practical expression of each approach in American policy is presented. Within administrations, different approaches compete for influence, though one approach is usually dominant.

The Parameters and Underpinnings of United States Policy

All American approaches to the Israeli-Palestinian conflict have adopted positions on the core substantive final-status issues that fit within six parameters. First, since supporting the United Nations Partition plan in 1947, the United States has consistently supported the partition of what was British Mandate Palestine (1920–1948); either between Israel and Jordan (1967–1988) or between Israel and the Palestinians (1989–). Second, since 1967, the United States has envisioned the demarcation of partition as relatively close, though not identical, to the line that existed on the eve of the Six-Day War, a position encapsulated in the United Nations Security Council (UNSC) resolution 242 of November 1967. Third, Resolution 242 affirmed Israel's right to peace and security in return for territorial withdrawal. In this regard, the United States has consistently offered to boost its security relationship with Israel to encourage it to make concessions that enhance the prospects of an agreement. Fourth, the United States has never supported Israeli settlements, though the strength of that opposition and the willingness to accommodate realities created by Israel on the ground has varied considerably. Fifth,

DOI: 10.4324/9780429027376-34

on Jerusalem, the United States has traditionally favoured maintaining an open city, while expecting Israel to cede control over much or all of the Palestinian populated areas. Sixth, the United States has opposed an unlimited 'right of return' for all Palestinian refugees and their descendants to the State of Israel. Instead, it has preferred a compromise involving the refugees choosing between immigration to Israel (an option open only to a relatively small number of refugees such that it does not threaten Israel's Jewish majority), or compensation and refugees' integration into either the country of their current abode, resettlement in another state, or return to a Palestinian state. Furthermore, when it comes to managing the conflict, even the most pro-Israel administrations have applied pressure on Israel to constrain its military actions in order to prevent the escalation of the conflict, even when the other side is widely recognised as a radical terrorist organisation such as Hamas. Though some have applied greater pressure more quickly, others have given Israel more room for manoeuvre.

Within these parameters, United States policy to the conflict has varied considerably (Touval 1982; Spiegel 1986; Ben-Zvi 1993; Quandt 2005; Miller 2008, 125–321; Ross 2015). Below, four main approaches to the conflict are identified: the Palestine-centric approach, the Israel-centric approach, the strategic approach, and the diplomatic approach. Each has had a significant influence over American policy. These approaches are distinguished one from the other along two axes: the characteristics of the policy itself, and the relative weight given to various factors that underpin each approach.

Along the first axis – policy characteristics – the approaches are differentiated from each other by the answers they give to the following five questions. First, to what degree is the conflict considered a policy priority? Second, should the United States focus more on conflict management or conflict resolution? Third, when dealing with conflict resolution, should the United States prefer a comprehensive approach that seeks to settle all the final status issues in one package or should it take a step-by-step approach? Fourth, should the United States take what has been termed, an 'even-handed' approach to the conflict, or should it lean towards Israel? Fifth, how much pressure should the United States apply on the parties to the conflict? Should it seek to impose a solution, facilitate negotiations or some kind of mediation between these two poles?

Along the second axis, five factors underpin each approach. First, there are America's strategic interests. The Middle East is the source of more than a third of the world's oil and gas. Were supply of these resources to the global economy to be cut for a significant period, the ensuing economic and political chaos would reach America, even though the United States has never been dependent on Middle Eastern oil and is on the way to energy self-sufficiency by 2025. Thus, the United States has a major strategic interest in ensuring the supply of energy to the global economy. The United States also has a vital strategic interest in preventing a hostile power gaining control of a dominant share of regional energy resources. During the Cold War the United States feared that Soviet allies would gain control of oil production and that the Soviets would then be able to pressure Western Europe and Japan, who were dependent on Middle Eastern oil, to adopt a neutral stance, thereby shifting the global balance of power against America. Since the end of the Cold War, the United States has feared that Iraq under Saddam or the radical Iranian regime might achieve such a position and then leverage the massive increase of revenue into military power, which could generate a conflict in the Gulf that would block energy supplies and ultimately threaten the United States through terrorism and weapons of mass destruction (WMD). As such, the United States retains a vital interest in ensuring a stable pro-American balance of power in the Middle East (Mansour 1994, 1–44: Pollack 2008, 5–58; Rynhold 2019). The question is how does the Israeli-Palestinian conflict fit in with America's broader strategic interests? Is it a major threat to those interests?

And if the United States leans towards one side in the conflict, how would this affect America's strategic position?

The second factor underpinning approaches is their attitude towards the 'special relationship' with Israel. The special relationship is grounded in the cultural resonance of Israel for many Americans and the political influence of Israel's supporters in the American political system through elections and pro-Israel lobbying organisations, notably AIPAC – the America Israel Public Affairs Committee (Bard 1991; Mearsheimer and Walt 2007: Miller 2008, 75–123; Flesher 2009; Lieberman 2009; Rynhold 2010). One element of cultural resonance has its foundations in the Puritan-Protestant roots of the country, which emphasises the Hebrew Bible and the role of Israel in the Second Coming. The second element relates to shared democratic values and a pioneering spirit related to the 'American Creed' (Rynhold 2015, 9–31).

Third is the impact of bureaucratic politics (Halperin 1974) within the executive branch. Who is most responsible for making policy? Is it the president, the National Security Council, the State Department, the Pentagon, and so forth? If interested and involved, the president is the most important decision maker (Spiegel 1986; Quandt 2005). However, the president does not have the capacity to deal with everything. This can be important because presidents are more likely to be influenced by the 'special relationship', while the State Department has traditionally been more 'Arabist' in orientation, due in part to there being 22 American ambassadors in Arab states reporting on how to improve relations with their hosts, while there is just the one ambassador reporting from Israel. Rubin (1985, 136, 247) termed this 'clientitas'.

Fourth are two psychological traits common to many American leaders who have dealt with this issue: hubris – a belief that they are uniquely able to resolve the conflict where all others have failed, and with an inclination to base their initial approach to the conflict on a rejection of their predecessors' approach: that is, 'Anything but Clinton/Bush/Obama' (Ross 2015).

Fifth is the impact of policy feedback – the way the Israeli and Palestinian leadership relates to American interests and policies towards the conflict and the Middle East more broadly. For example, the pro-Israel Reagan Administration, which was generally hostile to the PLO, reversed course, opening a dialogue with the organisation when in December 1988 its leader, Yasser Arafat, recognised Israel's right to exist and renounced terrorism. His successor, George H. Bush, who was far less sympathetic to Israel, nonetheless ended that dialogue in the summer of 1990 when Arafat failed to denounce a terrorist attack in Tel Aviv, while backing Saddam Hussein's invasion of Kuwait.

Below, each of the four approaches is described in terms of their characteristics, their underpinnings and their practical expression in American policy towards the conflict.

The Palestine-Centric Approach

According to this approach, the comprehensive resolution of the Palestinian problem should be *the* United States policy priority in the Middle East. It favours heavy international mediation in the conflict, with the focus being on pressuring Israel, which is viewed as a strategic liability (Mearsheimer and Walt 2007, 58–77). The underlying premise here is that the Israeli-Palestinian conflict is the lynchpin of regional instability and anti-Americanism in the Middle East. Resolving the conflict will therefore remove the most important obstacle to good relations between the United States and the Arab world, while simultaneously removing the most significant cause of regional instability. Ross and Makovsky (2009) term this approach 'linkage' as it links every other cause of anti-Americanism and instability in the Middle East to the Israeli-Palestinian conflict, which is deemed to be at the core of all other trials and tribulations. The Palestinian issue is deemed the key because of its resonance in Arab nationalist mythology. This was viewed as constraining America's Arab allies from adopting pro-American policies, while simultaneously allowing America's opponents to rally support to their cause.

From the very beginning of the Arab-Israeli conflict, this approach was dominant within the executive branch bureaucracy. While Congress endorsed the 1917 Balfour Declaration – which called for the establishment of a Jewish homeland in Palestine – the State Department favoured the findings of the King-Crane commission published in 1922, which opposed Jewish statehood. Within the State Department, the Bureau for Near East Affairs has been responsible for relations with the Middle East. Aside from their perspective on the American national interest, many were also sympathetic to Arab nationalism and thus hostile to Zionism, for the bureau was largely staffed by the children and grandchildren of American missionaries to the Middle East. They grew up in the Arab world and even played a role in the development of Arab nationalism (Kaplan 1995; Oren 2006). By the late 1980s, such Arabist sympathies were no longer dominant in the State Department. However, its bureaucratic structure means that the weight attached to relations with the Arab world continues to outweigh relations with Israel in their calculations of the national interest. In addition, since the 1970s, the Palestinian cause has received support from the Left of the Democratic Party, notably President Jimmy Carter. They sometimes make the comparison between what they viewed as the victimhood of native Americans and the Palestinians (Rynhold 2015, 68–70).

Others support the Palestine-centric approach based on their belief in a defensive grand strategy (Walt 2005). They believe that direct American intervention abroad generates a nationalist backlash that causes greater instability than it was intended to prevent, and that in the Middle East American support for Israel is the central cause of this backlash. Paleo-conservatives like Pat Buchanan, and academics like Mearsheimer and Walt (2007) were hardcore advocates of this approach. Advocates of a softer version of this approach have included decision makers associated with the Defensive Realist school, such as Brent Scowcroft (Brzezinski and Scowcroft 2008, 21–29, 57–59, 77–78), Colin Powell and Robert Gates, as well as defensive Liberals such as Bill Clinton's National Security Advisor, Sandy Berger (Berger and Baker 2012), and Barack Obama's chief of staff, Dennis McDonough (Rynhold 2015, 31–94).

In 1946–1947, the State Department and the Defense Department strongly opposed the creation of a Jewish state. However, they lost the bureaucratic battle within the administration. President Truman was deeply committed to helping Holocaust survivors stuck in Displaced Persons (DP) camps in Europe, and when the Arab side rejected any compromise, including the idea of allowing 100,000 to immigrate into Palestine in the context of a binational state, Truman began to get behind partition. He was distrustful of the State Department in general and was not persuaded by them that the Arab states would support the Soviets if the United States backed the creation of Israel. Indeed, the King of Saudi Arabia had admitted to an American military officer that, despite his fiery rhetoric, in the end, Palestine would not affect Saudi relations with America (Hahn 2004, 30). Once Truman felt sure the United States forces would not get bogged down in protecting the fledgling state on the ground, he felt able to follow his pro-Zionist instincts and his domestic political interests and support the creation of the State of Israel (Cohen 1987; Radosh and Radosh 2008).

In contrast, the first Eisenhower Administration unreservedly adopted the Palestine-centric approach. They sought to pressure Israel into a settlement of the conflict, known as 'Alpha', which would have meant Israel surrendering territory in the Negev, while limiting Jewish immigration and the size of the Israeli army. They also supported Egypt in the 1956 Suez-Sinai War by successfully pressuring Israel to withdraw from Sinai unconditionally. Despite Eisenhower's attempts to gain favour with the Arab side at Israel's expense, he could not get them to unite behind the United States against the Soviets. In fact, Republican Nasserite forces allied with the Soviet Union threatening the conservative Arab monarchies allied with the United States, causing Eisenhower to abandon the Palestine-centric approach during most of his second term (Ben-Zvi 1998).

Throughout the 1960s, the State Department continued to promote the Palestine-centric approach, but it only came to the fore again in 1969 and 1970, when Secretary of State William Rogers initiated plans to work with international partners, including the USSR, to reach a comprehensive resolution of the Arab-Israeli conflict. Implementing the plan would have required heavy pressure on both sides. At this stage, independent Palestinian representation was not envisaged, though the Palestinian refugee issue was addressed. However, President Nixon was not truly committed to Rogers' plans. Consequently, Rogers lost the bureaucratic battle for control over policy to National Security Advisor Henry Kissinger, whose 'strategic approach' to the conflict dominated policy-making until he left office in 1976 (Quandt 2005, 55–93).

In 1977 the Carter Administration adopted the Palestine-centric approach, both because of its perception of the United States national interest and because of the president's sympathy for the Palestinians. Carter shifted United States policy on the conflict by declaring that the Palestinians deserved 'a homeland', a deliberately vague phrase borrowed from the Balfour Declaration that thereby implied the possibility of a sovereign Palestine state (Pressman 2013). Carter initially sought to create an international framework together with the Soviet Union, focused on pressuring Israel. However, President Sadat of Egypt, fearing this framework would lead to a stalemate, flew directly to Jerusalem to break the logjam. Subsequently, State Department Arabists warned President Carter against brokering a separate Egyptian-Israeli peace, arguing that this would lead America's Arab allies to distance themselves from the United States (Quandt 1986; Spiegel 1986, 315–380; Stein 1999). In fact, it set the scene for Jordan to pursue secret peace talks with Israel in the 1980s and for Saudi Arabia to launch its own Arab-Israeli peace plan in 1981 in an attempt to ensure American support against Iran.

From 1983 until the 1988 Presidential election, the influence of the Palestine-centric approach declined substantially. Nonetheless, in the twilight between administrations in December 1988, the United States opened an official diplomatic dialogue with the PLO, when, after substantial coaxing and coaching, Arafat publicly recognised Israel's right to exist and renounced terrorism (Quandt 2005, 277–285). Subsequently, a softer, lite version of the Palestine-centric approach surfaced under Secretary of State James Baker (1989–1993), notably when the administration refused to guarantee an Israeli loan of $10 billion unless Israel froze settlement activity, which its right-wing government refused to do. However, there was no attempt to heavily pressure Israel into a comprehensive settlement.

After that, the Palestine-centric approach was largely eclipsed until Barack Obama entered the White House in 2009. During his first year in office, President Obama focused on drawing closer to the Palestinians and Muslim world. However, despite pressuring Prime Minister Netanyahu into a ten-month settlement freeze and a public endorsement of Palestinian statehood, the Palestinian side showed little interest in negotiations, and the Arab states refused to provide the confidence-building measures requested by the administration. This failure, combined with the Arab uprisings and negotiations over the Iranian nuclear program, led the administration to downgrade the resolution of the conflict as a practical priority (Ross 2015, 342–392).

The Israel-Centric Approach

According to the Israel-centric approach, working for a resolution to the Israeli-Palestinian conflict should not be the number-one priority for the United States and, when dealing with the issue, the United States should lean towards Israel. In terms of American national interests, the underlying premise is that anti-Americanism and instability in the Middle East are not primarily a function of the Israeli-Palestinian conflict. Rather the main cause of these problems lie in the anti-democratic culture, ideologies and theologies that are prevalent in the region, be it the fascistic Ba'athism of Saddam Hussein, the theocratic revolutionary regime in Iran, or Islamist extremist groups like al Qaida and ISIS. They seek to 'roll-back' these forces as part of an assertive interventionist grand strategy. In this scheme, Israel is viewed as sharing a Western democratic identity with America, which is in turn viewed as accounting for the fact that the two countries share common enemies in the region (Rynhold 2015, 39–47). Given that Israel is a militarily powerful and reliable ally that shares core interests with the United States, it is viewed as a strategic asset. In this vein, President Bush (2010, 422) was pleased when Israel destroyed the secret Syrian nuclear reactor in 2007. But that is not to say that the United States supported every Israeli policy – indeed they came out very firmly against Israeli arms sales to the People's Republic of China (Benn 2004).

A nascent version of this approach was apparent under President Lyndon Johnson. Johnson was a believer in the special relationship with Israel. As a Texas Congressmen during World War II, he was pro-Zionist and one of the few members of Congress to speak out against the Nazi extermination of European Jewry. He also admired Israel's pioneering ethos and its democratic values, both of which he saw as reflecting America's own values (Sohns 2017). These considerations influenced his willingness to be the first American president to supply Israel with offensive weapons, and his de facto acceptance of Israel becoming a nuclear power (Rabinowitz 2014, 78–87: Cohen and Burr 2006). However, strategic calculations were at least as influential in his decision to supply advanced weapons to Israel (Rodman 2007). Moreover, in the prelude to the Six-Day War, despite his personal feelings, Johnson was unable to actively assist Israel, with the United States already bogged down in an unpopular war in Vietnam (Gat 2003; Shalom 2012; Spiegel 1986, 118–165). After Israel's victory, Johnson worked with the British to craft UNSC 242, which – unlike in 1957, when Eisenhower forced Israel into an unconditional withdrawal – conditioned an Israel withdrawal on the Arab side giving Israel peace and security in return. By not specifying that Israel had to withdraw from all the territories captured in the war, the British and Americans hoped to provide Israel with some bargaining leverage (Ashton 2015). At this stage, the Palestinian issue was still viewed internationally as a humanitarian refugee issue, with Jordan and Egypt identified as the partner for negotiations over the West Bank and Gaza.

In the wake of its speedy and overwhelming victory, Israel was increasingly viewed by hawkish Democrats as a strategic asset. In 1980 a group of such Democrats, previously associated with Senator Henry 'Scoop' Jackson, moved across to the Republican Party due to their opposition to Jimmy Carter's dovish foreign policy. They became known as the neoconservatives. They had some influence over Reagan's foreign policy, but it was only in the wake of 9/11, under President George W. Bush that they came to dominate United States foreign policy (Velasco 2010). With regard to the peace process, they opposed Israeli concessions to radical regimes and backers of terrorism, like Syria under the Assads and the PLO under Yasser Arafat. They believe that such 'appeasement' of dictators would not only weaken Israel, but also the overall United States position in the Middle East. They are willing to engage in peace diplomacy if they perceive that there is a pro-Western Arab partner who aspires to move in a more liberal-democratic direction and accepts Israel's right to exist. In this sense, their approach is impacted by the way the Palestinian side responds to their outlook, though even here they remain more sensitive to Israeli concerns (Rynhold 2015, 41–51).

In 2001, George W. Bush came into office on the back of the collapse of the peace process and the beginning of the Second *Intifada*. Bill Clinton told Bush he primarily blamed Arafat for this, and warned Bush not to trust him. This reinforced Bush's own inclinations to downgrade American attempts to resolve the Israeli-Palestinian conflict (Rubin and Kolp-Rubin 2003, 213). Following 9/11, Israel came to be viewed as a frontline ally in the war against terrorism and extremism. A victory for Israel was a victory for America. Defeat for Israel would be defeat for America. Nonetheless, Bush came out in favour of Palestinian statehood on condition that Arafat end the terrorist campaign. When evidence was provided that Arafat was behind the upsurge in terrorism, and that he had sought to obtain arms from Iran, the president refused to work with him any longer. Instead, in June 2002, Bush conditioned progress towards Palestinian statehood on internal political reform in the Palestinian Authority. Subsequently, Bush worked closely with the moderate reformist Palestinian Prime Minister Mahmoud Abbas during his brief tenure in the summer of 2004 (Rynhold 2005). After Abbas' resignation, Bush backed Prime Minister Sharon's disengagement from Gaza by issuing a letter to Israel in February 2005, which adopted several pro-Israel positions, such as implicitly recognising that Israeli settlement blocs would remain under Israeli control in any peace deal and ruling out any 'right of return' for Palestinian refugees and the ancestors of the State of Israel. While the administration did not pressure Israel into compromises on final-status issues, it did pressure Israel to allow Palestinian elections in Gaza in December 2005, as part of its democratic reform agenda. The result brought Hamas to power and, with the descent into chaos in Iraq and the collapse of the pro-Western government in Lebanon in 2007, the neoconservative agenda for the region lay in tatters.

Aside from interest-based logic, the Israel-centric approach, which has become prevalent in the Republican Party since the mid-1990s, is also underwritten by an ideological and theological commitment to the special relationship. For neoconservatives such as leading former Republican officials Elliot Abrams, Doug Feith and Paul Wolfowitz, commitment to the special relationship is underwritten by Israel's identity as a democracy and the sense that having failed to prevent to Holocaust, 'American exceptionalism' requires the United States to protect Israeli security. While many neoconservatives are Jewish, many are not. For others in the Republican Party, such as President George W. Bush (2001–2008) and Secretary of State Mike Pompeo (2018–2021), evangelical theology informs their pro-Israel approach, particularly their commitment to Israel's security. Many evangelicals view the foundation of Israel as part of a messianic process involving Armageddon before the 'Second Coming'; they oppose any territorial compromise by Israel. However, President Bush and the neoconservatives supported Israel's withdrawal from Gaza and the President backed Israeli Prime Minister Olmert's peace plan, which involved Israeli withdrawal from virtually all of the West Bank, the dismantling of most settlements, and the division of Jerusalem (Rynhold 2015, 45–46; Bush 2010, 409–410).

This pro-Israel approach to the conflict is also influenced by domestic political considerations. Since the late 1990s, evangelicals have become the largest part of the Republican base and since 9/11 support for taking Israel's side in the conflict has soared (Rynhold 2015, 52–54). This consideration has played a central role in President Trump's very one-sided approach to the conflict. Trump himself did not share either the strategic or the ideational commitment to Israel. However, to please his Republican base he was strongly supportive of the right-wing Israeli government led by Netanyahu, such that the Palestinian Authority refused to deal with him. Trump expressed this support in publicly symbolic acts, such as moving the American embassy to Jerusalem and recognising the Golan Heights, which were captured from Syria in 1967, as Israeli. However, on practical strategic matters concerning Iran and Syria, Trump's isolationist inclinations were of concern to the Israeli security establishment.

The Strategic Approach

According to the strategic approach, the most important American interest related to the Israeli-Palestinian arena is conflict management. The primary interest is to prevent the conflict escalating into a regional war that could threaten the supply of oil to the world economy, lead to the use of nuclear weapons, or shift the regional balance of power against the United States and its allies. The Israeli-Palestinian conflict is but one of many conflicts in the Middle East that poses a threat to these interests. Thus, in contrast to the Palestine-centric approach, the conflict's resolution is not singled out as the permanent policy priority. Indeed, because the Palestinians lack the military and political power of a state, the strategic approach has generally paid them less attention than the inter-state component of the Arab-Israeli conflict, which has greater direct potential to affect the balance of power and the stability of the Middle East as a whole. In terms of the degree of United States diplomatic activity and whether to pressure or reassure Israel or the Arab side, the answers to these questions are determined by their reading of the regional strategic context at any given moment. This approach views Israel, given its military power, political stability and reliability as a strategic asset. Consequently, when mediating peace negotiations, adherents of this approach seek to preserve Israel's security. However, it is willing to heavily pressure Israel to make diplomatic and territorial concessions if this will shift the overall regional balance in America's favour.

As befits its name, the strategic approach is based primarily on an assessment of American national interests. It seeks to minimise the impact of culture, ideology and domestic politics. It dominated United States policy-making in two periods, from late 1957 until the end of the second Eisenhower Administration (Ben-Zvi 1998, 59–96) and during the Nixon and Ford administrations, when Henry Kissinger was the driving force behind United States policy. By late 1957 experience had taught the Eisenhower administration that the Palestinian issue was not the key strategic dynamic in the region, and that the Soviet-backed Nasser was set on undermining America's allies, the conservative Arab monarchies. With the Arab world divided between hostile Nasserite forces and weak pro-American allies, Israel emerged as, in the words of Eisenhower, 'the only strong pro-West power left in the Middle East' (Ben-Zvi 1998, 81). Subsequently, the administration used the implied threat of Israeli intervention in the West Bank to deter Nasser from overthrowing the pro-Western King Hussein (while simultaneously warning Israel not to do so). Instead of pressuring Israel to make concessions and seeking to resolve the Arab-Israeli conflict, the administration sought instead to manage the conflict so as allow it to concentrate on the containment of Nasserite forces in the region.

During his tenure, President Kennedy (1961–1963) came to adopt a softer, modified version of the strategic approach. As before, the main objective was conflict management. To this end the administration became the first to supply Israel with defensive weapons – the surface-to-air Hawk missile. At the same time, in the wake of the Cuban missile crisis, Kennedy was determined to prevent nuclear proliferation. Consequently, he personally applied heavy pressure on Israel to open up the Dimona nuclear reactor to inspection, without giving weight to domestic political considerations (Cohen 1998). Although conflict resolution was not a priority, Kennedy tried to take a step in this direction by promoting the Johnson Plan to resolve the problem of Palestinian refugees, a humanitarian issue of personal importance to him prior to becoming president. Kennedy offered incentives to the parties but was not prepared to apply serious pressure. Neither Israel nor the Arab side were enthusiastic about the compromises involved in the plan and, when the Arab side finally rejected it, Kennedy dropped it (Bick 2006). Unlike Eisenhower, domestic politics influenced Kennedy's policy towards the conflict, as the Jewish community was much more important to the Democratic Party than to the

Republicans. In the conduct of foreign policy in general, Kennedy was also inclined to give greater weight to his own White House advisors over the State Department. Both these factors helped to tilt policy in a pro-Israel direction. However, strategic factors related to the Soviets' supply of weapons to Egypt and Nasser's support for anti-Western forces in the Yemeni civil war were more important in determining policy (Ben-Zvi 1998, 97–131; Bass 2003).

On coming to power in 1969, and with half a million United States troops bogged down in Vietnam, President Nixon and his National Security Advisor, Henry Kissinger, concluded that the United States was strategically over-stretched. Subsequently, the 'Nixon Doctrine' emphasised burden-sharing with allies in place of additional direct United States military intervention in Asia. Israel and the Shah of Iran were considered the American allies best placed to play this role in the Middle East. Israel's victory in the Six-Day War had demonstrated its strength and its designation as a strategic asset was sealed in September 1970, after Israel saved the pro-American regime in Jordan from collapse at the hands of the PLO and Syria, then Soviets allies (Rubinovitz 2010). In the aftermath, the administration increased American aid to Israel tenfold, cementing America's post-1967 role as Israel's main arms supplier. As such, Kissinger sought to demonstrate to the Arab states that American weaponry and diplomatic leverage was greater than that of the Soviet Union. The implication being that the road to the return of their territory captured by Israel ran through Washington rather than Moscow (Spiegel 1986, 166–218)

Still, viewing Israel as a strategic asset did not mean giving it unconditional support. During the Yom Kippur War in October 1973, the administration delayed resupplying Israel with arms in order to 'soften up' Israel for post-war concessions (Gutfeld and Vanetik, 2016; Levey 2008). During and after that war, the United States put enormous pressure on Israel to accept a cease-fire in order to contain the threat of escalation to a global nuclear confrontation with the Soviet Union, Subsequently, and despite Israel's military victory, further United States pressure was applied to force Israel to withdraw from some territory on the Golan Heights and in the Sinai in disengagement agreements mediated by Kissinger using 'shuttle diplomacy'. This was done in order to entice Egypt to switch sides in the Cold War. By succeeding in this regard, Kissinger achieved two goals. First, he shifted the regional balance of power in a pro-American direction. Second, he greatly improved the prospects for conflict management. With both Egypt and Israel now dependent on American support, the United States had obtained unprecedented leverage to restrain its allies. Moreover, with Egypt effectively sidelined, Israel could concentrate its forces in the East, greatly enhancing its deterrence in that theatre. Kissinger wanted a militarily strong but diplomatically compliant Israel. Therefore, he compensated Israel for its withdrawals by greatly increasing aid, arms supplies, and strategic cooperation in tandem with the Sinai II disengagement agreement in 1975. The State Department had hoped to use the post-war situation to forward an international conference with Soviet involvement to pressure Israel into a comprehensive solution, including a new emphasis on the Palestinian dimension of the conflict. However, Kissinger absolutely opposed the idea, as it would increase the involvement and influence of the Soviets and their allies. Instead, he adopted a step-by-step approach designed to exclude the Soviets by focusing on Egypt and promising Israel that the United States would not negotiate with the Soviet-backed PLO as long it refused to recognise Israel and renounce terrorism (Spiegel 1986, 219–314; Lasensky 2007; Miller 2008, 129–156).

While the Carter Administration adopted an 'anything but Kissinger approach', at the beginning of the Reagan Administration (1981–1988), Secretary of State Alexander Haig returned to the strategic approach. Haig had served as Deputy National Security Advisor under Kissinger. He promoted a policy of 'strategic consensus', which aimed to develop strategic cooperation between Israel and America's Arab allies prior to a full resolution of the Israeli-Palestinian conflict. With President Reagan not functioning at full capacity following an assassination attempt, Haig had significant leeway, and he reached a secret understanding with Israeli Defense Minister Ariel Sharon, to back an Israeli invasion of Lebanon on the condition that it come in the wake of the PLO committing an internationally recognised terrorist incident (Haig 1984, 326–327). From Haig's perspective, the objective was to weaken Soviet allies – Syria and the PLO – in Lebanon. This would then open the way for American-sponsored peace talks between American allies Israel and Jordan, with Palestinian (though not PLO) involvement. However, with Reagan returning to full function, Haig paid for the fact that he had not taken the President into his confidence and he was thus forced to resign following Israel's invasion of Lebanon in June 1982. Israel then rejected the Reagan Peace Plan, with AIPAC limiting United States pressure on Israel in this regard. In any case, by February 1983, the plan collapsed as King Hussein felt unable to proceed, given Arafat's opposition. When the May 1983 peace agreement between Israel and Lebanon fell apart within a few months of its signing under Syrian pressure, Secretary of State George Shultz decided that the United States would no longer initiate grandiose peace plans unless the parties requested it (Lewis 1988; Shultz 1993, 439). Doing otherwise damaged American prestige by associating it with failure.

With the demise of the USSR in 1991, the United States became the dominant power in the Middle East, greatly reducing the potential for the Israeli-Palestinian conflict to escalate region-wide. In the wake of the 2003 Iraq War and the global financial crisis of 2008, the Obama Administration adopted a strategy of retrenchment designed to lessen America's military commitments in the region. Despite being polar opposites in most respects, President Trump's approach was at one with Obama's in this regard. With America retrenching, the progress of the Iranian nuclear program and the gains made by both Iran and *jihadi* groups like ISIS following the Arab Uprisings, America's allies in the Gulf began cooperating strategically with Israel to counter these common threats. Under the Trump Administration, the President's highly influential son-in-law, Jarred Kushner, sought to consolidate and expand on this by encouraging the Gulf States to begin normalising relations with Israel prior to a full resolution of the Israeli-Palestinian conflict. The fact that the Palestinians refused to engage with the administration's plan for 'the deal of the century' was not critical for Trump's team. They expected Palestinian President Mahmoud Abbas to reject their plan. Their objective, instead, was to make the plan generous enough to get Gulf States, especially Saudi Arabia, to engage. Unlike with Eisenhower and Kissinger, under Trump the strategic approach was severely constrained by domestic political considerations. Trump leaned heavily towards Israel and coordinated his moves closely with the right-wing Israeli government led by Benjamin Netanyahu in order to maintain the support of evangelicals who made up the bulk of his base of support. Moreover, Kushner had long-standing family ties with Netanyahu, while one of the other key players, United States Ambassador to Israel David Friedman, was a longtime supporter of the Israeli settler movement (Rynhold and Yaari 2019).

The 'Diplomatic Approach'

The motto of the 'diplomatic approach' can be summed up thus: the United States should remain intimately engaged in the peace process, but it cannot want peace more than do the parties. This maxim was repeated publicly in various iterations by every administration from George H. W. Bush to Barack Obama (Rynhold 2008). According to the diplomatic approach, the United States should always be engaged in promoting the peace process between Israel and the Palestinians. Maintaining a process is important as a mechanism for managing the conflict. It prevents the development of a political vacuum that could lead to a violent escalation of the conflict. There is also a genuine commitment to trying to resolve the conflict. Yet, while reaching a permanent resolution of the conflict is viewed as highly desirable and the ultimate objective, it is not viewed, in a fundamental sense, as *the* priority.

In general, the diplomatic approach focused on facilitation rather than on pressure. It sought to preserve America's role as the leading external power involved in the peace process, though it is happy to involve other actors in an auxiliary role. It will increase the intensity and level of United States mediation if it surmises that the parties desire this, but it will not seek to impose a settlement. The logic is that even if the United States surmises could impose a peace plan, any peace agreement would collapse unless the parties themselves are deeply committed to maintaining it (Ross and Makovsky 2009).

The diplomatic approach leans towards Israel. Being even-handed is not viewed as the key to successful mediation. What is important is the ability of the mediator to help extract the required concessions. Reassurance of Israel is critical in this context, since it is Israel that will be making the bulk of the tangible concessions (Ross and Makovsky 2009). Indeed, taking as a guide the 'Clinton Parameters' for a permanent settlement (December 2000), this approach envisages Israel withdrawing from the overwhelming majority of the West Bank (including land swaps) and dividing Jerusalem more or less along ethnic lines. In return, the United States was willing to massively boost its strategic relationship with Israel (Riedel 2002; Ross 2004, xxv–xxvi, 801–805).

Given these positions, it is not surprising that the diplomatic approach's tilt to the Israeli side is usually confined to an Israeli government that is perceived to be ready to advance the peace process. In such cases, adherents of the diplomatic approach will co-ordinate their diplomatic strategy with the Israeli government's, as the Clinton Administration did with Labour Prime Ministers Rabin and Peres in 1992–1996 and Ehud Barak in 1999–2000. The United States administration even tried to help Peres indirectly in the 1996 election. Since that failure, they have been disinclined to repeat the exercise. When the conservative Netanyahu became prime minister, 1996–1999, the focus was on preserving the peace process, and this required tightening the relationship with the Palestinian side (Rynhold 2008).

In terms of the American national interest, management of the conflict is important to prevent the contagion of instability across the region. Maintaining American primacy in mediating the conflict is viewed as preserving American prestige and thereby assisting in regard to the regional balance of power. Resolution of the conflict would be even more beneficial, as it would also further the values associated with the liberal internationalist grand strategy, which most adherents of the diplomatic approach support (Rynhold 2015: 61–65).

The diplomatic approach utterly rejects the idea that American support for Israel is the key cause of anti-Americanism in the region (Ross and Makovsky 2009; Miller 2008). Nonetheless, proponents accept that progress in the peace process is helpful to America's Arab allies. Thus, in the 1990s, they argued that the Israeli peace process weakened Iran and Iraq's ability to manipulate the conflict to their advantage. At the same time, the 'dual containment' of Iran and Iraq improved the prospects for peace-making by weakening opponents of the peace process (Indyk 2009).

Supporters of the diplomatic approach are also deeply committed to the United States' special relationship with Israel, and as a consequence, they strongly support the American commitment to Israel's security. They tend to have more personal ties with, and professional knowledge about, Israel than the Palestinians. At the same time, as liberal internationalists, they are committed to the general principle of national self-determination and democracy. These values inform their commitment to using the peace process to find a way to make Palestinian self-determination and dignity compatible with a secure, Jewish, and democratic Israel.

In the second half of the 1980s, Secretary of State George Shultz became the first to fully adopt the diplomatic approach. Shultz institutionalised and upgraded the strategic relationship with Israel, to both reinforce the special relationship and to reassure Israel and thus encourage Israeli willingness to make territorial concessions (Puschel 1992, 81–99). He also tried to help Israel, Jordan, and moderate Palestinians begin formal peace negotiations. Shultz coordinated diplomatic moves with Prime Minister Shimon Peres (1984–86). However, having been burnt by previous failures, Shultz was unprepared for the United States to pressure the parties, and neither side was strong enough domestically to move forward (Lewis 1988; Shultz 1993, 438–451). In April 1987 King Hussein and Peres, now foreign minister in a national unity government headed by the right-wing Yitzhak Shamir, reached an agreement in London to open peace negotiations. In order to pressure Shamir to provide the required assent, the plan was for the United States to present the agreement as its own. However, Shultz refused to get entangled in Israeli domestic politics and thus, despite his personal support for the London agreement, a major opportunity for a breakthrough was lost (1993, 937–942).

The high-water mark of the diplomatic approach's dominance over United States policy came in the 1990s during the Clinton Administration (1993–2000). The officials in charge of the peace process, Dennis Ross and Martin Indyk, were its two most influential representatives. They were given a lot of latitude by the political decision makers (Ross 2004; Indyk 2009). They did not initiate the Oslo Accords between Israel and the PLO, but they adopted them enthusiastically and remained deeply engaged in the process. In 2000, when the Israelis pushed for final status agreements, President Clinton became directly involved in mediating both the Israeli-Palestinian and the Israeli-Syrian tracks. However, in both instances, he failed, and the peace process collapsed.

This led to much criticism of the diplomatic approach. But, although George W. Bush came into office determined to strike out on a different path, towards the end of his presidency, he essentially adopted a lite version of it at the Annapolis peace conference in 2007 and during the subsequent Israeli-Palestinians negotiations in 2008. President Obama also came into office determined not to adopt the approach of his two immediate predecessors. Nonetheless, in 2013 Secretary of State John Kerry ended up adopting a modified version of the diplomatic approach. Kerry had a long track record as a pro-Israel senator, and he felt a strong personal urge to resolve the conflict. Much of Kerry's team preferred an even-handed approach but, in practice, Kerry spent much more time engaged with Prime Minister Netanyahu than with the Palestinian leader, Mahmoud Abbas, who was not enthusiastic about the negotiations. Netanyahu, notwithstanding his scepticism and his strained relations with the administration, was prepared to move forward on the basis of the Kerry proposal, but Abbas refused to endorse it, despite a personal plea from the President (Birnbaum and Tibon 2014).

Conclusion

Strategic considerations have been the most important ingredient in all American approaches to the Israeli-Palestinian conflict. Since Israel and the Gulf States began cooperating to combat the Iranian threat in the 2010s, the interest-based case underpinning the Palestine-centric approach has been severely weakened. At the same time, the Israeli-centric approach is also losing ground. America's special relationship with Israel is an article of faith for the Republican Party. However, on the other side of the aisle, the close association between the conservative Netanyahu and the despised Trump, combined with the long-term liberal trend in the Democratic Party, has led to a sharp decline in their sympathy for Israel (Rynhold 2019). If this trend continues, it will have consequences for the American approach to the Israeli-Palestinian conflict whenever there is a Democrat in the White House. Finally, despite America's increasing reluctance to remain deeply engaged in the Middle East, it would not be surprising if future leaders are tempted to pursue the 'deal of the century' in the belief that they can succeed where all others have failed. One can only wish them well.

Recommended Readings

Hahn, P. 2004. *Caught in the Middle East: U.S. Policy toward the Arab-Israeli Conflict, 1945–1961*. Chapel Hill, NC: University of North Carolina Press.

Miller, A. D. 2008. *The Much Too Promised Land: America's Elusive Search for Arab-Israeli Peace*. New York: Bantam.

Quandt, W. 2005. *Peace Process: American Diplomacy and the Arab-Israeli Conflict since 1967*, 3rd ed. Washington, DC: Brookings.

Ross, D., and D. Makovsky. 2009. *Myths, Illusions and Peace: Finding a New Direction for America in the Middle East* New York: Viking.

Rynhold, J. 2015. *The Arab-Israeli Conflict in American Political Culture*. Cambridge: Cambridge University Press.

Questions for Discussion

(1) What has been the most important consideration underpinning American approaches to the Israeli-Palestinian conflict?
(2) What are the main causes of changes in the United States approach to the Israeli-Palestinian conflict?
(3) Is the United States capable of imposing peace on the Israelis and Palestinians?
(4) Should seeking to resolve the Israeli-Palestinian conflict be the top priority for United States Middle East policy?
(5) Which of the approaches delineated above, is best suited to dealing with the Israeli-Palestinian conflict?

References

Ashton, N. 2015. "Searching for a Just and Lasting Peace? Anglo-American Relations and the Road to United Nations Security Council Resolution 242." *International History Review* 38:1, 24–44.

Bard, M. 1991. *The Water's Edge and Beyond: Defining the Limits to Domestic Influence on United States Middle East Policy*. New Brunswick, NJ: Transaction.

Bass, W. 2003. *Support Any Friend: Kennedy's Middle East and the Making of the American-Israeli Alliance*. New York: Oxford University Press.

Benn, A. 2004. "Pentagon Official Wants Yaron Fired. *Ha'aretz*, 16 December.

Ben-Zvi, A. 1993. *The United States and Israel: The Limits of the Special Relationship*. New York: Columbia University Press.

Ben-Zvi, A. 1998. *Decade of Transition: Eisenhower, Kennedy, and the Origins of the American-Israeli Alliance*. New York: Columbia University Press.

Berger, S., and J. Baker. 2012. "Forward." In *Pathways to Peace: America and the Arab-Israeli Conflict*, ed. D. Kurtzer. New York: Palgrave Macmillan, vii–xii.

Bick, E. 2006. "Two-Level Negotiations and US Foreign Policy: The Failure of the Johnson Plan for the Palestinian Refugees." *Diplomacy and Statecraft* 17:3, 447–474.

Birnbaum, B., and A. Tibon. 2014. "The Explosive, Inside Story of How John Kerry Built an Israel-Palestine Peace Plan – and Watched It Crumble." *New Republic*, 21 July. Available at: https://newrepublic.com/article/118751/how-israel-palestine-peace-deal-died.

Brzezinski Z. and B. Scowcroft. 2008. *America and the World*. New York: Basic Books

Bush, G. W. 2010. *Decision Points*. New York: Crown.

Cohen, A. 1998. *Israel and the Bomb*. New York: Columbia University Press.

Cohen, A., and W. Burr. 2006. "Israel Crosses the Threshold." *Bulletin of the Atomic Scientists* 62:3, 22–30.

Cohen, M. 1987. *The Origins and Evolution of the Arab-Zionist Conflict*. Berkeley, CA: University of California Press.

Flesher, D. 2009. *Transforming America's Israel Lobby*. Sterling, VA: Potomac.

Gat, M. 2003. "Let Someone Else Do the Job: American Policy on the Eve of the Six Day War." *Diplomacy and Statecraft* 14:1, 131–158.

Gutfeld, A, and B. Vanetik 2016. "'A Situation That Had to Be Manipulated': The American Airlift to Israel During the Yom Kippur War." *Middle Eastern Studies* 52:3, 419–447.

Hahn, P. 2004. *Caught in the Middle East: U.S. Policy toward the Arab-Israeli Conflict, 1945–1961*. Chapel Hill, NC: University of North Carolina Press.

Haig, A. 1984. *Caveat: Realism, Reagan and Foreign Policy*. New York: Macmillan.

Halperin, M. 1974. *Bureaucratic Politics and Foreign Policy*. Washington, DC: Brookings.

Indyk, M. 2009. *Innocent Abroad: An Intimate Account of American Peace Diplomacy in the Middle East*. New York: Simon & Schuster.

Kaplan, R. 1995. *The Arabists: The Romance of an American Elite*. New York: Free Press.

Lasensky, S. 2007. "Dollarizing Peace: Nixon, Kissinger and the Creation of the US-Israeli Alliance." *Israel Affairs* 13:1, 164–186.

Levey, Z. 2008. "Anatomy of an Airlift: United States Military Assistance to Israel during the 1973 War." *Cold War History* 8:4, 481–501.

Lewis, S. 1988. "The United States and Israel: Constancy and Change." In *Ten Years after Camp David*, ed. W. B. Quandt. Washington, DC: Brookings, 217–257.

Lieberman, R. 2009. "The 'Israel Lobby' and American Politics." *Perspectives on Politics* 7:2, 235–257.

Mansour, C. 1994. *Beyond Alliance: Israel in US Foreign Policy*. New York: Columbia University Press.

Mearsheimer, J., and S. Walt. 2007. *The Israel Lobby and US Foreign Policy*. New York: Allen.

Miller, A. D. 2008. *The Much Too Promised Land: America's Elusive Search for Middle East Peace*. New York: Bantam.

Oren, M. 2006. *Power, Faith and Fantasy: America in the Middle East 1776 to the Present*. New York: Norton.

Pressman, J. 2013. "Explaining the Carter Administration's Israeli–Palestinian Solution." *Diplomatic History* 37:5, 1117–1147.

Pollack. K. M. 2008. *A Path Out of the Desert: A Grand Strategy for America in the Middle East*. New York: Random House

Puschel, K. 1992. *US-Israeli Strategic Co-operation in the Post-Cold War Era*. Tel Aviv: Jaffe Centre.

Quandt, W. B. 1986. *Camp David: Peace-making and Politics*. Washington, DC: Brookings.

Quandt, W. B. 2005. *Peace Process: American Diplomacy and the Arab-Israeli Conflict since 1967*, 3rd ed. Washington, DC: Brookings.

Rabinowitz O. 2014. *Bargaining on Nuclear Tests: Washington and Its Cold War Deals*. Oxford: Oxford University Press.

Radosh, R., and A. Radosh. 2008. *Safe Haven: Harry S. Truman and the Founding of Israel*. New York. HarperCollins.

Riedel, B. 2002. "Camp David – The US-Israeli Bargain." *Bitter Lemons*, 26. 15 July. Available at: www.bitterlemons.org/previous/bl150702ed26extra.html.

Rodman, D. 2007. *Arms Transfers to Israel: The Strategic Logic*. Eastbourne: Sussex Academic Press.

Ross, D. 2004. *The Missing Peace: The Inside Story of the Fight for Middle East Peace*. New York: Farrar, Straus and Giroux.

Ross, D. 2015. *Doomed to Succeed: The US-Israel Relationship from Truman to Obama*. New York: Farrar Straus and Giroux.

Ross, D., and D. Makovsky. 2009. *Myths, Illusions and Peace: Finding a New Direction for America in the Middle East*. New York: Viking.

Rubin, B. 1985. *Secrets of State: The State Department and the Struggle Over U.S. Foreign Policy*. Oxford: Oxford University Press.

Rubin, B., and J. Kolp-Rubin 2003. *Yasir Arafat: A Political Biography*. Oxford: Oxford University Press.

Rubinovitz, Z. 2010. "Blue and White 'Black September': Israel's Role in the Jordan Crisis of 1970." *International History Review* 32:4, 687–706.

Rynhold, J. 2005. "Behind the Rhetoric: President Bush and US Policy to the Israeli-Palestinian Conflict." *American Diplomacy*. November. Available at: https://americandiplomacy.web.unc.edu/2005/11/behind-the-rhetoric/.

Rynhold, J. 2008. "The US and the Middle East Peace Process." In *US-Israeli Relations in a New Era*, eds. E. Inbar and E. Gilboa. London: Routledge, 140–158.

Rynhold, J. 2010. "Is the Pro-Israel Lobby a Block on Reaching a Comprehensive Peace Settlement in the Middle East?" *Israel Studies Forum* 25:1, 29–49.

Rynhold, J. 2015. *The Arab-Israeli Conflict in American Political Culture*. New York: Cambridge University Press.

Rynhold, J. 2019. "The Special Relationship Shoring Up Declining Sympathy for Israel Among Democrats." *Fathom*. September. Available at: http://fathomjournal.org/the-special-relationship-shoring-up-declining-sympathy-for-israel-among-democrats/.

Rynhold, J., and M. Yaari. 2019. "The Quiet Revolution in Saudi-Israeli Relations." *Mediterranean Politics*. DOI: 10.1080/13629395.2019.1699267.

Shalom, Z. 2012. *The Role of US Diplomacy in the Lead-up to the Six Day War: Balancing Moral Commitments and National Interests*. Eastbourne: Sussex Academic Press.

Shultz, G. 1993. *Turmoil and Triumph: My Years as Secretary of State*. New York: Scribner.

Sohns, O. 2017. "The Future Foretold: Lyndon Baines Johnson's Congressional Support for Israel." *Diplomacy and Statecraft* 28:1, 57–84.

Spiegel, S. 1986. *The Other Arab-Israeli Conflict: Making America's Middle East Policy, from Truman to Reagan*. Chicago: University of Chicago Press.

Stein, K. 1999. *Heroic Diplomacy: Sadat, Kissinger, Carter, Begin, and the Quest for Arab-Israeli Peace*. New York: Routledge.

Touval, S. 1982. *The Peace Brokers: Mediators in the Arab-Israeli Conflict, 1948–1979*. Princeton, NJ: Princeton University Press.

Velasco, J. 2010. *Neoconservatives in U.S. Foreign Policy under Ronald Reagan and George W. Bush*. Baltimore, MD: Johns Hopkins University Press.

Walt, S. 2005. *Taming American Power: The Global Response to U.S. Primacy*. New York: Norton.

29

THE ISRAEL LOBBY AND RELATIONS BETWEEN THE AMERICAN JEWISH COMMUNITY AND ISRAEL

Shaiel Ben-Ephraim

Introduction

For two countries without immediately similar cultural and linguistic backgrounds, Israel and the United States share a uniquely close relationship. The United States provides Israel with more direct foreign military aid than any other country, roughly 3.8$ billion per year. This allows it to maintain its qualitative military advantage over its regional rivals. In addition, the United States regularly exercises its veto power to protect Israel from adverse United Nations Security Council resolutions. The close strategic partnership with its great-power patron is essential to the maintenance of Israeli security (Weinberg 2014). The primary explanation for the closeness of the relationship is the existence of a "special relationship" engendering mutual emotional resonance within both societies. A cultural affinity based on perceived similarities of religious heritage, mutual commitment to democracy, and comparable patterns of settler-based state-building has often been noted (Kaplan 2018; Rynhold 2015; Stephens 2006). Those who analyze the relationship from this perspective believe that the domestic political supporters of Israel in the United States are merely promoting a deep pre-existing relationship that they manage rather than create (Rynhold 2015, 159–180).

The school of thought stressing the role of the "Israel lobby" disagrees. They believe an efficient group of lobbyists corrals the United States into pursuing pro-Israeli policies with detrimental consequences to American interests (Findley 1985; Hixson 2019; Mansour 1994; Mearsheimer and Walt 2007; Rubenberg 1986; Tivnan 1987). They see the Israel lobby as an almost monocausal explanation for the closeness of the relationship and for United States policies in the Middle East. According to the best-known work on the topic, "the overall thrust of U.S. policy in the region is due almost entirely to U.S. domestic politics, and especially the activities of the Israel Lobby" (Mearsheimer and Walt 2007, 1).

There is little doubt that the pro-Israel community in the United States has wielded influence since the establishment of the State of Israel, though they did not have as high a profile as they would enjoy in later years (Aridan 2017; Hixson 2019). Their first significant public victory took place during negotiations over the second disengagement agreement (SINAI II)

DOI: 10.4324/9780429027376-35

between Israel and Egypt in 1975. Israel proved reluctant to agree to withdraw from the strategic passes in the Sinai Peninsula in return for a partial agreement. President Gerald Ford threatened "an immediate reassessment of U.S. policy in the area" and shipments of fighter jets to Israel were correspondingly delayed. Pro-Israeli organizations circulated a letter supporting the Israeli position while calling for continued military aid. It was signed by 75 senators, constraining the ability of the Ford Administration to pressure Israel (Lazarowitz 2014). However, it should be noted that despite their impressive ability to obtain Congressional backing, the Sinai II agreement that followed saw Israel acquiescing to the terms it had mobilized the "lobby" to avoid (Stein 1999, 179).

Since then their reputation as one of the most fearsome lobbies on Capitol Hill has only grown (Mearsheimer and Walt 2007, 117–118). The leaders of the Israel lobby became more assured and, by the mid-1980s, they were well established as one of the top lobbies inside the Beltway, and easily the most influential in the field of foreign policy (Thomas 2007, 18–40). Steven Rosen, former director of foreign-policy issues at the American Israel Public Affairs Committee (AIPAC) boasted, "You see this napkin? In twenty-four hours, we could have the signatures of seventy senators on this napkin" (Goldberg 2005).

Lobby influence is facilitated by the American political system, which allows pressure groups easy access to legislators. This allows its primarily Jewish and evangelical Christian constituencies to maximize influence. Influence is considerable since both groups traditionally punch above their weight. Evangelical groups are a key component in the voting coalition of the Republican Party (Clark 2007; Fitzgerald 2017). Meanwhile, Jews contribute disproportionately to both parties and make up an essential component of the Democratic Party coalition (Wald 2015). Therefore, the lobby wields significant influence on both parties.

Despite its importance, the Israel lobby explanation is controversial. It is disturbingly similar to prevalent antisemitic narratives. A central claim in the *Protocols of the Elders of Zion*, amongst other antisemitic sources, is that Jewish political and financial power wields outsized malevolent influence (Hasian 1997; Laqueur 2006, 91–106). However, there is enough empirical substance to warrant discussion of the claim that the Israel lobby enjoys undue influence.

Existing Literature on the Israel Lobby

The debate over the influence of the Israel lobby goes back to the 1980s, when its significant role in American politics began to be acknowledged (Curtiss 1990; Findley 1985; Rubenberg 1986; Tivnan 1987). However, the publication of Mearsheimer and Walt's essay in 2006, and book the following year, were a watershed in the conversation (Mearsheimer and Walt 2006; Mearsheimer and Walt 2007). Though the claims were not new, the unimpressive American role in the Oslo Peace Process and the Second *Intifada* uprising that followed, engendered increased awareness towards the conflict and the role of the Israel lobby in it. In addition, Mearsheimer and Walt were two of the most well-known International Relations scholars of the time. Since the publication of their book, discussion of the Israel lobby has been central to the analysis of American policy in the Middle East.

Some works published since concurred with the main claims of their book, while adding nuance (Hixson 2019; Little 2008). However, the majority of analysis has disagreed with the main premise. The most immediate backlash to the Mearsheimer and Walt book characterized it as essentially antisemitic (Foxman 2007; Feingold 2008). A more empirical approach acknowledged the power of the lobby but noted its influence was limited and situational (Jackson 2015; Rynhold 2010). Other empirical works focused on divisions within the pro-Israeli community and their adverse influence on its lobbying capabilities (Ben-Ephraim 2020; Divine 2010; Waxman 2010). Another stream focused on the role of the Israeli government in lobbying, exposing the limits of the pro-Israeli organizations as autonomous actors (Aridan 2017; Ganin, 2005). Meanwhile, theoretically minded detractors noted that Mearsheimer and Walt's conceptualization of the influence of pressure groups was at odds with the literature on the topic (Fishman 2008; Lieberman 2009). The weight of these critiques has successfully undermined the almost monocausal claim that the Israel lobby can explain the general thrust of American policy in the Middle East. However, it has not altered the understanding that the pro-Israeli community plays an important, albeit limited, role in shaping bilateral relations.

What is the Israel Lobby?

Everything about the Israel lobby is controversial, even the definition. Mearsheimer and Walt define it as "organizations or individuals consistently promoting a pro-Israeli agenda in the U.S" (Mearsheimer and Walt 2007, 112). This is problematic, as it does not differentiate between lobbyers and the lobbied. Dov Waxman defines the lobby as a group of "formal organizations that try to influence American policy toward Israel in a direction that they believe is in Israel's interests" (Waxman 2016, 150). This definition is wider than necessary. It includes organizations sympathetic to Israel, yet focused primarily on unrelated issues, such as evangelical groups or conservative think tanks. I define the Israel lobby as formal organizations primarily concerned with influencing American foreign policy in a direction they believe is beneficial to Israel.

The Israel lobby is made up of several categories. The official Israel lobby consists of groups with stated lobbying functions focused mostly on Israel. Most powerful amongst these is the centrist American Israel Public Affairs Committee (AIPAC), which is considered the flagship of the lobby. There are lobbying organizations to the right and left as well. The main organization on the left is J-Street, which believes the United States should apply more pressure on Israel to withdraw from the territories. On the right, the Zionist Organization of America (ZOA) opposes a Palestinian state (Waxman 2010). Notably, the core of the lobby disagrees on the most desirable policy towards the Palestinians.. A second category encompasses organizations designed to promote general Jewish interests while spending significant resources lobbying for Israel. Notable in this category is the Conference of Presidents of Major American Jewish Organizations. Traditionally, they are charged with lobbying the executive branch (the White House) while AIPAC works Capitol Hill (Alteras 1985; Rossinow 2018).

The Israel lobby also includes organizations promoting the improvement of the image of Israel without direct lobbying. Examples include the Israel Project and Stand with Us. Some think tanks, such as the Washington Institute for Near East Policy, the Saban Center for Middle East Policy and the Jewish Institute for National Security of America also qualify due to their focus on proscribing policies perceived as beneficial to Israel.

Evangelical organizations focused on Israel form another component. Christians United for Israel (CUFI) is the largest pro-Israeli group, numbering eight million members. CUFI aspires to be the "evangelical AIPAC" and are certainly as enthusiastically supportive as any Jewish group (Salleh and Zakariya 2012). However, they do not have the same sway on Capitol Hill. In addition, evangelical influence within the Republican Party has diminished for demographic reasons, and due to an intra-movement turn towards populism (Goldman 2018, 173–178). Though many supporters of Israel are not Jewish, the current influential core of the Israel lobby is overwhelmingly Jewish.

American Jews and the Israel Lobby

Due to its mainly Jewish character, the Israel lobby cannot function without taking its main constituency into account. This complicates its mission, as the attitude of American Jews towards Israel is complex. Many feel a kinship with their Israeli brethren worldwide, as Judaism has a strong sense of peoplehood alongside its religious aspects (Lederhendler 2017). However, the relationship with Israel is particularly significant. The existence of a prominently controversial state claiming to be the Jewish homeland in an area of immense religious and sentimental importance to its tradition has forced Jews to reckon with Israel as a component of their identity. In the view of many non-Jews, American Jews gradually became associated with Israel whether they liked it or not (Cohen 2003, Raider 1998). As a result, the pro-Israel community represents not only the perspective of the Israeli government but also the interests of American Jewry in navigating its own identity.

What are these interests from an American Jewish perspective? Israel often treats American Jews as a source of funds and influence over the American government. On the face of it, American Jews are more altruistic and sentimental in their approach to Israel as evinced by their generous contributions to Israel as well as their impressive record of philanthropy (Sasson 2014, 62–88). However, the well-being of the community is undermined by two significant anxieties and concerns. Attitudes towards Israel are best understood within the context of efforts to cope with them.

First, the threat of assimilation has long been a major concern for American Jews. In 1997, Alan Dershowitz wrote that "American Jews – as a people – have never been in greater danger of disappearing" (Dershowitz 1998, 1). The problem has exacerbated since. The communal birth rate stands below the replacement rate, while intermarriage rates rose from 13 per cent in the 1960s to 58 per cent in recent years. This trend is consequential, as most children of dual-religion parents do not self-identify as Jews (Stammer 2003). As a result, absolute numbers of Jews recently declined by 5 per cent, while the share in the population has fallen from close to 4 per cent in the 1950s to around 2 per cent at present (Pew 2013). Over time this may render the community less influential and more vulnerable.

This trend renders the second threat – that of antisemitism – all the more dangerous to the community. Although antisemitism has historically been a less pressing concern for American Jews than for their brethren elsewhere, it has nonetheless been a constant cause of anxiety. Early in the twentieth century American colleges and universities enforced quotas on the number of Jews admitted. Fatal incidents from the lynching of Leo Frank in 1913 to the Overland Park shooting of 2014 loom large. Recently, the salience of the problem increased, and today more hate crimes are committed against Jews than any other religious group (Fisher 2018). The 2018 attack on the Tree of Life synagogue in Pittsburgh was the deadliest antisemitic attack in United States history. Even before the spike in attacks, 94 per cent of American Jews reported concerns over the issue (Wexler 2007, 276). Antisemitism is a serious problem in America.

Zionism has at different times either played a role in exacerbating or alleviating these anxieties. In the early years of the Zionist movement, many American Jews kept their distance, as they did not wish to open themselves to charges of "dual loyalty." And with good reason: according to a poll taken in 1938, 60 per cent of Americans believed Jews were greedy, dishonest, untrustworthy and pushy (Cople 2002, 230). As many non-Jews already believed Jews did not have the best interests of America at heart, most members of the community did not want to exacerbate the problem by pledging allegiance to nationalist aspirations elsewhere. Therefore, before the foundation of Israel in 1948, most Jews were either non-Zionists or anti-Zionists (Cohen 2003; Raider 1998).

Even after the State of Israel was established, Jewish American attitudes towards it remained guarded and lukewarm. The United States government kept Israel at arm's length in order to maintain good relations with the Arab countries and contain Soviet influence in the Middle East (Little 1993). The Conference of Presidents and AIPAC were formed in the 1950s but faced backlash. In 1962, the Senate Committee on Foreign Relations launched an investigation into the American Zionist Council, which led to the dismantling of the organization (Lazarowitz 2011). The hostile atmosphere deterred open American Jewish support for Israel.

The Israeli victory in the 1967 Six-Day War was a watershed in solidifying American government support for Israel. This was matched by high levels of public support, lasting for decades (Bar Siman Tov 1998). The support for Israel proved robust enough to overcome several crises, most notably the Jonathan Pollard affair: suspicions of "dual loyalty" towards the community was reignited in 1985 when Pollard, a Jewish American intelligence officer was arrested and later convicted of spying for Israel. The storm passed and did not lead to deterioration of bilateral relations or long-term increase in antisemitism (Raviv and Melman 1994, 283–288). Americans remained widely and robustly supportive of Israel (Gallup 2020). Supporting Israel in the benign political environment helped American Jews cement an important role for the community as a vital link with a new strategic ally.

The 1967 War and its aftermath created the context in which Israel became an overwhelmingly positive element in Jewish American identity. Israeli victory helped engender pride in Jewish identity by countering the prevalent stereotype that they were physically weak and unathletic. As Judith Elizur put it,

> gentile praise caused a sea change in the self-image of many conflicted individuals, who until then had viewed their Jewishness negatively through the eyes of non-Jews. Now, sharing vicariously in the success of Israel enabled them to identify publicly as Jews for the first time in their lives.
>
> *(Elizur 2001, 21)*

As attendance in synagogues decreased, activities in Jewish institutions increasingly focused on Israel. It also increasingly served as an anchor for Jewish communal life. The Taglit-Birthright Israel initiative to fund guided trips to Israel for young diaspora Jews was designed to counter assimilation and has been remarkably successful in this regard (Saxe et al. 2011, 159). It is no coincidence that in this period, support for Israel was described as "the new civic religion for American Jews" (Woocher 1986).

The vast majority of American Jews still profess emotional attachment to Israel. In addition, there are more intercommunal ties than ever before on both the civil society and individual levels (Sasson 2014, 144–164). However, over the last ten years or so there has been a steady erosion in support for the policies of the State of Israel, particularly amongst young Jews. For example, only 25 per cent of Jews aged 18–29 believe that Israel is sincere in attempts to make peace with the Palestinians (Pew 2013). This is often explained through ideological differences. The most common explanation is American Jewish dissatisfaction with Israeli policies towards the Palestinians and the Reform and Conservative streams of Judaism (Beinart 2012, Rosenthal 2001).

These are significant concerns dividing the two communities, but they do not fully explain the change. Contrary to common wisdom, Israeli policy on both issues has improved somewhat (although clearly not as much as American Jews would like). Israel has always treated its Palestinian citizens abominably, subjecting them to martial law until 1966. Discrimination persists but has lessened somewhat (Degani 2014). Meanwhile, the occupation has persisted brutally since 1967 (Gazit 2003). However, one could argue that since the creation of the Palestinian Authority in 1994 and the Israeli withdrawal from Gaza in 2005, the occupation is less direct. In terms of religious tolerance, Israel has always given precedence to the ultra-orthodox rabbinate and repressed Jewish pluralism. Nevertheless, in the last few years, the Israeli Reform and Conservative streams have grown, and new avenues of more lenient conversion have gained acceptance (Waxman 2013). Performance in these metrics has certainly not deteriorated to an extent justifying significant readjustment of attitudes towards Israel.

Changes in attitudes towards Israel are instead rooted in cultural and political developments in the United States, particularly on the left. Traditionally, ethnic minority groups, including the Jews, supported the Democratic Party due to its focus on equality. In recent years a progressive version of liberalism stressing multicultural diversity and racial equality has gradually displaced the classical liberal ideology on the left-wing of the party (Fukuyama 2018, 97–99). The progressive worldview portrays weak and victimized groups as possessing virtue and those with power as morally corrupt. Due to the tragic racial history of the United States, Americans tend to associate this disparity of power and morality with differences in skin colour (Horwitz 2018).

In the imagination of many progressives, the Israeli form of ethnic democracy is currently associated with white supremacy. When Temple University professor and former CNN commentator Marc Lamont Hill stated that Zionism is "a white supremacist, ethno-nationalist project" he was speaking for many on the left (Bernstein 2019). In recent years Zionists have been shunned by organizers of progressive political events, such as the Dykes March and the Women's March (Weiss 2019, 84–130). In particular, this attitude has taken hold on many college campuses, where Zionism is often synonymous with racism and colonialism (Nelson 2018; Pessin and Ben-Atar 2018).

To make matters worse for left-wing American Jewish supporters of Israel, support for the Jewish state has become associated with the Republican Party. Former Prime Minister Benjamin Netanyahu's enmity towards the Obama Administration and support for then President Trump helped create a wedge between the Israeli government and the Democrats (Rynhold 2015, 31–57). In an atmosphere of increased polarization in American politics, this takes on a special significance. In the current climate, Americans increasingly manifest distaste verging on hatred for the political opposition (Iyengar and Westwood 2015; Rosenthal, Poole and McCarty 2016). It is not surprising therefore that 18 per cent of Democratic voters have a positive view of Netanyahu, as opposed to 65 per cent of Republicans (Saad 2019). While older Democrats still maintain high levels of support for Israel, for younger Democrats this often translates into lessened overall support. One poll found that Democrats under 34 favour the Palestinians over Israel by 11 points (Beinart 2018). From the perspective of many left-leaning American Jews, Israel is on the wrong side of a bitter partisan divide. These developments have rendered progressive circles inhospitable for supporters of Israel.

These changes have begun to affect the attitudes of the Democratic Party leadership. In previous cycles, Democratic presidential nomination candidates fell over themselves making statements supportive of Israel. However, candidates for the 2020 nomination acted quite differently. Some have raised the possibility of withholding military aid to Israel, while both Bernie Sanders and Beto O'Rourke called Netanyahu a racist. In addition, most candidates avoided attending the annual AIPAC conference (Siddiqui 2019). In the House, at least two recently elected Representatives support the movement to Boycott, Divest and Sanction (BDS) Israel (Olesker 2019). While there is no lack of traditional supporters of Israel in the Democratic Party, the tide is notably shifting.

The polarization of American politics is poison to the mission of middle-of-the-road pro-Israeli organizations. AIPAC defines itself as "America's bipartisan pro-Israel lobby" and has always acted to promote strong relations with both parties (AIPAC n.d.a). However, left-leaning Jews are veering away from AIPAC, which they associate with the Likud and the Republican Party and are moving towards J-Street. Further left, there is a proliferation of non-Zionist and anti-Zionist groups, such as IfNotNow and Jewish Voice for Peace. Meanwhile, right-leaning groups, such as the ZOA, have supported the Trump Administration and annexationist policies unacceptable to most American Jews. In an effort to maintain strong ties with the Jewish community and both major parties, AIPAC is likely to avoid unduly controversial stands on Palestinian issues. The prospects of a strong united Israel lobby influencing the peace process seems unlikely if trends of polarization in American politics continue apace.

The Israel Lobby and the Israeli-Palestinian Conflict

The United States has been half-hearted in its efforts to end the Israeli occupation. Various administrations insisted that the settlements are detrimental to the peace process and declared support in principle for an independent Palestinian state. However, in practice, the United States has mostly refrained from pressuring Israel into making concessions. As a result, the American government has been accused of acting as "Israel's lawyer" (Hammond 2016; Khalidi 2014).

The Trump Administration has gone further than most in tilting towards the Israeli position by recognizing Jerusalem as its capital and its annexation of the Golan Heights. In addition, Trump has taken anti-Palestinian measures, such as cutting funding to the United Nations Relief and Works Agency (UNRWA) and closing the Palestine Liberation Organization (PLO) office in Washington, DC. However, even the Obama Administration, which was considered quite sympathetic to the Palestinian cause, worked to suppress its nationalist aspirations. For example, after a two-and-a-half-year halt in talks, the Palestinian Authority attempted to gain unilateral recognition of a Palestinian state in the United Nations. Despite no progress being made in talks, the ostensibly even-handed Obama Administration vetoed the resolution on the pretext that progress could only be made through negotiations. (Cooper 2011; Siniver 2011). The context and reasons change, but the United States has consistently enabled continued Israeli occupation.

The biased American position is undoubtedly encouraged by the Israel lobby. AIPAC and other pro-Israeli groups supported the erection of an illegal wall in the West Bank and have consistently opposed the Israeli refusal to divide Jerusalem (Mearsheimer and Walt 2007, 204–228; Seliktar 2002, 87–118). These are just some of the countless examples of the Israel lobby encouraging the American adoption of Israeli positions antithetical to Palestinian interests. Throughout this process, AIPAC and other groups have encouraged donors to fund the campaigns of candidates supporting these positions (Mansour 1994, 237–285; Mearsheimer and Walt 2007, 151–167).

However, when various administrations have turned against the Israeli occupation and the policies involved, the Israel lobby has been hesitant to confront the White House too strenuously. This is due to a long-standing lack of consensus amongst their prime constituency. In the first decade or so of the settlement enterprise, most American Jews supported the settlements for their ostensible security role (Harris Poll 1978). However, under successive Likud governments, the purpose of the settlements shifted from security to the suppression of Palestinian nationalism (Peleg 1987, 95–142; Sandler 1993). Doubts arose and, since the 1990s, a plurality of American Jews have consistently supported the removal of most settlements (American Jewish Committee 2020). By 2013 a mere 17 per cent of American Jews believed the continued construction of settlements furthered Israeli security, while 44 per cent believed they were detrimental to it (Pew 2013). Accordingly, the Israel lobby cannot support Israel whole-heartedly on settlement construction.

American Jewish attitudes towards Palestinian self-determination similarly have evolved. Palestinian statehood was opposed for decades, due to a belief that the PLO was a terrorist organization posing serious security risks to Israel (American Jewish Committee 2020). A 1980 Harris poll found that 49 per cent of American Jews supported Palestinian statehood, while 36 per cent opposed it. However, only 6 per cent approved of a state run by the PLO (Seliktar 2002, 62). When the PLO renounced terrorism and recognized the State of Israel in 1988, the attitudes of many American Jews shifted. Since then, a majority or plurality of the community have supported a PLO-controlled Palestinian state (American Jewish Committee 2020).

Though disagreements persist, the pro-Israeli community's stance on Palestinian statehood shifted accordingly. For the last two decades, AIPAC has supported a demilitarized Palestinian state (AIPAC n.d.b). Meanwhile, J-Street was created in 2008 in order to support a two-state solution. The ZOA persists in its opposition, insisting a Palestinian state would be a "Jew-hating base of terrorist operations for Iran" (ZOA 2018). However, it is fair to say that the American Jewish community and the Israel lobby generally support a Palestinian state despite ongoing disagreements over the terms. Previous opposition and current apprehensions over Palestinian statehood in the pro-Israeli community mostly stem from genuine (though possibly misguided) concerns over Israeli security.

With this in mind, it is not surprising that the few attempts made by the Israel lobby to confront an administration on the settlements and Palestinian issues ended in abject failure. For example, when the George H.W. Bush administration organized the first official face-to-face Israeli-Palestinian negotiations in the Madrid Conference in 1991, they were concerned that continued Israeli settlement construction would undermine talks. To prevent this, the White House conditioned a $10 billion loan guarantee – that Israel required to settle Jewish immigrants from the Soviet Union – on a settlement freeze in the occupied territories (AP 1991). The Bush Administration framed the settlements as an impediment to a peace process crucial to the national interest. AIPAC tried to mobilize pro-Israeli senators to pass a bill providing the loan guarantees (AIPAC 1991), but American public opinion supported the freeze and the administration's position. Ultimately, AIPAC and the pro-Israeli senators who sponsored the bill backed down. As columnist Thomas Friedman put it, "the Bush Administration had trounced Israel and its Congressional supporters (Friedman 1991)." The guarantees were not provided until the hard-line Likud lost to Labour at the 1992 general elections. In a post-mortem of the failure to block the move, AIPAC lamented that it could not take a strong position since "our community is split on settlements; therefore, it is impossible for us to take a position either way" (Bard 1991a).

The Israel Lobby and Israeli-Palestinian Negotiations

Considering the difficulty the American pro-Israel community has in taking strong positions on the Israeli-Palestinian conflict, what role does it have in negotiations? The truth is, the pro-Israel community has had little opportunity to influence directly the Israeli-Palestinian peace process. Most peace initiatives between the sides were stillborn or faltered quickly. The Oslo Process was a remarkable exception. It resulted in several important agreements, significantly altering the status quo in the occupied territories. Therefore, it was far and away the most promising and successful period of Israeli-Palestinian negotiations (Behrendt 2007; Ross 2004; Savir 1999).

The Oslo Process is particularly useful for examining the limits of the influence of the Israel lobby. During this period the lobby was at the peak of its influence. AIPAC had already cemented its fearsome reputation and, during this period, was considered to be "unquestionably the premier ethnically based foreign policy lobby in Washington" (Dumbrell 2009, 150). The Oslo process also predated the split within the ranks of the Israel lobby, signalled by the rise of J-Street (Thomas 2007, 18–40; Waxman 2010). Considering the power of the pro-Israeli community at that time and the importance of the negotiations taking place, it is the best case for examining the limits of its influence on an active peace process with a significant chance of success.

What is most notable about the engagement of the Israel lobby in the Oslo process is how often it sat on the sidelines. Talks were launched through an Israeli-Palestinian initiative launched without direct American involvement. As the Clinton Administration increased its involvement, they rarely disagreed substantively with the Israeli negotiation position (Dumbrell 2009, 149). Preferring to deal directly with the friendly Clinton Administration, Prime Minister Yitzhak Rabin and Foreign Minister (and later interim prime minister) Shimon Peres bypassed AIPAC and other lobby groups as intermediaries (Rynhold 1997, 111–132). With nothing to oppose, the AIPAC leadership declared it "will support this and support this enthusiastically because it's been arrived at by the Israelis of their own volition" (Niebuhr 1993). ZOA and other right-wing organizations opposed the process, but with limited success. As a *Washington Post* report put it, "the harshest attacks came from newly formed groups with letterheads and advertising budgets and little else" (Gellman 1996). For the most part, the mainstream pro-Israeli community did not try to substantially influence negotiation positions.

The role of the Israel lobby in the peace process changed in 1996, when Netanyahu was elected prime minister. The Israeli strategy shifted from initiating progress in the peace process to taking an uncooperatively reactive stance. Following partial withdrawal from Hebron in January 1997, talks stalled over the depth of further Israeli redeployment (FRD) required in the Oslo II agreement. The new Israeli government was unwilling to withdraw from more than 2.7 per cent of the West Bank and the Clinton Administration believed this was a non-starter (Freedman 1999, 57). The severe disagreement that followed placed the pro-Israeli community in the position of being asked to defend Israeli positions at odds with the White House.

Netanyahu had natural allies in this endeavour due to his strong working relations with the Republican Party and evangelical right (Caspit 2017, 12). The prime minister attempted to use his ties to undercut the Clinton Administration, alienating them in the process. Secretary of State Madeline Albright recalled in her memoirs that Netanyahu's meeting with Reverend Jerry Falwell, who had spread a video implicating Clinton in murder, was seen as a "direct slap in the face of the President" (Albright 2013, 299). This put the pro-Israeli community in the awkward position of being forced to pick sides between the administration and the party controlling both chambers of Congress.

Tensions came to the fore in mid-1998, when Albright suggested a 13 per cent withdrawal, which Palestinian leader Yasser Arafat accepted and Netanyahu turned down. Clinton threatened that if the terms were not accepted "we will have to reexamine our approach to the peace process" (Gellman 1998a). This placed Netanyahu in a bind. He feared the Israeli right-wing would bring him down if he acquiesced. However, he was equally concerned that the United States would blame him if talks faltered, threatening his popularity with centrist voters. Dennis Ross recalls in his memoir that Netanyahu uncharacteristically yelled at him, "this borders on the absurd … you will break my coalition … you cooked a deal with them" (Ross 2004, 391).

The prime minister did his best to rally the "Israel lobby" to support him. Netanyahu sent foreign policy adviser Dore Gold to strategize with the Conference of the Presidents. Following the meeting, Conference vice-chairman Malcolm Hoenlein warned, "when it comes to second guessing Israel on security, you cross a very delicate line, and I think the administration understands that" (Gellman 1998b). Representatives of the major Jewish organizations held several conversations with Albright and urged her to cease the pressure (Lippman 1998a). AIPAC and the Israeli embassy in Washington began to work their magic on Capitol Hill. They helped craft two letters, one signed by 150 members of the House and a second signed by 81 Senators, supporting the right of the Israeli government to determine its own security policy (Erlanger 1998). Republican Speaker of the House Newt Gingrich went one step further and declared "as Israel celebrates its 50th anniversary, the Clinton administration says, 'Happy birthday. Let us blackmail you on behalf of Arafat.'" (Lippman 1998b). The "Israel lobby" managed to put significant pressure on the Clinton Administration to avoid presenting Israel with an ultimatum.

This worked in terms of removing the immediate threat. Clinton wrote to the Conference of Presidents that "at no time have I given an ultimatum to either party" (Gellman 1998a). However, the position that Israel should withdraw from 13 per cent of the territory was maintained. In order to settle the issue out of the public eye, talks over the next FRD were finally scheduled to convene at Wye Plantation in October 1998 (Ross 2004, 401–402). The American delegation to Wye intended to obtain concessions through private negotiations rather than public decelerations.

Netanyahu had every reason to be optimistic, having won the public spat preceding negotiations. Clinton was in a tough spot politically as, two weeks earlier, the House voted to commence impeachment proceedings over his conduct in the Monica Lewinsky affair (Rudalevige 2016). With the mid-term elections in the United States just days away, Netanyahu hoped to strengthen his negotiating position by keeping in close contact with the pro-Israel community throughout the negotiations (Gellman 1998c).

None of this mattered in determining the outcome. Arafat and Clinton agreed Israel should withdraw from 13.1 per cent of the territory and release 750 Palestinian prisoners, and the pressure was on Netanyahu to acquiesce. After several days of contentious talks the Israeli delegation agreed, in exchange for security assurances from the PA and the elimination of the articles in the Palestine National Charter calling for Israel's destruction. Netanyahu also demanded the release of Jonathan Pollard in order to save face (Freedman 1999, 60). The other terms were granted, but Clinton was unwilling to release the spy.

Netanyahu asked for support from the pro-Israel community and his Congressional allies, but to no avail. AIPAC and the Conference of Presidents were hesitant to get involved (Freedman 1999, 60; Ross 2004, 457). Congressional Republican leaders took a stand against the demand, warning that if Pollard were released "he would resume his treacherous conduct" (Risen 1998). The prime minister was forced to agree to the 13 per cent withdrawal without receiving political cover. In his autobiography, Clinton noted that Netanyahu "had gone beyond his political safety zone at Wye River and his future was uncertain" (Clinton 2004, 833). Indeed, the withdrawal agreement ultimately led to the collapse of his right-wing government (Lochery 2000, 232–233). The Netanyahu government's attempt to create leverage through the support of the Israel lobby during the actual negotiations was ultimately unsuccessful.

After Netanyahu lost the 1999 elections, the Clinton Administration enjoyed a closer relationship with his successor, the Labour leader Ehud Barak. The new Israeli government was motivated to conduct negotiations on a resolution to the conflict and generally agreed with the United States on the scope of concessions to be made (Clinton 2004, 591–598; Ross 2004,

495–758). The mainstream Israel lobby generally did not try to alter the negotiation position of the Clinton Administration and left that to the groups on the right and left-wing fringes. While the collapse of the Oslo process has been blamed on all parties to the negotiation, the Israel lobby has been notably absent from that conversation (Aronoff 2009).

The role of the mainstream Israel lobby in the Oslo process was peripheral. When the Israeli government was a willing partner in negotiations, it was relegated to the sidelines and did not wish to interfere in a process that strengthened the bilateral relationship. When the Israeli government was reluctant to cooperate, the pro-Israel community opposed what it felt was excessive pressure on security issues. However, they avoided fully supporting the Israeli territorial position and could not prevent Israel from acquiescing to American demands in negotiations. Even Clinton's rivals on Capitol Hill did not support the more exorbitant Israeli demands. In fact, it could be argued that the Israeli government fared better in negotiations when it shut the Israel lobby out of negotiations and worked directly and openly with the Clinton Administration.

There is little evidence that the pro-Israel community has ever been instrumental in derailing a promising peace process. It has difficulty taking a stand on issues at the centre of the conflict, since its constituents disagree fiercely on the issues. Even when it has taken a stand, it has run into difficulty. It is easier to lobby the legislature than the executive, since there is more competition for the attention of the White House, which is more selective in terms of access. The White House is also less responsive to concentrated regional and special interests (Cole 2000, 285–291). However, peace initiatives are run by the executive, and the legislature enjoys only a peripheral role in funding them. Aside from this difficulty, there are also higher political costs to confronting the White House. Peace initiatives are often flagship administration initiatives and opposing them can sabotage the goal of promoting robust bilateral relations. For these reasons, there is little evidence of the lobby perceptibly altering American diplomacy (Bard 1991b; Thomas 2007).

This is not to say that the "Israel lobby" has no influence on the peace process. The pro-Israel community has had a strong influence on the discourse surrounding the conflict. One method defenders of Israel have used traditionally is to accuse critics of Israel of anti-Semitism. The fear of backlash leads to self-censorship amongst American politicians. This can inhibit policymakers from voicing opinions and taking initiatives they fear will displease the Israel lobby (Findley 1985; Mearsheimer and Walt 2007, 168–198). This certainly provides Israel with a degree of leeway in its occupation policies. Influence on the discourse influences policy in an amorphous yet important way. However, it is not tantamount to control over American policy towards the conflict.

Where the Israel lobby does enjoy immense success, is in the facilitation of military aid to Israel. It is more effective at this for two reasons. First, it enjoys firm bipartisan support in the pro-Israeli community. Even the dovish J-Street believes that "maintaining Israel's qualitative military edge is an important anchor for a peace process based on providing Israel with the confidence and assurance to move forward" (J-Street, n.d.). Second, it can be achieved by lobbying the more accessible legislature, which has the power of the purse. The argument that the Israel lobby has an outsized influence on policy derives to a great extent from its success in obtaining aid (Thomas 2007).

Conclusion

The Israel lobby has often been unhelpful to the peace process and protected Israel from pressure, particularly by wielding a chilling influence on the discourse and by shielding Israel from the discontinuation of military aid. However, the focus in some literature on the pro-Israel community as the central cause of failure in the Israeli-Palestinian peace process is flawed. This explanation does not take into account that the pro-Israel community has often avoided taking a strong unified stand and, when it has, it has often failed to substantially influence peace initiatives.

The Israeli government has been unserious in its approach to the peace process for quite some time, and the occupation of the West Bank seems disturbingly permanent. However, the pro-Israeli community is not the most significant cause of this. The majority of the Jewish community and the wider American public are disturbed by the uncomfortable reality on the ground. Therefore, the pro-Israeli community (from AIPAC and leftwards) will continue to avoid supporting Israel fully in its continued construction of settlements and the denial of Palestinian self-determination. As the case of the Oslo process indicates, in the event of a serious peace process that takes Israeli security concerns into account, the Israel lobby is unlikely to scuttle progress.

While the potential influence of the Israel lobby on the peace process has never been decisive, it is likely to be even less significant in the future. Political polarization has weakened the pro-Israel community by facilitating a split into competing factions, reducing its cohesion. It has also placed the centrist faction in an existential dilemma. Due to the sharp partisan divide, left-leaning American Jews are unwilling to support the policies of right-wing Israeli governments. This means AIPAC and the Conference of Presidents face a choice between opposing Israeli expansionism or risking losing the support of the majority of their constituency, replacing it with a less influential coalition of Orthodox Jews and Christian evangelicals. These developments have weakened the effectiveness of the Israel lobby in recent years.

The likely role of the pro-Israeli community in scuttling a future deal pales in comparison to the regional obstacles it faces. Israel is trending to the right. The Palestinians do not have a unified and legitimate government. There is more support than ever in both Palestine and the United States for a one-state solution rather than a two-state solution (PCPSR 2019; Telhami and Rouse 2018). In the meantime, serious American mediation seems like a far-fetched proposition, as it has lost the trust of the Palestinian side as a mediator and, in the longer term, its regional influence appears to be steadily eroding (Pillar 2019). It is unclear when there will be another serious peace process and, if one emerges, whether the United States will be able to play its traditional role of mediator.

The Israel lobby never held decisive influence over Israeli occupation policies or the peace process. If current trends in the American Jewish community continue, the leverage of AIPAC and other organizations will be further undercut. However, the good news – and the bad news – is that ultimately the outcome will continue to depend on the capabilities and political will of Israelis and Palestinians.

Recommended Readings

Hixson, W. 2019. *Israel's Armor: The Israel Lobby and the First Generation of the Palestine Conflict*. Cambridge: Cambridge University Press.

Lieberman, R. 2009. "The 'Israel Lobby' and American Politics." *Perspectives on Politics* 7:2, 235–257.

Mearsheimer, J., and S. Walt. 2007. *The Israel Lobby and U.S. Foreign Policy*. New York: Farrar, Straus and Giroux.

Rynhold, R. 2010. "Is the Pro-Israel Lobby a Block on Reaching a Comprehensive Peace Settlement in the Middle East?" *Israel Studies Forum* 25:1, 29–49.

Thomas, M. 2007. *American Policy Toward Israel: The Power and Limits of Beliefs*. London: Routledge.

Questions for Discussion

(1) What is the correct amount of influence for lobbyists in a democratic country? If the role of the Israel lobby exceeds this, what reforms should be made to the United States political system and how would they influence the ability of different sectors to be a part of the conversation?
(2) The Israel lobby has been accused of having great influence on the discourse on the Israeli-Palestinian conflict and silencing critics. How important is the content of the discourse in shaping American foreign policy towards the conflict?
(3) How will the polarization in American politics influence the role of the Israel lobby? Is polarization a long-term or short-term trend? What sort of influence will this have on American policy in the region?
(4) There is an argument that if the Israel lobby did not exist, Israel would be forced into making concessions to the Palestinians, such as ending the occupation and ceasing settlement construction. Can the parties be forced to the negotiation table, or for negotiations to succeed, do the sides need to arrive of their own volition?
(5) There are a number of reasons the Israeli-Palestinian conflict has yet to be resolved. How important is the Israel lobby in comparison to other factors? If other factors were resolved would the pro-Israel community remain a serious obstacle?

References

Albright, M. 2013. *Madam Secretary: A Memoir.* New York: Harper.

Alteras, I. 1985. "Eisenhower, American Jewry, and Israel." *American Jewish Archives Journal* 37:2, 258–274.

AIPAC. 1991. *Near East Report*, Vol. 35, no. 38. 23 September.

AIPAC. N. d.a. "Our Mission." Available at: www.aipac.org/about/mission.

AIPAC. N. d.b. "Peace Process." Available at: www.aipac.org/learn/issues/issue-display/the-peace-process.

American Jewish Committee. 2020. "Annual Polls." *Jewish Virtual Library.* Available at: www.jewishvirtuallibrary.org/american-jewish-opinion-polls.

Aridan, N. 2017. *Advocating for Israel: Diplomats and Lobbyists from Truman to Nixon.* Lanham, MD: Lexington.

Aronoff, M. 2009. "Camp David Rashomon: Contested Interpretations of the Israel/Palestine Peace Process." *Political Science Quarterly* 124:1, 143–167.

Associated Press. 1991. "Excerpts from President Bush's News Session on Israeli Loan Guarantees." *New York Times*, 13 September, A10.

Bard, M. 1991a. "The Settlement Maelstrom." *Near East Report* 35:41, 4–5.

Bard, M. 1991b. *The Water's Edge and Beyond: Defining the Limits to Domestic Influence on United States Middle East Policy.* New Brunswick, NJ: Transaction.

Bar Siman Tov, Y. 1998. "The United States and Israel since 1948: A "Special Relationship?" *Diplomatic History* 22:2, 231–262.

Behrendt, S. 2007. *The Secret Israeli-Palestinian Negotiations in Oslo: Their Success and Why the Process Ultimately Failed.* New York: Routledge.

Beinart, P. 2012. *The Crisis of Zionism.* New York: Times Books.

Beinart, P. 2018. "Rashida Tlaib and Her 'Squad' of Israel Critics Own the Future." *The Forward*, 5 December. Available at: https://forward.com/opinion/415482/rashida-tlaib-and-her-squad-of-israel-critics-have-the-future-on-their/.

Ben-Ephraim, S. 2020. "Therefore They Shouldn't Exist': The Carter Administration, the 'Israel Lobby' and the Sinai Settlements." *International History Review* 42:1, 1–18.

Bernstein, J. 2019. "Netroots Panel Equates Zionism and White Supremacy." *Pittsburgh Jewish Chronicle*, 17 July. Available at: https://jewishchronicle.timesofisrael.com/netroots-panel-equates-zionism-and-white-supremacy/.

Caspit, B. 2017. *The Netanyahu Years.* New York: St. Martins Press.

Clark, V. 2007. *Allies for Armageddon: The Rise of Christian Zionism.* New Haven, CT: Yale University Press.

Clinton, B. 2004. *My Life.* New York: Knopf.

Cohen, N. 2003. *Americanization of Zionism, 1897–1948.* Hanover, NH: University Press of New England.

Cole, N. S. 2000. "Pursuing the President: White House Access and Organized Interests." *The Social Science Journal* 37:2, 285–291.

Cooper, H. 2011. "Obama Says Palestinians Are Using Wrong Forum." *New York Times*, 21 September. Available at: www.nytimes.com/2011/09/22/world/obama-united-nations-speech.html.

Cople, J. F. 2002. *The Jews and the Nation: Revolution, Emancipation, State Formation, and the Liberal Paradigm in America and France*. Princeton, NJ: Princeton University Press.

Curtiss, R. 1990. *Stealth Pacs: How Israel's American Lobby Took Control of U.S. Middle East Policy*. Washington, DC: American Educational Trust.

Degani, A. 2014. "The Decline and Fall of the Israeli Military Government, 1948–1966: a Case of Settler-Colonial Consolidation?" *Settler Colonial Studies* 5:1, 84–99.

Dershowitz, A. 1998. *The Vanishing American Jew: In Search of Jewish Identity for the Next Century*. New York: Simon and Schuster.

Divine, D. R. 2010. "The Israel Lobby: Mantra Versus Analysis." *Israel Studies Forum* 25:1, 50–56.

Dumbrell, J. 2009. *Clinton's Foreign Policy: Between the Bushes 1992–2000*. London: Routledge.

Elizur, J. 2001. "The Fracturing of the Jewish Self-image: The End of 'We are one?'" *Israel Affairs* 8:1–2, 14–30.

Erlanger, S. 1998. "Jewish Groups Go to Capitol Squabbling Among Themselves." *New York Times*, 7 April, A15.

Feingold, R. 2008. *Jewish Power in America: Myth and Reality*. London: Transaction.

Findley, P. 1985. *They Dare to Speak Out: People and Institutions Confront Israel's Lobby*. Chicago: Lawrence Hill.

Fisher, A. 2018. "NYC Hate Crimes Target Jews More than Other Groups Combined in 2018." *The Forward*, 27 December. Available at: https://forward.com/fast-forward/416681/nyc-hate-crimes-target-jews-more-than-other-groups-combined-in-2018/.

Fishman, B. 2008. "The 'Israel Lobby': A Realistic Assessment." *Orbis* 52:1, 159–180.

Fitzgerald, F. 2017. *The Evangelicals: The Struggle to Shape America*. New York: Simon & Schuster.

Foxman, A. 2007. *The Deadliest Lies: The Israel Lobby and the Myth of Jewish Control*. New York: Palgrave Macmillan.

Freedman, R. 1999. "U.S. Policy Toward the Middle East in Clinton's Second Term." *Middle East Review of International Affairs* 3:1, 55–79.

Friedman, T. 1991. "Bush Makes Aid to Israel Subject to Conditions." *New York Times*, 6 October 6, A3.

Fukuyama, F. 2018. "Against Identity Politics: The New Tribalism and the Crisis of Democracy." *Foreign Affairs* 97:5, 90–115.

Ganin, Z. 2005. *An Uneasy Relationship: American Jewish Leadership and Israel, 1948–1957*. Syracuse, NY: Syracuse University Press.

Gallup. 2020. Gallup in Depth, "Middle East." January. Available at: https://news.gallup.com/poll/1639/Middle-East.aspx.

Gazit, S. 2003. *Trapped Fools: Thirty Years of Israeli Policy in the Territories*. London: Routledge.

Gellman, B. 1996. "At the Crossroads." *The Washington Post*, 26 May, W15.

Gellman, B. 1998a. "Clinton Asks Albright to Meet with Netanyahu." *The Washington Post*, 12 May, A14.

Gellman, B. 1998b. "U.S. Gives Israel a Deadline; Summit Invitation Is Keyed to Acceptance of Peace Proposal." *The Washington Post*, 6 May, A01.

Gellman, B. 1998c. "U.S. Barely Averts Walkout by Israel." *The Washington Post*, 22 October, A01.

Goldberg, J. 2005. "Real Insiders: A pro-Israel Lobby and an F.B.I. Sting." *New Yorker*. 26 June. Available at: www.newyorker.com/magazine/2005/07/04/real-insiders.

Goldman, S. 2018. *God's Country: Christian Zionism in America*. Philadelphia: University of Pennsylvania Press.

Hammond, J. 2016. *Obstacle to Peace: The US Role in the Israeli-Palestinian Conflict*. Cross Village, MI: Worldview Publications.

Harris Poll. 1978. *Israeli State Archives*, 6727–9/FM. 29 March.

Hasian, M. 1997. "Understanding the Power of Conspiratorial Rhetoric: A Case Study of *the Protocols of the Elders of Zion*." *Journal of Communication Studies* 48:3, 195–214.

Hixson, W. 2019. *Israel's Armor: The Israel Lobby and the First Generation of the Palestine Conflict*. Cambridge: Cambridge University Press.

Horwitz, R. 2018. "Politics as Victimhood, Victimhood as Politics." *Journal of Policy History* 30:3, 552–574.

Iyengar, S., and S. J. Westwood. 2015. "Fear and Loathing Across Party Lines: New Evidence on Group Polarization." *American Journal of Political Science* 59:3, 690–707.

J-Street. N. d. "Us-Israel Special Relationship & Security Aid." Available at: https://jstreet.org/policy/us-israel-special-relationship-security-aid/#.W76GLWhKi00.

Jackson, G. 2015. "The Showdown That Wasn't: U.S.-Israeli Relations and American Domestic Politics, 1973–75." *International Security* 39:4, 130–169.

Kaplan, A. 2018. *Our American Israel: The Story of an Entangled Alliance*. Cambridge, MA: Harvard University Press.

Khalidi, R. 2014. *Brokers of Deceit: How the U.S. Has Undermined Peace in the Middle East.* Boston: Beacon Press.
Laqueur, W. 2006. *The Changing Face of Anti-Semitism: From Ancient Times to the Present Day*. Oxford: Oxford University Press.
Lazarowitz, A. 2011. "A Southern Senator and Israel: J. William Fulbright's Accusations of Undue Jewish Influence over American Foreign Policy in the Middle East." *Journal of Southern Jewish History* 14, 112–136.
Lazarowitz, A. 2014. "American Jewish Leaders and President Gerald R. Ford: Disagreements Over the Middle East Reassessment Plan." *American Jewish History* 98:3, 175–200.
Lederhendler, E. 2017. *American Jewry: A New History*. Cambridge: Cambridge University Press.
Lieberman, R. 2009. "The "Israel Lobby" and American Politics." *Perspectives on Politics* 7:2, 235–257.
Lippman, T. 1998a. "Clinton Pressure on Israel Attacked." *The Washington Post*, 7 May, A01.
Lippman, T. 1998b. "Israel Urged to Accept U.S. Terms; Albright Calls Effort on Talks Balanced." *Washington Post*, 13 May, A19.
Little, D. 1993. "The Making of a Special Relationship: The United States and Israel, 1957–68." *International Journal of Middle East Studies* 25:4, 563–585.
Little, D. 2008. "David or Goliath? The Israel Lobby and Its Critics." *Political Science Quarterly* 123:1, 151–156.
Lochery, N. 2000. "The Netanyahu Era: From Crisis to Crisis, 1996–99." *Israel Affairs* 6:3–4, 221–237.
Mansour, C. 1994. *Beyond Alliance: Israel in US Foreign Policy.* New York: Columbia University Press.
Mearsheimer, J., and S. Walt. 2006. "The Israel Lobby." *London Review of Books* 28:6, 23 March. Available at: www.lrb.co.uk/the-paper/v28/n06.
Mearsheimer, J., and S. Walt. 2007. *The Israel Lobby and U.S. Foreign Policy*. New York: Farrar, Straus and Giroux.
Nelson, C. 2018. *Israel Denial: Anti-Zionism, Anti-Semitism, and the Faculty Campaign Against the Jewish State*. Bloomington, IN: Indiana University Press.
Niebuhr, G. 1993. "American Jewish Groups Generally Hail Agreement; Arabs, Muslims in U.S. Are More Cautious." *Washington Post*, 1 September, A28.
Olesker, R. 2019. "Delegitimization as a National Security Threat." *Israel Studies Review* 34:2, 33–54.
PCPSR. 2019. "Public Opinion Poll No (71) Press-Release. Available at: http://pcpsr.org/en/node/747.
Peleg, I. 1987. *Begin's Foreign Policy 1977–1983: Israel's Move to the Right.* New York: Greenwood Press.
Pessin, A., and D. Ben-Atar, eds. 2018. *Anti-Zionism on Campus: The University, Free Speech, and BDS.* Bloomington, IN: Indiana University Press.
Pew. 2013. "A Portrait of Jewish Americans." 1 October. Available at: www.pewforum.org/2013/10/01/jewish-american-beliefs-attitudes-culture-survey/.
Pillar, P. 2019. "The Kushner Plan: Keeping Israeli-Palestinian Peace Out of Reach." *Journal of Palestine Studies* 48:4, 113–120.
Raider, M. 1998. *The Emergence of American Zionism*. New York: NYU Press.
Raviv, D., and Y. Melman. 1994. *Friends in Deed: Inside the U.S.-Israel Alliance*. New York: Hyperion.
Risen, J. 1998. "G.O.P. Leaders in Congress Oppose Letting Pollard Go Free." *New York Times*, 28 October, A14.
Rosenthal, S. 2001. *Irreconcilable Differences?: The Waning of the American Jewish Love Affair with Israel.* Waltham, MA: Brandeis University Press.
Rosenthal, H., K. Poole, and N. McCarty. 2016. *Polarized America: The Dance of Ideology and Unequal Riches*. Cambridge, MA: MIT Press.
Ross, D. 2004. *The Missing Peace: The Inside Story of the Fight for Middle East Peace*. New York: Farrar, Straus and Giroux.
Rossinow, D. 2018. "The Edge of the Abyss": The Origins of the Israel Lobby, 1949–1954." *Modern American History* 1:1, 23–43.
Rubenberg, C. 1986. *Israel and the American National Interest*. Urbana, IL: University of Illinois Press.
Rudalevige, A. 2016. "The Broken Places: The Clinton Impeachment and American Politics," in *42: Inside the Presidency of Bill Clinton*, eds. M. Nelson, et al. eds., Ithaca, NY: Cornell University Press, 123–151.
Rynhold, J. 1997. "Realism, Liberalism, and the Collapse of the Oslo Process: Inherently Flawed or Flawed Implementation?» in *The Failure of the Middle East Peace Process?*, ed. G. Ben-Porat. London: Palgrave Macmillan, 111–132.
Rynhold, J. 2010. "Is the Pro-Israel Lobby a Block on Reaching a Comprehensive Peace Settlement in the Middle East?" *Israel Studies Forum* 25:1, 29–49.

Rynhold, J. 2015. *The Arab-Israeli Conflict in American Political Culture*. New York: Cambridge University Press.

Saad, L. 2019. "Americans, but Not Liberal Democrats, Mostly Pro-Israel." *Gallup*. 6 March. Available at: https://news.gallup.com/poll/247376/americans-not-liberal-democrats-mostly-pro-israel.aspx.

Salleh, M. A., and H. Zakariya. 2012. "The American Evangelical Christians and the U.S. Middle East policy: a Case Study of the Christians United for Israel (CUFI)." *Intellectual Discourse* 20:2, 139–163.

Sandler, S. 1993. *The State of Israel, The Land of Israel: The Statist and Ethnonational Dimensions of Foreign Policy*. London: Praeger.

Sasson, T. 2014. *The New American Zionism*. New York: NYU Press.

Savir, U. 1999. *The Process: 1,100 Days that Changed the Middle East*. New York: Vintage.

Saxe, L., et al. 2011. "Intermarriage: The Impact and Lessons of Taglit-Birthright Israel." *Contemporary Jewry* 31:2, 151–172.

Seliktar, O. 2002. *Divided We Stand: American Jews, Israel, and the Peace Process*. Westport, CT: Praeger.

Siddiqui, S. 2019. "Democratic Candidates Debate Using Aid to Israel as Leverage in Policy Disputes." *Wall Street Journal*. 31 October. Available at: www.wsj.com/articles/democratic-candidates-debate-using-aid-to-israel-as-leverage-in-policy-disputes-11572519601.

Siniver, A. 2011. "Change Nobody Believes In: Obama and the Israeli–Palestinian Conflict." *Diplomacy & Statecraft* 22:4, 678–695.

Stammer, L. 2003. "American Jews See Population, Birthrate Drop." *Los Angeles Times*. 11 September. Available at: http://articles(.latimes.com/2003/sep/11/nation/na-jews11.

Stein, K. 1999. *Heroic Diplomacy: Sadat, Kissinger, Carter, Begin and the Quest for Arab-Israeli Peace*. New York: Routledge.

Stephens, E. 2006. *US Policy Towards Israel: The Role of Political Culture in Defining the "Special Relationship."* Brighton: Sussex Academic Press.

Telhami, S., and S. Rouse. 2018. "American Views of the Israeli-Palestinian Conflict." *Critical Issues Poll – University of Maryland*. Available at: https://sadat.umd.edu/sites/sadat.umd.edu/files/UMCIP%20Questionnaire%20Sep%20to%20Oct%202018.pdf.

Thomas, M. 2007. *American Policy Toward Israel: The Power and Limits of Beliefs*. London: Routledge.

Tivnan, E. 1987. *The Lobby: Jewish Political Power and American Foreign Policy*. New York: Touchstone Books.

Wald, K. 2015. "The Choosing People: Interpreting the Puzzling Politics of American Jewry." *Politics and Religion* 8:1, 4–35.

Waxman, C. 2013. "Multiculturalism, Conversion, and the Future of Israel as a Modern State." *Israel Studies Review* 28:1, 33–53.

Waxman, D. 2010. "The Israel Lobbies: A Survey of the Pro-Israel Community in the United States." *Israel Studies Forum* 25:1, 5–28.

Waxman, D. 2016. *Trouble in the Tribe: The American Jewish Conflict over Israel*. Princeton, NJ: Princeton University Press.

Weiss, B. 2019. *How to Fight Antisemitism*. New York: Random House.

Weinberg, D. A. 2014. "Israel and the United States: An Alliance Like None Other." In *Israel and the World Powers: Diplomatic Alliances and International Relations beyond the Middle East*, ed. C. Schindler. London: I.B. Tauris, 61–91.

Wexler, R. 2007. "United States of America." In *Israel, the Diaspora and Jewish Identity*, eds. D. Ben-Moshe and Z. Segev. Brighton: Sussex Academic Press, 260–280.

Woocher, J. 1986. *Sacred Survival: The Civil Religion of American Jews*. Bloomington, IN: Indiana University Press.

ZOA. 2018. "Press Release." 28 September. Available at: https://zoa.org/2018/09/10378569-palestinian-state-would-be-another-arab-terrorist-state/.

30

RUSSIA AND THE ISRAEL-PALESTINE CONFLICT

Derek Averre

Introduction

Russia's involvement in the Israel-Palestine issue has long been an important aspect of its broader foreign policy in the Middle East. From initial support for the new state of Israel, the USSR switched to an alignment with Arab nationalist states in the Khrushchev and Brezhnev eras; this was partly fuelled by antagonism with the United States during the Cold War, though Soviet policy in the Middle East generally was marked by an uneasy combination of ideology and realism. The Gorbachev and Yeltsin leaderships, beset by domestic problems and seeking a new national ideology free of the logic of Cold War competition, took up a more even-handed position between Israel and the Arabs, as Russia began to redefine its national interests (see Herrmann 1994, 455). Over the last two decades, which were scarred by the US-led intervention in Iraq and the upheaval of the Arab Spring, the Putin leadership has followed a Middle East policy largely free of ideology, instead adopting a hard-headed pragmatism aimed at maintaining stability in the region while looking after Russian interests. At the same time, structural changes have taken place in Russia-Israel relations – including the increasing role played in Israeli politics and society by the community of émigrés from the USSR/Russia – to produce a shift in Moscow's approach to the Israel-Palestine dispute. While Russia affirms its continued commitment to the international legal aspects of the two-state solution, in practical terms it is forging a closer relationship with Israel that may well endure in the foreseeable future.

This chapter first examines the Cold War-era background to the USSR's role in the Israel-Palestine issue before going on to analyse developments in the first two post-Soviet decades, when Russia – recognising the growing political and security challenges presented by the Middle East generally and the Palestinian cause in particular, following the Second *Intifada* in 2000 – attempted gradually to recover its influence in the region. Russia became a member of the Quartet on the Middle East upon its foundation in 2002 and subsequently played a more active diplomatic role in the Israel-Palestine peace process. We then turn our attention to the period of the Arab Spring and consider how Russia's more extensive involvement in the Middle East – reflected both in its intervention in the Syrian civil war and in interceding in regional conflicts – has had to contend with the unpredictability of the Trump Administration, the volatility of political alignments in the region, and the failure to address regional challenges collectively, amid pervasive mistrust. The Middle Eastern powers in many respects exert greater

DOI: 10.4324/9780429027376-36

leverage than ever in a regional system marked by intractable power rivalries that often operate independently of external actors. We argue that Moscow's immediate aims are limited to being accepted as a credible and legitimate actor while working to avert – and indeed, avoid being drawn into – major conflicts among the regional powers. One casualty of this situation is the Palestinian cause. With international attention fixed firmly on Israel's rapprochement with moderate Sunni Arab states and hostility to Iran's power projection across the region, the chances for a settlement that favours the interests of the Palestinian people are receding.

Soviet Engagement in the Israel-Palestine Conflict

As outlined in the introduction, Russia's engagement with the Israel-Palestine issue has its roots in the Soviet period. The USSR backed the United Nations' (UN) Palestine Partition Plan and the founding of Israel, and in fact supplied weapons to the new state during its conflict with the Arab nations in 1948. However, Ben-Gurion's courting of the United States and Europe – in the context of increasing East–West tensions, as Cold War rivalry intensified – soon led Moscow to support Israel's antagonists in the Middle East. Soviet political backing for Egypt and Syria, and for the Palestinian cause, was accompanied by the provision of heavy weaponry in their short wars with Israel in 1956, 1967, and 1973 (Cohen 2012). The Soviet leadership was, however, cautious about extending its support to direct military involvement in the hostilities; following the Six-Day War, when Moscow broke off diplomatic relations with Israel, the realities on the ground – Israel's superior war-fighting capability and internal cohesion, and the extensive assistance provided to it by the United States – prompted the USSR to try to isolate Israel politically rather than undermine it militarily (Laqueur 1969, 304).

Despite the onset of a period of détente between the United States and the USSR, which included the 1972 Basic Principles Agreement – accords intended inter alia to attenuate rivalry between the superpowers, based on non-intervention and regulation of the use of force (see Herman 1996, 290–291) – tensions in the Middle East remained high, exacerbated by mistrust in the wake of the 1973 war. However, both the Americans and the Soviets meant to avoid an escalation that might lead to military engagement between them; moreover, neither side wanted destabilisation of the region that might lead to interference with navigation through the Mediterranean and the Suez Canal and disruption of oil supplies. Following the 1974 US-brokered agreement on the Golan Heights, Moscow became more active diplomatically, proposing various iterations of a peace plan that would include Israel's withdrawal from the territories captured in 1967 and the establishment of a Palestinian state in Gaza and on the West Bank – which would have the added attraction for Moscow of providing another Soviet foothold in the region – in return for Arab recognition of Israel's right to exist.

From the late 1960s, the Soviet position on the Palestine problem – grounded in the Marxist-Leninist idea of the struggle against colonial exploitation and imperialist aggression – had begun to change, from perceiving the issue in terms of the rights of refugees into the demand for a guarantee of the legal rights of the Palestinian people to self-determination, national independence, and sovereignty, as recognised in United Nations General Assembly resolution 3236 (1974). A Palestine Liberation Organisation (PLO) office was established in Moscow in 1976; the PLO was recognised as the sole legal representative of the Palestinian people by the USSR soon after the signing of the Camp David accords and was given diplomatic status in 1981 (Nosenko, Isaev and Melkumyan 2017, 115–116). Little progress was achieved in resolving the Israel-Palestine dispute, however, given the differences between Soviet and United States views on the future of the region. Two events weakened the USSR's position even further: first, the Camp David accords and peace treaty between Egypt and Israel, which brought to an end Israel's isolation, and second, the ill-fated Soviet invasion of Afghanistan, which drew both Western condemnation and widespread censure in the Arab world, provoking a crisis of confidence among Soviet foreign policy elites that eventually proved to be a contributing factor to the collapse of the USSR (Herman 1996, 295–296).

By the mid-1980s, closer political and military ties between Ronald Reagan's America and Israel (although not without their problems), as well as shifts towards Egypt in the positions of Jordan and Yasser Arafat's wing of the PLO, completed an unfavourable turn of events for Soviet interests (Freedman 1990, 133–134). But it was domestic developments in the USSR, with the advent of Mikhail Gorbachev as leader, that proved decisive in shifting its approach in the Middle East. Moscow, recognising the need to restore constructive relations with Israel as a means of reversing the decline of Soviet influence in the region, initiated talks with Israel, which ultimately led to the re-establishment of full diplomatic relations in 1991. Moscow co-sponsored the Madrid conference in that same year and hosted multilateral negotiations between Israel and a Jordanian-Palestinian delegation in January 1992. Despite the fundamental shifts in the USSR's foreign policy-making under Gorbachev – which introduced not only a more even-handed approach to the Israel-Palestine question but also attempts to forge amicable relations with as many regional states as possible – Soviet political and military elites still perceived the Palestinian cause through the lens of national liberation rather than terrorism (Kull 1992, 108–109, 115–116; Nosenko, Isaev and Melkumyan 2017, 118). However, the break-up of the USSR at the end of 1991 – and with it the demise of Soviet foreign policy ideology – led to the emergence of a Russia prepared, at least initially, to work within the framework of liberal internationalism.

Russia, the Middle East Quartet and the Israel-Palestine Issue 1992–2010

This more favourable state of affairs overshadowed the fact that Russia's influence in the Middle East remained weak. Under the presidency of Boris Yeltsin, the country played a secondary role to the United States in peace negotiations between the Arab states and Israel, the Oslo talks leading to the Declaration of Principles signed by Yasser Arafat and Itzhak Rabin in 1993, and the 1995 Interim Agreement that established the Palestinian National Authority, following a partial withdrawal of Israeli forces from the West Bank and Gaza. Russia continued the Soviet Union's support for the Palestinian cause; Yeltsin received Arafat in 1994 – a diplomatic coup for the latter, who was coming under increasing pressure from Hamas and Islamic Jihad – though stopped short of pledging immediate recognition of Palestinian statehood, seeking a more balanced approach that would sustain cooperation with the United States. In fact, opinion was divided within Russia's foreign policy establishment, with Yeltsin recognising the importance of developing positive relations with Israel – Ariel Sharon subsequently paid three visits to Moscow – while the foreign ministry under Evgenii Primakov, a noted academic Arabist, advocated strong support for Palestinian statehood.

Despite several points of contention, a closer relationship between Russia and Israel began to develop, aided by significant Jewish emigration in the 1990s. Several Russian speakers born in the USSR were to become Israeli ministers (Rabkin 2013, 12–13). Indeed, one source notes that Arafat "was quick to realize the future impact of this huge wave of immigrants, one of the main reasons he decided to proceed with Oslo Accords before they arrived and changed Israel", as Soviet/Russian-born immigrants generally had a prejudiced attitude towards Arab citizens

(Galili 2020, 3–4). Many of these Russophone Israelis retained close cultural and family ties with Russia and depended largely on their own broadcast, print, and social media, giving them an insight into Russian foreign policy and a desire to see Moscow play a more influential role in the Middle East (see Primakov 2004, 199).

The establishment of the Quartet coincided with the advent of a more activist foreign policy under Vladimir Putin, whose first two administrations from 2000 to 2008 began gradually to rebuild Russia's influence in the region, driven by concerns over Islamist militancy – Russia fought a bitter war with Chechen Islamist insurgents between 2000 and 2004 – and by the aim of improving Russian political and trade links. Moscow initiated a calculated policy of equitable and pragmatic relations with the leading Middle Eastern countries, in spite of the complex political and security challenges it faced, that has endured into Putin's third and fourth administrations. This was complemented by an even-handed approach to dealing with Israel and the Palestinian authorities. Moscow was critical of Israel's plan to build a security wall with the West Bank, underlining the importance of the peace process and holding fast to the two-state solution. In April 2005 Putin visited Mahmoud Abbas in Ramallah, after Abbas's inauguration as head of the Palestinian National Authority (PNA), pledging economic aid and calling on the Palestinian leadership to fight terrorism, while continuing to lay emphasis on a political settlement with Israel. Despite Moscow's recognition of the PNA's legitimacy, it was forced to acknowledge the political and military clout of Hamas following the latter's emergence as the biggest party in the January 2006 elections to the Palestinian Legislative Council. Hamas delegations – recognised by Moscow as elected representatives of the Palestinian people (Rabkin 2013, 20–21) – visited Moscow in March that year for exploratory talks with Putin. However, Hamas's continuing refusal to recognise the state of Israel led to Russia joining the other Quartet members in placing an economic embargo on its government. At the same time, in response to rocket strikes Russia criticised large-scale Israeli attacks on Gaza in 2006. Increasing tensions between Israel and Iran, over the latter's nuclear programme and support for Hezbollah and Hamas, complicated the wider regional situation even further.

Putin's policy of diversifying Russia's foreign policy links in the Middle East was reflected in his 2005 visit to Israel, the first ever by a Russian leader. Tel Aviv had demonstrated sympathy for Moscow's campaign in the second Chechen war and its ongoing struggle against North Caucasus Islamist insurgents carrying out terrorist attacks on Russian territory. Positive relations with Israel were reinforced through bilateral agreements on counterterrorism, military-technical and intelligence cooperation, as well as through the promotion of trade links (Dannreuther 2012, 547–548). In a mark of its commitment to its relationship with Russia, Israel discontinued military cooperation with Georgia during the Russia–Georgia conflict in 2008.

Visa-free travel between the two countries from 2008 and closer cultural-historical, religious, and family ties, founded largely on the integration of the émigré Russian-Jewish community in Israel, completed the picture of a relationship transformed within a period of little more than twenty years (Katz 2018, 104–105). One Russian expert assessment based on survey data concluded that, in Russia, "social representations of Israel are in the process of rapid transformation[;] … the new image of Israel is without doubt related to immigration from Russia and other former Soviet republics". One consequence was that a majority of Russian citizens had begun to support Israel, though they opposed the use of military force by both Israel and the Palestinians, and to believe that Russia should be involved in mediation of the conflict (Kolossov 2003, 143). Put simply, Moscow had realised that "there is significant Russian social capital in Israel which can and should be utilised to benefit the Russian economy" (Dannreuther 2012, 551).

The Arab Spring and the Marginalisation of the Israel-Palestine Issue

The turbulence that swept across the Middle East and North Africa (MENA) with the inception of the Arab Spring in 2010–2011 led to shifts in the political priorities and strategic alignments of actors both within and external to the region. The inconsistency of Washington's policy there, and the decline in the prestige of the United States left open opportunities for the various state and sub-/non-state actors to prosecute their interests. One outcome is that Russia has been able to assume a more influential role as a mediator in regional conflicts and as a trade or security partner for the major regional powers. At the same time, the Russia-United States relationship is no longer the key determinant of MENA security; the response of both powers to the complicated and erratic nature of events, exacerbated by the weak institutionalisation of the region, is often reactive and cautious, serving their immediate interests but with little sense of a clear strategy. This has impacted on their approach to the Israel-Palestine issue.

The peace process stalled under Obama and went into reverse under Trump. It was on the agenda at the Non-Aligned Movement summit in Tehran in August 2012, attended by the leaders of 120 countries, including China and India as members and Russia as a guest country. Although the event was criticised by the Obama Administration, the three states voted for the upgrading of Palestine's status at the United Nations (Rabkin 2013, 22–23). In November 2012, a considerable majority of states at the United Nations General Assembly, including Russia, passed a resolution granting observer status to Palestine, which introduced a new factor into the process; this resolution boosted Abbas's standing but changed little in the situation on the West Bank, given the US's continuing rejection of the recognition of Palestine. Russian experts argued at the time that Moscow had experience of civil diplomacy and suggested that a Russia-United States commission involving high-profile figures could have returned the talks to interim steps envisaged in the road map, imparting "an important direction in Russia's policy on the Middle East. Today, this direction is virtually non-existent" (Naumkin et al. 2013b, 18–19).

However, the turmoil resulting from the Arab Spring has diverted the attention of Russia's support for the Palestinian cause and mediation between Fatah and Hamas (Naumkin et al. 2013a, 33, 54). Russian scholars have argued that

> the threats stemming today from the destabilisation of the Arab world, the disintegration of state formations and appearance of new non-state structures claiming power and resources in the region, resorting to terrorism far beyond the region's borders, pose for Russia a more dangerous challenge that the non-resolution of the Palestine problem.
>
> *(Nosenko, Isaev and Melkumyan 2017, 121)*

Moscow has been unwilling or unable to prioritise the Israel-Palestine issue in the face of more urgent objectives: – preventing regime change and averting the destabilisation of Syria through political and, ultimately military, support for Bashar al-Assad; carrying the fight to pan-regional Islamist extremists (authoritative estimates put the number of Russian-speaking "foreign fighters" allied to Islamic State or Al-Q'aeda and their affiliates in Iraq and Syria between 2,900 and 5,000); and using its diplomatic heft to avert an intensification of inter-state tensions fraught with the prospect of a major conflict. Russia has also had to look after its relationship with the Netanyahu government in the face of the Trump Administration's attempt to stamp its own radical pro-Israeli, pro-moderate Arab, and anti-Iranian template on regional affairs. Beyond rhetorical calls for a Middle East peace conference, Moscow has recognised that, in the current volatile environment, this is not the time for grand designs: the Putin leadership has limited its ambitions to safeguarding and extending its trade and energy interests, diversifying its partnerships and pursuing incremental improvements in relations with regional states.

Russia's management of Israel's antagonistic relations with Iran, amid concerns over the expansion of the latter's military presence across the region, has become a central aspect of its security policy. Tehran's aim of cementing an "axis of resistance" though political-military links with Syria, bolstered by its influence in Lebanon and Iraq and with the support of Hezbollah and Hamas – condemned by Israel for inciting Palestinian youth demonstrations in the Gaza strip – not only poses a direct challenge to Israel and the Arab Gulf states but also – notwithstanding Moscow's Astana agreement with Tehran and Ankara in seeking a resolution to the Syrian civil war – militates against Russia's objective of maintaining a stable balance of forces and interests among the major Middle Eastern powers and furthering its trade and security partnerships with Israel and Gulf states. The Golan Heights, claimed by Israel as its sovereign territory, remain a bone of political contention, despite the continuing presence of the United Nations Disengagement Observer Force there, with regular violations that threaten to escalate into a military confrontation between Israeli and Syrian forces, again with the involvement of Iran. Russian sources report that, prior to Russia's military intervention in Syria in September 2015, Moscow tried to reassure Tel Aviv that Tehran and Damascus were not conspiring to create a front against Israel in the Golan Heights and sought to persuade Iran and Syrian Shi'ite forces to withdraw their heavy armaments from the demarcation line with Israel (Barmin 2018, 7, 10). However, in February 2018, after an Iranian drone was launched into Israeli territory from Syria, the Israeli air force carried out a large-scale attack against Syria's missile defences, with the loss of one of its fighter aircraft. In May 2018, Iranian forces fired missiles at the Golan Heights, again from Syrian territory, drawing an Israeli response targeting a number of military facilities.

With increasing United States hostility to Iran and its proxy forces in the region, one Russian expert has described these exchanges as "a harbinger of what the confrontation between Iran and Israel will look like in the event of an asymmetric response of the Iranian leadership to the actions of the United States"; Netanyahu has alerted Putin to the dangers of a much more robust military response from Tel Aviv if Iranian and its allied forces take root in Syria and establish positions adjacent to its border with Israel (Barmin 2018, 12–13). A series of further attacks by the Israeli air force in Syria in November 2019, including one aimed at the house of the commander of the Palestinian Islamic Jihad group in Damascus, were a reminder of the ongoing dangers presented by these clashes. Moscow's emphasis to date has been on deconfliction; it has tried to limit the provocative Iranian and Syrian presence near Israel's borders and has tolerated limited military retaliation by the latter as long as Russian forces are not harmed or Assad's leadership is not destabilised (Lund 2019, 30). Despite the risks involved, Moscow has gained credibility in Tel Aviv as the external power on a par with the United States in terms of preventing the conflict with Tehran from turning into a full-scale war (Barmin 2018, 4). At the same time, the prospect of Tehran making substantive concessions, and avoiding asymmetric retaliation to United States and Israeli actions, is likely to depend on Israel's relationship with a post-Trump United States administration and a relaxation of tensions stemming from agreement to revive the Joint Comprehensive Plan of Action to regulate Iran's nuclear programme (see Aksenyonok 2018). The Putin leadership has to resort consistently to agile diplomacy in response to changing circumstances, but a political solution to accompany a reduction in military tensions appears unlikely in the short term; Moscow risks losing its credibility if efforts to manage Israel-Iran tensions fail.

A direct consequence of this state of affairs is that, whereas Russia has sought a more influential role as a mediator in the Palestine question – both Abbas and senior Hamas officials are frequent visitors to Moscow, and the Russian foreign ministry has also met smaller Palestinian groups – its diplomatic capacity is still being absorbed by the Syrian civil war and the challenges posed by Iran's fraught relationships with Israel and the Arab states. It remains to be seen to what extent Trump's 'deal of the century' in support of Netanyahu's nationalist policies – the intention to claim sovereignty over Palestinian settlements on the West Bank, in defiance of United Nations Security Council resolution 2334, which states that they have "no legal validity, constituting a flagrant violation under international law and a major obstacle to the vision of two States living side-by-side in peace and security, within internationally recognized borders" (United Nations 2016), and United States recognition of Jerusalem as the capital of Israel – will in the longer term fuel regional tensions.

Russia and the Israel-Palestine Issue Today

At the time of writing, the Quartet appears to be losing its relevance. The US-Israel "deal", together with Israel's rapprochement with moderate Arab leaderships, effectively sidelines the PLA and disregards key elements of the peace process. Russia understands that the Palestinian cause remains a central aspect of Arab self-understanding and continues to support the principle of the Palestinian people's right to self-determination, the reversal of the occupation of Arab lands by Israel, and the establishment of an independent Palestinian state. In April 2017, the Russian foreign ministry for the first time recognised West Jerusalem as the capital of Israel and East Jerusalem as the capital of the State of Palestine (Barmin 2018, 16–18); in December that year Russia supported a United Nations Security Council (UNSC) draft resolution, proposed by Egypt on behalf of the Arab Group, affirming

> that any decisions and actions which purport to have altered the character, status or demographic composition of Holy City of Jerusalem have no legal effect, and calls upon all States to refrain from the establishment of diplomatic missions in the Holy City of Jerusalem, pursuant to resolution 478 (1980) of the Security Council.
>
> *(Ministry of Foreign Affairs [MFA] 2017)*

The UNSC failed to adopt the resolution after the United States voted against it. However, Moscow's capacity to move the peace process forward and secure its position as an influential regional actor, as part of its calculus of interests in the wider region, hinges on persuading an Israeli leadership sensitive to external threats to make concessions over issues vital to its national security.

Three factors determine the centrality of Israel in Moscow's Middle East policy. The first factor, analysed earlier in this chapter, relates to the Russian-Jewish diaspora in Israel. That part of the Soviet/Russian-Jewish population which emigrated to Israel in the late 1980s and 1990s and their descendants – today accounting for around 15 per cent of the population and nearly a quarter of the non-Arab inhabitants – has become deeply integrated into its political, economic, and social structures. Russian foreign minister Sergei Lavrov has stated,

> We see our ties with Israel *as strategic in nature*. Almost one and a half million citizens [of Israel] hail from the former Soviet Union or the Russian Federation. As you may already know, there is a political party over there, Our Home is Israel, which mostly relies on Russian-speaking voters.
>
> *(MID 2019; emphasis added)*

Russian speakers have formed "a large secular nationalist political camp that secures right-wing rule to this day", and that may even with time constitute an important part of Israel's future elite (Galili 2020, 1–2).

Second, Russia's trade turnover with Israel has been running at between $2.2 and $3.5 billion over the last ten-year period, up from just over $1 billion on 2000, though there was a dip in the aftermath of the Ukraine crisis in 2014 before a steady recovery took place (Russian Foreign Trade. n.d). Although Turkey is overwhelmingly Russia's principal trade partner in the MENA region, with Algeria and Egypt also ahead of Israel, thanks partly to sales of Russian armaments, Russia's trade with Israel currently outstrips that of other Middle Eastern states. There are longer-term prospects for reciprocal tourism and the development of high technologies (energy storage and transmission technology, nanotechnology, the digital economy), including dual-use defence-related goods, and for cooperation over joint projects with third countries (including with India, Russia's biggest export market for defence goods and technologies).

Third, despite Washington's pre-eminence as Israel's principal partner among the major powers and differences in Russian and Israeli positions on Iran and Syria, consultation and cooperation on military and intelligence matters and regional security developments have cemented a strong bilateral Russia-Israel relationship. Moscow's role as an intermediary in Israel's long-running enmity with Iran and Syria – as noted above, fraught with the risk of a ruinous inter-state conflict – has become an important factor in mitigating regional tensions. Events have also conspired to produce a closer alignment between Russia and Israel over important issues in the Middle East beyond the Iran-Syria issue. They share a dread of extremist Sunni Islamism. The military coup in Egypt in 2013 that brought Abdel Fattah al-Sisi to power at the expense of the elected Muslim Brotherhood, perceived as a potential threat to Israel, was seen by both Tel Aviv and Moscow as conducive to stability, despite the al-Sisi government's domestic repression and disregard for democracy and human rights. Egypt is also an important mediator between Fatah and Hamas and maintains a close diplomatic alignment with Russia on this matter (Kremlin.ru 2018). Both Russia and Israel are building relations with the leaderships of moderate Gulf Arab states and Turkey, although problems remain (see Katz 2018, 105–106).

An additional element of the Russia-Israel relationship centres on individual-level explanations of agency: the policy preferences of national leaders based on a common understanding of the political and security environment. A prominent Russian commentator argues that Putin and Netanyahu "share a basic realpolitik-influenced view of international relations, have little time for short- or medium-term democratic transition in the Arab world, and see Islamist terrorism as their major enemy" (Trenin 2016, 4). Other sources have referred to the "personal chemistry between Putin and conservative Israeli leaders" (Katz 2018, 103) that has resulted in frequent and intensive talks between the Russian president and Netanyahu over the last decade or so. Indeed, the latter's ties with Moscow go back to the Yeltsin period; in his memoir, Primakov noted that, from the early years of his first premiership from 1996, Netanyahu valued the political investment of Russia in mediating in the Palestine question (Primakov 2004, 197, 199). This has resulted in a deeper appreciation of each other's core national security concerns, as well as a responsiveness to developing crises and preparedness to allow each other a certain degree of leeway in dealing with them.

Conclusion

Writing in 2004, Primakov concluded that

> because so much blood has been shed, so many destinies have been broken, so much fury has accumulated, and so many eyes have been blinded by hatred, I am convinced

> that a Middle East settlement is impossible without active intervention from the outside.
>
> *(Primakov 2004, 190)*

The same sentiment – with the added proviso that a lasting resolution of the conflict cannot be achieved by the United States or Russia alone – prevails today in Russian thinking. In diplomatic rhetoric Moscow still holds fast to the notion that "the long-standing Israeli-Palestinian conflict lies at the epicentre of the upheavals in the Middle East" and that collective efforts must be coordinated on a multilateral basis and rooted in a political process leading to a two-state solution, underpinned by the international legal framework, particularly UNSC resolution 2334 and other existing agreements. Russia has repeatedly called for an urgent resumption of the work of the Quartet, stalled due to the United States position, and progress on the intra-Palestinian dialogue (MFA 2020). At the same time, Israel, confident in its security ties with Moscow, discerns little real damage arising from Russia's diplomatic backing for the Palestinian cause, which is unlikely to be translated into significant material support.

A prominent European commentator has argued that Russia's current policies in the Middle East are a "game changer: by vastly expanding its diplomatic outreach and by setting up permanent military bases in the region[,] … Russia has altered several strategic parameters in the Middle East region to its advantage" (Pierini 2019). Historically warm relations between Russia and the Palestinian leaders on the one hand and Russia's evolving relationship with Israel on the other mean that Moscow undoubtedly has a role to play as a legitimate and credible actor in the Israel-Palestine settlement. However, the factors impeding a more influential strategic position for Russia, both in the Israel-Palestine issue and the Middle East as a whole, are considerable. The wider regional environment, characterised by complexity, antagonism, and distrust, mean that the prospects for a settlement have been overshadowed by conflicts in Syria, Iraq, Yemen, and Libya. At the same time, the two-state solution is threatened by the loss of Palestinian territory, continuing divisions between moderate and more hard-line Palestinian factions, and the rapprochement between Israel and moderate Sunni Arab states, driven by their common perceptions of an increasingly assertive Iran projecting its power into Iraq, Syria, and Lebanon. Moscow's cooperation with Washington continues, but has been waylaid by the Trump Administration's "deal of the century", exacerbated by United States reduction of humanitarian assistance to the Palestinian population, as well as its pressure on Arab states to end the isolation of Israel, all of which threatens to change materially the facts on the ground and narrows the space for Russian involvement in an international settlement (Holmes 2020). Authoritative Russian experts have concluded that

> Palestine does not consider the Middle East Quartet in its current composition an impartial and effective organization… progress on the Palestinian track depends not only on the eventual resumption of bilateral Palestinian–Israeli negotiations; it requires changes in the regional context.
>
> *(Kuznetsov et al. 2018, 26–27)*

To conclude, Russian policy is highly contingent and context-dependent, intent on avoiding becoming embroiled in regional conflicts. Rather than acting as a power broker in the region, Moscow aims to limit further destabilisation and promote deconfliction, where possible through cooperation with major external and regional actors. Russia's regional interests – pursued through incremental tactical steps in the context of strategic change – have left it precariously positioned at times; this is accompanied by a cautious outlook that places further constraints on its influence in the region and limits the extent of its material, as distinct from diplomatic, support for the Palestinians.

Recommended Readings

Barmin, Y. 2018. *Russia and Israel: The Middle Eastern Vector of Relations*. Working Paper 42, 24 October. Moscow: Russian International Affairs Council.

Galili, L. 2020. *The Other Tribe: Israel's Russian Speaking Community and How It Is Changing the Country*. Washington, DC: Foreign Policy at Brookings.

Herrmann, R. K. 1994. Russian Policy in the Middle East: Strategic Change and Tactical Considerations. *Middle East Journal* 48:3, 455–474.

Kuznetsov, V., V. Naumkin, and I. Zvyagelskaya. 2018. *Russia in the Middle East: The Polyphonic Harmony*. Valdai Discussion Club, May. Available at: https://valdaiclub.com/events/announcements/polyfonic-harmony/

Naumkin, V. V., et al. 2013. *Russia and the Greater Middle East*. Russian International Affairs Council, No. 9. Available at: https://russiancouncil.ru/upload/Russia_Middle_East_En.pdf

Questions for Discussion

(1) How does the Israel-Palestine issue fit into Russia's broader contemporary strategy in the Middle East?
(2) In what ways has the emergence of a large émigré Russian-Jewish community in Israel shaped bilateral Russia-Israel relations?
(3) How might Russia seek to mitigate its antagonistic relations with the United States and other Western powers in order to improve diplomatic relations over the Israel-Palestine peace process?
(4) What are the central factors determining Russia's role in the Israel-Palestine issue at the current time?

References

Aksenyonok, A. 2018. *Steep Turns in the Middle East Policy. The US Can Become Hostage of Regional Powers Interests*. Valdai Discussion Club, 16 May. Available at: http://valdaiclub.com/a/highlights/steep-turns-of-the-middle-east-policy-the-us/.

Barmin, Y. 2018. *Russia and Israel: The Middle Eastern Vector of Relations*. Working Paper 42, 24 October. Moscow: Russian International Affairs Council.

Cohen, A. 2012. *How the US Should Respond to Russia's Unhelpful Role in the Middle East*. Heritage Foundation.

Dannreuther, R. 2012. "Russia and the Middle East: A Cold War Paradigm?" *Europe-Asia Studies* 64:3, 543–560.

Freedman R. O. 1990. "The Superpowers and the Middle East." In *Superpower Competition and Crisis Prevention in the Third World*, eds. A. R. and P. Williams. Cambridge: Cambridge University Press, 121–143.

Galili, L. 2020. "*The Other Tribe: Israel's Russian Speaking Community and How It Is Changing the Country*. Washington, DC: Foreign Policy at Brookings. Available at: www.brookings.edu/wp-content/uploads/2020/09/FP_20200921_other_tribe_galili.pdf.

Herman, R. G. .1996. "Identity, Norms, and National Security: The Soviet Foreign Policy Revolution and the End of the Cold War." In *The Culture of National Security: Norms and Identity in World Politics*, ed. P. J. Katzenstein. New York: Columbia University Press, 271–316.

Herrmann, R. K. 1994. "Russian Policy in the Middle East: Strategic Change and Tactical Considerations." *Middle East Journal* 48:3, 455–474.

Holmes, O. 2020. "Pompeo's Settlement Visit Gives Stamp of Approval to Israeli Military Occupation." *The Guardian*, 20 November, 29.

Katz, M. N. 2018. "Russia and Israel: An Improbable Friendship." In *Russia's Return to the Middle East: Building Sandcastles*, eds. N. Popescu and S. Secrieru, eds. Chaillot Paper 146, July, 103–108.

Kolossov, V. 2003. "'High' and 'Low' Geopolitics: Images of Foreign Countries in the Eyes of Russian Citizens." *Geopolitics* 8:1, 121–148.

Kremlin.ru. 2018. *Press Statements Following Talks with President of Egypt Abdel Fatah el-Sisi*. Sochi, 17 October. Available at: http://en.kremlin.ru/events/president/news/58842.

Kull, S. 1992. *Burying Lenin: The Revolution in Soviet Ideology & Foreign Policy*. Boulder, CO, and Oxford: Westview Press.

Kuznetsov, V., V. Naumkin, and I. Zvyagelskaya. 2018. *Russia in the Middle East: The Harmony of Polyphony*. Valdai Discussion Club, May. Available at: http://valdaiclub.com/files/18375/.

Laqueur, W. 1969. "Russia Enters the Middle East." *Foreign Affairs* 47:2, 296–308.

Lund, A. 2019. "Russia in the Middle East." *The Swedish Institute of International Affairs Utrikespolitiska institutet Paper, 2*. Stockholm: The Swedish Institute of International Affairs, 42–44.

MFA. 2017. Comment by the Information and Press Department on United States veto of United Nations Security Council Draft Resolution on Jerusalem, 19 December. Available at: www.mid.ru/en/foreign_policy/news/-/asset_publisher/cKNonkJE02Bw/content/id/2996544.

MFA. 2020. *Deputy Foreign Minister Sergei Vershinin's Remarks on Behalf of Foreign Minister Sergey Lavrov during an Open Debate in the UN Security Council on the Situation in the Middle East, Including the Palestinian Question*, 26 October. Available at: www.mid.ru/en/foreign_policy/news/-/asset_publisher/cKNonkJE02Bw/content/id/4406453.

MID. 2019. *Foreign Minister Sergey Lavrov's Remarks and Answers to Media Questions Following the High-Level Week of the 74th Session of the UN General Assembly*, New York, 27 September. Available at: www.mid.ru/en/foreign_policy/news/-/asset_publisher/cKNonkJE02Bw/content/id/3822554.

Naumkin, V., et al. 2013a. Islam v politike: ideologiya ili pragmatizm? [Islam in politics: ideology or pragmatism?]. Valdai Discussion Club analytical report, August. Available at: http://valdaiclub.com/files/11450/.

Naumkin, V., et al. 2013b. *Russia and the Greater Middle East*. Russian International Affairs Council, 9. Available at: https://russiancouncil.ru/upload/Russia_Middle_East_En.pdf.

Nosenko, T. V., V. A. Isaev, and E. S. Melkumyan. 2017. Palestinskaya problema v blizhnevostochnoi politike SSSR/Rossii (The Palestine Problem in the Middle Eastern Policy of the USSR/Russia). *Vestnik MGIMO-Universiteta* 4(55), 113–126 [in Russian].

Pierini, M. 2019. *Four Game Changers in Europe's South*. Carnegie Europe, 26 February. Available at: https://carnegieeurope.eu/strategiceurope/78447.

Primakov, E. 2004. *Russian Crossroads: Toward the New Millennium*. New Haven, CT: Yale University Press.

Rabkin, Y. M. 2013. "Russia, China and India and the Israel–Palestine Conflict." *Holy Land Studies* 12:1, 9–24.

Russian Foreign Trade. N. d. https://en.russian-trade.com/countries/israel/.

Trenin, D. 2016. *Russia in the Middle East: Moscow's Objectives, Priorities, and Policy Drivers*. Task Force on US Policy Toward Russia, Ukraine, and Eurasia. New York: Carnegie Endowment for International Peace. Available at https://carnegieendowment.org/files/03-25-16_Trenin_Middle_East_Moscow_clean.pdf.

United Nations 2016. *Israel's Settlements Have No Legal Validity, Constitute Flagrant Violation of International Law, Security Council Reaffirms*. UN Meetings Coverage and Press Releases, SC12657, 23 December.

PART VI

The Other Images of the Conflict

31

ISRAELI AND PALESTINIAN PUBLIC OPINION AND THE TWO-STATE SOLUTION

Paradigm or Window?

Dahlia Scheindlin

At the close of the second decade of the 2000s, political prospects for a two-state solution to the Israeli-Palestinian conflict appeared to have been completely exhausted. Throughout the decade, Israel's right-wing leadership expanded settlements and infrastructure in the Palestinian territories designated for a state, laid the political foundations for annexation in the West Bank, and maintained a strict closure and separation policy for Gaza. During the same period, Palestinian political leadership was divided and ineffective, with no leverage to advance a negotiated solution, or even to preserve the conditions for two states in the future. The American government, which had supported a two-state solution in principle, essentially reversed policy under the Trump Administration. After 2016, the United States government openly supported Israel's annexationist trends in the region and in international forums, by recognising Israeli annexation of the Golan Heights and hinting that annexation in parts of the West Bank was acceptable, moving the United States embassy to Jerusalem, and declaring that settlements did not contravene international law (Halbfinger 2019). By the end of the decade, these political and physical changes had fundamentally undermined the main paradigm for a solution among political elites, and on the ground.

This chapter examines another realm (one beyond political elites), and the physical realities on the ground: the public on both sides. What do the Israeli and Palestinian people think about these developments? Does the end of the two-state solution represent a betrayal of the regular people who would have embraced peace through a final-status accord separating the populations into independent states? Or perhaps the opposite: Does the end of the two-state paradigm reflect the true will of the people, a deeper level of resistance that belied the willingness of both sides to compromise on the surface?

This chapter examines the rise and fall of the two-state solution in the public mind, tracking both sides during the relevant years. The inquiry is structured both chronologically and thematically. Alongside the central question above, several secondary, derivative questions should be kept in mind: How did the two-state solution originally emerge to become a vision for peace among the Israeli and Palestinian publics? How much did each side embrace it, and were the two sides aligned? Which were the prime years of public support, how deep and genuine was

DOI: 10.4324/9780429027376-38

the support – did it include details or just the general concept? When and why did support wane, and was the two states solution replaced by a different goal for peace by either side?

The chronological stages are presented in four parts: (1) The emerging proposition stage, when the idea of a Palestinian state becomes part of policy discourse and public attitudes, mainly from the late 1980s, through the Madrid conference in 1991 and up to 1993; (2) The legitimisation stage, beginning from the Oslo Accords of 1993 through the remainder of the decade. During this time, the concept of a Palestinian state as the foundation for two states steadily gathers legitimacy; (3) The peak years, from roughly the Camp David negotiations of 2000, lasting most of that first decade, when the two-state solution becomes paradigmatic as a concept and both sides show their highest levels of support for specific elements of a peace plan; (4) The sunset phase, when support for the solution declines steadily over the course of the next decade, from roughly 2010 to the present.

The analysis here also highlights some key themes regarding the interaction between public opinion and policy-making, public opinion in conflict, alongside certain analytic claims that appear in popular discourse. These include: Does public opinion lead or follow policy-making (Foyle 1997)?[1] Does public opinion influence leaders in a democracy but have less impact or import in non- or partial democracies? Does force and violence increase support for reaching a peace agreement, or support for concessions towards an agreement (Thrall, 2017)? Is one side inherently more pro-peace or consistently more opposed to peace and supportive of hostilities in an "entrenched" way than the other (Polisar, 2015), and if so, what might be the reasons? The conclusion assesses two final questions: Is the two-state solution salvageable in the public mind; and does the public envision the alternative emerging paths?

This chapter is not a quantitative methodological examination of each question. Instead, it highlights which findings and observations form the basis of these claims, and how strongly those claims seem to hold up in light of the comprehensive picture provided here. The analysis is based on publicly available data sources, including some of the author's material, from credible polling and research organisations.

Pre-peace Process: An Emerging Scenario of Two States

The first official talks between Israelis and Palestinians took place at the Madrid Conference of 1991; the Palestinian representation fell under the Jordanian delegation and were not PLO representatives, following American pressure to exclude the PLO.[2] However, this was the first international forum in which a Palestinian delegation was allowed to represent the Palestinian people, with the participation of Israel and all stakeholder countries, to discuss the possibility of peace. The Madrid process collapsed before reaching any agreement, but it would not have been possible at all save for changes in political positions that had occurred prior to 1991.

Historically, the pre-state Zionist leadership had accepted the Partition Plan (United Nations General Assembly Resolution 181). However, the idea of an independent Palestinian state had long been suppressed in Israeli political discourse. During the negotiations held at Camp David in 1978, which resulted in the accord with Egypt, Israeli prime minister Menachem Begin had considered an autonomy plan for the Palestinians, but these did not advance and were not part of the final accords (Quandt 1986). From 1988, Israel was led by a hardline leader, Yitzhak Shamir of the Likud Party, who gave little credence to Palestinian claims. The term "two-state solution" would not become common for at least another ten years.

The attitudes of Israeli Jews – the only group in Israel for which data is available for that time – reflected widespread dismissal: 80 per cent of Israeli Jews surveyed in 1987 opposed the idea of establishing a Palestinian state – with 54 per cent who said this should "definitely" not be agreed to (Arian, Shamir, and Ventura 1992). Rejection of this concept was sufficiently shared by leaders and people alike that it would be difficult to discern a causal direction.

Palestinian public opinion from this era shows the symmetry of hardline positions between the two parties to the conflict. Very few Palestinians in the years prior to the First *Intifada* supported two states, before the term "two-state solution" was commonly used. Historically, Palestinians were committed to reclaiming and returning the entire area between the Jordan river to the sea, and this was the goal espoused by the political leadership that eventually emerged in the wake of 1948. In a 1986 survey in the West Bank and Gaza, 78 per cent of Palestinian respondents supported a "democratic Palestinian state in all of Palestine," as their preferred solution. This was akin to the goal articulated by the PLO and Fatah up to that point. In the same question, just 16.9 per cent preferred a democratic Palestinian state within the West Bank and Gaza (Shadid and Seltzer 1988), an area that would form the basis of a limited Palestinian state existing alongside Israel.

In the same survey, a plurality of Palestinians, nearly 30 per cent, preferred a state based on an Arab nationalist government with some Islamic character, while the second-highest preference (26.5 per cent) was a state based on Islamic law (Sharia).[3] The two responses "democratic secular" and "democratic Palestinian" government received a combined total of 31.5 per cent (Shadid and Seltzer 1988).

Furthermore, Palestinians in the West Bank and Gaza were in a fighting mood: The same poll also showed deep rejection of all Israeli political intervention in governing their society, and a strong majority supported the PLO-led struggle for self-determination, including the use of violence.

Interestingly, in the mid-1980s a survey was also conducted of Palestinians living in the United States. The results showed similar consensus support for the PLO as the leading representative of the Palestinian people. At the same time, negotiations were considered the top means of achieving political goals, ranking higher than civil disobedience and the use of force, which ranked lowest. Further, a clear majority of these diaspora Palestinians in the United States, 69 per cent supported "mutual recognition between Israel and the PLO" as a necessary precondition for peace (Moughrabi and El-Nazer 1989). While the American Palestinian community is far smaller than Palestinian communities in the Middle East, this group maintained close ties with those Palestinians and undertook political activity in the United States; in this case, they appeared to be a harbinger of political attitudes that Palestinians in the territories would embrace a few years later.

During the 1980s Israel made little attempt to advance a solution; contact with the PLO was illegal; Israel invaded Lebanon in 1982 to expel the PLO from Beirut, generating disarray in the Palestinian leadership. However, the next watershed event came from within the occupied territories: the outbreak of the Palestinian Intifada, in 1987. This unexpected turn of events challenged the unrivalled status of the PLO, now relocated in Tunis, as the representative of the Palestinian political cause. Suddenly, a grassroots, ground-up, nearly leaderless movement, was taking the initiative, leaving the PLO leadership a step behind the people it claimed to represent. In 1988, the PLO shifted its political goal from the idea of reconquering all of historic Palestine and bringing all exiled Palestinians back, to supporting the liberation of the people living under direct Israeli occupation, through national independence on part of the land and renouncing violence as the mode of struggle.[4]

The 1988 PLO declaration of independence for the Palestinian state on the basis of the United Nations Partition Plan was somewhat of a rupture in Palestinian politics. The new vision shifted the political focus to Palestinians living in the occupied territories rather than to refugees scattered around the world. In the same declaration the PLO also renounced the use of violence as the main means of struggle, further transforming the nature of the Palestinian political cause. Calling for a state within the 1949 Armistice lines following the 1948 war, or the pre-1967 areas, meant giving up on the demand for all of historic Palestine, and was ultimately a recognition that Israel exists in the pre-1967 areas. In a clarification shortly afterwards, Arafat told Western reporters that the PLO "accepted the existence of Israel as a state in the region. … We accept two states, the Palestine state and the Jewish state of Israel" (Lohr 1988).

Did the 1987 Intifada or the 1988 declaration change Israeli attitudes? Arian et al. (1992) found mixed results between surveys from 1987 and 1988, with some rise in conciliatory attitudes: opposition to a Palestinian state declined by four points, alongside a rise in militant approaches – including a decline in support for peace negotiations, decline in support for a peace conference with international powers, decline in willingness to negotiate with the PLO.

However, over the next few years, data collected among Israelis indicates an incremental rise from a low starting point of just 21 per cent support for the establishment of a Palestinian state – in the all-Jewish samples surveyed by the Jaffee Center/Institute for National Security Studies (INSS) – in 1987, to a peak of 32 per cent in 1991, which fell but rose again to 35 per cent in 1993, the year the Oslo Peace Process began. While the increase during those years is notable, even the high mark of 1993 is still a minority, just over one-third, of Jewish Israelis who accepted the principle of a Palestinian state, with a majority of Israeli Jews opposed (Ben Meir and Bagno-Moldavsky 2010, 76); between 42–52 per cent were "strongly" opposed (Arian 1995).

A second shift can be seen from the period of the late 1980s and early 1990s among the Israeli Jewish public: rising support for the idea of returning land in exchange for peace. In early 1987 (just prior to the Intifada), 63 per cent opposed returning anything, or favoured the return of only small portions of land. In November 1989, this total had declined to 55 per cent who gave those responses (Arian 1995).

While the explanation for this change is a matter of speculation, even by the authors of those studies, many assume that Israelis were reacting to the First Intifada as a sustained expression of Palestinian national frustration and political demands. One explanation that has generated a certain traction among observers of the Israeli-Palestinian conflict is that the use of force propels Israelis to support concessions. An alternate explanation is that the Intifada, combined with the PLO's 1988 declaration of independence within the West Bank and Gaza, rather than all of historic Palestine, clarified to Israelis the nature of Palestinian national demands for a state within their own territory, and the resilience of those demands to both force and time – leading more Israeli Jews to conclude that concessions were ultimately necessary. In hindsight, the First Intifada would be viewed as the least violent of Palestinian collective popular actions, though it would be difficult to gauge whether it was viewed at the time as a violent action or a mostly non-violent movement.

However, the 1988 declaration was a political watershed for the PLO leadership, which was widely considered to be the sole representative of the Palestinian people at the time (In the 1986 survey, 95 per cent of Palestinians in the West Bank and Gaza agreed that the group represented them, Shadid and Seltzer 1988). The Israeli leadership might have rejected the PLO's declaration formally, but it is also possible that Israelis began to internalise that not only had the PLO compromised its maximalist demand, which for Jews was synonymous with destroying Israel, but that it had renounced violence and begun to lead as a political organisation rather than a terror group. This would certainly become the case in the 1990s, when more Jewish Israelis told pollsters that Yasser Arafat was a statesperson, than those who considered him more a terrorist (40 and 34 per cent, respectively). The question was only asked in 1996, but the process might have begun earlier (Peace Index, January 1996).

Further, it is not clear that the Intifada was a singular turning point in which resistance to compromise dropped. Fully two decades earlier, between 1968 and 1978, the portion of Israeli Jews who rejected territorial concessions in the West Bank, for example, dropped 31 points, from a near-consensus of 91 per cent who supported returning nothing or just a small portion, to 60 per cent in 1978 – perhaps influenced by peace-gestures such as Egyptian President Sadat's visit to Jerusalem or the Camp David accords, rather than war. Regarding Gaza, these rejectionist attitudes dropped nearly forty points (from 85 to 46 per cent) in the same period (Arian 1995).[5]

A more banal explanation than either the effects of force or the PLO's conciliatory declaration is that Israelis might have simply observed that Palestinians did not abandon or forget their national goals as the decades went by. Simply maintaining the struggle over a sustained period – and shifting away from the maximalist territorial goal – may have eventually had an impact on Israelis who concluded that peace through concessions might be the only viable response.

At the same time, the PLO declaration was a rupture among Palestinians themselves. While this is commonly indicated anecdotally, quantitative data among Palestinians is scant following 1988 and prior to Oslo. However, when more systematic data began to appear from the time of the signing of the Oslo Accords, reviewed in the next phase, Palestinian attitudes reflected significant openness to creating the new paradigm of two states.

To summarise the "emerging proposal" phase, the mid-1980s trends represent the great gaps between the positions of the two sides prior to the Madrid process. Both sides' people and both sides' leaders called for maximalist or rejectionist approaches with a certain symmetry. Neither public was a driving force for peace in this stage. Any leader who would seek to advance peace along the lines of two states – whether in 1988 or in 1993 – would essentially be contradicting public opinion and would have required both personal vision and powerful political backbone to face possible backlash.

At the same time, the years before Oslo were a time when neither leadership had articulated or openly supported a political framework representing "peace" that their publics could conceivably debate and support. The Palestinian leadership advocated primarily for a single Palestinian state in all of historic Palestine, and when the goal shifted to a state next to Israel, there was no vision or discussion of a bilateral negotiated solution, only a unilateral declaration. The Israeli leadership kept a generally non-committal, ambiguous approach, but one that was categorical nonetheless in its rejection of the idea of Palestinian self-determination in the form of an independent sovereign state. If the publics did not support peace based on a two-state solution, this must be seen within a context that did not offer a clear, articulated vision of a future peace to support.

The Oslo Years: Legitimisation of an Idea

Immediately after the signing of the 1993 Declaration of Principles, known as Oslo I, a breakthrough moment – a poll of West Bank and Gaza Palestinians from September 1993 – became the first to test their attitudes towards the accord. Nearly two-thirds said they supported the "Gaza-Jericho First" agreement. When asked if this agreement would ultimately help to achieve a Palestinian state and thereby fulfil Palestinian rights, 45 per cent, a plurality, said they thought it would. A smaller number, 34 per cent, said the agreement would not help achieve Palestinian goals, and 21 per cent did not know. Any doubt about the intention behind Palestinian political goals was clarified in a later question asking whether respondents supported or opposed changing the PLO Charter to include mutual recognition between the PLO and Israel; a majority of 57 per cent supported this (Center for Palestine Research and Studies, 1993/1).

Yitzhak Rabin was not an obvious pioneer for Palestinian self-determination. Given his role in advancing the Oslo Accords, which opened the road to the two-state solution, Rabin appeared to take a major risk in contradicting the majority within Israeli public opinion who rejected a Palestinian state. However, Rabin was also cautious: whether public opinion acted as a constraint or due to his own political discomfort, the Oslo Accords never mentioned a Palestinian state, and it was never clear that this was the outcome Israel supported during that time. Avoiding the commitment to a Palestinian state likely reflected the positions of the leadership, but was also aligned – coincidentally or not – with the majority of Israelis who opposed the idea.

Israeli Jews showed other internal contradictions: the vast majority supported the peace process in general under Rabin: 89 per cent favoured continuing the process in 1993 in total (strongly or somewhat). However, just 43 per cent support the "Gaza and Jericho First" plan as the first stage of agreements (Arian, 1995). The substantial contrast between the theoretical support for peace and negotiations and lower support for the actual agreements, becomes a recurring theme in later dynamics among both populations, at various times.

Nevertheless, a notable trend would appear within the Israeli public attitude throughout the 1990s. Again, although the Jaffee Center study presents a Jewish-only sample, the consistent tracking question about Palestinian statehood is instructive: From the initial and uneven rise starting in 1987, by 1993 support for a Palestinian state marched consistently upwards. This continued despite unrelenting turmoil during the 1990s, ranging from both Jewish and Palestinian terror, the assassination of Prime Minister Rabin and the election of right-wing leader Benjamin Netanyahu, who opposed the accords. Despite all this, support among Israeli Jews for a Palestinian state reached 50 per cent for the first time in the year after Netanyahu was elected. With minor anomalies, the Jewish public continued to show majority support of 50 per cent or higher from that point onwards, at least through 2009 – the phase following 2009 will be reviewed in the next section (Ben Meir and Bagno-Moldavsky 2010, 76).

Thus, the 1990s, or the early years of the Oslo agreements, were poised to be a time when both populations were slowly converging towards the idea of two states living side by side, rather than maximalist demands by Palestinians, or rejectionist positions by Israel regarding Palestinian self-determination.

However, beneath the surface of support for the agreement and the process, lay less-consistent and more-complex attitudes within both populations. On the one hand, each side did begin to legitimise the two-state compromise. But when the fledgling peace process went into implementation, and each side experienced reality in negative ways, their attitudes split into reactions against what the process had brought, mitigating their desire to keep supporting the ideal and the goal the peace process was intended to reach.

Palestinians under Oslo

Under Oslo, Palestinians engaged in proto-state-building through national institutions, alongside a revised political goal built on a historic compromise relative to their original goals. As noted above, strong public support for the Oslo process in its earliest days indicated the willingness to embark on this path. However, Palestinians quickly felt a negative impact of the accords on their lives. Within one year, 41 per cent reported that their economic situation had deteriorated; half said it had not changed. Just 9 per cent reported improvement. The trend was worse in Gaza, which had seen the earliest transfer of power to the Palestinian Authority (PA): there 49 per cent said their economic situation had gotten worse, and just 40 per cent said it had stayed the same (CPSR 12, 1994). By the end of the decade, a majority of 51 per cent said their economic situation had gotten worse compared to before the peace process (CPSR 45, Dec. 1999)

Still, a majority – nearly 52 per cent – expressed support for the Oslo process, responding that their support had either increased or remained supportive as in the past (CPSR 12, 1994). In an election simulation, Palestinians supported Fatah, the dominant party in the PLO, which was coming to be associated with the Oslo process, by more than four-to-one against Hamas (43 per cent versus 10 per cent respectively), which opposed the process (CPSR 12, 1994). In April 1997, when asked about a final status plan, a majority of 52 per cent supported a demilitarised Palestinian state established in 95 per cent of Gaza and the West Bank (CPSR 27, 1997).

By February 1995, Palestinian attitudes had taken a decisive negative turn. This poll was conducted one year after the massacre committed by Israeli settler Baruch Goldstein against Palestinian civilians in Hebron; following the attack, Israel had further restricted movement of Palestinians, already constrained by the new division of territory under the Oslo agreements (Btselem 2011).

By 1995, over 80 per cent opposed continuing the negotiations if settlement expansion continued simultaneously. A plurality of 46 per cent supported armed attacks against Israel, and support for Hamas had risen four points compared to the poll six months earlier (to 14 per cent). Still, a majority of 55 per cent believed that the process begun with the Oslo Accords would eventually lead to an independent Palestinian state in the West Bank and Gaza (CPSR 15, 1995). Palestinians showed frustration with the lived reality, moved towards conditionalism about the process, but still supported that same process as the path to reaching statehood.

Israeli Jews under Oslo.

The Israeli public reflected the duelling forces of heightened security fears, even as they internalised the shifting political vision. Some polls reflected grave anxiety: In March 1995 (following severe terrorist attacks in Tel Aviv), nearly two-thirds (64 per cent) of Israelis said their personal security had gotten worse since the start of the process. Yet the feeling appeared to reflect immediate experiences; by July of that year, following a phase of relatively few attacks, that number declined by 16 points, to 48 per cent (Peace Index, July 1995). The fast, reactive shifts of opinion were consistent within the July survey: the portion of those who believed the PA was working to discourage attacks rose 17 points (to 38 per cent), and those who felt Palestinians were not fulfilling the spirit of the accords fell 11 points (to 45 per cent) during the same interval, when attacks subsided for a few months (Peace Index, July 1995).

While the spams of violence produced jumpy attitudes, Israeli Jewish society was more consistent in its opposition to some of the major components that need to be addressed in a final status accord – which was not yet on the table, but in the air. For example, just over one-fifth accepted the idea of evacuating all settlements for an agreement (Peace Index, July 1995). Most other core issues were not yet being tested.

At the same time, within one year after Oslo, Israeli Jews began to assess that a Palestinian state would come into being, regardless of whether they supported it. The percentage who believed a Palestinian state would come into being doubled, a dramatic shift, from 37 per cent prior to the first accord to a 74 per cent majority in 1994 (Arian 1995). In 1996, the Labour Party changed its platform to remove its opposition to a Palestinian state. Once again, the question of whether force results in concessions is complicated by the fact that violence was perpetrated by Jewish Israelis during this time as well (the Goldstein massacre and the assassination of Rabin); and that the dramatic rise in the public's assessment that Palestinian statehood could become a reality occurred in the context of a historic peace process that looked, for a phase, like it would be irreversible.

Hence during this phase, both sides came to legitimise the idea of separation, apparently (if not explicitly) into two states within historic Palestine as the broad goal. But each was already experiencing the dissonance of supporting the trajectory overall, while becoming embittered about their experiences in daily life. Unsurprisingly, in public discourse, each would come to blame the other for violating the terms and the spirit of the peace process; neither would assume responsibility for their own role. In February 1998, a steady 60 per cent of Jewish Israelis believed that Arabs (in general) had "not come to terms with the existence of the State of Israel and would destroy it if they could" (Peace Index, Feb. 1998) This is almost identical to the 63 per cent who said the same of Palestinians in particular, in 1996 (Peace Index, February 1996). Among Palestinians, by December 1999 just 18 per cent trusted the new Israeli government of Ehud Barak to advance peace, though he had run on a platform of reviving the peace process (CPSR 45, 1999). Yet in the same survey, fully three-quarters continued to support this peace process.

The Paradigmatic Years

Ironically, the history of public opinion research testing the term "two state solution," at least on the Israeli side, is an apt metaphor for the fate of this solution. The negotiations that would begin in Camp David in July 2000 and the subsequent formal and informal rounds through 2003 (a phase that included Camp David, the Taba negotiations, and the civil society-led Geneva initiative) represented the best chances of reaching a final status accord on two states. But polling on the term "two-state solution," or questions describing this concept in an explicit way, appeared consistently in the years following the failure of those negotiations.

In other words, by the time the concept of a final status agreement based on two states or the "two-state solution" became sufficiently common for researchers to begin asking the question clearly, and a solid majority of the public on both sides expressed support for this approach in surveys, the best chance of reaching it had already passed.

Israeli Jewish Society

As noted above, in the 1980s and 1990s the INSS/Jaffee Center studies asked about support or opposition to a Palestinian state; this question's wording did not include a solution, nor any sense of mutuality. Only in 2006 – long after the failure of Camp David and even after the Second Intifada had largely died down – did INSS researchers begin asking, "Do you support or oppose the solution of two states for two peoples?" Without the singular focus on a Palestinian state, but articulating the concept of a comprehensive conflict resolution, support among the Jewish samples rose to fully 70 per cent in 2006, 63 per cent the following year, and back up to nearly three-quarters (74 per cent) in 2009 (Ben Meir and Bagno-Moldavsky 2010, 77).

During this decade, pollsters began testing the detailed items of an agreement, that had been elaborated during the various rounds of the negotiations. The Israeli public would begin to support these substantive elements as well, in addition to conceptual approval for two states. For example, on one of the most sensitive issues of any two-state agreement, of dividing Jerusalem, support ranged from 37–41 per cent; not a majority but a large minority (Shamir 2007, 37). Critically, support for dismantling settlements for the sake of peace rose following the collapse of Camp David. In July 2000, in a poll taken immediately following the Camp David summit, just under half of all Israelis in 2000 (44 per cent) supported "the dismantling of most settlements" as per the language of the survey; by mid-2001, support climbed to 58 per cent, during the first year of the Second Intifada (Shamir and Shikaki 2010, 93). Prime Minister Ariel Sharon began building his case for dismantling settlements in Gaza from 2003 (Sharon 2003). Support for settlement evacuation reached a peak of roughly two-thirds just prior to, and during, the dismantling of settlements from Gaza, then fell again shortly after (Shamir and Shikaki 2010, 93).

This trend can be considered among the hardest examples of the presumed causal link between the use of force (considering the violence of the Second Intifada) and support for concessions. However, it also followed a major normalisation of the two-state separation advanced at the Camp David summit, which broke new ground for discussing final-status issues, and reached its highest point as the country's leader gave unprecedented legitimacy to the idea of dismantling settlements. Were these or the violence the causal force behind the shift? The data do not give a clear answer.

Palestinian Society

Among Palestinians, tracking polls conducted by the Jerusalem Media and Communications Center (JMCC) throughout the decade are the most indicative. These studies asked a question providing several main options:

> Some believe the two-state formula is the favoured solution for the Israeli-Palestinian conflict, while others believe that historic Palestine cannot be divided and thus the favoured solution is a binational state on all of Palestine with equal rights for Palestinians and Israelis. Which of these do you prefer?
>
> *(JMCC 2001–2010)*

Respondents were allowed to say "none" or "other" and some volunteered additional responses, including an "Islamic state" or "Palestinian state." Nevertheless, in all 21 surveys conducted from 2001 through 2010, the large majority or a plurality chose the two-state solution. In 11 of these studies, the two-state solution was favoured by an absolute majority. Notably, the highest level of support (69 per cent) was in January 2001. Support then dropped sharply to 44 per cent in April, and remained just below half for most of the years of the Second Intifada – raising further questions about the thesis that the use of force leads to greater conciliation, on either side (JMCC 2001–2010).

Indeed, during the year before and after the disengagement, support again topped half in the JMCC polls, and for most of the polls to follow. PSR surveys showed similar results, with a strong majority later in the decade, though the question was asked in different forms. A study from March 2007 (following the elections, but prior to the Hamas takeover of Gaza in June of that year) showed that a strong majority of 72 per cent supported the Arab League's Peace Initiative (a version of the two-state solution), and 71 per cent supported a process of negotiations leading to the establishment of a Palestinian state in most of the West Bank and Gaza, even prior to a final status solution. Also similar to the Israeli public, Palestinian polling showed significant, if not always majority, support for the substantive details of a two-state agreement. When considering each item separately, support was uneven but rose for all items during the years of the Second Intifada.

The idea of a demilitarised Palestinian state never achieved a majority but still rose, from under 20 per cent in 1996 to more than double – nearly 40 per cent – in 2003, before going down to just under 30 per cent, still higher than the starting point. Support for the border compromise (including the dismantling of outlying settlements), refugees, and security compromises would reach a majority at least once between 2000–2006; support for the compromise to divide Jerusalem ranged from 33–46 per cent among Palestinians (Shamir 2007, 37).

Thus, the first decade of the 2000s saw both sides embracing the two-state solution, in name and in substance, just as this approach became the paradigm supported openly by the leadership of both sides and embraced by the international community – primarily the United States and Europe. However, the data shows that support for the actual details of the plan was not stable; in fact, mutual support for the detailed plans occurred at points in time rather than forming a solid basis over the years. Starting from the end of the Camp David talks, the Joint Israeli-Palestinian polls regularly tested the specific items as discussed at Camp David and later elaborated by the negotiators, through to the Geneva Initiative. After each item was tested, the two polls would ask respondents whether they supported or opposed the final status agreement on the basis of those items. Israeli support ranged from 47–64 per cent from 2003 through 2006. During this same time, Palestinian support ranged from 39 to 54 per cent.[6] But the only phase during which both sides showed a majority of support for the whole detailed package was late 2004/early 2005 (Shamir 2007).

Still, the broader concept of the two-state solution was accepted more consistently by a majority within each society, if not the detailed package. In December 2005, for example, nearly two-thirds of Israelis (65 per cent) and 60 per cent of Palestinians – a clear majority in both cases – supported the American framework known as the "Road Map," a framework for the peace process that was explicitly designed to reach a two-state solution (Truman/PCPSR, JIPP #18, 2005).[7]

In 2007, 60 per cent of Palestinians and 64 per cent of Israelis supported "mutual recognition of Israel as the state for the Jewish people and Palestine as the state for the Palestinian people" (Truman/PCPSR, JIPP #24, 2007). This approach remained fairly consistent despite a deep and abiding chasm within Palestinian society – the 2006 elections that brought Hamas to a prominent position, and later takeover of Gaza. These events laid the groundwork for a leadership rift that continues to this day and could have been expected to legitimise the rejectionist approach to two-states espoused by Hamas. Yet, in the March 2007 PSR survey, 63 per cent supported the mutual recognition according to the language above. Similarly, among Israelis, support for negotiations towards a two-state solution remained high during this period, ranging from 61–72 per cent support during the decade (Peace Index surveys).

In other words, the trends among the two populations mirrored each other: widespread acceptance of the two-state solution, and substantial but inconsistent support for the major compromise components. Each item received different levels of support, and at no point did either side express majority support for all the elements of the final status package. After hearing all the details, there was only one phase when a majority on both sides supported the overall package for a final status accord (late 2004/early 2005).

Still, this was the most auspicious decade for the solution in terms of the three-way support from the public, domestic political leadership of both sides (at least in theory and official rhetoric), and international support. And yet countervailing forces meant that despite this wide support for a two-state solution, actual progress towards reaching a final status agreement slowed. The violence of the Second Intifada soured Israelis politically, sending many further to the right-wing of the political map, and eviscerating the political left. Israel's disengagement from Gaza was a dramatic moment but it was a unilateral action rather than the product of bilateral negotiations; Ariel Sharon's own advisors stated even before the disengagement took place that it was intended to freeze rather than advance the process, though it is debatable whether the Israeli public viewed it this way (Shavit 2004).

The isengageement also led to a divided Palestinian leadership, casting all future negotiations into doubt. The 2008 negotiations held under Israeli leader Ehud Olmert and the successor to Yasser Arafat, Mahmoud Abbas (Abu Mazen), appeared to reach an advanced stage of potential agreements, but the political conditions were poor from the start: Olmert was already facing pressure at home due to corruption investigations, and the Palestinian leadership was already split between Fatah and Hamas, to name a few elements burdening the talks. The failure of those negotiations led to a deep decline in the public's faith that a bilateral process could possibly bring peace. The ironic alignment of all political forces formally and normatively in favour of a two-state solution combined with the total failure to achieve the goal is a historic loss for this approach. As public expectations rose – with greater or lesser enthusiasm – over this decade, the empirical failure led to deep despair about both the desirability, and feasibility, of both the process and its goal in the next decade.

The Decline: Disintegration of Process, Faith, and Support

The start of 2009 saw two defining events that can be seen as either causal factors or at least turning points marking the next phase in the lifespan of the two-state solution. In late 2008, war erupted between Israel and Hamas in Gaza, which continued through early 2009. Almost simultaneously, in early 2009, Likud won the Israeli election (coming in second place, but ultimately responsible for forming the coalition government) and Benjamin Netanyahu returned to power. These events frame the beginning of a shift into the current phase of a slow decline for the two-state solution, which continues, incrementally, to the present.

Support on both sides for the broad concept of a two-state solution began to waver and diverge from the upward trajectory of the 1990s, then the high plateau of the 2000s. Between 2008 and 2009, support on the Israeli side dropped ten points (from 69 to 59 per cent), and seven points among Palestinians (from 68 to 61 per cent). Among all Israelis, this support became volatile: it rose again in 2010, then declined unevenly over the next years.[8] Palestinians, meanwhile, showed a consistent, incremental downward trend in support for the broad idea of a two-state solution, dipping below half for the first time in 2014, with only small adjustments in the years to follow. In 2018, both Israeli Jews and Palestinians showed, in a general sense, a new low of just 43 per cent support for the two-state solution (Shikaki and Scheindlin 2018; see Figure 31.1).

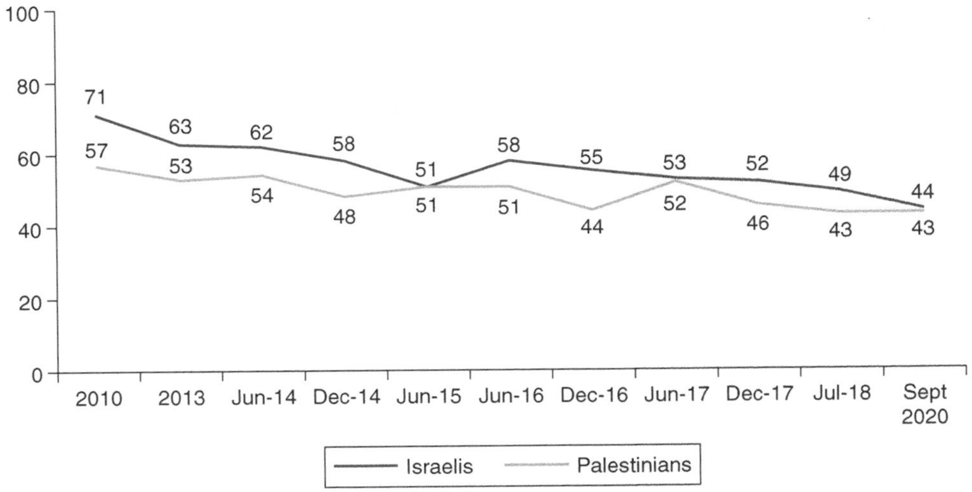

Figure 31.1 PSR and TAU Palestinian-Israeli Pulse.

It should be noted that different surveys continue to ask variations on this question, receiving different results. For example, the Tel Aviv University Peace Index from October 2019 asked only, "do you support or oppose the establishment of an independent Palestinian state next to Israel," without mentioning the two-state solution or any agreement. Just 41 per cent of Jews supported this, compared to 59 per cent of Arab citizens of Israel (Peace Index, October 2019). By contrast, the Institute for National Security Studies (INSS) continued to conduct an annual poll, asking only "do you support or oppose a two-state solution," without specifically mentioning the Palestinian state; the 2019 INSS survey showed higher support – 58 per cent among Jews (INSS 2019). However, the INSS survey presents a time series for the question, which shows a key finding: a decline over the course of the decade matching the same erosion seen in the joint Israeli-Palestinian surveys during the same time, with the peak support in 2006 (71 per cent), 69 per cent support at the start of the decade, and an 11-point decline by 2019.

Why did public support on both sides decline so steadily, with such mirror-image consistency on both sides? Is it sufficient to say that the hardline right-wing Israeli leadership and the demoralisation following "Operation Cast Lead" in Gaza (2008–2009) caused this? These factors may be correct, but they do not sufficiently parse the contributing factors.

One obvious additional reason was the ongoing escalation: Operation Cast Lead was soon followed by two further wars in Gaza between Israel and Hamas, known as operations "Pillar of Defence" (2012) and "Protective Edge" (2014) – eventually followed in 2021 by yet another Israel-Hamas war called "Guardian of the Walls." The former was relatively limited, but Protective Edge caused vast destruction and took a massive toll on lives in Gaza, with 2,200 people killed, of which nearly two-thirds were non-combatants (Btselem 2016).

Among Palestinians, the idea that high costs of force yield conciliatory attitudes is not borne out, judging by polls showing political preferences. PCPSR surveys from this time testing support for Palestinian political factions are indicative: after each war, support for the hard-line Hamas presidential candidate (Ismail Haniya) increased, with a corresponding decline in support for the Fatah candidate (Abu Mazen) – the party associated with negotiations and the two-state solution, rather than military force (see Figure 31.2). However, this dynamic tended to reverse by the time of the next study, giving Fatah a tenuous lead for some of this time.

As the decade drew to a close, the Palestinian Authority suffered a dramatic and fundamental loss of legitimacy among Palestinians. In a September 2019 survey, 61 per cent said they would like President Mahmoud Abbas to resign; in a potential presidential election, the

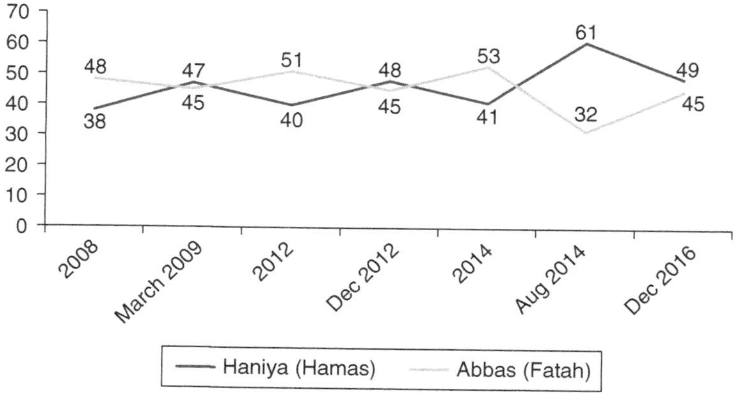

Figure 31.2 Support in Presidential vote, data from PSR surveys.

Fatah and Hamas candidates (Abbas and Ismail Haniye, respectively) were nearly tied. In a consistent finding, the September 2019 PSR survey (of Palestinians only), showed that about three-quarters were dissatisfied with the job performance of the PA, specifically with regard to its failure to address Israel's home demolitions in a West Bank neighbourhood. This highlights the fact that assessments of the PA are inextricably linked with attitudes towards the situation with Israel. Similarly, dissatisfaction with the PA is an indicator of declining support for the two-state solution – first, because the two-state solution is the policy associated with Fatah, who leads the PA; and second, because of growing concerns that a Palestinian state would be based on current government structures, characterised by high corruption levels and dysfunction and thus leading to a malfunctioning, defective state.[9] Correspondingly, despite a modest rise, support for the two-state solution went back down to 42 per cent in the September survey.

During this decade, Israelis mostly continued to support a process in name only. Based on Peace Index surveys, a majority (generally hovering above or below 60 per cent) continued to support negotiations. However, the portion of those who believed such negotiations would actually reach a solution began the decade at about one-third, and broadly declined, reaching as low as 22 per cent in 2017 (Peace Index surveys).

Among Jewish samples, attitudes to the main compromises for a two-state solution declined along with the broad conceptual support. On the most sensitive core issues of Jerusalem and refugees, the same basic concepts tested in the 2000s, the public expressed a steep decline in support: the elements of compromise over Jerusalem were supported by one-quarter of Jews by the joint survey in 2018, and just 20 per cent supported the refugee compromise (Shikaki and Scheindlin, 2018). These figures are steady and low; Israelis mainly supported the idea of a demilitarised Palestinian state and the optimistic notion of mutual recognition (among Jews, 59 per cent and 61 per cent, respectively).

The most striking decline, perhaps, relates to settlements. From a peak of nearly 70 per cent support for dismantling "most" settlements for peace in the mid-2000s, surveys during the second decade show that settlements are the clearest fault-line in Israeli Jewish society, dividing even centrist Israelis completely in half between those who support or oppose settlements, in various questions. For example, when asked if settlements help or harm Israeli security, data collected for Btselem showed how the issue polarises left and right, among other groups; in total, just 42 per cent express an attitude against settlements (see Figure 31.3).

Few surveys explicitly test Israeli willingness to dismantle settlements during the latter part of the decade; another indicator that the idea was less prominent in political discourse. The

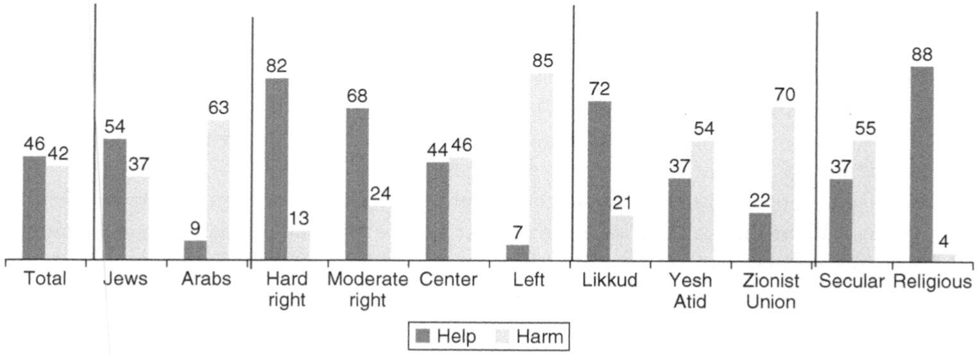

Figure 31.3 Settlements, by sector.

main settlement items tested in the joint Palestinian Israeli survey showed slightly less support than in the past: 36 per cent of Israeli Jews supported the following basic compromise: "The Palestinian state will be established in the entirety of West Bank and the Gaza Strip, except for several blocs of settlement which will be annexed to Israel in a territorial exchange. Israel will evacuate all other settlements."

Public disinterest and loss of faith in the process was mirrored by the political leadership on both sides. There have been no formal peace negotiations since the 2013–2014 process led by United States Secretary of State John Kerry, which hardly raised expectations from the start (Ben Zion 2013). In the numerous political campaigns that have been held on the Israeli side during this decade, the issue of peace, or conflict-resolution in any form, barely appears in campaign rhetoric. During the Trump era, bilateral negotiations were replaced altogether by a new form of diplomacy, a sort of US-Israeli mutual agreement to advance annexationist steps that undermined a two-state solution and the Palestinian leadership, while the external mediator – the United States – developed a plan on its own. In this context, it is little surprise that nearly two-thirds of Palestinians and a 45 per cent plurality of Israeli Jews believe that the two-state solution is no longer viable (Palestinian-Israeli Pulse, September 2020).

Conclusion

In conclusion, the data over time provide insight into some of the guiding questions and propositions posed at the beginning of this chapter.

- Parallel processes/mirror images: While Israeli and Palestinian societies differ greatly in their history and identity, they share some uncanny patterns of opinion with relation to the conflict. Both held hardline or maximalist positions prior to the late 1980s. Both saw increasing legitimacy for the two-state idea during the 1990s, embracing it more deeply during the 2000s; the decline of support is almost a mirror image during the second decade. Mirror images are not limited to peace-process questions; for example, both aspire to build a society that blends democracy and a particular religiously grounded national identity: In the 1980s, Palestinians envisioned their society's identity as a mixture of democratic and Islamic character – at almost exactly the same rate that Israeli Jews saw their country's preferred identity, containing both a Jewish and democratic character, in 2018.
- The question of whether the use of force is the decisive factor pushing both sides towards reconciliation has no conclusive answer from this examination of opinion trends juxtaposed with events. At each point where opinion became more conciliatory against the background of violence, it turns out there was also a context of compromise or a peace process that could be an equally powerful explanation, such as the First Intifada, alongside the first major Palestinian compromise of 1988; or the terror waves in the 1990s, alongside a peace process that seemed destined to advance. In the 2000s, violence appeared to have the opposite effect – causing both sides to express increased support for right-wing political forces that promised more militant approaches to the conflict.
- Is one side more committed to peace than the other? Only one project tracks identical questions about the issues at stake throughout two of the four periods observed here: the joint Israeli-Palestinian surveys. Broadly, these surveys show that both sides accept the overall concept of a two-state solution at higher rates than they support the detailed plans. Responses to individual items vary; during most of the project's nearly 20 years, support tended to be higher on the Israeli side for some items (mutual recognition, demilitarised Palestinian state), and higher on the Palestinian side for others (the refugee compromise).

Both sides showed low support for the division of Jerusalem in the various questions. When Jewish samples were compared to Palestinians' in recent years, support for the full package after hearing all the details was similar, with each side showing just slightly higher support at points. But in recent years the basic pattern of declining support for the concept, discouragement at the details and despair at the feasibility, holds for both.

As to the question at the heart of this inquiry: Does the "loss" of the two-state solution reflect or contradict public will? Given the consistently high support for the concept itself, it would be wrong to suggest that the leaders followed the public in distancing the two sides from an agreement. However, as support slid, and the specific compromises for peace lost their basis on both sides, it became clear that the public would not be a leading force for peace.

Finally, is the decline definitive or reversible? Here it is important to note that despite the broad downward trend, the two-state solution is still the preferred solution relative to others that were tested in various ways throughout nearly all the polls here. None of these surveys have shown another vision – one equal state, one unequal state in which one side is dominant, or even the status quo – overtaking the two-state solution in terms of public support. Further, under the right conditions and incentives, including adjustments and additions to the details of the plan, the joint survey research has shown repeatedly that more people can still be won over to support a two-state solution. Failing renewed negotiations and significant new energy to update the basic ideas, the current trends can be expected to continue.

Recommended Readings

Ben Meir, Y., and O. Bagno-Moldavsky. 2010. *Vox Populi: Trends in Israeli Public Opinion on National Security 2004–2009*, Memorandum 106. Tel Aviv: Institute for National Security Studies.

Data Israel: Archive of Israeli public opinion research, from 1940s to the present, collected through Israel Democracy Institute: https://dataisrael.idi.org.il/.

Key, V. O. Jr. 1964. *Public Opinion and American Democracy*. New York: Alfred Knopf.

Putnam, R. 1988. "Diplomacy and Domestic Politics: The Logic of Two-Level Games." *International Organization* 42:3, 427–460.

Shamir, J., and K. Shikaki. 2010. *Palestinian and Israeli Public Opinion: The Public Imperative and the Second Intifada*. Bloomington and Indianapolis, IN: University of Indiana Press.

Survey Archive of Palestinian Center for Policy and Survey Research. www.pcpsr.org/en/node/105.

Trumbore, P. F. 1998. "Public Opinion as a Domestic Constraint in International Negotiations: Two-Level Games in the Anglo-Irish Peace Process." *International Studies Quarterly* 42:3, pp. 545–565.

Notes

1 Foyle surveys numerous research studies on this question, specifically on issues of foreign policy. There is equally extensive literature regarding the impact of public opinion on domestic policy. Since decision-making on the conflict includes considerations more akin to foreign policy dilemmas, the foreign-policy literature is more relevant for the purposes of this chapter.

2 Office of the Historian, The Madrid Conference, 1991–1992. Department of State. https://history.state.gov/milestones/1989-1992/madrid-conference.

3 The finding shows a fascinating parallel with modern-day conceptions of Israel's preferred character, according to Jewish participants: Nearly 56 per cent of Palestinians in total supported a state with a national or partly (30 per cent), or fully Islamic (26.5 per cent) character in 1986; in the 2018 Israel Democracy Index, 26 per cent of Jews said the Jewish component of Israel should be dominant, and 38 per cent supported a combination of Jewish and democratic (Israel Democracy Institute 2018).

4 Palestinian 1988 Declaration of Independence: https://ecf.org.il/media_items/845.

5 This kind of finding makes it tempting to conclude that war causes Israelis to support concessions in greater numbers, by pointing to the Yom Kippur War of 1973 as the cause for the decline. However,

the first 15-point drop in support for the hardline position occurred between February and March of 1968; it is true that between 1974 and 1975, shortly after the war, support dropped 30 points to a new low of 36 per cent who supported just minimal or no land concessions in the West Bank, but this figure then rose precipitously to 68 per cent in 1976. There is little in Arian's data to indicate a clear causal link between war itself and concessions (though it can be hypothesised that perceptions of victory or near-defeat might influence attitudes towards concessions, with higher perception of victory (1967) associated with less inclination to compromise, and given the deep existential fear of defeat in 1973, the reverse might be true.

6 Palestinian support appears generally lower than Israeli overall support. However, it should be recognised that Arab citizens of Israel are included in the Joint Poll samples, and all studies show that they support all elements of the peace process at a far higher rate than Jews, raising the weighted average. Jewish-only data is not available during this phase, but is analyzed separately in the final section of this chapter.

7 Full text of the "Roadmap" available at Israel Foreign Ministry website: https://mfa.gov.il/mfa/foreignpolicy/peace/guide/pages/a%20performance-based%20roadmap%20to%20a%20permanent%20two-sta.aspx.

8 Roughly during the 2000s, polling studies worked more consciously to include Arab samples relative to the earlier decades. However, this is not to imply that volatility is the result of the full representative samples. In general, Arab citizens of Israel show the most stable support for a two-state solution and its component parts. Support for the general concept generally reaches 80 per cent or higher; therefore shifts during this time mainly refer to the Jewish respondents.

9 This has been the explanation of Dr. Khalil Shikaki, who conducts the PSR surveys – conversations with author.

Questions for Discussion:

(1) What is the direction of influence in policy-making, negotiations, and international conflict decision-making? Does public opinion drive leadership decisions, or vice versa, or is the relationship reciprocal and responsive?

(2) Do negotiation breakthroughs only occur following an escalation of violence? Is escalation of violence likely to be followed by concessions/breakthrough in negotiations, via changes in public opinion – that is, does violence lead conflict parties to support concessions?

(3) Is the two-state solution a consensus paradigm in Israeli and Palestinian society, if so, when and why?

(4) What do the questionnaires, topics, and wording of questions say about the political discourse over time?

(5) Is public opinion on conflict issues fixed or dynamic? What kinds of factors cause public opinion to change over time?

References

Arian, A., M. Shamir, and R. Ventura. 1992. "Public Opinion and Political Change: Israel and the Intifada." *Comparative Politics* 24:3, 317–334.

Arian, A. 1995. *Security Threatened: Surveying Israeli Public Opinion on Peace and War*. Cambridge Studies in Political Psychology and Public Opinion, Cambridge University Press; Tel Aviv University: Jaffee Center for Strategic Studies.

Ben Meir, Y., and O. Bagno-Moldavsky. 2010. *Vox Populi: Trends in Israeli Public Opinion on National Security 2004–2009*, Memorandum 106. Tel Aviv: Institute for National Security Studies.

Ben Zion, I. 2013. "Press-imism abounds over renewed talks." *Times of Israel*, 21 July. Available at: www.timesofisrael.com/press-imism-abounds-over-renewed-talks/.

Btselem. 2011. "17 years after Goldstein Massacre, Hebron city center paralyzed." 3 March. Available at: www.btselem.org/hebron/20110303_hebron_17_years_after_goldstein_massacre.

Btselem. 2016. "50 Days: More than 500 Children: Facts and figures on fatalities in Gaza, Summer 2014." 20 July. Available at: www.btselem.org/press_releases/20160720_fatalities_in_gaza_conflict_2014.

Center for Policy and Survey Research (CPSR). 1993. "Public Opinion Poll #1: The Palestinian-Israeli Agreement: "Gaza-Jericho First." 10–11 September. Available at: http://pcpsr.org/sites/default/files/Results%20of%20Public%20Opinion%20Poll%20English%20table%201.pdf.

Center for Policy and Survey Research (CPSR). 1994. "Public Opinion Poll #12: The West Bank and Gaza Strip." 29–30 September. Available at: http://pcpsr.org/sites/default/files/Results%20of%20Public%20Opinion%20Poll%20English%20table%2012.pdf.

Center for Policy and Survey Research (CPSR). 1995. "Public Opinion Poll #15: Armed Attacks, Negotiations, 'Separation,' Elections, Unemployment, and Palestinian-Jordanian Relation.," 2–4 February. Available at: www.pcpsr.org/sites/default/files/Results%20of%20Public%20Opinion%20Poll%20English%20table%2015.pdf.

Center for Policy and Survey Research (CPSR). 1999. "CPSR 27: PA and PLC Performance, Democracy, Armed Attacks, Local Councils and a Permanent Status Plan," 10–12 April. Available at: www.pcpsr.org/en/node/544.

Center for Policy and Survey Research (CPSR). 1999. "CPSR Public Opinion Poll 45: The Peace Process, Israeli Debate about Refugees, Safe Passage, Events in Nazareth, Refugees in Lebanon, Hamas and Jordan, Corruption and Democracy, Elections for the President and Vice-president, and Political Affiliation," 2–4 December. Available at: www.pcpsr.org/en/node/507.

Foyle, D. 1997. "Public Opinion and Foreign Policy: Elite Beliefs as a Mediating Variable." *International Studies Quarterly* 41:1, 141–169.

Halbfinger, D. 2019. "U.S. Ambassador Says Israel Has Right to Annex Parts of West Ban." *New York Times*. 9 June. Available at: www.nytimes.com/2019/06/08/world/middleeast/israel-west-bank-david-friedman.html.

Harry S. Truman Research Institute for the Advancement of Peace at the Hebrew University of Jerusalem and the Palestinian Center for Policy and Survey Research. 2005. "Joint Israel Palestine Poll (JIPP) #18: Stable Majority Support for Clinton's Final Status Package Among Israelis but Decline in Support Among Palestinians. Large support in both publics for the extension of the cease fire," December. Available at: www.pcpsr.org/en/node/436.

Harry S. Truman Research Institute for the Advancement of Peace at the Hebrew University of Jerusalem and the Palestinian Center for Policy and Survey Research. 2007. "Joint Israel Palestine Poll (JIPP) #24: In the Backdrop of the Gaza Takeover by Hamas, Israelis and Palestinians Share Grim Expectations of the other Side's Leadership and the Chances for the Resumption of Negotiations," June 2007. Available at: www.pcpsr.org/en/node/426.

Institute for National Security Studies (INSS). 2019. *National Security Index: 2019*. Available at: www.inss.org.il/wp-content/uploads/2019/01/%d7%9e%d7%93%d7%93-%d7%94%d7%91%d7%99%d7%98%d7%97%d7%95%d7%9f-%d7%94%d7%9c%d7%90%d7%95%d7%9e%d7%99-%d7%91%d7%90%d7%a0%d7%92%d7%9c%d7%99%d7%aa-2019.pdf?offset=undefined&posts=undefined&outher=undefined&from_date=undefined&to_date=undefined.

Jerusalem Media and Communication Center (JMCC). 2001–2010. Polling from 2001–2010. Available at: www.jmcc.org/imagesfolder/45_57_14_20_4_2010.jpg.

Lohr, S. 1988. "Arafat says PLO accepted Israel." *New York Times*, 8 December. Available at: www.nytimes.com/1988/12/08/world/arafat-says-plo-accepted-israel.html.

Moughrabi, F., and P. El-Nazer. 1989. "What Do Palestinian Americans Think? Results of a Public Opinion Survey." *Journal of Palestine Studies* 18:4, 91–101.

Palestinian Center for Policy and Survey Research and Evens Program for Conflict Mediation and Management (Tel Aviv University). 2020. "Palestinian-Israeli Pulse: A Joint Poll Summary Report," August 2020. Available at: www.pcpsr.org/en/node/823

Polisar, D. 2015. "What do Palestinians Want?" *Mosaic Magazine*. Available at: https://mosaicmagazine.com/essay/israel-zionism/2015/11/what-do-palestinians-want/.

Quandt, W. B. 1986. "Camp David and Peacemaking in the Middle East." *Political Science Quarterly* 101:3, 357–377.

Shadid, M., and R. Seltzer. 1988. "Political Attitudes of Palestinians in the West Bank and Gaza Strip." *The Middle East Journal* 42:1, 16–32.

Shamir, J. 2007. *Public Opinion in the Israeli-Palestinian Conflict: From Geneva to Disengagement to Kadima and Hamas*. Washington, DC: United States Institute of Peace.

Shamir, J., and K. Shikaki. 2010. *Palestinian and Israeli Public Opinion: The Public Imperative in the Second Intifada*. Bloomington and Indianapolis, IN: Indiana University Press.

Sharon, A. 2003. "Address by PM Ariel Sharon at the Fourth Herzliya Conference Dec 18- 2003." Israel Foreign Ministry Website. Available at: www.mfa.gov.il/mfa/pressroom/2003/pages/address%20by%20pm%20ariel%20sharon%20at%20the%20fourth%20herzliya.aspx.

Shavit, A. 2004. "Top PM Aide: Gaza Plan Aims to Freeze the Peace Process." *Haaretz*, 6 October. Available at: www.haaretz.com/1.4710372.

Shikaki, K., and D. Scheindlin. 2018. "Role of Public Opinion in the Resilience/Resolution of the Palestinian-Israeli Conflict." *Palestinian-Israeli Pulse: A Joint Poll (2016–2018) – Final Report.* Ramallah: PSR and Tel Aviv University: The Tami Steinmetz Center for Peace Research.

Tel Aviv University, Peace Index (prior to 2010). Poll data available through database search of specific questions (Hebrew) at https://dataisrael.idi.org.il/ July 1995, February 1996, February 1998.

Tel Aviv University, Tami Steinmetz Center for Peace Resarch, 2019. "Peace Index Findings, October 2019." (Hebrew). Available at: https://social-sciences.tau.ac.il/sites/socsci.tau.ac.il/files/media_server/resolution/%D7%9E%D7%9E%D7%A6%D7%90%D7%99%D7%9D%20%D7%9E%D7%93%D7%93%20%D7%94%D7%A9%D7%9C%D7%95%D7%9D%20%D7%90%D7%95%D7%A7%D7%98%D7%95%D7%91%D7%A82019%20%D7%9C%D7%90%D7%AA%D7%A8.pdf

Thrall, N. 2017. *The Only Language They Understand: Forcing Compromise in Israel and Palestine.* New York, Metropolitan Books.

32

POPULAR CULTURE IN ISRAEL/PALESTINE

Anastasia Valassopoulos

Introduction

> The violence and catastrophe that so frequently prevail in the landscape of Palestine and Israel give added weight to analytical tendencies to read culture as outside of or strictly determined by the realm of the political, and thus of subsidiary importance to the radical scholarly agenda.
>
> *(Stein and Swedenburg 2005, 7)*

Stein and Swedenburg, in their indispensable 2005 edited collection, *Palestine, Israel and the Politics of Popular Culture*, argue that "attention to popular culture configures both politics and history differently, providing a significant alternative to some of the political narratives and paradigms that have dominated academic, activist, and popular discourse on Palestine and Israel" (Stein and Swedenburg 2005, 11). Rather than read the historical debates – local, regional, and international – into the popular culture and see that culture as reflecting the socio-economic conditions on the ground, the debates in this chapter build on Stein and Swedenburg's work to actively advance the specificity of popular culture and its ability to speak differently to the context of occupation and to shape its experience.

Helga Tawil-Souri, in her 2011 work on Palestinian cultural studies, reveals the difficulty with the critical and discursive move described above. Overhearing a conversation between two men at an art exhibition in Ramallah, Tawil-Souri is reminded of the particular weight of representative expectations. The men, she recalls, rather than explore the meaning behind some of the conceptual art on display, bemoaned the fact that "the photographer had chosen to focus on colourful textiles rather than the ugliness of Palestinian refugees' lives" (Tawil-Souri 2011, 136). Speaking of the complexities in contextualising Arab cultural studies (but insisting on the necessity of doing so), Tarik Sabry reminds us of the extent to which "pan-Arab intellectuals [were] shaped by key historical events: the occupation of Palestine in 1948, the nationalisation of the Suez Canal by Nasser in July 1956, and the Arab-Israeli wars of 1967 and 1973" (Sabry 2011, 6). In other words, Arab culture is, more often than not, too heavily refracted and evaluated through its perceived engagement with these landmark events. Tawil-Souri's observations that the cultural events she most often encountered reproduced "jingoistic" presentations, "wallowing in Palestinian losses since 1948" (Tawil-Souri 2011, 137), and reflect

DOI: 10.4324/9780429027376-39

the difficulty for some artists and cultural actors – and indeed their audiences – to move away from the expectations that they engage with explicit socio-historical material in ways that make clear their political and ethnic allegiance. The fact that "the cultural records of Palestine only reflected its political horrors, with occupation, exile, loss, violence" (Tawil-Souri 2011, 138) is perhaps, on reflection, disappointing but not surprising. Tawil-Souri makes an important point that we must be attentive to: no matter how far we might seek to valorise or give value to the radical engagement that we see in contemporary popular culture, many Palestinians remain unimpressed with the array of "photographs, feature films, graffiti, musical compositions, when their themes do not directly portray the everyday experiences or 'political realities'" (Tawil-Souri 2011, 138).

It is useful to keep these issues in mind as we examine the contemporary popular culture that deals with the experience of Palestinians today, whether in the occupied territories or in Israel. The elevation of radically conceptual popular culture, critically and aesthetically, is a positive endeavour, but it sits within an often understandably conservative context. *Understandably*, because of the open question of Palestinian statehood, and *conservative*, because of the desire, by critics and intellectuals of Palestine, to often depict a unified vision around the representation of self-determination. Popular culture in all its various forms opens up a multitude of questions that then encourage participants and viewers to drill down into what it means to be creative, to be influenced, to be culturally hybrid. These forms do not always sit comfortably alongside a need to maintain an orthodox view towards the goal of statehood, global recognition, full human rights, reliable infrastructure, education and health facilities, and security.

Popular culture continues nevertheless to push forward in representing these concerns in unexpected and memorable ways. The popular culture produced in and for Israelis – both Jewish and Arab – and Arab Palestinians of various religious and ethnic configurations, points to the contiguous changes in the understanding of the past and the potential to influence and shape the future. Whereas I am sympathetic to the stance taken by Stein and Swedenburg, there is also a need to take into consideration a more materialist, and even essentialist, view and engage with forms of culture that remain determined in their quest to represent fear, rage, and anger within a mainstream political context. We can also acknowledge that our mode of engagement might be compromised and limited. To view and engage with the popular culture of Israel/Palestine is to familiarise oneself with public discourse and to appreciate how cultural forms choose to explore themes that affect every day. This must be done, on occasion, with a full understanding of personal and political limitations that both influence and, indeed, structure our perspective.

In other words, there is much at stake when various forms of culture are submitted for collective consumption in the Israel/Palestine context. Outside of artistic, filmic, and commercial considerations, what often works alongside the reception and critique of popular culture in the context of Israel/Palestine is the extent to which contemporary culture engages with these older, though still very pertinent, political debates. There is also something else here to consider: that the question of Palestine has always been, in different and often controversial ways, intimately connected to the wider Arab world.

In order to consider some of these issues, we need to take a look at some recent popular culture and attempt a reading within a particular context while at the same time remaining sensitive to the genre and broader framework being addressed, as well as attempt to see how these speak to the broader political questions, even when these appear to be over-familiar or essentialist. Here, I deal with television, music, documentary, cinema, and short video in order to productively engage a variety of themes and genres. We start with the 2015 Israeli political thriller show, *Fauda* (2015), written for Netflix by Lior Raz and Avi Issacharoff and acted in Arabic and Hebrew to explore the representation of an Israeli undercover unit working in the West Bank. "It's the first TV series that showed the Palestinian narrative in a way that you can actually feel something for someone who acts like a terrorist" (Stern cited in Shabi 2018). This celebrated "evenhandedness" of the show is worth exploring to understand what issues are perceived to require fair and equal treatment in popular culture. We then move to Jackie Salloum's 2008 documentary, *Slingshot Hip Hop*, a story of Palestinian-Israeli musicians who mould themselves in the image of "America's oppressed black urban youth" and, eventually, as DAM, "begin performing Arabic-language raps celebrating Palestinian literary figures, and decrying the realities of Palestinian life under Israeli rule in front of ever-growing crowds of Palestinian youth" (Murphy, 2008). DAM come to represent internally displaced Palestinians and work hard to make connections across the Palestinian territories as well as the Diaspora.

Next, we look at the Palestinian film *Wajib*, Annemarie Jacir's 2017 film set in the largest Arab-majority town in Israel – Nazareth. Here, a very subtle intergenerational struggle unravels that shows up the conflicting, and often surprising. expectations between a son and his father in relation to their engagement with the historical enmities between the two cultures. Whilst Shadi is an angry young Palestinian of the Diaspora, geographically distanced but emotionally obsessed with the idea of his homeland, his father has learnt to compromise, form friendships and contribute to a reconciliation of sorts with his surroundings. These tensions make for riveting viewing as they reveal the more complicated and nuanced consequences of everyday conviviality. *In Between*, Maysaloun Hamoud's fast-paced 2016 film about three Palestinian-Israeli women living in Tel Aviv examines how constraints can take many forms: societal; gendered; professional. Shared homes, aspirations, dreams and disappointments all take place against the backdrop of older embedded histories around home and belonging.

Finally, installation and video artist Larissa Sansour's science fiction trilogy captures an imaginary futuristic Palestinian reality that involves space exploration, architectural advancements that appear to solve the question of a Palestinian homeland, and an imaginary landscape that seems to create an artificial but necessary mythical past in order to secure a just future. Using much talked-about and ubiquitous symbols of the Palestinian homeland, Sansour builds landscapes that are both cavernous and claustrophobic, suggesting through her videos that the present condition of Palestine suffers from material lack and symbolic excess.

It is useful here to reassert the broader point behind looking closely at popular culture in this context. The material examined here certainly evokes a strong sense of engagement with the topics that are emerging as the most crucial of the contemporary moment: the price of security; the relationship to the Diaspora; an intimate look at Palestinian-Israeli citizens; youth cultures and their interpolation of history; empowerment through alternative genres and ultimately, participation *in* and engagement *with* a *global* cultural economy. These materials not only reveal a vibrant commitment to tackle the socio-political conditions head-on but also show how unremittingly those conditions impinge on the communal daily experience.

The challenge here, of course, is to remain attuned to the various structural inequalities that frame cultural production. Where TV shows such as *Fauda* benefit from solid entertainment foundations and distribution privileges through connections with streaming giant Netflix, funding is more of a challenge to independent filmmakers such as Jackie Salloum and Larissa Sansour who, however, enjoy Internet and art festival patronage respectively. A quick look at Jacir's funding and production credits reveals a vast international funding and distribution cohort, as does the work of Hamoud. The circulation and availably of the works is also a very significant consideration and impacts heavily on the on-going struggle for the visibility of multiple stories gaining traction on the international scene.

> In the global landscape, Palestinians' history is still marginal and often actively marginalised ... Palestinians continue to be vulnerable victims of history, belonging to a world politics larger than themselves, in which they have very little control over their own image.
>
> *(Tawil-Souri 2011, 143)*

In his article on the narrative power of "victimhood," Smulders notes how *both* the Israeli and Palestinian "claims to victim status' have enabled them to [create] collective identities and narratives around this status" (Smulders 2013, 179). Our brief look at some cultural productions that do not shy away from some of these vulnerabilities and actually seek to represent them will, however, go some way to redressing the assumed status of Palestinians only as "victims," for this too is something worth exploring. Writing of the importance of cultural work and its critique, Matar and Harb (2013, 5) argue that this approach enables a legitimate

> rethinking of culture as a crucial terrain for the struggle between hegemonic powers and subaltern counter-hegemonic forces and one that takes place across a vast array of space and modern institutions, including media institutions and other cultural forms and practices.

How conflict is understood and *narrated* forms the crux of Matar and Harb's overall argument. In this case, both the conflict and its *arrangements* in culture are crucial. Attention to this arrangement of ideas gives us the tools required to navigate the particular account of conflict and to better understand the shape of hegemony and the practice of counter-hegemony.

Undercover

Fauda is a thrilling, fast-paced Netflix drama based on an Israeli undercover counter-terrorist team that sets out to break up Palestinian nationalist groups and contribute to ongoing security measures seen as essential and crucial. They seem able to infiltrate Arab Palestinian spaces easily and can assimilate into any situation, be it a mosque or a wedding. This fact of swift assimilation is the crux around which much of the action hangs, and it plays very effectively on the often-repeated notion of the *similarities* between the two communities. Notwithstanding the nuance that is lost in such observations, the trope is used effectively to facilitate covert operations through which much is revealed about the current prevailing political ideologies. The ability of the Israeli team to "pass" as Arab Palestinians is what makes the show intriguing, whilst the characteristics that in turn make the Arabs visible need to be re-imagined so that they can be different from the Israelis. In a recent Netflix drama, *The Spy* (2020), based on the story of Israeli clerk Eli Cohen – recruited by the Mossad to be an undercover spy in Syria in the 1960s – the protagonist Eli bemoans his lack of status in a contemporary Israel, undermined by his "Arab" looks. After a party at which he is mistaken for a waiter, Eli remarks to his wife that the reason for their being invited is that they give colour to the party and that colour is "Brown." His assertion that, although he is Jewish, he will only ever be seen as "Arab" weighs heavily in his decision to take up the challenge to give up his life for his country: as though to *prove* his allegiance.

In *Fauda*, this ability to cross over and pass is a significant asset, and yet it produces an odd effect where the drama has to work hard to produce the difference that underpins the strife. In two scenes in particular, certain issues relating to language and dress serve to further confuse viewers, searching perhaps for stark contrasting imagery that might further illuminate the ongoing socio-political crisis. Instead, what they get is Israeli undercover agents who speak near-flawless Arabic in the interrogation rooms and who use turns of phrases and allusions commonly understood and referenced by Arabs. In an early scene in season one, an officer trying to elicit information from the arrested Palestinian pleads with him by saying, in Arabic, "Ali, I've got five children, may God keep them safe" using the Arabic term "Allah." In this performance of sameness, the interrogator nevertheless attempts to threaten the Palestinian to give up crucial information, using his love for his children as a coercive tactic in his attempt to convince Ali to give up information in exchange for his sick daughter having access to adequate medical care that only Israeli hospitals can provide. The impetus behind this short scene is repeated across *Fauda*: that cultural referents and convincing tropes are easily accessed and can be used to mimic empathy. When it comes to resources, however, it is clear who holds the power. *Fauda* is keen to reveal the extent of these surveillance resources that work to keep track of danger: perceived, real, or otherwise.

These mediated images amplify the implied fear that in turn requires sophisticated tracking techniques. Aerial cameras follow suspects and keep records of who moves in and out of spaces. The machinery and manpower required to do this is impressive and reveals a well-financed and smoothly run operation. In antithesis to this, the Palestinian freedom fighters work in safe houses and are either in hiding or constantly on the run. Their perceived lack of infrastructural support is laid bare as they concentrate instead on ideology and ill-conceived plans to cause chaos and disruption to the Israeli state. On the flip side, however, some of the most intriguing and memorable aspects of the show is the filming of the great lengths to which the Israeli operatives will go to look "Arab." Beards are blackened, hair is greased, eyebrows and sideburns are exaggerated, tattoos are concealed, tight t-shirts removed and replaced by vests and white collared t-shirts and, of course, *keffiyehs* are donned. This more pedestrian form of preparation works to contrast the more sophisticated technology required for tracking and following both operators and their victims in real-time. The difference between these two worlds is stark, and its representation does nothing less than reveal the wide technological gap between the two warring communities. Backed by this surveillance technology, however, the team seamlessly integrate into whatever context they wish and perform Arabness in plain view, safe in the knowledge that they are being monitored and protected. *Fauda* is uniquely set up to demonstrate the intricate needs of undercover work: earpieces, computers, mobile signal blocking, costumes, but most of all a thorough understanding and mimicking of the "other" and his mannerisms. Across the action in this TV drama, Palestinian men and women dress up as Palestinian women, and Israeli men pretend to be all types of Arab men: from poor delivery men to middle-class affable visitors. Their impeccable Arabic allows them to fool even the shrewdest of Palestinians. The show does not shy away from revealing the consequence of continued Israeli intervention on Palestinian families and, in particular, on Palestinian women whilst it continues to contextualise it within the broader context of a continued fight for national self-determination on both sides. In this way, *Fauda* is in tune with contemporary narratives of security and fear while it attempts to show the various ways in which these interests play out in social and political contexts.

Revolutionary Sounds

Jackie Salloum's *Slingshot Hip Hop* (2008) combines music, special effects, photography and video to tell the story of the development of hip-hop in Palestine. The film begins with American hip hop artist Chuck D interviewing the Palestinian-Israeli rap group DAM (made up of Tamer Nafar, Suheil Nafar and Mahmoud Jrere), promoting the relevance of the music and its dedication to politics. "When they ask us, 'What is Palestinian Hip Hop' we say that Hip Hop is our CNN" say DAM. For them, the opportunity to perform hip-hop is synonymous with having a political voice. As Abdel-Nabi et al. (2004, 232) argue, "artists [in the Arab world] have become the people's most important and trusted politicians." And, they remind us that "the struggle for Palestine plays a central role in Arab consciousness [and] is relived, reconstructed and collectively mourned in the space of popular music" (2004, 247). As Sherifah Zuhur argues, "the role of music [is] vital and circumscribed in the region and is, to an extent, that of a cultural guardian" (Images of Enchantment, 10). In the film, DAM perform this song:

> DAM have arrived
> from Palestine
> I was born in a 'hood called
> "I don't give a damn"

DAM provocatively make the connection with the origins of hip-hop and cite Public Enemy's 1990 album *Fear of a Black Planet*, reinterpreting this as *Fear of an Arabic Nation* all the while making associations and connections with African-American minority politics. The DAM's influences are extraordinary though: "How could we not love hip hop?" they say. Influences range from Tupac Shakur's "All Eyes on Me," The Fugees, DMX, Big Pun, Snoop Dog, The Notorious B.I.G., Talib Kweli, Woo Tang, Outkast, and then Edward Said and Mahmoud Darwish, Ahlem Mostaghanemi, Nawal El Saadawi, Nizar Qabbani and Hanan Al-Skaykh. DAM describe themselves as made up of 30 per cent musical influences, 30 per cent literature and 40 per cent environment (out there, they say, as they point beyond the bars to their window). In other words, the interaction of the intellectual and the creative must go hand in hand and be put to practice in the service of the context, and that context is the everyday lived experience of Palestinians.

The tools required to navigate this everyday context are reconstituted from a wide range of materials, however, and show the unpredictable destination and manipulation of cultural creations. Where Edward Said meets Nawal El Saadawi meets Tupac is in their articulation and representation of the disenfranchised and politically marginalised. Where Hanah Al-Shaykh and Mahmoud Darwish and Public Enemy might be said to converge is in their undermining of the dynamics of power and authority. In this way, DAM are able to arm themselves and converge on how best to communicate frustration and discontent whilst simultaneously providing images of resilience and survival. Joseph Massad writes about the continuing potential of music and notes (2003, 37), that "songs both express and register the changing dynamics of the Palestinian struggle, reflecting which segment of the Palestinian people is most salient at the moment and which form of struggle is imagined as most effective." Reflecting specifically on more contemporary forms, David A. McDonald argues (2013a, 71) that

> aesthetic experimentation, collaboration, and the expansion of public modes of consumption reflect[s] an awakening of sorts, a radical reconceptualisation of national subjectivity away from the intractable past towards an imagined future … in various modes of public performance, engagement with the national Other serve[s] to sustain and accelerate new forms of identity and intelligibility.

Speaking of DAM, in particular, McDonald argues that they "create spaces where traditional conceptions of Palestinian-ness are reconfigured to include media, aesthetics, and technologies from the non-Arab cosmopolitan world" (2013b, 239).

Salloum's film further extends these aesthetics to encompass engaging animated forms for telling the very particular story of Palestinians living in Israel, the so-called '48 Palestinians who struggle to visit or cross into Gaza or the West Bank. Footage from, for example, Tupac Shakur's 1993 music video "Holler if Ya Hear Me" is folded in to show the extent to which Tupac's hometown of Baltimore and the deprivation coupled with police surveillance remind DAM of their own context. These non-Arab influences are important as they perform a radical imagined solidarity against various forms of – if not equal, at least similarly debilitating – forms of oppression. DAM's political commitments intensified with the development of the Second Intifada. Documentary footage of this era is woven into *Slingshot Hip Hop* and placed alongside DAM's development as an artistic group. Importantly, the film shows the incremental understanding of the place of Palestinian-Israelis in a broader context: the realisation that they are cut off from the wider Palestinian community, that their experience includes daily interactions with Jewish-Israeli communities with whom profound engagement is a way of life and, most importantly, that they communicate proficiently in both Arabic and Hebrew. Other groups and individual artists are profiled in the film, all of whom consider their work in relation to innovation and political effectiveness. Infographics and short animated sequences populate the film to give a clear visual accompaniment to the complicated geographical manoeuvring required daily of Palestinians. The rap group Palestinian Rapperz from Gaza are shown having to address their particular aesthetic "look," how they dress and move, which falls out of line with conservative Palestinian dress codes.

Salloum is very attentive to the various opportunities available to the performers: to their ability to introduce new audiences to a long-standing political and social stalemate with a new idiom. Yet, her film also comprehends the frustration over lack of opportunity, the long waits at Israeli checkpoints (within Gaza itself, for example) that make artistic collaboration almost impossible and the sometimes claustrophobic sense that if it were not for the music these mostly-young men may lose sight of any ambition or courage. Mohammed, a rapper from Gaza, articulates this best when he says: "I wasn't rapping at the beginning of the Intifada. It was the time I suffered the most. It was a time that made me feel I wasn't human, I was totally demoralised." Whilst he reminisces, Salloum folds in scenes of young men and boys running away from rapid-fire gunshots whose origin remains invisible. One of the many strengths of Slingshot Hip Hop is that it does not show a homogeneous perspective that is pitted against a vague Israeli opponent. Rather, it allow the images, words, animated shorts, performances and music, interviews and many other visual cues to construct a complex response to the various experiences of everyday oppression. An earlier 2003 film by Anat Halachmi, *Channels of Rage* (2003), saw the gradual identification of DAM with Palestinian radical politics and tracks their disconnect from Israeli Jewish hip-hop artists, such as Shadow (Yoav Eliasi) and Subliminal (Kobi Shimoni). In *Slingshot Hip Hop* we witness the complicated nature of Palestinian performers from Gaza struggling to meet with Israeli-Palestinian performers: this only compounds and extends existing frustrations for both performers' communities. Salloum's film firmly establishes the politicised nature of contemporary Palestinian hip-hop and its ability to inspire creativity and activism in Palestinian youth but also reminds us at every turn of the labour that goes into both of these terms: *Palestinian* and *hip-hop*. Neither of these is easy to define, and both have thorny roots and untold potential.

New Cinema

Following Livia Alexander's call to examine Palestinian cinema in the context of how "national affiliations and international awareness affect film production in a society dominated by national conflict" (2005, 151), I look at Annemarie Jacir's 2017 film *Wajib*, and Maysaloun Hamoud's 2016 film *In Between*, to trace how a new, unexpected and "intellectually complex notion of Palestinianness that supersede[s] defined geographical boundaries" (Alexander 2005, 151) arises and takes shape. Nurith Gertz and George Khleifi chronicle, periodise, and thematise film production in the region in their *Palestinian Cinema: Landscape, Trauma and Memory* (Gertz and Khleifi 2008), reading the evolution of Palestinian cinema in line with perceived political and social gains and losses. These include broad categories such as silence, exile, and return. These are useful categories in the mapping of the general preoccupations that fuelled the purpose and content of Palestinian cinema as it sought to both conserve and archive local experiences of the occupation at the same time as it attempted to participate in broader international cinematic aesthetics. Edward Said's introduction to Hamid Dabashi's *Dreams of a Nation: On Palestinian Cinema* (2006), calls for a specific way of seeing Palestinian cinema – as having grown out of the impulse to act against "invisibility" at the same time as it needed to "stand against the stereotype in the media … a visual identity associated with terrorism and violence" (2006, 3). Dabashi himself identified certain features with Palestinian cinema: "subdued anger, a perturbed pride, a sublated violence" (2006, 11), suggesting both simmering unexpressed emotion and unrecognised repression of loss.

These pervading themes observed in the films alongside the dominant features governing cinematic production have only grown more complicated as the very *concept* of Palestinianness comes under scrutiny in contemporary film. *Wajib* and *In Between* are set in Nazareth and Tel Aviv, respectively and, thus, alongside the films of Elie Suleiman (*Divine Intervention* and *The Time that Remains*, in particular), go some way to shaping a cinematic aesthetic that is sensitive to the experiences particular to Palestinian citizens of Israel but also familiar and recognisable to Palestinians everywhere. The themes have now broadened to include issues around religiosity, piety, feminist empowerment, sexuality beyond the heteronormative, and labour. Alongside these, familiar concerns around intergenerational tensions, diasporic experiences, nostalgia, Palestinian politics of self-determination, and the burden of keeping the Palestinian dream alive are all dynamically animated in the films. Furthermore, many of the frustrations at the lack of gains on the international political scene are often dramatically played out in the context of Israeli-Palestinians who reside and labour in Israel but whose daily lives are structured by a Palestinian-Arab framework that requires constant performance. Maha Nassar's book, *Brothers Apart: Palestinian Citizens of Israel and the Arab World*, describes the complex process of ensuring that Palestinian citizens of Israel "become fully integrated into the Palestinian national narrative" and the work required to ensure that "their social and political concerns have also become integrated into the Palestinian national agenda" (2017, 187). Speaking of their physical isolation from those living in the West Bank and Gaza, Nassar argues that "as a result of these dynamics, there remains a great deal of confusion in the Arab world about how to regard this community" (2017, 187). Dabashi, in discussing the films of Elie Suleiman, notes how his cinema finds "emancipatory aesthetic solutions to otherwise debilitating political dead-ends" and aims to "universalis[e] the particulars of Palestine" (2006, 144). Whilst this certainly stands, Jacir and Maysaloun's film also shows the complexities that arise when these social conventions are troubled and questioned, and how these come into conflict with a national narrative that does not always have the capacity to incorporate or respond to societal changes and conventions. The question of loyalty – to this or that *vision* of a future Palestine – is in constant struggle with the expression of loyalty to particular locales where communities live and work.

Jacir's *Wajib* articulates the above in multiple scenes between a returning son, Shadi, and his father over the course of a day as they distribute wedding invitations in person – a Nazarene Christian tradition. The intergenerational dynamic that is set up works to reveal the huge gulf that exists between those who live in and navigate the everyday nature of the occupation and the idealism and frustration present in the rhetoric and ideology of the son who arrives from Italy – an idealism that is informed and sustained by the broader Palestinian Diaspora at large. As the father and son travel through Nazareth, visiting relatives and friends, a dialogue unfolds between them that reveals the various *wajib* – or duties – that are required of all people in whatever context they might reside. Furious that his father wants to invite an Israeli official to his sister's wedding, Shadi argues for purity and single-mindedness in Palestinian politics, a position that his father cannot accept and will not abide by, having learnt to make difficult compromises all his life in order to provide stability for his family. The film homes in on quite a fragile ecosystem where personal, structural, and financial needs collide to make the engagement with the occupation malleable and unpredictable. Whilst Shadi's father is busy trying to uphold tradition as he navigates the precarious nature of living as a Christian Palestinian in Nazareth, Shadi holds forth on the sacrifices of the PLO, whose glory days are long over. The film is astute on the politics of adaptation and looks closely at the sacrifices endured for relative peace. It is perhaps not surprising that Shadi is disturbed and angry at everything he perceives as dysfunctional: traffic, disorganised people, the desecration of beautiful buildings, soldiers, rubbish everywhere.

Though it is tempting to distance the preoccupations of father and son as somehow signalling a generational rift between the idealised revolutionary past and the compromised present, we do catch a glimpse of the desire for the memory of a pastoral and romantic Palestine. Forced to describe Nazareth on the phone to an exiled Palestinian PLO member, Shadi's father covers up the truth of what he is looking at: rubble, bins, and half-rebuilt ruins, and instead describes the non-existent orange trees and vineyards, totems of a lost past for all Palestinians that function almost as a common language and shared heritage (see Figure 32.1). In a poignant and heart-breaking argument between father and son at the end of the film we finally realise the huge effort required by both to keep the dream of an imagined unified Palestine alive and the equally exhausting attempt to continue existing in the present.

Figure 32.1 *Wajib* (2017), © Annemarie Jacir.

Maysaloun Hamoud's film *In Between* reveals the complexities of attempting to live a life of agency and empowerment, one that is however governed by both visible and invisible social and communal expectations. Three Palestinian-Israeli women – Salma, Laila, and Nour – share a flat in Tel Aviv and navigate multiple expectations: to be good daughters, workers, students, partners, and to uphold sexual and moral standards not of their own making. The film is quite refreshing in its pragmatism around the various possibilities available to the women though it also, in similar ways to *Wajib*, shows up the manoeuvres required to side-step an encroaching conservatism disguised as duty. Salma is a young lesbian DJ who in the course of the film is threatened by her parents and decides she must leave Israel. Laila appears to be the person least tied to rules around propriety but is caught out when a lover expresses his desire for her to be more traditional if they are to continue their relationship. When she confronts what she sees as his old-fashioned ideas he lets her know that this is the way it must be, and that they alone cannot hope to change societal expectations. Nour, a devout Muslim, adheres to the requirements set up by her fiancé to live a modest and virtuous life. He nevertheless rapes her when she does not agree to his every decree. His hypocrisy as a servant of god and a pious man of the community is revealed in the film, but at great cost to Nour. *In Between* encourages a critical look at what it might mean to live in a liminal space between what continues to be expected of young Palestinian women – discreet, modest and acquiescent – and the opportunities they might avail themselves of living in a city such as Tel Aviv. The choices are not easy, and the terrain is complex and dangerous. Identity politics are crucial, but so are friendships and solidarity beyond politics and nationalism. The in-between here may not entirely indicate the in-between space of ethnic and civic duties versus personal desires, but rather point to the *living* that must and does take place in between *all* of these dynamics. Music, dancing, drugs, drinking, parties, and joy as well as tears, tragedy and pain, make up the spaces in between difficult family dynamics, gender politics, and the requirements of work. *In Between* and *Wajib* encourage us to consider the representation of Palestinians and Palestinianness in film as evolving, a representation that requires the courage to consider new themes – not being afraid to challenge the idealism of the past, looking closely at the material realities of the present across the *entire* population, and considering the cost of doing so against an aesthetic that would seek to only represent Palestinians as victims of one form of political occupation, ignoring all other types of constraints that play out daily. Where it was once necessary and even crucial to commend Palestinian cinema in its prioritisation of themes that both educated viewers and acted as receptacles of cultural memory, films such as *Wajib* and *In Between* reveal instead the importance of contemporary intergenerational and interethnic dynamics that contribute to a wider transnational debate around the potential of cinema to both reflect and shape our understanding and appreciation of an evolving socio-political reality.

Next, the Stars

In a 2019 interview on the publication of a collection of science fiction short sorties by Palestinian authors, writer Sami Hadad noted that "Palestine is such a rich canvas for science fiction, all these themes we deal with as Palestinians [...] questions of the past and the present and ideas of memories and alternative realities, what might have been" (Hada cited in Flood 2019). Futuristic tales and their treatment are certainly at the core of Palestinian filmmaker and installation artist Larissa Sansour's work. Defined as an artist whose work "employs the genre of science fiction as a means of providing an alternative perspective on current social and political issues" (McNay 2019), Sansour deploys signifiers of Palestinianness, both past and present, in order to contribute to a new canvas of potential future associations with the history and legacy of the region. Her work, however, does not rely on a preconceived knowledge of the political and social impasse. Rather, her role seems to be to recreate emblematic notions associated with the geographical and historical context in order to offer alternative ways of thinking about them.

There are a few ways to approach the work of Sansour: as dystopic, as futuristic, as embedded in the temporal twists of science fiction narratives. Sansour's sci-fi trilogy has been seen as "advanc[ing] a specifically Palestinian anti-colonial dystopic poetics" (Hochberg 2018, 35). This move, argues Hochberg, "broadens our understandings of sci-fi dystopia as a mode of de-colonial artistic and political imagination" (2018, 35). Sansour's work, therefore, has the potential to expand the field of sci-fi aesthetics by using local context to reframe and reimage the sci-fi landscape. Though this argument is seductive, the three films, *A Space Exodus* (2008), *Nation Estate* (2012). and *In the Future They Ate from the Finest Porcelain* (2015) as well as "focus[sing] on the future as a setting for discussing Palestine-in-becoming" (Hochberg 2018, 40) bring us closer towards what art discourse has named "Arab Futurism" (Jussi Parikka 2018, 40), which seeks to "articu[late] histories of dispossession as part of imaginary futures" (Parikka 2018, 41). Set against a Gulf futurism that seeks to understand the consequences of urbanism, commodity, and temporality, we might see works such as Sansour's contributing to an Arab futurism that "articulate[s] a cultural politics of time, a chronography of power" (2018, 42). Looking to set up a different configuration of time *and* place, place across time and time across place can reveal the extent to which "the generative power of time functions as a way to invent different horizons of existence as well as to connect them to the lived genealogies of dispossession" (2018, 43). All three films are interested in putting together images and narratives that are not often seen together and that force the viewer to see a radically different combination of objects and spaces: a Palestinian space traveller reaching the moon; a high tech vertical building that houses Palestinians and encompasses a simulacrum of their geopolitical reality, but in a glossy and peaceful environment; a futuristic project where counterfeit archaeology is designed to be discovered in the future in order to finally be able to act as proof of an ancient Palestinian settlement. *In the Future* "explores the role of myth in establishing history, fact and national identity" (*In the Future*, 2017). In this film, "science fiction becomes a way to articulate the necessity to think of futures as part of a horizon of struggles" (Parikka 2018, 53), but to even look at these films is to partake in glossy, sharp focused images and palimpsest experiences. There are no representations here that partake of the catalogue of images already associated with the context of Palestine/Israel. What we see are concepts taking shape, possibilities becoming visible, discourses being formed so that they can be ready to use when needed.

It is indeed productive to view Sansour's work as coming to terms with the problem of *knowledge production* itself, and with the complexities involved in imparting technological and scientific advancement to the world when your socio-historical context has set up your presumptive nation as incapable of such achievements. Viewing Sansour's work is an act of locating, producing, and representing knowledge. Lebanese artists Joana Hadjithomas and Khalil Joreige, in the leaflet that accompanied their film, *The Lebanese Rocket Society* (2016), provides us with a framework within which we can entirely reconceptualise the popular history of the Middle East. Their research turns up an actual rocket society "that was mysteriously erased from Lebanese history: the active participation of a group of Lebanese scientists in space research during the 1960s, and the construction of rockets in Lebanon" (Joreige and Hadjithomas 2016). This remarkable story opens up the possibility of technological progress as a legitimate pursuit and gives us another way to conceptualise Sansour's work in the context of Palestine. Here, we might see her intervention as one that pushes at the boundaries of the genre but also at the boundaries of what *might* have been (and what in some instances *was*, as seen in the Lebanese context), but for the right resources and institutions. Having to imagine such achievements in the guise of science fiction film is not a nostalgic performance. Rather, the ideas and concepts that take shape in these films permit hitherto seemingly incompatible discourses to come together. In *Nation Estate*, Palestinians have built tunnels and an impossibly large skyscraper – they have resources and are involved in local trade. These illusions are stark to see because they do not exist in Palestine, but they *do* exist elsewhere. What might look ordinary in New York or Frankfurt looks positively Martian in the occupied territories. In turn, this shows up the significant gap between developed and underdeveloped spheres. In many ways, Sansour's films operate as sharp reminders of the ways in which disciplines and institutions such as space programmes, architecture, engineering and archaeology, among others, can flourish in certain contexts and come to shape nations. Where these disciplines are stunted and their development compacted, they can be envisioned to have continued through the work of art. This is not to imagine them because they do not exist, but rather to articulate *why* they do not exist.

Conclusion

The examples used here bring together a variety of contemporary cultural moments that can help shed light on the continuing development of popular culture in the Israel/Palestine context. There are many forms of culture, from TV to music to cinema and installation art, among others, that contribute to an ongoing conversation about how representation has broadened to encompass the many different ways in which lives are lived and experiences navigated. What is also clear is that in some cases a different idiom has emerged that allows us to better appreciate the various forms of struggle situated at the juncture between the reality of the socio-political conflict and the no less valuable materiality of those who must inhabit it.

Recommended Readings

Gertz, N., and G. Khleifi. 2008. *Palestinian Cinema: Landscape, Trauma and Memory*. Edinburgh: Edinburgh University Press.

McDonald, D. A. 2013. *My Voice is My Weapon: Music, Nationalism, and the Poetics of Palestinian Resistance*. Durham, NC: Duke University Press.

Parikka, J. 2018. "Middle East and other Futurisms: Imaginary Temporalities in Contemporary Art and Visual Culture." *Culture, Theory and Critique* 59:1, 40–58.

Sabry, T. 2010. *Cultural Encounters in the Arab World: On Media, The Modern and the Everyday*. London and New York: I.B. Tauris.

Stein, R. L., and T. Swedenburg, eds. 2005. *Palestine, Israel, and the Politics of Popular Culture*. Durham, NC: Duke University Press. https://larissasansour.com/.

Questions for Discussion

(1) Consider how TV programmes can popularise the conflict. Can you see any potential problems with this move?

(2) How does the hip hop genre help articulate the current context of the Israel/Palestine conflict?

(3) How are intergenerational conflicts represented in contemporary popular culture in Israel/Palestine?

(4) How does cinema contribute to our understanding of the various Palestinian communities across Israel and the occupied territories?

(5) How does science fiction challenge the viewer's popular perception of Palestine?

References

Abdel-Nabi, S., et al. 2004. "Pop Goes the Arab World: Popular Music, Gender, Politics and Transnationalism in the Arab World." *Hawwa* 2:2, 231–254.

Alexander, L. 2005. "Is There a Palestinian Cinema? The National and Transnational in Palestinian Film Production." In *Palestine, Israel, and the Politics of Popular Culture*, eds. R. L. Stein and T. Swedenburg. Durham, NC: Duke University Press, 150–172.

Dabashi, H., ed. 2006. *Dreams of a Nation: On Palestinian Cinema*. London: Verso Books.

Flood, A. 2019. "What Will Palestine be like in 2048? Writers Turn to Sci-fi for the Answer." *The Guardian*. 25 July. Available at: www.theguardian.com/books/2019/jul/25/what-will-palestine-be-like-in-2048-writers-turn-to-sci-fi-for-the-answer.

Gertz, N., and G. Khleifi. 2008. *Palestinian Cinema: Landscape, Trauma and Memory*. Edinburgh: Edinburgh University Press.

Hochberg, G. Z. 2018. "'Jerusalem, We Have a Problem': Larissa Sansour's Sci-Fi Trilogy and the Impetus of Dystopic Imagination." *Arab Studies Journal*, 26:1, 35–58.

In the Future they Ate from the Finest Porcelain. (2017). [Exhibition]. Bluecoat, Liverpool, 5 May – 24 June.

Massad, J. 2003. "Liberating Songs: Palestine Put to Music." *Journal of Palestine Studies* 32:3, 21–38.

Matar, D., and Z. Harb. 2013. "Approaches to Narrating Conflict in Palestine and Lebanon: Practices, Discourses and Memory." In *Narrating Conflict in the Middle East: Discourse, Image and Communications Practices in Lebanon and Palestine*, eds. D. Matar and Z. Harb. London: I.B. Tauris, 1–37.

McDonald, D. A. 2013a. "Imaginaries of Exile and Emergence in Israeli Jewish and Palestinian Hip Hop." *TDR: The Drama Review* 57:3, 69–87.

McDonald, D. A. 2013b. *My Voice is My Weapon: Music, Nationalism, and the Poetics of Palestinian Resistance*. Durham, NC: Duke University Press.

McNay, A. 2019. "Larissa Sansour: Interview." *Studio International*. 16 November. Available at: www.studiointernational.com/index.php/larissa-sansour-interview-danish-pavilion-venice-biennale-2019.

Murphy, M. C. 2008. "Film Review: Slingshot Hip Hop." *Electronic Intifada*. 10 September. Available at: https://electronicintifada.net/content/slingshot-hip-hop-comes-lebanon/7671.

Nassar, M. 2017. *Brothers Apart: Palestinian Citizens of Israel and the Arab World*. Stanford, CA: Stanford University Press.

Parikka, J. 2018. "Middle East and other Futurisms: Imaginary Temporalities in Contemporary Art and Visual Culture." *Culture, Theory and Critique* 59:1, 40–58.

Said, E. W. 2006. "Preface." In *Dreams of a Nation: On Palestinian Cinema*, ed. H. Dabashi. London: Verso, 1–5.

Sansour, L. 2017. "In the Future They Ate from the Finest Porcelain." *Bluecoat: Liverpool's Centre for the Contemporary Arts*. 6 May–24 June.

Shabi, R. 2018. "The Next Homeland? The Problems with Fauda, Israel's Brutal TV Hit." *The Guardian*. 23 May. Available at: www.theguardian.com/tv-and-radio/2018/may/23/the-next-homeland-problems-with-fauda-israel-brutal-tv-hit.

Shakur, T. 1993. "Holler if Ya Hear Me." YouTube, 5 July 2011, www.youtube.com/watch?v=zAtqb3T5CHE.

Smulders, K. N. 2013. "The Battle for Victimhood: Roles and Implications of Narratives of Suffering in the Israeli-Palestinian Conflict." In *Narrating Conflict in the Middle East: Discourse, Image and Communications Practices in Lebanon and Palestine*, eds. D. Matar and Z. Harb. London: I.B. Tauris., 164–182.

Stein, R. L., and T. Swedenburg, eds. 2005. *Palestine, Israel, and the Politics of Popular Culture*. Durham, NC: Duke University Press.

Tawil-Souri, H. 2011. "The Necessary Politics of Palestinian Cultural Studies." In *Conceptualising Cultural Studies and Media Studies in the Arab World: Mapping the Field*, ed. T. Sabry. London: I.B. Tauris, 150–176.

Zuhur, S. 1998. "Introduction." In *Images of Enchantment: Visual and Performing Arts of the Middle East*, ed. S. Zuhur. Cairo: The American University in Cairo Press, 5–20.

Filmography

A Space Exodus. 2008. Directed by Larissa Sansour. mec film.
Channels of Rage. 2003. Directed by Anat Halachmi.
Fauda. 2015. Netflix.

In Between. 2016. Directed by Maysaloun Hamoud.
In the Future They Ate from the Finest Porcelain. 2015. Directed by Larissa Sansour, Soren Lind. mec film.
Nation Estate. 2012 Directed by Larissa Sansour. mec film.
Slingshot Hip Hop. 2008 Directed by Jackie Reem Salloum.
The Spy. 2020. Directed by Gideon Raff.
The Lebanese Rocket Society. 2016. Directed by Joane Hadjithomas and Khalil Joreige.
Wajib. 2017. Directed by Annmarie Jacir.

33

BOYCOTT, DIVESTMENT, AND SANCTIONS (BDS) AND THE ISRAELI-PALESTINIAN CONFLICT

Maia Carter Hallward

Introduction

Few topics are as contentious in general discussions related to Israel/Palestine as the boycott, divestment, and sanctions (BDS) movement. On the surface, this is puzzling, given that boycott, divestment, and sanctions are time-honoured nonviolent methods used by politicians and civil society activists alike. Further, boycotts are in and of themselves value-neutral – they attain moral weight through their usage, which can be for causes deemed good or bad. Upon further investigation, however, it is not the use of BDS per se that is the problem for opponents of BDS. Instead, it is the portrayal of Israel as a violator of human rights and/or as a colonial and apartheid regime that troubles the Israeli government and supporters of its policies, since this stands in stark contrast to the public image they present of Israel as a bastion of democracy and a safe haven for Jews from the evils of global anti-Semitism. When Israeli officials portray BDS as an "existential" threat, it is to this identity that they refer, not to Israel's economic or physical security.[1] This chapter reviews the role of boycott, divestment, and sanctions in the context of Israel/Palestine.[2] It first defines the Palestinian-led BDS movement and its component parts and then engages in a discussion of the various perspectives of BDS among actors concerned with Israel/Palestine. Finally, the article analyzes the implications of the BDS movement for transnational politics related to Israel and Palestine, particularly in recent times, where the United States administration, under the Trump presidency, has changed the course of decades of United States policy vis-à-vis the status of Israeli settlements.

The Palestinian-led boycott, divestment, and sanctions (BDS) movement was officially launched on 9 July 2005, although Palestinians have a much longer history with boycott efforts, including the Arab Boycott of 1936–1939 during the British Mandate period and a range of boycott efforts during the First *Intifada* in the late 1980s (Qumsiyeh 2010; Hallward 2013). The 2005 call was issued on the first anniversary of the International Court of Justice (ICJ) advisory opinion on the "Legal Consequences of the Construction of a Wall in the Occupied Palestinian Territory" (ICJ 2004), which determined that the wall being constructed by Israel was contrary to international law, called on Israel to dismantle the wall and make reparation

DOI: 10.4324/9780429027376-40

for damages caused, and called on states party to the Fourth Geneva Convention to hold Israel accountable to abiding by international humanitarian law (ICJ 2004, 70). As no states had taken action to hold Israel accountable, and construction of the wall (also called the separation barrier or the security fence) had continued, 170 Palestinian civil society organizations representing Palestinians in the West Bank and Gaza Strip (occupied Palestinian territories), Palestinian refugees, and Palestinian citizens of Israel, called on "international civil society organizations and people of conscience all over the world to impose broad boycotts and implement divestment initiatives against Israel similar to those applied to South Africa in the apartheid era" (BDS Movement 2005). Specifically, the call identifies three goals, based on international law: an end to Israel's occupation and dismantlement of the wall; full equality for Arab-Palestinian citizens of Israel, and "respecting, protecting and promoting the rights of Palestinian refugees to return to their homes and properties as stipulated in UN resolution 194" (BDS Movement 2005).

The three components of BDS have different foci. Boycotts involve a withdrawal of support for cultural, academic, and economic institutions that are "engaged in violations of Palestinian human rights," while divestment targets organizations such as churches, pension funds, and universities to "withdraw investments from the State of Israel and all Israeli and international companies that sustain Israeli apartheid" (BDS Movement, n. d.). In contrast to these first two sets of methods, which focus on civil society actors, sanctions require state pressure, such as ending free trade deals or suspending Israel's membership in international forums, such as United Nations bodies. It is important to note that the methods of boycott, divestment, and sanctions pre-exist the 2005 Palestinian call, and that the methods are widely used by a range of actors around the world with diverse political, social, and economic views. Various forms of boycott and divestment are described and explained in Gene Sharp's 1973 classic treatise on nonviolence, *The Politics of Nonviolent Action*, and such methods were used by famous social movements including not only the campaign against South African apartheid cited in the Palestinian call, but also by the United States Civil Rights movement and Gandhi's campaign for India's independence from Great Britain.

Key Debates Surrounding BDS

If boycott, divestment, and sanctions are time-tested nonviolent tactics used across time and space by a wide array of actors, why does BDS become so highly charged in the context of Israel/Palestine? There are several reasons for this, to be discussed in subsequent sections, including the history of anti-Semitism and psychological reactions of the Jewish community to anything that hints of anti-Semitism, the perceived effectiveness of BDS campaigns, and the desire of Israel to preserve its international image as a rights-upholding democracy. Also inherent in these debates are rival interpretations of international law, conceptions of justice, and varying understandings of root and contemporary causes of the conflict between Israelis and Palestinians.

The launching of the BDS call was groundbreaking in several ways. First, it was a nonviolent call to action in the midst of the Second Intifada, which claimed the lives of thousands of Palestinians and Israelis.[3] Second, the call brought together, for a common purpose, Palestinians from across the political, legal, and psychological divides that long separated those living in the occupied territories, Israel, and the diaspora. As a result of this unification of Palestinians from the West Bank, Gaza Strip, Jerusalem, and inside Israel, some even suggest that the BDS movement is a fundamental challenge to the Oslo paradigm (Maira 2018, 12–13). Whereas Palestinians framed their activism in terms of nonviolence and international law, Israeli officials forcefully denounced the movement as a form of terrorism by other means, a high-level security threat aimed at delegitimizing the State of Israel (Hallward and Shaver 2012; Hallward 2013).

The Question of Anti-Semitism

One of the major criticisms of BDS opponents is that BDS is anti-Semitic, even though a number of Jewish organizations and individuals support BDS as a way to hold Israel accountable to international law and its espoused values of democracy and human rights. However, Israelis and Jewish diaspora groups who have supported tactics of boycott, divestment, and sanctions – although not all have signed on to the BDS movement per se – have been targeted as "anti-Semitic" or as "self-hating Jews." In a much-read op-ed published in the *Guardian*, Israeli professor Neve Gordon stated that "for the sake of our children, I am convinced that an international boycott is the only way to save Israel from itself" (Gordon 2009). Describing Israel as an apartheid state with differential treatment for Jews and Palestinians under Israeli control between the Mediterranean and the Jordan River, Gordon suggests international pressure is the only way to counter the apartheid trend (Gordon 2009). While Gordon acknowledges that the question of boycott carries undertones of anti-Semitism and that other human rights violating countries are not being boycotted, he argues that other efforts to bring political change in Israel have not brought results. Shortly after the *Guardian* op-ed was published, "wealthy Jewish Americans who donate tens of millions of dollars to keep BGU [Ben Gurion University] alive and growing … find themselves saying, 'If BGU professors feel free to invite the world to boycott Israel, then perhaps the time has come to boycott BGU.'" (Russo 2009). Pressure mounted on Gordon and other Israeli academics as a result of a donor boycott of the university. At present, Gordon and other outspoken academic critics of Israel's policies, such as Ilan Pappé, who left Israel in 2006 after a series of death threats, teach in other countries, such as the United Kingdom.[4]

In a 2019 debate by Intelligence Squared, Melanie Phillips linked the BDS movement to both anti-Zionism and anti-Semitism, asserting the terms are synonymous (Intelligence Squared 2019). However, while the BDS movement is explicitly anti-Zionist – Palestinians are opposed to an exclusivist state that occupies them militarily and does not recognize their human rights – the BDS movement also "categorically opposes as a matter of principle all forms of racism, including Islamophobia and anti-Semitism."[5] In the same debate, Mehdi Hassan asserted that Zionism is an ideology by definition, distinct from religious or national affiliation and that Israel's efforts to conflate anti-Zionism with anti-Semitism distracts attention from the anti-Semitism of Israeli prime minister Benjamin Netanyahu's right-wing supporters such as Steve Bannon. A number of Jews and Israelis identify themselves as anti-Zionist, in part due to what Allan Brownfield calls "the corruption of Judaism, as a religion of universal values, through its politicization by Zionism and by the replacement of dedication to Israel for dedication to God and the moral law" (Bronwfield 2001).

Supporters of BDS note that the accusation of BDS as "anti-Semitic" often serves as a red herring to divert attention from the issues at play. While some BDS activists may be anti-Semitic, the tactics of boycott, divestment, and sanctions in and of themselves are not anti-Semitic, and portrayal of the movement as anti-Semitic taps into generations of Jewish psychological trauma as well as gut-level emotional reactions. Mark Goldfeder, for example, when arguing that anti-BDS laws are constitutional, shifts the terminology away from a target on Israel's occupation and human rights abuses – including international corporations profiting from Israel's occupation – to a focus on "Jews" (Goldfeder 2018, 208). Many anti-BDS pieces are built almost entirely on such emotional appeals and lack factual support – opponents of BDS often intentionally divert away from engaging with the facts, since often the facts of human rights violations and the existence of separate laws for Jewish Israelis and Palestinians living next to them (the definition of apartheid) are difficult to refute, whereas emotional reactions cannot be disputed (Hallward 2013). One common argument of those opposing BDS is that it targets Israel unfairly, and consequently must be anti-Semitic since Israel is the only Jewish state. For example, Sheskin and Felson (2016, 272) assert:

> How else can one explain the vitriol aimed at Israel by the BDS movement when there are so many countries around the world that have human rights records that are far, far worse than Israel? Witness the treatment of women and gays throughout much of the Muslim world, or the treatment of Tibetans, Uighurs, and Mongolians in China, or the genocide in Darfur. Why have these academic organizations not called for BDS in these and many other places?

Arguments such as these shift the focus away from two of the primary arguments of the Palestinian BDS movement. First, because states have not responded to international law, for example United Nations Resolution 194 regarding the rights of Palestinian refugees or the 2004 ICJ ruling calling for Israel to dismantle the wall, global civil society activists must themselves exert pressure. Further, Israel receives special treatment from countries in Europe and the United States; its citizens do not require visas to enter these countries, it is part of European cultural programs like Eurovision, partner of the Euro-Mediterranean Partnership, and an associate member of the European Union (European Commission 2009). Israel receives over $3 billion in foreign aid (mostly military, to maintain a "qualitative military edge") plus additional loan guarantees and other benefits from the United States every year, which is more aid than the United States gives to any other country in the world (Sharp 2019). Given that states have put pressure on Darfur, for example with the joint UN-African Union mission, and on China, such as the October 2019 statement by United States Secretary of State Mike Pompeo pointing to "enormous human rights violation" in Xinjiang Province, there is not the same need for civil society to engage in BDS (although civil society movements have also been active in both of these cases).[6] Second, countries such as Saudi Arabia, the Sudan, and China do not claim to be human rights-upholding democracies, whereas Israel invests much time and energy into its image as "the only democracy in the Middle East." The Palestinian call for BDS explicitly states that its goal is to hold Israel accountable to the international laws to which it purportedly ascribes. Additionally, as Palestinians and their supporters note, the focus for Palestinians is understandably Israel, their oppressor, and not China, Sudan, or Saudi Arabia, who do not directly contribute to their lack of freedom and self-determination. The BDS call is specifically a call by Palestinians to change their circumstances, and that requires pressure on Israel specifically.[7]

Opponents of BDS often draw on centuries of Jewish persecution through emotional appeals that intentionally divert attention from the factual arguments raised by BDS activists. In the Intelligence Squared debate, for example, Melanie Phillips roused emotions through a discussion of Israeli democracy that was only loosely based on fact. The argument that Arabs and Jews have equal rights within a democratic Israel omits the fact that as a Jewish state, Israel focuses on the 75 per cent of its population that is Jewish while neglecting the 25 per cent that is not (Masri 2017). While Israel is indeed a democracy for its Jewish citizens, the Palestinian minority – over one-fifth of Israel's citizens – has never been invited to be part of the government, and over 65 Israeli laws discriminate directly or indirectly against Palestinian citizens of Israel (Adalah 2017). In this sense, Israel is what some have called an "ethnocracy," a state that privileges one ethnic group over another (Yiftachel 2006). The passage of the Nation-State Law in July 2018 defines Israel as the nation state of the Jewish people, and that the "exercise of the right to national self-determination in the State of Israel is unique to the Jewish People" (Sa'di 2019, 164). The same law demoted Arabic from one of Israel's official languages and emphasized Israel's responsibility to all members of the Jewish people, wherever they may live, thereby privileging Israel's Jewishness over its democratic credentials. Supporters of BDS suggest that identifying such laws and policies as exclusivist and racist is based on an analysis of the policies and laws themselves, and is not inherently anti-Semitic. However, the conflation of anti-Zionism with anti-Semitism as pushed for by supporters of Israel in countries around the world renders accusations of anti-Semitism easy to make (Harkov 2019). At the same time, some Jews – in Israel and in the Diaspora – have criticized the move to denounce all criticism of Israel and the Zionist ideology as "anti-Semitic," arguing that it empties the term of meaning at a time when genuine anti-Semitism is on the rise in right-wing, populist movements throughout Europe and elsewhere. The threat, they and supporters of BDS claim, is not from the left, but from the right, and by framing the BDS movement as the "bad guys," they are creating dangerous space for the right (Haaretz 2019; Scribd 2019).

The Question of Academic Freedom and Free Speech

While debates surrounding BDS are often contentious, opponents often particularly hone in on the specific components of an academic and cultural boycott. Further, such discussions are a clear example of how supporters and opponents of BDS portray the movement using oppositional frameworks. The Palestinian Campaign for the Academic and Cultural Boycott of Israel (PACBI) was instituted in 2004, thus predating the broader BDS call. PACBI "advocates for a boycott of Israeli academic and cultural institutions for their deep and persistent complicity in Israel's denial of Palestinian rights that are stipulated in international law."[8] Supporters of academic boycott, particularly within the United States context, view the Palestinian BDS call in the context of "antiracist, anticolonial, feminist, queer, and academic labor movements" (Maira 2018, 7). Opponents of BDS, in contrast, denounce the intersectional approach taken by BDS activists. One such opponent contends that "apart from their proclaimed status as victims, Palestinians and African Americans have little in common and would derive no particular benefit from joining together for a common strategy to improve their lives" (Divine 2019, 6). Such statements deny marginalized populations the agency to determine their own problems, and they seek to isolate movements, since together they are stronger. This move parallels Israel's historic preference for bilateral rather than multilateral diplomacy. For example, Israel has peace treaties with Egypt and Jordan that have lasted decades, but never responded to the Arab Peace Initiative proffered by the Arab League in 2002 and again in 2007 (Podeh 2014).[9]

In addition to denouncing intersectionality, opponents of the academic and cultural boycott reframe the issues in a way that obscures the rights of Palestinians. Arguments that the boycott undermines "academic freedom" erase the severe restrictions placed on Palestinian students and academics, many of whom have to cross multiple military checkpoints each day simply to obtain an education. It also ignores IDF surveillance of Palestinian educational institutions (Maira 2018; Zelkowitz 2014). Not all of the means of control are as visible as military checkpoints or arrests of students: between 2017 and 2019 four full-time and three part-time international lecturers at Birzeit University, outside of Ramallah, have been forced to leave Palestine due to Israel's refusal to renew their visas; in 2019 Israel also denied entry to two international lecturers with Birzeit contacts (Redden 2019). This policy denies Palestinian students from receiving instruction from diverse faculty and from those with expertise unavailable in Palestine. Further, supporters of BDS note, the academic boycott does not target the academic freedom of Israeli (or international) professors and students; it is an institutional boycott aimed at official state institutions, and explicitly does not target individual Israeli academics.[10]

Supporters and opponents of academic boycotts also paint radically different pictures of the university context in regard to Israel/Palestine, particularly in the United States. Divine (2019, 2), for example, suggests that university professors "earn … cultural capital for their anti-Israel words and deeds" without providing detail regarding what this "cultural capital" entails or evidence that it exists. Talking points circulated to students in Berkeley in advance of a student government vote on divestment, for example, encouraged students to focus on emotional appeals rather than responding to factual information (Hallward 2013), and talking points from the StopBDS website encourage students to paint the picture of a "culture of intimidation" on college campuses that makes Jewish students cry (StopBDS, N. d.). The irony of such statements is that, despite the picture painted by opponents of BDS, it is the anti-BDS activists, such as the Canary Mission, who have put significant pressure on faculty and students who are seen as supportive of Palestinian rights and/or BDS efforts. Faculty who have been advocates of boycott have been threatened by outside groups, and students who have been involved in campus organizing have experienced severe anxiety as a result of pressure from such groups (Kane 2018). Numerous faculty members have been denied tenure or been put under extensive pressure by well-funded groups such as the AMCHA initiative and the Canary Project for taking political stands related to the academic boycott, including Steven Salaita, Norman Finkelstein, and two University of Michigan professors who refused to write recommendation letters for students applying to study abroad in Israel (Maira 2018; Schrank 2019). The Canary Mission and other such endeavours are well funded, often by Jewish foundations and some by the Israeli government. At times individuals are penalized not only for what they themselves have said or done but, as in the recent case of a Palestinian Harvard student who was prevented from entering the United States in August 2019 (although he was later allowed to enter), because of what friends posted on social media (Svrluga 2019).

Discourses surrounding a student walkout in protest of a talk on the legal strategy of Israeli settlements, given by an Israeli envoy at Harvard in November 2019, illustrate the issues at play in academic boycott. As the Consul General to New York, Dani Dayan is an official representative of Israel and was chairman of the Yesha Council, an alliance of Israeli settlements. Therefore, Dayan was not acting as an individual, but as an institutional representative. Further, he was advocating the construction of Jewish settlements in Palestinian territory, which is a violation of international law according to the Geneva Conventions, which are signed by 196 states. Opponents framed the walkout, which was largely silent, as an attack on free speech (MEMO 2019), although the talk proceeded as planned to a small audience. In contrast, when critics of BDS put pressure on institutions having Palestinian speakers, they do not frame their discontent in terms of free speech, but rather "balance," suggesting it is not okay for a Palestinian to speak on their own without an Israeli or Jewish perspective, although Israelis often speak on the issue without any "balancing" Palestinian voice (Abu-Laban and Bakan 2019). Thus, a dual narrative surrounds the role of the academy in regards to Israel/Palestine, narratives that are often linked to broader ideological struggles related to the neoliberalization of the university, which go far beyond debates on Israel/Palestine (Maira 2018).

Israel's International Image: The Legitimacy Wars

Critics of BDS often deride the movement for being unable to bring economic pressure to bear on Israel due to its diverse and high-tech economy. However, these same critics view

BDS as one of the greatest strategic threats faced by Israel, perhaps because it "has ruptured the sanctioned narrative about Palestine-Israel, which occludes the history of colonization and displacement of the Palestinian people" (Maira 2018, 5). It is the delegitimization of the narrative of Israel as "the only democracy in the Middle East" and the reframing of its founding story from one of triumph under attack to one that involved displacing another people that has proven especially unsettling to supporters of Israeli government policies.

Perhaps one of the most challenging issues surrounding the discourse of BDS is that the tactics of boycott, divestment, and sanctions – neutral in and of themselves – are conflated with a highly diverse and decentralized "movement," much as the Israeli government conflates the state and its policies with the fate of Jews all around the world. Because of the linkage between the Israeli state and the fate of the Jewish diaspora – which retains existential fears due to the Holocaust and millennia of Jewish persecution – even those critical of Israeli state policies against Palestinians denounce BDS because of the existential threat they see it posing to Israel as a Jewish state. While BDS may not pose an existential threat to Israel's existence as a *state* in the neutral sense of the term, it explicitly challenges the structure of Israel as a Jewish state that privileges Jewish citizens at the expense of non-Jewish citizens, not to mention the privileging of Jews living in the West Bank over Palestinians who are living under Israeli military control without citizenship, and the privileging of Jews living in the diaspora with citizenship in other countries having rights and privileges related to Israel that are not afforded to Palestinian refugees whose families lived in Palestine/Israel for generations. While Israel's Law of Return (1950) grants citizenship privileges to Jews living in the Diaspora who wish to make *aliya*, Israel refuses to allow Palestinian refugees the right of return, barring them even from visiting relatives who remain either in Israel or the Palestinian Territories.

Natan Sharansky, an Israeli politician and former chair of the Jewish Agency, offers a "3-D" test for defining anti-Semitism, and for distinguishing it from what he considers legitimate criticism of Israel: demonization, which Sharansky considers is at play when Israelis are compared to Nazis; double standards, which Sharansky illustrates through pointing to the United Nations singling out Israel for human rights abuses when others are not mentioned; and delegitimization, such as "presenting [the Jewish state] as, among other things, the prime remnant of imperial colonialism" (Sharansky 2005). This framing denies, however, legitimate fact-based historical comparison between practices by the Israeli government and practices by the German government in the 1930s, as has, for example, been done by some Holocaust survivors (Knight 2019). In terms of double standards, BDS supporters point to the historic support of Israel by the United States in the United Nations Security Council over the decades, with repeated vetoes in support of Israel, or the special loan guarantees and military aid packages that Israel receives (Middle East Eye 2017). Opponents of BDS argue that the United Nations is biased against Israel, pointing to the many resolutions against Israel as evidence of this fact (Abrams 2018).

Prospect theory, often used in the fields of economics and international policymaking, is a useful tool for understanding how activists on each side of the BDS debate approach the issue. While prospect theory is often a tool for decision-making, its basic assumptions are relevant in this case, notably the characteristics of "*reference dependence*, meaning that people make decisions not based on the final outcome but relative to a reference point, oftentimes the status quo" (Vis and Kuijpers 2018, 577, emphasis in original). Consequently, the framing of the reference point is critical to what decisions follow, particularly in terms of whether individuals demonstrate risk-seeking behaviour (when moderate losses are presented) or risk-aversion behaviour (when moderate gains are presented), since prospect theory presumes that people tend toward loss aversion, demonstrating more sensitivity to losses than to equivalent gains (Vis and

Kuijpers 2018). Critics of BDS approach the context generally from a domain of loss, whereas supporters of BDS come from a domain of gain when looking at broader power dynamics and ways the situation is framed – see, for example, the discussion of the anti-Semitic framing which particularly targets generational trauma for Jews.

In contrast, BDS activists see themselves as the allegorical "David" against an Israeli "Goliath," pointing to the international power of Israel under the right-wing government of Benjamin Netanyahu, who has worked with Republican and Christian evangelical allies in the United States to advance Likud Party objectives, including United States' recognition of Jerusalem as Israel's capital and recognition of Israeli settlements. These kinds of actions have contributed to a shift in Israel's international image, from "an embattled Middle Eastern democracy and a haven for the oppressed Jewish people … [to] a military giant that is occupying Palestinian territory and breaking up peaceful Palestinian protests using force" (Beauchamp 2019). In response to BDS opponents who claim Israel is being unfairly singled out, BDS supporters say yes, because Israel itself claims special status, whether as the "only democracy in the Middle East" or as the recipient of special political, military, and financial arrangements with the United States and Europe. Using prospect theory to identify the framing of the issue helps explain why Israel engages in strong attack strategies against BDS efforts – it is operating from a domain of loss.

The Palestinian "legitimacy" war and the "lawfare" response by Israeli hardliners, as described by eminent international law scholar and international relations scholar Richard Falk, can also be understood in light of prospect theory. According to Falk (2010), the legitimacy strategy "seeks popular mobilization on the basis of nonviolent coercion to achieve political goals, relying on the relevance of international law." In contrast, the lawfare strategy seeks to discredit international law and criminalize dissent through tools such as BDS.

Lawfare in Action

Lawfare attacks against BDS have been waged in the context of domestic and international legal systems, not only in Israel but also in the United States and Europe. In 2011 the Israeli Knesset passed the "Law for Prevention of Damage to the State of Israel through Boycott," which allows any individual or organization proposing a boycott to be sued, without evidence, by any individual or organization claiming it would be damaged by such a call (Sherwood 2011). In May 2017 the Israeli Knesset passed a law banning entry to foreigners who call for a boycott of Israel or settlements. Numerous individuals have been prevented entry on these grounds, including United States Congresswoman Rashida Tlaib, who was prevented from entry in 2019, and Human Rights Watch's Israel and Palestine director Omar Shakir, who was deported in November 2019 on the grounds that he had supported boycott, divestment, and sanctions efforts based on statements and social media posts that predated his employment for Human Rights Watch (BBC 2019).

Not only has BDS activism been outlawed in Israel, but over two dozen states in the United States have passed bills to make boycotting Israel illegal, and the United States Congress has also debated bills criminalizing boycott activity (Hauss 2018; Thrall 2018). In states including New York, Texas, Rhode Island, and South Carolina, state laws require businesses contracting with the state – from software companies to those providing educational services – to affirm they are not participating in a boycott of Israel (Beauchamp 2019). In a recent example of the use of law to shut down criticism of Israel, in December 2019 President Donald Trump passed an executive order aimed at combatting anti-Semitism in schools and on college campuses using the International Holocaust Remembrance Alliance (IHRA) definition used by the Department of State. The executive order is widely seen as an effort to shut down Palestinian activism, including BDS actions; however, the equation of Jewish identity with a race or nationality is troubling to many American Jews (Brenner 2019; Ward and Levin 2019; Schraub 2019). Two illustrative examples of anti-Semitism in the IHRA definition are particularly relevant to this discussion: "Denying the Jewish people their right to self-determination, e.g., by claiming that the existence of a State of Israel is a racist endeavor," and "Holding Jews collectively responsible for actions of the state of Israel" (State Department, n. d.). The first example decouples the abstract idea of the "state" from the real-world policies of Israel, including the Nation-state Law which defines the State of Israel in explicitly racist terms that privilege one ethno-national group over another. The second example fails to acknowledge that Israel itself claims to speak on behalf of all Jews everywhere and give rights to Jews solely for being Jews and not having ever lived in the historic territory of Israel/Palestine. BDS activists explicitly seek to point out facts such as these in their appeals to international law, seeking equality for Palestinian citizens of Israel, for example, and calling for the application of international agreements regarding Palestinian refugees who do have a historic connection to the territory of Israel/Palestine but who are denied return. Further, while those opposing Jewish self-determination based on a model of dominance over non-Jews are seen as anti-Semitic, Palestinians calling for their own self-determination are often portrayed by those same actors as uncivilized, violent, and (also) anti-Semitic (Masri 2017, 402), illustrating the double standard applied in this context.

Effectiveness of BDS Campaigns

Inevitably, arguments around BDS turn to questions of "effectiveness" as one way of evaluating their worth. Further, "while Israel is winning one war due to its military dominance and continuous establishment of "facts on the ground," Palestine is winning what in the end is the more important war, the struggle for legitimacy" (Falk 2015, 19). The question of legitimacy is tied not only to what is seen as "effective" in terms of economic and political outcomes, such as putting an economic strain on the Israeli economy such that it withdraws from the occupied territories, but also what is "effective" in terms of wider perceptions of acceptable activism. Supporters of BDS point to numerous successes, including encouraging a boycott of Eurovision when it was held in Israel in 2019. According to Omar Barghouti, a leading figure in the BDS movement, only 4,000–5,000 people came to the performances instead of the expected 40,000–50,000, and Israel had to give away tickets to soldiers to improve the optics of empty arenas (Barghouti 2019). The BDS movement lists a number of successes on its website (bdsmovement.net/impact), including Chile suspending free-trade agreement talks with Israel as a result of the 2014 attacks on Gaza, Security services company G4S selling its Israeli subsidiary, and the Israeli state water company Mekorot losing contracts in European and South American countries. A number of mainline Protestant churches in the United States have also passed divestment resolutions in line with denominational policies regarding morally responsible investment (Hallward 2019).

However, some who are against Israel's occupation of the Palestinian territories, such as spiritual progressive Rabbi Michael Lerner, or the pro-Israel, pro-peace political advocacy group J Street, argue BDS is not effective due to its tendency to alienate possible allies. Some of these critics suggest that BDS causes a "circle the wagons" response that empowers right-wing elements within Israel and therefore is counterproductive to those seeking to strengthen Israeli and Palestinian peace efforts. Some members of the Israeli Left express concern that broadly defined BDS campaigns isolate Israeli civil society working to end the occupation. However, pro-Israel, two-state solution advocates such as Rabbi Lerner and Peter Beinart advocate for the use of "targeted, moral-witness BDS" that focuses explicitly on the Israeli occupation, selecting targets that profit from the occupation or products produced in Israeli settlements (Beinart 2012; Lerner 2012, 326), as a potential means for changing the status quo.

While the Israeli government and other opponents of BDS point to the strength of the Israeli economy and the many critical ways its high-tech products – such as semiconductors and other computer parts – are critical to the world economy as a way of discounting the BDS movement, for many activists, BDS campaigns are avenues for education and social change. Thus, rather than measuring success in dollar terms, BDS campaigns seek symbolic impact, informing the general public about the Israeli occupation and the daily reality of the situation on the ground for Palestinians, as a means of shifting public opinion and influencing foreign policy in the region (Hallward 2013). In this way, BDS activists are waging the so-called legitimacy war as described by Falk. Some also point to the intensity of the response to BDS – through the funnelling of tens of millions of dollars into counter campaigns and task forces, such as the international Maccabee Task Force funded by Sheldon Adelson, and an Israeli government not-for-profit organization – as a measure of its effectiveness (*Times of Israel* 2017; Cortellessa 2019). Were the movement not making strides in shifting public opinion on Israel/ Palestine such a response would not be required, they argue.

Conclusion

More than fifteen years after the launch of PACBI, the BDS movement continues to draw attention and punitive measures. Israel has denied entry to United States Congresswomen, academics, human rights officials, and former student leaders based on their prior or current involvement in BDS campaigns. With anti-BDS legislation on the books in increasing numbers of US states, and a new executive order against anti-Semitism that targets BDS activism on college campuses, the movement continues to pose a threat to the status quo. In November 2019, in what was heralded as a victory by the BDS movement, the European Court of Justice ruled that European Union countries must identify products made in Israeli settlements on their labels. While some critics suggest that this was "a new kind of yellow star on Jewish-made products" the differentiation of settlement products allows consumers to engage in targeted purchasing rather than a blanket boycott of all items with the "made in Israel" label (*The Guardian* 2019).

Opponents of BDS call on Palestinians to reject violence and embrace nonviolent action as a means to achieve self-determination, and many even recognize that BDS is "a nonviolent, yet coercive strategy" (Lerner 2012, 326). Yet, if opponents reject BDS as a form of "delegitimization" or "new anti-Semitism," what options exist for Palestinians who seek equal human rights under international law and who seek self-determination, freedom and justice, just as Jews around the world have sought in their own struggles over the years? Although there are individuals and groups who engage in the tactics of boycott, divestment, and sanctions who are anti-Semitic, they do not represent the movement as a whole, which denounces all forms of anti-Semitism and racism. It is critical to recognize that many of those Christian opponents of BDS and erstwhile supporters of Israeli policy are themselves anti-Semitic, and much of the outrage against Trump's December 2019 executive order was precisely because of the potential for anti-Semitic backlash in the way the order was framed. Thus, the selection over what modes of activism are deemed "anti-Semitic" is itself a reflection of power politics and strategic framing. There is no question that anti-Semitism is on the rise, particularly on the political right; however, attacks on the BDS movement, which largely emerge from the political left, will not address this danger. What is clear is that those benefiting from the current status quo in Israel do not want either militant or non-violent resistance to their power. BDS activism, precisely because it is nonviolent and grounded in international law, claims a type of legitimacy that armed struggle does not. Further, while Israel has the military might to squash armed resistance, its anti-BDS efforts – through lawfare and well-funded counter campaigns – have not yet managed to quell civil society pressure for political change.

Recommended Readings

Babbin, J., with H. London. 2014. *The BDS War Against Israel*. New York: The London Center for Policy Research.

Barghouti, O. 2011. *Boycott, Divestment, Sanctions*. Chicago, IL: Haymarket Books.

Dawn, A., and B. V. Mullen, eds. 2015. *Against Apartheid: The Case for Boycotting Israeli Universities*. Chicago, IL: Haymarket Books.

Hallward, M. 2013. *Transnational Activism and the Israeli-Palestinian Conflict*. New York: Palgrave Macmillan.

Maira, S. 2018. *Boycott! The Academy and Justice for Palestine*. Oakland, CA: University of California Press.

Notes

1 Opponents of BDS consistently walk this tightrope between arguing that BDS is not effective – that it is impossible to boycott all of the many high-tech products that Israeli companies invent and produce, and that Israel has one of the strongest militaries in the world – and that it is a leading strategic threat. For one such analysis that suggests that Israel's economy is less susceptible to boycotts and that the threat is more psychological and cultural, see Bahar and Sachs (2018).

2 While some might reference the "Israeli-Palestinian conflict," others would specify the "Israeli occupation of Palestine," as the term "conflict" often suggests parity of players whereas Israel is an internationally recognized state with one of the world's most powerful armies, and Palestine, while it is an observer state at the United Nations, lacks recognition by the Security Council, has no control over its borders, airspace, or coast, and has only a police force with powers approved by Israel. The asymmetry between the parties in this sense, as well as the disparity in terms of day-to-day experience of the "conflict," are significant, as most Israelis are untouched by it on a daily basis, whereas it is a constant presence for almost all Palestinians.

3 According to the Israeli human rights organization B'Tselem, in the decade following the start of the Second Intifada in September 2000, Israeli security forces killed 6,371 Palestinians, of whom 1,317 were minors, and at least 2,996 of whom did not participate in hostilities when killed. In the same time period, Palestinians killed 1,083 Israelis, 124 of whom were minors and 741 of whom were civilians. See B'Tselem (2010).

4 For more on Ilan Pappe's experience, see Winstanely (2010).

5 See FAQ page, (BDS Movement). Available at: https://bdsmovement.net/faqs#collapse16241.

6 See "Top US diplomat keeps up pressure on China over Muslim Uighurs." *Al Jazeera*. 9 October 2019. Available at: www.aljazeera.com/news/2019/10/top-diplomat-pressure-china-muslim-uighurs-191010013239989.html; United Nations-African Union Hybrid Operation in Darfur (UNAMID), with information about this international mission to Darfur. https://unamid.unmissions.org/. Civil society activists have also worked for human rights in locations such as these two mentioned in the article; "NGO Letter Regarding the Human Rights Situation in Sudan." *Human Rights Watch*. Last modified 8 September 2016. Available at: www.hrw.org/news/2016/09/08/ngo-letter-regarding-human-rights-situation-sudan#.

7 Halbfinger, David, Michael Wines, and Steven Erlanger. "Is B.D.S. Anti-Semitic? A Closer Look at the Boycott Israel Campaign." (*The New York Times* – Breaking News, World News & Multimedia). Last modified 27 July 2019. Available at: www.nytimes.com/2019/07/27/world/middleeast/bds-israel-boycott-antisemitic.html. The authors of this piece also note that "Palestinians who feel no ill will toward Jews but yearn for self-determination in the land of their forebears may rightly argue that to disparage that yearning is a form of bigotry." Omar Barghouti, a co-founder of the BDS movements also notes, "[Y]ou don't choose your oppression, your oppressor chooses you. … Palestinians didn't choose to be under Israel" (Barghouti 2019).

8 *Palestinian Campaign for the Academic and Cultural Boycott of Israel* (BDS Movement). Available at: https://bdsmovement.net/pacbi.

9 The strategic move of isolating various Palestinian populations – separating Jerusalemites from the West Bank, distinguishing the Gaza Strip from the West Bank (and cantonizing areas within the West Bank), as well as dividing Palestinian citizens of Israel and refugees from the remainder of Palestinians – has also been challenged by BDS. This coming together of all various Palestinian populations into one is part of the strategic threat as viewed by Israel.

10 See, for example the American Studies Association (ASA) explanation of the boycott resolution it passed. "What Does the Boycott Mean?" ASA. Available at www.theasa.net/what-does-boycott-mean; and the academic boycott guidelines from the BDS movement are also explicitly focused on institutions and not individuals. "Why Boycott Israeli Universities?" (BDS Movement). Available at: https://bdsmovement.net/academic-boycott#guidelines. Similar to earlier-mentioned tactics, critics of academic boycott, such as the one writing this piece in *Forbes Magazine*, shift attention away from the facts of the case of Israel to suggesting that other countries (China and Botswana in this case) should be boycotted instead. The author also removes agency from oppressed populations, speaking on behalf of Tibetans, and calling it "silly" not to speak on their behalf and ignoring Palestinian voices entirely (Gerstmann 2019).

Questions for Discussion

(1) How do rival conceptions of *Zionism* – defined as one of many different ideologies or as a movement for Jewish self-determination – impact perceptions of BDS activism and the extent to which it is "anti-Semitic"?

(2) Opponents and proponents of BDS claim that it seeks to "delegitimise" Israel. What does each of these perspectives mean by this portrayal and with what implications?

(3) To what extent is the use of boycott, divestment, and sanctions tactics in the case of Israel similar to and/or different from other uses of these tactics, such as in the anti-Apartheid campaign in South Africa, the tea boycott of the American Revolution, Israeli Jewish boycotts of cottage cheese in 2011, or the Nazi boycott of Jewish shops? How does one determine when such tactics are just and appropriate?

(4) How can one determine if BDS is "effective" or not?

(5) Critics and supporters of BDS approach international law from very different vantage points. How does each view international law and how does that affect their framing of the issues and appropriate action?

References

Abrams, E. 2018. "The UN's Automatic Majority against Israel is Fraying." *Council on Foreign Relations*. 16 June. Available at: www.cfr.org/blog/uns-automatic-majority-against-israel-fraying.

Abu-Laban, Y., and A. B. Bakan. 2019. *Israel, Palestine and the Politics of Race: Exploring Identity and Power in a Global Context*. London: Bloomsbury Publishing.

Adalah. 2017. "The Discriminatory Laws Database." 25 September. Available at: www.adalah.org/en/content/view/7771.

Bahar, D., and N. Sachs. 2018. "How Much Does BDS Threaten Israel's Economy?" *Brookings Institution*. 26 January. Available at: www.brookings.edu/blog/order-from-chaos/2018/01/26/how-much-does-bds-threaten-israels-economy/.

Barghouti, O. 2019. "Omar Barghouti, BDS and the Palestinians' Right to Resistance." *RTP News*. 2 December. Available at: www.rtp.pt/noticias/mundo/omar-barghouti-bds-e-o-direito-dos-palestinianos-aresistencia_v1189031.

BBC. 2019. "Israel's Deportation of Human Rights Watch Activist Condemned." *BBC World News*. 25 November. Available at: www.bbc.com/news/world-middle-east-50545733.

BDS Movement. N.d. *Overview: What is BDS?* Available at: https://bdsmovement.net/what-is-bds.

BDS Movement. 2005. *Open Letter: Palestinian Civil Society Calls for Boycott, Divestment and Sanctions against Israel Until It Complies with International Law and Universal Principles of Human Rights*. 9 July. Available at: https://bdsmovement.net/call.

Beauchamp, Z. 2019. "The Controversy over Laws Punishing Israel Boycotts, Explained." *Vox*. 9 January. Available at: www.vox.com/policy-and-politics/2019/1/9/18172826/bds-law-israel-boycott-states-explained.

Beinart, P. 2012. "To Save Israel, Boycott the Settlements." *The New York Times*. 18 March. Available at: www.nytimes.com/2012/03/19/opinion/to-save-israel-boycott-the-settlements.html.

Brenner, M. 2019. "Why President Trump's Executive Order to Fight Anti-Semitism Is Dangerous for Jews." *Washington Post*. 15 December. Available at: www.washingtonpost.com/outlook/2019/12/15/why-president-trumps-executive-order-fight-antisemitism-is-dangerous-jews/.

Brownfield, A. 2001. "The Origin of the Palestine-Israel Conflict," 3rd ed. *Jews for Justice in the Middle East*. Available at: https://ifamericansknew.org/download/origin_booklet.pdf.

B'Tselem. 2010. "10 Years to the Second Intifada - Summary of Data" (Israeli Information Center Human Rights in the Occupied Territories). 27 September. Available at: www.btselem.org/press_releases/20100927.

Cortellessa, E. 2019. "Anti-BDS Group Backed by Adelson Heads to 6 Countries Outside US." *Times of Israel*. 7 October. Available at: www.timesofisrael.com/anti-bds-group-backed-by-adelson-heads-to-6-countries-outside-us/.

Divine, D. R. 2019. "Word Crimes: Reclaiming the Language of the Israeli-Palestinian Conflict." *Israel Studies* 24:2, 1–16.

European Commission. 2009. "Israel – Trade." Available at: https://ec.europa.eu/trade/policy/countries-and-regions/countries/israel/.

Falk, Richard. 2010. "The Palestinian 'Legitimacy War.'" *Al Jazeera*. 24 December. Available at: www.aljazeera.com/indepth/opinion/2010/10/20101021113420124418.html.

Falk, Richard. 2015. "On 'Lost Causes' and the Future of Palestine." *Nation* 300:1, 18–24.

Gertsmann, E. 2019. "Why An Academic Boycott of Israel Is Hypocritical." *Forbes*. 26 February. Available at: www.forbes.com/sites/evangerstmann/2019/02/21/why-an-academic-boycott-of-israel-is-hypocritical/#43769ef05f04.

Goldfeder, M. 2018. "Stop Defending Discrimination: Anti-Boycott, Divestment, and Sanctions' Statutes Are Fully Constitutional." *Texas Tech Law Review* 50:2, 207248.

Gordon, N. 2009. "Time to Boycott Israel." *The Guardian*. 23 August. Available at: www.theguardian.com/commentisfree/2009/aug/21/israel-international-boycott.

Haaretz. 2019. "LISTEN: Anti-Semitism Is Not a Jewish Problem. Israel Is." *Haaretz Weekly Podcast*. 4 November. Available at: www.haaretz.com/israel-news/podcasts/listen-anti-semitism-is-not-a-jewish-problem-israel-is-1.8068566.

Hallward, M. 2013. *Transnational Activism and the Israeli-Palestinian Conflict*. Basingstoke: Springer.

Hallward, M. 2019. "Mainline Protestants and Divestment as International Economic Activism." *Oxford Research Encyclopedia of Politics*. 25 February. Available at: https://oxfordre.com/politics/view/10.1093/acrefore/9780190228637.001.0001/acrefore-9780190228637-e-689.

Hallward, M. C., and P. Shaver. 2012. "War by Other Means" or Nonviolent Resistance? Examining the Discourses Surrounding Berkeley's Divestment Bill." *Peace & Change* 37:3, 389–412.

Harkov, L. 2019. "French Parliament Decides Anti-Zionism is Antisemitism." *The Jerusalem Post*, 4 December. Available at: www.jpost.com/Diaspora/Antisemitism/French-parliament-decides-anti-Zionism-is-antisemitism-609764.

Hauss, B. 2018. "The New Israel Anti-Boycott Act Is Still Unconstitutional." *American Civil Liberties Union*. 7 March. Available at: www.aclu.org/blog/free-speech/rights-protesters/new-israel-anti-boycott-act-still-unconstitutional.

Intelligence Squared. 2019. *Anti-Zionism Is Anti-Semitism*. Available at: www.intelligencesquared.com/events/anti-zionism-is-anti-semitism/.

International Court of Justice (ICJ). 2004. *Legal Consequences of the Construction of a Wall in the Occupied Palestinian Territory, Advisory Opinion*, I. C. J. Reports 2004.

Kane. 2018. "'It's Killing the Student Movement?: Canary Mission's Blacklist of Pro-Palestine Activists Is Taking a Toll." *The Intercept*. 22 November. Available at: https://theintercept.com/2018/11/22/israel-boycott-canary-mission-blacklist/.

Knight, C. 2019. "Nine Holocaust Survivors Compare Zionist Policies to those of the Nazis." 30 *Labour Briefing*. 30 July. Available at: https://labourbriefing.org/blog/2019/7/30/six-holocaust-survivors-compare-zionist-policy-to-that-of-the-nazis.

Lerner, M. 2012. *Embracing Israel/Palestine*. Berkeley, CA: Tikkun Books.

Maira, S. 2018. *Boycott!: The Academy and Justice for Palestine*. Oakland: University of California Press.

Masri, M. 2017. "Colonial Imprints: Settler-colonialism as a Fundamental Feature of Israeli Constitutional Law." *International Journal of Law in Context* 13:3, 388–407.

Middle East Eye. 2017. "The 43 Times US Has Used Veto Power against UN Resolutions on Israel." Available at: www.middleeasteye.net/news/43-times-us-has-used-veto-power-against-un-resolutions-israel.

Middle East Monitor (MEMO). 2019. "*Harvard Students Walkout of Israel Envoy Talk*." 15 November. Available at: www.middleeastmonitor.com/20191115-harvard-students-walkout-of-israel-envoy-talk/.

Podeh, E. 2014. "Israel and the Arab Peace Initiative, 2002–2014: A Plausible Missed Opportunity." *The Middle East Journal* 68:4, 584–603.

Qumsiyeh, M. B. 2010. *Popular Resistance in Palestine: A History of Hope and Empowerment*. London: Pluto Press.

Redden, E. 2019. "Groups Protest Israeli Visa Policies for Foreign Academics Teaching in the West Bank." *Inside Higher Ed*. 26 July. www.insidehighered.com/news/2019/07/26/groups-protest-israeli-visa-policies-foreign-academics-teaching-west-bank.

Russo, Y. M. 2009. "The Battle of the Boycotts [on Neve Gordon]." *Campus Watch*. 26 September. Available at: www.meforum.org/campus-watch/16128/the-battle-of-the-boycotts-on-neve-gordon.

Sa'di, A. H. 2019. "The Nation State of the Jewish People's Basic Law: A Threshold of Elimination?" *Journal of Holy Land and Palestine Studies* 18:2, 163–177.

Schrank, A. 2019. "Why One Small SoCal College is at the Center of the Israel Boycott Debate." *LAist*. 4 January. Available at: https://laist.com/2019/01/04/why_one_small_socal_college_is_at_the_center_of_the_israel_boycott_debate.php.

Schraub, D. 2019. "Why Trump's Executive Order on Anti-Semitism Touched Off a Firestorm." *The Atlantic*. 12 December. Available at: www.theatlantic.com/ideas/archive/2019/12/dilemma-jewish-identity/603493/.

Scribd. 2019. "Call by 129 Jewish and Israeli Scholars to the French National Assembly: Don't Support Resolution Equating Anti-Zionism with Anti-Semitism and Endorsing IHRA Definition." 27 November. Available at: www.scribd.com/document/437713274/Call-of-129-Jewish-and-Israeli-Scholars-to-French-Parliament-About-Resolution-on-Anti-Semitism.

Sharansky, N. 2005. "Antisemitism in 3-D." *The Jewish Forward*. 21 January. Available at: https://forward.com/opinion/4184/antisemitism-in-3-d/.

Sharp, G. 1973. *The Politics of Nonviolent Action: The Methods of Nonviolent Action*. Manchester, NH: Extending Horizons Books.

Sharpe, J. M. 2019. "U.S. Foreign Aid to Israel." *Congressional Research Service*. Last modified 16 November. Available at: https://fas.org/sgp/crs/mideast/RL33222.pdf.

Sherwood, H. 2011. "Israel Passes Law Banning Citizens from Calling for Boycotts." *The Guardian*. 11 July. Available at: www.theguardian.com/world/2011/jul/11/israel-passes-law-boycotts.

Sheskin, I. M., and E. Felson. 2016. "Is the Boycott, Divestment, and Sanctions Movement Tainted by Anti-Semitism?" *Geographical Review* 106:2, 270–75.

State Department. N. d. *Defining Anti-Semitism*. Available at: www.state.gov/defining-anti-semitism/.

StopBDS. N. d. *A Toxic Campus Environment*. Available at: www.stopbds.com/?page_id=4.

Svrluga, S. 2019. "Palestinian Student Originally Denied Entry to U.S. Now Allowed in to Attend Harvard." *Washington Post*. 3 September. Available at: www.washingtonpost.com/education/2019/09/03/palestinian-student-originally-denied-entry-us-now-allowed-attend-harvard/.

The Guardian. 2019. "Products from Israeli Settlements Must be Labelled, EU Court Rules." 12 November. Available at: www.theguardian.com/world/2019/nov/12/products-israeli-settlements-labelled-eu-court.

Thrall, N. 2018. "BDS: How a Controversial Non-violent Movement Has Transformed the Israeli-Palestinian Debate." *The Guardian*. 24 August. Available at: www.theguardian.com/news/2018/aug/14/bds-boycott-divestment-sanctions-movement-transformed-israeli-palestinian-debate.

Times of Israel. 2017. "Israel Okays $72 Million Anti-BDS Project." 29 December. Available at: www.timesofisrael.com/israel-okays-72-million-anti-bds-project/.

Vis, B., and D. Kuijpers. 2018. "Prospect Theory and Foreign Policy Decision-making: Underexposed Issues, Advancements, and Ways Forward." *Contemporary Security Policy* 39:4, 575–589.

Ward, M., and D. Levin. 2019. "Anti-Semitism or Free Speech? College Students Cheer and Fear Trump Order." *The New York Times*. 18 December. Available at: www.nytimes.com/2019/12/15/us/trump-anti-semitism-order-college-students.html.

Winstanely, A. 2010. "The Last Chance Salon: Why Ilan Pappe Left Israel." *Ceasefire Magazine*. 3 February. Available at: https://ceasefiremagazine.co.uk/book-review-pappe/.

Yiftachel, O. 2006. *Ethnocracy: Land and Identity Politics in Israel/Palestine*. Philadelphia: University of Pennsylvania Press.

Zelkovitz, I. 2014. "Education, Revolution and Evolution: The Palestinian Universities as Initiators of National Struggle 1972–1995." *History of Education* 43:3, 387–407.

34
THE CONFLICT ON CAMPUS

Matthew Berkman

Introduction

Given their role as sites of critical discourse and incubators for the political and economic elite, college and university campuses have been a primary battleground on which the Israeli-Palestinian conflict has played out. While the volume of campus activism is likely greater today than at any point in the history of the conflict, contestation around the policies and legitimacy of the State of Israel dates to at least the early 1950s. The question of Palestine achieved particular prominence during the student uprisings of the late 1960s, and engagement with it has waxed and waned with political currents ever since. Notwithstanding similar contemporary trends in Canada (Kates 2013), the United Kingdom (Bicchi 2018), Latin America (Bisharat 2019), and elsewhere, this chapter focuses on the United States campus conflict due to its unique scale and breadth of historical context. Over the 70-year period since the creation of Israel, the terms of the debate on American campuses have evolved with developments on the international stage and in the domestic political arena. Yet we find a dearth of scholarship analysing the major actors and core dynamics of that debate, even as pro-Palestinian activism has increasingly become a target of intervention by United States elected officials. For that reason, this chapter draws on a combination of secondary literature and original primary research to offer a historical overview of United States campus advocacy around the Israeli-Palestinian conflict since 1948,[1] with a focus on institutional development, shifting discursive repertoires, and the role of state repression. It traces the ebb and flow of pro-Palestinian organizing and identifies two "waves" of solidarity activism on United States college campuses: first in the late 1960s, with the rise of the New Left, and again following the emergence of the global Boycott, Divestment, and Sanctions (BDS) movement in 2005. Paying close attention to Jewish institution building, the chapter charts the pro-Israel countermobilization and proliferation of organizations dedicated to monitoring and policing real and perceived "anti-Israel" activity among college and university students and faculty. It then concludes with an account of pending legislation and recent government action aimed at curtailing such activity under the rubric of combatting antisemitism on campus.

DOI: 10.4324/9780429027376-41

Early Interventions: From Statehood to the Six-Day War

The earliest campus activity bearing on the State of Israel was organized under the aegis of the Intercollegiate Zionist Federation of America (IZFA) – a joint project of the Zionist Organization of America (ZOA) and Hadassah, the two largest national Zionist agencies – and centred mainly on the promotion of Jewish cultural expression and youth immigration to Israel (*aliyah*) (Pins 1952, 199). The leading role of official Zionist agencies was short-lived, however. Not long after 1948, Israeli prime minister David Ben-Gurion adopted a deliberate policy of marginalizing the ZOA, fearing that an independent American Zionist movement would obstruct the state's diplomatic relations (Urofsky 1979, 83). The decline of the ZOA in the early 1950s mirrored a similar drop-off in the number of organized Zionist students on campus: from around 10,000 members in 1948, the IZFA, "lacking adequate financial support and experienced leadership," shrank to 1,700 members by 1953, the year it ceased operations (Solender 1954, 148; Jospe 1964, 144). Reconstituted the following year as the Student Zionist Organization (SZO) under the sponsorship of the American Zionist Youth Foundation, a branch of the Jewish Agency, the campus Zionist movement continued to attract minimal engagement. By 1963, the SZO's national membership amounted to around 2,500 out of a total of 275,000 Jewish students on United States college campuses (Jospe 1964, 133, 144). Through the mid-1960s, campus Zionism maintained its cultural and *aliyah*-oriented focus, even as political activism by Arab students and their supporters intensified.

As is the case today, the main organization cultivating Jewish student life in the postwar decades was the B'nai B'rith Hillel Foundations.[2] By the mid-1950s, there were more than 200 Hillel affiliates on United States campuses (Freeman 1956). Consistent with scholarship depicting the first two decades after 1948 as a time of comparative American Jewish disinterest in Israel, Hillel records from the 1950s reveal little of the Israel-centricity that emerged in force during and after the Six-Day War of 1967 (Waxman 2016, 33–35; National Jewish Monthly 1959). At most, as Emily Alice Katz (2015) has shown, the pre-1967 period was one of cultural exchange between the world's two largest Jewish communities. Thus, in the early 1950s, Israeli folk dancing, lectures on Hebrew literature, and fundraising for humanitarian causes in Israel marked the limits of Hillel-based student engagement with the Jewish state.[3] By the second half of the decade, however, Hillel chapters had begun to play a more active role in organizing Israeli Independence Day celebrations, and in 1960 the Hillel Foundations launched a national speaking program for Israeli government officials (BBHF 1968). This increased pro-Israel activity coincided with concern on the part of local Jewish Community Relations Councils (JCRCs) – the public affairs arms of the Jewish philanthropic federations – with the growth of anti-Israel activism on college campuses. JCRCs across the country had begun reporting a "tremendous stepping up of pro-Arab propaganda" advanced "largely through the activities of exchange students from Arab countries" (NCRAC 1955). The communal response that followed was the beginning of a broader expansion of organized pro-Israel advocacy on the part of non-Zionist Jewish agencies, a response that gradually accelerated after Israel's 1956 invasion of Egypt and climaxed with the Arab-Israeli wars of 1967 and 1973 (Berkman 2018).

While likely overestimated by American Jewish organizations, a relatively systematic public relations campaign aimed at fostering positive US-Arab relations and drawing attention to the plight of Palestinian refugees did, in fact, coalesce in the early 1950s. Those efforts were spearheaded by the American Friends of the Middle East (AFME), a non-profit organization established in 1951 by celebrity journalist Dorothy Thompson at the instigation of Kermit Roosevelt, a longtime United States intelligence operative. A CIA front group, the AFME received the bulk of its funding from "pass-through" foundations controlled by Roosevelt, and from the United States (now Saudi) oil company Aramco. Throughout the 1950s, AFME staged lectures, sponsored exchange students from the Middle East, supported Arab student organizations in the United States, and ran an extensive publishing operation (Levin 2019). In 1952, it helped initiate the Organization of Arab Students (OAS), "which became the most politically active Arab organization nationwide for much of the 1950s and 1960s" (Levin 2019, 30). Though its politics radicalized in subsequent decades, the OAS initially evinced a progressive but mainstream, even "pro-American," political outlook befitting the elite pedigree of its mostly foreign-born members at the time. Advocating "economic planning and political unity among the Arab states, educational development, land reform, and commitment to constitutional rights," OAS was united above all by its dedication to the Palestinian cause, a topic on which it organized frequent campus lectures and presentations for local civic and church groups (Pennock 2017, 50). In its early years, OAS maintained close ties with Arab government envoys, the Arab League's Washington-based Arab Information Center, and the anti-Zionist American Council for Judaism. Influenced by the latter, it drew sharp distinctions between Judaism and Zionism and criticized Israel for obstructing a geopolitically strategic Cold War partnership between the United States and the Arab world.

By the mid-1950s – whether fairly or not – American Jewish leaders came increasingly to believe that Arab student activists were casting Jewish commitment to Israel as a form of "dual loyalty." At an emergency meeting of Jewish agencies held in 1956, a representative from the Anti-Defamation League (ADL) lamented the "immeasurable" impact on United States public opinion of "hundreds of cases in ADL files of Arab students speaking before such groups as Kiwanis, Rotary, etc." Esther Herlitz, an Israeli consular official, expressed her "fear that we are losing the battle for the intellectual mind" and emphasized "the need for more coordinated planning rather than the fire extinguisher approach" to Arab activism. A more sceptical position was voiced by Alfred Jospe, director of programs for the B'nai B'rith Hillel Foundations. Having surveyed over two-hundred Hillel affiliates and found "meager" evidence of a crisis situation, Jospe "felt that the entire problem may be exaggerated" (Freeman 1956). Nonetheless, a communal strategy for college campuses soon appeared in the 1956–1957 Joint Program Plan of the National Community Relations Advisory Council (NCRAC, est. 1944), an umbrella body uniting local and national Jewish defence agencies. The plan called for

> [d]evelopment of programs on college campuses and in secondary schools to counteract the propaganda being disseminated by Arab students, [including] training and placement of qualified Jewish and non-Jewish students [to speak] before student body associations such as fraternities, sororities, Newman Clubs, etc.
>
> *(NCRAC 1956)*

By then, JCRCs had already begun surreptitiously monitoring Arab student activity at local universities and, when necessary, organizing pro-Israel rejoinders.[4] The following year, several national Jewish agencies joined a "Campus Coordinating Committee," the first of several umbrella groups that would attempt to harmonize communal strategy vis-à-vis college campuses (Levin 2019, 168–169). Anticipating the use of state power against pro-Palestinian activists in the decades ahead, a 1958 report by the American Jewish Congress noted the problem of Arab exchange students and urged that "[a]ny person present in the United States on a student visa who engages in public anti-Jewish activities aimed at American citizens should have his student visa terminated" (American Jewish Congress 1958).

Despite these alarm bells and external interventions, it was only in the late 1960s that defence of Israel became a defining feature of Jewish campus life. Politicized by the civil rights and anti-war movements, Jewish students reacted with passion to the Six-Day War of June 1967. While some embraced the anti-Zionist politics of the New Left, many more rallied behind Israel as it confronted what was widely portrayed as an existential threat. At the same time, Arab and Arab-American student activism crested in response to Israel's military victory and subsequent occupation of Arab lands. Already by the early 1960s, OAS had begun to advance a more left-leaning politics of solidarity with national liberation struggles against European colonialism and United States imperialism in Asia and Africa. As the decade wore on and American students became increasingly mobilized against the Vietnam War, the stage was set for the first of two historic waves of Palestine solidarity activism on college campuses.

The First Wave: 1967 and Its Aftermath

By the time the Six-Day War erupted on 5 June 1967, Hillel chapters had already commenced what one internal document called "a vast mobilization for Israel" at universities across the country (BBHF 1967, 1). In late May, as border tensions between Israel and Egypt threatened to boil over, B'nai B'rith issued a memo to all Hillel directors urging "you, your students, your community leaders, campus leaders, faculty, Jews and non-Jews, [to] send telegrams to the President, the Governor of your state, [and] your Senators and Congressmen" in support of Israel (Kahn and Jospe 1967). Over the next month, Hillel staffers organized teach-ins, staged rallies, circulated petitions, and crafted model letters of support for Israel along with instructions for dispatching telegrams to elected officials. At Tulane University, Hillel Director Jay Krause launched a "campus-wide drive to get the university community to send wires to the United States government and the United Nations" (BBHF 1967, 7). Hillel directors secured thousands of faculty signatures for a pro-Israel declaration in the *New York Times* (UCLA alone recruited nearly 400 professors). In late June, after the war subsided, signatories of the *Times* statement established American Professors for Peace in the Middle East, a chapter-based pro-Israel organization that "work[ed] with and through the Hillel Foundation and the Hillel Director," according to a B'nai B'rith memo (Kahn 1967). Campus groups also mobilized material support for the Israeli war effort. The University of Michigan's Herman Jacobs was one of many Hillel directors who recruited students for "a special summer work program in Israel" intended to "alleviate [the] shortage of manpower" resulting from the May-June military mobilization (Jacobs 1967). At the University of Maryland, Hillel "set up an office in Washington in front of the Israel Embassy to process students volunteering to work in Israel" (BBHF 1967, 5). On the fundraising front, Hillel directors helped solicit tens to hundreds of thousands of dollars in Israel bond purchases and donations to the United Jewish Appeal from students, faculty, and university staff.

This unprecedented campus mobilization for Israel was the product of several factors. First, as I have described elsewhere, the organizational infrastructure of the Jewish community had undergone a significant expansion in the years between 1948 and 1967 (Berkman 2018). By fostering the development of new JCRCs and linking them more systematically with national Jewish organizations, NCRAC formed a mechanism for coordination among agencies that had previously operated in isolation or conflict with one another. Hillel, both nationally and locally, comprised key nodes in this network. Second, American Jews (and Americans in general) had been exposed to nearly two decades of positive representations of Israel, of which the bestselling novel *Exodus* (1958) and its blockbuster film adaptation (1960) are perhaps the most famous examples. In depicting the Jewish state as a bastion of American values in a hostile region, these representations enhanced Jewish pride in Israel and enabled American Jews to reconcile pro-Israel activism with the idea of undivided loyalty to the United States (Kaplan

2018). Finally, the mass movements of the 1960s had normalized new forms of political activism. Whereas earlier campaigns on behalf of Jewish causes had bred conflict among Jews regarding the political wisdom of visible Jewish activism, the eruption of the Black freedom and women's liberation movements, and the overall waning of national authority occasioned by the Vietnam War, diminished the perceived liabilities of identity-based mobilizations (on these issues, see Dollinger 2000 and Jacobson 2006). In May and June 1967, the intersection of these developments with widespread fears about the imminent threat of a "second Holocaust" drew American Jewish students into a formidable political and fundraising effort on behalf of Israel.

Reactions to the war among Jewish students were by no means uniform, however. Like their non-Jewish peers, some Jews adopted the emerging anti-Zionist outlook of the New Left (Staub 2002). While OAS had long cast Israel as an extension of Western imperialism, it was only after the Six-Day War, when Israel's military conquests brought millions of stateless Palestinians under its control, that major New Left groups like Students for a Democratic Society (SDS) began to visibly integrate Palestine solidarity into their broader anti-imperialist agenda. According to one SDS leader, "Iranian and, to some degree, Palestinian, students were influential in stimulating campus interest in the Arab-Israeli conflict" following the June war (Fishbach 2020, 26). Most influential, however, were the actions of Black radicals. Starting with a fiery (and at points antisemitic) denunciation of Israel by the Student Nonviolent Coordinating Committee (SNCC) in the summer of 1967, Black Power organizations took up the Palestinian cause with vigour, inspiring white leftists to do the same (Fishbach 2020, 9–10, 26). In 1968, the Black Panther Party initiated an enduring relationship with the Palestine Liberation Organization (PLO) and its leading faction, Fatah. PLO statements appeared in the party's newspaper, and Panther leaders met with Fatah's Yasser Arafat on more than one occasion (Lubin 2014; Feldman 2015). For its part, OAS underwent a process of "Palestinianization" after 1967. Shifting allegiances from the Arab states to the PLO, OAS exchanged frequent communications with Fatah and echoed revolutionary calls for "Liberation War" against Israel (Pennock 2017, 54). These developments triggered a wave of pro-Palestinian activism uniting Arab and non-Arab students (including some anti-Zionist Jews) beginning in early 1969, as dozens of campuses hosted "Palestine Week" actions and students began forming the earliest dedicated solidarity groups (Fishbach 2020, 26–28). Working with the newly established Association of Arab American University Graduates, OAS "sponsored teach-ins and staged rallies at universities across the country and mobilized demonstrations at Arab embassies and venues hosting Israeli leaders" (Pennock 2017, 57). Enlivened by the New Left's embrace of Palestine, the first wave of solidarity activism persisted into the 1970s before losing momentum in the second half of the decade (discussed below).

As historian Michael E. Staub has shown, many left-wing Jewish students rejected the New Left's anti-Zionist turn, splitting with SDS to form "radical Zionist" groups dedicated to both Israel *and* world socialist revolution. Appropriating a Black nationalist aesthetic, radical Zionists used images of shackled fists to symbolize Jewish oppression and branded anti-Zionist Jews "Uncle Jakes" (Staub 2002, 207–214). While much of this activity was self-directed, the Israeli government and major Jewish agencies adapted and intensified their campus interventions in response to challenges from the left. In 1968, Israel's Midwest Consul General warned Jewish leaders of the

> approximately 10,000 Arab students in the United States who are fairly well organized on a national basis. Since they are subsidized by Arab governments … [they] have the time to devote themselves to propagandizing, with the results that generally, Arab

> propaganda on campus is effective. … [Their approach] is now slanted toward current problem groups in America, such as the Negro, the New Left, etc.
>
> *(JCRC-C 1968)*

Estimating that Jews comprised upwards of 30 per cent of the New Left, the Jewish Agency's American Zionist Youth Foundation (AZYF) established a department aimed at cultivating pro-Israel activism among left-wing Jewish students. By mid-1969, it counted 110 recently formed Zionist groups on North American campuses (Fishbach 2020, 34–35). To facilitate communication and consensus, the AZYF launched the North American Jewish Students' Network that same year, bringing together left- and right-leaning students around a common program of transnational Jewish solidarity. In addition to hosting "Israel Appreciation Week," the Network held annual conventions, created a Jewish student press agency, and served as a platform for a variety of political initiatives (Network 1979; Bronznick 1978). Not to be outdone, Hillel set up a Department of Israel Affairs to facilitate the creation of dedicated campus "Israel committees" to "combat Arab propaganda" and "develop affirmative programs favorable to Israel" (BBI 1970, 6). In response to demand, Jewish federations increased their annual allocations to Hillel from $650,000 to $3 million between 1969 and 1977 (BBI 1977). JCRCs and national organizations like the ADL also expanded their student outreach programs.

In sum, the Six-Day War and its aftermath brought the Israeli-Palestinian conflict to American college and university campuses in a singularly dramatic way. By reorienting the priorities of the organized Jewish community around the defence of Israel, the war stimulated substantial investment in pro-Israel campus infrastructure. At the same time, Israel's conquest of Arab lands catapulted Palestine to a place of prominence in the eyes of the New Left, generating a flurry of pro-Palestinian student activity. The late 1960s and early 1970s were thus an expansionary period for both sides of the conflict. Moving into the 1980s, however, the trajectories of the two camps would diverge: while political trends only further enhanced Jewish commitment to the campus as an ideological battleground, a combination of domestic and international developments would yield diminished prospects for Palestine solidarity organizing through the end of the century.

Repression and Reconfiguration: From the 1973 War to the End of Oslo

On 5 June 1968, exactly one year after the outbreak of the Six-Day War, Senator Robert F. Kennedy was assassinated at the Ambassador Hotel in Los Angeles. Arrested, tried, and convicted for the murder was Sirhan Bishara Sirhan, a young Palestinian Christian allegedly motivated by Kennedy's support for Israel. According to historian Pamela E. Pennock,

> Suspicion of Arab supporters of Palestine … heightened after [the assassination]. Gerald Ford [then Speaker of the House] fanned these flames in an incendiary speech to the American Israel Public Affairs Committee (AIPAC) in 1969. Associating Kennedy's assassination with "Peking-trained agitators from the Middle East" on America's college campuses, Ford demanded that the government monitor all Arab students in the United States. Within days of Sirhan's sentencing, leaders of the Anti-Defamation League (ADL) of B'nai B'rith made similar charges and demands.
>
> *(Pennock 2017, 145)*

The CIA and FBI soon launched investigations into potential ties between Arab students and foreign terrorist groups. While their probes yielded no evidence of illegal behaviour, government scrutiny returned following the murder of Israeli athletes by Palestinian militants at the 1972 Munich Olympics. In response to the attack, President Nixon instructed Immigration and Naturalization Services (INS) to monitor all United States residents of Arab extraction. The ensuing INS operation, dubbed "Operation Boulder," "set out to track down and question every Arab student in the United States with the expressed purpose of verifying their visa status but with the unstated goal of investigating the students' political views" (Pennock 2017, 149). By early 1973, the agency had investigated 3,500 Arab residents – including 1,000 students – and filed deportation proceedings against 68 of them for visa violations (see also Yaqub 2016, 99–100). The Association of Arab American University Graduates (AAUG), a group that produced scholarly research on the Middle East and fielded speakers for OAS events, was targeted for FBI surveillance and an Internal Revenue Service audit of its tax-exempt status. According to Pennock, the federal government's campaign of harassment against politically active Arab Americans continued for decades, receiving assistance from both the ADL and Israeli intelligence services (Pennock 2017, 104).

Like the FBI's COINTELPRO operations, which targeted Black radicals and left-wing groups more generally, Operation Boulder took a toll on pro-Palestine student organizing in the United States. By the end of the 1970s, the declining fortunes of secular pan-Arabism in the Middle East, along with mounting factionalism related to internal Palestinian politics, combined with government repression to weaken OAS and AAUG. Several OAS chapters continued to exist into the 1980s, but the primary responsibility for Palestine solidarity organizing on campus shifted to the Muslim Students Association and the General Union of Palestinian Students, an international organization affiliated with the PLO (Pennock 2017, 76, 202 n.6). While there are no detailed scholarly accounts of pro-Palestine student organizing in the 1980s, scattered evidence suggests that periodic educational and protest activity continued at scores of colleges and universities across the country, even as the left, in general, had become more disorganized and marginal since its heyday in the late 1960s. If opposition research by the American Israel Public Affairs Committee can be trusted, campus pro-Palestine organizing in the 1980s was still led primarily by foreign-born Arab and Muslim students, in alliance with other international solidarity groups and far-left sectarian organizations like the Spartacus Youth League and the Worker World Party (Kessler and Schwaber 1984, 5–18). Operating both on and off campus, these students made common cause with the movement against South African apartheid, drawing parallels that would become a rhetorical staple of Palestine activism in later years (Abdulhadi 2004, 242; Barrows-Friedman 2014, 53).

While the collapse of the New Left sapped some of the potency from Palestine work, pro-Israel institution building continued apace, receiving boosts from every subsequent Arab-Israeli confrontation. NCRAC, for example, responded to Israel's 1982 invasion of Lebanon by (among other things) using an emergency fund set up during the 1973 war to establish the Campus Advisory Committee (CAC). This new operation "brought together, for the first time on a permanent basis, over a dozen diverse Jewish agencies that have operated independently on American campuses for years." In addition to serving as a "clearing-house and coordinating center for Israel support," the CAC developed a series of "strategy manuals" for countering university appearances by the country's "top ten Arab propagandists" (NCRAC 1983). In 1979, AIPAC decided to augment an already crowded field by launching its own campus outreach initiative. Less than four years later, the Political Leadership Development Program had involved 4,500 students from 375 campuses in "regional and state-wide political education and propaganda response workshops and national political leadership training seminars." The program's director, Jonathan Kessler, devoted special attention to Jewish fraternities and sororities, which he called the "greatest untapped pool of potential pro-Israel political activists," given their "dynamic students" and "hierarchical structure." In addition to political education, AIPAC connected students to particular electoral campaigns, such as Richard Durbin's successful 1982 challenge to United States Representative Paul Findley – a victory for which Kessler took some credit (Zorn 1983).

The late 1970s and early 1980s also witnessed the first relatively systematic efforts by pro-Israel groups to police university curricula and other aspects of academia related to the Middle East. As a result of surging oil prices following the Yom Kippur War, American Jewish organizations became increasingly concerned with the reinvestment of Arab oil profits in United States institutions of higher learning. In a 1979 report entitled "Arab Petrodollar Influence on the American Campus," the ADL warned that "Arab governments, or their supporters or beneficiaries, may in some cases gain effective control or undue influence over academic activities or conditions and may otherwise threaten American values and traditions" (ADL 1979). That same year, the American Jewish Congress announced it was conducting a study of university endowment funds and called on JCRCs to dispatch special committees

> to visit the college and university campuses in your area, to review the various courses in international and Middle Eastern affairs offered by the schools, and to ascertain the scope and magnitude of Arab participation in the financing and development of the programs of study.
>
> *(Baum 1979)*

In 1982, Boston-area activist Charles Jacobs launched the Committee for Accuracy in Middle East Reporting in America (CAMERA), a right-leaning media monitoring outfit that soon expanded to college campuses, where it instructed pro-Israel students to demand the removal of "offensive" library books (Kaidy 1993). Efforts to publicly "out" and denounce campus critics of Israel also made their earliest appearances. In 1984, both AIPAC and the ADL came under fire from the Middle East Studies Association for "listing factually inaccurate and unsubstantiated assertions that defame specific students, teachers and researchers as 'pro-Arab propagandists,' who 'use their anti-Zionism as merely a guise for their deeply felt anti-Semitism'" (Slabodkin 1992).

But even as unprecedented effort and resources flowed into pro-Israel campus advocacy, cracks soon began to appear in the post-1967 façade of American Jewish unity. The Yom Kippur War triggered the formation of *Breira* (Hebrew for "alternative"), the first in a series of organized challenges to Jewish communal taboos against public criticism of Israel's military and security policies. According to Michael Staub,

> Breira drew considerable support from numerous Hillel Foundations across the US While they would later be mocked as "incubators of Breira," Hillels across the country indeed proved remarkably receptive to this new peace initiative; at least eight Hillel directors (including those at UCLA, Dartmouth, Carnegie-Mellon, Adelphi, Temple, and Yale) served on Breira's advisory committee.
>
> *(Staub 2002, 291)*

Adopting positions similar to those of the nascent Israeli peace movement, Breira called on Israel to relinquish occupied territory, recognize the legitimacy of Palestinian national aspirations, and negotiate what would come to be known as the "two-state solution" (Waxman 2016, 74–75). After a promising initial period of activity, Breira came under sustained attack by right-wing elements in the Jewish community, including threats of professional retaliation against

Breira-affiliated Hillel employees. Not resilient enough to cope, the fledgling peace group suffered high-level defections and slid into bankruptcy by 1978. While neither Breira nor its immediate successors – Americans for Peace Now, the New Israel Fund, and New Jewish Agenda – were student groups per se, their growing popularity signalled disaffection with communal priorities among younger American Jews, a trend that only intensified with Israel's disastrous 1982 invasion of Lebanon and the start of the first Palestinian *Intifada* in 1987. Yet, even as internal dissent became more vociferous, the Jewish peace movement's liberal Zionist orientation precluded fruitful alliances with the pro-Palestinian left, which continued to regard the PLO and its anti-Zionist program as the locus of international solidarity (Obenzinger 2008, 240).

Ideological configurations began to shift after 1988, however, when the PLO declared its acceptance of an independent Palestinian state alongside Israel. That historic compromise paved the way for an Israeli-Palestinian peace process and the signing of the Oslo I accord on the White House lawn in 1993. The Oslo period, as the remainder of the 1990s was known, both weakened the legitimacy of the PLO among Palestine organizers and elevated previously anathematized liberal Zionist prescriptions (negotiations with the PLO, Palestinian statehood) to a position of dominance in the American Jewish establishment. Not long after the peace accords were signed, the General Union of Palestinian Students in North America dissolved. While the precise reasons for its collapse are unclear, many Palestinian-American activists viewed the PLO's transition from anti-colonial resistance to state-building as a betrayal of refugee rights and diasporic participation in the Palestinian collective (Abdulhadi 2004, 250–251). Additionally, as part of the Oslo process, the United States criminalized "material support" for Palestinian factions that had opposed the peace agreements. As one activist notes, that decision "reshaped Palestinian organizing in the United States, segregating those in exile here from their counterparts in Palestine and elsewhere in the Arab world by creating barriers to common political affiliation and support" (Kates 2014). For these reasons, and perhaps because many believed that peace was around the corner, the Oslo period saw a sharp decline in campus activism around the Israeli-Palestinian conflict.

The Second Wave: BDS and Its Discontents

The collapse of the Oslo process and the subsequent outbreak of the second, more violent Intifada in September 2000 triggered the rebirth of Palestine solidarity activism. In 2001, the first chapter of Students for Justice in Palestine (SJP) was established at the University of California, Berkeley. The following year, Berkeley students hosted a national conference launching the Palestine Solidarity Movement (PSM), a short-lived umbrella group. Several years before the Palestinian call for boycott, divestment, and sanctions (BDS), PSM's inaugural conference called for a "national day of divestment" in which student groups from approximately thirty universities participated. Before it collapsed in the second half of the decade, PSM held four additional conferences and represented several hundred member groups (Barrows-Friedman 2014, 61–62). The setback would only prove temporary, however. In 2005, a broad coalition of Palestinian civil society organizations issued the call for BDS, self-consciously modelled on the South African anti-apartheid struggle. Motivated by frustration with the terms and consequences of the Oslo process, the authors of the BDS call sought to supersede the PLO as the primary locus of international solidarity and broaden Palestinians' potential coalition by reframing the conflict around questions of human rights and international law (Barghouti 2011). The gambit was a success. Over the next 15 years, the BDS vision – in conjunction with events in the Middle East – would propel a second great wave of pro-Palestinian organizing.

With a wider range of participants and more mainstream appeal than past iterations, the new campus solidarity movement would provoke a more intense pro-Israel counterreaction than ever before.

The years 2008–2010 were a watershed for BDS on college campuses. While additional SJP chapters had developed since 2002, moral outrage at Operation Cast Lead – the first of three Israeli wars in Gaza between 2008 and 2014 – delivered a jolt of energy to the movement. The country's first BDS conference was held at Hampshire College in 2009, followed in close sequence by the formation of an SJP umbrella group in 2010, a national SJP convention in 2011, and a second major BDS conference at the University of Pennsylvania in 2012. These networking opportunities facilitated the creation of new SJP chapters, which by 2014 numbered 130 (Barrows-Friedman 2014, 62–63; Abunimah 2014, 194). At the time of writing, National SJP claimed approximately 200 affiliated chapters (National SJP n. d.). Unsurprisingly, Arab and Muslim students, many of them first- or second-generation, remain a significant presence in Palestine organizing given their higher likelihood of familial or religious connections to the issue. As in earlier decades, progressive Black, international, and other student groups led by people of colour form a regular part of pro-Palestinian coalitions on campus (Bailey 2015; Medina and Lewin 2015). One major difference from the past, however, is the greater presence today of Jewish students in the Palestine solidarity fold, whether as members of SJP or Jewish Voice for Peace (JVP), a national organization with 15 student chapters as of 2019. Jewish BDS activists remain a small minority of the overall Jewish community, but the growth of JVP reflects (among other things) the broader appeal of a Palestine solidarity framework grounded in universal human rights claims (as opposed to nationalist ones). More common than JVP on today's campuses are members of J Street U, a liberal Zionist group that describes itself as "pro-Israel, pro-Palestinian, and pro-peace," and Open Hillel, which protests the exclusion of anti-Zionist Jewish student groups and speakers by Hillel International. Though neutral or hostile with respect to BDS, these two organizations nonetheless challenge dominant pro-Israel norms in the Jewish campus community (Waxman 2016, 80–88).

SJPs and their allies utilize a range of tactics, from staging mock dormitory "evictions" meant to simulate the demolition of Palestinian homes by the Israeli military, to silently protesting, walking out of, or occasionally disrupting presentations by pro-Israel advocates. One widely observed annual event is "Israeli Apartheid Week," first held in Toronto in 2005. In addition to arranging film screenings and lectures on the conflict, SJPs will mark the occasion by erecting a mock "apartheid wall" resembling Israel's West Bank separation barrier (Barrows-Friedman 2014, 75–87). By far the most potent tactic in the SJP repertoire, however, is the campus divestment campaign, which lobbies student government bodies to pass resolutions calling on universities to divest their endowment's from companies implicated in Israeli human rights violations. According to data from the United States Campaign for Palestinian Rights and the pro-Israel AMCHA Initiative, more than fifty colleges and universities have passed divestment resolutions since 2005, with a rate of passage of just over 50 per cent between 2015 and 2019. A handful of student governments have also passed resolutions calling on their universities to boycott an Israeli product (most frequently Sabra hummus) or cut ties with study abroad programs in Israel (USCPR n. d.; AMCHA n. d.). In almost all cases, trustees and administrators have simply ignored these non-binding declarations. Nonetheless, divestment hearings are often fiercely contested affairs involving emotional oratory and the recruitment of outside support by activists on both sides (Zoll 2015). The symbolic impact of divestment is thus considered at least as important as any material effects it might have. In addition to student activism, there has also been faculty BDS activism, typically aimed at learned societies or professional organizations. Since 2013, when the American Studies Association became the first learned society to endorse the academic boycott of Israel, at least seven other associations have followed suit, while at least five have defeated boycott resolutions placed before them (USCPR n. d.).

The reaction to BDS on the part of pro-Israel organizations, Jewish communal agencies, and the Israeli government has been intense and wide-ranging. It built on an existing pattern of re-investment in pro-Israel infrastructure that started in the wake of the Second Intifada, several years before the BDS call, and has now far surpassed the prodigious investments of the 1970s and 1980s. A defining feature of the Jewish institutional landscape in the last two decades has been the outsized role of individual megadonors and private family foundations (Wertheimer 2019). Whereas earlier investments in pro-Israel campus advocacy had derived mainly from Jewish federations and moderately sized direct contributions to legacy and membership organizations, most advocacy projects in recent years have taken the form of foundation-funded non-profits or partnerships between megadonors and communal institutions. (The one noteworthy exception is the Israel Action Network, a $6 million initiative of the Jewish Federations of North America, est. 2010.) The two-fold result has been the proliferation of Israel advocacy non-profits accountable to no identifiable social constituency and the growing influence of right-leaning megadonors over Jewish communal affairs. A comprehensive account of the anti-BDS campaign waged by these organizations and the many pro-Israel students with whom they work is beyond the scope of this chapter, but we can identify at least three broad areas of institutional activity: (1) education, training, and resources; (2) monitoring and subversion; and (3) legislation and lawfare. The first category is the most straightforward, resembling previous efforts to counteract "pro-Arab propaganda." Groups like the Hasbara Fellowships (est. 2001), StandWithUs (est. 2002), the Israel on Campus Coalition (est. 2002), the David Project (est. 2002 and now merged with Hillel), CAMERA on Campus (an offshoot that evolved in the early 2010s), the Louis D. Brandeis Center for Human Rights Under Law (est. 2012), and the recently re-capitalized Zionist Organization of America all provide microgrants, educational missions to Israel, and/or paid Israel advocacy "fellowships" to university students, along with nonstop flows of interpretive information. Undergraduate trainees subsequently work with and through Hillel to combat divestment initiatives, often with on-the-ground support from Israel advocacy professionals (Zoll 2015; Palestine Legal 2015).

The second category – monitoring and subversion – includes activities that range from relatively innocuous statistical accounting to Nixonian "dirty tricks." On the more benign end of the spectrum is the work of the AMCHA Initiative (est. 2011) in compiling extensive databases on divestment campaigns, academic boycotts, and anti-Israel incidents on campus. Inching towards the opposite pole, we find campus reporting initiatives like the online magazine *The Tower* (created by the now-defunct Israel Project, est. 2002) and training programs aimed at cultivating pro-Israel college journalists (Zeveloff 2012). More scurrilous in nature are public blacklists targeting students and faculty, which, as we have seen, date back to the 1980s. The first major post-Oslo blacklisting project was Campus Watch (est. 2002), a website that compiles critical dossiers about university professors known to criticize Israel. While Campus Watch is associated with the right-leaning think tank Middle East Forum and run by identifiable scholars, the more recent online blacklist, Canary Mission (est. 2015), operates under a veil of anonymity and targets student activists with the express purpose of diminishing their post-college career prospects. Reporting in the Jewish newspaper the *Forward* revealed that Canary Mission had received hundreds of thousands of dollars in donations through the Jewish Community Federation of San Francisco and the Jewish Community Foundation of Los Angeles (Nathan-Kazis 2018c, 2018d).

Uniting elements from across the spectrum and exemplifying current trends in anti-BDS advocacy is the Israel on Campus Coalition (ICC), established in 2002 as a collaboration between Hillel and the Charles and Lynn Schusterman Family Foundation. Initially, the ICC served as a broad umbrella for pro-Israel campus groups, coordinating responses and rigorously monitoring anti-Israel activity. Around 2014, however, the organization ended its formal partnership with Hillel and was taken over by a board of Jewish foundations and megadonors. While it still "plays air traffic control among anti-BDS groups," the ICC – with a 2017 budget of $14 million, up from $2–3 million every year before 2014 – has since "transformed into a highly sophisticated political operation, with some of Washington's top Republican operatives on its payroll" (Nathan-Kazis 2018a). A series of reports by the *Forward* and *ProPublica* found that the ICC, in coordination with Israel's Ministry of Strategic Affairs, had used political consultants to create a network of anonymous websites and Facebook pages, some of them posing as college students, to accuse pro-Palestinian campus activists of "terrorism" and "anti-semitism" (Nathan-Kazis 2018a, 2018e; Elliott and Nathan-Kazis 2018). Donor materials also revealed the ICC to have conducted surveillance on the Jewish student group Open Hillel (Nathan-Kazis 2018b; on Hillel's policies see JVP 2015). Like Canary Mission, which the ICC praised in its 2016–2017 annual report as helping establish "a strong deterrent against anti-Semitism and BDS activism," this pattern of clandestine activity follows a widely disseminated blueprint published in 2010 by the Reut Institute, a major Israeli think tank (Nathan-Kazis 2017). To combat the delegitimization of Israel, Reut counselled pro-Israel organizations to

> systematically expos[e] information about delegitimizers, their activities, and the organizations that they operate out of, … [with the goal of] fram[ing] them, depending on their agendas, as anti-peace, anti-Semitic, dishonest purveyors of double standards.
> *(Reut Institute 2010, 17)*

Given the expansive campaign just described, it should come as no surprise that pro-Palestinian activists have complained of widespread harassment, vilification, and suppression. Beyond the effects of blacklisting, there have been numerous reported instances of pro-Israel groups and donors bringing external pressure to bear on university administrators to cancel speaking engagements or deny positions or tenure to faculty members (see, inter alia, Petersen-Overton 2011; Abunimah 2014, 169–225; Mearsheimer 2015; Salaita 2018). In addition to private pressures, elected officials have also repeatedly intervened in campus controversies. One of the most dramatic cases occurred in 2010–2011, when ten Muslim students were arrested and eventually convicted for verbally disrupting a speech at the University of California, Irvine, by Israeli ambassador Michael Oren. Critics, including university administrators, described the district attorney's decision to prosecute the students as politically motivated (Williams et al. 2011). In 2013, after the Political Science department at Brooklyn College decided to co-sponsor a discussion of BDS, ten New York City Council members issued a letter to the administration urging the event's cancellation and making none-too-subtle references to the school's public funding (Taylor 2013). A few years later, the New York State Senate likewise threatened to decimate educational funding, this time for the entire CUNY system, in retaliation for ongoing student and faculty BDS activism (Vilensky 2016).

While neither threat came to fruition, these episodes point to the third and final category of pro-Israel activity: legislation and lawfare. Since 2014, pro-Israel legislators working with a loose coalition of Jewish and Christian Zionist organizations have introduced over a hundred bills at the local, state, and national levels aimed at curbing BDS activism. At the time of writing, 28 states had approved anti-BDS legislation, and similar bills had been proposed in 13 others (Palestine Legal n. d.). When not strictly rhetorical, state-level anti-BDS measures have focused primarily on government contracts with private companies, but a small handful have targeted funding for colleges and universities whose student or faculty organizations endorse BDS. None of the latter have passed, however, due in part to persistent opposition from civil liberties groups. More successful have been "lawfare" efforts, which use civil rights litigation to achieve pro-Israel political objectives. Palestine Legal, an organization that offers free legal support to Palestine solidarity activists, reported responding to 292 "incidents of censorship, punishment, or other burdening of advocacy" in 2014 and the first six months of 2015 alone. The vast majority of those incidents occurred on college campuses and involved "false accusations of antisemitism" (Palestine Legal 2015, 5). While there can be no doubt that antisemitic ideas are occasionally expressed by pro-Palestinian activists – just as pro-Israel advocates sometimes express anti-Arab racism or Islamophobia – the proliferation of accusations of antisemitism on campus reflects an increasingly successful lawfare strategy aimed at prosecuting anti-Zionism as a form of anti-Jewish discrimination under the 1964 Civil Rights Act.

Attempts to rearticulate antisemitism to encompass opposition to Israel's "right to exist" or its character as a Jewish state date back to the 1970s, when the Anti-Defamation League first popularized a discourse on "the new antisemitism" (see Forster and Epstein 1974; on the subsequent development of that discourse see Judaken 2008). The identification of anti-Zionism with antisemitism has long been de rigueur in Jewish communal and broader pro-Israel circles, but only in the last two decades have Israel advocacy groups endeavoured to establish it as a principle of United States anti-discrimination law. The earliest step in this direction was taken in 2004, when Kenneth L. Marcus, the Assistant Secretary of Education for the Office for Civil Rights (OCR) under President George W. Bush, issued a game-changing policy guidance letter empowering OCR staff, for the first time, to investigate complaints under Title VI of the Civil Rights Act alleging pervasive antisemitism on college campuses. While Title VI does not prohibit religious discrimination, the memorandum argued that anti-Jewish harassment could also constitute discrimination on the basis of "national origins," a protected category that Marcus argued was equivalent to ancestry (Marcus 2010, 30–35). Marcus's interpretation was reaffirmed by the Obama administration in 2010 and remains the official Department of Education policy (Ali 2010). But the 2004 policy guidance failed to specify exactly what forms of behaviour fall under the rubric of ancestry-based antisemitic discrimination, and a series of Title VI test cases soon followed.

Shortly after Marcus issued his memorandum, the Zionist Organization of America filed a Title VI complaint against the University of California (UC), Irvine, alleging that a combination of classically antisemitic and anti-Israel events on campus had created a "hostile educational environment" for Jewish students. The first of its kind, the UC Irvine case was eventually dismissed for technical reasons. In 2009, Tammi Rossman-Benjamin, a professor at UC Santa Cruz, filed a similar complaint against her own university. Once again, the OCR dismissed the case, this time on the grounds that anti-Israel activity constituted "expression on matters of public concern," not anti-Jewish harassment (Palestine Legal 2015, 37). Nonetheless, Rossman-Benjamin continued to initiate litigation as director of the campus monitoring and lawfare organization the AMCHA Initiative. In conjunction with the Louis D. Brandeis Center for Human Rights, a new Israel advocacy group headed by none other than Kenneth Marcus, AMCHA filed or threatened to file Title VI complaints against a number of additional universities. While those efforts were legally unsuccessful, they did force universities to exert greater control over pro-Palestinian activism. As Marcus wrote in an op-ed,

> At many campuses, the prospect of litigation has made a difference. If a university shows a failure to treat initial complaints seriously, it hurts them with donors, faculty,

political leaders and prospective students. No university wants to be accused of creating an abusive environment.

(Marcus 2013)

The initial wave of pro-Israel lawfare actions made clear that the success of a Title VI strategy would depend on the willingness of the Department of Education (DOE) to interpret anti-Israel pronouncements as antisemitic, rather than as mere "expression on matters of public concern." In 2016, the likelihood of such an interpretation increased dramatically when the United States State Department adopted a "working definition" of antisemitism developed by the International Holocaust Remembrance Alliance (IHRA). The IHRA's core definition was broad but included a list of examples of antisemitic conduct, among which was "[d]enying the Jewish people their right to self-determination, e.g., by claiming that the existence of a State of Israel is a racist endeavor" (US State Department n. d.). In light of this and other examples related to Israel and Zionism, the IHRA definition, and by extension the State Department, could plausibly be seen as ratifying the equation of anti-Zionism and antisemitism. Seizing the opportunity, pro-Israel legislators, supported by AIPAC, the ADL, and other Jewish organizations, soon introduced the Anti-Semitism Awareness Act of 2016, a bill advising the DOE to consult the State Department definition when adjudicating Title VI complaints. The bill met with objections from civil liberties groups and eventually fell into legislative limbo, but its necessity was eclipsed by subsequent events. In 2018, President Trump re-appointed Kenneth Marcus as Assistant Secretary of Education for Civil Rights. The following year, Trump issued an executive order instructing the DOE to utilize the State Department definition, thereby effectively circumventing Congress. Before stepping down in June 2020, Marcus reopened an Obama-era discrimination case against Rutgers University, launched new investigations into anti-Zionist student activity, and threatened to withhold federal funding from a Middle East studies centre deemed insufficiently "balanced" with respect to Israel (McLean 2020; Green 2020). Thus, at the time of publication, the stage has been set for a renewed legal offensive against pro-Palestinian activity on campus.

Conclusion

Since at least the early 1950s, the Israeli-Palestinian conflict has commanded the attention, energy, and resources of American university students and faculty alike. Warfare abroad and political tumult at home have stimulated activism on the part of Arabs and Jews, Muslims and Christians, Black and white. But just as the passion of student activists cannot be gainsaid, neither can the preponderant influence of outside actors. In the conflict's first decade, United States government agents lent material support to "pro-Arab" initiatives, recruiting foreign exchange students and promoting their organized self-expression. Local and national Jewish agencies, in turn, pumped substantial resources into counteracting "pro-Arab propaganda" on campus. By the early 1970s, political realignments had turned the American state decisively against Arab activists and their allies, giving rise to a campaign of government surveillance and harassment that targeted students in particular. Following a period of retrenchment and then collapse during the Oslo Peace Process of the 1990s, campus Palestine organizing re-emerged in force in the late 2000s, driven by renewed violence in the Middle East and the strategic reorientation of the BDS call. Yet that energy has been matched if not overwhelmed by the ever-escalating investments of pro-Israel megadonors and heightened threats to the civil liberties of pro-Palestinian students and faculty. Regardless of the direction that American politics takes in the short term, it is clear that external forces will continue to wield outsized, and largely one-sided, influence over the conflict on campus for some time to come.

Recommended Readings

Barrows-Friedman, N. 2014. *In Our Power: US Students Organize for Justice in Palestine*. Washington, DC: Just World Publishing.

Pennock, P. E. 2017. *The Rise of the Arab American Left: Activists, Allies, and Their Fight against Imperialism and Racism, 1960s–1980s*. Chapel Hill, NC: University of North Carolina Press.

Staub, M. E. 2002. *Torn at the Roots: The Crisis of Jewish Liberalism in Postwar America*. New York: Columbia University Press.

Waxman, D. 2016. *Trouble in the Tribe: The American Jewish Conflict over Israel*. Princeton, NJ: University Press.

Notes

1 While campus advocacy for and against Zionism stretches back to the birth of the Zionist movement at the turn of the twentieth century, I focus here on the period since the establishment of the State of Israel in 1948 – that is, on campus advocacy as it relates to the "Israeli-Palestinian conflict" proper.

2 Established in 1923, the organization dropped its B'nai B'rith affiliation in 1994 and legally changed its name to Hillel: The Foundation for Jewish Campus Life. In 2014, it again rebranded as Hillel International, though without legally modifying its name.

3 See, *inter alia*, various Hillel documents in Western Reserve Historical Society, Jewish Community Federation of Cleveland records MS4835, Series II, Box 102, Folder 2978.

4 See, *inter alia*, various reports in AJA, Jewish Community Relations Council of Cincinnati records MS-202, Box 40, Folders 5 and 6.

Questions for Discussion

(1) What role has the United States government played in debates over the Israeli-Palestinian conflict on university campuses?

(2) How has the response of the organized Jewish community to pro-Palestinian activism change over time?

(3) How have events in the Middle East impacted the behaviour of Jews and Arabs/Palestinians on American campuses?

(4) How does one's definition of antisemitism shape how one understands today's campus conflicts over Israel-Palestine?

References

Abdulhadi, R. 2004. "Activism and Exile: Palestinianness and the Politics of Solidarity." In *Local Actions: Cultural Activism, Power, and Public Life in America*, eds. M. Checker and M. Fishman. New York: Columbia University Press, 231–254.

Abunimah, A. 2014. *The Battle for Justice in Palestine*. Chicago: Haymarket.

Ali, R. 2010. "Dear Colleague Letter." US *Department of Education, Office for Civil Rights*. 26 October. Available at: www2.ed.gov/about/offices/list/ocr/letters/colleague-201010.pdf.

AMCHA. N. d. *Divestment Resolutions*. Available at: https://amchainitiative.org/israel-divestment-vote-scorecard/#divestment-resolutions/search-by-date/.

American Jewish Congress. 1958. "The Arab Campaign Against American Jews." American Jewish Archives (Henceforth AJA), World Jewish Congress Collection MS-361, Box 15, Folder 12.

Anti-Defamation League of B'nai B'rith (ADL). 1979. "Arab Petrodollar Influence on the American Campus." AJA, Oscar Cohen papers MS-294, Box 5, Folder 2.

Bailey, K. D. 2015. "Black–Palestinian Solidarity in the Ferguson–Gaza Era." *American Quarterly* 67:4, 1017–1026.

Barghouti, O. 2011. *BDS: Boycott, Divestment, Sanctions: The Global Struggle for Palestinian Rights*. Chicago: Haymarket Books.

Barrows-Friedman, N. 2014. *In Our Power: US Students Organize for Justice in Palestine*. Washington, DC: Just World Publishing.

Baum, P. 1979. "Petrodollars on the Campus." Memo, 2 February, to CRCs and Federations et al. AJA, Jewish Community Relations Council of Cincinnati Collection MS-202 (JCRC-C), Box 152, Folder 11.

Berkman, M. 2018. "Coercive Consensus: Jewish Federations, Ethnic Representation, and the Roots of American Pro-Israel Politics." PhD Dissertation, University of Pennsylvania. Available at: https://repository.upenn.edu/edissertations/3093/.

Bicchi, F. 2018. "The Debate about the Occupation of Palestinian Territories on UK Campuses, from Politicization to Re-writing the Rules." *Global Affairs* 4:1, 89–100.

Bisharat, R. 2019. "The Palestinian Diaspora and Latin American Solidarity with the Palestinian Cause." *Latin American Perspectives* 46:3, 102–113.

B'nai B'rith Hillel Foundations (BBHF). 1967. "The Response of the Academic Community to the Israel Crisis, May-June 1967." American Jewish Historical Society (henceforth AJHS), Near East Crisis Collection I-18, Box 4, Folder 13.

BBHF 1968. *CAMPUS: A Hillel Newsletter.* Western Reserve Historical Society, Jewish Community Federation of Cleveland records MS4835, Series II, Box 102, Folder 2980.

BBHF. 1977. "Allocations by Welfare Funds to Youth Services Appeal," AJHS, Council of Jewish Federation and Welfare Funds records I-69, Box 470, Folder 3.

B'nai B'rith International (BBI). 1970. Board of Governors Meeting Minutes, 17–19 January. AJA, B'nai B'rith International Records MS-900 (BBI), Box C1–1, Folder 5.

Bronznick, S. 1978. "Death of the North American Jewish Students Network." *Response: A Contemporary Jewish Review* 1:3, 25–28.

Dollinger, M. 2000. *Quest for Inclusion: Jews and Liberalism in Modern American.* Princeton, NJ: Princeton University Press.

Elliott, J., and J. Nathan-Kazis. 2018. "D.C.-Based Pro-Israel Group Secretly Ran Misleading Facebook Ads to Target Pro-Palestinian Activist." *ProPublica.* 12 September. Available at: www.propublica.org/article/dc-pro-israel-group-ran-facebook-ads-to-target-pro-palestinian-activist.

Feldman, K. P. 2015. *A Shadow Over Palestine: The Imperial Life of Race in America.* Minneapolis, MN: University of Minnesota Press.

Fishbach, M. R. 2020. *The Movement and the Middle East: How the Arab-Israeli Conflict Divided the American Left.* Stanford, CA: Stanford University Press.

Forster, A., and B. R. Epstein. 1974. *The New Anti-Semitism.* New York: McGraw-Hill.

Freeman, J. 1956. "Memo to Working Subcommittee of the NCRAC Committee on the Community Relations Aspects of Developments in the Middle East." 24 October. AJHS, National Community Relations Advisory Council Collection I-172 (NCRAC), Box 53, Folder 6, New York, NY.

Green, E. 2020. "Education Dept.'s Civil Rights Chief Steps Down Amid Controversy." *New York Times.* 27 July. Available at: www.nytimes.com/2020/07/27/us/politics/kenneth-marcus-education-department.html.

Jacobs, H. 1967. "Letter to Students." 2 June. AJHS, Near East Crisis Collection I-18, Box 4, Folder 13.

Jacobson, M. F. 2006. *Roots Too: White Ethnic Revival in Post-Civil Rights America.* Cambridge, MA: Harvard University Press.

Jewish Community Relations Council of Cincinnati (JCRC-C). 1968. "Israel and Middle East Affairs Committee Minutes." 5 December. AJA, JCRC-C, Box 40, Folder 1.

Jewish Voice for Peace (JVP). 2015. *Stifling Dissent: How Israel's Defenders Use False Charges of Anti-Semitism to Limit the Debate Over Israel.* Available at: https://jewishvoiceforpeace.org/wp-content/uploads/2015/09/JVP_Stifling_Dissent_Full_Report_Key_90745869.pdf.

Jospe, A. 1964. "Jewish College Students in the United States." *American Jewish Year Book* 65, 131–145.

Judaken, J. 2008. "So What's New? Rethinking the 'New Antisemitism' in a Global Age." *Patterns of Prejudice* 42:4–5, 531–560.

Kahn, B. M. 1967. "Memo to Directors and Counselors." 22 June. AJHS, Near East Crisis Collection I-18, Box 4, Folder 13.

Kahn, B. M., and A. Jospe. 1967. "Memo to Hillel Directors and Counselors." 24 May. AJHS, Near East Crisis Collection I-18, Box 4, Folder 13.

Kaidy, M. 1993. "Israel's US Influence Network: CAMERA and FLAME; Pressuring US Media." *Washington Report on Middle East Affairs* 12:2, 29.

Kaplan, A. 2018. *Our American Israel: The Story of an Entangled Alliance.* Cambridge, MA: *Harvard University Press.*

Kates, C. 2013. "New Cross-Canada Student Coalition Looks to Build on BDS Victories." *Mondoweiss.* 8 March. Available at: https://mondoweiss.net/2013/03/student-coalition-victories.

Kates, C. 2014. "Criminalizing Resistance." *Jacobin*. 27 January. Available at: www.jacobinmag.com/2014/01/criminalizing-resistance.

Katz, E. A. 2015. *Bringing Zion Home: Israel in American Jewish Culture, 1948–1967*. Albany: SUNY Press.

Kessler, J. S., and J. Schwaber. 1984. *The AIPAC College Guide: Exposing the Anti-Israel Campaign on Campus*. American Israel Public Affairs Committee.

Levin, G. P. 2019. "Another Nation: Israel, American Jews, and Palestinian Rights, 1948–1977." PhD Dissertation, New York University.

Lubin, A. 2014. *Geographies of Liberation: The Making of an Afro-Arab Political Imaginary*. Chapel Hill, NC: University of North Carolina Press.

Marcus, K. L. 2010. *Jewish Identity and Civil Rights in America*. New York: Cambridge University Press.

Marcus, K. L. 2013. "Standing up for Jewish Students." *Jerusalem Post*. 9 September. Available at: www.jpost.com/Opinion/Op-Ed-Contributors/Standing-up-for-Jewish-students-325648.

McLean, D. 2020. "This US Official Is Leading the Charge Against Anti-Semitism on College Campuses. Here's What You Should Know About Him." *Chronicle of Higher Education*. 3 February. Available at: www.chronicle.com/article/This-US-Official-Is-Leading/247956.

Mearsheimer, J. 2015. "Israel and Academic Freedom." In *Who's Afraid of Academic Freedom?*, eds. A. Bilgrami and J. Cole. New York: Columbia University Press, 316–333.

Medina, J., and T. Lewin. 2015. "Campus Debates on Israel Drive a Wedge Between Jews and Minorities." *New York Times*. 9 May. *Available at:* www.nytimes.com/2015/05/10/us/campus-debates-on-israel-drive-a-wedge-between-jews-and-minorities.html.

Nathan-Kazis, J. 2017. "Shadowy Blacklist of Student Activists Wins Endorsement of Mainstream Pro-Israel Group." *The Forward*. 3 October. Available at: https://forward.com/news/national/383938/shadowy-blacklist-of-student-activists-wins-endorsement-of-mainstream-pro-i/.

Nathan-Kazis, J. 2018a. "A New Wave of Hardline Anti-BDS Tactics Are Targeting Students, And No One Knows Who's Behind It." *The Forward*. 2 August. Available at: https://forward.com/news/407127/a-new-wave-of-hardline-anti-bds-tactics-are-targeting-students-and-no-one/.

Nathan-Kazis, J. 2018b. "Campus Pro-Israel Group 'Monitored' Progressive Jewish Students." *The Forward*. 25 September. Available at: https://forward.com/news/410757/campus-pro-israel-group-monitored-progressive-jewish-students/.

Nathan-Kazis, J. 2018c. "Revealed: Canary Mission Blacklist Is Secretly Bankrolled by Major Jewish Federation." *The Forward*. 3 October. Available at: https://forward.com/news/national/411355/revealed-canary-mission-blacklist-is-secretly-bankrolled-by-major-jewish/.

Nathan-Kazis, J. 2018d. "Second Major Jewish Charity Admits Funding Group Tied to Canary Mission Blacklist." *The Forward*. 11 October. Available at: https://forward.com/news/national/411895/second-major-jewish-charity-admits-funding-canary-mission-blacklist/.

Nathan-Kazis, J. 2018e. "When Jewish Leaders Decide to Harass College Kids – To 'Support' Israel." *The Forward*. 31 December. Available at: https://forward.com/news/416569/why-did-jewish-leaders-think-they-should-target-college-kids-to-help/.

National Community Relations Advisory Council (NCRAC). 1955. "Jewish Community Relations and Anti-Israel Propaganda." June. AJHS, NCRAC, Box 83, Folder 7.

NCRAC.1956. "Joint Program Plan for 1956–1957." AJHS, NCRAC, Box 53, Folder 7.

NCRAC. 1983. "1984 Budget." AJHS, NCRAC, Box 20, Folder 2.

National Jewish Monthly. 1959. "A pictorial review of the program of the B'nai B'rith Hillel Foundations." Available at: www.hillel.org/docs/default-source/historical/national-jewish-monthly-(1959).pdf.

National Students for Justice in Palestine (National SJP). N. d. *About*. Available at: www.nationalsjp.org/about-nsjp.html.

North American Jewish Students' Network (Network). 1979. "Questions and Answers about the North American Jewish Students' Network." AJA, American Jewish Committee records MS-780, Box G11, Folder 36.

Obenzinger, H .2008. "Palestine Solidarity, Political Discourse, and the Peace Movement, 1982–1988." *CR: The New Centennial Review* 8:2, 233–252.

Palestine Legal. 2015. *The Palestine Exception to Free Speech: A Movement Under Attack in the US*. Available at: https://palestinelegal.org/s/Palestine-Exception-Report-Final-jpjy.pdf.

Palestine Legal. N. d. *Legislation*.Available at: https://palestinelegal.org/righttoboycott.

Pennock, P. E. 2017. *The Rise of the Arab American Left: Activists, Allies, and Their Fight against Imperialism and Racism, 1960s–1980s*. Chapel Hill, NC: University of North Carolina Press.

Petersen-Overton, K. J. 2011. "Academic Freedom and Palestine: A Personal Account." *Arab Studies Quarterly* 33:3/4, 256–267.

Pins, A. 1952. "Youth and Recreational Services." *American Jewish Year Book* 53, 198–209.

Reut Institute. 2010. *Building a Political Firewall against the Assault on Israel's Legitimacy London as a Case Study*. Available at: www.reut-institute.org/data/uploads/PDFver/20101219%20London%20Case%20Study.pdf.

Salaita, S. 2018. "A Palestinian Exception to the First Amendment? The Pain and Pleasure of Palestine in the Public Sphere." In *With Stones in Our Hands: Writings on Muslims, Racism, and Empire*, eds. S. Daulatzai and J. Rana. Minneapolis, MN: University of Minnesota Press, 3–15.

Slabodkin, G. D. 1992. "The Secret Section in Israel's US Lobby That Stifles American Debate." *Washington Report on Middle East Affairs* 11:2, 7.

Solender, S. 1954. "Services to the Community and Its Youth." *American Jewish Year Book* 54, 142–153.

Staub, M. E. 2002. *Torn at the Roots: The Crisis of Jewish Liberalism in Postwar America*. New York: Columbia University Press.

Taylor, K. 2013. "Mayor Backs College's Plan to Welcome Critics of Israel." *New York Times*. 6 February. Available at: www.nytimes.com/2013/02/07/nyregion/bloomberg-defends-brooklyn-colleges-right-to-bds-talk.html.

Urofsky, M. I. 1979. "A Cause in Search of Itself: American Zionism After the State." *American Jewish History* 69:1, 79–91.

US Campaign for Palestinian Rights (USCPR). N. d. *US BDS Victories*. Available at: https://uscpr.org/campaign/bds/bdswins/.

US State Department. N. d. "Defining Anti-Semitism.' Office of International Religious Freedom. Available at: www.state.gov/defining-anti-semitism/.

Vilensky, M. 2016. "Fight Over CUNY Funding Takes Unforeseen Turn." *Wall Street Journal*. 17 March. Available at: www.wsj.com/articles/fight-over-cuny-funding-takes-unforeseen-turn-1458173768.

Waxman, D. 2016. *Trouble in the Tribe: The American Jewish Conflict Over Israel*. Princeton, NJ: Princeton University Press.

Wertheimer, J. 2019. *Giving Jewish: How Big Funders Have Transformed American Jewish Philanthropy*. Avi Chai Foundation.

Williams, L., et al. 2011. "Students Guilty of Disrupting Speech in 'Irvine 11' Case." *Los Angeles Times*. 24 September. Available at: www.latimes.com/local/la-xpm-2011-sep-24-la-me-irvine-eleven-20110924-story.html.

Yaqub, S. 2016. *Imperfect Strangers: Americans, Arabs, and US-Middle East Relations in the 1970s*. Ithaca, NY: Cornell University Press.

Zeveloff, N. 2012. "Circle of Pro-Israel Writers Rises." *The Forward*. 31 July. https://forward.com/news/160010/circle-of-pro-israel-writers-rises/.

Zoll, R. 2015. "Anti-Israel Divestment Push Gains Traction at US Colleges." *Associated Press*. 28 February. Available at: https://apnews.com/8769ec23564a4954b935a3ee9cd5b169/anti-israel-divestment-push-gains-traction-us-colleges.

Zorn, C. 1983. "A Counter-Offensive on Campus." *Israel Today*. 15 July. AJA, JCRC-C, Box 152, Folder 7.

35

TEACHING AND LEARNING ABOUT THE ISRAELI-PALESTINIAN CONFLICT IN ISRAEL

Ayman K. Agbaria and Aline Muff

Introduction

By nature, education is political and has always been an arena for political struggle. This is particularly pronounced in conflict-ridden societies such as Israel, where education can act as either a facilitator or a barrier for peacebuilding efforts (Bush and Saltarelli 2000). According to Bush and Saltarelli (2000), at its best, when given appropriate and sustainable support, education has the potential to challenge structures of violence but, at its worst, education can be manipulated to preserve ethnic privilege, to promote violence and intolerance and become a tool of cultural repression.

The literature is rife with examples of ways in which the state harnesses the education system to sociopolitically engineer a hegemonic collective memory in service of nation state-building processes, longstanding hierarchies, and political interests of the dominant groups (Zajda 2005 and 2007; Quaynor, 2012). In their review of history education in 14 case studies from different parts of the world, Nakou and Barca (2010) found as a common thread that the subject is seen as important because it usually conveys an "approved story," binding people together through a particular national, political, ethnic, or religious story that justifies the status quo and the dominance of a privileged group. On the other hand, they argue that history education is important precisely because it cannot tell a single approved story, but partial truths, and can accommodate ethnic diversity, reflect rival narratives, and serve competing political interests. Similarly, the literature is full of examples that outline how the education field has indeed been a central arena for disadvantaged groups such as indigenous and ethnic minorities, to demand cultural recognition and group-based rights (May, Modood, and Squires 2004; Zajda 2009), and to oppose cultural domination and stereotypical representations (Fraser, 2000).

Alongside the issues of cultural representation and collective rights, teaching and learning about the conflict itself are other major challenges in conflict-affected societies. As indicated above, education in these societies can focus on a unifying official standardized narrative that conveys an unreflective nationalism that emphasizes the group's own victimhood and delegitimizes the rival group's claims to the status of victim (Bar-Tal et al. 2014; Bar-Tal and

DOI: 10.4324/9780429027376-42

Halperin 2013; Bar-Tal and Salomon 2006). This might find expression in curricula that glorify the nation's history and achievements, while omitting or even censoring violence and crimes committed in the past as well as ongoing issues of injustice and discrimination. Indeed, Quaynor (2012) found in her literature review on the state of citizenship education across different post-conflict societies that discussions of controversial issues related to the recent conflict – inequality, and discrimination based on gender, race, or disability – were mostly absent.

In this chapter, we discuss the various ways through which the current educational system in Israel reproduces the Israeli-Palestinian conflict by focusing on the national identity-building school subjects of civics and history. First, the chapter presents a brief review of the literature to highlight how these subjects function as main carriers of the Zionist narrative while endorsing a strong nationalistic ethos. Second, the chapter underscores two shifts in Israeli politics: the rise of religious-ethnonationalism and the influence of neoliberalism. Both have been moulding the design and instruction of the two subjects in Israeli schools, in ways that amplify and reinforce the denial of cultural and national recognition of the Palestinian minority, and contribute to the censoring and avoidance of alternative and critical discourses about the conflict.

The Conflict in Citizenship and History Education in Israel

Before discussing how the Israeli-Palestinian conflict is framed, rendered, and served in the Israeli education system in general, and in history and citizenship education in particular, it is important to note that although the majority of schoolchildren in Israel are enrolled in the state education system, they are highly segregated. Despite the growing interest in bilingual and binational schools, these remain marginal in terms of their numbers, and the vast majority of the Jewish and Arab schoolchildren still attend different schools. This segregation reflects the structure of the education system, which is separated into four subsystems: (1) the general state educational system, serving mainly the Jewish secular population; (2) the religious state educational system, which caters to the Jewish-national religious population; (3) the Arab educational system (which is further divided into Arab, Druze, and Bedouin subsystems), serving the Arab minority; and (4) the independent ultra-orthodox religious school system (Svirsky and Dagan-Bozaglo 2009). Therefore, it is safe to argue that, to a large extent, education in Israel is segregated along the lines of nationality, religion, and degree of religiosity (Agbaria 2018a).

Over the last decades, the national identity-building subjects of civics and history have become increasingly subject to many controversies in academia and Israeli politics. After the 1948 war and the establishment of the State of Israel, the educational vision was generally dominated by the nation-building project of the Zionist state that sought to instill loyalty and attachment in its Jewish citizens while imposing a policy of control on its Arab population (Mahamid 2017). This policy was reflected in the early history curricula, published in 1954, which were fully in service of the national enterprise (Yogev 2010), inculcating nationalistic and religious values, and shaping a collective memory in an ethnocentric manner based on the Zionist narrative (Kizel 2008). In terms of the conflict, a discussion of the situation of Arab-Palestinians in Israel was absent in the early history curricula, and narratives were simplistic, one-sided and distorted, conveying a Zionist historiography that further served to legitimize the claim to the land of Israel (Podeh 2000). Textbooks, curricula and views that deviated from this narrative were delegitimized, which for Arab schools meant that any reference to Arab nationalism in history or geography was banned and, generally, that there was no reference to the conflict as a complex and multi-sided issue (Mahamid 2017).

A change in the ethnocentric focus of the history curriculum and its one-sided portrayal of the conflict only occurred during the 1970s, fuelled by an academic discourse that increasingly demanded a distinction between the heritage approach and critical analysis in history, a growing awareness of the Israeli-Palestinian conflict as well as an increasing demand among Arab-Palestinian citizens for equal rights and recognition (Matthias 2005; Yogev 2010). The subsequent history curricula were characterized by important revision, such as reducing ethnocentrism, stereotypical representations of Arab-Palestinians, and a more balanced account of the Jewish-Arab conflict (Podeh, 2000; Yogev 2010), including more aspects of Arab and Palestinian history in Jewish and Arab schools specifically (Podeh 2010). The term Palestine, Arab names of places (Barghouti 2009), recognition of Arab-Palestinian students belonging to a collective people, Arab nation and culture, and an Arab-Palestinian narrative were introduced for the first time in Arab schools (Mahamid 2017).

Yet, despite these improvements in the objectives of teaching history, these positive changes have been limited. The curriculum, textbooks, and teaching practice remain constrained to a focus on an ethnocentric narrative (Naveh and Yogev 2002), the omission of chapters of history and the histories of others, such as Arab-Palestinian and more general history (Kizel 2008). The final version of the curriculum from 2003 calls for recognizing different points of view, yet this is not reflected in the textbook and practice (Podeh 2010) and controversial content that could challenge the Zionist narrative is omitted (Yogev 2010). Another example for this revisionism is that Education Minister Yuli Tamir's attempt to introduce the term *Nakba* (the Arab-Palestinian term for the outcome of the 1948 war) into the curriculum of Arab schools was halted by the authorities, and a decision has been made to ban commemorations of events that refer to collective Palestinian memories, such as the *Nakba*, land day, or the *Intifadas* (Mahamid 2017).

Civics did not exist as an independent subject but was part of other subjects like history, geography, and extra-curricular activities such as memorial ceremonies and field trips that foster nation-building (Cohen 2019). According to Cohen, the first independent civics curriculum was only introduced in 1976 and focused on the teaching of formal knowledge about political procedures and institutions in Israel. During the 1990s, this curriculum was seen as outdated and criticized for covering only formal knowledge, and therefore it was revised to promote also democratic values and to be inclusive of all its citizens (Cohen 2019). However, as Cohen stated, the election of a right-wing government in 2009 brought a change to the educational agenda, which became more nationalistic, by emphasizing that Israel is the nation-state of the Jewish people. Even though the curriculum has also become more sensitive to the language of human rights and individual liberties (Ichilov, Salomon, and Inbar 2005), the continuous efforts to advance a particularistic hyper-ethnonationalist ideology in the Israeli education system and the total segregation between Jews and Palestinians in the school system have eroded the liberal and democratic sensibilities among Jewish youth (Gordon 2012). Cohen (2019) argued that civics in Israel is not a unifying subject matter that provides a framework for democratic discussion but rather is a means to advance sectarian political views. In this regard, the recent works on citizenship education (Agbaria 2018b; Cohen 2019; Muff and Bekerman 2019; Zohar and Cohen 2016) reflect a wide consensus with regard to its failing role in Israel in promoting an inclusive and shared civic culture for all citizens.

Like civics, history education has been subject to a turbulent and inconsistent "pendulum," alternating between expressive populist ethnocentricity on the one hand and critical inquiry and diversity on the other (Goldberg and Gerwin 2013). Yet, be it at the liberal or the conservative side, the pendulum has been consistent in underscoring the Jewish nature of the state, in normalizing the "Jewish and democratic" state framework, and in marginalizing the inclusive ideal of Israel as a state for all of its citizens. In the following, recent political developments are discussed in more detail – developments that halt progress toward more inclusive civic and history education in Israel.

Recent Developments

The Ethno-religious Shift

On 19 July 2018, the Israeli parliament (Knesset) completed legislation for the highly debated Nation-State Bill, which is officially known as the Basic Law: Israel – The Nation State of The Jewish People (Knesset 2018). In a nutshell, this law establishes that the State of Israel is the nation-state of the Jewish people, while stipulating that the exercise of the right to national self-determination in the State of Israel is unique to the Jewish people. Furthermore, the law, which has a constitutional status, sets the development of Jewish settlements as a national priority, downgrades the official status of Arabic, and specifies the state's symbols, calendar, and memorial days as Jewish. This law anchors the Zionist narrative on state-building in law, granting it indisputable constitutional status. It asserts further that the "State of Israel" (a political entity that exists in reality) was founded in the "Land of Israel" (a biblical landscape with no definite borders). By doing so, the law casts the real into the imaginative, the political into the religious, the known into the fantasy, obscuring the relation between these two concepts. It exemplifies to what extent Israeli politics has been infused with religious rhetoric of the ethno-religious politics in Israel.

This political shift is an expression of "ethnonationalism" that is distinguished from regular nationalism by its perception of the "nation," not in terms of citizenry but of ethnicity that is often based on descent from shared ancestors (Agbaria 2018a). Membership in the nation-state is conditioned upon belonging to a specific ethnic community that is perceived to be entitled to have absolute authority over the state's affairs (Travis 2013). Yet, Agbaria (2018b, 23) elaborated that Israeli ethnonationalism is in particular due to its emphasis on religion, it

> is distinguished by being based on a transcendent set of ideals and norms that gives ethnonational values, politics and identities a seal of sanctity and inevitability. It is an all-explaining ideology that imbues national identities with zeal, absolutism and historical justifications in the name of an imagined collectivity that is often conceived as superior, sacred, pure and with a long-standing historic mission.

This political ideology is promoted by neo-Zionist forces that are aligned with the settler movement and the extreme right-wing parties in Israel in which this ideology is anchored (Ram 2000). These forces hold a messianic political theology, according to which the biblical Land of Israel is a superior aspiration that supersedes the democratic principles in its importance to the Jewish people. More specifically, followers of this political theology believe that full redemption can be achieved only when the entire "People of Israel" come to live in the Land of Israel under exclusive Jewish sovereignty. Accordingly, the religious narrative of the Bible is presented through populist politics as a factual account of the Jews' role as God's chosen people. For Illouz (2014a), this narrative legitimizes the ethnic and religious superiority of Jews over non-Jews and justifies the seizure of land by merging and framing both the past and the future in a self-righteous, ethnocentric narrative. In this manner, Israeli settlers in the Palestinian West Bank rationalize their superiority by sanctifying the land and themselves on the basis of biblical narratives, in which they see themselves as executing God's will and justice – compared by some to the ideology of slave owners in the United States from the start of the seventeenth to the mid-nineteenth century (Illouz 2014b; Ohana 2009).

This political theology is becoming more prominent in the education system in general, but particularly in the ultra-orthodox religious subsystem. According to the State Education Law from 1953, this system enjoys administrative and pedagogical autonomy, especially with respect to the content of its Jewish education curriculum. Yet, it was not until 1998 that the law was amended to state specifically that the purpose of the state's religious education system is to educate in the spirit of religious Zionism. In 2008, the Ministry of Education explained what this spirit precisely means, stating that the religious Zionist viewpoint "sees the revival of the Jewish people in its land and the establishment of the State of Israel as the beginning of redemption" (Barak 2014, 5). Since the late 1990s, and especially after the unilateral withdrawal of Israel from Gaza in 2005, the state religious education system has been witnessing a process of radicalization, in which the state's authority is increasingly challenged and debated vis-à-vis Halakhic laws, which are perceived as equally important and, at times, as superseding the laws of the State (Saragossi 2013).

In the last decade, the ultra-ethnonationalistic trend has been increasingly taking hold of general Israeli education (see examples in Agbaria, et al. 2015). Commenting specifically on the expanding place of religion in the Israeli education system, Schnell (2012, 117) argued that "the sharp focus on the national identity as a religious identity has not been restricted to Gush Emunin (a Jewish national religious organization) and the religious Zionist movement, but has pervaded many other sectors in Jewish society." One of the recent programmes, for example, that draws on a plethora of religious texts and references to religious symbols and ceremonies is a new subject in the school curriculum, called "Jewish-Israeli culture." *Haaretz* reported, based on internal ministry documents, that the programme aims to develop and shape a Jewish-Israeli identity and develop a feeling of belonging and responsibility towards Jewish-Israeli heritage via a pluralistic, open, and critical approach by studying, for example, values of the Sabbath, Jewish prayers, legends, and fables (Kashti 2014). It is important to note that this programme is intended for the secular state education system, which exemplifies how the political right seeks to expand its sphere of influence. According to Peled and Peled (2018), since 2015, under Naftali Bennett as education minister, an increasing budget has been allocated to "Jewish culture" organizations and activities (almost 20 per cent of the ministry's budget), including a large proportion to orthodox NGOs that focus on promoting a religious Jewish identity. The religious shift is recent (Turner 2011), expressed in a "religionization" of education, as a public space (Peled and Peled 2018). Peled and Peled described the process of religionization as an increasing manifestation of Jewish religion as the basis of Jewish nationality and Zionism, as well as the weakening of more liberal, universalist aspects in the "secular" Jewish educational system.

In civics, this shift has been illustrated by the major revision of the civics textbook, *Being a Citizen in Israel,* towards a neo-nationalistic religious discourse that prioritizes the Jewishness of the state over democratic principles (Pinson 2019). The textbook omits Arab or Palestinian connections or historical claims to Israel's territory; it does not discuss Israeli settlements in the West Bank, portrays non-Jewish immigrants as a threat to the realization of the ethno-cultural nation-state (Pinson 2019, 45), and recognizes neither Arab-Palestinians as a collective national group nor their narratives (Ministry of Education 2017). Moreover, the textbook highlights the importance of the religious Jewish population and downplays that of the secular population, justifying the existence of the nation-state and Jewish sovereignty of Israel as a religious value.

The Neoliberal Shift

Conservative approaches that seek to instill a strong cultural and national authority have been paired with neoliberal market-based policies, deregulation and privatization processes, and new managerial and technical approaches; a combination that Apple (2001) has termed conservative modernization. These processes or shifts reinforce each other by claiming to address social and political issues such as achievement gaps by reinforcing individual responsibility and maximizing performance (Apple 2004; Giroux 1997).

The neoliberal shift comes at a price. It has been argued that these policies decrease teachers' professional autonomy (Barton et al. 1994), "de-professionalize" them by replacing teaching as an intellectual discipline with a focus on the acquirement of technological competence and skills (Connell 2009), and finally pressure teachers to focus on the knowledge that will be tested in the examination (Apple 2004). The focus on exam knowledge and performance has created a market driven by parental choice and competition that increasingly individualizes achievement (Hursh 2005). Instead of creating equal opportunities, it has been argued that these policies reinforce existing inequalities and achievement gaps in education by encouraging selection and benefiting higher-performing schools and students with more resources while neglecting those from less-privileged backgrounds (Gilborn and Youdell 2000; Hursh 2005; Tomlinson 1997).

Since the 1970s and 1980s, a neoliberal agenda has increasingly altered the education system in Israel, through promoting school autonomy, school-based management, parental choice, and accountability (Berkovich 2014; Resnik 2011). Neoliberal reforms have considerably changed educators' work in Israel. Yonah, Dahan, and Markovich (2008) have argued that while it seems that the state increasingly retreats from educational affairs through these processes of privatization and deregulation, at the same time it increases its control over education by determining uniform standards of achievement, cultivating values of neoliberal globalization, and establishing a national value system intended to raise loyal citizens. They continue that the reality of the conflict that demands loyalty and individual sacrifices from its citizens (such as compulsory military service) and the safeguarding of ethno-national characteristics, reinforce the perceived need to inculcate a strong sense of belonging and national solidarity among its Jewish citizens.

As has happened in other places, these reforms have exacerbated existing socio-economic gaps in education through processes of privatization and individualization (Yonah, Dahan, and Markovitch 2008). In addition, the reforms focus on the goal to unify and control education through a national curriculum, which enforces that teachers instruct values of loyalty and a standardized national narrative. The reforms have particularly negative effects on the Arab education sector for two reasons: first, because they exacerbate an already-existing gap in achievement as Arab students have relatively lower grades compared with Jewish students in international tests, the national threshold, and evaluation exams (Agbaria 2016); and, second, because the reforms further reinforce a traditional culture of control of the Arab-Palestinian population (Agbaria et al. 2015) –also now more readily from within, as it allows new coalitions of local Palestinian stakeholders and Israeli authoritative forces to join together to control Arab education in the name of "professionalism" and "progress." Under neoliberal policies, the de-politicization of Arab education has deepened, the sociopolitical role of Arab schools is diminished, and the collective voice of Arab teachers and pupils is subdued. As it cultivates aggressive individualism and social Darwinism, the neoliberal discourse has the potential to weaken the Palestinian pupils' and educators' sense of solidarity and collectivity and to produce a privatized Arab public sphere that is emptied of its own collective content and transformed into an agglomeration of private troubles and worries. In such a reality, as Israeli segregation, discrimination, and surveillance remain in place, the tension between control and mobility intensifies as follows: The more pupils believe in the neoliberal ethics of individual success at the expense of collective solidarity, the more they will be frustrated and alienated, as upon graduation they will soon find that their opportunities in the Israeli higher education system and in the labour market are still scarce, to say the least.

While neoliberal policies affect identity-making processes in both Arab and Jewish education, it seems that they have a greater impact on Arab education. The reason for this differential impact is that, for Jewish pupils and educators, the public sphere is still dominated by the Jewish hegemonic group's ideals and interests, and sources of collective identity formation are more powerful and more available. In parallel to the education system, Jewish identity is nourished and augmented with extracurricular programmes offered by the Israeli army, various highly politicized youth movements, and numerous civil society organizations.

Responses to the Ethnonational and Neoliberal Shifts

Teachers' Resistance against Censoring and Avoidance

The ethnonational and neoliberal shifts appear to reinforce two trends that were already present in the Israeli education system: censoring and avoidance. Teachers are censored mainly in two ways: first, through the ethno-national discourse that is presented as the only valid narrative, and, second, through a neoliberal culture that prioritizes student performance in exams over other pedagogical goals.

Regarding the ethno-national-religious discourse, the education system upholds three taboo areas whose importance cannot be curtailed: religion, the Holocaust, and the military. These were explicitly named in a statement by the past education minister, Shai Piron, in 2014, in response to a heated public debate on freedom of speech and the role of teachers in citizenship education following a case in which a civics teacher, Adam Verete, faced dismissal after describing the Israeli army as "immoral." Piron's statement called on schools to steer clear of "cultural land mines." These, according to the statement, insulted religion, offended individuals and/or communities, denied the Holocaust, and questioned the legitimacy of the Israeli army. The statement outlines the boundaries of class discussion (Misgav 2014).

Some of these taboos have been legally institutionalized. For example, the Knesset passed a bill in 2011 that allows the Ministry of Finance to decrease or even to withhold and withdraw funding from institutions that commemorate *Nakba* Day as a day of mourning. This bill is justified through the rationale that the teaching of the Nakba would politicize Palestinian children, as it reminds them of the loss of their land (Peled-Elhanan 2012). Additionally, in 2016, the Ministry of Education published a circular with guidelines for discussing controversial issues, allowing the ministry to discipline teachers who criticize state institutions, including the military (Ministry of Education 2016).

Tamir (2015) argued that civics teachers' insecurity about how to deal with the contradictions in the curriculum (for example, the mainstream Zionist perspective is seen as more "neutral" than human rights and liberal values) and the fact that controversial issues are avoided in the textbook leads to omitting those altogether. Muff (2019) found in her case study of a secular Jewish state school where civics teachers in Israel indeed avoid discussions about identity and the conflict, that focused generally on perspectives that portray their own group as the victim. Yet, it needs to be acknowledged that teachers and students are largely restricted by the demands of teaching and learning for the matriculation exam as well as censored by the national ethos. Processes of censoring through neoliberal policies that depoliticize political education, impose restrictions on schools and teachers to criticize or question essential aspects of the Jewish and democratic state, as well as the fear of students' and parents' reactions, and complaints lead many teachers to avoid important but critical content.

This form of avoidance or self-censorship was also reported in other studies. For example, Nets-Zehngut, Pliskin and Bar-Tal (2015) found that members of institutions in Israel that provide educational historical resources self-censor themselves from providing more accurate and alternative narratives about the conflict that might challenge dominant mainstream narratives. Similarly, even though they acknowledge the importance of discussing controversial issues, both teacher educators and teachers side-step these issues (Cohen 2020; Pollak, et al. 2018). Cohen (2020) argued that the avoidance of controversial issues among educators stems from a wider political discourse in Israel, one that emphasizes educators' professional loyalty to the Ministry of Education over political discussions.

While these processes of censoring and avoidance affect Arab-Palestinians and other minorities in particular, they also affect Jewish teachers who do not identify with the mainstream Zionist perspectives or who seek to introduce students to other perspectives and knowledge. Exemplary of this is the case of Jewish civics teacher Adam Verete, mentioned above, or the case of civics coordinator Adar Cohen, who was dismissed from his post because he was not perceived as supportive enough of the ethno-national religious ideology of the Ministry of Education at that time. These cases have heightened a culture among civics teachers of fearing the loss of their jobs, of not fulfilling the school's expectations, of social isolation and sanctions due to being considered disloyal (Cohen 2020).

Muff and Bekerman (2019) demonstrated in their study about Jewish civic teachers that, whereas many of them reproduce the dominant hegemonic discourse that promotes loyalism and patriotism, some also draw on counter-hegemonic strategies to rebel against it, for example through developing their students' critical thinking and introducing them to Palestinian narratives of the conflict. Similarly, Sheps (2019) reported from his interviews with teachers of Jewish history and civics that some try to resist the ethno-national content. Yet, both studies report that due to the censoring that they face from the curriculum, the authorities, and their students, they mostly feel powerless to provide more balanced or nuanced perspectives on the conflict and other polarizing topics.

In addition, a range of studies discussed teachers' resistance against neoliberal reforms in Israel (Berkovich 2011; Reichman and Artzi, 2012). For example, some teachers protested through resistance strikes and online petitions (Berkovich 2011). Importantly, by depoliticizing teachers' work through the focus on performance, the neoliberal shift is complicit with the ethno-national shift, since both contribute to the censoring and avoidance processes in civics and history education.

The Arab-Palestinian Struggle for Recognition

As indicated above, many minorities around the world undergo policies and practices of misrecognition that involve: cultural domination (being subjected to patterns of interpretation and communication that are associated with another culture and are alien and/or hostile to one's own); non-recognition (being rendered invisible by means of authoritative representational, communicative and interpretative practices); and disrespect (being routinely maligned or disparaged in stereotypic public cultural representations and/or in everyday life situations) (see Power & Frandji 2010).

This is also the case in Israel. According to Yair Bäuml (2010), the state of Israel is still dominated by policy principles that were designed in its early history to control the

Arab-Palestinian minority, including defining them as a security risk, expropriating their land, denying the development of a Palestinian collective identity, exercising discrimination, and excluding Palestinians from public spheres such as culture, education, law, communication, and national symbols. In particular, it seems that the field of education has been subjected to a double-edged policy of "supervised abandonment," in Bäuml's words. At the same time, as the "abandoning state" discriminates against Arab education by differential allocation of resources and creates persistent disparities between Arab and Jewish education across all socio-economic spheres, the "surveillance state" closely supervises and controls this education to ensure that the state's discriminatory policies do not generate a collective consciousness or resistance. The mechanisms include close surveillance of the system, elimination of any national content from the curriculum, and co-option of Arab academics and turning them into technocratic and apolitical teachers (Golan-Agnon 2004:79–80; Mazawi 1994).[1]

Accordingly, the literature is full of research accounts that demonstrate how the Arab-Palestinian education system in Israel has been controlled through policies and practices that result in the unequal allocation of state resources, lack of recognition of the Palestinian minority's cultural needs, and marginalization of the Arab leadership's influence on education policy (e.g., Abu-Asbe 2007; Abu-Saad 2004 and 2006; Agbaria 2013; al-Haj 1995; Amara and Mar'i 2002; Arar and Abu-Asbe 2013; Jabareen and Agbaria 2010; Makkawi 2002; Mazawi 1994; Rouhana and Ghanem 1998). In this regard, Mar'i argued that the Arab education system in Israel is set "to instill feelings of self-disparagement and inferiority in Arab youth; to denationalize them, and particularly to de-Palestinize them; and to teach them to glorify the history, culture, and achievements of the Jewish majority" (Mar'i 1978, 37). Zureik (1979, 200) pointed to the "implementation of an effective system of co-option, and control which segments an already sectionalized Arab society." For Zureik, the "asymmetrical relationship between the Arab and the Jewish population[s] is magnified by maintaining complete closure in the educational, cultural, and residential facilities of the settler group vis-à-vis the indigenous population" (Zureik 1979, 29). Among the features of settlers' societies that he viewed as applying to the study of the Arab minority in Israel, Zureik pointed to "the creating of a justificatory ideology based on the dehumanization of the culture and way of life of the indigenous population" (ibid), including the manipulation of cultural and national symbols that characterize Arabs and their history.

Despite the fact that Arab schools teach in Arabic, the literature is consistent in observing the absence of recognition of the Palestinian collective identity in school curricula and textbooks, which are void of any substantial engagement with Palestinian history and culture (Agbaria 2016). Specifically, the civics curriculum in Israel, which is standardized across the secular Jewish and the Arab educational sectors, is committed to upholding the Jewishness of the state and its national ethos. It is worth noting that civics is called *medaniyyat* (meaning "civilities" in Arabic), thus its name signals an emphasis on the disciplining civility and conforming civic virtues required to be a loyal and cooperative citizen.

However, the literature mentioned above lags behind the new realities created by the power of identity politics and the forces of globalization and economic liberalization in Israel. As the Palestinian minority's capacity to resist Israeli direct and overt methods of control has expanded dramatically, and as the state needs to accommodate its control technologies to the market-driven and highly ethnically politicized education system, the notion of control can no longer be solely perceived as the embodiment of state-centred, top-down, and unidirectional strategies of power, as traditionally presented in the literature on Arab education in Israel.

Literature from other contexts reported that many minorities counter misrecognition with oppositional strategies that attempt not only to invert their inferior status and affirm the value of their previously undermined identity (Simmons and Dei 2012), but also to cultivate their own societal culture in ways that would eventually be officially endorsed by the state (Kymlicka 1995). For misrecognized groups, the remedy for the denial of the expression of their societal culture in the public sphere lies with official, yet meaningful, equality, and recognition.

The above-mentioned neoliberal policies are inherently intertwined with the recent ethno-national turn in the evolution of Palestinian political activism in Israel to end Jewish ethnic hegemony (Haklai 2011). This new ethno-national political discourse among the Palestinians in Israel is characterized by a growing emphasis on the indigenousness of the Palestinian minority as a platform to demand national recognition and collective rights, including in the field of education (Jamal 2008). In practice, Arab-Palestinian teachers have developed counter-strategies by focusing on students' individual socio-economic mobility, their success in the matriculation exam, teaching about individual rights against discrimination and the legal aspects of citizenship, character education, democratic values, and civic action in their local communities (Agbaria and Pinson 2019). Agbaria and Pinson (2019) argued that in this way teachers have managed to restore to some extent the community's identity and cultural spaces and practices. Moreover, while Arab-Palestinian students are generally marginalized and alienated by official civic education (Pinson 2008), it appears that some students learn about their identity, culture, and narratives outside of the school context, through their families, peers, and extra-curricular activities in their communities (Muff 2019).

Consequently, the curricula for the subjects of history and civics have become fertile ground for political conflict in which the regulative and normative powers of the state collide with the counterforce of Arab civil society organizations (Agbaria 2013). During the past two decades, as these organizations have been deeply involved in empowering the Palestinian minority vis-a-vis the state by promoting processes of mobility, development and democratization (Jamal 2007 and 2008), they have likewise become more proactive in mobilizing initiatives of politics of recognition in the education field (Agbaria 2010 and 2013). As politics become more divided, the economy more privatized, and civil society more diverse, the central government's capacity to impede minority mobilization for equality and recognition, including in the field of education, has considerably diminished (Haklai 2011). Yet, as Dahan and Yonah (2005) argued, having receded from the socio-economic spheres under neoliberal policies, the state subsequently seeks increased control over the cultural arena.

Against these efforts to render the hegemonic Israeli narrative as canonical and shared by all ethnic and cultural groups in Israel, efforts which were often devised without significant public deliberation or involvement of the Palestinian minority, counter and "insurgent discourses" emerged to contest "the given symbols of authority" (Bhabha 2004, 277). These counter and anti-colonial discourses have become more prominent as the Palestinian civil society in Israel has become more proactive in linking civic equality to national recognition, placing more emphasis on the indigenousness status of the Palestinian minority in Israel to justify demands for collective rights (Jamal 2007 and 2008).

Conclusion

The goal of this chapter is to analyse the status quo of teaching about the Israeli-Palestinian conflict in Israel through the identity-building subjects of civics and history. The existing literature points towards two trends: on the one hand, an increasing ethno-nationalization and neoliberalization of education that deepens existing divisions in Israeli society, strengthens right-wing national and religious ideologies, and increasingly curtails opportunities for alternative views and narratives as well as critical thinking. Yet, on the other hand, we can observe resistance among Arab and Jewish educators who object to the government's ethno-national and neoliberal agenda, as well as a broader resistance from within Arab-Palestinian civil society and their political demands for recognition.

While it is important to recognize these resistance efforts, the current practice of teaching about the Israeli-Palestinian conflict, if it is taught at all, reinforces existing divisions between Jewish-Israelis and Arab-Palestinians as well as within these groups. By silencing alternative perspectives and narratives of the conflict, by refusing to recognize the other's collective national identity and belonging to the land, and by denying responsibility for historical and ongoing violence and oppression, current educational policies in Israel lag far behind from addressing the substantial issues that fuel the Israeli-Palestinian conflict; on the contrary, they serve to sustain the conflict and various divisions in Israel's society.

As the historical development of civics and history education in Israel has shown, a shift toward a more inclusive, multicultural, and transformative educational agenda would depend on the change of the dominant ideology of the political establishment and a substantial rethinking among Israel's society that remains dominated by an ethno-national-religious discourse. In this regard, the two school subjects – history and civics, are illustrative examples as to how Israeli education is infused with religious rhetoric that mobilizes teachers and pupils to replace Israeli patriotism with Jewish patriotism, while endowing the conflict with the Palestinians with religious significance. What is at stake here is that the education system in Israel is increasingly becoming a locus of religious reproduction, which repels not only the incorporation of secular ideals and values but also democratic principles and human-rights sensibilities (Gordon 2012).

Moreover, neoliberal policies in education are often entwined with various strands of neoconservative and religious fundamentalism (Apple 2000). Since states began to act as competitive entities in the world market, Harvey (2007) argued, they have increasingly faced the problem of finding alternative ways to secure citizen loyalty. For Harvey and Varga (2013), renewing the brand of nationalism was the answer. In Israel, the politics of the right have shaped the education system to become more particularistic and nationalistic. The radical right has further penetrated the education system, widening and deepening the divide between Arabs and Jews. On the one hand, Jewish pupils are educated with the aim of having a strong Jewish identity. On the other, Palestinian pupils are educated in schools that promote the idea that education should be strictly professional, allowing little space, if any, for shoring up pupils' collective identities.

Put differently, the two shifts, the religious-ethnonational and the neoliberal, are indeed constitutive to each other. In the neoliberal agenda, the state plays two dialectic roles: the "weak state" and the "strong state" (Yonah, Dahahn, and Markovich 2008), or, as Chana Katz and Erez Tzfadia (2010) put it, the "abandoning state" and the "surveillancing state." In education, the weak state reveals itself through policies and practices of privatization and depoliticization, while securing its control not so much by the volume of direct authoritarian production of incentive and sanctions, but rather through shaping the behaviour of a self-regulating, choice-making, self-reliant individual or citizen (Fisher 2003). Conversely, the strong state role is exercised by imposing practices, such as standardization, core curriculum, accountability measures, and placing heavy emphasis on what Beck (2003) has coined "renationalization," which is the attempt to revive national and particularistic identities against the forces of neoliberalism. In Israel, as the state has abdicated its traditional welfare state responsibilities, two twin competing educational strategies have emerged: education for a greater individualization of society, and education for strong ethno-religious collective identity.

The neoliberalization and nationalization of the teaching of the Israeli-Palestinian conflict have the effect of silencing and avoiding critical discussions about it and thus impede the potential of conflict transformation. Instead, the identity-building subjects contribute to normalizing the status quo of structural and institutional racism, privilege, and oppression – which sustain the conflict, even during times when levels of violence are moderate. As Davies (2004) stated, schools in conflict-ridden societies are at risk of inciting a culture of fear, nationalism, and obedience. Marginal resistance is usually crushed by the state apparatus that advances processes of censoring, by sanctioning those who seek to challenge existing power relations and structures of privilege. Yet, it has been argued that to some extent positive conflict or escalation is necessary to bring about constructive change in a conflict-ridden society like Israel (Lederach 2014). A transformative approach would seek to address social structures and relationships that sustain conflict by reducing underlying structural causes and patterns of violence, and also increasing justice. We argue that exposure to different narratives – perspectives that question the status quo – and critical discussion of existing structures of privilege and oppression can promote positive and constructive engagement with the conflict.

In the Israeli education system there is a need for two processes that can contribute to a more critical and sustainable approach towards teaching about the conflict: first, the need for collective rights of minorities, such as Arab-Palestinian citizens, to have their narratives, identities, and culture recognized by the education system and to be genuinely included in the decision-making processes of educational policies; and, second, a space for a critical pedagogy in the identity-building subjects of history and civics, a space that allows for the challenging of dominant ideologies that sustain the violent conflict and existing unequal structures in Israel's society.

Recommended Readings

Agbaria, A. K. 2018a. "The 'Right' Education in Israel: Segregation, Religious Ethnonationalism, and Depoliticized Professionalism." *Critical Studies in Education* 59:1, 18–34.

Al-Haj, M. 1995. *Education, Empowerment and Control: The Case of the Arabs in Israel.* Albany: State University of New York Press.

Cohen, A. 2019. "Israel's Civic Education Wars: A Review of the Literature and Theoretical Implications." *Educational Review* 71:3, 287–305.

Mar'i, S. K. 1978. *Arab Education in Israel.* Syracuse, NY: Syracuse University Press.

Peled-Elhanan, N. 2012. *Palestine in Israeli School Books: Ideology and Propaganda in Education.* New York: I. B. Tauris.

Note

1 See a petition to the Israeli Supreme Court against the interference of the Israel Security Agency (Shabak) in the staff appointments in Arab schools (see H.C. 8193/04 Union of Parents of Arab Students in Israel, et. al. v. The Ministry of Education, et. al. [petition withdrawn]. Available at: www.adalah.org/admin/DownLoads/SPics/ 8016370.pdf.

Questions for Discussion

(1) How is the Israeli education system related to the Israeli-Palestinian conflict? In what ways has the structure of this system and its curricula been sustaining the Israeli-Palestinian conflict?
(2) How has the rise of ethno-religious politics in Israel influenced the Israeli education system?
(3) How has the dominance of neoliberal policies in education influenced the Israeli education system?
(4) How have the influences of the ethno-religious politics and the neoliberal policies in Israel been encountered in the Arab education system in Israel?
(5) As the chapter argues that the Israeli education system has been used to serve the purposes of the Jewish nation-state building, do you think a similar situation exists in Palestinian education in the Occupied Territories of 1967, which is administrated by the Palestinian National Authority? What might be the similarities and differences between the two cases?

References

Abu-Asbe, K. 2007. *Arab Education in Israel: Dilemmas of a National Minority*. Jerusalem: Floersheimer Institute for Policy Studies. [In Hebrew].

Abu-Saad, I. 2004. "Separate and Unequal: The Role of the State Educational System in Maintaining the Subordination of Israel's Palestinian Arab Citizens." *Social Identities* 10:1, 101–127.

Abu-Saad, I. 2006. "Palestinian Education in Israel: The Legacy of the Military Government." *Holy Land Studies: A Multidisciplinary Journal* 5:1, 21–56.

Agbaria, A. K. 2010. "Civic Education for the Palestinians in Israel: Dilemmas and Challenges." In *Citizenship Education and Social Conflict: New Insights and Lessons from Israel*, eds. H. Alexander, H. Pinson, and Y. Yonah. New York: Routledge Press, 217–237.

Agbaria, A. K. 2013. "Arab Civil Society and Education in Israel: The Arab Pedagogical Council as a Contentious Performance to Achieve National Recognition." *Race Ethnicity and Education* 18:5, 675–695.

Agbaria, A. K. 2016. "Ethno-National Politics of Citizenship Education in Israel and the Counter-Knowledge of Palestinian Teachers." In *Global Migration, Diversity, and Civic Education: Improving Policy and Practice*, eds. J. Banks, M. Suárez-Orozco, and M. Ben-Peretz. New York: Columbia University Teachers College Press, 156–176.

Agbaria, A. K. 2018a. "The 'Right' Education in Israel: Segregation, Religious Ethnonationalism, and Depoliticized Professionalism." *Critical Studies in Education* 59:1, 18–34.

Agbaria, A. K. 2018b. "Israeli Education and the Apartheid in South Africa: Ongoing Insights." *Intercultural Education* 29:2, 218–235.

Agbaria, A. K., et al. 2015. "In Your Face Democracy': Education for Belonging and its Challenges in Israel." *British Educational Research Journal* 41:1, 143–175.

Agbaria, A. K., H. Pinson. 2019. "Navigating Israeli Citizenship: How do Arab-Palestinian Teachers Civicize Their Pupils?" *Race Ethnicity and Education* 22:3, 391–409.

Al-Haj, M. 1995. *Education, Empowerment and Control: The Case of the Arabs in Israel*. Albany: State University of New York Press.

Amara, M. H., and A. Mar'i. 2002. *Language Education Policy: The Arab Minority in Israel*. Dordrecht, Netherlands: Kluwer Academic Publishing.

Apple, M. W. 2000. "Between Neoliberalism and Conservatism: Education and Conservatism in a Global Context." In *Globalization and Education: Critical Perspectives*, eds. N. Burbules and C. A. Torres. New York: Routledge Falmer, 57–78.

Apple, M. W. 2001. "Comparing Neo-liberal Projects and Inequality in Education." *Comparative Education* 37:4, 409–423.

Apple, M. W. 2004. *Ideology and Curriculum*. New York: Routledge.

Arar, K., and K. Abu-Asbe. 2013. "'Not Just Location': Attitudes and Perceptions of Education System Administrators in Local Arab Governments in Israel." *International Journal of Educational Management* 27:1, 54–73.

Barghouti, S. 2009. "Palestinian History and Identity in Israeli Schools." *Badil Resource Center for Palestinian Residency & Refugee Rights*. Available at: www.badil.org/en/al-majdal/item/1265.

Barak, M. 2014. *Political Education in Israel*. Jerusalem, Molad: The Center for the Renewal of Israeli Democracy. [In Hebrew].

Bar-Tal, D., and E. Halperin. 2013. "The Psychology of Intractable Conflicts: Eruption, Escalation, and Peacemaking." In *The Oxford Handbook of Political Psychology*, eds. L. Huddy, D. O. Sears, and J. S. Levy. Oxford: Oxford University Press, 923–956.

Bar-Tal, D., et al. 2014. "Sociopsychological Analysis of Conflict-supporting Narratives: A General Framework." *Journal of Peace Research* 51:5, 662–675.

Bar-Tal, D., and G. Salomon. 2006. "Israeli-Jewish Narratives of the Israeli-Palestinian Conflict: Evolvement, Contents, Functions and Consequences." In *Israeli and Palestinian Narratives of Conflict: History's Double Helix*, ed. R. I. Rotberg. Bloomington, IN: Indiana University Press, 19–46.

Barton, L., E. Barrett, G. Whitty, S. Miles, and J. Furlong. 1994. "Teacher Education and Teacher Professionalism in England: Some Emerging Issues." *British Journal of Sociology of Education* 15:4, 529–543.

Bäuml, Y. 2010. "61 Years of Surveilled Abandonment-Deciphering the Code of Israeli Establishment Policy toward the State's Arab Citizens." In *Abandoning State – Surveillancing State: Social Policy in Israel, 1985–2008*, eds. C. Katz and E. Tzfadia. Tel Aviv: Resling, 35–54.

Beck, U. 2003. "Toward a New Critical Theory with a Cosmopolitan Intent." *Constellations* 10:4, 453–468.
Berkovich, I. 2011. "No We Won't! Teachers' Resistance to Educational Reform." *Journal of Educational Administration* 49:5, 563–578.
Berkovich, I. 2014. "Neo-liberal Governance and the 'New Professionalism' of Israeli Principals." *Comparative Education Review* 58:3, 428–456.
Bhabha, H. 2004. *The Location of Culture*. London and New York: Routledge.
Bush, K., and D. Saltarelli. 2000. *The Two Faces of Education in Ethnic Conflict: Towards a Peacebuilding Education for Children*. Florence: UNICEF.
Cohen, A. 2019. "Israel's Civic Education Wars: A Review of the Literature and Theoretical Implications." *Educational Review* 71:3, 287–305.
Cohen, A. 2020. "Teaching to Discuss Controversial Public Issues in Fragile Times: Approaches of Israeli Civics Teacher Educators." *Teaching and Teacher Education* 89, 103013.
Connell, R. 2009. "Good Teachers on Dangerous Ground: Towards a New View of Teacher Quality and Professionalism." *Critical Studies in Education* 50:3, 213–229.
Dahan, Y., and Y. Yonah. 2005. "The Dovrat Report: On the Neo-liberal Revolution in Education." *Theory and Criticism* 27, 11–38.
Davies, L. 2004. *Education and Conflict: Complexity and Chaos*. London: Routledge.
Fisher, F. 2003. *Reframing Public Policy*. New York: Oxford University.
Fraser, N. 2000. "Rethinking Recognition: Overcoming Displacement and Reification in Cultural Politics." *New Left Review* 3 (May–June), 107–120.
Gillborn, D., and D. Youdell. 2000. *Rationing Education: Policy, Practice, Reform and Equity*. Buckingham: Open University Press.
Giroux, H. 1997. *Pedagogy and the Politics of Hope: Theory, Culture, and Schooling*. Boulder, CO: Westview Press.
Golan-Agnon, D. 2004. "Why Are Arab Students Discriminated against in Israel?" In *Inequality in Education*, ed. D. Golan-Agnon. Tel Aviv: Babel Publications, 70–89. [In Hebrew].
Goldberg, T., and D. Gerwin. 2013. "Israeli History Curriculum and the Conservative-liberal Pendulum." *History Education Research Journal* 11:2, 111–124.
Gordon, N. 2012. "The Geography and Political Context of Human Rights Education: Israel as a Case Study." *Journal of Human Rights* 11:3, 384–404.
Haklai, O. 2011. *Palestinian Ethnonationalism in Israel*. Philadelphia: University of Pennsylvania Press.
Harvey, D. 2007. *A Brief History of Neoliberalism*. Oxford: Oxford University Press.
Hursh, D. 2005. "Neo-Liberalism, Markets and Accountability: Transforming Education and Undermining Democracy in the United States and England." *Policy Futures in Education* 3:1, 3–15.
Ichilov, O., G. Salomon, and D. Inbar. 2005. "Citizenship Education in Israel–A Jewish-Democratic State." *Israel Affairs* 11:2, 303–323.
Illouz, E. 2014a. "Where was the Left When the Settlers Hijacked Zionism?" *Haaretz*. 19 December. Available at: www.haaretz.com/.premium-where-was-the-left-when-the-settlers-hijacked-zionism-1.5348941.
Illouz, E. 2014b. "47 Years A Slave: A New Perspective on the Occupation." *Haaretz*. 7 February. Available at: www.haaretz.com/.premium-47-years-a-slave-1.5319717.
Jabareen, Y., and A. Agbaria. 2010. *Education on Hold*. Nazareth and Haifa University: Dirasat and the Arab Minority Rights Clinic. [In Hebrew].
Jamal, A. 2007. "Strategies of Minority Struggle for Equality in Ethnic States: Arab Politics in Israel. *Citizenship Studies* 11:3, 263–282.
Jamal, A. 2008. "The Counter-hegemonic Role of Civil Society: Palestinian–Arab NGOs in Israel." *Citizenship Studies* 12:3, 283–306.
Kashti, O. 2014. "Bringing Secular Israelis Closer to the Bible." *Haaretz*. 13 August. Available at: www.haaretz.com/news/national/.premium-1.610226.
Katz, C., and E. Tzfadia, eds. 2010. *Abandoning State – Surveillancing State: Social Policy in Israel*, 1985–2008. Tel Aviv: Resling.
Kizel, A. 2008. *Subservient History: A Critical Analysis of History Curricula and Textbooks in Israel, 1948–2006*. Tel Aviv: Mofet Institute. [In Hebrew].
Knesset. 2018. Basic Law: Israel – The Nation State of The Jewish People. Available at: https://knesset.gov.il/laws/special/eng/BasicLawNationState.pdf.
Kymlicka, W. 1995. *Multicultural Citizenship: A Liberal Theory of Minority Rights*. Oxford: Clarendon Press.
Lederach, J. 2014. *Little Book of Conflict Transformation: Clear Articulation of the Guiding Principles by a Pioneer in the Field*. New York: Good Books.

Mahamid, H. 2017. "History Education for Arab Palestinian Schools in Israel." *Journal of Education and Development* 1:1, 37–47.

Makkawi, I. 2002. "Role Conflict and the Dilemma of Palestinian Teachers in Israel." *Comparative Education* 38:1, 39–52.

Mar'i, S. K. 1978. *Arab Education in Israel*. Syracuse, NY: Syracuse University Press.

Mathias, Y. 2005. "Curriculum between Politics and Science: The Case of History in Israel after the Six-Day War." *Political Crossroads* 12:1, 47–65.

May, S., T. Modood, and J. Squires. 2004. *Ethnicity, Nationalism, and Minority Rights*. Cambridge: Cambridge University Press.

Mazawi, A. 1994. "Teachers' Role Patterns and the Mediation of Sociopolitical Change: The Case of Palestinian Arab School Teachers." *British Journal of Sociology of Education*. 15:4, 497–514.

Ministry of Education. 2016. "The National Programmes for Meaningful Learning – the Educational Discourse on Controversial Issues." [In Hebrew].

Ministry of Education. 2017. *Being Citizens in Israel*. Jerusalem: Ministry of Education Israel. [In Hebrew].

Misgav, U. 2014. "Israeli Education Minister's Creed: God, the Holocaust, and the Military." *Haaretz*. 6 February. Available at: www.haaretz.com/opinion/.premium-piron-s-creed-god-holocaust-idf-1.5319471.

Muff, A. 2019. "Citizenship Education and Identity: A Comparative Study Across Different Schools in Northern Ireland and Israel." Doctoral Dissertation, Queen's University Belfast.

Muff, A., and Z. Bekerman. 2019. "Agents of the Nation-state or Transformative Intellectuals? Exploring the Conflicting Roles of Civics Teachers in Israel." *Education, Citizenship and Social Justice* 14:1, 22–39.

Nakou, I., and I. Barca. 2010. *Contemporary Public Debates over History Education*. Charlotte, NC: Information Age Publishing.

Naveh, E., and E. Yogev. 2002. *Histories: Towards a Dialogue with the Israeli Past*. Tel Aviv: Bavel.

Nets-Zehngut, R., R. Pliskin, and D. Bar-Tal. 2015. "Self-censorship in Conflicts: Israel and the 1948 Palestinian Exodus." *Peace and Conflict: Journal of Peace Psychology* 21:3, 479–499.

Ohana, D. 2009. *Political Theologies in the Holy Land: Israeli Messianism and Its Critics*. London: Routledge.

Peled, Y., and H. H. Peled, H. H. 2018. *The Religionization of Israeli Society*. London: Routledge.

Peled-Elhanan, N. 2012. *Palestine in Israeli School Books: Ideology and Propaganda in Education*. New York: I.B. Tauris.

Pinson, H. 2019. "The New Civics Curriculum for High Schools in Israel: The Discursive Construction of Palestinian Identity and Narratives." *Education, Citizenship and Social Justice* 15:1, 22–34.

Podeh, E. 2000. "History and Memory in the Israeli Educational System: The Portrayal of the Arab-Israeli Conflict in History Textbooks (1948–2000)." *History & Memory* 12:1, 65–100.

Podeh, E. 2010. "Univocality within Multivocality: The Israeli-Arab-Palestinian Conflict as Reflected in Israeli History Textbooks, 2000–2010." *Journal of Educational Media, Memory, and Society* 2:2, 46–62.

Pollak, I., et al. 2018. "Teaching Controversial Issues in a Fragile Democracy: Defusing Deliberation in Israeli Primary Classrooms." *Journal of Curriculum Studies* 50:3, 387–409.

Power, S., and D. Frandji. 2010. "Education Markets, the New Politics of Recognition and the Increasing Fatalism towards Inequality." *Journal of Education Policy* 25:3, 385–396.

Quaynor, L. J. 2012. "Citizenship Education in Post-conflict Contexts: A Review of the Literature, Education." *Citizenship and Social Justice* 7:1, 33–57.

Ram, U. 2000. "National, Ethnic or Civic? Contesting Paradigms of Memory, Identity and Culture in Israel." *Studies in Philosophy and Education* 19:5–6, 405–422.

Reichman, R. G., and S. Artzi. 2012. "The Road Not Taken' – Israeli Teachers' Reactions to Top-Down Educational Reform." *The Qualitative Report* 17:33, 1–29.

Resnik, J. 2011. "The Construction of a Managerial Education Discourse and the Involvement of Philanthropic Entrepreneurs: The Case of Israel." *Critical Studies in Education* 52:3, 251–266.

Rouhana, N., and A. Ghanem. 1998. "The Crisis of Minorities in Ethnic States: The Case of Palestinian Citizens in Israel." *International Journal of Middle East Studies* 30:3, 321–346.

Saragossi, S. 2013. "Between Opposing Pulling Forces: The State Religious Education between Halachik Law and Democracy." In *Civic Education in Israel*, ed. D. Avnon. Tel Aviv: Am Oved, 202–235. [In Hebrew].

Schnell, I. 2012. "Geographical Ramifications of the Occupation for Israeli Society." In *The Impacts of Lasting Occupation: Lessons from Israeli Society*, eds. D. Bar-Tal and I. Schnell. Oxford: Oxford University Press, 93–121.

Sheps, S. W. 2019. "History and Civics Education in Israel: Reflections from Israeli Teachers." *Critical Studies in Education* 60:3, 358–374.

Simmons, M., and G. Dei. 2012. "Reframing Anti-colonial Theory for the Diasporic Context." *Postcolonial Directions in Education* 1:1, 67–99.

Svirsky, S., and N. Dagan-Bozaglo. 2009. *Separation, Inequality and Faltering Leadership*. Tel Aviv: Adva Center.

Tamir, Y. 2015. "Teachers in the Social Trenches: Teaching Civics in Divided Societies." *Theory and Research in Education* 13:1, 121–136.

Tomlinson, S. 1997. "Diversity, Choice, and Ethnicity: The Effects of Educational Markets on Ethnic Minorities." *Oxford Review of Education* 23:1, 63–76.

Travis, H. 2013. *Genocide, Ethnonationalism, and the United Nations: Exploring the Causes of Mass Killing Since 1945*. New York: Routledge.

Turner, B. S. 2011. *Religion and Modern Society: Citizenship, Secularisation and the State*. Cambridge: Cambridge University Press.

Varga, S. 2013. "The Politics of Nation: Branding Collective Identity and Public Sphere in the Neoliberal State." *Philosophy & Social Criticism* 39:8, 825–845.

Yogev, E. 2010. "A Crossroads: History Textbooks and Curricula in Israel." *Journal of Peace Education* 7:1, 1–14.

Yonah, Y., Y. Dahan, and D. Markovich. 2008. "Neo-Liberal Reforms in Israel's Education System: The Dialectics of the State." *International Studies in Sociology of Education* 18:3–4, 199–217.

Zajda, J. 2005. *International Handbook on Globalisation, Education and Policy Research: Global Pedagogies and Policies*. New York: Springer.

Zajda, J. 2007. "The New History School Textbooks in the Russian Federation: 1992–2004." *Compare* 37:3, 291–306.

Zajda, J. 2009. "Teachers and the Politics of History Textbooks." In *The New International Handbook of Research on Teachers and Teaching*, eds. L. Saha and A. Dworkin. New York: Springer, 373–387.

Zohar, A., and A. Cohen. 2016. "Large Scale Implementation of Higher Order Thinking (HOT) in Civic Education: The Interplay of Policy, Politics, Pedagogical Leadership and Detailed Pedagogical Planning." *Thinking Skills and Creativity* 21, 85–96.

Zureik, E. 1979. *The Palestinians in Israel: A Study in Internal Colonialism*. London: Routledge and Kegan Paul.

36

STUDYING THE ISRAELI-PALESTINIAN CONFLICT

Imogen Watson

Whilst studying at the University of Birmingham in late 2018, selecting a 20-hour post-graduate module entitled "The Politics of the Arab-Israeli Conflict" was, in hindsight, only ever going to be a challenge with so few hours to study a conflict that spans decades, incorporates numerous issues, and involves many players. Quickly I learned my main key to understanding the conflict was my actively wanting to understand it; otherwise, the breadth and depth of the conflict would have been a deterrent. For me, this subject was the only one about which I was adamant from the moment I applied for the degree programme, and it was this that provided me with the ammunition to keep reading beyond the recommended texts, outside of class and study hours, and long after the module ended. The discovery for me of a new culture that came from reading, studying, visiting, and loving the region also made studying the conflict so rewarding.

The focus of this chapter is distinct from academic analysis of the details of the Israeli-Palestinian conflict, examining instead the rewards, difficulties, and experiences which come with studying it, as well as an account of the experience of visiting Israel and Palestine after studying the conflict. Written from the accounts of only one student, it is inherently a personal perspective but includes elements certainly experienced by others on the module studied, and therefore likely to be experienced more widely by students of the conflict. This chapter begins by charting my motivations for studying the Israeli-Palestinian conflict, followed by what I found to be the conflict's most challenging elements and the rewards of studying it. Subsequently, the chapter explores my experience of visiting the region following the end of the module with a developed understanding of the conflict.

My intrigue began in a third nation, in the Hashemite Kingdom of Jordan. Prior to the module, I had spent a week in the Middle East, travelling alone around Jordan in the September before the module began. I had been inexplicably drawn to Jordan for years; I was desperate to visit, despite knowing nobody there, knowing no one who had visited and having no family connections to the region. It started by wanting to visit Petra, but the more I researched, the more I wanted to see. On my first day after arriving, I visited the border with the West Bank, watching Jewish religious ceremonies on the other side of a division rope in the middle of the River Jordan, which formed an international border, itself only yards from the baptismal site of Jesus Christ to which we had been driven past Jordanian military checkpoints by licenced guide – the only permitted way to visit the spot. It was a substantial piece of evidence of the

DOI: 10.4324/9780429027376-43

significance of the area. When our Jordanian guide gestured across into the distance, beyond the border and towards the town of Jericho, and asked what was there, multiple voices said simultaneously: "Palestine", "Israel", "the West Bank". The Star of David fluttered in the breeze. The guide said diplomatically that it was for someone else to decide.

Later that evening in my hotel on the edge of the Dead Sea, a narrow waterbody that separates Jordan from the West Bank, my recently purchased Jordanian SIM card, struggling to maintain consistent signal, alerted me to repeated, alternate messages about network charges, each either beginning with a friendly "Welcome to Palestine" or "Welcome to Israel" (and reassuringly the occasional "Welcome to Jordan"). A little signal trouble demonstrated a political problem: Is the West Bank Jewish or Arab? Which should it be?

These events, coupled with the knowledge gained from one long book I had read about the Middle East before the trip, showed that the land on the other side of the water was significant and hotly contested, but at this stage I was unable to explain in much detail the reasons why, the feelings of all involved, and how the situation had been reached. Wandering through the streets of Amman one evening towards the end of the week, and using my phone to find a popular Jordanian sweet shop, I met a Palestinian-American man who worked as a tour guide, although then off-duty. Displaying a generous and hospitable welcome that I later discovered to be typically Arab, he then showed me a few important sites in the city and talked a little of his experience as the son of a refugee, though I really had few reference points for his stories. Wanting not only to eliminate my ignorance of the Israeli-Palestinian conflict and the wider region, but to discuss and analyse its future, were driving forces throughout my studies. I had anticipated loving my trip, but I failed to foresee the positive impact it would have on my degree and my academic mindset.

One: Studying

My immediate feeling beginning the module was of being overwhelmed by its complexity, particularly the number of names and alliances with which it seemed I needed to become familiar. That is a defining problem of studying a period of history several decades in and one which continues to evolve. From David Ben Gurion to Benjamin Netanyahu, and through Moshe Sharett, Golda Meir and Ariel Sharon, over seven decades of Israeli prime ministers, foreign and defense ministers, and their political allegiances and priorities have changed numerous times, and Palestinian leaders have also come and gone, with the domestic support and fluctuating willingness of each to come to an agreement. Keeping track of these is one issue, but Palestinian factions and organisations complicate the matter, and mentally organising Fatah, Hamas, Islamic Jihad, the Palestinian Authority, the Palestinian Liberation Organisation, and particularly how they interact at any given time, at first seemed like a daunting task. Understanding the political contexts of each party to better appreciate the choices seemed like an overwhelming long-term project.

The situation felt even more complex when the Israelis' and Palestinians' neighbours were included. Not only have they long had a reasonable strategic interest in what happens in the Israeli-Palestinian conflict on their borders, but Syria, Egypt, and Jordan are members of the wider Arab-Israeli conflict, invading Israel after its declaration of independence in 1948 and sometimes partaking in subsequent Arab-Israeli wars across subsequent decades. They remain important players when it comes to the future of resolving issues, with large portions of the Jordanian population being of Palestinian refugee descent, and with a key interest in the future of Jerusalem; although Egypt and Jordan have lasting peace agreements with Israel, Syria and Israel technically remain at war. Secret relations between Arab nations and majority-Jewish

Israel have not been unheard of; simplifying this complex Middle Eastern web is not possible by simply assuming all Arabs are good friends and against the Israelis; during an early seminar we were introduced to the "Middle East Friendship Chart" (Keating and Kirk 2014), a table of predominantly red "enemy" faces, some yellow "it's complicated" faces, and fewer green "friends" faces. These countries and their leaders, have their own complex relations with each other as well as with Israel and Palestinians.

Yet at the heart of the conflict are issues that underpin the lack of resolution thus far. It is easier to start with the fundamental problems, gradually layering knowledge in relation to these. Examining these component problems appears to be a simpler path to understanding the conflict, but it also raises questions and reactions.

Jerusalem

Jerusalem has great holy significance to three major religions, and particularly to the Jewish and Arab sides in this conflict. Whilst I have sympathy with arguments over religious prominence of Jerusalem – it is both the holiest city of Judaism and the third most holy in Islam – these arguments avoid the crucial point: regardless of any consensus on "who came first" or "who stayed longest", no group is willing to rescind its claim to Jerusalem and allow the others to have it. Since 1980, Israeli Basic Law has enshrined Jerusalem as its "complete and united" capital, repeated in Israel's 2018 "Nation-State" Basic Law, making undertaking negotiations on Jerusalem's future legally and politically next to impossible for any Israeli government. The Palestinians claim at least East Jerusalem with its Muslim holy sites as the capital of its future state. Division is not a popular subject, and international control out of the question. Even if division could be agreed, the important parts of the Old City to each group are directly next to each other in a space smaller than one square kilometre; the Jewish Western Wall and the Muslim Haram al-Sharif are almost exactly on top of each other. My feelings staring at a map of the city during seminars can be summarised as utter frustration at an unresolvable situation, a feeling with which, like most observers, I would grow increasingly familiar.

Refugees

The history of Palestinian refugees quickly demonstrated the role of perspectives in this conflict; there is no single version of the story that can be told in order to have a complete understanding of how the current situation has evolved. The 1948 War, following the British withdrawal from its Mandate for Palestine and Israel's declaration of statehood, saw the departure of approximately 700,000 Palestinians from what had until then been known as Mandatory Palestine. The claims of official Israeli sources that Arab leaders ordered Palestinian withdrawal contradict those of Palestinians (such as Khalidi 1988), who argue that Israelis forced them out as part of a pre-designed plan, an incident the Palestinians call the *nakba* (the Arabic word for *catastrophe*). The historiography is resultingly complex, too, with traditional Israeli historians (such as Karsh 2010) defending the official Israeli position that this Palestinian exodus was at the hands of Arab leaders and no pre-designed plan ever existed, and "new historians" (such as Morris 1988; Shlaim 2001; Shlaim 2009; Flapan 1987) using Israeli archives to demonstrate greater Israeli responsibility for widespread attacks on Palestinian Arabs, forcing them from their lands, and the destruction of Palestinian Arab homes, but no consensus on the existence of a plan.

Hundreds of thousands of Palestinians no longer permitted to retain their homes and livelihoods, often not welcomed in by their Arab neighbours, either, understandably provoked anger and created in Palestinians a national identity which barely existed before, the Palestinians never having had their own official state. The departure of so many Palestinians has created a group which, even generations after the original refugees of 1948 and 1967, continues to consider itself refugees and maintains claims to land now internationally considered part of the Israeli state, increasing friction between the two groups. Palestinians have no single status of nationality – some are Jordanian, British, or American, and some have no official citizenship, while others hold foreign travel documents. This reinforces the image of being a refugee, even for those born outside of Palestine, a powerful image which binds Palestinians together as a stateless people facing injustice, a group that had previously been rather disparate.

Land

The discussion of borders swiftly raised the issue of historical claims to the land and the question of whose claim is more legitimate. Does an older claim have more legitimacy? Does more recent habitation of the land make a claim stronger? Does the amount of time spent living on the land cement a more convincing claim? These are all extremely difficult questions to answer, as different individuals hold different beliefs about them.

The Jewish biblical claim to the area historically known as Palestine, as the land promised to the Jewish people by God, naturally demands questions about the role of religion in the conflict. Should religion be used as a justification for the expansionism seen during war, particularly the Israeli annexation of East Jerusalem in 1967 and expansion beyond the 1949 Armistice Agreement's lines? Religion has been always quick to surface during extracurricular debates and discussions on the subject of Israel and Palestine with my mother, an Anglican priest with excellent theological and Biblical knowledge, including the history of the Jews in this period, as we grapple with questions about religion in the modern-day part of the conflict. I wonder if, as an increasingly irreligious Western society, it is perhaps more difficult to grasp the strength of feeling towards a religious belief about the fundamental significance of a specific piece of land that has survived through generations, a belief in a promised homeland that contributed to the survival of the Jewish diaspora across centuries, but it is undoubtedly one that endures within present-day Israeli Jewish society.

Security

Security and borders are inherently tied together: Where are the borders and who will protect them? Security is a cyclical issue. Wherever one begins in the cycle, each action seems to perpetuate a spiral of insecurity. For example, when Palestinian terrorist attacks injure and kill Israeli citizens, Israel justifies its own need for more settlements and more military presence, or for quicker building of the Separation Wall, or more bombings in Gaza. In turn, this reinforces Palestinian belief in the Israelis as occupiers of their land, and reinforces resistance towards them, sometimes hostile. As tensions rise, so does violence. The security spiral is extremely frustrating from the outside view; while no perfect solution to all of the issues at the centre of the conflict exists, when each side does something that will inevitably ramp up the tension – whether a bombing raid on Gaza, exchange of gunfire at the border, a new settlement in the West Bank, or an attack on Israeli citizens – it is extremely difficult not to be frustrated by the inevitability of the coming reaction.

Studying a live conflict has its advantages. Its steadily unfolding current affairs are excellent study material. During the module, Israel and Hamas exchanged extensive rocket fire and bombings following a failed Israeli intelligence raid within Gaza, which saw several – both Israeli and Palestinian – dead. During the writing of this chapter, Israel fired rockets into Gaza, killing a senior commander of the Palestinian group Islamic Jihad, allied with Hamas. This assassination prompted Palestinian rocket fire into southern and central Israel, with school and work being cancelled for many Israelis. The benefit of studying a live conflict is seeing it in action rather than in the abstract, which helps to show it as a real set of circumstances that affects real lives.

Security is also quite naturally an emotive subject; anyone would want to protect themselves and their families from attack. Politicians often draw on the emotional response their citizens experience when flare-ups occur, stoking the nationalism that keeps them engaged. But that the natural human response to violence, separation, encroachment or any other act that takes place in the Israeli-Palestinian conflict, is to protect oneself and one's loved ones from harm by the person perceived to be doing any of these things demonstrates a unnecessary ahead crucial point: both sides of this conflict are human. Depending on one's perspective, elements of one side, the other, or both have been radicalised, but at its heart this conflict is sad and tragic. Two groups of people want to live and to prosper in this land, but they believe that the other is their enemy – that is fundamentally tragic.

Two: Psychology

Understanding the psychological barriers at play in this conflict was the next key to understanding why it continues to be intractable, acting as the underpinning factor of why each side perceives the other as the aggressor and the enemy, and why so far the tangible issues have been insurmountable.

Investigating the psychology and the emotionality of the history between the Israelis and Palestinians was a rewarding but difficult task, having personally experienced a very different kind of life not surrounded or shaped by violent conflict. Studies such as those by Bar Tal (2001) demonstrate that large parts of Israeli culture – whether textbooks, news, literature – is anti-Arab and perpetuates stereotypes about them. Certainly, Palestinians have targeted Israeli citizens specifically, both within internationally recognised Israel and living in Israeli settlements (B'Tselem 2017), and those Palestinians living in close proximity to Jewish settlements and the Green Line as well as those who seek to cross the border to work in Israel see first-hand the evidence which leads them to a belief of Israelis as occupiers.

Living surrounded by an intractable conflict, where significant parts of one's culture encourage these beliefs, the logic of these psychological barriers is easy to follow, but it is a specific task to understand the depth of feeling and emotion that comes with them. It was made somewhat easier by visiting both Israel and Palestine, a subject I will discuss in greater detail later in this chapter, but in the abstract, it is quite hard to empathise with emotional and psychological perspectives even if a logical process by which those perspectives have been reached is clear. Understanding the existence and spread of these barriers is important in overcoming them and finding solutions to the problem; when one sees the other as the enemy, it is impossible to negotiate with them. Almost nothing in this situation that either party can say or do is positively received. When these barriers begin to crumble, common ground will be more easily achieved, and negotiations can proceed more readily – although negotiation certainly does not become simpler. Though these perceptions of each other are largely embedded in culture, politicians' repetition of imagery can activate these belief systems; it is common worldwide to see politicians who repeat a message to convince their constituents, whether of their integrity, the correctness of their beliefs or actions, or of the flaws of their opponents. Keeping these psychological beliefs active makes it easier to justify conflict and primes any actions that may be taken that otherwise people might disapprove.

These psychological barriers, for me, demonstrate the tragedy of the conflict once again. Because the two sides generally perceive the other as the enemy, there is little willingness to compromise – what government would be willing to be seen to compromise with the enemy? Whilst researching for an assignment about the conflict's psychological nature, I found polling figures from 2016 that reported that of those Israeli Jews and Palestinians who had had an encounter with each other in the months prior to the survey being taken, 94.8 per cent of Israeli Jews and 71.1 per cent of Palestinians described it as positive, both significant majorities. The greater problem, however, was that only 23.1 per cent of Israeli Jews and 11.5 per cent of Palestinians had had such an encounter (PCPSR 2016). The tragedy is that it seems as though when the two sides meet, largely they can see the humanity in each other, but simply not enough opportunities occur for this to have much long-term effect on a wide enough scale.

Three: Discussion

I anticipated that this subject would open a world of difficult debates and discussions, but my experience so far is that the more infuriating conversations have been those outside the classroom, the classroom largely remaining, quite surprisingly, an uncontroversial zone. Discussing these issues in the context of a United Kingdom university campus was a largely productive and enjoyable affair. It has been divided between those who are sufficiently knowledgeable about the conflict to be aware of its nuances and subtleties and even to debate them, and those who are willing to accept their ignorance and actively question to better understand it.

Outside of the module itself, as part of a week of mediation training, I was one of 30 participants involved in a two-day simulation exercise roleplaying the Hebron negotiations in the 1990s; the group was split into Palestinian and Israeli factions (the Palestinian Authority, Police and Hamas, and the Israeli government, military and settlers) and a group of mediators, and each group had specific instructions to which it had to stick rigidly. The purpose of the exercise was largely about enacting mediation skills, but also about playing the roles as accurately as possible; although one or two – knowing my affection for the region – asked me some questions in coffee breaks, many participants knew little about the conflict, and I found it incredibly frustrating that the group as a whole managed ultimately to reach an agreement within half an hour of the Hamas walkout from the international negotiation table. Yet the flaw in the exercise was not fuelled by the participants' own refusal to accept subtleties in the real conflict, but by the participants' lack of knowledge and their resultant willingness to behave and acquiesce in ways that would not have happened so easily in real life. For example, the Hamas walkout demonstrated the Palestinian Authority's inability to control them, and yet the Israeli groups remained willing to reach an agreement without so much as a pause, despite Hamas on the outside actively trying to cause problems.

The more stressful conversations have been those in the wider world and often those observed on social media. It seems to be fashionable at the time of writing that if you are left-wing, you must support the Palestinian cause and, if you do so, it must be at the expense of also supporting the existence of an Israeli state. There are many criticisms that can be made of social media, one of which is that a reduced number of characters, such as on Twitter, or the increased confidence it gives people to share their opinions due to increased anonymity and physical distance from an audience, removes any need for nuance. It seems prevalent in the Israeli-Palestinian conflict, where many with an interest often decide that if you are pro-Palestinian you must also be anti-Israel, or that if you believe in the right of Israel to exist, you must also therefore oppose the Palestinian claim to statehood. This lack of permitted subtlety decreases the quality of discussions, reducing them to mere sound bites and black-and-white beliefs, which is so far from the reality of the situation. Posting a photo on Instagram from my holiday, with the location accurately tagged as "Tel Aviv, Israel", I received a comment from an acquaintance that it was "not very Labour" of me to call it Israel (I had previously been a member of the Labour Party). It was an attempt to anger me, and one indicative of the wider problem: nuanced "grey area" understandings and beliefs about the conflict where both Israeli government expansionism and Palestinian terrorism are wrong, and a wish for both states to exist alongside each other, are unfashionable ones and can get you into arguments.

Four: Neutrality

Both during academic assignments and wider discussions, the difficulty of neutrality arose. I discovered that commonly used names in English for the Arab-Israeli wars, in which important shifts in regional influence and power took place, can imply bias. For example, calling the 1967 War the "Six-Day War" can emphasise the swiftness of the Israeli victory and thereby indicate a preference for the Israeli side of the argument; referring to the "Yom Kippur War" in 1973 can also imply an allegiance with the Israeli side because of its emphasis on the commencement of the Arab attack during the Jewish holy day. Of course, these perspectives are different depending on to whom you speak and would not be out of place in many contexts, but studying the conflict makes one alive to the language used and the sensitivities around it. The Israeli-West Bank wall is another example; different groups prefer different terms based on perception of its intentions. Is it a separation barrier, a security barrier, or an apartheid wall?

Regarding academic writing, I became extremely aware of my choice of sources because of this potential bias problem. Although my work would not be disseminated widely and would not get me into trouble with anyone, I was conscious of wanting to ensure that my arguments were not undermined by either my choice of language or by reliance on overly biased sources. I became much more conscious of the word choices of both my media and academic sources, and consciously chose to refer to the major wars by their year rather than by any other name assigned to them; I checked the backgrounds and other works of authors I was hoping to cite, and verified facts and claims across multiple sources. This behaviour is obviously good academic practice, but I felt an enhanced compulsion to do it because of the highly sensitive issues involved.

Benefits

Grappling with the difficulties has made the benefits more worthwhile. Studying the Israeli-Palestinian conflict provides the student with a greater understanding of the modern world, one in which the conflict remains both salient and contentious. Discussions about the merits or otherwise of boycotting Israel, or products it creates in West Bank settlements, are still prevalent. The Western world has seen a rise of anti-Semitism and an inappropriately common conflation of Israeli governmental action and Jewish beliefs, and understanding the conflict allows for a better understanding of why the two are not the same thing. Studying the conflict provides a context for these public debates that many simply do not have; it also provides the frustration with those who are unable to accept any nuance in the situation, who parrot viewpoints without critical engagement with them.

Studying this conflict has also enhanced my ability to appreciate other international relations. By accepting both that existence of nuance and deeply felt emotions and by taking the time to explore them in more depth means I have greater insight into the roles these might play in other conflicts far from the Middle East, even down to analysing areas with no physical or violent war, such as the ongoing Brexit debate in my own country and the emotions and psychological barriers among South African citizens with a South African friend.

A greater understanding of the conflict has given me joy and an affection for a part of the world I barely knew, and opened a path of my own intellectual interest that I previously did not know existed. My keenness encouraged me to pursue Middle Eastern politics for my dissertation, studying a wide range of primary accounts and secondary analyses of the Israeli-Egyptian peace agreements and the attempts to reach Israeli-Syrian deals, examining the role of psychological barriers in both sets of relations through a lens of international rivalry theory.

Visiting the Region

Undoubtedly, the most rewarding part of my studies was visiting Israel and the Palestinian Territories with my new knowledge in mind, expanding upon the understanding of the Israeli-Palestinian conflict that I had had during my time in Jordan. Without question, my studies allowed me to appreciate my experiences in more depth than had I not undertaken them. This section of the chapter outlines some of the most crucial experiences and perspectives I gained during my short time there.

The Israeli siege mentality, the understandable fear of outside attack, which has stemmed from centuries of Jewish persecution, the Holocaust, and the Arab invasion in 1948, all seemed to be in action from the very start of my trip, on my arrival at London Luton Airport and being questioned about my motives for travelling by two individual Israeli agents who reported back to a senior member standing in the corner, separately from my friend. I had prepared for these questions and others about the Jordanian stamps in my passport to be asked on arrival at Tel Aviv. Yet these answers needed to be given before I got to the gate, and in Tel Aviv nothing was asked at all; it seemed the Israeli fear of attack prompts them to ask the questions before anyone leaves non-Israeli territory in the direction of Israel. I had travelled to the United States and experienced something a little similar, but found it more intense when travelling to Israel. Then, having reached the gate, the four non-Jewish members of our group were separated from the Jewish person to have our shoes and luggage inspected a second time, after the normal airport security; whilst I recognised in these detailed checks the Israeli siege mentality, I confess I still found it intensely frustrating when some of us were kept waiting beyond the flight departure time despite having been punctual, having got so close but still unaware if we were allowed on the plane. I was the penultimate person allowed to board, and I have to say the experience was not at all relaxing or welcoming.

Our first day in Israel was greatly different from my first in Jordan; rather than visiting the birthplace of Jesus Christ and watching religious ceremonies in the River Jordan, we watched the Tel Aviv Pride Parade and joined the revellers in the sunshine with beers. This was my first experience of the modern Israel that would contrast significantly with later parts of the trip. Tel Aviv felt largely like a young Mediterranean city; in many respects I could have been in Barcelona, if Barcelona featured London prices. The two major cities in Israel differ greatly. I found Jerusalem far calmer and, even outside of the Old City, more aware of its historic presence. In general, I observed Israel to be more Western than what I had experienced in Jordan, more developed and quite surprisingly so for such a young country.

The level of emotion I felt upon arriving at the Old City of Jerusalem took me by surprise. The memory of turning a corner and catching my first glimpse of the Western Wall with the al-Aqsa Mosque behind it is still vivid, I needed to stop and absorb the site for a few moments. It was a beautiful day, but what struck me was the stark reality of these beautiful and incredibly significant places in both Judaism and Islam being essentially on top of each other. The fact had been stated in the classroom by the few who had visited prior, but it is hard to fully comprehend the problem until it is staring directly at you.

The strength of religious attachment to the area was also hard to understand until I witnessed it. Being neither Jewish nor strongly of any other religion, I held back from touching and praying at the Western Wall and observed instead its importance from the fact that on an ordinary day of no particular holiday, it was very busy, and multiple people were praying from copies of the Torah. Our visit to the Haram al-Sharif, or Temple Mount, the following day, due to its restricted visiting times for non-Muslims, was equally enlightening for me. The entrance from the Jewish Quarter is only up a ramp and through a doorway, but I felt the accompanied change in atmosphere almost immediately. Prayers had only recently finished at the al-Aqsa Mosque, and the modest clothing rules were strictly enforced. The Dome of the Rock is undeniably stunning, its golden roof glistens from every angle and represents the strength of faith and significance of the site for Muslims too. The experience clearly demonstrated the intense difficulties of sharing this space whilst antagonism is high (Israelis being forbidden from the quarter containing Muslim holy sites in an attempt to keep peace). Only a few weeks after our perfectly peaceful visit violence broke out in Temple Mount on the coinciding Jewish and Muslim holy days of Tisha B'Av and Eid al-Adha respectively, when Jewish worshippers were permitted into the site.

I was determined to visit the Palestinian Territories in addition to Israel; the day in Bethlehem was one of the most engaging. Having a Christian upbringing, an idealised version of Bethlehem was in my mind's eye, much like many others who spent their childhoods at the very least doing nativity productions every Christmas. Because we were entering Area A of the Palestinian Territories, where Israelis are forbidden under Israeli law (which is stated in Hebrew, Arabic, and English on red signs on roads leading in that direction), our guides were Palestinian. Only our driver had permission to cross the border from the Palestinian Territories into Jerusalem; our guide had to be collected from his home. On our journey to Bethlehem from Jerusalem we drove past an Israeli settlement that from a distance resembled a town; I recalled a former classmate's observation that the size and defensive measures of such settlements meant they were not likely to be dismantled, and had to agree with her. My first few mental images of a "settlement" had been rather more like shanty towns, but the real thing is substantially larger and more reinforced.

I find it difficult to maintain a level of neutrality when reflecting upon the differences between Israel and the Palestinian Territories. Even accounting for bias that one would anticipate from a Palestinian guide not allowed to enter Jerusalem, there is no mistaking the visible differences between the two places despite the lack of much distance between them. There were unfinished buildings throughout, and most homes had water tanks on the roof, as the water in the Territories is controlled by Israel and we were informed it costs too much for Palestinians to buy it back. Aspects such as the lack of infrastructure and the resulting litter by the sides of the roads is one notable example of the difference between the two nations. I would not seek to totally entirely absolve the Palestinian Authority of responsibility and lay it all at the feet of the Israeli government, but it is hard to deny that the restrictions on movement and goods make life substantially more difficult.

Following years of news reports about the Palestinian Territories, I admit I had downgraded significantly my expectations of Palestinian towns, but I feel now as if that was somewhat unjust. Central Bethlehem was not as run-down as I had been primed to anticipate. We drove past a small boutique hotel and were amused by the fake version of Starbucks in town, though it differed substantially from the areas of Jerusalem I had seen; I was conscious that its tourist appeal as the home of the Church of the Nativity may be somewhat helpful in a way in which many other Palestinian towns could not benefit. Despite the quaint old town and the Palestinian welcome and generous lunch, it was impossible to mistake that Bethlehem is a town with problems. The restaurant owners explained that business was tough, as many tourists move straight from the bus to the church via the tourist centre, not stopping to interact with locals, possibly for fear that the area is unsafe.

Moreover, I struggle to accept that the Israeli–West Bank wall (the name itself sparks political reaction) can in the long-term play anything but a negative role in the conflict. The wall section I saw stood metres high, topped with metal fencing, and the guard towers had been abandoned following Palestinian attack. It was covered in graffiti and artwork by locals and visitors from across the world, the most impressive of which was an incredibly lifelike rendering of Ahed Tamimi, the Palestinian teenage girl who has become the symbol of freedom fighters for many, known for her appearances in viral videos confronting Israeli soldiers. The wall prevents terror attacks (which also threaten any chances of resolution) in the areas where the concrete stands several metres high, but it fosters more hostility in the hearts and minds of those separated by it, for those who are affected economically, by familial ties, or by cultural and historical attachment to the land. It is an ugly, physical and offensive manifestation of how tribalism and enemy images spiral negatively into an oppressive stalemate. Where it fails to follow the Green Line, the wall provokes even more antagonism from Palestinians. For those looking for a real, durable solution, the barrier cannot possibly be it. Learning about it was one thing, but seeing it is another. Good fences do not make good neighbours.

During our stop at the Aida Refugee Camp, I was able to witness the Palestinian narrative I had thus far discussed only in the abstract brought to life. Before anything else, over the road on arrival is an archway in the shape of a keyhole with its correspondingly huge key fashioned on top, symbolic of the homes and property the Palestinians believe to have been stolen from them during the 1948 War, the *nakba* as they name it, or "catastrophe". Keys represent the belief passed down between generations of the right to those homes, often destroyed or owned now by Israeli Jewish families. Our camp guide, a descendant of Palestinian refugees and a youth worker in the camp, gave an introductory talk to the tour group, outlining the origins of the Palestinians' plight. Despite not being old enough to have experienced the initial fleeing personally, it was clear that the emotions, tradition, and Palestinian history are passed down between generations. There were factual inaccuracies too; I wished to offend nobody, so I did not seek to correct the camp guide for claiming that the British and Jews had been partners against the Arabs, although I thought immediately of the 1946 Jewish terrorist attacks on the British administrative headquarters in the Jerusalem King David Hotel. Again, there was no room for nuance, and I reflected upon the narrative that those in the wider group with less knowledge of the conflict would be understanding without alternative explanations also being given.

I confess to being quite shocked by the buildings in the refugee camps; as the population had grown over several decades, new storeys had been built on top of old ones with no real foundations, and people continue to live in them. The frustration I described earlier settled here, as we stood with our backs to these buildings and listened to the guide explain the paintings of Palestinians on a section of the wall, commemorating individuals who were almost celebrated for being imprisoned for having killed Jewish soldiers. The barrier is atrocious, but so is murder; as an outsider to the conflict, it is so difficult to reconcile these contradictory feelings of sympathy, understanding, and anger towards each "side" of the conflict, and whilst knowing the breadth and complexity of opinions towards the conflict within each group. It can only be more difficult for those caught up inside it. Later, members of the group heavily criticised the Palestinians for their actions without acknowledging any understanding for their situation and the history behind it; I could not help but feel the weight of history wrapped up within psychological hatred. I found myself taking a position that I often seem to do in discussions that feel one-sided – playing the part of the representative of the side of the story which seems to be missing from the conversation, the job of someone who appreciates both parts and assigns victimisation and blame to both.

The Church of the Nativity itself was another twinge of sadness for me. Despite the belief that this spot was the birthplace of Jesus, crucial to one of the world's major religions and faith of millions, and that the Church had been the site of a siege between Israelis and Palestinians less than two decades prior only demonstrated to me once more the absolute desperation of the situation between the two parties. No matter to whom one assigns the responsibility, and the group later hotly discussed this with the help of the Internet, the visible bullet holes in doorframes and walls of a place with such deep significance and religious meaning to so many were deeply upsetting, not even this place was sacred or exempt from the conflict.

The politics of the region played significantly on my mind throughout our trip, even down to the itinerary itself. In this respect, I would say that studying the conflict impeded my ability to enjoy my holiday as just a holiday; I was often aware of the implications and evidence of the conflict during our stay.

Returning from Bethlehem, we hired a car to leave Jerusalem for Ein Gedi. The Jewish member of my group and I had held several discussions in advance on which routes to take whilst driving, and she reached out to Israeli family for advice about speed versus safety. We debated whether it was safe to take routes 1 and 90 in the West Bank, and whether our car hire company would permit us to do so to reach Ein Gedi from Jerusalem, just south of the border between the Palestinian Territories and Israel. The alternative route only through Israel proper is significantly longer, and as I was our only experienced overseas driver, I picked up the car in the early evening. We feared, following numerous violent and fatal attacks on highway 60, another West Bank route, that West Bank driving might be risky. I felt both relieved and uncomfortable when the car hire advisor told us roads in Areas B and C were permitted; taking these roads would make our journey certainly quicker but meant taking roads through the Palestinian Territories on which we, as British tourists in an Israeli-plated car, were allowed to drive unimpeded, but on which Palestinian-plated cars have only restricted access. On greater reflection, I cannot say I would take these roads again: I felt even more uneasy as we merged onto Route 1, and I fully realised it seemed no different from driving in Israel proper, and that had I not known these were the Palestinian Territories, I could have mistaken them for still being in Israel. Later in the trip, taking route 90 from Ein Gedi through the length of the West Bank to the edge of the Golan Heights, we saw only a few Palestinian-plated cars. Although I felt uncomfortable then about using roads which so divide Palestinian areas from each other, with familial, economic and psychological damage, and which Palestinians cannot themselves use freely, I feel even more so now. Not at the expense of the current state of Israel, I believe in the right for Palestinians who have long lived on this land to be able also to do so, and these roads very much infringe their freedoms.

On our early morning sunrise hike to the top of Masada, I was able to witness the exquisite beauty of the area. This was an observation I was frequently struck by, but it came with a corresponding sadness that a land with such historical and religious significance has been the source of so much warfare and hatred, and now has two groups of people who want to live there but who struggle to live alongside each other. I thought of the ordinary people who ideally just want a peaceful and fair chance to live. I was thankful that we arranged the holiday so that we could meet quite a few of such people – the Israeli Jewish family of my friend, and some of their friends who kindly invited us for a delicious Shabbat dinner, one of whom shared with us her positive experience of her national service in the Israeli Defence Force (she could not tell us exactly what she had been doing!), the multiple Palestinian tour guides and Bethlehem restaurateurs. Above all, the trip allowed me to appreciate more physically how life unfolds in Israel and, talking to ordinary people who live there allowed me to do this.

One of the most difficult aspects of the trip was visiting the Golan Heights, a long-contested piece of land between Israel and Syria. Although tangential to the Israeli-Palestinian conflict, I reference it here because of its highly developed Israeli presence, with wineries, local businesses and Israeli towns scattered throughout. From the viewpoint at Coffee Annan (a café in the demilitarised UN-peacekeeping zone), looking into the land of Syria from the Golan Heights, I felt its connection to the occupation of and control over significant parts of the Palestinian Territories, and how such actions seemed only ever to perpetuate hostility, antagonism, and long-term insecurity. Israel states that it needs these territories, the checkpoints, walls, early warning stations, for its own security – or for some because of religious claim to the whole land – but the perception of its actions by those who live in that land is not of defence but offence, a feeling of "the Israelis are taking our land again". It will only ever cause antagonism and hostility, feeding into that long-term cycle of insecurity. I confess to feeling very frustrated standing there, with information points describing the Israeli view on the Golan Heights. I do not claim that everything they said was wrong, nor do I argue or question the courage of individual Israeli soldiers, but I wanted to see depictions of the Syrian perspective too. That feeling of wanting to defend the missing voice reared its head.

Conclusions

The Israeli-Palestinian conflict is inherently complex, and I cannot deny the high levels of frustration I have felt from studying it, from the wealth of information to read, the names to remember, the ease with which it is possible to demonstrate partiality, or from observing the participants' own behaviour and being able to see the inevitable consequences that stem from it. Studying this conflict has given me a new lease on intellectual life, in a region I did not anticipate becoming a passion for me, and I am proud to be a Middle East enthusiast. Visiting Israel and the Palestinian Territories was such a privilege, and the best way to grasp how life works there. I intend to return to the Middle East as soon as I can.

Fundamentally, the Israeli-Palestinian conflict is one that can aid understanding the importance of the role of psychology and the necessity of empathy and humanity in international relations. Understanding, or trying to understand, the variety of perspectives among Israelis and Palestinians is no easy task, being as many as there are, but it is a rewarding one.

Recommended Readings

Halperin, E., et al. 2010. "Socio-psychological Implications for an Occupying Society: The Case of Israel." *Journal of Peace Research* 47:1, 59–70.

Nets-Zehgnut, R. 2014. "The Israeli and Palestinian Collective Memories of Their Conflict: Determinants, Characteristics and Implications." *The Brown Journal of World Affairs* 20:2, 103–121.

Schori-Eyal, N., E. Halperin, and D. Bar-Tal. 2014. "Three Layers of Collective Victimhood: Effects of Multileveled Victimhood on Intergroup Conflicts in the Israeli-Arab Context." *Journal of Applied Social Psychology* 44:2, 778–794.

Shlaim, A. 2009. *Israel and Palestine: Reappraisals, Revisions, Refutations*. London and New York: Verso.

Questions for Discussion

(1) Is it ever possible to be fully unbiased when studying and discussing the conflict?
(2) Which elements of the conflict are the most difficult to understand?

(3) To what extent are you convinced that psychology is the most important factor in the conflict?
(4) Is religion relevant to the modern-day debate? If so, in what ways?

References

B'Tselem. 2017. "Targeting of Israeli Civilians by Palestinians." 11 November. Available at: www.btselem.org/israeli_civilians.

Bar-Tal, D. 2001. "Why Does Fear Override Hope in Societies Engulfed by Intractable Conflict, as It Does in the Israeli Society?" *Political Psychology* 22:3, 601–627.

Flapan, S. 1987. "The Palestinian Exodus of 1948." *Journal of Palestine Studies* 16:4, 3–26.

Karsh, E. 2010. *Palestine Betrayed.* New Haven, CT: Yale University Press.

Keating, J. and Kirk, C. 2014. "The Middle East Friendship Chart." *Slate.* 17 July. Available at: www.slate.com/blogs/the_world_/2014/07/17/the_middle_east_friendship_chart.html.

Khalidi, W. 1988. "Plan Dalet: Master Plan for the Conquest of Palestine." *Journal of Palestine Studies* 18:1, 4–33.

Morris, B. 1988. *The Birth of the Palestinian Refugee Problem, 1947–1949.* Cambridge: Cambridge University Press.

Palestinian Center for Policy and Survey Research (PCPSR). 2016. "The Palestinian-Israeli Pulse: A Joint Poll." December. Available at: www.pcpsr.org/sites/default/files/Table%20of%20Findings_English%20Joint%20Poll%20Dec%202016_12Feb2017.pdf.

Shlaim, A. 2001. *The Iron Wall: Israel and the Arab World.* London: Penguin Press.

PART VII

Conclusion

37

SAMSON'S FALL AND SOLOMON'S JUDGEMENT

Feelings and Fairness in the Israeli-Palestinian Conflict

Uriel Abulof

Introduction

While the grey Covid clouds were just starting to gather, I gave my last public talk on the Israeli-Palestinian Conflict (IPC) before the viral rain, in Haifa. I was reckless enough to try to be funny. I took the stage in front of several hundred Israelis and, in the calmest voice I could muster, solemnly opened, "Let's start with a joke – *Shalom*!"

Happily, for me, the crowd burst into laughter. Sadly for all, the joke is on us. As the audience well knew, the Hebrew word *shalom* carries the double meaning of "hello" and "peace." In the first sense, it is widely used; in the second, hardly anymore. My greeting provoked what Israelis and Palestinians have experienced over the past generation: peace has become a laughing matter. Some celebrate its demise, others lament it, but overwhelming majorities among both peoples see peace as a lost cause, an aspirational relic – whether naïve or dangerous – from a bygone era. Why?

Accounts abound, and here I focus on two pieces of the puzzle: emotions and morality. Both matter much, overall and specifically in the IPC (Abulof 2014a; Bar-Tal 2011). Here the chapter briefly sketches both themes, and elaborate elsewhere (Abulof forthcoming). To that end, I employ what I term, "mythic contemporaries": foundational fables that inform current processes and may help us understand them. Specifically, I turn to two biblical stories that capture the parts played by feelings and fairness in the IPC, the tales about Judge Samson and King Solomon, respectively.

The moral of the Samson story, especially its ending, is the heavy, humiliating cost of trusting Others, who may tempt but ultimately betray you. The price: stripping you of your power and pride. Only the Almighty is to be trusted to the bitter end. The Judgement of Solomon rules between two women who both claim to be the mother of a child. The moral of the story is, for some, the dangerous allure and illusion of "fair compromise." Justice is not about fairness but about ownership and, in matters of life and death, ownership should be exclusive, absolute. Compromise becomes an obstacle both to survival (since only the strong survive) and to peace

DOI: 10.4324/9780429027376-45

(since compromise preludes a bloodbath). The attempt to satisfy both rivals is the harbinger of the greatest evil.

I argue that both Israelis and Palestinians have effectively beheld their conflict through this dual, biblical, lens: both peoples regard themselves as Samson, following his omnipotent fantasy, fearing his fate, embracing his fury; both peoples also consider themselves the "real mother" of their living land, urging Solomon, with his wit and might, to make it right. I draw on two kinds of discourse: public and poetic, the former mainly in the case of Israel, the latter in the Palestinian case, as "poetry became the ultimate reference point for Palestine's national ethos and myths" (Ghanim 2009: 23).

Samson's Fall

Samson is the last of the twelve biblical "judges," each from a different tribe, who led the Israelites before the establishment of the united monarchy. Throughout most of the period, the Israelites feared and fought against their sworn enemy and existential threat: the Philistines. Their name's Semitic root (p-l-s designates "to invade") conveys the Philistines' supposed foreignness to the land, which God had promised to the Israelites. Divinely endowed with immense strength, Samson led the struggle against the Philistines of Gaza, but was betrayed by Delilah, delivered to the Philistines, had his eyes gouged out, and was put on humiliating display. In the temple of Gaza, Samson asked God to restore his strength for the last time, and he brought the temple down. The tale helps us grasp four key emotions that underpin the IPC: the fantasy of power, the fault of trust, the fear of humiliation, and the faith-fuelled fury against enemies.

The Fantasy: Omnipotence

Samson is the only biblical, and one of the world's first, superheroes, possessing a metaphysical, indeed superhuman strength, slaying a lion with his bare hands and an entire army of Philistines with a donkey's jawbone. The pursuit and possession of power, even omnipotence, is arguably an ongoing human drive. For Nietzsche (1907 [1886]: §259), "life simply is will to power." For Adler (1998), contra Freud, people seek power, not pleasure, to compensate for their infant sense of fragility. This pursuit, however, may go astray when a fantasy fed by an ongoing sense of inferiority breeds a pathological hunger for excessive power. Both Zionists and Palestinians have entertained this fantasy, and suffered its pathologies.

Among the biblical tales that have inspired Zionism, the story of David and Goliath takes pride of place. The Israelite shepherd boy who defeated the Philistine giant with a simple slingshot inspired a widespread Israeli self-perception: the small outsmarting the strong. Yet Zionists equally sought strength, fancying themselves Samson. Prime Minister Levi Eshkol was one of the first to explicitly, and ironically, draw on this imagery in 1963 when he suggested that Israel be portrayed as "poor Samson" (*Shimshon der nebechdikker*): Israel grew increasingly powerful, yet it wished to project a feeble image so as to impress upon others the need for aid.

Since then, Israel's power has only mounted. Most symbolic is the transformation of the proverbial slingshot into a highly advanced army – and a vast nuclear arsenal, which, in its region, Israel allegedly alone possesses. It also forged an effective alliance with a global superpower, the United States, which fostered Israel's peace treaties with two of its fiercest enemies, Egypt (1979) and Jordan (1994) and, more recently, diplomatic relations with the United Arab Emirates, Bahrain, Sudan, and Morocco (2020). Israel emerged victorious in all its key military engagements and effectively subdued the two Palestinian *Intifadas* (1987–1991, 2000–2004). In the wake of the Arab Spring (2011–2013), Israel's Arab neighbours, especially Syria, became much weaker. Moreover, Israel's economy has grown dramatically, becoming robust enough to contain, in the 2000s, the ill effects of the Second Intifada and the global financial crisis. With recent natural gas discoveries, Israel has also become more energy self-reliant than ever.

However mighty Israel has become, many Israeli Jews still fantasize about attaining (more) power, to assure its survival and, for some, domination. In military expenditure as a percentage of GDP, Israel continues to occupy the top of the scale (Tian et al. 2020). Its driving, subjective sense of inferiority draws not only on past trauma (see below) or fear of the future, but on objective assessments of the present. Its precarious nuclear monopoly notwithstanding, it remains vulnerable: geographically and demographically small in a region where, largely, leaders and publics still wish to see the Jewish state vanquished and vanished. Like the sense of inferiority, the fantasy of power too draws on the past – not the times of trauma but the days of glory: the ancient golden eras of Jewish polities, notably the biblical monarchies or the Maccabee/Hasmonean dynasty. In the Zionist narrative, national unity (e.g., the kingdoms of David and Solomon) and heroism (e.g., Bar Kokhba) underpin moments of political omnipotence – and are to be cherished and celebrated (Zerubavel 1995).

Palestinians foster their own fantasies of power, underscoring glorious epochs of might, unity and heroism. The Palestinian national movement is embedded in a larger kin-civilization, nurturing both Arab-Muslim political myths. The mediaeval Golden Age (eighth–thirteenth centuries) remains a key reference point in these modern fantasies of power, both material and spiritual (Renima et al. 2016).

The eminent figure of Saladin is especially pertinent. The Ayyubid sultan led the twelfth Muslim military campaign against the Crusader states in the Levant, recapturing Jerusalem, and with it the Arab popular imagination and collective memory. Modern prose, poetry, films, and TV shows have celebrated Saladin as a pan-Arab, and then as a pan-Muslim, (super)hero, who united the Arab-Muslim world to restore the holy land to its rightful owners (Sayfo 2017). Arguably, such Arab-Muslim unity should have given the Palestinians the "super power" to overcome Zionism.

The Palestinian fantasies of power attach specific Palestinian symbols to such myths of "martyrdom" and heroism. Thus, for example, during the Second Intifada, Palestinians and Lebanese in Beirut demonstrated against Israel, carrying posters comparing the PLO chairman, Yasser Arafat, to Saladin (Khalili 2007: 94). Similarly, the 1968 battle of Karameh – the semi-failed IDF operation against Arafat and the PLO – was integrated into the Palestinian political mythology and compared to the Battle of Hattin (1187), forming an "unbroken chain of heroism" (Khalili 2007: 152; Terrill 2001).

Notably, while Israel may be "poor Samson" – objectively powerful but subjectively frail – contemporary Palestinians can truly only fantasize about a Samson-like prowess or fancy themselves a Palestinian David contending with an Israelite Goliath. "I don't have tanks like you do, / ridden by soldiers to chew up Gaza. / Firing bombs from an Apache isn't on my CV," writes poet Marwan Makhoul (*An Arab at Ben-Gurion Airport*).

Ultimately, if Samson is the "strongest man in the world," there cannot, by definition, be two Samsons. The dual fantasy of omnipotence turned Israelis and Palestinians into almost "incompossible" peoples: the realization of one fantasy obliterates the other.

The Fault: Trust and Betrayal

A Herculean-like figure, Samson had his secret Achilles heel: his long hair, the extension of his Nazirite vow. Without his hair, Samson's power is gone. His lover, Delilah, covertly working for the Philistines, eventually coaxed him into divulging the source of his strength and, as he slept, had a servant cut off his hair, then turned the enfeebled Samson over to the Philistines. The moral of the story is clear: Samson's real vulnerability was not his hair but his submission to temptation, trusting others and being betrayed in return. Samson's fantasy and fault entwine to produce his downfall: if what matters is power, without it, one is lost; help from others is chimeric.

Samson's fault resonates in the annals of the Jewish people, carrying the scars and lessons of anti-Semitism. The Holocaust brought it to a devastating culmination. From the Jewish point of view, the fact that the enlightened world stood by and did not act, both in the lead-up to World War II (e.g., the 1938 Évian Conference) and throughout the war, compounded Nazi crimes with the offence of global indifference.

The deep-seated Zionist mistrust of the world lingered even after Israeli's establishment (1948). The young state became a target of existential delegitimization: countries worldwide, especially in Israel's own region, rejected its very existence, morally and practically. This international delegitimization reached a new peak when the UN General Assembly determined that "Zionism is a form of racism and racial discrimination" (Resolution 3379, passed on 10 November 1975). A generation later, the Second Intifada amplified this mistrust, often seen as "siege mentality," Zionists beholding the world – bar the Jewish diaspora and occasionally the United States – as innately hostile to the Jewish state (Bar-Tal 2013: 235–244). Public opinion polls continue to show that for the vast majority of Israeli Jews, "the whole world is against us," regardless of what Israel does (The Israel Democracy Institute 2018, May 2010).

The "trust no one" imperative, however, is often directed at not merely enemies from without but at traitors within. The clearest case is the 1995 assassination of Israeli PM Yitzhak Rabin by an Israeli ultranationalist, inspired by religious leaders to subject Rabin to "Din Moser" and "Din Rodef" (the laws on informers and pursuers, respectively). More recently, right-wingers have increasingly turned to name and shame the "domestic Delilah," lambasting Israel's left (Jews and Arabs), the media, the courts, and various NGOs for undermining Israel's standing. Thus, for example, throughout the 2014 Gaza crisis (in the wake of the kidnapping and murder of three Israeli teenagers by Hamas), radical right-wing activists protested in the streets and in the social media against left-wing Israeli Jews, whom they condemned as "traitors" to the Jewish and Zionist cause (*Eretz Acheret*, 71, July 2014).

Palestinians too have partaken in the blame game of exposing traitors to the cause. The *Nakba* (Arabic for "catastrophe") is the axis; the 1948 displacement of hundreds of thousands of Arabs by the emergent Jewish state is the Palestinians' defining moment – a national identity forged by trauma and its collective memory. The Nakba is the threshold in the Palestinian national narrative. Life before it was safe and familiar; in its wake, life became fragile and foreign.

A sense of lost omnipotence underpins the Nakba trauma. For most Palestinian Arabs at the time, Zionism stood little chance against the overwhelmingly stronger Arab countries; united, utilizing their full force, the Arabs should have defeated the Zionists. These seemingly obvious odds, and the shocking outcome, summoned a shameful narrative of paralysis, cowardice, and betrayal. Fawzi al-Qawuqji's volunteer Arab Salvation Army, for example, was depicted as cowardly, fleeing the battlefield. "The Salvation Army is escaping to the North," wrote the poet Samih al-Qasim, "The rescue army is throwing down its weapons / To the mud it sends its signs of honour and heroism / The rescue army! / Shames of man!"

Palestinian naming and shaming was directed more fiercely at certain Arab leaders. In the Palestinian mythology of 1948, Jordan's King Abdullah figures as a Delilah of sorts. Reined in by Britain, he allegedly colluded with Zionist leaders to crush Palestinian national aspirations, leading to the Nakba. Scholarship mostly rejects the narrative of Abdullah's treacherous plot

(Sela 1992). Some, like Karsh (2010), go further to portray Palestinian leaders as betraying their own people. But the Palestinian narrative mostly eschews responsibility for the Nakba, occasionally portraying it as "an irresistible natural disaster," even supernatural: "God ... appeared during the events as pathetic and useless" (Ghanim 2009: 23).

In the wake of the Nakba for two long decades, the Palestinians largely kept relying on the Arab world to redeem their land. The promise of Pan-Arabism, championed by Egypt's anti-colonialist leader, Gamal Abdel Nasser, glowed brightly: with Arab power restored, many hoped, so would Palestine be restored to its rightful owners. It was after the 1967 *Naksa* (Arabic for "setback"), Israel's Six-Day War victory and the demise of the pan-Arab dream, that Palestinians drew a larger lesson from Samson's fault: trusting Arab leaders is to no avail; they are inept or renegade. Thus, as for Zionists, the primacy of power went hand in hand with the imperative of self-reliance.

Believing that trust often ushers in betrayal, both Israelis and Palestinians rarely trust others, let alone one another. In *Identity Card*, Mahmoud Darwish's signature poem, he tells the Israeli office interrogating him at the checkpoint, "You have stolen the orchards / of my ancestors / And the land / which I cultivated." Tellingly, when the poem was read by IDF radio station in an intellectual discussion about Darwish's work, the reaction was swift: Israeli ministers of culture and defense vehemently decried the broadcast, the minister of defense comparing Darwish's poetry to Hitler's *Mein Kampf* (Haaretz 2016).

The Fear: Humiliation and Death

Having captured the incapacitated Samson, the Philistines gouged out his eyes and forced him to grind grain in a Gaza mill, then summoned him to the temple of their deity, Dagon, to be jeered by thousands of spectators. Samson's downfall is about the loss of power, control and physical strength, leaving the Israelites at the mercy of their enemies. But it is also about the loss of pride, and the resultant dread of humiliation and eventual death, engendering a frustrating gap between the fantasy of power and the fear of humiliation. Scholars have noted the importance of humiliation in understanding world politics (MoïSi 2009), and Middle Eastern politics in particular (Fattah and Fierke 2009). The IPC is another chapter in this emotional saga.

The defining humiliating experience of Zionism (and indeed of modern Jews, worldwide) is plainly the Holocaust. Of the many atrocities committed, one pre-war incident in Vienna should suffice: the so-called *Reibpartien* (scrubbing squads). On the night before, and especially in the weeks and months after, the 1938 *Anschluss* (union) of Austria by Nazi Germany, the city's Jews were forced to clean the streets and pavements of political slogans with brushes, sometimes toothbrushes, under the gloating eyes of the Viennese crowd. The Nazis subsequently used photos of the humiliating spectacle to demonstrate the subhuman status of Jews.

Decades later, Alfred Hrdlicka's sculpture, *Street-washing Jew*, used that degenerate imagery – depicting an orthodox Jew lying low on the pavement he is scrubbing – to trigger guilt among contemporary Austrians. To no avail; the artwork confirms rather than alters the perception of "the other" (Schult 2018). The tale of Samson may explain why the Philistines blinded him – to avoid their own shame lest his gaze fell upon them. For Levinas (1969 [1961]: 213), people's "face-to-face" encounters affirm their joint humanity, for the face, in its fragile nudity, pleas for peace – humanity itself looks at us through the eyes of others. Becoming blind, blindfolded, forcefully humbled (etymologically, lowering to *humus* – ground, earth, dirt) paves the path to humiliation without guilt, to turn humans into playthings.

Fast forward generations, May 2004, dozens of IDF soldiers were crawling on the sands of Rafah in the Gaza Strip, sifting earth in search of the remains of their comrades who were killed by the Hamas. It was a vivid, almost visceral, demonstration of both power and humiliation. The most powerful army in the Middle East, fighting against a rather weak organization, was literally brought to its knees. Though evidently demonstrating care for the dead and their families, the striking imagery was hard to shake off (Asher 2010), reminiscent of the haunting imageries of the 2000 Ramallah lynching at the onset of the Second Intifada (Liebes and First 2003: 63). Throughout, Israel's inability, despite its great might, to protect its citizens and soldiers (often conflating the roles of both) have kept the humiliating fear and frustration alive.

The frustrating, humiliating gap between omnipotence and impotence has haunted the Palestinians too – since the Nakba. The latter has become a moment of "paradise lost," a collective experience of expulsion and abandonment, turning the present into purgatory (Ismael 1981). A sense of desolation and death hovers over another one of Darwish's most notable poems, *A State of Siege*: "We are alone. We are alone to the point / of drunkenness with our own aloneness, / with the occasional rainbow visiting." Besieged, the Palestinians are taken with "black carnations. ... To the abyss of life within me."

In other poems, Palestine itself, whatever it may mean, becomes its people's prison (see, for example, Dareen Tatour, *A Poet Behind Bars*; Ashraf Fayadh, *Cracked Skin*). In impotence, fear is omnipresent, Palestine – and Palestinians – becoming a plaything. Salem Jubran describes how "Dusky was ... the night of Nakba / No light, but that of the bombs / Falling on the villages that didn't fight / But why my homeland? Frightened eyes asked / And never understand."

The romantically desperate "But why my homeland?" turns bitter and enraged in other Palestinian poems. The land, the lover, becomes a hub of honour undone, humiliation searing. This is not general honour (*Sharaf*), but family honour (*'ird*), determined by the sexual behaviour of the woman (here, the land), which man must then protect. In some cases, the poetic accusation is levelled against those who sold their land to Zionists, violating it. "You sold the braid of the olive tree," accuses Rashid Husayn in *She, The Land*, "You humiliated the honour of the garden at the market. / You betrayed the love of the garden."

Often enough, the homeland itself is disloyal, an unfaithful woman who gave herself up to the Zionist usurpers. Taha Muhammad Ali thus writes of

> the adulterous land / land has not maintained its love / land is a prostitute ... offering her hips to whomever wants / land denies us/betrays us ... and it bears no sign that it has ever been ours.
>
> *(Cited in Ghanim 2009: 34)*

Darwish too portrays the homeland as unfaithful, indeed a killer: "Do you love her? Well, I loved her before you. Furthermore, I was swinging on her flowing braids. She was beautiful. Nevertheless, she danced on my grave" (*Sadness and Anger*, 1964).

The Palestinian sense of humiliation starts with, but goes well beyond, the Nakba. The ongoing occupation of the West Bank and the Gaza Strip has created a climate of constant humiliation in the daily experiences of many. The main trigger of humiliation is the wait in line at checkpoints, followed by farmers banned from reaching their fields, and the wall encircling Palestinian land (Ginges and Atran 2008: 285). Nevertheless, in an honour-based society such as the Palestinian, one should expect reluctance to admit humiliation; it likely runs even deeper than surveys disclose.

Both Israelis and Palestinians were caught up in a mutually reinforcing spiral of fear and frustration, of honour and humiliation. Their sense of dignity has thus become dependent upon, and often enough tarnished by, the very existence of the other, whether mighty or weak-yet-lethal. Existentially fearing the Other, boldly reaching out to the latter is unlikely. In the face of such *dead*lock, it is easy to sense the temptation to rage and revenge.

The Faith-fueled Fury: Killing in the Name of God

The fourth and final chapter in Samson's fall is literal. The blinded, ridiculed Samson leaned against the temple's support pillars and prayed to God, "remember me, and restore my strength for one last time, oh God, and I shall avenge one of my two eyes." And so Samson did. Calling "Let my soul die with the Philistines," he brought the temple down upon them and himself – a sacrificial suicide.

Samson's suicidal move summons up another mythical tale – Masada: a Jewish stronghold during the Zealots' revolt against the Romans (66–73 AD), culminating in their mass suicide. Zionists have employed the myth to inspire resilience in the face of tough odds, making it a portal to the movement's memory-making (Zerubavel 1995). On one occasion the Masada myth became an actual plan, the 1942 "Masada on Mount Carmel," designating the *Yishuv*'s desperate determination to fight to the bitter end an impending Nazi invasion of Palestine (Gelber 1990). Yitzhak Tabenkin, a Zionist activist, expounded the rationale:

> We must stand here to the end for the future right, self-respect, and historic loyalty of the Jewish people. So we are told by Masada and even before Masada. … We must have no illusions: We face annihilation.
>
> *(Cited in Shavit 2013)*

Annihilation and, as previously mentioned, humiliation, engendering the imperative, "never again," expressing "the firm decision that we Jews must never again reach a situation of humiliation and persecution that the Jews of the Diaspora suffered" (Luz 2003: 57).

Israel developed its ultimate "never again" measure in its second decade: a highly advanced, and arguably militarized, nuclear capacity. Instead of Masada – "rather die than be defeated" – Israel chose *Samson's option*, a term used by policymakers and analysts to designate the country's nuclear strategy: its survival threatened, Israel's last resort is to bring down the temple with a massive nuclear retaliation that would likely lead to mutual destruction (Hersh 1991). Military historian Martin van Creveld thus responded to the potential Iranian nuclear threat: "We have the capability to take the world down with us. And I can assure you that that will happen before Israel goes under" (Hirst 2003: 119).

While the nuclear *Samson's option* translates its protagonist's fury into possible all-out annihilation, it neglects his faith, Samson's source of (super)power. Israeli society, however, has not lost its religion, and moreover has been undergoing "religionization" (Peri et al. 2012). Like Samson in his final moments, many Israeli Jews predicate their collective's political fate on their religious faith – a patent deviation from the founding, secular Zionism (Abulof 2014b). It may transpire as folklore, that is, bumper stickers reading "Israel trusts in the Lord" or "We can count on no-one apart from Our Father in Heaven" (Shain and Bristman 2002: 54).

Other folklore, however, features faith-fuelled fury, some explicitly relating to Samson's fall. A notable example is "Remember Me," a popular Hasidic rock song reciting Samson's vengeful words to God (above). First performed in 1996, the song became increasingly popular in the Second Intifada (issued in Dov Shurin's aptly entitled 2002 album *Vengeance*) (Sheleg 2005). It was notoriously sung at a 2015 wedding, celebrating not only marriage but the burning and murder of a Palestinian family by Jewish zealots, some of the wedding participants dancing while stabbing a photo of the murdered 18-month-old Ali Dawabsheh (Ben Kimon et al. 2015).

Israeli faith-fuelled fury has also become institutionalized, occasionally translated into a "holy war" sentiment. That much became apparent at the onset of Protective Edge Operation, when IDF colonel Ofer Winter's "battle call" echoed Samson's plea, asking for God's help in "fighting (against) the terrorist 'Gazan' enemy which abuses, blasphemes and curses the God of Israel's battles" (*Ha'aretz*, 12 July 2014). Humiliation calls for revenge: In the wake of the 2004 Rafah attack (above), Israel retaliated with massive house demolitions (Human Rights Watch 2004). Notably, however, the belief that Jews are "the chosen people" may be in decline: from 64 per cent of all Israeli Jewish respondents in a 2013 survey (Hermann 2013: 62–73) to 40 per cent in 2019 (Hermann 2019: 125).

While Zionist faith-fuelled fury largely lacks Samson's willing suicide, the radical wing of the Palestinian national movement made it for a time one of its signature actions. Palestinian suicide attacks began in the 1990s, gathering lethal momentum mid-decade as the peace negotiations advanced, and culminating during the Second Intifada. Most of the attacks were carried out by devout individuals or through religious organizations, mainly the Hamas and the Islamic Jihad. For many scholars, suicide attacks stem from "the urge to seek revenge for the death or injury of a close friend or family member, or the real or perceived humiliation brought about by Israeli occupation" (Moghadam 2006: 68).

There is an ongoing debate about the success rate and motivation of suicide attacks (Brym and Araj 2008; Moghadam 2006). The nexus between humiliation and violence is especially thorny and potentially paradoxical. On the one hand, violence typically requires a sense of power and agency, which humiliation undermines; on the other, "members of different militant groups often attribute their own violent acts to personal or collective humiliation experienced at the hands of their oppressors" (Ginges and Atran 2008: 282).

The psychodynamics of Samson's fall may help resolve the puzzle. First, while humiliation undermines the sense of power, the fantasy of power, especially when recalled and nourished by grievances (see below) can sustain agency. Second, humiliation can push one to inflict violence, not only on the other, but upon the self as well, redeeming one's honour through the ultimate sacrifice – especially when amounting to martyrdom, death as a religious sacrifice. "Martyrdom is a duty and a right," said one volunteer for performing a suicide attack, "There is no humiliation like that of living under the occupation" (cited in Moghadam 2006: 73). We should note, however, that while Palestinian wrath was driven by religious conviction, as for Samson, some narratives subvert God's role as protector. In face of the Nakba, Palestinian poet Rashid Husayn speaks of the "disappearance of God," and "God is a refugee" (Ghanim 2009: 29).

Can fury express faith in a secular human agency? Indeed, perhaps there is also a sense of liberation in humiliation when nearing death, the freedom to hope and resist. Darwish implies that much, speaking for Adam, made of earthly clay: "On the verge of death, he says, / 'I have no more earth to lose / Free am I, close to my ultimate freedom, I hold my fortune in my own hands.'" Masculinity rekindled: "To resist: that means to ensure the health / of heart and testicles, and that your ancient disease / is still alive and well in you / a disease called hope" (*A State of Siege*, 2002).

In hopeful resistance, "the sentimental longing for an idealized past is replaced by angry frustration" (Ismael 1981: 46), and by defiance: "Talk about exile – I defy / silence my argument with chains / and a foolish prison cell / I defy" (Sameeh al-Qassem, *I Defy*). In *Identity Card*, the humiliating checkpoint becomes a hub of rage. Darwish concludes his communication to the Israeli interrogating officer with an admonition: "[I]f I become hungry / The usurper's flesh will be my food / Beware. / Beware. / Of my hunger / And my anger!" And so does Makhoul conclude his humiliating search at the airport: "He searches me / for anything that could pose a threat / but this stranger is blind / forgetting the more grievous and important devices within: / my spirit, my defiance," and resumes the fantasy of power, "below me a big lie of tin-can history / like Ben-Gurion become as always, as always, as always / below me" (*An Arab at Ben-Gurion Airport*).

From the fantasy of power through the fault of trust and the fear of humiliation to lethal fury – the tale of Samson's fall resonates with the chronicles of the IPC and its seemingly endless vicious vortex. But all this does not, in itself, disclose the origins of the ongoing impasse. One way to address this puzzle is to reconsider its starting point: Why fantasize about power to begin with? Sensing one's own weakness only begs the question, for why would weakness be so bad (and power so good)? The answer is far from obvious and invites us to entwine feelings with fairness, might with right, moving on to another biblical story.

Solomon's Judgement

Samson was the last of the twelve judges to rule over the Israelite tribes, their inner strife propelling the establishment of the united Israelite kingdom, first under Saul, then David and, eventually, before the kingdom's demise, under his son, Solomon. If Samson was the strongest, King Solomon was allegedly the wisest. That much is conveyed in a key story, the king being approached by two women who gave birth on the same day. Only one baby survived, and each mother claimed it as hers. Solomon ordered the living baby split in two, each mother receiving half. One woman pleaded with the king to keep her son alive and give him to the other woman while the latter accepted the verdict. Solomon judged the former to be the true mother and gave her the baby.

Solomon's judgement reveals the limitations of the prevalent liberal, Rawlsian position on "justice as fairness," suggesting that every individual has an equal right to basic liberties, including "personal property" (Rawls 2001). In Solomon's judgement, there is no equal basic right. Righteousness is right: the mothers are not equally entitled to the baby; one mother is real, the other pretending, one should have it whole, the other nothing at all. This *is* justice, and there can be no compromise. The existential imperative is likewise clear: division is death. Some things cannot be shared, let alone divided, and are thus beyond negotiation. They constitute "sacred values," immune to material incentives (Atran and Ginges 2012).

Many Zionists and Palestinians have effectively sanctified the land, anthropomorphizing it into a baby wholly belonging to one people, never the other, making territorial compromise sacrilegious. Scholars aware of this predicament often prescribe pragmatism. "Justice will destroy all of us, so let's think of less than justice" (cited in Bar-Siman-Tov 2010: 178): since justice and fairness are barriers to peace, we should move beyond morality to practicalities, postponing justice to the phase of reconciliation, well after the conflict is pragmatically resolved.

Pragmatism, however, may be the very thing that perpetuates the conflict. After all, skirting morality turns power into the ultimate arbitrator of conflict. And when might makes right, the fantasy of (super)power is only to be expected; it becomes the only way to truly settle the conflict, to have it all. Moreover, psychological experiments indicate that for both Israelis and Palestinians who treat contested issues as sacred values, material incentives to coexistence backfire – they trigger more, not less, violent opposition to peace (Ginges et al. 2007). The result, as discussed above, is the IPC vicious vortex of Solomon's fall.

Here I will only briefly note some key signs of the Zionist and Palestinian submission to Solomon's judgement, with the focus on the personification and sanctification of the land in discourses, both prosaic and poetic.

Solomon's judgement surfaced in Zionist discourse in key moments of territorial decisions, as early as the 1937 Peel Commission deliberations (e.g., Haolam 1937: 932) and in the lead-up to the 1947 UN partition plan (e.g., Haolam 1946). On both occasions, if the land of Palestine/Israel is a baby, mainstream Zionism is the pretended mother, typically favouring demography (Jewish majority) over geography (the complete land). Many protested. For example, Yigal Alon (1960), a military commander and a Labour Party leader, stressed the dangers of retreating to the 1947 partition lines, accusing Jewish leaders of agreeing at the time to "appear as the pretended mother in Solomon's judgement."

The discourse against partition rose dramatically in the wake of the 1967 war, Israel taking over vast territories from Egypt, Syria, and Jordan. A month after the war, leading public thinkers on both the left and the right, secular and religious, formed the "Movement for Greater Israel." The English translation is somewhat misleading. In Hebrew *Eretz Yisrael HaSheleima* literally means "the complete Land of Israel" and should be understood as thus. The Movement's members regraded the newly acquired territories as part of the nation's integral *body politic*, which must never be divided. "The complete Land of Israel," reads the Movement's (1967) manifesto,

> is now in the hands of the Jewish People, and as we have no right to give up the State of Israel, so we are directed to hold on to what we received from her: the Land of Israel. ... We are bound by loyalty to the wholeness of our Land, to the past and the future of the Jewish People, and no government may give up this wholeness.

Even a most moderate leader like Foreign Minister Abba Eban highlighted the existential peril, submitting that, "The June [pre-1967] map is for us equivalent to insecurity and danger. I do not exaggerate when I say that it has for us something of a memory of Auschwitz" (*Der Spiegel*, 27 January 1969).

The insistence on the territorial integrity of the Land underpins the post-1967 discourse of religious Zionism, whose leader, Rabbi Tzvi Yehuda Kook, strongly proclaimed:

> There are no Arab territories here, only Israelite lands, the eternal possession of our forefathers, which others have come and built upon them without our permission and presence[;]... we are tasked with liberating them, and shall never abandon, nor disengage, them.
>
> *(Cited in Rot 2009: 44)*

The claim for the Jews' divine endowment over the land often couches a survival imperative: the dismembering of the land would murder the nation, indeed as it would a baby (e.g., Schneerson and Gruner 2012). Thus, for example, Rabbi Shlomo Aviner (2021), one of the spiritual leaders of Religious Zionism, suggested that the Israeli Supreme Court, in occasionally accommodating Palestinian appeals regarding land and houses, are like the false mother for "they have no problem dismembering a baby." While many religious Zionists arguably favour the integrity of the people over the land (Rot 2009), their willingness to submit territorial compromise to a plebiscite is typically limited to all-Jewish, rather than all-Israeli, referendum (Hermann 2013: 62–73).

The Palestinians too have imagined the land as an indivisible living entity. In a defining moment of the Palestinian national movement, Arafat (1974) addressed the UN General Assembly, and delivered the gist of the movement's doctrine, "bearing," as he proclaimed, "an olive branch and a freedom-fighter's gun." Appealing to the international community's sense of justice, he invoked Solomon's judgement. Scolding the 1947 UN resolution 181, Arafat explained:

> The General Assembly partitioned what it had no right to divide – an indivisible homeland. When we rejected that decision, our position corresponded to that of the natural mother who refused to permit King Solomon to cut her son into two when the unnatural mother claimed the child for herself and agreed to his dismemberment.

The personification of Palestine reverberates in poetry too, where patriotism and patriarchy fuse to "present the fall of Palestine as an act of 'rape' (*ightesab*) that brought collective shame (*A'ar*)" (Ghanim 2009: 34). Redeeming the land's honour and its ownership, Palestinian poetry professes its people's grounded authenticity. It validates the pre-Nakba existence as just and normal, the post-Nakba predicament as abnormal and abominable.

Danger lurks: a homeless people alienated from their land. The antidote: a sacrifice to sanctify the people–land union; bond by blood. "We shall not depart," writes Tawfiq Zayad, "Here we shall spill our dearest blood, / Here we have a past, / A present, / A future" (*The Impossible*; cited in Ismael 1981: 49). As in Arafat's speech, the olive tree's roots often symbolize the Palestinian native attachment to their land and their *Sumud*, "steadfast perseverance," in the face of existential adversities (Rijke and Toine Van 2014).

"If one day we stumble / our roots will stand us straight," Zayad confidently proclaims, adding that time is on the Palestinians' side: "[M]y country has known a thousand conquerors and they know that the thousand have all melted away like driven snow" (*They Know*; cited in Ghanim 2009: 37).

In Darwish's poetry, Palestinians' deep roots prescribe patience and perseverance: "Patient in a country / Where people are enraged / My roots / Were entrenched before the birth of time" (*Identity Card*). The patient attachment to the land becomes an existential imperative, for persistence ensures permanence, belonging and unity. "Always here. Eternally here, / we have one aim and one aim only: to continue to be … / Beyond that aim we differ in all" (*A State of Siege*, 2002). Lady Land becomes alive, life itself, even the very reason for living: We have on this earth what makes life worth living: on this /earth, the Lady of Earth, / the mother of all beginnings, the mother of all endings. She was called / Palestine. She came to be called / Palestine. O Lady, because you are my Lady, I am worthy of life (*On this Earth*).

While Palestinian poetry personifies Palestine and sanctifies the bond to the land, actual religious-national discourse further insists on its divine indivisibility. It portrays Palestine as *waqf*, a holy Islamic patrimony; its lands an endowment from God, "inalienable in the sense that they could not be sold or transferred to non-Muslims, and particularly not to Jewish Zionists" (Reiter 2007: 195). Though religious, this novel political myth, based on a *hadith* interpretation, has swiftly percolated into mainstream national discourse. Hamas skilfully employed the waqf claim to condemn Arafat's putative willingness to compromise the land, but with mounting obstacles on the path to peace, especially since the collapse of the 2000 Camp David negotiations, the waqf rhetoric became a useful outlet for Arafat too – to both legitimate his stand and consolidate his rule (Reiter 2007).

Solomon's judgement captures the framing of fairness by many Israeli Jews and Palestinians. For them, rejecting partition proposals is not missing chances for peace; rather, rejectionism evinces true love for the land, which should be rewarded by full possession. By sacrificing for sovereignty, dispensing with the material comforts of compromise, these radical forces strike deep moral and emotional chords among their peoples. Consequently, among both peoples, peace-spoilers effectively hold an emotional-moral veto right over compromise, leaving the moderates to defend their views by resorting to the apologetics of practicalities and realpolitik.

Conclusions: From Existential Conflict to Coexistence?

For generations, the IPC has been spinning in an existential vortex, emotional and moral. Both peoples have submitted themselves to Solomon's judgement: embracing a collective sense of righteousness, both secular and religious, to proclaim exclusive ownership over the entire land. Failing to achieve their "righteous" goal, realizing that right may not make might, they sought the reverse – make right through might – and have thus fallen with Samson: Seeking absolute power over their foes (mission impossible), distrusting adversaries from within and without (undermining collaboration), basking in dread of humiliation and death (forgoing bold moves), and opting for faith-fuelled fury (resorting to violence). These dynamics underpin the IPC's existential dimension. In the mindset of both peoples, the conflict does not merely pit Zionists versus Palestinians, but creates an "either/or" trap: "It's either us or them; the land is not big enough for both of us."

Another existential outlook on "either/or" is more hopeful: mustering the courage to choose anew, rather than yielding to extant narratives, biblical or modern (Kierkegaard 1992 [1843]). We may, for example, choose to read these two stories differently. Samson trusted Delilah despite being betrayed, again and again, by his former wives and by his own people. Could his real – human, not divine – power be that of trust, even to his own detriment? As for Solomon's judgement, we should recall that the true mother got her son only after showing a willingness to give him entirely to the other mother so that he might live. We should recall that no land is human, and that saving people might actually require material apportionment. Ultimately, a key to Solomon's judgement was his ability to convince the mothers of his plan, thereby prompting them to choose and take responsibility. By turning the dispute into a moral dilemma, Solomon's judgement awakened their freedom, and conscience.

Could Israelis and Palestinians undergo such an emotional and moral awakening? Can they freely choose a different path lest peace, and justice, remain laughable?

Recommended Reading

Abulof, U. 2015. *The Mortality and Morality of Nations*. New York: Cambridge University Press.

Atran, S., and J. Ginges. 2012. "Religious and Sacred Imperatives in Human Conflict." *Science* 336 (6083):855–857.

Bar-Siman-Tov, Y. 2010. *Barriers to Peace in the Israeli-Palestinian Conflict*. Jerusalem: Jerusalem Institute for Israel Studies.

Bar-Tal, D. 2011. *Intergroup Conflicts and Their Resolution: A Social Psychological Perspective*. New York: Psychology Press.

Ghanim, H. 2009. "Poetics of Disaster: Nationalism, Gender, and Social Change among Palestinian Poets in Israel after Nakba." *International Journal of Politics, Culture, and Society* 22:1, 23–39.

Questions for Discussion

(1) Consider one conflict, historical or contemporary, and one emotion – how do both entwine?
(2) Do you think that might makes right, or right makes might? Explain and give examples.
(3) If emotional and moral factors can foster conflict – can they also help make peace? How?
(4) What other mythic tales can shed light on the conflict?
(5) Write your own mythical story – one that can inspire rivals to make peace.

References

Abulof, Uriel. 2014a. "National Ethics in Ethnic Conflicts: The Zionist 'Iron Wall' and the 'Arab Question'." *Ethnic and Racial Studies* 37:14, 2653–2669.

Abulof, U. 2014b. "The Roles of Religion in National Legitimation: Judaism and Zionism's Elusive Quest for Legitimacy." *Journal for the Scientific Study of Religion* 53:3, 515–533.

Abulof, U. Forthcoming. *Killing Humanity: From Existential Clash to Coexistence in Israel/Palestine*. New York: Routledge.

Adler, A. 1998. *Understanding Human Nature*. Translated by C. Brett. 1st American ed. Center City, MN: Hazelden.

Alon, Y. 1960. "Preventing Another Partition [in Hebrew]." *LaMerhav*, 29 April 1960, 2.

Arafat, Y. 1974. "UN General Assembly Speech." United Nations General Assembly, 29th Session [A/PV.2282 and Corr.1; 13 November 1974].

Asher, I. 2010. "A Decade to the Intifada: Comradeship on Philedelphy Axis [Hebrew]." *NRG (Makor Rishon)*.

Atran, S., and J. Ginges. 2012. "Religious and Sacred Imperatives in Human Conflict." *Science* 336:6083, 855–857.

Aviner, S. 2021. "The Trial of Nobody against Ofra [Hebrew]." *Judaism in Love (YahadothbeAhava)*, 27 January 2021.

Bar-Siman-Tov, Y. 2010. "Justice and Fairness as Barriers to the Resolution of the Israeli-Palestinian Conflict." In *Barriers to Peace in the Israeli-Palestinian Conflict*, ed. Y. Bar-Siman-Tov. Jerusalem: Jerusalem Institute for Israel Studies.

Bar-Tal, D. 2013. *Intractable Conflicts: Socio-Psychological Foundations and Dynamics*. New York: Cambridge University Press.

Ben Kimon, E., K. Nahshoni, Y. Zayton, and I. Eichner. 2015. "A Wedding of Hatred: Celebrating and Stubbing a Photo of the Baby Dawabsheh [Hebrew]." *Ynet*, 24 December 2015.

Brym, R. J., and B. Araj. 2008. "Palestinian Suicide Bombing Revisited: A Critique of the Outbidding Thesis." *Political Science Quarterly* 123:3, 485–500.

Fattah, K., and K.M. Fierke. 2009. "A Clash of Emotions: The Politics of Humiliation and Political Violence in the Middle East." *European Journal of International Relations* 15:1, 67–93.

Gelber, Y. 1990. *Masada: Defending Israel During World War II* [Hebrew: "Metsadah"]. Ramat-Gan: Bar-Ilan University.

Ghanim, H. 2009. "Poetics of Disaster: Nationalism, Gender, and Social Change among Palestinian Poets in Israel after Nakba." *International Journal of Politics, Culture, and Society* 22:1, 23–39.

Ginges, J., and S. Atran. 2008. "Humiliation and the Inertia Effect: Implications for Understanding Violence and Compromise in Intractable Intergroup Conflicts." *Journal of Cognition and Culture* 8: 3–4, 281–294.

Ginges, J., S. Atran, D. Medin, and K. Shikaki. 2007. "Sacred Bounds on Rational Resolution of Violent Political Conflict." *PNAS* 104:18, 7357–7360.

Haaretz. 2016. "Darwish and the Dwarfs." *Haaretz*, 2 July 2016. Available at: https://www.haaretz.co.il/opinions/editorial-articles/1.3014490.

Haolam. 1937. "The Partition Plan [in Hebrew]." *Haolam: The World Zionist Organization Weekly*, 15 July 1937, 929–934.

Haolam. 1946. "The 22nd World Zionist Congress [in Hebrew]." *Haolam: The World Zionist Organization Weekly*, 19 December 1946, 116–126.

Hermann, T. 2013. *Israeli Democracy Index 2013*. Jerusalem: Israeli Democracy Institute.

Hermann, T. 2019. *Israeli Democracy Index 2019*. Jerusalem: Israeli Democracy Institute.

Hersh, S. M. 1991. *The Samson Option: Israel's Nuclear Arsenal and American Foreign Policy*. 1st ed. New York: Random House.

Hirst, D. 2003. *The Gun and the Olive Branch: The Roots of Violence in the Middle East*. New York: Thunder's Mouth Press/Nation Books.

Human Rights Watch. 2004. *Razing Rafah: Mass Home Demolitions in the Gaza Strip (October #17, 2004)* [cited. Available from www.hrw.org/report/2004/10/17/razing-rafah/mass-home-demolitions-gaza-strip].

Ismael, J. S. 1981. "The Alienation of Palestine in Palestinian Poetry." *Arab Studies Quarterly* 3:1, 43–55.

Israel Democracy Institute. 2018. *War and Peace Index, 1994–2018*. Edited by IDI's Guttman Center for Public Opinion and Policy Research and the Evens Program in Mediation and Conflict Resolution. Tel Aviv: Tel Aviv University.

Karsh, E. 2010. *Palestine Betrayed*. New Haven: Yale University Press.

Khalili, L. 2007. *Heroes and Martyrs of Palestine: The Politics of National Commemoration*. Cambridge and New York: Cambridge University Press.

Kierkegaard, S. 1992 [1843]. *Either/Or: A Fragment of Life*. New York: Penguin Books.

Levinas, E. 1969 [1961]. *Totality and Infinity; an Essay on Exteriority*. Pittsburgh: Duquesne University Press.
Liebes, T., and A. First. 2003. "Framing the Palestinian-Israeli Conflict." In *Framing Terrorism: The News Media, the Government, and the Public*, eds. P. Norris, M. Kern and M. R. Just. New York: Routledge, 59–74.
Luz, E. 2003. *Wrestling with an Angel: Power, Morality, and Jewish Identity*. New Haven, CT: Yale University Press.
Moghadam, A. 2006. "Suicide Terrorism, Occupation, and the Globalization of Martyrdom: A Critique of Dying to Win." *Studies in Conflict and Terrorism* 29:8, 707–729.
MoïSi, D. 2009. *The Geopolitics of Emotion: How Cultures of Fear, Humiliation, and Hope Are Reshaping the World*. 1st ed. New York: Doubleday.
Movement for Greater Israel. 1967. "For the Complete Land of Israel [Hebrew]." *Maariv*, 22 September 1967, 24.
Nietzsche, F. W. 1907 [1886]. *Beyond Good and Evil, Prelude to a Philosophy of the Future*. New York: Macmillan.
Peri, Y., T. Hermann, S. Fischer, A. Cohen, B. Susser, N. Leon, and Y. Yadgar. 2012. "The 'Religionization' of Israeli Society." *Israel Studies Review* 27:1, 1–30.
Rawls, J. 2001. *Justice as Fairness: A Restatement*. Cambridge, MA: Harvard University Press.
Reiter, Y. 2007. "'All of Palestine Is Holy Muslim Waqf Land': A Myth and Its Roots." In *Law, Custom, and Statute in the Muslim World: Studies in Honor of Aharon Layish*, eds. A. Layish and R. Shaham. Boston: Brill, 173–197.
Renima, A., H. Tiliouine, and R. J. Estes. 2016. "The Islamic Golden Age: A Story of the Triumph of the Islamic Civilization." In *The State of Social Progress of Islamic Societies: Social, Economic, Political, and Ideological Challenges*, eds. H. Tiliouine and R. J. Estes. Cham: Springer International Publishing, 25–52.
Rijke, A. and T. V. Teeffelen. 2014. "To Exist Is to Resist: Sumud, Heroism, and the Everyday." *Jerusalem Quarterly* (59):86.
Rot, A. 2009. "Religious Zionism Facing Statism: From Kfar Maymon to Amona [Hebrew]." In *Disengagement Plan – an Idea Shattered*, ed. Y. Bar-Siman-Tov. Jerusalem: The Jerusalem Institute for Israel Studies.
Sayfo, O. 2017. "From Kurdish Sultan to Pan-Arab Champion and Muslim Hero: The Evolution of the Saladin Myth in Popular Arab Culture." *The Journal of Popular Culture* 50:1, 65–85.
Schneerson, M. M., and Y. Gruner. 2012. *I Called and There Is No Answer* [Hebrew]. Jerusalem: Malkhot haKeter.
Schult, T. 2018. "The Performative Power of a Problematic Public Work: Art-Interventions at Alfred Hrdlicka's Memorial against War and Fascism in Vienna." *Public Art Dialogue* 8: 2, 231–257.
Sela, A. 1992. "Transjordan, Israel and the 1948 War: Myth, Historiography and Reality." *Middle Eastern Studies* 28: 4, 623–688.
Shain, Y., and B. Bristman. 2002. "The Jewish Security Dilemma." *Orbis* 46:1, 47–71.
Shavit, A. 2013. *My Promised Land: The Triumph and Tragedy of Israel [Ebook]*. 1st ed. New York: Spiegel & Grau.
Sheleg, Y. 2005. "A New Habit in Religious Zionism: Revenge Songs [Hebrew]." *Haaretz*, 6 November 2005.
Terrill, W. A. 2001. "The Political Mythology of the Battle of Karameh." *Middle East Journal* 55:1, 91–111.
Tian, N., A. Kuimova, D. L. Da Silva, P. D. Wezeman, and S. T. Wezeman. 2020. *Trends in World Military Expenditure, 2020*. Stockholm: Stockholm International Peace Research Institute (SIPRI).
Zerubavel, Y. 1995. *Recovered Roots: Collective Memory and the Making of Israeli National Tradition*. Chicago: University of Chicago Press.

INDEX

Note: Page numbers in **bold** refer to tables and *italics* refer to figures